The Company of the Preachers

A History of Biblical Preaching from the Old Testament to the Modern Era

The
Company
of the
Preachers

*A History of Biblical Preaching from
the Old Testament to the Modern Era*

David L. Larsen

kregel
PUBLICATIONS

Grand Rapids, MI 49501

The Company of the Preachers: A History of Biblical Preaching from the Old Testament to the Modern Era

Copyright © 1998 by David L. Larsen

Published by Kregel Publications, a division of Kregel, Inc., P.O. Box 2607, Grand Rapids, MI 49501. Kregel Publications provides trusted, biblical publications for Christian growth and service. Your comments and suggestions are valued.

For more information about Kregel Publications, visit our web site at www.kregel.com.

Cover illustration: Patrick Kelley
Cover design: Alan G. Hartman

Library of Congress Cataloging-in-Publication Data
Larsen, David L.
    The company of the preachers: a history of biblical preaching from the Old Testament to the modern era / David Larsen.
        p.   cm.
    Includes bibliographical references and indexes.
    1. Preaching—History. I. Title.
BV4205.L37   1998   251'.009—dc21   97-10242
                                                                                CIP

ISBN 0-8254-3128-x

Printed in the United States of America

1 2 3 / 03 02 01 00 99 98

For the churches we have served
and the students we have taught.

*Because of the truth that lives in us
and will be with us forever.*
—2 John 2

Contents

Preface

The Lord gives the command; great is the company of those who bore the tidings.

—Psalm 68:11 (NRSV)

To undertake a history of preaching in any form is to be aware of indebtedness to so many who have gone before on this journey of inquiry and evaluation. Broadus and Dargan (even as updated by Turnbull) are now out of print; Webber, while massive in its attention to the English-speaking world, does not go beyond it; Perry and Wiersbe have given us *The Wycliffe Handbook of Preaching and Preachers,* which is mainly skeletal and anecdotal; and numerous brief monographs by Brillioth, DeWitte T. Holland, and Paul Scott Wilson all whet our appetite for a contemporary work that is both descriptive and analytic. The forthcoming works of O. C. Edwards and Ronald E. Osborne have not been available to me as I have engaged in this study, but our perspectives are different.

Preaching in our time is in a dither. Questions and challenges and interest abound, and we are wrestling with so many issues about direction and thrust. This then is the hour in which we need the perspective of history and the sense of what preaching really is over against its biblical and historical roots. My focus has not been upon preaching in a generic sense but more narrowly upon biblical preaching, upon the endeavor to communicate the supernatural written Word of God. My viewpoint is unabashedly that of classical biblical Christianity.[1] Necessarily and often regrettably no living persons as of the date of this writing can be included in the history. The decisions regarding inclusion or exclusion of representative preachers in a given age have often been obvious and easy but, in other cases, tortuous and difficult.

My deepest thanks to the Regents of Trinity Evangelical Divinity School for sabbatical time to work on this project; to my colleagues and students for their interest and input; to my precious life-partner for over forty years, Jean, for her understanding and encouragement; and to my son Dan, a history teacher himself, for his willingness to serve as my technical helper again and again. Preaching the Word of God has been my calling and my life. I have been preaching for more than fifty years and still find indescribable fascination in the intricacies of the craft. For many years in parish ministry and in pulpits around the world, my hunger for greater effectiveness in expounding Scripture has led me to look at the history of preaching over the centuries for such clues and insights as may be afforded by a consideration of the able practitioners of the calling over time. What have been the schools of preaching and how can we trace the evolution of sermonic form? The history of preaching has been one of my favorite courses in my years of teaching preaching at Trinity. It is my prayer and desire that this work will inflame and ignite interest and dedication for some of the preachers of our time. *Ad Gloriam Dei.*

---

1. Cf. J. N. D. Kelly, *Early Christian Doctrines,* rev. ed. (New York: HarperCollins, 1978). Kelly demonstrates that the early church held (as in Tertullian, for instance) to Scripture's "absolute authority"; "whatever it teaches is necessarily true and woe betide him who accepts doctrines not discoverable in it" (39); "Scripture is the doctrinal norm" (42); the primary task is "the exposition of the Bible" (46). Kelly shows their great reverence for the Old Testament (52) with a strong insistence on the unity of both Testaments (65). The full inspiration of Holy Scripture is assumed as their premise (64). What I have called classical biblical Christianity starts with these premises and then builds, and this is where I have also begun.

INTRODUCTION

The Postulates of Preaching

The goal of preaching is the glory of God in the glad submission of his people. . . .

—John Piper in *The Supremacy of God in Preaching*

"But let him who boasts boast about this: that he understands and knows me, that I am the LORD, who exercises kindness, justice and righteousness on earth, for in these I delight," declares the LORD.

—Jeremiah 9:24

The focus of this study is biblical preaching, the central concern of which is to communicate and apply what the Bible teaches. Thus, biblical preaching necessarily must be defined and developed in relationship to the nature and character of God.

The widespread focus on humanity's horizontal relationships and psychological experience in the preaching of our time reflects the increasingly pervasive banishment and exile of God from Western culture—even in the enclaves of conservative Christianity. The contemporary thinning and vivisection of evangelical theology make this study all the more imperative.[1] In spite of this growing aversion to normative theological constructs or the notion of orthodoxy itself, all human activity is to be doxological in nature, including preaching in and for the Christian church. Preaching, therefore, as an act which brings ultimate glory to God himself, should and must reflect both the objective truths of God's very nature and his character as expressed in the vertical relationships of Creator to creation and Redeemer to the redeemed.

The basic premises and essential presuppositions which will govern this study, therefore, need to be clearly stated at the outset.

The Importance of the Word of God

The voice of the LORD is powerful; the voice of the LORD is majestic.

—Psalm 29:4

You have exalted above all things your name and your word.

—Psalm 138:2b

Your word is truth.

—John 17:17b

The God of the Bible is a speaking God. The God of the Bible has revealed himself in nature and in the person of Jesus Christ. The Holy Scriptures give written and propositional interpretation to the mighty acts of God. What the Scriptures represent as fact and truth is indeed fact and truth. The words of Scripture are the words of God, and therefore the Scripture's assertions are totally trustworthy and reliable (John 10:34–36).

Moses declaimed "the word of the Lord" (Deut. 5:5). The speaking God is not silent (Ps. 50:1–3a). The Lord tells Isaiah, "I have put my words in your mouth" (Isa. 51:16). Again and again the servants of God announce, "Thus says the Lord!" Haggai is a case in point. Four times we read of the prophet's mediation of what God says and then the resultant positive response to "the voice of the LORD their God and the message of the prophet Haggai" (Hag. 1:12). To understand what a sunflower is, we need to make a primary induction—we need to look at a sunflower. To understand what the Bible is, we need to make a similar primary induction. We must examine the Bible's claim itself to be in truth the Word of God.

Christ and the apostles taught a *doctrine* of Scripture (cf. 2 Tim. 3:16–17). They submitted themselves to the text of Scripture. The Word of God was seen as "living and powerful" and confidently guaranteed to have an effect (Isa. 55:10–11). How this Word of God "spread rapidly and was honored" (2 Thess. 3:1) is chronicled in Acts and has been confirmed and corroborated down through the centuries. Our study of the history of preaching is grounded on the undying conviction of the absolute authority and total sufficiency of the Bible as the inerrantly and infallibly inspired Word of God.

The secularism of the Enlightenment mounted a relentless assault on the authority of Scripture. Every vestige of the supernatural was jettisoned. Other movements within Christendom have de-emphasized text in favor of experience. In the postmodern period, we now face a massive attack on the very notion of meaning itself and a denial of the fixity of any text. Today the interpreter is elevated over the author. The result has been a recession of the Bible in the church, indeed "a famine of hearing the words of the LORD" (Amos 8:11).[2] Our perspective here is the orthodox and received doctrine of the full inspiration of the Holy Scriptures.

The Importance of the Preaching of the Word of God

And we also thank God continually because, when you received the word of God, which you heard from us, you accepted it not as the word of men, but as it actually is, the word of God, which is at work in you who believe.

—1 Thessalonians 2:13

This conviction that the message comes from God is fundamental to effective preaching.

—Leon Morris

Preach the Word . . .

—2 Timothy 4:2

What we believe about the Bible shapes our view of what preaching is to be. The undercutting of authority and meaning generally in our culture and the undercutting of the authority and meaning of the biblical texts more specifically have had a marked impact upon preaching in our time. If, as many argue, "theology must begin not with revelation or an authoritative tradition but with ordinary human experience" enriched with some "signals of transcendence," then preaching is bound to be groping, hesitant and flat.[3] But if what the Bible says God says, then the preaching of the Word of God becomes an incredibly exciting enterprise.

So central and pivotal is preaching that it would not be overstatement to say that the history of the Christian church is the history of preaching. The day on which the church was born was a day of epochal preaching (Acts 2). When Jesus Christ drew upon the legacy of the seers and prophets of the Old Testament, he became the original preacher. Although beginning with the apostles and continuing down through successive historic periods, preaching has had its diverse styles and forms, its ups and downs, its traumas and its triumphs. Like the church itself which stands just one generation from extinction, so preaching has threatened to self-destruct with its own excesses or to be snuffed out by external foes and pressures. Yet preaching survives and underscores the abiding validity of P. T. Forsyth's classic aphorism, "With its preaching Christianity stands or falls."

The concentration of this study is not on preaching in a generic sense, however, but on biblical preaching as such. John Stott puts it with admirable succinctness: "To preach is to open up the inspired text with such faithfulness and sensitivity that God's voice is heard and God's people obey him."[4] A sermon is biblical when it says what the Scripture says. This may be done in topical, textual-topical, textual or expository form, to use the most basic nomenclature. The form employed, however, is no guarantee of biblical content (later in our study we shall examine the use and the abuse of all of these forms). Only exegetical conscience and the illumination of the Holy Spirit can keep the preacher from wandering away from the Word of God.

Yet the slant of this study cannot be disguised. An expository sermon uses a natural thought unit of biblical text (often in *lectio continua,* a series, as over against *lectio selecta,* not in a series) and seeks to make the sermon say what the specific text says in its actual context. The history of preaching bears out the acute dangers of preaching out of a text rather than preaching the text. Respect for authorial intention may be under siege currently, but it must be seen as the hermeneutical high ground which must not be surrendered. Finding truth in a text is quite different from finding the truth of the text. Given our understanding of what the biblical text in fact is—the very Word of God—what can be more honoring and pleasing to God than the communication of his truth in every possible setting, the resultant conversion of sinners, and the renewed commitment and worship of his people?

The Importance of the History of the Preaching of the Word of God

In every age of Christianity, since John the Baptist drew crowds into the desert, there has been no great religious movement, no restoration of Scripture truth, and reanimation of genuine piety, without new power in preaching both as cause and effect.

—John Broadus

Decline of spiritual life activity in the churches is commonly accompanied by a lifeless, formal, unfruitful preaching, and this partly as cause, partly as effect. On the other hand, the great revivals of Christian history can most usually be traced to the work of the pulpit.

—E. C. Dargan

Preaching has always been the life-blood of the Christian church. The average preacher spends countless hours in preparing messages and multiplies hundreds of thousands of words in conveying the everlasting gospel. Certainly exegesis of the scriptural text "is the central task of biblical exposition."[5] Technical homiletical concerns with form, structure, and delivery are essential. Warren Wiersbe has well said, "Homiletics is the science, of which preaching is the art, and the sermon is the product." It is a fascinating process by which the preacher moves from the then to the now, striking the preaching arc from the Word as written to the world in which the hearers live. We are not the first to walk on these trails of interpretation and application, and historical reflection provides a very significant and immensely rich perspective on how this has been done from the beginning until now.

Every discipline is well served by historical investigation and reflection. In contrast to industrialist Henry Ford who viewed history as "bunk," philosopher George Santayana well argued that "those who cannot remember the past are condemned to repeat it." Philosophy is enhanced by the history of philosophy. Art and sculpture are enhanced by appreciation of the schools and styles of the past. Theology and preaching need the history of doctrine. It is unimaginable that a preacher can practice his craft for a lifetime without historical references and context. Impatience or indifference to history is a regrettable oversight that will exact a loss in effectiveness and impact in preaching.

Reading the sermons of master preachers humbles us as we survey the high standards of many who have preceded us; realizing that even the best had their own weaknesses and were children of their times encourages us. While we should not read sermons in order to imitate them (or worse, appropriate them), we do find special friends and companions in our own pastoral journey and marvel at the diversity of the preaching which God has blessed. The history of preaching helps us understand the task with which we struggle and agonize every week. We are assisted in our quest for variety and enlightened to see contextualization in action. We garner new insights from familiar texts and glimpse into the wealth of unfamiliar texts. We are reminded of the importance of preaching and inspired by the lives and experiences of others who are part with us in "the royal order of the pulpit."

Some very effective practitioners are intuitive in their preaching and function well without a knowledge of preaching's history. More commonly, however, there are significant advantages to those who will reflect on the craft. They will examine issues of proper construction and the use of the various components of the sermon. They will familiarize themselves with the schools of preaching. A sense of such historical perspective develops caution as we trace wrong roads taken by others as well as provides consolation in our missteps. G. Ray Jordan sharpens the point when he observes, "The fact that many preachers do not diligently study the history of preaching is a major reason for so many failures in the pulpit."[6]

Laypersons as well need the history of preaching. There is no such thing as great preaching if there is not great listening, what Aaron Copeland called "talented listening." Laypersons need to know something of the history of biblical communication in order to reflect in an intelligent and spiritually insightful manner on the current crisis in the evangelical pulpit. Just as the crucial issues in contemporary missiology require reflection on the history of missions (as set forth, for instance, in Kenneth Scott Latourette's massive *A History of the Expansion of Christianity*), so we need broadened awareness of what the Holy Spirit has done in the two thousand years of Christian proclamation. If preaching is as important as we are arguing that it is, then the history of preaching assumes an importance rarely accorded it in our time.

The Importance of the History of the Preaching of the Word of God in Our Time

The fundamental issue is the issue of the truth.
—Carl F. H. Henry in *God, Revelation and Authority*

When the church gives to prayer and preaching their true biblical priority, she is able, under God, to meet the challenge of every generation.
—D. Martyn Lloyd-Jones

I do not envy those who have to fight the battle in Christianity in the twentieth century.

—Marcus Dods

This study advances, then, on the premise of the priority of the Word of God and its proclamation. Our times present some very special and perhaps some unique challenges for the preacher. The prevailing preference for the nonverbal is itself formidable. The average person in the United States receives twenty-eight hundred messages in advertising and general communication daily. The grand revolt against design in science and the runaway river of immorality and indecency in contemporary society make the preacher's task all the more difficult. Christians are enmeshed as well as non-Christians. J. I. Packer gives his opinion that at no time since the Reformation are so many Christians "unsure, tentative and confused."

The corroding doubts of twentieth-century thought have tended to undermine all structures of authority. Mounting biblical illiteracy and an increasingly acerbic struggle for attention confront us constantly as we seek to maintain that Christianity and the Bible are true. The all-too-common caricature of "the Bible totin' Scripture quotin' preacher" is unseemly to many. The pluralistic, multicultural venue of secularism introduces the need for further nuances. Ours is the era of political correctness, to the point of politically correct bedtime stories. The shift from the age of exposition to the age of entertainment injects new strains as the whole fate of reading in the Electronics Age seems up for grabs.[7]

How then has preaching fared in the recent past and how will it fare in the future? We are undeniably in another of those time periods when the basic idea of preaching is being challenged in some quarters, and the call for a minimalist approach comes ominously from many quarters. Some evangelical leaders disparage preaching as only the dessert of the meal. Others totally ignore preaching in the interest of small group experiences and the "meta-church." Some, in the wake of an upsurge of narrative and story, seem ready to toss out doctrine and direct application in total concession to the anti-propositional and anti-authority mood of modernity.[8] Clearly, some in the church are in an illicit affair with secular culture. The emphasis on marketing and management seems to hold sway over those who have not already been seduced by psycho-babble, and the result, as David Wells observes, has been "the virtual collapse of biblical preaching in the contemporary church."[9]

Evidence does exist of a paradigm shift underway in evangelical preaching from text-driven and text-dependent preaching to need-driven and market-driven preaching.[10] Some signs in homiletical training programs and recent homiletical publications reinforce the contention that serious attention and dialogue-in-depth are needed right now as we consider where we are and where we ought to go. There has never been a time when we had a greater need for the perspectives and patterns that can be drawn from the history of biblical preaching. In that interest and with that concern, we commence our journey into the fascinating and exciting terrain that looms before us.

1. N.B. the two thought-provoking volumes by David F. Wells: *No Place for Truth* (Grand Rapids: Eerdmans, 1989) and *God in the Wasteland: The Reality of Truth in a World of Fading Dreams* (Grand Rapids: Eerdmans, 1994).
2. James D. Smart, *The Strange Silence of the Bible in the Church* (Philadelphia: Westminster, 1970).
3. Peter L. Berger, *A Rumor of Angels: Modern Society and the Rediscovery of the Supernatural* (Garden City: Doubleday, 1969).
4. John R. W. Stott, *The Contemporary Christian: Applying God's Word to Today's World* (Downers Grove, Ill.: InterVarsity Press, 1992), 208.
5. Elliott E. Johnson, *Expository Hermeneutics: An Introduction* (Grand Rapids: Zondervan, 1990), 154.
6. G. Ray Jordan, *You Can Preach* (New York: Revell, 1951), 46.
7. Neil Postman, *Amusing Ourselves to Death: Public Discourse in the Age of Show Business* (New York: Penguin, 1985); and Sven Birkerts, *The Gutenberg Elegies: The Fate of Reading in an Electronic Age* (Boston: Faber and Faber, 1994).
8. Marsha G. Witten, *All Is Forgiven: The Secular Message in American Protestantism* (Princeton, N.J.: Princeton University Press, 1993) which states that based on a study of sermons by preachers in a number of denominations there is widespread cashiering of God's wrath and the need for repentance in preaching today and that God is in fact being refashioned and the message being made more palatable for complacent, comfortable hearers. Here is prima facie evidence of the ascendancy of the therapeutic gospel.
9. David F. Wells, *God in the Wasteland,* ibid., 196.
10. Gerald L. Nelson in a most significant Doctor of Ministry project for which I was mentor, shares the empirical data, cf. Preaching: A New Model for the Twenty-First Century (Deerfield, Ill.: Trinity Evangelical Divinity School, 1994).

CHAPTER ONE

The Gestation Period of Biblical Preaching

Your word, O LORD, is eternal; it stands firm in the heavens.
—Psalm 119:89

The LORD is faithful in all his words, and gracious in all his deeds.
—Psalm 145:13b (NRSV)

Every word of God is flawless; he is a shield to those who take refuge in him. Do not add to his words, or he will rebuke you and prove you a liar.
—Proverbs 30:5–6

The underlying metaphor in this study of the history of preaching is that, as several have suggested, preaching is more like birthing babies than it is like building buildings. A high view of Scripture requires a high view of preaching. The Second Helvetic Confession boldly says: *Praedicatio verbi dei est verbum dei* ("The preaching of the Word of God is the Word of God"). That is to say, to the degree that a sermon says what the Word of God says, that sermon is the Word of God. And thus, as the Word of God is "living and powerful," so the sermon should partake of that same vitality and liveliness through the Holy Spirit. There is order, structure, and architectonic balance to a sermon as there is to a building, but this form must be made alive through the life-giving Spirit.

In applying the metaphor of birth to the history of preaching, we may well ask a pregnant question: what is the genetic background of the preached word? What are the biblical genes and chromosomes that shape and determine the sermonic outcome? What is the spiritual DNA that makes the sermon what it is supposed to be?

Strangely, many treatments of the history of preaching succumb to a Marcionite attitude toward the Old Testament or at least ignore two thirds of the Bible. Christian proclamation has an Old Testament ancestry. The genealogy of preaching, like the genealogy of our Savior, can be traced through the Old Testament. Christ and the apostles were heirs to a legacy in communication. There is a primary tradition to which they and we are greatly indebted. A careful review of the Old Testament yields critical precedents and crucial preparation for the later development of preaching.

1.1 THE INITIATIVES OF THE SPEAKING GOD

My hand has made both earth and skies and they are mine. Yet I will look with pity on the man who has a humble and a contrite heart, who trembles at my word.

—Isaiah 66:2 (TLB)

I would have him take the best and most irrefragable of human theories, and let this be the raft on which he sails through life—not without risk, as I admit it, if he cannot find some word of God which will more surely and safely carry him . . .

—Plato's *Phaedo,* 85

In the past God spoke to our forefathers through the prophets at many times and in various ways.

—Hebrews 1:1a

Presume upon the veracity of God. . . .

—John Calvin

The God of the Bible is a speaking God. We read in Genesis 1 of the Creator of all that "God said," "God saw," "God called," and "God blessed." The triune God has from all eternity been in conversation within the mysterious counsels of the Godhead (Gen. 1:16; 11:7). Humankind as created in the image of God are likewise communicating beings. Everything in the history of preaching hinges on the univocal point of contact between God and humankind by virtue of the *imago dei*.

As God thinks, speaks, and acts so do we, although we exist on a finite and limited plane. God made our minds to work in an organized way according to thought patterns. After all, Greek philosophers did not invent the law of contradiction without which meaningful communication cannot take place. Thoughts consist of words. There cannot be thoughts without words anymore than there can be music without notes. Helen Keller, the deaf and blind woman who mastered so admirably the various aspects of discourse, maintained that a wordless thought is impossible.

That propositions may be true or false is a critical foundation for civilization and civil discourse. Truth is ultimately correspondence to the mind of God. J. G. Hamann, the German philosopher who was converted to pietistic Christianity (1730–88), vehemently argued that "Where there is no word, there is no reason—and no world."[1] For Hamann, if there is no text, there is nihilism. The three pounds of gray matter we call the brain are like a computer with experience, making new synapses to appear. Professor Pinker is certainly right at this point when he urges that "the language instinct is innate and universal, and that all human beings can, from a very early age, express themselves with more or less equal skill, unless they incur brain damage."[2] Indeed Professor Shevoroshkin of the University of Michigan is leading many linguists in search of the original "mother tongue" out of which all five thousand human languages have sprung.[3] The divine origin of speech steadies us gyroscopically in a time of the depreciation of words when images seem more attractive than ideas. The French social critic and philosopher Jacques Ellul characterized our times as the age of "the humiliation of the word."[4]

Preaching can then be called a "word-event." The common Hebrew term for "word" is *dabar* which is used three hundred and ninety-four times in the Old Testament for the revelation of God, and is translated "the word of God" in that familiar phrase. *Dabar* is both word and deed.[5] Words were seen as actions and God's word as powerful and proactive (Isa. 55:10–11). God's power attaches to the word. Indeed, from the Hebrew *amar* derives the Aramaic *memra* or "word" which is substituted for the name of the Lord one hundred and seventy times in the Targum of Onkelos alone as in Genesis 3:8, 10, and 24 and Deuteronomy 33:27, among other references.

The inscripturation of God's speech can then rightly be called "God's written voice" or "God's voice put to print."[6] Notwithstanding the culturally conditioned nature of language and the noetic effects of sin upon the human mind, language is sufficient to bear clear meaning. This is the assumption of all concourse and commerce. Words cause things to happen. William Safire reminds us of the pragmatic reality, "with words we govern men." Words have limitation even for God. There is, after all, that which can only be described as the "ineffable" and the "unspeakable."

While from the biblical perspective words are an event, we must strenuously hold that divine events and deeds necessitate an interpretive word. As J. I. Packer well argues: "The biblical position is that the mighty acts of God are not revelation to man at all, except in so far as they are accompanied by words of God to explain them."[7] God not only acts but God also speaks. This is the prolegomena to preaching. Preaching is in its essence sharing this word God has spoken.

Clearly, we recognize the primary nature of oral speech and then its complement, the written form of the spoken word. No scholar has been more helpful in showing how we need both the written word and the spoken word than Walter Ong. The word is first the impinging of sound. Ong is correct in insisting on "the strongly oral cast of the Hebrew and Christian Scriptures."[8] "Faith comes from hearing" (Rom. 10:17) is still the fact of the matter. "The air was full of the word of God" is normative.[9] The word needs to be preserved and propagated and hence must be written. But that word needs to be proclaimed and preached. The assertion of primitive orality can only reassure and comfort the preacher.

God, then, is the original proclaimer, and preaching from the beginning is listening to God speak, responding to God speaking, and then sharing what God has spoken. In a time like ours when the notion of a "sermon" often seems suspect and the very idea of preaching passé, we need to be reminded of the roots of the calling. Richard Weaver, the gifted rhetorician, defines rhetoric as "persuasively presenting choices." The title of his lead essay and the volume containing it is suggestively titled *Language Is Sermonic*.[10] The foundation stones of preaching are seen in the nature and character of God and in the reality of words and language as God has graciously given them to his creatures.

---

1. Isaiah Berlin, *The Magus of the North: J. G. Hamann and the Origins of Modern Irrationalism* (New York: Farrar, Strauss and Giroux, 1994).
2. Stephen Pinker, *The Language Instinct: How the Mind Creates Language* (New York: Morrow, 1994).
3. Harvey Hagman, "Tracking Mother of 5000 Tongues," in *Insight* (February 5, 1990): 54–55.
4. Jacques Ellul, *The Humiliation of the Word* (Grand Rapids: Eerdmans, 1986).
5. James G. S. S. Thompson, *The Old Testament View of Revelation* (Grand Rapids: Eerdmans, 1960), 57ff.
6. Charles Fuller, "Preaching and Education" in ed. Michael Diduit, *Handbook of Contemporary Preaching* (Nashville: Broadman Press, 1992), 470.
7. J. I. Packer, *Fundamentalism and the Word of God* (Grand Rapids: Eerdmans, 1952), 92.
8. Walter Ong, *The Presence of the Word* (Minneapolis: University of Minnesota, 1967, 1981), 317.
9. Ibid., 268. Another splendid title by Ong is *Orality and Literacy* (New York: Routledge, 1982).
10. Richard M. Weaver, *Language Is Sermonic: Richard M. Weaver on the Nature of Rhetoric* (Baton Rouge: Louisiana State University Press, 1970), 201.

1.2 THE INITIATION OF PEOPLE WHO SPEAK FOR GOD

My heart grew hot within me, and as I meditated, the fire burned; then I spoke with my tongue.

—Psalm 39:3

They took copies of *The Book of the Law of the Lord* to all the cities of Judah, to teach the Scriptures to the people.

—2 Chronicles 17:9 (TLB)

Hilkiah said to Shaphan the secretary, "I have found the Book of the Law in the temple of the LORD." . . . Hilkiah and those the king had sent with him went to speak to the prophetess Huldah . . . She said to them; "This is what the LORD, the God of Israel, says . . ."

—2 Chronicles 34:15, 22–23

Who speaks for God? The question seems almost too audacious and presumptuous were it not that God obviously calls and employs human beings in the pro-

cess of communicating his truth. God wants to convey sentences and propositions, and he both speaks and writes (cf. Exod. 20:1; 31:18). Human beings in
complicity with God both speak and write (cf. Exod. 34:27–28). Thus from the
very beginning, it is clear that what we call preaching is God's word to humankind, not humankind's word about God.

Even prior to the deluge, two figures are identified from primal history as
spokesmen for God. In each case the delivery of the message was highly confrontational. Of Enoch, who walked with God, Jude tells us (quoting from the
ancient but noncanonical book of Enoch—a practice utilized by others in Scripture), "Enoch, the seventh from Adam, prophesied about these men: 'See, the
Lord is coming with thousands upon thousands of his holy ones to judge everyone, and to convict all the ungodly of all the ungodly acts they have done in the
ungodly way, and of all the harsh words ungodly sinners have spoken against
him'" (Jude 14–15). The four occurrences of *ungodly* reflect the collision course
that this godly man faced with his generation (Gen. 4:21–24; Heb. 11:5). Enoch
did not so much speak words about God as indeed the words that God gave to
him.

Noah, who lived in the same antediluvian decadence, was likewise a person
who knew God personally and intimately (Gen. 6:9). For one hundred and twenty
years he testified to his contemporaries as he built the ark, and is called consequently "a preacher of righteousness" (2 Peter 2:5). Noah's work is not evaluated numerically but in terms of his faithfulness and the practicality of his obedient
construction of the ark. "The days of Noah" according to the words of the Lord
Jesus are seen as typical of the apostasy of the end-time (Luke 17:26–27), but in
all of this Noah preached righteousness and practiced what he preached.

Both Enoch and Noah were exercising the prophetic office, although Abraham
is the first person called "a prophet" (Gen. 20:7; Ps. 105:15). A prophet is one
who authoritatively represents God and speaks God's word. The much-discussed
Hebrew word *nabhi* means "one who tells forth, announces, proclaims."[1] The
prophet is God's messenger or God's herald. The prophet both foretells and
"forthtells." Prophetic utterance is always predicated on the call of God and communion with God (Gen. 18:17ff.). The prophet or prophetess (which are also
numerous in the Scriptures) stands before people because he or she has stood
before God.

Moses must be seen as the model for the whole line of prophetic succession
which includes Jesus Christ (Deut. 18:15, 18; Acts 3:25–26; 7:37). Moses is the
trailblazer in challenging an idolatrous culture (Isa. 45:20–22). John Calvin discerned that the human mind is an idol factory, and this means that from the very
beginning prophetic preaching is conducted in a hostile environment. Moses'
exposition of the divine law laid bare what Richard Mouw has called "a divine-
command morality" which has had rough sledding in modern ethical theory.[2] With
regard to the idols of our culture, the prophet-preacher has the ministry of spiritual interpretation. The promise to the prophet is ever the same: "I will put my
words in his mouth, and he will tell them everything I command him" (Deut.
18:18b).

In the Balaam cycle we see, among many interesting phenomena, a donkey to which speech is given (Num. 22:28ff.). Our inadequacies do not stymie our great enabling and empowering God. Balaam himself becomes the prototype of the false prophet who is mostly interested in profit, who sells out (cf. Num. 31:8, 16). Balaam is presented as both poet and orator, the master of blessing and cursing (Num. 22–24). Balaam spoke under divine endowment but ultimately would not pay the price for acting as God's prophet (2 Peter 2:15–16; Jude 11b). Undeniably the purpose of those who share the "oracles of God" (the *oi logoi*), is not primarily to help people with their problems, it is to speak for God who is ultimately the only help. Human beings "have been entrusted with the very words of God" (Rom. 3:2).

Early on Moses was very uneasy about his speaking role (Exod. 6:12; 7:1ff.).[3] Was this the result of immense discouragement with the children of Israel or an unrealistic feeling of inferiority? It is hard to say, but certainly Moses developed and grew in his communicative skills as one of whom it was later said, "Moses was educated in all the wisdom of the Egyptians and was powerful in speech and action" (Acts 7:22). Nowhere do we see this more strikingly than in Moses' valedictory address, which we know as Deuteronomy. The book of Deuteronomy is in point of fact a series of sermons. In his superb commentary on Deuteronomy, J. Ridderbos shows how "the reminiscences and the exhortations give the book the character of a sermon."[4] Here we have a series of discourses calling the people of God back to covenant renewal.

The rediscovery of this lost book in the days of young King Josiah and its reading and interpretation by the prophetess Huldah led to one of the most remarkable spiritual awakenings in the history of God's ancient people (cf. 2 Chron. 34:14ff.). To be sure, the Bible gives us many examples of effective speaking such as Judah pleading for Benjamin before Joseph (Gen. 44) or Jotham's brief speech which is essentially secular in content (Judg. 9). When we read Joshua's two farewells, ponder Nathan's dramatic appeal to David, marvel at David's eloquence in the Psalter, or consider Solomon's address at the Dedication of the Temple, we are standing again in the tradition of the God-intoxicated discourse of Moses as he bid the children of Israel farewell.

Although we shall deal extensively with the New Rhetoric in succeeding chapters, it is necessary to call attention to more recent trends in Old Testament study which have emphasized the rhetorical tenor of much of the Old Testament materials. In his work *The Great Code,* Northrop Frye demonstrates that the essential idiom of the Bible is oratorical. That is to say that the Bible has an oral and linear quality.[5] The resurgence of interest in literary criticism and rhetorical criticism has reinforced the declamatory and suasive aspects of the biblical material.[6]

In his epochal work, *The Pentateuch as Narrative,* John Sailhamer calls us boldly to the text of Scripture.[7] His work shows the striking literary and verbal parallelisms; the word plays; the numerical symbolism; the mixture of narrative and instruction; and the chiastic coordination—all of which buttress the essential unity of the five books and support the literary and rhetorical nature of the basic materials. In his similar argument for the evidence of the skilled storyteller in 1 and 2 Chronicles, Sailhamer shows how, for instance, 2 Chronicles 36:14–21 is a sermon, emphasizing how "the LORD, the God of their fathers, sent word to them through his messengers" (2 Chron. 36:15).[8]

These earliest preachers, in whose succession preachers of today truly stand, were mostly occasional preachers or messengers of God. Before the coming of the canonical or writing prophets, we see prophetic mountain peaks when Elijah or Elisha spoke for God with great drama and the corroboration of mighty signs. Spurgeon was right in saying that good preaching is always controversial; it must always face up to our accommodationist habits. Then there are undulating valleys as in the times described in 1 Samuel 3:1, "In those days the word of the LORD was rare; there were not many visions."

The persons who speak for God are in the category of witness. Indeed the Lord Jesus is called "the faithful witness" (Rev. 1:5; 3:14). Scripture warns about the false witness (Deut. 19:16; Prov. 6:14; 19:5, 28; 21:28, etc.). We are to bear witness and "a truthful witness does not deceive" (Prov. 14:5). Indeed "a truthful witness gives honest testimony" (Prov. 12:17). We are accountable in our witness to the Lord who ponders the heart and who weighs the spirits.

At the conclusion of his masterful survey of the pursuit of happiness, the teacher or preacher *(Koheleth)* in the book of Ecclesiastes describes his procedure. He writes, "Not only was the Teacher wise, but also he imparted knowledge to the people. He pondered and searched out and set in order many proverbs. The Teacher searched to find just the right words, and what he wrote was upright and true. The words of the wise are like goads, their collected sayings like firmly embedded nails—given by one Shepherd. Be warned, my son, of anything in addition to them" (Eccl. 12:9–12a).

The angel Gabriel spoke the good news as one who stood in the presence of God and was sent to speak (Luke 1:19). The angel in Revelation was "flying in midair, and he had the eternal gospel to proclaim to those who live on the earth" (Rev. 14:6).

This is the familiar track of preachers down through the centuries, even for these, the very earliest messengers of a holy God—an awesome pursuit and a high calling. All of those who to this hour stand in this succession are not so much entitled to their position as they have been entrusted with a legacy.

---

1. Walter Conrad Klein, "Prophecy, Prophets" in Hastings, *Dictionary of the Bible*, rev. ed. (New York: Scribner's, 1962), 802.

2. Richard J. Mouw, *The God Who Commands* (South Bend, Ind.: University of Notre Dame Press, 1990).

3. For a truly rich study of Moses' call, see James Hardee Kennedy, *The Commission of Moses and the Christian Calling* (Grand Rapids: Eerdmans, 1964).

4. J. Ridderbos, *Deuteronomy* in the *Bible Student's Commentary* (Grand Rapids: Regency/Zondervan, 1984), 3.

5. Northrop Frye, *The Great Code; The Bible and Literature* (New York: Harvest/HBJ, 1982), chap. 1.

6. David M. Howard Jr., "Rhetorical Criticism in Old Testament Studies," in *Bulletin for Biblical Research* 4 (1994), 87–104.

7. John Sailhamer, *The Pentateuch as Narrative* (Grand Rapids: Zondervan, 1992); see also my *Telling the Old, Old Story: The Art of Narrative Preaching* (Wheaton, Ill.: Crossway, 1995).
8. John Sailhamer, *I and II Chronicles* (Chicago: Moody Press, 1983).

1.3 THE EXTRAORDINARY INSPIRATION OF THE ANCIENT PROPHETS OF GOD

The Lord said to me, "I knew you before you were formed within your mother's womb; before you were born I sanctified you and appointed you as my spokesman to the world."

—Jeremiah 1:4–5 (TLB)

But who will listen when I warn them? Their ears are closed and they refuse to hear. The word of God has angered them; they don't want it at all.

—Jeremiah 6:10 (TLB)

And I can't quit! For if I say I'll never again mention the Lord—never more speak in his name—then his word in my heart is like fire that burns in my bones, and I can't hold it in any longer.

—Jeremiah 20:9 (TLB)

"Whatever happened to prophetic preaching?" was the doleful lament of an ecumenical preacher nostalgic for the days of preaching on social issues, "debatable, arguable, oppositional, global, national or local societal problems. Nobody gets hanged for talking about pastoral care. But prophetic sermons get preachers into hot water."[1] The tragedy of this kind of "prophetic preaching" in its heyday was not that the preachers did not find a kind of inspiration in the fiery counter-cultural passion of the canonical prophets, but rather that their confrontation was so often devoid of the supernaturally authoritative revealed word from God. One such beacon light apologized to a conference on solidarity with the Liberation Struggle for possibly offending anyone by referring to God in his invocation.

The spiritual Olympians we call the canonical prophets flourished in Israel and Judah during a period of four hundred years of abysmal moral and spiritual disintegration. Of course they are unique and unrepeatable as part of that once-for-all, segmented strand of history in which God revealed himself and his will as miraculously preserved in Holy Scripture. These prophets preached (as John Broadus exclaims, "The prophets were preachers!") under an amazing sense of God's call and authority. They were God's messengers and the "messenger formulas" abound in their recorded utterance—"thus says the Lord" and "the burden of the Lord." We do not replicate this role, but we likewise have no word of our own to share but are totally dependent on the biblical repository of supernaturally revealed truth. Thus prophetic preaching is to proclaim God's word as given by the inspiration of God canonically as in their case or to proclaim God's

Table 1: The Canonical Prophets as Preachers

	ethos ηθος—The Speaker	pathos παθος—The hearers	logos λογος—The message
Before the End Pre-exhilic: to Nineveh– **Jonah**	A super-patriot who defied God, then broke contritely under God's chastening hand. Mightily used in preaching (Matt. 12:41), he was out-of-sorts with a compassionate God.	The cruel and rapacious Assyrians and their powerful capitol, Nineveh, were simultaneously the objects of the goodness and the severity of God. God in mercy sends a preacher to warn them.	A real historical situation (as Jesus established, cf. Matt. 12:40f.; Luke 11:30). The rustic, bleached prophet comes striding through the city with his brief message (8 words in English, 5 in Hebrew) of impending doom. The result of this epochal day of preaching was radical repentance.
to Israel– **Joel**	As is not infrequent, we know little or nothing about the messenger; we have but the message. The dating is uncertain. The preacher uses bold and descriptive imagery and makes strong appeal.	An horrendous horde of locusts invades the land and devastates agriculture (chap. 1). "The word of the LORD" through the prophet sees this scenario as symbol of foreign invasion and the Day of the Lord.	An impassioned call for repentance ensues (2:12–17, a genuine and authentic repentance). Promise is given of an outpouring of the Spirit (fulfilled on Pentecost) and description of eschatological judgments and a final invasion of the land at the end of the Tribulation with the assurance of ultimate victory for God's people.
Hosea	A husband and a father in a marriage commanded by God (1:2), but Gomer his wife (like Israel) was unfaithful. He is instructed to buy her back from slavery. His marriage becomes the symbolic illustration of his message.	For sixty to seventy years Hosea addresses the deplorable spiritual and moral decline of Israel. "Israel has forgotten his maker" (8:14). Spiritual infidelity is analyzed and addressed. Baalism is choking the modern church—the gods of the land.	Using powerful figures of speech (especially the agricultural) and lyrical style (along with rhetorical repetitions and chiasms). Hosea preaches chesed (God's loyal covenant love), of a piece with the N.T. disclosure of love. The summons is to repentance (14:1–3) and the promise is restoration (14:4–8). God's love is triumphant over sin—both Paul and Peter pick up on this poignant preaching.
Amos	"The LORD has spoken—who can but prophesy?" (3:8). Amos, from Tekoah near Jerusalem, cared for sheep and had to do with sycamore-figs. The Lord took him and pressed him into prophetic ministry to Judah (7:10–17).	In a time of social and economic transition and upheaval, the rich were getting richer and the exploited poor were becoming poorer. The thirst for luxury, mounting injustice, and spiritual idolatry were objects of Amos' excoriating preaching.	The sermons of Amos (from within the perspective of God's ancient covenant) were a blistering challenge to the festive mood and frothy religiosity of the time. He used sarcasm, irony, and many rhetorical stratagems, "The lion has roared!" The final positive promise of the rehabilitation of the house of David (9:11–14) projects the pattern of a future and permanent reoccupation of the Land of Promise.
Nearing the Abyss to Edom— **Obadiah**	The name *Obadiah* (meaning "the servant of the Lord") was a common name—there being a dozen other Obadiahs in the O.T. We know virtually nothing about this prophet from Jerusalem who has given us this very slender but provocative piece.	This message of judgment is directed to the Edomites, descendants of Esau, who lived in Mt. Seir, south of the Dead Sea, and whose chief fortified city was Sela (later called Petra). Dated in relationship to some sack of Jerusalem earlier or later.	Snug and proud in their impregnable fortress, Edom watched Judah's discomfiture with glee. Using a typical messenger formula (v. 1) the prophet launches a scathing exposé of Edom's pride and arrogant self-sufficiency. The doom of Edom presages the eschatological Day of the Lord. The prophecy about the coming messianic kingdom is embedded in the text (v. 17) and is consistent with the general representation in all the prophets.

to Judah–

	ethos ηθος—The Speaker	pathos παθος—The hearers	logos λογος—The message
Isaiah	Isaiah, the prince of the prophets, lived in and around Jerusalem. When King Uzziah died after 52 years of rule, Isaiah had a transforming vision and call (chap. 6). His wife was a prophetess (8:3) and his children had symbolic names. He is called "the evangelical prophet."	Isaiah's sermons were addressed to kings and the common people. There is much political and diplomatic intrigue. The themes of holiness, the remnant, and Immanuel—the child King, virgin-born, who will save and rule—are oratorically directed to the hearers.	The prophet's theme is "salvation is of the Lord," which is the meaning of his name. Chapters 1–39 are heavy with indictment of Judah's neighbors and of Judah herself for spiritual declension in a time of great prosperity. Chapters 40–66 contain the messianic servant songs and speak with great specificity of Messiah's substitutionary death. The sermons conclude with a magnificent vignette of the perfected kingdom of God.
Micah	While Isaiah impacted the Jerusalem area, Micah reached a rural area in the same time-frame. "The word of the LORD came to him" (1:1). He spoke in the Spirit—"I am full of power by the spirit of the LORD" (3:8). A sensitive and feeling person (1:8–9), he knew loneliness and desolation for God.	Ministering during the tenure of three kings (one strong, two weak), he spoke of Jerusalem's destruction (2:6–7) and diagnosed the injustice, oppression of the poor, and spiritual apostasy that made it inevitable. Assyria besieges Jerusalem as a foreshadowing of what is coming.	His style is exquisitely ordered and compact. His sermons included judgment oracles and a great prophetic oracle that envisioned the coming of the child from Bethlehem who would shepherd the remnant and the nations (5:2–4). Exposition of what God requires (6:8) is coupled with a magnificent cameo of God's forgiving mercy (7:19). God spoke, yet Judah would not hear. This is always the preacher's grief.
Nahum	Nahum ("full of comfort"), a "village prophet" from Elkosh (1:1), probably in Judah. His work may date about 654 B.C. Bishop Lowth spoke of Nahum's "sublimity, ardor, and daring style." Some of the best poetry in the O.T.—used vivid language and "photographic description." Both assonance and alliteration.	Written to encourage God's people about the fate of Nineveh, "the bloody city," which did fall in 612 B.C. Insisting on the unswerving justice of God, Nahum's objective is to focus on God and foster faith in him (1:7). This is ever the source of comfort and consolation for the people of God.	The prophecy commences with a victorious ode celebrating the Lord's mighty power. The last two chapters describe the destruction of Nineveh. Dr. Walter Maier's peerless study identifies 22 specific prophetic predictions made by Nahum, everyone of which was literally and historically fulfilled. Elaborate archaeological evidence is cited to demonstrate the extraordinary accuracy and precision with which the prophet wrote and spoke.
On the Edge			
Habakkuk	Habakkuk has been called "the man with honest questions." He lived at "wit's end corner," and sought out God i"the watchtower (2:1). The posture must be "the just living by faith" (2:4)—a jewel picked up both by Paul in Romans and Galatians and in Hebrews. The principle is age-abiding.	Not sermons to others—"the private journal of a confused preacher." His problem is the "problem of history." How can a Holy God (1:13) tolerate and countenance such a wicked world power as Babylon? The taunt song of five "woes" directed shows the ultimate outcome of judgment for the oppressors.	As is always the case, an understanding and compassionate God speaks to the doubting and despairing prophet. God seeks to help him to understand the situation. The consequence is the outpouring of prayer (3:1–19) climaxing in a triumphant and confidence-exuding song of praise! Habakkuk 3:16–19 was John Newton's sermon text for his wife's funeral. The emergence of confidence and poise is a most beautiful and bracing example of the Lord's address to our needs.

Zephaniah	Probably the first prophet to speak after the wicked reign of Manasseh (before the renewal in the days of Josiah in 621 B.C.). Seemed to be a resident of Jerusalem from a respected old family (1:1). Possibly a religious official, he draws on Psalms, Amos, and Isaiah. One of the most neglected of the prophets in the O.T.	Manasseh and his son Amon were so desperately depraved. Then most unexpectedly King Josiah sought after God. And with the recovery of the Word of God (Deuteronomy) there was a great turning to God and the celebration of the greatest Passover since the days of Samuel (2 Chron. 35:18).	As a contemporary of Jeremiah, Zephaniah is facing impending judgment. He shares judgment speeches ever with an eye toward the ultimate Day of the Lord, in the light of which he calls to repentance. He closes with an upbeat projection of the perfected kingdom of God and its great joy: "He will rejoice over you with singing" (3:17). Ellison well argues: "Judgment on Israel is always linked, explicitly or implicitly, with ultimate restoration and blessing."
Jeremiah	Called "the prophet who wouldn't quit," from a family of priests living at Anathoth; for fifty years lived out his divine call (chap. 1). His "confessions" show his deep struggles (chap. 20). Aspects of his life and ministry have resemblance to Jesus (Matt. 16).	Jeremiah preached a series of sermons (as in the temple gate in chap. 7) that warned Judah of her spiritual decline and danger. He was imprisoned as a traitor and was a witness to the destruction of Jerusalem (cf. Lamentations). He was kidnapped and taken to Egypt where he died.	Contending with false prophets and faithless kings (to say nothing of a fickle populace), Jeremiah spoke of the perpetuity of God's ancient people and the glories of the new covenant (chap. 31). Biography and prophecy blend beautifully. His figures are poignant—"breakup your fallow ground," "circumcise your hearts," "broken cisterns," etc. He has given our language the word "jeremiad," which refers to a doleful and passionate lament.
Out of the Depths Exilic:			
Ezekiel	Ezekiel, from an old priestly family, was taken into exile in 597 B.C. (when he was 25, cf. 1:1). He was called to be God's spokesman to the captives in Chebar in the context of a visit by the throne-chariot of the Lord (chaps. 1–3). He spent the balance of his life and ministry with the exiles. He lived and spoke God's message.	Ezekiel showed the exiles why God judged Judah (chap. 8). He pressed their responsibility for their plight (chap. 18). Six months after the destruction of Jerusalem, the news came to Chebar (586 B.C.), but he had previously disclosed it in connection with his wife's death (25:15–24). Ezekiel used many visuals and symbolic acts in his communication.	Along with indictments of the nations and of the false shepherds of Judah (chap. 34), Ezekiel shares concerning the ultimate restoration to the land (chaps. 35–36), the physical and spiritual resurrection of God's people (chap. 37), various enemies and battles of the end-time (chaps. 38–39), and the millennial temple in a radically reconfigured Holy Land (chaps. 40–48). The visions of this "mystic" among the prophets are dazzling. He speaks of Job, Noah, and Daniel—among others.
Daniel	Daniel as a youth went into Babylonian captivity where he took a principled stand (1:8); interpreted the king's dream (chap. 2). He outlasted the Babylonians and persisted in a leadership role into Persian hegemony. He was a man of unflinching prayer (chaps. 6, 9–10). As far as we know he never returned home to eretz Israel.	Objectionable to critics because of his true prophecy and apocalyptic material, Daniel is endorsed by Jesus (Matt. 24) and by Hebrews (chap. 11). While not directly addressing his people, his testimony is to the glorious victory and rule of the sovereign God—the wild beasts are overcome in the coming of the Son o' Man (chap. 7).	Chapters 1–6 give narratives from Daniel's life and times; chapters 7–12 share prophetic vistas of near-range (chaps. 8, 11—Antiochus Epiphanes) and far-range (chap. 7—the coming of the kingdom, chap. 9—a great chronological prophecy of the Messiah, chap. 12—the final events of space-time history). The N.T. (particularly Revelation) draws heavily on Daniel. The seven-year time interval, in two 3 1/2 year periods (corresponding to 42 months and 1,260 days), is the backbone of both books. The last chapter is replete with a magnificent promise of resurrection and an ominous warning.

	ethos ηθος—The Speaker	pathos παθος—The hearers	logos λογος—The message
Prisoners of Hope Post-exilic: **Haggai**	Called simply "the prophet" in 1:1 and in Ezra 5:1; 6:14. Among the remnant in 520 B.C. who had to face the unfinished temple. Publicly proclaimed God's Word—four of his sermons preserved (chap. 1; 2:1–9; 2:10–19; 2:20–23). God stirred the hearts of his people—the temple was rebuilt.	Conditions for the remnant were at low-ebb—returning home in 538 B.C. and laying the foundation of the new house—but distracted by a poor economic situation, their own selfish pursuits, and paralyzed by despair, the temple project languished. Some verses have poetic form.	Only two chapters and thirty-eight verses, Haggai preaches to the issue of priorities. Baldwin cites his favorite imperatives: consider (1:5, 7; 2:15, 18), take courage (2:4). Referred to earlier prophets and an apt metaphor (1:6e) as well as a dialogical illustration (2:10–12). The temple was rebuilt and dedicated in 516 B.C. a momentous little fragment. An eschatological overlay looks forward to the time when the Lord shakes heaven and earth, sea and dry land (2:6).
Zechariah	A book of visions from Zechariah, grandson of Iddo, a priest (1:1). Seems to have had a longer ministry than Haggai. The people needed to repent (1:1–6), needed to fast for God, not themselves (7:6). In the early section (chaps. 1–8), we have eight visions. The prophet is instructed to "cry out" (1:14). He does so.	Like Haggai he seeks to encourage the builders to the temple and looks forward to the Day of the Lord. There were tensions in the vassal province, external and internal. Both the high priest Joshua and the civil leader Zerubbabel faced challenge (chaps. 3–4). Haggai was practical—the man of action; Zechariah was the visionary. He shares his burdens for the future (chaps. 9–14).	Jerome wrote: "The most obscure and the longest of the Twelve . . .". Quoted most in the passion narratives and with 9–14 apocalyptic, very influential on Revelation. Seventy quotes or allusions in N.T. Some scholars see chiastic structure in 9–14. He depicts the coming of God's King in contrast to Alexander the Great (9:1–10). But God's Shepherd is rejected (11:4–17). The prophet describes how the enemy will besiege Jerusalem in the end, how God's people will repent when they confront the One who is pierced (12:10), and how the Lord will come in power and glory to the Mt. of Olives (14:1–15).
Malachi	Malachi ("my messenger" or "my angel") is probably a title for the anonymous prophet, not a proper name. The last of the canonical prophets moved in temple circles during or just after Nehemiah's time. His prophecy is termed an oracle or burden for Israel (1:1; as Zech. 9:1; 12:1). Short sentences and direct style.	The post-exilic community was disillusioned. High expectations were not realized; religion was a dull routine. The people were adrift in uneventful times. "Generations were dying without receiving the promises—Hebrews 11:13—many were losing their faith" (Baldwin). Uses disputation—quoting his antagonists and giving answers. Gives 47 first-person addresses from the Lord to Israel.	The over-arching theme is "God's unchanging love" (Kaiser). The sermonic sections treat their relationship to God, the quality of their worship, matters of marriage and divorce, the issue of justice, the practice of tithing, honoring God, and serving him. In all of this he summons the people to truly seek God in a context of God's love ("I have loved you"). Malachi emphasizes divine protection for God's people in a day of judgment (3:13–4:3). God's day is coming. The final plea for repentance comes in the setting of the prophecy of Elijah's coming prior to the final spasm of the time-space history.

word as given through the illumination of the word written through the agency of the Holy Spirit. (Some too facilely equate the prophetic office with the preaching office of today. We shall address that question when we consider the relationship of the prophetic gift in the primitive church to preaching.)

Very clearly the vitality of this prophetic tradition is virtually without parallel and without analogy as Leon Wood argues in his substantive work on the prophets.[2] Micah, Isaiah's country contemporary, laid bare the spiritual dynamic of prophetism: "But as for me, I am filled with power, with the Spirit of the Lord, and with justice and might, to declare to Jacob his transgression, to Israel his sin" (Mic. 3:8). The fundamental reliance of all who speak for God is reiterated again and again in the Old Testament (cf. 1 Sam. 10:10; 19:23; 2 Chron. 15:1ff.; 20:14; Ezek. 2:2; 3:12, 14; 37:1ff.; Neh. 9:30; Zech. 4:12; 7:1).

The prophets in faithfully representing God's message of judgment and grace used rational discourse. If they were among us today, they would not join those who denigrate rational consistency, empirical verification as a test of truth, or the valid if limited benefits of general or natural revelation. Even so, the prophets were not image poor but used symbolic acts and object lessons, that is to say "visuals."[3] They were not only concerned to communicate the insights God gave them but to make them clear, compelling, and convincing. Rhetorical criticism has assisted us in appreciating the attention given to form in discourse. What James Muilenberg, the father of rhetorical criticism, termed "structural patterns," are to be seen in remarkable diversity. Thus from the very outset of the history of preaching, we see precedent for attention to effective form as being an important and necessary ally of right content.

Just as the Psalter contains seven alphabetical psalms and two partially alphabetic psalms (for communicative and mnemonic reasons), so we see such devices as inclusio and clusters used extensively in Isaiah. We discern chiasms in Jeremiah.[4] Rhetorical components shape the parts and the whole of discourse. Concern for form can become obsessive (as subsequent chapters will examine), but as in worship, having no form is bad form. The challenge is always to find the optimally beneficial and appropriate form. We are facing the rhetorical nature of biblical theology.

We know very little of "the company of the prophets" and the schools of the prophets that apparently had their inauguration in Samuel's time (cf. 1 Sam. 10:5–10; 19:10). They came more prominently to the fore in Gilgal, Jericho, and Bethel, "the very seats of idolatry" in the time of steepest decline in the northern kingdom (cf. 2 Kings 2:3–7, 15–18; 4:38; 6:1–2). The courageous loneliness of the prophetic role, particularly as the prophets stood against the false prophets—the hirelings, the time-servers, the servile bootlickers—is quite impressive. Micaiah, the son of Imlah, seems to be the first to square off against the false prophets in his courageous stand. "As surely as the LORD lives, I can tell him only what the LORD tells me" (1 Kings 22:14).[5] The free-wheeling, far-ranging address of these venerable pioneers of preaching is remarkable as they addressed the whole nation, the religious establishment, and the civil leaders as a "sinful nation," "rebels," "oppressors," "godless," "drunkards," "faithless," "stupid children," "lusty stallions," and "lying sons."[6]

A recent study of the prophets which is of inestimable value for this endeavor is aptly titled *The Prophets as Preachers*. Author Gary V. Smith effectively analyzes how this ancient preaching transformed people and what it involved theologically, communicationally, and sociologically.[7] Each of these servants of God has a distinctive style and allows us to see his own life's anguish in the process of communication. Isaiah, the prince of prophets, has such a rich series of messianic vignettes and is on the whole quite personally recessive.[8] Jeremiah is psychological and confessional, and Ezekiel is mystical and visionary. Daniel is godly and apocalyptic. Reflect on Hosea's gripping figures of speech, Joel's use of the locust plague, and the oratory of Amos—"The lion has roared—who will not fear? The Sovereign LORD has spoken—who can but prophesy?" (3:8).

Jesus spoke of the preaching of Jonah (Matt. 12:41). God's servant Obadiah launched a scathing indictment against the pride and self-sufficiency of the Edomites. We marvel at the relevancy of Habakkuk's theodicy in his "wit's end corner," and the practical poignancy of Haggai's sermons delivered to the remnant which returned to build the second temple. Each one is uniquely appropriate and effective. These are the forebears and genetic roots of those who now seek to preach messages from God's Word that will be transforming and proactive in the face of our own cultural collapse. Long and loving personal reflection on God's servants, the prophets, will be amply repaid.

Studying Jeremiah is a case in point. His forty years in prophetic ministry spanned some indescribably trying times for Judah, including her capture and destruction. His skilled use of the question and answer pattern, his ability to reach a diverse audience (note the three audiences of Jeremiah 27), his sensuous imagery are all so instructive for us as his message is potent for us. Whether we look specifically at the sermon delivered at the Benjamin Gate, the sermon on the potsherd, or the sermon in the court of the Lord's house, we marvel. His third sermon preached on the subject of "The Temple of the Lord" (Jer. 7) is a classic in communication.[9] But along with his "jeremiads" of denunciation, there was also a broken and compassionate spirit. No wonder that some thought our Lord Jesus Christ was Jeremiah come back to life (Matt. 16:14).[10]

---

1. Richard C. Devor, "Whatever Happened to Prophetic Preaching?" in *Christian Ministry* (July–August 1990), 9; cf. also ed. Earl Shelp and Ronald Sunderland, *The Pastor as Prophet* (New York: Pilgrim Press, 1985).

2. Leon J. Wood, *The Prophets of Israel* (Grand Rapids: Baker, 1979), 674.

3. Elouise Renich Fraser, "Symbolic Acts of the Prophets," in *Studia Biblica et Theologica* (October 1974), 45–53.

4. Jack R. Lundbom, *Jeremiah: A Study in Ancient Hebrew Rhetoric* (Missoula, Mont.: Society of Biblical Literature and Scholars Press, 1975).

5. Several helpful studies of the false prophets include Dwight Stevenson, *The False Prophets* (Nashville: Abingdon, 1960); James Stalker's fourth lecture on "The Preacher as a False Prophet" in his Yale Lectures of 1891 titled *The Preacher and His Models;* and a very poignant address by G. Campbell Morgan on God's rebuke of Hananiah, a false prophet, "The Lord has not sent you; but you make this people

to trust in a lie" (Jer. 28:15) in his *Searchlights from the Word* (Old Tappan, N.J.: Revell, 1977), 247.

6. Otto J. Baab, *Prophetic Preaching: A New Approach* (Nashville: Abingdon, 1948), 24.

7. Gary V. Smith, *The Prophets as Preachers: An Introduction to the Hebrew Prophets* (Nashville: Broadman and Holman, 1994). The whole treatment is superb. Note also "The Prophets as Great Preachers" in Andrew W. Blackwood, *Preaching from Prophetic Books* (Nashville: Abingdon, 1951), 11–23.

8. An example of the positive value of rhetorical criticism is Robert B. Chisholm Jr., "Structure, Style and the Prophetic Message: An Analysis of Isaiah 5:8–30" in *Bibliotheca Sacra* 143 (January–March 1986): 46–60.

9. Especially tantalizing here is John Guest's commentary on Jeremiah in the *Communicator's Commentary Series;* see also on the third sermon, G. Ernest Wright, *The Rule of God* (New York: Doubleday, 1960), 77–92, which he entitles *Security and Faith.*

10. Still my favorite on the prophets as a whole is Edward J. Young, *My Servants the Prophets* (Grand Rapids: Eerdmans, 1952).

1.4 THE INCEPTION OF INSTITUTIONAL STRUCTURES FOR PREACHING

For Ezra had devoted himself to the study and observance of the Law of the LORD, and to teaching its decrees and laws in Israel.

—Ezra 7:10

And all the people listened attentively to the Book of the Law. Ezra the scribe stood on a high wooden platform built for the occasion. . . . Ezra opened the book. All the people could see him because he was standing above them; and as he opened it, the people all stood up. . . . The Levites . . . instructed the people in the Law while the people were standing there. They read from the Book of the Law of God, making it clear and giving the meaning so that the people could understand what was being read.

—Nehemiah 8:3b–5, 7–8

(The Jews) are taught, so to speak, from their swaddling clothes by their parents, teachers and those who bring them up, even before instruction in the sacred laws and unwritten customs, to believe in God the one Father and the Creator of the world. . . .

—Philo

Worship and didactic instruction are always central to the spiritual journey of the people of God. In all time periods, the people of God are to be both doxological and pedagogical. Worship fulfills preaching, and preaching fuels worship. While biblical fact and faith are fundamental to each, the actual structures employed in worship and preaching are historically contingent and relative. With the destruction of Solomon's temple in 586 B.C., the worship cultus had to decentralize.

Although there was a return after captivity by some and the rebuilding of a new temple, many Jews never lived in proximity to the Holy House again, and its destruction in 70 A.D. completed the temple era to this day. Significantly, the prophets in their exposure of the emptiness and hollowness of external ritual by itself seem to anticipate Christ's words about the locus of worship (John 4:21–24), the argument of Stephen in Acts 7, and the Epistle to the Hebrews in regards to the danger of absolutizing time-bound structures.

What is more, the four hundred years between the Testaments were a very turbulent and troubled time for those in the land of Israel as successive invasions upended the familiar stabilities. The Persians yielded to Alexander and the Greeks and ultimately the Roman colossus held power. After Malachi, the last of the writing prophets, the virtual disappearance of prophetism either in the land or in the diaspora occasion produced grave anxiety (cf. 1 Macc. 4:46; 9:27; 14:41).

The advancing waves of Hellenistic influence particularly threatened at times to inundate the frail surviving spiritual fabric. From within and from without, God's ancient people faced what seemed to be insuperable odds and obstacles. In this time-frame, some new structures came into being that more adequately addressed the crisis of decentralized worship and the need for strong teaching. The synagogue is a very strategic test-case, the first in a series, that helps us see stylistic and structural adaptations as necessary but potentially perilous. Since many of us stand liturgically and ecclesiastically in the synagogue-prophet-pulpit tradition rather than in the temple-priest-altar tradition, the rise of the synagogue is critical.

Such examples demonstrate that the authoritative message as given must be contextualized, that is, translated into the idiom and understanding of a given people and situation. Inspired Scripture is translatable and every serious preacher is involved in the process although no two communicators will pursue the process in identically the same way. The Oxford method of translation seeks to give the full idiom, while the Cambridge method of translation stresses great verbal accuracy at the expense of some literary attractiveness. We shall argue in this study that there is not a single informing rhetoric for biblical preaching, but in fact, there are many rhetorical models. There may be and indeed must be adaptations and shifts in many of the culturally conditioned aspects of biblical application (distinguishing between the normative pole which is the Bible and its theology and the relative pole which is culture or context).

Sources on the origin of the synagogue (literally, the "gathering together place") are sparse. The synagogue as such is not in the Old Testament but probably did strike its roots in the experience of the Babylonian exile. Without access to a central sanctuary, the Jews gathered in little clusters for worship and instruction. Had not the Lord promised to be their sanctuary in the nations to which they were scattered? (Ezek. 11:16). Perhaps early antecedents are to be seen in meetings conducted by the prophets for prayer (2 Kings 4:23) and the emphasis in Solomon's dedication prayer on the House of Prayer (cf. 1 Kings 8:27–30, also Ps. 99:6).[1] Ezekiel met with elders from among the exiles while at Babylon (cf. Ezek. 8:1; 14:1; 20:1). What is described so movingly in Nehemiah 8 in the public reading and interpretation of the Word of God reflects the serious intent of the people to hear God's Word.

Synagogue buildings began to proliferate throughout the diaspora. The two essential features were an ark or closet for the scrolls and a raised platform with a lectern for the reader of Scripture and for the leader of prayers. The service consisted of an invitation to prayer and then prayers, the lesson from the Torah (in a three-and-a-half-year cycle with an Aramaic interpretation since few knew Hebrew), a reading from the Prophets, after which someone present would give "an exposition of one or both of the passages,"[2] and then the service closed with the benediction. Actually the synagogue in the dispersion became not only the worship center, but the communal center and the school house for the instruction of children.

The rise of the synagogue has been pivotal for Christianity. When we come to the New Testament, we find thirty-four references to synagogues. The diaspora was far larger in the first century than the resident Jewish population in the land. There were apparently hundreds of synagogues in Alexandria, Egypt, a great Jewish center. By the first century A.D. synagogues were established throughout Palestine with thirteen in Tiberias, and according to the rabbis, four hundred and thirty-eight in Jerusalem.

The centrality of the reading of Scripture and its subsequent exposition are critical since demonstrably, the early Christian believers organized themselves for worship, prayer, and benevolence after the synagogue pattern. Most significantly, the sermon was also for Christ and the apostles very much in the tradition of the synagogue sermon.[3] Those who read the Scripture stood, and those who expounded it sat (cf. Luke 4:16–20). This address or discourse *(Deresha)* was given by a rabbi, visiting dignitary, or some qualified person in the congregation. Edersheim does not overstate the matter when he says, "Jewish tradition uses the most extravagant terms to extol the institution of preaching."[4] Usually at the end of the sermon the preacher would refer to the messianic hope. Fairweather concludes that this "homiletical discourse"[5] could be either thematic or, strictly speaking, expository, the latter being more analytical and didactic.[6]

The words *homiletics* and *homily* are from the Greek and have to do with speaking, discussing, and conversing (for which the Latin is *sermo, sermonis*) although Lloyd Perry has argued a derivation from *homo/laleo* meaning to speak the same thing as (the text). A sermon has always properly been talk about a text just as we see in the synagogue. Sandmel has maintained that even before the first century A.D. the structured homily emerged from random *halakic* (exegetical data) or *haggadic* (applicable data) inquiry connected with the reading of Scripture.[7] In fact *haggadic* material—the folk tales, narratives, and parables used by the rabbi for a text—really represent the "earliest extant synagogue homilies."

A case can be made for some influence of the Greek and Roman rhetorical diatribe on synagogue preaching. J. B. Lightfoot, in his notable essay on "St. Paul and Seneca," argued that since the principal Stoic teachers came from the East, this philosophical perspective had certain affinities with Judaism and Christianity.[8] The Stoic diatribe was a rhetorical genre, a "stylistic convention—an extension of moral sentiment so that the ethos of the speaker may abide in the mind of the hearer."[9] This was in a time when "public preaching was a prominent phenomenon in Greco-Roman society."[10] Cicero used the diatribe as did Philo and Paul. It was deeply embedded in Hellenistic communication. Romans and James reflect diatribal style, and certainly many who used it were not self-consciously aware of their usage. Many have equated the sermon or homily as being equivalent in some senses to diatribe. Certainly the moral sermons of Epictetus were called diatribes.

Surely in this time of immense flux and ferment, we see a virtual explosion of new forms and structures usable by the Spirit of God for the dissemination of the truth of God. The synagogue itself was a revolutionary development, and the synagogue sermon represented the institutionalization of "prophetism." But there were fresh and forceful formative influences that helped propel the Christian gospel out into the Greco-Roman world. When we come to the early pages of the New Testament, we find the synagogue in place and throughout the empire as the launching pad for the tremendous spiritual detonation described in Acts. At the heart of the synagogue worship and liturgy is the sermon, the opening and expounding of the text of Holy Scripture as read.

1. Louis Finkelstein, "The Origin of the Synagogue," in ed. Joseph Gutman, *The Synagogue: Studies in Origin, Archaeology and Architecture* (New York: Ktav, 1975), 49.
2. Bruce M. Metzger, *The New Testament: Its Background, Growth and Content* (Nashville: Abingdon, 1965), 59.
3. The general course and nature of Jewish preaching through the ages is beyond the purview of this study, but a very helpful survey of the subject is to be found in Raphael Levine, "Preaching in the Jewish Tradition," in ed. Ralph G. Turnbull, *Baker's Dictionary of Practical Theology* (Grand Rapids: Baker, 1967), 31–33; a representative Jewish work in homiletics can be seen in Henry Adler Sosland, *A Guide for Preachers on Composing and Delivering Sermons* (New York: Jewish Theological Seminary in America, 1988). Another ancillary thread of more than ordinary interest is the teaching and preaching in the Qumran Community as reflected in the Dead Sea Scrolls, cf. F. F. Bruce, William S. LaSor, and other perceptive writers on this theme.
4. Alfred Edersheim, *The Life and Times of Jesus the Messiah, Volume I* (Grand Rapids: Eerdmans, reprint, 1953), 446.
5. William Fairweather, *The Background of the Gospels: Judaism in the Period between the Old and New Testaments* (Edinburgh: T & T Clark, 1908), 26.
6. Bo Reicke, *The New Testament Era: The World of the Bible from 500 B.C. to 100 A.D.* (Philadelphia: Fortress, 1964), 123.
7. Samuel Sandmel, *The First Christian Century in Judaism and Christianity* (New York: Oxford University Press, 1969), 73.
8. J. B. Lightfoot, "St. Paul and Seneca," in *St. Paul's Epistle to the Philippians* (Grand Rapids: Zondervan, reprint 1953), 299.
9. George L. Kustra, *Diatribe in Ancient Rhetorical Theory,* No. 22 (Berkeley: The Center for Hermeneutical Studies, Graduate Theological Union/University of California, 25 April 1976): 7.
10. Ibid., 38.

CHAPTER TWO

The Glorious Birth of Christian Preaching

Preaching is the supreme work of the Christian minister.
—G. Campbell Morgan

Church history is the history of the exposition of Scripture.
—Gerhard Ebeling

The most urgent need in the church today is true preaching.
—D. Martyn Lloyd-Jones

Old Testament believers who eagerly awaited the coming of the Messiah found fulfillment in the advent of Jesus Christ the God-man. Christianity is Christ. The redemption he accomplished and announced is the moral and spiritual epicenter of history.

The downplaying of the accuracy of the New Testament documents and the historicity of Jesus Christ threaten to become the death knell of biblical Christianity. P. T. Forsyth was on target in his Yale Lectures on Preaching in 1907 when he argued for the historic Redeemer:

All the amateur philosophandering of the hour is fumbling to escape from a historic, positive, evangelical Christianity, and to preserve before God a remnant of self-respect, self-possession, and self-will. But the prime content both of Christian and human experience is the Savior, triumphant, not merely after the Cross, but upon it. This cross is the message that makes the preacher.[1]

Apart from the historic events of Christ's incarnation, atonement, and bodily resurrection there is nothing to preach and no gospel! (cf. 1 John 1:1–3).

Immediately we are struck by the prominence and importance of preaching in the New Testament. Careful studies of the documents indicate 221 references to preaching in the New Testament. The Greek vocabulary to describe preaching extends to thirty-seven different verbs. The Savior himself was a preacher, but he came so that there would a gospel to be preached. His coming into the world and the birth of Christian preaching to communicate his splendor and excellency now become the focus of our inquiry.

---

1. P. T. Forsyth, *Positive Preaching and the Modern Mind* (New York: Hodder and Stoughton, 1907), 71.

2.1 THE PREPARATORY PREACHING OF JOHN THE BAPTIST, THE FORERUNNER

A voice of one calling: "In the desert prepare the way for the Lord; make straight in the wilderness a highway for our God."

—Isaiah 40:3

"See, I send my messenger, who will prepare the way before me. Then suddenly the Lord you are seeking will come to his temple; the messenger of the covenant, whom you desire, will come," says the Lord Almighty.

—Malachi 3:1

In those days John the Baptist came, preaching in the Desert of Judea.

—Matthew 3:1

He must become greater; I must become less.

—John 3:30

What prepares the way for the manifesting of the glory of the Savior is preaching. The prolonged prophetic silence of the intertestamental period is suddenly shattered as angels from heaven articulate messages of climactic fulfillment and as the daring and dramatic preaching of John the Baptizer captivates and enthralls the nation.

2.1.1 The Essential Continuities in the Preaching

And he will go on before the Lord, in the spirit and power of Elijah, to turn the hearts of the fathers to their children and the disobedient to the wisdom of the righteous.

—Luke 1:17

John the Baptist has been called the clasp of the two Testaments. He is the link and bridge between them. Like the fearless prophets of the Old Testament, John comes to declare the Word of God. His methodology, his distinctive dress and diet were doubtless shocking to the stiff and staid, but he broke the "grand and awful silence" with a ministry of proclamation from the edge of the sacred Jordan river to the villages and even possibly to Jerusalem itself.[1] His message, like that of the prophets before him, is explained in that "the word of God came to John son of Zechariah in the desert" (Luke 3:2). His mission was "to call Israel to submit to the reign of God, about to be manifested in Christ."[2] A. T. Robertson says: "The Spirit of God put a live coal upon his lip. The fire burned in his heart. He felt the woe of the true preacher upon him if he did not speak. He had to speak even if no one heard."[3]

---

1. Carl H. Kraehling, *John the Baptist* (New York: Scribner's, 1951), 64.
2. Alfred Edersheim, *The Life and Times of Jesus the Messiah* (Grand Rapids: Eerdmans, 1953), 1:270.
3. A. T. Robertson, *John the Loyal: Studies in the Life of John the Baptist* (New York: Scribner's, 1915), 34.

2.1.2 THE EXCITING DISCOVERIES IN THE PREACHING

The next day John saw Jesus coming toward him and said: "Look, the Lamb of God who takes away the sins of the world!"

—John 1:29

John stands in the succession of the prophets who went before him, but his was the joyful privilege of announcing, "He is here!" John spoke as "a friend of the bridegroom," and thus he spoke with overpowering joy (John 3:29), but without accompanying miracles (10:41). He proposed genuine repentance as the remedy for the nation and offered baptism to all Jews as an external expression of the heart's contrition (Luke 3:3). Their response was like Nineveh's repentance (Matt. 3:5–6). His simple, direct language and his practical application for religious leaders and others who interacted with him were critical in understanding his impact (Luke 3:10–14). Robertson correctly judges, "His sermons hit the center."[1] Marcus Loane's assessment is also accurate: "The vehemence and violence of his mighty preaching had set the land afire" (cf. Matt. 11:7–15).[2]

---

1. A. T. Robertson, *John the Loyal: Studies in the Life of John the Baptist* (New York: Scribner's, 1915), 92.
2. Marcus L. Loane, *John the Baptist as Witness and Martyr* (London: Marshall, Morgan, and Scott, 1968), 106.

2.1.3 THE EMBLEMATIC LEGACIES OF THE PREACHING

To this John replied, "A man can receive only what is given him from heaven."

—John 3:27

John's clarion call for decision stood in stark contrast with the endless disputes of contemporary Judaism. One critical scholar has strongly affirmed that "John's ministry was essentially a preaching one. . . . The primacy of preaching was thus one of the most marked features of John's ministry."[1] John's was a kerygmatic role, to use Walter Wink's phrase. Even Josephus characterizes John's call for virtue, justice, and piety as given with "great persuasiveness."[2]

John's ministry was not long; we possess less than two pages of the message he proclaimed. Yet the commendation of Christ and the lingering echoes of John's ministry (cf. Acts 19:4) require our underscoring the importance of the character of those who speak for God. We are told that "Herod feared John and protected him, knowing him to be a righteous and holy man. When Herod heard John, he was greatly puzzled; yet he liked to listen to him" (Mark 6:20). John had his dark valleys (cf. Matt. 11:2ff.). Yet he saw Christ as above all (John 3:31), as the coming One "mightier than I," whose ministry is both of judgment and restoration.[3] Who then is the preacher? The preacher is "a voice crying in the desert."

---

1. Charles H. H. Scobbie, *John the Baptist* (Philadelphia: Fortress, 1964), 209–10.
2. Josephus, *Antiquities of the Jews* 18.116–19.
3. Robert L. Webb, *John the Baptizer and Prophet: A Socio-Historical Study* (Sheffield: JSOT Press, 1991), 263.

2.2 THE POWERFUL PREACHING OF JESUS CHRIST THE SAVIOR

In principio erat sermo. ("In the beginning was the Word.")
—John 1:1, Latin translation by Erasmus

No one ever spoke the way this man does.
—the guards in John 7:46

For I gave them the words you gave me and they accepted them. . . . I have given them your word and the world has hated them. . . . I pray also for those who will believe in me through their message.
—John 17:8, 14, 20

Increasing recognition has been given in recent years to the oratorical style of Scripture.[1] The homiletical qualities of the gospel narratives are of special interest to us. But more central is the fact that Jesus Christ, God's only Son, must be seen as a preacher *par excellence*. Teaching and preaching were basic components of Christ's ministry. That "the good news is preached to the poor" is one of the proofs of his authenticity (Matt. 11:5). The apostle Paul summarizes Christ's ministry like this: "He [Jesus Christ] came and preached peace to you who were far away and peace to those who were near" (Eph. 2:17). The apostle Peter speaks of what may have been a ministry of Jesus immediately after his death in his descent into hades: "He went and preached to the spirits in prison who disobeyed long ago when God waited patiently in the days of Noah while the ark was being built" (1 Peter 3:19b–20a).

In what sense is Jesus our model and paradigm in preaching? No one will ever reproduce his ministry because of the uniqueness of who he is and what he came to do. Questions about format and structure of worship services and sermons cannot be answered from the New Testament documents. But what basic principles and patterns may we establish from the pages of Scripture that will serve as a reasonable model for Christlike ministry?

---

1. Northrop Frye, *The Great Code: The Bible as Literature* (New York: Harvest/HJB, 1982), 216.

2.2.1 PREACHING AS A METHODOLOGY OF JESUS

From that time on Jesus began to preach, "Repent, for the kingdom of heaven is near."

—Matthew 4:17

Jesus Christ came into the world "to seek and to save what was lost" (Luke 19:10) and "to serve, and to give his life as a ransom for many" (Mark 10:45). In support of these objectives Jesus utilized the ministry of communication (he preached and taught), the ministry of compassion (he healed), and the ministry of companionship (he made disciples). It is difficult to rank these in importance and impossible to assign appropriate allocations of time. They all are complementary and crucial.

Just as the Gospels all speak of the preaching ministry of John the Baptist, so do they record the preaching aspect of Jesus' public ministry. Christ came preaching and teaching. (The words are used interchangeably, although we shall note the distinctions between *kerygma* and *didache* in the next section; N.B. Matt. 9:35). He used a variety of communicative forms and strategies, but his constant mission was to preach the kingdom of God.

Perhaps the best example of that preaching is the Sermon on the Mount (Matt. 5–7). This may be a collection of the sayings of Jesus, given when he sat down and taught as the second and greater Moses. The Sermon on the Mount might well be called the constitution of the kingdom, and ends with Jesus' exhortations to respond appropriately to his message (Matt. 7:24–27). The crowds were amazed by the authority evident in his teaching (Matt. 7:29).

Jesus deputized the Twelve to perpetuate the pattern. "As you go, preach this message: 'The kingdom of heaven is near'" (Matt. 10:7). The task is clear: "What I tell you in the dark, speak in the daylight; what is whispered in your ear, proclaim from the roofs" (Matt. 10:27). Indeed, to receive those whom Christ has commissioned is to receive Christ himself, and those who speak will obtain a prophet's reward (Matt. 10:40–41).

The discourses of Jesus are interspersed throughout the Gospels. Jesus' preaching in the synagogue in Nazareth (Luke 4:14–30) shows us another venue he utilized for proclamation. Both the "law and the prophets" were read in the synagogue. Our Lord's reading from Isaiah 61 is the earliest historical instance of a *haftarah* reading (a reading from the prophets).[1] Jesus had apparently announced a most exceptional Year of Jubilee ("the year of the Lord's favor"). The sermon seems brief, but the clause *he began to say* is in the Greek imperfect, "which could simply mean that 'he was talking to them.'"[2] The engaging move to contemporary application is clear when Jesus says, "Today this scripture is fulfilled in your hearing" (Luke 4:21). The pattern seems to be that Jesus the preacher takes a text of Scripture, reads it, explains it, and applies it. This is biblical preaching, and it was a central methodology employed by the Savior in his earthly ministry.

---

1. Michael Hilton with Gordian Marshall, *The Gospels and Rabbinic Judaism* (Hoboken, N.J.: Ktav, 1988), 45.
2. Ibid., 46. This section from Isaiah is omitted in the cycle of synagogue readings "probably because of its association with Jesus."

2.2.2 PREACHING AND THE MESSAGE OF JESUS

> The Spirit gives life; the flesh counts for nothing. The words I have spoken to you are spirit and they are life.
>
> —John 6:63

Everywhere Jesus went, people crowded around him "listening to the word of God" (Luke 5:1). Again we note a marked characteristic of the discourses of Jesus: "They were amazed at his teaching, because his message had authority" (Luke 4:32). This teaching was always rooted firmly in the Old Testament.

A key premise for Christ was "the Scripture cannot be broken" (John 10:35). John Wenham has masterfully shown that "belief in the Bible comes from faith in Christ," that is, "to Christ, what Scripture says, God says."[1] Jesus constantly quotes from the Old Testament and uses Old Testament narrative as straightforward records of fact. Jesus does not nullify the Old Testament in the "but I say to you" passages of Matthew 5, he deepens and enlarges the message and application because he has supernatural knowledge. Wenham is on target when he asserts, "When the moment came for his ministry to begin, he knew who he was, what his task was and what were the limitations of his human nature. With this authority he summoned his hearers to obedience to his word; with this authority he authenticated the Old Testament."[2]

This base of revealed knowledge in the Old Testament Scriptures helps us to understand why our Lord and the apostles kept underscoring the fulfillment of the Old Testament promises (Matt. 5:17–18). Repeatedly we see passages in the Gospels that make use of the "that it might be fulfilled" formula (Matt. 1:22; 2:15; 4:14; 8:17 and others). The kingdom of God depicted by the inspired prophets of the Old Testament (in both its material and spiritual dimensions)[3] was at hand, and both John the Baptist and Jesus took that prophetic definition as valid and built upon it without negating it. The time of fulfillment has come in Christ (Matt. 11:4–6); the powers of the age to come are breaking into this present evil age (Matt. 12:28; Heb. 6:5).

Jesus warned against the teaching of the Pharisees and Sadducees (Matt. 16:12). In contrast, Christ's teaching was new, and his listeners found it astonishing (Matt. 22:33; Mark 1:27; 11:18). Jesus developed a body of teaching (Mark 4:2) that was essentially the fulfillment of the Old Testament in his own person, life, deeds, sacrificial death, and resurrection.

Jesus speaks of this developing corpus when he says, "My teaching is not my own. . . . If anyone chooses to do God's will, he will find out whether my teaching comes from God or whether I speak on my own" (John 7:16–17). The content of this teaching was the subject of inquiry by the enemies of Jesus (John 18:19).

By the time we come to Acts, the gospel is called "the apostles' teaching" or "the apostles' doctrine" (Acts 2:42). In the writings of Paul it becomes "the faith" and "sound doctrine." This is the message Jesus preached. It has been called the *kerygma* or message of salvation (from "to proclaim," used sixty-one times in the New Testament). C. H. Dodd delineated the content of this heralded message (although he overstated the distinction between *kerygma* and *didache,* as we shall later discuss).[4] A. H. Hunter has instructively demonstrated that the content of the *kerygma* is essentially "Jesus Christ" (Rom. 16:25).[5] So Jesus explained to the disciples on the road to Emmaus, "And beginning with Moses and all the Prophets, he explained to them what was said in all the Scriptures concerning himself" (Luke 24:27).

The *kerygma,* or the gospel (virtually synonymous), is thus "a proclamation containing good news, the good news of an event, the event, the saving Act of God in Jesus Christ whereby 'He has visited and redeemed his people.'"[6] This body of teaching, this received tradition of fact, was first lodged in preaching. The good news is Jesus in his life, death, resurrection, and exaltation as fulfilling the Scriptures and summoning all of humankind to repentance and faith for the forgiveness of sin. This was the foundational message taking shape in the preaching of Jesus and reflected more fully in the preaching of the apostles.

So from the beginning, preaching has never been mere human words about God so much as God's words to humanity. We begin to see the relationship between the living Word (Christ Jesus), the written Word (the Scriptures), and the preached Word. Jesus Christ is himself the preacher above all other preachers, and in his majestic and powerful message we have the prototype of what all preaching is to be.

---

1. John W. Wenham, *Christ and the Bible* (Downers Grove, Ill.: InterVarsity Press, 1972), 6, 12.
2. Ibid., 60.
3. David L. Larsen, *Jews, Gentiles, and the Church: A New Perspective on History and Prophecy* (Grand Rapids: Discovery House, 1995), 11–27.
4. C. H. Dodd, *The Apostolic Preaching and Its Development* (London: Nisbet, 1936).
5. A. H. Hunter, *The Message of the New Testament* (Philadelphia: Westminster, 1954), 25.
6. Ibid., 25.

2.2.3 PREACHING AS THE MEDIUM OF JESUS

The large crowd listened to him with delight.

—Mark 12:37b

Jesus went into Galilee," we read in the gospel narrative, "proclaiming the good news of God" (Mark 1:14); for indeed as our Lord said, "Let us go somewhere else—to the nearby villages—so I can preach there also. That is why I have come" (Mark 1:38).

Even some evangelicals seem surprisingly skeptical about the trustworthiness of the representations made by the Evangelists. For example, some critics question if our Lord himself used the Trinitarian baptismal formula in the Great Commission of Matthew 28:18–20, or was it added later by a redactor? The verbal variations in the reporting of Christ's utterance in relation to the *ipssima verba* of Christ may be variously explained, but we must insist that the gospel report is reliable and true. We may be confident, as Carl F. H. Henry expresses it, "There is to be sure, no reason to question that the writers preserve the thought and teaching of Jesus with singular precision and accuracy."[1] Professor Linnemann rightly laments that "the authority of God's Word is undermined by the systematic exercise of a critical predisposition to reduce the Word of God to literary-theological construction, instead of seeing it as the revelation of our creator and redeemer."[2]

The parable of the sower and the seed in Matthew 13 shows us the importance of the Word of God (Luke 8:11). Here we wrestle with responses to the declaration and dissemination of the message of the Word. The sower and the four kinds of soul-soil show that Jesus carefully considered his audience. The audience criticism of J. Arthur Baird impressively establishes the fact that both Jesus and the Evangelists are concerned about who is being addressed. Several identifiable audiences must be considered: the twelve disciples, the crowd of disciples, the opponent crowd, and the opponents. Fascinatingly, "the Evangelists identify the audience in 98 percent of all the Synoptic logia and in 94 percent of all the Huck-Lietzmann units."[3] The nature of multilayered audiences is carefully spelled out.

The skill and acumen of the teaching approach of Jesus confronts us on every side.[4] Raymond Bailey is right when he says, "Jesus used every figure of speech and literary device imaginable."[5] He used metaphor (Matt. 5:13); simile (Matt. 10:16); hyperbole (Matt. 7:3–5; 19:24; 23:24); rhetorical questions (Luke 6:32; Matt. 6:27; 11:7; 18:12). He asked a total of 168 questions. And what shall we say about the incomparable parables of Jesus? And the double parables? And the allegories? And the visual object lessons? And the epigrams? Conversely, in the Gospel of Thomas we find 114 sayings but not a single story. The pattern of assertion, argument, illustration, and application is persistent in the discourses of Jesus.

Our Lord's view of the authority of Scripture—"You are in error because you do not know the Scriptures or the power of God" (Matt. 22:29)—assumes universals and principles. Biblical preaching is always a blend of inductive and deductive elements, but Christ's lead-in was generally inductive. He moved from the familiar to the unfamiliar, typically using an inductive pattern that began where the listeners were and led them to the principle and universal.

But Christ's preaching is supremely noteworthy not primarily because of his utilization of model technique. "The preaching of Jesus was distinctive for its great themes."[6] For centuries the sublime themes and powerful imagery of the discourses of Jesus have engaged the minds and hearts of young and old, rich and poor, educated and unlettered.

---

1. Carl F. H. Henry, *God, Revelation, and Authority* (Waco, Tex.: Word, 1979), 3:90. For an exceedingly competent treatment of these issues, see Ned B. Stonehouse, *Origins of the Synoptic Gospels: Some Basic Questions* (Grand Rapids: Eerdmans, 1963).
2. Eta Linnemann, *Is There a Synoptic Problem?* (Grand Rapids: Baker, 1992), 15.
3. J. Arthur Baird, *Audience Criticism and the Historical Jesus* (Philadelphia: Westminster, 1969), 33ff.
4. Herman Harrell Horne, *Jesus: The Master Teacher* (Grand Rapids: Kregel, 1964). On the content of Jesus' teaching, see G. Campbell Morgan, *The Teaching of Jesus* (New York: Revell, 1913).
5. Raymond Bailey, *Jesus the Preacher* (Nashville: Broadman, 1990). Analysis of Jesus' style in terms of adaptation, clarity, and impressiveness is revealing and positive; see Samuel S. Pan, "A Stylistic Analysis of Jesus' Teaching as Presented in the Canonical Gospels for Application to Contemporary Preaching" (Ph.D. dissertation, Penn State University, August 1990).
6. Francis J. Handy, *Jesus the Preacher* (Nashville: Abingdon-Cokesbury, 1949), 118. Other classic pieces in this area are Albert Richmond Bond, *The Master Preacher: A Study of the Homiletics of Jesus* (New York: American Tract Society, 1910); T. Alexander Hyde, *Christ the Orator* (Boston: Arena, 1893).

2.2.4 PREACHING AND THE MIGHTINESS OF JESUS

"Where did this man get these things?" they asked. "What's this wisdom that has been given him, that he even does miracles!"
—Mark 6:2b

The Christ we encounter in the gospel record is a supernatural Christ.[1] It is "the genius of the gospels," to use Merrill Tenney's apt phrase, to present in four matchless portraits the Lord of Glory, the God-man. There can be no accounting for his preaching and teaching apart from supernatural endowment. Thus in what we may call "the Bethlehem of preaching," essential foundations are laid for all subsequent preaching. Jesus notes these foundations when he speaks to the crowd about John (Matt. 11:7–19), excoriating the unrepentant cities of Galilee (vv. 20–24). As he is about to extend a tender invitation to the weary and burdened multitude (vv. 28–30), he consults with his Father and refers directly to their unique relationship:

> All things have been committed to me by my Father. No one knows the Son except the Father, and no one knows the Father except the Son and those to whom the Son chooses to reveal him.
>
> —Matthew 11:27

The total reliance of the Son upon the Father must be viewed as a model and a paradigm. This principle is apparent in John's gospel:

> The one who comes from above is above all; the one who is from the earth belongs to the earth, and speaks as one from the earth. . . . For the one whom God has sent speaks the words of God, for God gives the Spirit without limit.
>
> —John 3:31, 34

> Jesus gave them this answer: "I tell you the truth, the Son can do nothing by himself; he can do only what he sees his Father doing, because whatever the Father does the Son also does. For the Father loves the Son and shows him all he does."
>
> —John 5:19–20

> Just as the living Father sent me and I live because of the Father, so the one who feeds on me will live because of me.
>
> —John 6:57

> I am one who testifies for myself; my other witness is the Father, who sent me.
>
> —John 8:18

> I have much to say in judgment of you. But he who sent me is reliable, and what I have heard from him I tell the world.
>
> —John 8:26

> I do nothing on my own but speak just what the Father has taught me.
>
> —John 8:28b

> Though you do not know him, I know him. If I said I did not, I would be a liar like you, but I do know him and keep his word.
>
> —John 8:55

> He who does not love me will not obey my teaching. These words you hear are not my own; they belong to the Father who sent me.
>
> —John 14:24

> If you obey my commands, you will remain in my love, just as I have obeyed my Father's commands and remain in his love.
>
> —John 15:10

I have called you friends, for everything that I learned from my Father I have made known to you.

—John 15:15b

All that belongs to the Father is mine. That is why I said the Spirit will take from what is mine and make it known to you.

—John 16:15

The pattern of dependency is clear. While Christ is unique in his economic subordination to the Father in the days of his flesh, he has marked out the way that the preacher in every age must walk. We shall examine further the anointing of the Spirit in relation to preaching, but surely if the Son of God needed to learn of his Father, how much more do we?[2] Of the majestic discourse of Jesus, no one ever said it more effectively than did John Broadus: "We know that preaching deserves the highest excellence since it is the chosen instrument of the Savior of the world, who himself came preaching."[3]

---

1. Wilbur M. Smith, *The Supernaturalness of Christ: Can We Still Believe in It?* (Boston: W. A. Wilde, 1940).
2. A salutary reawakening of interest in this subject is reflected in Dennis Kinlaw, *Preaching in the Spirit* (Grand Rapids: Frances Asbury, 1985); James Forbes, *The Holy Spirit and Preaching* (Nashville: Abingdon, 1989); Tony Sargent, *The Sacred Anointing: The Preaching of Dr. Martyn Lloyd-Jones* (Wheaton, Ill.: Crossway, 1994).
3. John Broadus, *On the Preparation and Delivery of Sermons* (New York: Harper, 1870), 5.

2.3 THE PROPULSIVE PREACHING OF THE FOLLOWERS OF JESUS

I have revealed you to those whom you gave me out of the world. They were yours; you gave them to me and they have obeyed your word.

—John 17:6

We will . . . give our attention to prayer and the ministry of the word.

—Acts 6:3–4

Those who had been scattered preached the word wherever they went.

—Acts 8:4

The bridal church that Jesus Christ promised to build (Matt. 16:18) was founded on Christ himself, the Son of the living God, and upon the testimony of "the apostles and prophets" (Eph. 2:20). The church came into being through the death and resurrection of Christ and was born on Pentecost in a great outpouring of the Holy Spirit. A vast spiritual explosion occurred, and led to exponential growth that multiplied the members of Christ's body from a mere handful to about one million believers by the end of the first century. Acts 1:8 maps the course of this extraordinary phenomenon.

Energizing this expansion was the Holy Spirit of God (mentioned one hundred times in Acts). Also prominent was the preaching of the Word of God in the power of the Spirit. Roland Allen captures the reality: "The Holy Spirit was given: forthwith the apostles began to preach Christ. They began to preach Christ to those who did not believe."[1]

Many scholars who write about the sermons in Acts are skeptical about the historicity of Luke's report, but our analysis advances on the premise that we have accurate reporting of what was said.[2] Curiously, many secular writers have given greater support to the historical worth of Acts than have many religious writers. But what does Acts tell us about the preaching?

---

1. Roland Allen, *The Ministry of the Spirit* (Grand Rapids: Eerdmans, 1960), 22.
2. Everett F. Harrison, *Interpreting Acts: The Expanding Church* (Grand Rapids: Zondervan, 1986), 24ff. N. B. W. Ward Gasque, *Sir William Ramsay* (Grand Rapids: Baker, 1966) and the whole collection of Ramsay's books and research, which while older, strongly buttress the case for the historicity of the Book of Acts.

2.3.1 The Diverse Threads in the Tapestry

So the word of God spread. The number of disciples in Jerusalem increased rapidly, and a large number of priests became obedient to the faith.

—Acts 6:7

Those who "from the first were eyewitnesses" were also "servants of the word," Dr. Luke states (Luke 1:2). Jesus the great proclaimer becomes the proclaimed. C. K. Barrett is right when he insists that "New Testament Christianity was a proclaimed faith."[1] Acts is full of many kinds and genres of preaching. The Greco-Roman rhetoricians stressed adaptability in discourse. This is noticeable in Acts, where we detect "the necessity of presenting the Gospel in a form which will appeal to each particular audience."[2] Preaching is so prominent in Acts that Bailey goes so far as to say that "one of the purposes of the writer of Acts was to instruct readers in the art of preaching."[3]

In Acts we see instructions to leadership from both Peter and Paul. We have preaching in the precincts of the temple and in synagogues to Hellenistic Jews. We have messages to heathen in the provinces and on the Areopagus to the intellectual upper crust. Paul's speeches at the trial afford us glimpses into proclamation under exceedingly difficult circumstances. So we shall focus on some very different personalities in a variety of situations but all under the unction of the Holy Spirit.[4] Nowhere do we see the need and promise of Christian preaching any clearer than in the narratives of the Book of Acts. Let us examine some of these strands.

Peter as a Preacher

1. Acts 1:16–22. Peter addresses the followers of Jesus before Pentecost.
2. Acts 2:14–36. Keyed to the audience, saturated with Scripture, definite arrangement.
3. Acts 3:12–26. On the occasion of the healing of the lame man; the mission of Christ.
4. Acts 4:8–12, 19–20. To the Jewish leadership. Moves strongly to the person of Christ.
5. Acts 5:29–32. Another response to pressure that moves clearly to Jesus' death.
6. Acts 10:34–43. The great kerygmatic sermon on the house of Cornelius.
7. Acts 11:5–17. Peter's effective message in Jerusalem explaining Caesarea.
8. Acts 15:7–11. Peter's statement at the Jerusalem Council on Gentile salvation.

Stephen as a Preacher

Acts 7:2–53. A new kind of preacher (out of Hellenistic culture). Long historical survey from the Old Testament. Climaxes in salvation. Anticipates the argument of Hebrews.

Philip as a Preacher

Acts 8:4–8, 26–40. Philip preaches Christ to a city and to a solitary listener.

James as a Preacher

Acts 15:13–21. Powerful use of Amos 9 as authority. He speaks of how Moses "is preached in every city from the earliest times." Others besides Christians also preach.

Paul as a Preacher

1. Acts 9:20, "At once he began to preach in the synagogues that Jesus is the Son of God."
2. Acts 13:13–47. To Hellenistic Jews—Jesus is Savior (v. 23); Jesus is King (v. 22); Jesus is the Son (v. 33).
3. Acts 14:8–18. To pagan Gentiles—spoke of general revelation and ended with stoning.
4. Acts 17:15–34. To the Greek intellectuals; cites philosophers and poets; begins with the inscription on the statue. God is Creator. God is Sustainer. God is Judge.
5. Acts 20:15–38. To the elders of the assembly in Ephesus, "I have not hesitated to preach anything that would be helpful to you" (v. 20).
6. Acts 21–26, Paul's speeches at the trial;[5]
    a. on the steps of the castle, 21:27–22:29;
    b. before the council, 22:30–23:10;
    c. before Felix, 24:1–27. Paul shares vivid knowledge of the events.
    d. the appeal to Caesar, 25:1–12;
    e. before Agrippa, 25:13–26:32. The conversion testimony of Paul repeated three times. The messages here "more personal in tone and character."[6]

In the light of this data, Dibelius does not overstate the facts when he observes about Paul, "Preaching was in fact his calling, and with a fine single-mindedness he made it his life's work, everything else being subordinated to it."[7] We turn now to assay the message of the preaching in Acts.

---

1. C. K. Barrett, in Joseph A. Fitzmyer, "Preaching in the Apostolic and Subapostolic Age," in *Preaching in the Patristic Age,* ed. David G. Hunter (New York: Paulist, 1989), 24ff.
2. Maurice Jones, *St. Paul the Orator* (London: Hodder and Stoughton, 1910), 28.
3. Raymond Bailey, *Paul the Preacher* (Nashville: Broadman, 1991), 11.
4. F. Dale Bruner, *A Theology of the Holy Spirit* (Grand Rapids: Eerdmans, 1970). This is one of the richest and most satisfying treatments of this theme in the last half of the twentieth century.
5. Jones, *St. Paul the Orator.* Another important and solid study of this data is found in John Eadie, *Paul the Preacher* (London: Richard Griffin, 1859).
6. Jones, *St. Paul the Orator,* 164.
7. Martin Dibelius, *Paul,* as quoted in Bailey, *Paul the Preacher,* 87.

2.3.2 THE DYNAMIC THEMES OF THE STORY

But the word of God continued to increase and spread.

—Acts 12:24

The object of the apostles was to preach the Word of God everywhere (Acts 16:6). After all, there is no good news unless it is told. They varied their approach to suit their audience.[1] Lake and Cadbury have demonstrated Paul's distinctive style before the Areopagus (his use of neuters, particles, alliteration, repetitions, and various idiomatic expressions).[2] If this is so, the issue yet remains: Was there a common and shared message that, although adapted, did not change?

We have already argued our agreement with C. H. Dodd that there was a defined and identified core of preaching material used by all of the apostles in their proclamation. While there is a distinction between preaching and teaching *(kerygma and didache),* it is generally felt that Dodd overstated the distinction.[3] The essence of the message is Jesus Christ (cf. 1 Cor. 15:1–3). In what seems to be a curious disparagement of doctrinal assertion, Michael Green inveighs against "a fixed *kerygma.*"[4] Granted the variations to which we have already alluded, we are assisted by Mounce's observation that the *kerygma* is "not the outline of a particular sermon" or "a ready-made proclamation that was delivered on every occasion."[5] The *kerygma* is rather "a survey of primitive Christology arranged as such." It is "the theology of the primitive church."[6] Mounce argues well for a pre-Pauline *kerygma* and effectively speaks to Green's concerns. Mounce well concludes that preaching involves the miraculous contemporizing of the Christ-events "and moves the individual to respond in faith."[7]

The unchanging theme of Christian preaching then is Jesus Christ. The Old Testament is seen as promising Christ; the preacher heralds the fulfillment. Building on Wilhelm Vischer's *Christological Exegesis of the Old Testament,* G. C. Berkouwer concludes: "Either the Old Testament is full of Christ or the writers of the New Testament have simply, on the basis of their Christian faith, read Christ into the Old Testament—an undeniable falsification of history."[8]

The discourses of Acts are studded with reference to Christ. Even in the supposedly atypical sermon in Athens, Paul preaches Jesus and the Resurrection. If the Christian were to preach a sermon from an Old Testament text that a Jewish rabbi could preach, then that sermon is not Christian proclamation. The theme of the ministry of the Holy Spirit is ever our Lord, and the theme of Christian preaching under the tutelage of the Holy Spirit is Jesus Christ (cf. John 15:26–27; 16:13–15). If Christ is the only way to the Father, then we are not surprised he is the subject and focus of apostolic preaching (Acts 4:12).

Jesus anticipated the worldwide proclamation of the good news (Matt. 26:13), which we watch take place in Acts. The early believers could not be silenced in their testimony, insisting "we cannot help speaking about what we have seen and heard" (Acts 4:20). Even the remembrance of the Lord in Communion was a proclamation of his death (1 Cor. 11:26, *katangello*). All believers properly shared in the proclamation (1 Cor. 14:26; 1 Peter 2:9). The themes are "the wonders of God," the work of God in Christ, the death and resurrection of Jesus, and the necessity of faith and repentance. The pattern is first vertical—what God has done; then horizontal—what God expects us to do. This is the pattern found in the Epistles, as we shall see in the next section. In the light of these building blocks, we can underscore the contention of John Bright: "The strength of the church lies in the gospel it proclaims—thus in its preaching today. . . . The church lives, let it be repeated, in her preaching—always has and always will."[9]

1. F. F. Bruce, *The Defense of the Gospel in the New Testament* (Grand Rapids: Eerdmans, 1959); Abraham J. Malherbe, *Paul and the Thessalonians* (Philadelphia: Fortress, 1987). Both afford splendid insights.
2. K. Lake and H. J. Cadbury, *The Beginnings of Christianity* (London: Macmillan, 1933), 1:209.
3. Supplying appropriate critique and correction for C. H. Dodd are Robert H. Mounce, *The Essential Nature of New Testament Preaching* (Grand Rapids: Eerdmans, 1960); Jesse Burton Weatherspoon, *Sent Forth to Preach: Studies in Apostolic Preaching* (New York: Harper, 1954); Robert C. Worley, *Preaching and Teaching in the Earliest Church* (Philadelphia: Westminster, 1969). A very helpful study is Everett F. Harrison, "Some Patterns of the New Testament Didache," *Bibliotheca Sacra* 119, no. 474 (April 1962): 118–28.
4. Michael Green, *Evangelism in the Early Church* (Grand Rapids: Eerdmans, 1970), 60.
5. Mounce, *Essential Nature of New Testament Preaching,* 64.
6. Ibid.
7. Ibid., 153.
8. G. C. Berkouwer, *The Person of Christ* (Grand Rapids: Eerdmans, 1954), 129.
9. John Bright, *The Authority of the Old Testament* (Nashville: Abingdon, 1967), 162, 164.

Table 2: Greek Words Used in the New Testament for Preaching and Communication

1. LEGŌ	preaching as "face-to-face direct-personal speech"	John's gospel uses LEGŌ 266 times—emphasizing the spontaneous character of Jesus' discourse
2. LALEŌ	outward utterance, speech, talk	John's gospel uses LALEŌ 60 times, not so much the substance of discourse
3. ERŌ, EIPOV	to say, speak, use language, command	often used in reporting what the Old Testament prophets said, now being fulfilled
4. EUANGELIZŌ	to announce and emblazon the good news	Matt. 11:5; Luke 4:18; 7:22; Acts 8:25; Rom. 1:15; 10:15; 15:20; 1 Cor. 1:17; 9:16
5. KĒRUSSŌ	to herald, proclaim, publish, announce	1 Cor. 1:21, 23; 2 Cor. 4:5. "No appeal without proclamation; No proclamation without appeal."[1]
6. ANANGELIZŌ	to announce, make known, report, rehearse	Acts 14:27; John 16:13–15; 1 John 1:5; Rom. 15:21; Acts 16:38; 2 Cor. 7:7
7. APANGELLŌ	to bring word, to report, proclaim	1 Thess. 1:9; 1 John 1:2; Acts 26:20; Heb. 2:12; Luke 8:34
8. HOMILEŌ	to converse with, to talk with	Luke 24:14, 17; Acts 20:11; 24:26
9. MARTUREŌ	witness, preaching as born of experience	John 1:7–8, 15, 32, 34; 3:26; 5:33; Acts 10:43; 23:11; 1 Cor. 15:15
10. KATANGELLŌ	to announce, to proclaim publicly, publish	Acts 13:5; 17:13; 1 Cor. 2:1 (with the idea of celebrating, commending)
11. DIDASKŌ	to teach, instruct, to give instruction	Matt. 4:23; 9:35; Rom. 12:7; 1 Cor. 4:17; 1 Tim. 2:12; 4:11
12. PROPHETEUŌ	to prophesy, to be a prophet, to foretell	1 Cor. 11:4–5; 13:9; 14:1, 3–5, 24, 31, 39; Rev. 11:3; 1 Peter 1:10; Jude 14
13. PARAKALEŌ	to beg, beseech, console, comfort	Acts 20:2; Rom. 12:8; 2 Tim. 4:2; Acts 25:2; 1 Cor. 16:12; Acts 21:12
14. PRO-EVANGELIZŌ	to announce good news beforehand	Gal. 3:8 (before the event by which the promise is made good)
15. DIANGELLŌ	to tell or announce thoroughly	Luke 9:60; Acts 21:26; Rom. 9:17 (to carry a message through)
16. PROKĒRUSSŌ	to cry or proclaim beforehand	Acts 3:20, 24; 13:24 (to proclaim by herald, cf. kĒrussō)
17. PARRĒSIAZOMAI	to be free in speaking, to have boldness	Acts 9:27, 29; 18:26; 19:8 (n.b. also Acts 13:46; 26:26; Eph. 6:20)

1. Cf. John Stott, *The Preacher's Portrait* (Grand Rapids: Eerdmans, 1961). A marvelous chapter on "The Herald," pp. 33–59.

18. PARAMUTHEOMAI	to address, calm, encourage, console	John 11:31 (also 16:19); 1 Thess. 2:12 (for the purpose of arousing)
19. NOUTHETEŌ	to admonish, warn, exhort, put in mind	Acts 20:31; Rom. 15:14; 1 Cor. 4:14; Col. 1:28; 3:16; 1 Thess. 5:12, 14
20. DIALOGIZOMAI	to bring together reasons, deliberate	Acts 20:7 (Luke 1:29; 5:21; Heb. 12:5), a more conversational word
21. PHĒMI	to make known one's thoughts, to say	2 Cor. 10:10; Luke 7:44; Acts 10:28; 16:1; 1 Cor. 10:15, 19
22. PROLEGŌ	to say beforehand, to predict	2 Cor. 13:2; Gal. 5:21; 1 Thess. 3:4 (PRO may have the sense of plainly)
23. PLĒROŌ	to fulfill, to fully preach	Rom. 15:19; Col. 1:25 (to cause to be everywhere known)
24. AKOĒ	the word of hearing	Heb. 4:2, what is heard by the ear
25. PEITHŌ	to persuade, to convince, to win over	often used of Paul's preaching in Acts (13:43; 17:2–4; 18:4; 19:8, 26; 26:28)
26. DIALEGOMAI	to discourse, argue, discuss	Acts 17:2, 17; 24:12; Heb. 12:5 (preached in Acts 20:7, 9 AV)
27. SUZĒTEŌ	to discuss, dispute, reason with	Acts 28:29 (Luke 24:15; Mark 8:11); Acts 11:29 (examine together)
28. PARAINEŌ	to exhort, admonish, recommend	Acts 27:9, 22 (with the addition of LEGŌ + direct discourse)
29. PROTREPŌ	to urge forward, exhort, encourage	Acts 28:27. From Homer down, but only once in the N.T.
30. GNŌRIZŌ	to make known, to cause to be recognized	Luke 2:15; John 15:15; 17:26; Rom. 9:22; 2 Cor. 8:8; Eph. 3:5, 10; 6:21
31. DĒLOŌ	to make manifest by relating, declare	1 Cor. 1:11; 3:13; Col. 1:8; Heb. 12:27; 1 Peter 1:11; 2 Peter 1:14
32. DIĒGEOMAI	to recount, to relate in full, set forth	Acts 8:33; 9:27; 12:17; Heb. 11:32 (cf. Mark 5:16; Luke 8:39; 9:10)
33. EKDIĒGEOMAI	to narrate in full or wholly, tell, declare	Acts 13:41; 15:3 (cf. Hab. 1:5 LXX), used in Aristotle's *Rhetoric*
34. EXĒGEOMAI	to recount, rehearse, to lead out	Acts 10:8; 15:12; 21:19 (cf. Luke 24:35). To unfold—John 1:18.
35. PHRAZŌ	to indicate plainly, make known, declare	Matt. 13:36; 15:15. To explain—as the thought in a parable.
36. PROSLALEŌ	to speak to or with someone	Acts 13:43; 28:20. Preaching is certainly acoustical as Luther said.
37. PLĒROPHOREŌ	to fulfill, accomplish, to fully proclaim	2 Tim. 4:17, with kerygma (mg. proclamation)

2.3.3 THE DRIVING THRUSTS OF SPIRITUAL URGENCY

> In this way the word of the Lord spread rapidly and grew in power.
> —Acts 19:20

Before us then is the high-density mass of apostolic preaching in Acts, a corpus of sentences and propositions about Jesus the Messiah and his redemptive works.[1] Though they are varied and often contrasting in format and nuance, a common core of fixed truth is evident. The purpose of this proclamation was not simply to inform minds of truth but to transform lives by the power of God. The ministry of the Holy Spirit who is ever "in, with and under the Word" is highlighted.

Peter's preaching on Pentecost is most instructive. Surely one of the most gripping miracles of Pentecost was the boldness and scriptural competence of Peter, who so recently had quailed in cowardice before a servant girl and seemed to be in a fog regarding the crucifixion and resurrection of the Lord. Now he is filled with the Holy Spirit. The narrative describes what happened: "Then Peter stood up with the Eleven, raised his voice and addressed the crowd" (Acts 2:14). In this sermon, as is evident again and again in Acts, the preacher is preaching for a verdict.

Powerful preaching is accompanied by response, both positive and negative. The aftermath is as supernatural as is the utterance itself. F. F. Bruce reminds us, "The worthlessness of the vessels is evidence of the transcendent power which attends the preaching of the gospel, the change which it effects in human lives is God's and not the apostles'."[2] In a most impressive climactic conclusion, Peter affirms the crucified one as both "Lord and Christ" (Acts 2:36). The result is stated: "When the people heard this, they were cut to the heart" (v. 37). The verb *(katanusso)* is strong, meaning to prick or pierce, to sting to the quick, to pain the mind sharply, to agitate it vehemently. This is a fulfillment of Jesus' prediction of the convicting work of the Holy Spirit (John 16:8–11).

We see joined in this sermon and its consequences the total sovereignty of God and the complete responsibility of humans in response. In the call to repentance (in the plural) and in the call for baptism to make the commitment visual and public (in the singular) we see clearly what is involved in obtaining the forgiveness of sins and the gift of the Holy Spirit (Acts 2:38–39). Peter warns and pleads "with many other words" (v. 40). The consequence of his urgent plea, "Save yourselves from this corrupt generation," was the baptism of three thousand persons. The pattern here is with regard not only to the truth conveyed but also to the power energizing the communication and its follow-up. The sermon Peter preached in Solomon's Colonnade after the healing of the beggar closes with the accent on conversion—"turning each of you from your wicked ways" (3:26)—and not surprisingly results in the further swelling of the ranks of those who believed (4:4).

Apostolic discourse is always disruptive and disturbing. It raises questions (Acts 4:15–17). The status quo is interrupted and the messengers become the objects of resentment and anger. "When they heard this, they were furious and wanted to put them to death" (5:33). To proclaim Christ is to enter the spiritual battle. It is warfare. But of the apostles we read, "Day after day, in the temple courts and from house to house, they never stopped teaching and proclaiming the good news that Jesus is the Christ" (v. 42).

Stephen's preaching elicited an even more drastic response. Of his efforts it is recorded, "They could not stand up against his wisdom or the Spirit by whom he spoke" (Acts 6:10). The radiance of his demeanor (v. 15) and the steadfastness of his vision of the living Christ (7:55–56) were part of his impression even on the uncircumcised hearts and ears. If indeed preaching is an extension of the ministry of Jesus, we see a marked resemblance of the servant to his Master in his martyrdom (see vv. 59–60). Jesus himself knew so painfully the agony of rejection and negative response even as Isaiah described it (cf. John 12:37–41).

The preaching of Paul corroborates these findings. Each of the apostle's sermons centers around a single thought, and that thought is invariably Jesus Christ and the redemption he purchased for us. Paul did not preach *like* Jesus, he preached *Jesus*. Like all of the apostolic preachers, Paul sought a faith-hearing and faith-response. (The word *faith* occurs two hundred times in Paul's writings.) The mood of the sermon corresponds to the situation. In this he and John, although so contrastive, are in accord. Paul's theology is a conversion theology.[3] His preaching was part of the eternal call of God to errant humankind (cf. 2 Thess. 2:13–14). Reception and refusal bring us to the drama of the proposal, and in this process we see hearing, acceptance, rejection, learning, obedience.[4]

Paul's preaching again and again rises out of the Old Testament but focuses on the Good News (Acts 14:21). After Paul ministered for three consecutive Sabbaths in Thessalonica ("reasoned . . . explaining . . . proving" [17:1–3]), the house was divided. Some were persuaded. Eadie is right in observing of this effort: "His argument lay in his exposition."[5] In Athens similarly, some hearers sneered, some equivocated, and some believed (17:32–34). We see the same in Corinth, Ephesus, and wherever Paul ministered. The same is true down to this present preaching hour.

Fascinatingly, at the conclusion of Acts (28:30–31), we again have the Isaiah oracle about the hardening of hearts in response to the truth. (It also occurs in Matthew 13 and in John 12.) Human resistance to the truth comes to a point where preaching itself hardens and makes the hearer impervious. But all of this is in the context of the relentless wooing and striving of the Holy Spirit (Gen. 6:3). God will not break down the door to the human heart, but will eternally accommodate those who choose not to welcome him into their lives. And so the Acts concludes with the apostle Paul preaching the gospel in Rome itself. We now turn to study the apostolic understanding and theology of the preaching event.

---

1. One cannot help being impressed with the sheer bulk of this material when examining this data in the pages of Rudolf Stier's massive work, *The Words of the Apostles* (Edinburgh: T & T Clark, 1860).

2. F. F. Bruce, *1 and 2 Corinthians* in the *Century Bible* (London: Oliphant, 1971), 197.

3. See my book *The Evangelism Mandate: Recovering the Centrality of Gospel*

Preaching (Wheaton, Ill.: Crossway, 1992) for a discussion of Paul's own conversion and a conversion theology.

4. Jerome Murphy-O'Connor, *Paul on Preaching* (New York: Sheed and Ward, 1963).

5. John Eadie, *Paul the Preacher* (London: Richard Griffen, 1859), 163.

2.4 THE PROFOUND PREACHING OF THE NEW TESTAMENT WRITERS

"Everyone who calls on the name of the Lord will be saved." How, then, can they call on the one they have not believed in? And how can they believe in the one of whom they have not heard? And how can they hear without someone preaching to them? And how can they preach unless they are sent? . . . Faith comes from hearing the message, and the message is heard through the word of Christ.

—Romans 10:13–14, 17

The Bible is truly the treasury of preaching. It is the document that establishes what preaching is and what it is intended to be. The Scriptures overflow with instructive narratives that describe various kinds of communication used by God. Preaching and testimony persist throughout the Canon all the way to the end of God's great plan as revealed in the Book of Revelation.[1]

Yet narrative does not yield doctrine or theology. Theology is reflection and rigorous rumination on the meaning of deeds and behavior, both divine and human. The Gospels give us the facts of Jesus' suffering and death with a body of predictive prophecy and a few glimmers of interpretive comment (such as Mark 10:45). But it is in the Epistles that inspired interpretation is shared, establishing the vicarious, substitutionary nature of Christ's redemptive death.

We turn now to the wealth of teaching by the apostles as stored up in their Epistles. Here we shall discern the critical understanding of preaching and its place as set forth by the apostolic preachers themselves. The awesome nature of the preaching task is described strikingly by Peter, who says, "If anyone speaks, he should do it as one speaking the very words of God" (1 Peter 4:11).

---

1. A valuable study of one aspect of preaching in Revelation can be seen in Rodney L. Petersen, *Preaching in the Last Days: The Theme of "Two Witnesses" in the Sixteenth and Seventeenth Centuries* (New York: Oxford University Press, 1993).

2.4.1 CATCHING THE IMPERATIVE OF PREACHING

To the New Testament writers, preaching stands as the event through which God works.

—Haddon Robinson

The apostle Paul's preaching came before his writing. Personal and private reading of the Scripture is not enough. That word must be spoken. Selwyn argued that much of the New Testament material was catechetical in nature.[1] Beyond that it may be asserted that many of the Epistles are written sermons or notes of sermons. The epistle of James is a prime example of this. Hebrews with all of its exhortations is surely a sermon-epistle, a blending of exposition and admonition that can be called a homily (Heb. 13:22).

Preaching was absolutely central to Paul. Karl Barth is perceptive when he sees preaching as a language event that is "God's activity, his address to each of us personally."[2] Preaching is the true translation of the text. "The task of the sermon is to make space for the Word of God."[3] This is why Barth argues so strenuously that preaching must be exposition of Scripture, not something lifted out of the Bible, but what the Bible says.[4]

In writing to the Galatians, Paul traces his conversion and call: "But when God, who set me apart from birth and called me by his grace, was pleased to reveal his Son in me so that I might preach him among the Gentiles, I did not consult any man" (Gal. 1:15–16). The gospel is at the core of ministry (1:11). That is why "another gospel is a contradiction in terms."[5] The standard for preaching is the gospel. So we understand that the obligation of the preacher rises out of "the essential authoritative nature of the gospel."[6] Paul solemnly intones, "If anybody is preaching to you a gospel other than what you accepted, let him be eternally condemned!" (1:9).

Similarly in the Corinthian correspondence, Paul makes his prioritization clear: "Christ did not send me to baptize, but to preach the gospel" (1 Cor. 1:17). The great themes are the preaching of the cross (vv. 17–25), the resurrection (15:1–12), and the lordship of Christ (2 Cor. 4:1–6).[7] Consistent with this sense is what A. T. Robertson called "the glory of the ministry—Paul's exultation in preaching." Paul stoutly insists, "Woe to me if I do not preach the gospel!" (1 Cor. 9:16). This necessity and compulsion were supernaturally laid upon the apostle.

In this light a helpful definition of preaching emerges. "Preaching is an act which fulfills the will of the sovereign in a public proclamation."[8] This explains Paul's passion to preach in Rome, Spain, and the regions beyond. He says, "I am so eager to preach the gospel also to you who are at Rome" (Rom. 1:15). He is not embarrassed by the gospel because of its power to save (vv. 16–17).

The Epistle to the Romans is the classic exposition of that gospel. Thus we understand why it is that "the gospel requires the immediacy of the oral voice" of the preacher.[9] Here we face the incomparable privilege, the agony and the ecstasy, of being entrusted with "the ministry of reconciliation" (2 Cor. 5:18). "And he has committed to us the message of reconciliation. We are therefore Christ's ambassadors, as though God were making his appeal through us. We implore you on Christ's behalf: Be reconciled to God" (vv. 19b–20).

In a time that F. F. Bruce describes as "a landslide away from apostolic teaching," the apostle John, writing in 1 John with "conscious authority," summons his hearers back to the "apostolic tradition," and in so doing puts the function of preaching in bold relief.[10] Some have maintained that the theme of 1 John is "the apostolic proclamation of the Word of Life."[11] In the first paragraph of the epistle we see the pattern:

What we have heard . . . we proclaim to you (1:1–2).
What we have heard . . . we proclaim to you (1:3).
The message we have heard . . . we announce to you (1:5).[12]

Thus the message that is eternal life in Christ and its communication are at the front of John's thinking and sense of purpose, as was the case with Paul and should be with all who follow in their calling.

---

1. E. G. Selwyn, *The First Epistle of Peter* (London: Macmillan, 1946), essay 2, 363ff.
2. Karl Barth in John William Beaudean Jr., *Paul's Theology of Preaching* (Macon, Ga.: Mercer University Press, 1988), 3.
3. Karl Barth, *Homiletics* (Louisville: Westminster/John Knox, 1991), 122.
4. Ibid., 49.
5. Beaudean, *Paul's Theology of Preaching,* 69.
6. Ibid., 86.
7. Ibid., 88.
8. Ibid., 153.
9. Ibid., 208.
10. F. F. Bruce, *The Epistles of John* (Grand Rapids: Eerdmans, 1970), 14, 17.
11. Gary Derickson, "What Is the Message of 1 John?" *Bibliotheca Sacra* 150, no. 597 (January 1993): 99.
12. Charles P. Baylis, "The Meaning of Walking in Darkness," *Bibliotheca Sacra* 149, no. 594 (April 1992): 219.

2.4.2 CONSIDERING THE IMPRESSIVENESS OF PREACHING

For what I received I passed on to you.

—1 Corinthians 15:3

The city of Corinth was an intimidating field of ministry for the apostle Paul (Acts 18:9–10). A notoriously wicked seaport (which has given the expression "to Corinthianize" to our language, a synonym for debauchery and licentiousness), Corinth was the milieu for an eighteen-month ministry in which "Paul devoted himself exclusively to preaching" (Acts 18:5). The response led to baptisms and a congregation of notable import. The soundness and legitimacy of Paul's gospel was never at issue in Corinth, but there were those in the assembly who criticized his appearance and his speaking style ("In person he is unimpressive and his speaking amounts to nothing" [2 Cor. 10:10]). This scathing and biting criticism set the stage for an informative and significant discussion by Paul of the relationship between preaching and rhetoric or style.

Rhetoric according to Aristotle is "giving effectiveness to speech." We shall have occasion to speak at greater length about Aristotle's influential book *Rhetoric* and the thinking of other Greco-Roman rhetoricians. Rhetoric is essentially how ideas are packaged for communication, and as such the word does not bear the generally pejorative sense in which the word is used today (e.g., "That is mere rhetoric!"). Aristotle's axiom is "For it is not enough to know what we ought to say; we must also say it as we ought."

We have already traced varying rhetorical styles in the prophets. We have seen diverse influences shaping synagogal rhetoric (i.e., how the truth of Scripture was conveyed or communicated). George A. Kennedy speaks of the *kerygma* as "a mode of rhetoric" and shows examples of deliberative rhetoric (Sermon on the Mount); epideictic rhetoric, the oratory of praise or blame (John 13–17); and judicial rhetoric (2 Corinthians). A variety of forms is used in the New Testament documents and proclamation.[1]

Rhetoric had to be important in Greco-Roman society. Duane Litfin has shown that there were two kinds of rhetoric: primary or functional and secondary or decorative. Unfortunately "the decorative or showcase declamation" seemed to be winning in the struggle between the two kinds of rhetoric.[2] The Corinthians tended to judge Paul by the standards of secondary or decorative rhetoric. They were prone to overdo just about everything. The Corinthian arch with its rows of leaves and its pairs of scrolls meeting at the corner in spiral volutes was the most elaborate and ornate of all the arches. Paul in his classic argument in 1 Corinthians 1–2 thus readily concedes that he did not come to Corinth with an impressively ornate rhetoric—"I did not come with eloquence or superior wisdom as I proclaimed to you the testimony about God" (2:1).

But what to the Corinthians seemed unimpressive and plain matched "the foolishness" of the cross which was "a stumbling block . . . and foolishness" but indeed "the power of God and the wisdom of God" (1 Cor. 1:21, 23–24). The Corinthians were not contesting the content of his preaching, but were finding fault with his form. Apollos, the Greek orator, was more to their liking. Paul wanted to avoid words of human wisdom and preach that bloody cross "with a demonstration of the Spirit's power" (2:4). The Corinthians were of the opinion that the only way to be wise was to be eloquent.[3] Paul did not repudiate rhetoric or proper concern for form. Rather, he warned against placing undue emphasis on form, which would make the gospel herald vulnerable to distortion and distraction.

Some have argued, in error I believe, that Paul is repenting of his Areopagus address in Athens as he writes these words to the Corinthians. As we have already noted, the content is correct at Athens and the rhetorical flexibility commendable. Both in his use of sources and quotations and in his style and strategy, we have a model to emulate in Paul on the Areopagus.[4] There is no inconsistency with 1 Corinthians 1–4, where Paul is essentially countering the lionization of secondary rhetoric.

Also consistent in 1 Corinthians is the apostle's preference for the gift of prophecy over the more flamboyant gift of glossalalia or speaking in tongues (1 Cor. 14:5). Paul lays stress on the communication of content and intelligibility. Thomas Gillespie has recently argued that prophecy is preaching, basically the interpretation of the apostolic *kerygma*.[5] It would seem closer to the facts not to equate prophecy with preaching but rather to emphasize that the charism of prophecy is a gift of special illumination of a truth of Scripture and its application. With the canon of Holy Scripture closed, we deny continuing revelation in the root sense. Yet the Spirit affords insight and wisdom in the Scripture. This is a gift that some preachers manifest but it is a gift that all Christians may exercise (cf. 14:31ff.; 11:4–5). To equate prophesying with "exhortatory preaching" is to ignore the more unstructured kinds of sharing insights from the Word in the life of a normal Christian assembly (14:26ff.). Such insights ought to appear in the content of preaching but in every case "the others should weigh carefully what is said" (v. 29). Obviously the gift of prophecy as discussed in 1 Corinthians has both continuity and discontinuity with the canonical prophets of the Old Testament and prophetic utterance found in other places in the New Testament. An immense literature has arisen in recent years on thorny aspects of the use and misuse of this charism of the Spirit.[6] The inclusion of 1 Corinthians 13 in the discussion of these gifts which speak the Word further buttresses Paul's earlier argument that the truth and its inward grasp and our motivation and spirit are more critical than outward appearance and impression (13:1–3).

---

1. George A. Kennedy, *New Testament Interpretation Through Rhetorical Criticism* (Chapel Hill: University of North Carolina Press, 1984). Another important treatise is Amos N. Wilder, *Early Christian Rhetoric: The Language of the Gospel* (London: SCM Press, 1964).
2. Duane Litfin, *St. Paul's Theology of Proclamation: 1 Corinthians 1–4 and Graeco-Roman Rhetoric* (Cambridge, Mass.: Cambridge University Press, 1994), 110.
3. Ibid., 245.
4. For useful treatments of the Areopagus address see Ned B. Stonehouse, *The Areopagus Address* (London: Tyndale, 1949); Kenneth O. Gangel, "Paul's Areopagus Speech," *Bibliotheca Sacra* 127, no. 508 (October 1970): 308ff.; John R. W. Stott, "The Paroxysm of Paul: Summary of a Sermon," *The Pulpit* (July–August 1964): 21–22.
5. Thomas W. Gillespie, *The First Theologians: A Study in Early Christian Prophecy* (Grand Rapids: Eerdmans, 1994), 165.
6. Wayne A. Grudem, *The Gift of Prophecy in 1 Corinthians* (Lanham, Md.: University Press of America, 1982). For a thoughtful response to Grudem, see Robert L. Thomas, "Prophecy Rediscovered?" *Bibliotheca Sacra* 149, no. 593 (January–March 1992). It is difficult for me to see an exegetical case for cessationism.

2.4.3   CONFIRMING THE IMPACT OF PREACHING

. . . in truthful speech and in the power of God.

—2 Corinthians 6:7

The scene is the pagan world of the first century with all of its sights, sounds, and sins.[1] The Book of Acts concludes with an open-ended picture of Paul at Rome. "For two whole years Paul stayed there in his own rented house and welcomed all who came to see him. Boldly and without hindrance he preached the kingdom of God and taught about the Lord Jesus Christ" (Acts 28:30). The gospel was spreading and the church was growing explosively and exponentially.

The dynamics of this growth are clear, and Michael Bullmore's nuanced study of Paul's theology of preaching in 1 Corinthians 2:1–5 contrasts "the traveling orators in which the power lay in the speaker and his stylistic virtuosity"[2] with Paul's dedication to the plain style (as over against the grand style preferred by the Corinthians). Paul was not rhetorically unaware. Like other writers in the New Testament he would occasionally indulge in beautiful Greek prose (cf. Eph. 1 or the writer to the Hebrews' magnificent period sentence in Heb. 1:1ff.), yet he diligently sought to avoid any stylistic artifice that might obstruct the proclamation of the crucified One.

Paul had preached to the Corinthians and they had received the message (1 Cor. 15:1–2). Preaching was the instrument used by the Holy Spirit to reach the lost. Ernst Fuchs insists that in this sense preaching "participates in God's omnipotence."[3] The impact of preaching is unequivocally clear when Paul states, "Our Gospel came to you not simply with words, but also with power, with the Holy Spirit and with deep conviction" (1 Thess. 1:5). In the following chapter the pattern is clear:

> The gospel is spoken—"We dared to tell you his gospel" (2:2).
> The gospel is shared—"Delighted to share the gospel" (2:8).
> The gospel is preached—"We preached the gospel of God" (2:9).
> The gospel is recognized as the Word of God—"You received the word of God" (2:13).[4]

In summary, "There is a divine, creative energy released in the act of listening to the orally proclaimed gospel,"[5] for "we speak not in words taught us by human wisdom but in words taught by the Spirit, expressing spiritual truths in spiritual words" (1 Cor. 2:13).

The whole "proclamatory interaction" must be seen as taking place in a fierce spiritual battle (2 Cor. 4:3–4). The assured ultimate triumph (2:14) cannot eclipse the reality of the division between "those who are being saved and those who are perishing" (2:15). In our preaching, "To the one we are the smell of death; to the other, the fragrance of life" (2:16). In all of this "our competence comes from God" (3:5b). The stakes are so high and the issue of eternity so weighty that Paul warns, "Do not peddle the word of God for profit" (2:17), and "do not use deception, nor . . . distort the word of God" (4:2). We are called as preachers to "speak before God with sincerity, like men sent from God" (2:17). Also, "by setting forth the truth plainly we commend ourselves to every man's conscience in the sight of God" (4:2). We are not to "preach ourselves, but Jesus Christ as Lord, and ourselves as your servants for Jesus' sake" (4:5). The Word of God will then illuminate and transform (4:6). We must not get in the way of or impede the work of the Holy Spirit in blessing the word of God. Preaching is ever "I, yet not I."

This section in the Corinthian correspondence (2 Cor. 2:12–4:6) is like a capstone to all that Paul shares with us about what preaching is and should be. G. Campbell Morgan says of this portion, "Perhaps nowhere in the New Testament is the subject of the ministry set forth in its sublimity as it is here."[6] On the basis of these steady and enduring foundations, Ralph Turnbull asserted a generation ago, "In spite of the ferment and the new forms of ministry devised by the church, the heart of the ministry of the past half century was, as it ever has been, the proclamation of the good news, the gospel, and its claim upon the whole life as taught by our Lord."[7]

1. E. M. Blaiklock, *The Christian in Pagan Society* (London: Tyndale Press, 1951).
2. Michael A. Bullmore, *St. Paul's Theology of Rhetorical Style: An Examination of 1 Corinthians 2:1–5 in the Light of First Century Graeco-Roman Rhetorical Culture* (San Francisco: International Scholars publications, 1995), 169f., 205–222.
3. Ernst Fuchs in John William Beaudean Jr., *Paul's Theology of Preaching* (Macon, Ga.: Mercer University Press, 1988), 17. Fuchs insists, "Proclamation requires the text, because it only continues what was revealed through Jesus, the event of God's word."
4. Ibid., 54.
5. Ibid., 56.
6. G. Campbell Morgan, *The Corinthian Letters of Paul* (New York: Revell, 1956), 234.
7. Ralph Turnbull, *A History of Preaching,* vol. 3 of Dargan (Grand Rapids: Baker, 1974), 14.

CHAPTER THREE

The Infancy and Childhood of Biblical Preaching (A.D. 70–450)

The law of the LORD is perfect, reviving the soul. The statutes of the LORD are trustworthy, making wise the simple. The precepts of the LORD are right, giving joy to the heart. The commands of the LORD are radiant, giving light to the eyes. The fear of the LORD is pure, enduring forever. The ordinances of the LORD are sure and altogether righteous. They are more precious than gold, than much pure gold; they are sweeter than honey, than honey from the comb. By them is your servant warned; in keeping them there is great reward.

—Psalm 19:7–11

We often hear nostalgic sighs for the worship practices of the early church. Doubtless there are some worship principles that are always relevant. But we must recognize the absence of evidence for a uniform liturgy in the early church.

Certainly there was no wedge between Jesus and Paul. The apostles enjoyed doctrinal harmony, and a rich diversity of expression existed among them as well. Yet there were differences and tensions. Recall the discussion in Galatians 2.

As we move beyond the apostolic age into the patristic period, material evidence is somewhat sparse, but we can see a common heritage preserved while variation in expression continues. The preaching Fathers are still deeply indebted to the Old Testament and are indeed *Benai-Tanakh* (children of the Scriptures).[1] They are the legatees of the developing New Testament canon, consisting of accounts of Jesus (Luke 1:1–4) and the expanding collection of apostolic correspondence among other items.

Just as God's revealed truth was expressed variously during the Exile, the return, and the intertestamental period, so the Fathers adapted to an ever-shifting kaleidoscope of circumstances. Just as the synagogue sermon that accompanied the reading of Scripture could be topical or expository, so we shall discern a similar variation among the preaching Fathers.[2] But whatever the environment for proclamation, Scripture was highly regarded. In the first-century synagogue, the reading could not be too long lest the expositor get away from the text, nor could the exposition be given more loudly than the reading of the text lest greater prominence be given to the interpretation.[3] The emphasis remained on the text. We now move to a more detailed examination of preaching among the Fathers.

---

1. A lovely expression coined by Bernard and Sue Bell.
2. Everett Ferguson, *Backgrounds for Early Christianity* (Grand Rapids: Eerdmans, 1987), 461.
3. Isaac Levy, *The Synagogue: Its History and Function* (London: Vallentine Press, 1963), 102.

3.1 THE UNEVEN LANDSCAPE OF PREACHING IN THE EARLY CHURCH

Much of our preaching in church at the present day would not have been recognized by the early Christians as *kerygma*.

—C. H. Dodd

Then the disciples went out and preached everywhere, and the Lord worked with them and confirmed his word by the signs that accompanied it.

—Mark 16:20

We can discern a continuity in preaching from New Testament times to the fifth century.[1] Three principal settings are in view in the postapostolic period: (1) kerygmatical or missionary preaching; (2) catechetical or instructional preaching; and (3) liturgical or preaching for the worshiping community. While A. T. Robertson in his *Types of Preachers in the New Testament* and others have underscored the rich variety of spokesmen for the gospel from the very beginning, early preaching was cut from the same piece of cloth. It is text-dependent.[2]

The preparations for the coming of Christ into the world are also to be seen as preparations for the promulgation of the gospel message Christ made possible. Speaking of the first-century world, Paul Johnson is graphic: "The world was intellectually ready for Christianity . . . it was waiting for God."[3] The early Christian proclaimers confronted a Greco-Roman world in decline and which was moving toward its demise before the barbarian hordes. Her divisions and debaucheries rendered her increasingly helpless and hopeless. The gospel message was vibrant with hope and power and made an immediate and revolutionary impact. Johnson aptly characterized the early church as "a loosely organized revivalistic movement awaiting the *parousia* (the second coming of Christ)." The place of preaching in this expansion is now before us.

----

1. Robert D. Sider, *The Gospel and Its Proclamation* (Wilmington, Del.: Michael Glazier, 1983), 14.
2. John Ker, *Lectures on the History of Preaching* (New York: Armstrong, 1889), 54.
3. Paul Johnson, *A History of Christianity* (New York: Atheneum, 1976), 7.

3.1.1   PREACHING AND THE ENLARGEMENT OF VISIBILITY

Preaching carries the church.

—Elizabeth Achtemeier

Organizational patterns began to shift with the death of the apostles. Volz concludes, "It is certain that by the end of the first century the Pauline multiplicity of ministries given by the Spirit has developed into the threefold offices of bishop, presbyter (or elder), and deacon. Yet there was considerable overlap between the two triads and within them."[1] There is a sense of order and proper authority (1 Clement 44:1–6, c. A.D. 96).

Without church buildings and with the synagogues less available, many meetings were held in homes, the discourse informal. We have fragments of the preaching but little extant preaching from before the middle of the third century. Laypersons, bishops, and itinerant evangelists preached. Howden characterizes it all: "Early Christian preaching was biblical preaching," in which Scripture was cited as authority and Scripture was applied, usually explicitly.[2]

The geographical extension of Christianity through North Africa and up into the Rhone Valley in Europe made the increase in visibility and influence a vexing problem for Imperial Rome.[3] Serious inroads were being made into all classes in society. Sporadic local outbursts of persecution and a series of empire-wide persecutions followed.

Amid all this tumult, preaching continued. Wayne Meeks, who has concentrated on the early urban Christians, concedes the point: "Beside exposition of Scripture, preaching in the assemblies must have included other things, preeminently statements about Jesus Christ, and inferences, appeals, warnings, and the like, connected logically or rhetorically with these statements."[4] Michael Smith likewise concludes: "From what we can tell, Bible reading and preaching composed much of the programme of the public meetings of the Christian congregations."[5]

Eusebius, the first church historian, describes the action in the province of Asia around the turn of the first century: "Many, who amplified the Message, planting the saving seed of the heavenly kingdom far and wide in the world . . . evangelizing with God's help and favor . . . [relying] not on plausible, clever argument but on manifestations of the Holy Spirit and of supernatural power."[6] With cascading numbers of conversions, enemies of Christianity from within and without were hard at work.[7]

The believers needed to be alert to false prophets and false teachers. The *Didache* (c. A.D. 100) warns against false prophets and contrasts them with genuine prophets (11:3). The Shepherd of Hermas (c. A.D. 100–150) speaks of "apostles and teachers who preached unto the whole world" (15:1) and focuses on purity in the church. Polycarp to the Philippians (c. A.D. 108 or 116) is full of scriptural allusions. The Epistles of Ignatius (c. A.D. 107 or 115) center on the unity of the church and pastoral holiness.

Generally considered the oldest surviving sermon manuscript from this period is the anonymous homily called Second Clement (c. A.D. 120–140). Based on Isaiah 54:1, the homily is described by Hatch as "inspired by a genuine enthusiasm, it is rather more artistic in its form than a purely prophetic utterance is likely to have been."[8] Somewhat Pauline in tone, it ends with a splendid ascription. The writer calls his hearers to "pay attention while we are being exhorted by the Elders, but also when we have gone home let us remember the commandments of the Lord" (17:3–5).[9]

What leaves us uneasy in our survey of this foundational time is a perceptible weakening of the gospel message itself. We listen in vain to hear the kerygmatic proclamation of the death, burial, and resurrection of Christ. In his doctoral work, T. F. Torrance surveyed *The Doctrine of Grace in the Apostolic Fathers* and found that the doctrine of grace which was absolutely pivotal in the New Testament "did not have that radical character" in this expression.[10] A teaching of salvation by works or hypersacramentalism seeps in insidiously. We have seen the shape of what is to come.

---

1. Carl A. Volz, *Pastoral Life and Practice in the Early Church* (Minneapolis: Augsburg, 1990), 19.
2. William D. Howden, "Preaching," in *Encyclopedia of Early Christianity*, ed. Everett Ferguson (New York: Garland, 1990), 748.
3. Kenneth Scott Latourette, *The First Five Centuries* (Grand Rapids: Zondervan, 1970), 65–113.
4. Wayne A. Meeks, *The First Urban Christians: The Social World of the Apostle Paul* (New Haven, Conn.: Yale University Press, 1983), 146.
5. Michael Smith, *From Christ to Constantine* (Downers Grove, Ill.: InterVarsity Press, 1971), 39.
6. Eusebius *Ecclesiastical History* 3.37, quoted in Ramsay MacMullen, *Christianizing the Roman Empire* (New Haven, Conn.: Yale University Press, 1984), 25.
7. Robert L. Wilken, *The Christians As the Romans Saw Them* (New Haven, Conn.: Yale University Press, 1984). A thoughtful study of the early Christians.
8. Edwin Hatch, *The Influence of Greek Ideas and Usages Upon the Christian Church* (London: Williams and Norgate, 1901), 106.
9. In *Twenty Centuries of Great Preaching*, ed. Clyde Fant Jr. and William M. Pinson Jr. (Waco, Tex.: Word, 1971), contains the entire sermon, 1:19–25, and characterizes it as the "oldest surviving sermon manuscript." The next sermon in this fine collection is from Origen.
10. Thomas F. Torrance, *The Doctrine of Grace in the Apostolic Fathers* (Grand Rapids: Eerdmans, 1959), 133ff.

3.1.2 PREACHING AND THE EXPLORATION OF IDENTITY

> On the day called Sunday, there is a meeting for "all in one place," according to the city or the countryside where one lives . . . the Memoirs of the Apostles or the Writings of the Prophets are read as long as there is time, and when the reader has ceased, the president in an address gives a reminder and a challenge to imitation of these good things.
> —Justin Martyr *Apology I* 67

As the gospel message moved powerfully into the Greco-Roman world, the church faced the pressures of Greek influence and thought. Western civilization is built both on a Christian and a classical legacy. Cultural conflict provided the backdrop against which the church sought to forge a sense of her identity in Christ. Already in 1 Clement to the Corinthians (A.D. 80–100), a pastoral concern for staying with the Holy Scriptures appears. "You have studied the Holy Scriptures, which are true, and given by the Holy Spirit. You know that nothing unjust or counterfeit is written in them" (45:2–3).[1]

Evidence of Greek rhetorical influence can be seen in Melito of Sardis (c. A.D. 150) in his *On the Pascha:* "For born Son-like, and led forth lamb-like, and slaughtered sheep-like, and buried man-like, he has risen God-like, being by nature God and man." Thomas Carroll discerns new elements of Greek influence here, but rhetoric is still servant and not master.[2]

An important early defender of the purity of the message was Justin Martyr (d. about A.D. 166). Justin was born in Palestine and converted in Ephesus. He shows significant Greek influence but defended Christianity from both Jewish and Greek attack. A layman himself, he yet pleaded, "Everyone who can preach the truth and does not preach it, incurs the judgment of God."

Justin must also be seen as an important interpreter of Christian worship, especially baptism and communion and their relationship to preaching. Also critical is his rejection of Marcionism (that is, the rejection of the Old Testament) and his insistence that "all Scripture came through the Logos, centered on the Logos, and led back to the Logos," the Logos being Jesus Christ.[3] He is apparently responsible for the well-known gloss on Psalm 96:10, "The Lord has reigned from the tree." The final paragraph of his *Dialogue with Trypho* (142) discloses the heart of the communicator:

> And I in turn prayed for them, saying, "I can wish you no greater blessing than this, gentlemen, that, realizing that wisdom is given to every man through this Way, you also may one day come to believe entirely as we do that Jesus is the Christ of God."

Another key leader who labored to coalesce Christian and classical components was Clement of Alexandria (A.D. 150–215). Clement is at the vortex of the mingling of Greek gnostic thinking, Philonic Jewish exegesis, and emerging Christian theology. With his student, Origen, Clement is responsible for a school of biblical interpretation with immense implication for preaching.

Clement was active in the worshiping communities of cosmopolitan Alexandria. He may have been the first thinker to speak of the written Old Testament and written New Testament as such.

He has left us only one sermon, a message titled "Who Is the Rich Man Who Can Be Saved?" based on Mark 10:17–31. Some of the wealthy were being drawn to Christianity, and Clement warns them but argues that money is essentially value-neutral.

Clement was quite possibly influenced in his sermon by *The Epistle to Diognetus,* which is addressed to an inquirer after the truth (possibly the Diognetus who was tutor to Marcus Aurelius). The preaching here begins with the prologue of John's gospel and moves quickly to John 3:16. He holds forth Christ the eternal One as the Savior.[4]

While *The Epistle of Barnabas* reflects early feuds between Christians and Jews, some fragments of the life of Bishop Papias of Hierapolis also survive and contribute to our grasp of the developing situation. Irenaeus attributes to him the authorship of *Expositions of the Oracles of the Lord.* Eusebius notes how Papias used *Gospel* and *Epistle* and related the story of Jesus before the woman accused of many sins. Papias wishes to purge Christianity of gnosticism.[5] But another factor must be considered.

---

1. The source of most of these quotations is J. B. Lightfoot, *The Apostolic Fathers* (Grand Rapids: Baker, 1980) or *The Apostolic Fathers,* ed. Kirsopp Lake, in the Loeb Classical Library (Cambridge, Mass.: Harvard University Press, 1952) in two volumes.
2. Thomas K. Carroll, *Preaching the Word: Messages of the Fathers of the Church* (Wilmington, Del.: Michael Glazier, 1984), 37.
3. Walter H. Wagner, *After the Apostles: Christianity in the Second Century* (Philadelphia: Fortress, 1994), 164.
4. John Foster, *After the Apostles: Missionary Preaching of the First Three Centuries* (London: SCM Press, 1951), 82.
5. Edward H. Hall, *Papias and His Contemporaries* (Boston: Houghton Mifflin, 1899).

3.1.3   PREACHING AND THE EXPERIENCE OF AGONY

The blood of the martyrs is the seed of the church.

—Tertullian

The ministry and outreach we have described is set in intense conflict. In his classic work, H. E. W. Turner shows how the early church sought to keep the teachings of the Lord Jesus and the traditions of the apostles undefiled. He argues that the development of Christian theology is "the interaction of fixed and flexible elements, both of which are necessary."[1]

Equally as bruising for the life of the church organism was its persecution. There were those who cowered and quailed before pressure, but the example and nobility of so many sufferers made a deep and indelible impression upon the world. Their testimony became a sermon for their generation.

Christianity was a destabilizing force in its challenge to emperor worship and its leveling of social stratification. The relentless evangelism seemed only to be fueled by persecution (cf. "On that day a great persecution broke out against the church at Jerusalem, and all except the apostles were scattered throughout Judea and Samaria. . . . Those who had been scattered preached the word wherever they went," [Acts 8:1, 4]).

Such oppression prevented the church from becoming "at ease in Zion." As Clement of Alexandria put it in the dialogue between Rusticus the Prefect and Justin: "We would rather suffer now and please the Lord, than please you and suffer on that day."[2]

Workman observes that the suffering foundations of the Christian church were laid "deep in Calvary."[3] A theology of suffering has always been a necessity for the church. Christian proclamation of the gospel inevitably brought the early church on a collision course with constituted authority and culture. Seneca said of both slaves and Christians that anything was lawful against them. Tacitus described some of the scenes of suffering:

> Mockery of every sort was added to their deaths. Covered with the skins of beasts, they were torn by dogs and perished, or were nailed to crosses, or were doomed to the flames and burnt, to serve as a nightly illumination when daylight had expired. Nero offered his gardens for the spectacle, and was exhibiting a show in the circus, while he mingled with the people in the dress of a charioteer or stood aloft in a car.
> —*Annals* 15.44

And in all of this the preaching of the Word continued under the outpoured blessing of the Spirit of God.

---

1. H. E. W. Turner, *The Pattern of Christian Truth* (London: Mowbrays, 1954). Another key volume is the superb treatment by Harold O. J. Brown, *Heresies* (Grand Rapids: Baker, 1984).
2. David Winte, *100 Days in the Arena* (Wheaton, Ill.: Shaw, 1977), day 80.
3. Herbert B. Workman, *Persecution in the Early Church* (Nashville: Abingdon, 1906, 1960), 11.

3.2 SOME SHINING LIGHTS AMONG THE PREACHERS

> The preaching of the truth shines everywhere and enlightens all men that are willing to come to a knowledge of the truth. This preaching, as cited, and this Faith, as forementioned, the Church although scattered in the whole world, diligently guards as if it lived in one house, and believes, like the above, as if it had but one mind and the same heart, and preaches and teaches and hands on these things harmoniously, as if it had but one mouth. And although there are different languages in the world, the force of the tradition is one and the same.
> —Irenaeus *Adversus Haereses* 1.10

Christianity was born into the matrix of Greco-Roman and Jewish tension. Mediterranean culture helped create an uneven fusion between the classical heritage and the Judeo-Christian heritage. In intellectual centers like Alexandria, there is an almost overmastering Greek influence, as we can trace in a Jewish thinker like Philo. In other areas the authentic message of historic Christianity is distinctively preserved.

When after 250 years of persecution the church came under imperial favor, even more pressure was brought to bear upon her to conform to the prevailing culture as a whole. This tension affects preaching in two particular areas: (1) hermeneutically, that is, in terms of understanding and interpreting the Scripture; and (2) homiletically, that is, in terms of preaching and communication of the truth. We shall examine some leading preachers of the time and how they demonstrate diverse approaches in the developing synthesis.

3.2.1 TERTULLIAN—THE CHAMPION OF TRUTH

We assemble to read our sacred writings, if any peculiarity of the times makes either fore-warning or reminiscence needful. However it be in that respect with the sacred words, we nourish our faith, we animate our hope, we make our confidence more steadfast; and no less by inculcations of God's precepts we confirm good habits.

—Tertullian *Apologeticus* 1.118

Although we have no extant sermons from Tertullian, he is apparently the first to give the name *sermon* to the Christian address. He was born about 150 in Carthage in North Africa, the son of a Roman centurion. He studied law in Rome and was attracted to Stoicism, which may have led him to study Christianity. He was converted in 193 and ultimately came under the influence of Montanus, who began to prophesy against the formalism and sinfulness of the church in Asia about 170.[1]

Tertullian was a doughty defender of orthodox Christology and Trinitarian theology. He addressed contemporary issues like divorce and remarriage and Christian participation in the shows with fiery discourse. He criticized the academy and asked, "What has Athens to do with Jerusalem?" He contrasted knowledge in general (such as philosophical knowledge) with divine revelation. Jerome called him a man of "sharp and vehement temper."

Danielou characterizes the Latin Christianity Tertullian influenced as having "a realism which knows nothing of the Platonic devaluation of matter; a subjectivity which gives special prominence to inner experiences; and a pessimism which lays more stress on the experience of sin than on transfiguration."[2] Obviously Tertullian is a forerunner of Augustine.

Robert Payne speaks of Tertullian as "the thunderer." He is witty and eloquent. He hates deeply and feels keenly. "In that overheated world where Tertullian explores his own anger, there are occasional moments of coolness, of an unexpected tenderness. At such moments the lawyer's tricks fall away."[3] In his puritanism and Montanism he took a firm stand against strangulating sacramentalism and vapid intellectualism.

1. Timothy David Barnes, *Tertullian: A History and Literary Study* (Oxford: Clarendon, 1971) is the best overall study of Tertullian and his times that I have seen.
2. Quoted in Thomas K. Carroll, *Preaching the Word: Messages of the Fathers of the Church* (Wilmington, Del.: Michael Glazier, 1984), 138. Also, Robert Dick Sider, *Ancient Rhetoric and the Art of Tertullian* (New York: Oxford, 1971).
3. Robert Payne, *The Fathers of the Western Church* (New York: Viking, 1951), 47.

3.2.2 IRENAEUS—THE CHURCHMAN ALWAYS

This, beloved, is the preaching of the truth, and this is the manner of our salvation, and this is the way of life, announced by the prophets and ratified by Christ and handed over to the apostles and handed down by the church in the whole world to her children. This must be kept in all security, with good will and by being well-pleasing to God through good works and sound moral character.

—Irenaeus, Proofs, 98

The worthy bishop at Lyon in the Rhone Valley, Irenaeus (135–202?) ministered in the administrative center of all Gaul. He was born in Smyrna and heard the sermons of the great leader and martyr Polycarp. He speaks of the New Testament as a gathered collection and refers to the preaching of both Paul and Peter in Rome as well as the character of the four gospels (*Adversus Haereses* 3.1.1). His ecclesiology reflects great pastoral concern and traces four dispensations from Adam and Eve until Christ. His doctrine of Christ and his *Christus Victor* have enjoyed new popularity in our own time. He insisted that the God of the Old Testament and the God of the New Testament arc the same.

Irenaeus fought the gnostics who made inroads on his own congregation and seduced away the wife of one of his deacons. He conceded that his preaching was not eloquent, but he maintained that it was without distortion. He preached in the outdoor markets of Lyons as well as in the villages in the general area (preface to *Adversus Haereses* 1.1). He preached to the Celts in their own language and apologized because his Greek had become rusty. His absorbing concern was for the unity of the church, and he sought to clarify the implications of Montanism. God used his ministry and message to establish the church in southern France.[1]

---

1. For an important study of Irenaeus, see J. Barton Payne, "The Biblical Interpretation of Irenaeus," in *Inspiration and Interpretation* (Grand Rapids: Eerdmans, 1957). For Irenaeus, the words of Scripture are the words of God.

3.2.3 HIPPOLYTUS—THE CHARGE AGAINST HERESY

Feed the holy flock.
—Hippolytus Apostolic Tradition, the first duty of the ordained

Hippolytus (c. 150–235) was apparently a disciple of Irenaeus who served in the church of Rome. He was inspired by Irenaeus to engage in lifelong combat with the gnostics and other heretical groups. He is considered one of the four ranking theologians of his time, along with Tertullian, Clement of Alexandria, and Origen. His description of a worship service in Rome makes mention of the reading of Scripture and the exposition of the lessons. Also among his legacies are examples of eucharistic prayers, catechetical forms, discussions on baptism (even to such practical matters as not wearing jewelry during baptism), the role of deacons in assisting the bishop, and even a baptismal liturgy from which the Apostles' Creed may have developed.[1]

A controversialist, Hippolytus even wrote a defense of apostolic authorship of the Fourth Gospel and the Book of Revelation. We have his sermon "In Sanctam Theophaniam," based on Matthew 3:13–17. Garvie observes that this preaching justifies the title Eusebius gave him, "man of the word."[2] The sermon artfully uses analogy and is highly rhetorical in form. Thus Hippolytus takes his stand in the enlarging circle of witnesses to the nature of the early preaching.

---

1. F. F. Bruce, *The Spreading Flame* (Grand Rapids: Eerdmans, 1958), 254.
2. Alfred Ernest Garvie, *The Christian Preacher* (New York: Scribner's, 1923), 68ff.

3.2.4 CYPRIAN—CUSTODIAN OF THE MIDDLE

> Thus the Church, filled with the light of the Lord, sends forth her beams over the whole earth; the light which is diffused over all places, being one, and the unity of the body unbroken. So the Church expands her boughs over the whole world in the rich results of her exuberance, and scatters, with beneficent hand, onward-flowing streams; yet is there one head, one source, one mother, whose abundance springs from her own fruitfulness.
>
> —Cyprian, *Treatises,* 5

Cyprian (c. 200–258) was born to an upper-class family near Carthage in North Africa. He was well educated and served for years as a teacher of rhetoric. He was converted in 246 and made bishop of Carthage, where he served from 248 until his martyrdom in 258. With Tertullian, after whom he modeled himself, he presents us with examples of the earliest Latin exegesis and preaching.

Greatly concerned about the unity of the church, he fled from persecution in the early Decian massacres. The persecution was followed by a devastating plague. Cyprian ultimately died a martyr's death, the first North African bishop to be slain for the gospel.

While lacking the fire of Tertullian, Cyprian was a generous and self-giving leader, notwithstanding his social origin and the apparent fact that he was a senator. We do not have any of his sermons but do possess fourteen treatises, eighty-one epistles, and a short memoir by his deacon. These all reflect the flavor of his often ornate but effective discourse. He dealt with the critical issues in polity and church life, insisting strongly, for instance, that presbyters "be well-informed in the Word and exemplary in life."[1] While he held to a high view of the power of the episcopate, he was merciful and generous to the "lapsed."

Cyprian describes his missionary preaching in the marketplaces during the time of persecution. His writings have the sound of sermons, such as his address to "insincere repentance" (Treatise 6), or "The Christian's Native Land" on heaven (Treatise 9 on Mortality).[2] In the face of schism and imminent death, Cyprian preached faithfully and finally laid down his life for Christ.[3]

---

1. Edward P. Echlin, *The Priest As Preacher: Past and Future* (Notre Dame, Ind.: Fides, 1973), 42.
2. William Wilson, *Popular Preachers of the Ancient Church* (London: James Hogg and Sons, n.d.), 40ff.
3. Kurt Aland, *A History of Christianity* (Philadelphia: Fortress, 1985), 1:156–61.

3.2.5   ORIGEN—THE CRAFTSMAN OF THE TEXT

All in whom Christ speaks, that is to say every upright man and preacher who speaks the word of God to bring men to salvation—and not merely the apostles and prophets—can be called an arrow of God. But what is sad, I see very few arrows of God. There are so few who so speak as to inflame the heart of the hearer, drag him away from his sin, and convert him to repentance. Few so speak that the heart of their hearers is deeply convicted and his eyes weep for contrition. There are so few who unveil the light of the future hope, the wonder and glory of God's Kingdom to such effect that by their earnest preaching they succeed in persuading men to despise the visible and seek the invisible, to spurn the temporal and seek the eternal. There are all too few preachers of this calibre.

—Origen *Commentary on Psalm 36*

Born in a Christian home in Alexandria (his father was martyred in 202), Origen (185–254) may be viewed as the father of Greek preaching and a figure of significance for theology. Matriculating in Clement's academy, Origen became a teacher and a lay preacher. From childhood he was severely ascetic, owning but one coat and no shoes, drinking no wine, and sleeping on the bare floor.[1] Thomas Carroll points out that Origen wrestled with the whole Bible and with the Bible as a whole.[2]

To Origen the preaching of the Word was emphasized over the sacraments. He was the first to speak of taking a text and explaining it. Justin Martyr described the use of a text, but Origen speaks of it by name. He traveled widely, mastered Hebrew, and was finally ordained, moving to Caesarea in 233. He wrote a number of commentaries and left many homilies (mainly from the Old Testament). Jerome asked, "Has anyone read everything that Origen has written?"

According to his biographer, Origen preached virtually every day. He spoke to the eucharistic assembly on Sunday, for the Wednesday and Friday eucharist at 3 P.M., and every day but Sunday for early morning services in which the Scripture was read in a three-year cycle and preached in series.[3] He preached without notes and often ended abruptly with a doxology. He attempted to "explain the Bible with the Bible." F. W. Farrar claimed, "He was by general admission the greatest, in almost every respect, of all the great Christian teachers of the first three Christian centuries." His recorded sermons were widely circulated.

Origen must be seen as both debit and credit theologically and exegetically. He was the first to formulate clearly the doctrine of the eternal generation of the Son, and yet his unblushing optimism led him to foresee a totally Christian world (*Contra Celsum* 8.68–72) and the ultimate salvation of all persons. Unduly influenced by Greek ideas, he denied the bodily resurrection and taught the Platonic preexistence of the soul. He never expressed concern for authorial intentions.[4]

Like Justin, Origen accused the Jews of an opaque literalism in interpreting the Old Testament, for instance, failing to see that reference to "God's hands" is anthropocentric language. This legitimate concern, however, led him to espouse Philo's overly allegorical approach to Scripture.

Origen was by no means the first Christian expositor to emphasize allegorization. As early as The Epistle of Barnabas (c. 130) we see allegorical explication of the Old Testament. Certainly there is allegorization in the interpretative efforts of the Qumran community, and in Justin and Hippolytus on Daniel, or Heracleon on the Fourth Gospel. Our Lord himself uses allegory in his discourse on the vine and the branches in John 15 and in his words shortly before the cross in Matthew 21:33–41. Paul makes use of carefully controlled allegory in Galatians 4:21–31.

Origen's Greek-influenced hermeneutic must be seen as part of an apologetical strategy. But it was also his conviction that the literal involves insoluble contradictions. He sees Scripture as verbally inspired,[5] indicating that "The wisdom of God has penetrated to all the inspired Scripture even as far as the slightest letter." Origen saw three levels of meaning in Scripture:

1. the literal, earthly, sensual, carnal—of minimal significance—the body;
2. the moral, religious, doctrinal, practical—more important—the soul;
3. the spiritual, heavenly, allegorical, mystical, speculative—the greatest—the spirit.

Allegorical preaching loses control in the interpretation of the text when it disregards the author's purpose. The conflict between the Alexandrian allegorists and the Antiochian advocates of historico-grammatico exegesis is one of the key watersheds in the history of interpretation.[6]

Gregory, the "wonder worker," was led to Christ and discipled by Origen. In his *Panegyric,* he reflects on Origen's teaching:

Like some spark it came dropping into my inmost soul. And there, being kindled and catching fire, was love: Love toward the Word (Logos) Himself, most alluring to all by reason of beauty unspeakable, the holy, the most lovely. And love toward this man, His friend and representative. By this love sore wounded, I was induced to give up all the aims which I was proposing to myself, for my affairs and education, among other things, even my law-studies of which I was proud; yes, fatherland and family, both relatives in Caesarea and those left behind at home. I had one regard, one passion—theology, and this godlike man, master therein.

Origen encouraged itinerant preaching and the opening of Scripture. Yet his overly-allegorical approach still yields a negative effect today. Any sermon may be striking. Yet the important question to ask is, Does the text really say what the sermon claims? Put more colorfully, if the text had a contagious disease, would the sermon catch it?

1. A. H. Newman, *A Manual of Church History* (Philadelphia: Judson, 1899), 28.
2. Thomas K. Carroll, *Preaching the Word: Message of the Fathers of the Church* (Wilmington, Del.: Michael Glazier, 1984), 49.
3. Joseph T. Lienhard, "Origen as Homilist," in *Preaching in the Patristic Age,* ed. David G. Hunter (New York: Paulist, 1989), 40.
4. Eugene de Faye, *Origen and His Work, The Olaus Petri Lectures for 1925* (New York: Columbia University, 1929), 37.
5. R. P. C. Hanson, *Allegory and Event: A Study of the Sources and Significance of Origen's Interpretation of Scripture* (Richmond: John Knox, 1959), 187.
6. Milton S. Terry, *Biblical Hermeneutics* (Grand Rapids: Zondervan, n.d.), 639–41.

3.2.6 THE CAPPADOCIAN CLOVERLEAF—CONNOISSEURS OF COMMUNICATION

My only affection was eloquence, and long did I apply myself to it with all my might; but I have laid it down at the feet of Christ, and subjugated it to the great word of God.

—Gregory of Nazianzen

With the aging of Hellenism, increasing syncretism, the weakening of Imperial Rome, and the growing dominance of Greek rhetoric, Christian preachers faced new challenges in keeping Scripture and sermon in sync. Three noteworthy preachers bear analysis in this context. They are often called the Cappadocian cloverleaf because they all came from that region of modern Turkey and have striking natural and spiritual linkages.

Basil the Great (329–379), a rigorous ascetic and skilled rhetorician, became the bishop of Caesarea (370). He lived in the waning days of Constantine and saw the bizarre reign of Julian the Apostate (361–363). His grandmother was known for her great love for Scripture and had been a follower of Gregory of Thaumaturgus. A devotee of Origen, Basil shows profound influence by Greek philosophy and rhetoric. His sermons are based on biblical texts and show orderly arrangement and simple ideas. Rhetorically, he is the least extravagant of the three. His sermons are strong in application and practical import. He inveighs against profiteers and the indifferent rich in a time of famine.[1] In a well-known passage, Basil speaks to the affluent:

> The bread that you hold back belongs to the hungry; the coat that you hoard in your cupboard belongs to the naked. The shoe that is gathering mildew in your home belongs to the unshod; the money you have hoarded belongs to the poverty-stricken. Thus you are oppressing as many people as you could have helped with your possessions.

His nine sermons on the six days of creation (Hexaemeron) are classic, showing careful adherence to the text but a commanding commitment to the unity of the sermon. Other memorable sermons include "Spiritual Work and Warfare" and "The Peril of Procrastination."[2]

Gregory of Nazianzen (329–389), a friend of Basil, was a leader of whom it was said, "His words were thunder; his life lightning." He was a true rhetorician and a poet. He has been described as having a "nervous rhetorical nature." His emphasis on style has prompted some critics to say that his lectures were "more oratorical masterpieces than sermons on Bible texts."[3]

Gregory of Nyssa (335–395) was the brother of Basil and himself a philosopher and rhetorician. He was Platonic in his philosophy and Origenistic in his interpretation. We see this particularly in his fifteen notable *Homilies on the Song of Songs*. He had great admiration for the pagan rhetorician Libanius. In a great passage on pride, Gregory takes a tour of a cemetery and asks, "Where in these bones are all these things about which you are now so greatly puffed up?"[4] He has left us beautiful homilies on the Beatitudes of Jesus and the Lord's Prayer. He also wrote passionately of yearning for God *(epiktasis),* and said, "The true sight of God consists in this, that the one who looks up to God never ceases in that desire."

Other respected preachers in the Greek tradition were Cyril of Jerusalem, who has left us twenty-four sermons preached to the catechumens of Jerusalem, and Athanasius, bishop of Alexandria (328–375), whose took a strong stand for orthodox Christology. His homilies focus on the incarnation of Christ.

With the growing dominance of Greek rhetorical form, the church would soon face a more balanced and judicious blending. Content and form are both essential and inescapable.

But the most powerful preaching of the period is yet to be surveyed. We see the hardening of a kind of Byzantine scholasticism at this juncture in which "Greek theology gradually suffocated by its own traditionalism."[5] It was left powerless to face Islam.

---

1. Hans von Campenhausen, *The Fathers of the Greek Church* (London: Adam and Charles Black, 1963), 91.
2. William Wilson, *The Popular Preachers of the Ancient Church* (London: James Hogg, n.d.), 196.
3. von Campenhausen, *The Fathers of the Greek Church,* 103.

4. Carl A. Volz, *Pastoral Life and Practice in the Early Church* (Minneapolis: Augsburg, 1990), 127.
5. von Campenhausen, *The Fathers of the Greek Church,* 175.

3.2.7 JEROME—THE ICONOCLAST OF THE COMPANY

> When teaching in church, seek to call forth not plaudits but groans. Don't be a ranter, one who gabbles without rhyme or reason. Show yourself versed in the mysteries of God. To astonish an unlettered crowd with oratorical skill is a sign of ignorance. Season your speech with frequent reading of Scripture.
>
> —St. Jerome to a young preacher

Jerome (345–420) is considered one of the Four Doctors of the Latin Church. Born in Dalmatia, Jerome studied in Rome and traveled widely. When he was in Antioch he had a vision and fell ill. The experience led him to spend six years as a hermit in the desert. He returned to Antioch and was ordained in 379. He studied later under Gregory of Nazianzus and was commissioned by Pope Damascus to translate the Scriptures. This translation, the Vulgate, became widely used. In 385 he went to Bethlehem, where he labored in translation and commentary writing for thirty-five years. His friend Sulpicius Severus said of him, "He is always reading books . . . he is always either reading something or writing something."[1]

Jerome was outspoken, prickly in disposition, and extremely opinionated, but he was a scholar of the Word. He wrote poems and letters and preached against "the purple-clad harlot" of Rome."[2] He detested Ambrose of Milan because of his patrician background, cursed the rhetoricians, and shuddered at the news of distant invasions and wars. He carried on a contentious correspondence with Augustine, although they stood together against Pelagius. We possess ninety-six of his sermons. His chief significance in the history of preaching beyond his work in translation is his concern about Greek rhetorical influence on preaching. His advice to Nepotian is typical: "Let the presbyter's preaching be based on his reading of the Scriptures. I do not want you to be a declaimer, or argumentative, or longwinded."[3]

1. Robert Payne, *The Fathers of the Western Church* (New York: Viking, 1951), 87.
2. Ibid., 114.
3. Carl A. Volz, *Pastoral Life and Practice in the Early Church* (Minneapolis: Augsburg, 1990), 120ff.

3.2.8 AMBROSE—THE COUNSELOR OF THE CONFRATERNITY

> We have given a daily sermon on morals, when the deeds of the Patriarchs or the precepts of the Proverbs were read, in order that, being informed and instructed by them, you might become accustomed to enter upon the ways of our forefathers and to pursue their road, and to obey

the divine commands, whereby, renewed by baptism, you might hold to that manner of life which befits those who are washed.

—Ambrose in *De Mysteriis*

With the Latin fathers we sense at once that style becomes more direct and concise. Ambrose (340–397) is a case in point. His role as the preacher who gripped and moved Augustine guaranteed him a lofty niche in the company of the preachers.

Born to the ruling class, at the age of twenty-nine Ambrose was appointed governor of the province of which Milan was the chief city. When he was not yet baptized, he was appointed bishop of Milan in a time of crisis and confusion. Orthodox in his theology, he clashed repeatedly with the emperor and empress. He loved music and wrote hymns, several of which are still part of the western liturgy ("O Splendor of God's Glory Bright" and "O Trinity Most Blessed Light").

Ambrose was influenced by Platonic ideas and was thoroughly allegorical in his approach to the text.[1] Often deep in his books or involved in discussion and debate with others, he was not easily accessible. Yet Augustine testifies: "I first began to love him . . . as a man who showed me kindness."[2] Peter Brown describes the man who so touched Augustine as "a passionate little man . . . a frail figure . . . clasping the codex of the Scriptures, with a high forehead, a long melancholy face, and great eyes."[3]

His sermons on the six days of creation in Genesis particularly moved Augustine, who up to this time had a distinct aversion to the Old Testament. His treatment of the sacraments and his two volumes on repentance in relation to Novatian practice reflect his preaching style. His address about drunkenness *(De Elia et Jeiunio)* illustrates his appealing discourse:

> Strong drink alters the senses and the forms of men. By it they are turned from men into neighing horses. A drunken man loses voice, he changes color, he flashes fire from his eyes, he pants, he snorts, he goes stark mad, he falls into a foaming pit. . . . Hence come also vain imaginings, uncertain vision, uncertain steps: often he hops over shadows, thinking them to be pits. The earth acquires a facial expression and nods to him; of a sudden it seems to rise and bend and twist. Fearful, he falls on his face and grasps the ground with his hands or thinks that the mountains close in on him. There is a murmur in his ears as of the surging seas; he hears the surf booming on the beach. If he spies a dog he imagines it a lion and takes to his heels.

Thus Ambrose preached and steeped himself in Scripture with the end that his hearers would confront Christ, for indeed it is Jesus Christ "to whom no price or ornament can be compared. Take as your counselors Moses, Isaiah, Jeremiah, Peter, Paul, John and the greatest counselor of all, Jesus the Son of God, that you may gain the Father."

Gibbon in his classic history of the Roman Empire observes that "The custom of preaching, which seems to constitute a considerable part of Christian devotion" was to be found everywhere in the Roman Empire. Indeed, "The pulpits of the empire were now filled with sacred orators who possessed the advantage of not being questioned without danger of interruption or reply."[4] And the two most powerful and significant preachers of this age are now before us.

---

1. For helpful discussion of typology in relation to allegory, see F. F. Bruce, *Hebrews* (Grand Rapids: Eerdmans, 1990), 96–97; Leonard Goppelt on "tupos" in *Theological Dictionary of the New Testament,* ed. G. Kittel and Gerhard Friedrich (Grand Rapids: Eerdmans, 1972), 246–59.
2. Augustine *Confessions* 5.13.23. Cf. also Neil B. McLynn, *Abrose of Milan: Church and State in a Christian Capital* (Berkeley: University of California Press, 1995).
3. Peter Brown, *Augustine of Hippo* (Berkeley: University of California, 1967), 83.
4. Edward Gibbon, *The Decline and Fall of the Roman Empire* (J. B. Bury Edition of 1909) 20:6.

3.3 THE EXPLOSIVE LUSTER OF CHRYSOSTOM, JOHN OF ANTIOCH

Preaching makes me well; as soon as I open my mouth to speak, my weariness is forgotten.

—Chrysostom

Before us now is unquestionably the greatest preacher of the early church. John of Antioch, or Chrysostom (meaning the "golden-mouthed," a name given him 150 years after his death), lived from 343 to 407. At the pinnacle of his ministry, he was the archbishop of Constantinople. He suffered greatly at the hands of the rulers of the eastern empire. Chrysostom was preeminently a biblical preacher whose approach to Scripture was Antiochene rather than Alexandrian.

Mediterranean society was in a state of drift and division in the fourth century. Constantine's Edict of Milan of 313 legalized Christianity. With Constantine's death in 337, however, a new period of disorder ensued. The empire was under severe strain, and the church was torn by doctrinal controversies. Now patronized rather than persecuted, the church tasted of power and sought more, prompting Chrysostom to write, "The desire to rule is the mother of heresies." With the death of Theodosius, the empire grew unwieldy and split into two segments in 395. Yet the preaching of Chrysostom rises above the chaotic times.

3.3.1 CHRYSOSTOM—THE PILGRIM

You praise what I have said, and receive my exhortations with tumults of applause; but show your approbation by obedience; this is the only praise I seek.

—Chrysostom

John was born in Antioch into a devout home. His father, Secundus, died when

John was young, and his mother, Anathusa, dedicated herself to rearing her gifted son. R. A. Krupp reminds us that John was "a chauvinist raised by a woman."[1] When he was twenty years of age he began to study law under the famous pagan rhetorician Libanius, who highly regarded John and considered him a prospect as his successor.

While in his youth John had "plunged into the whirlpool of the world." But he came to Christ and was baptized. He served as a reader in the church in Antioch but was soon inclined to go to the mountains as a hermit. When his mother pleaded with him not to leave her, he changed their home into a monastery where he stayed until her death. A strong ascetic streak is apparent in his life and teaching.[2]

John then spent four years as a monk in company with an aged hermit and another two years alone in a cave. A slight man whose health was permanently affected by his extreme asceticism, he returned to Antioch where he was ordained as a deacon at the age of thirty-seven and began to preach two or three times weekly to increasing audiences. Steeped in the classics, polished as an orator, but fashioned as a disciple of Christ, he was ready for one of the most remarkable ministries the world has ever seen. He had virtually memorized the Scriptures and preached systematically and consecutively through book after book of the Bible. He condemned empty oratory but used the finest skills of his age in opening the Word of God.

After twelve years as chief presbyter in Antioch, John was coerced into becoming archbishop of Constantinople, where he served for six years in running controversy with the empress Eudoxia, but with a resoundingly effective pulpit ministry in St. Sophia's. Twice banished because of his unwillingness to compromise on principle, Chrysostom died in exile. Because of Chrysostom's commitment to biblical preaching and his fiery zeal, Bishop Kallistos Ware has recently written of him, "He can be truly called an evangelical."[3] We shall trace the significance of his attachment to "the literal and historical meaning of the text."

---

1. R. A. Krupp, *Shepherding the Flock of God: The Pastoral Theology of John Chrysostom* (New York: Peter Lang, 1991), 1. This is an exceedingly valuable and helpful treatment by my former colleague at Trinity Divinity School. Vying for this niche is J. N. D. Kelly's new *Golden Mouth: The Story of John Chrysostom, Ascetic, Preacher, Bishop* (New York: Cornell University Press, 1995).
2. For a superb work of historical fiction, nothing is better than F. W. Farrar, *Gathering Clouds: A Tale of the Days of St. Chrysostom* (New York: Longmans, Green, 1895). The classic work on the life of Chrysostom remains F. Chrysostomos Baur, *John Chrysostom and His Time* (Westminster, Md.: Newman, 1960), translated from German in two volumes.
3. Bishop Kallistos Ware of the Antiochene Orthodox Church in the splendid issue on Chrysostom in *Christian History* 44:13 (November 1994), 36.

3.3.2 CHRYSOSTOM—THE PERSONALITY

> Or do you not know what a passion for oratory has nowadays infatuated Christians? Do you not know that its exponents are respected above everyone else, not just by outsiders, but by those of the household of the faith? How, then, can anyone endure the deep disgrace of having his sermon received with blank silence and feelings of boredom, and his listeners waiting for the end of the sermon as if it were a relief after fatigue; whereas they listen to someone else's sermon, however long, with eagerness, and are annoyed when he is about to finish and quite exasperated when he decides to say no more?
>
> —Chrysostom on Priesthood

Although both Syrian Antioch and Constantinople were about half Christian, they were cesspools of depravity. This in part explains John's ascetic bent.[1] The church was hideously corrupt. Such a deeply feeling person as John recoiled from the sinful scenes and inclined to monastic seclusion. Just forty miles east of Antioch was the pillar on which Simon Stylites lived for thirty-seven years in protest of the wickedness of his day.

But this kind of monastic severity spawns the intense individualism we see again and again in John. Described by one scholar as a "choleric ascetic," his enemies thought him hard, arrogant, morose, overly passionate. He heaped up illustrations and metaphors, and his vocabulary was undisciplined. His first sermon is described as "embroidered rhetoric gone wild."[2]

Despite a possible touch of Pelagianism, he is on the whole steadfastly orthodox. In preaching on Hebrews 10:9, he insists, "We do not offer another sacrifice, but we make a commemoration of a sacrifice." He confronts the drift of his times as "the dementation before doom." Krupp shows how he preached against excesses at wedding celebrations, spoke against abortion, critiqued aspects of slavery,[3] protested the abuses of wealth and power, and opposed gluttony, drunkenness, and class distinctions. His occasionally irritable nature showed itself in unfortunate anti-Semitic outbursts.[4]

John wrestled with why people did not come to church, especially in the summer months. "I hear them saying, 'The heat is excessive; the scorching sun is intolerable; we cannot bear to be crushed in the crowd and to be oppressed by the heat and confined space.'"

Chrysostom essentially wrote the eastern liturgy, which even in this century has inspired the great Russian composer Sergei Rachmaninoff ("Liturgy for the Holy Communion: Liturgy of John Chrysostom, Patriarch of Constantinople," written 1910–11). Many Christians are familiar with his invocation: "Almighty God, unto whom all hearts are open, all desires known, and from whom no secrets are hid; cleanse the thoughts of our hearts by the inspiration of your Holy Spirit, that we may perfectly love you, and worthily magnify your holy name, through Christ our Lord."[5]

1. John Heston Willey, *Chrysostom: The Orator* (Cincinnati: Jennings and Graham, 1906), 45.
2. Ibid., 62.
3. R. A. Krupp, *Shepherding the Flock of God: The Pastoral Theology of John Chrysostom* (New York: Peter Lang, 1991), 188.
4. Robert L. Wilken, *John Chrysostom and the Jews: Rhetoric and Reality in the Late Fourth Century* (Berkeley: University of California, 1983).
5. Quoted in Carl A. Volz, *Pastoral Life and Practice in the Early Church* (Minneapolis: Augsburg, 1990), 127.

3.3.3   Chrysostom—The Preacher

I cannot let a day pass, without feeding you with the treasures of the Scripture.

—Chrysostom *Homilies from Genesis* 1.82.2

Chrysostom stands tall among preachers as one whose sermons took the text of Scripture with utmost seriousness. His question was never, Is this a suitable occasion for preaching? but rather, Why should not this be a suitable occasion for preaching?[1]

We have more than seven hundred of Chrysostom's sermons, including twenty-one given during the infamous tax revolt in Antioch in A.D. 387. His address on the nature of homiletics in *On the Priesthood* focused on the fact that "Preaching is a work for God and its object must never be forgotten." His devotion to the text led him to produce running commentary, and he systematically expounded whole books of the Bible, among them Genesis (75 sermons), the Psalms (144), Matthew (90), John (88) and a number of Paul's epistles (244). His fifty-four messages on the Acts constitute what may be the first real commentary on that book. He generally preached for an hour.

Chrysostom did not divide the text for preaching but typically added an applicatory section to his exegetical address. No wonder that John Calvin chose to write a preface to an early edition of Chrysostom's sermons in which he lauds Chrysostom for excelling the other Fathers in seeking the true sense of the scriptural text.[2]

Personally wed to careful Bible study, Chrysostom urged personal and family study and application of the Word. In his preaching, he "works steadily through the chosen passage . . . he tries to let it speak to himself, and hopes that in this way it will speak to his hearers . . . the sermon is a real exposition of the Word of God."[3] T. Harwood Pattison quotes Macgilvray's description of Chrysostom in action:

As he advanced from exposition to practical appeals, his delivery became gradually more rapid, his countenance more animated, his voice more vivid and intense. The people began to hold in their breath. The joints of their loins were loosened. A creeping sensation like that produced by a series of electric waves passed over them. They felt as if drawn toward the pulpit by a sort of magnetic influence. Some of those who were sitting rose from their seats; others were overcome with a kind of faintness as if the preacher's mental forces were sucking the life out of their bodies, and by the time the discourse came to an end the great mass of that spellbound audience could only hold their heads and give vent to their emotions in tears.[4]

The style of the preaching was direct and homely. The preacher did not have an extraordinary voice. He used rhetorical and linguistic skills in shaping discourse.[5] Often he carried on what seems to be a dialogue with his congregation, with question and response. He preferred his ambo, or pulpit, rather than the bishop's throne because it was closer to the people. He was sometimes criticized for being too dramatic.

John Chrysostom's sermons were quoted by preachers up to the Reformation. His influence can be traced clearly in Fénelon's *Dialogue on Eloquence.* Themes he developed included the truthfulness of the Holy Scripture (with a pronounced harmonistic tendency[6]); Christ dying for all, even those who reject him; the free will of man; male headship. He saw homosexuality as a detestable perversion and took exception to certain Mariological trends.[7]

The quest for holiness was uppermost for Chrysostom. Little wonder that Dante in *Paradisio* puts him between Nathan, who rebuked sin in King David's court, and St. Anselm of Canterbury.

In his own time he was known as the golden lyre of the Holy Spirit. As Thomas Carroll describes it, "For Chrysostom preaching was essentially the interpretation of a text from Scripture and its application to a particular congregation. Exegesis is, therefore, the starting point of his preaching as exhortation is its conclusion."[8]

He could be especially sharp in his denunciations. He spoke of the empress: "Again Herodias raves; again she rages; again she dances; again she asks for the head of John [Chrysostom] upon a charger." This spelled the end for the preacher. But in his final sermon, which meant exile and death, he preached:

> The waters are raging and the winds are blowing but I have no fear for I stand firmly upon a rock. What am I to fear? Is it death? Life to me means Christ and death is gain. Is it exile? The earth and everything it holds belongs to the Lord. Is it loss of property? I brought nothing into this world and I will bring nothing out of it. I have only contempt for the world and its ways and I scorn its honors.[9]

---

1. As quoted in E. M. Blaiklock, *The Pastoral Epistles* (Grand Rapids: Zondervan, 1972), 119.
2. R. A. Krupp, *Shepherding the Flock of God: The Pastoral Theology of John Chrysostom* (New York: Peter Lang, 1991), 234.
3. Stephen Neill, *Chrysostom and His Message* (London: Lutterworth, 1962), 17.

4. T. Harwood Pattison, *The History of Christian Preaching* (Philadelphia: American Baptist Publication Society, 1903), 71.
5. Paul Scott Wilson, *A Concise History of Preaching* (Nashville: Abingdon, 1992), 46.
6. Krupp, *Shepherding the Flock of God,* 73.
7. Ibid., 169.
8. Thomas K. Carroll, *Preaching the Word: Message of the Fathers of the Church* (Wilmington, Del.: Michael Glazier. 1984), 114.
9. Ibid., 126–27.

3.3.4 *CHRYSOSTOM—THE INTERPRETER*

> When a king made his entrance into a city, certain ones among the dignitaries, the chief officials and those who were in the good graces of the sovereign would go forth from the city in order to meet him, while the guilty and the criminals are kept within the city where they await the sentence which the king will pronounce. In the same manner, when the Lord will come, the first group will go forth to meet him with assurance in the midst of the air, while the guilty and those who are conscious of having committed many sins will await below their judge.
> —Chrysostom on the *parousia* in a sermon from 1 Thessalonians 4:17

The importance of Chrysostom for preaching derives not only from his devotion to the exegesis of the text and its forceful proclamation but also from his careful and exemplary hermeneutical principle. Hermeneutics (not an exact science) is our method of interpreting the Scripture. The word comes from the name of Hermes, who in the pantheon of Greek gods was the messenger. We may have the highest view of scriptural authority, but if we cannot get at the meaning of the text, our esteem for it is in vain. If the author's intent is inaccessible, we are left with the reader-response approach to meaning so rife today, which says in effect that the meaning of a text is in our own imaginations.

The spiritualization of a text can be useful in avoiding apologetical discussion of a historical Garden of Eden or ark of Noah. But if Scripture has hidden spiritual meanings, we have reserved its interpretation for the elite and torn it from average believers—and we have done so contrary to apostolic representation (cf. 2 Peter 1:19–21; 1 John 2:26–27).

Allegory is extended metaphor. Indeed, modest allegory is found in Scripture, but it is clearly identified as such (Matt. 21:33–46, labeled as parable; John 15:1ff.; Gal. 4:21–31, in which Sarah and Hagar are seen as figurative in a careful and restrained contrast). But the influence of the Alexandrian hermeneutic was widespread and devastating. The heirs of the allegorists let imagination run rampant, and allowed Job's three thousand camels to represent the depraved Gentiles. Ruth's lunch in the field of Boaz came to symbolize the Lord's Supper. The three baskets on the baker's head in Joseph's interpretation of the dream were said to represent the Trinity; the twopence given by the Good Samaritan represented baptism and the Lord's Supper; Elijah's four barrels of water symbolized the four gospels; the ship in which Jesus crossed Galilee described the Church of England and the "other ships" the nonconformist groups. We shall see vestiges of this overallegorization in Augustine and through the Middle Ages. Such a fine witness and careful commentator as Ephrem the Syrian (306–373) was misled by Origen's views and arrived at some outlandish interpretations.[1]

In our own day the hypertypologists (who see Abraham's servant's seeking a wife for Isaac as setting forth forty characteristics of the ministry of the Holy Spirit) and the allegorists have surrendered up the text. We can lose scriptural authority in adopting a wrong hermeneutic.[2]

Staunchly poised against the Alexandrian allegorists was the Antiochene school, originating in the very city where believers were first called Christians (Acts 11:26). This school emphasized a literal, simple meaning of the text. This is not, as some have alleged, "A wooden-headed literalism," but rather a dedication to finding the author's purpose in the text and its literal meaning wherever possible. The interpretation of a text must take into account its literary genre. Precursors to the Antiochene approach abound in individuals such as Theodorus of Antioch, who championed the historical sense in the Genesis account, Julius Africanus in Palestine, Dorotheus in Antioch, and Lucian in Edessa and later of Antioch. All of these were known as strong biblical expositors.[3] Also in this lineage was Eusebius of Emesa, known for his adherence to "the historical sense of Scripture."

The prime mover in the Antiochene school was Diodorus (d. 394), who later became bishop of Tarsus. He argued that the prophetic predictions of the Old Testament "were at the same time both historical and Christocentric,"[4] the phenomenon of prophetic perspective. Diodorus was the teacher of both Theodore of Mopsuestia (350–428) and John Chrysostom. Both of these influential leaders learned historical exegesis from their mentor.

Chrysostom recognized types and figures in the biblical text, but Origen rejected any reference to physical bread in the petition "Give us this day our daily bread" and argued that this was a reference to Christ himself. Chrysostom urged that we understand the text as being a plain and natural reference to daily nutriment.

Influenced more by the empiricism of Aristotle than the rational idealism of Plato, Chrysostom and the Antiochene school stressed the historical, grammatical, and literal meaning of a text. What is called the Antiochene *theoria,* or idea of a supernatural insight given the inspired writers by the Holy Spirit and the illuminating ministry of the Holy Spirit for biblical exegetes and readers, is clearly based on a commitment to the plenary and verbal inspiration of the autographs.[5] Nassif speaks of the *theoria* in exegesis as "that prophetic vision whereby the prophet saw and recorded both the present historical and future Messianic meanings under one literal and hyperbolic mode of expression without division."[6] This asserts that texts may have a double meaning (as the Gospel of John is built on a series of double meanings), and there may be a mild *sensus plenior* in a text (see 1 Peter 1:10–12). Yet the base and control are always historical, literal, and grammatical in a text. This is where Chrysostom stood, and this became the launching pad for his public proclamation of the Word of God. The contrast with the contemporary "new hermeneutics" is clear and painful. The difference is demonstrated in a comment made by Chrysostom interpreting Isaiah 2:5–6:

We are not the lords over the rules of interpretation, but must pursue Scripture's interpretation of itself and in that way make use of the allegorical method. . . . This is everywhere a rule in Scripture: when it wants to allegorize, it tells the interpretation of the allegory, so that the passage will not be interpreted superficially or be met by the undisciplined desire of those who enjoy allegorization to wander about and be carried in every direction.[7]

Clearly, Chrysostom's hermeneutical framework is critical to the whole proclamatory enterprise.[8] A final word from him seems relevant to our times: "The church is not a theater, that we should listen for amusement. With profit ought we to depart hence, and some fresh and great gain should we acquire before we leave."

---

1. Frederic W. Farrar, *History of Interpretation, The Bampton Lectures of 1885* (Grand Rapids: Baker, 1961), 209ff.
2. For a superb study, see David S. Dockery, *Biblical Interpretation: Then and Now* (Grand Rapids: Baker, 1992). Also worthwhile in this area is Karlfried Froehlich, *Biblical Interpretation in the Early Church* (Minneapolis: Fortress, 1984).
3. Milton S. Terry, *Biblical Hermeneutics* (Grand Rapids: Zondervan, n.d.), 644.
4. Dockery, *Biblical Interpretation,* 107.
5. Bradley L. Nassif, *Antiochene Theoria in John Chrysostom's Exegesis* (Ann Arbor: UMI Dissertation Services, 1991), 157.
6. Ibid., 158.
7. Dockery, *Biblical Interpretation,* 117.
8. For a fascinating comparison of the exegesis of Chrysostom, Augustine, and Origen on Romans 1–11, see Peter Gorday, *Principles of Patristic Exegesis* (Lewiston, N.Y.: Edwin Mellen Press, 1983).

3.4 AUGUSTINE—THE STELLAR LUMINARY AMONG HOMILETICIANS

To have to preach, to inveigh, to admonish, to edify, to feel responsible for every one of you—this is a great burden, a heavy weight upon me, a hard labor.

—Augustine

Preaching never enjoyed great prominence in the Eastern church. Worthy of note, however, is an eighth century movement in Isauria, in the western part of what we know today as Turkey. In the so-called Isaurian Dynasty there arose an iconoclastic move against elaborate liturgy and in favor of bringing the Word to the people.[1] But by and large, preaching has not been strongly highlighted in Orthodoxy. To find out why, we must turn to the Western church and the preacher who had such influence in shaping it theologically and homiletically. These facts merit our review:

1. Alexandrian allegorization carried the day in the East. Its triumph was adverse to biblical preaching.
2. From early on, the church in the West was more institutional and consistent with characteristically Roman efficiency and organization. Thinkers like Novatian and Cyprian tilted the Western church toward an order that esteemed preaching. In contrast, a standard history of the Eastern church did not include a single reference to preaching.[2]
3. The Eastern church's theology of glory put the liturgy essentially out of sight of the congregation with an emphasis on "a continuum reaching into eternity."[3] The stress was on the incarnation of Christ; in the West the atonement of Christ was accented. Tertullian in *De Resurrectione* stresses "order and simplicity in theology," going "hand in hand with the concern for the institutional life of the church."[4] The Western emphasis was more pastoral; hence, preaching loomed larger.
4. Tertullian's reservations about Greek philosophy were part of his crusade against all paganism, Greek or Latin. While he is more indebted to Stoicism than he acknowledges, he is critical of Platonism.[5] The Eastern church was Platonic and mystical while the Western church was Aristotelian and empirical. The monasticism of the East seemed sharper and more severe than in the West. All this shaped the place of preaching.
5. While Chrysostom is virtually unexcelled as a preacher, what promised to be a reflection on preaching in *On the Priesthood* actually focused more on purity and the morality of the clergy. The West had Augustine, who gave us our first textbook on homiletics.

It is our contention that Augustine's contextualizing synthesis of biblical truth and classical rhetoric is a defining hour for preaching. We shall trace how Augustine's contribution helps explain the prominence of preaching in the West.

---

1. Research on these aspects of the Isaurian Dynasty by Walter Persson of Stockholm and Thonos Karbonis of Athens is slated to take book form in the future.
2. Aziz S. Atiya, *History of Eastern Christianity* (Notre Dame, Ind: University of Notre Dame Press, 1968).
3. Danielou, *The Origins of Latin Christianity,* 471.
4. Ibid., 474.
5. Ibid., 224.

3.4.1 THE SPIRITUAL JOURNEY OF AUGUSTINE

I do not care whether you expect some well-turned phrases today. It is my duty to give you due warning in citing the Scripture.
—Aurelius Augustine

Aurelius Augustine was born November 13, 354 in Tagaste in Roman Numidia (modern Souk Ahras in Algeria), North Africa. His parents were poor, but his father, Patricius (a pagan until shortly before his death in 372), and his mother, the saintly Monica, shared a driving aspiration for their son. His early years of study in Madaura and Carthage were years of sin and license. His unnamed concubine bore him a son, Adeodatus, who died at the age of seventeen. For eleven years he was a traditional school teacher who increasingly longed to go to Rome.

As her son moved successively from dualistic Manichaeism and its austerities to a more philosophical neo-Platonism, Monica lived in agony. She would stay for days in a chapel to fast and pray for her wayward son.[1] To her dismay, in 383 Augustine sailed for Rome and then on to Milan, where he was appointed professor of rhetoric in the fall of 384. The following spring Monica pursued him to Milan.

Augustine was "a master of the spoken word" and had the ability and the training to produce what Brown calls "verbal fireworks . . . with sudden meteorites."[2] He soon came under the influence of the sermons and exhortations of Ambrose in Milan. In 386 he was converted and then baptized by Ambrose in 387, abandoning his career as a rhetorician and professor.

After the death of his mother, Augustine went back to North Africa where he was ordained in Hippo in 391. His powerful preaching and prolific writing gave him a special place in the doctrinally divided and politically imperiled area. He was consecrated as a bishop in 395 and established what was in effect a theological seminary. For thirty-five years he labored as a spiritual leader, finally dying in 430.

The conversion of Augustine, so powerfully chronicled in his famous *Confessions,* must be seen as the outcome of his dear mother's ceaseless intercession, the preaching of the Word by Ambrose, the influence of friends, and his own reading of Romans 13:13–14. On the day of his conversion he heard the famous words *tolle, lege,* or "Take up and read." He never got away from the grip of Holy Scripture, as is clear from the *Confessions.*[3]

Augustine supplied us with works still profitably read today, including *On Free Will* (in which he defends free moral agency against Manichaean determinism) or *On the Trinity* (one of the choicest expositions of the triune nature of God ever written) or *The City of God* (his magnificent philosophy of history as the Roman Empire disintegrates). He can justly be called the father of systematic theology. As Rudolph Eucken described him, "The single greatest philosopher on the basis of Christianity proper the world has had." Harnack termed him "the incomparably greatest man in the Church between St. Paul and Luther," and Souter called him "the greatest man who wrote in Latin." But no less impressively, we see Augustine as an outstanding preacher and exegete who shaped aspects of preaching both in his own time and yet in ours.

---

1. Peter Brown's rich and magnificent treatise *Augustine of Hippo* (Berkeley: University of California Press, 1967).
2. Ibid., 22–23.
3. R. L. Ottley, *Studies in the Confessions of St. Augustine* (London: Robert Scott, 1919). Another superb anthology is *St. Augustine: His Age, Life and Thought* (New York: Meridian, 1957). An old landmark is B. B. Warfield, *Calvin and Augustine*

(Philadelphia: Presbyterian and Reformed, 1956), especially 305–477. The entire issue of *Christian History* 6:3 is devoted to Augustine.

3.4.2 THE PREACHING STORY OF AUGUSTINE

My preaching almost always displeases me. For I am eager after something better, of which I often have an inward enjoyment before I set about expressing my thoughts in audible words. Then, when I have failed to utter my meaning as clearly as I conceived it, I am disappointed that my tongue is incapable of doing justice to that which is in my heart. What I myself understand I wish my hearers to understand as fully; and I feel I am not so speaking as to effect this. The chief reason is that the conception lights up the mind in a kind of rapid flash; whereas the utterance is slow, lagging and far unlike what it would convey.
— Augustine in *De Catechizandis Rudibus* (chapter 2)

Augustine's ministry took root amid widespread cultural decay. An inner rottenness had gutted the once proud empire, and even though the emperor Theodosius declared Christianity the state religion, the church was unresponsive to the events swirling about her. Even as Augustine lay dying at the age of seventy-six, the Vandals surrounded Hippo and were in the process of torching the city. Rome was sacked in 410.

Augustine had battled the Manicheans, the Donatists, and the Pelagians in the interest of biblical integrity. He had written 230 books. He was to be the fountainhead from which Luther, Calvin, and Jansenius drank. But he was most of all a consummate preacher. The focus of his life and ministry was the Word of God. He held stoutly to verbal inspiration.[1] In a letter to Jerome, Augustine wrote, "For I confess to your charity that I have learned to defer this respect and honor to those scriptural books only which are now called canonical, that I believe most firmly that no one of these authors has erred in any respect of writing."[2] We are not surprised then to hear him say (again to Jerome, who claimed Paul might have used a white lie in Galatians):

It seems to me that most disastrous consequences must follow upon our believing that anything false is found in the sacred books: that is to say that the men by whom the Scripture has been given to us and committed to writing, did put down in these books anything false. If you once admit into such a high sanctuary of authority one false statement, there will not be left a single sentence of those books, which, if appearing to any one difficult in practice or hard to believe, may not by the same fatal rule be explained away as a statement, in which, intentionally the author declared what was not true.[3]

Further influencing Augustine's preaching was his early vocation as a schoolmaster and his high regard for teaching. In the New Testament, preaching and teaching are used virtually interchangeably. Yet there is a useful distinction when we recognize that a good preacher will use much teaching and a good teacher will at some point preach. Teaching is absorbed primarily with a subject; preaching tilts toward obsession with an object.

Augustine argued for the significance of verbal signs in achieving understanding. He reasoned that since Christ is prophet and teacher, the believer is in union with him and is to share in that office. Not only the bishop is to preach; Christ speaks through his messengers.[4]

Thus we see the man who as a youth had loved to steal pears, who early on prayed "Give me chastity but not yet," whose sexuality was subliminated in his disputations, who saw the world "as a sea in which men devour one another like fish." In appearance Augustine was a brother of the Berbers of the North African desert, "tall and long limbed, thin chested, with sloping shoulders . . . long nose, high forehead, thick lips, tremendous black eyes . . . his skin a kind of dark bronze."[5] This was the preacher.

Dressed in street clothes, he preached without manuscript or notes. We have 685 of his sermons, some of which consumed an hour and some of which were very brief. He was sparse with illustration but fond of pithy aphoristic sayings, loved rough Punic words, and was noted for his logic and rhetorical devices such as alliteration and rhyme. He explained and repeated the text, although he was guilty of horrendous misinterpretation on occasion. His delivery had striking beauty and effect.

Augustine was highly doctrinal in his preaching. He used spacious themes and spoke of the mysteries without being patronizing or condescending. He could weep in the pulpit. Occasionally he indulged in gross allegorization, yet he held to the literality of Genesis 1 but not creation in seven literal days of twenty-four hours. Typical discourse is from a sermon on Proverbs 10:

> Thus our summer is the advent of Christ, our winter his concealment in heaven. Our summer is the revelation of Christ. In a word, to good and faithful trees, the Apostle addresses these words: "You are dead, and your life is hid with Christ in God." Certainly dead, but dead in appearance, living at the root. Fix your eye on the season of summer that is to come; mark how it follows: "When Christ, who is your life, shall appear, then shall you also appear with Him in glory."[6]

Peter Brown emphasizes that Augustine seldom preached from "without" to his beleaguered congregants but rather from "within" the flock. As he puts it, "This is the secret of Augustine's enormous power as a preacher. He will make it his first concern to place himself in the midst of the congregation, to appeal to their feelings for him to react with immense sensitivity to their emotions, and so, as the sermon progressed, to sweep them up into his own way of feeling."[7] Eye to eye with those who stood in the front rows, "For Augustine and his hearers, the Bible was literally the 'word' of God."[8]

"Let me try to winkle out the hidden secrets of this Psalm we have just sung; and chip a sermon out of them, to satisfy your ears and minds,"[9] he would seductively say in tones resonating with excitement and thrill. His sermons on the

Psalms are especially impressive. Apparently his voice became even richer and more dulcet in his late middle age (when he preached *The City of God*). Little wonder that Spurgeon called Augustine "the quarry from which nearly every preacher of note has dug." The old proverb stands apropos, "A sermon without Augustine is as a stew without bacon."[10]

---

1. David W. Kerr, "Augustine of Hippo," in *Inspiration and Interpretation,* ed. John Walvoord (Grand Rapids: Eerdmans, 1957), 73.
2. *Epistolae* 82.3.
3. *Epistolae* 28.3. For an very important study see A. D. Polman, *The Word of God According to St. Augustine* (Grand Rapids: Eerdmans, 1961), especially "The Word of God as Holy Scripture," 39–122.
4. Edward J. Hughes, *The Participation of the Faithful in the Regal and Prophetic Mission of Christ According to Saint Augustine* (Mundelein, Ill.: St. Mary of the Lake, 1956), 52.
5. Robert Payne, *The Fathers of the Western Church* (New York: Viking, 1951), 139.
6. Sermon 212 on Proverbs 10.
7. Peter Brown, *Augustine of Hippo* (Berkeley: University of California, 1967), 251. Also of relevance is Brown's more recent *Power and Persuasion in Late Antiquity* (Madison: University of Wisconsin, 1994).
8. Ibid., 253.
9. Ibid., 254.
10. T. Harwood Pattison, *The History of Christian Preaching* (Philadelphia: American Baptist Publication Society, 1903), 63.

3.4.3 THE RHETORICAL ODYSSEY OF AUGUSTINE

It is better that we should use these barbarisms and be understood by you than be artists in speech and talk past you.
—Augustine in *De Doctrina Christiana*

Augustine's hermeneutic was somewhat eclectic. Although he did lapse into the allegorical mode, we must still view him as the dean of preachers in the Western church, standing head and shoulders above his noteworthy contemporaries. These included Hilary, bishop of Poitiers (d. 368), whose reverent use of Scripture can be traced in his sermons on Matthew and in his twelve volumes on the Trinity; Zeno of Verona (d. 380), from whom we have ninety-three well-illustrated tractates; and Pacianus, bishop of Barcelona (d. 392), who is favorably mentioned by Jerome; and Gaudentius of Brescia (d. 410), who corresponded with Chrysostom.[1]

In every age communicators must grapple with the culturally appropriate and conditioned form that will most effectively transmit the "everlasting gospel." The question of form is the question of rhetoric. Today, rhetoric bears the largely negative connotation of meaning "empty talk." A rhetorical question requires no answer. "That is just so much rhetoric," is dismissive. Against that reductionism,

Lischer is correct in asserting that "Rhetoric is the theory and practice of purposive discourse."[2] Aristotle proposed five divisions of rhetoric:

1. Invention—the composition of content
2. Arrangement—"beauty is a kind of order"
3. Style—elocution, selection of words, grammar
4. Delivery—the actual communication of content
5. Memory—freedom from dependence on written material

The Romans learned from Greek rhetorical style and in turn produced Cicero (d. 43 B.C.), whose *De Oratore* so shaped Augustine. Like Aristotle, Cicero valued *ethos* (or the character of the speaker) more than *logos* or *pathos*.[3] Augustine was the Ciceronian man as set forth in Cicero's Brutus, well rounded and inspiring.

Also very influential in this field was Quintilian (d. 120), whose twelve-volume manual *Institutes of Oratory* is even more finished than Aristotle. In *The Schoolmaster,* Quintilian argues typically: "I dare affirm that even a mediocre speech will be more effective, if delivered well, than the best speech, if poorly delivered."[4] We have already detected the influence of the Athenian School of Rhetoric on Chrysostom through his teacher Libanius, but other schools in Constantinople and in Gaza exerted extensive influence. Their counterparts were in the West.[5]

Edwin Hatch argues that Greek rhetoric created the Christian sermon and in the process effectively killed it.[6] Others have claimed that Greek philosophy exerted only a deleterious influence on Christian thought. But it is inaccurate to issue a wholesale condemnation of Greek rhetorical influence on the sermon. Cicero's contention that style should always be adapted to purpose is sound and was strongly commended to Augustine and by Augustine.

Thus we must concur with an approach to preaching that speaks of "The Preacher as Rhetorician"[7] or a treatment of preaching style that probes rhetorical and traditional sources.[8] The significance of Augustine here is his clear thinking on the relationship between the cultural significance of contemporary rhetorical categories and the Word of God he was committed to proclaim. In the next section we shall examine his *De Doctrina Christiana,* in which he advances a balanced solution to the dilemmas of the Christian communicator. In essence, Augustine baptized Aristotle's rhetorical approach through Cicero into the Christian church. The gospel of Christ made oratory Christian.

---

1. E. C. Dargan, *A History of Preaching* (Grand Rapids: Baker, 1954), 93ff.
2. Richard Lischer, *Theories of Preaching* (Durham, N.C.: Labyrinth, 1987), 209.
3. James M. May, *Trials of Character: The Eloquence of Ciceronian Ethos* (Chapel Hill: University of North Carolina Press, 1989).
4. Marcus Fabius Quintillianus, *The Schoolmaster* (Nashville: George Peabody University Press, 1951), 1:294. This is the book title used for *Institutio Oratorio.* I am indebted to my former student, Dr. Don Whitney, for the reference.
5. George A. Kennedy, *Greek Rhetoric Under Christian Emperors* (Princeton, N.J.: Princeton University Press, 1983).

6. Edwin Hatch, *The Influence of Greek Ideas and Usages on the Christian Church* (London: Williams and Norgate, 1901), 113ff.
7. Lester De Koster, "The Preacher as Rhetorician," in *The Preacher and Preaching: Reviving the Art in the Twentieth Century,* ed. Samuel T. Lorgan Jr. (Phillipsburg, N.J.: Presbyterian and Reformed, 1986), 303–30.
8. William H. Kooienga, *Elements of Style for Preaching* (Grand Rapids: Zondervan, 1989), 19ff.

3.4.4   THE HOMILETICAL THEORY OF AUGUSTINE

We must beware of the man who abounds in eloquent nonsense, and so much the more if the hearer is pleased with what is not worth listening to, and thinks that because the speaker is eloquent, what he says must be true . . . A man speaks with more or less wisdom to the extent he has made more or less progress in the knowledge of the Scripture, not just in knowing them but especially in understanding them correctly . . . It is more important to speak wisely than eloquently.

—Augustine in *De Doctrina Christiana*

Some have called Chrysostom's *On the Priesthood* the first book on homiletics, but this tome really addresses the character of the preacher rather than the craft of preaching. It is Augustine's *On Christian Doctrine* that can legitimately claim to that title. Books 1–3 of his treatise, written in 397, address the Scriptures and a proper hermeneutic. His final section, written thirty years later, concerns the methodology of preaching. Britannica's *Great Books* (volume 18, 621–98) contains this work in an able translation by J. F. Shaw.

Augustine sets forth the necessity of an inquiring spirit: "What says the Scripture?" He seeks an environment in which people can "feed on the good bread of the Lord." While Scripture is veiled to the non-Christian, Augustine sees it as a river in which an elephant can swim and a little child can wade. He maintained that a lifetime of studying the Bible would leave him "still making progress in discovering their treasures."[1]

In what Peter Brown maintains is "one of the most original [books] that Augustine ever wrote,"[2] we mark a strong emphasis on "the words of Scripture." Augustine sees words as signs, and grapples with the inadequacy of language. He underscores what he calls "the primary principle" on interpretation, seeing every part in relation to the teaching of Scripture as a whole as relating to God's redeeming love for humanity and humanity's response to God.

In Book 4 Augustine turns to effective rhetoric. Classical rhetoric can enhance preaching, he argues, but rhetorical skill can be gained from the careful study of Scripture itself.

Content is more than form, maintains Augustine. Content is the foundation, but the Christian expositor is to combine wisdom with eloquence.[3] Drawing upon his Ciceronian roots, Augustine agrees that the purpose of the speaker is "to teach, to delight and to move . . . of these teaching is the most essential."[4] He strongly reinforces the necessity of prayer[5] and underscores the importance of a consistent life.[6]

In the closing movement of this landmark, Augustine urges, "But whether a man is going to address the people or to dictate what others will deliver or read to the people, he ought to pray God to put into his mouth a suitable discourse."[7]

Augustine thus stakes out a position that effectively models a prudent use of stylistic forms in the interest of valid communication of the changeless gospel. Erich Auerbach describes Augustine's approach as generally using *sermo humilis* (or down-to-earth speech) but on occasion using when appropriate a more elevated style.[8] Above all, Augustine maintained his determination to stay close to the text. Was this not the practice of the apostle Paul?

"More heavily than all rhetorical brilliance on the one hand, or the displeasure of the grammarians because of unpolished diction on the other hand, there weighed on Augustine the duty of explaining the Word of God in so plain a manner that the less gifted could also grasp it."[9]

---

1. Augustine, *Epistolae* 137.3.
2. Peter Brown, *Augustine of Hippo* (Berkeley: University of California, 1967), 264.
3. Augustine, *De Doctrina Christiana* 4.5.8.
4. Ibid., 12.27.
5. Ibid., 15.32.
6. Ibid., 27.59.
7. Ibid., 30.63.
8. Erich Auerbach, *Literary Language and Its Public,* quoted in William H. Kooienga, *Elements of Style for Preaching* (Grand Rapids: Zondervan, 1989), 28–29.
9. Thomas K. Carroll, *Preaching the Word: Message of the Fathers of the Church* (Wilmington, Del.: Michael Glazier, 1984), 196.

CHAPTER FOUR

The Adolescence of Biblical Preaching (A.D. 450–1450)

Jesus of Nazareth . . . a prophet, powerful in word and deed before God and all the people.   —Luke 24:19

He said to them, "How foolish you are, and how slow of heart to believe all that the prophets have spoken! Did not the Christ have to suffer these things and then enter his glory?" And beginning with Moses and all the Prophets, he explained to them what was said in all the Scriptures concerning himself.

—Luke 24:25–27

They asked each other, "Were not our hearts burning within us while he talked with us on the road and opened the Scriptures to us?"
—Luke 24:32

He told them, "This is what is written: The Christ will suffer and rise from the dead on the third day, and repentance and forgiveness of sins will be preached in his name to all nations, beginning at Jerusalem."
—Luke 24:46–47

The important thing is that in every way . . . Christ is preached.
—Philippians 1:18

After Augustine, preaching entered its adolescence. Civilization settled uneasily into the Middle, or Dark Ages, and feudalism took root. It was a time of violence and disorder, of introversion and gloom. And yet it was not a period of unrelieved darkness. The preaching of the Word retained certain vital qualities. As Professor Bark argued, "Nothing better attests to the creative genius, the capacity both to learn and to originate, of western civilization, *even in the period of its youth,* than the mighty product of its religious art, which combined spiritual aspiration, warm human feeling and artistic excellence, in a way unknown to pagan, classical antiquity."[1]

After the death of Constantine in 337, the Roman Empire gradually disintegrated. In 395, the empire split in half, and a process of barbarization began. Cicero saw the empire as "a picture fading because of old age." Ambrose preached that "we are indeed in the twilight of the world."[2] Eusebius had been optimistic about the ultimate victory of the empire, but Augustine in *De civitate dei* delineated the need for the separation of the church from the state.[3] Augustine proved prophetic. Sin and corruption within and the barbarian hordes without eroded the structures of government. In 476, the last emperor, the boy Romulus Augustulus, had the crown taken from him and placed on the head of Odovacar.

The irreversible decline of the Roman Empire has been explained by Professor Trevor-Roper:[4]

1. The ruralization of Europe, the decline of the cities, exhaustion of the soil, economic depression, the prolonged effects of slavery, insufficient numbers of soldiers for defense in the face of hired mercenary barbarians, the loss of promise and hope.
2. The incursions of new religions from the East, including Christianity, which "stabilized on a rural base." Religious syncretism undercut vitality. Clovis of the Franks (466?–511) provides us with a colorful example. Clovis promised God he would become a Christian if he won a great battle. He was subsequently baptized with three thousand of his warriors but tellingly held his battle ax out of the water.
3. The invasion of the barbarians, who did not destroy the empire but continued many aspects of it. First were the Arians, followed by the Arabs, and ultimately the Vikings, who swept across Europe amid a vacuum of governmental institutions, violence, and chaos.[5]

For an example of sermons from this tumultuous era, we turn to Quodvultdeus, bishop of Carthage, who faced the Vandal conquest. He was a mighty preacher of repentance, and saw God as punishing Rome and the Christians for their sins. He urged his hearers not to put their hope in this world but to look forward to the joys of heaven.[6]

The sense of devastation and defeat was profound, but the resultant power vacuum presented an opportunity for the Christian church. Thus Professor Bark sees a "frontier quality" in the early Middle Ages, the emergence of something new in place of shattered antiquity. Professor von Campenhausen, in a memorable post-World War II address titled "Augustine and the Fall of Rome," called for theology to maintain its historic and God-given role to assert divine truth to all of its pagan opponents, no matter how tragic history may have become.[7] We now survey preaching in the Middle Ages.

---

1. William Carroll Bark, *Origins of the Medieval World* (Palo Alto, Calif.: Stanford University Press, 1958), 70ff. The italics are mine.
2. Santo Nazzarino, *The End of the Ancient World* (New York: Knopf, 1966).
3. Bark, *Origins of the Medieval World,* 109.
4. Hugh Trevor-Roper, *The Rise of Christian Europe* (New York: Harcourt Brace, 1965).
5. Richard E. Sullivan, *Heirs of the Roman Empire* (Ithaca, N.Y.: Cornell University Press, 1960), 45.
6. Robert B. Eno, "Christian Reaction to the Barbarian Invasions and the Sermons of Quodvultdeus," in *Preaching in the Patristic Age,* ed. David G. Hunter (New York: Paulist, 1989), 153.
7. Bob Patterson, ed., *Makers of the Modern Theological Mind: Pannenberg* (Waco, Tex.: Word, 1973).

4.1 THE LOWERING OF THE LIGHTS AND THE GATHERING OF THE GLOOM

See what has befallen Rome, once mistress of the world. She is worn down by great sorrows, by the disappearance of her citizens, by the attacks of her enemies, by numerous ruins. Thus we see brought to fulfillment what the prophet [Ezekiel] long ago pronounced on the city of Samaria.
—Gregory I (593 or 594)

With the catastrophic collapse of the effective structures of governance in the empire, the world braced for three developments:

1. The rise of the Byzantine Empire, in which preaching was virtually nonexistent. Some spiritual leaders fled to the west, such as Maximus the Confessor, whose labors in Carthage (614–638) were exegetically and hermeneutically important. His anti-Origenistic bent gives him special significance.[1]
2. The birth of Islam and the new civilization it brought, as well as the strange absence of a vigorous evangelistic effort to win Muslims to Christ.
3. The stirrings of Western European civilization as the church became the preserver and guarantor of the revealed truth of Scripture through a dismal time.

At first the church seemed paralyzed by what has been termed "despondent passivity." A marked decay in the arts and letters took place. The middle class was hounded out of existence and the growing peasantry was "reduced to total dependency."[2] The sacerdotalism of the clergy removed them from preaching and the people were increasingly ignorant and illiterate. Dean Milman characterized the situation: "Actual preaching had fallen into disuse."[3] The peasant class might see a priest once a year in order to receive the sacraments.

Education and the reading arts were confined to the monasteries. One conservative estimate indicates 90 percent of the literate men in the Middle Ages received their instruction in a monastic school.[4] The effective loss of the Bible and its truth with the related demise of biblical preaching spelled curtains for Christian vitality. Who and what kept the light shining in this darkness? We sense in our own time "a famine of hearing the words of the LORD" (Amos 8:11) and a growing biblical illiteracy among churched people. Some beacon lights of resistance to the drift of the period require consideration.[5]

---

1. Paul M. Blowers, *Exegesis and Spiritual Pedagogy in Maximus the Confessor* (Notre Dame, Ind.: Notre Dame University Press, 1991). Maximus was Christocentric in his interpretation of Scripture with an emphasis on the indwelling of Christ in the believer's life. He was concerned about both the *theoria* and *praxis* of scriptural truth.
2. William Carroll Bark, *Origins of the Medieval World* (Palo Alto, Calif.: Stanford University Press, 1958), 64.
3. Quoted in Arthur H. Smith, *Preachers and Preaching* (Philadelphia: United Lutheran Publication House, 1925), 12.
4. Norman F. Cantor, *The Civilization of the Middle Ages* (New York: HarperCollins, 1993), 153.
5. We seem to be facing a similar move from the Scriptures and text-driven preaching in our time, and it will have identical ramifications. One prominent pulpiteer recently explained to a Christian media convention: "You'll notice that I don't have a Bible. I've stopped using a Bible in the pulpit. People don't want sermons; they want to hear what God means to us in our own hearts." This retreat from Scripture will be as disastrous now as it was long ago.

4.1.1   LEO THE GREAT—PREACHER OF COURAGE

Love your Bible and you will not fulfill the lusts of the flesh.

—Jerome

He who knows his Bible, as men ought to know it, is offended at nothing that befalls him, but bears all things with noble endurance.

—Chrysostom

The church fathers placed considerable focus on the Scriptures, both in study and proclamation. For Augustine, "Bible study is the highest kind of Christian learning."[1] It was also a time of writing many commentaries. Such leaders as Cyril of Alexandria (d. 444), Theodore of Mopsuestia (d. 428), and Theodoret of Cyrus in Syria (d. 460) wrote significant commentaries. (Interestingly, the cults have never been much interested in writing Bible commentaries.)

A great drawback of the era was that it was left to bishops and prelates to do the preaching. As late as 692 the Council of Quinisext advised that the bishop had the responsibility of preaching to both clergy and laity as follows:

It behooves those who preside over the churches, every day but especially on the Lord's Day, to teach all the clergy and people words of piety and right religion, gathering out of Holy Scripture meditations and determinations of the truth, and not going beyond the limits now fixed, nor varying from the tradition of the God-bearing fathers.[2]

Bishops then were critical in preserving and promulgating biblical truth. Among the early bishops who did this commendably was Leo the Great (390–461). Born south of Pisa, he was a true Etruscan aristocrat. While on a mission in Gaul, he was was informed that he had been chosen bishop of Rome (440). Leo was a doughty defender of the faith, both against Manichaeism and Pelagianism, but also against a Paulinianism "formulated in the context of the ancient liturgy."[3] Paulinianism was a kind of adoptionist Christology. Leo also took vigorous leadership on behalf of the full deity and humanity of Christ, the victory of the Cross, the Resurrection, and the Ascension, and the principles of the new life in the believer. He had great courage and withstood both Attila the Hun and Genseric the Vandal to spare Rome from destruction. He exerted strong influence on the Council of Chalcedon to abide by his position on the fully divine and fully human natures of Christ without debate (451).

Leo the Great was dedicated to preaching. He was saturated in the Scriptures and preached sermons from the whole liturgical cycle. He held to "the unyielding truth of the gospels,"[4] emphasizing that what the apostles preached the prophets had previously announced. Murphy stresses the depth of his theological perception, his unmistakable social consciousness, and his "homiletical omnicompetence."[5] We have a fair sample of extant sermons.[6]

Examination of the sermons indicates they are more homilies than full-blown expositions. Leo quoted much Scripture. The sermons were Christocentric and he did not hesitate to engage falsehood and heresy. He emphasized personal union with Christ as the wellspring of the sanctified life. His passiontide sermons strongly underscored God's strict justice in redemption along with God's mercy.[7] While his claims for the Petrine priority of the Roman bishopric are exaggerated, we must see his energetic pursuit of sound doctrine, liturgical purity, and biblical preaching as pivotal in a time of drastic transition.

---

1. Beryl Smalley, *The Study of the Bible in the Middle Ages* (Notre Dame, Ind.: University of Notre Dame Press, 1964), 26.
2. James J. Murphy, *Rhetoric in the Middle Ages: A History of Rhetorical Theory from St. Augustine to the Renaissance* (Berkeley: University of California, 1974), 284.
3. Louis Bouyer, *A History of Christian Spirituality: The Spirituality of the New Testament and the Fathers* (Minneapolis: Seabury, 1960), 529.
4. Francis X. Murphy, "The Sermons of Pope Leo the Great: Context and Style," in *Preaching in the Patristic Age,* ed. David G. Hunter (New York: Paulist, 1989), 186.
5. Ibid., 195.
6. Trevor Jalland, *The Life and Times of St. Leo the Great* (New York: Macmillan, 1941), 495–514, 525.

7. William Bright, *Select Sermons of St. Leo the Great* (London: J. Masters and Co., 1886).

4.1.2 GREGORY THE FIRST—PREACHER OF CONVICTION

> The martyrs preached, till their bodies were dissolved in death; their bodies were dissolved in death, that they might shine forth with miracles; they shone forth with miracles, that they might overthrow their enemies with divine light; so that they might no longer stand up and resist God, but submit to, and be afraid of, Him.
>
> —Gregory *Moralia* 30.76

Born in a turbulent time to patrician parents, Gregory I, or Gregory the Great (540–604), rose quickly to Roman preferment. At age thirty-three he was made prefect or mayor of Rome and rode in a chariot pulled by four snow-white horses. Coming into contact with some of the disciples of the monastic St. Benedict, he dedicated his life to Christ and subsequently had a monastic tinge to his yearning to have "the odor of all flowers" pervading his life.[1] Dispositionally he tended to be bipolar ("I am all honey and stings"), and he served a stint as Roman representative in Constantinople. Gregory never learned Greek, and his Latin grammar was atrocious, yet he was made bishop of Rome in 590.

Gregory was a key figure in defining the evolving role of the papacy. He regarded the Western church as a ship which "creaked shipwreck." He founded monasteries and sent out missionaries while establishing strong ties with emerging monarchies.[2]

Gregory saw himself as "servant of the servants of God" and gave himself to the improvement and development of the clergy. His extended sermon on the Book of Job, the *Moralia,* runs to two thousand pages. The treatise has a powerful section on the resurrection of the flesh. His simple Latin writing style made this a classic. John Milton read this work deeply and drew upon it when he formed *Samson Agonistes*.

Gregory called preachers to the Scripture. In his own preaching he took a text step-by-step. In the *De cura pastorali,* he gave practical pointers to preachers. He wrote, "It is indeed difficult for a preacher who is not loved, however well he may preach, to be willingly listened to. He then that is over others, ought to study to be loved, to the end that he be listened to."

Yet at the heart of his commitment to preaching was a deathless conviction of the centrality of Scripture. Walker says that Gregory's attitude toward Scripture "is completely fundamentalist" (i.e., he believed of the Book of Job that "It is very pointless to ask who composed this volume, since we believe loyally that its author was the Holy Ghost").[3] He was concerned "to erect on the foundation of history a spiritual edifice." He summoned those called to the cure of souls to daily meditate, to feed on the Word of God, and to obey it. "We hear the Words of God if we act upon them," he argued. Of the preacher he says:

For it is true that whosoever enters on the priesthood undertakes the office of herald, so as to walk, himself crying aloud, before the coming of the judge who follows terribly. Wherefore, if the priest knows not how to preach, what voice of a loud cry shall the mute herald utter? For hence it is that the Holy Spirit sat upon the first pastors under the appearances of tongues (Acts 2:3); because whomsoever He has filled, He himself at once makes eloquent.[4]

The exact status of the Second Dialogue of Gregory the Great (with Benedict) is highly controverted, but here we have representations consistent with what we have been ascribing to the man some call "the father of the medieval papacy."[5]

Gregory broke new ground in his extensive audience analysis. A master storyteller, he may have been the first to introduce a sequential story for illustrative purposes in his sermons. He recommended that officiants read a patristic sermon, which may have tended to further fossilize preaching for many. His own preaching was often thunder and lightning and frequently reflected his conviction that the end of human history was near. The recession of the Parousia was not in evidence in his discourse (*Homillae in Ezechielem* 2.8):

Fiery swords, which reddened with the blood of mankind, and soon after flowed in streams were seen in the heavens before Italy became the prey of the Lombards. Be watchful and alert! Those who love God should shout for joy at the end of the world. Those who mourn are they whose hearts are rooted in love for the world, and who neither long for the future life, nor have any foretaste of it within themselves. Every day the earth is visited by fresh calamities. You see how few remain of the ancient population: each day sees us chastened by new afflictions, and unforeseen blows strike us to the ground. The world grows old and hoary, and through a sea of troubles hastens to approaching death.

Other preachers of the day, like the oratorical Peter Chrysologus of Ravenna (d. 451), tended to be moralistic. Maximus of Turin (d. 465) was known as a gifted extempore preacher who used word pictures skillfully. Caesarius of Arles (d. 542) argued that "the Word should not be honored less than the Body of the Lord" but tended to borrow heavily from Augustine. Others make us appreciate all the more the gifts and convictions of Gregory, who was often called "the last of the Romans."[6] Bible preaching was slipping away.

---

1. Robert Payne, *The Fathers of the Western Church* (New York: Viking, 1951), 201. For a vivid description of Gregory in action, see 199.
2. Norman F. Cantor, *The Civilization of the Middle Ages,* rev. ed. (New York: HarperCollins, 1963, 1993), 153.
3. G. S. M. Walker, *The Growing Storm: Sketches of Church History from A.D. 600 to A.D. 1350* (Grand Rapids: Eerdmans, 1961), 13.
4. James J. Murphy, *Rhetoric in the Middle Ages: A History of Rhetorical Theory from*

St. Augustine to the Renaissance (Berkeley: University of California Press, 1974), 292.

5. Pearse Cusack, *An Interpretation of the Second Dialogue of Gregory the Great* (Lewiston, N.Y.: Edwin Mellen Press, 1993). This is volume 31 in the series Studies in the Bible and Early Christianity.

6. Thomas K. Carroll, *Preaching the Word: Message of the Fathers of the Church* (Wilmington, Del.: Michael Glazier, 1984), 206ff.

4.1.3   SAINT PATRICK—PREACHER OF CONVERSION

That is why I am now ashamed and am seriously afraid of revealing my unskilfulness, the fact that I cannot hold forth in speech to cultivated people in exact language.

—Confessions 10

Who am I, Lord, and what is my calling since you have worked with me with such divine power?

—Confessions 34

But I see that I have been promoted beyond measure by the Lord in this present age and I was not worthy nor the kind of person to whom he might grant this.

—Confessions 55

Even without embellishment, Patrick (389–461) stands as a spiritual giant. He may never have driven the snakes out of Ireland or proved the doctrine of the triune nature of God with a shamrock, but he is the first British churchman whose writings have come to us. We are just now learning of the animistic and totemistic worship of the Druids. Pre-Christian religion in the British Isles was gross and dismal.

Christianity arrived in Roman Britain sometime after A.D. 100. Britons soon were making significant contributions. Alban (c. 208) was martyred when he refused to denounce Christ. Athanasius reported that British bishops stood with him in Nicea (325). Pelagius (354–418) was a Welshman whose teachings troubled the British scene, although his controversies with Augustine followed his departure from Britain. Christian churches were also springing up across the stormy Irish Sea in Ireland (Hibernia to the Romans).

Patrick was born on the west coast of England or Wales and reared in an aristocratic home. His father, Calpurnius, seems to have been a municipal officer and a deacon in the church. At the age of sixteen (405) Patrick was kidnapped by Irish pirates and worked six years in County Mayo as a slave caring for sheep. He escaped across country to Wexford or Wicklow and returned to England. In 430 he returned as bishop and poured the balance of his life into vigorous evangelization. It was this role that ensured his place in the history of biblical preaching.

Patrick traveled widely, planting about 365 churches and winning some 120,000 converts to Christ.[1] He also won the man whose slave he had been, as well as many Irish kings.[2]

In conjunction with prayer, the Scripture was primary for Patrick and Celtic Christianity. He was said to have prayed one hundred times a day. Hanson describes his constant quoting from the Latin Bible, which "impregnated his mind and dominated his thought."[3] He loved the promises of the Old Testament but most frequently quoted from Romans. He had a good grasp of justification by faith alone,[4] and his interpretation was generally balanced and sound. He experienced the Holy Spirit praying in him.[5] Patrick's conviction with regard to Scripture was clear: "That which I have set out in Latin is not my words but the words of God and of his apostles and prophets who of course have never lied."[6]

In his Letter to Coroticus he indicates his conviction that the last days of history are upon the church. He wrote that toward this end the gospel must be preached "as a testimony to all nations"[7] (Matt. 24:14). The flavor of Patrick's preaching may be tasted in a piece from his famous *Hymn Before Tara* (Tara being the High King of Ireland), called St. Patrick's Breastplate, or the Deer's Cry:

> At Tara today
> May God be my stay.
> May the strength of God now nerve me!
> May the power of God preserve me!
> May God the Almighty be near me!
> May God the Almighty espy me!
> May God the Almighty hear me!
> May God give me eloquent speech!
> May the arm of God protect me!
> May the wisdom of God direct me!
> May God give me the power to teach and to preach!
> May the shield of God defend me!
> May the host of God attend me,
> And ward me.[8]

---

1. For the overall picture of this period, see V. Raymond Edman, *The Light in Dark Ages* (Wheaton, Ill.: Van Kampen, 1949), 97–103; Kenneth Scott Latourette, *The First Five Centuries,* volume 1 in *A History of the Expansion of Christianity* (Grand Rapids: Zondervan, 1937, 1970), 216–23; F. F. Bruce, "The Apostle of Ireland," in *The Spreading Flame* (Grand Rapids: Eerdmans, 1958), 371–83. A very choice study: Thomas Cahill, *How the Irish Saved Civilization* (New York: Doubleday, 1995). Shows "The Untold Story of Ireland's Heroic Role from the Fall of Rome to the Rise of Medieval Europe."
2. James Bulloch, *The Life of the Celtic Church* (Edinburgh: Saint Andrew Press, 1963); Kathleen Hughes, *Early Christian Ireland* (Ithaca, N.Y.: Cornell University Press, 1972); Donald E. Meek, "Modern Celtic Christianity: The Contemporary 'Revival' and Its Roots," *Scottish Bulletin of Evangelical Theology* 10 (spring 1992), 6–31. I am indebted to my former teaching fellow Jeffrey Sickles for introducing me to these titles.
3. R. P. C. Hanson, *The Life and Writings of the Historical Saint Patrick* (New York: Seabury, 1983), 45.

4. Ibid., 39.
5. Ibid., 48.
6. Ibid., 46.
7. Ibid., 68.
8. Saint Patrick: Apostle of Ireland in *Notre Dame Lives of the Saints* (London: Sands, 1911), 252. We still have the sermon as more of a homily than oratio. This is contrary to Edwin Hatch's frequently cited lament that Christian preaching was handicapped early on by adopting Greek and Roman rhetorical forms such as introduction, division of the matter, and conclusion; see Edwin Hatch, *The Influence of Greek Ideas and Usages upon the Christian Church* (London: Williams and Norgate, 1901), 107ff. Hatch actually argues most curiously that the tragic development was the replacement of prophesying by preaching. D. Martyn Lloyd-Jones endorses this notion in his *Knowing the Times* (Edinburgh: Banner of Truth, 1989), 270. We must be wary of a knee-jerk reaction against the influence of Greek rhetoric which is not historically discerning and careful with the facts.

4.2 PRESERVING POINTS OF LIGHT—PREACHING IN THE GLOOM

He who realizes the living place which preaching in its most vital forms has ever taken in the spiritual life of the Church will need no further assurance of its great importance. He will not fail to note that the preacher's message and the Church's spiritual condition have risen or fallen together. When life has gone out of the preacher it is not long before it has gone out of the church also. On the other hand, when there has been a revival message of life on the preacher's lips there comes as a consequence a revived condition of the Church itself. The connection between these two things has been close, uniform and constant.

—John Brown, Puritan Preaching in England

The interrelationship of the health of the church, the health of biblical awareness, and the health of preaching is nowhere more striking than in the Middle Ages. All three were at an abysmally low ebb. The role of preaching was explicitly clear in the Gallican Rite (sixth century French Ecclesiastical Rule) and in Gregory's *Moralia*. Yet in practice preaching was nonexistent for most, and where it did exist it was gravely defective.

But God had not abandoned his beleaguered people. A multiplicity of movements reflected his faithfulness. The Bible was yet preserved, and in fascinating and fruitful ways it was yet proclaimed.

A wealth of research in recent years has taken issue with the long-prevailing view that the Bible was of little consequence during these one thousand years. This reversal is largely due to the studies of Beryl Smalley and her mentor, F. M. Powicke. In Professor Powicke's tenure at Manchester and Oxford and in his lectures on Stephen Langton at Oxford in 1927, he argued for the influence of the theology of the schools on medieval life. Smalley gave a lifetime to the study of the biblical commentaries of the Middle Ages and to the identification of the *Glossa Ordinaria,* a compilation of biblical text commentary begun by Walafrid

Strabo, a ninth-century German monk, and continued by such luminaries as Stephen Langton in Paris, Anselm of Laon, Andrew of St. Victor, and Herbert of Bosham. Several of these scholars were eminent Hebraists, and the work was generally based on a literal exegesis of Scripture.[1]

The *locus classicus* embodying this research may be seen in Smalley's incomparable *Study of the Bible in the Middle Ages.*[2] Here is evidence indicating how the Bible was preserved in a decadent period and how the light of the Scripture glimmered out of the monasteries in an ever-increasing brilliance until the dawn of the Reformation in the sixteenth century. What a debt of gratitude we owe to those who nourished and fed that flame. Our analysis must touch a variety of movements and influences.

---

1. R. W. Southern, "Beryl Smalley and the Place of the Bible in Medieval Studies, 1927–84" in *The Bible in the Medieval World* (Ecclesiastical History Society, Oxford: Blackwell, 1985), 1–16.
2. Beryl Smalley, *The Study of the Bible in the Middle Ages* (Notre Dame, Ind.: University of Notre Dame Press, 1964).

4.2.1 POINTS OF LIGHT—THE PREACHING OF THE MONASTICS

Let us pray that what is hidden may be revealed to us, and let us by no means desist from our studies.

—Cassiodorus

The instinct to withdraw in time of peril to seek purity is a two-sided coin. There *is* a biblical summons to separation (Rom. 12:2; 2 Cor. 6:17–18), but this must not entail isolation (John 17:15). We withdraw so that we may reenter refreshed and renewed. The Sabbath principle enshrines the soundness of going in and going out.

The earliest monastics, the so-called Desert Fathers, were responding to a situation of external decline and internal desire. **Anthony of Egypt** (d. 356) began as a solitary hermit in order to battle the Devil and later founded a community of hermits. He took literally Christ's command, "Go sell all that you have." Athanasius' great treatise on *The Life of St. Anthony* gave a significant boost to the monastic way of life.

Pachomius (290–346) brought together thousands of Egyptian Christians in communities of work and obedience. Helen Waddell's memorable observation is to the point, "These men [the North African ascetics] stamped infinity on the imagination of the West." All of this has immense implication for preaching.

Athanasius (328–373), the stalwart defender of orthodox Christology and bishop of Alexandria, brought the monastic ideal to the West in his Italian exile (c. 340).

Two early planters of monasteries in Gaul, **Martin of Tours** (316–397) and **St. John Cassian** (360–432), were not only contemplative but also evangelistic, in contrast to the Egyptian ascetics. Preaching was important to Martin of Tours, though it was not his strength. Cassian had sought admission to the Cave of the Nativity in Bethlehem, knew Chrysostom personally during his several years in Constantinople, and after a sojourn in Rome planted two monasteries in Marseilles (c. 410).[1]

Cassian's *Institutes and Conferences* give insight into the life of the community. The sacrament was shared daily. Scripture was basic. "The mind, in its course of growth, is to be filled and conditioned by meditations upon Scripture."[2] Wrestling with the meaning of texts, understanding the Scripture first in its literal or historical sense, pursuing moral application—these encapsulate the rhythm of monastic life. The copying of manuscripts was crucial. The Irish monks from the sixth century on preserved western culture in a very real sense as the world was overrun by barbarians. Cassian's monks copied and recopied the manuscripts.

Basil of Caesarea (330–379) struck a balance between biblical and theological study and the necessity of outreach by exposition and hospice work.

Benedict of Nursia (480–547), author of the influential Benedictine Rule, renounced the world in his fourteenth year. Born in Rome (and very much a Roman in his approach to all things), Benedict eventually established the great monastery at Monte Cassino.[3] His Rule not only governed the Benedictines but by the ninth century dominated all other rules and was the basis for the establishment of the Cluniacs and Cistercians. The Rule was hard law, and set forth twelve rungs of humility and seventy-two spiritual tools to be used in monastic ritual.

"The art of the Benedictine scribe" was instrumental in saving civilization through its copying of manuscripts. In the daily vigils there was great emphasis on Scripture, on "holy reading," on the library with its scrolls.[4] "St. Benedict's doctrine was based upon the Holy Scripture, so profoundly meditated upon and assimilated that his quotations enter easily and naturally into his text."[5] He was a prayerful man who practiced the praying of Scripture.[6] Benedict's emphasis on Scripture and the life of devotion, as well as his blend of preaching, education, and the arts for maximum cultural impact, became paradigmatic for centuries to come.

Cassiodorus in the mid-sixth century and **Boethius** (480–524) were significant because of their formative influence on the shaping of the monastic schools. Cassiodorus' volume on *Divine and Secular Learning* was critical in keeping education and literacy alive.

Another stellar figure reflecting the virility of Anglo-Saxon preaching was the monk known as **The Venerable Bede** (673–735). This worthy lived, preached, and died in the north of England, at the Church of Ceolfrith, in Jarrow, almost in the shadow of Hadrian's Wall. Fluent in Latin and an author of Anglo-Saxon poetry, his *Ecclesiastical History of the English Nation* remains an invaluable guide to understanding the advance of Christianity. *Liber de schematibus et tropis* is considered the first book of rhetoric written in England, and Bede's *De arte metrica* deals with grammatical lore. **Alcuin** (735–804) extended Bede's concerns on the Continent.[7]

Bede's chief distinctiveness, however, resided in his great love for Scripture and his dedication to preaching. Cloistral preaching (i.e., preaching within a monastery), like cloistral learning, was central to the survival of biblical communication. But Bede also preached to the people. His homilies were not long and frequently indulged in painful allegorization, but they were based on Scripture. G. F. Browne describes his method: "He took a passage of some considerable length, one of the lessons for the day, for example, and went through it, verse by verse, expounding rather than preaching."[8] He may have been the first preacher to use the church year in projecting his sermons.

The better preaching of this period has great resemblance to the popular Bible reading or running commentary which came into such vogue in the nineteenth century and continues on into our own time. Yet Jenkins observes correctly, "No reader of Bede can fail to observe his insistence, repeated and manifold, on the blessing which attends preaching . . . a blessing not only for the hearers but also for the preacher himself."[9]

Tradition has it that when Bede was dying, he was translating John's gospel into Anglo-Saxon and urged his amanuensis to "write quickly." He wanted "one more sentence" and was given the next verse from John 19, "It is finished," to which he replied, "Aye, it is finished." And he died.

Amid the deplorable moral and spiritual collapse, some of the monastics began to reach out in preaching missions into the cities and countryside, such as **Leander** and **Isidore** in Spain. The preaching was generally in Latin, but interpreters were beginning to be employed. In 762 **Chrodegang**, archbishop of Metz, in his *Regula Canonicorum* stipulated that there must be preaching at least twice every month in every parish, hopefully on every feast day and on every Lord's Day, and "that the preaching must be such as the people can understand."[10] Similarly in Charlemagne's *Capitularia,* as early as 769 priests are "forbidden to feign and preach to the people out of their own understanding and not according to the Sacred Scriptures, new or uncanonical things."[11]

One of the foremost examples of monastic preaching must be that of **St. Bernard of Clairvaux** (1091–1153), called "the last of the Fathers," and "the mellifluous doctor" by Pius XII at the eighth centenary of his death in 1953. Luther regarded him as "the most pious of all the monks," and said of him, "He preached Christ most charmingly. I follow him wherever he preached Christ, and I pray to Christ in the faith in which he prayed to Christ."[12] Erasmus paid tribute to Bernard's fiery eloquence in his *Art of Preaching,* saying, "Bernard is an eloquent preacher, much more by nature than by art; full of charm and vivacity, and knows how to reach and move the affections."

Brought up near Dijon in an aristocratic family, Bernard early in life entered the Cistercian abbey at Citeaux, where at the end of his first year he could not recall whether the ceiling was vaulted or if there were two or three windows in his cell. He was a man of singular discipline. In time he established Clairvaux in the Burgundian hills. His organizational genius, his writing and preaching, his involvement in the Second Crusade (Christendom's highly flawed military effort to combat Muslim expansionism, described by Professor Trevor-Roper as "a deplorable outburst of fanaticism and folly"), and his rescue of the papacy from the Great Schism are all most remarkable. His conflict with Peter Abelard is the stuff of fiction.[13] We would love him if only for "O Sacred Head Now Wounded" and "Jesus the Very Thought of Thee."

Yet here we note particularly his strong biblical preaching. Two daily sermons were given to "the white monks" in this tradition. Bernard's preaching was influential through the written transcripts circulated far and wide. The eighty-six sermons he preached from the Song of Solomon are of special significance, as are his preaching on the love of God and his extraordinary sermons on conversion.

The sermons of Bernard are the first to divide discourse into sections. He typically took a text and then studded his message with Scripture.[14] Clear throughout is his high view of biblical inspiration. Like a skilled physician, he analyzes the "hidden sores of mankind," but then he insists that "[we] must rely upon grace and not upon nature, nor even upon sincere efforts. [We] must turn toward the Word, because the affinity which links [our] soul to Him is not illusory. The proof of this kinship is the likeness which remains."[15] Even his sermons on "Various Meanings of the Kiss" and "The Breasts and Their Perfume" from the Canticles, while a bit of a stretch, are yet full of devotion to Christ. "To know Jesus and Him crucified is the sum of my philosophy," he would argue. His preaching on conversion is aggressive and clear and he would often ask for a response after the message.[16]

Bernard's life and testimony exerted a profound influence on his own and subsequent times. He inveighed against the doctrine of papal infallibility, monastic corruption, the doctrine of the immaculate conception of Mary, and atrocities against the Jews. Conservative and controversial, he was a servant of Christ.

We must consider one more monastic, the Cistercian from southern Italy, **Joachim of Fiore** (1135–1202). He was the abbot of the monastery of Curazzo in Calabria. Joachim loved the exposition of Scripture and emphasized the essential agreement of the Old Testament and the New Testament in his widely read *Liber concordie*. He advanced the idea of the future conversion of the Jews and advocated the establishment of preaching orders.

With a strong following up into the sixteenth century, Joachim has bequeathed us "his great lyrical outbursts on the glories of the Age of the Spirit."[17] Unlike Thomas Aquinas, who taught that hope is a transcendent virtue and that the fulfillment of promise would not be in time/space history, Joachim taught the overlap of the two ages and a chiliastic age in which all of the Old Testament promises will be fulfilled. Moltmann argues that Joachim is more alive and relevant today than Aquinas.[18] Wycliffe quoted him often, and his influence on the Franciscans has been traced. His preaching rhythms move right into the Renaissance. The biblical and spiritual resources preserved and promulgated through the monastic system are a resounding testimony to God's gracious providence.

---

1. Owen Chadwick, *John Cassian* (Cambridge, Mass.: Cambridge University Press, 1968), 10, 19, 23.
2. Ibid., 101.
3. For a superbly researched historical novel about St. Benedict, see Louis de Wohl, *Citadel of God* (San Francisco: Ignatius, 1959).
4. T. F. Lindsay, *Saint Benedict: His Life and Work* (London: Burns and Oates, 1949), 119.

5. Ibid., 149.
6. Ibid., 163.
7. James J. Murphy, *Rhetoric in the Middle Ages: A History of Rhetorical Theory from St. Augustine to the Renaissance* (Berkeley: University of California Press, 1974), 76ff.
8. G. F. Browne, *The Venerable Bede: His Life and Writings* (London: SPCF, 1930), 232.
9. Claude Jenkins, *Bede As Exegete and Theologian,* ed. A. H. Thompson (New York: Atheneum, 1966). For a fascinating probe of Bede's exegesis for preaching, see Judith McClure, "Bede's Notes on Genesis and the Training of the Anglo-Saxon Clergy," in *The Bible in the Medieval World,* essays in memory of Beryl Smalley (Oxford: Blackwell, 1985), 17–30. He also plumbed deeply into Ezra and Nehemiah to parallel his own times.
10. E. C. Dargan, *A History of Preaching* (New York: Hodder and Stoughton, 1905), 1:134.
11. Ibid.
12. James M. Houston, ed., *The Love of God by Bernard of Clairvaux* (Portland, Oreg.: Multnomah, 1983), 19–20.
13. Denis Meadows, *A Saint and a Half: The Remarkable Lives of Abelard and St. Bernard of Clairvaux* (New York: Devin-Adair, 1963). Meadows sees Bernard as a joyous mystic.
14. Jean Leclercq, *Bernard of Clairvaux and the Cistercian Spirit* (Kalamazoo, Mich.: Cistercian Publications, 1976), 129ff., on "Bernard the Biblical Preacher"; M. Basil Pennington, ed., *Saint Bernard of Clairvaux: Studies Commemorating the 8th Century of His Canonization* (Kalamazoo, Mich.: Cistercian Publications, 1977), 101ff.
15. Bernard of Clairvaux, *On the Song of Songs,* 3 vols. (Spencer, Mass.: Cistercian Publications, 1971).
16. Bernard of Clairvaux, *Sermons on Conversion* (Kalamazoo, Mich.: Cistercian Publications, 1981).
17. Marjorie Reeves, *The Influence of Prophecy in the Later Middle Ages* (London: Oxford, 1969); also Marjorie Reeves, *Joachim of Fiore and the Prophetic Future* (New York: Harper, 1976).
18. Jurgen Moltmann, *History and the Triune God: Contributions to Trinitarian Theology* (New York: Crossroad, 1992), 92ff.

4.2.2 POINTS OF LIGHT—THE PREACHING OF THE MISSIONARIES

> But you will receive power when the Holy Spirit comes on you; and you will be my witnesses in Jerusalem, and in all Judea and Samaria, and to the ends of the earth. . . . One of these must become a witness with us of his resurrection.
>
> —Acts 1:8, 22b

In analyzing the place of preaching in the essentially chaotic period of the Dark Ages we are pursuing subjects of more than antiquarian interest. In our time we hear Charles Colson and Alasdair MacIntyre saying that "the new dark ages are already engulfing us." Leslie Newbigin opines, "It is hard to see any future except collapse." Carl Henry tells us, "The barbarians are coming." How relevant, then, is it for us to understand what took place in the Dark Ages! The preservation and preaching of Scripture are the significant actions of the Middle Ages. We want also to note what forces and forms tended to impede scriptural advance.[1]

Preaching could not be limited to the daily *collatio,* where the abbot preached to the monks and the monks asked questions. Such was the tradition of Augustine in *De Doctrina Christiana.* Teaching and preaching are exegesis, and exegesis is teaching and preaching.[2] Here we are viewing the high regard for Scripture reflected in Gregory the Great's attitude toward the Bible, the *lectio divina,* the *sacra pagina.* But the monks were thrust out of seclusion (which was an essential denial of the gospel, cf. Matthew 5:12–14) into the highways and byways of public concourse, as evidenced in the ministry of St. Bernard, who become a public preacher of considerable distinction.

The early Middle Ages were a time of population migration and dislocation. In 596 Gregory the Great dispatched Augustine, prior of the monastery of St. Andrew on the Caelian Hill in Rome, to lead a party in the evangelization of England. His interest in the Britons had been kindled when he saw some fair-haired youth in the Forum and learned they were "Angles." He is supposed to have said, "A good name, too, for they look like angels and they ought to be joint-heirs with the angels of heaven."[3]

In all of this, we see a remarkable spread of the gospel, with preaching at the forefront. This expansion of the faith is doubly impressive in light of the fact that Christianity was a diminishing presence in large parts of the Near East and the Mediterranean right up to 732, when Charles the Hammer halted the Saracen advance at the Pyrenees.[4]

While evangelistic efforts did emanate from Rome, the most potent thrusts for renewal came from the outposts of Celtic Christianity, where Scripture was cherished (e.g., the illuminated manuscripts such as *The Book of Kells,* which can still be seen at Trinity College, Dublin). The missionary breakthroughs of this period were led by preaching.

The role of preaching in Christianity is unique, as Dargan points out: "There was nothing in ancient oratory corresponding to our lecture platform or pulpit."[5] A preaching ministry was an indispensable aspect of the remarkable growth of Christianity "in a crumbling world."[6] Pointing out how Christianity utilized many viable rhetorical forms familiar within the culture, Professor Latourette argues: "In the fourth and fifth centuries eloquent preaching which conformed to these models won loud acclaim from huge audiences."[7]

With the Frankish church in decline, the fire came from Ireland (largely because of its bibliocentric tradition). According to Bede, **St. Ninian** brought the gospel to the Picts of Southern Scotland in the fifth century and **St. David** to Wales in the sixth century. But it was the brave Irishman **Columba,** who with twelve others landed on the island of Iona in 563 and declared their resolution to stay by burning their boats. A bit of the flavor of his preaching can be sensed in his hymn "Altus Prosator," written to describe the day of doom:

The Day of God's provings, King over kings,
The Day of His anger loud, darkness and cloud,
The Day of the thunder's sound, heard in the heavens around,
The Day in mourning clad, bitter and sour and sad.
When women's love lies dead, and men now have fled
All lust and petition of this world's ambition.

Then stand we shall trembling before the Lord's judging
To account for our actions, our sins, laws infractions;
Then shall we see nearby our wickedness clearly,
The book of our conscience shall look in our face.
Into weeping we break forth, all hope we forsake,
Gone now is the hour once held in our power.[8]

In 633–34 King Oswald of Northumbria sent to Ireland for a bishop who would come to preach. Ultimately the godly **Aidan** was sent. He entered into evangelization on horseback, "Preaching, baptizing, doing all a mission bishop's work."[9] Still another Irish missionary monk of impact was **Columban** from Bangor, who in the sixth and seventh centuries exerted himself in frenetic preaching in France, Italy, and Switzerland. Following forays of monks to the Orkney Islands, the Shetlands, and Iceland, evangelization soon moved to the European continent. Bede (1.26) described how missionary work began in a part of England:

> There was on the east side of the city, a church dedicated to the honour of St. Martin, built whilst the Romans were still on the island, wherein the Queen, who, as has been said before, was a Christian, used to pray. In this they first began to meet, to sing, to pray, to say mass, to preach, and to baptize, till the king, being converted to the faith, allowed them to preach openly, and build or repair churches in all places.

We must remember that while all of this was going on in the West, missionary advance in the East was limited due to doctrinal conflict, the Muslim explosion, and what Dargan characterizes as "continuous decline in preaching."[10] Ker is undoubtedly correct in alleging, "A great torpor has benumbed the preaching of this church for centuries. No great name stirring the hearts of the masses and shining out to lands beyond has appeared for more than a thousand years."[11]

Still another luminous herald of the gospel, **Wilfrid of Northumbria,** started out for the continent in 678 and evangelized Friesland. Bede records: "He was honorably received by that barbarous people and their King Aldgist, to whom he preached Christ, and instructed many thousands of them in the word of truth, washing them from their abominations in the laver of salvation. Thus he there began the work of the gospel which was afterwards finished by Willibrord" (5.19).

Willibrord was trained by Wilfrid and left in 692 to do evangelism along the southern shores of the North Sea. The devastating raids by the pirates of Scandinavia pointed to the urgent need to bring the gospel to those farther east.

Willibrord succeeded in enlisting thirty Danish boys to be trained as future missionaries in their homeland and to the north.

Born in Devon in England in 675 and influenced by Wilfrid and Willibrord, **Winfrid** (later called **Boniface**) spearheaded the gospel advance to the pagan Germans. He courageously challenged the pagan gods, felling the notorious pagan symbol of the Oak of Thor and building a monastery at Fritzlar out of its timbers.[12] He was used mightily to spread the church in Bavaria, Thuringia, and Hesse. Winfrid's sermons were rich with Scripture, his appeals were seethed with earnestness:

> Apply yourselves to learn the Lord's Prayer and the Creed, and teach them to your children. Fast, love righteousness, resist the devil, receive communion at the appointed seasons. Believe that Christ will come again, that there will be a bodily resurrection, and a general judgment of all men. Then the evil will be divided from the good, and the one will go to eternal burning, the other to eternal bliss, to enjoy life everlasting in God with no more death, light without darkness, health without suffering, joy without fear, happiness without sorrow; peace there shall be forevermore, and the righteous shall shine like the sun, for eye hath not seen, nor ear heard, neither hath it entered into the heart of man to conceive what things God has prepared for them that love Him.[13]

Known as the apostle of the north, **Anskar** or **Ansgar** (known to the Scandinavians as Oscar) was born in 801 in northern France. He was first master and preacher at a monastic school in Westphalia. Anskar went to Denmark as a missionary and established a mission in Schleswig in 827. Appointed bishop of Hamburg and all of the north, he survived the destruction of Hamburg by the king of Denmark, then regrouped and advanced into Denmark and Sweden with the preaching of the Word of God. Facing an opportunity to preach in the court of King Harald of Sweden, he and his party were set upon by bandits en route and robbed of all of their possessions. They persevered and won converts in their preaching mission. Again and again there were setbacks and discouragements. But Anskar was a man of God. He loved the Psalms especially and sang them day and night. The great spiritual tide would not reach Scandinavia as a whole until 1000, but the seeds had been sown in his faithful preaching labors. In the next section we shall consider the revitalization of the Frankish church and its outreach into Bohemia and Jugoslavia.

Some of the most powerful sermons in all of history have been preached by dedicated missionaries. Often unnoted in the annals of homiletics and frequently performed in the face of grave danger, the torch of divine truth has been lifted high again and again by Christ's special servants, the foreign emissaries of the gospel.

---

1. For further background of the Middle Ages one can read the historical novels of Sir Walter Scott, such as *Ivanhoe* or *The Talisman*. A diary from the Middle Ages such

as Louise Collis, *Memoirs of a Medieval Woman: The Life and Times of Margery Kempe* (New York: Harper Colophon, 1964) is also helpful. One can also learn from well-researched novels of suspense like those by Ellis Peters depicting Brother Cadfael or the splendid works of Edward Marston, P. C. Doherty, or (by the latter's pen name) C. L. Grace. The finest collection of the art and architecture of the Middle Ages in the US is at the Cloisters, a branch museum of the Metropolitan Museum of Art, located in Fort Tryon Park, New York.

2. Beryl Smalley, *The Study of the Bible in the Middle Ages* (Notre Dame, Ind.: University of Notre Dame Press, 1964), 35.

3. F. F. Bruce, *The Spreading Flame* (Grand Rapids: Eerdmans, 1958), 397.

4. For a delightful survey of this theme, see Eleanor Duckett, *The Wandering Saints of the Early Middle Ages* (New York: W. W. Norton, 1959).

5. For a discussion of this point, see my "Does Preaching Have a Future?" in *The Anatomy of Preaching* (Grand Rapids: Baker, 1989), 11–21.

6. Kenneth Scott Latourette, *A History of the Expansion of Christianity: The Thousand Years of Uncertainty* (Grand Rapids: Eerdmans, 1938), 2:252.

7. Ibid., 2:328.

8. Duckett, *The Wandering Saints,* 86.

9. Ibid., 101.

10. E. C. Dargan, *A History of Preaching* (New York: Hodder and Stoughton, 1905), 1:157.

11. John Ker, *Lectures on the History of Preaching* (New York: Armstrong, 1889), 79.

12. G. M. S. Walker, *The Growing Storm: Sketches of Church History from* A.D. *600– A.D. 1350* (Grand Rapids: Eerdmans, 1961), 30.

13. Ibid., 32.

4.2.3 POINTS OF LIGHT—THE PREACHING OF THE SCHOOLMEN

> The Holy Spirit makes use of the human tongue as an instrument, but it is He who perfects the work within us.
> —Thomas Aquinas in *Summa Theologica* 2a, 2ae, 177, 1

In tracing the epochal expansion of Christianity across these centuries, Professor Latourette characterizes the pattern as one of advance and recession.[1] We have seen that even in the Dark Ages there was considerable light both in the monasteries as well as on the frontier of missionary proclamation, in both cases evidencing quite a commitment to exegetical preaching. Yet there was an appallingly widespread ignorance and superstition, as we see when Gregory I sent a little filing dust from the alleged chains of the apostle Paul to the Eastern empress to help her face a crisis!

Public worship centered on "the doctrinally undefined sacrifice of the mass" in the Latin language, meaning that "missionary preaching, the marriage ceremony and confession were the only rites of Christianity performed in the language of the people."[2] Worshipers attended church weekly and received the sacrament three times a year. In the East the sacrament totally overpowered preaching; there was little emphasis on evangelism or missions. Yet at this very dire time, we see a movement of renewal known as the Carolingian Renaissance (756–882) under **Charles the Great** (or Charlemagne) and its counterpart, the Revival in Britain (871–899) under **King Alfred,** the greatest of the Anglo-Saxon kings.

The catalytic influence on Charlemagne was an Englishman, **Alcuin of York,** a spiritual heir of Bede (735–804), who had headed the Cathedral School in York. Alcuin went to work for Charlemagne as his personal tutor and advisor, and had spearheaded the revival of learning. This revival brought needed discipline for the clergy, helped establish schools, and sparked a renewal in preaching. The vast Frankish kingdom[3] thus saw marked change under the aegis of a spiritual leader who saw all of Scripture as "divinely inspired."

Under the Decree of 789 every local parish was to operate a school open to all children. If people were to read the Bible, they needed to know how to read. Alcuin set himself to purge all corruption from the Vulgate, and presented the revision to Charlemagne at his coronation in 800. He insisted that new converts be instructed in the Christian faith before being baptized.

Following Augustine's essential prescription from *De Doctrina Christiana* and the method of the Venerable Bede, Carolingian scholars collated Scripture with extracts of patristic interpretation. The result is called the Gloss, and did not take final shape until the twelfth century.

Two of the most prominent commentators in the ninth century were **Paschasius Radbertus** (c. 830) and **John Scotus Erigena** (born in Ireland about 810). John insisted, "The authority of Scripture in all things is to be followed," and spoke of "the unshakable authority of Holy Scripture."[4] Though an unconventional genius, John the Scot introduced theological discussion that shaped the preaching of the time.[5] Theological discussion was becoming part of exegesis. This is proper since we must proceed with a sense of theological construct. Yet it is dangerous if our theological presuppositions alter and determine our exegetical outcomes. John the Scot urged that "the Fathers stood below the divine authority of Scripture."[6]

Another theologian who was influential in the movement toward and within the monastic and cathedral schools was **Haimo,** who wrote commentaries (840–860) and gathered a rough concordance of texts. **Heiric of Auxerre** was a strong exponent of literal exegesis. **Remigius'** comments were crisp and concise. Like Jerome, he made important comparisons with the Hebrew. **Theodulf,** bishop of Orleans, was another proponent of linguistic studies. Although the preaching of the day often consisted of reading these extracts in relation to a text, they had the strength of being strongly biblical and highly exegetical.

After 908 this process was interrupted. Not a single commentary emerged for a century and a half. Smalley rightly argues that this regrettable hiatus cannot be explained simply in terms of wars and Viking invasions.[7] Liturgy preempted textual study and proclamation (a recurrent danger for the church). So much creative energy went into liturgical poetry and drama that there was precious little left for preaching. Smalley shows how the Cluniac abbots "in their sermons and meditations concentrate on the dramatic and emotional aspects of Scripture."[8] Thus, in our survey of the undulating story of medieval preaching, we have come to another trough.

In England at this time, we do have superb examples of more exegetical preaching from **Aelfric,** Abbot of Eynsham near Oxford (appointed in 1005), and **Wulfstan,** bishop of Worcester and archbishop of York (appointed in 1002). They flourish as part of the ripple effect of the Carolingian renewal experienced in Britain. But the lights were again dimming as the Danish King Canute established himself in their domains. Aelfric's homilies, or postils (since each homily began with the words *Post illa verba textus,* "after these words of the texts"), generally adhered to the literal and historical text. The preaching of both of these expositors was heavily eschatological.[9]

Also in this time, called the Ottonian period in Germany, we have **Liudprand of Cremona,** whose notable Easter sermon (delivered c. 960) on central tenets of the Christian faith is found in Bishop Abraham's collection and brings us into the central drama of the Christian faith.[10] He includes imaginary dialogue and persuasive argument.

In the eleventh and twelfth centuries we witness another resurgence of exegetical productivity in the schools. By this time the cathedral schools, forerunners to the universities in Paris and at Oxford, were more prominent than the monastic schools. An honor roll of outstanding teachers and exegetes must include **Fulbert of Chartres,** so concise in his literal exposition; his pupil **Berengar of Tours,** whose exegetical labors in Paul's epistles have been described as demonstrating "strenuous vigilance in understanding and expounding Scripture";[11] and Archbishop **Lanfranc,** the teacher of Anselm of Canterbury. By now, scholarly work was being centralized in Paris. The marginal and extralinear notes which would comprise the Gloss were nearly complete.

The central figure among these glosatores is **Anselm of Laon.** Along with others, he sought to merge the various glosses which had developed into Magna Glosatura to be used as a supplement for preachers.[12] But a problem arose, blunting the move back to the text. Smalley concedes that the tendency toward endless theological dialectic and philosophical hair-splitting led the cathedral schools away from "old-fashioned Bible study."[13]

The consequences for preaching were lamentable. The promise of the eighth and ninth centuries was the identification of theology with exegesis; now we find exegesis identified with theology and a diminishing exegetical scholarship.[14] Smalley lists the rediscovery of Aristotle, canon law interest, reason, speculation, and endless discussion of abstruse issues (all good in themselves) combining to discourage and reduce concentration on the Scriptures. But then came a renewal of biblical scholarship, a "back to Scripture framework" in the twelfth century.

The Bible was in fact the textbook of the Middle Ages. It was an Age of Faith, in which the biblical worldview informed cultural and societal thought. The authority of the Bible was final. Sir Maurice Powicke of Oxford saw the twelfth-century renaissance as significant as the later Italian renaissance. The scriptural body of truth informed all of life and presented a *preparatio evangelica,* a preparation and presentation of the Good News, in terms of which a medieval preacher observed: "Many throughout all the world have eagerly received faith in the Savior and His teaching, and so they shall do continually until the end of the world."[15]

The loss of focus on Scripture in the schools and in preaching is a downturn; the recovery of exegetical focus is an upswing.

The center of this crucial recovery was the Abbey of St. Victor in Paris, founded by **William of Champeaux** in 1110. Here **Hugh of St. Victor** (the second Augustine, d. 1141), his thought saturated with Scripture, called the church back to *De Doctrina Christiana*. He was a champion of the literal, historical sense and urged interpreters not to take the text "as an excuse for preferring our own ideas to those of the divine authors."[16]

Another stalwart in this school was **Andrew of St. Victor** (d. 1175). He combined vigorous study of the text of Scripture with "cataracts of eloquence" in expressing its truth. He was called "the second Jerome," but quoted secular sources such as Horace, Ovid, Virgil, Juvenal, Lucan, and Josephus. Andrew had interest in the geography and chronology of the Old Testament and exerted much influence on the Cistercians, Roger Bacon, and the English monastics. He was quoted often by Stephen Langton of Paris, who divided the Bible into chapters. Andrew's work is requisite background for understanding the biblical scholarship of the later preaching orders of friars. He insisted:

> The whole context must be carefully considered and expounded, lest we who rebut the errors of others, if it be done more carelessly, be ourselves rebutted.[17]

We shall meet later his famous student in another connection, **Herbert of Bosham,** secretary and biographer of Thomas Becket.

In a moving chapter titled "Masters of the Sacred Page," Professor Smalley shows how the Victorines fostered "new devotion to the letter of Scripture." Signal contributors here were the Paris masters: **Peter the Comestor** (d. 1169),[18] **Peter the Chanter** (d. 1197), and **Stephen Langton** (d. 1228). All stressed literal exposition in *lectio* (lectures), *disputatio* (debates), and *predicatio* (sermons). They stressed also the spiritual sense or application of the text. Their sermons were recorded by stenographers *(reportatio),* which meant some distinct reportorial differences in the style such as St. Bonaventure's "University Sermons at Paris between Easter and Whitsuntide, 1273."[19]

Langton urged his students to preach to the people where they are and not just as they would to their fellow students. He himself was a popular preacher. An excerpt from a sermon on Shamgar's ploughshare out of Judges 3 illustrates several points:

> See! This makes clear that a preacher should not always use polished, subtle preaching, like Aod's sword, but sometimes a plough-share, that is, rude and rustic exhortation. Very often a popular story *(exemplum vulgare)* is more effective than a polished, subtle phrase. Aod killed one man only with a two-edged sword, Shamgar six hundred with a plough-share; so, whereas the laity are easily converted by rude, unpolished preaching, a sermon to clerks will draw scarcely one of them from his error.[20]

We wince at aspects of this thrust but identify with the point being made. Langton's motivation was ever, "The Word of the Lord must be turned into deed, we must act on what we have heard or read."

These preachers also developed another homiletical tool replicated frequently in the twelfth century and afterward. This new method involved building a sermonic skeleton by collecting all references through Scripture to a given theme or image. This was called a *distinctio*.[21]

Clearly we are in a fertile and fruitful time for biblical preaching and will not be surprised to discover some fascinating homiletical implications. The core of the issue is the thesis of Professor Powicke, who writes, "The legacy of medieval Christianity to later ages was the problem of authority," that is, what is to be the basis of life and trust.[22] Thus the critique of the prolific medieval historian G. G. Coulton is to the issue when he faults the medievals for their bibliolatry, although he concedes they received it from the Jews. He rejects God as the author of Scripture and the noncontradictory nature of the biblical text.[23] But the answer to the question of biblical authority shaped the approach to preaching as here described. Our answer shapes our preaching. The belief in the literal and historical truth of Scripture led further to the founding of two great preaching orders in the medieval church. That is our next area of inquiry.

---

1. We are immensely in the debt of Professor Latourette's magnificent study, but we should not be oblivious to certain regrettable premises in his work; see John D. Hannah, "Kenneth Scott Latourette—A Trailblazer," *Grace Theological Journal* 2:1 (spring 1981): 3–32.
2. William Ragsdale Cannon, *History of Christianity in the Middle Ages* (New York: Abingdon, 1960), 50.
3. An invaluable tool in these studies is Charles S. Anderson, *Augsburg Historical Atlas of Christianity in the Middle Ages and Reformation* (Minneapolis: Augsburg, 1967). For a readable and reliable overview of this complex period, see Brian Tierney and Sidney Painter, *Western Europe in the Middle Ages, 300–1475* (New York: Knopf, 1970).
4. G. S. M. Walker, *The Growing Storm: Sketches of Church History from a.d. 600 to a.d. 1350* (Grand Rapids: Eerdmans, 1961), 53.
5. Bernard McGinn and Willemien Otten, eds., *Eriugena: East and West, Papers of the Eighth International Colloquium of the Society for the Promotion of Eriugenian Studies, 1991* (Notre Dame, Ind.: University of Notre Dame, 1994).
6. Beryl Smalley, *The Study of the Bible in the Middle Ages* (Notre Dame, Ind.: University of Notre Dame, 1964), 39.
7. Ibid., 44.
8. Ibid., 45.
9. Milton McC. Gatch, *Preaching and Theology in Anglo-Saxon England: Aelfric and Wulstan* (Toronto: University of Toronto, 1977).
10. Karl Leyser, "Liudprand of Cremona, Preacher and Homilist," in *The Bible and the Medieval World* (Oxford: Blackwell, 1985), 43.
11. Drogo in Smalley, *The Study of the Bible,* 47.
12. Ibid., 63.

13. Ibid., 76.

14. Ibid., 77.

15. Maurice Powicke, *The Christian Life in the Middle Ages* (Oxford: Oxford University Press, 1935), 83.

16. Smalley, *The Study of the Bible,* 94. The five senses of Scripture are (1) literal and historical; (2) allegorical; (3) tropological, holds the mirror up to us, satirical; (4) anagogical or mystical; (5) moral.

17. Ibid., 128.

18. David Luscombe, "Peter Comestor," in *The Bible in the Medieval World,* 109–29.

19. Smalley, *The Study of the Bible,* 208.

20. Ibid., 253–54.

21. Ibid., 248. This technique is used by all preachers on occasion but was particularly popular among the Brethren preachers and was widely published in the works of F. E. Marsh, in many volumes such as *Illustrated Bible Studies* (New York: Revell, n.d.). In a sermon outline on "whatsoever you shall ask" (Matt. 21:22):
    1. Asking in prayer, Matthew 7:7–11
    2. Asking for help, Luke 6:30
    3. Asking for water, John 4:9–10
    4. Asking for light, Acts 26:29
    5. Asking for wisdom, James 1:5
    6. Asking for filling, Colossians 1:9
    7. Asking for a murderer, Matthew 27:20; Acts 3:14 (cf. 186–87)

22. Powicke, *Christian Life in the Middle Ages,* 1.

23. G. C. Coulton, "Medieval Panorama," in *The Twelfth-Century Renaissance,* ed. C. Warren Hollister (New York: Wiley, 1969), 154.

4.2.4   *Points of Light—The Preaching of the Mendicants*

> Masters, I could have told you, said this friar . . . after the texts of Christ and Paul and John . . . such torments that your hearts would shake with dread, albeit by no tongue can half be said, although I might a thousand winters tell, of pains in that same cursed house of Hell. But all to keep us from that horrid place, watch, and pray Jesus for His holy grace.
>
> —Chaucer, "The Friar's Tale" from
> *Canterbury Tales in Modern English*[1]

Some of the sunshine and deep shadows of this time are reflected in Chaucer's characters, such as the Monk, the Friar, the Pardoner, and the Nun's Priest. Chaucer (1340–1400) pictured those who journeyed to Canterbury in unforgettable vignettes of medieval life. The preaching friars were part of the preaching effort before all the people and were recognized for their preaching, but they were not all exemplary:

> Oh, how the friar behaves himself / Full wisely can they preach and say / When he comes to the house of a poor man! / But as they preach nothing do they.[2]
>
> Oh, well he knows how to preach![3]

This realism, as Pattison pointed out, was the theme of Henry Wadsworth Longfellow's "Golden Legend," in that "through the darkness and corruption of the Middle Ages ran a bright deep stream of faith strong enough for all of the exigencies of life."[4]

The setting for the revival of preaching through the friars was a great ferment and flux which must take into account:

1. The depletion of the Crusades (although the Crusades stimulated the growth and renewal of the cities). **Urban II** launched the first crusade with a mighty sermon at the Council of Clairmont in southern France in 1095. One historian calls it "one of the most skillful and effective examples of rhetoric in European history." **Bernard of Clairvaux** preached the second crusade in 1144. **Peter the Hermit** enlisted a great following. This huge popular response reflects "the millennial and apocalyptic outlook of the lower and middle classes of European cities" at this time.[5]
2. The Great Schism between the Eastern and Western churches in 1054.
3. The rapid growth of the cathedral schools as such leaders as **Anselm of Canterbury, Abelard,** and **Peter Lombard** press toward the emergence of the universities which become the centers for the friars and their revival of preaching in Paris, Lyons, Cologne, Florence, and Bologna.
4. The reforms of **Hildebrand,** or Gregory VII (1073–1085) emphasized the mission of the church. In 1074 he wrote to Herman of Metz, "We have a mission to evangelize mankind—woe be to us if we preach not the gospel." This is an important phase in the development of the power of the papacy.
5. The conversion of Russia and the fruit of Anskar's ministry in the conversion of the Scandinavian countries, with the baptism of King Olof Skotkonung near Skara in 1008.
6. The intensification of church-state tensions as the papacy seeks to be all-encompassing in its power, as when **Henry II** and **Thomas Becket** faced off in England. The institution of the Inquisition in this period was a significant step.
7. The twelfth-century scholastics and their controversies with the rediscovery of Aristotle, in which discussions no one seemed to take a more balanced view than **John of Salisbury** (1125–1180), an Englishman who was to become prominent in the School of Chartres.[6]

In this period a portentous revival of preaching providentially took place. The need for more and better preaching was apparent. Preaching aids had become a business.

Two-tiered sermons were seen in embryonic form (in which there is first a basic and elementary statement supplemented by deeper and more technical material). Since the days of **Paul the Deacon** (eighth century), we have an annual cycle for the church year in which the passage for the day is called the pericope. We are beginning to see "macaronic preaching," in which Latin and the vernacular were blended. **Albertano of Brescia** (1250) numbered his points. The *florilegium,* or collections of sermons, are seen early.[7] Under the driving influence of

Innocent III (1198–1218) the Fourth Lateran Council ordered more frequent preaching and more popular preaching. Preaching was beginning to be seen as part of the *vita apostolica* (apostolic life of the church).

Innocent was genuinely concerned about preaching. In 1213 he deposed a bishop because he was too aged and infirm to preach. Innocent's own preaching has been characterized as "dignified and scriptural, but brilliant rather than profound."[8] Out of this matrix came the two powerful preaching orders, the Dominicans and the Franciscans. Moving out from their university bases, they traveled through the countryside, towns, and cities preaching, sometimes with the approval and sometimes with the opposition of the regular clergy.[9]

The Dominicans were founded by the Spanish-born **Domingo de Guzman (Dominic),** born in 1170 and died in 1221. The order he established was called by the pope "the brethren preachers," or Friar Preachers. The Dominicans were more intellectual in a time when the systematizing of knowledge was popular. We can see this emphasis in two great schoolmen of this order, **St. Albert the Great** and **St. Thomas Aquinas.** The Rule of St. Augustine was adopted by the order. The purpose was "for the sake of preaching and the salvation of souls." The foundation was *missio a Deo*. Great stress was placed on contemplation and proclamation *(infusio* and *effusio)*. An insightful theme was ever before these preachers: *sine periculo non praedicatur* (preaching is a dangerous occupation). Emphasis was placed on both the grace of preaching *(gratia praedicantionis)* and the preaching of grace. **Hugh of St. Cher** (d. 1264) argued that the commission of John 20:21–23 was to preach, and **Humbert** (1200–1277) contended that "preachers are the mouth of God. No human activity is so noble as talking, because it is in this especially that man excels the animals. So preaching, being an activity of the mouth, is a noble task."[10] For the Dominicans, the contemplative basis for preaching was foundational.

Among the outstanding members of this "order of the prophets" were such gifted preachers as **John Bromyard, Meister Eckhart** (1260–1327), **Henri Dominique Lacordaire** (1802–1861), **Peter Martyr** (1200–1252), whose preaching led to the conversion of so many Catharists, **Johannes Tauler** (1300–1361), and **Vincent Ferrer** (1350–1419). Ferrer was a fiery preacher described as "a heavy-built old man with a bad leg, wearing an old green hat or a bonnet of black wool armed with a crucifix and perched on the back of a little ass. Yet the moment he spoke it seemed as if an angel entered into him."[11] He loved to preach to the Jews in Spain. The order also had units for women among which was the celebrated mystic and lay preacher, **Catherine of Sienna** (d. 1380). Catherine was one of only two women named Doctor of the Church. Her testimony was "Jesus died for me. This is the true science."[12] **Humbert of Romanis,** later General of the Order, argued in *De Eruditione Praedictaorum* that the sermon is of a higher order than is the mass. The unknown author of a thirteenth-century work titled *Tractatus de Arte Praedicandi* (A Treatise on the Art of Preaching) differentiates three kinds of preaching: topical, textual, and expository.

The greatest influence to emanate from the Dominicans was certainly **Thomas Aquinas** (1225–1274), of whom his mentor Albert said "It is a grace of preaching that enables a dumb ox to fill the whole world with his bellowing."[13] Like

Albert, Thomas took Scripture in a literal and historical sense. He believed canonical Scripture to be God-authored and inerrant. Besides his extraordinary theological treatises, he wrote an extensive series of solid Bible commentaries.[14] He said, "Holy Scripture sets up no confusion, since all meanings are based on one, namely, the literal sense. From this alone can arguments be drawn . . . nor is anything lost from Sacred Scripture on this account, for nothing that is necessary for faith is contained under the spiritual sense which is not openly conveyed by the literal sense elsewhere."[15]

The Angelic Doctor, as he was called, was a gifted preacher. He was also a poet and hymn writer. "He preached plain, powerful sermons, always in the vernacular of the people, keeping his eyes shut and his mind directed toward heaven while he spoke."[16]

If preaching is now aimed at winning souls as Gilson so well insists, then he is right in asserting that the move from fine-lined reasoning and disputation to preaching must take place. In the new method seen within these orders, reasoning was far less formal. Divisions were being made in the discourse (*primo, secundo, tertis, quarto,* etc.) to help hearers to fix in their minds easily what is being presented.[17] Such categorizations did not derive from Aristotle or Cicero but from the scholastic penchant for division and subdivision. Only one authority should be quoted in each division, as **Richard of Thetford** maintained, "lest it should appear that in dividing he has invented the members" (i.e., that what the text itself says should be obscured by imposition of external ideas). Interestingly, Dante was a student of the Dominicans and held to the highest doctrine of biblical inspiration himself.

The founder of the Franciscans, **Francis of Assisi** (1182–1226), was born the son of a cloth merchant. He has become exceedingly appealing in his austere wedding to poverty and preaching. He renounced all for Christ and urged his followers to possess nothing and to beware of learning. The Franciscans were more emotional than were the Dominicans. Of the life and legend of St. Francis and his preaching we have beautiful *residuum*.[18] He emphasized living the life one preaches. He was so unconventional as on one occasion after severe illness he was led before the people naked to preach to them.[19] He led the bandits to Christ who came to waylay him. He stressed the prayers and tears of those who would win others to Christ. He set the example by doing the humblest of tasks. He faced the most vexed opposition to his preaching. "Let every friar make his own life a sermon to others," he urged. His advice to the preachers was succinct:

> I warn and remind friars that whenever they preach, their words are to be well chosen and pure, so as to help and edify the people, and to define virtues and vices, punishment and glory. And let them be brief, for the Lord Himself while on earth was brief.[20]

The word of the Franciscan to the leper and to the sultan was "repent." Evangelical preaching was the way to win all people everywhere to Christ.

We have little that remains of Franciscan preaching because it was ad hoc in nature. We do have "The Sunday Sermons" (*Sermones Dominicales*) of

Bonaventure (1221–1274), successor to Francis as governor general of the order. The man called Good Fortune (his actual name was John Fidanza) was somewhat mystical. He studied with **Alexander Hales** in Paris and was a close friend to Thomas Aquinas. When Thomas visited and asked to see his library, Bonaventure pointed to the cross on the wall and said: "This is where I learned everything I know." He felt that too many preachers put learning before holiness. The Franciscans widely employed *exempla,* or illustrative stories and anecdotes, mixing in popular proverbs as "spice for the exegesis." Bonaventure wrote a small but useful volume on *The Art of Preaching.*

Up until the time of the great plague and the Black Death, there were upwards of two thousand Franciscans in Britain alone. While they had houses at Oxford and Cambridge and elsewhere, they wandered and evangelized over the countryside.[21] They would preach in churches, or in the fields and squares if they were denied access to the churches. Their preaching was forceful and popular.

A superb example of Franciscan roving was **Anthony of Padua** (1195–1231), born in Lisbon. He joined the Franciscans after seeing the remains of two Franciscans who were martyred in Morocco. Anthony ministered in Africa and throughout Italy. Up to thirty thousand people would listen to him preach outdoors. He divided the sermons under headings and used extensive illustration. He lit huge bonfires after the messages to burn up playing cards and similar items. He was known everywhere as "the friend of the poor." Another outstanding Franciscan was **Berthold of Regensburg** (1220–1272), whose lively and imaginative style was heard throughout Germany and Switzerland. The axiom of Jean de Verdi catches the heart of this resurgence in popular and effective preaching: "Lectures are to instruct the intellect, but preaching is to educate the heart."

A modern listener can scarcely imagine the impact of the preaching of an itinerant friar upon ignorant and isolated people. Huizinga describes the impression made by the Franciscan friar Richard, who preached in Paris in 1429 for ten consecutive days. "He began at five in the morning and spoke without break till ten or eleven, for the most part in the Cemetery of the Innocents. When, at the close of his tenth sermon, he announced that it was to be his last, because he had no permission to preach more, 'great and small wept as touchingly and as bitterly as if they were watching their best friends being buried; and so did he.' Thinking that he would preach once more at Saint Denis on the Sunday, the people flocked thither on Saturday evening, and passed the night in the open, to secure good seats."[22]

Reportedly, Francis received the stigmata after forty days of fasting. He then wrote his famous "Hymn to the Sun," so full of joy and praise to God. His sense of mission is reflected in his famous dedication:

> Lord, make me an instrument of Thy peace;
> Where there is hatred, let me sow love;
> Where there is injury, pardon;
> Where there is doubt, faith;
> Where there is despair, hope;
> Where there is darkness, light;
> Where there is sadness, joy.

O Divine Master, grant that I may not so much seek
To be consoled as to console,
To be understood as to understand,
To be loved as to love;
For it is in giving that we receive;
It is in pardoning that we are pardoned;
It is in dying that we are born to eternal life!

The same passion that typified the Franciscan preachers was also true of the Dominicans. Note this response to the Dominican Vincent Ferrer: "When he spoke of the Last Judgment, of Hell, or of the Passion, both he and his hearers wept so copiously that he had to suspend his sermon till the sobbing had ceased. Malefactors threw themselves at his feet, before everyone, confessing their great sins."[23] One friar put decaying corpses about the pulpit as he preached on death; another drew a human skull from within the folds of his robe to make a particularly dramatic point. With all of its spurts and spasms, this was a time of glorious promise for preaching.

1. Geoffrey Chaucer, *Canterbury Tales in Modern English* (New York: Garden City Publishing Co., 1934), 355. Chaucer (1340–1400) was a genius in the portrayal of daily medieval experience.
2. Edith Rickert, *Chaucer's World* (New York: Columbia University Press, 1948), 373.
3. Ibid., 378.
4. Henry Wadsworth Longfellow, *The Complete Poetical Works* (Boston: Houghton Mifflin, 1899), 516. Longfellow also has a striking poem on "The Abbot Joachim" of Flora (or Fiore) which closes with the trenchant lines,

   Love is the Holy Ghost within;
   Hate the unpardonable sin!
   Who preaches otherwise than this
   Betrays his Master with a kiss! (514–15).

5. Norman F. Cantor, *The Civilization of the Middle Ages* (New York: HarperCollins, 1993), 293.
6. Michael Wilks, ed., *The World of John of Salisbury* (Oxford: Blackwell, 1984).
7. R. H. Rouse and M. A. Rouse, *Preachers, Florilegia and Sermons: Studies on the Manipulus Florum of Thomas of Ireland* (Toronto: University of Toronto Press, 1979).
8. G. S. M. Walker, *The Growing Storm: Sketches of Church History from A.D. 600 to A.D. 1350* (Grand Rapids: Eerdmans, 1961), 163.
9. D. L. d'Avray, *The Preaching of the Friars* (Oxford: Clarendon, 1985). A choice treatment.
10. Simon Tugwell, O.P., *The Way of the Preacher* (Springfield, Ill.: Templegate, 1979), 27, 30.
11. Ibid., 75.
12. A. T. Pierson, *Catherine of Sienna* (New York: Funk and Wagnalls, 1898).

13. G. K. Chesterton, *Saint Thomas: The Dumb Ox* (Garden City, N.Y.: Doubleday/Image, 1956).
14. Thomas Aquinas, *St. Paul's Epistle to the Ephesians* (Albany, N.Y.: Magi, 1966).
15. Ibid., quote from *Summa Theologiae,* 15.
16. Walker, *The Gathering Storm,* 203.
17. d'Avray, *The Preaching of the Friars,* 177.
18. G. K. Chesterton, *Saint Francis of Assisi* (Garden City, N.Y.: Doubleday/Image, 1957); for a recent important title, see Duane W. H. Arnold and C. George Fry, *Francis: A Call to Conversion* (Grand Rapids: Zondervan, 1988).
19. Leo Sherley-Price, trans., *St. Francis of Assisi: His Life and Writings As Recorded by His Contemporaries* (New York: Harper, 1959), 74.
20. Ibid., 233. An intriguing book and film about the Franciscan William Baskerville's visit to the abbey of Melk in Italy may be found in Umberto Eco's *The Name of the Rose.*
21. John R. H. Moorman, *The Grey Friars in Cambridge, 1225–1538* (Cambridge, Mass.: Cambridge University Press, 1952).
22. J. Huizinga, *The Waning of the Middle Ages* (London: Edward Arnold, 1924), 4.
23. Ibid., 5. Concerning the itinerant ministry of Peter Waldo and his followers, a contemporary, Friar Steven de Borbonne, wrote: "A rich man in Waldensis, hearing the Gospels, and having a little learning, desirous to know their contents, made a bargain with these priests, that one should translate the Gospels into the vernacular language, and the other should write under the dictation of the first. . . . Now the same citizen, after reading those writings and learning them by heart, resolved to keep evangelical perfection as the Apostles did. He sold everything he had . . . and preaching the Gospels . . . succeeded in gathering together men and women; and teaching them the Gospels induced them to do the same. They were called to account by the bishop of Lyons who commanded them not to dare to explain the Scriptures nor to preach any more. They defended themselves with the answer of the Apostles from Acts 5." From T. J. Bach, *Vision and Valor* (Grand Rapids: Baker, 1963), 28.

4.2.5 *POINTS OF LIGHT—THE PREACHING OF THE PARISH MINISTERS*

The preacher of the Gospel, who, like the Apostle, ought not to be ashamed of the Gospel . . . ought every Sunday to set before the faithful peoples specified sections of the Gospel . . . like the specified measures of wheat.

—Bertrand de la Tour (a fourteenth-century Franciscan)

It should be considered that everything which ought to be put over successfully will be introduced into the mind of the hearer much better through similitudes, than through the simple naked truths.

—Thomas of Cobham
(probably identical with Thomas of Salisbury, c. 1238)

The status of biblical preaching in local parishes was uneven and spotty. Archbishop Pecham of Canterbury made a stipulation in 1281 ordering parish ministers to expound fourteen articles of faith, the ten commandments, the gospel, seven works of mercy, seven deadly sins, seven chief virtues, and the seven sacraments in the vernacular four times a year.[1] The archbishop of York duplicated the expectation. In many quarters there was gross ignorance among both clergy and laity. As late as 1551 one bishop found that nine of his priests did not know how many commandments there were; thirty-three did not know where they occurred in the Bible (Matthew was the primary guess); thirty-four did not know who wrote the Lord's Prayer and ten were not able to recite it.

Yet preaching was now more generally practiced than previously. Alexander Carpenter in the fifteenth century wrote, "Now, in many places, there is greater abundance of preaching of the Word of God than was customary before our time."[2] Berthold of Regensburg in the thirteenth century advised his listeners, "Although you lay folks cannot read as we priests can, yet God has given you two books to read . . . one is the heavens, and the other the earth."[3] The confidence of the preacher is seen in the words of a twelfth-century homilist: "Many throughout all the earth have eagerly received faith in the Saviour and his teaching, and so they shall do continually until the end of the world."[4]

Listening to preaching in a vast Gothic cathedral did inculcate a sense of religious exaltation. Winchester Cathedral can only be described as "ordered, magnificent stability" in a time when people genuinely felt upended and insecure.

The sermon was evolving from the rambling, ad hoc homily to something more cohesive and structured. Anthony of Padua carefully divided his sermons under *mains* (as in Revelation 14: the debt of nature; the merit of grace; and the reward of glory).[5] Thematic preaching made its appearance in the thirteenth century, the same century that produced hundreds of manuals on theoretical preaching.

The influence of the roving preaching orders had a salutary effect upon many local clergy. St. Francis scored heavily in his insistence on personal piety and a walk with the Lord. "No purse—no scrip—as you go, preach!" was his watchword. When he penetrated a camp of Saracens, he announced fearlessly: "I am not sent of man, but of God to show you the way of salvation."[6]

No one has served us better in our analysis of thirteenth-century parish preaching in England than has G. R. Owst of Cambridge in his two classic volumes, *Preaching in Medieval England* (1926) and *Literature and Pulpit in Medieval England* (1933). Owst contends that the local preacher was the chief mediating cultural influence in the Middle Ages. The prototypes of John Bunyan lived. Yet there was always a struggle to preserve the sacred page from the abuse of allegorization, bizarre numerology, and extensive moralization.[7]

Parish preaching demonstrated a growing interest in biblical characters, a highly developed demonology, and elaborate and vivid teaching about hell. Hagiography also hung heavily over the preaching scene. The use of *exempla*, or sermon illustrations, was typical. Even *narratio jocosa* (witticisms) were used, along with riddles and plays on words. **Robert of Holyard** used the properties of a magnet to illustrate his point on sin and salvation. Satire was common. Anglo-Norman verse-making was in evidence in local preaching. Miracle and morality plays would serve as the antecedents of Elizabethan drama.

Under the influence of the preaching orders, application of the Word to the political and social mind-set of the time was strong. The English Dominican **John Bromyard** (thirteenth into the fourteenth century) castigated the rich and oppressive nobility. "They provide for their dogs better than for the poor," he protested.[8] He flayed the aristocracy and criticized the jousting tournaments. He rebuked the vices of the clergy as well. Bromyard called for justice and denounced all its corrupters.[9]

The literature of the clergy helped lead the way as well. "Piers Ploughman" was a poem likely written by a peasant priest named **William Langland,** who created a Dickensian clergyman called Parson Sloth. Langland denounced high fashion, the use of oaths in conversation, and the follies of the inebriate. The drunkard's homecoming is seen as "a peep into hell" and the tavern as "the devil's church."

Owst maintains that "the medieval pulpit was a creative center,"[10] with the Shepherd's Plays depicting the Last Judgment and the terrors of death. Shakespeare's "seven ages of man" clearly built on the common pulpit discourse of the prior century. In Langland, it was the angelic figure of the preacher who dared to speak out, but what we see is preaching that is stronger in application but weak in Scripture. The brighter lights on the local parish scene addressed the pressing needs, as they well ought to, but if their prescription for the problems is denatured Scripture, what would save them from vapid moralism and mere good advice?

In a most remarkable survey of preaching on the continent in this period, Larissa Taylor shows that in France also "the pulpit was the mass medium of the era."[11] Although printed sermons were not always as preached, five thousand volumes of sermons were published in the period 1460 to 1500. Twenty-five percent of all religious books were sermonic. Earlier in the Middle Ages preaching had almost disappeared in the Mass; now there was an extraordinary upsurge of preaching. The bishop of Meaux "urged preaching in a more biblical manner."[12] Large towns would sometimes employ a preacher. "When a great preacher came to town, representatives of all classes and occupations would turn out to greet him at the city gates."[13] Styles ranged from the colloquial and racy, to the plain, to the ornate. Open-air preaching was not uncommon.

Jean Vitrier, who preached up to seven times daily, usually for an hour at a time, was a typically popular preacher. His homilies were "filled with Scripture, for he knew how to preach nothing else." His sermons were more thematic and unified than the earlier medieval preaching had been. He used illustrations and stories as parables with a decided entertainment value. His style embraced histories and legends, contemporary events and recollections, fables, and descriptions of animals.[14]

Illyricus was another noted preacher who preached literally hours every day. He claimed, "I preach to you for the health of your souls. Whoever wants to hear philosophy preached will have to seek from someone else." **Guillaume Pepin** preached amid considerable eschatological ferment. The Black Death and a poor quality of life contributed to a profound sense of dislocation. Pepin spoke of the three provinces of the afterlife: heaven, hell, and the present world.[15]

The quality of preaching was lacking, however, as Heath shows in his analysis of John Myrc's work in his *Festial,* a collection of sermons for feast days.[16] Myrc cautioned, "For little of worth is the preaching if you be of evil living," but we must express disappointment that his own preaching on the high holy days is so lacking in clear proclamation of the gospel of Christ. There is a massive dose of sacramentalism, too many fables, too little exegesis, too much Mariolatry, too much bizarre spiritualization. A major recovery of Scripture was needed.

Yet there were in fact local clergy like the Parson of Chaucer's depiction:

> There was a good man of religion, too,
> A country parson, poor, I warrant you;
> But rich he was in holy thought and work . . .
> Who Christ's own gospel truly sought to preach;
> Devoutly his parishioners would he teach.
> He had no thirst for pomp or reverence,
> Nor made himself a special, spiced conscience,
> But in Christ's own lore, and His apostles' twelve
> He taught, but first he followed it himself.[17]

1. Peter Heath, *The English Parish Clergy on the Eve of the Reformation* (Toronto: University of Toronto Press, 1969), 93.
2. Ibid., 94.
3. Maurice Powicke, *The Christian Life in the Middle Ages* (Oxford: Clarendon, 1935), 78.
4. Ibid., 83.
5. Robert D. Sider, *The Gospel and Its Proclamation* (Wilmington, Del.: Michael Glazier, 1983), 102ff. The most trenchant analysis of this shift is found in the new and massive study of H. Leith Spencer's *English Preaching in the Late Middle Ages* (Oxford: Clarendon, 1993), 228–268.
6. T. Harwood Pattison, *The History of Christian Preaching* (Philadelphia: American Baptist Publication Society, 1903), 105.
7. G. R. Owst, *Literature and Pulpit in Medieval England: A Neglected Chapter in the History of English Letters and of the English People* (Cambridge, Mass.: Cambridge University Press, 1933), 76.
8. Ibid., 327.
9. Ibid., 345.
10. Ibid., 469.
11. Larissa Taylor, *Soldiers of Christ: Preaching in Late Medieval and Reformation France* (Oxford: Oxford University Press, 1992), 4. Exploring a parallel in Italy cf., Augustine Thompson, *Revival Preachers and Politics in Thirteenth Century Italy: The Grand Devotion of 1233* (Oxford: Oxford University Press, 1992).
12. Ibid., 16ff.
13. Ibid., 28. Note the classic study: Allan Temko, *Notre Dame de Paris* (New York: Viking, 1952).
14. Ibid., 68.

15. Ibid., 96. This powerful book concludes with an invaluable series of brief biographical sketches of a number of the more noteworthy of these preachers, 235–42.
16. Heath, *The English Parish Clergy,* 94ff.
17. Geoffrey Chaucer, *Canterbury Tales in Modern English* (New York: Garden City Publishing Co., 1934), 15–16.

4.3 PUNCHING HOLES IN THE DARKNESS

Do your best to present yourself to God as one approved, a workman who does not need to be ashamed and who correctly handles the word of truth.

—2 Timothy 2:15

The unifying structure of Scripture is the structure of redemptive history. The Bible does not have the form of a textbook, and the witness to Christ unfolds with the progressive epochs of revelation which in turn are grounded in the successive periods of redemption.

—Edmund Clowney

After 1270 we begin to see the decline of the medieval papacy. The Great Schism and the Babylonian Captivity discredited the ecclesiastical behemoth of the Middle Ages.[1] The papacy of the Borgias had ceased to be a spiritual power by 1500. Protests by heretical movements like the Albigensians, who dominated southern France, and the Cathari, along with the Bogomils in the Balkans, sapped further strength. Many orthodox critics of the papacy such as Bernard of Clairvaux became a growing chorus of dissent. The corruption of certain of the monastic orders and the greed and cruelty of the Templars ate away at the heart of piety.

Peter Waldo of Lyon, a wealthy merchant, was moved to rise up in protest, reflecting the anticlericalism and the antisacerdotalism of the time. Securing a translation of the Bible in French, Waldo defied prohibitions to preach. The Waldensians were condemned and excommunicated. Still they went out two by two to preach the gospel of Christ. Something of the apocalypticism of Joachin of Fiore, who had disapproved of the Crusades and urged Christians "not to fight but to preach,"[2] can be seen among the Waldensians. John Milton's beautiful "Sonnet 15" is a fitting tribute to these champions of the faith who fled into the mountains of northern Italy.

Historians trace the dissolution concluding the Catholic Middle Ages, a dissolution that was fomented by economic depression, the Hundred Years' War, the plague and pestilence of the Black Death, and "the little ice age"—the unusually heavy winters of the fourteenth century. Yet a great change was taking place. Cantor quotes Johan Huizinga's great dictum: "A high and strong culture is declining, but at the same time and in the same sphere new things are being born. The tide is turning, the tone of life is about to change."[3]

It was, of course, the Renaissance. Many factors brought about the end of medieval winter. One cannot draw a sharp line between the Middle Ages and the Renaissance, but the new classical learning took root. The power vacuum in the empire and in the papacy opened up new opportunities. Italianization was more Platonic than Aristotelian.[4] Travel, exploration and discovery, mail service, and the invention of printing with the circulation of books were all part of it. The gothic was supplanted by the baroque. We see the rebirth of all the arts, as art again became realistic. The merchant class rose with power. It was an age of "more."[5] We see renewed interest in the natural sciences, philology, and aesthetics. Hale talks about a "genius for the use of words."

Developments in preaching were an integral part of this rebirth. We shall trace the impact of the Reformation, the greatest recovery of the power of biblical preaching in the history of Christianity. Faithful practitioners of the craft of preaching had been hard at work. They were instrumental in the recovery from the panic of the Black Death in the middle of the fourteenth century "by making the Gospel story as real as possible to them." This "was achieved chiefly through anecdotal and story-telling sermons and homilies."[6]

Yet, as Francis Schaeffer has pointed out, the seeds of serious spiritual sedition were also sprouting. The parity of divine revelation and human reason had been given to Western civilization largely by the scholastics, who placed humankind at the center. Hence, the Renaissance was the birth of a new humanism. The concept of autonomous man took root. The Copernican revolution no longer saw the earth as the center of the universe, but man became the new center of the universe of thought.[7] It was a time of great horizontalization, as in our own time.

The "man at the center" would later be enshrined and ensconced in the Enlightenment. He is man as Thomas Aquinas understood him, only "partly affected by the fall." As Schaeffer observes, "The intellect was not affected."[8] Bishop Cannon makes the same observation: "Yet the total depravity of man, stressed so vigorously by Augustine, got weak and half-hearted support from the scholastics. Human nature, they felt, is not totally corrupted by sin."[9] The Reformers and their forerunners had their work cut out for them. Rapid societal change and positive progress on the whole do not always make the task of the Christian proclaimer any easier.

---

1. C. Warren Hollister, *Medieval Europe: A Short History,* 5th ed. (New York: John Wiley, 1982), 326–27.
2. G. S. M. Walker, *The Growing Storm: Sketches of Church History from a.d. 600 to a.d. 1350* (Grand Rapids: Eerdmans, 1962), 146.
3. Norman F. Cantor, *The Civilization of the Middle Ages* (New York: HarperCollins, 1993), 562.
4. Jacob Burkhart, *The Civilization of the Renaissance in Italy,* 2 vols. (New York: HarperColophon, 1958).
5. John Hale, *The Civilization of Europe in the Renaissance* (New York: Athenaeum, 1994).
6. Ibid., 226.
7. Francis A. Schaeffer, *How Should We Then Live? The Rise and Decline of Western Thought and Culture* (Old Tappan, N.J.: Revell, 1976). The seminal volume is Schaeffer's *Escape from Reason* (Downers Grove, Ill.: InterVarsity Press, 1968) particularly 9–19.

8. Ibid., 52.
9. William Ragsdale Cannon, *History of Christianity in the Middle Ages: From the Fall of Rome to the Fall of Constantinople* (New York: Abingdon, 1960), 266.

4.3.1   THE RETOOLING OF THE PATTERN

> The Bible is an eloquent preacher, much more by nature than by art; full of charm and vivacity, and it knows how to reach and move the affections . . .
> —Erasmus in his *Art of Preaching*

During the approximately one thousand years of medieval Christianity, preaching had been conducted for the most part on the Augustinian definition. At its best, medieval preaching used patristic exposition as its model, Augustine's eclectic heremeneutic as its guide, and the Augustinian modus operandi with classical rhetoric as its standard. **Michael Psellus** (1018–1072) illustrates this accommodation well:

> I soon mastered the rhetoric enough to be able to distinguish the central theme of an argument and logically connect it with my main and second points. I also learned not to stand in complete awe of the art, nor to follow its precepts in everything like a child . . . I acquainted myself sufficiently with the art of reasoning, both deductive and inductive.

While there were abundant examples of the egregious abandonment of the text and much outlandish interpretation, there were conspicuous examples of powerful biblical preaching. The German bishop **Rabanus Maurus** (776–856) reiterated Augustine's analysis (quoting him seventy-eight times) in his widely used work *On the Institution of the Clergy.* But Perry is right that little attention was given to homiletical theory.[1] **Guibert's** (1053–1124) *Book on How a Sermon Is to Be Given* was more on scriptural interpretation than on preaching itself.

Faithful and loyal Christian proclamation took place here and there, as is demonstrated in the missionary passion and gifts of **Raymond Lull**. Born on the island of Majorca in 1232, his life was transformed by a vision of the crucified Christ. He followed after the Dominicans. After mastering Arabic, Lull became an apologist and missionary to the Muslim world. He used visuals skillfully, and wrote *On the One Hundred Names of God,* showing that Christianity exceeded Islam by one. He wrote 250 books, and urged the church to set aside 10 percent of its funds for missions.[2]

The outburst of preaching in the thirteenth century through the Dominican and Franciscan orders required new attention to the theory and form of the sermon. We are not caught unawares, then, that with all of the preparations for the strong recovery of the Scriptures for preaching in the Reformation, we have at this time the first formal consideration of preaching and its cultural forms since the time of Augustine nearly one thousand years earlier. The leading figure here was **Alan of Lille** (d. 1202), a Cistercian, influenced greatly by Gilbert of Poitiers and

William Thierry of Chartres. His *Art of Preaching* and his *Sermons* were defining for medieval preaching to follow. Here we see the scholastic desire for order and exactness. The legacy of Alan long survived him in the history of preaching, and its echoes are heard even in our own century.

Alan crystallized the method of taking a theme and text and dividing it. In the introduction, or protheme, the preacher sought the good will of the listeners and invited them to join him in prayer. The narrative usually was divided into three parts, with a rhyming scheme to help preacher and listener remember. The dilation of the argument utilized such techniques as *digressio, correspondentia, circulatio, unitio,* and *convolutio.* Conceding that "little has been said of this,"[3] he argued that the amplification of the proposition can be achieved by the constant reintroduction of the theme.

The definition of preaching given by Alan was clear: "Preaching is an open and public instruction in faith and behavior, whose purpose is the forming of men; it derives from the path of reason and from the fountainhead of the 'authorities'" *(Scripture and the Patristics).*[4] He differentiated between preaching and teaching. He also urged "weight in the thought of a good sermon," not to be dissipated by too much childish jesting.

> Preaching should not glitter with verbal trappings, with purple patches, nor should it be too much enervated by the use of colorless words: the blessed keep to a middle way.[5]

Concerned about the variegated congregations to be addressed, Alan tenaciously insisted that the object of the preaching was true repentance. "So the preacher should come to the exposition of the proposed text, and bend everything he says to the edification of the listener . . . let him not begin with a text which is too obscure or too difficult . . . nor in the expounding of his authority should he move too quickly away from his text."[6] He advocated the careful selection of a good blend of illustration. Alan emphasized the importance of a right life and godly example on the part of the preacher. Much good can be discerned in his conceptualization. The torrent of writers who followed him on this subject expose a totally new genre by 1220: books on preaching, the influence of which has continued down through the centuries.

Alexander of Ashby (c. 1200) allowed for only the briefest recap in the conclusion and insisted urgently that the Scripture must furnish the material of the sermon. **Thomas Chabham** or **Thomas of Salibury** (c. 1219) argued for the "artistic sermon," with preachers more like poets. A clear theme was essential, and division was necessary. **Richard of Thetford** (c. 1245) wrote about the art of amplifying thought in sermons using a triplex *divisio.* **Robert Basevorn** (c. 1322) wrote on *The Form of Preaching,* and **Thomas Tode** (c. 1380) wrote about its rhythms.

The French General of the Dominicans, **Humbert de Romanis** (d. 1277), spoke of preaching as an extension of the dialogue of heaven. He contended that preaching was superior to the mass and all liturgical expression. He urged the Dominicans to preach the gospel of Christ as the fundamental responsibility of the clergy. As Paul urged in 1 Corinthians 14:9, "Unless you speak intelligible words with your tongue, how will anyone know what you are saying? You will just be speaking into the air." Humbert asserted that the dish (the form) is far less important than the food (the Word). The renewed interest in preaching must be seen as preparatory for the Reformers and their forebears.

Why do we not see more full-blown expository preaching of natural thought units from the Scripture in *lectio continua*? The reasons at this point would seem to be that

1. preaching was frequently in a liturgical straight-jacket, subordinated to sacraments;
2. tradition often undermined *sola Scriptura;*
3. the persistence of the allegorical method in interpretation (still with us);
4. the historico-grammatico approach to exegesis was not tuned up;
5. preaching tended to be quite moralistic, not sufficiently God-centered;
6. the widespread ignorance of the clergy.

These issues all cried for attention. The Reformation would address them shortly.

---

1. Warren W. Wiersbe and Lloyd M. Perry, *The Wycliffe Handbook of Preaching and Preachers* (Chicago: Moody, 1984), 31.
2. G. S. M. Walker, *The Growing Storm: Sketches of Church History from A.D. 600 to A.D. 1350* (Grand Rapids: Eerdmans, 1962), 227. A priceless new study of Lull's preaching: Mark D. Johnston, *The Evangelical Rhetoric of Roman Lull: Lay Learning and Piety in the Christian West Around 1300* (Oxford: Oxford University Press, 1996). Professor Johnston shows Lull's commitment to preaching as "the paramount exercise of eloquence." The division of the text and the arrangement of the sermon are critical for him.
3. Alan of Lille, *The Art of Preaching* (Kalamazoo, Mich.: Cistercian Publications, 1981), 16. It is interesting that Dargan does not mention Alan of Lille, nor is he descriptive or analytic with respect to this transition.
4. Ibid., 16–17.
5. Ibid., 18.
6. Ibid., 21–22.

4.3.2   THE RENEWAL IN DEVOTION

We improve the preaching by improving the preachers.
—Warren Wiersbe and Howard Sugden

A minister of Christ is often in highest honor with men for the performance of one half of his work, while God is regarding him with displeasure for the neglect of the other half . . .
—Richard Cecil

Take heed to the ministry which thou hast received in the Lord, that thou fulfil it.

—Colossians 4:17 (KJV)

The quality of preaching is directly correlated with the godly character and compassion of the preacher. The Reformation touched not only technical aspects of sermonic form but also the well-springs of the inner life of devotion and intimacy with Christ. We have seen how vital Francis of Assisi's vision of the crucified Christ was for his subsequent ministry. Now we turn to a crucial movement of spiritual renewal. William Blake observed, "The inner world is all-important." Dag Hammarskjold believed, "The longest journey is the journey inward." George Herbert opined, "The greatest and hardest preparation is within."

The spiritual movement that made such dynamic impact on northern Europe and on the Reformers was known as The Brethren of the Common Life, or *devotio moderna* (the new devotion). The movement had its roots in the concern for clerical reform by **Jan van Ruysbroeck** (1293–1381) from Brussels. Taking the Rule of St. Augustine, he and several friends established a priory to which both Tauler and Groote came.

The founder of the Brethren of the Common Life was **Gerard Groote** (1340–1384), a Carthusian who was born in Deventer in the Netherlands and trained at the University of Paris. He was gloriously converted and began to preach against decadent scholasticism. Not a solitary like van Ruysbroeck, Groote established schools and houses even after he was forbidden to preach. By the middle of the next century there were more than one hundred such houses in the Low Countries and Germany. The fruit of this movement included **Thomas à Kempis, Wessel Gansfort** (who had a profound influence on Martin Luther), and **Erasmus** (who studied with the Brethren of the Common Life for twelve years).

In his definitive study, Professor Hyma describes Groote's ministry: "He preached the gospel of repentance . . . like John the Baptist 'laying the axe to the root of the tree.' His magnetic personality, burning zeal to win souls, and power of conviction carried their message straight to the heart."[1] He would preach in Latin to the clergy but in the vernacular to the people, who came from miles around. He would sometimes preach outdoors because the churches could not contain the crowd. Groote emphasized the intensely personal nature of Christian experience.

Originating in the beautiful Yssel Valley in the Netherlands, this movement spurred what is called the Christian Renaissance, something unrelated to the Italian Renaissance. The life and preaching of it were focused on the Cross of Christ,[2] the centrality of the Word, which laymen were encouraged to read,[3] the nonsacramental confession of sins,[4] and the true church of the little flock as compared with the organizational outer court.[5]

The essential message of the movement can be seen in Thomas à Kempis' *Imitatio Christi,* undoubtedly the most widely read book of Christian devotion in the world. It has gone into six thousand editions. Thomas, born Thomas Hammerken in Kempen (1379–1471), called people to the way of the Cross. He joined the Augustinian order, and preserved and published many of Groote's works. Another leader in the movement was **John Cele,** whose school at Zwolle was the model for the gymnasia of John Sturm at Strasbourg and John Calvin at Geneva. **Wessel Gansfort** (1419–1489) gave the Scripture authoritative standing above the pope and preached powerfully against indulgences in the church. In this he blazed the trail for Luther, who spoke of him as "that most Christian author." Luther also said, "If I had read his works earlier, my enemies might think that Luther had absorbed everything from Wessel: his spirit is so in accord with mine."[6]

Luther paid immense tribute to the Brethren of the Common Life. The influence of this positive "Christ-mysticism" (as contrasted with the often pantheistic metaphysical mysticism of a Jacob Boehme, for instance) had a long and powerful impact on French believers, even up to Port Royal and the Jansenists. Others who benefited from Wessel's work included Nicholas of Cusa, Ignatius of Loyola, John Calvin, and Zwingli. It was a defining movement in terms of the Word, salvation, the Cross in justification, and sanctification.

The roots of *devotio moderna* were solidly in the biblical preaching of Groote. Hyma contends, "The Christian Renaissance may be said to have had its birth in Groote's first sermons, preached early in 1380."[7] And indeed Luther quotes Groote in his seminal lectures on Romans.[8] "We do not believe the Gospel for the Church's sake,"[9] Gansfort argued. Many reforming insights abound in this movement. The worship style of the Brethren of the Common Life beyond question influenced Bucer, Calvin, and Zwingli. Calvin declared his desire "to follow Bucer, man of holy memory,"[10] and Bucer was an intimate of *devotio moderna.* The influence on Zwingli was through Erasmus, who visited him in 1516, two years before he heard of Luther.[11] The flame of this fervent fellowship also spread to England through the Brownists and the Barrowists, who had a colony at Kampen on the Yssel. In summation, we can accurately represent a most significant visit of the Holy Spirit through a bibliocentric movement of piety and devotion prior to the Reformation. God was at work. The pieces of the mosaic are fitting into place.

---

1. Albert Hyma, *The Christian Renaissance* (New York: Century, 1924), 13. A long-time professor at the University of Michigan, Hyma also wrote *The Brethren of the Common Life* (Grand Rapids: Eerdmans, 1950).
2. Ibid., 54, 58.
3. Ibid., 69, 93ff.
4. Ibid., 78.
5. Ibid., 107.
6. Ibid., 191.
7. Ibid., 303.
8. Ibid., 309, 318.
9. Ibid., 323.
10. Ibid., 337.
11. Ibid., 342.

4.3.3   THE REKINDLING OF PASSION

> Preaching is Christian only when it is passionately, uncompromisingly biblical, that is, when it sets forth faithfully what the Bible teaches on a given topic.
>
> —Richard Allen Bodey

> "Is not my word like fire," declares the LORD, "and like a hammer that breaks a rock in pieces?"
>
> —Jeremiah 23:29

In any time of spiritual decay we can mark a tendency to turn toward the cultivation of the inner life, as in the case of monastic spirituality early in the Middle Ages. In the deepening shadows of dissolution we see the same countercultural phenomenon in mystical spirituality. Church history is replete with instances of undue subjectivity in some mystics in which the Creator/creature distinction is in danger of being obliterated. Yet a solid "Christ-mysticism" (to use Deissman's expression) is certainly consistent with Galatians 2:20 and a host of other passages.

Several medieval English mystics began to exert an inordinately positive influence. Among these are **Richard Rolle** (1300–1349), given to excessive alliteration and misogyny, yet whose *Incendium* argues against the overcerebralization of the Christian faith. Then there was the unknown author of *The Cloud of Unknowing,* who so profoundly explores the treasures in the dark clouds of human anguish. **Walter Hilton** (d. 1396), an Oxford don and an Augustinian, testified to an experience of the Holy Spirit and likened the Christian life to a pilgrimage toward maturity. **Dame Julian of Norwich** (1342–1420) had a sense of the great love of God that was overpowering.[1] But here we want to focus on **Johannes Tauler** (1300–1361), whose ministry in Strasbourg, Cologne, and Basle was mightily owned of God and who must be considered one of the premier preachers among the mystics.

Tauler was born into a family of means (his father was a senator) in a time that the historian Barbara Tuchman describes as disaster—plague, war, taxes, brigandage, bad government, insurrection, and schism in the church.[2] He became a Dominican, renouncing the world, and matriculated at the University of Paris. Dissatisfied with the subtleties of the dialecticians, he began to identify with the movement known as The Friends of God, who under the influence of Ruysbroeck sought spiritual rather than formalistic piety.[3] Tauler was also much influenced by **Meister Eckhart** (1260–1328), the noted Dominican mystic, who twice served stints at the University of Paris.

We have about one hundred of Eckhart's sermons, preached in Latin to the clergy and in the vernacular to the laity. Often quite abstract, his burden in preaching was on target:

> When I preach, I am careful to speak about detachment and that a person should become free of self and of all things. Secondly, that one should

be re-formed in the simple good that is God. Thirdly, that one should think of the great nobility which God has placed in the soul, so that a person may thereby come to God in a wonderful way. Fourthly, concerning the purity of divine nature—there is such brilliance in it that it is inexpressible.[4]

Eckhart preached in Strasbourg, and his searing sense of sin along with his tendency to speculate always seemed to land him in ecclesiastical hot water. The contemporary apostate Roman Catholic thinker, Matthew Fox, has latched onto something of the creation spirituality in Eckhart and run it into the ditch. Contemporary New Age spirituality deifies nature and worships Mother-Earth *(Gaia),* often within a pantheistic framework.

Tauler enjoyed considerable success in preaching to the Rhenish states before his remarkable conversion in 1338. Then a mysterious layman confronted him with the ultimatum: "You must die, Dr. Tauler! Before you can do your greatest work for God, the world, and this city, you must die to yourself, your gifts, your popularity, and even your own goodness, and when you have learned the full meaning of the Cross, you will have new power with God and man."[5] Consequently, his preaching evidenced more searching application and trembled with much greater sorrow over sin.[6] When the Black Death visited Strasbourg in 1348, all saw Tauler's great zeal for discipline and self-denial. He was walking the way of the Cross.

Possessing about eighty of his sermons, we can well appreciate the impression made upon Christina Ebner, a contemporary: "His fiery tongue kindled the entire world."[7]

This preacher rocked a nation with reverberations that would reach to the time of Martin Luther, who read and annotated his sermons. Tauler blended the two main forms of preaching popular at time—the exegetical homily and the more thematic sermon based on the university sermon model. In the thema, the topic and text were announced in Latin and then immediately rendered into the vernacular. This was frequently followed by the prothema with an amplification of the biblical theme. In "Sermon I for Christmas," based on Isaiah 9:6, we see a threefold division of the text. Tauler did not give equal treatment to the three mains, and the third main did not relate in clear fashion. Yet he stayed close to the biblical images and evinced a sense of close relationship to the congregation.[8]

A computer-aided analysis of syntactic patterns and idiosyncrasies has been made on the styles of Eckhart, Tauler, and Suso. Tauler is shown to plough his own furrow, using short sentences in an oral pattern, and stressing logical disposition amid reflective units and application.[9] Clearly Tauler must be recognized as one of the most gifted and influential preachers of this time. His sermons had a profound impact upon the Reformers.

An impressive example of the effect of impassioned preaching upon a city may be seen in the utterance of **Girolamo Savonarola** (1452–1498). To the great disappointment of his physician father, Savonarola entered a Dominican monastery in Bologna in 1475 after writing an essay, "The Contempt of the World." As a child he had loved the Bible. Disappointed in love and in his studies in philosophy at the university, he heard the call of the Nazarene (Matt. 11:28). Savonarola followed, joining the Dominicans, the *Domini cani,* the hounds of the Lord.

Savonarola was born to preach—"he was enlightened in order to illuminate."[10] Still his initial efforts in preaching were dismal. He struggled at San Marco and failed again at San Lorenzo. One professor worked with him to add an oratorical dimension to his discourse, but the struggle was too painful. Discouraged, Savonarola determined to leave the pulpit forever. Then the Count of Mirandola took an interest in him. His preaching was transformed. Soon he was preaching from a strong and deathless conviction deep with in him. He itinerated for about three years before returning to San Marco in Florence. One biographer describes his preaching:

> A new man . . . dominated by an overpowering personal emotion that inspired him with daemonic energy. He preached like a man fighting for life; he struck, exhorted, appealed, menaced; the words poured forth in a rhapsodic stream; he leaned over the pulpit, as if to seize the dense inimical mass at his feet and breathe into it his passion, to hypnotize it with his emotion, and to force it to feel with him. Like a castaway, gesticulating, exclaiming, struggling to rejoice humanity, he struggled for communion and response; and only when it came, only when he felt at last the hostile mass moving to his dictating emotion, he paused and drew breath—a long breath of victorious relief. For it was a triumph—the response came in a tide of exclamations and sighs; he had sprung the secret of the revivalist; he had tapped a great undertow of popular emotion; and henceforth he was to be its master and its creature.[11]

Savonarola was drawn to the wrathful and the apocalytpic, chiefly enjoying the Old Testament. He particularly loved preaching from Genesis and Haggai, and in the New Testament from the Book of Revelation. He was given to *lectio continua* (consecutive book exposition). He saw himself as a "reviver of scripturalism,"[12] and called Florence back to the Word of God. He stood in contrast to the popular humanistic orators of his time. Summoned to "quicken the sluggish conscience of the age,"[13] he found his former doubts vanishing when he stood in the pulpit. Boldness became his stock in trade.

In the fall of 1494, Charles VIII of France drew near to Florence with forty thousand soldiers and one hundred siege guns. Savonarola picked up his accustomed Advent theme of the coming fifth age when the Antichrist would appear, Christ would conquer, and the Turks and pagans would be baptized. This was a variation of the Christian apocalypticism of Joachine of Fiore (Joachite prophecy). Savonarola blended both the optimism of Augustinian eschatology (the final victory of God and his own) with a realistic pessimism about the human prospect (influenced by the Joachites). Throughout the crisis, Savonarola preached daily in the cathedral "to swollen and frightened crowds."[14] He was a patriot and a peacemaker, because it was he who confronted the French king and ordered him to depart. He did.

Savonarola was supreme for three and a half years. He was the most articulate theorist and spokesman of republican liberty in Florence. His early-morning audiences outgrew the Duomo, and a wooden amphitheater was put up against the walls. He gave a famous ultimatum to Lorenzo the Magnificent on the latter's deathbed. He relentlessly attacked Rome and its abuses and corruption. With his vigilantes, he launched moral crusades against sodomy, gambling, insufficient apparel for women, and certain kinds of art. And yet the foremost artists of the time read his sermons and painted his versions of doomsday. Michelangelo's "The Last Judgment" carries Savonarola's theme right into the Vatican.[15] Of course many, like Machiavelli, dismissed him as a "windbag," but others saw him as God's special preacher of repentance and divine wrath upon a decadent civilization. Bartolomeo Redditi testified, "I believed and I believe, because his preaching made Florence a paradise on earth."[16]

The conflicts deepened, and finally Savonarola was excommunicated. The following day, the pope died. The new pope put the city under interdict, and the people turned against him. Savonarola defied the ban and was brought to trial. He was tortured and hung on May 23, 1498, his body burned and his ashes flung into the river. Savonarola spent his last nights poring over the prophecy of Jeremiah, the man of God whose last days in Egypt were with those who rejected the Lord and his counsel. In his last sermon, Savonarola spoke to himself, as it were:

O Father, we are little scandalized that you should submit your decision to men. If your preaching or not preaching depends on God, it does not seem proper that you should yield to men, and we believe no longer . . . I told you that God recommended my preaching and perseverance; but I told you also that it was not His purpose to grant you salvation against your will; and there I consented to your councils and agreed to observe their decisions, because the Lord will not force your welfare upon you . . . but when I mounted the pulpit, I could not contain myself, I could not do otherwise. The Word of the Lord became, in this place, like a consuming fire devouring my heart and my marrow; I could not gainsay it, I must needs utter it, for I burn with it utterly, I feel myself inflamed with the Spirit of the Lord.[17]

Certainly critical questions must be raised about Savonarola's message and methods. Did he too uncritically identify the kingdom of God with the republic of Florence? Did he see the Florentines as "God's chosen" in too cavalier a fashion? If so, he was not the first nor the last to do so of a beloved country or society. Did this fiery preacher become too embroiled in the political process of the republic? Did he curtail his spiritual ministry by too much involvement in the machinations of power? Every preacher who would significantly address the issues of the times faces this dilemma.

Savonarola's end-time scenario for his powerful preaching reconfigured daily life and experience in Florence. Professor Weinstein, who is not given to careless overstatement, is right that the Savonarola movement must be seen in relation to the Protestant Reformation ready to break out over Europe as "a harbinger of things to come."[18]

1. For what is in my opinion the best overview of Christian spirituality and spiritual formation over the centuries, see Cheslyn Jones, Geoffrey Wainwright, Edward Yarnold, eds., *The Study of Spirituality* (Oxford: Oxford University Press, 1986). This runs to more than six hundred pages and is a gem!
2. Cited in Josef Schmidt, "Introduction," Johannes Tauler, *Sermons* (New York: Paulist, 1985), 3. This is in The Classics of Western Spirituality series.
3. Susanna Winkworth, *The History and Life of Doctor John Tauler* (London: Allennson, 1905), 131. This volume is our sentimental favorite on Tauler and is replete with John Greenleaf Whittier's great poem on Tauler and an introductory preface by Charles Kingsley, the eminent preacher and novelist.
4. Jill Raitt, ed., *Christian Spirituality: High Middle Ages and Reformation* (New York: Crossroad, 1987), 147.
5. F. B. Meyer, *Five Musts of the Christian Life* (Chicago: Moody, 1927), 41.
6. Winkworth, *Doctor John Tauler*, 142–43.
7. Schmidt, "Introduction," xi.
8. Ibid., 17.
9. Ibid., 17ff.
10. Ralph Roeder, *Savonarola: A Study in Conscience* (New York: Brentano's, 1930), 26.
11. Ibid., 46. George Eliot has a striking description of Savonarola's preaching in *Romola*, 2:xxiv, "Inside the Duomo."
12. Donald Weinstein, *Savonarola and Florence: Prophecy and Patriotism in the Renaissance* (Princeton, N.J.: Princeton University Press, 1970), 183. A recent and very important study is Lorenzo Polizzotto's *The Elect Nation: The Savonarolan Movement in Florence* (Oxford: Oxford University Press, 1995).
13. Roeder, *Savonarola*, 96.
14. Weinstein, *Savonarola and Florence*, 114.
15. Roeder, *Savonarola*, 181.
16. Weinstein, *Savonarola and Florence*, 239.
17. Roeder, *Savonarola*, 266ff.
18. Weinstein, *Savonarola and Florence*, 377; and Augustine Thompson, *Revival Preachers and Politics in Thirteenth-Century Italy: The Great Devotion of 1233* (Oxford: Oxford University Press, 1993). Savonarola picked up the cues left by the "alleluia preachers" of 1233.

CHAPTER FIVE

The Reformation—
Preaching Comes of Age

How can a young man keep his way pure? By living according to your
word.

—Psalm 119:9

I have hidden your word in my heart that I might not sin against you.

—Psalm 119:11

Open my eyes that I may see wonderful things written in your law.

—Psalm 119:18

My soul is weary with sorrow; strengthen me according to your word.

—Psalm 119:28

Then I will answer the one who taunts me, for I trust in your word.

—Psalm 119:42

How sweet are your words to my taste, sweeter than honey to my mouth!

—Psalm 119:103

Your word is a lamp to my feet and a light for my path.

—Psalm 119:105

All your words are true; all your righteous laws are eternal.

—Psalm 119:160

Of all the actions of the Christian ministry, preaching is the highest, and the test of our reverence for our profession is our performance of the preacher's duty.

—Bishop Hensley Henson

Baring Gould characterized the preaching of the Middle Ages: "We find that preaching consisted chiefly in scriptural exposition, the only order being observed being the sacred text."[1] Whether the simpler homilies or the more complex university sermons, solid scriptural preaching did manage to bubble to the surface. But it is the Protestant Reformation that must be seen as one of the most fertile and forceful times of biblical preaching.

Some preachers fixated on form, as St. Victor of Paris observed: "There are many who, when they come to the sermon—do not care what the preacher says; but only how he says it."[2] This was in part due to the dominance of the medieval papacy. The Scripture fairly suffocated under the dead weight of ecclesiastical structures and politics. The sacramental system held Scripture at bay. Tradition was choking and stifling the Word of God.

The "flying wedge" we call the Reformation was the insight and doctrine of the Reformers, who restored preaching to its proper place in the church and its life.[3] The centrality accorded to the Word and its proclamation ignited an unparalleled revival of preaching. Preachers long "wearied of conventional restraints" began to preach the Word with freedom and fire. They "spoke from their hearts" the marvelous Word of God.[4] The Reformers insisted that the Word always be expounded in the administration of the sacraments but also held that the Word of God could be proclaimed without the sacraments. This is a key insight.

Certainly the spiritual turnaround did not take place in a vacuum. We shall examine three persons out of the fourteenth century who are direct antecedents of the Reformers. We will see how the growth of national consciousness prepared the way for the German princes' support of Luther.[5] With the papacy seemingly bent on self-destruction, England, France, Bohemia, and even Italy pulled away from subordination to the pope.

Yet Aland is right when he points to something altogether new at the heart of the Reformation—the universal priesthood of all believers.[6] This emphasis on access to the Scriptures, along with the invention of the printing press, opened new doors of opportunity and obligation. What McLuhan and Postman speak of as a "print culture" made "the age of exposition" possible.[7]

The Reformers subscribed to a view of scriptural authority which made biblical preaching a necessity. As Schaeffer characterizes them: "They refused to accept the autonomy of human reason."[8] Thus, "At its core, therefore, the Reformation was the removing of the humanistic distortions which had entered the church."[9] While far from perfect, the Reformers have bequeathed us a legacy which we dare not squander.

---

1. S. Baring Gould, *Post-Medieval Preachers* (London: Riverton's, 1865), 7.

2. Charles Smyth, *The Art of Preaching: A Practical Survey of Preaching in the Church of England 747–1939* (London: SPCK, 1940), 41.
3. D. Martyn Lloyd-Jones, *Knowing the Times* (Edinburgh: Banner of Truth, 1989), 102.
4. Gould, *Post-Medieval Preachers,* 22.
5. Kurt Aland, *A History of Christianity* (Minneapolis: Fortress, 1985), 1:352.
6. Ibid., 357.
7. Neil Postman, *Amusing Ourselves to Death: Public Discourse in the Age of Show Business* (New York: Viking Penguin, 1985), 63.
8. Francis A. Schaeffer, *How Should We Then Live?* (Old Tappan, N.J.: Revell, 1976), 81.
9. Ibid., 82.

5.1 THE QUICKENING OF EXPECTATION

> The reason for the great weight that the Reformers laid on preaching was not educational or social but theological.
>
> —T. H. L. Parker

Preaching is a theological act. Karl Barth says, "Theology is the conscience of preaching." But homiletical theology means more than that. If the Bible is supremely authoritative, the translation of Scripture into the language of the people must follow. Then, given the accessibility of Scripture, the necessity for the preaching and dissemination of the truth of the Word of God must follow that. Preaching then is not chiefly rhetorical or communicational but theological.

The growing respect for the authority of the Word over ecclesiastical structures would culminate in the Reformation. Somewhat ahead of his time, University of Paris chancellor **John Gerson** (1363–1429) protested corruption and abuses in the church and called for biblical preaching:

> Many believe that sermons should be delivered only that the people may learn and know something they did not know before. Hence their scornful saying, "What is preaching to me? I already know more good than I am willing to do!" But these people are in error; for sermons are not delivered for this reason only, that one may learn something, but also for this reason, to move the heart and inclination so that they shall love, desire, and accomplish that which is good. Therefore the apostle desires not so much that one should learn what is in Christ, as that he should be like-minded with him. They, however, who attend sermons only to learn something new are like those of whom the apostle writes, that they are ever learning and yet know nothing.[1]

Others who would shape the coming Reformation included **Richard Grosseteste** (1175–1253), bishop of Lincoln and an eminent preacher who taught homiletics at Oxford. He influenced Wycliffe with his urgent appeal to the authority of Scripture. In his last illness, Grosseteste castigated the papacy with these words frequently quoted by the Reformers.[2] "But what is the cause of this hopeless fall of the Church? Unquestionably the diminution in the number of good shepherds . . . no wonder, for they preach not the Gospel of Christ with that living word which comes forth from living zeal for the salvation of souls, and is confirmed by an example worthy of Jesus Christ."[3]

William of Occam (1285–1347), a philosopher and theologian, taught at Oxford and influenced all of the Reformers. He argued that popes and church councils may err but Scripture may not err, for the Scripture alone has universal validity. William maintained that the pope was a heretic and that even the lowest peasant may be guided by the truth of the Bible. He saw that the propositions of theology cannot be established by reason but are derived from special revelation. Not surprisingly, William was excommunicated.

These were the ideas that filled the air when Wycliffe was at Oxford. Like subsequent Reformers, he found them congenial. Also shaping Wyclifffe's Augustinian bent was **Thomas of Brandwardine** (1290–1349). Appointed archbishop of Canterbury shortly before his death, Thomas was initially Pelagian in his inclinations but came to see "God's free and unmerited grace in the conversion and salvation of man."[4] Here was a herald of grace a full century before the Reformation! And now to the three towering figures of the time.

---

1. Alfredo E. Garvie, *The Christian Preacher* (New York: Scribner's, 1923), 123ff.
2. F. R. Webber, *A History of Preaching in Britain and America* (Milwaukee: Northwestern, 1952), 1:144–45. Webber's two volumes are an invaluable and exceedingly sound study, though they are limited to the English-speaking world.
3. W. L. Watkinson, *John Wycliffe* (Mobile, Ala.: R E Publications, n.d.), 10–11.
4. Ibid., 30.

5.1.1   THE GOLDEN FINGERS OF THE DAWN—JOHN WYCLIFFE

The highest service that men may attain to on earth is to preach the Word of God . . . hereby should they produce children to God, and that is the end for which God has wedded the Church. And for this cause Jesus Christ left other works, and occupied Himself mostly in preaching; and thus did His Apostles, and for this God loved them. Jesus Christ, when He ascended into heaven, commanded it especially to all His Apostles, to preach the Gospel freely to every man. In this stands the office of the spiritual shepherd.

—John Wycliffe

John Wycliffe (1320 or 1325–1384) has a special niche among those who preceded the Reformation. John Milton said of him, "He was honored of God to be the first preacher of a general revelation to all Europe."[1] We know little of his life; we do know that he earned his B.A. at Oxford in 1356 and became a Doctor of Theology in 1372. He had a distinguished academic career at Oxford[2] and wrote several learned philosophic tomes which gave him considerable academic prestige. In one of his books, *On the Truth of Holy Scripture,* he defended the doctrine of the literal inspiration of Scripture. Here he writes: "Holy Scripture is the faultless, most true, most perfect, and most holy law of God, which it is the duty of every man to learn, to know, to defend, and to observe, inasmuch as they are bound to serve the Lord in accordance with it, under the promise of an eternal reward."

Wycliffe's view of Scripture led him to translate the Bible from the Latin Vulgate into the English language, "the very first to give the whole of Revelation to his countrymen."[3] He regarded the Bible as the Christian's Magna Carta and gave his life to making that Word so filled with Christ available to the rank and file. In this we see striking parallels with Luther, who did much to shape the German language with his translation. Workman says he was "irresistibly driven into translation."[4]

Out of this great reverence for Scripture came his compunction to preach it. Innis puts Wycliffe's dedication in context: "Preaching the Word was the efficient means of extending the Kingdom in Apostolic times—every awakening has seen the marked increase and amount and intensity of the public exposition of Scripture."[5]

Wycliffe began to preach during his student days in 1361. He longed for the purity of the church and treasured the message of salvation by grace. He repeatedly reiterated that the first duty of the clergy is to preach.[6] The Scripture was the living seed and was to be preached openly to the people, and Wycliffe insisted on serious exposition for himself and those whom he trained to preach.[7] His sermons were revolutionary in that he drew back from the popular overuse of *exempla,* or fables, which had begun to consume discourse. Yet he did make use of illustrations, often from the science of optics.

Wycliffe's eloquent and moving sermons against the corruption and worldliness of the church and its clergy quickly got him into trouble. He opposed the worship of the Virgin, the invocation of the saints, the veneration of relics, the infallibility of the pope and the church. Ultimately he did come to see the error of transubstantiation, but he never renounced the doctrine of purgatory. He sent his Lollard missionaries out through the countryside, and congregations were established for his preachers.

When the peasants rebelled, national leaders turned against Wycliffe (cf. Luther and the Peasant's Rebellion). He was summoned to St. Paul's Cathedral for trial in 1377. He refused to go to Rome but returned to his beloved parish in Lutterworth, where a granite pillar in his honor now bears the words *Search the Scriptures.*

Wycliffe parted company with the mendicants of Oxford because they invariably served the cause of papal absolutism. He was the object of five papal bulls. In his latter years he was in constant peril and danger. He died of a violent stroke on December 31, 1384. Let us remember Wycliffe in his prime, preaching the gospel as he loved to do it:

> A tall thin figure, covered with a long light gown of black cloth, with a girdle about his body, the head adorned with a full flowing beard, exhibiting features clean and sharply cut, the eyes clear and penetrating, the lips firm closed in token of resolution, the whole man wearing an aspect of lofty earnestness, and replete with dignity and character.[8]

Preaching was soon to have seismic repercussions on the Continent, even to central Europe. In the decades after Wycliffe's death his teaching found "widespread acceptance."[9] Eventually he was condemned posthumously by the Council of Constance in 1415. His body was disinterred and burned, and his ashes scattered on the River Swift. When the converts of Wycliffe were burned at the stake, Wycliffe's Bible was put around their necks and burned with them. Luther wrote a hymn with obvious reference to Wycliffe's life and ministry:

> Fling to the heedless winds,
> On the water cast,
> Their ashes shall be watched,
> And gathered at the last.
>
> And from the scattered dust
> Around us and abroad,
> Shall spring a plenteous seed,
> Of witnesses for God.
>
> Jesus hath now received
> Their latest, dying breath.
> Yet vain is Satan's boast
> Of victory in their death.
>
> Still, still, though dead, they speak,
> And triumph-tongued proclaim,
> To many a waking land
> The one availing name.[10]

1. George S. Innis, *Wycliffe: The Morning Star* (Cincinnati: Jennings and Graham, 1907), 15.
2. K. B. McFarland, *John Wycliffe and the Beginnings of English Nonconformity* (London: English University Press, 1952), 5.
3. W. L. Watkinson, *John Wycliffe* (Mobile, Ala.: R E Publications, n.d.), 151.
4. Herbert B. Workman, *John Wycliffe* (Oxford: Clarendon, 1926), 2:155, 185. Two classic volumes.
5. Innis, *Wycliffe*, 143.
6. Douglas C. Wood, *The Evangelical Doctor: John Wycliffe and the Lollards* (Welwyn Herts, England: Evangelical Press, 1984), 88.
7. Workman, *John Wycliffe*, 213.
8. Innis, *Wycliffe*, 212.
9. McFarland, *John Wycliffe*, 129.
10. Quoted in W. A. Criswell, *Expository Sermons on Revelation* (Grand Rapids: Zondervan, 1962), 1:134.

5.1.2 Gracious Foregleams of the Coming Day—John Huss

But I hope that God will send after me champions stronger than I, who will better bare the sin of Anti-christ, and who will expose themselves to death for the truth of the Lord Jesus Christ, who will give to you and to me eternal glory. . . . I hope that the life of Christ, that I painted through His Word at Bethlehem in the hearts of men, and that His enemies have tried to destroy by forbidding all preaching at the chapel and wishing to raze it to the ground; I hope, I say, that this same life will be better drawn in the future by preachers more eloquent than I, to the great joy of the people who cling with all their hearts to Christ.

—John Huss

In my opinion, John Huss bought with his own blood the gospel which we now possess.

—Martin Luther

At Worms in Germany, there stands an imposing statue paying tribute to the Reformation. The forerunners of the Reformation are represented and they are three: John Wycliffe, John Huss, and Savonarola. **John Huss** (1369–1415) must have a place in this chronicle as a Reformation statesman and as a great and gifted preacher. Despite being born of peasant stock, he matriculated at the University of Prague, which by 1400 had thirty thousand students, many from outside Bohemia. Here he successively took his B.A. in 1393, his Th.B. in 1394 and his M.A. in 1396. He became a public teacher at the university. Even with his Wycliffian ideas, Huss was so popular he was named dean of the philosophy faculty in 1401 and rector of the university in 1402.

Students in Prague frequently debated with students from Oxford. (**Jerome of Prague,** the young, brilliant contemporary of John Huss, studied at Oxford for a time.) Huss became an avid student of Wycliffe, saying, "I confess before you here that I have read and studied the works of the Master, John Wycliffe, and I have learnt from them much that is good."[1]

"Wycliffe was the original and bolder mind—the pathfinder."[2] As early as 1399, Huss publicly defended the propositions of Wycliffe at the university. He became an articulate part of that crescendo of criticism protesting the oppressive hierarchy of the papacy and the unsound teachings emanating from the papal chair.

Even in tiny Bohemia there were fiery preachers who roused the populace to concern and commitment. **Conrad of Waldhausen** (d. 1369) preached on the true nature of sin and its overbearing pride, insisting that outward religious ritual and form could not insure salvation.[3] **Militz of Kremsier** (named by Neander as the first Reformation preacher in Bohemia) was a millennial type who attracted a huge following. **Matthias of Janow** was influential through his writings, such as *Studies on True and False Christianity.* He delineated the signs of the approaching antichrist. These preachers pioneered the impetus to protest in Bohemia.

Also assisting the ferment in favor of Wycliffite teaching was Anna, the sister of the Bohemian King Wenzel, who married Richard II of England and personally encouraged Wycliffe in his immense task of Bible translation.

Like Wycliffe, Huss and his followers ascribed ultimate and absolute authority to the Scriptures alone. David Schaff says, "He followed Wycliffe in demanding that the Scriptures should be in the hands of the people and that the priest's first duty is to expound their teachings to all men alike."[4] The Bible, the incontrovertible authority, is the Book of Life *(liber vitae)*. Like Wycliffe and Luther, Huss also translated Scripture, revising an old Bohemian version. In the face of scrutiny and hatred, Huss was a man of "irreproachable personal conduct" and was never faulted by his critics.

The locus of Huss's powerful preaching ministry was the famous Bethlehem Chapel (meaning "House of Bread" in Hebrew) in Prague. This vast structure was built in 1391 largely through the influence of Militz of Kremsier and Matthias of Janow in Prague's old town. Gregory XII indicated that its purpose was "for the preaching of the Word of God" in the Czech language. It was not a parish church but featured worship services and preaching on the Lord's Day, during the week, and on holy days. It was destroyed by the Jesuits in 1786.

Huss's early preaching was done in St. Michael's parish church in Prague. We possess none of these early sermons but can deduce that they were eminently biblical and full of Christ. He was called to be the fourth person to fill the office of preacher at Bethlehem in which he functioned simultaneously with his work at the university. He lived in a dwelling room in the chapel, with a staircase directly to the pulpit.[5] In his preparation he steeped himself in Scripture and laced all discourse with the Word. Overflow crowds jammed the chapel to hear him. The fawning discourses of the friars *(blandis sermonibus)* had little appeal now.[6] Sometimes Huss enjoyed audiences of close to ten thousand. He wrote to England of what was happening in Bohemia:

> The people will hear nothing but the Scriptures, especially the gospels and epistles. And wherever, in town, village, house or castle, a preacher of the sacred truth appears, there the people flock together in crowds. Lo, I have but touched the tail of Anti-christ, and it has opened its mouth that it may swallow me up with my brothers . . . Our Lord the king and his whole court, queen, barons, and common people are all for the word of Jesus Christ . . .[7]

Yet clearly Huss was on a collision course. The first lesions with the hierarchy surfaced when Huss was appointed to be part of an official commission of inquiry. He was adverse to the miracle of Wilsnack, one of a series of superstitions. His identification with Wycliffe incurred the wrath of Pope John XXIII, who determined to close all private chapels and forbade Huss to preach. Needless to say he continued to preach. The tension was exacerbated when Huss and his compatriots took a stand against the sale of indulgences by Wenzel Tiem in 1412. Huss went briefly into exile at Austi, which later on became a center of Taborite life.

Even though he believed the tribunal of Christ was higher than the tribunal of the church, Huss traveled to the Council of Constance with a promise of safe conduct, but this was broken. Huss was imprisoned and finally burned at the stake in 1415, as was Jerome of Prague. The same council deposed John XXIII.

The shadow of the life and death of John Huss was very much over Martin Luther. Luther found a volume of the sermons of Huss at Erfurt and observed, "On reading, I was overwhelmed with astonishment. I could not understand for what cause they had burnt so great a man, who explained the Scriptures with so much gravity and skill."[8] At Leipzig, Eck accused Luther of being a Hussite.

After the martyrdom of Huss, his followers broke into two groups: the Calixtines, or Utraquists; and the Taborites, or radicals, who were very much like the Puritans of England. Much influenced by Joachim of Fiore, they were distinctly millennial. The tragic Bohemian wars and the Thirty Years' War decimated the population of Bohemia from about four million to seven or eight hundred thousand. Still the *Unitas Fratrum,* or Brethren group (out of which Jan Amos Comenius [1592–1640] came; he was once invited to become president of Harvard[9]), and the Moravian church survive as a tribute and evidence of the faithful testimony and witness of God's servant, John Huss.

1. Herbert B. Workman, *The Age of Huss* (London: Charles H. Kelly, 1902), 130.
2. David S. Schaff, *John Huss: His Life, Teaching and Death* (New York: Scribner's, 1915), 44.
3. Oscar Kuhns, *John Huss: The Witness* (Cincinnati: Jennings and Graham, 1907), 31ff.
4. Schaff, *John Huss,* 282.
5. Workman, *The Age of Hus,* 120.
6. Schaff, *John Huss,* 35.
7. Workman, *The Age of Hus,* 148.
8. Ibid., 117.
9. An entire issue of *Christian History* 6:1 is devoted to Comenius, great leader and Christian educator.

5.1.3 MR. FACING BOTH WAYS—ERASMUS

> I have tried to call back theology, sunk too far in sophistical subtleties, to the sources and to ancient simplicity.
> —Erasmus to Jean Gachi, October 1527

> So keep on believing what you have been taught from the beginning. If you do you will always be in close fellowship with both God the Father and his Son.
> —1 John 2:24 LB

His name is virtually a synonym for the Renaissance. He was "an enormous celebrity" in his time but a tragic figure. **Desiderius Erasmus** (1467–1536) was born in Rotterdam in the Netherlands in the difficult circumstance of illegitimacy. Early cast adrift, he was educated at Gouda and by the Brethren of the Common Life in Deventer. In 1486 he entered the Augustinian monastery at Steyn and was ordained in 1492. He traveled as secretary to the bishop of Cambrai, but soon began his study of Scripture at the University of Paris. He spent time in England where he came under the influence of **John Colet,** the New Testament lecturer of Oxford, and **Thomas More,** the author of *Utopia.* Erasmus spent two years in More's home while he wrote *In Praise of Folly,* a debunking of the pretensions of the medieval church. Often in dire poverty, he traveled extensively and spent his last years in Basle.

Erasmus was a genius whose thoughts lent themselves to the kind of circulation now made possible through the printer's art. His *Enchiridion* is a manual for spiritual warfare and a lusty call back to the Scripture.[1] He was revulsed by the methods of scholasticism, yet he was no systematic theologian and could be unguarded in his expression. He adulated the philosophy of Christ (i.e., the basics of Christian belief and loving conduct). Who he really was and where he really stood are matters of great controversy and difference. As Huizinga says of his first pamphlet, Erasmus was not "fervent" and took an "ambiguous position."[2] Yet this teacher of teachers is germane to our narrative for three reasons.

One, Erasmus was a linguist whose Latin was impressive and who learned Greek for the sake of reading the Greek New Testament. He was committed to the text of Scripture. He suffered under some six hundred mistranslations in the Vulgate, and set himself to identifying the true text of the New Testament through what we would call today the science of lower criticism. While greatly limited in his tools from our standpoint, his *Novum Instrumentum* in 1516 has been strikingly influential. Some of his "caustic notes stirred the ire of the priests,"[3] but this publication was the standard for three hundred years.

While the debates between John William Burgon and Westcott and Hort about the *textus receptus* are beyond the scope of our present discussion, we who hold to the inerrancy of the original autographs treasure the laborious work of textual critics who have collated and compared the thousands of extant manuscripts and vouchsafed to us the substantial accuracy of our present text. In this tedious but important work Erasmus must be seen as a pioneer. He had profound knowledge of Scripture and believed that the Bible is "divinely inspired and perfected by God its Author."[4] He wrestled with seeming contradictions, as did Luther after him, with reference to the Book of James,[5] and was keenly interested in text.[6]

Two, Erasmus influenced the Reformers, though it is exaggeration to say that "Erasmus laid the egg of the Reformation and Luthered hatched it." He was a very inward man, a believer who never had a Damascus Road experience like St. Paul. He wanted to get back through the medieval accretions to the Fathers and the simplicity of the gospel.

Many have pointed to the influence of Erasmus on the young Luther. Indeed, Erasmus criticized indulgences fifteen years before Luther did.[7] He also had ties with Zwingli, who wrote in 1516, "The Swiss account it a great glory to have seen Erasmus."[8] He was not at all confrontational and hated dissension, coming to the conclusion that Luther was using "extreme remedies." He and Luther broke sharply over the issue of the freedom of the will, prompting Erasmus to speak of "the Lutheran tragedy."

Erasmus found it hard to champion any cause.[9] Preserved Smith faults him for not really supporting the Reformation. His language was always qualified; he certainly was not the stuff of which martyrs are made. He was too perceptive to support Catholicism and too evasive to support Protestantism. Erasmus tended to shade his yes until it was no, and then burnish his no until it became yes, as someone has put it. Yet Bainton argues that the whole English Reformation was in its early stages Erasmian.

Three, Erasmus is also relevant because he skillfully used the art of rhetoric in Christian communication. He said of the training of preachers, "If elephants can be trained to dance and lions to play and leopards to hunt, surely preachers can be taught to preach." *On Preaching* (1535) urges that the introduction be close to the theme and that the sermons be divided. The basic outline of his treatment is

I. The dignity of the preaching office;
II. Doctrines and precepts on the art of preaching;
III. Particular subjects for pulpit treatment (to awaken feeling, one must feel).[10]

Like many scholastics, Erasmus was lost in allegorism early on. Yet as he turned more to Jerome as his pattern, he made a radical shift to "go to the sources themselves to deduce from that which precedes and from that which follows, the natural sense of the Scriptures."[11] Luther followed suit. He wrote to John Lang in 1517 that he was reading Erasmus, "And it pleases me that he constantly condemns both monks and priests for their inveterate ways and stupid ignorance."[12] Although he was to show considerable disdain for Erasmus later on (as he did to Karlstadt and Zwingli), Luther acknowledged his debt to him:

There has never been a great revelation of the word of God unless He has first prepared the way by the resurgence and prospering of languages and letters, as though they were John the Baptists.

To Oecolampadius, Luther wrote, "Erasmus has recalled the world from godless studies and reinstated the ancient languages, though, like Moses, he could not himself enter the promised land."[13]

In his declining years Erasmus became increasingly conservative. In many ways he disappoints us. Nonetheless, his work was essential.

---

1. Johan Huizinga, *Erasmus and the Age of Reformation* (Princeton, N.J.: Princeton University Press, 1924, 1984), 51.
2. Ibid., 31.
3. A. T. Robertson, *An Introduction to the Textual Criticism of the New Testament* (Nashville: Broadman, 1925), 18.
4. John C. Olin, *Six Essays on Erasmus* (New York: Fordham University Press, 1979), 6.
5. Bruce Ellis Benson, "Erasmus and the Correspondence with Johann Eck: A Sixteenth-Century Debate over Scriptural Authority," *Trinity Journal* 6 n.s. (1985): 157–65.
6. Marjorie O'Rourke Boyle, *Erasmus on Language and Method in Theology* (Toronto: University of Toronto Press, 1977); also Marjorie O'Rourke Boyle, *Rhetoric and Reform: Erasmus' Civil Dispute with Luther* (Cambridge, Mass.: Harvard University Press, 1983). These are both worthwhile studies.
7. James McConica, *Erasmus* (Oxford: Oxford University Press, 1991).

8. Huizinga, *Erasmus and the Age of Reformation*, 96.
9. Olin, *Six Essays on Erasmus*, 62.
10. Roland H. Bainton, *Erasmus of Christendom* (New York: Scribner's, 1969), 268ff.
11. John William Aldridge, *The Hermeneutic of Erasmus* (Richmond: John Knox, 1966), 30.
12. Ibid., 35.
13. Ibid., 37.

5.2 MARTIN LUTHER—THE EXPONENT OF THE GOSPEL OF GRACE

The Lord God is the real preacher.

When one for the first time mounts the pulpit, no one would believe how very afraid one is! One sees so many heads down there! Even now when I am in the pulpit I look at no one but tell myself they are merely blocks of wood which stand there before me, and I speak the word of my God to them.

—Martin Luther

We have seen that Erasmus felt the truth-unity tension but unwisely veered toward unity. We now consider a company of preachers who opted strongly for truth. Their stand would become the Protestant Reformation of the sixteenth century.

Luther, Calvin, and Zwingli loom large in this company. Professor Aland helpfully underscores how different each was:

1. Luther, the prophet and interpreter of Scripture; German profundity;
2. Calvin, the scholar and church leader; French clarity;
3. Zwingli, the Christian humanist and preacher; Swiss practicality.[1]

Yet they hold historic orthodoxy with one voice. Most particularly, "They develop their common understanding of the primacy of the newly discovered and newly understood Scriptures."[2]

The outgrowth of this common view of Scripture was the high view of preaching, which was an inevitable concomitant of a high view of Scripture. The primacy of the preaching of the Word would become one of the identifying marks of the Reformation.

The German theologian Christlieb points out the Roman Catholic devaluation of preaching historically and the contrasting Reformation emphasis on didactic preaching "built on the basis of the text alone."[3] Standing squarely in the Reformation tradition, he critiques Schleiermacher's "devotional-aesthetic" conception of preaching and pleads for active and passionate preaching for a decision, which has as its objective conversion, "fruit for the Kingdom of God."[4] As one the Reformers recognized "the supreme and ultimate act to be exposition of the Word of God."[5] The result was painful, but led to some improvements in Roman Catholic preaching.

---

1. Kurt Aland, *A History of Christianity* (Philadelphia: Fortress, 1986), 2:17.

2. Ibid., 18. I am using Aland chiefly among others as the check on the complex histo-riography of this period.
3. Theodor Christlieb, *Homiletic: Lectures on Preaching,* trans. C. H. Irwin (Edinburgh: T & T Clark, 1897), 93–94, 101.
4. Ibid., 111.
5. Edward P. Echlin, *The Priest As Preacher: Past and Future* (Notre Dame, Ind.: Fides, 1973), 60. This Roman Catholic lecturer at Durham makes the case for preaching as the priest's primary mission (p. 72) and calls for a renewed dedication to the minis-try of preaching.

5.2.1   LUTHER AND SALVATION

I am not good and righteous, but Christ is.

When I became a Doctor I did not know we cannot expiate our sins.

The Cross is the safest of all things. Blessed is the man who understands this.

—Martin Luther

God's man in God's hour for the Reformation was the earthy, courageous, and gifted **Martin Luther** (1483–1546). A child of his turbulent times, Luther was truly a medieval, but the great step for him was his break with medieval soteriology. Luther saw all of humanity "locked in a profound conflict between God and the Devil while the Last Judgment rapidly approached."[1]

This millennial cast is not new to us, but it is the context in which Luther's personal struggles and battles must be seen. He has learned of no gracious God in his parental home or in his schooling. His resort to the monastery came out of fear. The fear of God's wrath upon him eternally drove him desperately. Educa-tion as such (he received his Th.D. in 1512) did not ameliorate his anguish. In-volvement in the church and in its ministry could not palliate his agony (he was ordained in 1507). All of the frenetic works of supererogation could not bring peace to his troubled soul. He visited Rome as part of a delegation from the Au-gustinian Hermits but found no solace there. In fact, the shallowness and super-cilious mood there depressed him all the more, and he exclaimed, "If there is a hell, Rome is standing on it."[2]

When he stood at the altar as an officiant, "a deep fear dismayed him."[3] A se-ries of significant appointments as professor of Bible at Wittenberg, as monas-tery preacher, and as successor to **Johann von Staupitz** as head of the Augustinian Hermits did nothing to placate his sense of spiritual estrangement and alienation. His early sermons and lectures were very much in the pattern of the medieval scholastics. He was very probing of the biblical text. And this is what brought him to his Damascus Road.

Luther was very conscious of his sin, and spoke of the plague of his own heart. He saw sin as man *incurvatus en se,* or turning in upon oneself. Setting himself to study the Scriptures for his lectures and sermons, he was in his tower-study.[4]

No one tells of Luther's evangelical experience as does Roland Bainton, who describes his attention to the Psalms, Romans, and Galatians. Staupitz had directed him "to the wounds of the sweet Savior." Luther saw the cross of Christ in Psalm 22.[5] Then in Romans and Galatians he saw how wrath and love fuse on the cross. "The All Terrible Is the All Merciful." He wrote to his mother that the Word of God teaches us to trust only in Christ. To use Luther's own words:

> I greatly longed to understand Paul's Epistle to the Romans and nothing stood in the way but that one expression, "the justice of God" . . . . Night and day I pondered until I saw the connection between the justice of God and the statement that "the just shall live by faith." Then I grasped that the justice of God is that righteousness by which through grace and sheer mercy God justifies us through faith. Thereupon I felt myself to be reborn and to have gone through open doors into paradise. The whole of Scripture took on a new meaning.[6]

The relationship of his liberating experience of grace to his exegetical insight and his theological understanding of the meaning of the Cross is clear. Indeed he had formerly hated God and was angry with God, but now he was convulsed with love for God and his Word. His writings from 1518 have a new tone and dimension.

Luther's new forensic understanding of "justification by faith apart from the works of the law" was for him "the summary of all Christian doctrine." The traditional Lutheran preaching pattern of beginning with law and moving to grace has its genesis in Luther's own spiritual journey (although perhaps the real order is grace-law-grace). Luther described the transactual nature of Christ's work on the cross—in which Christ takes our sins and we take his righteousness by faith— as that "sweet exchange." So thus the believer in Christ is "at once righteous and a sinner" *(simul iustus et peccator)*.[7] This message was a total breach with the semi-Pelagianism endemic in the medieval world which threatens the message of grace and salvation in all ages.

Luther's discovery of the righteousness of God led to the formulation of a *theologia crucis*. Alister McGrath brilliantly demonstrates the scope of Luther's theological breakthrough. On justification he was a true Augustinian, and "the cruciality of the Cross embedded itself more and more deeply" into the man and into his message.[8] "The Cross alone is our theology" *(Crux sola est nostra theologia)* was his confession (Wa. 5.176.32–33). The whole medieval notion of accumulating merit before God was destroyed.[9] Out of this radical revolution in his thinking come deep and deathless convictions about his sources and authority and the proclamation which must be made. Spurgeon quotes Luther as to why he preached justification constantly: "Because the people would forget it; so that I was obliged almost to knock my Bible against their heads, to send it into their hearts."[10]

---

1. Heiko A. Oberman, *Luther: Man Between God and the Devil* (New Haven, Conn.: Yale University Press, 1989), 61ff.

2. Kurt Aland, *A History of Christianity* (Philadelphia: Fortress, 1986), 2:38.

3. Ibid., 35.

4. Some have been influenced by psychoanalytic theorists like Erik Erikson in *The Young Man Luther* (1958) to see Luther's tower experience as his moving from anal retentive to anal explosive (incorrectly translating *cloaca* as "privy" rather than the study in the tower above the privy). This is another example of extreme psychobiography.

5. Roland H. Bainton, *Here I Stand* (New York: Mentor, 1950, 1977), 47.

6. Ibid., 49.

7. Timothy George, *Theology of the Reformers* (Nashville: Broadman, 1988), 71.

8. Alister E. McGrath, *Luther's Theology of the Cross* (London: Blackwell, 1985), 26.

9. Alister E. McGrath, *Iustitia Dei: A History of the Christian Doctrine of Justification* (Cambridge, Mass.: Cambridge University Press, 1986).

10. Charles H. Spurgeon, "The Carnal Mind Enmity Against God," in *Spurgeon's Sermons* (New York: Funk and Wagnalls, n.d.), 1:248.

5.2.2 LUTHER AND THE SCRIPTURES

I simply taught, preached, wrote God's Word . . . otherwise I did nothing . . . the Word did it all.

Now let me and everyone who speaks of the word of Christ freely boast that our mouths are the mouths of Christ. I am certain indeed that my word is not mine, but the word of Christ. So must my mouth be the mouth of him who utters it.

—Martin Luther

Our doctrine of the Scripture determines the direction and nature of our theology and ministry. Up to age twenty, Luther had apparently not even seen a Bible. While he was a student at Erfurt he discovered the Bible and was given his own copy when he entered his novitiate. He began studying Hebrew in 1507 (Reuchlin's Hebrew text was published in 1506) and made considerable progress, followed then by his study of Greek.[1] Vivian Green helpfully observes, "The Sacred Scriptures in which his mind became so saturated formed the central feature of his study."[2] As he read the Scriptures the light began to dawn. Everything soon changed. He concurred with Augustine, "Everything written in Scripture must be believed absolutely."[3] Subsequently, everything for Luther hinged on his conviction, *sola Scriptura*. He rested his entire argument on Scripture. His indictment of his frequent adversary Eck lays out the issue:

I regret that the holy doctor penetrates the Scriptures as deeply as a spider does the water: in fact, he runs away from them as the devil from the cross. Therefore, with all my regard for the fathers, I prefer the authority of the Scriptures, which I commend to those who will judge me."[4]

We marvel at what has been called the kerygmatic exegesis of Luther the commentator on Scripture. His work is voluminous, extending to about one hundred volumes. He broke loose from the medieval "four senses of Scripture" to reinstate the original text and its literal sense.[5] As with Wycliffe and Huss, he saw the necessity of translating the Scripture into the language of the people, and his German Bible became the "keystone of the Reformation." The Bible became the people's book. Luther did not see the Scripture as a "waxen nose" to be twisted this way and that, and he warned against the "spiritualizers" among his own followers.

Professor Prenter's classic study of Luther's concept of the Holy Spirit shows that he did not regard the Holy Spirit as a warm feeling but as the one on whom we rely for understanding and preaching of the Word of God. "The Word is the means of the Holy Spirit."[6] The sacraments are seen as visible words.

All sides in the modern theological debate about Scripture have tried to claim Luther, but Pelikan is surely right that for Luther the Bible is the Word of God and does not become the Word when we believe. It has ontic status as the Word of God whether or not we believe it.[7] Worthies such as Reinhold Seeberg and Philip Watson espoused the more subjective idea of biblical inspiration. J. Theodore Mueller,[8] A. Skevington Wood, J. Michael Reu, Herman Sasse, and Klaas Runia all take seriously Luther's words when he argues for the objective nature of biblical revelation.[9] Listen to Luther:

> So then the entire Scriptures are assigned to the Holy Ghost (St.L. 3, 1890);

> The Holy Scriptures have been spoken by the Holy Ghost (St.L. 3, 1895);

> In the Book of the Holy Ghost, that is Holy Scripture, we must seek and find Christ (St.L. 9, 1775);

> In the Scripture you are reading not the word of man, but the Word of the most exalted God (St.L. 9, 1818);

> The Scriptures have never erred (St.L. 9, 356).[10]

Luther's radical Christocentrism simply recognized the mediatorial office of Christ in its rich, full sense and took seriously the teaching of Scripture itself (cf. Luke 24:27; John 5:39). The difficulty Luther had with several portions of Scripture was not in relation to inerrancy but rather in relation to canonicity. His view of the inerrant and infallible nature of scriptural authority led him to some issues with respect to the canon. Since Scripture cannot be contradictory, and wondering if James did not contradict Paul on "justification by faith apart from the works of the law," he called James "a right strawy epistle." Rather than creating a problem about a noncontradictory Scripture, Luther's position supported the view that Scripture is noncontradictory. "The Scriptures cannot lie," remained his stand.

Holy Scripture was thus his sword and his light. At the Diet of Worms in 1521 he declared to the emperor and five thousand people: "Unless I am convicted of error by the Holy Scriptures, I neither can or dare retract anything; for my conscience is held captive by God's Word. Here I stand, I can do no other. God help me. Amen." The Word always afforded him the most amazing confidence and courage, as he later wrote:

> That word above all earthly powers, no thanks to them, abideth:
> The Spirit and the gifts are ours Thro' Him who with us sideth.
> Let goods and kindred go, this mortal life also; The body they may kill:
> God's truth abideth still, His kingdom is forever.

Such a view of Scripture inescapably gives rise to a perception and practice of preaching.

---

1. Luther was always strong for the mastery of the biblical languages, as when he insisted: "Languages are the sheath in which hides the Sword of the Spirit—so although the faith of the gospel may be proclaimed by a preacher without the knowledge of the languages, the preaching will be feeble and ineffective. But where the languages are studied, the proclamation will be fresh and powerful, the Scripture will be searched, and a faith will be constantly rediscovered through ever new words and deeds" (cited from Peter Meinhold in Fred W. Meuser, *Luther the Preacher* [Minneapolis: Augsburg, 1983], 42ff.).
2. A. Skevington Wood, *Captive to the Word: Martin Luther: Doctor of Sacred Scripture* (London: Paternoster, 1969), 42. This choice volume is Wood's Ph.D. dissertation at the University of Edinburgh.
3. Ibid., 39.
4. Ibid., 70.
5. Ibid., 78.
6. Regin Prenter, *Spiritus Creator: Luther's Concept of the Holy Spirit* (Philadelphia: Muhlenberg, 1953). One must beware of a severe Barthian tinge throughout the work.
7. Jaroslav Pelikan, *From Luther to Kierkegaard* (St. Louis: Concordia, 1950), 18.
8. J. Theodore Mueller, "Luther and the Bible," in *Inspiration and Interpretation,* ed. John Walvoord (Grand Rapids: Eerdmans, 1957).
9. Wood, *Captive to the Word;* James Atkinson in *The Great Light: Luther and the Reformation* (Grand Rapids: Eerdmans, 1968) holds that "Luther's soul was saved by an unyielding and uncompromising faith in the Bible" (20).
10. Mueller, "Luther and the Bible," 97ff.

5.2.3   *LUTHER AND THE SERMON*

Always preach in such a way that if the people listening do not come to hate their sin, they will instead hate you.

It is disgraceful for the lawyer to desert his brief; it is even more disgraceful for the preacher to desert his text.

> To preach simply is a great art . . . Christ understood it and practiced it
> . . . He speaks only of the ploughed field, of the mustard seed, and uses
> only common comparisons from the countryside.
>
> My best craft is to give the Scripture with its plain meaning; for the plain
> meaning is learning and life.
>
> —Martin Luther

"Luther's influence was due to the wide-ranging character of his evangelical preaching"[1] claims one Luther scholar. The data suggest this is not an overstatement. At the Leipzig debate with Eck in 1519, Luther contended that the true church exists where the Bible is preached, the sacraments are administered, and faith, hope, and love exist. His insights into the Scripture were embedded in his sermons, such as his crucial "Treatise on Good Works." His direct, Spirit-anointed preaching touched the hearts of the masses. John Ker depicts the scenario:

> On the way to Worms to meet the Diet, he could not escape from the
> crowds. At Erfurt the church was so crowded they feared it would fall.
> At Zwickau, the marketplace was thronged by 2,500 eager listeners and
> Luther had to preach from a window. He continued to preach to the end
> of his life though so broken in health that he often fainted from exhaus-
> tion. To the end he retained his wonderful power. The last time he en-
> tered the pulpit was February 14, 1546, a few days before he died.[2]

Protestantism was a movement in which the pulpit was literally higher than the altar. In the Wittenberg church where Luther often preached, the schedule was 5–6 A.M., exposition of the Pauline Epistles; 9–10 A.M., exposition of the Gospels; afternoon, the morning theme continued or the catechism, and then preaching every day. He would often preach four times on Sunday. We possess about 2,300 of his sermons, delivered in German but transcribed by his friends in Latin.[3] As in his famous *Table Talk,* his preaching abounds with German sayings and peasant crudities. He would speak of how Mary took baby Jesus "and wiped his bottom before putting him to her breasts."

Preaching the church year was important to Luther. Though his was a "theology of the cross," the resurrection of Christ was prominent among his themes. On one occasion, when things seemed very bleak, he was seen tracing on a table with his finger the words *Vivit, vivit,* "He lives, he lives!"[4] Preaching for Luther was an outcropping of the eschatological battle. The pulpit was a battlefield.

Luther would take his concept or his basic schema with him into the pulpit but would sometimes move entirely away from it. He strongly emphasized the spiritual preparation of the preacher, urging that to pray well is to study well. As with all of the Reformers, he believed that the text should control the sermon—the main point or *hertzpunkt* to which the preacher is to come back again and again. Structure as such was not strong in Luther's preaching, but his running commentary was directed by the central thought. As he put it, "In my sermons I bury myself to take just one passage and there I stay so the hearers may be able to say 'That was the sermon.'"[5] He held to the real presence of Christ in preaching and that the preaching of Christ is Christ preaching. There can be no higher view of preaching than this.

Luther said he would rather be a preacher than a king, but when he was wrung out he would become discouraged and weary. He saw the preacher as both soldier and shepherd. "He must nourish, defend and teach; he must have teeth in his mouth and be able to bite and fight." Sometimes the drained and depleted Luther wanted to quit, and told his congregation he was going to do so.

Yet he loved the tension of dialectic in preaching. "When I preach a sermon, I take an antithesis."[6] And that he did in pressing law/gospel; God/Satan; sin/grace. He always aimed at both the heart and mind of his hearers.[7] Although he confessed timidity (always appropriate for the preacher in dependence on the Lord), his delivery was forceful and sometimes bombastic. He frequently offended by language and action. He spoke of "stink" and "manure" from the pulpit. At Eisenach on one occasion he hammered away at a text while preaching so that he split a three-inch board.[8]

As we have pointed out there was what Meuser calls a kind of "heroic disorder"[9] in Luther's preaching, which is only to say that he exalted the Word and generally disdained the form. Still well worth reading, the sermons of Luther have great mood swings and sudden surges. He was immensely pictorial in his preaching.[10] But in all of this the Word of God dominated and directed and determined. Luther was not in comparison with Calvin a systematic thinker. He was far more a feeling preacher but under the text. As he put it, "A little word of God makes the whole world too narrow for me."

While always in reaction against that which was too fine or too ornate, Luther defined the preacher as "a logician and a rhetorician."[11] In his *Table Talk* he indicates that a preacher should have these qualities: (1) to teach systematically; (2) to have a ready wit; (3) to be eloquent; (4) to have a good voice; (5) to have a good memory; (6) to know when to make an end (Luther could be very brief as well as extended); (7) to be sure of his doctrine; (8) to venture and engage body and blood, wealth and honor in the Word; (9) to suffer himself to be mocked and jeered of everyone.[12]

Luther's famous sacristy prayer lays bare his own soul as he prepared to preach:

O Lord God, dear Father in heaven, I am indeed unworthy of the office and ministry in which I am to make thy glory and to nurture and to serve this congregation. But since thou hast appointed me to be a pastor and teacher, and the people are in need of the teaching and the instruction, O be thou my helper and let thy holy angels attend me. Then if thou art pleased to accomplish anything through me, to thy glory and not to mine or to the praise of men, grant me, out of thy pure grace and mercy, a right understanding of thy Word and that I may also diligently perform it. O Lord Jesus Christ, Son of the living God, thou shepherd and bishop of our souls, sent thy Holy Spirit that he may work with me, yea, that he may work in to will and to do through thy divine strength according to thy good pleasure. Amen.[13]

1. D. Olivier, *Luther's Faith: The Cause of the Gospel in the Church* (St. Louis: Concordia, 1982), 110.
2. John Ker, *Lectures on the History of Preaching* (New York: Armstrong, 1889), 152ff.
3. Roland H. Bainton, *Here I Stand: A Life of Martin Luther* (New York: Mentor, 1950, 1977), 272–81.
4. Cortland Myers, *Making a Life* (New York: Revell, 1900), 142.
5. Fred W. Meuser, *Luther the Preacher* (Minneapolis: Augsburg, 1983), 47. Meuser points out that the Franciscans and Dominicans gave up the cruciform church building and took the huge hall churches with the pulpit on one of the middle pillars, thus sparing the Reformers the necessity of developing their own architectural style. He also shows how Tauler influenced Luther on the need for the sermon to be "centered." This influence on Luther was more telling than even Augustine's homiletical form (cf. 91).
6. A. Skevington Wood, *Captive to the Word: Martin Luther: Doctor of Sacred Scripture* (London: Paternoster, 1969), 91.
7. Meuser, *Luther the Preacher*, 38.
8. Charles H. Spurgeon, *Lectures to My Students* (Grand Rapids: Zondervan, 1954, 1979), 282.
9. Meuser, *Luther the Preacher*, 57.
10. Ibid., 78.
11. Thomas S. Kepler, ed., *The Table Talk of Martin Luther* (New York: World, 1952), 251.
12. Ibid., 238.
13. Meuser, *Luther the Preacher*, 51. For a delightful sampling of Luther's sermonic material in all of its vigor, see *Martin Luther, Day by Day We Magnify Thee: Daily Readings for the Entire Year* (Philadelphia: Fortress, 1982).

5.3 JOHN CALVIN—THE EXEGETE OF GOD'S WORD

When the Word of God is rightly expounded, the faithful are not only edified, but if an unbeliever come into the church and hear the doctrine of God he is reproved and judged.

When the gospel is preached in the name of God, it is as if God spoke in person.

The office of the Spirit promised to us is not to form new and unheard of revelations . . . but to seal on our minds the very doctrine which the gospel recommends.

—John Calvin

Two sharply different traditions in preaching vie for adherents in our time and through the last several hundred years. Preaching in the tradition of the Reformation is God-centered with vertical dominance; preaching in the tradition of the Enlightenment is anthropocentric with horizontal dominance. F. W. Boreham relates a comment of a parishioner to his departing pastor: "I never had but one objection to you—your preaching was always too horizontal."[1] At the aorta of the Reformation, that was seldom the problem.

Ulrich Luz has observed that "until the Enlightenment, the scholarly and the homiletical interpretation of the Bible were closely related—witness, for example, the influence of the homilies of Chrysostom or the relationship between the lectures and sermons of Luther—but since the Enlightenment they have been diverging more and more, leading to a far-reaching divorce between text and sermon, as becomes apparent very often in homileticial practice and sometimes even in homiletical theory."[2]

The result is "the empty pulpit," as Nigel Watson describes it, and urges on us a definition of preaching to counteract it. Preaching is "an act of worship which seeks, in dependence on the presence of God, to bring this passage of Scripture, or this aspect of Christian doctrine, to life as a word of importance for the members of this congregation."[3] The preacher must be an exegete of the text. We now turn to John Calvin, whose genius as an exegetically savvy preacher has set the standard since Reformation days.

---

1. F. W. Boreham, *The Luggage of Life* (London: Charles H. Kelly, 1912), 183.
2. Ulrich Luz as cited in Nigel Watson, *Striking Home: Interpreting and Proclaiming the New Testament* (London: Epworth, 1987), 15ff.
3. Ibid., 120.

5.3.1 CALVIN—IN HIS SAVIOR

Grant, Almighty God, that as Thou hast been pleased to set before us an example of every perfection in Thine only-begotten Son, we may study to form ourselves in imitation of Him, and so to follow not only what He has prescribed, but also what He really performed.
—Calvin's prayer after a lecture on Jeremiah

Many would agree that **John Calvin** (1509–1564) "gave the ablest, soundest, clearest expositions of Scripture that had been seen in one thousand years, and most of the Reformers worked in the same direction."[1] Luther excelled at grasping the one great central truth of a text and pounding it home. But Calvin, fragile in contrast to the emotionally volatile "wild boar" of Saxony, was like a skilled surgeon with the text of Scripture, cool and lucid in his analysis of revealed truth.

In both Luther and Calvin, "the force of their character gave great force to their utterance."[2] Our challenge is to probe what made John Calvin so utterly God-centered in his preaching and so committed in his exegesis. William J. Bouwsma's recent well-received study of Calvin is amazingly destitute of reference to his theology.[3] Bouwsma sees Calvin as a troubled and anxious man in a troubled and anxious age, caught between his medieval scholasticism and his Renaissance humanism. But this distinguished scholar does not allow for the reality of the supernatural in Calvin's life, apart from which his ministry is indeed inexplicable.

John Calvin was born in Noyon in beautiful Picardy, France, the son of a lay diocesan official. Both Calvin's father and brother died as excommunicates because of their questioning of church practices. John was sent to Paris by his father in 1523 to study law (an intriguing parallel with Luther) and then to Orleans, where he earned his doctorate in 1533.

By training he was a skilled rhetorician. His first publication was on the rhetoric of Seneca.

In 1533 he fled Paris because he had written an oration sympathetic to Reformation ideas, which was given by the rector of the University of Paris, Nicolas Cop.

In 1534 he experienced the crisis of "conversion." Later he described it, "At last, God turned my course in a different direction by the hidden bridle of his providence . . . by a sudden conversion *(subita conversione)* to docility, he tamed a mind too stubborn for its years."[4] Bouwsma denigrates real significance in Calvin's conversion,[5] but soon thereafter Calvin resigned his benefices in the church to take a dramatically different course.

At the age of twenty-six, he wrote his famous *Institutes* in Basel in 1535, revising and expanding these throughout his life. (We must note that Calvin and Calvinism are not the same, as McGrath and R. T. Kendall remind us with regard to the doctrine of limited atonement, which they assert is the product of Beza, for example.) Regardless of our own particular theological perspective, the *Institutes* are a beautiful, precise, and focused work. Kenneth Scott Latourette calls the work "the most influential single book of the Protestant Reformation." Book 1 is *The Knowledge of God the Creator;* Book 2 is *The Knowledge of God the Redeemer;* and Book 3 is *The Mode of Obtaining the Grace of Christ.* Sections on our knowledge of God in creation and on the illuminating work of the Holy Spirit are classic.[6] Calvin was a God-intoxicated man!

Calvin fed deeply on the writings of Martin Luther. Our argument is that because the Reformers had such a strong vertical theology, they readily yielded to the supremacy of the Word. Their preaching arose out of their theology. In the *Institutes* we see how Calvin has imbibed Luther, as is demonstrated by his eloquence on justification by faith alone.

Calvin's personal preference would have been to live a scholar's life in Basel, but the God he knew through Christ had called him to preach, to teach, and to lead. His two stints in Geneva and the four intervening years in Strasbourg give proof of his obedience to that call.

Bucer urged him to find a wife, and in 1540 he married a widow, Idelette de Bure. She bore him three children, all of whom died. She herself died nine years later. Calvin also knew oppressive illness and physical weakness, but these did not impede his prodigious labors in preaching, writing, and administration. We see him at a disputation in Lausanne in 1536, where Farel and Viret are the protagonists. When the Romanists accuse the Protestants of neglecting the church fathers, it is Calvin who rises to his feet.

He suggested that the Romanists might read the Fathers before they mentioned them, and quoting one Father after another in exact content, he argued his case with unerring certainty. Men realized that there stood in their midst not a man who had memorized catenae of the Fathers but one who had read them, understood them and set them forth in their proper relation to true catholicism.[7]

Certainly John Calvin was a child of his times, but what is ignored by those who rail against him in caustic caricature and crass condemnation is the unmistakable evidence of the reality of God in his life and his dogged insistence on "the utter gratuity of grace." Apart from this, nothing that he said or did finds explanation. As he himself stressed: God selects vile and worthless persons to instruct and warn us, in order to subdue our pride. Indeed, God employs many in the publishing of His Word "who are not quite so agreeable to the human mind."[8]

1. Leroy Nixon, *John Calvin, Expository Preacher* (Grand Rapids: Eerdmans, 1950), 29.
2. Ibid., 31.
3. William J. Bouwsma, *John Calvin: A Sixteenth-Century Portrait* (Oxford: Oxford University Press, 1988).
4. Alister E. McGrath, *A Life of John Calvin* (Oxford: Blackwell, 1990), 70.
5. Bouwsma, *John Calvin,* 10–12.
6. John Calvin, *Institutes* (Grand Rapids: Eerdmans, 1953), 43–45, for instance, where Calvin graphically pictures the "audacious despiser of God" as in fact "most easily disturbed, trembling at the sound of a falling leaf."
7. James Atkinson, *The Great Light: Luther and the Reformation* (Grand Rapids: Eerdmans, 1968), 162.
8. As cited from commentaries and sermons in Ronald S. Wallace, *Calvin's Doctrine of the Word and Sacrament* (Grand Rapids: Eerdmans, 1957), 117.

5.3.2 CALVIN—IN HIS STUDY

Christ hath therefore been appointed by the Father, not to rule after the manner of princes, by the force of arms and by surrounding Himself with other external defenses, to make Himself an object of terror to His people; but His whole authority consists in doctrine, in the preaching of which He wishes to be sought and acknowledged.

The Scriptures are thus sufficient in themselves to furnish the people of God with all the inspiration and knowledge they require apart from any other source. Through them the Spirit leads us into all truth, and to imagine that this needs supplementing is "to do grievous injury to the Holy Spirit."

—John Calvin

Vadian's famous evaluation of Erasmus—that "he was strong in expression but weak in substance"—could never be offered concerning Calvin because of his total sense of call to be an interpreter of Scripture. Calvin lived and breathed the inspired text, and his commentaries, treatises, and sermons show it. When he first went to Geneva in 1536 under pressure from **William Farel,** he went not in any pastoral capacity but as a "reader in Holy Scripture." He led Bible studies. Although he was never ordained, Calvin's gifts and leadership were soon recognized. He wrote *Ordinances of the Church in Geneva,* in which he saw the pastoral office as "proclaiming the Word of God and instructing believers in wholesome doctrine."

In his first stay in Geneva, a burgeoning republic of about ten thousand people, Calvin was constantly embroiled in controversy. Yet he gave himself wholly to the study of Scripture. He would sleep little, and begin his day of study about 5 or 6 A.M. His sermons were built out of the commentaries and his commentaries are sermonic. His magnificent commentary on Romans came in 1539.

Underlying Calvin's herculean labors was his conviction that "the Bible is true."[1] In his invaluable treatment of Calvin and the Bible, Kenneth Kantzer shows that "Calvin's loyalty to the written Scriptures knows no bounds."[2] While indebted to general or natural revelation, Calvin saw special revelation as "a surer and more direct means" to the knowledge of God as Creator and the only means of knowledge of God as Redeemer. He was convinced of the "divine authority" of the self-authenticating Scripture, and made it clear that this view is the universal view. As a foundation for the Westminster divines and others who followed, Calvin stressed the witness of the Holy Spirit to the authority, accuracy, and sufficiency of Scripture as decisive.[3] Kantzer adds, "According to [Calvin] the human authors of Scripture were controlled by God in every detail of what they wrote."[4] The Scriptures are like spectacles to give us "a clear view of the true God." He saw the sacraments as seals of the divine Word, bringing into the senses what has been thought in the mind. They are extensions of the preached Word and in this respect are to be considered a form of preaching (cf. 1 Cor. 11:26).

When Calvin returned to Geneva in 1541, he spent a great part of his time exegeting and writing commentaries. He delivered Bible readings on the basis of his commentary work several afternoons each week. In his epochal volumes on the commentaries, T. H. L. Parker pays tribute to Calvin's scholarly work.[5] The commentaries demonstrate the application of Calvin's inerrancy to exegesis.[6] Even Jacob Arminius praised Calvin's commentaries, saying that his work was "incomparable in the interpretation of the Scripture."[7] Arminius recommended Calvin's commentaries next to the Bible itself.

Calvin was always concerned about the question of canonicity (again reflecting Luther), and held to the perspicacity (clarity and wisdom) of Scripture. He saw the doctrine of salvation as clear in the Scripture even for the unconverted, but maintained that comprehending the full meaning of the text always relied on the collaboration of the Holy Spirit.[8] He advocated what he called "the natural" meaning of the text. Like Luther, Calvin abandoned the medieval hermeneutic, and pleaded, "Don't use fanciful allegories."[9]

Using Greek and Hebrew with ease, Calvin has given us commentaries on almost all of the New Testament books and many Old Testament books. He had a great love for the Old Testament and emphasized preaching Christ from it (as did Luther). Calvin saw Christ foreshadowed everywhere in the Old Testament, especially in the sacrifices, priesthood, and ritual of the tabernacle and temple. Of the Old Covenant people, Calvin wrote, "The manifestation of Christ was the goal of the race which God's ancient people were running."[10] The inscripturated Word and the preached Word give meaning to the signs which God has given. Commenting on 2 Timothy 2:15, Calvin remarks:

> This is a beautiful metaphor. Since we ought to be satisfied with the Word of God alone, what purpose is served by hearing sermons every day, or even the office of pastors? Has not every person the opportunity of reading the Bible? But Paul assigns to teachers the duty of dividing or cutting, as if a father in giving food to his children were dividing the bread and cutting it in small pieces.[11]

Thus Calvin observed that it was Philip, not an angel, who opened the Word to the Ethiopian on the Gaza road.

In four happy years in Strasbourg, Calvin served as chair of exegesis. Only reluctantly did he go back to Geneva to battle for the integrity of the Word of God. When he did return to Geneva in 1541, he was made head pastor and gave much to his people. From 1550–1559 he performed 270 weddings and 50 baptisms out of St. Pierre's Church. Still, in a one typical year during his second tenure in Geneva, he preached 286 sermons and gave 186 lectures. In his last years he ate a single meal daily and on some days would walk only in his room. "The feeble-looking Frenchman," as he was called, suffered from asthma, weak digestion, and numerous other complaints. Ironically, his wheezing made it easier for those who transcribed his discourses because his pace was necessarily slower. Of his preaching Beza said: "Every word weighed a pound."

---

1. Kenneth S. Kantzer, "Calvin and the Holy Scriptures," in *Inspiration and Interpretation,* ed. John F. Walvoord (Grand Rapids: Eerdmans, 1957), 145.
2. Ibid., 155.
3. Bernard Ramm, *The Witness of the Spirit: An Essay on the Contemporary Relevance of the Internal Witness of the Holy Spirit* (Grand Rapids: Eerdmans, 1959). Ramm wrestles with the origin of Calvin's doctrine, opining that it may derive from his personal study of Scripture along with his own experience in conversion. The Word of God is objective revelation in Scripture for Calvin, but because of the noetic effects of sin the ministry of the Holy Spirit is necessary and essential.
4. Kantzer, "Calvin and the Holy Scriptures," 140. Another Genevan professor of some years later argues the same case; see L. Gaussen, *Theopnuestia: The Inspiration of the Holy Scriptures* (Chicago: Moody, 1949).
5. T. H. L. Parker, *Calvin's Old Testament Commentaries* (Louisville: Westminster/John Knox, 1986); *Calvin's New Testament Commentaries* (London: T & T Clark, 1971). Parker shares Karl Barth's praise of Calvin's exegesis to Eduard Thurneysen: "Calvin is a cataract, a primeval forest, a demonic power, something directly down from Himalaya, absolutely Chinese, strange, mythological; I lack completely the means, the suction cups, even to assimilate this phenomenon, not to speak of presenting it

adequately. What I receive is only a thin little stream and what I can then give out again is only a yet thinner extract of this little stream. I could gladly and profitably set myself down and spend all the rest of my life just with Calvin" in *Calvin's Old Testament Commentaries*, frontispiece.

6. Kantzer, "Calvin and the Holy Scriptures," 140.
7. Timothy George, *Theology of the Reformers* (Nashville: Broadman, 1988), 187.
8. Kantzer, "Calvin and the Holy Scriptures," 152. That even the unregenerate can understand clear language and its meaning can be seen in E. D. Burton's great commentary on Galatians in the old ICC. Burton pointed out that the apostle Paul clearly believed in the substitutionary atonement and taught it in Galatians, but Burton himself held another view.
9. Ibid., 152.
10. Ronald S. Wallace, *Calvin's Doctrine of the Word and Sacrament* (Grand Rapids: Eerdmans, 1957), 59.
11. Ibid., 115.

5.3.3   CALVIN—IN HIS PULPIT

Let the preachers attempt nothing by their own brains; let them bring forth, as coming from God, all that they proclaim.

Therefore lest, like giants, we make war against God, let us learn to hearken to the ministers by whose mouth He teaches us.

The office of a good and faithful shepherd is not barely to expound the Scripture, but he must use earnestness and sharpness, to give force and virtue to the Word of God.

God sometimes connects Himself with His servants and sometimes separates Himself from them . . . He never resigns to them His own office. . . . When God separates Himself from His ministers, nothing remains in them.

—John Calvin

Scholarship in this century has tended to emphasize Calvin as pastor and preacher. His conviction about Scripture and his indefatigable labors in exegesis climaxed in the pulpit communication of Scripture. He exalted preaching because "this incomparable treasure set in our midst by the grace of God . . . the Word which is able to save the human soul."[1] Calvin spoke of "my beloved Holy Scriptures." As early as his stay in Paris he was exposed to powerful preaching by the evangelical **Gerard Roussel,** who drew "large crowds with his preaching during Lent 1533."[2] The sermons of Roussel commanded the attention of the nation, including the king.

During Calvin's four years in Strasbourg when he pastored the French church, he preached nearly every day and twice on Sundays. Until he died, the pulpit was the heart of his ministry. When summoned back to Geneva in 1541, he resumed his exposition on the next verse from the place where he had stopped. The pattern of preaching twice on Sundays and in alternate weeks at a daily evening service continued in Geneva. He preached extempore, that is, without a manuscript. (Calvin faulted the English for using manuscripts.) A paid stenographer recorded his sermons.

He moved consecutively through book after book. We possess about a thousand of his sermons, many of which have not been translated. Yet this signal preaching ministry was always conducted in the face of strong opposing forces. In Geneva, "He was insulted in the streets, and fireworks were put in his door, while lewd louts sang obscene songs in his window at night."[3]

He was encouraged by an influx of French immigrants who fled religious tensions in France. He appealed to them to come and help him, and the population of Geneva swelled to upwards of 19,000. The presence of so many émigrés complicated the already tense political situation for Calvin's implementation of his dream of a Christian commonwealth.

Building on his magisterial analysis of Calvin's commentaries, Parker has recast his brilliant *The Oracles of God: An Introduction to the Preaching of John Calvin* (1947) in the magnificent successor volume, *Calvin's Preaching* (1992). He shows how Calvin moved away from the "pick and choose" approach to scriptural truth by systematic verse by verse exposition.[4] Calvin's sermons then are more like the homilies of Augustine than the structured university sermons of Alan of Lille in the High Middle Ages. The price Calvin paid for this is frequently a lack of unity in the sermon. Division implies unity. Here, perhaps, the commentator has overpowered the preacher. Then too, there is a danger "to exalt the expounding above what is expounded."[5] Yet the strength of Calvin's content and his application tended to compensate.

Each of Calvin's sermons was about an hour long. He used language simply and directly, and had a remarkably retentive mind, but he was utterly destitute of imagination and humor.[6] He employed no introduction to the sermon, and would invariably launch into the text by saying, "We saw yesterday" or "We have seen this morning." His conclusion amounted to "Therefore we see now" or "We will have to save the rest until tomorrow."[7]

The context was critical for Calvin. He delighted in word studies but never quoted the Hebrew or Greek in the sermon. He insisted, "I do not willingly accept interpretations which can only be fitted to the words by twisting the words to them."[8] He used virtually no anecdotes and had little sense of climax or crescendo, and was weak in image and metaphor. From Sermon XVI in the 2 Samuel series we glean his viewpoint:

> When we have access to the preached Word, God speaks to us in a common and ordinary fashion. It is an illustration of his condescension. Hence the preaching of the Gospel is like a descent which God makes in order to seek us. We must not abuse this simplicity of the Word of God by disdaining it. Rather we must receive it all the more, recognizing that he indeed deigns to transfigure himself, so to speak, that we might approach him. He is not content with giving us his word, but adds baptism to it . . . the point is of course that since God has come down to us, we must go up to him.[9]

Many were irresistibly drawn to the teaching and preaching ministry of Calvin—John Knox from Scotland sat entranced with many other clergy and political figures in St. Pierre's. He said that Calvin's Geneva was "the most perfect school of Christ that ever was in the earth since the days of the Apostles."[10] This remarkable appeal may be found in the biblical richness and substance which Calvin set as a feast for his hearers. It was this content, carefully and skillfully applied, that drove the biblical truth into the heart of the hearers. The movement in the sermon was from the exegesis to the application to the exhortation, from the "then" of biblical revelation to the "now" of present daily life.[11] John Leith frames the issue succinctly:

> First of all, Calvin understood preaching to be the explication of Scripture. The words of Scripture are the source and content of preaching. As an expositor, Calvin brought to the task of preaching all the skills of a humanist scholar. As an interpreter, Calvin explicated the text, seeking its natural, its true, its scriptural meaning . . . Preaching is not only the explication of Scripture, it is also the application of Scripture. Just as Calvin explicated Scripture word by word, so he applied the Scripture sentence by sentence to the life and experience of the congregation.[12]

Calvin used words artfully. He used the expressions of the people. He read them well and knew how to get them to listen. He was well schooled in Quintilian and he quoted Cicero. But he insisted that this by itself is not enough. Calvin used an intensely personal conversational style he called *familiere*. He did not use long sentences. He employed question and answer and objection and reply as bridges in his communication.

Parker helpfully catalogues the course of his preaching.[13] The consistency and clarity of Calvin's expositions, along with the gravity and earnestness of his delivery, make him one of the sterling models of biblical preaching in the history of the Christian church. In what Dargan called "the mighty wave of reformatory preaching," John Calvin was the master preacher.

---

1. Ronald S. Wallace, *Calvin's Doctrine of the Word and Sacrament* (Grand Rapids: Eerdmans, 1957), 89.
2. Alister E. McGrath, *A Life of John Calvin* (Oxford: Blackwell, 1990), 63.
3. James Atkinson, *The Great Light: Luther and Reformation* (Grand Rapids: Eerdmans, 1968), 164.
4. T. H. L. Parker, *Calvin's Preaching* (Louisville: Westminster/John Knox, 1992), v.
5. Ibid., 20.
6. Leroy Nixon, *John Calvin: Expository Preaching* (Grand Rapids: Eerdmans, 1950), 31ff.
7. John Bishop, "John Calvin: Character in Preaching," *Preaching* (January–February 1993), 60–61.
8. Douglas F. Kelly, "Some Aspects of the Preaching of John Calvin," *Evangel* (autumn 1987), 11.
9. Ibid., 13.

10. Timothy George, *Theology of the Reformers* (Nashville: Broadman, 1988), 167.
11. As so classically articulated in John R. W. Stott, *Between Two Worlds: The Art of Preaching in the Twentieth Century* (Grand Rapids: Eerdmans, 1982). McGrath incisively demonstrates how Calvin addressed "real and specific situations—social, political, and economic—with all the risks that such precision entails" (*Life of John Calvin*, 220ff). He explains Calvin's appeal but also the vicious antagonisms he confronted.
12. John H. Leith in "Calvin's Doctrine of the Proclamation of the Word and Its Significance for Today in the Light of Recent Research," *Review and Expositor* 86 (winter 1989), 33, quoted in Harold T. Bryson, *Expository Preaching: The Art of Preaching Through a Book in the Bible* (Nashville: Broadman and Holman, 1995), 17.
13. Parker, *Calvin's Preaching,* 150ff.

5.4 HULDRYCH ZWINGLI—THE EXPOSITOR OF SCRIPTURE

No matter who a man may be, if he teaches you in according with his own thought and mind his teaching is false. But if he teaches you in accordance with the word of God, it is not he that teaches you, but God who teaches him. For as Paul says, who are we but ministers of Christ and dispensers or stewards of the mysteries of God? Again, I know for certain that God teaches me, because I have experienced the fact of it: and to prevent misunderstanding this is what I mean when I say that I know for certain that God teaches me. When I was younger, I gave myself overmuch to human teaching, like others of my day, and when about seven or eight years ago I undertook to devote myself entirely to the scriptures I was always prevented by philosophy and theology. But eventually I came to the point where led by scripture and the word of God I saw the need to set aside all these things and to learn the doctrine of God direct from his own word. Then I began to ask God for light and the scriptures became far clearer to me—even though I read nothing else—than if I had studied many commentators and expositors. Note that is always a sure sign of God's leading, for I could never have reached that point by my own feeble understanding. You may see then that my interpretation does not derive from the overestimation of myself, but the subjection.

—Huldrych Zwingli

The rallying cry in the Reformation from Luther on was to preach God, not man. Yet one lingering vestige of medieval preaching continued to be problematic. Both Calvin and Zwingli tended to moralizing preaching on occasion.[1] Moralism is a heavy dose of exhortation; it is attaching branches to an umbrella stand rather than seeing branches grafted into a living organism. It is preaching from the circumference of duty without sufficient attention to the dynamic center. The apostle Paul's practical admonitions followed his doctrinal delineation of who God is and what He has done (as in Romans and Ephesians). The thirteen hortatory "let us" references in the Epistle to the Hebrews always build upon doctrine. Much hortatory preaching tends to moralism. How growth in the sense of God-centered reality and discourse altered Zwingli's preaching is now before us.

1. Ulrich Gabler, *Huldrych Zwingli: His Life and Work* (Philadelphia: Fortress, 1986), 33, for the early preaching of Zwingli as consisting chiefly of "moral admonitions." Cf. T. H. L. Parker, *Calvin's Preaching* (Louisville: Westminster/John Knox, 1992), 20.

5.4.1 Zwingli's Personal Pilgrimage

But we, to whom God himself has spoken through his Son and through the Holy Spirit, are to seek these things not from those who are puffed up with human wisdom, and consequently corrupted what they received pure, but from the divine oracles.

For as often as by the use of clear passages of scripture they are driven to the point of having to say, I yield, straightway they talk about "the Spirit" and deny scripture . . . As if indeed the heavenly Spirit were ignorant of the senses of scripture which is written under his guidance or were anywhere inconsistent with himself.

The word of God is so sure and strong that if God wills all things are done the moment that he speaks his word. For it is so living and powerful that . . . things both rational and irrational are fashioned and despatched and constrained in conformity with its purpose.

—Huldrych Zwingli

Although he was not of the stature of Luther and Calvin, **Huldrych Zwingli** (1484–1531) was the leader of the Swiss German Reformation and a pivotal figure in the unfolding drama we call the Protestant Reformation. He was born the oldest of nine children to a rural chief magistrate and his wife in the Toggenburg Valley in the Swiss Confederation. He studied at the University of Vienna and learned his Aristotelian texts at the University of Basel, where he took his M.A. His first pastorate was in Glarus (1510–1516), where he wrote a political tractate against alliance with the French in the form of a poetic fable about an ox. He felt unsettled about his early more moralistic preaching, and began to move from absorption in the commentaries themselves to the text of Scripture. In 1516 he was one of the first to get the new Greek text from his friend Erasmus. The influence of the biblical text and Augustine's writings on the Fourth Gospel moved him to begin preaching Christ and the gospel.

Zwingli's next pastorate was in Einsiedeln (1516–1518), which was also the site of "an image of the Black Virgin" and a place to which many pilgrims came. As Potter reports, "Many visitors came home to report that the preacher was saying new things and introducing passages from the Bible, and particularly of the New Testament, into his discourses . . . he made a passionate appeal for a direct approach to God the Father through God the Son."[1]

Zwingli was more Erasmian than any of the other Reformers. His personal library of some 350 volumes contained many classics and patristic works. When the position of people's priest opened at the Great Minster in Zurich in 1518,

Zwingli was at the apex of his power, and desirable in the political complexity of the time because of his hostility to France. One impediment loomed, and it was that he had yielded to the advances of a common prostitute. Gabler speaks of the resolution of this problem: "In an unreservedly candid letter to Henrich Utinger, dated December 5, 1518, Zwingli confessed to the errors of youth, stressed the secrecy of his actions, spoke of his repentance and vowed never again to touch a woman."[2]

Thus at age thirty-five, on January 1, 1519, he began his preaching ministry in the famous collegiate church in Zurich, a church that dated back to the eighth century. Zwingli announced that on the following Sunday he would start an extended series of expositions from Matthew's gospel, the pattern throughout his ministry in Zurich.

Potter asserts, "Even more than Luther, Zwingli valued preaching very highly and was indefatigable in the pulpit."[3] He practiced and urged the simple exposition of Scripture in the pulpit. About this time, Zwingli experienced a spiritual crisis in which, influenced by Lutheranism, he turned from Erasmian humanism to a new commitment to the Bible as "the direct Word of God." It is possible that nearly dying of the plague in 1519, when two thousand of Zurich's seven thousand people died, may have motivated his about-face. Or perhaps it was his own revitalized experience in the Word. Bullinger, his successor, related that Zwingli had memorized the entire Greek New Testament.

Throughout these years Zwingli also served as a chaplain in the Swiss army, which was valued everywhere for its mercenaries. (It survives to this day as the Swiss Guard in the Vatican.) He both ministered to the troops and fought in military engagement himself.

Described as a "cheerful, sanguine, short-sighted priest," Zwingli found his stride as a preacher who was "fast becoming Scripture-dominated"[4] and who preached Christ and the cross as the essence of the gospel. He loved to speak of "the reborn Christ" in every believer. Needless to say, he was on a collision course with Rome. His first rift with Rome came over the issue of fasting during Lent and indulgences. Even though a cardinal's hat was dangled before him, he soon became an ardent Reformer. Under the influence of his new view of Scripture and its priority, Zwingli renounced his papal pension, ate sausages during Lent,[5] and got married. He argued in *The Clarity and Certainty of the Bible* for the need of positive scriptural evidence for church practice, and hence he challenged images, prayers to the saints, the mass as performed, purgatory, and distinctive clergy dress.

No longer were popes or councils to steer the church—it must be Christ and the Bible alone. In his Sixty-seven Articles of 1523 he advances the convictions *sola Scriptura, sola Christus*. He did not question the canon, and held that "the very words directly inspired by the Holy Spirit were those for them to read."[6]

He engaged in many public disputations at this time and urged that only the gospel be preached. The Zurich council ordered that all preachers were to follow Zwingli's example. Monasteries and nunneries were emptying. He reorganized the minster and set up a Latin school in order to institutionalize sound exegesis. As Professor Aland concludes: "The means by which the Reformation took hold among the populace was the reading and exposition of the Bible—the 'reading' or the Prophezei."[7]

The Marburg Colloquy in 1529 was the opportunity for Luther and Zwingli to unite in common cause. Disagreement over the Lord's Supper made the desired convergence impossible. Philip of Hesse had catalyzed the conference, but Luther came "overconfident and abusive" and Zwingli did not get the recognition he craved.[8] Luther quickly categorized Zwingli as being like Karlstadt and the "spiritualists." Throughout their discussions Luther kept calling him "Zwingel" and angrily denounced him and his "rabble." He described Zwingli as a heathen,[9] even though Zwingli's good friend and Luther's cohort Melancthon seemed to indicate that Augustine favored Zwingli's position.[10] Zwingli understood the phrase "this is my body" to mean "this *signifies* my body." That was unacceptable to Luther, whose doctrine of consubstantiation is a curious stopoff on the way from transubstantiation. Luther felt the commemorative view of the Supper involved a denial of the full deity of Christ and the Trinity. This was the death knell of any hope for unity. Luther summed up his contentions with Zwingli by saying: "You have a different spirit than we."

Zwingli was an effective shepherd of souls, and spoke of the pastoral office as that of shepherd or watchman. He wrote copiously on many subjects theological and practical, including a splendid analysis of pastoral work in 1525 titled *The Shepherd.* He detested what he called "noisy hymns" in the worship service.

Serfdom was a widespread grievance that led to the great Peasants' War in 1525. According to the scholar Peter Blickle, the impact of Zwingli's ministry may be seen in the conflict. Many Roman Catholic thinkers have blamed Luther for this tragic uprising which led to the slaughter of more than one hundred thousand peasants. In his general aversion to chaos of any kind, Luther took the side of the nobility.

But Blickle argues that Zwingli and other Reformers must bear some responsibility for the war. Zwingli's preaching of the Word of God presented a mandate for freedom. Blickle points out, "What united the peasants and the townspeople was the Gospel."[11] Some of the key leaders in the movement were disciples of Zwingli. Indeed, Zwingli had categorically stated, "The most peaceful and God-fearing regime will be found where the Word of God is preached most purely."[12] The Revolution of 1525 must then be seen as part of the unfolding of the Reformation and its message. The desire for freedom is the fruit of the gospel. Serfdom was abolished in Zurich and Bern, and the free election of pastors became the practice.

In the Second Kappel War between Catholics and Protestants, Zwingli was killed on the battlefield on October 11, 1531. The issue in the conflict for Zwingli was "the free preaching of the word of God."

Even at this time, Calvin was experiencing his conversion in Paris and Orleans and would soon inherit the leadership of the Swiss French Reformation.

---

1. G. R. Potter, *Zwingli* (Cambridge, Mass.: Cambridge University Press, 1976), 42. A rewardingly rich study.

2. Ulrich Gabler, *Huldrych Zwingli: His Life and Work* (Philadelphia: Fortress, 1986), 44.
3. Potter, *Zwingli*, 61.
4. Ibid., 62.
5. Kurt Aland, *A History of Christianity* (Philadelphia: Fortress, 1986), 2:167.
6. Potter, *Zwingli*, 64.
7. Aland, *A History of Christianity*, 171.
8. Potter, *Zwingli*, 329.
9. E. J. Furcha and H. Wayne Pipkin, eds., *Prophet, Pastor, Protestant: The Work of Huldrych Zwingli after Five Hundred Years* (Allison Park, Pa.: Pickwick, 1984), 77ff.
10. W. P. Stephens, *The Theology of Huldrych Zwingli* (Oxford: Clarendon, 1986), 21n.
11. Peter Blickle, *The Revolution of 1525: The German Peasants' War from a New Perspective* (Baltimore: Johns Hopkins University Press, 1977), 115.
12. Ibid., 159.

5.4.2 ZWINGLI'S PROWESS IN PREACHING

> This is the seed I have sown. Matthew, Luke, Paul and Peter have watered it, and God has given it splendid increase, but this I will not trumpet forth, lest I seem to be canvassing my own glory and not Christ's.

> Whithersoever, then, prophets or preachers of the word are sent, it is a sign of God's grace that he wishes to manifest the knowledge of himself to his elect; and where they are denied, it is a sign of impending wrath.

> The work of prophecy or preaching I believe to be most holy, so that above any other duty it is in the highest degree necessary. For in speaking canonically or regularly we see that among all nations the outward preaching of apostles and evangelists or bishops has preceded faith, which we nevertheless say is received by the Spirit alone. For alas! we see very many who hear the outward preaching of the gospel, but believe not, because a dearth of the Spirit has occurred.
>
> —Huldrych Zwingli

The vacuum of vapid moralism in the early preaching of Zwingli and the Reformers was soon filled with the wonder of Scripture and an expansive sense of the greatness and majesty of a holy and merciful God. Zwingli preached from the Gospels with the Greek text of the New Testament before him. One listener in Zurich named Thomas Platter was so euphoric in hearing the bracing exposition of the text that he felt he was "being pulled by the hair on his head." Zwingli's determination was clear from the outset:

> The life of Christ has been too long hidden from the people. I shall preach upon the whole of Matthew's gospel, chapter by chapter, according to the inspiration of the Holy Ghost, without human commentaries, drawing solely from the fountain of Scripture, according to its depths, comparing

one passage with another and seeking for understanding by constant and earnest prayer. It is to God's glory, to the praise of His holy Son, to the real salvation of souls, and to their edification in the true faith that I shall consecrate my ministry.[1]

Typical of the Reformers, Zwingli had a great love for the Old Testament. Both Zwingli and Calvin would abandon the prescribed pericope texts in favor of book exposition *lectio continua*. Zwingli preached more from the Old Testament than from the New. He preached 134 sermons on the Book of Deuteronomy alone. Professor Reu's deft analysis of the Reformers' use of the Old Testament shows the refreshing balance and soundness of their approach.[2] God's people in all times need the older and larger Testament as well as the New.

"Preaching is the sign of the true pastor" Zwingli maintained, and a veritable epidemic of evangelical and biblical preaching followed his example.[3] This was so because he had submitted to "the tyranny of the Book."

Unfortunately, we do not possess many of Zwingli's sermons, because they were delivered extempore and no stenographers took them down. Occasionally he would transcribe a sermon from memory, but these tended to be unduly long. He filled himself with the truth through careful preparation and prayer and then burst into the pulpit.

His exegetical works give us the substance of his preaching,[4] and a careful and thorough inventory of his scriptural citations fully discloses his real biblicality.[5] Close examination of his pulpit ministry during the critical year 1522 shows how adroitly he used the biblical text to relevantly address the controversial questions and practical issues of the time.[6]

Zwingli's sermons would begin with the reading of the biblical text, then a wrestling with its meaning with adaptation to the hearers and their situation. He used homely illustrations and borrowed from the classics. He loved farm illustrations we might consider crude, and made artful use of humor as a bridge to reach his audience. He preached with little gesture in an unadorned style. His voice was on the weak side. When he preached in Strasbourg many complained they could not hear him. He had none of the bombast of Luther, nor did he have the extraordinary brilliance of Calvin, but he preached the Word with power for the changing of human hearts.

Zwingli never divided the text for purposes of exposition as in the homilies that were common among the Reformers. James McGraw points out the vulnerability of this approach:

> The principal criticism of Zwingli's sermons is that they are somewhat formless in their composition. The scriptural examples are unnecessarily numerous, and in them there are many exegeses of passages which are not directly related to the main theme. In spite of these homiletical weaknesses, there is a fine power and freedom in his development of the subject.[7]

This is only to say that high-density exegesis without sufficient attention to form and communication can be detrimental. It is most striking, however, that as different as the three great continental Reformers were, they shared an avid dedication to biblical exposition. Zwingli, like his compatriots, saw grave danger in elevating tradition over Scripture or being too subjectivistic and individualistic in interpretation. He argued for a kind of *analogia fidei* in the expression of his pastoral concern:

> How dare you introduce innovations into the church simply on your own authority and without consulting the church? I speak only of those churches in which the word of God is publicly and faithfully preached. For if every blockhead who had a novel or strange opinion were allowed to gather a sect around him, divisions and sects would become so numerous that the Christian body which we now build up with such difficulty would be broken to pieces in every individual congregation. Therefore no innovations ought to be made except with the common consent of the church and not merely of a single person. For the judgment of scripture is not mine or yours, but the church's.[8]

1. Quoted in John Bishop, "Ulrich Swingli: the Swiss Reformer," *Preaching* (January–February 1994), 61.
2. M. Reu, *Homiletics* (Grand Rapids: Baker, 1924), 279ff.
3. G. R. Potter, *Zwingli* (Cambridge, Mass.: Cambridge University Press, 1976), 135.
4. Ulrich Gabler, *Huldrych Zwingli: His Life and Work* (Philadelphia: Fortress, 1986), 161.
5. E. J. Furcha and H. Wayne Pipkin, eds., *Prophet, Pastor, Protestant: The Work of Huldrych Zwingli after 500 Years* (Allison Park, Pa.: Pickwick, 1984), 57–58.
6. Ibid., 59–61.
7. Bishop, "Ulrich Swingli," 61.
8. W. P. Stephens, *The Theology of Huldrych Zwingli* (Oxford: Clarendon, 1986), 266.

5.5 BIBLICAL PREACHING AMONG THE ENGLISH REFORMERS

> The visible Church of Christ is a congregation of faithful men, in which the pure Word of God is preached, and the Sacraments be duly ministered according to Christ's ordinance.
> —Nineteenth Article of the Thirty-nine Articles

> By the preaching of God's Word the glory of God is enlarged, faith is nourished, and charity increased. By it the ignorant is instructed, the negligent exhorted and incited, the stubborn rebuked, the weak conscience comforted . . . by preaching also due obedience to Christian princes and magistrates is planted in the hearts of subjects.
> —Archbishop Edmund Grindal

The Reformation in England is such an integral part of this narrative, and yet it baffles us with its complicated and intricate turns. Here we see almost without parallel how preaching shaped the life of a nation.

Wales had furnished England with the ruling house of the Tudors, out of which came **Henry VII,** a shrewd and irenic statesman. In 1509, his ambitious son **Henry VIII** ascended the throne. Henry's divorce was the precipitating factor of the English Reformation but it was not the cause. The papacy had lost the respect of Christendom as a whole but nowhere more obviously than in England.[1] Much antipapal feeling and deep anticlericalism were felt in England, where by the sixteenth century there was clearly "long-standing aloofness to Rome."[2] Lollardism (the preaching movement initiated by John Wycliffe, cf. 5.1.1) had never really died on the island nation.

Thus while there was much political machination on the part of Henry VIII and his early cohort Cardinal **Thomas Wolsey,**[3] as well as his powerful secretary, **Thomas Cromwell,** we sense the genuine spiritual aspirations of Cranmer, Latimer, and Ridley. Henry wanted a Roman Catholic Church, but without the authority of the pope to challenge him. Social and economic variables must be also be factored in, as well as a huge dollop of nationalism.

Cranmer, Hooker, and Ridley were Wycliffite in their sympathies and were subsequently exposed to Luther's writings. Preaching was at low ebb in the kingdom, but as the spiritual movement quickened so did theological reconstruction and the call for biblical preaching. By 1536 Archbishop Cranmer successfully petitioned for a Bible in the vernacular. Thus during all of the intrigue of the king's six marriages, significant reformatory progress was being made. When Henry died in 1547, it was Cranmer he called to his deathbed.

Under the impetus of Cranmer and company, we see the Protestant movement flourishing during the reign of young **Edward VI** (1547–1553). Cranmer preached Edward's coronation sermon, in which he acclaimed the boy as "a new Josiah who was to reform the worship of God, destroy idolatry, banish the bishop of Rome, and remove images."[4] Many refugees from the Continent assisted Cranmer in publishing and preaching ventures which laid firm foundations for Protestantism.

But the reaction under **Queen Mary** (1553–1558) saw the reimposition of all the medieval ceremonies and rites in detail. The Protestant bishops were imprisoned and martyred. Some four hundred gave their lives for Christ at this time.

Upon Mary's death her half-sister **Elizabeth I** (1558–1603) came to the throne. Elizabeth had lived all her life "under the shadow of the block," and while she was not personally devout, she was politically shrewd. She perceived that England would increasingly become Protestant. Out of the conflict between the Romanists on the one hand—whom Elizabeth detested—and the Puritans on the other hand—who always displeased her—the Church of England emerged. The "Anglican Compromise"[5] in a sense did not please anyone fully, but it was a *modus vivendi* in which all sides conceded the primacy of preaching. After all, preaching was "the tap-root" of the Reformation. Not only were crosses, images, and altars removed from St. Paul's and other London churches, but biblical preaching began to thrive in England once again. [6]

---

1. L. Elliott-Binns, *The Reformation in England* (London: Duckworth, 1937), 16.

2. James Atkinson, *The Great Light: Luther and the Reformation* (Grand Rapids: Eerdmans, 1968), 194.

3. See the invaluable two volumes on Wolsey by Charles W. Ferguson, *Naked to Mine Enemies* (New York: Little, Brown 1958).

4. Elliott-Binns, *The Reformation in England,* 97.

5. Atkinson, *The Great Light,* 258.

6. My favorite treatment of Elizabeth and her times is Elizabeth Jenkins, *Elizabeth the Great* (New York: Coward-McCann, 1958). The queen did not require thirteen thousand learned preachers for England but "honest, sober and wise men and such as can read the Scriptures and the Homilies well unto the people" (289).

5.5.1 THOMAS BILNEY, THE PRELUDE

Thomas Bilney (1495–1531) is significant to the Protestant preaching that followed him. Born near Norwich, he studied at Trinity Hall, Cambridge, and came under the influence of Luther's writings and was considered a disciple of Erasmus. Tormented by lack of the assurance of salvation, he found deliverance in 1 Timothy 1:15 out of the Greek New Testament. Justification by faith alone became his song. He preached with growing popularity and often attacked Romish practice. Imprisoned in the Tower by Wolsey in 1526, he was released to preach again. God used Bilney to bring Hugh Latimer to Christ at Cambridge. Bilney often preached to great crowds in the open fields. He was burned at the stake in the Lollards' Pit near his hometown of Norwich, saying to Dr. Warner, who accompanied him, "Feed your flock, so that when the Lord cometh he may find you so doing."[1]

1. F. R. Webber, *A History of Preaching in Britain and America* (Milwaukee: Northwestern, 1952), 1:176–79.

5.5.2 JOHN ROGERS, THE PIONEER

John Rogers, otherwise known as Thomas Matthew from Matthew's Bible (1500–1555), was born near Birmingham and took his degree from Cambridge. He served Holy Trinity Church in London before becoming chaplain to the Merchant Adventurers in Antwerp. There he met William Tyndale and gave his life to Christ. Upon the arrest of Tyndale in 1535, Rogers finished Tyndale's translation under the pseudonym of Thomas Matthew.[1] He served a congregation in Wittenberg for eleven years and returned to England during the reign of Edward VI but got in trouble because of his vehement preaching in Mary's years. He was the first to be martyred under Mary. He served as prebendary (salaried preacher) at St. Paul's, and was burned at the stake in February of 1555.

Although we do not possess any of Rogers' sermons, we understand from his contemporaries something of the quality of his biblical and controversial preaching. His wife and children urged him to remain courageous as he walked to the place of execution. The French ambassador who witnessed the martyrdom wondered about the man because he went to his death as one might go to his or her wedding.[2]

---

1. David Daniell, *William Tyndale: A Biography* (New Haven, Conn.: Yale University Press, 1995). This extraordinary new work underscores the need for the Scriptures in England.
2. E. C. Dargan, *A History of Preaching* (New York: Hodder and Stoughton, 1905), 1:484–86.

5.5.3 THOMAS CRANMER, THE PRIME MOVER

The doctrinal heavyweight in the English Reformation was **Thomas Cranmer** (1489–1556), who was born near Nottingham and matriculated at Cambridge. After his ordination, he was appointed university preacher and a teaching fellow. He traveled to Germany and there married the niece of Osiander, the German reformer. Always influenced by Lutheran thinking, Cranmer favored continental connections for the English Reformation. He recommended that Henry VIII seek the counsel of university faculties rather than the pope in his marital dilemmas and as a result was appointed archbishop of Canterbury in 1532.[1] He was forthright in his opposition to Rome, on one occasion preaching for two hours out-of-doors at Paul's Cross with a bad cold and cough. He called the pope the Antichrist, and anathematized images, adoration of the saints, purgatory, and monasteries.[2]

In 1547, Cranmer issued *The Book of Homilies,* consisting of a series of topical homilies. Of these he authored several himself, including the first, titled "A Faithful Exhortation to the Reading and Knowledge of Holy Scripture." Ultimately there were two such volumes.[3] Illustrations and classical allusions abounded in them. Cranmer was also responsible for "The Order of Communion in English" and the Prayer Books of 1549 and 1552. Both show his "unrivaled skill in composing collects."[4] The 1552 volume known as *The Book of Common Prayer* was written with the collaboration of Bucer and Peter Martyr, and was more acceptable to the Reformation party.[5] He also authored the Forty-two Articles (later to become the Thirty-nine Articles). Commendably, he promoted the publication and reading of the Bible by the laity.

Bromiley has shown the Reformation orthodoxy of Cranmer's views, demonstrated in his writing and preaching.[6] During the Marian restoration, Cranmer stood adamantly against the reinstitution of the Mass. He did not agree with Luther on the Lord's Supper, but they were in accord on justification by faith alone. He conducted the funeral of the deceased young king Edward VI in Westminster Abbey according to the Reformed ritual.[7] Meanwhile, Mary celebrated a requiem for her brother in the Tower. The following month, Cranmer and Ridley stood against eleven Romanists at Oxford in a debate over eucharistic doctrine. They were afterward remanded to custody. Although he recanted, Cranmer publicly renounced his recantation and was martyred in March of 1556. His theology and leadership were critically formative in the English Reformation, even if he disappointed at times with inconsistent leadership.

1. Jasper Ridley, *Thomas Cranmer* (Oxford: Clarendon, 1962), 50ff.
2. Ibid., 98.
3. J. W. Blench, *Preaching in England in the Late Fifteenth and Sixteenth Centuries* (New York: Barnes and Noble, 1964), 87.
4. L. Elliott-Binns, *The Reformation in England* (London: Duckworth, 1937), 105.
5. Samuel Leuenberger, *Archbishop Cranmer's Immortal Bequest* (Grand Rapids: Eerdmans, 1990). The Swiss scholar argues that *The Book of Common Prayer* of 1552 is a model of soundness on the Scriptures and is indeed an evangelistic and revivalistic liturgy. He contrasts it with the Oxford Group's later abandonment of *sola Scriptura*.
6. G. W. Bromiley, *Thomas Cranmer Theologian* (New York: Oxford University Press, 1956).
7. Elliott-Binns, *The Reformation in England,* 120.

5.5.4   HUGH LATIMER: THE PREACHER'S PREACHER

> Take away preaching and take away salvation . . . Preaching is the thing the devil hath wrestled most against . . . This office of preaching is the only ordinary way that God hath appointed to save us all.
>
> —Hugh Latimer

Born in Leicestershire and receiving his B.D. from Cambridge, **Hugh Latimer** (1485–1555) was the most able all-round preacher of this time. After defending his dissertation, which was a full-press assault against Melancthon's teachings, Latimer was visited by Thomas Bilney, who led him to see Luther's doctrine of justification and brought him to conversion. As Latimer describes it:

> Master Bilney, or rather Saint Bilney, that suffered death for God's word sake—the same Bilney was the instrument whereby God called me to knowledge; for I may thank him, next to God, for that knowledge I have in the Word of God. For I was as obstinate a papist as any was in England . . . he came to me afterwards in my study and desired me to hear his confession. I did so; and to say the truth, by his confession I learned more than before in many years. So that from that time forward I began to smell the Word of God and forsook the school doctors and such fooleries.[1]

His preaching began to draw quite a following, and he was successively expert on canon law, chaplain to the queen, and bishop of Worcester. His faithful servant, Augustine Bernher, recorded many of his sermons, and these have been preserved for us. Latimer often preached before King Henry and on one reported occasion began augustly: "Latimer, Latimer, King Henry is listening." Then after a pregnant pause he continued: "Latimer, Latimer, Almighty God is listening!" Then he preached boldly against marital infidelity. He was fearless but exceedingly shrewd and adaptive to the audience and the immediate situation.

Latimer has been called the father of English preaching. His effectiveness grew out of his scriptural soundness combined with a likableness and an encouraging manner that endeared him to his listeners. Children even followed him through the streets.[2] Organization of discourse was not his forte, but he displayed good variety. On occasion he would use visual aids. Blench lauds him as "the greatest pulpit exponent of the colloquial style in the century."[3] He used humorous stories, proverbs, and exempla.

Latimer was relentless in his condemnation of abuses and superstitions in the church. He referred to "strawberry prelates" who preached only seasonally. In and out of favor, he began to preach again with the accession of Edward. His legendary Sermon on the Plough was especially timely. Here he spoke of the Devil as the most diligent preacher in England, always at his plough. His series of sermons on The Card are creative and compelling. Since the people played so many card games at Christmas, he wanted to show them how to play with Christ's cards and come out winners.[4] He tended to implement long introductions, running applications, and brief, direct conclusions. John Brown says of him, "Other preachers have excelled him in rhetoric, refinement and accuracy; but few have proved his equals in broad, forceful influence over all classes of people, and his sermons remain prose classics to this day."[5]

When he preached at St. Margaret's, Westminster, the crowds were so great that they broke the benches. He was often heard in St. Paul's Cross, "the most celebrated pulpit in England." In his final imprisonment, Latimer read his New Testament through seven times. When he and Ridley were burned at the stake on October 16, 1555, he made his famous statement and testament: "Be of good comfort, master Ridley, and play the man. We shall this day light such a candle by God's grace in England, as I trust shall never be put out."[6]

---

1. E. C. Dargan, *A History of Preaching* (New York: Hodder and Stoughton, 1905), 1:488.
2. Jay E. Adams, *Sermon Analysis* (Denver: Accent, 1986), 97. A fine workbook with model sermons.
3. J. W. Blench, *Preaching in England in the Late Fifteenth and Sixteenth Centuries* (New York: Barnes and Noble, 1964), 142.
4. T. Harwood Pattison, *The History of Christian Preaching* (Philadelphia: American Baptist Publication Society, 1903), 152.
5. F. R. Webber, *A History of Preaching in Britain and America* (Milwaukee: Northwestern, 1952), 1:167.
6. For a satisfying biography of Latimer, see Harold S. Darby, *Hugh Latimer* (London: Epworth, 1953).

5.5.5 NICHOLAS RIDLEY, THE PEDAGOGUE

The man who died beside Latimer was his colleague and friend **Nicholas Ridley** (1500–1555). From Northumbria, Ridley was trained at Cambridge, often the center of the English Reformation. Cambridge may have produced Cranmer, Latimer, and Ridley, but they burned at Oxford.[1]

Ridley was an effective preacher, perhaps second only to Latimer, but he was preeminently a theologian and teacher. He studied at both the Sorbonne and at Louvain. In 1533 he became senior proctor and university chaplain at Cambridge.[2] Eventually he aspired to master of Pembroke Hall, then chaplain to the king, bishop of Rochester, and ultimately bishop of London. His was the sermon at St. Paul's Cross announcing the death of the young Edward VI. It was in this sermon that Ridley declared both Mary and Elizabeth illegitimate, in the hope of the succession of Lady Jane Gray and the Protestant succession.[3]

He had once preached such a forceful sermon before young Edward VI about the poor of London that a subsequent interview with the king led to the establishment of three new London hospitals.[4] Ridley had significant influence on Cranmer and *The Book of Common Prayer* and was beyond doubt the intellectual genius of Reformation theology in England. He spent long hours memorizing the New Testament Epistles as he walked his "famous orchard walk" at his college.[5] A leading ecclesiastic observed, "Latimer leaneth to Cranmer, Cranmer leaneth to Ridley, and Ridley to the singularity of his own wit." John Foxe of martyrs' fame described Ridley's preaching:

> Every holiday and Sunday he preached in some place or other, unless hindered by weighty business. The people resorted to his sermons, swarming about him like bees, and coveting the sweet flowers and wholesome juice of the fruitful doctrine which he did not only preach, but showed the same by his life.[6]

Such was a tribute and testimony every preacher might cherish.[7]

---

1. L. Elliott-Binns, *The Reformation in England* (London: Duckworth, 1937), 47.
2. F. R. Webber, *A History of Preaching in Britain and America* (Milwaukee: Northwestern, 1952), 1:183.
3. J. W. Blench, *Preaching in England in the Late Fifteenth and Sixteenth Centuries* (New York: Barnes and Noble, 1964), 277.
4. E. C. Dargan, *A History of Preaching* (New York: Hodder and Stoughton, 1905), 1:495.
5. Elliott-Binns, *The Reformation in England*, 47.
6. Dargan, *A History of Preaching*, 495ff.
7. An excellent biographical survey is J. G. Ridley's, *Nicholas Ridley: A Biography* (London: Longmans, Green, 1957).

5.5.6 JOHN BRADFORD, THE PROCLAIMER

It was **John Bradford** (1510–1555) who first uttered the immortal words when seeing someone being led off to execution, "There but for the grace of God goes John Bradford." Reared in Manchester, he served with the British forces in France. Later in London he came under deep conviction through the preaching of Hugh Latimer. While an older student at Cambridge, he wrestled with the call to preach. Among the many foreign scholars at Cambridge at this time was Martin Bucer, the Reformation leader in Strasbourg. He urged Bradford to enter the ministry because he saw his preaching gifts. Bucer told him, "If you don't have fine manchet bread, then give the people barley bread."[1] Ridley appointed Bradford a prebendary at St. Paul's in London, and he also served as one of six traveling preachers during the reign of Edward VI who gave themselves to evangelistic labor throughout the kingdom.

A contemporary description of Bradford's preaching gives the following sketch:

> A master of speech, his eloquence native, masculine, modest, in one word, heavenly, for if you mark him he favors and breathes nothing but heaven; yea, he sparkles, thunders, lightens; pierces the soft, breaks only the stony heart.[2]

Two volumes of his sermons have been preserved, including stellar efforts on "The Lord's Supper," with three careful divisions, and "Repentance," likewise deftly divided into three parts. In a style influenced by Melancthon and Erasmus,[3] Bradford was highly doctrinal in his preaching. He made artful use of humor, alliteration, word lists, and agricultural metaphors.[4] His messages abounded with scriptural quotation and allusion. Ridley said of him, "He was a man by whom God hath and doth work wonders in setting forth his word."[5]

Bradford had a tremendous passion to preach even during his long imprisonment in the Tower. He was so trustworthy that he was occasionally permitted to leave the Tower to perform good deeds. He was burned at the stake in Smithfield Market in 1555 in the Marian persecution (cf. 5.5). At these martyrdoms, formal sermons were preached by direction of the Crown.

John Brown said of Bradford:

> A man of bold and daring energy who had great power of command over an audience. Filled with the Spirit of God and with a passionate love for Christ and the souls of men, wherever he was announced to preach the people crowded around him, their beating hearts responding to his burning words.[6]

---

1. E. C. Dargan, *A History of Preaching* (New York: Hodder and Stoughton, 1905), 1:499.
2. T. Harwood Pattison, *The History of Christian Preaching* (Philadelphia: American Baptist Publication Society, 1903), 148.
3. While Melancthon, Luther's systematician, did not feel called to preach, he pressed for biblical preaching in his famous *Loci communes*. N.B. Joseph Stump, *A Life of Philip Melancthon* (Reading: Pilger, 1897).
4. J. W. Blench, *Preaching in England in the Late Fifteenth and Sixteenth Centuries* (New York: Barnes and Noble, 1964), 155.
5. Dargan, *A History of Preaching*, 502.
6. F. R. Webber, *A History of Preaching in Britain and America* (Milwaukee: Northwestern, 1952), 1:192.

5.5.7 JOHN HOOPER, THE PURITAN

Different in many ways but one with the illustrious champions of the Reformation in England is **John Hooper** (1495–1555), who came from comfortable circumstances in Somersetshire and took his degree at Oxford in 1519. He apparently became a Cistercian monk. When his abbey was closed he went to London. Through the influence of the writings of Zwingli and Bullinger, Hooper began to study the Pauline Epistles and became committed to the Reformation position. He visited Strasbourg, Basel, and Geneva.[1] He came back to England tilted not only toward the Reformation view but toward an even more drastic position on vestments, foreshadowing the convictions of those who would be called Puritans. He quickly became spokesman for the Reformers on the right, and had running encounters with the more conciliatory Cranmer and Ridley.

Hooper's preaching was somewhat gruff and austere, but he preached with marked effect. He gained considerable favor when he presented a series of expositions on the Book of Jonah before young King Edward VI. Although he was embroiled in controversy, he was consecrated as bishop of Gloucester in 1550. Hooper was proactive in his approach to every aspect of the life of the diocese. His wife complained to Bullinger that her husband "preached four or at least three times every day and I am afraid lest these over-abundant exertions should cause a premature decay."[2]

At times his theological burdens intruded unnaturally into his exposition. He used extensive Scripture quotation, very short sentences, and few illustrations. We see in Hooper the embryonic development of what would increasingly be the Puritan sermon form with two main sections: doctrine and its uses.

Hooper was imprisoned in 1553 and brought to trial two years later. He was burned at the stake in front of the cathedral in Gloucester. The execution was handled clumsily and he suffered unspeakably.

---

1. F. R. Webber, *A History of Preaching in Britain and America* (Milwaukee: Northwestern, 1952), 1:179.
2. E. C. Dargan, *A History of Preaching* (New York: Hodder and Stoughton, 1905), 1:497.

5.5.8 MILES COVERDALE, THE PUBLISHER

A significant contribution to the cause of the English Reformation was made by **Miles Coverdale** (1488–1568). The Coverdale Bible was well known and widely disseminated, furthering the cause of biblical preaching by putting the Scriptures in the language of the people.

Coverdale came from Yorkshire and graduated from Cambridge, becoming first an Augustinian friar. He traveled as an itinerant and then surfaced in 1535 with his translation of the first complete Bible in English.[1] He also worked on the Great Bible while he was in Paris in 1538, and he edited Cranmer's Bible in 1540. Coverdale served as a Lutheran pastor in Germany, returning to England in 1551 to become chaplain to the king. In 1551 he was appointed bishop of Exeter but was imprisoned by the queen. The king of Denmark persuaded the queen to release Coverdale, who traveled to Denmark and later Germany.[2] He did return to England in the Elizabethan settlement but turned down bishoprics because of his growing Puritan convictions. Coverdale was pastor of St. Magnus Martyr near London Bridge until his seventy-eighth year.[3] Regarded as a strong biblical preacher, for Coverdale conviction always took precedence over ecclesiastical preferment.

---

1. F. R. Webber, *A History of Preaching in Britain and America* (Milwaukee: North-western, 1952), 1:168.
2. James Atkinson, *The Great Light: Luther and the Reformation* (Grand Rapids: Eerdmans, 1968), 224n.
3. Webber, *A History of Preaching,* 1:169. Among the memorable translations is Coverdale's rendition of Genesis 39:2, "And the Lorde was with Joseph in so moch that he became a luckye man" or Isaiah 24:9, "The beer shall be bitter."

5.5.9 MATTHEW PARKER, THE PRELATE

With the coronation of Elizabeth I in 1558, the spiritual and religious situation in England was mottled. Because of the increased circulation of the Bible and *The Book of Common Prayer,* there was a vast increase of scriptural knowledge. Yet there was confusion and consternation in the churches. The nation teetered on the brink of civil war; the Counter-Reformation was in full force; many foreign states were hostile; and the queen's claim to the throne was somewhat sullied.[1] Elizabeth and her men were determined to steer a middle course between Rome and Geneva. Parliament opened with a sermon by Dr. Cox, who was a moderate Protestant.

A pressing priority was the appointment of a new archbishop of Canterbury—the reluctant **Matthew Parker** (1504–1575), who was from Norwich and who took his degree at Cambridge in 1525. He had been a Master at Cambridge and Dean of Lincoln. He had lost his preferments during Mary Tudor's reign but did not lose his life even though his convictions were with the German Reformers and his associations were with Bilney and Latimer. He was consecrated at Lambeth in 1559.[2] Other new appointments to the episcopal bench at this time were Grindal for London, Cox for Ely, and Jewel for Salisbury.

Parker was a thoughtful and scholarly leader, not a great preacher but always well heard. He set himself to a recasting of the Articles and their revision out of which emerged the Thirty-nine Articles, the release of another *Book of Homilies,* the publication of The Bishops' Bible, and the collection of 6,700 other manuscripts still to be found at Cambridge. All of this was critical to build up the churches and to increase the number of available preachers. The complaint was lodged, "There is hardly one in a hundred who is both able and willing to preach the Word of God."[3] To these gaping needs Matthew Parker gave himself and the resources of his office.[4]

1. James Atkinson, *The Great Light: Luther and the Reformation* (Grand Rapids: Eerdmans, 1968), 236ff.
2. L. Elliott-Binns, *The Reformation in England* (London: Duckworth, 1937), 153.
3. F. R. Webber, *A History of Preaching in Britain and America* (Milwaukee: Northwestern, 1952), 1:185.
4. Rich research has been uncovered in recent years on the state of local church life in A. Tindal Hart, *The Country Clergy in Elizabethan and Stuart Times* (London: John Baker, 1958) and *The Man in the Pew: 1558–1660* (London: John Baker, 1966). Also Alan Fager Herr, *The Elizabethan Sermon: A Survey and a Bibliography* (New York: Octagon, 1969).

5.5.10 EDMUND GRINDAL, THE PERSISTENT

When the archbishop of Canterbury, Matthew Parker, died in 1575, Queen Elizabeth appointed **Edmund Grindal** (1519–1583) as new titular head of the Church of England. Grindal hailed from Cumberland and was trained at Cambridge, where he became proctor of the University in 1548 and Lady Margaret Preacher in 1549.[1] Later he was chaplain to Ridley and to Edward VI, and then prebendary at Westminster. When Mary Tudor came to power he fled to the Continent, where he lived first at Strasbourg. After Elizabeth's accession, Grindal served as bishop of London, bishop of York, and then as the archbishop of Canterbury. Manifestly he was not political enough for the delicate balancing act required for his job. Perhaps Elizabeth appointed him because he was unmarried. Why else we cannot see.

The situation for preaching was erratic. There were not many effective preachers to begin with, and Elizabeth clamped down on what she felt were the "impertinent babblings" of both Catholics and Protestants.[2] Court sermons continued, and more than one preacher discoursing before the queen was told to "stick to the text!"[3] The Act of Uniformity was further constrictive in effect. Some services were held in secret. After so much exposure to the Continental Reformers, Grindal was quite Puritan in his leanings. He refused to dampen the meetings for "prophesying," so popular among those inclined to Puritanism. When the queen asked Archbishop Grindal to subdue these "subversive" gatherings, he refused and was suspended for five years of disgrace, finally to be restored shortly before his death.

Grindal was himself well received as a Reformation preacher of grace and gave special attention to the pulpit at St. Paul's Cross where up to six thousand people would convene in the churchyard.[4] In his own preaching he used a modification of the classical sermon with careful divisions of the sermon and evidence of the Puritan adjustment. We shall analyze this development at greater length in our attention to Hyperius in the next chapter.[5] Upon Grindal's death, he was succeeded by **John Whitgift,** an ultra-Calvinist to the point of being supralapsarian (believing that the decree for damnation was from all eternity) but who believed in "the supreme importance of the episcopacy."[6] Whitgift was hard on the Puritans, as was Elizabeth, who did not care for them. He served until after the queen's death.

1. F. R. Webber, *A History of Preaching in Britain and America* (Milwaukee: North-western, 1952), 1:207.
2. Alan Fager Herr, *The Elizabethan Sermon: A Survey and a Bibliography* (New York: Octagon, 1969), 12.
3. Ibid., 38.
4. Ibid., 23–25.
5. J. W. Blench, *Preaching in England in the Late Fifteenth and Sixteenth Centuries* (New York: Barnes and Noble, 1964), 100ff.
6. L. Elliott-Binns, *The Reformation in England* (London: Duckworth, 1937), 167.

5.5.11 JOHN JEWELL, THE PROTECTOR

The most polished preacher in the Elizabethan era was **John Jewel** (1522–1571), who came from Devonshire and did his academics with great acclaim at Oxford. There he was particularly impressed by the new Regius Professor of Divinity, **Peter Martyr Vermigli,** the close associate of Bucer, who was at Cambridge. On Mary's coming to the throne, Jewel fled to the Continent. After hearing John Knox, Jewel became convinced of the merit of the Reformation. In 1559 he returned to England and preached in London, often at St. Paul's Cross. The following year he was made bishop of Salisbury.[1]

Jewel was an ardent controversialist who did not shrink from the burning issues. He was displeased when he learned that the queen had a crucifix, candles, and clergy with vestments in her royal chapel. He preached his famous "challenge sermon," first at St. Paul's Cross, later before royalty, and then made a direct assault on Romish practices. He promised that if anyone could prove Catholic practices by Scripture or by any teacher of the church for the first six hundred years after Christ, he would personally adhere to the Roman Catholic Church again. He then wrote his classic *Apology for the Church of England,* which goes right to the jugular of the issue of authority for the church in all ages.[2]

Jewel was a servant of Christ who had immense intellect and learning and who consecrated these gifts to his Lord. His sermons were meticulously crafted and full of Scripture. He preached in cadences similar to those of the Prayer Book and the King James Version which was yet forty years in the future. Like Grindal, Jewel often used the modified version of the modern style, "Short but elegant," as Blench summarized it.[3] Sensitivity to climax is evidenced in his emotional outline. He maintained extensive correspondence for many years with Bullinger and others. Early in his life he preached a sermon on 1 Peter 4:11. The subject: preaching. His divisions were simple but profound: (1) that the preacher should preach; (2) what he should preach; (3) how he should preach.[4] That was his life and ministry. His health finally broke, and he passed on in 1571.

---

1. F. R. Webber, *A History of Preaching in Britain and America* (Milwaukee: North-western, 1952), 1:208.

2. W. M. Southgate, *John Jewel and the Problem of Doctrinal Authority* (Cambridge, Mass.: Harvard University Press, 1962), 49ff., 146ff.

3. J. W. Blench, *Preaching in England in the Late Fifteenth and Sixteenth Centuries* (New York: Barnes and Noble, 1964), 102ff.

4. E. C. Dargan, *A History of Preaching* (New York: Hodder and Stoughton, 1905), 1:509.

5.5.12 RICHARD HOOKER, THE PURIST

The strains between the more episcopal and the more Puritan in the Church of England were intensifying. In the last several decades of the sixteenth century, no one better epitomized the Episcopalian than **Richard Hooker** (1553–1600). He was born in Exeter in Devonshire, and with Bishop Jewel as his patron he went to Oxford to study. Ordained in 1581, he served a parish in Lincolnshire and was made a Master of the Temple in 1585. His counterpart there was a stolid Puritan, Walter Travers. Out of their ongoing debates Hooker wrote several volumes in defense of the Elizabethan settlement and the Church of England.

On of his works is the famous *Laws of Ecclesiastical Polity*. In opposition to Travers and **Thomas Cartright** (1535–1603), who was called "the earliest complete incarnation of Puritanism on its controversial and theological side," Hooker argued for the episcopacy. Whether one agrees with him or not, one is forced to recognize that no one has ever stated the position more skillfully.[1] The tone of his polemic was reasonable.[2] He argued that the forms of worship are not stipulated in Scripture and pleaded for liberty of conscience.

Richard Hooker was considered one of the foremost preachers of the end of the sixteenth century. His sermons were replete with Scriptures usually taken in the literal sense. He denied that Paul and James contradict each other,[3] and used the modification of the modern form described briefly in Grindal and Jewel. His sermons are the most ornate that we have considered thus far. He reproduced the Ciceronian period more aptly than any other preacher of note. He was poetic and classic but with evidence of the Anglican maturity we have felt missing early on in this turbulent history.[4] Blench speaks of "a new wholesomeness of tone" and a "fragrant spirituality" in his pulpit discourse. Hooker would say:

> I am not in ignorance whose precious blood hath been shed for me; I have a Shepherd full of kindness, full of care, and full of power: unto him I commit myself; his own finger hath engraven this sentence in the tables of my heart, "Satan hath desired to winnow thee as wheat, but I have prayed that thy faith fail not": therefore the assurance of my hope I will labor to keep as a jewel unto the end; and by labor, through the gracious mediation of his prayer, I shall keep it.[5]

Blench asserts that the Anglican piety of Hooker and Andrewes is the fountain from which flowed the stream so vital for George Herbert and T. S. Eliot.

1. L. S. Thornton, *Richard Hooker: A Study of His Theology* (London: SPCK, 1924); Robert K. Faulkner, *Richard Hooker and the Politics of a Christian England* (Berkeley: University of California, 1981). Thornton is a good interaction with the man and his message, and Faulkner probes the *Zeitgeist.*
2. F. R. Webber, *A History of Preaching in Britain and America* (Milwaukee: Northwestern, 1952), 1:218.
3. J. W. Blench, *Preaching in England in the Late Sixteenth and Seventeenth Centuries* (New York: Barnes and Noble, 1964), 64.
4. Ibid., 228.
5. Ibid., 320.

5.5.13 Bernard Gilpin, the Protestant

Renowned in the north country as the apostle of the north, **Bernard Gilpin** (1517–1583) is recorded in the annals of preaching as a powerful preacher of the gospel of grace. Nurtured in a well-to-do home in Westmoreland, Gilpin studied at Oxford, graduated in 1540, and was ordained in 1549. His discussions with Peter Martyr at Oxford rattled his Roman Catholic foundations. Deeply disquieted by the state of the church, he went abroad to study at Louvain and Antwerp. Here he came to a deeply Protestant persuasion.[1] When he returned to England in 1556, his uncle Bishop Tunstall secured several parishes for him where he preached with extraordinary fervor and was known as a gifted preacher and tender shepherd.

The cross of Christ was one of Gilpin's favorite themes, but his preaching incurred the displeasure of the establishment and he was summoned to appear before Queen Mary. In an accident en route to London he broke his leg. While he recuperated, the queen died. He was never tried. Thereafter several offers of episcopal preferment came to him, but he always declined them because of his sense of call to preach and his reservations about the episcopacy.

Gilpin's sermons were simply constructed. He made use of classical quotations and went right to the heart of "popery," which he felt should be sent packing to Rome. He was deeply concerned about social injustice and the lack of schools for children, and he built schools in his parishes.[2] The countryside was rough, but he did not hesitate to enter situations of great peril. His eloquence, piety, and "the graces of his character" cause him to loom large in this cadre of preachers, truly a Westminster Abbey of the heroes of faith from a tumultuous time.[3]

1. F. R. Webber, *A History of Preaching in Britain and America* (Milwaukee: Northwestern, 1952), 1:193–94.
2. J. W. Blench, *Preaching in England in the Late Fifteenth and Sixteenth Centuries* (New York: Barnes and Noble, 1964), 271.
3. E. C. Dargan, *A History of Preaching* (New York: Hodder and Stoughton, 1905), 1:504.

5.6 THE SUSTAINED EXPRESSION OF REFORMATION PREACHING

God was reconciling the world to himself in Christ, not counting men's sins against them. And he has committed to us the message of reconciliation. We are therefore Christ's ambassadors, as though God were making his appeal through us. We implore you on Christ's behalf: Be reconciled to God.

—Paul in 2 Corinthians 5:19–20

Finally, brothers, pray for us that the message of the Lord may spread rapidly and be honored.

—2 Thessalonians 3:1

What began incipiently as a hole in the dike rapidly became a tidal wave which threatened to inundate the whole of Europe. In a sense, many readers of this chronicle are part of a ripple effect of the Reformation and its exaltation of the Scripture and the preaching of the Scripture. Each of the Reformers had a drove of followers who walked in his footsteps. Dargan describes **Heinrich Bullinger** (1504–1517), who succeeded Zwingli in Zurich, as "tall of form, with a flowing beard, a benevolent and intelligent expression, a pleasing voice, a dignified yet animated bearing." He reports that between 1549 and 1567 Bullinger preached 100 sermons on Revelation, 66 on Daniel, 170 on Jeremiah, and 190 on Isaiah.[1]

Names on the honor roll must also include the Petri brothers in Sweden, Hans Tausen in Denmark, Myconius and Oecolampadius in Switzerland, Augustino Cazalla and Juan Gil in Spain, Bernardino Ochino of Italy, and on and on. Three particular personalities command our attention before we leave the sixteenth century.

---

1. E. C. Dargan, *A History of Preaching* (New York: Hodder and Stoughton, 1905), 1:414.

5.6.1   THE DYNAMIC JOHN KNOX OF SCOTLAND

Give me Scotland or I die.

I would most gladly pass through the course that God hath appointed to my labors . . . giving thanks to His Holy Name; for that it hath pleased His mercy to make me not a Lord-like Bishop, but a painful preacher of His blessed Evangel.

—John Knox

Now we turn to Scotland to pick up the thread of the Reformation and its preaching in the tapestry of this rugged and vital land. The story of this people and their "intense individualism, fierce stubbornness, prickly pride and suspicion of each other's motives," along with their fondness for "religious and metaphysical argument" spring naturally from their true Celtic origin and their ancient Celtic religious tradition.[1] The Roman Catholic Church made slow headway, especially in the Highlands, but when it was established, Scottish Catholicism was highly reactionary and impervious to challenge. In the sixteenth century Scotland was four centuries behind the rest of Europe.[2]

Except for a handful of preaching friars, preaching was almost nonexistent. Nary a bishop could preach, except Bishop James Kennedy of St. Andrews, who died in 1465, and at Ayr, the bishop of Glasgow attempted to do so:

> It proved a fiasco, for he had uttered only a few sentences when he had to apologize to his audience saying, "They say we should preach: why not? Better late thrive than never thrive. Have us still for your bishop, and we shall provide better for the next time." The bishop had desired to counter the preaching of George Wishart in Ayr. Instead he hastily left the town, and did not attempt to preach there again.[3]

So the inert clergy, "dumb dogs," and "idle bellies" as they were termed, were no positive factor, but some Lollards and students from Wittenberg along with writings of the Reformers began to seep in. Tyndale's Bibles also began to infiltrate. The "evangelical themes of sin and salvation began to stir men's hearts."[4]

The first of the Scottish martyrs was **Patrick Hamilton**. He was born to a noble family, and studied at Paris and the Louvain. Soon he came under the influence of John Major and Erasmus. His ideas were not well received at St. Andrews, where he was on faculty, and he took refuge at Marburg University, an important evangelical center. He returned to Scotland to preach, was tricked by Archbishop Beaton, and burned at the stake, February 27, 1528. He carried his beloved Bible in his hand to his death.

Likewise **George Wishart,** a highly focused preacher who introduced systematic Bible exposition to Scotland and translated Bullinger's Helvetic Confession, ran afoul of now Cardinal Beaton and was consigned to the stake March 1, 1546. These unpopular executions were a crossing of the Rubicon for the Roman Catholics.

Young **John Knox** (1505 or 1513–1572) was born near Haddington and matriculated at St. Andrews in 1529, the year after Patrick Hamilton's martyrdom. He also heard George Wishart's last sermon before his arrest in 1546. Knox defended Wishart and began to receive what he called some "lively impressions of the heart." Ordained in 1540, he began to share expositions from John's gospel in the Castle Chapel at St. Andrews and introduced the public celebration of the sacrament according to the Reformed ritual. For nineteen months he was consigned to galley service as a punishment, but was released to spend time in England (1549–1554) as a minister at Berwick-on-Tweed (where kneeling for communion was discontinued) and as chaplain for Edward VI. He was especially enamored with the high-priestly prayer of Jesus in John 17 and considered John 17:3 as his anchorage even to the time of his death.[5]

From 1554 to 1559 Knox was in France, Switzerland, and Germany. He came back to Scotland briefly but then spent another year in Geneva where John Calvin was his mentor and model.

The Scottish Parliament established the Reformed Church by law during Knox's absence, and structures emerged "to maintain the Word of God and His Church and to seek ministers of Christ's gospel and sacraments to serve His people."[6] House churches proliferated. The appeal went forth to Knox to return and take leadership, which he did in 1559 after writing his celebrated "First Blast of the Trumpet Against the Monstrous Regiment of Women" (1558). The diatribe had been aimed at Mary Tudor, but Elizabeth Tudor took umbrage.

Upon his return to Scotland, Knox expounded Scripture daily in St. Giles, Edinburgh, where he had been appointed pastor. He preached a vehement sermon in Perth against idolatry and again in St. Andrews on "Cleansing the Temple." In the years 1561 to 1563 he had five recorded interviews with Queen Mary, a dedicated Roman Catholic. The intrigues and tangles of the politics and Scottish nationalism of the time are stranger than fiction.[7] Mary, queen of Scotland (and now also queen of France as wife of Francis II) used French troops to subjugate the Protestants. Queen Elizabeth, because of no liking for Knox but out of detestation of the French, gave her full backing to the Protestant cause. The courage of Knox and his strong preaching were critical during this time.

The Scots Confession (1560) was largely the work of Knox and anticipated in many ways the Westminster Confession of 1647. In 1560, the first General Assembly of the Church of Scotland was convened. Despite the great shortage of good preachers, the Church of Scotland always insisted on "a high standard of preaching."[8] Knox measured up.

The preaching of John Knox was incredibly stirring. When he preached Moray's funeral at St. Giles, he moved the entire company to tears. A marked apocalyptic and eschatological edge to Knox's preaching was clear.[9] James Melville, who heard Knox preach in 1571, a year before his death, testified:

> Of all the benefits I had that year was the coming of that most notable prophet and apostle of our nation, John Knox, at St. Andrews. I heard him teach the prophecies of Daniel that summer and the winter following. In the opening of his text he was moderate the space of a half an hour, but when he reached the application he made me tremble so much that I could not hold the pen to write. He wielded this power when in bodily weakness, for he had to be helped into the church and lifted into the pulpit where he had to lean on his first entry. But when he came to his sermon he was so active and vigorous that he was like to beat the pulpit into pieces and fly out of it.[10]

One thoughtful student of the preaching of Knox identifies six features to be emulated:

1. True preaching must be doctrinal. Knox always preached within a clear sense of theological structure.

2. True preaching must be empathetic. He knew where his people were and utilized gripping illustrations of truth.
3. True preaching must be pointed. He was not afraid to confront the issues of the times and in human life.
4. True preaching must ring with urgency. "Knowing therefore the terror of the Lord . . ." (1 Cor. 5:11).
5. True preaching must be realistic. He was not in denial in relation to the dangers and heartaches faced.
6. True preaching must be victorious. He kept focusing on the God of Scripture who maintains his cause on earth.[11]

The English ambassador Randolph wrote William Cecil after hearing Knox preach: "The voice of one man is able in one hour to put more life in us than five hundred trumpets continually blustering in our ears."[12] In 1570 Knox suffered a stroke which hindered his speech. He moved to St. Andrews, where he appeared in the pulpit for the last time on November 9, 1572. He died November 24, 1572. The Regent Morton said at his grave, "Here lyeth a man who in his life never feared the face of man."

---

1. For a helpful survey of the Scottish background to the Reformation, see Nigel Tranter, *Robert Bruce: The Steps to the Empty Throne* (London: Hodder and Stoughton, 1969); *The Stewart Trilogy* (London: Hodder and Stoughton, 1976); also *Unicorn Rampant* (London: Hodder and Stoughton, 1984), this being a study of James Stuart, who became James VI of Scotland and James I of England. Recent cinema such as *Braveheart* (on William Wallace) and *Rob Roy* afford marvelous scenery and superb historical representation.
2. James Atkinson, *The Great Light: Luther and Reformation* (Grand Rapids: Eerdmans, 1968), 222.
3. A. M. Renwick, *The Story of the Scottish Reformation* (Grand Rapids: Eerdmans, 1960), 17.
4. Atkinson, *The Great Light,* 223.
5. F. W. Boreham, "John Knox's Text," in *A Bunch of Everlastings* (Nashville: Abingdon, 1920), 110ff.
6. Atkinson, *The Great Light,* 226.
7. For solid biographies of John Knox, see Henry Cowan, *John Knox: The Hero of the Scottish Reformation* (New York: Knickerbocker, 1905); W. Stanford Reid, *Trumpeter of God* (New York: Scribner's, 1974).
8. Richard G. Kyle, *The Mind of John Knox* (Lawrence, Kans.: Coronado, 1984), 215ff. This book is flawed in its understanding of the relationship between the Word of God and the words of Scripture, which are the same.
9. Quoted in John Bishop, "John Knox: The Thundering Scot," *Preaching* (September–October 1992), 74.
10. Renwick, *Story of the Scottish Reformation,* 110.
11. Kevin Reed, "John Knox and Faithful Preaching," *Banner of Truth* (November 1984): 5–7.
12. Quoted in Renwick, *Story of the Scottish Reformation,* 83.

5.6.2 *THE DOCTRINALLY SENSITIVE JACOB ARMINIUS OF THE NETHERLANDS*

We declare, therefore, and we continue to repeat the declaration till the gates of hell re-echo the sound, that the Holy Spirit, by whose inspiration holy men of God have spoken this word, and by whose guidance they have as his amanuenses consigned it to writing—that this Holy Spirit is the author of that light by the aid of which we obtain a perception and an understanding of the divine means of the word and is the effector of that certainty by which we believe those meanings to be truly divine, and that he is the necessary Author, the all-sufficient Effector.

There are two stumbling-blocks against which I am solicitously on my guard—not to make God the author of sin, and not to do away with the freedom inherent in the human will.

—Jacob Arminius

Three systems of theology spring from the Reformation: the Reformed, the Lutheran, and the Arminian. The latter has had extensive impact upon parts of Evangelical Anglicanism (John Jewel, Lancelot Andrewes), the Wesleyan movement (Wesley's periodical was called *The Arminian Magazine*), and many other still viable and vital parts of Christ's church to this very day. The spur to the formulation of the Arminian system came out of discussions and controversies over how to understand what the Bible says about predestination. These topics had long been discussed and debated—even Dante has a lively discussion on free will in Canto XVI of *Purgatorio*.

Jacob Arminius (1559–1609) was born in Oudewater on the Ijseel River in South Holland. His father died when he was an infant, and his mother and siblings were slaughtered by the Spanish Papists when Oudewater was destroyed in 1575. The tyranny of the duke of Alva is a sad and melancholy tale. Young Arminius was studying in Marburg and had come under the spell of the logic of Peter Ramus. Ramus challenged the rigidities of Aristotle and exerted a profound influence on many of the Puritans, particularly on William Perkins, as we shall see in the next chapter.[1] Arminius was a brilliant and retentive student. He studied at the New Free University in Leiden, established by King William, prince of Orange, and graduated in 1581 at the age of twenty-two. One of his teachers there was the uncle of Hugo Grotius, the noted jurist who had reservations about Calvin's teachings.

Through the patronage of friends, Arminius was able to study for six years in Geneva, Padua, and Basel. The rector at Geneva was **Theodore Beza,** Calvin's successor. Beza was a linguist and controversialist who had come to hold a "derivative Calvinism," that is, something beyond that held by the master himself. Beza was an unabashed *supralapsarian:* he believed that God made the decree to elect some to heaven and damn some to hell even before the decree to create. Arminius did not challenge the sovereignty of God but held that his was a sovereignty of moral supremacy.[2] He felt that Beza's view in effect made God the author of sin and made God's love and mercy problematic. Beza's extreme view (which is sometimes called "hard Calvinism") was not in the Belgic Confession of 1561 or the Heidelberg Catechism of 1563, but it did surface at the Synod of Dort in 1618–19. Many of the subsequent controversies had to do with the effort to require Arminius to subscribe to a view not even in the earlier symbols. He stoutly resisted the whole idea of making any creedal statement as of the same level as Holy Scripture itself.

When Arminius returned to Holland in 1587 it was to begin fifteen years of pastoral ministry in Amsterdam. The preachers in Amsterdam circulated among the churches and generally preached consecutive book studies. The sermons were about half an hour long. Arminius was warmly pastoral and much appreciated, especially by the Amsterdam merchants. He began conducting evening services in the Old Church where he was ordained in 1588. His preaching became very popular, as one listener described him:

> This flattering reception ought to excite no wonder; for—I speak before those who knew him well—there was in him a certain incredible gravity softened down by a cheerful amenity; his voice was rather weak, yet sweet, harmonious, and piercing. . . . He disdained to employ any rhetorical flourishes, and made no use of the honeyed sweets collected for this purpose from the Greeks.[3]

After an extended series on Jonah, we have record of a series of sixty-nine sermons on Malachi. Arminius married Lijsbet in 1590. He was a good family man and upright citizen. In 1603 he was appointed to a professorship in Leiden, and in 1605 he was made rector of the University. The controversies that arose in the Reformed Church that gave birth to the Remonstrants were questions about predestination and the order of decrees, free will, and the nature of original sin. Beyond question, Arminius stood in the mainstream of the Reformation on Scripture, *sola gratia,* justification, and the propitiatory nature of Christ's atonement.[4] He stood with Melancthon for a more moderate understanding of predestination based on foreknowledge. He did not believe that knowledge is causal. One of his staunch allies was Professor Hemmingsen, a student of Melancthon at the University of Copenhagen. A series of vicious colds wasted him away, and he died of consumption in 1609.

The ideal situation for Arminius was Free Churches based only on the Holy Scriptures.[5] The independent Robert Browne group that lived in Holland in the 1590s did not much care for Arminius and his sense of order in the church. The collected works of Arminius show him to be an erudite student of Scripture (as per his superb study of Romans 9). He was a godly man, a gifted teacher, and an able preacher. In his message on the occasion of receiving his doctorate, he prayed: "Sprinkle thou our spirits, souls and bodies, with the most gracious dew of thy immeasurable holiness."[6] His exposition that day on "The Priesthood of Christ" is chock full of Scripture. His treatment divides into three logical parts. His discourse is full of Christ and the blood atonement of Christ.[7] "He being dead yet speaks."

1. We have a choice biography, Carl Bangs, *Arminius: A Study in the Dutch Reformation* (Grand Rapids: Francis Asbury/Zondervan, 1971).
2. A. Skevington Wood, "Understanding Arminius: Origins of His Theology," in *Life of Faith* (July 8, 1972), 9–11.
3. Bangs, *Arminius,* 114.
4. Richard A. Muller, *God, Creation, and Providence in the Thought of Jacob Arminius* (Grand Rapids: Baker, 1991).
5. Gerald O. McCulloh, ed., *Man's Faith and Freedom* (Nashville: Abingdon, 1961), 15.
6. Jacob Arminius, *The Writings of Arminius* (Grand Rapids: Baker, 1956), 19.
7. Ibid., 2ff.

5.6.3   THE DARINGLY ASSERTIVE MENNO SIMONS OF THE NETHERLANDS

Faith firmly believes and lays hold upon and acknowledges every word of God, the threatening Law as well as the comforting Gospel, to be dependable and true. Whereby in turn the heart is pierced and moved through the Holy Ghost with an unusual regenerating, renewing, vivifying power, which produces first of all the fear of God.

And we, before God and His angels, seek nothing on this earth but that we may obey the clear and printed Word of the Lord, His Spirit, His example, His command, prohibition, usage, and ordinance (by which everything in Christ's kingdom and church must be regulated if it is to please Him) according to our weakness in all subjection and obedience.

The Word of Christ remains and is the word of the cross; all who accept it in power and truth must be prepared for the cross. This both the Scriptures and experience teach abundantly.

—Menno Simons

The Anabaptists are another important wellspring of Reformation vitality. The movement abounded with laypersons and was reordinationist, that is, it did not accept the validity of any other ordination. Strong opposition surfaced against absolute predestination and the notion of the invisible church. The emphasis was on believers' baptism, the gifts of the Spirit, regeneration, sanctification, and the believers' church. Professor George Williams in his irreplaceable work on "the radical Reformation" characterizes their preachers as "literalistic preachers of repentance."[1] Luther was unnerved by the Zwickau Prophets and the unstable Thomas Muntzer and his experiment in Munster (his millennialism fueled by Joachim of Fiora's earlier teaching).

In the mainstream, however, the Anabaptists stressed the preaching of the Word. **Casper Schwenckfeld** (1489–1561) and **Balthaser Hubmeier** (1485–1528) both preached in fields and anywhere available. The latter would hold eight-day meetings with preaching every evening. His messages were full of stories. The fiery **John Hut** preached the imminence of Christ's return,[2] and **Clement Ziegler** in the Alsace had a great burden for the Jews in the latter days, as per Malachi 4:5. Ziegler preached his message mainly in churchyards.

Although he was not the first Mennonite as such (the Swiss Brethren in Zwingli's domain antedated him), the primary light of the regrouping after the Munster debacle was **Menno Simons** (1496–1561). Simons was born in West Frisia in the Netherlands. He studied for the priesthood in the Franciscan Monastery in Bolsward and was ordained in 1524. He was not overly serious in his priestly duties, indulging freely in "card playing, drinking and all manner of frivolous diversions."[3]

One day while officiating at Mass, he was overcome with doubts about Transubstantiation. For an extended period of time he agonized, and finally was rebaptized by Obbe Philips of the evangelical Anabaptist Brotherhood. He actually lived a double life for some time, preaching evangelical truth from a Roman Catholic pulpit. He finally made the break and was reordained as an elder in 1537. Wenger says, "His great work was the proclamation of the gospel of Christ," through which many souls were saved.[4] Simons felt his earlier preaching was not sufficiently loving, but was redirected to the Word and Christ, who transforms from within. He wrote twenty-four books and pamphlets, the chief of which was his influential *The Foundation Book,* written in 1540, of which Loeschen says sixty percent is Scripture itself.[5]

Menno Simons, after whom part of the movement was named, held a high view of the preaching office. He believed that the preacher must be called and ordained. The conduct and uprightness of the preacher are indispensable. "It is not enough that in appearance a man speaks much of the Word of the Lord. It must also be verified by devout and unblamable conduct, as the Scriptures teach."[6] The preaching is to be without "perverting glosses, without the admixture of leaven," for the Word of God "preached without admixture in the power of the Spirit is the only right and proper Seed from which truly believing and obedient children of God are born."[7]

Menno Simons was ultimately called as Shepherd of the Brotherhood and preached throughout Holland, northwest Germany, and Holstein in Denmark. One biographer says of his preaching: "Menno's greatness lay not so much in his eloquence, although he was a good preacher, nor in his literary craftsmanship, although he could write well for the common man. He was no great theologian, although he knew how to present the plain teachings of the Bible with force and clarity. He was not even a great organizer, although he rendered a real service in the guidance which he gave to the bishops and ministers of the growing church." His greatness is to be seen in his character, his writings, and his message. "He merely caught a clear vision of two fundamental Biblical ideals: the ideal of practical holiness, and the ideal of the high place of the church in the life of the believer and in the cause of Christ."[8]

Simons and his wife and family were mercilessly hunted. In 1542 the Emperor Charles V issued an edict against him. Even the Reformers were harsh and cruel. Calvin said of him: "Nothing could be more arrogant and more impudent than this donkey."[9] At last he died, broken in body but not in spirit.

Anabaptism as a movement sprang from a return to the Scripture and a concern for a more thorough reformation of the church. Simons claimed he had never read the Bible until two years after his ordination as a priest. Then he read with a passion and preached the Scriptures. He had problems with infant baptism because he did not see it in the Bible. He constantly stressed the new birth. Simons believed that "while all persons inherited a corrupt nature which inevitably leads to actual sins, the death of Christ on the cross removed the guilt of original sin for everyone!"[10] Like all the Anabaptists, Simons had "a stiff aversion to the twin doctrines of predestination and the bondage of the will."[11] But "God's infallible Word" was his firm foundation, and on the Word and its careful exegesis all of the Reformers stood united and, thus, their collective emphasis on the essentiality of biblical preaching.

1. George Huntston Williams, *The Radical Reformation* (Philadelphia: Westminster, 1962), 124.
2. Ibid., 163.
3. John Horsch, *Mennonites in Europe* (Scottsdale, Pa.: Herald Press, 1942), 185.
4. J. C. Wenger, *Glimpses of Mennonite History and Doctrine* (Scottsdale, Pa.: Herald Press, 1947), 78.
5. John R. Loeschen, *The Divine Community: Trinity, Church and Ethics in Reformation Theologies* (Kirksville, Mo.: The Sixteenth Century Journal Publishers, 1981), 68.
6. Menno Simons, *The Complete Writings of Menno Simons* (Scottsdale, Pa.: Herald Press, 1956), 169.
7. Ibid., 164.
8. Ibid., 28–29.
9. Wenger, *Glimpses of Mennonite History and Doctrine*, 80.
10. Timothy George, *Theology of the Reformers* (Nashville: Broadman, 1988), 268. This application of Romans 5:12–21 is the basis of the approach Menno Simons and the Wesleys took to the vexed issue of infant salvation.
11. Ibid., 271.

CHAPTER SIX

The Ripening Maturity of Biblical Preaching in the Seventeenth Century

... who have tasted the goodness of the Word of God. . . .

—Hebrews 6:5

It is not as though God's word had failed.

—Romans 9:6

As for God, his way is perfect; the word of the LORD is flawless.

—2 Samuel 22:31

The Spirit of the LORD spoke through me; his word was on my tongue.

—2 Samuel 23:2

Indeed, to them you are nothing more than one who sings love songs with a beautiful voice and plays an instrument well, for they hear your words but do not put them into practice.

—Ezekiel 33:32

Let the word of Christ dwell in you richly as you teach and admonish one another with all wisdom. . . .

—Colossians 3:16

This hearing of the Word of God, hearing what the Lord of the Church wants to say to His Church in its actual situation, is the primary task of the church, the basic human action in worship.

—C. E. B. Cranfield

The translation of the Bible and "the living preaching of the Word of God" (to use the rich expression from the Heidelberg Catechism) are logically and properly complementary and intertwined. In his massive work, *The English Bible and the Seventeenth-Century Revolution,* Christopher Hill documents the explosive results of letting the Word loose.[1] In previous centuries translators had been martyred for their labors. Even prelates had warned that the Word of God "causeth insurrection and teacheth the people to disobey . . . and moveth them to rise against their princes, and to make all common, and to make havoc of other men's goods." One observer commented, "The Bible in English under every weaver's and chambermaid's arm hath done much harm." In this sense the Scripture was a dangerous dynamic unleashing societal change and challenge.

The English language was at the peak of its utility for prose and poetry. "Those Elizabethans had a sense of diction," Matthew Arnold commented.[2] This was amply demonstrated by Shakespeare, Spenser, Sydney, Raleigh, and Bacon. At the Hampton Court Conference convened by James I in 1604, the Puritan leader Dr. John Reynolds proposed a new translation of the Bible without notes. The king was taken with the project and promoted it. The result was the so-called Authorized Version of 1611, whose stately cadences and rhythms have been such a blessing down to the present.[3] The history of the English Bible with its parallels in other languages through the centuries is a narrative of romance and risk. The Bible is a miracle book, and its extraordinary power and vitality can be chronicled from the turbulent seventeenth century or any other century to the praise of God.[4]

---

1. Christopher Hill, *The English Bible and the Seventeenth-Century Revolution* (New York: Penguin, 1994).
2. T. Harwood Pattison, *The History of Christian Preaching* (Philadelphia: American Baptist Publication Society, 1903), 163.
3. F. F. Bruce, *The Books and the Parchments: Some Chapters on the Transmission of the Bible* (London: Pickering and Inglis, 1950), 217ff.
4. Gwynn McLendon Day, *The Wonder of the Word* (Chicago: Moody, 1957); Lawrence E. Nelson, *Our Roving Bible: Tracking its Influence Through English and American Life* (Nashville: Abingdon, 1945). Nelson quotes the great Yale scholar William Lyon Phelps: "The Bible has been a greater influence on the course of English literature than all other forces put together" (9).

6.1 GROWING IN MATURE REFLECTION ON THE PREACHING CRAFT

Let a lawful and a godly seigniory look that they preach, not quarterly or monthly, but continually.

—Thomas Cartright

A veritable torrent of biblical preaching was unleashed in the Reformation. In form the Reformers reverted to the ancient Augustinian pattern of the personal, conversational homily. They seemed weary of the traditional restraints and gave little attention to structure. They were medieval in agreeing with **Robert of Basevorn** (1322) that preaching is the second act of God after creation (i.e., after creating man, God preached) and with **Humbert of Romanis** (d. 1277) that preaching carries on the discourse of heaven.[1] English preachers like John Colet, John Fisher, and Bishop Tunstall tended to use the ancient form which had no particular scheme.

The other option for them would have been the university sermon with its divisions and subdivisions as described in our treatment of Alan of Lille. While *divisio* was overdone by some, as in **Jean Raulin** (b. Toulouse 1443), whose sermons were clogged with divisions and subdivisions, the dividing of the sermon and the text does promote unity. The process of principalization and contemporization present some risk, but are effective with the use of divisions.[2] The use of a protheme (introduction) and theme are aids to understanding and recollection. Amplification of this form was further supplied by **William of Auvergne** (bishop of Paris, 1228–1249) and by English writers and preachers such as **Thomas Waleys** (c. 1349) from Oxford and **Ranulph Higden** of Chester (d. 1364). Most noteworthy is **Simon Alcock** (d. 1459), whose work *On the Mode of Dividing a Theme for Dilating Sermon Material* was exceedingly influential.[3] Preachers like Tauler, Erasmus, Hugh Latimer, John Bradford, John Jewel, Richard Hooker, and Stephen Baron used this form.

The revival of preaching inevitably fostered reflection and experimentation on form and structure. Two new forms came into existence at this time. What Professor Blench calls "the modified modern style" soon became popular. This bridging form employed divisions but with considerably greater freedom. This form was used by Grindal, often by Jewel, and by its chief exemplar, the silver-tongued **Henry Smith,** who will be considered shortly. A key advocate of this modification, one whom we will analyze in our next section, was **Andrew Hyperius** of Marburg.

The argument for the use of divisions arises out of the tendency for a homily to be a rambling cluster of sermonettes, much like unwinding a ball of twine. John Oman flinched from the sermon whose divisions were only pauses. He advocated a plot and a plan, a sequencing, the artful interruption and sustaining of discourse without slavish adherence to a skeletal structure.[4]

Yet another form was emerging, which was really a subdivision of the basic modification referred to by Blench above. We have already observed it in John Hooper, and it became dominant in Puritan preaching. Its chief theoretician was **William Perkins,** and it proved to be a major formative influence in the logic of **Peter Ramus**. Clearly, the seventeenth century was a time of unusual fecundity and homiletical formulation.

---

1. James J. Murphy, *Rhetoric in the Middle Ages: A History of Rhetorical Theory from St. Augustine to the Renaissance* (Berkeley: University of California Press, 1974), 270.
2. For an illuminating probing of this issue, see Ramesh Richard, *Scripture Sculpture* (Grand Rapids: Baker, 1995), 163.
3. Murphy, *Rhetoric in the Middle Ages,* 339.

4. John Oman, *Concerning the Ministry* (Richmond: John Knox, 1936), 209–13. Trenchant discussion of *lucidus ordo* can also be found in M. Reu, *Homiletics* (Grand Rapids: Baker, 1924, 1967), 456–85; R. L. Dabney, *On Preaching* (Edinburgh: Banner of Truth, 1870, 1979), 214–32.

6.1.1   ANDREW HYPERIUS—THE THINKER

> How he stampt and took on I cannot tell, but crash quoth the pulpit, and there lay Hubberd in the middest of his audience.
>
> —John Foxe, the martyrologist

As Augustine's work dominated for a thousand years, so now we detect new hands and minds shaping the preaching. **Andreas Gerard** (1511–1564), or as he was more widely known, **Andrew Hyperius,** has been called "the father of the later Reformation preaching."[1] He was born in Ypres in Flanders, hence his more common name. His father, who died when Andrew was yet a boy, had been a prominent lawyer. His father had laid out a program for his son's education which led him to the University of Paris and on to England, where he was much influenced by Reformed ideas. In 1542, he was made a professor in Marburg in Germany. He was widely respected for his theological acumen.

Hyperius authored two books on preaching, the first of which, *Topica Theologica,* was a survey of preaching themes and how they could be handled. The more homiletically significant work was *De Formandis Concionibus Sacris (On the Making of Sacred Discourses).* No less than von Harnack called this piece "the first really scientific treatise on the theory of preaching."[2] It was titled *The Practice of Preaching* when it was "Englished" by John Ludham in 1577. Since neither Luther nor Calvin bequeathed their followers any systematic statement of principles for preaching, this volume loomed large as an influence both on the Continent and in Britain.

Bridging between the ancient homily and the university sermon of Thomistic order and structure, Hyperius adapted the latter for more common and general use. He was not indifferent to matters of form, but was freer and more direct in his approach. Hyperius typically began with the reading of the Scripture lesson, gave an invocatory prayer, introduced his theme, developed the proposition with possible divisions, and moved to the conclusion. Traditional sections of confirmation and confutation were frequently omitted.[3] There is increased flexibility and adaptability in this modified form. Interestingly, in Dietrich Bonhoeffer's lectures on preaching at the Confessing Church Seminary at Finkenwalde in the 1930s, he stresses the importance of Hyperius and his modification of Augustine.

Hyperius also stipulated some general axioms for preaching the Word:

1. the sermon is to be adapted to the capacity of the hearers;
2. theological questions which excite curiosity rather than edification are to be avoided;
3. the doctrines to be taught are to be confirmed from the prophetic and apostolic writings;

4. time, place, and audience are to be considered in developing the doctrinal explanation;
5. only the canonical writings are to be used in confirming what is taught;
6. the proofs used are to be simple and direct;
7. preference is to be given to the simple sense;
8. figurative language is to be used sparingly, types and allegories seldom, and neither are to be used for proof;
9. the mode of expression should not provoke contradiction;
10. when a doctrine is taught, it should be practically applied both in regard to the church and the individual.[4]

The relevancy and applicability of these axioms for preaching in an age of great controversy are evident. The strong emphasis on audience is an obvious effort to overcome the excessively scholarly preaching of the *oratio* and the emphasis on doctrine a clear foreshadowing of the great Reformed and Puritan emphasis on doctrine with its possible perils. We now want to see how this translates in parish preaching.

---

1. John Ker, *Lectures on the History of Preaching* (New York: Armstrong, 1889), 174.
2. Warren W. Wiersbe and Lloyd M. Perry, *The Wycliffe Handbook of Preaching and Preachers* (Chicago: Moody, 1984), 50.
3. J. W. Blench, *Preaching in England in the Late Fifteenth and Sixteenth Centuries* (New York: Barnes and Noble, 1964), 102.
4. Hering's *Lehrbuch der Homiletik* as quoted in A. E. Garvie, *The Christian Preacher* (New York: Scribner's, 1923), 142.

6.1.2 HENRY SMITH—THE PRACTITIONER

> None ought to take upon them the function of preaching in the church, unless they have their warrant or authority from God, as Aaron had, Heb. 5:4. And although they have not their authority in that form and manner as Jonah had his, namely, as it were, by word of mouth even from God himself, "Arise, and go to Nineveh," yet they must have their warrant from him, else their calling is unlawful.
> —Henry Smith in the sermon "The Calling of Jonah"

Called "the most popular Puritan preacher of the Elizabethan era,"[1] **Henry Smith** (1560–1609 or 1613) was born to a wealthy family in Leicestershire. Smith illustrates and embodies choice aspects of strong biblical preaching. He took his M.A. in 1583 at Oxford, where he was esteemed "for his prodigious memory and for his fluent, eloquent and practical way of preaching."[2] Drawn to Puritan ways and tending to be anti-episcopal, he declined to take a benefice, choosing preaching over patrimony. One of his early sermons preached in 1582, "The Lost Sheep Found," is a model of direct and clear statement.

In 1587 Smith was appointed lecturer at St. Clement Danes in London. We shall describe later the critical function of the Puritan lectureships of the day, but suffice it to say that they were a means for bypassing certain ecclesiastical strictures unfavorable to the Puritan wing in the Church of England. Archbishop Whitgift dismissed him from his post after one year, but he was soon reinstated and continued for an extended period of time. The church was always full when he preached, with people standing in the alleyways outside to hear. J. B. Marsden said that Smith was "probably the most eloquent preacher in Europe."[3] Many regarded him as "the first preacher of the nation."[4] Quaint Thomas Fuller, who wrote his biographical memoir, spoke of him as "the silver-tongued preacher," one metal below Chrysostom.[5] His sermons were so sought after that they were widely pirated. Smith finally collected fifty-six of them in an edition we possess today.

Plagued with ill health, Smith always considered himself a moderate in the Church of England and eschewed separatists like the Brownists and the Barrowists. He exemplified what he called "living sermons." For Smith, the sermon was central to worship. Those who read homilies he termed "dumb dogges." He fretted over the tendency for preachers to turn from the grand themes of Scripture to ecclesiastical politics and sensational antics. He would concur with Archbishop Sandy's diagnosis of the situation:

> The preacher is gladly heard of the people, that can carp the magistrates, cut up the ministers, cry out against all order and set all at liberty. But if he shall reprove their insolency, pride and vanity, their monstrous apparel, their excessive feasting, their greedy covetousness, their biting usury, their halting hearts, their muttering minds, their friendly words and malicious deeds, they will fall from him then. He is a railer, he doteth, he wanteth discretion.[6]

Henry Smith proved that faithful biblical preaching will draw the audiences. Key to Smith's listenability was his use of variety. Occasionally he used the ancient homily form. He avoided the developing New Puritan Form as we have described it. Chiefly he used the modified modern form as espoused by Andrew Hyperius. In terms of his style, he preferred the plain but most often blended it with an ornate style even within the same sermon. Blench includes him in a quartet of preachers "whose richly colored style reaches out towards the fully ornate mode, forming a bridge between it and the plain style."[7] Here is an example:

> There is no salt but may lose his saltnesse, no wine but may lose his strength, no flower but may lose his scent, no light but may be eclipsed, no beauty but may be stained, no fruit but may be blasted, nor soule but may be corrupted, we stand all in a slippery place, where it is easie to slide, and hard to get up, like little children which overthrow themselves with their cloaths, now up, now downe at a straw, so soone we fall from God, and slide from his word and forget our resolutions, as though we had never resolved.[8]

The richness of his imagery, his masterful use of homely similes, his occasional employment of classical reference bespeak his ability to utilize effective variation. His most famous sermon, "Dialogue Between Paul and King Agrippa," climaxes in a powerful exposé of "the almost Christian." Other examples of his hardy and sturdy preaching include such titles as "The Trumpet of the Soul Sounding to Judgment," "The Sinful Man's Search," "The Sweet Song of Old Father Simeon," "The True Trial of the Spirits," and "The Art of Hearing." Of ill-trained preachers Smith inveighed:

> None should meddle with the word (which is the law of God) but they which are fit, lest they make it despised. Hannah said, "I will not offer the child to God before he be weaned," 1 Samuel 1:22, that is, before he be taken from the dug; but now they offer their children to God before they are weaned, before they can go, before they can speak; and send them to fight the Lord's battles before they have one stone in their hand to sling at Goliath, that is, one scripture to resist the tempter.[9]

In Henry Smith we see giftedness and spiritual endowment. But an undoubted aspect of his strength and appeal is seen in his sensitive adaptation of form and the utilization of variety in setting forth and framing the scriptural text to which he had great devotion. In this he models wisdom and exemplary vision.

---

1. R. B. Jenkins, *Henry Smith: England's Silver-Tongued Preacher* (Macon, Ga.: Mercer University Press, 1983), 1.
2. Ibid., 11.
3. Ibid., 16.
4. Ibid., 20.
5. F. R. Webber, *A History of Preaching in Britain and America* (Milwaukee: Northwestern, 1952), 1:215.
6. Jenkins, *Henry Smith*, 45.
7. J. W. Blench, *Preaching in England in the Late Fifteenth and Sixteenth Centuries* (New York: Barnes and Noble, 1964), 182.
8. Ibid., 184–85.
9. Jenkins, *Henry Smith*, 77–78.

6.1.3 WILLIAM PERKINS—THE PROSPECTOR

> When being young, I heard worthy Master Perkins, so preach in a great assembly of students, that he instructed them soundly in the truth, stirred them up effectually to seek after godliness, made them fit for the kingdom of God; and by his example showed them what things they should chiefly intend, that they might promote true religion, in the power of it, unto God's glory, and other's salvation.
> —William Ames, student and admirer of William Perkins

For to leave the right handling of scripture is the way to bring in all error and barbarism in religion.

—William Perkins

In turning to **William Perkins** (1558–1602) we are looking at a pivotal figure in both theology and homiletics. He is often called the greatest of the sixteenth-century Puritan theologians or the prince of the Puritan theologians. Ian Breward described him as "the most widely known theologian of the Elizabethan church."[1] He had international standing rivaling that of Luther and Calvin. Samuel Morison maintained that the "typical Plymouth Colony library comprised a large and small Bible, Ainsworth's translation of the Psalms, and the works of William ('Painful') Perkins, a favorite theologian." For our purposes, not at all incidentally, he authored what may be the first homiletics book in English and a volume that exerted tremendous influence, *The Art of Prophesying*.

William Perkins was born in Warwickshire and attended Cambridge, where he earned his M.A. in 1584. In his early years he was given to drunkeness and astrology but was converted after overhearing a father point him out to his child as "that drunken Perkins."[2] He later served as a jail chaplain with such effectiveness that townspeople would come up to the prison to hear him preach. Greatly touched by Puritan influences at Cambridge, he was, like Henry Smith, a moderate who would not himself be called a "Puritan."[3] Although much dissatisfied with church government and worship in the Church of England generally, he refused to separate. He was heavily burdened by the slowness of the Reformation and the shortage of Bible preachers in the established church. In 1603 there were 9,244 parishes but only 4,830 preachers licensed to preach. Perkins' inner life of devotion was exceedingly rich (in fact it was his felicitous fusion of theology and piety which really made him) and evinces affinity for the much earlier Walter Hilton and his widely read *The Ladder of Perfection*.

Influencing Perkins' homiletical persuasion were Augustine, Erasmus, and Hyperius. But we cannot understand Perkins or the Puritan mode of preaching without first examining **Peter Ramus** (1515–1572). Ramus was born in northern France in a family of modest means but achieved a fine education where he became professor of dialectic. He wrote sixty books on logic and philosophy and coauthored thirteen with his colleague Taleus.[4] Ramus protested against Aristotelian scholasticism's domination in the sixteenth century and opted for Platonism instead. He inclined to deductive approaches to reality and posited a universe of order, "a copy of an ordered hierarchy of ideas existing in the mind of God."[5] He made charts and diagrams setting forth the logical pairings found everywhere in reality. While arrangement was important to Ramus, the subject matter reigned supreme. (The Puritans generally and William Perkins specifically downplayed rhetoric.) In 1562 Ramus converted to Protestantism, and in 1572 he was killed in the massacre of St. Bartholomew's Day in France, when up to fifty thousand Huguenots (French Protestants) were slain.

Ramian logic and rhetoric triumphed throughout England, especially at Cambridge and most particularly through the increasingly influential William Perkins. There were many translations of Ramus into English, including one by John

Milton. The dialectic of dichotomies and their harmonization is seen in Perkins' approach to preaching, which began with the reading of the text and comments on the background and exegesis of the passage, then doctrinal propositions followed by "uses" or application. Like Ramus, Perkins loved charts and diagrams.[6] The weaknesses in the Ramean formulation are seen in the Puritans' overemphasis on introspection and the tendency to an extreme authoritarianism in which certain select minds will decide.

The last commentary Perkins wrote was his great masterpiece on Galatians. This is the material he preached at Great St. Andrew's Church in Cambridge and was refined in its final form by Perkins' good friend, Ralph Cudworth, the well-known Cambridge Platonist, after Perkins' death. In his discussion of Galatians 3:1 and "plain style preaching," Perkins lays out not only his approach to the commentary but to all preaching:

> The first is, true and proper interpretation of the Scripture, and that by it selfe: for Scripture, is both the glosse, and the text. The second is, savorie and wholesome doctrine, gathered out of the Scriptures truly expounded. The third is, the Application of the said doctrine, either to the information of the judgement, or to the reformation of the life.[7]

On Scripture Perkins stood stalwartly for the authority of the literal sense of the Bible. He saw preaching as central in God's plan, for "in the preaching of the Word and in the administration of the sacraments men could see."

> The great and glorious account which God makes of the word of his ministers, by them truly taught and rightly applied; namely that he, as it were, tieth his blessing to it: for ordinarily till a man know his righteousness by the means of an interpreter, God hath not mercy on him.[8]

Perkins's *The Art of Prophesying* is well worth reading. Chapter 3 is on the Word and the Christocentricity of true preaching. He analyzes the nature of authentic persuasion. Preparation of preaching involves two processes:

1. interpretation of the Scripture
2. the right cutting or dividing of the Scripture (2 Timothy 2:15)

He speaks magnificently of the kinds of application and the spiritual life of prayer and worship necessary for the communication God owns.[9] The sermon is not a parade of the preacher's learning, and indeed Perkins is responsible for the wise counsel, "It is also a point of art to conceal art."

All Puritans in a sense follow Perkins, although he had special influence on William Ames, Thomas Goodwin, George Herbert (not a Puritan), John Robinson, Richard Baxter, and Bishops Joseph Hall and James Ussher. Although Perkins was a staunch Calvinist and crossed polemical swords with Arminius himself, he wavered on some of Beza's extreme ideas (as did Peter Baro, Samuel Barsnet, Richard Hooker, and John Cotton).[10] From many vantage points, William Perkins is a seminal figure, not least in his laying of the foundations for so much of the Puritan preaching of all time.

---

1. Ian Breward, ed., *The Works of William Perkins* (Berkshire: Sutton Courtenay Press, 1970), xi.
2. F. R. Webber, *A History of Preaching in Britain and America* (Milwaukee: Northwestern, 1952), 1:220.
3. Breward, ed., *The Works of William Perkins,* 22.
4. William H. Kooienga, *Elements of Style for Preaching* (Grand Rapids: Zondervan, 1989), 37. Perry Miller in *The New England Mind: The Seventeenth Century* (Cambridge, Mass.: Harvard University Press, 1939), 338–39, argues that the Puritan sermon is *de novo* the product of Peter Ramus, but there is evidence of antecedents for this form from much earlier. Perkins and the Puritans are also indebted here to the Latin commentaries of Musculus (Wolfgang Muesslin, 1497–1563); see J. W. Blench, *Preaching in England in the Late Fifteenth and Sixteenth Centuries* (New York: Barnes and Noble, 1964), 101; see Walter J. Ong, *Ramus: Method, and the Decay of Dialogue* (Cambridge, Mass.: Harvard University Press, 1958). A solid study.
5. Ibid., 37.
6. Breward, ed., *The Works of William Perkins,* for example the elaborate chart on "A Golden Chain," 168.
7. William Perkins, *A Commentary on Galatians* (New York: Pilgrim, 1989). Cf. for instance, Galatians 3:13.
8. Breward, ed., *The Works of William Perkins,* 41.
9. Ibid., 323–49.
10. R. T. Kendall, *Calvin and English Calvinism to 1649* (Oxford: Oxford University Press, 1982). An instructive study of Beza, the first to make predestination central, Amyraut's position (1596–1644), and Perkins' vacillation.

6.1.4 JEAN CLAUDE—THE FORMULATOR

> When too little text is taken, you must digress from the subject to find something to say; flourishes of wit and imagination must be displayed, which are not of the genius of the pulpit: and in one word, it will make the hearers think, that self is more preached than Jesus Christ; and that the preacher aims rather at appearing a wit, than at instructing and edifying his people.
>
> —Jean Claude

A significant conduit of mature reflection on preaching is the Frenchman **Jean Claude** (1619–1687). Here is a parish pastor who developed great strength in preaching and left a rich legacy of homiletical instruction for subsequent generations in a series of remarkable divine providences. Part of the severely decimated French Protestant remnant, Claude was born in a small village in southern France, the son of a pastor who was dedicated to the spiritual and pastoral education of his son. Claude may have had some theological training at Montauban[1] and served congregations at St. Afrique, Nimes, and Charenton. He became embroiled in controversies with the Roman Catholics, wrote a powerful tome titled *Defense of the Reformation,* and debated the eminent Bossuet publicly. When the Edict of Nantes was revoked in 1685, he was forced to leave the country within twenty-four hours and spent his last several years working and preaching among the refugees in the Hague. Even his opponents called him "ce fameux M. Claude."

While his early preaching tended to be like the ancient homilies, Claude made the transition to what we have called the modified modern approach in which principalization and division of the text convey what the text says with appropriate application. Claude's own powerful preaching exerted an influence on even the great court preachers in France. What can be called the French model usually had two or three main points with relaxed development and emphasis on subpoints. Peter Bayley's classic study identifies Claude as a model of this tradition.[2]

The most conspicuous contribution of Claude has been his *Essay on the Composition of a Sermon.* This skillful work was translated into English by the eminent Cambridge preacher Robert Robinson and has continued to wield its effect to this day in several respects. It shaped **Charles Simeon,** one of the great fathers of the evangelical wing of the Church of England. We shall note Simeon's immense contribution later, but here we want to register the influence of Claude on his thinking.

Simeon's multiple-volumed expository sermons, *Horae Homileticae,* still in print, contains Claude's piece which Simeon himself indexed.[3] Here Claude explored the choice of a text and warned against selecting one too short or too long. He pled for serious exegesis and explication of the whole text, that is, in its context. He urged "perpetual application" of the text.[4] Claude dwelt on the divisions of the text and in the sermon, urging consideration of the genre or character of the passage as a whole. He dealt with the elucidation or amplification of the text, with the exordium and introduction, and commended conclusions which are "lively and animating, full of great and beautiful figures, aiming to move the Christian affections."[5]

When we read Simeon's admonition in relation to the proposition, we hear echoes of Jean Claude. Listen:

> Reduce your text to a simple proposition, and lay that down as the warp;
> and then make use of the text itself as the woof; illustrating the main idea
> by the various terms in which it is contained. Screw the word into the minds
> of your hearers. A screw is the strongest of all mechanical powers . . . when
> it has turned a few times, scarcely any power can pull it out.[6]

As we revel in the preaching of the seventeenth century, we must be mindful of this serious reflective work on preaching and its formulation, so basic to what was happening at the time.

---

1. E. C. Dargan, *A History of Preaching* (New York: Hodder and Stoughton, 1912), 2:124ff.

2. Peter Bayley, *French Pulpit Oratory: 1598–1650* (Cambridge, Mass.: Cambridge University Press, 1980), 110.
3. Charles Simeon, *Horae Homileticae* (Grand Rapids: Zondervan, 1955), 22:291ff.
4. Ibid., 297.
5. Ibid., 408.
6. As quoted in John R. W. Stott, *I Believe in Preaching* (London: Hodder and Stoughton, 1952), 226.

6.2 THE TUDOR AND CAROLINE DIVINES AND THE RISE OF THE CRAFT

> Beware, beware, ye diminish not this [preaching] office; for if ye do, ye decay God's power to all that do believe. We must be ready to hear God's holy word; we must have good affections to hear God's holy word; and we must be ready to make provision for the furtherance of the preaching of God's holy word, as far forth as we be able to do.
>
> —Hugh Latimer

The preaching of the seventeenth century in England arose out of the turbulence and tumult of the previous century. The legacy of biblical preaching had instilled a great hunger for the Word of God. Latimer and all the cohorts of the Reformation left a testimony and testament to the Word of God. How much it would be needed!

The first Stuart king, **James I,** was in many ways a despicable human being. Those in the stream of the Reformation were hopeful because the king had been raised a Scot, but he was "physically repellent . . . a pedant . . . [with] a crude, boyish humor . . . a drunkard and a sex pervert"[1] and yet cunningly able to ingratiate himself. The temptation for ecclesiastics was to fawn and flatter the royal presence, and into this trap Bishop Bancroft and Bishop Whitgift and even John Donne fell.[2]

James professed love for the sermon, and whenever he entered the chapel the preacher went into the pulpit, thus interrupting the flow of worship. Archbishop **William Laud** was the sycophantic advisor and confidante of James's son, **Charles I,** and continued to press the insane efforts for religious uniformity and to persecute and hound all nonconformists. The ultimate beheading of the king in 1649[3] and the years of the Puritan Commonwealth under Oliver Cromwell were the unfamiliar terrain over which England and her preachers traversed. Four years earlier Laud had been executed for "high treason."[4] Still, the restoration of the monarchy did not seem to resolve the religious tensions and strains of the period.

Yet for all this there was much preaching and avid attention to preaching in many quarters. Caroline Richardson has given us a splendid study of the preparation of clergy for preaching.[5] All classes went to church, and personal diaries show considerable interaction and comment with the sermon. Samuel Pepys, the most eminent of all the diarists, was an inveterate churchgoer, sometimes attending two or three different churches on a Sunday. Preaching was in vogue. He was well disposed toward the Puritans and comfortable in the Church of England. It is now to some more focused attention on preachers of this period that we turn.

1. Sidney Dark, *Seven Archbishops* (London: Eyre and Spottiswoode, 1944), 121.
2. T. Harwood Pattison, *The History of Christian Preaching* (Philadelphia: American Baptist Publication Society, 1903), 170.
3. C. V. Wedgewood's trilogy on *The Great Rebellion* is classic. These volumes are *The King's Peace, The King's War,* and especially *A Coffin for King Charles* (New York: Macmillan, 1964). A particularly helpful study of the Civil War of recent vintage is Christopher Hibbert, *Cavaliers and Roundheads: The English Civil War, 1642–1649* (New York: Scribner's, 1993).
4. Dark, *Seven Archbishops,* 141.
5. Caroline Francis Richardson, *English Preachers and Preaching 1640–1670* (New York: Macmillan, 1928).

6.2.1 THE POINTMAN OF THE PREACHERS—LANCELOT ANDREWES

I need more grief, I plainly need more of it. I am far from that which I ought to have. I can sin much! I cannot repent much. My dryness! My dryness! Woe unto me! Would that I had such grief, or even more! But of myself I cannot obtain it. I am parched, I am parched like a spotsherd. Woe is me! Thou, O Lord, O Lord, a fountain of tears. Give me a molten heart.

—Lancelot Andrewes in his classic
Preces Privatae (Private Devotions)

Lancelot Andrewes (1555–1626) was the primary court preacher in the time of James I *stella praedicantium,* a brilliant star in a lustrous firmament. He was born in London, the oldest of fourteen children born to a merchant family. From the beginning, he was precocious. Throughout his life he rose at 4 A.M. to study. He knew fifteen languages and could write better in Greek and Latin than in English.[1] He studied at Cambridge, where he was exposed to Puritan influence, and at Oxford. He was lecturer at Pembroke College, Cambridge, and served as one of the translators of the King James Version of the Bible. Andrewes was among the group translating the Pentateuch and Joshua through 2 Chronicles. He was successively prebend of St. Paul's, Dean of Westminster (he shared in the funeral of Queen Elizabeth I and the coronation of James I), and then bishop of Chichester, Ely, and Winchester.

T. S. Eliot, who acknowledged a great debt to both Lancelot Andrewes and John Donne, said of Andrewes' sermons, they "rank with the finest English prose of their time, any time."[2] Critics like Canon Wellsby allege undue servility to King James I. Eminence poses its own perils. He was a close friend of Francis Bacon. Charged to refute the errors of Cardinal Bellarmine in debate, he acquitted himself splendidly. His preaching always seemed to have a lifting effect upon the king. "The atmosphere changed when Lancelot Andrewes appeared."[3] *Lex ordandi, lex credendi* (how we pray is what we really believe) is borne out in Andrewes because his life was prayer and his theology flourished through it. His classic devotions and prayers continue to be widely used, and indeed Charles I used them just before his death.

Andrewes was a "preacher's preacher, very theological and very dependent on the Scripture." Mueller says that Andrewes tended to underplay and Donne to over-play.[4] Donne used a more varied rhythm while Andrewes had a staccato, elliptical quality in his preaching. Examination of his sermons shows "the profoundly liturgical character of his preaching."[5] F. E. Brightman has shown the vital linkage of prayer and celebrative worship in the preaching of Andrewes. As one of the evangelical Arminians, he was critical of strict Calvinism's denial of free will[6] and stressed the work of the Holy Spirit in preaching. This emphasis on the Holy Spirit is not all that common in the history of preaching.[7] He was strongly Trinitarian and Christocentric in his pulpit discourse. Lossky's priceless study leads us through the Christmas sermons of Andrewes on through Lent to Easter and then to Whitsuntide (or Pentecost, the greatly neglected festival of the church). His fifteen sermons on the Holy Spirit are doctrinally rich, as when he says:

> "Another Comforter" . . . "Another;" which word presupposes one besides, so that two there be. One they have already; and now another shall have, which is no evil news. For thus instead of a single, they find a double comfort. But they both are needed . . . Christ was one; was, and is still. Christ had been their comforter . . . but expedient it was He should go, for expedient it was they had one in Heaven; and expedient withal, they had one in earth, and so another in his stand.[8]

Andrewes still clung to allegorization, and he could moralize with the best of them. But he divided the text and the sermon very much in the modified modern style, with three main points and ordered subdivisions. He tended to be more chaste in his ornamentation than many, although he did use patristic citation. He loved to recreate the Christmas and Easter scenes.[9] He possessed a good sense of humor and enjoyed puns.

Eliot's essays on Lancelot Andrewes indicate the nature of the moral and spiritual impact Andrewes made on his life. His poem "The Journey of the Magi" was inspired by a sermon of Andrewes preached in Whitehall in 1622.[10] The wholesome spirituality and intensity in the inner spiritual life of Andrewes is impressive. Ophelia's complaint to Laertes in *Hamlet* has often been reiterated, but it has no application to Lancelot Andrewes:

> Do not, as some ungracious pastors do,
> Show me the steep and thorny way to heaven:
> Whilst like a puff'd and reckless libertine
> Himself the primrose path of dalliance treads,
> And recks not his own rede.

—Shakespeare's *Hamlet,*
first performed in London in 1603

1. Thomas S. Kepler, ed., *The Private Devotions of Lancelot Andrewes* (New York: World, 1956), xvii.
2. Nicholas Lossky, *Lancelot Andrewes: The Preacher (1555–1626)* (Oxford: Clarendon, 1991), 1.
3. Ibid., 24.
4. William R. Mueller, *John Donne: Preacher* (New York: Octagon, 1977), 235.
5. Lossky, *Lancelot Andrewes,* 28. One of his choice Christmas sermons, "The Sign to the Shepherds," is included in Wilbur M. Smith, *Great Sermons on the Birth of Christ* (Natick, Mass.: W. A. Wilde, 1963), 132–55.
6. Ibid., 332.
7. Ibid., 331, 333. Several more recent volumes have spoken to this lucuna: Dennis F. Kinlaw, *Preaching in the Spirit* (Grand Rapids: Frances Asbury/Zondervan, 1985); James Forbes, *The Holy Spirit and Preaching* (Nashville: Abingdon, 1989); Tony Sargent, *The Sacred Anointing: The Preaching of Dr. Martyn Lloyd-Jones* (Wheaton, Ill.: Crossway, 1994).
8. Ibid., 214.
9. J. W. Blench, *Preaching in England in the Late Fifteenth and Sixteenth Centuries* (New York: Barnes and Noble, 1964), 205ff.
10. Russell Kirk, *Eliot and His Age* (LaSalle, Ill.: Sherwood Sugen and Co., 1971), 136.

6.2.2   THE WORDMAN OF THE PREACHERS—JOHN DONNE

> Batter my heart, three-personed God, for you
> As yet but knock, breathe, shine and seek to mend;
> That I may rise and stand, o'erthrow me, and bend
> Your force to break, blow, burn and make me new. . . .
> Take me to you, imprison me, for I
> Except you enthrall me, never shall be free,
> Nor ever chaste, except you ravish me.

These moving lines reflect a deep spirituality, and are the work of **John Donne** (1572–1631). Donne was one of the noted "metaphysical poets" of this time and an English writer who has been rediscovered and celebrated in this century as few others. T. S. Eliot, while preferring "the cool, cultivated medieval temper" of Lancelot Andrewes, was yet taken with Donne's "flashing brilliance" and gave himself to reading his sermons.[1] For indeed as Frank Warnke describes him, Donne was "the greatest preacher of the greatest age of English pulpit oratory." Ten volumes of his sermons have been published by the University of California Press at Berkeley.[2]

John Donne was born to a distinguished Roman Catholic family in London which traced its lineage back to Sir Thomas More. Privately tutored at Oxford starting in 1584 but debarred from any degree because of his religious affiliation, he was much influenced in his early years by St. Teresa of Avila and St. John of the Cross. This was not an easy time to be a Roman Catholic in England, and Donne was witness to the execution of the brilliant young Edmund Campion in 1581 (memorialized in the book by Evelyn Waugh in 1935). He studied further at Cambridge and for the law at the Inns of Court and traveled abroad. He was restless, and his early poetry was quite erotic. In 1596 he was part of a military expedition with Essex and Raleigh to Cadiz in Spain. He was feeling among other things the dissolution of the medieval synthesis. To use his own words, "'Tis all in peeces, all cohaerence gone."[3]

Clearly in much stress and strain, Donne was in process of passage to Protestantism. He became secretary to Sir Thomas Edgerton, Keeper of the Seal, and secretly married his niece in 1601. Consequently he was in everyone's disfavor and soon unemployed. During this time he wrote his *Biathanatos,* which sought to rationalize suicide. At some point he was converted to Christ, and ultimately, at age forty-three, he took holy orders and was ordained in 1615.

A current Roman Catholic critic, John Carey of Oxford, disparages him and impugns his motives by alleging that Donne really wanted to be ambassador to Venice. For Carey, Donne was "self-advancing . . . pitiless . . . egotistical . . . with an urge to dominate women . . . [and] relishes dwelling on God's destructive purposes."[4] But this preacher-poet began to find a wide hearing for his rich biblical discourse. He preached at Paul's Cross in 1617, and in 1621 was appointed dean of St. Paul's in London, where he remained until his death.

Both his preaching and his poetry show his deeply-fixed theological roots. Donne was a follower of Augustine in many respects. Potter and Simpson mark a curve of positive and striking sermonic development.[5] Izaak Walton, one of his parishioners, called him "another Ambrose." Walton's description is telling:

> Preaching the Word so, as shewed his own heart was possest with those very thoughts and joys that he laboured to distill into others. A Preacher in earnest; weeping sometimes for his Auditory, sometimes with them: always preaching to himself like an Angel from a cloud, but in none; carrying some, as St. Paul was, to Heaven in holy raptures, and inticing others by a sacred Art and Courtship to amend their lives; here picturing a vice so as to make it ugly to those that practised it; and a vertue so as to make it beloved even by those that lov'd it not; and all this with a most particular grace and an unexpressible addition of comeliness.[6]

Donne saw himself as a trumpeter of the Word. He was a strong advocate of careful preparation, insisting on careful reading of the original text of Scripture. He used irony, satire, wit, and macabre images.[7] He employed diminuendo and crescendo. He spoke of "The Book of the World," "The Seal of the Sacrament," and "The Eyes of the Soul." Such epigrammatic language as endures can be seen in his phrases, "For whom the bell tolls," "No man is an island," or "Go and catch a falling star." Torrential eloquence can be marked along with a sense of dramatic immediacy and great personal intensity. He had a profound sense of calling to preach, a *vocatio radicalis,* in terms of which he stated: "It becometh me to make my selfe as acceptable a messenger as I can, and to infuse the Word of God into you, as powerfully from the Word of God it selfe, quickened by his Spirit."[8] Donne's unshakable persuasion was that the center of all preaching is "Christ Jesus and him crucified; and whosoever preaches any other Gospell, or any other things for Gospell, let him be accursed" (4.231).

Donne saw preaching as art and drama as well as exposition. The Puritans would have none of this. Much later Archbishop Davidson remarked that "sermons are often without real substance, deficient in intellectual quality, and unable to arouse interest or response in their hearers."[9] It is in the address to the latter of these challenges that the Donnean sermon is so instructive. His sermons were dramatic and dialogic. He used powerful metaphors and linguistic elevation. His hands and his voice were important for him. He used rhetorical device as did the prophets, Christ, and the apostles. The suspicion always is in some circles that anything too well ordered must be insincere. How does this follow?

Of the plain, middle, and ornate styles, Donne is actually quite middle. Certainly sermons in this era tended to be florid. But the danger of the plain style is that the sermon becomes a lecture without undulation or hills and valleys at all. The problem for the preacher is suggested in what Chips writes about her church in a recent Robertson Davies novel:

> What gets my goat is the sermon. . . . Then you come down with a bang from all the splendor of the Prayer Book and the really super prose of Cranmer to hear what some chap thinks it would be good for you to hear.[10]

John Donne addressed that issue in one way. We shall now inspect others. Donne's preaching and poetry show an obsession with death. Quite early on his young wife died, as did six of their twelve children. While he was at St. Paul's three waves of the Black Death swept over London with forty-thousand people dying in the last. Thirty-two of his fifty-four songs and sonnets are about death. His great sermon "Death's Duell" is a classic. Donne himself died after a long, lingering illness. He had hoped to die in the pulpit, yet he found Christ sufficient in his extremity. His personal experience validates his preaching.[11] In his last sermon he brought his hearers to Calvary:

> We leave you in that blessed dependency, to hang upon Him that hung upon the cross. There bathe in his tears, there suck of his wounds, and lie down in peace in his grave, till he vouchsafes you a resurrection and an ascension into that kingdom which he hath purchased for you with the inestimable price of his incorruptible blood.[12]

1. Alzina Stone Dale, *T. S. Eliot: The Philosopher Poet* (Wheaton, Ill.: Shaw, 1988), 90, 72.
2. George R. Potter and Evelyn M. Simpson, eds., *The Sermons of John Donne,* 10 vols. (Berkeley: University of California Press, 1953–1962). A top selection is also in the Modern Library's *The Complete Poetry and Selected Prose of John Donne* (New York: Modern Library/Random House, 1952). A sampling is in Erwin Paul Rudolph, ed., *The John Donne Treasury* (Wheaton, Ill.: Victor, 1978).

3. Michael Francis Moloney, *John Donne: His Flight from Medievalism* (Urbana: University of Illinois, 1944), 109.

4. John Carey, *John Donne: Life, Mind and Art* (New York: Oxford University Press, 1981), 95, 123.

5. Gale H. Carrithers Jr., *Donne at Sermons* (Albany: State University of New York Press, 1972), 78.

6. William R. Mueller, "The Sermons of John Donne," *Christianity Today* (September 28, 1962): 1203. Mueller also is the author of a fine study, *John Donne: Preacher* (New York: Octagon, 1977).

7. Winfreid Schleiner, *The Imagery of John Donne's Sermons* (Providence, R.I.: Brown University Press, 1970).

8. Robert B. Shaw, *The Call of God: The Theme of Vocation in the Poetry of Donne and Herbert* (Cambridge, Mass.: Cowley, 1981).

9. Quoted in Charles Smyth, *The Art of Preaching: A Practical Survey of Preaching in the Church of England* (London: SPCK, 1940), 1.

10. Robertson Davies, *The Cunning Man* (New York: Viking, 1994), 316.

11. Philip Yancey, "A Wrestling Match with the Almighty," *Christianity Today* (September 8, 1989): 22ff.

12. T. Harwood Pattison, *The History of Christian Preaching* (Philadelphia: American Baptist Publication Society, 1903), 176f.

6.2.3 The Pictureman of the Preachers—George Herbert

> Lord, how can man preach Thy eternall word?
> He is a brittle crazie glasse:
> Yet in Thy temple Thou dost him afford
> This glorious and transcendent place,
> To be a window, through Thy grace.

In these lines of the parson-poet we meet **George Herbert** (1593–1633), a skilled artisan of the craft. Born into a wealthy and titled family, Herbert studied at Cambridge, where in 1619 he was made orator of the university. He developed high tastes and obtained the notice of even James I, whose court he often attended. Disappointed in politics, he sensed God's call to preach and took a small congregation at Bemerton near Salisbury. Notwithstanding what might seem to be a meager opportunity, Herbert was determined:

> And though the iniquity of the late times have made clergymen meanly valued, and the sacred name of priest contemptible; yet I will labor to make it honorable, by consecrating all my learning, and all my poor abilities to advance the glory of that God who gave them; knowing that I never can do too much for him, that hath done so much for me as to make me a Christian. And I will labor to be like my Saviour, by making humility lovely in the eyes of all men.[1]

Consumed by ill health, he did not have long to serve. In contrast to Donne's fire and complexity, we cannot but be impressed by Herbert's gentleness and simplicity.

Described as "not witty or learned or eloquent but holy," George Herbert preached the Word. He also wrote 169 poems collected in *The Temple,* using many verse forms and ranging over many Christian doctrines, including election and eschatology. He reflected on affliction and his sense of vocation. He wanted to be fruitful "like the orenge tree" for his Lord.[2] His is a highly sacramental theology, but he chose the plain style for his discourses, worrying that "overheated imagination can obscure the heavenly glory."[3] He did not disdain the ministrations of the country parson who

> holds the Rule, that Nothing is little in God's service: If it once have the honour of that Name, it grows great instantly. Wherefore neither disdaineth he to enter into the poorest cottage, though he even creep into it, and though it smell never so lothsomely. For both God is there also, and those for whom God dyed . . .[4]

Preaching that is "speech alone" is bereft of blessing, and as he insisted on his deathbed, all "must be sprinkled with the blood of Christ."

While much of his poetry was written in Latin and Greek, Herbert divulged some of the richness of his inner life and communication in his extended series of verses in reply to the Scot Andrew Melville's *Accusations.* This is also evident in some of his charming and moving poems on Christ's passion.[5]

The Carolingian preachers give us a heightened appreciation for their diversity and the beauty and symmetry possible in the craft of preaching.

---

1. M. C. Allen, "George Herbert: Poet to the Clergy," *The Pulpit* (September 1964): 7–10.
2. Robert B. Shaw, *The Call of God: The Theme of Vocation in the Poetry of Donne and Herbert* (Cambridge, Mass.: Cowley, 1981), 78.
3. Ibid., 98.
4. Ibid., 90. Two other poet-preachers of note are Robert Herrick and Richard Crashaw.
5. Also note Mark McCloskey and Paul R. Murphy, trans., *The Latin Poems of George Herbert* (Athens: Ohio University Press, 1965).

6.2.4 *THE MARKSMAN OF THE PREACHERS—JEREMY TAYLOR*

> If homilies or sermons be made upon the words of Scripture, you are to consider whether all that be spoken be conformable to the Scriptures; for, although you may practice for human reasons, and human arguments, ministered from the preacher's art, yet you must practice nothing but the command of God, nothing but the doctrine of Scripture; that is, the text.
> Let not the humours and inclinations of the people be the measures of your doctrines, but let your doctrines be the measure of their persuasions.
> —Jeremy Taylor

Sometimes called the poet of the preachers, **Jeremy Taylor's** (1613–1667) sermons stand as great English literature. He was called the English Chrysostom. One pulpit observer commented, "We have no modern sermons in the English language that can be considered as very eloquent . . . for eloquence we must ascend as high as the days of Jeremy Taylor."[1] Coleridge called him "the most eloquent of divines." Similar accolades have come from Ralph Waldo Emerson and James Russell Lowell. His critic Robert Southey described him: "From whose mind of its treasures redundant streams of eloquence flowed, like an inexhaustible foundation."[2] Was he too grandiose? Too ornate? The more florid and oratorical among us must constantly ask ourselves, Am I becoming too convoluted and turgid?

Taylor was born the son of a barber and baptized in Holy Trinity Church in Cambridge. In 1626 he entered Cambridge, taking orders in 1629. He lectured at St. Paul's in London, where he was an instant favorite, for "no one had preached in St. Paul's with such impassioned eloquence since the great Dean [John Donne] who had been dead three years."[3] Here he caught the attention and favor of Archbishop Laud, whose protégé he became along with George Herbert. **William Laud** (1573–1645), successively bishop of London and archbishop of Canterbury as well as key advisor to King Charles I, sponsored Taylor on a fellowship at Oxford and then saw him placed at age twenty-five in Uppingham, a small country church. Laud, a high churchman, Arminian but a strong Anselmian, pressed for Scottish uniformity. As a result, Parliament effectively abolished the episcopacy and Laud was accused of "high treason" in 1640. Some of the Puritan complaints were laughable, such as Laud's positive attitude toward plays which were "accompanied by lust-provoking music and profuse exorbitant laughter."[4] He was beheaded in 1645.

Taylor survived the civil war in Golden Grove, where he wrote and preached, steadfast in his loyalty to the crown and the Church of England. He was imprisoned a number of times. In the Restoration he was consecrated as a bishop in the Church of Ireland at St. Patrick's Cathedral in Dublin, where he also served as vice chancellor of the University of Dublin. These were ecclesiastically stormy and personally sorrowful years for Taylor, who died in 1667.

Taylor was a controversialist but wisely counseled preachers, when preaching "do not trouble your people with controversies."[5] As one who shrank from hyper-Calvinistic ideas, particularly the doctrine of reprobation as preached by some Puritans, he was called Arminian Taylor. His treatise *The Liberty of Prophesying* was to freedom of speech and tolerance what Milton's *Areopagetica* was to freedom of the press. Taylor was best known for his great personal piety and his devotional writings, such as *The Rule and Exercises of Holy Living* (1650) and *The Rule and Exercises of Holy Dying* (1651), are still circulated. These are actually portions of his preaching.

A master of English prose, Taylor was known above all for his great integrity and character. He pled for "an upright and holy life." His influence on John Wesley was profound, and Wesley acknowledged that his acquaintance with Taylor when he was in his twenty-third year was defining for him.[6]

Taylor's preaching utilized long sentences. He loved homely illustrations. He preached vividly on heaven and hell, death and judgment, God's mercy and

God's severity. He warned of relying on deathbed repentance, and abhorred the doctrines of extreme unction and prayers for the dead. Sixty-four of his sermons have been preserved, including a most striking series on "Christ's Advent to Judgment," which graphically depicts the wicked in their confusion and believers in the house of feasting. Allusions, metaphors, and similes abounded in his preaching. Horton Davies, speaking of Puritan preaching, lamented that "the wit of South, the brilliant and quaint imagination of Donne, the sustained metaphors of Jeremy Taylor or the racy language of Latimer are not to be found there."[7]

While we have two distinct styles here, is it entirely fair to say of Taylor that "he delights but does not move"?[8] He was a child of his age and effective in his setting, as were the Puritans. Webber decries Taylor's description of the fallen angels which he contrasts with the simplicity of the biblical statement, but is not Taylor's treatment defensible? Taylor's own words are: "The angels themselves, because their light reflected home to their orbs, and they understood all the secrets of their own perfection, they grew vertiginous, and fell from the battlements of heaven."[9] Perhaps he overused quotations as in his declamation, "Aelian tells of the geese flying over the mountain Taurus; that for fear of eagles, nature hath taught them to carry stones in their mouths, till they be past their danger."[10] In a funeral sermon for the archbishop of Armaugh, he waxed eloquent in his tribute. "For in him were visible the great lines of Hooker's judiciousness, of Jewel's learning, of the acuteness of Bishop Andrewes."[11] Overdone? Possibly, but memorable. Jeremy Taylor remains an uncommon preacher still read in our times.

---

1. Thomas S. Kepler, ed., *Jeremy Taylor's The Rules and Exercises of Holy Living* (New York: World, 1956), xx.
2. Ibid., xxii.
3. W. J. Brown, *Jeremy Taylor* (London: SPCK, 1925), 10.
4. Sidney Dark, *Seven Archbishops* (London: Eyre and Spottiswood, 1944), 134.
5. Frank Livingstone Huntley, *Jeremy Taylor and the Great Rebellion* (Ann Arbor: University of Michigan, 1970), 6.
6. H. Trevor Hughes, *The Piety of Jeremy Taylor* (London: Macmillan, 1960), 175.
7. Ibid., 116.
8. F. R. Webber, *A History of Preaching in Britain and America* (Milwaukee: Northwestern, 1952), 1:246.
9. Ibid., 247.
10. Caroline Francis Richardson, *English Preachers and Preaching 1640–1670* (New York: Macmillan, 1928), 84.
11. Ibid., 103.

6.2.5   THE CROSSMAN OF THE PREACHERS—JOSEPH HALL

He [Bishop Hall] never durst climb up into the pulpit to preach any Sermon, whereof he had not penned every word in the same order, wherein he hoped to deliver it: although in his expressions he was no slave to syllables, neither made use of his notes.

—John Lightfoot at Bishop Hall's funeral

We are surveying what are sometimes called the metaphysical preachers, so-called because of their classical learning and the wit, imagination, and learning characterizing their sermons.[1] In these preachers the extravagance of the age is clearly reflected (in general contrast to the Puritans). Classical rhetoric was still the basis of the educational system, and even the Puritans had rhetorical leanings,[2] although their interest in rhetoric was more for the explication of the scriptural text than the composition of the sermon. We have been looking at "the luscious style" of Jeremy Taylor and his "witty preaching," which caused Coleridge to place him with Shakespeare, Milton, and Bacon. As we shall see, Richard Baxter, the Puritan yet within the Church of England, chose the plain style of preaching. But several of the Caroline divines cut a unique swath. We turn to them now.

Joseph Hall (1574–1656) was born in Leicestershire, graduated from Cambridge in 1592, and taught rhetoric there for two years. He was ordained in 1601 and began his parish ministry in Halsted, Suffolk.[3] In his storied career he was successively chaplain to the Prince of Wales, chaplain in France to the British ambassador, in the retinue of James I in his ill-conceived visit to Scotland to impose the English liturgy on the Scottish people, rector at Waltham for twenty-two years, a Royal Commissioner to the Synod of Dort, and bishop of Exeter and bishop of Norwich. Hall was of the Calvinistic persuasion but was also disliked by Laud for his views on the toleration of the Puritans. Finally he was deprived of his bishopric by the Long Parliament, imprisoned in the Tower of London, and stripped of all his possessions. His final days were lived in poverty but in peace.[4]

Hall was renowned as a preacher of the Word. Twelve volumes remain of his collected works, which include much preaching and his poetry. He preached three times a week and loved to preach biblical characters and biographical sermons. He did careful work out of the original languages, loved proverbs and quotations, and used wit in a way that the Puritans did not. In arguing against veneration of relics, he said:

> But to dig up their holy bones, that I may borrow Luther's word, out of their quiet graves and to fall down before these worm-eaten monuments of the Saints, to expect from them a divine power, whether of cure or of sanctification, equally to respect Francis's cowl, Anna's comb, Joseph's breeches, Thomas's shoe, as Erasmus complains, with the Sone of God Himself, can seem no better to us than a horrible impiety.[5]

Hall advocated thoughtful use of the church year as an instructive device. He did research on the history of heraldry to illustrate aspects of truth in an outstanding sermon. He had a great love for Scripture, and one of his enduring memorials is his book of sermonic material titled *Contemplations Upon the*

Principal Passages in the Holy Story. He was called the English Seneca for his eloquence.

Hall's reputation as a gifted and effective preacher focused on his preaching of Christ and his Cross. His preaching on the seven last words of Christ is monumental. Hall stands in an enviable succession of preachers who concentrated their best work on the sufferings of our Lord and the meaning of his atonement. One such sermon at Paul's Cross on Good Friday, April 14, 1609, was on John 19:30 and includes the following meditation on the anguish of the suffering Savior:

> That head, which is adored and trembled at by the angelical spirits, is all raked and harrowed with thorns; that face of whom it is said, Thou art fairer than the children of men, is all besmeared with filthy spittle. . . . and furrowed with his tears; those eyes, clearer than the sun, are darkened with the shadow of death; those ears, that hear the heavenly concerts of angels, now are filled with the cursed speakings and scoffs of wretched men; those lips, that spake as never man spake, that command the spirits both of light and darkness, are scornfully wet with vinegar and gall; those feet, that trample on all the powers of hell (his enemies are made his footstool) are now nailed to the footstool of the cross; those hands, that freely sway the sceptre of the heavens, now carry the reed of reproach, and are nailed to the tree of reproach; that whole body, which was conceived by the Holy Ghost, was all scourged, wounded, mangled: this is the outside of his sufferings.[6]

1. Horton Davies, *Like Angels from a Cloud: The English Metaphysical Preachers 1588–1645* (San Marino, Calif.: Huntington Library, 1986), 49. A joyous piece of careful research!
2. W. Fraser Mitchell, *English Pulpit Oratory from Andrewes to Tillotson: A Study of its Literary Aspects* (London: SPCK, 1932), 69, 95.
3. F. R. Webber, *A History of Preaching in Britain and America* (Milwaukee: Northwestern, 1952), 1:229.
4. E. C. Dargan, *A History of Preaching* (New York: Hodder and Stoughton, 1912), 2:153.
5. Davies, *Like Angels from a Cloud,* 318.
6. Ibid., 374–75.

6.2.6   THE SPOKESMAN AMONG THE PREACHERS—THOMAS FULLER

In explaining why he concluded a sermon somewhat abruptly: "These things deserve larger Prosecution; but this is none of Joshua's day, wherein the Sunne standeth still; and therefore I must conclude the time."

About the Puritans: "I never knew nor heard of an Army all of Saints, save the Holy Army of Martyrs; and those, you know, were dead first."

> Defending wit in sermons providing: "The sweetnesse of the sauce spoile
> not the savourinesse of the meat."
>
> —Thomas Fuller

One of the most extraordinarily popular preachers in this golden age of preaching was **Thomas Fuller** (1608–1661), who when preaching at the Savoy in the Strand attracted so many outside visitors that his own people had difficulty finding seating. It was said that he always preached to two congregations—one in the sanctuary and the other outside the windows of the church. His father was rector at St. Peter's, Aldwincle, and he was educated at Cambridge, where he graduated in 1624. He served a succession of posts, including Inns of Court and the Savoy. As all of these preachers now before us, he was a staunch loyalist and royalist and in the difficult years he was at Oxford and Exeter. After the Restoration, Fuller was appointed chaplain to King Charles II.

Two volumes of his printed sermons remain, and his influential books, *Church History of Britain* and *History of the Worthies of England,* were widely circulated in his time and subsequently. He was known as a jovial Calvinist who used humor, puns, and playful banter with his congregation—a tactic that is usually difficult and sometimes dangerous.[1]

Charles Lamb called him a great storyteller, and his very appearance, "corpulent, ruddy, cheerful and head adorned with a comely light-colored haire which was so by nature exactly curled,"[2] made him like a big teddy bear to his adoring listeners. Gifted with an amazing memory, he stressed literal exegesis over allegorization, but pooh-poohed rigid literality.

> Besides, Christ at his death spake no other language than what his tongue
> and his Disciples were used to in his life time: I am the Vine, I am the
> Way, I am the Doore. Hee who is so sottish as to conceive that Christ
> was a materiall Doore shoeweth himself to be a post indeed.[3]

Earlier on he delighted in consecutive book exposition in his preaching. His sermons were more like the Puritan style of selecting a thematic doctrine from the text and tracing its uses. Some of his unforgettable epigrams linger with us, such as "You cannot repent too soon because you do not know how soon it will be too late" or "God's children are immortal while their Father hath anything for them to do on earth" (possibly the source for Mark Twain's famous quote).

Fuller was a man of quirks and quaintness; hence, we are not surprised to find these qualities in his preaching. His wit sprang from "that genuine observance of similitudes,"[4] which informed his notion of amplification in the sermon; he sought out "the untold wonders of association, which a phrase or often a single word suggested to him, and which he immediately shared with his hearers."[5] The grave peril which Fuller faced and of which all preachers must beware is any ostentatious effect which draws attention to itself and away from the compelling biblical subject. His sermons were heard well and they read well. These qualities are commendable, but cause us to walk a fine line.

1. John W. Drakeford, *Humor in Preaching* (Grand Rapids: Zondervan, 1986).
2. Horton Davies, *Like Angels from a Cloud: The English Metaphysical Preachers 1588–1645* (San Marino, Calif.: Huntington Library, 1986), 172.
3. Ibid., 118.
4. W. Fraser Mitchell, *English Pulpit Oratory from Andrewes to Tillotson* (London: SPCK, 1932), 233.
5. Ibid., 236.

6.2.7   THE OARSMAN AMONG THE PREACHERS—JOHN TILLOTSON

Of Tillotson's preaching it was said: "He was not only the best preacher of the age, but seemed to have brought preaching to perfection; his sermons were so well liked that all the nation proposed him as a pattern and studied to copy after him."

—Bishop Burnet

The firmament was bright with preachers in seventeenth-century England. We have yet to consider the Puritan school with its immense contribution. Worthies mentioned in this galaxy must include **Edmund Calamy** (1600–1666), known for his careful craftsmanship in preaching. Calamy opposed the execution of Charles I but did adopt nonconformist views and spent time in prison after the Restoration. **Herbert Palmer** (1601–1647) could read the Bible at age four. He was fluent in French, a member of the Westminster Assembly of Divines, and wrote much of the Shorter Catechism. Palmer burned himself out in his preaching. **William Chillingworth** (1602–1644), famous for his words, "The Bible, I say the Bible only is the religion of Protestants," was a strong expositor of Scripture and highly intellectual. **Isaac Ambrose** (1604–1663) suffered much for his Puritan views but is most remembered for his beautiful study, *Looking unto Jesus*.[1] Archbishop **James Ussher** (1581–1656) was primate of the Church of Ireland (Protestant). He was a learned and tolerant Calvinist, and author of the famous Ussher's chronology which put the creation at 4004 B.C. Ussher was opposed to florid preaching, and introduced plain style preaching at Oxford and Westminster. He used poignant imagery and metaphor, and was especially gifted in his preaching on the cross.[2] Bishop **John Pearson** was an effective court chaplain in the Restoration. Pearson was a linguist, and a friend of Baxter at the Savoy Conference. He is remembered for his classic work on the Apostles' Creed. **William Gurnall,** who gave us his sermonic work on *The Christian in Complete Armour,* was reordained in the Church of England.

Amid the ecclesiastical complexity of this age, a key figure is **John Tillotson** (1630–1694), a popular preacher in London. Fourteen volumes of his sermons are extant. Admired by Addison and praised by Doddridge for his clarity, Tillotson became archbishop of Canterbury in 1690, and for a few short years exerted immense influence on church life and preaching. His style was persuasive, not polemic.[3] His sermons were logical and intellectual but memorable, as was his famous sermon on "The Reasonableness of the Resurrection." He was such a smooth stylist that the poet Dryden said of him, "if he had any talent for English prose it was owing to his having often read the writings of the great Archbishop Tillotson."[4] Tillotson's sermons were like literary essays, in which each word was carefully considered, with a general sense of the text neglected and no division of the text.[5]

This was the age of the reaction of the Cambridge Platonists against the Puritans on the one hand and the extreme embellishment of the metaphysical preachers and the high churchmanship of Laud on the other. Such luminaries as Benjamin Whichcote, Ralph Cudworth, Henry More, and Nathaniel Culverwell were all effective preachers but veered toward a sterile, rationalistic preaching. Meanwhile, Robert South lurched toward clever political preaching. South was more courtier than preacher. The two sermons for which he is remembered were one preached against extemporaneous prayer and another in memory of Charles I.[6]

The result of these developments was decline in the English pulpit to the end of the century.

Archbishop Tillotson bears some of the culpability for the diminution of biblical preaching, despite his love for the Scripture and his Puritan upbringing. Tillotson admirably appealed to reason and common sense, but the great danger was that his sermons became highly polished moral essays. His sermons took on a read rather than a spoken quality, and no longer plumbed the biblical text.

The essay sermon is still with us today, particularly in mainline and liturgical circles. Such sermons are smooth and controlled, never succumbing to panting passion or the rarified air of the mountain peak. Thus preaching lost momentum by the end of the century. As Smyth argues, it would be the evangelists of the next century who restored the powerful preaching of the Cross of Christ.[7]

---

1. Helpful sketches of these preachers will be found in F. R. Webber, *A History of Preaching in Britain and America,* vol. 1 (Milwaukee: Northwestern, 1952).
2. Horton Davies, *Like Angels from a Cloud: The English Metaphysical Preachers 1588–1645* (San Marino, Calif.: Huntington Library, 1986), 164–68.
3. Webber, *A History of Preaching,* 1:267.
4. Ibid., 208. For a good sampling, see James Moffat, *The Golden Book of Tillotson* (London: Hodder and Stoughton, 1926). Note particularly "The Bible a Plain Book," 67–68. Striking and appropriate literary quotations.
5. Charles Smyth, *The Art of Preaching: A Practical Survey of Preaching in the Church of England 747–1939* (London: SPCK, 1940), 99, 106.
6. T. Harwood Pattison, *The History of Christian Preaching* (Philadelphia: American Baptist Publication Society, 1903), 208ff.
7. Smyth, *The Art of Preaching,* 173.

6.3 FRENCH PULPIT ORATORY AND THE REFINEMENT OF THE CRAFT

To preach is the publication and declaration of God's will, made to men by one lawfully commissioned to that task, to the end of instructing and

> moving them to serve his divine Majesty in this world so as to be saved
> in the next.
>
> —Francis of Sales

With the waning of Spanish and Portuguese power, especially after the defeat of the Spanish Armada in 1588, England and France come increasingly to the fore, and their very position and power in the seventeenth century mean inevitable clash between them. It was a time of greatness for France. Henry of Navarre (Henry IV) with the aid of the Duke of Sully reduced taxes and oversaw impressive economic growth. He also signed the Edict of Nantes in 1598, giving a degree of freedom of worship to the persecuted Protestants, the Huguenots. Henry was himself a Huguenot but became a Roman Catholic to achieve peace in 1593.

Louis XIII, his son, became king on his father's assassination in 1610, and, under the dominant leadership of Cardinal Richelieu, saw the establishment of an absolute monarchy. All Huguenot political power was destroyed as power centralized in the hands of the king. Thousands of Huguenots fled. When Louis XIII died in 1642, he was succeeded by his five-year-old son, Louis XIV, who ruled for seventy-two years. He was known as Louis the Great or the Grand Monarch. His chief minister was Cardinal Mazarin. Louis XIV fought four major wars. The final conflict, the War of the Spanish Succession, was lost largely through the English and left France prostrate just before his death. Through the malignant influence of his chief mistress, Madame de Maintenon, Louis XIV revoked the Edict of Nantes in 1685 and fiercely persecuted the Huguenots. Even though France bled seriously through the flight of so many prosperous and upstanding citizens, the king remained unbearably headstrong, declaring, "I am the state!" France's strength and leadership were visibly reduced. At the time of Louis XIV's death, France was a shadow of what she had been before. Yet even in such stressful times, God and His Word were not silent.

6.3.1   THE SHAPING INFLUENCES ON FRENCH PREACHING

> We must preach the Word of God. . . . Preach the Gospel says the Master. . . . St. Francis explains this when he commands frairs to preach on virtues and vices and on hell and paradise. There is sufficient matter in Sacred Scripture for all of that; nothing further is needed.
>
> —Francis of Sales

Pattison asserts that "the pulpit eloquence of France in the seventeenth century was distinguished by extraordinary richness of thought and splendor of diction . . . to the present hour the great sermons of that era remain the classics of the language."[1] Dargan called it "the classic age" or "the golden age" of the French pulpit. We know that Tillotson studied the court preachers of France, but it is of interest that we find such striking parallels between England and France.

For a sense of the often tense environment for preaching at this time, we may peruse the biography of **René Descartes**. Born in 1596 near Tours, Descartes was trained in a Jesuit college where the need for reform was obvious.[2] The essential purpose of education was to "pour [persons] forth to preach and teach the Word of God to the masses" to counteract increasing Protestant influence.[3] Using his notion of "clear and distinct ideas," Descartes developed a psychological theory of cognitive grasp which eventuated in his famous *Cogito, ergo sum* (I think, therefore I am).

While in contact with Cardinal Berulle, who championed a revival of Augustinianism emphasizing a radical dependence on God (which Descartes could never accept), he relished the freedom of Protestant Amsterdam. He was especially stung by the condemnation of Galileo in 1633[4] and turned from his brilliant and productive labors in physics to metaphysics. He met the sixteen-year-old genius Pascal at this time, but troubled in his own personal affairs and in conflict with Protestant theologians like Voetius at Utrecht, he finally took the patronage of Queen Christina of Sweden, moving there in his midfifties. Descartes died in Stockholm in February of 1650. His biographer calls him "a zealous Roman Catholic who feared the displeasure of the Church above all else."[5]

The flurry of interest in preaching theory from the time of Alan of Lille in the twelfth century stands in contrast to the paucity of biblical preaching at this time. Yet there were those who strove to uphold solid preaching. One of the princely figures of the time was **Francis of Sales** (1567–1622), who went to Geneva to attempt to convert Beza. He served as prince bishop of Geneva in exile at Annecy. He authored several widely influential works on Christian spirituality, including *The Introduction to the Devout Life* and *Treatise on the Love of God,* and preached powerfully. His great burden was "a call to universal holiness."[6] His work was read by Jeremy Taylor and John Henry Newman. He attempted to fuse the Tridentine decrees on preaching (which affirmed the classical canons) with his personal affection for the instructional emphasis of **Charles Borromeo** of Italy.

Borromeo's book, which recommends elucidation of the Scripture and simple rhetorical devices, was approved by the Council of Bordeaux in 1624.[7] Also influential was the book written for the new diocesan seminaries by the bishop of Verona, **Agostino Valiero**. His work appeared in 1574 and argued the difference between the homily and the classical oration.[8] Spanish and Jesuit theorists were also at work. And De Sales himself wrote a famous letter to Andre Fremiot, bishop-designate of Bourges, addressing the craft of preaching.[9] We quote from this letter at the beginning of each of these sections.

Other spiritual movements beyond the French School of Cardinal Berulle contributed to the spiritual venue of preaching. Above all was **Cornelius Jansen** (d. 1638), a convinced Augustinian, who settled around Port Royal des Champs, which would become a stronghold of Scripture and gospel purity. Port Royal des Champs was the chief influence shaping **Blaise Pascal** (1623–1662), the brilliant apologist for the Christian faith. Calvary was the great divide in Pascal's search for truth. Pascal was a Christian layman imbued with a supernaturalistic worldview which was bibliocentric. Cailliet says, "At the heart of Christianity he saw Christ Himself . . . . All our virtue and felicity."[10]

The crushing of Port Royal and the condemnation of Antoine Arnauld, who was head of the Jansenists, were ominous signs. They foreshadowed the fact that "spiritual life in France was threatened by authoritarian proceedings copied from the Inquisition, and all morality was threatened at the same time."[11] Yet this would provide the spiritual milieu for an astounding outburst of preaching in the most unlikely places. God was yet at work, and He would bless his holy Word.

---

1. T. Harwood Pattison, *The History of Christian Preaching* (Philadelphia: American Baptist Publication Society, 1903), 214.
2. Stephen Gaukroger, *Descartes: An Intellectual Biography* (Oxford: Clarendon, 1995), 27.
3. Ibid., 39.
4. For important studies of the bearing of Galileo's controversy with the church at Rome, see Giorgio De Santillana, *The Crime of Galileo* (Chicago: University of Chicago, 1955); James Reston Jr., *Galileo: A Life* (New York: HarperCollins, 1994). Touching description of visits to the dying old man by Thomas Hobbes and John Milton.
5. Gaukroger, *Descartes,* 291.
6. Cheslyn Jones, Geoffrey Wainwright, Edward Yarnold, *The Study of Spirituality* (New York: Oxford, 1986), 381.
7. Peter Bayley, *French Pulpit Oratory* (London: Cambridge University Press, 1980), 45.
8. Ibid., 48.
9. Francis of Sales, *On the Preacher and Preaching* (Chicago: Henry Regnery, 1964).
10. Emile Cailliet, *Pascal: The Emergence of Genius* (New York: Harper Torchbooks, 1945, 1961).
11. Ibid., 201.

6.3.2 THE SHINING INSTANCES OF FRENCH PREACHING

Preaching must be spontaneous, dignified, courageous, natural, sturdy, devout, serious, and a little slow. But to make it such what must be done? In a word, it means to speak with affection and devotion, with simplicity and candor, and with confidence, and to be convinced of the doctrine we teach of what we persuade. The supreme art is to have no art. Our words must be set aflame, not by shouts and unrestrained gestures, but by inward affection.

—Francis of Sales

Francis always insisted that the test of a sermon was not whether a congregation responded, "What a beautiful sermon," but whether they departed saying "I will do something." We shall soon see some extraordinary preaching, but to preach on parade is perilous. Eloquence can never be a goal in itself, but we must never forget, as John Donne observed, "There are not so eloquent books in the world, as the Scriptures."[1]

King Louis XIV led an especially strong Counter-Reformation, not only against the Huguenots but also against Jansenism within the church. The stamping out of these renewal movements led to moral laxity in the nation, which ultimately brought France to the French Revolution and the Enlightenment. There were no

Pietists to ameliorate the radicality of the Enlightenment in France.[2] Of course
the French church always had a unique relationship to the Roman pontiff
(Gaullicanism). We will scrutinize the spheres and subjects of French preaching
in this period, for as Huizinga maintained, preaching can show us the "structure
of feeling" of a whole civilization.

1. Peter Bayley, *French Pulpit Oratory 1598–1650* (Cambridge, Mass.: Cambridge University Press, 1980), 3.
2. Kurt Aland, *A History of Christianity* (Philadelphia: Fortress, 1986), 2:267.

6.3.2.1 Roman Catholic Preaching by Parish Priests and Primates

> What soul is so unfeeling that it does not take very great pleasure from
> learning the path to heaven in so good and holy a way, and does not feel
> the greatest consolation in love of God? There is another kind of delight
> . . . this is a sort of tickling of ears, which derives from a certain secular,
> worldly and profane elegance and from various affectations and arrange-
> ments of ideas, words and phrases . . . it depends wholly on artifice . . .
> they do not preach "Jesus Christ crucified"; they preach themselves.
>   —Francis of Sales

The contemporary Cambridge scholar Peter Bayley has given us an invaluable study of the preaching of fifty or sixty preachers in this period.[1] Some preachers made minimal comments in conjunction with the Mass, but there was some
significant preaching on the part of some in the Roman Catholic Church. Then
there were the Protestant preachers for whom preaching was at the core of the
worship experience. The earlier preaching in this period was more in the plain
style. **Jean Bertraut** of Caen (1552–1611), the well-known poet, was one such
preacher. Another was the Franciscan **Jean Boucher** of Poitiers (1560–1631).
Their style reflected the influence of the essays of Montaigne. Their sermons
possessed some decorative features, but were nothing to compare with the "thesaurus sermons" which came into vogue, packed with "anecdotes, illustrations
and analogies."[2]

Reacting against the tendency to monotony and flabbiness in this style was
Jean-Pierre Camus (1584–1652), bishop of Belley and friend of Francis of Sales.
He developed what Bayley calls "catenary prose," the use of long examples,
"breathless, inchoate," with little regard for elocution.[3] Predictably, a rhetorical
reaction set in, as is seen in the preaching of Etienne Molinier of Toulouse (d.
1647). He moved back into more traditional rhetoric. The emphasis on *le naturel,*
and more "orchestrated prose" will be seen more prominently among the Protestant preachers surveyed in the next section.

But the master preacher who emerged out of this flux was doubtless **Jacques
Benigne Bossuet** of Dijon (1627–1704). Reared in a large, middle-class family,
he had a transforming experience early in his life when he discovered the Book of
Isaiah in his uncle's study. It was the first time he had read the Scripture, and it

began a lifelong journey of study in the Word. Bossuet received his doctorate and was ordained in 1652. Very much drawn to Augustine (whose commentaries he always carried with him), he was also greatly influenced by the gracious and gentle **Vincent de Paul,** with whom he held a memorable retreat after his ordination.[4]

Serving at first in Paris and then as dean in Metz, Bossuet was soon marked as a powerful preacher. His first major visibility came in a Lenten course of sermons at the Louvre in 1662. Over his lifetime, he delivered five courses of Lenten sermons and three courses of Advent sermons in Paris, although the state of his surviving sermons is not good. He loved the work of Pascal, and observed that if he could write anything that would last, he would wish to write the *Pensees.*

Elevated to the episcopacy, Bossuet was appointed bishop of Condom before serving as the bishop of Meaux with 230 parishes. Bossuet was a champion of the Gallican insistence on the uniqueness of the French church in Catholicism. He preached a famous sermon to the Assembly of the French Clergy in 1681 on the subject of Christian unity and service. He was uneasy about papal power. He pursued dialogue with leading Protestants like Paul Ferry and Jean Claude and kept abreast of trends in the Church of England.[5] He was critical of Richard Simon, early pioneer of biblical criticism, and battled with Fénelon over Madame Guyon and Quietism (the unacknowledged "offspring" of St. Teresa of Avila), which he adamantly opposed.

Bossuet was invited to preach in the royal court because of his friendship with Queen Anne, but he was quite bold before the king and his invitations to preach decreased. He gave the funeral oration of Queen Anne as well as that of the widow of the English King Charles I. He anguished over the profligacy of the French court and pleaded with the king to repent of his backsliding. He served as tutor to the Dauphin of France, and became known as "The Eagle of Meaux" for his great ministry. The following observations can be made about his preaching:

1. He studied constantly, keeping the light on in his room all night and arising to study often.
2. He quoted much Scripture in his sermons.
3. The sermons were elaborately written and outlined.
4. His preaching was highly theological.
5. He loved to preach on John the Baptist and particularly the humility of the Forerunner.
6. He preached often on the Cross and the believer's death with Jesus. Typical is an outline on "Today you will be with me in paradise": (1) Today—what swiftness; (2) with me—what companionship; (3) in paradise—what rest![6]
7. Bossuet was strong on the relationship of the Word and the eucharist.
8. He was known for his funeral orations, "in a class by themselves."[7]

There was something collegial about Bossuet, as we mark in his extensive contacts with the German Protestant philosopher Leibniz. At the same time there was a regrettable narrowness, as when he welcomed troops into his diocese to root out the Huguenots. On balance, however, he was a positive influence on preaching because of his conviction to "speak the Scripture."

1. Peter Bayley, *French Pulpit Oratory 1598–1650* (Cambridge, Mass.: Cambridge University Press, 1980).
2. Ibid., 77.
3. Ibid., 88.
4. H. L. Sidney Lear, *Bossuet and His Companions* (London: Rivertons, 1876), 42.
5. W. J. Sparrow Simpson, *A Study of Bossuet* (London: SPCK, 1937), 115.
6. Ibid., 135.
7. Ibid., 145.

6.3.2.2 Preaching Among the Protestants

I say the same thing about language. It must be clear, simple and natural, without display of Greek, Hebrew, novel or fancy words. The structure must be natural, and without prefatory and ornamental phrases. I approve of saying "firstly," "on the first point," and "secondly," "on the second point," so that the people may see the order followed. . . . We must be on guard against introducing conversations between characters in the episodes unless they are in words taken from Scripture or very probable.

—Francis of Sales

Reference has already been made to the anguish and persecution of the French Protestants, the Huguenots. By mid-sixteenth century they were a numerically and politically potent force. Kings, nobles, and military (Admiral de Coligny) were staunch Huguenots. Caught in the coils of domestic intrigue between the Medicis and the Guisess, thousands were slain in the massacre of 1572. They enjoyed some reprieve in the Edict of Nantes in 1598 but again felt persecution in the seventeenth century. Although they dominated in seventy-five cities of France, they were forced to flee, and many took refuge in England. Here they were instrumental in building the English textile industry. Toleration was not achieved until Napoleon's concordat with the pope in 1801.

We have already noted the significant homiletical contribution of **Jean Claude** (1619–1687), who was forced to flee to the Netherlands. Bossuet was wary of Claude, because, as he put it, "I feared for those who heard him." The Huguenot preachers "drew their inspiration largely from the expositions of Scripture which form the greater part of the Reformers' writings."[1] They followed Hyperius, who insisted a sermon be based on a scriptural text. Like Keckerman, they believed in strong persuasion but essentially preached biblical commentary with application.

While an earlier preacher like **Charles de Beauvais** (c. 1636) used three main headings with thirty-two sections in a sermon, Claude advocated a less cumbersome form with great care for thematic clarity and unity. Eloquence was always a watermark of French preaching, as was the case in the popular preaching of **Pierre du Moulin** (1568–1658). **Moses Amyraut** (1596–1664) impressed even Richelieu and Mazarin,[2] and the widely heard controversialist and stylist, **Jean D'Ailly** (1619–1687), has been considered the greatest leader in the French church since John Calvin.

Professor Vinet, who wrote two centuries later, asserted that there were at this time "great theologians, great controversialists, great diplomats, and above all, great Christians."[3] Yet this strong, vital church was to be decimated and nearly destroyed, leaving a negligible remnant which over the years became for the most part theologically concessive and liberal.

Bayley in his invaluable study uses **Jean D'Ailly** (1594–1670), pastor in Saumur and Charenton and later moderator of the Synod of Loudun, as a good example of the Protestant preaching of the day. Daille balanced careful use of the scriptural text with rhetorically sensitive discourse.[4] For Roman Catholic preachers, the text was merely a starting point "or even a purely decorative element, stripped of any analytic function."[5] But for Protestant preachers, a close inspection and analysis of the text was mandatory. Another greatly used preacher was **Pierre Du Bosc** (1623–1692) from Normandy, who served his entire ministry in Caen. Du Bosc was respected by friend and foe alike. After he had appealed to King Louis XIV on a matter related to Protestant persecution, the king remarked to the queen, "Madam, I have just heard the best speaker in my kingdom." Broadus cautions us to remember that he had not yet heard Bourdaloue or Massillon. Du Bosc was highly educated and an avid student. He surpassed even Claude in the forcefulness and power of his discourse. He fled to Rotterdam just prior to the revocation of the Edict of Nantes, where he ministered to the refugees.

Counted among the giants of French Protestant preachers was **Jacques Saurin** (1677–1730), who was reared in Nimes, where his father was a Protestant minister. He fled with his family to Geneva at the revocation. After a stint in the English military fighting against France, Saurin was educated under the great Turretin at Geneva. For five years he served a refugee congregation in London, where he had an unhappy marriage. He served in the Hague in the Netherlands, and always seemed to be in the center of some turbulence. His preaching was less formal and more soaring than Claude's, but not as textually rooted and grounded. As a preacher he was sometimes tedious and onerous, at other times like a bird in flight.[6] Yet Robinson, who has translated Saurin, pays glowing tribute to his subject:

> In the introduction of his sermon, he used to deliver himself in a tone modest and low; in the body of the sermon, which was adapted to the understanding, he was plain, clear and argumentative; pausing at the close of each period, that he might discover by the countenances and motions of his hearers whether they were convinced by his reasoning. In his addresses to the wicked, Saurin was often sonorous, but oftener a weeping suppliant at their feet. In the one he sustained the authoritative dignity of his office; in the other he expressed his Master's and his own benevolence to bad men, "praying them in Christ's stead to be reconciled to God." In general, his preaching resembled a plentiful shower of dew, softly and imperceptibly insinuating itself into the minds of his numerous hearers, as the dew into the pores of plants, till all the church was dissolved, and all in tears under his sermons.[7]

It would yet be one hundred years before there is much stirring among French-speaking Protestants. Then we shall have Caesar Malan, L. Gaussen, d'Aubigne and Alexandre Vinet as well as the Swiss Monods. Yet in the darkest and most difficult days, God is never without his witness.

---

1. Peter Bayley, *French Pulpit Oratory 1598–1650* (Cambridge, Mass.: Cambridge University Press, 1980), 61.
2. B. G. Armstrong, *Calvinism and the Amyraut Heresy* (Madison: University of Wisconsin, 1969). The great preponderance of Baptists are not five-point Calvinists but rather Amyrauldian, holding perhaps two or three of the five points. This explains the importance of Amyraut, who deserves much more study than is ordinarily given him.
3. E. C. Dargan, *A History of Preaching* (New York: Hodder and Stoughton, 1912), 2:118.
4. Bayley, *French Pulpit Oratory 1598–1650,* 117.
5. Ibid., 102–3.
6. A. E. Garvie, *The Christian Preacher* (New York: Scribner's, 1923), 173.
7. T. Harwood Pattison, *The History of Christian Preaching* (Philadelphia: American Baptist Publication Society, 1903), 219.

6.3.2.3 Preaching in the Royal Court Before the Potentates

I said that our preaching must be a spontaneous action, in contrast to the constrained and studied action of the pedants. I said dignified, in contrast to the rustic ways of some preachers who make a show of striking their fists, feet, and stomach against the pulpit, shout and utter howls that are strange and often improper. I said courageous in contrast to those who have a certain fearful way of acting as if they were speaking to their fathers and not to their pupils and children. I said natural, in contrast to all artificiality and affectation. I said sturdy, in contrast to a kind of dead, soft, ineffectual action. I said devout, to avoid obsequious and worldly acts of flattery. I said serious, in contrast to those who doff their caps so many times to the audience, make so many signs of respect, and perform so many little tricks by showing their hands or surplices, and aming other such indecorous movements. I said a little slow, to avoid a kind of curt and brusque way that diverts the eyes rather than pierces the heart.

—Francis of Sales

Throughout history, God's spokesmen have addressed a royal court, including Joseph before Pharaoh, Daniel before Nebuchadnezzar, prophets like Micaiah the son of Imlah before Ahab and Jehosophat, and the apostle Paul before King Agrippa. Those who preached before Henry VIII or Elizabeth I did not have an easy road, nor did the court preachers in Germany such as Father Abraham of Vienna or Krummacher, whom we shall consider subsequently. No situation, however, lent itself less to flattery or ease than did the royal court of Louis XIV of France. Yet the Lord raised up one of the brightest and most brilliant array of preachers to articulate his truth for this very opportunity. No doubt rhetorically overwrought at times, this preaching was often ornate, and is frequently called French lacquer style because of its elegance.

The history of preaching shows many curious venues for the proclamation of the truth of God. We return to Bossuet, who did preach at court but was not one of the favorites. Bossuet first came to the attention of high society through an impromptu sermon preached to nobility in the salon of Rambouillet.[1] We now move on to consider the court preachers who emerged in the strategy of divine providence.

None was more lustrous than **Louis Bourdaloue** (1632–1704), a Jesuit born in Bourges, the son of a lawyer. Early on he earned a reputation as one whose preaching missions swayed throngs of hearers. When Bossuet retired from court preaching, Bourdaloue was selected to take his place. For thirty-four years he filled the post as the prime preacher of France and was known as "king of preachers and preacher to kings." Louis XIV loved to hear preaching, and told Bourdaloue that he would rather hear him repeat his sermons every two years than to hear someone else preach new ones.[2]

Bourdaloue did not have the poetic flair of Bossuet, but he had strong personal appeal and impeccable personal integrity. As a teacher first of all, his appeal was to reason. "My design is to convince your reason," he would say. He exhibited strong biblical preaching. The Jesuit John Reville depicts him as logic—force—fire! His messages were "masterpieces of anatomical dissection." He used two or three mains with subs and then a closing peroration for the final assault. His was a manliness of expression, a clarity and earnestness which rushed on "like a swollen stream."

Feugere said of him that he was "as the royal serpent which with velvet coils slowly surrounds the object of its prey, softly, indeed, but in such a way that the captured animal cannot escape."[3] Like Nathan to King David, Bourdaloue preached against the vices of the court specifically. Often he preached with his eyes closed so that he would not be distracted and would open them to powerful effect. On one occasion the king stated after the sermon, "The preacher has done his duty; it is for us to do ours." In a personal interview after an especially probing sermon on sin, Bourdaloue urged the king, "May God in his infinite mercy grant me to see the day when the greatest of monarchs shall be the holiest of kings."[4]

Bourdaloue preached mightily on the passion of Christ. Twin addresses titled "Christ Judged by the World" and "The World Judged by Christ" are particularly incisive. In preaching on impurity and reprobation, he emphasized that the reprobate soul after death faces darkness, disorder, slavery, and remorse.[5] He also preached on Christ's words to the women of Jerusalem who witnessed his crucifixion. Here is his outline:

I. Sin caused the passion;
II. Sin renews the passion, "crucifying Christ afresh";
III. Sin defeats the passion; it breaks the heart of Jesus.

One can only marvel in reading a sermon like "Perverted Conscience" at how apropos his messages were for his audience and how fearless he was. His prayer to the Holy Spirit was: "O Spirit of my God, fountain of all grace, author of all holiness, come! Enlighten and strengthen us. Come! Sanctify this house, which is devoted to you, and which would not be governed but by you, because any other spirit but you would not keep up the regularity, harmony and perfect charity, which have always maintained the peace of God in it."[6]

Another singularly used instrument of righteousness was **Francois de Fénelon** (1651–1715). Fénelon was from a noble family in the south of France. Louis XIV called him "the finest and most visionary thinker in the kingdom." He was trained at Cahors and Paris and served in parish ministry in St. Sulpice in Paris. From early on he had something of Port Royal's "obstinate rationality." He was more tolerant of Protestants than any of the others and known for his cultivation of the interior life. His treatise on *Christian Perfection* is a classic and reflects his drastic theocentricity.[7]

Fénelon taught how to live Christianly in a licentious setting like the royal court. He was noted as an educator of young women and as preceptor of the king's grandson, the Duke of Burgundy. He was deeply infused with Quietistic views and the inspiration of Molinos, the controversial Spanish thinker.

In 1695 Fénelon was named archbishop of Cambray. He and Bossuet tangled over the teachings of Madame Guyon, which according to Fénelon was like all the artillery of heaven firing against a little fly. Consequently Fénelon was banished from court. He retired to his diocese, where he preached and served the poor until his death.

His sermons were carefully written and then delivered from the heart without notes. He wrote a significant work on preaching titled *Dialogues on Eloquence* in which he opts for a simpler, more direct style. He was described as "a tall, thin man of a goodly shape with a large nose, eyes through which the mind poured like a torrent, and a countenance of which I never saw the like, and which, once seen, was never forgotten. It blended every quality, even the most opposite. It had gravity and gallantry, seriousness and gaity; in it you were aware of doctor, bishop and fine gentleman at once: what was most conspicuous in it, as in his whole person, was thought, wit, and graces, decorum, and above all, nobility. It required an effort to cease looking at him."[8]

Called by Saintsbury "the greatest preacher of France," **Jean Baptiste Massilon** (1663–1742) was known as the great searcher of hearts. He hailed from a humble background but became a teacher at both college and seminary levels. In 1693 he was appointed as the head of the seminary at Magloire. Massilon was the Advent preacher at Versailles in 1699 and deeply impressed the king, who said of him, "When I hear most preachers, I am contented with them; when I hear Massilon I am discontented with myself." Even Voltaire praised him for his daring. He preached with a gentle persuasiveness and "spoke to the heart in language always understood." But the domineering mistress of the king was offended by Massilon's preaching, and he did not sustain favor.

Massilon was appointed bishop of Clermont in 1717. His sermon on "The Woman That Was a Sinner" (Luke 7:37ff.) shows clearly why he made some at the court uncomfortable. Yet it was he who preached the funeral of Louis XIV. When he stood in the pulpit at Notre Dame, he paused emphatically and then spoke his first words, "Only God is great!"

Although conscious of Bourdaloue's influence, Massilon was determined to stake out his own turf. Sometimes he would breathe an audible prayer right in the middle of a sermon. Analysis of his sermons is rewarding.[9] Sermon 16 on "The Word of God" (based in Matthew 4:4) is characteristically broken down into mains and subs and colorfully develops the potency of the Word of God. Sermon 17 on "The Delay of Conversion" (based on John 1:23) is overtly evangelistic. Unfortunately neither the king nor his heirs really responded to these watchmen on the walls, and the next centuries were blood-soaked.

Only one preacher of this stature ever emerged in France, and he lived in a later era. Yet we refer now to **Henri Lacordaire** (1802–1861) because he stands squarely in this succession. A Burgundian with great reserve, he testified, "It was in my weary state of isolation and mental sadness that God came to seek me." Lacordaire became conscious of his call to preach but utterly failed in his first attempts. He lamented, "It is evident that I have neither the physical power, nor the mental flexibility, nor the knowledge of a world in which I have lived and always shall live apart; in short, I have nothing to the degree required to be a preacher in the full sense of the word."[10]

Yet Lacordaire stood on the shoulders of the giants, and discovered the reality: "The orator is like the rock of Horeb—until touched of God, it is a barren stone, but once let His finger be laid upon it, and it becomes a fertilizing spring."[11] He occupied the pulpit at Notre Dame in Paris (1843–1851) and was widely known for his conferences on chastity and humility of soul. He was frequently in tears at the cross, "frightened of all this success."[12] He was a member of the French National Assembly and knew de Tocqueville. His preaching conferences in Toulouse in 1854 were epochal. Some marked similarities with the earlier preachers set him apart from his compatriots.

---

1. E. Paxton Hood, *The Throne of Eloquence: Great Preachers, Ancient and Modern* (New York: Funk and Wagnalls, 1888), 9ff.
2. E. C. Dargan, *A History of Preaching* (New York: Hodder and Stoughton, 1912), 2:101.
3. A. E. Garvie, *The Christian Preacher* (New York: Scribner's, 1923), 178.
4. T. Harwood Pattison, *The History of Christian Preaching* (Philadelphia: American Baptist Publication Society, 1903), 230.
5. Dargan, *A History of Preaching,* 105.
6. Pattison, *The History of Christian Preaching,* 226.
7. Francois de Fénelon, *Christian Perfection,* ed. Charles F. Whiston (New York: Harper, 1947); and James Mudge, *Fénelon: The Mystic* (Cincinnati: Jennings and Graham, 1906).
8. Pattison, *The History of Christian Preaching,* 233.
9. *Sermons by John-Baptist Massilon* (Edinburgh: Archibald Allardice, 1824).
10. H. L. Sidney Lear, *Henri Dominique Lacordaire* (London: Rivingtons, 1882), 97.
11. Ibid., 100–101.
12. Ibid., 204.

6.4 GERMAN PREACHERS AND THE RESILIENCY AND RENEWAL OF THE CRAFT

The reformation work of Luther's was to be continued and the church which had become paralyzed in forms of dead doctrinal conformity was to be brought back to the living source of God's Word.
> —Joachim Justus Breithaupt, one of Francke's close associates

The Teutonic and Germanic people have been front and center for many centuries. Yet they did not achieve national unity until well into the nineteenth century. Until then they were largely a collection of highly competitive nobles and various smaller states. After the religious Peace of Augsburg (1555), which essentially endeavored to balance a status quo between Roman Catholics and Protestants, there continued to be intense debate as to its implementation.

The abdication of **Charles the Great** of the Holy Roman Empire in the same year concluded an era.[1] The fierce moves of the Roman Catholic Counter-Reformation complicated a fragile situation. Particularly vexed conflict led to the Thirty Years' War, which began in 1618 and finally ended with the Treaty of Westphalia in 1648. The second phase of this bloody conflict saw the victories of **Gustavus Adolphus** of Sweden, whose father, **Charles IX,** had finally established Protestantism in Sweden by shaking Sweden loose from Polish Catholic control.[2] In an unimaginable ordeal, over half the population of Germany perished in the war itself or through starvation. All of the powers of Europe used Germany as a battleground for vicious internecine slaughter.

---

1. Kurt Aland, *A History of Christianity* (Philadelphia: Fortress, 1986), 2:152ff.
2. Ibid., 213.

6.4.1 THE POST-REFORMATION MOOD IN THE GERMAN CHURCH

Pietism is undoubtedly the most significant movement which has happened within Protestantism since the Reformation.
> —Kurt Aland

Spener was the reformer of the life of the German church *(reformatio vitae),* as Luther was the reformer of its doctrine *(reformatio doctrinae).*
> —John Ker

The effect of the Thirty Years' War on the churches was numbing. Yet additional factors led to the decline of preaching in Germany from Luther's death until Philipp Spener. Germany was virtually a desert after this fratricidal futility. Controversy between Roman Catholics and Protestants and controversies between factions among the Protestants quenched vitality. Calixtus of Helmstadt was at the throat of Calovius of Koenigsberg in the so-called syncretism debate.[1] What is more, orthodoxy shriveled in arid speculation and a constrictive hardening of the categories. Doctrine and rigid confessionalization supplanted Scripture as the prime focus. The sermons dried up. Aristotelianism reappeared. Baptismal regeneration was central. Stoeffer in his classic analysis shows that *fiducia* became *assenus* and there was general ethical insensitivity.[2] One observer offered the comment: "Churchly oratory discards Scripture; this logic and polemic can not minister to edification."[3]

Garvie describes a volume of sermons from **Jacob Andrea** preached in 1658 in Esslingen: one quarter consists of sermons against the Papists; one quarter against the Zwinglians; one quarter against the Schwenkfeldians, the mystics and perfectionists of the times; and one quarter against the Anabaptists.[4] This is surely a stack of straw for hungry hearts!

Of course there were substantive issues often discussed as when **Andrew Osiander,** one of the pioneers in the Reformation, argued that justification was not forensic, nor was it imputed but infused (he confused justification with sanctification).[5] In all of this there was an unabated hunger for the Word of God. Forgetting the legacy of Hyperius, preachers turned to **Andreas Pancratius,** who advocated synthetic or topical preaching. He dismissed analytic preaching or the division of a text.

The answer to the extended spiritual drought came in the spiritual renewal called Pietism, which corresponded in some significant ways with Jansenism in France and Puritanism in England.

One who embodied the longing for spiritual life and who is often called father of German Pietism is **Johann Arndt** (1555–1621). This second phase of the Protestant Reformation has important linkage to English Puritans and to Jeremy Taylor. It also draws heavily on the mystical and relational emphases in Luther, who like Arndt loved Tauler, and *Theologia Germanica,* which emphasized the life of self-denial. Some have too strongly stated the roots of Pietism in medieval mysticism[6] and nudged Pietism too close to Boehme's pantheistic and Rosicrucian ties. There are tinges of Theosophy and Christadelphianism here.

Arndt avoided the exaggerated subjectivism of mysticism with a virile "Christmysticism" (to use Deissman's good phrase). He was a pastor's son but was orphaned early and reared by friends. While studying medicine, he was converted and felt God's call to ministry. His concern was with the practical Christian life. Arndt was a staunch advocate of daily Bible reading and devotions. He was troubled by what seemed to be a contradiction in Luther between "justification by faith alone" and baptismal regeneration. He strongly preached conversion in the churches he served. He stressed union with Christ. An overlay of amorous language from the Song of Solomon is perceptible in his style.

The most powerful of his written works, *True Christianity,* is an exposition of *unio mystica.*[7] Arndt at this point was influential in the thinking of Albert Schweitzer, who testified, "In my youth I gained from my mother a love for Arndt; he was a prophet of interior Protestantism."[8] Arndt's writings and sermons also helped mold Spener and others. He was firmly anchored in Scripture, as we note in "God's Word Must Demonstrate Its Power in Man through Faith and Become Living."[9] Arndt's thrust is plain: "God gave the whole of the Holy Scriptures in spirit and in faith and everything in them must happen in you spiritually."

Others who followed Arndt were the cousins **John Gerhard** (1582–1637), whose sermons were heavy yet warming, and **Paul Gerhard** (1607–1676), the great hymnwriter whose hymns are still sung, such as "O Jesus, Thy Boundless Love to Me."[10]

The glaciers were receding in this spiritual ice age. A thawing was taking place. It would soon be spring.

---

1. John Ker, *Lectures on the History of Preaching* (New York: Armstrong, 1889), 171. Ker is especially helpful on the German picture while totally neglectful of almost all else.
2. F. Ernest Stoeffer, *The Rise of Evangelical Pietism* (Leiden, Netherlands: E. J. Brill, 1965). A masterpiece!
3. E. C. Dargan, *A History of Preaching* (New York: Hodder and Stoughton, 1912), 2:64.
4. A. E. Garvie, *The Christian Preacher* (New York: Scribner's, 1923), 143–44.
5. Reinhold Seeberg, *Textbook of the History of Doctrines* (Grand Rapids: Baker, 1952, reprint), 2:369ff.
6. As Emil Brunner's statement, "Squeezed in between rationalism and orthodoxy, and mediating between them at the same time as it was marked off from both, a place was found for Pietism, a mode of understanding faith, the deepest roots must be sought in medieval mysticism," as given in Peter C. Erb, *Pietists, Protestants and Mysticism* (Metuchen, N.J.: Scarecrow, 1989), 1.
7. Peter Erb, trans., Johan Arndt's *True Christianity* (New York: Paulist, 1979).
8. Ibid., 1.
9. Ibid., 49ff.
10. The whole matter of artistic expression in relation to preaching is beyond our scope, but suffice it to say that paintings by Dürer and Grunewald and Rembrandt's magnificent "Christ Preaching" rendered in 1650 are significant ancillary considerations for our study as well as the hymns and oratorios. Note Jane Dillenberger, *Style and Content in Christian Art* (New York: Crossroad, 1986), 181ff.

6.4.2 THE POST-REFORMATION MOVEMENT OF SPIRITUAL AWAKENING IN THE GERMAN CHURCH

German Pietism was essentially a preaching movement.

—Martin Schmidt

With the Pietists everything began at the very beginning with the Exposition of Scripture.

—Kurt Aland

Of the Pietistic movement and the quickening it brought to Germany and Scandinavia and beyond,[1] John Ker writes:

For a whole century after the death of the leaders of the Reformation, Germany was in a state of spiritual hardness and coldness of the most distressing kind. The warmth and life were chiefly in polemical passion. Witnesses for the better kind of Christianity were rare, and they were subjected to bitter attacks as enthusiasts. Yet a genuine revival came in the course of the seventeen century, and we shall hope that another and a more lasting one will dispel the rationalism of the present day.[2]

The church was in large part "a magnificent neological ice palace," when the mighty breath of the Spirit arrived. Peter Erb calls it, "The most important development in Protestant spirituality."[3] The summons was to new life in Christ, to regeneration of the sinner, and the nurture of the spiritually newborn. As Van Oosterzee insisted:

> Spener did succeed in recalling to life the spirit of Luther and Arndt in many a pulpit, and in making the preaching a powerful embodiment of the theologia regenitorum.[4]

The result was a reshaping of theological education (and the establishment of Halle University). Preaching was stimulated, hymnody revitalized, the growth of family worship appeared, charitable institutions were built, and a whole new missionary impetus began. John Wesley was heir to the best in Pietism in his insistence: "Let us unite the two so long divided—knowledge and vital piety." There is much here in emphasis on personal relationship to Christ that replicates the English Puritans such as William Perkins, Henry Smith, Richard Sibbes, and Bishop Joseph Hall. Echoes of the same are seen on the Continent in Reformed circles represented by William Teelinck, William Ames (who fled to Holland), Jean de Labadie, and the hymnwriters and poets, Joachim Neander and Tersteegen. The focus was on meeting and knowing the living Christ through the Spirit by the Word.

Yet the word "Pietism" is virtually pejorative in many circles. Dale Brown calls Pietism "one of the least understood movements in Judeo-Christian history."[5] Barth had a strong aversion to it. Martin Marty argued that "Pietism was one of the major strides of Christian retreat from responsibility." Albrecht Ritschl in three volumes lobbed the charge that Pietism was too individualistic, too separatistic, and too anti-intellectual (despite the fact that Spener's M.A. was on Thomas Hobbes, and Francke was in much dialogue with the philosopher Leibniz). Troeltsch terms it a sect.

Pietists were immediately embroiled in dispute and controversy. Francke and friends were expelled from Leipzig and Erfurt. Aland concedes a kind of "narrowness" in early Pietism (one might add that this is found in any reforming wedge such as Puritanism or Jansenism),[6] but Francke and his cohorts were protesting against the absence of any lectures or studies on the exposition of Scripture. This was a Bible movement tingling with eschatological urgency. No wonder Cotton Mather in correspondence with Francke in 1715 fairly chortled:

> The world begins to feel a warmth from the fire of God which thus flames in the heart of Germany, beginning to extend into many regions; the whole world will ere long be sensible of it.[7]

But there was danger here. Webber worries about confessional erosion, about the replacement of justification by sanctification. The strong emphasis on holiness makes any good Lutheran skittish (remember Luther's problem with "good works" and the Book of James), but he overstates a bit when he says that "in its final stages Pietism degenerated into salvation by good works rather than by the grace of God in Christ."[8]

We cannot totally dismiss the concern. Immanuel Kant was raised a Pietist. Schleiermacher, "the father of German liberalism," who exchanged theology for psychology, along with his father was trained at Herrnhut and studied and taught at Halle (1787–1789), although he was much influenced by romanticism also.[9] Johan Semler, the rationalist and early higher critic, was an ardent Pietist who conducted family devotions with fervor.

The University of Halle was the first to succumb to rationalism. The peril in protesting against dead orthodoxy and emblazoning the appeal for new life is ultimately to exalt the ethical and demote the doctrinal. John Baillie argues that Kant's dictum "I must therefore abolish knowledge to make room for faith" betrays his Pietistic proclivity.[10] Neve concedes that "the pietistic way of life and theological liberalism may go a long way together." Paul Fuhrman's trenchant descriptive refers to "liberalism's insistence on the primacy of life over doctrine."[11] Neve well demonstrated that Baxterianism (Richard Baxter, to whom we shall refer at length in the next chapter) was "a theology which furnished doctrinal foundations for his type of ardent Pietism, but which after him contributed to breaking down the forms of doctrine and polity and conservative theology in England." Numbers of his followers became Arians and anti-Trinitarian.[12] Zinzendorf also veered toward some odd views on the Trinity, but J. A. Bengel corrected him. When under the influence of Pietism a brother pleads: "No creed, no loyalty oaths, no worship forms, no hierarchical traditions, no dogmatics," we know the fox is in the henhouse.[13]

Thus Ritschl's criticism of "separatism" and undue individualism is belied with but few early exceptions by subsequent history.[14] Pietists tended to become experience-oriented in their quest for ecumenism, and hence are quite broad. Pietistically based fellowships were not the only ones to be infected by liberalism and rationalism, but they were among the first to go. The achievement of balance between doctrine and life is not easy, but it is imperative. As R. V. G. Tasker says so well: "The appeal to live a Christian life must always be based upon Christian doctrine. . . . If Christian ethical standards are being abandoned, it must always be because Christian faith is weak."[15]

1. Valdis Mezezers, *The Herrnhuterian Pietism in the Baltic and Its Outreach into America and Elsewhere in the World* (North Quincy, Mass.: Christopher, 1975). In 1736 Zinzendorf went to Riga in Latvia; a great revival broke out in 1739, out of which hundreds of missionaries went forth.

2. John Ker, *Lectures on the History of Preaching* (New York: Armstrong, 1889), 180.

3. F. Ernest Stoeffler, *Classics of Western Spirituality: Pietists—Selected Writings* (New York: Paulist, 1983), ix.

4. Quoted in A. E. Garvie, *The Christian Preacher* (New York: Scribner's, 1923), 187.
5. Dale Brown, *Understanding Pietism* (Grand Rapids: Eerdmans, 1978). The thesis of this book goes to the point of "The Problem of Subjectivism in Pietism."
6. Kurt Aland, *A History of Christianity* (Philadelphia: Fortress, 1986), 2:226–245. An important discussion.
7. John T. McNeil, *Modern Christian Movements* (Philadelphia: Westminster, 1954), 74.
8. F. R. Webber, *A History of British and American Preaching* (Milwaukee: Northwestern, 1952), 2:281.
9. J. L. Neve, *A History of Christian Thought* (Philadelphia: Muhlenberg, 1946), 2:104.
10. John Baillie, *The Idea of Revelation in Recent Thought* (New York: Columbia University Press, 1956), 10.
11. Paul Fuhrman, *God-Centered Religion* (Grand Rapids: Zondervan, 1942), 21.
12. Neve, *A History of Christian Thought,* 31.
13. David L. Larsen, "The Perils of Pietism," a lecture to the Southern California Covenant Ministers, December 28, 1959, published in the *California Covenanter,* July 27, 1961, 4ff. John Sailhamer points out that Professor Sigmund Baumgarten of the University of Halle provided the "decisive turning point from a view of Scripture as revelation to a view of Scripture as a record of revelation in events"; see *The Pentateuch as Narrative* (Grand Rapids: Zondervan, 1992), 28 n. 32. This is a tragically significant paradigm shift.
14. Koppel S. Pinson, *Pietism as a Factor in the Rise of German Nationalism* (New York: Octagon, 1968).
15. R. V. G. Tasker, *The Gospel in the Epistle to the Hebrews* (London: Tyndale, 1950), 51.

6.4.3   THE POST-REFORMATION MESSENGERS OF THE WORD IN THE GERMAN CHURCH

While the older preachers made the teaching of orthodoxy and the refutation of gainsayers their principal end and aim, from Pietist pulpits there was heard little besides the sinfulness of man, the need of repentance, and the merits of Christ. That tares were mingled with the wheat in the field of Pietism, that some Pietists held extravagant opinions and that others were little better than hypocrites, seems to admit no doubt; but also it cannot be doubted that they infused a new life into the Lutheran community at a time when the lamp of Christian life burned very low.

—S. Cheetham, *A History of the Christian Church,* London, 1907

Having looked at certain of the proto-Pietists, we now turn to the patriarch of the Pietists, called by some the second Luther. **Philipp Jacob Spener** (1635–1705) was born in the Alsace into a godly and devout home. He was educated in Strasbourg, where among other studies he learned Hebrew from an erudite Jew. (Spener always had a great love for the Jews and believed in a great day of conversion and glory for the Jewish people.) He was by temperament a gentle man who spoke softly. He studied a year in Geneva and came to know **Jean Labadie** (1610–1674), who in quest of a pure church left the Reformed church.

Labadie's emphasis on small groups and his fiery preaching left a deep mark on Spener. He also had some contact with Geger the Waldensian in Geneva.

Some are very nervous about admitting Reformed influence on Spener and any kind of cross-fertilization at this time, but the lines do cross. No one has demonstrated this more adeptly than W. R. Ward, who points out that Francke and all the Protestants read Molinos. Puritan works flooded into Germany. John Bunyan was read at the Halle orphanage when no actual preacher was present.[1]

Spener subscribed to Lutheran orthodoxy, but he felt the Reformation was not finished. He stood unequivocally for "the absolute authority of Scripture" (F. E. Stoeffer) and "verbal inspiration" (Dale Brown). He promoted the exaltation of Scripture and encouraged a renewed interest in the biblical languages. Spener emphasized the necessity of a personal relationship with the Lord. Rebirth (or *wiedergeburt*) was the subject for one collection of sixty-six sermons.[2]

Spener commends the sentiments of the Lutheran theologian **David Chytraeus** (1531–1600), who was a professor at Rostock and whose important and thoroughly Anselmian work *On Sacrifice* has now been translated.[3] While Luther held to the imminency of Christ's second coming, it was Spener who introduced chiliasm, or the belief in the one thousand year millennial reign of Christ, into Lutheranism.[4] His doctoral dissertation was on Revelation 9:13–21 and shows his belief in the imminent wrap-up of human history. He was also a student of Joachim of Fiore.[5]

In 1666, Spener took a call to be senior minister in Frankfurt-am-Main. Here he developed his conventical groups and pushed confirmation as a requirement for the training of youth. He edged away from the preaching of the pericope toward something more solidly expository. Lutheran orthodoxy used several approaches in preaching but was greatly influenced by English preaching. Spener felt a keen affinity for the Epistles of Paul and preached them most frequently; for this he was faulted. From 1686 to 1691 he was Saxon court preacher in Dresden, where he had his first contacts with Francke. From 1691 to 1705 he was first minister at the St. Nicholas Church in Berlin, from which vantage point he shaped the new university in Halle. Sometime after blessing his godchild, Nicholas von Zinzendorf, he died at the age of seventy and was buried in the St. Nicholas Church, where his wife is also interred.

In his *Pia Desideria* (holy longings), an introduction he wrote for Arndt's *True Christianity,* he encapsulated the essential thrusts of Pietism:

1. spread the Word of God
2. emphasize the priesthood of all believers
3. cultivate the inner spiritual life
4. remember that truth can be lost in disputes
5. candidates for the ministry should be true Christians
6. sermons should edify the hearers

These symbolic points were augmented by detailed instructions against dancing and the like.[6] The ascetic strain in Spener also came to the fore in his lengthy statement on drinking in *Pia Desideria.*

Spener's own preaching tended to be lengthy. His exegesis was solid but he used no illustration to speak of. Contrary to prevailing practice, he did omit extensive Greek and Latin quotations. Clearly, he is not the colorful character that Luther was. His personal reserve is reflected in his sermons, but he made a positive impression:

> Not exceeding medium height, his physical form slim and yet equal to the task of the office, his pale face which created a sense of strength of judgment and a deep sense of contemplation, his very prominent brow with eyes clear and piercing, but moderated with a sweet modesty, his nose inclined somewhat to aquiline form, his mouth a little drawn apart, with the whole face reflecting a serene tranquillity with kindness.[7]

The golden age of Pietism was entrusted to **August Hermann Francke** (1663–1727), who was born in Lubeck and who found Arndt's *True Christianity* his companion through youth. He was converted in 1687 and drawn into the Spenerian circle. He stayed for awhile with the Speners and then moved to Halle. He "conserved and compacted Spener's insights," holding steadily the "Lutheran regard for the objective authority of Scripture."[8] Like Spener, he loved Hebrew and Greek, and one year read the Hebrew Old Testament through seven times under the guidance of a Jewish rabbi. In 1691 he became professor of Hebrew and Greek at Halle and pastor of St. George's Church in Glaucha to ensure adequate income.

Francke was a model pastor, enjoying pastoral calls and personal contact with his congregants (something quite innovative), and loving to preach three times a week. He was outstanding as an educator of children, and founded orphanages. He was a visionary for missions and corresponded with Leibniz about China. He influenced the schools of Russia through his contacts with Peter the Great, whose wife once visited the Halle institutions incognito.[9] Francke also sent quantities of Bibles to Swedish prisoners in Siberia (which was a factor in the spread of Pietism to Sweden).

In 1716, Francke was named vice-chancellor of the university and faced the massive incursions of the Enlightenment upon the simple faith of Halle Pietism. An activist in every respect and well designated the Melancthon of Pietism, Francke worked himself to exhaustion and died at the age of fifty-four.

Francke may have been a more effective preacher than Spener. His delivery was livelier, and he gave more thought to rhetorical aspects of communication. Like Spener, his sermons were long to the point of prolixity. His mighty message on "The Doctrine of Our Lord Jesus Christ Concerning Rebirth" (based on John 3:1–16) had a double introduction and five parts. His sermon on the rich man and Lazarus did not fixate on aspects of the afterlife but properly on Jesus' point, "Our Duty to the Poor."[10]

The contacts and outreach of Pietistic life and "the simple Halle Gospel" were astounding. The bottom line for Francke was conversion as an object: "Gospel preachers should constantly make it their aim and direction of their preaching to lead their hearers to Christ and to His grace."[11]

There were also radical Pietists, like **Gottfried Arnold** (1666–1714) from Saxony, who was influenced by Spener to enter pastoral ministry. Both Spener and Francke made immense spiritual impact on Arnold. Laxity among believers led Arnold into the radical camp. Ironically this movement veered toward separatism and indifference to basic theological formulation in matters touching universalism, Arianism, the church, and even a negative view toward Scripture.[12] As time passed, Arnold's pastoral instincts brought him back toward the center. However, with **Johan Dippel** (who substituted "Christ in us" for "Christ for us") and **Gerhard Tersteegen** (1697–1769, "the poet-laureate of the interior life" but termed "pagan mystic" by Ritschl), he remained on the fringes of Pietism.

Pietism in Wurtenberg centered at the University of Tubingen and flourished between 1680 and 1775. Spener visited often. Reuchlin (1660–1707) held a conventicle in his home.[13] Here **Johan Albrecht Bengel** (1687–1752) also held forth. His eschatologically oriented theology was shaped by the influences of Cocceius, Vitringa, and Lampe of Halle. John Wesley called him "the great light of the Christian world." He set the date of 1836 for the Second Advent of Christ.

Nicholas von Zinzendorf (1700–1760) was born in Dresden and reared by his maternal grandmother, who knew Spener. A brilliant student at Halle, Zinzendorf settled Moravian emigres at his ancestral estate, where he founded Herrnhut. He made many evangelistic tours, including a visit to America. Although his "blood and wounds cult" was extreme, we treasure his hymn "Jesus Thy Blood and Righteousness."

Revivals soon swept through central Europe and involved many children. The people were being "converted by revival preaching."[14] What was transpiring in Europe had effect elsewhere. Muhlenberg, the Lutheran leader in America, used so many Hallesian preachers that some of his followers went West to produce a pure church (the origins of the Missouri Synod). Doddridge's grandfather was from Bohemia. John Wesley, who visited Herrnhut and Halle, married a Huguenot widow. George I of England had a chaplain who was in close contact with Francke, as was George Whitefield. Trevacca, the training school of the Countess of Huntingdon, was derived from the Halle pattern, and John Fletcher, its great leader, was from Switzerland. Ward, who traces all of these cross-connections, reminds us that there was no insularity in what the Spirit of God was doing in this powerful time of preaching.

---

1. W. R. Ward, *The Protestant Evangelical Awakening* (Cambridge, Mass.: Cambridge University Press, 1992). A helpful note on Jean Labadie is found in John Ker, *Lectures on the History of Preaching* (New York: Armstrong, 1889), 199.
2. Manfred Waldemar Kohl, "Wiedergeburt as the Central Theme in Pietism," *Covenant Quarterly* (November 1974): 15ff.
3. John Warwick Montgomery, *Chartraeus on Sacrifice* (St. Louis: Concordia, 1962).
4. Ward, *The Protestant Evangelical Awakening,* 51.
5. K. James Stein, *Philipp Jakob Spener: Pietist Patriarch* (Chicago: Covenant, 1986), 67.
6. F. Ernest Stouffer, *The Rise of Evangelical Pietism* (Leiden, Netherlands: E. J. Brill, 1965). A brilliant study.

7. Stein, *Philipp Jakob Spener,* 268. It is significant that Richard Lischer in *Theories of Preaching: Selected Readings in the Homiletical Tradition* (Durham, N.C.: Labyrinth Press, 1987), 60ff. includes Philip Jacob Spener under the heading, "The Reform of Preaching," stressing the inner transformation of the preacher and his hearers.

8. F. Ernest Stouffer, *German Pietism During the Eighteenth Century* (Leiden, Netherlands: E. J. Brill, 1973). Invaluable.

9. Gary R. Sattler, *God's Glory, Neighbor's Good: A Brief Introduction to the Life and Writings of August Hermann Francke* (Chicago: Covenant, 1982), 77.

10. Ibid., for a choice collection of Francke's sermons, 113ff.

11. For analysis of this line of influence, particularly in the Danish mission to India, see Kenneth Scott Latourette, *A History of the Expansion of Christianity: Three Centuries of Advance* (Grand Rapids: Zondervan, 1970), 3:277–81; *The Great Century: Europe and the United States* (Grand Rapids: Zondervan, 1970), 4:90, 92. In thinking of the Danish-Halle mission, we must remember the Danish royal court was the most Pietistic at this time.

12. Peter C. Erb, *Pietists, Protestants, and Mysticism: The Use of Late Medieval Spiritual Texts in the Work of Gottfried Arnold* (Metuchen, N.J.: Scarecrow, 1989), 38.

13. F. Ernest Stouffer, *German Pietism during the Eighteenth Century* (Leiden, Netherlands: E. J. Brill, 1973).

14. Ward, *The Protestant Evangelical Awakening,* 112. This volume is a masterpiece of erudition and inspiration.

6.5 THE COUNTER-REFORMATION AND THE RIVALS IN THE CRAFT

It is the office of the ecclesiastical orator to open up for the people the truth and the secrets of God, to teach men and women how to live piously and innocently, to abolish those most repulsive errors, destructive superstitions, depraved customs, and compel men and women to the pious, true, and divine wisdom and to the Christian religion; to nourish the souls of their listeners with a knowledge of the truth (than which there is no more pleasant food). For the preacher, this is the proposed end: by persuading to increase the kingdom of God, to acquire souls for Christ, to adorn the holy Church, to lessen the tyranny of the devil, excite souls redeemed by the precious blood of Christ to eternal life and beatitude.
—Agostino Valiero, bishop of Verona (1531–1606)

After the Council of Trent (1545–1563), the Roman Catholic Church gave itself to the improvement of preaching, As in England, France, and Germany the seventeenth century, a "golden age of preaching," can be seen in Roman Catholic countries like Spain and Italy.[1] It was an age of eloquence throughout the West.

Even in staunchly Roman Catholic Italy, there were voices raised for the gospel of the grace of God, although any idea of justification by faith alone was quickly quashed. **Cardinal Contarini** (d. 1542), who was papal representative at the Colloquy of Ratisbon, agreed with the Reformers on justification.

Some in this circle fled, like **Peter Martyr,** and many were killed. **Juan de Valdes** (d. 1541), of Spanish nobility, fled from the Spanish Inquisition to Italy.

Ministering in Naples, Valdes wrote many books, including a solid commentary on Matthew and *The Spiritual Alphabet* (c. 1536), which trumpeted the doctrine of justification.[2] At the heart of his ministry was the cross of Christ and the doctrine of satisfaction.

A Benedictine monk and friend of Valdes, **Don Benedetto** (d. 1544) wrote *Benefit of Christ,* which was translated into French, German, English, and Croatian. These works are now available in English editions. The latter, as Leon Morris observes in an introduction to the treatise, majors in the finished work of Jesus Christ on the cross.[3] In Benedetto we also sense a radiant joy in Christ. But the momentum of the Counter-Reformation did not leave many vestiges of the gospel of grace in southern Europe.

In the current popularity of historical rhetoric we are seeing some remarkable studies, among which is certainly McGinness's thorough piece on the revival of sacred oratory in Rome. The success of Protestant preaching obviously spurred Roman Catholics to new emphasis on preaching. The Council of Trent specifically addressed its importance. The Fifth Lateran Council's concern about "the ills of preaching" had not made much difference.[4] Preaching was one of the keys of Protestant appeal, and efforts were now joined to rally Catholicism's dormant pulpits. The Council of Trent called on preachers above all "to concern themselves with the Gospel of Jesus Christ . . . that sermons be scriptural, and that preachers take up the Gospel everyday and 'never omit mentioning what occurred in that passage of the Gospel.'"[5]

Older medieval homiletical patterns were discarded, although there was still a considerable appeal to St. Francis and the resuscitation of preaching under his auspices. Preachers were urged to avoid scholastic debate and nit-picking in favor of "the matter necessary for salvation." Even preaching on the Second Coming of Christ was common in this eschatologically charged time. The object of preaching was to move the will, not simply to inform the mind and titillate the emotions. Persuasion was seen as essential to the process.[6]

Changing tastes in the Sistine Chapel indicate a preaching revival subsequent to the Council of Trent. The Catechism of the Council of Trent was published in 1566, and stressed doctrine and oratorical skills. All over Rome, preaching gained in popularity and in quality. But the message, while ostensibly concerning Christ, was highly synergistic as a whole, semi-Pelagian at best, and heavily moralistic.[7] Unmerited favor was in evidence in baptismal regeneration, but in so-called second justification human works and deeds were necessary to sustain a right relationship to God. The intrusion of the treasury of merit, Mariolatry, saints, and relics all conspired to dim any perception of the true nature of saving and sustaining grace.

Seventeenth-century preaching in Rome saw considerable refinement in the art of amplification in the sermon.[8] The technique of outdistancing in preaching, that is, having each point exceed the previous point in scope and size, was widely utilized. Of course some invective against the heretics flavored Catholic communication, and an increasingly triumphalistic tone put forth the pope as the only reliable guide. His dignity and jurisdiction were seen as undeniably *de iure divino*. Pancgyrics for the bishop of Rome were common. Preaching emphasized classical rhetoric and humanistic pursuits. The flurry of interest in the pulpit began to subside before the century was over.

The thrust of the Counter-Reformation was felt worldwide. Its chief architect, the Basque **Ignatius Loyola** (1491–1556), became a soldier for Christ in the Society of Jesus, which he founded after a cannonball fractured his right leg in battle in 1521. His *Spiritual Exercises* are still classic and record the single-mindedness of a man who dedicated himself to exterminating Protestants. The growth of his movement was phenomenal. Notwithstanding his fanaticism, Ignatius had a deep spiritual commitment, considering himself and his compatriots as "the companions of Jesus," although he maintained a special devotion to the Queen of Heaven.

Ignatius personally commissioned young **Francis Xavier** (1506–1552), who was born in Pamplona, Spain, of aristocratic parents. Trained at the University of Paris, Francis was ordained by Ignatius to propagate the gospel. Sponsored by the Portuguese, at thirty-five he went to India. Troubled that the Portuguese seemed to be in India only for pepper and pearls, he gave himself to preaching. Subsequently he went to Malacca in the East Indies, to Japan (where he was struck by the magnificent squalor of Kyoto), and close to China.

Preaching was primary for Francis, and he was unusually gifted at it.[9] De Wohl says of him, "Francis preached either in good French or in bad Italian. He had no inhibitions about speaking in a language of which he knew only a couple of thousand words, if that many. Somehow they understood him, he knew that."[10] What gripped Francis throughout was the Lord's question: "What shall it profit a man if he gain the whole world and lose his soul?" But as his mission work unfolded, "There was no time for preaching," and the abuses of mass baptisms took place.[11] Francis died at forty-five, exhausted and emaciated. If only his great gifts had focused on the "riches of God's grace" and "the riches of God's glory."

The danger in the preaching of this century was that of pulpit pretension and false finery, what Paxton Hood termed "pulpit pedantry." At what point do style and form distract from the biblical message? When does the packaging conceal the truth?

1. A probing study is Hilary Dansey Smith, *Preaching in the Spanish Golden Age* (Oxford: Oxford University Press, 1978). J. M. Neale mentions Antonio Vieyra (1608–1697), a Jesuit, who preached in the royal chapel in Lisbon and who ministered between Portugal and Brazil, where he died. His sermons were eminently biblical and occasionally tinged with great irony. In Spain, Paravicino, Francesco Blamas, and Francesco Labata are mentioned by Dargan.
2. James M. Houston, Juan de Valdes and Don Benedetto, *The Benefit of Christ,* in the Classics of Faith and Devotion Series (Portland, Oreg.: Multnomah, 1984).
3. Ibid., xiii.
4. Frederick J. McGinness, *Right Thinking and Sacred Oratory in Counter-Reformation Rome* (Princeton, N.J.: Princeton University Press, 1995), 34.
5. Ibid., 45.
6. Ibid., 56.

7. Ibid., 99.

8. Ibid., 105. Paul Scott Wilson introduces us to Alphonsus Liguori (1696–1787), a law-yer who became a gifted preacher and founded a preaching order, the Redemptorists. He wrote one hundred books and prescribed two- or three-week preaching missions. He also practiced street preaching. He used "the great sermon" for adults and "the small sermon" for children in another place so as not to strip the sermon of its sub-stance. See Paul Scott Wilson, *A Concise History of Preaching* (Nashville: Abingdon, 1992), 115–22. His critics complained his results were short-lived.

9. Louis de Wohl, *Set All Afire (Ignatius)* (San Francisco: Ignatius, 1953), 29, 39. A novel.

10. Ibid., 56. John W. O'Malley in his *The First Jesuits* (Cambridge, Mass.: Harvard University Press, 1993) shows how "itinerant preachers . . . engaged in a holiness ministry" made immense impact. Cf. also W. W. Meissner, *Ignatius of Loyola* (New Haven, Conn.: Yale University Press, 1992).

11. Jonathan D. Spence, *The Memory Palace of Matteo Ricci* (New York: Penguin, 1983). This is the skillful portrait of a Jesuit who went to China to minister to the Ming Dynasty. Since the Madonna and child were more appealing to the Chinese than the crucified Christ (even though Loyola's exercises called for the Jesuits to live as if Jesus Christ were being crucified before their eyes), they redrafted the gospel mes-sage to appeal to the refined tastes of the Chinese literati and omitted significant emphasis on the cross. Professor Hugh Trevor-Roper of Oxford observed that what was left was "an unobjectionable residue, with no divine power to win converts." How much better to share "Christ and him crucified" which is "the wisdom and power of God."

CHAPTER SEVEN

The Robust Days of the Puritan Pulpit

A man finds joy in giving an apt reply—and how good is a timely word!
—Proverbs 15:23

Jesus answered, "It is written: 'Man does not live on bread alone, but on every word that comes from the mouth of God.'"
—Matthew 4:4

It has always been my ambition to preach the gospel where Christ was not known. . . . Now to him who is able to establish you by my gospel and the proclamation of Jesus Christ, according to the revelation of the mystery hidden for long ages past, but now revealed and made known through the prophetic writings by the command of the eternal God, so that all nations might believe and obey him—to the only wise God be glory forever through Jesus Christ! Amen.
—Romans 15:20; 16:25–27

But as surely as God is faithful, our message to you is not "Yes" and "No." For the Son of God, Jesus Christ, who was preached among you by me and Silas and Timothy, was not "Yes" and "No," but in him it has always been "Yes."
—2 Corinthians 1:18–19

Now when I went to Troas to preach the gospel of Christ and found that the Lord had opened a door for me. . . . Unlike so many, we do not peddle the word of God for profit. On the contrary, in Christ we speak before God with sincerity, like men sent from God.
—2 Corinthians 2:12, 17

What they wanted in strength, they supplied in activity; but what won them repute was their ministers' painful preaching in populous places; it being observed in England that those who hold the helm of the pulpit always steer people's hearts as they please.

—Thomas Fuller, speaking of the Puritans

We have already noted the vital spiritual movements of the seventeenth century such as the Jansenists in France and the Pietists of Central Europe and surges of biblical preaching in England, France, Germany, and even Spain and Italy. Yet we have now before us one of the most extraordinary developments in the history of preaching, special in the depth of its biblicality, the scope of its address to the times, the sweep of its influence in Europe, and its spread with such vitality to the New World.

Puritanism has frequently been vilified as a failure of ideas, a fallback to reactionism, and a fiasco in society and culture. As we shall see, this is not an adequate representation. Puritanism was a reform movement in the Church of England, beginning in the sixteenth century and flourishing in the seventeenth, but still reverberating in our own time. Puritanism had theological, political, ecclesiastical, and polemical aspects. Puritans were not all cut from the same piece of cloth. There were Anglican and separatist Puritans; there were hyper-Calvinistic and Arminian Puritans; there were moderates and radicals. Puritanism was a revival movement, and it stirred generations for God. At its core was the preaching of the Word of God.

There are those who virtually beatify Puritanism. There are indeed happily many lines of interrelationship between Continental Pietism and Puritanism. Yet there are also blemishes and blight in Puritanism that we must face as we consider its preaching. We must also beware of the impossible and less than prudent dedication to recreating Puritanism in our own time. We can learn many lessons from our earlier brothers and sisters in all movements of God in the church, but the replication of any era (even the apostolic age in its fine-lined detail) is neither possible nor desirable.

7.1 THE GENEALOGY OF THE PURITANS

Promote preaching of the word of faith which is so powerful . . . for faith comes by the word preached.

—Thomas Watson

What power and efficacy the word hath . . . it is a word that changeth and altereth the whole man.

—Richard Sibbes

The roots of Puritanism trace back to John Wycliffe and the Lollards through the Reformers, via the theological insights of Cranmer and the preaching of Latimer. The Elizabethan Settlement in 1558–59 brought back Protestantism, but it was a compromise that did not please all. Those who wanted a cleaner sweep of Romish vestigial remains were first called Puritans in 1566, or precisions by some. Theirs was a simple biblical faith, a strong preference for low church and even free liturgy, and a nonhierarchical mode of church governance. It should not be supposed that Puritanism was a monolith since there was great divergence on many issues, but the unifying thread was the desire for the purification of the church and an abiding dissatisfaction with the Tudor modus operandi.

The initial issues were trivial: the use of the sign of the cross in baptism, the ring in marriage ceremonies, and the wearing of the surplice during the services (the Vestiarian controversy).[1] Differences in theology (Calvinism versus Arminianism); differences in polity (conflicts over the episcopacy versus Presbyterianism); and differences in practice (the Sabbatarian issue for instance) all became part of the simmering broth. Some plainly and simply opted for total separation, such as **Robert Browne** (1550–1633), whose Brownists cut loose completely and whose heirs included the Pilgrim Fathers. They went from Scrooby in England to Leiden in Holland under the leadership of William Brewster. They then went on to establish Plymouth Colony in the New World in 1620.[2]

Stoeffer sees Puritanism and Pietism as "the second phase of the Reformation," as experiential Protestantism.[3] Puritanism was a total worldview with implications for all of life and existence: a new piety, a new politics, a new person, the "citizen activist."[4] As those who had taken refuge on the Continent returned to England, their ideas seemed threatening to the queen and to the ecclesiarchs generally. When James I was crowned, he convened the Hampton Court Conference in 1604 to resolve the tensions between the Puritans and the High Church party entrenched in the Church of England. A few minuscule changes were made in the ritual, but apart from the authorization of the King James Version of the Bible the positions of the respective parties only hardened. M. Lloyd-Jones emphasizes Tyndale and his bibliocentrism and John Knox and his vehement preaching as profoundly formative in their influence (agreeing with Thomas Carlyle that Knox is "the founder of Puritanism").[5]

What Lloyd-Jones termed "a continuous and persistent sense of dissatisfaction"[6] led to endless conflict and ultimately to the civil war and the Puritan Commonwealth. Because of the unique centrality of the sermon in Puritanism, and because even though they were not a majority, the Puritan pulpit outdrew such pastimes as bearbaiting, Shakespeare, and Jonson.[7]

A fascinating ad hoc institutional structure was set up to enlarge preaching opportunity and exposure. These were the preaching lectureships. Lectureships were like sustained special meetings outside of a liturgical context. They were funded by the laity and allowed for "an extra clergyman to be attached to a parish for preaching purposes alone." There were cathedral lectureships, local parish lectureships, and borough corporation lectureships for which Puritans were often hired.

In the first generation, Thomas Cartwright, William Ames, and William Perkins all lectured. Before he became a bishop John Hooper lectured and wrote his old mentor Henry Bullinger in Zurich about his experience.

Great, great, I say, my beloved master and gossip, is the harvest, but the laborers are few . . . Such is the maliciousness and wickedness of the bishops that the godly and learned men who would willingly labor in the Lord's harvest are hindered by them; and they neither preach themselves, nor allow the liberty of preaching to others. For this reason there are some persons here who read and expound the holy scriptures at a public lecture, two of whom read in St. Paul's cathedral four times a week. I myself, too, as my slender abilities will allow me, having compassion upon the ignorance of my brethren, read a public lecture twice in the day to so numerous an audience that the church cannot contain them.[8]

The lectures were about an hour long and quite exegetical. Often the preacher would give a series on related texts, although there were instances where the preacher "followed never a whit of the text."[9] The Laudians fought the lectureships, but the Puritans obviously triumphed. The lectureships were the Puritan answer to the demand for a godly preaching ministry. By 1664, twenty-six or twenty-seven remained in London. Three hundred years later, a few still survive.

For years leading up to the Long Parliament of 1640, there flourished what was called the Puritan or Carolinian underground. A network of organized conventicles distributed literature in the interest of the promulgation of the Word and its exposition. Archbishop Laud tended not to differentiate among the Puritanically inclined, so he and his henchmen went after the leaders, such as the "Presbyterian man of war," Dr. Alexander Leighton. A Scot who was both a medical doctor and a preacher, Leighton was fearless and unflinching. He was apocalyptic in his message and wrote a treatise against high Calvinism. He was arrested in 1630 and appeared before the Star Chamber. He was mutilated and imprisoned for ten years for treason and sedition.

The story of the Puritan Triumvirate, William Prynne, John Bastwick, and Henry Burton, epitomizes the Puritan struggle.[10] Prynne's massive *Histriomastix,* a book against stage plays, seemed necessarily seditious to Laud, so he ordered Prynne's ears cut off and his confinement in the Tower. Burton was a master in the composition and circulation of anti-episcopal tracts (using Dutch printers). Henry Burton "preached a seditious sermon at his private church" and had the temerity to repeat it on a lecture day in Colchester. The trials were farcical, and the three were confined in their respective fortresses because of their opposition to growing ritualism and *jure divino* episcopal claims.[11]

Still another opportunity to inspect Puritan preaching is afforded us in the sermons preached to the Long Parliament and in London at a time when tensions were building toward civil war. In his original and creative study, Professor Stephen Baskerville shows us that the very act of preaching was of the essence in the Puritan movement toward freedom.[12] The famous Puritan plain style was an important aspect to the vehicle of massive societal and personal change. Baskerville quotes Samuel Hieron: "The exercise of preaching ought to receive from us all esteem . . . the preaching of God's holy word, though it be meanly esteemed by the world, it is the ministry of the Spirit."[13] Baskerville traces the pervasive themes in this preaching: divine providence, sin, covenant, faith, and the church.

Finally the gathering storm burst over England. It started with a riot at St. Giles in Edinburgh in Scotland against Laud himself when he was seeking to enforce uniformity. Extended military action, with plundering and abuse on both sides, saw the defeat of the Royalists and the institution of the rule of Colonel Cromwell and Parliament. Neither they nor England would be the same again. The Barebones Parliament of 1653, which yielded power to Cromwell, was named for one of its members, an Anabaptist preacher from London whose name was Praisegod Barebones (his two brothers were named Christ-came-into-the-world-to-save Barebones and If-Christ-had-not-died-thou-wouldst-be-damned Barebones, sometimes called Damned Barebones for short).

1. Paul S. Seaver, *The Puritan Lectureships* (Palo Alto, Calif.: Stanford University Press, 1970), 4.
2. The best study is that of George F. Willison, *Saints and Strangers* (New York: Time Reading Program, 1945, 1964).
3. F. Ernest Stoeffer, *The Rise of Evangelical Pietism* (Leiden, Netherlands: E. J. Brill, 1965).
4. Stephen Baskerville, *Not Peace But a Sword: The Political Theology of the English Revolution* (London: Routledge, 1993), 8.
5. M. Lloyd-Jones, *The Puritans: Their Origins and Successors* (Edinburgh: Banner of Truth, 1987).
6. Ibid., 56.
7. Seaver, *The Puritan Lectureships,* 5.
8. Ibid., 78.
9. Ibid., 144.
10. Stephen Foster, *Notes from the Caroline Underground: Alexander Leighton, the Puritan Triumvirate and the Laudian Reaction to Non-Conformity* (Hamden, Conn.: Archon, 1978).
11. Ibid., 47.
12. Baskerville, *Not Peace But a Sword,* 8.
13. Ibid., 47.

7.2 THE GENIUS OF PURITANISM

The minister may, yea and must privately use at his liberty the arts, philosophy, and variety of reading, whilst he is in framing his sermon, but he ought in public to conceal all these from the people and not to make the least ostentation. It is also a point of art to conceal art.

—William Perkins

Embrace every occasion which the Lord offereth in the public ministry of his word . . . get something from every sermon, from this which you have this day heard.

—John Brinsley

Probably no religious entity has ever been so grossly maligned and misunderstood as have the Puritans. To be puritanical in our culture is to be overly prudish, unbearably rigid, and spiritually snobbish. Undeniably there was an underside to Puritanism, but in the history of preaching we do have what is an almost unprecedented prominence of biblical preaching affecting an entire culture. Daniel J. Boorstin observed of Puritan New England, for instance, that "there was hardly a public event of which the most memorable feature was not the sermon."[1] In understanding this unparalleled phenomenon, we must inquire into those factors comprising the Puritan genius.

---

1. Quoted in Ralph G. Turnbull, *The Preacher's Heritage, Task and Resources* (Grand Rapids: Baker, 1968), 115.

7.2.1 THE PURITANS—THE ABSOLUTE INFALLIBILITY OF THE SCRIPTURE

Protestants suppose the Scripture to be given forth by God to be . . . a complete rule of . . . faith.

—John Owen

For over a millennium and a half, the church's view of the Scriptures was that the Bible is the authoritative Word of God. This is where the Puritans stood. John Eliot from Roxbury in Massachusetts assured his listeners that "the writings of the Bible are the very words of God."[1] Carden lists the designations of the Bible in Puritan sermons: "word of truth," "great store-house of truth," "Scriptures of truth," "ye eternal word," "the Holy Scriptures," "the Sacred Word," "the infallible Oracles," "his [God's] revealed will," "the Rule," "the purest spiritual milk," "a treasure."[2] The use of both Old and New Testaments in Puritan preaching corroborate their theological formulation—they loved and believed in the Bible!

The Puritans encouraged Bible translation and distribution. Laypeople were to study and know their Bibles. The family altar and reading of the Bible in the home were encouraged. Puritans were aware of the original autographs and their importance. The Scriptures as given were without error.[3]

Counseled Thomas Watson: "Think in every line you read that God is speaking to you."[4] This conviction is reflected in The Westminster Confession of Faith (1643), which speaks of the Holy Scripture and "our full persuasion and assurance of the infallible truth and divine authority thereof is from the inward work of the Holy Spirit, bearing witness, by and with the Word, in our hearts. . . . Nothing is at any time to be added—whether by new revelations of the Spirit or traditions of men." This firm grounding in the Scripture was the foundation and basis of everything Puritan. They were truly a people of the Book.

It follows from this view of Scripture that the exposition of the Word, the public gathering "to hear God speak," was the central focus of Puritan life. Professor Stout has shown us that the average colonial Puritan heard more than seven thousand sermons requiring some fifteen thousand hours of concentrated attention in a lifetime. Based on his study of sermon manuscripts, Stout has authentically grasped the heart of Puritanism. Wrote Stout:

> The ministers enjoyed awesome powers in New England society; they alone could speak for God in public assembles of the entire congregation. Their sermons were the only voice of authority that congregations were pledged to obey unconditionally. Yet because sermons had to be based on *Sola Scriptura,* even the ministers' authority was limited. Their authority was by virtue of their specialized knowledge of the Scriptures and their ordination, not through any special perfections or infallible inspiration.[5]

Preaching was pervasive in Puritan culture because of and through the Bible. Although the premise is an extension of the Reformation presupposition about the centrality of the Word and its proclamation, the permeation of a society by Scripture among the Puritans rarely if ever has been equaled in history.

---

1. Allen Carden, *Puritan Christianity in America* (Grand Rapids: Baker, 1990), 36.
2. Ibid., 36.
3. Leland Ryken, *Worldly Saints: The Puritans As They Were* (Grand Rapids: Zondervan, 1986), 142.
4. J. I. Packer, *A Quest for Godliness: The Puritan Vision of the Christian Life* (Wheaton, Ill.: Crossway, 1990), 99.
5. Harry S. Stout, *The New England Soul: Preaching and Religious Culture in Colonial New England* (New York: Oxford University Press, 1986), 19.

7.2.2   THE PURITANS—THE ESSENTIAL PRIMACY OF PREACHING THE SCRIPTURE

> What strong castles have been demolished by preaching, how many thousand enemies have been made friends by preaching, how many kingdoms have been subdued by preaching, how . . . the preaching of the word had gone into all the earth and unto the ends of the world and rent in pieces the kingdom of the devil. . . . In a word, preaching is that whereby Christ destroys the very kingdom of Antichrist. Though it is the devil's masterpiece laid the deepest in policy and founded not only states but in men's consciences, yet Christ destroys it by the "word of his mouth"—that is, the preaching of the gospel in the mouths of his ministers.
> —Stephen Marshall, "trumpet" of St. Margaret's Church, 1646

Whether ensconced in the Church of England or of Baptist, Congregational, Presbyterian, or Independent persuasion, for Puritans the pulpit and preaching were paramount. In building their own edifices, particularly in New England, the pulpit was physically front and center. The aim of preaching was the transformation of the individual and the reorganization of society. In what was called "the rhetoric of the Spirit," the objective of spiritual preaching was to "catch the conscience of the common man."[1] The Puritans were logicians and believed that reason was part of the *imago dei*. Their indebtedness to Peter Ramus and his emphasis on disjunction and careful use of hypothesis meant their preaching sought simplification, clarity, precision, and conciseness.[2]

Nearly all of the Puritan preachers were trained at Cambridge or Oxford. They were conversant with Hebrew, Greek, and Latin, and were often quite literary. Puritan culture flowered in writers like John Milton, John Bunyan, and Daniel Defoe. Harvard and Yale were established in New England for the primary purpose of training preachers. The Puritan sermon was a work of art, "a way of conceiving the inconceivable," to use Perry Miller's apt phrase.

The aura of the Word was over the culture. Literacy was widespread. Books were considered cordials like fasting and prayer. Some knew the Bible almost by heart.[3] Emory Elliott's analysis is that "the power of the Puritan sermon was in its symbolic and metaphorical meaning, which resulted from a dynamic interaction between the clergy and their people."[4]

In the new rhetoric of the Puritans there was a move away from reading the sermon in the interest of this "dynamic interaction" with the listeners.

Solomon Stoddard cautioned, "Sermons when read are not delivered with authority in an affecting way."[5] We shall see how Jonathan Edwards, who once read his sermons, endeavored to be delivered from his "paper." The Puritan sermon was really a subgenre of the so-called university sermon we have previously analyzed and of the Hyperian modified modern type (see 6.1.1, 6.1.2, 6.1.3 n. 5). All of the Puritans used divisions and subdivisions in the sermon. Their sermons began with exegetical observations, then the body was shaped in relation to a chief doctrinal subject or theme and applied in a series of uses. This is not classical exposition, in which the sermon is shaped by the very development within the text itself. F. R. Webber understood this:

> This method of homiletics led to a diffused sermon structure instead of unity and progress. Instead of constructing a sermon on the plan of several rivers, which unite and form one great stream that moves forward steadily toward a definite goal, the sermons of Puritan times were constructed on the plan of a tree. A general theme was stated, and then each one of its details was traced out in turn, as one might trace each limb and each branch of a tree. It was a mixed style. Some of the preachers of those days derived their divisions and subdivisions from the text, but more often than not, the divisions and subdivisions were based partly on the thoughts of the text and partly upon ideas suggested by the general nature of the subject. Often there was little actual advancement of thought, leading the hearers onward, and culminating in a powerful impression. Rather were the sermons of those days a number of minor truths tied together by the text. If as Dr. John Watson says, three detached sermonettes do not make done sermon, how can thirty or forty ideas result in unity?[6]

The subordination of the text to the doctrinal theme suggested within it is seen in a series of fifty-eight sermons Thomas Brooks preached on the theme, "The

Necessity, Excellency, Rarity and Beauty of Holiness." The thrust was powerful and the truth was stated, but the text of Scripture is minimized when so little text is exposed. We must prefer the Hyperian modification, which like the homily follows the order of the text but divides the text for exposition.

The Puritan sermon tended to be long and heavy, but it had the great advantage of being theological and doctrinal. Puritan preachers ranged over the theological encyclopedia. Our generation of preachers could profit from their example They preached from within a sense of doctrinal construct. We read their sermons to learn doctrine on sin, for instance. We see what every student of Puritan preaching notes as the persistent millennial or chiliastic strain, even in Jonathan Edwards, for whom the postmillennialist figure is the controlling metaphor in his epochal *Magnalia Christi Americana.*

Most of the Puritans were futurists and of a millennialist school that anticipated a great movement among the Jews to Christ. Indeed Oliver Cromwell invited the Jews to return to England, from which they had long been banned. This tradition was sustained down to Spurgeon himself, who affirmed, "Our hope is the personal, premillennial return of the Lord Jesus Christ in glory."[7] This is just a sample of the doctrinally rich and substantial issues addressed from the Puritan pulpits on both continents. But the text was not king!

1. William Haller, *The Rise of Puritanism* (Philadelphia: University of Pennsylvania Press, 1938), 19, 30.
2. Perry Miller and Thomas H. Johnson, eds., *The Puritans* (New York: Harper Torchbooks, 1938), 1:24, 29.
3. David L. Hall, *Worlds of Wonder, Days of Judgment: Popular Religious Belief in Early New England* (New York: Knopf, 1989), 219.
4. Emory Elliott, *Power and the Pulpit in Puritan New England* (Princeton, N.J.: Princeton University Press, 1975), 204. A delightful panegyric for Puritan preaching is by Peter Lewis, *The Genius of Puritanism* (Haywards Heath, England: Carey Publications, 1979), 19–52.
5. Donald Weber, *Rhetoric and History in Revolutionary New England* (Oxford: Oxford University Press, 1988), 26.
6. F. R. Webber, *A History of Preaching in Britain and America* (Milwaukee: Northwestern, 1952), 1:202–3.
7. Charles H. Spurgeon, *The Sword and Trowel* (London: The Preacher's College, 1891), 446. Solid studies of this theme are Iain Murray, *The Puritan Hope* (London: Banner of Truth, 1971); Peter Toon, ed., *Puritans, the Millennium and the Future of Israel: Puritan Eschatology* (Cambridge, Mass.: James Clarke, 1970). On the Jews more particularly, see my study, *Jews, Gentiles and the Church* (Grand Rapids: Discovery House, 1995). Perry Miller advanced the bizarre idea that Cocceius projected federal theology to blunt the pain of predestination. Federal theology, important to the Puritans, would seem to rise quite clearly from the biblical text as in Romans 5:12–21. Note also Charles S. McCoy and J. Wayne Baker, *Fountainhead of Federalism: Heinrich Bullinger and the Covenantal Tradition* (Louisville: Westminster/John Knox, 1991). This book has a helpful treatment of Johannes Cocceius as well as Bullinger.

7.2.3   The Puritans—The Inescapable Applicability of the Scripture

> God never proposed to leave his holy word to be no more but read, either privately in men's houses or publicly in our churches, but appointed there should be men ordained to expand the same by voice and apply it to the occasions and necessities of the people.
>
> This is the soul of prophesying and the very life of preaching. It openeth the scripture to show what it meaneth; it fits to the particular uses and necessities of the people.
>
> —Samuel Hieron

The practicality and profitability of the Scriptures have been an emphasis from the beginning of biblical preaching (cf. 2 Timothy 3:16–17), but few eras have been as plush and prolific in application as the Puritans. With much doctrinal exposition, the Puritans always concluded their sermons with an extensive section of "uses" which sought to bridge from the "then" to the "now." Since this has not been strong in the preaching of more recent years, we do well to analyze this aspect of Puritan preaching with some care. John Brown in his Beecher Lectures relates of one William Bourne, who

> seldom varied the manner of his preaching, which after explication of the text, was doctrine proof of it from Scripture, by reasoning and answering more and more objections; and then the uses, first, of information, secondly, of confutation of popery, thirdly of reprehension, fourthly of examination, fifthly, of exhortation, and lastly of consolation.[1]

All of this can add up to considerable complexity. John Owen is a case in point. His sermon on Habakkuk 3 had a fourfold division subdivided into "almost 150 observations, reasons, uses, particulars, etc."[2]

In an extensive analysis of Jonathan Edwards' sermons, Ralph Turnbull demonstrates the emphasis on application in Edwards' sermons.

1. "The Sovereignty of God": twelve pages of exposition, three pages of application;
2. "Sinners in the Hands of an Angry God": four pages exposition, five pages application;
3. "The Excellency of Christ": thirteen pages of exposition, nine pages of application;
4. "A Warning to Professors": five pages of exposition, five pages of application;
5. "True Saints, when absent from the body are present with the Lord": thirteen pages of exposition, three pages of application;
6. "The True Excellency of a Gospel Minister": nine pages of exposition, four of application;
7. "A Farewell Sermon": nine pages of exposition, ten pages of application.[3]

In *The Westminster Directory for the Publick Worship of God (Of the Preaching of the Word),* issued by the Westminster Assembly, great emphasis is placed on not resting "in general doctrine" but in moving the truth of the Word to the hearers, some of whom are asleep, some seekers, some young, some old, some fallen, some sad. A specific appeal was to be made to the mind, the affections, and the will in self-examination and encouragement.[4]

Such audience analysis in the interest of direct application must be distinguished from audience-centered preaching as it has arisen in our time. The compact application of the Puritans has given way to continuous application today.

Further evidence for the Puritan penchant for application can be seen in the widely acclaimed development of the Puritan work ethic. This was a consequence of the preaching of the Puritan doctrines of grace and godly living. In his recent masterful study, *Trust: The Social Virtues and the Creation of Prosperity,* the noted social theorist Francis Fukuyama leans on Max Weber's *The Protestant Ethic and the Spirit of Capitalism* to show that "the early Puritans, seeking to glorify God alone, and renouncing the acquisition of material goods as an end in itself, developed certain virtues like honesty and thrift that were extremely helpful to the accumulation of capital."[5] Fukuyama shows how these Puritan traits were replicated in Protestant converts in the Methodist revivals in the eighteenth and nineteenth centuries and among Protestant converts in Latin America in our time.[6] Not only Weber but also R. H. Tawney in his memorable *Holland Lectures* in 1922 mulls over the extraordinary impact of Puritan preaching and values in the shaping of an economic and political system. Observed Tawney:

> The growth, triumph and transformation of the Puritan spirit was the most fundamental movement of the seventeenth century . . . Puritanism was the schoolmaster of the English middle classes . . . a godly discipline was, indeed, the very ark of the Puritan covenant. . . . What is required of the Puritan is not individual meritorious acts, but a holy life—a system in which every element if grouped round a central idea, the service of God, from which all disturbing irrelevancies have been pruned, and to which all minor interests are subordinated.[7]

The great stress then on the practical application of the preaching of the Word can be seen as it translates so vividly and strikingly in the sinews of a society in its day-by-day experience.

---

1. John Brown, *Puritan Preaching in England* (New York: Scribner's, 1900), 60.
2. F. R. Webber, *A History of Preaching in Britain and America* (Milwaukee: Northwestern, 1952), 1:202.
3. Ralph G. Turnbull, *Jonathan Edwards the Preacher* (Grand Rapids: Baker, 1958), 168ff.
4. For further discussion of this, see David L. Larsen, *The Anatomy of Preaching* (Grand Rapids: Baker, 1989), 95ff.
5. Francis Fukuyama, *Trust: The Social Virtues and the Creation of Prosperity* (New York: Free Press, 1995), 37.

6. Ibid., 45. Fukuyama quotes David Martin's significant study, *Tongues of Fire: The Explosion of Protestantism in Latin America* (Oxford: Blackwood, 1990).

7. R. H. Tawney, *Religion and the Rise of Capitalism* (New York: Mentor, 1926), 164ff.

7.2.4 THE RADICAL INTERIORITY OF THE CHRISTIAN LIFE

Make my every sermon a means of grace to myself,
and help me to experience the power of thy dying love,
for thy blood is balm, thy presence bliss, thy smile heaven,
thy cross the place where truth and mercy meet.
When I preach to others let not my words be merely elegant and masterly,
my reasoning polished and refined,
my performance powerless and tasteless,
but may I exalt thee and humble sinners.
O Lord of power and grace,
all hearts are in thy hands, all events at thy disposal,
set the seal of thy almighty will upon my ministry.[1]

While the Puritans were devotees of one authoritative Book and set on preaching it and the doctrines it delineated, Puritanism was a movement of revival and the cultivation of the inner affections. Packer calls them "restless experientialists."[2] Stoeffer, in his classic study, roots the "rise of evangelical pietism" in the Puritan camp, with its quest for personal piety even stronger than its pursuit of institutional purity.[3] The genius of the Puritan pulpit was its balance, however precarious at times, between the propositional and the personal, the outer and the inner, the Spirit and the Word. When Puritanism began to flag, it was because this delicate balance was lost in favor of an ossified externalism which was devoid of life.

We can see this balance in **William Perkins** (cf. 6.1.3), who stressed the propriety of human learning, and then the acquisition of divine knowledge (revealed truth), and subsequently "that inward learning taught by the Spirit of God."[4] This emphasis is seen in the Westminster Shorter Catechism:

The Spirit of God maketh the reading, but especially the preaching of the Word, an effectual means of convincing and converting sinners, and of building them up in holiness and comfort, through faith, unto salvation (89).

G. F. Nuttall in his definitive study on the Holy Spirit in Puritan thought argues that the Puritans were not primarily dogmatic but experiential (compared to Calvin, who saw the Holy Spirit as a necessity of thought but not known overtly in experience).[5] For Richard Sibbes, the Spirit was in the Scripture inspiring it, but the Spirit was also in the believing reader and preacher of Scripture enlightening it. Thus it is that John Robinson, in his farewell to the Pilgrim Fathers, was reported to have said, "The Lord hath more truth and light yet to break forth out of his holy word."

The first to upset this equilibrium were the Quakers, who stressed the inner light of the Spirit in every person, including the unregenerate. Neither Baxter nor Owen would recognize infallible revelation apart from Scripture, while George Fox contended that he had independent revelation.[6] The hazard of this Spirit without the Word approach can be seen in the fact that Quakers frequently did not preach from a text at all.[7] This was also displayed in certain radical Puritans, the Ranters and the Shakers.

The Puritans believed in "immediacy in relation to God." Their illustrious political leader **Oliver Cromwell** (1599–1658) testified to "the full assurance of the Spirit's nearness," and stressed the inner transformation of the Spirit. "His presence hath been amongst us, and by the light of His countenance we have prevailed."[8] Both Richard Sibbes and Thomas Goodwin returned again and again to the grave danger of grieving the Holy Spirit. The Puritans were deeply into the life of prayer and communion with God, privately, in the family circle at home, and in public gatherings and worship. Their theology of the gifts of the Spirit and the Spirit's manifestation in prayer set them at odds with the Anglican habit of "set prayers." Worship and preaching directed by Scripture are enlivened by the Spirit.[9]

Puritan spirituality focused on conversion, cherished the Word and personal and corporate worship (with a strong emphasis on baptism and the Lord's Supper), and maintained high reverence for the Lord's Day.

Similar to the Caroline divines, the Puritans stressed "the mystical union" with Christ and loved to preach from the Song of Solomon. Wakefield cites **John Preston** (1587–1628), "Prince Charles' Puritan Chaplain," who composed a piece titled "The Soliloquy of the Devout Soul Panting after the Love of the Lord Jesus."[10] Apart from this arduous cultivation of the inner spiritual life there would never have been what we call Puritanism. Their preaching would have been sucked into the hot sands of secularism—as would ours as well.

---

1. From Arthur Bennett, *The Valley of Vision: A Collection of Puritan Prayers and Devotions* (Edinburgh: Banner of Truth Trust, 1975), 186.
2. J. I. Packer, *A Quest for Godliness: The Puritan Vision of the Christian Life* (Wheaton, Ill.: Crossway, 1990), 30.
3. F. Ernest Stoeffer, *The Rise of Evangelical Pietism* (Leiden, Netheralnds: E. J. Brill, 1965).
4. John Brown, *Puritan Preaching in England* (New York: Scribner's, 1900), 74.
5. Geoffrey F. Nuttall, *The Holy Spirit in Puritan Faith and Experience* (Oxford: Blackwell, 1946), 6.
6. Ibid., 54.
7. Ibid., 153. For an important study of the intellectual leader of early Quakers, see D. Elton Trueblood, *Robert Barclay* (New York: Harper and Row, 1968). Barclay (1648–1690) also confronted the celebrated lunatic **Lodowick Muggleton,** whose followers were called "Friends" and who bombastically castigated preaching, worship, and churches. The last of his followers died about midway in our century. William Blake's mother was a follower of Muggleton.
8. Ibid., 136. Still my favorite biography of Cromwell is by Antonia Fraser, *Cromwell: The Lord Protector* (New York: Knopf, 1973).

9. A magnificent study is Roy Walter Williams, *The Puritan Concept and Practice of Prayer* (Unpublished Ph.D. dissertation, University of London, 1982). A copy is in the library of Trinity Evangelical Divinity School, Deerfield, Illinois.

10. Gordon S. Wakefield, "The Puritans," in *The Study of Spirituality,* ed. Cheslyn Jones, Geoffrey Wainwright, Edward Yarnold (Oxford: Oxford University Press, 1986), 444. See also the choice study, Ted A. Campbell, *The Religion of the Heart* (Columbia: University of South Carolina, 1991).

7.3 THE GLORIES OF THE PURITAN PULPIT

Preaching of the Word, being the power of God unto salvation, and one of the greatest and most excellent works belonging to the ministry of the Gospel, should be so performed that the workman need not be ashamed, but may save himself and those that hear him.
— *The Westminster Directory for the Publick Worship of God*

The Bible, I say the Bible only.

—William Chillingworth

Puritanism was, as Perry Miller argued, a kind of "Augustinian piety." It was a deep-seated dissatisfaction with the terms of the Reformation embodied in the Elizabethan settlement. Puritanism's insistence on a conversion experience for every believer set Puritans against the sacerdotal. As Brauer said of the Puritan understanding of conversion, "They preached for it, sought it and testified of it."[1]

Within and against governmental restrictions and ecclesiastical controls, the Puritans forged their alliance. Laypersons were thrust to the fore. Puritans such as Thomas Adams and John White opposed the deposition of King Charles I (John Preston, the future Master of Emmanuel College, had been his chaplain while he was growing up), but the nation plunged into a bloody civil war in which one hundred thousand people were killed.

In the widening conflict, the Puritans became increasingly powerful. Preaching remained at the center of their worship.[2] They viewed preaching as the antidote to social and political disorder. Preaching was effective, from the Puritan perspective, in that "Growing awareness of the importance of consent in establishing social order underlay Puritan emphasis on the efficacy of preaching as a means of social control."[3] But many in the Establishment saw Puritans as the cause of insurrection and destablization.[4]

During the civil war (1642–1649), Puritan preachers saw the destiny of their nation in the drama of Scripture. They sponsored a series of "Humiliations and Thanksgivings" (1641–1642) to summon the nation to God. Throughout the Long Parliament, many of the outstanding Puritan preachers opened Scripture and preached to the members. Stephen Marshall brought an extended series on Psalm 102. In the parliamentary year 1648–1649, 125 different preachers addressed Parliament. Most of them belonged to the Westminster Assembly.[5] John Owen, though not in the Assembly, was extremely influential and preached the sermon in Parliament on the day following King Charles' death.

Analysis of these sermons yields invaluable insight into effective biblical communication.[6] However, Richard Baxter, "the loquacious Presbyterian" and an army chaplain himself, indicated that he was personally appalled by the language of some of the "hot-blooded sectaries." Still, preaching was unquestionably ascendant once again.

---

1. Jerald C. Brauer, "Conversion: From Puritanism to Revivalism," *Journal of Religion* (1958): 227–43.
2. David Zaret, *The Heavenly Contract: Ideology and Organization in Pre-Revolutionary Puritanism* (Chicago: University of Chicago Press, 1985), 62; for a full treatment of this, see Horton Davies, *The Worship of the English Puritans* (Westminster, London, England: Dacre, 1948), 182–202.
3. Zaret, *The Heavenly Contract*, 87.
4. Ibid., 75.
5. John F. Wilson, *Pulpit in Parliament: Puritanism During the English Civil Wars 1640–1648* (Princeton, N.J.: Princeton University Press, 1969), 108.
6. Ibid., 137ff.

7.3.1 GOSPEL TRAILBLAZERS—EARLIER PURITAN PREACHERS

They hould that the highest and supreame office and authoritie of the Pastor, is to preach the gospell solemnly and publickly to the Congregation, by interpreting the written word of God, and applying the same by exhortation and reproof unto them. They hould that this was the greatest worke that Christ and his Apostles did.

—William Bradshaw

The makers of Puritanism were almost all university men. Although a few came from Oxford, the great majority came from Cambridge, where early on Christ College and then Emmanuel College were great centers of Puritan activity. The latter was even known as "the nursery of Puritanism."

Even Oliver Cromwell put his son Henry at Emmanuel. **Laurence Chaderton** (1536–1640), from an old Roman Catholic family, went up to Cambridge in 1564 and met Christ there. For over fifty years he was afternoon lecturer at St. Clement's, where he consistently drew enormous crowds. He was deep into the Scriptures, and used the plain style with "the eloquence of the body." Chaderton exerted a seminal influence on his own brother-in-law, **Ezekiel Culverwell,** in whose congregation at Sudbury was the young **John Winthrop,** later the governor of Massachusetts Bay Colony. Chaderton also shaped **William Perkins,** who touched **John Cotton** and **John Robinson,** whose ministries would be in the New World.[1] Chaderton was also one of the translators of the King James Version and faithfully preached the Word into an advanced age.

We have already identified early Puritan trailblazers such as John Hooper (cf. 5.5.6), who visited and studied in Geneva, and **Archbishop Edmund Grindal** (cf. 5.5.9), whose exile in Germany reconfigured his views and ministry. Grindal much preferred the sermon to the homily, and sharpened the contrast in a famous letter:

> The Godly preacher is termed in the Gospel, a Faithful Servant, who knoweth how to give his Lord's family their apportioned food in season; who can apply his speech according to the diversity of times, places and hearers; which cannot be done in the Homilies: exhortations, reprehensions, and persuasions, are uttered with more affection, to the moving of the Hearers, in Sermons than in Homilies. Besides, Homilies were devised by the Godly Bishops in your Brother's time, only to supply necessity, for want of Preachers; and are by Statute not to be preferred, but to give place to Sermons, whensoever they may be had.[2]

Grindal undoubtedly brought the shape of the Puritan sermon back to England from Germany (cf. 6.1 n.5).

Other worthies in this early succession are **Thomas Cartright** (cf. 5.5.11 in relation to Richard Hooker), **Henry Smith** (cf. 6.1.2), so well and so widely heard, and of course the inimitable **William Perkins,** who instructed lucidly on the preaching craft (cf. 6.1.3).[3] Following this noble band were Bishop **Joseph Hall** (cf. 6.2.5) and **Richard Clifton** (1545–1616), who after serving as rector in Nottinghamshire joined the Puritans at Scrooby and succeeded John Robinson. Clifton ultimately fled to Amsterdam, where he had a noteworthy ministry. **John White** (1570–1615) came out of Cambridge and served in Manchester, where his reputation as a vehement preacher ripened. He was generally polemical, and espoused an extreme Calvinism and defended the monarchy.[4]

In this line of distinguished Puritan forefathers we must certainly see the eloquent **Thomas Adams** (1580–1653?), often called the Shakespeare of the Puritans. Solid in his conviction, he was immensely creative, and bore similarity to some of the more ornate Caroline divines. He argued, "It was not one for one that Christ died, not one for many: but one for all . . . and this one must needs be of infinite price."[5] Like the Caroline preachers, he was stoutly loyal to the monarchy.

The poetic Adams added to the Puritan homiletical legacy. When preaching out of the text, "Their poison is like the poison of a serpent, like the deaf adder that stops her ear," Adams used eleven characters to convey his point—among them salamanders, crocodiles, caterpillars, and lizards. His apt aphorisms flavored his messages:

> There be pirates in the sea, alas! but a handful to that huge army of them in the world. Take a short view of them, borrowed of a divine traveler. Fury fights against us like a mad Turk; fornication, like a treacherous Joab, in kisses it kills us; drunkeness is the master gunner that gives fire to all the rest; gluttony may stand for a corporal; avarice for a pioneer; idleness for a gentleman of the company; pride must be the captain. But the arch-pirate of all is the devil, that huge leviathan

that takes his pastime in the sea. And his pastime is to sink merchants' freight that are laden with holy traffic for heaven. Historians speak of a fish that is a special and oft-prevailing enemy of the whale, called the sword-fish. The most powerful thing to overcome this leviathan is the sword of the Spirit.[6]

Adams also preached on "The Three Divine Sisters—Faith, Hope and Charity," and published an expository commentary on 2 Peter which echoes his preaching on that Epistle. His published *Sermons and Expositions* (1630) are appreciated.

Stephen Marshall (1594–1655) often preached at St. Margaret's (the parish church at Westminster). He was one of the prime movers in the Westminster Assembly. Marshall was sent to Scotland to bridge the gap with the Scots, and was one of the authors of *Smectymnuus,* an important tract outlining the vision of nonconformity.[7] He attended Archbishop Laud before Laud's execution in 1645.

Marshall's preaching was powerful and effective. He loved to preach from both Testaments. Wilson adjudges him to be "without peer as preacher to the Long Parliament" and effective as a broker both before and behind the scenes.[8] Something of a clerical politician, he was more importantly a biblical preacher whose preaching made a vast difference. He was buried in Westminster and disinterred upon the Restoration.

As we turn to the more typical Puritan preachers, we shall adopt Professor Knight's bifurcation—two main categories in England that were then transferred to New England: (1) Perkins and Ames, those who stress cultivating true piety through spiritual discipline within a sense of covenantal obligation; and (2) Sibbes and those who emphasize the experience of the Spirit's indwelling and the "joys of Christian fellowship."[9] In the wake of certain tensions that arose on both continents, the Amesians were accused of legalism and the Sibbesians charged with of antinomianism. We shall now trace this important succession.

---

1. John Brown, *Puritan Preaching in England* (New York: Scribner's, 1900), 67ff.
2. Horton Davies, *The Worship of the English Puritans* (Westminster, London, England: Dacre, 1948), 187.
3. Brown, *Puritan Preaching in England,* 75.
4. F. R. Webber, *A History of Preaching in Britain and America* (Milwaukee: Northwestern, 1952), 1:222.
5. Brown, *Puritan Preaching in England,* 91ff.
6. T. Harwood Pattison, *The History of Christian Preaching* (Philadelphia: American Baptist Publication Society, 1903), 182.
7. Webber, *A History of Preaching,* 1:235.
8. John F. Wilson, *Pulpit in Parliament: Puritanism During the English Civil Wars* (Princeton, N.J.: Princeton University Press, 1969), 109.
9. Janice Knight, *Orthodoxies in Massachusetts: Rereading American Puritanism* (Cambridge, Mass.: Harvard University Press, 1994).

7.3.2 GOSPEL TRUMPETERS—ADVOCATES OF COVENANT AND DISCIPLINE

> The preaching of the Word is that lattice where Christ looks forth and shows himself to his saints.
>
> —Thomas Watson

The drumbeat of the more traditional Puritans emphasized strenuous preparation of the heart for reception of divine grace. It accented power and sovereignty as the essential divine attributes, and was furnished by the germinal thinker **William Ames** (1576–1633), student and follower of the great William Perkins. A graduate of Christ's College, Cambridge, Ames emigrated to Holland, where he attended the Synod of Dort. He became a professor at Friesland and died in Rotterdam. His famous *Marrow of Sacred Divinity* was a Puritan staple and exerted a profound influence on Puritan thinking. It was considered fundamental at Harvard and Yale in the seventeenth century. Ames shaped so much of the tone and texture of Puritan preaching. He saw theology as "the science of living to God," and stressed the nurture of a clear conscience in all details of life (especially in his *Cases of Conscience*). He wrote:

> But although divers parts of the Scriptures were written, upon some speciall occasion, and were directed to some certaine men, or asemblies: yet in God's intention, they doe as well pertaine to the instructing of all the faithfull thorough all ages, as if they had been specially directed to them.[1]

Thus sanction for morning and afternoon services was to be found in the double burnt offering of Numbers 28:9, etc. With this approach, Ames disparaged topical preaching:

> Ministers impose upon their hearers and altogether forget themselves when they propound a certain text in the beginning as the start of the sermon and then speak many things about or simply by occasion of the text but for the most part draw nothing out of the text itself.[2]

Not only in his fidelity to the text but also in his broad address in applying Scripture to every aspect of human life, Ames sets landmarks long observed. Sermon outlines must facilitate remembrance of the sermon. His famous epigram encapsulates the serious approach of the Puritan to Scripture: "The receiving of the word consists of two parts: attention of mind and intention of will." Ames is one of the formative pillars of Puritan orthodoxy.

---

1. Horton Davies, *The Worship of the English Puritans* (Westminster, London, England: Dacre, 1948), 5.
2. Leland Ryken, *Worldly Saints: The Puritans As They Really Were* (Grand Rapids: Zondervan, 1986), 98.

7.3.2.1 John Robinson—Pastor of the Pilgrims

> I charge you before God and his blessed angels to follow me no further
> than I follow Christ.
>
> —Pastor John Robinson in his farewell sermon
> to the Pilgrims, from Ezra 8:21

Another young Cambridge graduate, **John Robinson** (1575–1625), was apparently born near Lincoln and served several curacies but was expelled because of his separatistic bent. He became associated with the Scrooby separatists who met in William Brewster's house and fled to Amsterdam in 1608. From there he moved to Leyden, where he became pastor of a Puritan congregation that grew to three hundred constituents.[1]

The influence of William Perkins was evident in Robinson's doctrinal and homiletical views. The émigrés purchased a house which was remodeled to serve as a meeting house and parsonage and had a number of small cottages behind it for poor members of the congregation. Robinson preached to the appreciative congregants twice on Sunday and on Thursday evening and was considered a "commone father unto them."[2]

While properly labeled a separatist among the Puritans,[3] Robinson exemplifies the strong Puritan commitment to an emphasis on covenant, the preaching of the Word, and the prime requisite of conversion. The three volumes of his sermons demonstrate his high view of the preached Word. As Maclure states in his masterful study:

> For the Puritans, the sermon is not just hinged to Scripture; it quite literally exists inside the Word of God; the text is not in the sermon, but the sermon is in the text. . . . Put summarily, listening to a sermon is being in the Bible.[4]

The clear focus of Puritan preaching was salvation by grace alone (although this was later compromised in some quarters by a moralistic tendency).[5]

Members of the assembly took their places by 8 A.M. on the Lord's Day under the strict scrutiny of the deacon. Men, women, and children sat apart, thus "dignifying the meeting,"[6] and began the worship service with prayer. Pastor Robinson read from the Geneva Bible with expository comments (not mere "dumb reading"). After the singing of a psalm came a two-hour sermon, an exposition of the text "with a quiet and moving eloquence, a deep human understanding, and a wealth of apt illustration that held his brethren spellbound."[7] The singing of another psalm followed and the sacraments were administered when appropriate. The service closed about noon with the benediction. The afternoon service was less formal and featured "prophesying" by the pastor or ruling elder Brewster, likewise from a text.

Under continued pressure because of his publishing activities, William Brewster and others explored the possibility of a concession in Virginia by way of refuge. Because they further wanted to farm and did not want their children to grow up Dutch, they finally negotiated with some English merchants who agreed to sail them to the New World, where they arrived in Provincetown harbor on November 21, 1620. Pastor Robinson planned to join this segment of his flock but bade them farewell in a memorable address. He was never to see the 104 again. He wrote moving letters to encourage them in their dark hours. When he became ill in 1625, he insisted on preaching his customary two sermons on Sunday. He died a week later on March 1.[8]

---

1. F. R. Webber, *A History of Preaching in Britain and America* (Milwaukee: Northwestern, 1952), 1:232.
2. George F. Willison, *Saints and Strangers* (New York: Time Reading Program, 1945, 1964), 91.
3. Timothy George, *John Robinson and the English Separatist Tradition* (Macon, Ga.: Mercer University Press, 1982).
4. Millar Maclure, *The Paul's Cross Sermons, 1534–1642* (Toronto: University of Toronto Press, 1958).
5. C. F. Allison, *The Rise of Moralism: The Proclamation of the Gospel from Hooker to Baxter* (London: SPCK, 1966).
6. Willison, *Saints and Strangers,* 92.
7. Ibid., 93.
8. Ibid., 279.

7.3.2.2 Richard Mather—Founder of a Dynasty

The word of God is very plaine . . . [God] will give grace to whoever will receive it and come for it . . . it is a great encouragement and comfort that the righteousness of our God will move him and prevail with him, to pereform what he hath promised and so to give unto his the grace of faith.

There is an inseparable connection of the gifts and graces of Christ, so that if he give conversion and justification, he will sanctification also.
—Richard Mather

Of note both as a preacher and as a father of preachers, **Richard Mather** (1596–1669) was born in the village of Lowton near Liverpool. He became a teacher at a grammar school in Toxteth Park and eventually became master there. While there, he heard the preaching of the Word through Mr. Harrison of Hyton. Along with reading William Perkins, he came under deep conviction after one of Harrison's sermons on the new birth (from John 3:3, 5) and beside a Lancashire hedge he came to the assurance of salvation in 1614.[1] He had no particular ecstasy, but as Perkins stipulated, he should expect none.[2] Mather did matriculate briefly at Oxford but in 1619 took holy orders and returned to become the minister at Toxteth Park.

Already suspect for nascent Puritanism, Mather gave himself to preaching twice each Sabbath to his own charge and in surrounding churches during the week. He married, and in the next fifteen years had six sons. For the next fifty years, he never missed preaching on the Sabbath. His preaching drew heavily on the books of Samuel and Isaiah and the Epistles of Paul, with considerable reinforcement of the analogy between God's ancient chosen people and his faithful in the seventeenth century.[3]

Mather became increasingly convinced that congregationalism was correct, and predictably came into serious tensions with his bishop, who expelled him. He endured a period of much soul-searching and pondering of "England's apostasy," and reflected on the martyrdom of John Bradford. Mather soon moved with his family to New England, where he took up pastoral responsibilities in the Dorchester church in Massachusetts Bay Colony. Eventually he became president of Harvard. Yet in all his years in New England, Mather was a nostalgic exile.

As did all the Puritans, Mather preached with a sense of the impending end and Christ's soon appearing. He used Perkins' *The Art of Prophesying* as his model. Mather wrote books, such as his reply to Samuel Rutherford and the Scots who criticized New England congregationalism, and he made efforts to translate Psalms from the Hebrew. His many sermons and regular lectures display no "literary virtuosity,"[4] but he faithfully held forth "the undisputed word of Christ" in Puritan plain style. While typically given to much introspection and self-examination, the Puritan "frames," he took a staunch stand with Ames and Perkins and "the preparationists" who stressed God's work of preparing the elect for salvation through common grace. He opposed such notions as "the indwelling of the Holy Spirit"[5] and worried about the mystic manifestations of the antinomians.

Still, his ministry of fifty-two years was always with a thrust to heighten the awareness of the line between the saved and the unsaved. At times he seemed like a Calvinist in his study but an Arminian in his pulpit, and he came close to Richard Sibbes in subscribing to the validity of the universal call.[6]

When Mather's wife eventually died, he married the widow of the Reverend John Cotton. In his later years, he increasingly sounded the jeremiad from his pulpit as he witnessed a decline in faith and piety. His farewell exhortation was delivered from the observation of forty years of spiritual ebbs and flows and had the ring of authenticity in its depiction of the fall of nations and the hope of redemption.[7]

One of Mather's great legacies was his sons—two of whom returned to England and Ireland to minister, and Increase, who took his M.A. at Trinity College in Dublin after graduating from Harvard. In four generations this family had eleven well-known preachers who published five hundred books. Richard Mather is representative of Puritan preachers who combined intellectual and affective elements in a striking and stirring fashion.

1. B. R. Burg, *Richard Mather of Dorchester* (Lexington: University Press of Kentucky, 1976), 9.
2. Robert Middlekauff, *The Mathers: Three Generations of Puritan Intellectuals* (New York: Oxford University Press, 1971), 14.

3. Ibid., 16.
4. Burg, *Richard Mather of Dorchester,* 69.
5. Ibid., 41.
6. Norman Pettit, *The Heart Prepared: Grace and Conversion in Puritan Spiritual Life* (New Haven, Conn.: Yale University Press, 1966); John von Rohr, *The Covenant of Grace in Puritan Thought* (Atlanta: Scholars Press, 1986).
7. Burg, *Richard Mather of Dorchester,* 161.

7.3.2.3 Thomas Goodwin—Exemplar of Wholeness

Whereas some men are for preaching only extempore, and without study, Paul bids Timothy meditate and study, and give his mind wholly to these things.

The same Spirit that guided the holy apostles and prophets to write it must guide the people of God to know the meaning of it; and as he first delivered it, so must he help men to understand it.

—Thomas Goodwin

On every short list of the most admired and respected Puritan pastor-theologians is the name **Thomas Goodwin** (1600–1680). He was born in Norfolk and educated at Cambridge. Although dedicated by his parents to Christian ministry, he did not care for preaching until he came under conviction while attending a funeral and was converted. He describes his experience:

I observed of this work of God on my soul that there was nothing of constraint or force in it, but I was carried on with the most ready and willing mind, and what I did was what I chose to do. With the greatest freedom I parted with my sins, formerly as dear to me as the apple of my eye, yea, as my life, and resolved never to return to them more. And what I did was from deliberate choice; I considered what I was doing, and reckoned with myself what it would cost me to make this great alteration. What the world thought of these things hindered me not at all. The weeds that entangled me in those waters, I swam and broke through with as much ease as Samson did with his withes; for I was made a vassal and a captive to another binding, such as Paul speaks of.[1]

Goodwin served churches in Cambridge and London, but under the influence of John Cotton he became a Congregationalist, or Independent. When Laud made things too hot in England, he ministered to an English congregation at Arnheim in Holland for a brief while, returning to England in the Puritan ascendancy. Goodwin was a key member of the Westminster Assembly and exerted a prevailing influence on The Directory for Public Worship in Three Kingdoms.[2] In 1647 he accepted an invitation from John Cotton to come to minister in New England, and was about to sail when the pleas of his own dear congregation in

London dissuaded him and he remained as their pastor.[3] Cromwell appointed Goodwin as President of Magdalen College, Oxford, where he also preached in St. Mary's Church.

In sermonic form, Goodwin was among the best. John Brown advances the thesis that John Owen preached primarily to the mind, Richard Baxter to the conscience, and Thomas Goodwin to the spiritual affections. Goodwin was a traditional Calvinist, though not "exaggerated" in his beliefs.[4] In fact, he nearly became an Arminian because of acute depression stemming from uncertainty over his election.

Goodwin was influenced by Richard Sibbes, who once told him, "Young man, if you ever would do good, you must preach the Gospel and the free grace of God in Jesus Christ" (c. 1625). He was to Alexander Whyte, "The greatest pulpit exegete of Paul that has ever lived." His massive works, *The Objects and Acts of Justifying Faith* and *The Work of the Holy Spirit in Our Salvation,* are still in circulation by Banner of Truth Trust.

Though early on exposed to more elegant form at Cambridge and endowed with great gifts of natural eloquence, Goodwin had to fight a great battle against what he called his "master lust," the desire to impress. Sermons with "literary distinction" may be, to use his own words, "distinguished rather for ostentatious display of rhetoric than for clear statement of evangelical truth."[5] When once preparing to preach a university sermon at Cambridge, he had to excise the "purple patches" and preach a sermon which was "simple, earnest and faithful."

In his noted sermon on April 27, 1642, to the Commons Fast on "Zerubbabel's Encouragement to Finish the Temple" (from Zechariah 4:6–9), Goodwin saw the overarching apocalyptic implication for England of the analogy with Israel.[6] His great sermon on "The Heart of Christ in Heaven to Sinners on Earth" had the basic proposition "The living Christ is the same in character and purpose as the historical Jesus; and what He is in heaven that as universally present He also is to us on earth."[7] Goodwin was also a strong premillennialist, *a la* Joseph Mede, the "father of English premillennialism."[8]

1. John Brown, *Puritan Preaching in England* (New York: Scribner's, 1900), 102.
2. Horton Davies, *The Worship of the English Puritans* (Westminster, London, England: Dacre, 1948), 127.
3. F. R. Webber, *A History of Preaching in Britain and America* (Milwaukee: Northwestern, 1952), 1:237.
4. Brown, *Puritan Preaching in England,* 101.
5. D. Martyn Lloyd-Jones, *The Puritans: Their Origins and Successors* (Edinburgh: Banner of Truth, 1987), 384.
6. John F. Wilson, *Pulpit in Parliament* (Princeton, N.J.: Princeton University Press, 1969), 208–9.
7. A. E. Garvie, *The Christian Preacher* (New York: Scribner's, 1923), 157–58.
8. Mal Couch, ed., *Dictionary of Premillennial Theology* (Grand Rapids: Kregel, 1996), 250.

7.3.2.4 John Owen—Pillar of Orthodoxy

Protestants suppose the Scripture to be given forth by God to be . . . a perfect complete rule of faith.

The first and principal duty of a pastor is to feed the flock by diligent preaching of the word.

Scripture contains all things necessary to be . . . practiced in the worship of God.

—John Owen

Called the systematic theologian of Puritanism and the Calvin of England, **John Owen** (1616–1683) must be viewed as one of the heavyweights in the pulpit during this renaissance of preaching. He was the son of a clergyman, born in Oxfordshire of Welsh ancestry. He earned his M.A. at Oxford when he was only nineteen and preached before Parliament in 1649. J. I. Packer pays singular tribute to Owen by acknowledging him as the most formative influence in shaping his Christian life and theology.[1] D. Martyn Lloyd-Jones in both his style and emphasis is much like John Owen. In Owen we find one of the defining mentors for "the Doctor."[2]

"To scorn delights and live laborious days" had been the watchword for John Milton, who served the Commonwealth as a translator of Latin and Italian documents. Milton became a chief Puritan pamphleteer, not returning to his poetry until after the Restoration.

We see the same intense productivity in Owen, who shocked the sensibilities of some with his "powdered hair and cocked hat." When the civil war hit, Owen did not care to go into battle, serving instead as the reluctant chaplain to Cromwell. Later he became dean of Christ Church College, where he was called "the greatest of all the Deans of Christ Church College" by Professor Benjamin Jowett. Owen eventually served as chancellor of Oxford in 1651.

Among Owen's students were John Locke, Philip Henry, and William Penn. He was offered the presidency of Harvard and invited to First Church, Boston, but declined. As an Independent, he was deposed after the collapse of the Commonwealth in 1660. He served as *de facto* leader of the Independents after the Restoration, and was pastor of an independent church in London from 1673 until his death.[3]

John Owen's preaching style was "elaborate and exhaustive." We see in him the prolixity and pedantry that sometimes marred Puritan preaching. In his address to Parliament on the day after the decapitation of Charles I, Owen took Jeremiah 15:19d–20 as his text. His theme: "Treacherous Contrivances against the God of Heaven." In typical Puritan fashion, Owen did exhaustive work in excavating the text within its setting. He then developed a series of ten "propositions allegedly in the text," one of which he pressed more generally.[4]

His monumental seven volumes of exposition on Hebrews[5] is his magnum opus. His study of the Holy Spirit[6] and of *Apostasy from the Gospel*[7] are still available and widely read, though they are often tough slogging. In length and treatment he tended to be tedious. As Dargan observes, Owen had neither "the logical coherence" of Barrow and Howe, nor the popular tone of Baxter or the beauties of Jeremy Taylor.[8] Yet Alexander Whyte called Owen, "The most massive of the Puritans." Spurgeon labeled him "the prince of the Puritans," and advised, "To master his works is to be a profound theologian."

Like many of the Puritan preachers, when Owen was barred from his pulpit he wrote voluminously. A learned man, he laced his works with Latin and Greek quotations. He and Goodwin were contemporaries at Oxford and Baxter, Thomas Manton and John Bunyan were his friends. Allegedly he said of Bunyan, "Had I the tinker's abilities, I would gladly relinquish my learning." Like all Puritans he was dedicated to the practical application of the truth he preached.[9] When he died in 1683, he was buried in Bunhill Fields, London, the Westminster Abbey of nonconformity.

---

1. J. I. Packer in his introduction to John Owen, *Sin and Temptation* (Portland, Oreg.: Multnomah, 1983), xvii–xxx.
2. D. Martyn Lloyd-Jones, *The Puritans: Their Origins and Successors* (Edinburgh: Banner of Truth, 1987), 73–100.
3. Peter Toon, *God's Statesman: The Life and Work of John Owen, Pastor, Educator and Theologian* (Grand Rapids: Zondervan, 1973).
4. John F. Wilson, *Pulpit in Parliament* (Princeton, N.J.: Princeton University Press, 1969), 163.
5. John Owen, *The Epistle to the Hebrews*, 7 vols. (Edinburgh: Banner of Truth, 1992). A one-volume abridgment is *Hebrews: The Epistle of Warning* (Grand Rapids: Kregel, 1985).
6. John Owen, *The Holy Spirit: His Gifts and Power* (Grand Rapids: Kregel, 1954).
7. John Owen, *Apostasy from the Gospel* (Edinburgh: Banner of Truth, 1992).
8. E. C. Dargan, *A History of Preaching* (New York: Hodder and Stoughton, 1912), 2:179.
9. Sinclair B. Ferguson, *John Owen on the Christian Life* (Edinburgh: Banner of Truth, 1987). See also, David J. McKinley, "John Owen's View of Illumination: An Alternative to the Fuller-Erickson dialogue" in *Bibliotheca Sacra* 154 (January–March 1997): 93–104.

7.3.2.5 John Bunyan—The Storyteller of the Ages

I preached what I smartingly felt.

I never endeavored to, nor durst make use of other men's lines (although I do not condemn all that do), for I verily thought and found by experience that what was taught me by the Word and Spirit of Christ could be spoken, maintained and stood to by the soundest and best established conscience.

—John Bunyan

Justly renowned for his vastly popular *Pilgrim's Progress* and *The Holy War,* **John Bunyan** (1628–1688) was not only a noteworthy figure in the history of English literature but also was a preacher of no small accomplishment. Born in Elstow near Bedford, Bunyan followed his father's trade as a tinker, making and repairing pots and pans. He served in the Parliamentary army, closely escaping death on several occasions.

Known as something of a rake, he was influenced toward the things of the Lord by his first wife, who read to him from Arthur Dent's *The Plain Man's Path to Heaven* and Lewis Bayly's *The Practice of Piety,* popular books among the Puritans. He was further nudged toward the kingdom through Luther's commentary on Galatians ("most fit for a wounded conscience") and the ministry of John Gifford, pastor in Bedford.[1] After hearing three women talking about the joys of the Christian life, Bunyan sought the new birth. His protracted introspection and depression at this time are typically Puritan. At the time of his conversion he could not read or write.

Finally, like Christian at Mt. Calvary, the chains fell off. In 1653 Bunyan joined St. John's Church, a nonconformist fellowship in Bedford pastored by Gifford. Two years later he was called to be the pastor-preacher of the assembly, but "His call to be their preacher aroused the opposition of many who denied that he had a right to preach, since he had practically no education, no theological training, and of course, was never able to read any of the original languages."[2]

Yet his fame as a preacher grew and with the Restoration so did his problems with the Act of Uniformity. As a result, he was imprisoned for twelve years. This was a fruitful time of literary production. He was also permitted to preach in the jail and toward the end of his sentence even preached outside. To help his family, who visited him faithfully, he made lace while in prison. He said that his beloved blind daughter "lay nearer my heart than all I had beside."

Again in 1672 Bunyan assumed pastoral office in Bedford. In a second imprisonment he wrote *Pilgrim's Progress.* Professor Trevelyan writes of the leading character:

> That lonely figure with the Bible and the burden of sin is not only John Bunyan himself. It is the representative Puritan of the English Puritan epoch. The poor man seeking salvation with tears, with no guide save the Bible in his hands, that man, multipled, congregated, regimented, was a force by which Oliver Cromwell and George Fox and John Wesley wrought their wonders, being men of a like experience themselves.[3]

Soon his preaching was heard by throngs in London and elsewhere.

The helpful study by Professor Tindall of Columbia University has shown that while many of the Puritan preachers were university men, there were those like Bunyan who came from humble backgrounds.[4] On occasion Bunyan would boast that he was not like Pontius Pilate, who could speak Hebrew, Greek, and Latin. Yet Bunyan was steeped in Scripture, and once indicated that his library was only the Bible and a concordance.

Not only was his the plain style of the Puritans, but he was "folksy and colloquial . . . he had the gift of filling out the brief stories and sparse records of the Scripture with human detail."[5] He had an active imagination and sometimes over-allegorized Scripture.[6] An early sermon from 1658 opened up Luke 16:19–31, the story of the rich man and Lazarus. He titled the sermon "A Few Sighs from Hell; or, The Groans of a Damned Soul." He followed the order of the verses, made his argument, and gave five uses. We do not see homely language here, and the sermon may well have been edited by an admirer in order to make him seem more standard in his preaching.[7] In a later sermon (1678), "Come and Welcome to Jesus," Bunyan took the text "All that the Father giveth me shall come to me; and him that cometh to me I will in no wise cast out" (John 6:37) and made the words "shall come" into a character by that name. Wakefield points out the tender evangelical "warmth and emotion" that swept over the listeners as he expounded the last clause.[8]

Although he stands in the wake of Ames, Perkins, and Owen, as he grew older Bunyan became burdened about legalism and the excesses of some Sabbatarians. Some call the later Bunyan a Pietistic Puritan. Considered a Baptist, he still did not insist on immersion for church membership, rather respecting conscience in the matter of mode of baptism. Richard Muller argues that Bunyan (not unlike Richard Baxter at this point) "reformulated federalism" in a reaction against legalistic covenant theology, hoping to avoid the opposite danger of antinomianism.[9]

As a preacher, Bunyan stands (as does his statue in Bedford) with his eyes to heaven, the Book in his hand. His characters Evangelist, Watchful the porter who speaks the kindly word, and Greatheart, the servant of Interpreter, set forth his perception of the preacher's role.[10]

Bunyan wrote one hundred books and preached whenever and wherever possible.[11] He died in his fifty-ninth year, his life cut short by pneumonia contracted while on a mission of mercy. He was buried at Bunhill Fields, the dissenters' graveyard.

In a fitting epitaph, Froude says that for two centuries John Bunyan "affected the spiritual opinions of the English race in every part of the world more powerfully than any book or books except the Bible."[12]

---

1. John Bunyan, *Grace Abounding to the Chief of Sinners* (Grand Rapids: Baker, 1978).
2. Wilbur M. Smith in his introduction to *John Bunyan, The Holy War* (Chicago: Moody, 1948), 19.
3. Ibid., 28.
4. William York Tindall, *John Bunyan Mechanick Preacher* (New York: Columbia University Press, 1934).
5. Gordon Wakefield, *Bunyan the Christian* (London: Harper/Collins Religious, 1992), 38.
6. Ibid., 36ff.
7. Caroline Francis Richardson, *English Preachers and Preaching 1640–1670* (New York: Macmillan, 1928), 74.
8. Wakefield, *Bunyan the Christian,* 39.
9. Richard A. Muller, "Covenant and Conscience in English Reformed Theology: Three

Variations on a Seventeenth Century Theme," *Westminster Theological Journal* 42 (1980): 318, 321.

10. John Brown, *Puritan Preaching in England* (New York: Scribner's, 1900), 139.

11. John Bunyan, *The Works of John Bunyan,* ed. George Offor, 3 vols. (Edinburgh: Banner of Truth, 1853, 1862).

12. Smith, in *John Bunyan,* 33.

7.3.2.6 John Howe—Thinker Par Excellence

> But what I sensibly felt through the admirable bounty of my God and the most pleasant, comforting influences of His Spirit on October 22, 1704, far surpassed the most expressive words my thoughts can suggest. I then experienced an inexpressibly pleasant melting of heart, tears gushing out of mine eyes for joy that God had shed abroad His love abundantly through the hearts of men; and that, for this purpose, mine own heart should be so signally possessed of and by His blessed Spirit.
>
> —John Howe (comment inscribed on a blank page in his Bible and found at his death)

Standing as an able representative of the more conservative Puritans is **John Howe** (1630–1705), who was born in Leicestershire, the son of a clergyman who was ejected from the Church of England for his nonconformity. A brilliant thinker, Howe was trained at Cambridge and Oxford. He was a close friend of Henry More and Ralph Cudworth, of the Cambridge Platonists. His pastoral tenure at Great Torrington in Devon was a model in effective preaching and impact. He corresponded weekly with his father-in-law in Latin. He was called the Platonic Puritan. Tall and dignified in appearance,[1] Howe was summoned to be the chaplain for Oliver Cromwell and subsequently for Cromwell's son Richard. He was not happy to leave his parish for these duties, but report has it that Cromwell went to hear him at Whitehall Chapel and sent him a request for the treatment of a certain text. Howe then expounded upon it in a manner so appealing that Cromwell would not be denied in his desire for Howe as his chaplain.

On a typical fast day, Howe deported himself in this manner:

> It was his common way to begin about nine in the morning with a prayer for about a quarter of an hour, in which he begged a blessing on the work of the day and afterward read or expounded a chapter or psalm, in which he spent about three-quarters of an hour; then prayed an hour, preached another hour, and prayed again for half an hour. After this he retired and took a little refreshment for a quarter of an hour or more, the people singing all the while. He then returned to the pulpit, prayed for another hour, gave them another sermon of about an hour's length, and so concluded the service of the day, about four o'clock in the evening, with half an hour or more of prayer.[2]

After his service as chaplain, he returned to Great Torrington but was silenced by the Act of Uniformity. Destitute, in 1671 he went to Ireland where he was chaplain to Lord Masarene at Antrim Castle. He preached the funeral sermon for Richard Baxter in 1681. He emigrated to Utrecht in the Netherlands in another wave of persecution, but returned to finish out his days in an independent church in London after the Declaration of Indulgence in 1687. His purpose in ministry was ever "the promotion of practical godliness, and of Christian liberty and love, irrespective of all sectarian considerations."[3]

Howe always preached without notes and could be exceedingly lengthy. He preached five sermons weekly. His gesture was vehement and voice and diction somewhat affected. He preached fourteen sermons on "we are saved by hope" from Romans 8; seventeen sermons on 1 John 4:20; and eighteen on John 3:6. He tended to launch strongly, wane and ramble somewhat, and then end strongly. One parishioner commented that Howe spent so much time setting the table in his introduction that the audience fairly lost its appetite for dinner.

His admirable treatise on "Delighting in God" embodies all of these strengths and weaknesses. Especially striking are his sermons "Vanity of Man as Mortal" and "The Redeemer's Tears over Lost Souls." His collected works contain much of his pulpit utterance, and his sermon "Yield Yourselves to God" from Romans 6:13 is typical. Laced with Scripture and divided into mains, subs, and sub-subs, the sermon is heavy but vibrant. One of his best-remembered messages was his famous sermon on "Carnality of Religious Contention."

Robert Hall called him "the greatest of the Puritan divines" and said of him, "I have learned far more from John Howe than from any other author I have ever read . . . there is an astounding magnificence in his conceptions."[4]

---

1. E. C. Dargan, *A History of Preaching* (New York: Hodder and Stoughton, 1912), 2:180.
2. T. Harwood Pattison, *The History of Christian Preaching* (Philadelphia: American Baptist Publication Society, 1903), 200.
3. J. P. Hewlett, "A Life of the Author," in *The Works of Rev. John Howe* (Ligonier, Pa.: Soli Deo Gloria, 1990), 1:xix. This fine set is published in three volumes.
4. F. R. Webber, *A History of Preaching in Britain and America* (Milwaukee: Northwestern, 1952), 1:266.

7.3.2.7 Philip Henry—Contender for the Faith

Let your preaching be plain. Painted glass is most curious; plain glass is most perspicuous. Preach a crucified Saviour in a crucified style. Be a good crucifix to your people. Let your matter be substantial; wholesome food; God and Christ, and the gospel, faith, repentance, regeneration. Aim purely at God's glory and the salvation of souls. Study, as if there were no Christ; preach as if there had been no study. To this end get your sermon into your own souls. It is best, from the heart, to the heart. Get your sermons memoriter. How can you expect your people should remember, and repeat, if you read?

—Philip Henry

Taking his place in this lustrous succession is **Philip Henry** (1631–1696), whose son Matthew Henry has given us the story of his father's life. The Henry family had roots in Wales. Philip Henry was born in Whitehall, London, and knew Prince Charles and Prince James as "boyhood companions." He early listened to preaching. "He used to sit always upon the pulpit stairs, and it was his constant practice from eleven or twelve years old, to write, as he could, all the sermons he heard, which he kept very carefully, transcribed."[1]

Henry graduated from Christ Church, Oxford, in 1647. He served as tutor and preacher until he ran afoul of the authorities and was imprisoned on several occasions, preaching intermittently in Flintshire. Of his first parish it was said, "Here by his close and practical preaching he was made exceedingly useful, and wrought under God a wonderful change in the parish, which before was esteemed one of the most loose and profane places in all that county."[2]

Philip Henry was an avid student of Scripture and published a commentary on Genesis, as well as numerous sermons. Because of his limited opportunities under the Five-Mile Act, he frequently preached *gratis*. He tended to preach in a series *(lectio continua),* carefully aiming his discourse at his hearers and their situation, "fetching his similitudes for illustration from those things which were familiar to them. He did not shoot the arrow of the word over their heads in high notions or under their feet by blunt and homely expressions, but to their hearts, in close and lively applications."[3]

In his introduction he sought to make a point of contemporary contact, as when preaching on the conversion of Paul from Galatians 1:16, "He began his sermon with this remark, to raise attention: 'Much is said in story concerning the seven wonders of the world (and he named them); but I have been sometimes thinking, whether I could not name seven things which I would call the seven wonders of the church. And what do you think of these seven? (and he names seven, the last of which is the conversion of the Apostle Paul).'"[4]

Henry produced splendid sermon series on the Ten Commandments, the Lord's Prayer, types of Christ in the Old Testament, and forty sermons on the prodigal son from Luke 15 in 1673. He had his Bible re-bound with blank pages alternating with Scripture pages, and transcribed exegetical notes on them as an aid to sermon preparation. So rich were messages that he was known as "heavenly Henry."[5] Once he spent two months preaching the doctrine of the Lord's Supper and half a year preaching on the living Christ's letter to the Laodicean church.

The Puritan dedication to exegetical preaching within a strong sense of doctrinal construct is clearly seen in Philip Henry's pulpit labors. Concerning repentance he would often say, "If I were to die in the pulpit, I would desire to die preaching repentance; as if I die out of the pulpit, I would desire to die practicing repentance."[6] One Scripture verse which was particularly meaningful to him as a preacher was Isaiah 50:4, "The Sovereign LORD has given me an instructed tongue, to know the word that sustains the weary. He wakens me morning by morning, wakens my ear to listen like one being taught." This was the influence which touched so many and shaped his illustrious son Matthew.

1. Matthew Henry, *The Life of Rev. Philip Henry* (Edinburgh: Banner of Truth, 1974), 6.
2. F. R. Webber, *A History of Preaching in Britain and America* (Milwaukee: Northwestern, 1952), 1:270–71.
3. Henry, *The Life of Rev. Philip Henry,* 59ff.
4. Ibid., 241.
5. Webber, *A History of Preaching,* 1:271.
6. Henry, *The Life of Rev. Philip Henry,* 141.

7.3.3 GOSPEL TORCHBEARERS—ADVOCATES OF PROMISE

The preaching of God's holy word is the ministry of the Holy Spirit.

Preaching is the ordinance of God, sanctified for the begetting of faith, for the opening of the understanding, for the drawing of the will and affections to Christ.

—Richard Sibbes

We come now to the second grouping in Professor Knight's taxonomy: "The Sibbesians who set their clocks not on preparative disciplines but on the direct experience of the Spirit's indwelling, the joys of Christian fellowship and the divine attribute of overflowing love."[1] The Amesians and the Sibbesians clashed in the 1630s and later—the former being accused of legalism and the latter being accused of antinomianism. The tension was especially marked in New England.

This entire century in England was one of endless disruption and religious turmoil. Yet this is when preaching flourished in the culture as at perhaps no other time. We must take into account not only all of the acrimony leading up to the civil war and the subsequent emergence of the Puritan Commonwealth but also the fact that the Restoration picked up where events had been before.

Again the nation was plunged into chaos as the Stuarts persisted in their Romish-tilted policies, to the consternation of most of their subjects. The Cavalier Parliament (1661–1679) passed laws aimed directly at the Puritans: the celebrated Corporation Act (no Roman Catholic or Puritan could be a member of a municipal body); the Act of Uniformity (all clergy were to accept *The Book of Common Prayer*); the Five-Mile Act (two thousand clergy who refused to obey the Act of Uniformity were prohibited from coming within five miles of their former dwellings); and the Conventicle Act (all non-Anglican religious meetings were forbidden.).[2] Charles II prescribed listening to sermons as the remedy for insomnia, thus showing the general royal attitude toward the craft. Not until the Glorious Revolution and the enthronement of William and Mary in 1688 was any relief to be experienced.

Until the Revolution, any ministry outside the bounds of the established church was severely interrupted. Even those within the Church of England who were of Puritan bent were sent packing. An especially egregious case was the noted Puritan centrist **Thomas Watson** (1620–1686), whose preaching was among the most eagerly received in London.[3] Watson served St. Stephen's, Walbrook, for fifteen years with distinction before his ejection, when he experienced unspeakable hardship and privation.

But this was not uncommon and helps explain why many chose to move on to the New World. Our problem here is the ample supply of preachers who call for our attention. The level of sermonic discourse was amazingly high, even among the rank-and-file clergy.[4] Of course, there were the more eccentric preachers, some of whom were extraordinarily gifted. John Stoughton was given to bizarre sermon titles like "Baruch's Sore Gently Opened, and the Salve Skillfully Applied," or "The Church's Bowel Complaint." Then there was the "Spiritual Mustard Pot to Make the Soul Sneeze with Devotion," "The Snuffers of Divine Love," and "A Pack of Cards to Win Christ."[5] Nor are we particularly drawn to the book titled *Sermons to Asses, to Doctors of Divinity, to Lord's Spiritual and to Ministers of State,* or to John Haslebach, who expounded on a single chapter in Isaiah for twenty-one years. Another preacher served up an entire sermon on the letter O. These colorful characters aside, we now turn to one of the venerable patriarchs of the Puritans.

---

1. Janice Knight, *Orthodoxies in Massachusetts: Rereading American Puritanism* (Cambridge, Mass.: Harvard University Press, 1994).
2. David Green, *History of England* (Ames: Littlefield, Adams and Co., 1958), 128–29.
3. See Thomas Watson, *The Sermons of Thomas Watson* (Ligonier, Pa.: Soli Deo Gloria, 1990); *The Doctrine of Repentance* (Edinburgh: Banner of Truth, 1987). Curiously neither Dargan nor Webber mention Thomas Watson or Richard Sibbes.
4. John Chandos, ed., *In God's Name: Examples of Preaching in England 1534–1662* (London: Hutchinson, 1971). A splendid sampling of some of the lesser lights.
5. Paxton Hood, *The Throne of Eloquence* (New York: Funk and Wagnalls, 1888), 276.

7.3.3.1 Richard Sibbes—Teacher of Spirituality

Of this blest man, let this just praise be given, Heaven was in him, before he was in heaven.

—Izaak Walton of Richard Sibbes

The eminent Thomas Manton called him "the heavenly Doctor Sibbes"; Spurgeon said that "Sibbes never wastes the students' time; he scatters pearls and diamonds with both hands." Lloyd-Jones intones, "There are Puritans and there are Puritans . . . I shall never cease to be grateful to one of them called Richard Sibbes who was a balm to my soul at a period in my life when I was overworked and badly overtired, and therefore subject in an unusual manner to the onslaughts of the devil."[1]

Richard Sibbes (1577–1635) was born in Tostock, Suffolk, and matriculated at Cambridge at the same time as Jeremy Taylor. There he took successively his B.A., M.A., B.D., and D.D. degrees. He was named college preacher in 1609.

Peter Bayne (Perkins' successor) had led Sibbes to Christ at Cambridge, giving us an interesting succession in the Cambridge Lectureship: Perkins, then Bayne, then Sibbes, then John Preston, who was led to Christ by John Cotton, who was led to Christ by Richard Sibbes! And Richard Baxter came to Christ through a book of sermons by Sibbes purchased by his father.

Sibbes was lecturer at Cambridge until 1615, when Laud ousted him. He was then appointed preacher at Gray's Inn while Francis Bacon lived there. Bacon's famous "I am a bruised reed" undoubtedly was derived from Sibbes' sermon on that topic. Through Archbishop Ussher, Sibbes simultaneously served as provost at Trinity College, Dublin, and as Master of Catharine Hall, Cambridge (where John Milton was writing his sonnets on Sibbes' themes).

Thomas Manton spoke of Sibbes "sweet-dropping voice," and, in some respects, he was "sweet-natured to a fault."[2] He stammered noticeably when speaking, and shrank from separatism. Despite his timid nonconformist views, he never left the Church of England. Neither did he marry.

Sibbes is a seminal thinker for those holding that reason must be in subjection to the authority of the Spirit by the Word. Sibbes was influenced by mysticism of a healthy sort, as we see in his works *Bowels Opened* and *A Breathing after God*. He did not go as far as **Frances Rous** (1579–1659), who spoke of climbing the mystical ladder and who in his *Mystical Marriage* was much like St. Bernard of Clairvaux. Several have commented that only his Puritan biblicism saved him from extremes.[3] Yet Izaak Walton valued his books so highly, he left several marked volumes for his children to read.

Sibbes is the primary figure in Nuttall's study on *The Holy Spirit in Puritan Faith and Experience*. Sibbes insisted:

> There must be an infused establishing by the Spirit to settle the heart in this first principle . . . that the Scriptures are the word of God. . . . There must be a double light: so there must a Spirit in me, as there is a Spirit in the Scripture before I can see anything. . . . The breath of the Spirit in us is suitable to the Spirit's breathing in the Scriptures; the same Spirit doth not breathe contrary motions . . . as the spirits in the arteries quicken the blood in the veins, so the Spirit of God goes along with the word and makes it work.[4]

Though staunchly Calvinistic, Sibbes led those who were of a freer spirit and had a balanced view of experience and feeling.[5] His delivery was the plain style common among the Puritans. As one observer said, "Great affectation and good affections seldom go together."[6] Sibbes argued in his classic *The Bruised Reed:*

> The church of Christ is a common hospital, wherein all are in some measure sick of some spiritual disease or other; that we should all have ground of exercising mutually the spirit of wisdom and meekness.

Sibbes' memorable sermons on "The Sword of the Wicked" from Psalm 42:10 and "The Saint's Safety in Evil Times" (one sermon from Psalm 7:14 and another from 2 Timothy 4:16–17) are moving and enlightening. Although there were many divisions, he used the question/answer and the objection/answer technique as an aid to understanding and concluded with an impressive array of "uses."[7] All of his sermons blended short sentences with fairly complex structure and excellent devotional application.

Sibbes followed Thomas Goodwin as vicar of Trinity in Cambridge. He died on July 5, 1635, in his fifty-eighth year.

---

1. Alexander B. Grosart, "Memoir," in *Works of Richard Sibbes* (Edinburgh: Banner of Truth, 1973), xv–xvi.
2. Ibid., xi.
3. F. Ernest Stoeffer, *The Rise of Evangelical Pietism* (Leiden, Netherlands: E. J. Brill, 1965).
4. Geoffrey F. Nuttall, *The Holy Spirit in Puritan Faith and Experience* (Oxford: Blackwell, 1946), 23.
5. For significant studies, see Bert Affleck, "The Theology of Richard Sibbes" (Ph.D. dissertation, Drew University, 1968); Harold Palton Shelly, "Richard Sibbes: Early Stuart Preacher of Piety" (Ph.D. dissertation, Temple University, 1972). Both are available in the University of Michigan Microfilm 85–10.
6. W. Fraser Mitchell, *English Pulpit Oratory from Andrewes to Tillotson* (London: SPCK, 1932), 117.
7. Richard Sibbes, *Works of Richard Sibbes* (Edinburgh: Banner of Truth, 1973), 108ff., 119ff., 295ff., 314ff.

7.3.3.2 Richard Baxter—Master of the Puritan Pulpit

I preach as never sure to preach again, and as a dying man to dying men.

The Holy Spirit, by immediate inspiration, revealed unto the apostles the doctrine of Christ, and caused them infallibly to indite [compose] the Scriptures. But this is not that way of ordinary illumination now.

This trying the Spirit by the Scriptures, is not a setting of the Scriptures above the Spirit itself; but is only a trying of the Spirit by the Spirit; that is, the Spirit's operations in ourselves and his revelations to any pretenders now, by the Spirit's operations in the apostles, and by their revelations recorded for our use. For they and not we are called foundations of the church. We may be sure the inward testimony of the Spirit never is opposite to the outward testimony of his gospel which is the Spirit's testimony also.

—Richard Baxter

Perhaps the best-known of all the Puritan preachers is **Richard Baxter** (1615–1691), called by some "the most successful preacher and winner of souls and nurturer of won souls that England has ever had." Edmund Calamy spoke of him as "The most voluminous theological writer in the English language." Baxter wrote 160 works. Spurgeon highly regarded him as the tonic for his own sluggishness.[1]

Born in Shropshire in modest circumstances, Richard Baxter was largely self-educated. The young Baxter was not altogether sure when he was converted, but he sensed God's call to holy orders and was ordained by the bishop of Worcester. He did some teaching and preaching around Dudley, and in 1641 was made lecturer and curate at Kidderminster near Birmingham.

Kidderminster was a town of about four thousand souls. The area was desperately depraved and engulfed in an abysmal ignorance of spiritual truth. The resident vicar preached only quarterly and was known as a heavy drinker. Kidderminster's inhabitants were primarily weavers, and virtually none of them knew the Lord. Except for a brief stint with Cromwell's army, Baxter ministered faithfully from 1647 to 1660. He visited and catechized eight hundred families every year. He put forth the principle in his famous *The Reformed Pastor:* "The first and main point, which I submit to you is that it is an unquestionable duty of all ministers of the church to catechize and teach personally all who are submitted to their care."[2] Dean Stanley said of Baxter's "awakening ministry" in Kidderminster:

> There have been three or four parishes in England which have been raised by their pastors to a national, almost a world-wide fame. Of these the most conspicuous is Kidderminster: for Baxter without Kidderminster would have been but half of himself; and Kidderminster without Baxter would have had nothing but carpets.[3]

Although Baxter had opposed the deposition of the king, he could not adhere to the Act of Uniformity and was put out of Kidderminster. He was even offered a bishopric, but chose imprisonment rather than compromise. He was brought to trial before the infamous Judge Jeffreys and spent a year and a half in the Tower. Matthew Henry was among the many friends who visited him during his incarceration.

In appearance Baxter was tall and slender with "long tapering fingers," high forehead, and Roman nose. His eyes were described as "piercing."[4] His health was poor, and he was "seldom an hour without pain." But his consuming passion was to preach. Although he preached in Westminster Abbey and before the king and Parliament, his favorite venue was Kidderminster, where his preaching greatly moved his congregation. He returned most of his salary to the poor and never lived in the vicarage, allowing the aging incumbent to occupy it to his last days.

The outstanding characteristic of Baxter's preaching was his remarkable earnestness.[5] He often felt the lack of formal education and did not labor long on his manuscripts. Yet in one sermon he advanced sixty-six main points. The "uses" in another sermon filled thirteen pages.

Baxter often progressed through the presentation of competing ideas.[6] He tended to do his writing when in a state of physical collapse. His *A Call to the Unconverted* sold twenty-thousand copies in the first year. His classic *The Saints' Everlasting Rest* was equally popular. In all of his output he reflected his conviction that preachers need "the skill necessary to make plain the truth, to convince the hearers, to let in the irresistible light into their consciences, and to keep it there and drive all home; to screw the truth into their minds and work Christ into their affections . . ."

Although a controversialist by nature, Baxter was burdened for Christian concord.[7] He was bitterly disappointed when the Savoy Conference following the Restoration did not unite Anglicans and nonconformists. He was moderate in his own thinking, with "no Calvinist axe to grind,"[8] and rejected rigid Calvinistic extremism. This led some to describe him as fickle. His greatest strengths were his pastoral theology, his imagery in preaching, and his skill in application.[9] But some of his followers overemphasized these aspects, and Baxterism had some regrettable manifestations (cf. 6.4.2). The Kidderminster church is today a Unitarian assembly.

In his later years, Baxter developed considerable interest in the apocalyptic, and argued that Protestants need to take more interest in Bible prophecy.[10] He veered toward historicism in his prophetic hermeneutic. He wrestled much with the role of the Christian prince, and was crushed by the collapse of the Commonwealth. Baxter sought to reverse the Calvinist tide, advocated "free-will"[11] with Ussher on his side,[12] and fought the particular Baptists. (He denounced Bunyan as an "unlearned antinomian.") Baxter's was a middle way, and he craved consensus on what he called "mere Christianity," from whence C. S. Lewis obtained his famous title.

In all of this, the overmastering passion of Baxter's persuasive preaching was the conversion of the lost. His *A Call to the Unconverted* is a scalding meditation on Ezekiel 33:11 and well represents the communication which made Baxter so effective in the pulpit.[13] Closely reasoned and logical, it is studded with Scripture. In Richard Baxter we have a pastor whose influence moved Wesley, Doddridge, Spurgeon, Isaac Watts, Wilberforce, Whitefield, and ministers in our own day.[14]

---

1. Timothy Beougher and J. I. Packer, "Go Fetch Baxter," in *Christianity Today* (December 19, 1991): 26ff. Both of these scholars wrote most helpful doctoral dissertations on Baxter; cf. J. I. Packer, "The Redemption and Restoration of Man in the Thought of Richard Baxter: A Study in Puritan Theology" (D.Phil., Oxford University, 1954); Timothy K. Beougher, "Conversion: the Teaching and Practice of the Puritan Pastor with Regard to Becoming a 'True Christian'" (Ph.D. dissertation, Trinity Evangelical Divinity School, 1990).
2. Richard Baxter, *The Reformed Pastor* (Portland, Oreg.: Multnomah, 1982), 5.
3. John Brown, *Puritan Preaching in England* (New York: Scribner's, 1900), 169.
4. Charles F. Kemp, *A Pastoral Triumph: The Story of Richard Baxter and His Ministry at Kidderminster* (New York: Macmillan, 1948), 6.
5. Ibid., 23.
6. Caroline Francis Richardson, *English Preachers and Preaching 1640–1670* (New York: Macmillan, 1928), 73.
7. *Autobiography of Richard Baxter* (London: Dent, 1974 ed.).
8. Geoffrey F. Nuttall, *The Holy Spirit in Puritan Faith and Experience* (Oxford: Blackwell, 1946), 163.

9. N. H. Keeble, *Richard Baxter: Puritan Man of Letters* (Oxford: Clarendon, 1982).
10. William M. Lamont, *Richard Baxter and the Millennium* (London: Croom Helm, 1979), 51.
11. Ibid., 141. See also Peter Toon, *Puritans and Calvinism* (Swengel, Pa.: Bible Truth Depot, 1973), 83, 86, 89.
12. Ibid., 153.
13. Richard Baxter, *A Call to the Unconverted* (Grand Rapids: Baker, 1976).
14. Lamont, *Richard Baxter and the Millennium,* 286.

7.3.3.3 Thomas Manton—Anchor of Stability

> That knowledge is best which endeth in practice. . . . The hearer's life is
> the preacher's best commendation.
>
> —Thomas Manton

The Puritan penchant for practical application for daily life along with a bracing sense of doctrinal construct is seen vividly in one of the eminent Puritan preachers, **Thomas Manton** (1620–1677). Manton is a superb example of that fusion of warm piety and massive knowledge which characterized the Puritans.[1] He was born in Somerset, the son and grandson of ministers. Educated at Oxford, he served parishes at Stoke-Newington in Middlesex and Covent Garden in London. Functioning as chaplain and as examiner for the Protector, he was nonetheless uneasy about regicide, and urged the restoration of Charles II. He preached often to Parliament. His early preaching tended to be over the heads of his hearers. One poor man told him after a sermon:

> "Sir, I came with earnest desires after the word of God, and hopes of getting some good to my soul, but I was greatly disappointed; for I could not understand a great deal of what you said; you were quite above me." It is then reported that Manton replied: "Friend, if I did not give you a sermon, you have given me one; and by the grace of God I will never preach before my Lord Mayor in such a manner again."[2]

Although favored by the court in the Restoration, he refused to take the oath and was ejected in 1662. Imprisoned after preaching an illegal sermon, he continued to preach in the prison itself. Baxter, Charnock, and Ussher were his close friends. He died in 1677, with Dr. Bates preaching a memorable funeral sermon. One who attended his funeral spoke of him as "deservedly styled the King of Preachers." Appropriately his funeral was "attended with the vastest number of ministers of all persuasion that ever I saw together in my life. And the ministers walked in pairs, a Conformist and a Nonconformist."[3]

Manton's depth in exegetical work is seen in his still popular commentaries on James and Jude. He was well read in ancient and modern history. His pulpit expression was "natural and free, clear and eloquent, quick and powerful . . . inflamed by holy zeal."[4] Much of his preaching was published posthumously.

Manton was in the habit of repeating his main headings in his closing prayer and "was noted for his lively and affectionate administration of the Lord's Supper." Charnock paid tribute to him "the best collector of sense of the age." Barstow called him "one of the most elaborate and ingenious of all the Puritan preachers."

Manton's exposition of Psalm 119 is classic and ran to 190 sermons. Typical of his preaching are the exceedingly rich studies in John 17. Sermon 3 follows the standard Puritan pattern, beginning with exegetical highlights, proceeding to doctrinal affirmations, and concluding with the customary uses. A number of ancillary Scriptures were woven into the sermon's fabric. Manton's messages were high-density content with little *lucido ordo,* but they were forceful and full of Christ and the gospel.[5] His fluid prose style is evident here:

> The sum of the gospel is this, that all who, by true repentance and faith, do forsake the flesh, the world and the devil, and give themselves up to the Father, Son and Holy Spirit, as their creator, redeemer and sanctifier, shall find God as a father, taking them for his reconciled children, and for Christ's sake pardoning their sin, and by his Spirit giving them his grace; and, if they persevere in this course, will finally glorify them, and bestow upon them everlasting happiness; but will condemn the unbelievers, impenitent, and ungodly to everlasting punishment.[6]

---

1. Thomas Manton was at the forefront of the emphasis on personal piety, as noted by Dewey D. Wallace Jr., *The Spirituality of the Later Puritans* (Macon, Ga.: Mercer University Press, 1987), 2–3; for further substantive insights, see Greg K. Daniel, "The Puritan Ladder of Meditation: An Explication of Puritan Meditation and its Compatibility with Catholic Meditation" (M.A. thesis, Trinity Evangelical Divinity School, 1993). An important resource is Patrick Collinson, *The Elizabethan Puritan Movement* (Berkeley: University of California Press, 1983).
2. William Harris, "Memoir," in *The Complete Works of Thomas Manton* (London: James Nisbet, 1870), 1:xiii.
3. Caroline Francis Richardson, *English Preachers and Preaching 1640–1670* (New York: Macmillan, 1928), 31.
4. Harris, "Memoir," 1:xxii.
5. Thomas Manton, *An Exposition of John 17* (Evansville, Ind.: Sovereign Grace Book Club, 1958), 39ff.
6. Manton, *The Complete Works,* 2:102ff.

7.3.3.4 Stephen Charnock—Revitalizer of the Church

> A spiritual worshipper actually aspires in every duty to know God. . . . To desire worship as an end, is carnal; to desire it as a means for communion with God is spiritual, and the fruit of a spiritual life. . . . Evangelical worship is a spiritual worship, and praise, joy and delight

are prophesied of as great ingredients in attendance on gospel ordinances, Isaiah 12:3–5 . . . Delight in God in a gospel frame, therefore the more joyful, the more spiritual.

—Stephen Charnock

Stephen Charnock (1628–1680) was a rare and vital spirit among the Puritans. He was born in London, where his father was a solicitor in Chancery. While studying at Emmanuel College, Cambridge, he was powerfully converted. At first he became a preceptor with a wealthy family but then began his work as a parish minister in Southwark, where he saw many come to Christ. He went on to Oxford for an M.A. His unusual intellectual gifts were soon recognized, and he became a senior proctor in 1652.

Charnock served briefly as an assistant to John Owen before going to Ireland. There he served as chaplain to the governor, Henry Cromwell, son of the Protector. He preached every Lord's Day there and was given an honorary B.D. by Trinity College. With the collapse of the Protectorate, he lacked opportunity for some time, but in 1675 he joined Thomas Watson in a Presbyterian ministry in Crosby Square. It was here that he delivered his justly famous messages on "The Existence and Attributes of God." He died in his fifty-third year.

Charnock possessed an extraordinary mastery of the Greek and Hebrew originals. He always carried a book with him and wrote down any profitable thought that came to mind.[1] He was respected for his keen judgment and vivid imagination, and was capable of remarkable concentration.[2] His "reasonings and applications" were renowned. In 1666 he lost all of his books in the great fire of London, a deprivation he felt sharply. Through it all, "He excelled as a preacher."[3]

Initially Charnock preached without notes, but his eyes began to fail him and he had to read his sermons with a magnifying glass. He loved to preach on the cross of Christ and pleaded with sinners to "turn" to the crucified Savior. "Perspicuous plainness, convincing cogency, great wisdom, fearless honesty and affectionate earnestness are the chief characteristics of his sermons,"[4] Symington writes. Webber cites one of the most widely disseminated works of Charnock, *Discourses on Christ Crucified*, which was reprinted in America. In a notable sermon based on 1 Corinthians 2:2, his third main division was "The Fruits of His Death."

1. The death of Christ appeases the wrath of God for us;
2. The death of Christ satisfies the demands of the Law;
3. The death of Christ removes the guilt of sin;
4. The death of Christ conquers the power of Satan;
5. The death of Christ brings us sanctification;
6. The death of Christ opens the kingdom of heaven for us.[5]

This richly woven tapestry of biblical and theological truth was massive but magnificent. The republished sermons of Charnock are as fine an array of Puritan preaching as is available today.[6]

1. F. R. Webber, *A History of Preaching in Britain and America* (Milwaukee: North-western, 1952), 1:259.
2. William Symington, "The Life and Character of Stephen Charnock," in *Discourses upon the Existence and Attributes of God* (Grand Rapids: Baker, 1979), 1:11.
3. Ibid., 15.
4. Ibid.
5. Stephen Charnock, *Discourses on the Knowledge of God* (Edinburgh: Banner of Truth, 1985).
6. Webber, *A History of Preaching,* 1:261.

7.3.3.5 John Flavel—Model of Holiness

> The preaching of the gospel by Christ's ambassadors is the principal means appointed for reconciling and bringing home sinners to Christ. . . . A crucified style best suits the preachers of a crucified Christ. . . . Prudence will choose words that are solid, rather than florid. . . . Words are but servants to matter. An iron key, fitted to the wards of the lock, is more useful than a golden one that will open the door to the treasures. Prudence will cast away a thousand fine words for one that is apt to penetrate the conscience and reach the heart.
>
> —John Flavel

One of the godliest and most fragrant testimonies among the Puritan pastor-theologians was **John Flavel** (1630–1691), whose lineage traces back to fore-bears who came to England with William the Conqueror in the eleventh century. He was the son of Richard Flavel, a minister in Devon, who was roughly treated in the Restoration. Richard's two sons were both ministers of the gospel. John graduated from Oxford and in 1650 was made a probationer and assistant to a very ill clergyman in Diptford in Devon. In that same year he was ordained and became rector upon the death of the incumbent. Not long after, he went to Dartmouth, with which he was associated off and on through the Restoration period until his death in 1691. Here is one tribute to him:

> I could say much, though not enough, of the excellence of his preaching; of his seasonable, suitable and spiritual manner; of his plain expositions of Scripture, his talking method, his genuine and natural deductions, his convincing arguments, his clear and powerful demonstrations, his heart-searching applications and his comfortable supports to those that were afflicted in conscience. In short that person must have a very soft head, or a very hard heart, or both, that could sit under his ministry unaffected.[1]

John Flavel was "full and copious in prayer" and an ardent soulwinner. The dangerous times in which he ministered seemed only to burn off the dross in his life. While Flavel was preaching in the woods near Exeter, the constabulary came suddenly, and in the great confusion Flavel escaped.

He wrote extensively, the six volumes of his works often being reprinted. Among those who drank deeply of this spring are Jonathan Edwards and George Whitefield (who ranked him with John Bunyan and Matthew Henry), and later in Scotland, R. M. McCheyne and Andrew Bonar.[2] Other favorites are *Pneumatologia (Treatise on the Soul of Man)* and *The Method of Grace (How the Holy Spirit Works)*.

D. Martyn Lloyd-Jones types him as a "Christ-Mystic" who accented the objective bases of Christian experience. "He wrought it, though we wear it," Flavel liked to say. Yet he affirmed the subjective reality as well. Isaac Watts shares an anecdote from Flavel's life:

> There going on his way his thoughts began to swell and rise higher and higher like the waters in Ezekiel's vision, til at last they became an overwhelming flood. Such was the intention of his mind, such the ravishing tastes of heavenly joys, and such the full assurance of his interest therein, that he utterly lost all sight and sense of the world and all of the concerns thereof, and for some hours he knew no more where he was than if he had been in a deep sleep upon his bed. Arriving in great exhaustion at a certain spring, he sat down and washed, earnestly desiring, if it was God's good pleasure, that this might be his parting place from the world. Death had the most amiable face in his eye that ever he beheld, except the face of Jesus Christ which made it so, and he does not remember, though he believed himself dying, that he even thought of his dear wife and children or any earthly concernment. On reaching his inn the influence still continued, banishing sleep—still, still the joy of the Lord overflowed him and he seemed to be an inhabitant of the other world. He many years after called that day one of the days of heaven, and professed that he understood more of the life of heaven by it than by all the books he ever read or discourses he ever entertained about it.[3]

In his sermon "Crucifying the Flesh, or the Mortification of Sin," Flavel saw the text as the center of gravity in the sermon. He began with exegetical observations, identified and expounded the doctrine under five mains, and then inferentially draws out appropriate "uses" (i.e., motives, rules, and meditations which follow upon the truth). The last sermon he delivered in Dartmouth was from 1 Corinthians 10:12, "Wherefore let him that standeth take heed lest he fall." It was characteristically deeply moving, "tending to awaken careless professors, and to stir them up to be solicitous about their souls."[4]

---

1. "The Life of John Flavel" in *The Works of John Flavel* (Edinburgh: Banner of Truth, 1968), 1:vi.
2. Ibid.
3. Ibid., 1:xv.
4. John Flavel, *The Method of Grace* (Grand Rapids: Baker, 1977), 436ff.

7.3.3.6 Isaac Barrow—Watcher on the Wall

The insatiable appetite for laughter keeps itself within no bounds. Have you crowded to this place for the purpose of listening and studying and making progress, or only for the sake of laughing at this thing and making a jest of that other? There is nothing so remote from levity which you do not instantly transmute into mirth and absurdity, and let a discourse be such as to move no laughter, nothing else will pleasure, neither dignity, nor gravity, nor solidity, neither strength, nor point, nor polish.

—Isaac Barrow

Reinforcing the impression of the diversity among the Puritans is the singular ministry of **Isaac Barrow** (1630–1677). Barrow was not a pastor but a professor of Greek and mathematics. Yet he had a reputation as an Arminian preacher, albeit a long-winded one. He was born in London and reared in a merchant's home, often the despair of his father. He began to shine as a student at Cambridge and studied in Europe, particularly in Constantinople, "where he devoted a full year to the reading of Chrysostom in the original."[1] A loyalist to Charles I, he was successively professor of geometry and Lucasian Professor of Mathematics at Cambridge. Eventually he would yield that prestigious chair to his student and friend, Isaac Newton. Appointed chaplain to Charles II in the Restoration, Barrow was at the time of his passing the vice-chancellor of the university.

In appearance, Barrow was utterly unimpressive. As one witness to a sermon reported: "A pale, meagre, unpromising-looking man . . . dressed in a slovenly manner with his collar unbuttoned and his hair uncombed. It so happened that an alarm of fire was raised and most of the congregation went away. The preacher, unmoved by the commotion, gave out his text and went through his sermon to the two or three people present. Richard Baxter was one of those who remained . . . who declared that he had never heard a better discourse."[2]

Like Howe, Barrow could preach for an hour, give his congregation a break, and preach another hour. When preaching at Westminster one Lord's Day, the dean asked him to give only the first half of his sermon, which he did—and preached for almost two hours. On another occasion, a listener came to hear him and asked if the afternoon service had started. He was told that Barrow had not yet finished his morning sermon. Yet another account has the bellringers ringing the bells to stop him. King Charles II considered Barrow to be the best scholar in England but unfair as a preacher because he left nothing for others to say.

Barrow loved the church fathers, and occasionally quoted pagan moralists, but was most concerned with the Scripture. His sermons were not flowery, but were exhaustive in attention to the text. There was an attractiveness in his prose style,[3] and his strong personal devotion to Christ was his hallmark. He shared the Puritan view on the "naturalness and plainness" which should accompany preaching, and yet he was oratorically moving.[4]

Some called him the English Bossuet. Not unlike Chrysostom, Barrow had a remarkable ability to "reanimate attention while considering a topic from as large a number of angles as possible."[5] He knew how to usc "lively and apt images."

Mitchell calls him "the one great orator produced by England before Burke."[6] Tillotson has considerably revised many of his published sermons.

Broadus considers Barrow an example of intellectual richness. Many identify his great sermon on "The Crucifixion of Christ" as praiseworthy. It had five main divisions and twelve full applications after the Puritan manner. He argued that "this way of suffering had in it some particular advantages conducing to the accomplishment of our Lord's principal design." He preached movingly about the passion of our Lord and its place in the redemptive plan of God.

Barrow is properly remembered as an Anglican with a strong Puritan bent. A bust of him remains in Westminster Abbey.

<hr>

1. F. R. Webber, *A History of Preaching in Britain and America* (Milwaukee: Northwestern, 1952), 1:262.
2. T. Harwood Pattison, *The History of Christian Preaching* (Philadelphia: American Baptist Publication Society, 1903), 202.
3. W. Fraser Mitchell, *English Pulpit Oratory from Andrewes to Tillotson* (London: SPCK, 1932), 323.
4. Ibid., 323.
5. Ibid., 326.
6. Ibid., 400.

7.3.3.7 Joseph Alleine—Martyr in the Cause

> The distinctive principle of a true Puritan was reverence for the strict letter of Holy Scripture, as God's direct message to each individual man, and as forming our final and absolute authority in religion.
>
> —Charles Stanford

The last notable Puritan of the Sibbesian style is **Joseph Alleine** (1634–1668). He portrayed the turbulence and unsettledness of the Restoration. Before the Puritan Revolution, ecclesiastical pressures and political machinations led some to say:

> Men must content themselves and think it well
> If once a month they hear the sermon bell.

The rise of the Puritan lectureships and Puritan preaching began to redress that grievous situation. Joseph Alleine was born in Divizes in Wiltshire, where his father had been mayor. He entered "the so-called Puritan University" at Oxford in 1649 when Cromwell was chancellor and John Owen was dean of Christ College. Thomas Goodwin was the principal of the college. (Though a Puritan, Goodwin still used the magnificent organ in the chapel.) Alleine left before obtaining his degree to assist George Newton at St. Mary Magdalen Church in Taunton, Somerset. With his Bible in his hand, "His very appearance was a sermon," it was said. He defended illegal preaching. He was ordained a Presbyterian in 1655 and in that same year married Theodosia.[1]

Alleine dearly loved the flock at Taunton, urging that "If I should die 50 miles away, let me be buried at Taunton." His preaching had a "piercing directness, a powerful and charming eloquence." He was "insatiably greedy for souls"[2] and had as his compelling central theme "Jesus Christ and him crucified." Although he was a Calvinist, he "proclaimed a completed and gratuitous salvation to all who were willing to accept it."[3] He rose daily at 4 A.M. to spend time with God and then catechize the flock. He "had a poet's enjoyment of nature, but with a Puritan's love for the Bible."[4]

Alleine was among those who were unwilling to subscribe to the Act of Uniformity, and he was arrested and imprisoned. Taunton was singled out because of the sieges in the 1640s and Newton and Alleine were flung down. Presiding Judge Foster wanted to exterminate nonconformity. In his trial, Alleine was accused of preaching.[5] Of that much he was certainly guilty. When the jailer was late, he preached while waiting to be incarcerated. Through a series of imprisonments, he preached in the jail and from the jail window. Even though frail, he would preach up to fourteen times in a week. Finally his health broke. Even his wife and aged father were imprisoned. His last incarceration destroyed him, yet he continued to preach and fast.

Alleine's most powerful books were *An Alarm to Unconverted Sinners or The Sure Guide to Heaven* and his *Christian Letters,* in which he variously addresses his wife and the congregation at Taunton and expounds on the gracious love of God for sinners.[6] As his wife made clear, "He was very urgent with those who were unconverted."[7] He died at the age of thirty-four as a true martyr, and though he left no children, Alleine left a legacy of many spiritual sons and daughters.

----

1. Rich resources on Alleine's life are Richard Baxter, *The Life and Death of Joseph Alleine* (New York: Robert Carter, 1840) and the memorial volume written largely by his wife, *The Life and Death of that Excellent Minister of Christ Mr. Joseph Alleine* (London, 1671).
2. Charles Stanford, *Joseph Alleine: His Companions and Times* (Mobile, Ala.: R E Publications, 1861), 140.
3. Ibid., 143.
4. Ibid., 156.
5. Ibid., 227.
6. For excerpts from the letters, see Dewey D. Wallace Jr., ed., *The Spirituality of the Later English Puritans* (Macon, Ga.: Mercer University Press, 1987), 179–93.
7. Ibid., 56. He was such a kindly, gentle soul and sustained a cheerful disposition even under constant duress; see Caroline Francis Richardson, *English Preachers and Preaching 1640–1670* (New York: Macmillan, 1928), 285.

7.4 GEYSERS OF PURITAN PREACHING IN AMERICA

Mr. Cotton preaches with such authority, demonstration, and life that, methinks, when he preaches out of any Prophet or Apostle I hear not him; I hear that Prophet and Apostle; yea, I hear the Lord Jesus Christ speaking in my heart.

—observation by a listener

The work of the Spirit doth always go with the Word.

—Thomas Hooker

The experience of Puritan emigration in the seventeenth century must be understood in light of the persecutions and turbulences in England at that time.[1] In their courageous move from England to New England, the Puritans brought the centrality of the preached Word with them, but the ordeal was indescribable.[2] We now trace the contours of biblical preaching in the New England experience of the "come-outers" who settled those shores and aspired to be a "city set on a hill."

The tension between the Amesian piety and the Sibbesian piety as set forth by Professor Knight is transplanted directly to New England, where the embroiling conflict became more pronounced. The Ames/Perkins axis was represented in New England by Thomas Hooker, Thomas Shepard, and Peter Bulkeley, while John Cotton, John Davenport, and John Wheelwright comprised the Sibbesians.[3] We shall examine several of these leaders and through them pinpoint the centrality of biblical preaching in the New England experience.

---

1. John Brown, *The Pilgrim Fathers of New England and their Puritan Successors* (London: Religious Tract Society, 1895). Brown gave the Beecher Lectures at Yale on Puritan Preaching and served a church in Bedford.
2. Andrew Delbanco, *The Puritan Ordeal* (Cambridge, Mass.: Harvard University Press, 1989).
3. Janice Knight, *Orthodoxies in Massachusetts: Rereading American Puritanism* (Cambridge, Mass.: Harvard University Press, 1994).

3.4.1   JOHN COTTON—LEADER IN OLD BOSTON

I never yet observed any part of a Scripture . . . but without carnal affectation or straining of wit, it might holily be applyed both with power and profit and delight to an honest heart.

Knowledge is no knowledge without zeal.

Yet there is also an essential wisdom in us, namely, our Reason, which is not natural.

—John Cotton

Conspicuous in the pantheon of the early founders is **John Cotton** (1585–1652). He was a significant link between England and the new experiment in New England, and had "an early and clear prominence" in the affairs of

Massachusetts Bay. Perry Miller spoke of him as "the mouthpiece of the ruling oligarchy." He was above all things a preacher who has left us nineteen volumes of sermons and who epitomized what William Haller described as "English Puritanism, denied opportunity to reform the established church, wreaking its energy during a half century and more upon preaching."[1]

Born in Derby, Cotton went to Cambridge at age thirteen and studied at Emmanuel College, where he made his mark as "a witty, elegant preacher."[2] Here he was converted through the preaching of Richard Sibbes and adopted the plain style of Puritan preaching. Through his ministry, John Preston was converted, the later distinguished master of Emmanuel. Cotton himself served as dean and catechist at Emmanuel and then served twenty-one years as vicar of famous St. Botolph's in Boston, Lincolnshire. Though more and more a Puritan, he continued to use *The Book of Common Prayer* all of his life.

Cotton preached in his English days on Sundays and on Thursday and Friday mornings early and on Saturday afternoon. He loved to preach expository series through a book in the Bible. He studied and prepared twelve hours a day.[3] He loved Scripture and laced his sermons with verses ancillary to his text. In his children's catechism of sixty-two questions, he used sixty-six Old Testament citations and 106 from the New Testament. In a twelve-page treatment of the church, he used more than four hundred scriptural references. He was known for his evangelistic preaching. Although later he embraced a stricter Calvinism, earlier on he held to a kind of voluntarism in which the hearers of the gospel could either receive or reject it. John Preston would follow him in these views.

At age fifty, Cotton moved to Boston, where he commenced a twenty-year ministry at First Church. Cotton spoke out for the new form of church government emerging in New England. His commitment was to the gathered church, and yet he feared the separatism of Roger Williams and Williams' rejection of communion with English churches.[4] Anne Hutchinson, who had been one of his members in Lincolnshire in England, followed her pastor to New England and found early support from him. But in her drift to extreme views on private special revelation and her antinomian bent, Cotton and Hutchinson parted ways.

Cotton Mather, John's grandson, assessed his distinguished grandfather:

A man of might, at heavenly eloquence, To fix the ear and charm the conscience, As if Apollos were reviv'd in him, Or he had learned of a seraphim
(from *Magnalia Christi Americana*).

John Cotton was not as lively as Shepard and Hooker nor as severe. His style was only occasionally gripping. He was not an original thinker, yet he utilized much variety in his work. We discern a distinct eschatological tone in his preaching. He had interest in poetry and music. Governor John Winthrop, with whom Cotton worked closely, paid him tribute: In 1633 "more were converted and added to that church [Cotton's] than to all the other churches in the Bay . . . Divers profane and notorious evil persons came and confessed their sins, and were comfortably received into the bosom of the church."[5]

Interestingly, Cotton's Pauline sermons on the gospel and salvation became popular in New England. His emphasis may well have been pushed by Mrs. Hutchinson to deal with the antinomian extremism of freedom from all law.[6] In his widely read writings such as *The Way of Life, Christ the Fountaine,* and *God's Mercie Mixed with His Justice,* Cotton sets forth his convictions on conversion. His intriguing *An Exposition Upon the Thirteenth Chapter of the Revelation* speaks of the Book of Life:

> When the Lord wrote down thy name, or mine, or any man's name, who stood by His elbow (if I may so speak) to put Him in mind of my name or thine? He thought of us, if our names be there, and He set us down, and He delivered us to Christ Jesus by name. Whatever thy name is, He took notice of thy name. Such a man in such a place, he will live in this or that country. He is one; take notice of him; lay down a price for him. In fulness of time send a spirit into his heart. If he live in a popish country, save him from popery. If in a worldly country, save him from the world. Wherever he lives, save him from himself and bring him to my heavenly kingdom.[7]

John Cotton is a significant first-generational sample of Puritan biblical preaching.

1. William Haller, *The Rise of Puritanism* (Philadelphia: University of Pennsylvania Press, 1938), 15.
2. Everett H. Emerson, *John Cotton* (New York: Twayne, 1965), 33.
3. Ibid., 35.
4. Edwin S. Gaustad, *Liberty of Conscience: Roger Williams in America* (Grand Rapids: Eerdmans, 1991), 38–43, 72–85, 98–103. Gaustad also shows Williams' great love for the Jews and his intensified millennialism.
5. Emerson, *John Cotton,* 104.
6. Well analyzed in Emory Eliott, *Power and the Pulpit in Puritan New England* (Princeton, N.J.: Princeton University Press, 1975). See also Donald R. Come, "John Cotton: Guide of the Chosen People" (Ph.D. dissertation, Princeton University, 1948); Stephen K. Cottingham, "An Analysis and Evaluation of John Cotton's Apologetic against Seventeenth-Century Antinomianism" (Th.M. thesis, Dallas Theological Seminary, 1984). For background, see Gertrude Huehns, *Antinomianism in English History* (London: Cresset Press, 1951).
7. Emerson, *John Cotton,* 98.

7.4.2 INCREASE MATHER—SECOND GENERATION CONSERVATOR

> Yea it is a sad truth, that religion hath seldom been upheld in the power of it, for above one or two generations together.
> —Increase Mather

The power of the Puritan sermon was in its symbolic and metaphorical meaning, which resulted from a dynamic interaction between the clergy and their people.

—Emory Elliott

The most striking representative of the second-generation New England Puritans is **Increase Mather** (1639–1723). His father Richard was one of the founders who came from England (cf. 7.3.2.2) and served the Dorchester church near Boston. Here Increase was born, the youngest of six sons. Richard taught Increase to read as well as to handle Greek and Latin, so he was ready to enter Harvard at age twelve. He also studied at Trinity College, Dublin, and he served as a military chaplain on the island of Guernsey.

Increase Mather was precocious and always interested in scientific investigation. In 1693 he wrote a book about comets. He energetically supported inoculations for smallpox but was conservative theologically and politically. The Salem witchcraft trials troubled him and he put an end to them. He served as rector at Harvard (1685–1701) and spent four years in England (1688–1692) pleading with King William III for a new charter. He was instrumental in obtaining one, and effectively merged Massachusetts and Plymouth colonies in 1691.

Increase Mather preached his first sermon in his father's church in Dorchester in 1657. He had been converted two years earlier in a pattern not uncommon:

About which time the Lord broke in upon my conscience with very terrible convictions and awakenings. In the months of March, April, and till the latter end of May, 1655, I was in extremity of anguish and horror in my soul. Once at Dorchester when my Father was gone abroad on a public occasion and not to return for a day or two, I shut myself up in his study, and there wrote down all the sins which I could remember I had been guilty of, that lay as a heavy burden on my conscience. I brought them before God, and cried to him for pardoning mercy; and at night burnt the paper which in way of confession I had sorrowfully spread before the Lord.[1]

He went on to serve Second Church in Boston, usually called North Church, from 1664 until his death in 1723. His widowed father married John Cotton's widow, and Increase married Maria, daughter of the John Cottons and his stepsister. Desiring continuity with the vision of the founders, Increase and his generation lamented the spiritual drift in New England. He lambasted backsliding at Harvard, becoming somewhat bitter over trends and asserted that "Philistines had captured the ark." In one of his jeremiads, a style which he developed into a form, he preached on "Ichabod," from Ezekiel 9:3, "And the Glory of the God of Israel was gone up from the Cherub whereupon he was, to the Threshold of the House."[2]

The 1670s were the high point of Puritanism, and Increase Mather's sermons were widely heard (the parish had fifteen hundred souls) and widely published. He memorized all of his sermons and delivered them without notes. Mather had a good-sized library and read broadly. His theme increasingly became "the great radical apostasy of New England." One of his trademark jeremiads was his fast-day sermon in 1671, "The Day of Trouble Is Near," in which he argued that God "doth sometimes bring times of great trouble upon his people."[3] He felt the wars with the Indians, the outbreak of smallpox, and the scourge of fires were all chastening blows from God upon New England because of spiritual declension.

His were "muscular sermons" preached to issues like drinking and dancing. He preached three sermons on murder on the occasion of the execution of James Morgan. Mather also preached series on "practical truths" and on "The Duty of Parents to Pray for Their Children." He wrote a small book on witches and another on angels. In 1674 he preached a memorable series on "Some Important Truths about Conversion."[4] He saw the "storms of God's wrath" on the horizon and in a typical sermon, "The Times of Men," gave these directions to his flock:

1. Take notice of the hand of God in this that is come to pass.
2. Lay it to heart.
3. Let us adore the hand of God.
4. Let us labor to understand the Lord's mind and meaning in this awful Providence.
5. Let us repent of past and present iniquities.
6. Be prepared for a change of times.[5]

Not known for high commitment to pastoral ministry, Increase Mather gave himself to sixteen hours of study daily and to preaching, disregarding chronic health problems and periodic bouts of depression. He took his stand with Charles Chancey and John Davenport against the "Half-way Covenant," which was a relaxation of the requirement that both parents needed to be in the faith for a child to be baptized, adopted in 1662.[6] Increase broke with his own father over this but ultimately changed his own position years later and came to favor it.

Mather was a preacher of hellfire in a way revived in the next century by Jonathan Edwards. Mather would say:

Thy soul is hanging over the mouth of hell by the rotten thread of a frail life: if that breaks, the devouring Gulf will swallow thee up forever.[7]

He embraced the plain style and shrank from the kind of elegance his son Cotton found appealing, but beyond doubt Increase Mather was a preacher of considerable oratorical effect. One of his chief biographers calls him "The Last Puritan" because of his staunch adherence to the vision of the founders.

Not surprisingly his "rhetoric of wrath" caused him to move deeply into eschatology and apocalypticism (not unlike the later Richard Baxter). His rhetoric reverberated with eschatological urgency. When there was a stirring among the Jews in the Levant because of a false messiah, Mather saw this as a possible sign of the Second Coming. He wrote a tome titled *The Mysteries of Israel's Salvation* in which he argued that the Jews would miraculously return to Palestine at the end of the age. In this he was influenced by the thinking of Voetius,

Brightman, John Cotton, and Joseph Mede, who also influenced Thomas Goodwin. While Mather was in England, he visited with Richard Baxter over the millennial issues and the conversion of the Jews.[8]

Daniel and Revelation became important sources for the messages of judgment and impending doom as well as hope. The use of typology would become universal in the second and third generation, as the parallels between the Puritans in New England and ancient Israel were a fertile field for endless analogy. Yet all of this did not divert Increase Mather's longing to see "the pangs of the new birth," nor did he ever desist from his conviction that "Faith and repentance are the great duties required in the New Testament." For Mather, "This was the scope and sum of all the Apostle's preaching."

---

1. Mason I. Lowance, *Increase Mather* (New York: Twayne, 1974), 27.
2. Ibid., 140.
3. Everett Emerson, *Puritanism in America 1620–1750* (Boston: Twayne, 1977), 92.
4. Michael G. Hall, *The Last Puritan: The Life of Increase Mather* (Middletown, Conn.: Wesleyan University Press, 1988), 91.
5. Emory Elliott, *Power and the Pulpit in Puritan New England* (Princeton, N.J.: Princeton University Press, 1975), 116.
6. Peter Y. DeJong, *The Covenant Idea in New England Theology* (Grand Rapids: Eerdmans, 1945).
7. Robert Middlekauff, *The Mathers: Three Generations of Puritan Intellectuals 1596–1728* (New York: Oxford University Press, 1971), 91.
8. Hall, *The Last Puritan,* 274.

7.4.3   COTTON MATHER—MOVER AND SHAKER IN NEW ENGLAND

This day I likewise obtained of God that he would make use of me as of a John to be herald of the Lord's kingdom now approaching, a voice crying in the wilderness for preparation thereunto.

A great and general assembly was now called . . . By the providence of God it then fell unto me to preach . . . I ran the hazard of much reproach by testifying in that sermon against the persecution of erroneous and conscientious dissenters by the civil magistrate.

Should I tell, in how many forms the Devil has assaulted me, and with what subtilty and energy his assaults have been carried on, it would strike my friends with horror.

—Cotton Mather's diary

Clearly the leading scholar in Puritan New England was **Cotton Mather** (1663–1728). Described as "the real virtuoso of the new themes and language of the sermons of the last decades of the century," Cotton may have been the brightest star in the Mather galaxy. He was the most brilliant and prolific thinker of his times. His life motto was *fructuosus* (i.e., being fruitful). Never traveling very far from his birthplace in Boston, Mather entered Harvard at eleven years of age and began preaching soon after. He could give orations in Latin and wrote his M.A. thesis on the possibility of the divine origin of the Hebrew vowel pointings. Ultimately he would grow disappointed in Harvard and, along with Elihu Yale, became one of the founders of Yale College.

At eighteen, Cotton became his father's associate at North Church. Something of a stutterer as a young person, he overcame the problem. He preached two or three times a week, both at North Church and elsewhere. One month he spoke seventy-two times. We have seven thousand pages of his early sermon notes. Exegesis was not his forte, but his content was rich, theological, and well applied. He had an unusually effective ministry among the young people of Boston. While the quality of Puritan preaching was uneven and "the hourglass was often turned with resignation," even in printed form Mather's sermons have life.[1] His literary output was massive, running to 388 titles. He had a personal library of eight thousand volumes and read in many fields.

Cotton Mather came to the assurance of personal faith only with great struggle, seeing himself as "one of the filthiest creatures on earth."[2] He was a man of extraordinary personal devotion and prayerfulness. In a sense he was a kind of John the Baptist for the fourth-generation preacher Jonathan Edwards, who would so shake New England and rekindle the "preaching of intense zeal" after Mather's death.[3] Looking at Mather's huge *Magnalia Christi Americana* (with its controlling millennial metaphor), one is impressed with the contrast between the Virginia settlers who took such delight in high culture but were essentially receptors, and the Puritan mind which was so dedicated to expression and creation of thoughts and beliefs.[4] In Mather we see what the prominent Puritan scholar Barrett Wendell called "the passionate enthusiasm of their faith." He foresaw a brighter day ushered in ultimately by the return of the Lord Jesus Christ to set up his kingdom.[5]

Mather was much more attuned to pastoral ministry than was his father and advocated visitation and catechizing of families. His personal life was filled with much tragedy, including the deaths of two wives, the severe mental illness of his third wife and the deaths of thirteen of his fifteen children. His involvement in the Salem witchcraft debacle was not his greatest hour.[6] He wrote a manual for the preparation of pastors titled *Manductio ad Ministerium,* widely influential in his time. Like his father, he had scientific inclination, supported inoculation against smallpox, and was elected a member of the Royal Society in London.

Cotton Mather shows the complex interrelationship between Continental pietism and Puritanism. He stands with Richard Baxter and August Hermann Franke as the embodiment of cross-fertilization. Although he was a devout Calvinist, he was a preparationist who expected and called for conversions (cf. Thomas Shepard who believed the odds were 1,000 to 1 against a given conversion). Mather carried on an extensive correspondence with Franke.[7] This relationship began when the SPCK in London sent a copy of the *Magnalia* to Franke in Halle and Franke wrote a seventy-page letter to Mather in return. Professor Richard

Lovelace has shown the mutual enrichment which this relationship produced in terms of a sound balance between right theology and genuine experience. This did involve some move away from hyper-Calvinism on his part[8] and a healthy "Christ-mysticism."[9] Lovelace calls this "an eclectic spirituality" and cites Ritschl's phrase "the unitive tendency of Pietism" to describe the concern for Christian unity which captured Mather.

Other benefits we see in Mather are his emphasis on lay ministry (uncommon in Puritanism), his love for distribution of tracts and his "collects" of prayer for persons whom he saw on the street, his use of collegia, or small groups, after the manner of the pietistic conventicles,[10] his sensitivity to social issues and his "revivalistic expectation" in which he cites the Halle model. His prayer was

> Wherefore under a terror of God, it becomes us to labour fervently in our prayer that the glorious God of our Life would revive decayed piety . . . and that His quickening Spirit would not withdraw any further . . . Lord, revive thy work in the midst of the nations.[11]

Illustrative of this was his growing burden for missions and for outreach to the Indians (in view of the fact that Puritans did not ordinarily have missionary zeal) and his correspondence with Bartholomew Ziegenbalg, the Pietistic missionary to Malabar.[12]

The preaching of Cotton Mather always had a pronounced Christocentric thrust. He had a great love for Bible prophecy but guarded against date-setting. His appetite for scholarship dove into the deeper veins of Scripture. The ministry of the Word was for him "the principal agent in spiritual nourishment and awakening . . . and thus he still used long bouts of preaching and teaching as the basic protein of his ministry."[13]

Mather would preach for at least an hour, often an hour and three quarters. Once his pastoral prayer went for two hours, and he had to apologize. He did his exegesis and outlining in the typical Puritan form and valued illustrative anecdotes to help his audience get the picture. He spent considerable time internalizing his message because he neither read from a manuscript nor memorized his sermon. He typically took about seven hours for preparation. He spoke in free style, extempore. He attempted to begin slowly and quietly, using short sentences and emphasizing key words. He loved the use of exclamation marks in his writing, which tells us something about his flow.[14] If his goal was to use short sentences, he did not always succeed—the first sentence in his life of Governor Phips ran 254 words.

Benjamin Coleman described Mather's preaching:

> Here he excelled, here he shone; being exceeding communicative, and bringing out of his treasury things new and old, without measure. Here it was seen how his wit, and fancy, his invention, his quickness of thought and ready apprehension were all consecrated to God, as well as his heart, will and affections.[15]

Cotton Mather did depart from the plain style of the Puritans into what Professor Lovelace describes as "an opulent and humorous floridity—its puns, tropes, allusions, and encrustations of literary jewelry—Mather's style is constantly in danger of sounding ridiculous, whenever his taste, or ear, fails."[16] Yet notwithstanding, Lovelace quotes Sidney Mead, the Unitarian church historian, as saying that Mather's work "unknowingly was fanning the spark that eight years later would burst into flame in Jonathan Edwards' Northampton church."[17]

---

1. Thomas Jefferson Wertenbaker, *The Puritan Oligarchy: The Founding of American Civilization* (New York: Grosset and Dunlap, 1947), 79.
2. Kenneth Silverman, *The Life and Times of Cotton Mather* (New York: Columbia University Press, 1985), 29. This is the Pulitzer Prize-winning biography for 1985. Copious and clear, the study has spiritual limitations.
3. Wertenbaker, *The Puritan Oligarchy*, 82.
4. Ibid., 104.
5. Barrett Wendell, *Cotton Mather: The Puritan Priest* (New York: Harcourt and Brace, 1963). See the new introduction and evaluation of Wendell by Alkan Heimert, xxi.
6. Ibid., 65. The classic study here is Marion L. Starkey, *The Devil in Massachusetts* (New York: Time Reading Program, 1963).
7. Robert Middlekauff, *The Mathers: Three Generations of Puritan Intellectuals 1596–1728* (New York: Oxford University Press, 1971), 305.
8. Richard F. Lovelace, *The American Pietism of Cotton Mather: Origins of American Evangelicalism* (Grand Rapids: Christian University Press, 1979), 6.
9. Ibid., 181, 187.
10. Ibid., 220.
11. Ibid., 248.
12. Ibid., 34.
13. Ibid., 203.
14. Emory Elliott, *Power and the Pulpit in Puritan New England* (Princeton, N.J.: Princeton University Press, 1975), 188.
15. Lovelace, *The American Pietism of Cotton Mather*, 26.
16. Ibid., 288.
17. Ibid., 283.

7.4.4 *THOMAS SHEPARD—SOLDIER OF CHRIST*

Saints have an experimental knowledge of the work of grace, by virtue of which they come to know it as certainly . . . as by feeling heat, we know that fire is hot; by tasting honey, we know it is sweet.

As it is with conduit pipes, so here. . . . Let the pipes be laid ever so well, and laid ever so far up, yet if they are not laid wholly and all the way up to the conduit head, no water will ever come down to that family.

—Thomas Shepard

When he was heard by Edward Johnson, the author of *Wonder-Working Providence of Zion's Saviour in New England,* **Thomas Shepard** (1605–1649) was totally convincing: "All doubts and fears were swept away."[1] Jonathan Edwards was much influenced by Shepard, and quoted him often. He had a unique niche as pastor of the Cambridge church and as one of the founders of Harvard. Shepard came from Essex, as did John Eliot, the noted missionary to the Indians. He matriculated brilliantly at Emmanuel College, Cambridge, where John Preston had great influence on him. While at Cambridge, Shepard heard Thomas Goodwin preach on conversion and the ministry in a powerful way, but he castigated himself incessantly for his hesitation in taking action.

Shepard was such a staunch Calvinist that he urged those who were not of the elect to praise God for their damnation. Only on the matter of an incipient preparationism (the idea of steps and stages leading to conversion) did he deviate from the old Amesian line, as he spoke of "conviction, compunction and humiliation" as preliminary stages in the *ordo salutis* followed by "justification, reconciliation, adoption, sanctification and glorification."[2]

Shepard got himself into ecclesiastical troubles, and Laud called him "a prating coxcomb." On the eve of his departure for New England, he solemnly intoned, "It shall not be with us there as it is with the wicked Israelites who when they came into the good land of rest, they then forgot the Lord and all his works past."[3] But it was not long before he was denouncing "that inundation of abominable filthinesses breaking in upon us."[4]

The glass was always half-empty for Thomas Shepard. If there is truth in the characterization of Puritan society in New England in the seventeenth century as "harsh," we sense something in Shepard that was excessive. Giles Fermin termed him a "gloomy exclusionist," and he in fact denounced all toleration and debated endlessly with the Baptists (and just about anyone else). The more recent publication of his diary shows him as a man in great internal turmoil. His "tortured self-examination leads to no conviction, no real certainty."[5]

Shepard writhed with jealously when his wife reported the good sermon of a colleague.[6] He preached exclusively on prayer for such a long time and scolded his people so vehemently on their prayerlessness that some of his most prayerful saints left him.[7] He lamented his faults at great length, which were chiefly his too great love for his books, neglect of family worship, his failure to speak to his children about their spiritual life as he should have (although all three sons went into the ministry and called him blessed), and his natural gloom.

Yet despite his many flaws and his "raw-headed preaching," Shepard's sermons were monumental. Although severe, he was more vivid and lively than even John Cotton. He is not easy to read because of his "ragged style," but he was forceful. He expected results in his preaching and used analogy to great effect.[8] He testified, "I learned from Paul what it was to be spiritually-minded, and I learned from him also how to compare spiritual things with spiritual."[9] Samuel Blair demonstrated that in the Great Awakening the writings of "those old pious and experimental writers" like Thomas Shepard were revisited.[10]

In one of the most widely published sermons in New England history, "The

Sincere Convert," Shepard traced the path from remorse to repentance to saving faith, and spoke passionately about the issues:

> That God the Father of our Lord Jesus Christ may be honored by the performance of these duties, therefore use them. Christ shed his blood that he might purchase unto himself a people zealous of good works, (Titus 2:14), not to save our souls by them, but to honor him. O, let not the blood of Christ be shed in vain! Grace and good duties are a Christian's crown; it is sin only makes a man base. Now, shall a king cast away his crown, because he brought not his kingdom by it? No; because it is his ornament and glory to wear it when he is made a king. So I say unto thee, It is better that Christ should be honored than thy soul saved; and therefore, perform duties because they honor the Lord Jesus Christ.[11]

In this sermon he also trumpeted his confidence in the return of the Lord Jesus for his own. In his "Parable of the Ten Virgins" (from which he had preached for four years), he spoke of two future comings of the Lord.[12]

His own last words encapsulate the man: "O my sinful heart! O my often-crucified and never wholly mortified sinfulness! O my life-long damage and my daily shame. O my indwelling and so besetting sins, your evil dominion is over now! It is within an hour or two of my final and everlasting release! For I am authoritatively assured that by tomorrow morning I shall have entered into my eternal rest! And then, O my ransomed soul, one hour in heaven will make me forget all my hell on earth!"[13]

---

1. Thomas Jefferson Wertenbaker, *The Puritan Oligarchy: The Founding of American Civilization* (New York: Grosset and Dunlap, 1947), 209.
2. Andrew Delbanco, *The Puritan Ordeal* (Cambridge, Mass.: Harvard University Press, 1989), 49.
3. Ibid., 103.
4. Ibid., 206.
5. Everett Emerson, *Puritanism in America 1620–1750* (Boston: Twayne, 1977), 125.
6. Alexander Whyte, *Thomas Shepard: Pilgrim Father and Founder of Harvard, His Spiritual Experience and Experimental Preaching* (Edinburgh: Oliphant Anderson and Ferrier, 1909), 280.
7. Ibid., 228.
8. Harry S. Stout, *The New England Soul: Preaching and Religious Culture in Colonial New England* (New York: Oxford University Press, 1986), 43.
9. Whyte, *Thomas Shepard*, 94.
10. Iain H. Murray, *Jonathan Edwards: A New Biography* (Edinburgh: Banner of Truth, 1987), 214.
11. Stout, *The New England Soul,* 42.
12. Thomas Shepard, "The Parable of the Ten Virgins" (Ligonier, Pa.: Soli Deo Gloria, 1994), 24–25.
13. Whyte, *Thomas Shepard*, 144.

7.4.5 THOMAS HOOKER—ORATOR OF NEW ENGLAND

When there is a kind of spiritual heat in the heart, when there are holy affections, and the heart of the minister is answerable to that, he communicates and delivers to the people.

My brethren, it is all one, if hearing the Minister speak unto you the word of God, and bring home to you the reproofs and admonitions and counsels thereof, you kick his Word from you, and happily take up arms against him; it is all one (I say) as if you take up arms against God and despised him.

That rhetoric which we find in Scripture to be used by the Prophets and Apostles, hath great use in preaching if it be used with the like prudence . . . narratives, examples, precepts . . . because that manner doth make most for the common use of all kinds of men, and also most to affect the will and stir up godly motions, which is the chief scope of Divinity.

—Thomas Hooker

More than ninety Oxbridge graduates built and enriched the spiritual and intellectual life of New England. Among the most distinguished and influential of them was **Thomas Hooker** (1586–1647). Born into a middle-class family in the tiny hamlet of Marfield in Leiscestershire, he studied at Emmanuel College, Cambridge, where he received his B.A. in 1608 and his M.A. in 1611. More importantly, it is where he was converted. After serving in a fellowship at the university, he took a living in the Esher parish in rural Surrey, where he served with distinction and where also he married. His pastoral skills were sharpened especially through his dealings with an oppressed soul known as Mrs. Drake, of whose trials he wrote in *Poor Doubting Christian,* a book which brought him dramatically into the limelight. He began to be in demand as an occasional preacher in London and at this time assisted his friend Thomas Shepard in finding his first pulpit. In 1626 he was called as lecturer to St. Mary's, Chelmsford, where his reputation as a preacher of ability was greatly enhanced.

A man of choleric temperament, Hooker used the Ames and Perkins model for his preaching with exegetical comments followed by doctrine, reasons, and uses. He strongly emphasized headings and the "firstly" and "secondly" in his preaching to safeguard against wandering from the text and theme.[1] Recognizing the gifts and effectiveness of Hooker's preaching, Cotton Mather wrote:

Hereby there was a great reformation wrought, not only in the town, but in the adjacent country, from all parts whereof they came to "hear the wisdom of the Lord Jesus Christ," in his gospel, by this worthy man dispensed; and some of great quality among the rest, would often resort from far to his assembly; particularly the truly noble Earl of Warwick.[2]

Hooker was known for fire and lightning in the pulpit and was seen by many as a demanding if not a harsh preacher. Yet he gave assiduous attention to the overlapping roles of prophet and shepherd, seeing himself often as "an evangelizing prophet." He loved to be in his pulpit above all else.

In 1629 he was called to appear before Archbishop Laud's High Commission and was removed from pulpit ministry. He kept a small grammar school at Little Baddow, where John Eliot was his assistant. Continuing to preach illegally in homes, Hooker was once again summoned. He fled to the Netherlands with his family in 1631.

Living in Delft, Hooker found the climate neither physically nor ecclesiastically tolerable, and he migrated to New England. He settled in Newtown, where a covenant was established in 1633, but the community never became a commercial center. In 1636 he led about one hundred members and 160 head of cattle one hundred miles westward to settle in the beautiful Connecticut Valley. We know the settlement as Hartford.[3] He preached at the first session of the General Court in 1638 and was instrumental in shaping the first written constitution in the thirteen original colonies. The document is considered a milestone in the history of constitutional government in the United States.[4] Yet Perry Miller is right in his epochal work that Thomas Hooker is to be seen first and foremost as a preacher, not a founder.

Hooker was always in the eye of some storm, but was known as a steady and consistent Bible preacher. One observer described his pulpit presence:

> When he spoke his entire person was fired with enthusiasm, his eyes shone, his gestures were animated. He seemed to be inspired by the "divine relish" he had of his subject, "the sacred panting of his holy soul after the glorious objects of the invisible world" . . . "The distinct images of things would come so nimbly, and so fitly into his mind, that he could utter them with fluent expressions."[5]

Numerous instances are reported of those who came to hear "that bawling Hooker" in order to mock him but who remained afterward to pray. In Leicester the burgesses hired some fiddlers to play outside the church in order to drown out the preacher, "but the sound of his pleadings and warnings floated out of the door above the scrapings of the fiddlers." The chief burgess leaned forward to listen and became sincerely penitent.

Hooker was known for his "verbal wit and his ear for neatly balanced sentences."[6] He spoke often of the terrors of heaven and hell, and his preaching made use of narrative in a way not common at this time. Hooker used the journey of the sinner/saint resourcefully, with considerable typology and metaphor. His dramatization and skill in interrogative dialogue[7] were striking; his narrative was termed "epic-scale."[8] True, his inaccessible "language of Canaan" needed to be translated for subsequent generations, but it was effective for the times. He was a traditional Calvinist except for his strong insistence on the soul's preparation for the Spirit's work, and he developed a theology of preparation.[9]

Hooker's preaching was characterized by stupendous energy. He spent nearly a year in Acts 2:37. He was also known for his powerful and efficacious prayers.[10] Hooker warned against too much reliance on emotion, and urged: "Therefore away with your sense and feeling, and go to the promise." While preaching on the Holy Spirit, he would wait for the Spirit's working.[11] He periodically experienced "particular faith," or the settled assurance that this prayer would be specifically answered.[12] He did on occasion exercise the gift of prophecy.

Hooker's sermons were widely published and circulated. In a great sermon on Romans 4:12 titled "The Activity of Faith," he urged his hearers along this line:

> But look to it, wheresoever faith is, it is fruitful. If thou art fruitless, say what thou wilt, thou hast no faith at all. Alas, these idle drones, these idle Christians, the Church is too full of them. Men are continually hearing and yet remain fruitless and unprofitable; whereas if there were more faith in the world, we should have more work done in the world; faith would set feet and hands, and eyes, and all on work. Men go under the name of professors, but alas, they are but pictures; they stir not a whit; mark, where you find them in the beginning of the year, there you will find them in the end of the year, as profane, as worldly, as loose in their conversations, as formal in duty as ever. And is this faith? Oh, faith would work other matters, and provoke a soul to other passages than these.[13]

1. Frank Shuffelton, *Thomas Hooker 1586–1647* (Princeton, N.J.: Princeton University Press, 1977), 106.
2. Ibid., 75.
3. John Brown, *The Pilgrim Fathers of New England and Their Puritan Successors* (London: Religious Tract Society, 1895), 319ff. For a disclosure of the current spiritual state of the church in Hartford, see Gary Dorsey, *Congregation: The Journey Back to Church* (New York: Viking, 1995).
4. For a good selection of election sermons from this period, see A. W. Plumstead, ed., *The Wall and the Garden: Selected Massachusetts Election Sermons* (Minneapolis: University of Minnesota Press, 1968).
5. Thomas Jefferson Wertenbaker, *The Puritan Oligarchy: The Founding of American Civilization* (New York: Grosset and Dunlap, 1947), 81.
6. Sargent Bush Jr., *The Writings of Thomas Hooker: Spiritual Adventure in Two Worlds* (Madison: University of Wisconsin Press, 1980), 13.
7. Shuffelton, *Thomas Hooker 1586–1647*, 67.
8. Bush, *The Writings of Thomas Hooker*, 343.
9. Ibid., 154, 159.
10. Mason L. Lowance, *Increase Mather* (New York: Twayne, 1974), 56.
11. David L. Hall, *Worlds of Wonder, Days of Judgment* (New York: Knopf, 1989), 28.
12. Richard F. Lovelace, *The American Pietism of Cotton Mather: Origins of American Evangelicalism* (Grand Rapids: Christian University Press, 1979), 181.
13. F. R. Webber, *A History of Preaching in Britain and America* (Milwaukee: Northwestern, 1957), 3:38.

7.4.6   PETER BULKELEY—COVENANTER OF THE PURITANS

> If God be God over us, we must yield him universal obedience in all things. He must not be over us in one thing, and under us in another, but he must be over us in everything.

> The Lord looks for more from thee then from other people; more zeal for God, more love to his truth, more justice, and equality in thy ways; thou shouldst be a special people, an only people, none like thee in all the earth. Oh be so, in loving the Gospel and the Ministers of it . . . take heed lest for neglect of either, God remove thy Candlestick out of the midst of thee; lest being now as a city upon an hill, which many seek unto, thou be like a Beacon upon the top of a mountain, desolate and forsaken.
>
> —Peter Bulkeley

Daniel Boorstin rightly claims that preaching is "the characteristic Puritan institution." One of the eminent Puritan fathers who deserves notice in this history is **Peter Bulkeley** (1582–1646), the founder and first pastor of the congregation in Concord. Bulkeley hailed from Bedfordshire, where he followed his father as rector of Odell on the Ouse River. His was a strong family; his brother-in-law had been Cromwell's attorney general.[1] With a Cambridge M.A. (1608), Bulkeley was a person of broad reading and much learning. His interest in chemistry is reflected in the thirty-five volumes of notes, now found in the Walter R. Steiner Medical Library at Hartford, written largely by Bulkeley and his sons.[2]

In the face of mounting ecclesiastical pressure, Bulkeley emigrated to New England at the relatively advanced age of fifty-two. Purchasing land from the Indians, he led in the building of the famous colony on the banks of the Merrimac River. Known for his able preaching, Bulkeley was frequently cast into roles of significant leadership. He and Thomas Hooker jointly presided over the three-week inquiry into antinomian dissent in 1637. The concerns were John Cotton, Anne Hutchinson, and John Davenport (John Cotton had refused to attend Bulkeley's installation in Concord).[3] Bulkeley also played a prominent part in elections for Massachusetts political office.

Bulkeley was an outspoken preparationist. Hooker and he argued that the unconverted must make some significant response to the overtures and initiatives of grace, that the soul is not entirely passive, and that good works are a test of true salvation and sanctification. In advancing this argument, Bulkeley had to be careful that he did not move onto the ground of meritorious works. He clearly moved away from the doctrine of irresistible grace when he insisted that men "make the covenant of grace void unto themselves by neglecting and slighting the offers and tenders of grace which are made unto them."[4] Under Hooker and Bulkeley, the New England ministers gave definition to these concerns. As a result, they excluded Anne Hutchinson and came to terms with John Cotton, but utterly failed with John Wheelwright, who was also banished.

In distinction to John Cotton, Hooker and Bulkeley maintained that faith precedes justification. Bulkeley steadfastly followed John Preston in arguing that the process of preconversion work does not involve meritorious works. Cotton finally came to oppose Anne Hutchinson.

The most significant contribution of Bulkeley, however, is his sermons collected under the title *The Gospel-Covenant or The Covenant of Grace Opened* (although it was not published until 1641). In the judgment of Perry Miller, this is "the outstanding work" on this central doctrine from the Puritan founders. The idea of covenant is clearly a defining doctrine in both Old and New Testaments. Bulkeley insists there are three covenants: (1) the covenant between the Father and the Son; (2) the covenant of works with our first parents in innocence; and (3) the covenant of grace proffered because of the broken covenant of works. The idea of covenant and compact suffuses all of Puritan life. Undergirding the whole projection is the character of God, of whom Bulkeley said, "God cannot be a covenant-breaker." Both individual and corporate covenants (the latter included with so-called federal theology) "are proclaimed through the same medium—the sermon."[5]

The so-called covenant of grace is not without a condition, Bulkeley said. One's "calling and election" are made sure by evidence in the life (which is what the antinomians most dangerously denied). The sermon is critical because it is through the sermon that the terms of obedience are articulated. There is an element of voluntarism here, which comes close to a denial of the strictures of the Synod of Dort to the effect that grace is irresistible. Bulkeley insisted, "There is danger in sinning against the covenant of works, but it is more dangerous to sin against grace. For there is help for such as break the covenant of works, but no help for such as make void the covenant of grace in themselves."[6] The practical implications of the Puritan view of covenant extend to marriage and the rearing of children.[7]

Bulkeley's influence is seen especially in the life of Samuel Willard, who worked closely with Increase Mather and followed him to the presidency of Harvard. Willard's *Systematical Divinity* was one of the great Puritan landmarks. He sat under the ministry of Bulkeley in Concord, and prepared for entrance into Harvard while there.[8]

Once again, we see the centrality of the sermon in Puritan society.

1. John Brown, *The Pilgrim Fathers of New England and Their Puritan Successors* (London: Religious Tract Society, 1895), 314.

2. Thomas Jefferson Wertenbaker, *The Puritan Oligarchy: The Founding of American Civilization* (New York: Grosset and Dunlap, 1947), 262.

3. Andrew Delbanco, *The Puritan Ordeal* (Cambridge, Mass.: Harvard University Press, 1989), 118.

4. Everett Emerson, *Puritanism in America 1620–1750* (Boston: Twayne, 1977), 60.

5. Harry S. Stout, *The New England Soul: Preaching and Religious Culture in Colonial New England* (New York: Oxford University Press, 1986), 27.

6. Emerson, *Puritanism in America 1620–1750,* 60.

7. Edmund S. Morgan, *The Puritan Family: Religion and Domestic Relations in Seventeenth-Century New England* (New York: Harper Torchbooks, 1944, 1966), 91, 97, 161–62.

8. Ernest Benson Lowrie, *The Shape of the Puritan Mind: The Thought of Samuel Willard* (New Haven, Conn.: Yale University Press, 1974), 10–11.

7.4.7   *JOHN DAVENPORT—ELDER AMONG THE PURITANS*

That practice that exposeth the blood of Christ to contempt and baptism to profanation, the Church to pollution and the Commonwealth to confusion is to be admitted.

The porter looks well unto the doors of the Lord's House.

—John Davenport

Emblematic of the older generation of the founders who detected ominous spiritual slippage and who eloquently cried out against it is **John Davenport** (1597–1670). Born in Coventry, the son of the mayor, he was a graduate of Magdalen College, Oxford. Davenport began to preach at the age of nineteen in a noted ministry at St. Stephen's, Coleman Street, London. During this time he hid John Cotton. Davenport himself had to flee the pincers of Laud, and became copastor of the English church in Amsterdam. There he became embroiled in a fierce dispute when he opposed the baptism of children whose parents were not Christians.[1]

Davenport was dogged in his insistence on biblical authority: "The whole Scripture is breathed of God, and therefore infallible, and stamped with God's own authority in every sentence of it, 2 Timothy 3:16." He returned to England briefly and then migrated to New England, where he led a group of colonists to Quinnipiac in Connecticut. There he founded New Haven. He was elected pastor and served with powerful impact for thirty years. With John Cotton and Thomas Hooker, Davenport was invited back to England to be part of the Westminster Assembly, but none were able to go. He was one of the most well-heard ministers in New England and advanced with the understanding that "God's usual way which he will bless for the converting or turning of elect sinners to himself, is by sending his Ministers with a Message from himself to them, in their preaching God's Word unto them" (from *God's Call*).

In the antinomian controversy, Davenport argued for greater pastoral understanding of Anne Hutchinson. He desired to correct rather than condemn.[2] So recently arrived from England, Davenport stood more with the preaching of Sibbes and Cotton than with Hooker and Bulkeley. He preached the last sermon at the synod called to inquire into the problem, and issued a strong call to unity based on Philippians 3:16.

Twenty-five years later, however, in the divisive conflict over the Half-way Covenant, Davenport led the forces opposing Solomon Stoddard's crusade to relax baptismal requirements. Davenport was successful in enlisting the support of Increase Mather for the cause, though Mather later switched positions and identified with his own father's thinking. This shift was possibly more a function of broadening church control over more persons than it was the result of a theological stance. Davenport manifested the longing for a pure church, a desire that was common among the fathers.[3]

This issue divided First Church when Davenport was called to succeed the revered John Norton in 1668. Believing that his opposition to the Half-way Covenant made Davenport unsuitable, a strong minority opposed him. But Davenport desired the call to Boston, and once in place gave no ground to the dissenters. Richard Mather was chosen as mediator in the dispute but was not admitted by Davenport. The elder Mather soon died, possibly influencing Increase Mather in his change of heart on the issue.[4] Many problems now confronted Davenport. Ultimately, he planted another congregation.

The year before he died, he preached an election sermon and verbalized the burden of the founders:

> I shall conclude with a brief reminding you of the first beginning of this Colony . . . Churches were gathered in a Congregational way, and walked therein, according to the Rules of the Gospel . . . Now therefore take heed and beware, that the Lord may not have just cause to complain of us . . . lest you lose by God's punishing justice what you received from his free mercy . . . take heed and beware lest he remove the golden candlesticks, and the burning and shining lights in them, as he hath already done to many eminent lights; and woe to them for whom the Gospel is spurned, for their abusing it, and the messengers of it . . . And see that your fruitfulness is good, answereth the cost and pains that God hath been at with you in his Vineyard, lest the Lord be provoked to deal with us as he did with his ancient Vineyard (1669).

1. F. R. Webber, *A History of Preaching in Britain and America* (Milwaukee: Northwestern, 1957), 3:42.
2. Andrew Delbanco, *The Puritan Ordeal* (Cambridge, Mass.: Harvard University Press, 1989), 157.
3. Robert Middlekauff, *The Mathers: Three Generations of Puritan Intellectuals 1596–1728* (London: Oxford University Press, 1971), 56–57.
4. Michael G. Hall, *The Last Puritan: The Life of Increase Mather* (Middletown, Conn.: Wesleyan University Press, 1988), 78ff.

7.5 THE SCOTTISH PULPIT IN THE SEVENTEENTH CENTURY

> To the Presbyterians of the seventeenth century the Bible, as interpreted by them, was an absolutely infallible guide of religion and moral conduct.
>
> —Duncan Anderson

It is only with the realization of his implicit faith in the Bible as the infallible law in human conduct, so infallible that "if an angel from heaven should reveal anything contrary to the Scriptures, or offer to add anything to that perfect rule of faith and manners, he ought to be accursed, that

understanding comes of the motives which made fervent royalists take
up arms against their king.

—Duncan Anderson

He chose to give us birth through the word of truth. . . . Therefore, get
rid of all moral filth and the evil that is so prevalent and humbly accept
the word planted in you, which can save you.

—James 1:18, 21

The startling prominence and power of the Scottish pulpit in the eighteenth
and nineteenth centuries can be understood only in light of the legacy of biblical
preaching that **John Knox** (cf. 5.6.1) and **Andrew Melville** (1545–1622) bequeathed to their spiritual heirs. Holy Scripture was at the center of Scottish life
as even Robert Burns much later reflects in "The Cotter's Saturday Night." It
was Melville who took the king by the sleeve in 1596 and told him: "There is
twa Kings and twa Kingdoms in Scotland; there is King James, the head of this
commonwealth; and there is Christ Jesus the King and His Kingdom the Kirk,
whose subject King James the Sixth is."

The Scots Confession of 1560 came from the Reformation Parliament and was
foundational for the reconstituted Church of Scotland.[1] The confession "professed
and believed as wholesome, sound doctrine, grounded upon the infallible truth
of God's Word" was the platform from which "the true church is discerned from
the false by the true preaching of the Word of God, the right administration of
the sacraments, and ecclesiastical discipline uprightly ministered."[2] Later, Principal Rainy held, "Surely it is a striking thing that what so united the nation was
a resolution that God's authority, discerned by themselves in His Word, that and
nothing else, should set up institutions in their Church. That principle was written then on the fibre of the Scottish people in a manner that is legible yet."[3]

The biblical idea of covenant (three hundred times in the Old Testament alone),
flowered in covenant theology and its close cousin, federal theology, was developed by **Johannes Cocceius** on the Continent, (1603–1669).[4] The National Covenant of 1638 and the Solemn League and Covenant of 1643, along with the
Westminster Confession of 1647, solidified the theological stance of the Scottish Covenanters. After the fall of the Cromwellian commonwealth, virtually the
whole of Scotland united against the reestablishment of the episcopacy in 1661
under Charles II.

Many Scotsmen gave their lives in defiance when the Westminster Confession
was abolished and English troops were sent in 1666 to force people to go to the
established church. An uprising followed when an old man was roasted alive for
not paying his fine for nonattendance at church. Although conciliation was
attempted by Bishop Leighton, what was known as the "killing times" followed
and the Scottish people endured incredible oppression. Upwards of eighteen
thousand were martyred in a country with less than two million people. The
persecution ended in late 1688 when **William of Orange** took the throne in the
Glorious Revolution. William's trusted Scottish chaplain was the greatly loved
William Carstares, a Church of Scotland minister and son of a Church of

Scotland minister. At long last in 1689 came the Act Abolishing Prelacy in Scotland, and in the following year Presbyterian government was established in the Church of Scotland. Soon the Treaty of Union between England and Scotland was enacted, joining the two countries.

Throughout the trial, even while devout Scots met secretly in house churches, preaching was prominent.[5] The Bible was deeply interwoven with every facet of daily life, as Duncan Anderson has so well shown.[6] Family worship was deep-dyed in the customs of the time.[7]

Scottish sermons were generally given from memory, and delivered after considerable reading of Scripture "without any other colours than those that are peculiar to Faith and Reason." The objective was to evoke "a responsive thrill to the stimulus of the Scriptures."[8]

Great throngs came to hear preachers like **John Welsh** (1624–1681) of Irongay, the Covenanting field preacher and great-grandson of John Knox. Then there was the extraordinary preacher **Robert Bruce** (1554–1631), sometime minister in Inverness. He rebuked King James for talking during the service in St. Giles and was expelled from his pulpit by the king.

We now examine some sterling examples of Scottish preaching.

---

1. As a fantastic resource for every aspect of Scottish church history and practice, see Nigel M. de S. Cameron, ed., *Dictionary of Scottish Church History and Theology* (Downers Grove, Ill.: InterVarsity Press, 1993).
2. Ninian Hill, *The Story of the Scottish Church* (Glasgow: James Maclehose, 1919), 117.
3. Ibid., 164.
4. G. D. Henderson, *The Burning Bush: Studies in Scottish Church History* (Edinburgh: St. Andrew Press, 1957), 71. See C. S. McCoy, *The Covenant Theology of Johannes Cocceius* (New Haven, Conn.: Yale, 1957).
5. Hector Macpherson, *Scotland's Battles for Spiritual Independence* (London: Hodder and Stoughton, 1905).
6. Duncan Anderson, *The Bible in Seventeenth Century Scottish Life and Literature* (London: Allenson, 1936).
7. Ibid., 104.
8. Ibid., 94ff.

7.5.1 *Alexander Henderson—Designer of the National Covenant*

The badge of the Church of Scotland, a bush burning but not consumed, was as true a type of Scotland's inexpugnable defense of her ancient liberties, as it was of the Jewish people in their emergence from Egyptian bondage. And so the early history of the Presbyterian Church had been one long struggle of dogged resistance to superior power.

—Dean Stanley in 1872

You will know the truth, and the truth will set you free.

—John 8:32

Your word is truth.

—John 17:17b

There are divers among us that have had no such warrant for our entry to the ministry as were to be wished. Alas, how many of us have rather sought the kirk than the kirk sought us!

—Alexander Henderson

Third only in influence to John Knox and Andrew Melville was **Alexander Henderson** (1583–1646), "The scholarly and statesmanlikc" leader in the stand against the episcopacy.[1] Often called the Second Reformer, Henderson was born in Fifshire and in 1603 graduated with honors from St. Andrews, where he became a regent and a teacher of philosophy and rhetoric. Up to this point he supported the episcopacy, the system of church government by bishops. He was made pastor of the country church at Leuchars, but the members locked the doors on him when he arrived. Sometime soon after he went secretly to hear Robert Bruce, the avid follower of Andrew Melville, preach at Forgan church. The text was John 10:1, and Henderson was converted not only to Christ, but as reported, "He worshipped God and going away, reported that God was of a truth in whose ways were so opposite his own."[2] He was soon in the forefront of those who challenged the king.

Alexander Henderson is considered the chief architect of the National Covenant, the Magna Carta of Presbyterianism in Scotland. This battle cry of resistance and conviction was provoked by a series of riots caused by the forceful imposition of Laud's Liturgy. It all climaxed on Sunday, July 23, 1637, when the two archbishops and all of their retinuc made their way in their robes to St. Giles Cathedral in Edinburgh. Then it was that Jenny Geddes, a poor woman who kept an herb stall, "flung her stool with a curse at the head of the Dean."[3] An uproar ensued.

The next year the National Covenant was presented and in the churchyard at Gray Friars sixty-thousand Scots gathered. Henderson prayed fervently and read the covenant, and it was subscribed with many tears and great resolve.[4] Subsequently elected moderator of the Church of Scotland, Henderson continued in his country parish until he was fifty-four. He then successively served Gray Friars Church and Great St. Giles.

Henderson led the Scottish delegation to the Westminster Assembly and drafted the Solemn League and Covenant. Never married, he was small of stature, had dark hair with a pointed beard, and was never robust in health.[5] Yet he was a stately soul of great personal piety. One convert from Leuchars said to him: "I love you, Sir, because I think you are a man in whom I see much of the image of Christ."[6]

His courage did not falter even in the face of the direst dangers. In 1638 he preached to the assembly in Glasgow from Psalm 110:1, a solemn sermon called "The Bishops' Doom," followed by the intonation of their excommunication. He dissolved the historic assembly with the words: "We have now cast down the walls of Jericho; let him that rebuildeth them beware of the curse of Hiel the Bethelite."[7] At this same assembly, as part of many nights in prayer, Henderson led the great duke of Argyll to Christ. The duke was Scotland's first citizen and never wavered in his support of the Covenanters.[8]

Henderson's preaching was clear and expository. Only three sermons were printed in his lifetime, but posthumously many sermons were published. Webber confirms that Henderson's sermons were in the style of the day and were clearly divided with subdivisions and sub-subs. Especially to be noted are his series from Hebrews 11 and on the different pieces of the whole armor of God.[9] That the infallible Scriptures had the defining word to speak is demonstrated in the skillful use of the applied texts, as when Henderson preached before the Lord General at Berwick on the Lord's Day, May 26, 1639. He used as his text Exodus 17, the fight of the Israelites with "Amalek's ungracious progeny." His courageous ministry in the Word assured him a niche in the annals of great biblical preaching in Scotland.

1. J. H. S. Burleigh, *A Church History of Scotland* (Oxford: Oxford University Press, 1960), 215.
2. Marcus L. Loane, *Makers of Religious Freedom in the Seventeenth Century* (Grand Rapids: Eerdmans, 1961), 21.
3. Ibid., 27.
4. Alexander Smellie, *Men of the Covenant* (London: Andrew Melrose, 1905). An exquisite volume of the most spiritually radiant and provocative vignettes.
5. Loane, *Makers of Religious Freedom in the Seventeenth Century,* 49.
6. Ibid., 50.
7. Ibid., 39.
8. Smellie, *Men of the Covenant,* 63.
9. F. R. Webber, *A History of Preaching in Britain and America* (Milwaukee: Northwestern, 1955), 2:79.

7.5.2   DAVID DICKSON—THE DEFENDER OF PRESBYTERIANISM

> The Covenant of Grace. . . "a contract between God and men, procured by Christ upon these terms, that whosoever in the sense of their own sinfulness shall receive Christ Jesus offered in the Gospel shall have Him." . . . Grace is ordinarily bestowed by God by the preaching of the gospel, which is offered "indifferently to all hearers, that they may be tried, whether they pleased to receive the offer or not" . . . Grace is justly withheld from those who do not receive the offer, but is given by means of the condition of faith to the elect.
>
> —David Dickson, *Therapeutica Sacra*

Standing squarely in the front ranks of post-Reformation leadership with Alexander Henderson is the redoubtable **David Dickson** (1583–1663). He was born in a wealthy merchant's family in Glasgow and took his M.A. at the University of Glasgow in 1610. Thereafter he served as a professor of philosophy in his alma mater. He was ordained and took the pastorate in Irvine in Ayrshire, where he served for twenty-three years and was affectionately known as Dickson of Irvine. Like Henderson, he drew from a wide geographic area, and "Yea, not a few came from distant places and settled at Irvine that they might be under the drop of his ministry."[1]

As early as 1622 Dickson was in the vanguard of those protesting oppression and served as a chaplain for the Covenanters' military. Ultimately he was summoned to be professor of theology at Glasgow for a decade and for another ten years at the University of Edinburgh in a similar capacity during difficult years of sharp confrontation. Intermittently suspended from his charge because of his stand, he did not give way, although he and Rutherford broke over strategization in the fray.

Dickson was moderator of the church the year following the great Glasgow Assembly (1638), which was held in Edinburgh. He kept company with the duke of Argyll on his last two nights before his execution. He was a gifted exegete and wrote commentaries on Hebrews, Matthew, the Psalms, and all of Paul's Epistles. He also coauthored with his student James Durham the noted *Sum of Sacred Knowledge,* and translated the beloved hymn "O Mother Dear, Jerusalem."

But it was as a preacher that Dickson was most remembered. An English merchant related that he had heard Robert Blair preach in Fife, and Rutherford and then Dickson in Irvine. He reported that Blair "showed me the majesty of God," and "a little fair man [Rutherford] showed me the loveliness of Christ. Then I came and heard at Irvine a well-favored proper old man, with a long beard, and that man showed me all my heart."[2]

Unlike most preachers of his day, who preached four or five sermons from a single verse, Dickson would take three or four verses in a sermon, saying that "God's bairns [children] should get a good portion of His own bread."[3] He discouraged the use of Greek and Hebrew words in sermons and opposed the affectation of spending the first half of the sermon demolishing false and fanciful interpretations.

Dickson preached to the conscience, and there was revival in power at Irvine and Stewarton under his ministry. Indeed, G. D. Henderson remarks that "the emotional revivalist of Stewarton is not utterly lost in the exegete of the Gospel according to Matthew."[4] To him there was no nobler calling than that of preaching. When he was elected to the chair of theology at Edinburgh, he commented, "The professor of divinity at Edinburgh is truly a great man, the professor of divinity at Glasgow is a still greater man, but the minister of Irvine was the greatest man of all."[5]

1. Duncan Anderson, *The Bible in Seventeenth Century Scottish Life and Literature* (London: Allenson, 1936), 95.

2. Alexander Smellie, *Men of the Covenant* (London: Andrew Melrose, 1905), 192.

3. F. R. Webber, *A History of Preaching in Britain and America* (Milwaukee: Northwestern, 1955), 2:83.

4. G. D. Henderson, *The Burning Bush: Studies in Scottish Church History* (Edinburgh: St. Andrew Press, 1957), 106.

5. T. Harwood Pattison, *The History of Christian Preaching* (Philadelphia: American Baptist Publication Society, 1903), 185.

7.5.3 *SAMUEL RUTHERFORD—LOVER OF CHRIST AND HOLINESS*

> Fair Anwoth by the Solway,
> To me thou art still dear!
> E'en from the verge of Heaven
> I drop for thee a tear.
>
> Oh, if one soul from Anwoth
> Meet me at God's right hand,
> My Heaven will be two Heavens,
> In Immanuel's land.
>
> —Mrs. A. R. Cousin

> Oh, if I might but speak to three or four herd-boys of my Master, I would be satisfied to be the meanest and most obscure of all the pastors this land, to live in any place, in any of Christ's outhouses.
>
> —Samuel Rutherford

One of the most inspiring preachers in Scottish history is known to us through many biographers and through his amazing letters. We refer to **Samuel Rutherford** (1600–1661), born a gentleman's son near Nisbet in Roxburghshire. He was educated at Edinburgh, where he served as a tutor in Latin before being called as pastor in Anwoth, a small village in southwestern Scotland. John Welsh, son-in-law to John Knox, was an earlier incumbent in this parish. Here Rutherford preached and taught and visited and loved his people. He knew great personal sorrow at Anwoth in the death of his wife and two children.[1]

His publication of *Exercitationes Apologeticae pro Divina Gratia (An Apology for Divine Grace)* brought him censure and suspension. He did not return to Anwoth but moved on to a professorial chair at St. Andrews and then to be a main participant in the Westminster Assembly. He was a controversialist and polemicist of the first order. His antiroyalist *Rex Lex* was a bombshell that strained all of his relationships and got him into deep trouble. Even those who stood with him on most things rebuked him (including Oliver Cromwell and John Milton, the latter rebuking Rutherford in one of his sonnets).[2] In his last imprisonment after the Restoration, he repeated over and over the text, "Thy Word was found, and I did eat it, and it was to me the joy and rejoicing of my heart." He was martyred March 29, 1661.[3] His last words were reportedly, "Glory, glory, dwelleth in Immanuel's land."[4]

Through the Lowlands, Anwoth became the spiritual center for the whole of southwestern Scotland. The work started slowly for Rutherford; the sanctuary sat but 250 people. His beginning sermon was from John 9:39, "Jesus said, 'For judgment I have come into this world, so that the blind will see and those who see will become blind.'" Here Archbishop James Ussher visited him incognito, asking him how many Commandments there were. Discovering who his distinguished guest was, Rutherford asked him to preach on the Lord's Day, and he took as his text: "A new commandment I give to you, that you love one another."[5]

The glory of Rutherford's life and ministry must be seen as his constant "absorption in Christ," whom he worshiped as "the outset, the master-flower, the uncreated garland of heaven, the love and joy of men and angels."[6]

Alexander Whyte saw Rutherford as inspiring Scotland's best preaching for generations. His published *Quaint Sermons,* and his *Communion Sermons* (edited by A. A. Bonar) are passionate and poignant. "He hath neither brim nor bottom," Rutherford exclaimed of Christ. "Get love and no burden Christ will lay on you will be heavy."[7]

He could have had prestigious chairs in Dutch universities, but Rutherford felt the call in his homeland despite constant jeopardy. He saw himself as a Joshua sent ahead to spy the riches of the land and bring the news back to his persecuted brothers and sisters.

Rutherford was the spiritual father to Covenanters such as James Guthrie and his cousin William Guthrie. He was a staunch advocate of conventicles, "private men's liberty in public praying and expounding of Scripture."[8] Hungry saints would travel vast distances to a communion service where it was reported Rutherford would preach.[9]

His famous series of sermons on the names of Jesus Christ is especially memorable. "With a high-pitched voice, called in Scotland pulpit-skriech, and trembling with emotion, he would picture the beauties of the Rose of Sharon, the life-giving properties of the Bread of Life, the glory of the Bright and Morning Star, the fruitfulness of the Branch of Righteousness and the Root of Jesse, the invincibleness of the Lord of Hosts and the majesty of the King of Kings and the Lord of Lords."[10]

---

1. Warren W. Wiersbe, *Living with the Giants* (Grand Rapids: Baker, 1993), 13.
2. T. Harwood Pattison, *The History of Christian Preaching* (Philadelphia: American Baptist Publication Society, 1903), 185.
3. Alexander Smellie, *Men of the Covenant* (London: Andrew Melrose, 1905), 58.
4. Wiersbe, *Living with the Giants,* 17.
5. Marcus L. Loane, *Makers of Religious Liberty in the Seventeenth Century* (Grand Rapids: Eerdmans, 1961), 67.
6. Smellie, *Men of the Covenant,* 56. See Andrew A. Bonar, ed., *The Letters of Samuel Rutherford* (Edinburgh: Oliphant, Anderson, 1891).
7. Loane, *Makers of Religious Liberty in the Seventeenth Century,* 96.
8. G. D. Henderson, *The Burning Bush: Studies in Scottish Church History* (Edinburgh: St. Andrew, 1957), 58.
9. Duncan Anderson, *The Bible in Seventeenth Century Scottish Life and Literature* (London: Allenson, 1936), 91.
10. F. R. Webber, *A History of Preaching in Britain and America* (Milwaukee: Northwestern, 1955), 2:91.

7.5.4 John Livingstone—Seeker of the Lost

I found that much study did not so much help me in preaching as getting my heart brought to a right disposition; yea, sometimes I thought that the hunger of the hearers helped more than my own preparation.

—John Livingstone

As I began to speak, the Holy Spirit came on them.

—Acts 11:15a

The storms of persecution raged over the Scottish church during the seventeenth century. In many cases, "The flower of the clergy were driven from their charges."[1] The unremitting focus of preaching, however, remained "the great saving truths of the gospel."[2] Later critics faulted the lack of polish and ornament in this biblical preaching. They lambasted **James Renwick** (1662–1688) and other evangelicals for their fervor, their multiplied headings and involved subdivisions, their word pictures, and their allegorical biases.[3] But Renwick steadfastly preached the Word. He was executed in the Grassmarket in 1688.

Another firebrand was **John Livingstone** (1603–1672). Born in a minister's family in Stirlingshire, he was well-trained at Glasgow and St. Andrews. Although he was licensed to preach, he found it difficult to procure a charge of his own and went to Ireland, where he served briefly until his nonconformist views inclined him to go to America. Stormy seas caused the ship to return to port, and he served in Stranraer until called to Ancrum.[4]

Periodic revivals graced Livingstone's ministry. One particular sermon catapulted him to national prominence when at the age of twenty-seven he was asked to preach at Shotts. Young and unsure, he wandered in the fields until he "got good assistance." Braced with Ezekiel 36:25–26, he rose to preach to an immense throng.[5] His words "had the flame of the Holy Ghost glowing in them, and they conquered and captivated the souls of men."[6] After preaching for an hour and a half he was led to give an additional hour of tender exhortation and warning. The result was not fewer than five hundred men and women who "traced the dawn of their undying life," pressing forward to confess their sins and seek the Lord.

John Livingstone was a humble man whose spirit did not always please either his friends or his foes. Yet he appealed both to the upper class and the lower class. Deposed in the Restoration, he took exile in Rotterdam, where he developed his Orientalist gifts. Livingstone was skilled in Hebrew, Chaldee, Syriac, and Arabic, to say nothing of his abilities in French, Spanish, and Italian.[7] On his deathbed, his last words were, "I cannot say much of great services; yet if ever my heart was lifted up, it was in preaching of Jesus Christ."[8] He kept his charge and satisfied his God.

---

1. W. G. Blaikie, *The Preachers of Scotland: From the Sixth to the Nineteenth Century (The Cunningham Lectures)* (Edinburgh: T & T Clark, 1888), 155.

2. Ibid., 158.

3. Ann Matheson, *Theories of Rhetoric in the Eighteenth-Century Scottish Sermon* (Lewiston, N.Y.: Edward Mellon Press, 1995), 14.

4. F. R. Webber, *A History of Preaching in Britain and America* (Milwaukee: Northwestern, 1955), 2:92–93.

5. Ibid., 93.

6. Alexander Smellie, *Men of the Covenant* (London: Andrew Melrose, 1905), 99.

7. Webber, *A History of Preaching*, 2:94.

8. Smellie, *Men of the Covenant*, 104.

7.5.5 *JAMES FRASER OF BRAE—UPHOLDER OF THE FREE GOSPEL*

The great object of all their sermons was the presentation of Jesus Christ and Him crucified. Nothing can exceed the pathos with which they besought their hearers to be reconciled to God and to endure patiently His cause . . .We do not claim for them the highest scholarship, the profoundest thought, the most polished style, or the finest eloquence, but we do claim for them that they preached Christ most effectively, and that they drew for themselves, and exhorted all their hearers to draw, their motives for their daily conduct from the cross of their Redeemer.

—William M. Taylor in *The Scottish Pulpit*

James Fraser of Brae (1639–1699) stands among the field preachers, so-called because of their disenfranchisement amid the religious oppression. From a noble family and heir to vast estates, young Fraser studied law at Edinburgh before coming into a profound encounter with the Lord. His experience turned him to ministry. He began to expound the Scriptures but was condemned for it and imprisoned at Bass Rock. Described as "a huge mass of conglomerate rock rising from the waters of the North Sea," Bass Rock was a place of unbelievable misery.[1] In the winters the cells were filled with suffocating smoke. Yet Fraser continued to study Scripture and to teach from the black hole in which he was incarcerated. He also studied Greek and Hebrew, and wrote his famous *A Treatise on Justifying or Saving Faith*.

Thomas Hog (1628–1692), who had served near Dingwall, also languished at Bass Rock. He was a gifted preacher who spoke "with an unusual measure of life and power."[2] Hog spent his last years as pastor in Culross.

Alexander Whyte delivered twenty-eight lectures on Fraser, and termed his treatment of justification an evangelical classic. Fraser had access to an old book titled *Marrow of Modern Divinity,* which along with the writings of Samuel Rutherford and Thomas Shepard of New England markedly shaped his thinking. Fraser harked back to earlier Reformed views, and held that the assurance of salvation is inherent in saving faith. He believed that the gospel invitation could be given to all and that the unregenerate sinner has "a particular right to the promises of the gospel before closing with Christ."[3]

This stands in contrast to **Thomas Halyburton** (1674–1712), who did not feel any assurance could be held out to the sinner if he came.[4] Fraser was an advocate of the position we have previously described as preparation for grace, which holds that the preparatory work cannot be meritorious, since justification is by faith alone. His discussions anticipated the very important "Marrow controversy," which we shall consider in reviewing the next century. With only his Bible in his dungeon, Fraser concluded that the offer of grace is given to all persons impartially.

1. Alexander Smellie, *Men of the Covenant* (New York: Andrew Melrose, 1905), 390.
2. F. R. Webber, *A History of Preaching in Britain and America* (Milwaukee: Northwestern, 1955), 2:127.
3. David C. Lachman, *The Marrow Controversy 1718–1723* (Edinburgh: Rutherford House, 1988), 92. This is a Ph.D. dissertation done at St. Andrews University in Scotland.
4. Ibid., 121.

7.5.6 WILLIAM GUTHRIE—PREACHER IN THE FIELDS

In days of struggle a free pulpit was contended for as for dear life . . . a ministry free to utter the message of Christ was indispensable, and if it could not be enjoyed under the arches of the cathedral or the roof of the parish church, it must be sought in conventicles and chapels, or even among the mountains and moorlands, with sentinels all round to give warning of the dragoons.

—W. G. Blaikie

This is what we preach, and this is what you believed.

—1 Corinthians 15:11b

In the wake of the Restoration, the Glasgow Act of 1662 imposed the episcopacy upon Scotland and required all clergy to submit to bishops. Though they were ejected from their pulpits, more than four hundred clergy would not keep silent.[1] In some cases huge congregations would meet outdoors—in Fife on one day sixteen thousand people met for services.

Many preachers and laypersons were executed or sold as slaves. Among the field preachers and their honor roll of faith are such names as James Guthrie, Donald Cargill, Alexander Peden, and Richard Cameron (1648–1680). Out of the field preaching of Cargill and Cameron came the United Societies, or "the Cameronians," who, while never having many adherents, exerted an influence far greater than their numbers. By 1988 only five Cameronian congregations remain in Scotland (with about 150 members), but ties are maintained with the Reformed Presbyterian Church in Northern Ireland.

One of the inspirational founts of influence on the field preachers was the cousin of James Guthrie. "The little man who never bowed," **William Guthrie** (1620–1665), was the first pastor at Fenwick in Kilmarnock. The oldest son of landed gentry, he lived for a brief while in the ancestral castle but felt God's call and settled the estate on another brother in order that he might preach. He studied under Samuel Rutherford at St. Andrews and soon became a pacesetter in gospel causes, serving as moderator of the Protesting Synod of Glasgow and Ayr in 1654. Coming into a newly formed parish in which the people were steeped in ignorance and superstition, he saw literally thousands converted and confirmed. He was known as a man of extraordinary prayer and "the greatest practical preacher in Scotland."[2] He loved to fish and hunt and often turned these jaunts into innovative occasions of gospel proclamation. Though somewhat melancholy and sickly throughout his life, Guthrie would come in disguise to homes resistant to the gospel and spend the night. Once he stayed with a poacher who bragged he could earn half a crown on Sunday mornings when his neighbors were in church. Guthrie offered a half a crown if he would come to church. When he did, Guthrie led him to Christ. Crowds came to Fenwick, and of his ministry there it was said, "He had a strange way of persuading sinners to close with Christ, and answering all objections that might be proposed."[3]

His preaching was scriptural, delivered with great enthusiasm and vigor, and encased within a deeply satisfying sense of theological construct.[4] His well-known little book *The Christian's Great Interest* was prized by John Owen, who called it his *"vade mecum"* (a book carried as a constant companion). What Guthrie called "imperfect notes" of sermons were also sent forth under the title *A Clear Attractive Warning Beam of Light*. Blaikie quotes Kirkton's contemporary assessment of the church then:

> Every parish had a minister, every village had a school, every family almost had a Bible; yea, in most of the country, all the children at school could read the Scriptures, and were provided with Bibles either by their parents or ministers. Every minister was a very full professor of the Reformed religion, according to the large Confession of Faith framed at Westminster. None of them might be scandalous in their conversation, or negligent in their office, so long as a presbytery stood. I have lived many years in a parish where I never heard an oath; and you might have ridden many miles before you heard any. Also you could not, for a great part of the country have lodged in a family where the Lord was not worshipped by reading, singing and public prayer. Nobody complained more of our church-government than our taverners, whose ordinary lamentation was, that their trade was broke, people were too sober.[5]

When twelve soldiers came to depose him from his office, Guthrie's people were filled with sorrow and anger. He had preached the previous Wednesday after a great fast out of Hosea's mournful cry, "O Israel, thou hast destroyed thyself," but on the Lord's Day he took the softer word: "But in me is thine help."[6] Deprived of his parish pulpit, he preached on the grasses. Though he was not bitter, he was called from this life soon after at the age of forty-five.

---

1. F. R. Webber, *A History of Preaching in Britain and America* (Milwaukee: Northwestern, 1955), 2:107ff.

2. W. G. Blaikie, *The Preachers of Scotland from the Sixth to the Nineteenth Century* (Edinburgh: T & T Clark, 1888), 123.

3. Alexander Smellie, *Men of the Covenant* (London: Andrew Melrose, 1905), 123.

4. Blaikie, *The Preachers of Scotland,* 126.

5. Ibid.

6. Smellie, *Men of the Covenant,* 125.

7.5.7 ROBERT LEIGHTON—PEACEMAKER IN TURMOIL

> Beautiful spirit! fallen alas!
> On times when little beauty was;
> Still seeking peace amidst the strife,
> Still working, weary of thy life;
> Toiling in holy love,
> Panting for heaven above.
>
> —Walter Smith

Amid the debilitating dissensions which tore the fabric of Scotland in the seventeenth century, there were godly men and women who retained loyalty to the episcopacy. The most striking of these was **Bishop Robert Leighton** (1611–1684). Among his circle of influence was the remarkable **Henry Scougal** (1650–1678), the son of a minister who became bishop of Aberdeen, and himself a close friend of Leighton. Young Henry entered Aberdeen at age fifteen and graduated to serve a church and return to Aberdeen as a professor. Scougal wrote *The Life of God in the Soul of Man.* This remarkable volume stressed union with Christ and greatly shaped the Wesleys and led Whitefield to Christ. Scougal died of consumption at the age of twenty-eight.[1]

Leighton, who was known as the "sweetest and saintliest of the Puritans," was born in a minister's home. His father had suffered greatly—his ears had been cropped, his nose had been slit, he had stood in the pillory, and he had been in jail.[2] The younger Leighton matriculated at Edinburgh, though he spent some time studying abroad where he was influenced by the Jansenists in France. He was irenic in temperament. After serving a large parish, he became principal at the University of Edinburgh and preached often in English and Latin to large and appreciative congregations. After the Restoration, he took a bishopric in hopes of effecting unity and understanding in his homeland, though he insisted on the smallest and most insignificant of the bishoprics. Ultimately he became the archbishop of Glasgow.

Leighton made a strong impression in the pulpit with his deeply spiritual presence and his simple and direct preaching style. His magisterial commentary on 1 Peter is still used today. Bishop Burnett praised Leighton:

> He had the great elevation of soul, the largest compass of knowledge, the most mortified and heavenly disposition I ever yet saw in a mortal; he had the greatest parts as well as virtue, with the most perfect humility that I ever saw in a man; and had a sublime strain in preaching, with so

grave a gesture, and such a majesty both of thought, of language, and of pronunciation, that I never once saw a wandering eye when he preached, and have seen whole assemblies often melt into tears before him.[3]

Leighton opposed all persecution, yet he was seen as a wobbler by the Covenanters. Not all faithful preachers of the Word will see ecclesiastical issues exactly the same. Most rejected Leighton's efforts at accommodation. Perhaps he hated strife too much and too quickly sought to escape the cross of controversy. He found himself more and more at odds with several of his fellow bishops. When he retired, he spent the last decade of his life disengaged from the ecclesiastical scene. Even those who disagreed sharply with his position paid tribute to him as "attired in brightness like a man inspired" and a man "who seemed to be in a perpetual meditation."[4]

1. G. D. Henderson, *The Burning Bush: Studies in Scottish Church History* (Edinburgh: St. Andrew Press, 1957), 94ff.
2. T. Harwood Pattison, *A History of Christian Preaching* (Philadelphia: American Baptist Publication Society, 1903), 186.
3. Ibid., 187.
4. Alexander Smellie, *Men of the Covenant* (London: Andrew Melrose, 1905), 191.

7.6 THE DECLINE OF PURITANISM AND PURITAN PREACHING

The fatal error was that the "moderate" pulpit sought to accomplish these ends apart from the life-doctrine of Christianity—apart from its doctrine of salvation. The world was to be taken as it was, and made a friend of— it did not need to be first conquered to Christ. The Church was to bestow her blessing on all the forces and forms of culture around her, whatever might be the spirit in which they were carried on, and the objects at which they aimed.

—W. G. Blaikie

An indispensable aspect of the Puritan genius was the priority and quality of its biblical preaching. Few if any times in church history have exceeded it in terms of the impact and influence of its preaching. Yet undeniably Puritanism, though it leaves us with an impressive legacy, began to flag in the seventeenth century and with it the luster of its pulpit. While in the next century a new upsurge of preaching rolled over the British Isles and New England with ripple effects even in our own time, the Puritan hegemony would not be and could not be replicated.

What happened to weaken and waste Puritanism and the Puritan pulpit? We have no part with those who disparage Puritanism and its failures or give themselves to the endless vilification of Puritan ways, but in an age where we see the decline of preaching a careful analysis of the phenomenon of the Puritan decline is imperative.

1. *External and ideological factors.* The major paradigm shift in worldview called the Enlightenment beat heavily on theological orthodoxy as received down through the centuries. Orthodoxy was the apostolic core of doctrine transmitted across the centuries. Whatever ecclesiological differences may have existed, the supernatural gospel was recognized all but universally as true Christianity. Archbishop Leighton took a different trail in regard to the church but stood with orthodoxy in maintaining that justification means, "The sinner stands guiltless of any breach, yea, as having fulfilled the whole law."[1]

But now building on the humanistic impulses of the Renaissance and the "new science" of Copernicus and Isaac Newton, the Enlightenment is humankind's declaration of independence from God and the authority of His Word. Beginning in Britain with John Locke's attempt to bring all of Scripture within the bounds of human reason and with David Hume's empiricism, or the French "encyclopedists" and Voltaire and Rousseau, and on through Germany's Lessing and Herder and ultimately Immanuel Kant, this is to be the Age of Reason, secular life and existence and autonomous man.[2] Dogma and theology were undercut, and while in its earlier expressions Enlightenment thinking coexisted with religion, the later experience became bitter and acrimonious. The bottom line here is the systematic elimination of God from all of life. The Puritans ran head-on into this juggernaut.

We shall delve further into the effect of the Enlightenment and modernity upon preaching in the next chapter. Here we must cite an example of the deleterious effect of the rebellion against all authority—**Ralph Waldo Emerson** (1803–1882), the New England preacher, poet, and thinker. Not much is left of Emerson's Puritanism in the wake of his "modern disintegrative studies of the Bible."[3] Like Hawthorne, Melville, and Emily Dickinson, he broke with his past and Scottish common sense Realism and ultimately left the Unitarian ministry. Emerson built on the Schleiermachian legacy in which humanity is the starting point.[4] His second wife was a descendant of John Cotton, but that was about all that was left. His sermons were anthropological.[5] Puritanism and all of Christendom would never be the same.

2. *Historical and political factors.* The virtual identity of the medieval papacy as both spiritual and temporal ruler was on balance a negative. We can never underestimate the effects of human depravity. Both in England in Cromwell's Protectorate and in New England, church and state were hard to differentiate. The church is to be salt and light that infuses every sector of culture with spiritual tinge, but when the church becomes the government we lose the essential focus. The collapse of the Commonwealth, abruptly in England and gradually in New England, tended to have similar and extensive negative effect on both the ministry and the preaching of the Puritans. We are not Israel, as the Puritans sometimes forgot and as Dominion theologians and Reconstructionists also seem to forget in our time.

3. *Internal and spiritual factors.* Spiritual movements tend to expire because of their own excesses, as we shall be reminded again when we consider the great awakenings of the next century. The perpetuation of sound vitalities tends to be undermined by internal more often than external forces. Those Puritans we have called Sibbesian were accused of antinomianism but tended to emphasize the life

of the Spirit and tilted toward grace as over against law or works. Amesians like Bulkeley and Shepard triumphed in the antinomian controversy, and they tended to legalism. The result was a marked tendency toward moralism, and this is always a vapid futility for preaching.[6] The fixation on the Fourth Commandment and Sabbatarianism is proof of this. Nathaniel Mather came under the "great reproach of God" for whittling on a Sunday afternoon at the age of sixteen. Bunyan felt he could never be forgiven for playing "cat" after a Sabbath service.[7]

A further area of "hardening of the categories" is seen in the growing intolerance for any variation in views. We do not need to sacrifice an iota of conviction to allow for difference of opinion. The persecuted so soon become the persecutors. The whole Roger Williams episode is a case in point. Williams was banished from Massachusetts and founded Rhode Island where church and state were separate. He was the champion of the Indians as well as of freedom for Jews and Quakers. The Salem witchcraft trials are symptomatic of an unhealthy rigidity and turning inward. Missions seldom flourished in Puritanism (Alexander Duff who was born in 1806 was the first missionary sent out by the Church of Scotland), and evangelism waned.

Elliott-Binns argues that Puritanism was hard hit by "the loose morals which followed the Restoration" and the subsequent reaction against the Puritans, as well as by the "over-intellectualization which robbed Christianity of its life."[8] The Age of Reason found the Puritans exceedingly cerebral and rationalistic. The more whole-souled response to God is the best defense against massive intellectual assault by unbelief and skepticism. In this maelstrom of change and transition, not only Puritanism but also the preaching of Puritanism began a downward slide on the slippery slope. The next century would bring both solace and despair.

---

1. Happily quoted by D. Martyn Lloyd-Jones, *The Life of Peace: An Exposition of Philippians 3 and 4* (Grand Rapids: Baker, 1992). The Doctor did not often have good things to say about bishops.
2. Wilhelm Windelband, *A History of Philosophy* (New York: Harper Torchbooks, 1901, 1958), 2:437ff.
3. Robert D. Richardson Jr., *Emerson: The Mind on Fire* (Berkeley: University of California Press, 1995), 13–14.
4. Ibid., 98.
5. Wesley T. Mott, *The Strains of Eloquence: Emerson and His Sermons* (State College: Pennsylvania State University Press, 1990). This study documents Emerson's change in theology.
6. C. F. Allison, *The Rise of Moralism: The Proclamation of the Gospel from Hooker to Baxter* (London: SPCK, 1966).
7. Leland Ryken, *Worldly Saints: The Puritans as They Really Were* (Grand Rapids: Zondervan, 1986), 192.
8. L. E. Elliott-Binns, *The Early Evangelicals: A Religious and Social Study* (London: Lutterworth, 1953), 56.

CHAPTER EIGHT

Malaise and Revival: Preaching in the Eighteenth Century

Although I am less than the least of all God's people, this grace was given me: to preach to the Gentiles the unsearchable riches of Christ.

—Ephesians 3:8

Pray also for me, that whenever I open my mouth, words may be given me so that I will fearlessly make known the mystery of the gospel, for which I am an ambassador in chains. Pray that I may declare it fearlessly, as I should.

—Ephesians 6:19–20

And that you have already heard about in the word of truth, the gospel that has come to you. All over the world this gospel is bearing fruit and growing, just as it has been doing among you since the day you heard it and understood God's grace in all its truth.

—Colossians 1:5b–6

This is the gospel that you heard and that has been proclaimed to every creature under heaven, and of which I, Paul, have become a servant.

—Colossians 1:23b

And pray for us, too, that God may open a door for our message, so that we may proclaim the mystery of Christ, for which I am in chains. Pray that I may proclaim it clearly, as I should.

—Colossians 4:3–4

> Beware, beware, ye diminish not this office; for if ye do, ye decay God's power to all that do believe . . . we must be ready to hear God's holy word; we must have good affections to hear God's word; and we must be ready to make provision for the furtherance of the preaching of God's holy word, as far as we be able to do.
>
> —Hugh Latimer

> To preach is to open up the inspired text with such fruitfulness and sensitivity that God's voice is heard and God's people obey Him.
>
> —John R. W. Stott

For over a millennium and a half the absolute and infallible authority of the Bible was virtually uncontested in the church or in society. What Principal Rainy said of the Scottish church was true elsewhere: "Surely it is a striking thing that what so united the nation was a resolution that God's authority, discerned by themselves in His Word, that and nothing else, should set up institutions in their Church. That principle was written then on the fibre of the Scottish people in a manner that is legible yet."[1] Indeed both Protestants and Roman Catholics were in basic agreement on the inspiration of Scripture, as Professor Burtchaell observes:

> Despite a radical disagreement on these issues (i.e. the relationship of Scripture and tradition, etc.) both groups persevered in receiving the Bible as a compendium of inerrant oracles dictated by the Spirit. Only in the 19th century did a succession of empirical disciplines newly come of age begin to put a succession of inconvenient queries to the exegetes.[2]

Catholicism effectively lost her Bible as the uniquely inspired revelation from God when in the wake of the Council of Trent tradition assumed greater and greater significance. Protestantism began to lose her infallible Scripture in the face of the massive assault of unbelief and skepticism we speak of as "the Enlightenment" (or as the Germans call it, *Aufklarung*). This movement had its roots in Renaissance humanism and the stirrings of modern science. At first the challenge to authority was essentially philosophical. Sir Isaac Newton was a convinced theist who believed that God is the master mechanic of the universe.[3] Then the Scottish empiricist David Hume challenged the idea of first cause, and ultimately Immanuel Kant took God out of the sphere of knowledge as such.

What began in the British Isles became more radical in France and moved on to Germany, where Lessing argued that "accidental truths of history can never become the proof of necessary truths of reason." This is the "great broad ditch" which can never be transversed. The assertion of the primacy of human reason, the ultimacy of nature, and the relativity of all ethical premises soon confronted the church. If indeed "reason is the judge of all truth, even revelation,"[4] then we perceive a direct challenge to orthodox Christianity and all of her institutions, including preaching. The sixteenth century may have been "the century of genius," as Alfred North Whitehead insisted, but it spawned a corrosion of authority in the next century which we still feel.

The Enlightenment was hostile to Christian doctrine and authority.[5] The failures of the church along with Enlightenment preaching from the pulpit led to moral and ethical chaos. Hume's attack on miracles set up a life-and-death struggle for the church.

Discerning clergy and laity such as Edmund Burke fought against these poisonous philosophies.[6] Leibniz in Germany sought to save orthodoxy, but his Christianity was a modified one. For Leibniz, Christ's redemption had no real significance, and he totally lacked a doctrine of the Holy Spirit.[7] Enlightenment preaching took over in Germany,[8] going so far that one Christmas sermon was about stall feeding. "Christianity was watered down into nothing but ethics, instruction about how to lead an upstanding bourgeois life."[9]

In France the nucleus of the revolution was formed in Enlightenment thinking and the negation of the supernatural by intellectuals such as Voltaire. Principal **William Robertson** of Edinburgh (1721–1793) led the moderates' charge in Scotland and was supported by noted preachers such as **Hugh Blair** (1718–1800), whose elegant sermons were pure moralism. His platform was clear: "The end of all preaching is, to persuade men to be good."[10] It is a rhetoric of optimism:

> Of old, it was customary to preach upon controverted and mysterious points of divinity, but it is now hoped that the generality of the Clergy confine the subject of their preaching to what has a tendency to promote virtue and good morals, and to make a people peaceable and useful members of society.[11]

In England the preaching of **Archbishop Tillotson** (cf. 6.2.7) set the pace for neoclassical preaching and a glacial epoch which impeded dissent as well as the established church. The Arian blight, crass materialism, and moral decay were confronted by an impotent church whose preachers "let alone the mysterious points of religion, and preached to the people only good, plain, practical morality."[12] Paul Johnson shows how "the decline of clerical power in the eighteenth century" created a vacuum into which the secular intellectual stepped who really had nothing to say to the crying need of the hour.[13] Our task in this chapter is to show the faithfulness of a godly remnant in the time of a great malaise and the glorious visits of the Holy Spirit in revival preaching that reshaped history before the end of the century.

In a curious argument, David Bebbington asserts that the Enlightenment as such really started evangelicalism.[14] Doubtless it had both a positive and negative influence. But on balance the Enlightenment brought heavy losses to Christianity.

E. W. Hengstenberg (1802–1869) of Bonn became a rationalist under the impact of the Enlightenment. In fact he set forth the principles of rationalism for his university. The Lord touched his heart in a Moravian service through a simple Bible study, and he became a true follower of Christ. In his inaugural lecture as professor of Oriental languages at Berlin he stated:

It matters not whether we make a god out of stone or out of our own understanding, it is still a false god; there is but one living God, the God of the Bible.[15]

His last audible words were: "That is the nothingness of rationalism: the fundamental thing is Christ. . . . " And that is indeed the issue, the hinge of all history in time and in eternity.

1. Ninian Hill, *The Story of the Scottish Church from the Earliest Times* (Glasgow: James Maclehose, 1919), 164.
2. James Burtchaell, *Catholic Theories of Biblical Inspiration Since 1810: A Review and Critique* (Cambridge, Mass.: Cambridge University Press, 1969), 1–2.
3. Richard S. Westfall, *Never at Rest: A Biography of Isaac Newton* (Cambridge, Mass.: Cambridge University Press, 1980). This treatment is especially good on his religious crisis in 1662 and his Puritan cast. See also E. A. Burtt, *The Metaphysical Foundations of Modern Science* (Garden City, N.Y.: Doubleday/Anchor, 1954).
4. Kurt Aland, *A History of Christianity* (Philadelphia: Fortress, 1986), 2:272.
5. Crane Brinton, *Ideas and Men* (New York: Prentice-Hall, 1950). Brinton defines the Enlightenment as a cosmology which is "the belief that all human beings can attain here on this earth a state of perfection hitherto in the West thought to be only for Christians in a state of grace, and for them only after death" (2:113).
6. Russell Kirk, *The Conservative Mind from Burke to Santayana* (Chicago: Regnery, 1986); Russell Kirk, *Edmund Burke: A Genius Reconsidered* (Peru, Ill.: Sherwood Sugden, 1967, 1988), 128–91.
7. Aland, *A History of Christianity,* 2:283.
8. John Ker, *Lectures on the History of Preaching* (New York: Armstrong, 1889). Interestingly, Ker moves from the ossification of preaching in Protestant Scholasticism directly to the Enlightenment and "Illuminism," which he treats quite fully, lamenting its largely negative and destructive influence on German preaching.
9. Aland, *A History of Christianity,* 2:283, 291.
10. Ann Matheson, *Theories of Rhetoric in the Eighteenth-Century Scottish Sermon* (Lewiston, N.Y.: Edwin Mellen Press, 1995), 120.
11. Ibid., 143.
12. A. Skevington Wood, *The Inextinguishable Blaze: Spiritual Renewal and Advance in the Eighteenth Century* (Grand Rapids: Eerdmans, 1960), 7–25. For a similar sketch of the decomposition of morality and society in Hannoverian England, see L. E. Elliott-Binns, *The Early Evangelicals: A Religious and Social Study* (London: Lutterworth, 1953). He characterizes what passed for religion as "a savourless conception of religion." The debility of the Church of England was due to the death of Queen Anne—"a disaster"; the deistic controversy; the loss of the Puritans; the withdrawal of the nonjurors upon the accession of William and Mary; the decline and silencing of Convocation which hamstrung any response to the Methodists; more and more aristocratic bishops; the degenerate state of many local clergy-nonresident benefices.
13. Paul Johnson, *The Intellectuals* (New York: Harper and Row, 1988) quoted in E. Michael Jones, *Degenerate Moderns* (San Francisco: Ignatius, 1993), 14–15.

14. D. W. Bebbington, "Evangelical Christianity and the Enlightenment" in *Crux* (December 1989): 29ff. Bebbington, who is so insightful on many matters evangelical, disappoints on this and always in his lower view of inspiration and his bizarre notion that the Second Coming of Christ is no part of accepted doctrine; see his *Evangelicalism in Modern Britain* (London: Unwin Hyman, 1989), 87, 83.
15. Quoted in William Childs Robinson, "The Inspiration of Holy Scripture," *Christianity Today* (October 11, 1968): 6.

8.1 STANDING IN THE GAP

Why, Sir, you are to consider, that sermons make a considerable branch of English literature; so that a library must be very imperfect if it has not a numerous collection of sermons.

—Samuel Johnson

I read that Lady Yarmouth sold a bishopric to a clergyman for 5000 pounds. She betted him that he would be made a bishop and he lost, and paid her. As I peep into George II's St. James, I see crowds of cassocks rustling up the back stairs of the ladies of the court; stealthy clergy slipping purses into their laps; that godless old king yawning under his canopy in the chapel royal as the chaplain before him is discoursing. Whilst the chaplain is preaching the king is chattering in German almost as loud as the preacher; so loud that the clergyman actually burst out crying in his pulpit because the defender of the faith and dispenser of bishoprics wouldn't listen to him. No wonder that skeptics multiplied. No wonder that clergy were corrupt . . . No wonder that Whitefield cried out in the wilderness, that Wesley quitted the insulted temple to pray on the hillside.

—William Makepeace Thackeray

Preach the Word; be prepared in season and out of season.

—2 Timothy 4:2a

Pithy in utterance, eloquent in style, **Robert South** was an English preacher who represented conformity to rather than correction of the dangerous drift to *latitudinarianism*—the broad church commitment to pluriformity and, most often, doctrinal indifference. **Bishop Joseph Butler** of Durham (1692–1752), on the other hand, took up the cudgel against deism and unbelief with a vengeance. Born into a merchant's Presbyterian home, Butler chose the established church while in a brilliant academic career at Oxford. In the solitude of Stanhope, an isolated country parish, he wrote his famous *Analogy of Natural and Revealed Religion* and his *Fifteen Discourses.*[1]

Joseph Addison wrote of the English spirituality of the time that there was "less appearance of religion than in any neighboring state or kingdom whether it be Protestant or Catholic." Montesquieu said of France that "the subject of religion if mentioned in society excited nothing but laughter."[2] John Caird described the Georgian sermon as "having been constructed almost expressly to steer clear of all possible ways of getting human beings to listen to it."[3] Samuel Wesley's curate at Epworth had an absorbing theme in his preaching—the necessity of making a will. Moralism and politics dominated preaching as the Word of God slipped from prominence. Only a little flock treasured the spiritual patrimony. We want to look at them quite closely, particularly in England and Scotland.

---

1. Even William E. H. Lecky pays tribute to Bishop Butler for his analysis of moral judgments and his definition of conscience; see *History of European Morals* (New York: D. Appleton, 1877, 1913), 1:20–21, 32, 76, 83.
2. T. Harwood Pattison, *The History of Christian Preaching* (Philadelphia: American Baptist Publication Society, 1903), 247.
3. Ibid., 248.

8.1.1   PHILIP DODDRIDGE—PREACHING WITH CONVICTION

Some sense of sin, and some serious and humbling apprehension of our danger and misery in consequence of it, must need be necessary to dispose us to receive the grace of the Gospel, and the Saviour who is there exhibited to our faith.

What then is to be done? Is the convinced sinner to lie down in despair? to say, "I am a helpless captive, and by exerting myself with violence, may break my limbs sooner than my bonds, and increase the evil I would remove." God forbid! You cannot, I am persuaded, be so little acquainted with Christianity, as not to know, that the doctrine of divine assistance bears a considerable part in it . . . you have heard of "doing all things through Christ who strengtheneth us," (Philippians 4:15) whose grace "is sufficient for us," and "whose strength is made perfect in weakness" (2 Corinthians 12:9). Permit me, therefore, now to call your attention to this, as a truth of the clearest evidence, and of the utmost importance.

—Philip Doddridge

Indeed we have come to days "when Puritanism walked in shadows, spoke in whispers." Horton has drilled to the core when he observes: "Puritans began to lose their central focus—the gospel of grace—and allowed their reformist impulse to create a salvation by personal and social improvement, Christianity became the social glue: urbane, civil and less concerned with theology."[1] Yet some stood firm and valiantly.

One such champion was from among the independents (the Congregational-Presbyterian), **Philip Doddridge** (1702–1751). Born in London the youngest of twenty children, he was actually laid aside as stillborn. Only he and one sister survived, and they were orphaned when he was thirteen. The Duchess of Bedford offered to send him to Oxford or Cambridge if he would stay in the Church of England, but he declined. Friends helped him to enter a Dissenters' Academy at

Kibworth near Leicester, where he taught as well. He began to preach at twenty, and at twenty-seven he was called to the important Congregational church in Northampton, where he ministered for twenty-two years. Although he had met the Lord at sixteen it was only under the stirring appeals of Baxter that bona fide communion with God became a reality.[2] He transferred the academy to Northampton, where over the years he trained more than two hundred young preachers. We still have his "Lectures on Preaching" from these early years.

His biographers generally concede that while of ready and fervent speech, he did not "climb the Alps" in his preaching. He did have an eminent gift of prayer.[3] Moderately Calvinistic, he stressed the urgent necessity of preaching Christ. His best-known book, *The Rise and Progress of Religion in the Soul,* is an earnest outpouring to sinners with the grand object of getting them to the cross of Christ. One sensed in his preaching "quite a rush of love toward God and Christ." He longed for revival and quickening and believed that it would come.

Doddridge was deeply committed to the mastery of Latin, Hebrew, and Greek (and a knowledge of shorthand) for all ministers. One of his contemporaries described him as "not handsome in person; very thin and slender, in stature somewhat above the middle size, with a stoop in his shoulders; but when engaged in conversation or employed in the pulpit, there was a remarkable sprightliness in his countenance and manner, which commanded general attention." One of his students said of his preaching:

> His favorite topics of public discourse were the distinguishing doctrines of Christianity. He considered himself as a minister of the Gospel, and therefore could not satisfy himself without preaching Christ and Him crucified. He never puzzled his hearers with dry criticisms and abstruse disquisitions; nor contented himself with moral essays and philosophical harangues. He thought it cruelty to God's children to give them stones when they came for bread.[4]

He wrote many hymns, of which we have 374, most of them as conclusions to sermons he preached. Such rich favorites persist among us as "Awake, My Soul, Stretch Every Nerve," "O Happy Day that Fixed My Choice," "See Israel's Gentle Shepherd Stand," "Great God We Sing that Mighty Hand," and "My God and Is Thy Table Spread." He also published *Family Expositor,* a paraphrase and commentary on the New Testament which was widely used. Never strong in body, Doddridge began to fail and sought rest and recovery in Lisbon, where he died at the age of forty-nine. Doddridge's faithful heralding of Christ and the Cross in his methodical and orderly style touched many in his own lifetime and down to our own.[5]

---

1. Michael Scott Horton, *Made in America* (Grand Rapids: Baker, 1991), 20.
2. T. Harwood Pattison, *The History of Christian Preaching* (Philadelphia: American Baptist Publication Society, 1903), 254.
3. John Stoughton, *Life of Philip Doddridge* (London: Jackson and Walford, 1851).

4. F. R. Webber, *A History of Preaching in Britain and America* (Milwaukee: Northwestern, 1952), 1:315.

5. Philip Doddridge, *The Rise and Progress of Religion in the Soul* (Grand Rapids: Baker, 1977), 72. Here is the "gospel which I preach and proclaim." He brings his hearers right to the crucified One.

8.1.2 Matthew Henry—Preaching with Content

> Though the people at Chester are a most loving people, and many of them have had and have an exceeding value for me and my ministry, yet I have not been without discouragements there and those such as have tempted me to think my work in that place has been in large done. Many that have been catechized with us and many that have been long communicants with us have left us and very few have been added to us.
>
> —Matthew Henry

The terrain was rough and the grade steep even for such a gifted preacher as **Matthew Henry** (1662–1714). Born into a godly minister's home (cf. 7.3.2.6), he was inclined toward the ministry and Zion's way from an early age. He was converted under the preaching of his father before his eleventh year[1] and began to imitate preaching. He was well into Latin and Greek verses even earlier and studied at Dr. Doolittle's Academy in Islington. Nonconformists (those who communed outside of the established church, the Church of England) were not admitted to Oxford or Cambridge at this time. He heard **Edward Stillingfleet** and **Tillotson** preach but was not drawn to the established church. He studied for the law at Gray's Inn but was not diverted from his call "to make known the mystery of Christ."[2]

"Mercies received" was his testimony. Henry was ordained a nonconformist and shared his dedication as he commenced his ministry in the independent church in the charming, old walled city of Chester in the west of England near Wales:

> I purpose and resolve that, by the grace of God, I will abound more than ever in all manner of gospel obedience; that I will strive to be more humble, serious and watchful and self-denying, and live more above the world and the things of it; that I will pray with more life, and read the scriptures with more care, and not be slothful in business, but fervent in spirit, serving the Lord; that I will abound in good discourse, as I have ability and opportunity with prudence; endeavoring as much as I can "to adorn the doctrine of God my Saviour in all things."[3]

Matthew Henry knew much personal sorrow and ill-health, losing his first wife and several children in death. He was known for his unremitting preparation for preaching (in his study at 4 or 5 A.M. each day) and for his fervency in the pulpit. He was influenced early on by contacts both with Baxter in prison and by hearing John Howe (cf. 7.3.2.6). He usually preached seven times a week. His Sabbath (Sunday) morning service began at 9 A.M. with the singing of Psalm 100, brief prayer, exegetical findings from an Old Testament passage, singing another psalm, and praying for half an hour. Then came the one hour sermon from the text, followed by more prayer and then singing and the benediction. An afternoon and evening service followed. On Thursday there was always a Bible lecture. Known among his flock of about 350 for his frequent pastoral calls, he nonetheless studied deeply and thoroughly. As his biographer comments, "He then invariably conducted them to Calvary."[4]

Beyond his own congregation, Henry ministered regularly in the jails and in villages around Chester. Unlike some, such as **William Greenhill** (1571–1677), who spent almost a lifetime of preaching in Ezekiel, Henry took a variety of texts from all parts of the Bible. He would stick assiduously with the announced text and masterfully use biblical allusions to great effect.[5] He would spend Saturday afternoons catechizing in the manner of Richard Baxter. A new meeting house was built on Crook Lane in the course of the twenty-five years he ministered in Chester. Out of this rigorous study and the hundreds of sermons he preached has come of course his justly renowned devotional commentary, which he finished through Acts (and which various associates completed after his passing).

Still in print and influential, Matthew Henry's commentary is a good sample of his preaching and lecturing ministry. Spurgeon used to read it through regularly on his knees. His "expositions" were endorsed by Doddridge and Watts in his lifetime, by William Romaine and George Whitefield and by **Dr. Adam Clark,** who attributes his own commentary to the stimulus of Matthew Henry. His object in the "expositions" was "to give the sense, and cause men to understand the reading."[6] His is a more mild Calvinism, insisting on "faith" as a condition[7] (although not a meritorious work) and strong for inviting "all people to him."[8] Perhaps alliteration was overdone and there is some "quaintness" in application occasionally, but this is exceedingly rich fare. The subjects and series he preached during his time in Chester provided nourishment for his people and pointed to the way of salvation for the unsaved.[9]

At last he left Chester and took the call to serve a congregation of about one hundred people at Hackney. By this time he was showing severe symptoms of diabetes (frequent nephritical attacks). On his return to Hackney from a taxing ministry, he was thrown from his horse. He tried to preach once more but died a day later on June 22, 1714, at the age of fifty-two, leaving his second wife and seven children. What a beautiful ministry in a dry and difficult time! I never fail to be blessed by something in Matthew Henry. Recently in preaching from John 14:27 on Jesus' last will and testament, I began with Henry's description: When Jesus died he left his spirit with the Father, his body with Joseph of Arimathea, his garments with the soldiers, his mother with the apostle John—and he left us peace, his peace!

---

1. J. B. Williams, *Memoirs of the Life, Character and Writings of the Rev. Matthew Henry* (Edinburgh: Banner of Truth, 1828, 1974), 5.
2. Ibid., 31.
3. Ibid., 42.

4. Ibid., 121.
5. Ibid., 123.
6. Ibid., 251.
7. Ibid., 241.
8. Ibid., 244.
9. Ibid., 274.

8.1.3 ISAAC WATTS—PREACHING WITH CLARITY

> In Bach's sacred music . . . he wanted others to praise God with him . . .
> if so, he was to that extent a preacher as well as an artist.
> —Professor Garry Wills in *Certain Trumpets*

> To the law and to the testimony! If they do not speak according to this
> word, they have no light of dawn.
> —Isaiah 8:20

While **Isaac Watts** (1674–1748) can properly be called "the inventor of hymns in the English language" and "the father of the English hymn," he was also a preacher of distinctive gifts and influence. Up to this time mainly psalms were sung (and among Puritans, *only* psalms were sung—no organs, choirs, or stained glass). Watts was born in Southampton to a staunchly nonconformist family. His father was a schoolmaster and a deacon in Above Bar Congregational Church and knew time in prison because of his religious stand.

The oldest of eight children, Watts began to learn Latin at the age of four, Greek at nine, French at ten, and Hebrew at thirteen.[1] He enrolled at Thomas Rowe's Academy near London, a one-man institution of higher learning led by a minister ejected for his nonconformity. Watts was a genius with a flair for organizing and condensing vast amounts of learning.

He wrote his first hymn, "Behold the Glories of the Lamb," when his father urged him to do something positive rather than find fault with the "lifeless psalm-singing" of his day. His Scripture-based hymns were the substance of his *Horae Lyricae* and other collections of his work. While tutoring, he wrote many hymns including such classics as "O God Our Help in Ages Past," "Joy to the World," "Come Holy Spirit, Heavenly Dove," "Alas! and Did My Savior Bleed," "Jesus Shall Reign," "Am I a Soldier of the Cross," and "When I Survey the Wondrous Cross," which some call the most perfect hymn ever written in the English language. He also wrote books on logic which attracted the attention of Dr. Samuel Johnson. In 1702 he became pastor of Mark Lane Congregation in London where John Owen had once served. Never married and only five feet tall, Watts was never very well, yet God blessed the ministry of the Word at Mark Lane, and the congregation increased from sixty to four hundred.[2] Watts believed the preacher should make his message clear to the simple as well as convincing to the learned. Above all, the preacher should never forget the essential question for his hearers: "What must I do to be saved?"

Struck by a terrible fever in 1712, Isaac Watts took four years to make a partial recovery. During that time he was offered hospitality by the former Lord Mayor of London, Sir Thomas Abner. He stayed there for thirty-six years, continuing as pastor of Mark Lane until his death at the age of seventy-five. His reputation grew during these years, and he became "London's most important nonconformist minister."[3] Two Scottish universities gave Watts honorary doctorates; he handled his finances well; he enjoyed close correspondence with Zinzendorf, Cotton Mather, and Jonathan Edwards. He wrote *Divine Songs for Children* in 1715. In all he published fifty-five books and wrote more than six hundred hymns.

Watts' preaching was intense but not florid. One delightful collection of his sermons, *The World to Come,* treats "the glories of the resurrection for the saved and the sorrows of eternity without Christ for the lost." Discourse 12 on "The Nature of the Punishments of Hell" is indeed somber. Discourse 13 on "The Eternal Duration of the Punishments of Hell" is solidly scriptural in its argument. Discourse 4 is an especially charming message based on 2 Thessalonians 1:10, "Christ Admired and Glorified in His Saints." His main points are to show the reasons for the admiration and glorification of Christ in his saints.

I. That persons of all characters should have been united in one, and persuaded to believe in the same Savior and embrace the same salvation.
II. That so many wicked obstinate wills of men and so many perverse affections should bow down and submit themselves to the holy rules of the gospel.
III. That so many thousand guilty wretches should be made righteous by one righteousness, cleansed in one laver from all their iniquities, and sprinkled unto pardon and sanctification, with the blood of one man, Jesus Christ.
IV. That a company of such feeble Christians should maintain their course to heaven, through so many thousand obstacles.
V. That so many dark and dreadful providences were working together in mercy, for the good of all the saints.
VI. That heaven should be so well filled out of such a hell of sin and misery as this world is.
VII. That so many vigorous, beautiful and immortal bodies should be raised at once out of the dust, with their old infirmities left behind them.
VIII. That the saints shall all appear in that day, as so many images of his person and as so many monuments of the success of his office.

Then, as per the custom of the Puritan preachers, he follows the basic thought development with an impressive series of uses which he divides under five heads.[4] This is more like the inverted pyramid style of Donald Grey Barnhouse and D. Martyn Lloyd-Jones in our time, with the preacher using a small piece of text to supply the theme and then drawing upon the full range of scriptural revelation for the construction of the body of the sermon. Watts' preaching and correspondence suggest how he decried the decay of nonconformity in England and how he longed for a quickening. It was he and **John Guyse** of Hertford who first published Jonathan Edwards' narrative of revival in Northampton.[5] In the meantime, from his deathbed Samuel Wesley laid his hands on Charles and said that God would again visit the land. "I shall not see it, my son," said the elder Wesley, "but you will."[6]

---

1. S. Maxwell Coder, "Biographical Sketch of Dr. Isaac Watts," in Isaac Watts, *The World to Come* (Chicago: Moody, 1954), 18.
2. Ibid., 24.
3. Ibid., 26.
4. Ibid., "Christ Admired and Glorified in His Saints," 160–85.
5. A. Skevington Wood, *The Inextinguishable Blaze: Spiritual Renewal and Advance in the Eighteenth Century* (Grand Rapids: Eerdmans, 1960), 61–62.
6. T. Harwood Pattison, *The History of Christian Preaching* (Philadelphia: American Baptist Publication Society, 1903), 255.

8.1.4 JOHN NEWTON—PREACHING FOR CONVERSION

I am ashamed that I have done and suffered so little for Him that hath done and suffered so much for ill and hell-deserving me.

The more I looked at what Jesus had done on the cross, the more He met my case exactly. I needed someone or something to stand between a righteous God and my sinful self: between a God who must punish sins and blasphemies and myself, who had wallowed in both to the neck. I needed an Almighty Saviour who should step in and take my sins away, and I found such a one in the New Testament . . . I saw that because of the obedience and sufferings of Jesus, God might declare His justice, in punishing my sin, and declare His mercy also, in taking that punishment on Himself on the Cross, so that I might be pardoned.

—John Newton

So spiritually bleak were the times that the famous jurist Blackstone reported that he had visited church after church in London and "did not hear a single discourse which had more Christianity in it than the writing of Cicero." William Jay of Bath observed that "The Establishment was asleep in the dark and the Dissenters were asleep in the light." William Cowper depicted "the fashionable preacher of a city congregation" thusly:

> Behold the picture! Is it like? Like whom?
> The things that mount the rostrum with a skip
> And then skip down again, pronounce a text,
> Cry "Hem!" and reading what they never wrote
> Just fifteen minutes, huddle up their work,
> And with a well-bred whisper close the scene.[1]

"Holding forth the Word of Life" for twenty-eight years in London in this stygian darkness was **John Newton** (1725–1807), who like Doddridge and Watts before him was an accomplished hymnwriter as well as a preacher. His father was a Jesuit-trained seaman and his mother a dissenter. He was reared on Scripture, the catechism, the hymns of Isaac Watts, and the preaching of Dr. David Jennings of the Congregational church at New Stairs, Wapping. He learned from his dear mother that "the third mark of profaneness is to make jest of the Word of God, or preaching or prayer, or any part of true religion."[2] With his mother dead, he spent ten years at sea, enduring flogging and imprisonment before he took up slave trading.[3] Yet during this time he read the Scriptures and Thomas à Kempis. The Book of Proverbs particularly reproved him for his ungodly and wicked lifestyle.

During a fierce storm he yielded to Christ,[4] but still he plied the slave trade and was ultimately made surveyor of tides in Liverpool. Here he came under the influence of both Wesley and Whitefield as well as William Grimshaw, and married his beloved Mary while preparing for the ministry. Through the influence of the evangelical Lord Dartmouth, he was ordained and appointed to his first parish charge in Olney where he labored for sixteen years. Here he preached, wrote hymns, and collected the famous Olney Hymns, among them his own "Amazing Grace," "Glorious Things of Thee Are Spoken," "How Sweet the Name of Jesus Sounds," and "Safely Through Another Week." Here also he developed his friendship with that most peculiar curious Christian brother, **William Cowper** (1731–1800). Tillotson's moralistic preaching could not help Cowper, but Newton's plainer and more direct Christ-centered discourse deeply touched him. He wrote:

> The Spirit breathes upon the Word, and brings the truth to sight;
> Precepts and promises afford a sanctifying light.
> A glory gilds the sacred page, majestic like the sun;
> It gives a light to ev'ry page, It gives, but borrows none.

Cowper's bouts with mental illness and his relationship with Mrs. Unwin are long stories in themselves.[5]

Newton's first preaching was done shyly, as he quickly read his sermon manuscripts. Then he learned the value of eye contact. He was a small, quiet-voiced man, yet with a delightful sense of humor. He offered Sunday dinner to those who had come more than six miles to church. His warm and caring sermons were characterized by a clear organizational principle and were filled Scripture-filled.[6] His most famous preaching was a series of fifty sermons on the Scripture texts that were the basis of Handel's *Messiah*. Complementing his ministry was his extraordinary dedication to letterwriting.[7]

An avowed Calvinist, Newton nonetheless eschewed high Calvinism. Having become the real leader of evangelical forces in England, he was invited to become the pastor of St. Mary Woolnoth, where he served for twenty-seven years.

Newton built St. Mary Woolnoth to be the most significant ministry in London at the time. His preaching attracted the Lord Mayor of London. He preached an evangelistic crusade in Portsmouth every year for his holiday and helped establish the London Missionary Society. He and Mary had a beautiful marriage. His broad friendships and influence extended to young William Wilberforce, Hannah More, Charles Simeon, and to dissenters like William Jay, who visited often. Jay reports in his memoirs that Newton's study was in the attic of his home. Written above it were these words: "Remember that thou wast a bondman in the land of Egypt."[8]

Wilberforce records his impressions of the old man:

> Called upon Old Newton—was much affected in conversing with him—
> something very pleasing and unaffected in him . . . on the whole he en-
> couraged me—though got nothing new from him, as how could I, except
> a good hint. That he never found it answer to dispute . . . when I came
> away I found my mind in a calm, tranquil state, more humbled, and look-
> ing more devoutly to God.[9]

In advanced age, Newton became deaf and almost blind. In his last sermon he forgot where he was, and a curate had to come up and tell him. He said, "My memory is almost gone; but I remember two things: that I am a great sinner and that Christ is a great Saviour." His authentic experience of God's saving grace gave his preaching and his ministry an intrinsic credibility under God. The heart of it is clear by his own words:

> The union of a believer with Christ is so intimate, so unalterable, so rich
> in privilege, so powerful in influence that it cannot be fully represented
> by any earthly simile. The Lord, by His Spirit, showed and confirmed
> His love and made Himself known as He met me at the throne of Grace
> . . . . Wonderful are the effects when a crucified, glorious Saviour is pre-
> sented by the power of the Spirit, in the light of the Word, to the eye of
> faith.

1. Quoted from T. Harwood Pattison, *History of Christian Preaching* (Philadelphia: American Baptist Publication Society, 1903), 247–48.
2. Bernard Martin, *An Ancient Mariner: A Biography of John Newton* (New York: Abingdon, 1950), 11.
3. John Pollock, *Amazing Grace: The Dramatic Life Story of John Newton* (San Francisco: Harper, 1981), 63.
4. Martin, *An Ancient Mariner,* 52.
5. For a magnificent new study, see George M. Ella, *William Cowper: Poet of Paradise* (Durham, N.C.: Evangelical Press, 1993); also Hugh l'Anson Fausett, *William Cowper* (New York: Harcourt, Brace, n.d.).
6. David Lyle Jeffrey, ed., *A Burning and Shining Light: English Spirituality in the Age of Wesley* (Grand Rapids: Eerdmans, 1987), 393ff.
7. See his famous *Cardiphonia* (1787).
8. *The Autobiography of William Jay* (Edinburgh: Banner of Truth, 1854, 1974), 237.
9. Martin, *An Ancient Mariner,* 205.

8.1.5 THOMAS BOSTON—PREACHING WITH COURAGE

But yet seeing I am called out to preach this everlasting gospel, it is my
duty to endeavor, and it is my desire to be (Lord, thou knowest) a fisher
of men. But, alas! I may come in with my complaints to my Lord, that I
have toiled in some measure, but caught nothing, for anything I know,
as to the conversion of any one soul. I fear I may say, I have almost spent
my strength in vain, and my labor for nought, for Israel is not gathered.
O my soul, what may be the cause of this, why does my preaching so
little good? No doubt part of the blame lies on myself, and a great part
of it too. But who can give help and in this case but the Lord himself?
and how can I expect it from him but by prayer and faith in the promises
and by consulting his word where I may by his Spirit shining on my heart
(shine, O Sun of righteousness), learn how to carry, and what to do, to
the end the gospel preached by me may not be unsuccessful?

—Thomas Boston

The developing theological polarity in the Scottish church began with the decline of spiritual life, moved on to loose theology and conformity to the world,
and then inevitably to "cold, passionless preaching."[1] At first evangelical truth
was more ignored than opposed, as Blaikie shows in his classic analysis. The
old supernatural gospel passed away in many stylish circles in which Thomas
Boston's book *Human Nature in Its Fourfold State* (1720) was pilloried as "severe and reactive dogmatism."[2] The increasingly secular sermons of the moderates did nothing to dent the growing strength of deism; indeed, "moderate
preaching did not arrest its spread even among the clergy."[3] One of Blair's staunch
defenders says of his approach, "Blair made little use of supporting biblical evidence. He derived his proofs from the common experience of man, and the Bible
provided a secondary source by which to confirm them."[4]

At the forefront of "the twelve apostles" who led the biblical cause and who
were all ostracized by the General Assembly was **Thomas Boston** (1676–1732).
He was born in Berwickshire. As a boy, he often sat outside the prison where his
nonconformist father was incarcerated. He was converted under the preaching
of the godly **Henry Erskine** (1624–1696), whose texts on that occasion were
John 1:29 and Matthew 3:7. Boston recalled them: "By these, I judge, God spoke
to me. My lost state by nature and my absolute need of Christ, being thus discovered to me, I was set to pray in earnest."[5] He was "touched quickly" by this
preaching and at great sacrifice studied at Edinburgh. After a brief stint as a tutor, he took the pastoral charge at Simprin, where he stayed for eight years, and
then on to Ettrick in Selkirkshire, where he ministered with great distinction until
his death. He was "staked at Ettrick," as he put it, even though he might well
have moved to something far more prestigious.

While ministering to the ninety souls at Simprin, he discovered the old English
Puritan work, *Marrow of Modern Divinity,* in the home of one of his members.
Flying in the face of official opposition, Boston and his circle began to preach
universal grace.

Believing the Gospel offer was for all, that to mankind as sinners the call and overture of divine are to be addressed, the moderate Calvinists of the eighteenth century were animated and dominated by the missionary spirit of Christianity.[6]

The "Marrow-men," as they were called, used Preston's phrase as their watchword, "Go and tell every Man without exception, that there's good news for him, Christ is dead for him."[7] This is what Boston called "the authentick gospel offer."[8]

Boston was a gifted linguist and expert on Hebrew accents, but not a particularly skilled orator. His illustrations were homely, his sermons richly theological, thoroughly biblical, and sensitive. His *Soliloquy on the Art of Man-Fishing* was a masterpiece of passionate discourse.[9] He was a master of variety and the vivid. John "Rabbi" Duncan called him "a genius of the commonplace." When he preached on vital union with Christ, his outline was (1) a spiritual union; (2) a real union; (3) a close and intimate union; (4) though not merely a legal union, it is yet a union supported by law; (5) an indissoluble union; (6) a mysterious union.[10] Davidson of Braintree said of his preaching, "He was indeed one of the most powerful preachers of the Gospel I ever heard open a mouth."

---

1. W. G. Blaikie, *The Preachers of Scotland from the Sixth to the Nineteenth Century* (Edinburgh: T & T Clark, 1888), 216.
2. Ibid., 222.
3. Ibid., 240.
4. F. R. Webber, *A History of Preaching in Britain and America* (Milwaukee: Northwestern, 1955), 2:124.
5. Ibid.
6. A. E. Garvie, *The Christian Preacher* (New York: Scribner's, 1923), 168.
7. David C. Lachman, *The Marrow Controversy 1718–1723* (Edinburgh: Rutherford House, 1988), 204.
8. Ibid., 448.
9. Thomas Boston, *The Art of Man-Fishing* (Grand Rapids: Baker, 1977).
10. Blaikie, *The Preachers of Scotland,* 202.

8.1.6   *EBENEZER AND RALPH ERSKINE—PREACHING WITHOUT COMPROMISE*

An age of cold and feeble rationality, when evangelism was derided as fanatical and its very phraseology was deemed an ignoble and vulgar thing in the upper classes of society. A morality without goodness, a certain prettiness of sentiment, served up in tasteful and well-turned periods of composition, the ethics of philosophy or the academic chair rather than the ethics of the Gospel—the speculations of natural theology and perhaps an ingenious and scholar-like exposition of the credentials rather than a faithful exposition of the contents of the New Testament—these for a time dispossessed the topics of other days, and occupied that room in our pulpits which had formerly been given to the demonstrations of sin and the Saviour.

—Thomas Chalmers

The Marrow Controversy over the gospel (particularly as it focused on the heresy charges against Professor Simson) had its ecclesiological implications. Two gifted brothers were in the vanguard in the forming of the secession church, or the first Associate Reformed Presbytery, the sons of Henry Erskine, **Ebenezer Erskine** (1680–1754) and **Ralph Erskine** (1685–1752). Both were educated at Edinburgh with Ebenezer serving at Portmoak in Fife and then at Stirling, while Ralph spent his entire ministry in Dumfermline. Ralph came first into vital experience with Christ and Ebenezer later after he overheard a conversation between his brother and his wife about a firm ground on which to rest. His life was changed.[1] Ebenezer was one of the original twelve Marrow-men and led out in the formation of the secession church, to be followed in a few years by his younger brother. Both were gifted and able preachers in a time of theological confusion. Yet they drew back from association with George Whitefield because of Whitefield's fellowship with the established church. The evangelical wing of the Church of Scotland thus espoused Whitefield's cause and ministry while the moderates like Robertson and Blair scorned him.

Ebenezer has been described as "the more stately and dignified" preacher of the two and was widely heard, especially in Communion seasons when people would journey considerable distances to listen to the Word as he preached it. These were twice-yearly occasions of great solemnity and often great power.[2] A bit more joyous than Thomas Boston, Ebenezer was clear exposition of grace. Often he spoke from the Old Testament (thirty of fifty-one texts, particularly messianic portions) and with a tendency to stray from the text. He traveled extensively in the interests of the secession and preached throughout Scotland. Here are his main divisions in a sermon on Psalm 89:14 (we have excluded an amplitude of subs and sub-subs):

  I. A view of the throne of grace
 II. Its basis or foundation
III. The pillars supporting and surrounding it
 IV. Why justice and judgment are its foundations
  V. The application of the whole.[3]

Ralph's preaching was more fervent and passionately eloquent and was noted for its effective conclusion and final appeal. His critics then and now fault him for his verbosity and overwrought language and for his "uncomplicated system of eternal reward and punishment."[4] But while his sermons may have been overly enthusiastic, they remained faithful to the gospel. Ralph's preaching must be seen in the context of a large parish of five thousand souls. He maintained fellowship meetings throughout the parish and was a poet and master violinist.[5]

The Erskines thrived on the great fundamental doctrines of Scripture and Christian faith. John Brown of Haddington reported: "I can never forget those days when I traveled over the hills of Cleish to hear that great man of God [Ralph Erskine], whose sermons I thought were brought home by the Spirit of God to my heart. At those times I thought I met with the God of Israel, and saw Him face to face."[6]

1. W. G. Blaikie, *The Preachers of Scotland from the Sixth to Nineteenth Century* (Edinburgh: T & T Clark, 1888), 204. On the controversy involving Professor Simson, who argued from the goodness of God rather than the Bible that God would save the heathen without the knowledge of Christ, see Henry F. Henderson, *The Religious Controversies of Scotland* (Edinburgh: T & T Clark, 1905).
2. Nigel M. de S. Cameron, ed., *Dictionary of Scottish Church History and Theology* (Downers Grove, Ill.: InterVarsity Press, 1993), 200.
3. F. R. Webber, *A History of Preaching in Britain and America* (Milwaukee: Northwestern, 1955), 2:171.
4. Ann Matheson, *Theories of Rhetoric in the Eighteenth-Century Scottish Sermon* (Lewiston, N.Y.: Edwin Mellen Press, 1995), 274.
5. Cameron, *Dictionary of Scottish Church History and Theology,* 301–2.
6. Webber, *A History of Preaching,* 2:174.

8.1.7   JOHN BROWN OF HADDINGTON—PREACHING TO A COMMUNITY

To the Marrow men and those who lighted their torches at the same altar fire we owe the maintenance in Scotland of the evangelistic and evangelical succession at a time when the dominant party in the Church of Scotland, becoming heartless in a high and dry hyper-Calvinism, abandoned theology for morality, and so drifted into moderatism.

Of *The Marrow of Modern Divinity:* The design of the treatise is to elucidate and establish the perfect freeness of the Gospel salvation; to throw open wide the gates of righteousness; to lead the sinner straight to the Savior; to introduce him as guilty, impotent and undone; and to persuade him to grasp, without a moment's hesitation, the outstretched hand of God's mercy.

—A. E. Garvie

At a time when, as Cowper put it, "preaching and pranks share the motley scene," there were those who swam against the prevailing currents. One such preacher was **John Brown of Haddington** (1722–1787). Brown was born in Carpow in Perthshire in meager circumstances. Orphaned at eleven, Brown had only a few months of schooling, spending his early years tending sheep in the hills of Abernethy.

Despite his lack of formal training, Brown read Alleine (cf. 7.3.7), and William Guthrie (7.5.6), and the Bible in a little lodge he and another shepherd had built to protect themselves from the sharp winds. He taught himself Greek and Latin. His great longing was for a copy of the Greek New Testament. He walked twenty-four miles to St. Andrews to a bookstore where Professor Pringle listened to him read and gave him a copy.[1]

Brown's idiosyncratic ways brought him suspicion, false charges, and much misunderstanding in his home parish. He traveled as a peddler for five years and fought against the Pretender ("Bonnie" Prince Charlie of the Stuarts who drew some Scots to challenge the Hannoverians) in 1745. He listened to Ebenezer Erskine, whose emphasis on "God in Christ, a God of love," deeply moved him. He joined with the Erskines, studied briefly with Ebenezer, and finally took the call to Haddington church in 1751, serving there for thirty-seven years. Thomas Carlyle liked to remark that John Knox had been born at Haddington.

In the winter months, Brown preached morning and evening; the rest of the year he preached morning, afternoon, and evening. He visited every family annually and examined adults and children in the catechism.[2] For nineteen of his years in Haddington he did professorial work for the Burgher section of the secession church and wrote a two-volume Bible dictionary and his scholarly *Self-Interpreting Bible*. But it was his biblical preaching that made his mark. His preaching was characterized by "great plainness, faithfulness, seriousness and earnestness."[3] One professor who heard him reported:

> I well remember a searching sermon he preached from the Word, "What went ye out for to see? A reed shaken with the wind." Although at that time I had no experimental acquaintance with the truth as it is in Jesus, yet his grave appearance in the pulpit, his solemn, weighty and majestic manner of speaking, used to affect me very much. Certainly his preaching was close, and his address to the conscience pungent. Like his Lord and Master, he spoke with authority and hallowed pathos, having tasted the sweetness and felt the power of what he believed.[4]

Even David Hume enjoyed hearing him. When Hume was asked to explain, he replied that he liked to hear Brown because he preached as if Jesus Christ were at his elbow. Brown strongly opposed "the light sermonizing of the moderates." While their home was often full of visiting students, six of their eight children died young, and Mrs. Brown died also in 1771 at the age of thirty-eight. Both of his surviving sons became preachers of distinction. He maintained personal ties with Whitefield and the Wesleys through a long correspondence with Lady Huntingdon.[5] He was thus clearly not a scholastic Calvinist but an evangelical Calvinist. He had pronounced millenarian views and expected the conversion of the Jews after their reinstatement in their own land.[6] "Oh, to hate sin and the cause of it!" was his watchword. Ultimately the anti-burgher group of the secession and other seceders joined with the relief church founded by Thomas Gillespie and Thomas Boston (the younger) to form the United Presbyterian Church in 1847. The foundation of all of these movements is the unfettered Word in all of its pristine beauty and power.[7]

---

1. Robert Mackenzie, *John Brown of Haddington* (Edinburgh: Banner of Truth, 1918), 34.
2. F. R. Webber, *A History of Preaching in Britain and America* (Milwaukee: Northwestern, 1955), 2:185.
3. Mackenzie, *John Brown of Haddington*, 106.
4. Ibid., 106.

5. Ibid., 158.
6. Ibid., 206.
7. In a moving appeal for expository preaching based on sound exegesis, W. G. Blaikie draws the chief lesson from three hundred years of Scottish preaching, "that notion of sin which reaches deepest into the human conscience . . . which is taught at the cross of Christ . . . no sprinkling of rose-water on the surface . . . preaching which ignores the work of Christ as an atonement ignores the central truth of Christianity." See *The Preachers of Scotland from the Sixth to the Nineteenth Century* (Edinburgh: T & T Clark, 1888), 303–5. These are the Cunningham Lectures, 12th series.

8.2 SINKING INTO THE GLOOM

In the leading Protestant countries—Germany and England—and from them elsewhere, there was a cold wave of skeptical recoil from the religious enthusiasm of earlier times. Deism and latitudinarianism in England, philosophic skepticism (partly due to English Deism and partly to French infidelity) and rationalistic criticism in Germany, combined to make the eighteenth century the "dark age of Protestantism."

—E. C. Dargan

For Christ did not send me to baptize, but to preach the gospel—not with words of human wisdom, lest the cross of Christ be emptied of its power.

—1 Corinthians 1:17

The same harsh winds of unbelief that led moderates to deny the gospel in Scotland hit France and Germany with galelike velocity. The radicalism of the French Enlightenment was marked, and the drastic consequences of the celebration of autonomous man are seen nowhere more pathetically than in Germany, with a ripple effect in all of the surrounding countries. **Immanuel Kant** of Prussia (1724–1804) is rightly called the watershed thinker of the Enlightenment, because he worked on the basis of reason alone and was agnostic regarding ultimate reality. Remembering his Pietistic roots, we perceive how quickly theistic defenses were demolished and the tidal waves of unbelief and nihilism swept over Europe. The darkness which ultimately fell over Europe resulted in Nietzsche, world wars, the Holocaust, and deconstructionism.[1] A case study in the devastation wrought by Enlightenment antisupernaturalism can be traced in the Tubingen School of the atheistically inclined **F. C. Baur** and his student, **David Strauss,** who denied the historicity of Jesus.[2] Baur remained active in church until his death. **J. S. Semler** continued to have morning devotions with his family, but the supernatural gospel was gone. The fallout for pulpits throughout Germany is unimaginable.

Using an identical epistemology, some protested the sterility of rationalism and developed the imaginative, and the poetic, but even the romanticists had no more to offer than did the rationalists. Exalting feeling above thought was **Jean-Jacques Rousseau** (1712–1756), who was born in Geneva, the grandson of a Calvinistic minister. He argued that man is naturally good, yet he fathered five children out of wedlock. His "I feel, therefore I am" was as much under the tyranny of self-autonomy as the earlier "I think, therefore I am."[3]

In England the romantic **Samuel Taylor Coleridge** (1772–1834) was also the son of a clergyman. Apart from his gross plagiarism, he had "a profoundly religious impulse." While he was ultimately victimized by his opium addiction, he often preached in dissenting chapels, his voice "rising like a steam of rich, distilled perfume." Influenced by Eichorn at Gottingen in Germany, he was very close to **William Wordsworth.** Oddly enough, he had millennial overtones and cherished a great love for the Jewish people.[4] He ardently disliked the Enlightenment, remarking that "the Enlightenment was full of enlighteners but lacking in light." Some have called him the Schleiermacher of Anglican theology. This is all part of the avalanche that threatened to bury biblical faith and biblical preaching in the eighteenth century.

---

1. For a good analysis of these issues, see Ravi Zacharias, *Can Man Live Without God?* (Dallas: Word, 1994), 35ff. Zacharias vigorously argues that "Apart from God, chaos is the norm."
2. Horton Harris, *The Tubingen School: A Historical and Theological Investigation of the School of F. C. Baur* (Grand Rapids: Baker, 1975, 1990). He concludes that "biblical exegesis and interpretation without conscious or unconscious dogmatic presuppositions is impossible," 262.
3. Will and Ariel Durant, *Rousseau and Revolution* (New York: Simon and Schuster, 1967), 10:31ff.
4. Richard Holmes, *Coleridge* (New York: Viking, 1989), 219. Keats said it best for the romantics when he wrote: "O for a life of sensations, rather than of thoughts." See Daniel Hoffman, "S. T. Coleridge and the Attack on Inerrancy," *Trinity Journal* 7 n.s. (1986): 55–68.

8.2.1 JOHANN LORENZ MOSHEIM—THE MENACE OF MEDIATION

A sermon is a discourse in which, following the guidance of a portion of Scripture, an assembly of Christians, already instructed in the elements of religion, is confirmed in knowledge or aroused to zeal in godliness.

It should be in keeping with the dignity and importance of the subject; it should be lively and have as much ornament as does not interfere with clearness; and the language should as far as possible be that which is used in ordinary life among cultivated people.

—Johann Lorenz Mosheim

In the clash between historic Christian orthodoxy and Enlightenment rationalism or romanticism, some opt for a diluted supernaturalism and an appropriate communicational form. Mediating views of scriptural authority represent a desperate effort to salvage something of the Christian gospel, but inevitably satisfy neither side. Compromise on truth issues is always unsatisfactory; compromise on taste issues is necessary.

We have already seen Principal Robertson in Scotland and Archbishop Tillotson making an earnest but futile effort to stake out a middle ground. Now in Germany we see the brilliant and able **Johann Lorenz Mosheim** (1693–1755) make the same commitment. Born in Lubeck and serving as professor of history and chancellor at Gottingen, he was an exceedingly popular preacher.[1] Beamed to the more sophisticated classes, Garvie says that Mosheim "was too fluent; and so his sermons assumed an inordinate length, e.g. his funeral sermon for Frederick II fills eighty-three printed pages."[2] On occasion his audiences were so large that soldiers would be called to keep order. But Garvie observes: "He was lucid, but superficial; he was eloquent, but not fervent; his reasonableness and seriousness did not sound the depths of God or man."[3] His instincts were still orthodox, but Ker must say: "He tones down its strong features, and presents it in such a way that it awakens a sense of chill."[4] This is the bane of the mediating.

Mosheim was so congenial and collegial that he avoided confrontation. Analysis of his sermons shows that he was guided more "by the usefulness of religion" than by penetrating to "the marrow of the text—the excellency of the knowledge that I may win Christ and be found in Him."[5] The trend was to be selective in Scripture, accommodating interpretation to the antisupernaturalistic biases in vogue. "Most of this school took to 'moral preaching.' Sometimes they changed the language of the Bible in order to make it more rational. For conversion or regeneration they spoke of amendment of life; for justification of forgiveness on condition of repentance; for the Holy Spirit, of the exercise of the higher reason; for the atonement of Christ of the spirit of sacrifice which He has taught us by His example, and so on."[6] Such wholesale concessions to unbelief and infidelity please no one. This strategization did nothing to alleviate the increasingly raw situation. Evangelistic vision and passion were lacking. The cupboard was becoming bare.

---

1. Robert Browning in his marvelous "Christmas Eve" depicts the lecture hall at Gottingen, where the discussion is as to the derivation of the Christ myth, not at all concealing "the exhausted air-bell of the critic." See W. E. Williams, ed., *Browning,* (New York: Penguin, 1954), 161ff.
2. A. E. Garvie, *The Christian Preacher* (New York: Scribner's, 1923), 199.
3. Ibid.
4. John Ker, *Lectures on the History of Preaching* (New York: Armstrong, 1889), 242.
5. Ibid., 262.
6. Ibid., 247.

8.2.2 *Johann Albrecht Bengel—The Meaning of the Message*

Eat simply the bread of the Scriptures as it presents itself to thee; and do not distress thyself at finding here and there a small particle of sand which the millstone may have left in it. Thou mayest, then, dismiss all those doubts which at one time so horribly tormented myself. If the Holy Scriptures—which have been so often copied, and which have passed so often through the faulty hands of ever fallible men—were absolutely without variations, the miracle would be so great, that faith in them would no longer be faith. I am astonished, on the contrary, that the result of all those transcriptions has not been a much greater number of different readings.

Scripture is the foundation of the Church: the Church is the guardian of Scripture. When the Church is in strong health, the light of Scripture shines bright; when the Church is sick, Scripture is corroded by neglect; and thus it happens, that the outward form of Scripture and that of the Church, usually seem to exhibit simultaneously either health or else sickness; and as a rule the way in which Scripture is being treated is in exact correspondence with the condition of the Church.

Apply yourself wholly to the text and apply the text wholly to yourself.
—Johann Albrecht Bengel

Among those who stood valiantly for the faith was the heir of true Spenerian and Franckian Pietism, **Johann Albrecht Bengel** (1687–1752). Pietism, with its light touch on doctrine, was vulnerable to Enlightenment sorties, and indeed the notorious rationalist Semler was appointed to Halle in 1751. Not a glimmer of Pietism was seen at Halle by the end of the century save for "the venerable Georg Knapp, who remained faithful among the faithless."[1]

Bengel was born near Stuttgart and studied there and in Halle. He was an avid student of Scripture, and his magnum opus was his five-volume *Gnomon of the New Testament* (i.e., index finger), a Latin commentary on the text with a wide sphere of influence, including John Wesley, whose *Notes on the New Testament* are based on this work by Bengel.[2] Kaiser has shown how Bengel was the first to classify New Testament texts into families and how he explored biblical figures of speech (of which he identified one hundred in an epochal index).[3] His preaching was richly expository. He was greatly influenced by Vitringa on the Apocalypse and sadly veered toward date-setting (he set 1836 as the year of the "end"), but he lived with eschatological awareness.[4] He wrote:

My greatest burden is not my weak physical frame, or my relative afflictions, or the attacks made on me, though from all these I have suffered. It has been hidden in the heart, the burden of eternity. Eternity itself in its infinite moment has pressed upon me, and sometimes entered my soul like a sword.[5]

A whole school of preachers emanated from his wake, including Georg Conrad Rieger. He predicted increasing skepticism and unbelief as attacks on the supernatural became bolder with preaching becoming "bare morality." He saw a mounting desire for "the kernel without the husk" (i.e., Christianity without the Bible) and the introduction of "attractive tales" rather than Scripture. Bengel's own grandson, **Ernst Gottlieb Bengel,** who served at Tubingen, taught that Jesus was essentially an ethical teacher. The younger Bengel was the mentor who most shaped F. C. Baur.[6] Yet Johann Bengel expected a renewal and revival, and correctly assessed his own legacy: "I shall be forgotten at first, but I shall be remembered again."[7]

---

1. John Ker, *Lectures on the History of Preaching* (New York: Armstrong, 1889), 224.
2. Interestingly, Emil Brunner asserts that "Quite apart from its rejuvenation of the dried-up Protestant Church, what Pietism accomplished in the sphere of social amelioration and foreign missions is at the least the token of that Spirit which is promised in the Bible to those who truly believe, and is among the most splendid records of achievement to be found in Church history," in *The Divine-Human Encounter,* (Philadelphia: Westminster, 1943), 23.
3. Walter C. Kaiser Jr., *Toward an Exegetical Theology: Biblical Exegesis for Preaching and Teaching* (Grand Rapids: Baker, 1981), 62, 124.
4. C. John Weborg, "The Eschatological Ethics of Johann Albrecht Bengel," *Covenant Quarterly* (May 1978): 31ff. We sense the great influence of Johannes Cocceius in Bengel; see C. S. McCoy, *The Covenant Theology of Johannes Cocceius* (New Haven, Conn.: Yale University Press, 1957). G. Schrenk says: "Bengel without Cocceius is unimaginable."
5. Ker, *Lectures on the History of Preaching,* 228. Bengel's influence on Zinzendorf is addressed in Gottfried Malzer, *Bengel und Zinzendorf* (Witten, Germany: Luther-Verlag, 1968). For treatment of Zinzendorf, see 6.4.3.
6. Horton Harris, *The Tubingen School: A Historical and Theological Investigation of the School of F. C. Baur* (Grand Rapids: Baker, 1975, 1990), 1, 16, 139.
7. Ker, *Lectures on the History of Preaching,* 237.

8.2.3 FRANZ VOLKMAR REINHARD—THE MOUTHPIECE TO THE MONARCHY

If anyone is ashamed of me and my words, the Son of Man will be ashamed of him when he comes in his glory and in the glory of the Father and of the holy angels.

—Luke 9:26

I tell you, whoever acknowledges me before men, the Son of Man will also acknowledge him before the angels of God. But he who disowns me before men will be disowned before the angels of God.

—Luke 12:8

One of the ablest and most articulate preachers of this time, **Franz Volkmar Reinhard** (1753–1812), took his stand on the issues of his day:

I became a preacher at the time when our Illuminist theologians had succeeded in making the Christian doctrine so clear and intelligible that nothing remained but pure rationalism . . . I felt I must be either an out-and-out rationalist or a supernaturalist . . . if there was no consistent

middle path, and if I had to choose between rationalism and supernaturalism, I was obliged to hold by the Bible, and to accept what could be
proved from it. I honour all conscientious inquiry, I am open to all light,
but my rule of judgment, my guide in perplexity, is the Gospel of Christ.[1]

Called by Dargan "the leading preacher in Germany at the end of the eighteenth century," Reinhard was born into a devout Lutheran pastor's home in
the Duchy of Sulzbach. His father was a faithful preacher of the Word and taught
his son Scripture and Latin. He loved clear outlines and was able to reproduce
his father's sermons ten years after they were preached.[2] He studied at
Regensburg and was a bibliophile of the first order. He was drawn to the clarity and eloquence of Demosthenes. He studied further at Wittenberg (a great
center of the Bible movement), where he became a professor and preacher to
the university. In 1792 he was called to be court preacher at Dresden, where he
attained great distinction as a powerful preacher and as a disseminator of the
historic gospel.

The doctrine of the free grace of God was his absorbing theme. As he put it:

There are moments when the awakened conscience speaks with a re-
morseless claim; when it shows us our sins in all their magnitude; when
it makes us feel with deep conviction and with humbling power the want
of any good in us; when our guilt before God, and the punishment we
deserve, are set before us in a light that strikes us to the ground and leaves
us in a condition the most helpless. Woe then to the sinner who feels
himself so convicted, so condemned, so agonized, if he does not know
the hope of the Gospel, if it has not been proclaimed to him that we are
justified freely by His grace through the redemption that is in Christ Jesus!
Happy then all who know this Gospel and hope in it![3]

Ker wonders if Reinhard preached Christ "in us" as well as "for us,"[4] but the
evidence is that he was a faithful, balanced preacher on the whole. Still, Ker shows
the tension of his encounter with the influence of illuminism in his time.

With respect to the process of developing the trajectory of the sermon, Ker
remarks:

He worked out each sermon with the greatest care. First he sketched a
scheme in which the chief thoughts were outlined in logical order and
on this he set great value, both for its own sake and as an aid to his
memory. The sermon, in his view, is a piece of art, to which, as to its
outer form, both logic and rhetoric must contribute, but logic is the most
important. Its thoughts must come up in regular order, group themselves
in proportion, and lead to proper conclusions. The language should be
suited to this, simple, clear, pointed. The preacher must never forget that
he is above all a teacher; he who makes it his chief aim to awaken and
move robs his office of much of its value, for if we are to reach the heart,
it must be through the understanding.[5]

John Ker's lectures on the history of preaching seem top-heavy with analysis of German preaching but reflect the deep concern of this esteemed preacher and scholar about trends he saw in his own beloved Scotland.

---

1. John Ker, *Lectures on the History of Preaching* (New York: Armstrong, 1889), 286f.
2. E. C. Dargan, *A History of Preaching* (New York: Hodder and Stoughton, 1912), 2:228.
3. Ker, *Lectures on the History of Preaching*, 254–55.
4. Ibid., 256.
5. Ibid., 267–68.

8.2.4 *FRIEDRICH SCHLEIERMACHER—THE MIASMA OF MODERNISM*

[Speaking of the Moravian Brethren] There is no other place which could call forth such lively reminiscences of the entire onward movement of my mind, from its first awakening to a higher life, up to the point which I have at present attained. Here it was that, for the first time, I awoke to the consciousness of a higher world . . . Here it was that mystic tendency developed itself which has been of so much importance to me, and has supported me and carried me through all the storm of skepticism. Then it was germinating, now it has attained its full development; and I may say that, after all I have passed through, I have become a Herrnhuter again, only of a higher order.

—Friedrich Schleiermacher

It may be possible that erroneous conceptions of the significance of the baptismal estate may in part account for the perpetuation of this conception of preaching in Germany. A baptized congregation is assumed to be a Christian congregation and should be addressed as such. Perhaps this may in part explain the relative ineffectiveness of German preaching.

—Lewis O. Brastow

Nowhere do we see the disaster of the opening of the spiritual sinkhole we have been describing any more vividly or drastically than in the life and teaching of **Friedrich Schleiermacher** (1768–1834). He was born into the devoutly Pietistic home of a cavalry chaplain of the Reformed church in Breslau. Educated in Moravian Brethren schools, he ultimately went to Halle over the objection of his father and studied under Semler and other old rationalists. He jettisoned belief in everlasting punishment, Christ's deity and atonement, and the supernatural character of Christian faith. After much study in Kant, he turned toward this mystical modification we can call "the new rationalism."[1]

Schleiermacher served several pastoral charges and became widely known as a powerful communicator, setting as his model the Scottish moderate, Hugh Blair.[2] While serving as chaplain at the Charity Hospital in Berlin he issued a translation of the sermons of Blair. He added a romantic overlay to his Kantian thought (very much a la Goethe) and spent several years teaching at Halle. The fallout of the Napoleonic Wars necessitated Schleiermacher's relocation to Berlin, where he was a court preacher, professor, and pastor.

People would begin to gather at 7 A.M. to hear his Sunday sermon. He had a great disdain for the Old Testament generally and his ten-volume collection of sermons use only twenty Old Testament texts, chiefly from the wisdom literature and prophets. Imbibing Spinozistic pantheism, Schleiermacher had no supernatural revelation (for him, revelation was only "another name for human discovery"),[3] nor did he have a transcendent God.[4] Such a view of Scripture, as we have maintained, has a profound influence on preaching. Denying that the doctrine of the Trinity has any significance, and without any objective truth, Christianity becomes feeling. Preaching becomes a horizontal endeavor to sound a cheerful note.

Truly the father of modern liberalism, Schleiermacher never came to grips with the message of the Reformation. He had a "constant hankering after the pulpit"[5] and was very much like Beecher and Brooks in his preaching.[6] He was vague on Jesus but preached him warmly and greatly touched the great Neander's heart.[7] His appearance in the pulpit was arresting—"short of stature, and as to his shoulders slightly deformed; but he had a broad forehead, firm-set lips, strong Roman nose, a keen eye, and an altogether serious and vigorous countenance and a penetrating voice."[8] His oft-quoted sermon on "The Dying Saviour Our Example" is typical. The sermon is striking but based on the premise that dogma should not be allowed to obtrude "in the Good Friday service."[9] Schleiermacher correctly saw that preaching and theology are inseparably intertwined, but his theology with its egregiously deficient Christology is too thin.[10] For him Christmas meant "the feeling of immediacy in one's life."[11] The influence of these theological denials of the supernatural, and the strong emphasis on religion as feeling has resurfaced explosively in our times in an increasingly common approach to preaching. Is the purpose of preaching to make us feel good about God? And in such an anthropocentric approach, is this God really anyone other than ourselves?

---

1. The legacy of the Kantian bifurcation in epistemology is so foundational for understanding modern thought and preaching. Hence I recommend a work like S. Korner, *Kant* (New York: Penguin, 1955). The influence of Heidegger, the modern existentialist philosopher, cannot be followed apart from realizing he was trained in Marburg Kantianism; see Thomas Langan, *The Meaning of Heidegger* (New York: Columbia University Press, 1960).

2. Lewis O. Brastow, *Representative Modern Preachers* (New York: Macmillan, 1904), 11.

3. H. R. Mackintosh, *Types of Modern Theology* (New York: Scribner's, 1937), 71.

4. Karl Barth, *Protestant Theology from Rousseau to Ritschl* (New York: Harper, 1959); Karl Barth, *The Theology of Schleiermacher* (Grand Rapids: Eerdmans, 1983). This is based in large part on a study of Schleiermacher's sermons.

5. Mackintosh, *Types of Modern Theology*, 39.

6. Brastow, *Representative Modern Preachers,* 42–43.

7. Mackintosh, *Types of Modern Theology,* 54.

8. Brastow, *Representative Modern Preachers,* 43.

9. Ibid., 34.

10. Richard R. Niebuhr, *Schleiermacher on Christ and Religion* (New York: Scribner's, 1964), 14.

11. William Alexander Johnson, *On Religion: A Study of Theological Method in Schleiermacher and Nygren* (Leiden, Netherlands: E. J. Brill, 1964), 54.

8.2.5 *CLAUS HARMS—THE MODUS OPERANDI OF THE MIDDLE*

In those days the word of the Lord was rare; there were not many visions.

—1 Samuel 3:1b

We must pay more careful attention, therefore, to what we have heard, so that we do not drift away.

—Hebrews 2:1

I had to write and urge you to contend for the faith that was once for all entrusted to the saints.

—Jude 3b

Even in the face of such widespread and pervasive theological declension, there were voices crying in the wilderness. Among them were **Claus Harms** (1778–1855), born in the well-to-do home of a miller in the province of Holstein. The young Harms was inclined to spiritual things and made his way through the University of Kiel. At this time he tended toward the prevailing rationalistic ideas, but within that arid desert he thirsted for the reality of the Lord. His first step was Schleiermacher's *Discourses on Religion,* which he read ravenously and which with its discussion of Jesus led him to Christ. Now awakened, he began to dig into Luther and the Reformers and became a preacher of considerable conviction and forcefulness.

Preaching first as a student and then as a visiting pastor, he was well heard in a widening circle from the pulpit of St. Nicholas Church in Kiel, where he began as an archdeacon in 1816. The university snubbed him as "an obscurantist, a darkener of the light of reason, a retailer of old, worn-out ideas, he and his Bible and Luther!"[1] He was given the preaching time during the dinner hour, but gradually spiritually hungry people revised their dining time and even Professor Eckermann, "father of Kiel rationalism, never missed an afternoon service."[2] He won the war of the pamphlets and was even invited by the king of Denmark to preach in Copenhagen and by the emperor of Russia to come and settle in St. Petersburg. Most curious of all, he was invited by the king of Prussia to succeed Schleiermacher in Trinity Church, Berlin.[3] But he was determined to labor in the vineyard in Kiel.

Harms led a revival in confessionalism which shook all of Northern Germany. He attacked rationalism and set forth a new set of ninety-five theses in favor of the evangelical faith. He greatly stressed biblical preaching. His divisions of the text were clear. Dargan says of his ministry: "During his whole career he was the most powerful preacher in Northern Germany."[4] Harms wrote on the importance of a right spirit in the preacher nurtured by the Holy Spirit's power and the results of seasons of retreat and refreshing and waiting before God. He quoted Hamann, "The nearer the Scripture, the nearer the skies." (cf. 1.1 n. 1). A sample of his style as translated is striking:

> Who are the careless? We cannot seek them out or count them; but let each man step forward to the word with his heart. Who is the careless? The man who has behind him a youth full of sins, his riper years guilty without repentance, and who, because in old age he has been forced to give up some sins, is confident that all is right. Man! thou hast built their house upon a fire-vomiting hill, and thou dost not know it. Before thou art aware, in "a little while," it will burst out and hurl thee into an abyss where thou shalt no longer stand erect. Thou dost not fear this? Even that is thy carelessness—thy sinful carelessness—from a sermon on John 16:19, on "a little while."[5]

---

1. John Ker, *Lectures on the History of Preaching* (New York: Armstrong, 1889), 340.
2. Ibid., 340.
3. Ibid., 341.
4. E. C. Dargan, *History of Preaching* (New York: Hodder and Stoughton, 1912), 407.
5. Ker, *Lectures on the History of Preaching*, 347.

8.2.6   FRIEDRICH AUGUST THOLUCK—THE MAGNIFICENT MOLLIFIER

The Church theology and Christian life have had their progress and regress, counting back from the days of the Reformation to the days of their origin, from our times back to the sixteenth century; nor will it be otherwise with regard to the future development of the Church of Christ. Our understanding and our moral state will ever alternately move on and turn back, and, opposed to the Kingdom of the Lord, a realm of Antichrist will remain, and will continue to grow, until it be destroyed by the last victory. May the Lord give us clear eyes and warm hearts, in order that, from all the aberrations that His Church has undergone till now, there may redound to us an everlasting gain.

Every sermon should have heaven for its father and earth for its mother.
—Friedrich August Tholuck

Given the intensity and strain of the theological tug-of-war, it is not surprising to find a mediating school that would attempt a fence-straddling position. But is that really possible when the issue is the supernaturalism of biblical faith? Nonetheless, such well-known names as Neander, Dorner, Olshausen, and

Tholuck are in this group. We shall look at Tholuck because of his eminent preaching.

Friedrich August Tholuck (1799–1877) was born in Breslau, the son of a goldsmith. He studied at Berlin with particular interest in things oriental but turned to theology under the influence of Count Ernst von Kottwitz of the Moravian Brethren in Silesia. This mentor led him into the study of the Pauline Epistles, and "through the great mercy of God he found wisdom and life in Christ crucified."[1] Tholuck read about the life of Henry Martyn and dedicated his life to missions in the East. He intended to take a position with the British and Foreign Bible Society in Malta, but his health collapsed. He followed De Wette at Berlin, and in 1826 he took the place of the venerable Dr. Knapp at Halle. This fulfilled a great longing for Tholuck, since he had become much enamored by August Francke's example. The Halle faculty, led by the great Hebraist Gesenius, strongly opposed his coming—the school had become a "hot-bed of rationalism," with only five students out of nine hundred professing belief in the deity of Christ.[2]

Not only did Tholuck produce a substantial body of scriptural commentary (with noteworthy volumes on Romans, Hebrews, John, the Sermon on the Mount, and the Psalms) but also he won the hearts of the students. He "was an evangelist as well as an evangelical,"[3] and was considered the best preacher in all of Germany. Conspicuous for his conversational tone, Tholuck artfully flouted homiletical convention and made effective use of his vivid imagination. As chaplain to the university he drew not only students but also townspeople to his sermons. He truly preached the gospel message. One of his five volumes of university sermons has been translated under the title *Light from the Cross*. It is a choice treasure and must be considered one of the ten best collections of sermons on the cross of Christ ever published.[4] It is divided into two parts:

I. The Cross as a Revealer of the Hearts of Men. A series based on Luke 2:34–35 and probing into the lives and experiences of various personalities in relation to Calvary. Strong preaching on sin. His models were Luther, Hamann, and Bunyan.
II. The Sufferings and Death of Christ. Sermon 7 is especially outstanding on Luke 23:26–31, "Weep not for me but for yourselves." His messages on the seven last words of Christ are among the first of its kind.

Beyond question Tholuck was a true believer, and at the end of his life was in great peace, saying, "I fear not for myself; the death of Christ avails for me."[5] But there is something missing in the man and in his messages. He brings us to the Cross, but he does not share doctrine. He is theologically inarticulate. How can we preach the death of Jesus without theological construct? "Christ died for our sins" is heavily freighted with Anselmian and transactional implication. Is this the price middle-grounders must pay? Tholuck was neutered doctrinally.[6] In order to mollify his critics and take advantage of opportunities for ministry, he skimmed along the surface of a text with his eyes closed to theology. As a consequence, he left his heirs penniless.

1. John Ker, *Lectures on the History of Preaching* (New York: Armstrong, 1889), 318.
2. J. C. Macaulay, "Biographical Introduction," F. A. Tholuck, *Light from the Cross* (Chicago: Moody, 1952), 12.
3. Ibid., 13.
4. Ibid.
5. E. C. Dargan, *A History of Preaching* (New York: Hodder and Stoughton, 1912), 410.
6. The dilemma of the "mediating" is seen recurring through history. In the reorganization of Princeton Seminary in 1929 such basically conservative professors as Charles Erdman and others sought to avoid alignment but paid an immense price for their attempted neutrality. We can easily lose our influence and the respect of both sides.

8.2.7   HENRIC SCHARTAU—MESSENGER IN THE LAND OF THE MIDNIGHT SUN

We had poor preachers, poor in preaching or in life, but the great Shepherd of souls kept His promise, which in like cases He has given to His dearly bought sheep, even to those that have drifted away, "I shall shepherd them according to their need." During a wretched and careless altar address He gave me grace so that, while reading the confession, I had a living insight and conviction, especially at the words, "I therefore know that I am worthy of hell and eternal condemnation." I clearly understood . . . I would certainly be lost . . . but I also received grace to accept the words of absolution unto forgiveness . . . based on His bloody atonement. Since that day I have, by the power of God, and in spite of errors and much wavering, been preserved unto salvation.

When the Holy Scriptures are left to occupy the seat of honor and other writings are used as their footstool, then scriptural learning will be dominating in one's preaching without debasing one to copy the methods or idiosyncrasies of any particular school. One may then emulate the gifts of others without deviating from one's own high pattern.

—Henric Schartau

An influential preacher in southern and western Sweden in this time of enveloping shadows was **Henric Schartau** (1757–1825). Born in Malmo in Skåne, the son of a city clerk and councilman, Schartau grew up in a family where Scripture was highly valued. At fourteen, he enrolled in the University at Lund, where "fighting, drinking and gambling were very general."[1] But, to use his own words, "The wise hand which had grasped my heart led me likewise imperceptibly into the Word of God."[2] Schartau was led captive not only to the Word but also to Scrivner's *Treasury* (**Christian Scrivner,** 1629–1693, a widely-read German Pietist). He was also shaped by J. A. Bengel's works but was cool toward the accompanying Moravian Brethren emotionalism (although he was a great admirer of the Norwegian lay reformer, Hauge). At the core Schartau was a follower of Luther with a tinge of John Arndt. "Schartau indeed went deep into the mine of Holy Scripture . . . he brought out great treasures and thus built up his discourses."[3]

Like Luther, he preached law before he preached grace. His outlines were famous, and he worked hard at delineating the steps to salvation by grace, the *ordo salutis*. Sometimes under his intense preaching listeners would become so aware of the danger of hell and future judgment that they would cry out for everyone to repent.

Karl Olsson sees Schartau's "orders of blessedness" as a counteraction against "the non-confessional and unscriptural mood of the Enlightenment."[4] In all of this, Schartau was much maligned and vilified. Yet he urged that there be no quarreling in the pulpit. His style was rugged and perhaps legalistic, but we must remember he lived in an antinomian time. He was the quintessential Swede:

> His was an art, known by but few,
> Of being strong and gentle too.

In retrospect, this able preacher has risen in esteem. The Swedish Academy coined a memorial to him with the inscription: "He was a faithful shepherd of his flock and a true teacher."[5] His collected sermons show the function of a clear proposition, great dedication to the text, and a concern for clear and practical application.

---

1. Henrik Hagglund, *Henric Schartau and the Order of Grace* (Rock Island, Illinois: Augustana, 1928), 13.
2. Ibid., 14.
3. Ibid., 18.
4. Karl Olsson, *By One Spirit* (Chicago: Covenant, 1962), 664 n. 2.
5. Hagglund, *Henric Schartau and the Order of Grace,* 36. A fine collection of fifteen sermons is appended.

8.3 STIRRING UP THE GIFT

Quicken me, O Lord, according unto thy word.
—Psalm 119:107b (KJV)

Will you not revive us again, that your people may rejoice in you?
—Psalm 85:6

Lord, I have heard of your fame; I stand in awe of your deeds, O Lord. Renew them in our day, in our time make them known; in wrath remember mercy.
—Habakkuk 3:1

Although some held forth the word of life "in a crooked and depraved generation," shining "like stars in the universe" (Phil. 2:15), the eighteenth-century spiritual landscape was generally bleak. Times were reminiscent of the grim days of the Old Testament judges, but a sovereign God deigned to visit his people and stirred among them.

One of the most glorious visits of God to his people in all of history took place in the eighteenth century. It was the Great Awakening. At a time when a deistic poet like **Alexander Pope** was pushing the notion that "the proper study of mankind is man" and when the jurist **Blackstone** observed that it was impossible to tell from the sermons preached in English churches whether the preacher was Muslim, Confucian, or Christian, God came in mighty revival.

At the epicenter of any spiritual detonation is the recovery of the preaching of the Word of God. Revival, according to C. E. Autrey, is "the reanimation of God's people."[1] The people of God "felt a divine vibration."[2] The message was not new; the preachers were "enthusiastically orthodox,"[3] illustrating again the principle that the preaching of the Scriptures became central.[4] It was a revival of the Reformation in a real sense. As Skevington Wood argues, the irresistible authority of the Word under the unction of the Holy Spirit swept through in cyclonic force. "The note of authority returned to the pulpit: an authority springing from the Word and finding its corroboration in the heart of man."[5] He then quotes J. C. Ryle:

> The spiritual reformers of the last century taught constantly the sufficiency and supremacy of the Holy Scripture. The Bible, whole and unmutilated, was their sole rule of faith and practice. They accepted all its statements without question or dispute. They knew nothing of any part of Scripture being uninspired. They never allowed that man has any "verifying faculty" within him by which Scripture statements may be weighed, rejected or received. They never flinched from asserting that there can be no error in the Word of God; and that when we cannot understand or reconcile some parts of its contents, the fault is in the interpreter and not in the text. In all their preaching they were eminently men of one book. To that book they were content to pin their faith, and by it to stand or fall.

Antecedents and catalysts of various kinds were used of God to prepare the way:

1. Many faithful servants of Christ remained true to the gospel, often at great price.
2. Gifted apologists like Butler and exegetes like Bengel held the field for historic orthodoxy even under the withering fusillade of enemy fire.
3. The revival really began with the Pietists on the Continent; Spener and Francke helped "restore biblical preaching and Bible study."[6] W. R. Ward traces the awakening to Silesia and the children's prayer meetings. The revival of 1727 began with the conversion of an eleven-year-old girl. Much opposition was encountered, for only in New England "did the establishment take up with the revival."[7] Wesley visited Herrnhut and Halle and fellowshiped with Francke; Whitefield was also in touch with young Francke. Trevecca was derived from Halle as a model. Wesley's wife was a Huguenot. Bengel's

eldest daughter married a fervent Herrnhuter. Doddridge's grandfather was from Bohemia. All this shows that the revival was, as Ward contends, a pan-Protestant phenomenon.

4. Gifted devotional writers like **William Law** (1686–1761) addressed the needs of the heart and most significantly dealt with the root causes of widespread unbelief. His *A Serious Call to a Devout and Holy Life* had an immense effect on John Wesley, for instance. He has been called "a herald of the Evangelical Revival."[8]

5. Revival fires were kindled in the religious societies springing up everywhere by a series of awakening sermons, such as those delivered in the Savoy Chapel in London by **Dr. Antony Horneck.** Horneck came from the Rhineland, studied at Oxford, and was much used in societies dedicated to the promotion of scriptural holiness. Samuel Wesley had one of the most vigorous societies in his parish at Epworth.[9]

Yet, as Elliott-Binns insists, "[The revival] came without organization and almost without expectation." And really, after Continental Pietism and its relatives, the dawn first began to glimmer in beautiful and rugged Wales.

---

1. Earle E. Cairns, *An Endless Line of Splendor: Revivals and Their Leaders from the Great Awakening to the Present* (Wheaton, Ill.: Tyndale House, 1986), 54–55. Another key study is James Burns, *Revivals: Their Laws and Leaders* (Grand Rapids: Baker, 1909, 1960). See also my "The Corollary of Revival—Evangelism," *The Evangelism Mandate* (Wheaton, Ill.: Crossway, 1992), 164–174.
2. A. Skevington Wood, *The Inextinguishable Blaze: Spiritual Renewal and Advance in the Eighteenth Century* (Grand Rapids: Eerdmans, 1960), 236.
3. L. E. Elliott-Binns, *The Early Evangelicals* (London: Lutterworth, 1953), 91.
4. Wilbur M. Smith, *The Glorious Revival under King Hezekiah* (Grand Rapids: Zondervan, 1937), 23ff.
5. Wood, *The Inextinguishable Blaze,* 227.
6. Cairns, *An Endless Line of Splendor.*
7. Wood, *The Inextinguishable Blaze,* 112.
8. William Law, *A Serious Call to a Devout and Holy Life* (New York: E. P. Dutton, Everyman's Library, 1955).
9. Wood, *The Inextinguishable Blaze,* 30ff.

8.3.1 GRIFFITH JONES—THE DAYSTAR OF THE AWAKENING

Nothing was to be seen in almost every parish but young men and young women flocking together into the churches and churchyards and engaging in different gambols and pastimes such as ball playing, football, leaping, fighting and such like frolics. . . . Common preaching will not do to rouse sluggish districts from the heavy slumbers into which they are sunk. Indeed, formal prayers and lifeless sermons have also entered the Principality under the pretence of order. Five or six stanzas will be sung as dry as Gilboa, instead of one or two verses like a new song, full of God, of Christ, of the Spirit of grace, until the heart is attuned to worship . . . you are content with a preacher speaking so lifelessly and so low that you can hardly understand the third part of what he says; and you will call this decency in the sanctuary.

—Christmas Evans

Through the lovely valleys of Wales, where once the gospel message had reverberated with rejoicing, now the lassitudes prevailed. **William Wroth, Rees Prichard, Walter Cradock,** and the eloquent **Vavasor Powell** (1617–1670), who was imprisoned thirteen times for his field preaching, were the bright stars in the darkness. But the first preacher of the dawn was the venerable **Griffith Jones** (1683–1761) of Llanddowror. He was a shepherd boy who was called to preach in a dream. Born into "a religious and respectable family," he had the rare opportunity of education while many were illiterate. Jones was ordained in 1709 and served out his life preaching in the Vale of Taf.

The revival message he preached was not pleasing to all. He was accused of preaching outside the walls of a church (when the church could not hold the congregations in excess of four thousand). He saw the signs of spiritual starvation. He organized not only catechetical classes but schools to teach reading until over 215 such schools existed in South Wales. He sponsored the publication and distribution of more than thirty thousand Bibles in the Welsh language. He was responsible for a great effort of charity for the poor and dispossessed.[1] But gospel preaching was always his forte. He divided his sermons carefully, explicated the text with thoroughness, and "as he advanced, his subject fired him more and more."[2] Said one analyst of his style:

When he came to the application, he entered upon it with a solemn pause. He seemed to summon up all his remaining force; he gave way to a superior burst of religious vehemence and, like a flaming meteor, did bear down all before him. His voice broke silence and proceeded with a sort of dignified pomp. Every word was like a fresh attack, and carried with it a sort of triumphant accent. By his preaching the drunkards became sober; the sabbath-breakers were reformed; the prayerless cried for mercy and forgiveness; and the ignorant were solicitously concerned for an interest in the Divine Redeemer.[3]

Before the conclusion of his ministry he had met with both Wesley (he heard him preach outdoors at Bath) and Whitefield, and had forged a bond with the ministry and outreach of the Countess of Huntingdon. Not the least of his spiritual productivity can be seen in the lives of preachers he led to Christ and influenced. An arrogant young curate was soundly converted in one of his meetings in 1735 and became one of the flaming preachers of the Welsh awakening: **Daniel Rowland** (1713–1790). He was known for the great centrality to which he gave Christ in every sermon—his blood, his sacrifice, his righteousness.

Others influenced by Griffith Jones during this unparalleled time of great preaching in Wales was the lay preacher **Howell Harris** (1714–1773), who was converted in the same year as Rowland. At the advice of Jones, Harris gave himself to establishing societies in the Church of England. These became the nucleus of the Calvinistic Methodist Church of Wales. When he was denied ordination, Harris became an itinerant evangelist. His greatest years of fruitfulness were from 1735 to 1750. In his prime it was said that he preached on hell as if he had been there. Toughs would seek to rough him up, and on one occasion a musket was fired at him and narrowly missed.

Harris was one of Whitefield's closest friends and actually gave Whitefield the woman he loved rather than be tempted by her affection.[4] Yet he entered a period of dryness and broke with Whitefield when the latter would not tolerate the moral indiscretion of Harris. Harris also strayed in doctrine (1751–1753), going too deeply into "the felt Christ" of the Moravians and veering toward patripassionism.[5] These bypaths also strained his long relationship with Rowland. To the praise of God, Harris repented but never totally mended his ties with Whitefield. He was still mightily used as a preacher, and when he died at age fifty-nine, twenty thousand people attended his funeral.

Like many Welsh preachers, Harris's discourses erupted like molten lava. Here is how Whitefield described him:

> A burning and shining light has been in those parts; a barrier against profaneness and immorality, and an indefatigable promoter of the true Gospel of Jesus Christ . . . He is of a most catholic spirit, loves all that love our Lord Jesus Christ, and therefore, he is slighted by bigots and dissenters. He is condemned by all that are lovers of pleasure rather than lovers of God: but God has greatly blessed his pious endeavors. Many call him as their spiritual father; and I believe, would lay down their lives for his sake. He discourses generally in a field, from a wall, a table, or anything else, but at other times in a house. He has established near thirty societies in South Wales, and still his sphere of action is enlarged daily. He is full of faith and the Holy Ghost . . . Blessed be God, there seems to be a noble spirit gone out into Wales, and I believe ere long there will be more visible fruits of it.[6]

Still another in this sterling succession of revival preachers in Wales must be noted in the person of **William Williams** of Pant-y-celyn (1717–1791). Williams has been called the Charles Wesley of Wales. He began studying for medicine, but was converted after hearing Howel Harris preach in 1738. Soon Williams felt the call to preach himself. He traveled three thousand miles a year in revival ministry and wrote more than eight hundred hymns, including "Guide Me, O Thou Great Jehovah" and "O'er the Gloomy Hills of Darkness."[7] In Williams and his contemporaries, God's Spirit was clearly on the move.

---

1. A. Skevington Wood, *The Inextinguishable Blaze: Spiritual Renewal and Advance in the Eighteenth Century* (Grand Rapids: Eerdmans, 1960), 43.

2. F. R. Webber, *A History of Preaching in Britain and America* (Milwaukee: North-western, 1955), 2:560.
3. Wood, *The Inextinguishable Blaze,* 42.
4. Harry S. Stout, *The Divine Dramatist: George Whitefield and the Rise of Modern Evangelicalism* (Grand Rapids: Eerdmans, 1991), 157. This is the only treatment I can find of the moral wobbling of Howell Harris.
5. Robert Bennett, *The Early Life of Howell Harris* (Edinburgh: Banner of Truth, 1909, 1962).
6. Wood, *The Inextinguishable Blaze,* 51.
7. D. Martyn Lloyd-Jones, "William Williams and Welsh Calvinistic Methodism," in *The Puritans and Their Successors* (Edinburgh: Banner of Truth, 1987), 191ff.

8.3.2 JOHN WESLEY—THE DYNAMO OF THE AWAKENING

Let me be *homo unius libri.* (Let me be a man of one book.)

The Bible must be the invention of either good men or angels, bad men or devils, or of God. (1) It could not be the invention of good men or angels, for they neither would nor could make a book, and tell lies all the time they were writing it, saying "Thus saith the Lord," when it was their own invention. (2) It could not be the invention of bad men or devils, for they would not make a book which commands all duty, forbids all sin, and condemns their souls to hell to all eternity. (3) Therefore I draw this conclusion that the Bible must be given by divine inspiration.

I look on all the world as my parish. . . . God buries the workmen, but continues His work.

—John Wesley

The true end of preaching is to amend men's lives, not fill their heads with unprofitable speculation.

—Susanna Wesley

The human workhorse in the Great Awakening was **John Wesley** (1703–1791), who ministered tirelessly for sixty-six years. At his energetic peak, Wesley traveled five thousand miles per year, averaging three sermons a day. He published a four-volume commentary on all of Scripture, a dictionary of the English language, a five-volume work on natural philosophy, grammars on the Hebrew, Latin, French, and English languages, three books on medicine, six on church music, seven volumes of sermons, edited *The Arminian Magazine* and a library of fifty volumes of the classics called The Christian Library. He rose at 4 A.M. and worked until 10 P.M. In his eighty-sixth year he still rode thirty to fifty miles a day. "I know my commission," he said. "Courage mounteth with occasion."

The principal personalities of the Awakening differed on certain theological issues. (For instance, Wesley's Arminianism led to a break with the Calvinistic

Whitefield. Fortunately this wound was largely healed, and Wesley ultimately preached Whitefield's funeral.) But the basis of doctrinal agreement is impressive, particularly with reference to the authority of Scripture, the sinfulness of man, the absolute centrality of Christ's atonement, the necessity for the new birth, and so forth.[1] Whitefield was undoubtedly the more eloquent preacher and Wesley the more brilliant organizer, but both were evangelists who communicated with indisputable results.

John Wesley—the Believer

John Wesley was the fifteenth child of Samuel and Susanna Wesley. His father was a high church evangelical whose father and grandfather had been clergymen, while his mother was reared in Puritan nonconformity. Susanna's marriage to Samuel deeply alienated her nonconformist parents. Samuel was impulsive and imperious and dedicated twenty-five years to writing a Latin commentary on the Book of Job. Susanna gave herself with an identical pertinacity to the raising of her nineteen children (she was one of twenty-five children herself). She personally instructed her children in the Scriptures and with regard to their personal relationship to Christ. Susanna home-schooled her children and taught them Greek by their eighth year.

Samuel Wesley served the Epworth parish in Lincolnshire. Many in his congregation hated him, and he spent time in debtor's prison. To his chagrin, his wife conducted preaching services in the rectory during his incarceration. In John's sixth year, enemies burned the rectory down, and the lad was miraculously spared as "a brand from the burning."[2] John grew to believe God had something special for him.

Matriculating at Charterhouse School in London, John went to Oxford. Shocked by the profligacy of so many students, he gave himself to a hard regimen. He was made a don at Oxford and received ordination in 1725. With his brother Charles and others he founded the famous Holy Club. Wesley said of this time, "I preached much but saw no fruit of my labor." He was still struggling for spiritual light and in considerable bondage to the law. Discouraged, he went to Georgia in "the hope of saving my own soul."[3] His brief stint in America was not successful. He observed the inner peace of Moravian believers during a fierce storm on the sea, and upon returning to London sought out a Moravian chapel where he heard Luther's preface to his commentary on Galatians being read. Wesley entered into faith and assurance of salvation. Only three days earlier, Charles had been saved. This "strange warming of his heart" at Aldersgate was the turning point of his life and ministry. Of this Pentecost Sunday he told the archbishop:

> It is true that from May 24, 1738, whenever I was desired to preach, salvation by faith was my only theme . . . And it is equally true that it was for preaching the love of God and man that several of the clergy forbade me their pulpits.

John Wesley—the Preacher

Wesley loved to share his own personal testimony as he preached. "As soon as I saw clearly the nature of saving faith and made it the standing topic of my preaching, God then began to work by my ministry as He had never done before."[4] His friend from the Holy Club, George Whitefield, taught him to do field preaching. On Monday, April 2, 1739, he preached to three thousand people outdoors at Kingswood near Bristol, and it became his modus operandi. He loved to preach at 5 A.M. before the men went to work. Only five feet seven inches tall and weighing 122 pounds, the slender white-wigged preacher had a strong voice and never failed to be understood, even when in his eighties he spoke to thirty-three thousand people.

His style was calm and reasoned. Without humor or pathos, there was yet a moral earnestness about his preaching, a subdued intensity that gave him intrinsic credibility. His journal is fascinating, as he often records, "I gave them Christ!" He felt reservations about Whitefield's bombastic style and flamboyant gestures. He said Whitefield was too much like a Frenchman in a box. Wesley's own delivery was not dramatic but was "a combination of terror and tenderness." "But for an occasional lifting of his right hand, he might have been a speaking statue." As one interpreter puts it: the message was carried by what he said rather than how he said it.[5] He used the pause to good effect. He personified piety. Of course he preached "Christian perfection," which to him was having the mind of Christ, walking as he walked, nothing more and nothing less. Yet he never claimed to have reached it himself.[6]

Wesley was more textual than expository, demonstrated in his famous sermon on "The Great Assize" from Romans 14:10, preached at the time of assizes. The sermon was bare of illustration but rich with Scripture and metaphor.[7] Wesley was lucid and logical and never failed to give a clear proposition. In his sermon from 1 Corinthians 14:20, "The Poverty of Reason," he states: "Reason, however cultivated and improved, cannot produce the love of God . . . it cannot produce either faith or hope, from which alone this love can flow." He pleaded for a religion of the heart and conversion. His magnificent sermon on "The Scripture Way of Salvation" from Ephesians 2:8 is clear:

I. What is salvation?
II. What is that faith by which we are saved?
III. How are we saved by it?

While the interrogative outline is notoriously wooden and lacking in assertiveness, clearly Wesley is at the aorta of this great text. He urged his preachers:

> Preach our doctrine, inculcate experience, urge practice, enforce discipline.
> If you preach doctrine only, the people will be antinomians; if you preach
> experience only, they will become enthusiasts; if you preach practice only,
> they will become pharisees; and if you preach all of these and do not enforce

discipline, Methodism will be like a highly cultivated garden without a fence, exposed to the ravages of the wild boar of the forest.[8]

John Wesley—the Organizer

Whether the Great Awakening in England averted a bloodbath like that of the French Revolution is a matter of debate and scholarly discussion, but even the skeptical Lecky observed:

> Although the career of the elder Pitt, and the splendid victories by land and sea that were won during his ministry, form unquestionably the most dazzling episodes in the reign of George II, they must yield, I think, in real importance to that religious revolution which shortly before had begun in England by the preaching of the Wesleys and Whitefield.[9]

Along with his preaching, Wesley brought what has been rightly called an organizing flair to the ministry. In 1739 he preached for the first time on "Free Grace" at the Foundry in London, which became the headquarters for Methodism (a name first used of the Holy Club at Oxford). In 1740 the first of the societies was founded, and the first Annual Conference was held in 1744. The Wesleys never intended to leave the Church of England and remained officially within its ranks until their deaths. Wesley adapted from the Moravian bands (the Pietistic conventicles) his lay-led class meetings. Twenty percent also belonged to a band, committed to the fervent pursuit of holiness. In the whole structure lay pastors were working side by side with clergy.[10]

Wesley was quite high church throughout his long life, taking the Lord's Supper weekly.[11] He had a keen sense of the body of Christ and was burdened also for the abolition of slavery and the amelioration of bad conditions in prisons. His commitment to an itinerant ministry harks back to his own evangelistic experience, and while he never traveled to America again, he commissioned Thomas Coke and Francis Asbury to be superintendents in America. Asbury was the only one to stay in America during the revolution. He called himself a bishop with much disapproval of Wesley. Yet the sense of esprit and élan constantly comes through, as in a journal entry for Christmas Day, 1747:

> We met at four and solemnly rejoiced in God our Saviour. I found much revival in my own soul this day. . . . Both this and the following days I strongly urged the wholly giving up ourselves to God, and renewing in every point our covenant that the Lord should be our God.

In two areas Wesley never found satisfaction. His own marriage was desperately unhappy, ending when his shrewish wife left him. Neither was he able to plant Methodism in Scotland. Whitefield himself had his problems there, but Wesley's experience was especially sour.[12]

Still "the grand itinerant" persisted. How many heard him in church yards, fields, in the collieries! As John Nelson wrote when hearing him for the first time:

It made my heart beat like the pendulum of a clock and when he did speak, I thought his whole discourse was aimed at me. When he had done, I said, "This man can tell the secrets of my heart."[13]

1. Timothy L. Smith, *Whitefield and Wesley on the New Birth* (Grand Rapids: Frances Asbury/Zondervan, 1986).
2. A Methodist Preacher, *John Wesley the Methodist* (New York: Eaton and Mains, 1903), 3. A veritable gold mine is to be found in W. L. Doughty, *John Wesley Preacher* (London: Epworth, 1955). "Monotony is a great fault," he said.
3. F. R. Webber, *A History of Preaching in Britain and America* (Milwaukee: Northwestern, 1952), 1:337.
4. A. Skevington Wood, *The Inextinguishable Blaze: Spiritual Renewal and Advance in the Eighteenth Century* (Grand Rapids: Eerdmans, 1960), 113.
5. Richard P. Heitzenrater, *The Elusive Mr. Wesley* (Nashville: Abingdon, 1984), 2:83.
6. Harald Lindstrom, *Wesley and Sanctification* (Nashville: Abingdon, 1946). This study clearly shows Wesley's commitment to humanity's moral inability, to salvation by grace and to the gospel of ruin by the fall, redemption by the Cross, and regeneration by the Holy Spirit. See also George A. Turner, "John Wesley as an Interpreter of Scripture," in *Inspiration and Interpretation,* ed. John Walvoord (Grand Rapids: Eerdmans, 1957), 156–78.
7. Edward H. Sugden, ed., *John Wesley's Fifty-Three Sermons* (Nashville: Abingdon, 1983), Sermon 48.
8. P. Boyd Mather, "John Wesley and Aldersgate 1963," *The Christian Century* (December 18, 1963): 1581ff.
9. Quoted in T. Harwood Pattison, *The History of Christian Preaching* (Philadelphia: American Baptist Publication Society, 1903), 255.
10. Howard Snyder, *The Radical Wesley and Patterns for Church Renewal* (Downers Grove, Ill.: InterVarsity Press, 1980).
11. Ole E. Borgen, *John Wesley on the Sacraments* (Grand Rapids: Frances Asbury/Zondervan, 1972). A Swedish bishop's definitive study.
12. Samuel J. Rogal, "John Wesley at Edinburgh: 1751–1790," *Trinity Journal* 4 n.s. (1983): 18–34.
13. Quoted in Bill J. Leonard, "Preaching in Historical Perspective," in *Handbook of Contemporary Preaching,* ed. Michael Duduit (Nashville: Broadman, 1992), 31.

8.3.3 CHARLES WESLEY—THE DREAMER OF THE AWAKENING

I am not afraid that the people called Methodists should ever cease to exist, either in Europe or America. But I am afraid, lest they should only exist as a dead sect, having the form of religion without the power. And this undoubtedly will be the case unless they hold fast both the doctrine, spirit and discipline with which they first set out.

—John Wesley

My gracious Master, and my God, Assist me to proclaim, "To spread through all the earth abroad The honours of thy name."
—Charles Wesley (c. 1740)

Much of the vitality of the Great Awakening was certainly due to the giftedness of John Wesley and George Whitefield, but an indispensable factor was the preaching, praying, and praising of **Charles Wesley** (1707–1788). Charles was the eighteenth child of Samuel and Susanna Wesley, born in the Epworth rectory in Lincolnshire. At the age of eight he was sent to the Westminster School (by Westminster Abbey), where his older brother Samuel attended, and in due time went on to Christ Church, Oxford.

Like his older brother John, Charles (who was more mercurial in temperament) was not truly converted until after a frustrating experience in Georgia. Upon returning to England, Charles met the Lord, largely through the influence of his good friend from Oxford, George Whitefield, and through the insights of the Moravian Peter Bohler. Although previously he had been overcome by strong drink and fits of temper, his life changed dramatically.

He breaks the power of canceled sin, He sets the prisoner free;
His blood can make the vilest clean, His blood availed for me.

Though not yet understanding justification by faith alone, Charles Wesley was ordained in the Church of England.[1] He began to preach to the prisoners in Newgate and elsewhere. For the next sixteen years he traveled in itinerant ministry preaching the gospel of the grace of God. He ministered both in Wales and Ireland.

Charles' preaching was always with many tears, and his words came "in sentences which had the rush and impact of bullets."[2] Happily married, he preached even on his honeymoon. The great sorrow of his life was that his three children did not become Christians. These strenuous exertions were draining on his poetic nature, but as many have observed, he was overshadowed by his illustrious colleagues apart from whom he would have been better known as a mighty preacher of the Word of God. After he preached for two hours on John 3, many conversions were reported, including one notorious drunkard.[3]

Charles made Bristol his headquarters; John was centered at the Foundry in London. Charles often served as a liaison between his brother John and George Whitefield. Some strains developed as Whitefield moved more and more toward Calvinism.

Throughout these busy years he wrote nine thousand poems, many of which were set to music. He penned hymns such as "Hark, the Herald Angels Sing!" "Rejoice, the Lord Is King," "Jesus, Lover of My Soul" and "Christ the Lord Is Risen Today." The theological richness of these hymns is striking. Largely through Methodist influence, hymn-singing became an accepted part of worship. Other Methodist hymnwriters at this time included Oliver the converted shoemaker who wrote "The God of Abraham Praise," and Edward Perronent, who composed "All Hail the Power of Jesus' Name."[4]

A particularly close associate of both the Wesleys was **John William de la Flechere** or **Fletcher** (1729–1781), born in Nyon in Switzerland. Steeped in Holy Scripture, he served in Madeley, a mining village in Shropshire. He was an exceptionally gifted preacher who spoke with "great freedom of speech and enlargement of heart." He traveled often with the Wesleys and served as principal of the Countess of Huntingdon's school at Trevecca until they parted company over limited atonement. The students said that to have breakfast with Fletcher was like having the holy Communion, he was so full of the love of Christ. Long a consumptive, he poured out his limited energy in ministry. His famous *Checks to Antinomianism* needs a contemporary reissue.[5]

We sense that we are in the company of a select cadre of individuals who preached and lived in a most extraordinary time. "Lord, do it again" should be our earnest prayer.

Charles Wesley captured the sense of the Great Awakening in his lines:

> A charge to keep have I—a God to glorify,
> A never-dying soul to save and fit it for the sky.
> To serve the present age, my calling to fulfill—
> O may it all my powers engage, to do my Master's will!
> Arm me with jealous care, as in Thy sight to live,
> And O, Thy servant, Lord, prepare, a strict account to give.

---

1. Arnold A. Dallimore, *A Heart Set Free: The Life of Charles Wesley* (Wheaton, Ill.: Crossway, 1988), 45.
2. F. R. Webber, *A History of Preaching in Britain and America* (Milwaukee: Northwestern, 1952), 1:350.
3. Dallimore, *A Heart Set Free,* 86.
4. L. E. Elliott-Binns, *The Early Evangelicals* (London: Lutterworth, 1953), 416.
5. Joseph Benson, *The Life of the Rev. John de la Flechere* (New York: Methodist Book Concern, 1904); J. Marrat, *The Vicar of Madeley: John Fletcher* (London: Charles H. Kelly, 1902) shows how Charles Simeon desired to catch the glow of Fletcher's fire, 128.

8.3.4 GEORGE WHITEFIELD—THE DRAMATIST OF THE AWAKENING

I love those who thunder out the Word!

If thou canst prove, thou unbeliever, that the book which we call the Bible, does not contain the lively oracles of God; if thou canst shew that holy men of old did not write this book as they were inwardly moved by the Holy Ghost, then we must give up the doctrine . . . but unless thou canst do this, we must insist upon it . . . if for no other, yet for this one reason, because that God, who cannot lie, has told us so.

—George Whitefield

Great, warming currents were melting huge chunks of spiritual glaciation. The revival breezes came from Continental Pietism, touching Lutherans, the Reformed, and Anabaptists alike with Puritan flavor and revivalistic fervor. It was the time of "the religion of the heart."[1]

Invariably, spiritual awakening is intertwined with the recovery of the Word of God and its preaching. Edwards, in documenting his contention that "true revival is a revival of gospel preaching," cites many examples like that of Asahel Nettleton in America. His preaching was "vigorous and bold . . . warm, pungent and awakening."[2]

We now consider that great era of powerful preaching, full of Christ and his blood atonement. George Whitefield was at the vortex of it all.

George Whitefield—the Character

He has been called the Demosthenes of the pulpit. "He preached like a lion." He was the major influence on the Awakening in New England. Some have termed him the greatest evangelist since the apostle Paul. Lloyd-Jones called him "the greatest preacher England ever produced." **George Whitefield** (1714–1770) was born in Gloucester in the Bell Inn, a tavern owned by his father, to a family of six boys and one girl. His father died when he was two, and he suffered much in his mother's unhappy second marriage. When he was four he had measles. This resulted in permanent damage to his eyes for which he was often called Dr. Squintus. At fifteen he was taken out of school and tended bar, but all through this time Whitefield sought time to read the Bible. In 1732 he went to Oxford and served for three years as a servitor in Pembroke College (from which Samuel Johnson had just come). There he became acquainted with the Wesleys and joined the Holy Club.

Although Whitefield had a reputation as a drunkard and a thief, he seemed penitent. At Oxford, after reading William Law, August Francke, and Henry Scougal, and through the friendship of Charles Wesley, he was converted.[3] "God was pleased to remove the heavy load," he recalled. Later he went to Georgia, as did the Wesleys, and wherever he went, his ministry could be called "preaching that startled a nation." In all he made thirteen trips to America.

His preaching was powerful and dramatic. Reportedly, after his first sermon fifteen people went mad. C. S. Horne said of him, "We may accept the almost universal verdict that for dramatic and declamatory power he had no rival in his own age, and no superior in any age."[4]

Dallimore's two volumes convey the spiritual warmth and great godliness of Whitefield.[5] A typical exclamation: "Oh that we were all a flame of fire!" He was first and always a soulwinner, saying, "Oh, that I might catch them with a holy guile." Reading more and more of the old Calvinists, he drew away from the Wesleys but always insisted "we are ready to give a universal offer to all poor sinners."[6]

Whitefield's marriage was not fulfilling, and his only son died at four months. He himself was afflicted with frequent illness and always got sick just before he preached. At the age of fifty-six, George Whitefield died of asthmatic complications after preaching in Massachusetts. Wesley gave the funeral address in England. One of the mighty giants had fallen.

George Whitefield—the Communicator

A more striking contrast cannot be drawn than that between the calm dignity of John Wesley and the emotional and sprightly preaching of George Whitefield. He preached with great pathos, weeping in every sermon. He had a great faculty for description; his preaching abounded with anecdotes. Dallimore characterizes his preaching as biblical, doctrinal, and simple. Gillies, his first biographer, reports just some of the astonishing numbers:

1. The incredible extent of his preaching: forty to sixty hours a week
2. The number of times he preached: one thousand times a year for thirty years
3. The immensity of his audiences: Benjamin Franklin heard him preach to thirty thousand
4. The breadth of his appeal—peer and peasant alike loved him

Dallimore observes, "He had a most peculiar art of speaking personally to you in a congregation of four thousand people."[7] Another observer remarks: "He made them laugh, he made them moan, he swayed them like reeds in the wind. A surly old general who despised preachers followed the crowd, listened as the young preacher described a blind man stumbling nearer and nearer to the edge of a precipice, forgot himself and preacher-hate and shouted right out in the meeting, 'Good God, he's over!'"[8]

Whitefield used the three-point homiletic and spoke in an amazing voice. It was reported that a man leaning on a gate a mile away could hear enough and was saved. David Garrick, the actor, panted, "I'd give one hundred guineas to be able to say 'oh' like George Whitefield." With his interest in narrative and in portraying Christ and biblical characters (his Zacchaeus rendition was especially famous), Whitefield anticipated emphases which were uncommon in his day.

Some hagiographers of Whitefield have been uneasy over Harry Stout's recent *The Divine Dramatist,* which presents the great revivalist as a "born actor," as one who read plays as a youth but who turned on the worldliness of the theater later in life.[9] Stout points to the "dramaturgy" in the Church of England service which Whitefield never left (he always wore the gown in preaching, even in the fields).

Whitefield utilized imaginative flight, as in the frequent use of the metaphor of an ocean voyage,[10] and not always wisely, as when he purported to impersonate the marriage agent for Christ or when he hid a trumpeter to peal forth suddenly after a sermon on the Second Coming—and precipitated a panic and hysteria.[11] Whitefield did adapt to the fields and the marketplace in his time. And he did make use of his wealthy friend and his ornate carriage to drive through the town and invite people to the service.[12]

Stout is sadly out of balance in some of his criticisms, but we can hardly fault him for bringing us real aspects of Whitefield's preaching. Were we to fuse the hagiographic Dallimore with the realistic Stout we would have an effective blend.[13]

Whitefield cried out, "I'll preach Christ till I do to pieces fall!" This is almost literally what happened—he preached himself to death. Even here he was the actor, for he used his own physical maladies and miseries to portray the agonies of the damned.[14]

In terms of structure, Whitefield followed a modified Puritan pattern. Like the Wesleys, he broke away from reading manuscripts and especially loved free prayer. He wrote, "I find I gain greater light and knowledge by preaching extempore, so that I fear I should quench the Spirit did I not go on to speak as He gives me utterance."[15]

George Whitefield—the Intercontinental Commuter

Whitefield reminds us of the old adage: If we take care of the depth of our ministry, God will take care of the breadth. The Lord enlarged the scope of Whitefield's ministry geographically, ecclesiastically, and socially.

Though self-conscious of his meager origins in a society of great social stratification, Whitefield got along with almost everyone. His remarkable friendship with Benjamin Franklin, who became his American agent, is most telling. Franklin eulogizes Whitefield in his *Autobiography*.[16] Whitefield never stopped seeking to win Franklin to Christ. David Hume was reportedly so taken with Whitefield's message that "he forgot to sneer." Bolingbroke admitted, "He has the most commanding eloquence I have ever heard in any person." Whitefield's close ties with Jonathan Edwards were typical, and his ability to steer a middle course between the moderates and the separatists in Scotland extended his sphere of influence.

Whitefield's relationship to **Selina, Countess of Huntingdon** (1707–1791), bears out the point. Converted as a girl of nine when she saw a corpse her own age, she married the wealthy Theophilus Huntingdon and heard the Wesleys, Whitefield, Romaine, and Fletcher in her private chapel. She was well read in Scripture and theology and helped Charles Wesley see the error of excessive Moravian quietism. Her two sons died of smallpox in 1744, and her husband died in 1746. She lent support and encouragement to her friends, as well as to Watts and Doddridge and John Newton. She knew and influenced Georg Handel. It was her conviction that "on the character of ministers the prosperity of the churches will at all times greatly depend."[17] She sold all her jewels to sponsor Trevecca College and her spiritual enterprises, and was drawn more and more to Whitefield's theological slant. He was one of her chaplains and she helped build his London headquarters, the Chapel at Tottenham Court Road.

Whitefield was a true Puritan in some ways, but was his own man. He loved Christmas and preached a great sermon on "The Observation of the birth of Christ, the Duty of All Christians; Or, the True Way of Keeping Christmas." The argument is so biblical, so practical, so winsome, even to the appeal not to overindulge during the holy season and thus to "forget the Lord of Glory."[18] John Greenleaf Whittier commemorates Whitefield in these lines:

Lo! by the Merrimac Whitefield stands
In the temple that was never made with hands—
Curtains of azure and crystal wall,
And dome of the sunshine over all!
A homeless pilgrim, with dubious name
Blown about on the wings of fame;

Now as an angel of blessing classed,
And now as a mad enthusiast.
Possessed by the one dread thought that lent
Its goad to his fiery temperament,
Up and down in the world he went,
A John the Baptist crying—Repent!

---

1. Ted A. Campbell, *The Religion of the Heart* (Columbia: University of South Carolina Press, 1991). A rich study.
2. Brian H. Edwards, *Revival: A People Saturated with God* (Durham, N.C.: Evangelical Press, 1990), 102.
3. Timothy L. Smith, *Whitefield and Wesley on the New Birth* (Grand Rapids: Francis Asbury/Zondervan, 1986), 39ff.
4. A. E. Garvie, *The Christian Preacher* (New York: Scribner's, 1923), 217.
5. Arnold A. Dallimore, *George Whitefield: The Life and Times of the Great Evangelist of the Eighteenth-Century Revival,* 2 vols. (Wheaton, Ill.: Crossway, 1970, 1979). Stout calls this a "filiopietist" biography.
6. Dallimore, *George Whitefield,* 2:239.
7. Ibid., 2:482.
8. Frank S. Mead, "The Story of George Whitefield," *The Sword of the Lord* (January 31, 1992): 3–4.
9. Harry S. Stout, *The Divine Dramatist: George Whitefield and the Rise of Modern Evangelicalism* (Grand Rapids: Eerdmans, 1991), 7.
10. Ibid., 47.
11. R. T. Kendall, *Stand Up and Be Counted* (Grand Rapids: Zondervan, 1984), 87ff.
12. Stout, *The Divine Dramatist,* 72.
13. It is curious that Stout does not once mention Whitefield's conversion. Does he not understand the criticality of conversion? His stress on the effeminacy of Whitefield (24) is bizarre, and he certainly overstresses "marketing." How much of this was part of a conscious strategy in Whitefield? (cf. Frank Lambert, *"Pedlar in Divinity": George Whitefield and the Transatlantic Revivals, 1737–1770* (Princeton, N.J.: Princeton University Press, 1994). He gives heavy fire to Whitefield's "genius for self-promotion" and his "shameless ego-centricity."
14. George Marsden's review of Stout in *Christianity Today* (April 27, 1992): 60 is choice, and the review by William L. Sachs in *The Christian Century* (January 29, 1992): 104–5 is also full of good questions.
15. Jay E. Adams, *Sermon Analysis* (Denver: Accent, 1986), 118ff.
16. Stout, *The Divine Dramatist,* 222.

17. William Edward Painter, *Life and Times of Selina, Countess of Huntingdon* (London: Shirley, 1844).
18. *Whitefield's Sermons,* vol. 1 (London: Banner and Truth, 1959).

8.3.5 JONATHAN EDWARDS—DEEP THINKER OF THE AWAKENING

> Sinners should be earnestly invited to come and accept the Saviour—with all of the winning, encouraging arguments that the Gospel affords.
>
> Yet if in these sermons he shall find the most important truths exhibited and pressed home on the conscience with that pungency which tends to awaken, convince, humble and edify; if he shall find that serious strain of piety which, in spite of himself, forces upon him a serious frame of mind; if in the perusal, he cannot but be ashamed and alarmed at himself, and in some measure feel the reality and weight of eternal things; if, at least he, like Agrippa, shall be almost persuaded to be a Christian; I presume he will not grudge the time required to peruse what is now offered him. These, if I mistake not, are the great ends to be aimed at in all sermons, whether preached or printed, and are ends which can never be accomplished by those modern fashionable discourses which are delivered under the name of sermons.
>
> —Jonathan Edwards

For generations the words "Puritan" and "Puritanism" were pejorative terms, and no one was more anathemic than **Jonathan Edwards.** Oliver Wendell Holmes described Edwards' basic convictions as "barbaric . . . not only false but absurd." Mark Twain spoke of Edwards as a "drunken lunatic . . . a resplendent genius gone mad. . . . I was ashamed to be in such company."[1] Edwards' sermon "Sinners in the Hands of an Angry God" was to many a symbol of religious reaction, and even James Houston, a sympathetic friend and editor, speaks of it as a *faux pas,* excusing it as only one out of twelve hundred extant sermons.[2]

Yet in recent years there has come a tremendous renascence of interest in the Puritans and Edwards, starting with Perry Miller's work at Harvard on *The Puritan Mind.* Miller overplayed the influence of John Locke and Sir Isaac Newton in the shaping of Edwards and really did not understand evangelical conversion and revival in any biblical sense, but he was a sparkplug in Puritan studies. Academic dissertations on Edwards have exponentially increased in recent times. Noll points out that the three-volume *Encyclopedia of the American Religious Experience* has more references to Edwards than to any other person. The magnificent Yale edition of Edwards' complete works stands as a monument to this resurgence of interest.[3]

Now it is generally recognized that Jonathan Edwards was the most powerful and effective preacher ever heard in America. Many concede Edwards to be America's prime theologian and one of her most distinguished philosophers. His influence on other molders of thought is mind-boggling: Thomas Chalmers of Scotland in the next century spent a year in rapture over Edwards' concept of the magnificence of the Godhead, and James Orr of Scotland praised Edwards' "exalted vision of God."[4] Noll speaks of Edwards as "besotted with God." Others of his admirers, like D. Martyn Lloyd-Jones, contend that "Puritanism reached its fullest bloom in the life and ministry of Jonathan Edwards."[5] What mattered most to Lloyd-Jones was that "[Edwards] preached sermons . . . he did not deliver lectures."[6] Richard Lovelace speaks of him as "the greatest mind produced in America" as well as the theologian of revival.[7] Even Roman Catholic theologians have boarded the bandwagon, conveniently ignoring the antipathy Edwards felt for Roman Catholic doctrine and practice.[8] But what does this towering figure in biblical preaching mean to us?

Jonathan Edwards—the Man

Jonathan Edwards (1703–1758) was born to the manse, the son of Timothy and Esther Edwards, who were serving the Congregational church in East Windsor, Connecticut. The only son of eleven children, he was early marked as precocious, learning Greek, Latin, and Hebrew from his father beginning at age five. He wrote a treatise on flying spiders at age eleven. At thirteen, he entered Yale and graduated four years later as valedictorian.

In reaction to his father's high Calvinism,[9] Edwards read Locke's "Essay Concerning the Human Understanding" when he was fourteen. He came to "sweet delight in God" at Yale in 1721 while reading 1 Timothy 1:17.[10] He was commanded by "vehement longings for God" and set himself to read the Scriptures "steadily, constantly and frequently." He made a series of resolutions for his new walk in Christ and had a great interest in millennial ideas and unfulfilled prophecy.

After taking his M.A. at Yale, Edwards briefly pastored a small Scottish Presbyterian church in New York City, on Wall Street near Broadway, and a congregation in Bolton, Connecticut. He then returned to serve as a tutor at Yale. In 1727 he was ordained, and in July of that year married Sarah Pierrepont. His marriage always greatly strengthened him, and he and Sarah were parents of twelve children.

Although John Locke's influence over Edwards has been overstated, Locke's emphasis on a knowledge based on sensation and experience rather than innate ideas was important for him. Puritan preaching was often unemotional, but Edwards' "heightened imagination" rekindled "a warmer, more emotional preaching," even with a rather dull delivery.[11]

Edwards served as an assistant pastor to his maternal grandfather, Solomon Stoddard, who at eighty-three was winding up a sixty-year pastorate at Northampton, Massachusetts. Edwards' preaching was especially appreciated when the longtime pastor died. A vigorous twenty-three-year ministry ensued during which successive waves of revival and awakening swept over the Northampton church. It was to become the eye of a spiritual storm that reached to the ends of the earth.

Jonathan Edwards—the Mind

New England was on the way from *The Scarlet Letter* to *Peyton Place*. Its trademark Puritanism was in serious decline. The Half-way Covenant (an issue surveyed in 7.4.2), supported by Solomon Stoddard but opposed by Edwards (an issue which would ultimately cost him dearly), was intended to prop up a shaky church. In fact, it poisoned the church with unbelief and carnality.

Edwards did not embrace everything Calvinistic.[12] He advocated experiential religion. The sermon was to be the agent of conversion, which in turn served as the doorway into the experience.

> An increase in speculative knowledge in divinity is not what is so much needed by our people as something else. Men may abound in this sort of light and have no heat. . . . Our people do not so much need to have their heads turned as to have their hearts touched; and they stand in the greatest need of that sort of preaching which has the greatest tendency to do this.[13]

Harold Simonson argued that in *Religious Affections: How a Man's Will Affects His Character Before God* the more dominant influences on Edwards "were Augustine, Calvin, and the Scriptures."[14] Simonson's contention is that "true religion is a fixed engagement of the heart."

Although the Northampton church had experienced five revivals during Stoddard's time, it seemed to Edwards that the people heard the gospel preached as if they had never heard it before. In the spring of 1735, Edwards preached a series of sermons on "Justification by Faith," and there came a moving of the Spirit, stirring up the believers and bringing the unconverted to Christ. "There scarcely was a single person in the town, young or old, left unconcerned about the great things of the eternal world."[15]

Case histories of these conversions are deeply moving. Edwards' descriptions in *The Narrative* had immense impact on both sides of the Atlantic. Edwards, Whitefield, and the Tennents reported great "effusions" of the Spirit as the revivals spread. When Edwards preached "Sinners in the Hands of an Angry God" in Enfield on July 8, 1741, the people cried out so loudly that the sermon could scarcely be heard. In terrible agony, some chewed on carpet. Others tried to cling to the pillars of the church lest they slip into hell. Blacks and Indians alike were touched by the revivals. All told, there were four hundred converts.[16]

Jonathan Edwards—the Message

Picture the six-foot one-inch, emaciated figure standing in the pulpit, sermon notes held close to his eye because of his shortsightedness. In his other hand, he held a candle. His voice was weak and monotone. It could only be the Holy Spirit who energized such preaching.

Edwards used the typically Puritan plain style, simple and direct. He referred often to Scripture. In one set of fifteen sermons, he used 374 biblical quotations, an average of twenty-five per sermon.[17] Eighty-two percent of his words were fewer than five letters. He used *you* with great effect and artfully employed illustration and anecdote. Turnbull has helpfully categorized Edwards' sermons for us.[18] We appreciate the evangelist's adroit versatility as we consider his series of thirty sermons on Isaiah 51:7, "A History of the Work of Redemption." Listen as he preaches on God's wrath and judgment:

> The bow of God's wrath is bent, and the arrow made ready on the string, and justice bends the arrow at your heart, and strains the bow; and it is nothing but the mere pleasure of God—and that of an angry God, without any promise or obligation at all—that keeps the arrow one moment from being made drunk with your blood. Thus all of you that never passed under a great change of heart by the mighty power of the Spirit of God upon your souls; all of you that were never born again, and made new creatures, and raised from dead in sin to a state of new and before unexperienced light and life, are in the hands of an angry God. However you may have had religious affections, and may keep up a form of religion in your families and closets and in the house of God, it is nothing but his mere pleasure that keeps you from being this moment swallowed up in everlasting destruction.

But the revival began to wane, and the years 1743 to 1748 were years of conflict for Edwards. In 1750 he was overwhelmingly voted out of his church. His farewell sermon is a model of Christian love and charity, and he was willing to stay on for six additional months because the church had no supply. He then went to Stockbridge as a missionary to the Indians for seven years. While he was there he wrote several of his most piercing works. His scholarship was widely respected, and he was called to succeed his deceased son-in-law, Aaron Burr (father of the infamous statesman), as president of the College of New Jersey (later Princeton University). Soon after arriving in New Jersey he was inoculated for smallpox and died, being less than six months in his position. His last words to his loved ones were, "Trust in God and ye need not fear." What a preacher of grace indeed. The message may seem heavy to us and not always balanced, but we need to be reminded of his demeanor as he preached the message:

> A preacher of a low and moderate voice, a natural way of delivery; and without any agitation of body, or anything else in the manner to excite attention; except his habitual and great solemnity, looking and speaking as in the presence of God.[19]

The lingering lessons from the vital pulpit ministry and life of Jonathan Edwards are many. As one contemporary writer explained it: "While others preached self-reliance and sang the song of the self, Edwards drew nearer the truth—that nothing can be saved without confronting its own damnation, that the way to gain one's life is to lose it."

----

1. Mark Noll, "God at the Center: Jonathan Edwards on True Virtue," in *The Christian Century* (September 8–15, 1993): 856. Some scholars try to argue that the Great Awakening was the result of the last gasp of the "traditional, premodern, anti-capitalistic

values" of rural New England; see James German, "The Social Utility of Wicked Self-Love: Calvinism, Capitalism, and Public Policy in Revolutionary New England," *Journal of American History* (December 1995): 965ff.

2. James Houston, ed., *Religious Affections* (Portland, Oreg.: Multnomah, 1984), xv.

3. Noll, "God at the Center," 857.

4. Ibid., 858.

5. D. Martyn Lloyd-Jones, *The Puritans: Their Origins and Successors* (Edinburgh: Banner of Truth, 1987), 351.

6. Ibid., 359.

7. Richard F. Lovelace, "The Surprising Works of God," *Christianity Today* (September 11, 1995): 29ff.

8. Anri Morimoto, *Jonathan Edwards and the Catholic Vision of Salvation* (University Park: Penn State University Press, 1995). While helpfully pointing out that while Edwards was a theologian of the heart but not a "theologian of subjectivity," Morimoto fails to grasp the importance of forensic justification, which is both real and legal. This is a major sticking point between Roman Catholics with their "double justification" and historic Protestants. Morimoto gives in to "salvation for non-Christians," which is universes away from Edwards.

9. Ralph Turnbull, *Jonathan Edwards the Preacher* (Grand Rapids: Baker, 1958), 16.

10. Iain H. Murray, *Jonathan Edwards: A New Biography* (Edinburgh: Banner of Truth, 1987), 34ff. The best yet.

11. Turnbull, *Jonathan Edwards the Preacher*. Murray (ibid.) shows that Edwards ceased preparation of and use of a manuscript in preaching after 1741 (189).

12. John H. Gerstner, *Steps to Salvation: The Evangelistic Message of Jonathan Edwards* (Philadelphia: Westminster, 1960). Even Gerstner must concede that for Edwards people can seek after God, and he is "most optimistic about the outcome of genuine seeking," 96.

13. Houston, *Religious Affections,* xvi. In the Classics of Faith and Devotion series. A "must" to understand Edwards.

14. Harold Simonson, *Jonathan Edwards: Theologian of the Heart* (Grand Rapids: Eerdmans, 1974).

15. James A. Stewart, ed., *Jonathan Edwards—The Narrative* (Grand Rapids: Kregel, 1957), 25.

16. Professor Alan F. Segal, a Jewish scholar, has argued that Paul's conversion is the New Testament paradigm for revolutionary change. See his *Paul the Convert* (New Haven, Conn.: Yale University Press, 1990).

17. Jay E. Adams, *Sermon Analysis* (Denver: Accent, 1986), 107.

18. Turnbull, *Jonathan Edwards the Preacher,* 168ff.

19. Thomas Prince in John Piper, *The Supremacy of God in Preaching* (Grand Rapids: Baker, 1990), 102. Piper's lectures on the God-centered preaching of Edwards are luminous and exciting.

8.3.6   GILBERT TENNENT—THE DEVELOPER OF THE AWAKENING

In arguing for preaching terrors first and comforts second, Tennent pictures a neighbor who was sleeping securely and dreaming pleasantly while his house was afire.

You would not surely go to whisper in [your neighbor's] ear some soft round-about discourse, that his house was you feared not in the best condition possible; it might perhaps take damage if suitable care were not taken to prevent it. I say would I go thus about the bush with a poor man in a time of such danger? No, I believe not: I fancy you would take a rough method, without ceremony or grimace.

—Gilbert Tennent

Spiritual tides were at low ebb in the eighteenth century in the mid-Atlantic states as well as New England. Jonathan Dickenson concluded that in New Jersey "religion was in a decline, with most church members moribund and the body of the people careless and carnal."[1] Vital Christianity seemed to be in the death throes in Pennsylvania as well.

In the year 1720 a Dutch Reformed minister, **Theodore Freylinghuysen** (1691–1748), born in Germany near the Dutch border, began a revival ministry in the Raritan Valley of New Jersey. He preached with evangelical fervor and insisted on conversion and a changed life. The strategy of "the new lights" (or those in favor of revivals) was always more aggressive and confrontational than some of the old diehards could handle. In general the newer rhetoric of the Awakening sermons of this century involved moving away from reading manuscripts to a "more fragmentary mode of sermonic discourse."[2]

On occasion Freylinghuysen exchanged pulpits with members of the Tennent family, who served Presbyterian churches in New Jersey. **William Tennent Sr.** (1673–1746) was born in Northern Ireland, graduated from the University of Edinburgh, and was ordained in the Church of Ireland (Episcopal). In 1718 he came to the United States and was accepted by the Presbyterian synod, serving in Neshaminy, Pennsylvania, until his death. In 1726 he established a training school for ministers in his manse, called the Log College, where he trained his four sons and many others for the ministry.

Again we see the influence of Continental Pietism on the revivalists in this region. It was their aim "to rejuvenate sincere practical piety among the colonial laity."[3] William Tennent's message was directed against rebels who "resisted the Divine Sovereign by corrupting the Scriptures, by forsaking God's Word, or by refusing to 'improve' themselves after experiencing providential afflictions . . . still others revolted by relishing every sort of iniquity or by simply offering empty ecclesiastical performances."[4]

One of his sons, **Gilbert Tennent** (1703–1764), was born in Ireland, trained at the Log College, and received an honorary M.A. from Yale. After teaching at the Log College for a year, he took a Presbyterian charge in New Brunswick, New Jersey. Here in 1739 he welcomed Whitefield, and they became fast friends and travel companions. His brothers **John Tennent** and **William Tennent Jr.** had an unusual ministry at Freehold, New Jersey, where many were "taken in the gospel net." After strong biblical preaching, "the terror of God fell generally upon the inhabitants of this place; so that wickedness, as ashamed in a great measure, hid itself."[5] Gilbert's ministry was even more extensive. In one series in Boston, more than six hundred were converted. In 1743 he took the pastorate of the Second Presbyterian Church in Philadelphia, where he served until his death.

Between 1753 and 1755, he ministered in England and Scotland with Samuel Davies in the interest of raising funds for the College of New Jersey; he did raise a subscription from Lady Huntingdon, George Whitefield, and others. Davies, "an astonishing preacher" himself, has given us one of the most realistic descriptions of Whitefield's ministry in Moorfields.[6] Davies had the opportunity to preach before young George III and his queen, who expressed themselves as being enchanted but were rude and audible in their interruptions of the service. Samuel Davis fixed his eyes on the royal pair and boldly intoned the text: "When the lion roars, the beasts of the field tremble; when Jehovah speaks, let the Kings of the earth keep silence before him."

The die was cast in Gilbert Tennent's ministry as early as 1740, when he preached his famous sermon on "The Danger of an Unconverted Ministry" from Mark 6:34. Whitefield paid tribute to Tennent's preaching:

> I never before heard such a searching sermon. He [Gilbert Tennent] convinced me more and more that we can preach the Gospel of Christ no further than we have experienced the power of it in our own hearts. Being deeply convicted of sin, by God's Holy Spirit, at this first conversion, he has learned experimentally to dissect the heart of a natural man. Hypocrites must either soon be converted or enraged at this preaching. He is a son of thunder, and does not fear the faces of men.[7]

Tennent had also visited with Zinzendorf during the latter's one visit to America in the winter of 1741 to 1742. Tennent was troubled by Zinzendorf's perfectionistic tendencies and his tilt toward universal redemption, but he was especially concerned over Zinzendorf's depreciation of the role of the law and conviction for sin. Tennent also questioned Whitefield's participation with the Moravians.[8] He and Whitefield broke on this issue. Again we see that revivals tend to falter because of their own excesses. After lightning hit his house, threw him down, and scorched his feet, Tennent's adversaries saw God's hand of warning against their inveterate foe. He preached a memorable sermon in reply titled "All Things Come Alike to All."[9] The tensions with Whitefield exacerbated. At this time he led in the building of a new church (Arch Street Presbyterian Church). He continued to aid in the development of the College of New Jersey where he preached a notable revival. He died in 1764 and was buried in the center aisle of the church he had so long and ably served. he preached fire and judgment, but he could apply the "gospel balsam" with great skill and positive effect.

---

1. A. Skevington Wood, *The Inextinguishable Blaze: Spiritual Renewal and Advance in the Eighteenth Century* (Grand Rapids: Eerdmans, 1960), 54.

2. Donald Weber, *Rhetoric and History in Revolutionary New England* (Oxford: Oxford University Press, 1988), 150. Further relevant reading can be found in Leonard I. Sweet, ed., *Communication and Change in American Religious History* (Grand

Rapids: Eerdmans, 1993); Paul K. Conkin, *The Uneasy Center: Reformed Christianity in Ante-Bellum America* (Chapel Hill: University of North Carolina Press, 1995); Max Stackhouse, *Creeds, Society and Human Rights* (Grand Rapids: Eerdmans, 1984). Particularly suggestive on "Free Church Calvinists" or the Puritans (55–57).

3. Milton J. Coalter Jr., *Gilbert Tennent, Son of Thunder: A Case Study of Continental Pietism's Impact on the First Great Awakening in the Middle Colonies* (New York: Greenwood, 1986), xviii.

4. Ibid., 7.

5. Wood, *The Inextinguishable Blaze,* 58–59.

6. D. Martyn Lloyd-Jones, *The Puritans: Their Origins and Successors* (Edinburgh: Banner of Truth, 1987), 123ff.

7. Coalter, *Gilbert Tennent,* frontispiece.

8. Coalter, *Gilbert Tennent,* 108ff.

9. Ibid., 126.

8.3.7 WILLIAM McCULLOCH—THE DEFINER OF THE AWAKENING

The yearning for salvation and the sense of God's nearness break forth
at certain epochs simultaneously with over-mastering power and with
effects that are felt centuries and millennia later.
—Archbishop Nathan Soderblom of Sweden
in the Gifford Lectures of 1931

For the Scots, the Bible had been front and center from the days of the Scottish Reformation and John Knox. But the emerging spirit of great toleration gave rise to "lapse and languor." The Marrow-men and the seceders struck a blow for true faith, but a significant defining experience for biblical faith and preaching came in the controversial "Cambuslang Work" of 1742.[1]

Cambuslang was a village of six hundred near Glasgow. **William McCulloch** (1691–1771), the son of a schoolmaster in Whithorn, studied at Edinburgh and Glasgow universities and was ordained in 1731, when he assumed pastoral ministry in Cambuslang. Not noted for his preaching endowments, it was joked that McCulloch sent the men of the community to the alehouses when he preached. Yet he was learned in several languages and an authority in mathematics and astronomy.[2]

While his first years were uneventful, McCulloch sought to establish prayer societies in which intercession for awakening took place. "He spent much time in secret prayer, waiting with humble patience for a favourable return. He greatly encouraged private Christians to meet for social prayer, and particularly that God would revive His work everywhere."[3] Whitefield's first visit to Scotland had highlighted a style of preaching "that commanded and compelled attention."[4] McCulloch picked up the torch and soon began to preach law and grace with a rich sense of doctrinal construct. People began to crowd out the church.

All of this was in a context of deep internal problems for the parishioners—a terrible storm and a period of famine. Many were critical of the new style of preaching, but fifteen people found salvation.[5]

The people wanted more Bible lectures and more prayer meetings. Soon two hundred converts were listed. Sermons were preached every day, at 2, 6, and 9 P.M. with widespread symptoms of "uncontrolled distress." There were the phenomena of revival, including convulsions, prophecies, and tongues. Seekers were carried into the manse like wounded soldiers.[6] McCulloch sent for Whitefield, who made fourteen trips to Scotland in all.

Whitefield soon left the Tabernacle in the charge of his associate, John Cennick, and went straight to Glasgow, where he addressed twenty-thousand people. He then went to Cambuslang. On July 9, 1742, he preached to thirty-thousand. The sacrament was celebrated in the fields until 2 A.M. Old John Bonar, ancestor of the Bonar brothers, was one of those fired up for Christ. Communion tables were set up in the preaching tents. After one of these powerful communion services, Whitefield preached his famous sermon on "being married to Christ."[7]

News of the revival began to spread. Its effects were soon felt in Kilsyth under the ministry of Pastor **James Robe** (1688–1753), who endured a wicked and licentious community. Robe also began preaching on the doctrine of regeneration, and many were awakened and converted. Public worship sometimes began at 8:30 A.M. and continued for up to twelve hours.

The Erskines were critical of both McCulloch and Robe for remaining in the national church. In fact, the revivals arrested the drift toward secession. The Erskines spoke of Whitefield himself as "a limb of the anti-Christ" and said that he "trimmed and temporized" the message. Nonetheless "the fruits of it remain."[8] In 1751 McCulloch could still count four hundred in his parish who had been converted in the revival. The revival had a great influence on Thomas Chalmers and others who led "the great disruption" in 1843, upon English Anglicans, and on the work of foreign missions.

McCulloch corresponded extensively with Jonathan Edwards. Here we appreciate the networking of God's quickening Spirit through so many different cultures and personalities.

Yet another heroic champion of biblical preaching at this time was **John Erskine** (1721–1803), the long-time pastor of Grayfriars Church. Not related to the seceder Erskine brothers, he led evangelicals in the Church of Scotland and was a great friend of Whitefield's. Erskine wrote often to Jonathan Edwards, and like McCulloch was an ardent proponent of missionary outreach. The parents of Sir Walter Scott were members of his congregation. While Scott leaned toward the moderates, he gave a sympathetic portrayal of Erskine in chapter 37 of his novel *Guy Mannering*.

1. Arthur Fawcett, *The Cambuslang Revival* (Edinburgh: Banner of Truth, 1771). This very searching account needs to be set over against the contemporary drift in the Church of Scotland, which has fewer than eight hundred thousand members and loses some twenty thousand every year. Ian Bradley in *Marching to the Promised Land: Has the Church a Future?* points out that at this rate of decline the Church of Scotland will cease to exist in 2047.

2. F. R. Webber, *A History of Preaching in Britain and America* (Milwaukee: Northwestern, 1955), 2:220.

3. A. Skevington Wood, *The Inextinguishable Blaze: Spiritual Renewal and Advance in the Eighteenth Century* (Grand Rapids: Eerdmans, 1960), 120.

4. Ibid., 119.

5. Fawcett, *The Cambuslang Revival*, 100, 106ff.

6. Ibid., 114.

7. Harry S. Stout, *The Divine Dramatist* (Grand Rapids: Eerdmans, 1991), 149.

8. Fawcett, *The Cambuslang Revival*, 166ff.

8.4 SENT WITH THE GOSPEL

> He who goes out weeping, carrying seed to sow, will return with songs of joy, carrying sheaves with him.
>
> —Psalm 126:6

> The seed is the word of God.
>
> —Luke 8:11b

> As the rain and the snow come down from heaven, and do not return to it without watering the earth and making it bud and flourish, so that it yields seed for the sower and bread for the eater, so is my word that goes out from my mouth: It will not return to me empty, but will accomplish what I desire and achieve the purpose for which I sent it.
>
> —Isaiah 55:10–11

Where were Protestant missions during this time? The surging missionary passion of the early church and the throbbing courage of gospel emissaries during the Middle Ages do not find replication in the Reformers or the Puritans. Yet incubated in the bosom of Continental Pietism and ignited by the Great Awakening, missions were poised on the brink of a glorious explosion.

A return to the Lord always requires a new seriousness about what is on God's heart and what obedience to God entails. The Great Commission (in its five forms) mandates making disciples, preaching the gospel to every creature, preaching repentance and forgiveness of sins in Christ's name to all nations, being sent as Christ was sent, and being Spirit-empowered as witnesses in Jerusalem, Judea, Samaria, and to the ends of the earth. Preaching is an integral part of the Lord's plan for the expansion of the church. It is now our joy to pursue the action which came out of the mighty spiritual revival we call the Great Awakening.

8.4.1 BARTHOLOMEW ZIEGENBALG—GOING AFAR

> We missionaries on our own part are endeavoring, according to the Measure of Grace God Almighty has imparted to us, plentifully to spread abroad the Seed of the Word of God among the Heathen in their own

language, there being no other means for touching the hearts of the heathen in order to their conversion.

—Bartholomew Ziegenbalg

I am sending you to them to open their eyes and turn them from darkness to light, and from the power of Satan to God, so that they may receive forgiveness of sins and a place among those who are sanctified by faith in me.

—Acts 26:17b–18

We have seen that early Protestants had little sense of the world task of the church. Luther himself taught that the Great Commission was for the apostles alone. The Puritans with few exceptions did not evince any strong missionary impulse.

With Dutch independence and the advance of the Dutch East India Company, a training school for missionaries was set up in Leyden under the aegis of **Hugo Grotius,** whose *De Veritate Religionis Christianae (The Truth of Christianity)* spurred missionary enterprise. **George Candidius** went to Formosa to evangelize, as did others to Ceylon and India.

A new impetus to the world task arose out of Pietism and the Moravians from Herrnhut. Herrnhut, through Zinzendorf's efforts, became what Latourette calls "the center of a missionary enterprise which extended over much of the world."[1] Here was "an emphasis upon the conversion of individual non-Christians and a distrust of mass movements of whole communities."[2] Pivotal was the Danish outreach through the Halle Pietists and A. H. Francke with encouragement from the newly formed Society for the Propagation of Christian Knowledge (SPCK, founded in 1698).

King Frederick IV of Denmark was moved by the missionary passion of his court preacher, a German named **Franz Julius Lutkens,** and desired to send out missionaries. Francke was asked to recommend candidates since none could be found in Denmark. He nominated two godly students from Halle, **Bartholomew Ziegenbalg** (1683–1719) and **Henry Plutschau** (1677–1747). The two were ordained in Denmark and posted to the Danish colony at Tranquebar southwest of Madras in 1706.

In the face of stiff opposition, Ziegenbalg learned the Tamil language and with the help of a new recruit from Halle, **Johan Grundler** (Plutschau's failing health necessitated his return home), built a chapel, preached the Word, baptized converts, and translated the Scriptures into Tamil.[3] Assistance for the project came from the SPCK under the auspices of **Anton Wilhelm Boehm,** the German chaplain to Prince George, Danish consort to Queen Anne. Letters from India and Ziegenbalg came to Boehm in London onboard vessels of the East India Company. These were read in sessions of the SPCK in London and forwarded to royalty in Copenhagen. Francke and Cotton Mather shared much about this work, impressing us with the providential interconnectedness of gospel witness.[4]

Ziegenbalg died at thirty-six and endured unspeakable misunderstanding. Yet in his brief life, he oversaw a printer's ministry in the publication of Scriptures, catechisms, hymnals, and other works.[5] He left 350 native converts and many catechumens. He departed from this life singing "Jesus My Redeemer Lives."

The challenge of preaching cross-culturally is one we all face, but learning to preach in a second or third language poses unusual difficulty. The company of those who have surmounted the obstacles is great and noble.[6] We salute these spiritual pioneers and groundbreakers!

---

1. Kenneth Scott Latourette, *Three Centuries of Advance* (Grand Rapids: Eerdmans, 1939, 1967), 3:47.
2. Ibid., 51.
3. V. Raymond Edman, *The Light in Dark Ages* (Wheaton, Ill.: Van Kampen, 1949), 353.
4. Ernst Benz, "Pietist and Puritan Sources of Early Protestant Missions," *Church History* (June 20, 1951): 28–55.
5. T. J. Bach, *Vision and Valor* (Grand Rapids: Baker, 1963), 31.
6. Admirably and ably treated in David J. Hesselgrave, *Communicating Christ Cross-Culturally: An Introduction to Missionary Communication,* 2d ed. (Grand Rapids: Zondervan, 1991). A wealth of data for all communicators.

8.4.2 DAVID BRAINERD—GETTING DOWN

> I prayed privately with a dear Christian friend or two; and I think I scarce ever launched so far out on the broad ocean that my soul with joy triumphed over all the evils on the shores of immortality. I think that time and all its gay amusements and cruel disappointments never appeared so inconsiderable to me before.
>
> —David Brainerd

Another brilliant star flamed across the mission horizon. **David Brainerd** (1718–1747) enjoyed only four years of ministry, yet he bequeathed a magnificent legacy to Native Americans and to missions.

Brainerd was born on a farm in Haddam, Connecticut. His father died when he was nine, and his mother died five years later. He stayed with his pastor for a time and was converted in 1738. Beginning at Yale the next year, he heard Ebenezer Pemberton preach on missions and the love of Christ. Brainerd resolved "to be wholly the Lord's, to be forever dedicated to his service."[1]

As a New Light and in favor of the revivals that visited Yale, Brainerd commented about a tutor that "he had no more grace than a chair." Expulsion followed, but he sought further study in theology, was licensed by the Congregationalists, and was sent by the Scottish Society for the Propagation of the Gospel to work with the Indians in Stockbridge. Here he preached to the Indians with great passion. Turning down a large and wealthy church on Long Island, he went on to minister to the Delaware Indians north of Philadelphia. He soon burned himself out for the Lord.[2]

Brainerd did live to see revival come to the Indians. Forty-three adults and forty-two children were converted. When his health broke down in 1746, he went to the Jonathan Edwards' home, where Edwards' daughter Jerusha, his fiancée, cared for him until his death at the age of twenty-nine. David's brother John took over his work. Jonathan Edwards wrote a famous account of his ministry. He preached with great power and said of his preaching,

> I have frequently been enabled to represent the divine glory, the infinite preciousness of the great Redeemer, the suitableness of His Person and purchase to supply the wants and answer the utmost desires of immortal souls; to open the infinite riches of His grace and the wonderful encouragement proposed in the Gospel to unworthy, helpless sinners; to call, invite and beseech them to come and give themselves to Him and be reconciled to God through Him; to expostulate with them respecting their neglect of One so infinitely love and freely offered; and this in such a manner, with such freedom, pertinency, pathos, and application to the conscience as I am sure I never could have made myself master of by the most assiduous application of mind.[3]

Brainerd was consumed with missions. Listen as he pours out his heart in prayer: "All things here below vanished and there appeared to be nothing of any importance to me but holiness of heart and conversion of the heathen to God."

The legacy of this incendiary can be traced to the impact his life made on Henry Martyn, William Carey, Adoniram Judson, Robert Murray McCheyne, Thomas Coke, Samuel Marsden, and many others.

Jonathan Edwards preached Brainerd's funeral sermon:

> How much is there, in particular, in the things that have been observed of this eminent minister of Christ, to excite us, who are called to the same great work of the gospel-ministry, to earnest care and endeavors, that we may be in like manner faithful in our work, that we may be filled with the same spirit, animated with the like pure and fervent flame of love to God, and the like earnest concern to advance the kingdom and glory of our Lord and Master, and the prosperity of Zion! Oh that the things that were seen and heard in this extraordinary person, his holiness, heavenliness, labour and self-denial in his life, his so remarkably devoting himself and his all, in heart and practice to the glory of God, and the wonderful frame of mind manifested in so stedfast a manner, under the expectation of death, and the pains and agonies that brought it on, may excite in us all, both ministers and people, a due sense of the greatness of the work we have to do in the world, the excellency and amiableness of thorough religion in experience and practice, and the blessedness of the end of such a life, and the infinite value of their eternal reward, when absent from the body and present with the Lord; and effectually stir us up to endeavors that, in the way of such a holy life, we may at last come to so blessed an end.[4]

---

1. Earle E. Cairns, *An Endless Line of Splendor* (Wheaton, Ill.: Tyndale, 1986), 245.

2. T. J. Bach, *Vision and Valor* (Grand Rapids: Baker, 1963), 34ff. See Philip E. Howard

Jr., ed., *Jonathan Edwards, The Life and Diary of David Brainerd* (Chicago: Moody, 1949).

3. F. R. Webber, *A History of Preaching in Britain and America* (Milwaukee: Northwestern, 1952), 3:109f.

4. D. Martyn Lloyd-Jones, *The Puritans: Their Origins and Successors* (Edinburgh: Banner of Truth, 1987), 370–71.

8.4.3 WILLIAM CAREY—GLOBALIZING MISSION

Neglecting my business! My business, sir, is to extend the kingdom of Christ. I only make and mend shoes to help pay expenses.

I would rather win to Christ the poorest scavengers in Leicester than draw off to Harvey Lane the richest members of your flock.

Having so little acquaintance with ministers, I was obliged to draw all from the Bible.

Preach the never-failing word of the cross. Do not be above sitting down to the patient instruction even of one solitary native.

—William Carey

William Carey (1761–1834) was the father of modern missions. Spending more than forty years in pioneer work in India, Carey inaugurated a whole new era.

He was heir to an evangelical ecumenism. Hailing from a schoolmaster/weaver's home in Northampton, he was "born on the tidal wave of the Wesleys and Whitefield."[1] He became a Baptist but sought the blessing of the Anglican John Newton before he sailed for Bengal.

From early on he had a hunger for spiritual reality.[2] But he had also read about Captain Cook's voyages in the South Pacific and always felt the "lure of the South Seas."[3] He cobbled and studied Greek with a map of the world before him. Carey's studies were ultimately included in his significant work, *An Enquiry into the Obligations of Christians, to Use Means for the Conversion of the Heathens.*

Carey married Dorothy Plackett and served village chapels, where he preached with much verve. He avidly read about Moravian missions in "the Pietist advance," but Eliot and Brainerd ignited the torch for missions within him. Edwards' works he could hardly lay down. John Erskine's concerts of prayer in Scotland touched him.

The ultra-Calvinist John Ryland Sr. rebuked him with the words, "Young man, sit down. When God pleases to convert the heathen, He will do it without your aid or mine."[4] But Carey chose to follow Andrew Fuller and Robert Hall. Fuller believed in the offer of grace to all through his study of the Scriptures, the examples of Eliot and Brainerd, and a study of Edwards. Hall's sermon, "Help to Zion's Travellers," made a deep impression on Carey. Hall argued, "The way to Jesus is graciously open for everyone who chooses to come to him."[5]

Carey's sermon to the Association at Nottingham on May 31, 1792, is one of the great sermons of history. Taking as his text Isaiah 54:2–3, Carey poured eight years of vision and passion into the message. Carey pressed God's appeal: "Get up, find larger canvas, stouter and taller poles, stronger tent-pegs. Catch wider visions. Dare bolder programs. Dwell in an ampler world." His application: "Expect great things from God. Attempt great things for God."[6] Out of this gathering came the commission and the call to India. Soon Carey and John Thomas were off, never intending to return.[7]

The platform for Carey's ministry was clear: "I have God and His Word is true!"[8] He supported his family by raising indigo, and he quickly mastered languages that made possible the translation of the Bible into six tongues, parts of the Bible into twenty-nine more, and the development of seven grammars and three dictionaries. Yet he testified, "Preaching the gospel is the very element of my soul."[9]

Carey preached half-hour sermons in two hundred villages, traveling about twenty miles a day during one stretch. He struggled with the Home Board for years, especially after Fuller's death. He also taught languages at Fort William College and combated infanticide and suttee (the practice of burning the widow of a deceased man on his funeral pyre).

The three thrusts of his ministry were to preach the gospel, translate the Bible, and establish schools.[10] Amid much personal anguish and suffering, Carey was steady and unflinching in his determination to see the vision through.

----

1. S. Pearce Carey, *William Carey, Fellow of Linnaean Society* (London: Hodder and Stoughton, 1923), 9. This standard biography is written by his great-grandson.
2. Ibid., 10.
3. Timothy George, *Faithful Witness: The Life and Mission of William Carey* (Birmingham, Ala.: New Hope, 1991), 20.
4. Ibid., 53.
5. Ibid., 57.
6. Carey, *William Carey,* 83.
7. Ibid., 139.
8. Ibid., 154.
9. Ibid., 165.
10. George, *Faithful Witness,* 173.

8.4.4   HENRY MARTYN—GIVING ALL

> I prayed both before and after, that the Word might be for the conversion of souls, and that I might feel indifferent, except on this score.
>
> O what a snare the public ministrations are to me.
>
> —Henry Martyn

Out of the ferment and fire of the Great Awakening came the modern missionary enterprise. One of its great champions was the physically frail but spiritually hardy missionary to India and Persia, **Henry Martyn** (1781–1812).

Born in rugged Cornwall at Truro in the home of a former tin miner, Martyn was able to attend "the Eton of Cornwall" and went to St. John's College, Cambridge. There he took his B.A. and M.A. with highest honors, coming out as senior wrangler and first prizeman and earning a fellowship. While at Cambridge he came under the ministry of **Charles Simeon** and went on to be his curate. Simeon's parish, Holy Trinity Church, Cambridge, became a springboard for overseas missions.

Martyn helped found the Church Missionary Society, to whom he gave the challenge, "What can we do? When shall we do it? How shall we do it?" Martyn took his own challenge seriously, obtaining a position as chaplain for the East India Company. Ordained in 1803 in Ely, he left behind his lovely Lydia Grenfell, who stayed home when her mother refused to give her consent.[1] Martyn sailed for India in 1805.

First stationed at Dinapur, he gave himself to preaching to the English and mastering Hindustani. Webber observes, "His sermons attracted great attention and it was not uncommon for him to have eight hundred English people in his congregation."[2] Soon he was preaching to the nationals in their language.

Martyn became a close friend of William Carey. Upon his transfer to Cawnpur, he extended his ministry and translated the New Testament and *The Book of Common Prayer* into Hindi. One man who came to Christ under his preaching was to be the first Indian clergyman of the Church of England in India. Martyn soon translated the Scripture into Arabic and Persian, resolving to present a copy to the ruler of Persia.

In his diary, Martyn had exclaimed, "Now let me burn out for God." He undertook a journey by horseback to Persia and—he hoped—on to Constantinople. But his health was ravaged and his strength left him. He sent a message home urging, "Tell them to live more with Christ; to preach Christ; to catch His spirit, for the spirit of Christ is the spirit of missions. The nearer we get to Him, the more intensely missionary do we become." At the age of thirty-one, Henry Martyn died at Tokat in Persia.

---

1. George Smith, *Henry Martyn* (London: Religious Tract Society, 1892).
2. F. R. Webber, *A History of Preaching in Britain and America* (Milwaukee: Northwestern, 1952), 1:724–25.

8.4.5 ALEXANDER DUFF–GLORIFYING GOD

We must pay more careful attention, therefore, to what we have heard, so that we do not drift away.

—Hebrews 2:1

For we also have had the gospel preached to us, just as they did; but the message they heard was of no value to them, because those who heard did not combine it with faith.

—Hebrews 4:2

Humbly accept the word planted in you, which can save you.

—James 1:21b

Even in a time of doctrinal muddle and tension in the Scottish church, he was recognized not only as Scotland's first missionary but also as one of her greatest statesmen. **Alexander Duff** (1806–1878) was "one of the most convincing pulpit orators" of his age, a child of the revivals in "the finest flowering of missionary zeal in Scottish history." **Robert Murray McCheyne** said of him, "He kindles as he goes."

Duff was born in Moulin in the highlands of Perthshire. His father James, a farmer, was converted under the preaching of **Charles Simeon**. After nearly drowning in a swollen stream, Alexander came to trust in Christ's atoning blood and went on to St. Andrews to study in 1821. Here he came under the spell of **Thomas Chalmers** (cf. 9.1.3), whose lectures on moral philosophy were so enthralling that many students were too transfixed to take notes. Duff imbibed the story of Henry Martyn and consequently helped lead in the formation of a Missionary Society at St. Andrews.

As late as 1796, the Church of Scotland had turned down a proposal for a general collection for missions, but Chalmers and his student cohorts ignited a movement that led to an opening in India. The polarizing issue was the evangelical contention that "the preaching of morality without doctrine was insufficient."[1]

Chalmers' lectures instilled a deep conviction of God's love for those afar off. Chalmers conducted what amounted to an evangelistic laboratory for his students in which he led them in home visitation. "This is what I call preaching the gospel to every creature," he maintained.[2]

Duff and his fellows learned to give Bible expositions. In action, "six feet tall, ruddy of countenance, with a decided Scottish brogue," Duff preached the Word with great enthusiasm and excitement, his earnestness described as "apoplectic."[3] One of his most memorable addresses was as a young man of twenty-eight speaking to the General Assembly of the Church of Scotland—for three hours.

The death of a college friend, Urquhart, melted Duff. He surrendered to go to India. Ordained in 1829 at St. George's in Edinburgh, he sailed for Calcutta almost immediately. Latourette pays high tribute to the diverse missionary enterprises initiated by Duff.[4] The college he founded became the largest in India. Duff's mission strategy to win Hindu intellectuals was highly successful, and many high-caste Hindus came to Christ.

In 1843, the religious rift known as the disruption took place. It involved several issues, including patronage, but at its heart was the outgrowth of two entirely different theological tracks. The disruption forced the hand of Duff and the other missionaries, and they followed Chalmers to establish another college. By 1862, it boasted 1,723 students.

Duff's able preaching made his furloughs great times of rallying missionary motivation in the homeland. His best known sermon, "Missions the Chief End of the Christian Church," was widely heard and distributed. He addressed Parliament, and his visit to the U.S. in 1854 made an impact unlike any since

Whitefield's visits. When ill health required him to leave India permanently, Duff returned home to head up the missionary work of the Free Church and to become the first professor of missions at New College. Duff stands tall in the company of preachers.

---

1. Stuart Piggin and John Roxborough, *The St. Andrews Seven* (Edinburgh: Banner of Truth, 1985).
2. Ibid., 79.
3. F. R. Webber, *A History of Preaching in Britain and America* (Milwaukee: Northwestern, 1955), 2:364.
4. Kenneth Scott Latourette, *A History of the Expansion of Christianity: The Great Century, North Africa and Asia* (Grand Rapids: Zondervan, 1944, 1970), 6:116.

8.4.6 *ROBERT MORRISON—GLOWING IN THE GLOOM*

What peculiar fitness for the pulpit, qualifying me to commend myself to every man's conscience in the sight of God? With what stock of self-experienced texts and principles of inspiration am I entering this tremendous office? Has my soul ever tasted of the wormwood and the gall? What cords of infinite love have caught and held my heart? What oracles of heaven have I found and treasured up? Of what tests and truths could I now say, "I believe and therefore speak"? Say then, my conscience, as thou shalt answer at the judgment-seat of God; am I taking this honour to myself, or am I called of God as was Aaron? Is Christ sending me, and laying a necessity upon me to preach the Gospel? Am I thrusting myself into the office? Is He breathing on my soul, and causing me to receive the Holy Ghost? Is He enduing me with deep compassion to the souls of men and with a deep sense of my own unfitness?

I pant so much for the liberty to declare freely the unsearchable riches of Christ, and to teach fully the doctrines of the Christian religion, that I have often felt a wish to quit my present station and seek one less restricted.

—Robert Morrison

The father of Protestant missions to China, **Robert Morrison** (1782–1834), stood in the succession of Scots who were the heirs of the Great Awakening. He was born in humble circumstances; his family lived in one side of the house and the cow in the other. Ultimately the family, in which Robert was the youngest of eight, moved on to Newcastle in England.

The home was devout, and Robert's father became an elder in the High Bridge Presbyterian Church. Young Robert loved to study and knew Psalm 119 by memory at age twelve. As a boy, he played with George Stephenson of locomotive fame. Robert was converted at the age of fifteen, in a vivid, life-changing fashion.

The fear of death compassed me about, and I was led to cry mightily to God that He would pardon my sin, that He would renew me in the spirit of my mind. Sin became a burden. It was then that I experienced a change of life, and I trust a change of heart too. I broke off with my careless companions and gave myself to reading, to meditation, and to prayer. It pleased God to reveal His Son in me, and at that time I experienced much of "the kindness of youth and the love of espousals."

Young Morrison joined a prayer society. He mastered shorthand, which would be invaluable to him in future ministry, and learned Latin from the Rev. Adam Laidlaw. He attended Hoxton Academy and opened himself to the call of the London Missionary Society, either to Timbuktu or China.[1] He had a notable preaching mission in Newcastle in 1806, and set sail for China the next year.

Morrison translated for the East India Company but was restricted in his ministry. His duties placed him between Macao, where his family lived, and Canton, the great gateway city to China. Morrison turned down the opportunity to be a chaplain for the East India Company because it "would not afford him the opportunity of preaching the Gospel of Christ."[2] He carried on extensive correspondence with Carey and his coworkers at Serampore, all the while carrying on his translation work bolstered by the presence of a dear colleague, **William Milne,** who with his family joined the Morrisons in 1813.

Morrison initiated the Ultra-Ganges Mission, which did effective work in Malaya. In 1815 his family returned to England without him. He would not see them for six years.

Although Morrison shrank from publicity, he was increasingly known as the first China-scholar in Europe. In 1819 and the next year he completed the Old and New Testaments as well as a dictionary and catechism. But tragedies began to hound him, and Morrison took a furlough. He had never wavered from his commitment that "the end designed by the Missionary Society is to preach the Gospel to the heathen and convert the natives from Satan to God . . . to effect this end a knowledge of languages is an indispensable means."[3]

During his furlough, Morrison had contact with Edward Irving, Sir Walter Scott, and Dr. Adam Clarke as well as receiving the D.D. from Glasgow University. But his heart was in China, and he returned to Macao in 1826. White ants destroyed his library, yet he gave himself to preaching to Caucasians and Chinese and to the preparation of a Bible commentary in Chinese.

Though much maligned, Morrison gave himself unwaveringly to the task for twenty-five years, dying at his post. His life ended in his early fifties. Latourette observes, his body "had long been showing the effects of the adverse conditions but which the resolute will of its master had kept going until almost the very last."[4]

---

1. Marshall Broomhall, *Robert Morrison: A Master-Builder* (New York: George Doran, 1924); a fine sketch is also in J. Theodore Mueller, *Great Missionaries to China* (Grand Rapids: Zondervan, 1947), 39ff.

2. Broomhall, *Robert Morrison,* 68.
3. Ibid., 152.
4. Kenneth Scott Latourette, *A History of the Expansion of Christianity: The Great Century* (Grand Rapids: Zondervan, 1944, 1970), 6:299.

8.4.7 ROBERT MOFFAT—GROWING THE CHURCH

I have tried to look upon those hands and those feet streaming with blood. I have tried to look on that thorny crown that encircled the sacred head of the Son of God. I have tried to hear his voice; I have read in the words of eternal truth what he said, and I believed that he was the Son of God, and the Saviour of the world. I believed that what he said was true when, as he left the sacred mount of Olives to ascend his mediatorial throne, he said: "Go ye into all the world, and preach the Gospel to every creature."
— Robert Moffat in York Street Chapel, Walworth

Another case linking the preaching of the Great Awakening and the great century of missionary advance is the herculean career of **Robert Moffat** (1817–1870). Although one of his more modern biographers faults him for rigid theology and vanity, even he must concede that Moffat was the great pioneer missionary of southern Africa and that his many years of preaching, translating, and printing were signal years of gospel advance.[1]

Moffat was born in Ormiston, 26 miles from Edinburgh. His father was a ploughman and a member of the United Presbyterian Church. His mother read to him about Moravian missionaries in Greenland and Labrador. When he left home to take a position as a gardener in Cheshire in England, his mother admonished him to read his Bible twice daily. To the consternation of his parents he found great inspiration in a Methodist hall, and there was converted:

One evening while poring over the Epistle to the Romans, I could not help wondering over a number of passages which I had read many times before . . . turning from one passage to another, each sending a renovation of light into my darkened soul. The Book of God, the precious undying Bible, seemed to be laid open, and I saw what God had done for the sinner . . . I felt that, being justified by faith, I had peace with God through the Lord Jesus Christ.[2]

He was particularly moved by the ministry of **William Roby,** pastor of Grosvenor Chapel, Manchester (Congregational), and a member of the board of the London Missionary Society. Lapping up Roby's formally Calvinistic lectures on theology (his only formal education), he felt the call to missionary service. Roby spoke from the premise of "the divine authority of Scripture," which became Moffat's watchword for a lifetime. His theory of preaching mirrored Roby's: the sermon and its "ideas, words, phrases and sentences" should be "simple" and in the language of the people.[3]

Moffat was commissioned at a service in Surrey Chapel on August 31, 1816, and then sailed for Capetown, Africa.[4] He was married in Africa to his sweetheart, Mary Smith, in 1819; she was his faithful wife and partner in ministry for fifty-three years.

Moffat was known as a peacemaker among warring tribes and found himself in the middle of the great Boer trek northward. He gave immense investment to the translation of Scripture into Bechuana, the first draft of which was finished in 1838. The gospel stories were easier than the Epistles. When Moffat introduced the word *epistole,* the native preachers confused it with the much more familiar *pistols.*

Preaching almost continuously, Moffat one evening found himself as the guest of a wealthy farmer who asked him to conduct a service of divine worship. Moffat asked where the servants were, to which the old man said:

> Hottentots! Do you mean that, then! Let me go to the mountain and call the baboons, if you want a congregation of that sort. Or stop, I have it: my sons, call the dogs that lie in front of the door, that will do.

Moffat then preached from the gospel text, "Truth, Lord, but even the dogs eat of the crumbs that fall from the Master's table." The landowner interrupted him after a few minutes and announced, "He shall have the Hottentots." In came the slaves, who had never been in the master's house or heard a preacher. Moffat continued preaching. When all had left, the old man said to Moffat, "My friend, you took a hard hammer and you have broken a hard head."[5]

Moffat did pioneer work in Great Namaqualand and saw revival come to Kuruman, where he headquartered for forty years and initiated a ministry among the Matabele, south of the Zambesi. He led several great chiefs to Christ, most prominent of whom was the great Moselekatse. A picture of Moffat preaching from a wagon to the chief's people is powerful.[6]

On one foray, a chief and his retinue confronted the Moffats with an ultimatum to leave the area. Moffat pulled his tall frame even taller and, with Mrs. Moffat standing in the doorway with her baby in her arms, spoke in ringing tones:

> If you are resolved to rid yourselves of us, you must resort to stronger measures, for our hearts are with you. You may shed blood or burn us out. We know you will never touch our wives and children. Then shall they who sent us know, and God, who now sees and hears what we do, shall know that we have been persecuted indeed.[7]

The chief before dispersing is reported to have said: "These men must have ten lives, since they are so fearless of death; there must be something in immortality."

At age seventy-four, Moffat retired to England. The following year his wife died. He continued to speak and shape thinking on missions.[8] When he died in 1883, *The Times* of London spoke of his ministry: "The Bechuanas became new men . . . a proof that the ground was not barren and that even in South Africa the good seed might be trusted to spring up and to bring forth abundant fruit. The progress of South Africa has been mainly due to men of Moffat's stamp."[9] Such is another validation of the power of biblical preaching.

---

1. Cecil Northcott, *Robert Moffat: Pioneer in Africa* (New York: Harpers, 1961); also see the tribute in Kenneth Scott Latourette, *A History of the Expansion of Christianity: The Great Century* (Grand Rapids: Zondervan, 1970), 5:345.
2. Ibid., 20.
3. John S. Moffat, *The Lives of Robert and Mary Moffat* (London: Unwin, n.d.), 18–19.
4. Northcott, *Robert Moffatt*, 34.
5. Moffat, *The Lives of Robert and Mary Moffatt*, 23–24.
6. Northcott, *Robert Moffatt*, 233.
7. Ethel Daniels Hubbard, *The Moffats* (New York: Friendship, 1917, 1944), 91.
8. Moffat, *The Lives of Robert and Mary Moffatt*, 156.
9. Northcott, *Robert Moffatt*, 329.

8.5 SOWING IN GRACE

The fires of the Revival had been kindled from heaven, and before the accession of George III the Congregational churches had caught the flame. Their ministers were beginning to preach with a new fervour, and their preaching was followed with a new success. The religious life of their people was becoming more intense. A passion for evangelistic work was taking possession of church after church, and by the end of the century the old meeting-houses were crowded; many of them had to be enlarged, and new meeting-houses were being erected in town after town, and village after village, in every part of the kingdom.

—Dr. R. W. Dale

Not only a resurgence of missionary outreach but many positive developments emerged from the Great Awakening (1726–1756) and the Second Evangelical Awakening (1776–1810). We shall trace the rise of the evangelical wing in the Church of England, to which the history of preaching has such indebtedness, and the revitalization of nonconformity.

A new freedom in ministry found expression[1] and a new concept of the Christian minister came into focus. The doctrines of sin[2] and of the Holy Spirit were treated biblically. Hymns and liturgy became part of the changing landscape in a new way. Bible societies were founded. Social sensitivity and concerns for justice were seen in the Clapham Sect. **Robert Raikes** (1735–1811) popularized the Sunday school. Training schools for ministry flourished. In the Baptist tradition, the heirs of **Benjamin Keach** (1640–1704) and **John Gill** (1697–1771) the commentator, or the young and controversial **Augustus M. Toplady** (1740–1778), who was converted listening to a Methodist preaching in a barn, display the scope and sweep of this mighty series of movings of the Spirit. We shall proceed now to examine some of these pulpit princes.

1. John S. Simon, *The Revival of Religion in England in the Eighteenth Century* (London: Robert Culley, n.d.), 288.
2. Ibid., 275. The duchess of Buckingham wrote to the Countess of Huntingdon: "I thank your Ladyship for the information concerning the Methodist preaching; these doctrines are most repulsive and strongly tinctured with impertinence and disrespect toward their superiors in perpetually endeavoring to level all ranks and do away with all distinction, as it is monstrous to be told that you have a heart as sinful as the common wretches that crawl on the earth. This is highly offensive and insulting, and I cannot but wonder that your Ladyship should relish any sentiments so much at variance with high rank and good breeding."

8.5.1 WILLIAM ROMAINE—THE SEED WHICH IS SOUND

When I was about sixteen years of age, I heard Mr. Romaine preach a sermon in the city of Oxford, in which he advanced with great earnestness most of the principal gospel-doctrines. I was so completely exasperated at this mode of preaching, that I could have found it in my heart to have torn him to pieces. About ten days after under a sermon delivered by Dr. Hawes, my views of divine things, my sensations, the objects of my love and hatred, were all totally changed; and I cordially embraced and relished those very doctrines which before I detested and abhorred.

—Rev. Thomas Bliss, son of the professor of astronomy at Oxford

My Jesus hath contrived so much work for me in these parts, and he is so evidently and powerfully with us, that I cannot leave my neighbors, who crowd to hear far more than ever, and they are to me as my own soul. We are beyond all description happy in our lovely Lord. Such meetings I never knew—and twice a day—and many churches open. Oh! that I could but stay—I am so knit in heart to my neighbors and the most of them come and sit quietly to hear, that I know not how to leave them. But it must be.

—William Romaine of a visit to Hartlepool

At the heart of the revival was a proper view of Scripture and the gospel. As Bishop Ryle contends, "The instrumentality by which the spiritual reformers of the eighteenth century carried on their operations was of the simplest description . . . it was neither more nor less than the old apostolic weapon of preaching."[1]

They preached everywhere, they preached simply, they preached fervently and devoutly. A key figure in the movement was **William Romaine** (1714–1795). Born in Hartlepool in Durham of French Huguenot stock, he studied at a school founded by Bernard Gilpin (cf. 5.5.12) and then at Christ Church, Oxford. Romaine mastered the biblical languages, particularly Hebrew and the Hebrew Psalter, and sought to develop as a public speaker, even attending a performance of David Garrick "to improve himself in the graces of oratory."[2]

Early on, Romaine was high church and a Hutchinsonian (an obsessive fixation on Hebrew roots). All through his life he preached through the whole Bible with a particular love for the charms of the Old Testament. In dress he tended to be rough and careless, in habits fastidious and rigid, in temperament a Boanerges (like James and John, "sons of thunder"), controversial, aloof, lacking in personal warmth and friendliness. Yet he was an enormously effective preacher.[3]

Romaine experienced a spiritual crisis in which he was stripped of all of his familiar dependencies. He became more expository and devotional in his preaching and moved into the orbit of the Wesleys, Whitefield, the Countess of Huntingdon, and Henry Venn. Romaine married Mary Price in 1755; one son died in the military in Ceylon and another became a well-known preacher. Over a period of forty-five years of ministry, he was in and out of many London churches as a lecturer, becoming one of the most popular preachers in London. He even did a stint as a professor of astronomy.

Londoners were apprehensive about a possible French invasion and by the news of thirty-thousand fatalities in the Lisbon tidal wave. Romaine addressed their fears by preaching from Amos 4:12 on "Prepare to Meet Thy God," "An Alarm to a Careless World" and "The Parable of the Dry Bones" from Ezekiel 37. He understood the latter to speak primarily of the restoration of the Jews at the end of the age but secondarily as a figure of the need for revival in the church. In 1757 he issued his famous "An Earnest Invitation to the Friends of the Established Church for Setting Aside One Hour a Week for Prayer and Supplication During the Present Troublesome Times."

After Romaine preached in the Oxford University pulpit on "imputed righteousness," he was prohibited from preaching there again.[4] But his plain manners, coarse haberdashery, and introversion could not obscure his rich ministry in the Word nor deny him the post as "the leading pioneer Evangelical clergyman in the Church of England." He served as a chaplain for the Countess of Huntingdon and took many evangelistic tours. He deplored the increasing controversies between the Arminians of Wesley and the Calvinists of Whitefield, although he tilted toward the latter and as well to Sandeman's intellectual assent. Rowland Hill went to hear him preach and reported he had been fed "with the fat of the land."[5] The placid Newton felt Romaine veered close to antinomianism, but it was a time of polarization and extremes (among the worst of which was Madan's advocacy of polygamy).

Declining a call to Philadelphia, Romaine was appointed to St. Anne's, Blackfriars, where he labored for twenty-nine years. For a long time he was the only evangelical with a benefice in London. As Ryle asserts, in his ministry there he became "the rallying point for all in London who loved evangelical truth in the Church of England."[6] Within sight of St. Paul's and Westminster, he did not hesitate to take controverted stands, not always correctly, as on the Jewish Naturalization Act, or in the Gordon Riots where he and the Wesleys took opposite sides. Then there was his ill-advised "An Essay on Psalmody" (1775), in which he calls for the singing of the psalms only (something Romaine did not practice himself). John Newton expressed the wistful regret that the work had ever been published. Newton's coming to St. Mary Woolnoth greatly strengthened Romaine's ministry since this was a second pulpit for an evangelical in London.

Romaine enjoyed immense stature among conservative spiritual leaders in a mightily energized Church of England. So loyal was he to the established church that he would not preach in a dissenting setting. Davis claims that a chief asset of Romaine was his ability to preach doctrine interestingly and understandably. "To the amazement of the laity and the consternation of the clergy, he did not take it for granted that all who had been baptized in the Church of England were regenerated people."[7]

Not outward form but inward change was his insistence, with Christ crucified ever as his message. His delivered and printed sermons brought a great harvest of conversions. Such sermons as "A Method for Preventing the Frequency of Robberies and Murders," "A Discourse on the Self-Existence of Jesus Christ," and "The Duty of Watchfulness Enforced" suggest the burden of his heart. Romaine continued preaching four or five times a week until his death at eighty. He was greatly mourned in his passing. He is an important pillar in a growing edifice of vitality.

---

1. J. C. Ryle, *Five Christian Leaders* (London: Banner of Truth, 1960), 19.
2. Donald Gordon Davis, "The Evangelical Revival in Eighteenth Century England as Reflected in the Life and Work of William Romaine" (Ph.D. dissertation, University of Edinburgh, 1949), 19.
3. Ibid., 51.
4. Ibid., 105.
5. Ibid., 168.
6. Ryle, *Five Christian Leaders,* 76.
7. Davis, "The Evangelical Revival," 304.

8.5.2 WILLIAM JAY—THE SEED WHICH IS SPIRITUAL

The glorious Gospel of the blessed God our Saviour is the great object of our attention as minister and people; this only am I allowed to preach, this only are you allowed to hear. If you "hold the Head" you will not be "carried about by strange doctrines." A disposition for novelty in religious truth is the spring of error running through the flowery field of speculation into the gulf of apostasy. No system of doctrine will serve in the stead of that grace by which the heart is to be renewed and the life sanctified.

—William Jay

Some, like Romaine, were dedicated to seek renewal within the Church of England. Others, like the Wesleys, Whitefield, and the Countess of Huntingdon were determined to make every effort for such a rekindling but failed. Still others took the course of independency or dissent. Either their temperament or circumstances forced them to choose a separation. **William Jay** (1769–1853) exemplifies this course of action. For sixty-two years Jay served as pastor of the Argyle Chapel in Bath and was widely known as an expert exegete and expositor. He was born in a stonecutter's home in Salisbury and nurtured in a modest but pious context. Drawn by curiosity to Methodist preaching in his village and the announcement that "Christ Jesus came into the world to save sinners," he was wonderfully converted. He served as his father's apprentice for two years and then went on to study at an academy in Marlborough operated by a nonconformist minister. Soon after commencing study, he preached his first sermon at age sixteen at Ablington near Stonehenge from 1 Peter 2:3, "If so be ye have tasted that the Lord is gracious." His outline was simple but direct:

I. The Lord is gracious;
II. The best way to know this is to taste Him;
III. Such knowledge will have an influence.

He preached one thousand times before reaching the age of eighteen.[1] At nineteen he preached for Rowland Hill at Surrey Chapel in London and did so annually thereafter for fifty years. Throughout his life he was a relentless campaigner for total abstinence from alcohol.

Jay preached at several places until 1791, when he was ordained at Argyle Chapel in beautiful Bath. The chapel was twice enlarged to accommodate the audiences that wanted to hear the Word.[2] At Argyle, "the dipped and the sprinkled have dwelt in peace." Jay, although not physically robust, rose at 5 A.M. daily to study and pray and would seek before preaching to exercise out his nervous trepidations.[3] His desire was to come to the pulpit "anointed as with fresh oil."

He read widely with special interest in John Owen, Leighton, Newton, and Flavel. He was much involved in the outreach of the London Missionary Society and preached its annual sermon five times. In his preaching he confessed, "I always loved arrangement and division," and he dedicated himself to never preaching more than forty-five minutes.[4] He loved to preach and his audiences knew it. "Preaching has been the element of my heart and my head," he testified. In recognition of his solid ministry, Princeton bestowed an honorary degree on him in 1810. He was a textual preacher, not taking a long portion but staying within the parameters of that text. He was a moderate Calvinist and cherished fellowship in a wide circle of Bible-believing Christians.

Jay was especially close to Newton and Wilberforce, and his personal recollections of these worthies are a delight. He dined with and heard John Wesley. Joseph Parker paid him the tribute of saying that Jay "first and last kept to the Bible. He seemed to penetrate into its eternal meaning, and to apply that meaning to the immediate wants of the age."[5] His sermons were full of scriptural quotation and allusion. Sheridan spoke of his "manly oratory." Rowland Hill avowed that in preaching William Jay "blows the silver trumpet." One visitor from America claimed, "He seemed to chain each heart to his own and to draw the whole to the Saviour's feet."

1. William Jay, *The Autobiography of William Jay* (Edinburgh: Banner of Truth, 1854, 1974), 44.
2. F. R. Webber, *A History of Preaching in Britain and America* (Milwaukee: Northwestern, 1952), 1:451.
3. Jay, *Autobiography of William Jay,* 107. The collected works of William Jay run to fourteen volumes.
4. Ibid., 146.
5. Webber, *A History of Preaching,* 1:451.

8.5.3 ROWLAND HILL—THE SEED WHICH IS SCRIPTURAL

Preaching was indeed his element; it was an exercise necessary to the health and vigour of his mind, so that Mrs. Hill used frequently to say, in his declining years, "What I dread is, lest he should ever be so feeble as not to be able to preach—in that case, what would become of him I cannot tell."

—Edwin Sidney

If I may be permitted to drop one tear, as I enter the portals of the city of my God, it will be at taking an eternal leave of that beloved and profitable companion, repentance.

Of a preacher who knew the truth but hesitated to preach it fully: "He preaches the gospel as a donkey mumbles a thistle . . . very cautiously."

—Rowland Hill

We are looking at preachers whose preaching changed the course of a nation's history. As Wesley said of Grimshaw, we are looking at preachers whose lives made a nation tremble.[1] The same surely could be said of the saintly **Rowland Hill** (1744–1833). His father, Sir Rowland Hill, baronet of Hawkstone near Wales, was sheriff of Shropshire and a member of Parliament, as were two of Rowland Hill's brothers. The older Hill was a "zealous advocate of religious causes" and sent his son to Eton. The younger Hill was influenced by John Fletcher and William Romaine, and read Archbishop Leighton.[2] In fact, he was converted at Eton after reading a sermon by Bishop Beveridge. When Hill went up to Cambridge in 1764 he immediately began to preach and was zealous in ministry to the sick and imprisoned. He corresponded with Whitefield and loved John Berridge.

Because of his irregular preaching commitments, six bishops refused to ordain him as deacon. His father had grave reservations about his preaching to the colliers, as did John Wesley. Whitefield told him that "preaching should be part of the education of a student in divinity."[3] His style was "to present simple and forcible treatment of a scriptural text . . . lucid views of the doctrines of the gospel, mingled with sudden bursts of vivid, sublime and sometimes singular illustrations."[4]

After obtaining both his B.A. and M.A., Hill married. Soon he was ordained a deacon "without any promise or condition" by the bishop of Bath and Wells but was not allowed to proceed farther. He did take a curacy, but his preaching was more and more out of the loop of the established church. He "revived Whitefield's cause at the Tabernacle in Moorfields,"[5] and became known as an inspirational preacher who had a particular love for preaching to children and writings children's hymns.

In 1779 Hill founded the Surrey Chapel in St. George's Fields, a depraved neighborhood. Although open to ministers of all denominations, worship was conducted according to the ritual of the Church of England. Both organ and choir at Surry Chapel were outstanding. Hill fostered prodigious Sunday schools and pushed missionary concern, standing with the plate after a missionary day at the Surry Chapel. He was one of the first directors of the London Missionary Society, assisted in founding the Religious Tract Society, and was one of the anchors of the British and Foreign Bible Society. He preached for seventy years and was known for his powerful illustrations, his sublime images from nature, his high energy, and his powerful voice. He was generally opposed to long addresses but invariably gave vent to "bursts of eloquence" of an unusual quality.[6]

Rowland Hill had a propensity for humor. His *Village Dialogues* (chats on various practical issues) show him at his innovative best. As a moderate Calvinist, he was a great winner of souls, and had a spotless reputation for integrity and uprightness. Hill remained a thoroughly evangelical Anglican but was too broad in his churchmanship to be confined within the ecclesiastical straitjacket. He wanted his successor to be from the Church of England, but the search was difficult because Hill's solution to the ecclesiastical riddle did not fit any true loyalty to the established church. He died in his eighty-ninth year. His friend William Jay preached the funeral sermon out of Zechariah 11:2, "Howl, fir-tree, for the cedar is fallen." Jay had heard the old pilgrim singing as he walked through the chapel shortly before his passing:

> And when I die . . . receive me, I'll cry,
> For Jesus has loved me, I cannot tell why;
> But this I can find, We two are so joined,
> He'll not be in heaven and leave me behind.

Hill was a master craftsman, always drawing "his sermon fresh from a prayerful reading of the Bible."[7] A partisan of the view that "the fall must be preached as an introduction to the Gospel,"[8] Hill was heard in a variety of circles. Richard Sheridan said he went to hear Hill "because his ideas come hot from the heart."

Hill was an admirer of Thomas Chalmers and invited him to preach in his church. The Dean of Carlisle, **Isaac Milner,** went to Hill after a service to tell him: "Mr. Hill, Mr. Hill, I *felt* it today—'tis this slap-dash preaching, say what they will, that does all the good."

Once Lady Ann Erskine saw a crowd and hearing that Rowland Hill was preaching asked that the coachman drive near. Hill saw her and stopped in his discourse to deliver a quintessential Rowland Hill appeal.

"I have something for sale." The astonished listeners wondered of what he was speaking. "Yes, I have something for sale . . . it is the soul of Lady Ann Erskine. Is there anyone here that will bid for her soul? Ah, do I hear a bid? Who bids? Satan bids. Satan, what will you give for her soul? 'I will give riches, honor and pleasure.' But stop, do I hear another bid? Yes, Jesus Christ bids. Jesus, what will you give for her soul? 'I will give eternal life.' Lady Ann Erskine, you have heard the two bids—which will you take?" Lady Ann Erskine fell down on her knees and cried out, "I will have Jesus."

---

1. J. C. Ryle, *Five Christian Leaders* (London: Banner of Truth, 1960), 5.
2. Edwin Sidney, *The Life of the Rev. Rowland Hill* (London: Baldwin and Craddock, 1835), 14.
3. Ibid., 33.
4. Ibid., 74.
5. Ibid., 71.
6. Ibid., 205.
7. Ibid., 422.
8. Ibid., 443. We have only several complete sermons of Rowland Hill.

8.5.4 *CHARLES SIMEON—THE SEED WHICH IS SPLENDID IN HARVEST*

My endeavor is to bring out of the Scriptures what is true and not to trust in what I think may be there. I have a great jealousy on this head, never to speak more or less than I believe to the mind of the Spirit in the passage which I am expounding . . . I love the simplicity of the Scriptures and I seek to receive and inculcate every truth precisely in the way it is set forth in the sacred volume. . . . Reading one's own ideas into Scripture is not preaching God's truth.

I am willing that every part of God's Word should speak exactly what it was intended to speak . . . give every text its just meaning, its natural bearing and its legitimate use. . . . A screw is the most powerful of mechanical forces. The screw as it turns round again and again is forced deeper and deeper and gains such a hold that it is impossible to withdraw it. In my sermons the application is always another turn of the screw.

—Charles Simeon

While Romaine and Newton established an evangelical foothold in London and others sought to enhance evangelical strength in outlying areas, the most unexpected and far-reaching beachhead for evangelical advance was established and flourished in Cambridge under **Charles Simeon** (1789–1836). In fifty-four years of ministry at Holy Trinity Church in Cambridge, Simeon inaugurated what has been called "the Simeonite era of the Evangelical party."[1] The evangelical wing owed much to the Great Awakening (some have said "Methodism is the

Church of England felt"), for Methodists and Evangelicals shared the conviction that "the Bible is the supreme test of any doctrine."[2] Elliott-Binns assays the strength of evangelicals in every corner of England and sees them as those who hold to verbal inspiration, the centrality of conversion, the reality of heaven and hell, an understanding of satisfaction in the atonement, and the Reformation article of justification by faith alone.

Born in Reading, Charles Simeon was the fourth and youngest son of Richard Simeon, a prosperous attorney. At seven Charles Simeon went on to Eton, where there were some spiritual stirrings, and then on to King's College, Cambridge, at nineteen. Required to take communion, he read Bishop Wilson on the Lord's Supper, and concluded, "The Jews knew what they did when they transferred their sin to the head of their offering. . . . Accordingly I sought to lay my sins on the sacred head of Jesus."[3]

Simeon began instructing his father's servants when he was home, as he did the servants at King's College. He was ordained by the bishop of Ely in 1782 and served at St. Edwards, but longed for Holy Trinity Church. Through his father's influence, he obtained the appointment against the majority wishes at Holy Trinity. The parishioners locked their pews and the churchwardens locked the doors. For five years Simeon had very limited preaching. "I preached to bare walls," he said, and though the situation began to ease he had another five years of strenuous opposition. Believing that "the servant of the Lord must not strive," he gave himself to the improvement of his preaching and met in hired rooms for instruction classes.

In this time he discovered the French Huguenot Jean Claude (cf. 6.1.4), who convinced him to make his sermons more clear and to be more in illustration. "Write your own before you consult commentaries," Simeon would urge later.[4] In all of this, Simeon was, as Henry Venn observed, "exceedingly esteemed, exceedingly despised." As Charles Smyth remarked, "Simeon was almost the first man in the history of the English pulpit since the Middle Ages to appreciate that it is perfectly possible to teach men how to preach and to discover how to do so."[5] He had sermon parties every other Friday night and worked with students "to let the sermon come naturally from the text," he himself having "uncommon skill in arrangement."

While most Anglican preachers were Tillotsonian, Simeon gave thrust to biblical exposition. In the 2,537 sermon skeletons in *Horae Homileticae,* which is still in print, he attached Claude's lectures on preaching. His strategy was to avoid grammatical observations, critical observations, and historical and philosophical observations, and to advance discussion of the text through explication, observation, propositions, and perpetual application. His philosophy was to advocate unity in design, perspicuity in arrangement, and simplicity in diction. "The leading point of the passage is to be mainly regarded and subordinate parts only so far noticed as to throw additional light on the thought."[6] He put in on an average twelve hours per sermon.

Simeon regularly preached at the university in Great St. Mary's and began drawing large attendance at Holy Trinity. He instituted an evening service which was derided but quickly filled to overflowing. He was known for the discipline of his quiet time in which he found "marrow and fatness" for his own soul and the energy to preach. He practiced free style (extempore), believing that "there is a medium between such extemporaneous effusions and a servile adherence to what is written."[7] He preached with considerable zeal and fervor, "pounding the Scripture," as was said. He affirmed, "It is for the want of a good and impressive delivery that destroys the usefulness of a great proportion of pious ministers."[8]

Simeon's throbbing missionary passion was reflected in his curate, Henry Martyn. Simeon himself was one of the founders of the Church Missionary Society. He traveled hundreds of miles annually visiting pastors and preaching. He sought to preserve the established church. "Stay in the church," he counseled. There were secessions, but there would have been many more if Simeon had not been at Cambridge. Yet he would preach in Presbyterian churches or fill in for his friend John Fletcher of Madeley. He was also a friend of John Wesley, and felt there were extremes in both Calvinism and Armininism. A trenchant quote opens his view:

> The author is disposed to think that the Scripture system is of a broader and more comprehensive character than some very dogmatical theologians are inclined to allow; and that, as wheels in a complicated machine may move in opposite directions and yet subserve one common end, so may truths apparently opposite be perfectly reconcilable with each other and equally subserve the purposes of God in the accomplishment of man's salvation. The author feels it impossible to avow too distinctly that it is an invariable rule with him to endeavor to give to every portion of the Word of God its full and proper force, without considering what scheme it favours, or whose system it is likely to advance. Of this he is sure that there is not a decided Calvinist or Arminian in the world who equally approves of the whole of Scripture . . . who, if he had been in the company of St. Paul whilst he was writing his Epistles, would not have recommended him to alter one or other of his expressions.[9]

Simeon had a genius for problem-solving.[10] While there was a certain irritability in him, and he occasionally had great passions about small things, he was called the apostle by a great throng of admirers. He established a manufactory for the plaiting of straw as employment for the poor at Stapleford. He also had a great burden for the Jews, and spoke of "the absurd position of the non-restoration of the Jews."[11] Despite vacationing each summer in Scotland, he wore himself down by his pace. He preached his last Sunday morning sermon in his seventy-eighth year. Greatly weakened by a chill, Charles Simeon entered his rest on November 13, 1836. "Through evil report and good report he ceased not to preach Thy saving Word," as says the prayer quoted in King's College Chapel on the anniversary of his death. Simeon can rightly be called the father of modern evangelical homiletics.

---

1. L. E. Elliott-Binns, *The Early Evangelicals: A Religious and Social Study* (London: Lutterworth, 1953), 365.

2. Ibid., 385.
3. William Carus, ed., *Memoirs of the Life of the Rev. Charles Simeon* (London: J. Hatchard, 1847), 9. More recent and invaluable studies are H. C. G. Moule, *Life of Charles Simeon* (Chicago: InterVarsity Press, 1892), and Hugh Evan Hopkins, *Charles Simeon of Cambridge* (London: Hodder and Stoughton, 1977).
4. Ibid., 143. To this day Cambridge has lively churches (still including Holy Trinity) which feature expository preaching, N. B. Robert Benne, "Cambridge Evangelicals," in *Christian Century,* (October 27, 1933): 1036ff.
5. Charles Smyth, *The Art of Preaching: A Practical Survey of Preaching in the Church of England 747–1939* (London: SPCK, 1940), 175.
6. Carus, *Memoirs,* 532.
7. Ibid., 146.
8. Ibid., 685.
9. Quoted in A. M. Stibbs, *Understanding God's Word* (Chicago: InterVarsity Press, 1950), 36. Note also D. N. Samuel, ed., *The Evangelical Succession* (Cambridge, Mass.: James Clarke, 1979), 70ff.
10. Charles Smyth, *Simeon and Church Order: A Study of the Origins of the Evangelical Revival in Cambridge in the Eighteenth Century, The Birkbeck Lectures 1937–38* (Cambridge, Mass.: Cambridge University Press, 1940). Smyth also quotes Macaulay (1844): "If you knew what his authority and influence were, and how they extended from Cambridge to the most remote corners of England, you would allow that his real sway in the church was far greater than that of any primate," 7.
11. Carus, *Memoirs,* 635.

8.5.5   THE TRIUMVIRATE: GRIMSHAW, BERRIDGE AND VENN—THE SEED WHICH IS STRONG

They [the great evangelicals of the eighteenth century] gradually changed the whole spirit of the English Church. They infused into it a new fire and passion of devotion, kindled a spirit of fervent philanthropy, raised the standard of clerical duty and completely altered the whole tone and tendency of the preaching of the Ministers.

—William Lecky

Significant strides in evangelical advance were also made out on the hustings, as the case of **William Grimshaw** (1708–1763) clearly indicates. He was born in Brindle, Lancashire, attended Christ College, Cambridge on a scholarship because of his poor background, and served St. Mary's Chapel in Todmorden until 1742. There he drank too much and cursed in his reading for orders at Cambridge. The death of his wife and the suicide of a member sobered him with guilt, and he began to read the Bible and Owen on justification. This was his conversion. The clouds began to lift and the Bible became a new book to him. To Henry Venn he wrote:

I was now willing to renounce myself: every degree of fancied merit and ability: and to embrace Christ for my all in all. O, what light and comfort did I now enjoy in my soul, and what a taste of the pardoning love of God.[1]

In 1742 he was appointed to Haworth, a center of the combing industry in Yorkshire. (Haworth was where Rev. Patrick Bronte began his ministry in 1820 and where his daughter Charlotte wrote *Jane Eyre*.)[2] The powerfully built and colorful Grimshaw used marketplace language in reaching the uncouth and unpromising parish. The Haworth ministry was virtually defunct when he started with twelve communicants, but soon his effective pastoral skills and his powerful preaching were having effect. He wrote a friend about his launch in the primitive place:

> In that year our dear Lord was pleased to visit my parish. A few souls were affected under the Word, brought to see their lost estate by nature and to experience peace through faith in the blood of Jesus. My church began to be crowded, insomuch that many were obliged to stand out of doors. Here as in other places, it was amazing to see what weeping, roaring and agonies my people were seized with at their apprehension of the sinful state and the wrath of God.[3]

Grimshaw had a love for souls and was a giant in prayer. He had four special prayer times every day. It was said of him that he was a Calvinist on his knees and an Arminian on his feet. In doctrine "he was not numbered among the Calvinists" but held adamantly to a juridical view of the atonement.[4] In his powerful extempore prayers he took hold of the horns on the altar. He preached twenty to thirty times weekly. The fact that his parsonage was filled with Methodist preachers and that he sent his daughter to the Methodist School at Kingswood demonstrates the linkage between the Awakening and the evangelicals in the Church of England. Both Whitefield and John Wesley held meetings with him. Their strong desire was that the Methodists should not leave the church.

Grimshaw's preaching was legendary, though we do not possess any of his sermons. He was careful in dividing the text, and "He had a happy skill in teaching those around him spiritual lessons from the incidents of daily occurrence and the objects which were before their eyes."[5] He rebuked vice, and went into ale houses to haul people to the services. Little wonder that he was called Mad Grimshaw. Many of his "Timothys" became noncomformists, like John Fawcett who wrote "Blessed Be the Tie That Binds." Although he never preached in London, Grimshaw had Romaine as his dear friend and frequent pulpit supply. Fittingly, a Methodist minister preached Grimshaw's funeral service.

Another eccentric but vital part of this evangelical circle was **John Berridge** (1716–1793), who was so inept on his father's Nottinghamshire farm that his father threatened to send him to Cambridge to become "a light to the Gentiles." That is exactly what happened. If Berridge was a hapless farmer, he was a brilliant student, reading fifteen hours a day and using Greek and Latin like his mother tongue.[6] But through his first curacy and on into his thirty-eight-year ministry at Everton in Bedfordshire, he was not converted.

At the age of forty-two this all changed. Formerly his wit and cleverness carried him, but now he ceased reading manuscript sermons and began to preach Christ and justification. One thousand people with deep spiritual concerns visited him in his first year after conversion. Never married, he itinerated one hundred miles and preached a dozen times a week. He worked closely with Whitefield and the Wesleys. His message of justification by faith alone was so flaming that his bishop reprimanded him and threatened to imprison him, and would have except for the intervention of William Pitt. The "phenomena" were present in the great revival which came to Everton.[7]

John Berridge had immense influence on Rowland Hill. When Berridge had exhausted his resources in ministry, William Romaine "begged on his behalf."[8] His preaching had a "rustic homeliness." His main points were boldly underlined. Tall and thin in appearance, he had an iron constitution, but at the end he was alone, blind, and deaf. Yet Berridge testified, "Lord, if I have thy presence and love, that sufficeth."[9]

Simeon preached Berridge's funeral sermon and six clergy, including the Venns, carried the casket. We again witness quite an unusual confraternity of preachers of the gospel! All of the movers in the revival came to visit Everton, including John Wesley and the Countess of Huntingdon. On Berridge's grave were words of characteristic testimony:

> Here lie the earthly remains of John Berridge: Late Vicar of Everton, and an itinerant servant of Jesus Christ, who loved his Master and His work, and after running on his errands many years was called to wait on Him above.
> Reader: Art thou born again? No Salvation without New Birth![10]

Still another figure in this firmament was **Henry Venn** (1724–1797), who came from seven generations and 230 years of evangelical clergy testimony. Webber insists he must be included in a list of the ten greatest English preachers of the eighteenth century.[11] Venn had an excellent academic career at Cambridge, where he was known for his prowess at cricket. He was much taken with William Law but in danger of a fixation on works righteousness. Thus the Countess of Huntingdon wrote him:

> Oh my friend, we can make no atonement to a violated law; we have no inward holiness of our own; the Lord Jesus Christ is "the Lord our righteousness." Cling not to such beggarly elements, such filthy rags, mere cobwebs of Pharisaical pride; but look to him who hath wrought out a perfect righteousness for his people . . . now, my dear friend, no longer let false doctrine disgrace your pulpit. Preach Christ crucified as the only foundation of the sinner's hope. Preach him as the Author and Finisher as well as the sole Object of faith, that faith which is the gift of God. Exhort Christless sinners to fly to the City of Refuge.[12]

God used this correspondence to change Venn's preaching. He served in Clapham (1754–1759), and then up in Huddersfield for twelve years, where he preached

6,250 sermons to "the rough and ignorant weavers of Yorkshire."[13] Whitefield said of his preaching, "The worthy Venn is valiant for the truth, a son of thunder." So many came to hear Venn that he had to preach outdoors. He sent twenty-two men into the ministry. He had a dynamic impact on the whole community, like McCheyne's in Dundee. Marcus Loane observed, "Few parish ministers in English history have so moved and shaken town and county by the simple act of preaching."[14] In preaching, Venn often looked as if he were about to jump out of the pulpit. Ryle asks rhetorically, "Who can deny the immense effect of good delivery?"[15]

Venn's health finally broke at Huddersfield, and he took the charge at Yelling near Cambridge in 1771. Here he finished out his active ministry. Every Tuesday, he and Simeon would dine at Berridge's. His devotional writings and his preaching made a memorable mark. Venn felt he had "always been too much on the side of free grace for many Arminians and too much on the side of experimental religion for many Calvinists." At the suggestion of Charles Simeon, Venn organized the Church Missionary Society in 1799.

Henry Venn's son, John, was rector of Clapham (1759–1813). In turn, John's son, Henry, was a gifted and powerful preacher who served parishes with distinction, counted Thomas Chalmers as one of his closest friends, and who in 1846 became the CEO of the society.[16] He was a visionary and eminent missions statesman, and lived with his son, John, who was rector at Mortlake, in his last year. To his great anguish, he saw his son become doubtful about the supernatural and in 1864 break with the evangelicals. His father, Henry, had keen interest in the revival of 1859 and died in 1873. Much earlier when Cowper heard that old Henry Venn was very ill, he wrote Newton in 1791, "I am sorry that Mr. Venn's labors below are so near to a conclusion . . . I should envy him and Mr. Berridge and yourself, who have spent, and while they last, will continue to spend your lives in the service of the only Master worth serving. Labouring always for the souls of men, and not to tickle their ears as I do."[17] What a succession of preachers! The fruit of it all will be seen in the next century and in our own.

1. George G. Cragg, *Grimshaw of Haworth: A Study in Eighteenth-Century Evangelicalism* (London: Canterbury, 1947), 15.
2. For recent treatments of Rev. Patrick Bronte and his family, see Juliet Barker, *The Brontes* (New York: St. Martin's, 1994), a comprehensive work; Lyndall Gordon, *Charlotte Bronte: A Passionate Life* (New York: Norton, 1995). Bronte adapted to the church where the pulpit dominated the altar. Although "a little peculiar in his manner," Bronte developed "the assurance to preach without notes."
3. Cragg, *Grimshaw of Haworth*, 22.
4. Ibid., 70.
5. Ibid., 59.
6. J. C. Ryle, *Five Christian Leaders* (London: Banner of Truth, 1960), 120.
7. For a balanced and open address to the issue of the phenomena, see D. Martyn Lloyd-Jones, *The Sovereign Spirit: Discerning His Gifts* (Wheaton, Ill.: Harold Shaw, 1985).
8. Edwin Sidney, *The Life of the Rev. Rowland Hill* (London: Baldwin and Cradock, 1835), 56.

9. Ryle, *Five Christian Leaders,* 130.

10. Ibid., 132.

11. F. R. Webber, *A History of Preaching in Britain and America* (Milwaukee: Northwestern, 1952), 1:401.

12. Ryle, *Five Christian Leaders,* 158–59.

13. Earle E. Cairns, *An Endless Line of Splendor: Revivals and their Leaders from the Great Awakening to the Present* (Wheaton, Ill.: Tyndale, 1986), 64.

14. Marcus L. Loane, *Cambridge and the Evangelical Succession* (London: Lutterworth, 1951), 134.

15. Ryle, *Five Christian Leaders,* 177.

16. Wilbert R. Shenk, *Henry Venn: Missionary Statesman* (Maryknoll, N.Y.: Orbis, 1983).

17. George Melvyn Ella, *William Cowper: Poet of Paradise* (Durham, N.C.: Evangelical Press, 1993), 428.

8.5.6 ANDREW FULLER—THE SEED WHICH IS SPREAD

Carey, as it were said, "Well, I will go down if you will hold the rope."

One thing in particular I would pray for; namely, that I may not only be kept from erroneous principles, but may so love the truth as never to keep it back. O Lord, never let me, under the specious pretence of preaching holiness, neglect to promulgate the truths of Thy Word; for this day I see, and have all along found, that holy practice has a necessary dependence on sacred principle. O Lord, if Thou wilt open mine eyes to behold the wonders of Thy Word, and give me to feel their transforming tendency, then shall the Lord be my God. Then let my tongue cleave to the roof of my mouth, if I shun to declare, to the best of my knowledge, the whole counsel of God.

I preached a sermon to the youth last Lord's Day: For what is our hope, or joy, or crown of rejoicing? Are not even ye in the presence of our Lord Jesus Christ at His coming? For ye are our glory and our joy. I think I must have had nearly a thousand. They came from all quarters. My heart's desire and prayer for them is that they might be saved.

—Andrew Fuller

"The pulpit is an awful place; we preach for eternity." So wrote **Andrew Fuller** (1754–1815) in his diary. Raised and ministering his whole life among the Strict or Particular Baptists, Fuller was a great soul with a large vision. He was reared among the fens in a rural setting but early discovered and loved books. Highly athletic, he wrestled and skated with the best of them. Converted at fifteen, he was early embroiled in controversies generated by the hyper-Calvinism in his home church of Soham near Ely. At twenty-one he began to serve the church, and souls were saved. The shackles of hyper-Calvinism undercut the validity of the universal call. The issue was: can the preacher appeal to people to come to Christ? The old diehards denied that souls should be called to repentance and faith.[1]

Called and ordained in 1775, Fuller preached to his small congregation of about forty with great faithfulness. The disunity in the church discouraged him, and he became sick and almost died.[2] He studied the Scriptures to gain a proper theology. His motto was "Never be an imitator." Out of his agonies came his widely-read book, *The Gospel Worthy of All Acceptation,* in which he argues that it is not a matter of cannot but a matter of will not.[3] After two years of struggling with the call to move to Kettering in 1782 he took the charge in there, where he ministered for thirty-three years. He gained a wide reputation as a preacher-theologian, often being called the apostle Fuller.

Although a constant visitor among his people, Fuller was best-known for his Sunday morning expository preaching. He covered most of the Bible in his ministry. Sunday evenings and on special occasions he preached topically or textually. Pattison adjudges, "He had not the finish of Foster nor the splendour of Hall, but his simple and vigorous style expressed simple and vigorous thought."[4] Thomas Chalmers came to hear him, and, after sensing Fuller's freedom, resolved never again to preach from notes.

Fuller became a founder of the Baptist Missionary Society (cf. 8.4.3), and was the prime mover behind William Carey and the India Mission. Carey's crucial *Enquiry* really rose out of Fuller's *The Gospel Worthy.* Even with the death of his wife and many of his children, Fuller traveled widely for the mission, making five trips to Scotland, where he met and enjoyed the largess of the wealthy Haldane brothers.

Like many others, such as Charles Simeon, the Haldanes, Thomas Chalmers, and Rab Duncan, Fuller had a special love for the Jewish people and saw spiritual significance for them in the future.[5] He wrote a weighty challenge to deism and rationalism titled *The Gospel Its Own Witness.* This was the volume Wilberforce had on his table when William Pitt came to visit him.[6] Virtually unschooled, Fuller received honorary doctorates from Yale and Princeton. When Fuller passed on, Robert Hall the younger preached the funeral service. Augustus Hopkins Strong's *Systematic Theology* makes thirteen references to Andrew Fuller. Spurgeon, who himself was accused of Fullerism, called him "the greatest theologian of the century."[7]

---

1. Gilbert Laws, *Andrew Fuller: Pastor, Theologian, Ropeholder* (London: The Carey Press, 1942), 20.
2. Ibid., 34.
3. William Rushton, *A Defense of Particular Redemption: Wherein the Doctrine of Andrew Fuller Relative to the Atonement of Christ Is Tried by the Word of God* (Elom College, N.C.: Primitive Publications, 1831). The fact that the Primitive Baptists are still publishing this work indicates that the issue is far from settled for some.
4. T. Harwood Pattison, *The History of Christian Preaching* (Philadelphia: American Baptist Publication Society, 1903), 287.
5. Iain Murray, *The Puritan Hope* (London: Banner of Truth, 1971), 154ff.
6. Laws, *Andrew Fuller,* 94.
7. Ibid., 127. For a bit of a personal sense, see "Andrew Fuller's Text" in F. W. Boreham,

A Bunch of Everlastings (New York: Abingdon, 1920), 235ff. We shall meet Boreham as a preacher in his own right, but his sketches on the great texts of servants of Christ are outstanding, as are all of his essays which had amazing circulation and are now being reprinted by Kregel Publications in Grand Rapids.

8.5.7 ROBERT HALL—THE SEED WHICH IS SUFFICIENT

He always began with a prayer (sometimes of considerable length) uttered with great earnestness and simplicity, but injured in effective power from an apparent asthmatical difficulty of articulation. There was the same constitutional or organic difficulty in the commencement of his sermons. But the breathing of his sentences became more easy as he advanced, and before long there was a moral grandeur in his delivery which triumphed over all organic defect or physical weakness. While he rolled out his beautiful and purely constructed sentences one felt as if under the training of a higher nature. In occasional flights of imagination, in discussion of metaphysical subtlety, we were for a while amazed and almost in fear for the preacher. And then he would come down, with an eagle's swoop, upon the matter he had in hand, and enforce it with a power of eloquence such as I never felt or witnessed in the speaking of any other man. Such is my feeling now. Many a long year has passed away since I last heard Robert Hall. I have listened with admiration to many orators in the two Houses of Parliament, and to many good and heart-moving preachers, but I never heard one who was in my mind on the same level with Robert Hall.

—Prof. Adam Sedgewick

Robert Hall (1764–1831) was a most unusual preacher. Born into a minister's family in Arnesby, Leicestershire, his godly father, the elder Robert Hall, authored the well-known *Help to Zion's Travelers*. An inveterate reader from very early, he had read Edwards *On the Will* and Butler's *Analogy* by age nine. He attended Rylands' School in Northampton and there was exposed to massive doses of Latin, Greek, and rhetoric.

But Robert was virtually an invalid from childhood, which did not allow him to sit while studying, so he lay on the floor for hours. His breathing was often irregular. Despite his health problems, he preached an ordination sermon when he was sixteen, duly impressing the many ministers present.[1]

Hall studied at King's College, Aberdeen, taking his degree in 1784. Following that he assisted Dr. Evans at the Broadmead Church (Strict Baptist) in Bristol. He was much taken with the preaching of **Robert Robinson** (1735–1790), a young barber who had been converted under the preaching of Whitefield. Robinson had gone on to become pastor of a small Baptist church in Cambridge which grew exponentially. We know Robinson as the translator of Jean Claude's *Essay on the Composition of the Sermon* and the author of the hymn "Come Thou Fount of Every Blessing." Robinson followed his mentor **Joseph Priestly** into heterodox views on inspiration, the atonement, and the Trinity. Young Hall took Robinson's place in 1790, and endeavored to imitate the somewhat stilted form. The death of his own father sobered him,[2] and he left this bondage and also his addiction to the model of Dr. Samuel Johnson's "tea-table talk."

Hall began to preach the Bible and the historic faith with confidence. His sermons started slowly but built momentum. He elucidated profound truths simply and clearly. Hall would sometimes stop for a brief time of prayer before launching into the application of the sermon.[3] **John Foster** (1770–1843), who was himself a gifted preacher, evaluated the preaching of his good friend Robert Hall as being unusually imaginative and carefully prepared.[4]

Exhausted by his regimen, the frail Hall suffered a total physical and emotional collapse in 1805 and had to leave Cambridge. He drew closer to the Lord during this trying time, and soon articulated his famous "An Act of Solemn Dedication of Myself to God." He regained his strength and took the call to Harvey Lane, Leicester, in 1807 and then in 1826 the charge at Broadmead in Bristol.

Hall was a moderate Calvinist who believed in general redemption. He called Gill's formulations "a continent of mud" (Gill was a strict Baptist of great rigidity). His sermons were long, but he carried his audience with him through the sheer attraction of truth powerfully stated through the Spirit. The two most-remembered of his sermons were topical (a testimony to the power of relentless unity): "Modern Infidelity Considered" and "The Death of Princess Charlotte," from Jeremiah 15:9, "She hath given up the ghost; her sun has gone down while it is yet day."[5]

His sermon in the *Collected Works* on "The Lamb of God—His Character—His Sacrifice—and His Claim to Universal Attention" from John 1:35, 39 is Christocentric and evangelistic, taking as its central idea, "The justice of the Deity, not to be propitiated by any other means, pursues the transgressor on earth and in hell; nothing in the universe can arrest it in its awful career, until it stops in reverence at the cross of Christ!"[6] Likewise his messages on "The Joy of Angels over a Repenting Sinner," from Luke 15:7, and "The Glory of Christ's Kingdom" from Psalm 145:11 are ripe and rich discourse.[7] Professor Bebbington calls Hall "the most powerful of early nineteenth-century English preachers" and cites his greatest sermon as evidence, which was "a defence of the principle of the substitution of the innocent for the guilty."[8]

How do we correlate the uniqueness of this able preacher with his life experience and the power of God along the journey? What varied instruments God uses in all ages!

---

1. Olinthus Gregory, ed., *The Works of Robert Hall* (London: Henry C. Bohn, 1841), 6:8.
2. Ibid., 6:30.
3. Ibid., 6:56.
4. Ibid., 6:144, 150, 156.
5. E. C. Dargan, *A History of Preaching* (New York: George H. Doran, 1912), 2:502.
6. Gregory, *The Works of Robert Hall,* 6:300.

7. Ibid., 6:356ff., 123ff.
8. D. W. Bebbington, "Evangelical Christianity and the Enlightenment," in *Crux* 25:4 (December 1989): 30.

CHAPTER NINE

Starbursts and Sidetracks of the Victorian Pulpit

Part One: The Headwaters

Our gospel came to you not simply with words, but also with power, with the Holy Spirit and with deep conviction. . . . The Lord's message rang out from you . . .

—1 Thessalonians 1:5, 8

With the help of our God we dared to tell you his gospel in spite of strong opposition. . . . We speak as men approved by God to be entrusted with the gospel. We are not trying to please men but God, who tests our hearts . . . And we also thank God continually because, when you received the word of God, which you heard from us, you accepted it not as the word of men, but as it actually is, the word of God, which is at work in you who believe.

—1 Thessalonians 2:2b, 4, 13

Beyond all question, the mystery of godliness is great: He appeared in a body, was vindicated by the Spirit, was seen by angels, was preached among the nations, was believed on in the world, was taken up in glory.

—1 Timothy 3:16

This is my gospel, for which I am suffering even to the point of being chained like a criminal. But God's word is not chained. Therefore I endure everything . . .

—2 Timothy 2:8b–10a

But the Lord stood at my side and gave me strength, so that through me
the message might be fully proclaimed and all the Gentiles might hear it.
—2 Timothy 4:17

The office of the preacher is to smite the rock, that the living waters may
gush forth to satisfy the thirst of the age.
—Archbishop of York, W. C. Magee (1821–1891), considered
second only to Prime Minister William E. Gladstone as an orator

Good expository preaching does not impress the congregation; it feeds
them.
—Walter L. Liefeld

As the eighteenth century closed with the American Revolution and the barbarism of the French Revolution,[1] the nineteenth century loomed with promise and
change. The convulsions of the Napoleonic Wars,[2] the agricultural and industrial
revolutions, immigration, the era of colonial expansion, and Victorianism created a milieu for heroic preaching. Here we shall see much maturity and pulpit
potency, but here we shall also see the seeds of apostasy and a disappointing
hesitancy.

In his monumental work *The Birth of the Modern: World Society 1815–1830,*
Paul Johnson advances the thesis that the foundations were laid in these years
for the new ideas, inventions, and technological progress that would shape the
new world order to come.[3] Evangelical stalwarts like Wilberforce, Shaftesbury,
John Bright, and Prime Minister William E. Gladstone (a lay preacher in his own
right)[4] were front and center in England. James Madison, the fourth president of
the United States, must be seen as "America's most theologically knowledge-
able president." Madison graduated from the College of New Jersey (later to
become Princeton), and stayed an additional year to study Hebrew with President John Witherspoon. His political ideas were largely derived from New-Side
Presbyterians.[5]

Certainly the much maligned Victorians had inconsistencies and hypocrisies,
but their overall commitment was to virtue. Marriage and the family were important to them. Gertrude Himmelfarb has ably shown that the Victorians did
not take sin lightly.[6] She quotes the French historian Halevy to show how
Wesleyanism stimulated family values in part through its fostering of worshiping together as a family unit.[7]

Peter Gay's multivolume series, *The Bourgeois Experience: Victoria to Freud,*
shows the surviving influence of the Enlightenment on the nineteenth-century
bourgeois, but cannot dispute the continuing impact of revival and preaching upon
society in every echelon.[8] This is the context for our consideration of the promise that emanated from the Victorian pulpit.

---

1. For an important interpretation of the American Revolution, see Barbara Tuchman,
The First Salute: A View of the American Revolution (New York: Knopf, 1988 see

also Howard Fast, *Seven Days in June: A Novel of the American Revolution* (New York: Brick Lane Press, 1994). This focuses on the first military encounter of the Revolution in Lexington and Concord on April 19, 1775. The best background of the French Revolution on a modest scale is R. R. Palmer, *The World of the French Revolution* (New York: Harper and Row, 1971). An estimated two million Frenchmen died (cf. Rene Sedillot).

2. For a significant newer study, see David Hamilton-Williams, *The Fall of Napoleon: The Final Betrayal* (New York: John Wiley, 1994). Hamilton-Williams argues that Napoleon was overthrown not in battle but by treason, and was murdered by his friend Montchenu.

3. Paul Johnson, *The Birth of the Modern: World Society 1815–1830* (New York: Harper/Collins, 1991).

4. David W. Bebbington, *William Ewart Gladstone: Faith and Politics in Victorian Britain* (Grand Rapids: Eerdmans, 1993). Contains an important treatment of Gladstone's spirituality and his sermons, 68ff.

5. William Lee Miller, *James Madison: The Business of May Next and the Founding* (Charlottesville: University of Virginia Press, 1992). Miller shows how Madison got many of his political ideas from the New-Side Presbyterians.

6. Gertrude Himmelfarb, *The De-Moralization of Society: From Victorian Virtues to Modern Values* (New York: Knopf, 1994), 26. In a remarkable article, "Is America's Moral Crisis Irreparable?" in *Human Events* (December 1, 1995): 10ff., Himmelfarb argues that Puritan and Wesleyan spirituality caused a moral order to flourish in England.

7. Ibid., 55.

8. Peter Gay, *The Naked Heart: The Bourgeois Experience: Victoria to Freud,* vol. 4 (New York: Norton, 1995).

9.1 THE SCOTTISH TORRENT

How beautiful on the mountains are the feet of those who bring good news, who proclaim peace, who bring good tidings, who proclaim salvation, who say to Zion, "Your God reigns!"

—Isaiah 52:7

Again we must visit Scotland to find the red-hot core of great preaching. Considering the relative smallness of her scattered population, the preaching phenomenon is all the more astounding. The vitality of evangelicalism at the time must be seen as the product of the Cambuslang Revival of 1742 and the ministry of the American evangelists. But the Church of Scotland was becoming increasingly divided between the moderates and the children of the revivals, the evangelicals.

9.1.1 THE HALDANE BROTHERS—LAYING THE FOUNDATION

Disputes about election and predestination, or the extent of the atonement, are, amongst true disciples, generally little more than strifes of words, arising out of the partial restoration of spiritual eye-sight.

> The Scriptures contain a plain warrant to preach the Gospel to every crea-
> ture. There is no exception. "Whosoever believes" this testimony, may
> conclude with certainty that for him Christ died.
> —Alexander Haldane (representing the thoughts and convictions of
> Robert Haldane, his uncle, and James Alexander Haldane, his father)

Nonordained servants of Christ loom large throughout this narrative. **Hannah More** (1745–1833), the poetess and friend of Samuel Johnson, was one such lay-person. **David Garrick,** converted through John Newton's preaching and who established schools in Cheddar near Bristol in which twenty-five thousand students matriculated, was another.

The Haldane brothers provide us with a third example of effective lay preachers. They spent their fortune on evangelism and missions, only to be put out by the Kirk of Scotland. **Robert Haldane** (1764–1842) and **James Haldane** (1768–1851) were descendants of Danish chiefs and of the barony of Grayeagles. Their father was a wealthy sea captain and their mother a devout Christian who taught her sons to love Scripture. The two sons each pursued naval careers after schooling in Edinburgh. James sailed in and out of Macao and read Doddridge. Both were gloriously converted but were blocked in their aspirations to go to India as missionaries.

The Haldanes gave themselves to the study of Christian evidences at a time when the assaults of unbelief and the compromises of the moderates had left the Kirk of Scotland weak. When moderates opposed bringing the gospel to the heathen, old **John Erskine** (cf. 8.3.7) electrified evangelicals in the Assembly by demanding, "Moderator, rax me that Bible!" ("Reach me that Bible!"), and he read the Word to the abashed commissioners.[1]

The brothers were tireless in their preaching. Networking with John Newton, Charles Simeon, and Rowland Hill, they gave themselves to tract publication, the establishment of Sabbath schools, and a great preaching crusade in the Circus in Edinburgh. James traveled with Simeon on riding tours in 1794 and 1795 with revival breaking out here and there.

James made a memorable preaching tour of the Hebrides and the Orkneys.[2] Soon after, Robert sold the ancestral estate and was established as pastor of a tabernacle seating three thousand in Edinburgh. Tabernacles were also constructed in Glasgow, Dundee, and Perth. Training schools were held for young preachers. More than three hundred men known as Haldane preachers, several of whom were Gaelic-speaking, were sent forth.

In 1808, the brothers were immersed, and their followers became Baptists. "The church is in the wilderness," became their theme. Robert went to Geneva, Switzerland, and was followed by the English banker, Henry Drummond. There Haldane taught the Book of Romans with a great response among university students, and young pastors like d'Aubigne, Frederic Monod, Cesar Malan, Gaussen, and others (cf. 9.6) were converted.[3] This was the beginning of revival in both Switzerland and France. Wilberforce paid tribute to Robert and the "charms of his melodious eloquence." Chalmers himself used Robert Haldane on inspiration, which accounts in part for David Bebbington's irritation with

Haldane.[4] Meanwhile, James was itinerating extensively in Scotland and brought Andrew Fuller up for services.

The Haldanes' preaching was biblical and evangelistic, as an extract from Robert's commentary indicates:

> In the resurrection and exaltation of Jesus Christ, believers are taught the certainty of their immortality and future blessedness. Lazarus, and others who were raised up, received their life in the same state as they possessed it before; and after they arose they died a second time; but Jesus Christ in His resurrection, obtained a life entirely different. In his birth a life was communicated to Him which was soon to terminate on the cross. His resurrection communicated a life imperishable and immortal. Jesus Christ being raised from the dead, death hath no more dominion over Him . . .[5]

The Haldanes were also in touch with Bishop Edward Bickersteth, an outstanding evangelical, Andrew Thompson, the Scottish champion of plenary inspiration, and John Brown, the grandson of John Brown of Haddington in a delightful camaraderie of Bible preachers. How mightily God used the lives and utterances of the Haldane brothers.[6]

---

1. Alexander Haldane, *Memoirs of Robert Haldane and James Alexander Haldane* (Edinburgh: Hamilton, Adams, 1852), 131.
2. Ibid., 151.
3. Robert Haldane, *Exposition of the Epistle to the Romans* (Edinburgh: Banner of Truth, 1958). D. Martyn Lloyd-Jones regarded this commentary as one of his very favorite on Romans, so "warm in spirit and practical in application."
4. D. W. Bebbington, *Evangelicalism in Modern Britain* (London: Allen and Unwin, 1989), 87ff.
5. Ibid., 275.
6. A. T. Olson, *Believers Only* (Minneapolis: Free Church Press, 1964), 270. Olson shows how the Haldanes made an impact on Denmark and Sweden as well as Canada. The restoration movement in the U.S. reflects some Haldane features. In Gunnar Westin's *The Free Church Through the Ages* (Nashville: Broadman, 1958), we have frequent references to the Haldanes and their influence, as on 243, 265, 280, 285, 295, 329.

9.1.2   THE BONAR BROTHERS—LOOKING TO THE HILLS

I find myself in the cleft of the rock and preach about it every Sunday.

Very few ministers keep to the end the spark that was in their ministry at the beginning.

Make my sermons like quivers full of arrows dipped in love.

—Andrew Bonar

Of the seven sons in the Bonar family, three were outstanding preachers: **John Bonar** (1803–1891), **Horatius Bonar** (1808–1889), and the youngest, **Andrew Bonar** (1810–1892). All three graduated from the University of Edinburgh, in the city of their birth. John's ministry was largely at Greenock and then in the Free Church in 1843 at the Disruption. Horatius is best known as the writer of six hundred hymns, including "I Heard the Voice of Jesus Say," "I Lay My Sins on Jesus," and "Here, O My Lord, I See Thee Face to Face." He served with distinction at Kelso and then at Chalmers Memorial in Edinburgh. His was rich in the Scriptures and his preaching appealed especially to children.[1]

Both Horatius and Andrew served as moderators of the General Assembly. Andrew ministered first in Perthshire, and after the disruption pastored the Finnieston Free Church in Glasgow until his death. Like his brothers, Andrew was a fervent premillenarian and was part of the group that traveled to Palestine. The group, which included Robert Murray McCheyne, worked on behalf of the Church Mission to the Jews (1839). As a dear friend of McCheyne, Andrew wrote the highly charged *Memoirs and Remains of McCheyne*. He also edited Rutherford's letters (cf. 7.5.3).

Andrew was part of the so-called saints' school among Scottish evangelicals, explaining in part the vigorous upsurgence in Scottish preaching at the time. He was a warm, passionately revivalistic preacher who welcomed D. L. Moody to Scotland and visited Moody's Northfield Conference in the U.S. Andrew's confidence in the integrity of Scripture knew no bounds—while in his eighties he became deeply troubled over Marcus Dods' theological slippage. The depth of his exegesis can be seen in the *Book of Psalms* (1859), a choice example of what Bonar called "a dropping of the honeycomb."[2]

In his *Life and Letters,* Andrew pleads for "the necessity of preaching Christ in every sermon."[3] Indeed, he loved his calling so much that he asked the Lord to help him be "weaned from being too fond of preaching." With respect to his delivery style he testified: "I do not like paper."

Andrew always referred to his dear wife as "the desire of my eyes" in any public reference. W. Robertson Nicoll calls Andrew Bonar a "Prince of the Church" because his power was the power of prayer. "May every sermon be laid on the altar of incense," Bonar prayed. He reported of one Lord's Supper, "Every part of the Communion Service seemed to be under His smile . . . our objective being 'reclining on Christ's bosom.'"

1. Horatius Bonar, *God's Way of Holiness* (Chicago: Moody, n.d.).
2. Andrew Bonar, *Christ and His Church in the Book of Psalms* (London: Nisbet, 1859). A rich repository of exegetical and devotional thoughts.
3. Marjory Bonar, ed., *The Diary and Life of Andrew Bonar* (London: Hodder and Stoughton, 1894), 43.

9.1.3 ROBERT MURRAY MCCHEYNE—LIFTING THE TONE

A man cannot be a faithful minister unless he preaches Christ for Christ's sake.

What would my people do if I were not to pray?

Nothing is more needful for making a sermon memorable and impressive than a logical arrangement.

—Robert Murray McCheyne

He stands as one of Scotland's most brilliant and able preachers. Believing that every sermon represented "an inch of time in which to stand and preach Christ . . . and then the endless roll of eternal years follows," **Robert Murray McCheyne** (1813–1843) packed as much into his thirty short years as any man ever did.

Born in Edinburgh, he was so precocious he learned the Greek alphabet at age four and enrolled in the University of Edinburgh at fourteen. He studied divinity under Chalmers but was not converted until the death of his brother, David. With the prayer "less like myself, more like my Master," and "Lord, purify me,"[1] the writings of both Jonathan Edwards and David Brainerd, as well as the letters of Samuel Rutherford shaped him. McCheyne soon developed a profound desire to please God. He once criticized another's sermons, saying, "Some things are powerful, but I long to hear more of Christ."

McCheyne served with John Bonar in Larbert and Duniplace and there imbibed Bonar's premillennial insistence on the restoration of the Jews. "Regenerated Israel will be as a dew from the Lord." His eschatological orientation was reflected in the signature he attached to his letters, "Yours in Jesus our Hope."[2]

In 1836 he took the call to St. Peter's, Dundee, a newly organized congregation of some 1,100 members. His sermons tended to be lengthy but greatly supported by prayer. "What would my people do if I were not to pray?" he asked. He confessed of his own preaching, "I am just an interpreter of Scripture; and when the Bible runs dry, then I shall."[3]

Because of his missionary spirit he was asked by Dr. Candlish to accompany three other ministers on a mission of inquiry to Palestine in the interest of Jewish evangelism. He regretted he could not speak Arabic and witness to the Muslims. On this epochal trip, he studied Bonar on Leviticus. On the way home they established a ministry to the Jews in Budapest (to which John Duncan was later called).[4]

Never physically hardy, McCheyne became deathly sick in Bouja near Smyrna on the way back. In praying for their pastor, the folk in Dundee experienced a special visit of the Holy Spirit at the same time of the stirring at Kilsyth, where **William C. Burns** was the pastor and where thousands were gathering for renewal and salvation. Burns (called by Hudson Taylor "the man of the Book," and the first English Presbyterian missionary to China) filled the pulpit in Dundee while McCheyne was abroad. Revival fires began to burn, and when the pastor returned he found his congregation in the ferment of awakening. He preached extensively and lived in the flame of revival in his own church where thirty-five prayer meetings were held every week, five of which were children's prayer meetings. He wrote several hymns still sung today, such as "Jehovah Tsidkenu," with the marvelous opening line, "I once was a stranger to grace and to God."

Like all of these Scottish divines, he seemed to confess sin more and more and practice it less and less. He was known for his "communion sessions" when "the Lord gave tokens."

McCheyne inscribed on his letters, "The night cometh." "Live so as to be missed," he advised, and so he was when after a sudden fever he parted from this life just short of his thirtieth birthday. His printed sermons remain a fragrant memorial to his faithful preaching.[5] We have the notes of three hundred or so of his sermons preached to the weavers of Dundee. Notes taken by a parishioner on his messages from Revelation 2–3 were published as *Expositions of the Epistles to the Seven Churches* (1838). "His preaching was a giving out of his inward life," one observer noted. Almost always textual, crisply outlined, pulsating with spiritual power, they merit reading yet today. Of particular worth are "Time Is Short," from 1 Corinthians 7:29–31, and "A Time of Refreshing," from Isaiah 44:3–4. Blaikie wrote of McCheyne's style:

> McCheyne brought into the pulpit all the reverence for Scripture of the Reformation period; all the honor for the Headship of Christ of the Covenanter struggle; all the freeness of the Gospel offer of the Marrow theology; all the bright imagery of Samuel Rutherford; all the delight of the Erskines in the fullness of Christ. In McCheyne the effect of a cultured taste was apparent in the chastened beauty and simplicity of his style, if you can call it a style—in a sense he has no style, or rather it was the perfection of style, for it was transparent as glass. The new element he brought to the pulpit, or rather which he revived and used so much that it appeared new, was winsomeness . . .[6]

McCheyne's own counsel was:

> Get your texts from God—your thoughts, your words, from God . . . It is not great talents God blessed so much as great likeness to Jesus. A holy minister is an awful weapon in the hand of God. A word spoken by you when your conscience is clear, and your heart full of God's Spirit, is worth ten thousand words spoken in unbelief and sin.

---

1. Andrew Bonar, *The Life of Robert Murray McCheyne* (Edinburgh: Banner of Truth, 1844, 1962), 16ff.
2. Ibid., 78.
3. Alexander Smellie, *Robert Murray McCheyne* (London: National Council of Evangelical Free Churches, 1913). A rich resource!
4. Robert A. Peterson, "An Early Scottish Mission to the Jews," *Israel My Glory* (June–July 1989): 22ff. McCheyne's and Bonar's journal on this trip is now available, cf. ed. Allan Harman, *Mission of Discovery: The Beginnings of Modern Jewish Evangelism* (Fearne, Ross-shire, Scotland: Christian Focus, 1996). Very rich.
5. Robert Murray McCheyne, *Sermons of Robert Murray McCheyne* (Edinburgh: Banner of Truth, 1961).

6. W. G. Blaikie in F. R. Webber, *A History of Preaching in Britain and America* (Milwaukee: Northwestern, 1955), 2:392.

9.1.4 THOMAS CHALMERS—LEADING THE WAY

Enthusiasm is a virtue rarely produced in a state of calm and unruffled repose. It flourishes in adversity. It kindles in the hour of danger and rises to deeds of renown. The terrors of persecution only serve to awaken the energy of its purposes. It swells in the pride of integrity, and great in the purity of its cause, it can scatter defiance amid a host of enemies.
—Thomas Chalmers to four hundred or five hundred brethren
in 1842 on the eve of the Disruption

It would be difficult not to congratulate you on the unrivaled and un-bounded popularity which attended you in the metropolis . . . The attention which your sermons have excited is probably unequaled in modern literature.
—Robert Hall ("the greatest pulpit orator in England," cf. 8.5.7)
when Chalmers came to London

I suppose there will never again be such a preacher in any Christian Church.
—Thomas Carlyle

What Smellie calls "the long reign of moderatism" (both a theological and a political problem) was moving toward a necessary confrontation. McCheyne, who died before this denouement, had said in a letter: "You don't know what Moderatism is. It is a plant that our Heavenly Father never planted, and I trust it is now to be rooted out."[1]

The leader who moved more than four hundred clergy to leave the established church and form the Free Church in 1843 was **Thomas Chalmers** (1780–1847).[2] Born in Fifeshire, Chalmers was probably the most gifted and powerful preacher since John Knox in Scotland. The sixth of fourteen children, he was the son of a shipowner and merchant.

Early in life Chalmers was much exposed to the Bible and *Pilgrim's Progress.* He began studies at St. Andrews, the oldest university in Scotland, when he was twelve. He was raised among moderates, and his mind soon clouded with doubt. He pursued studies in mathematics and physics, and tutored until he was old enough to become a probationer, finally taking a charge in Kilmany, where he served from 1803 to 1815. His preaching was, as he described it, "blanched morality."

At thirty, after reading Jonathan Edwards and William Wilberforce and after experiencing a severe illness, he wrote an article on Christianity for an encyclopedia. Soon he was wondrously converted, some say while preaching in his own pulpit.[3] Immediately he turned to preach the Bible, was married (1812), and soon gained acclaim as a pulpiteer of excellence. Now, "he has seen the reality of

Christ's atonement, and of the work of the Holy Spirit, and found a new value in prayer, and a new use of the sacred Scriptures."[4]

In 1815, Chalmers accepted a call to the Tron Church in Glasgow (with a parish of eleven or twelve thousand people) and took the teeming masses of the great city by storm. After four years he transferred to St. John's, where **Edward Irving** was his gifted associate in a great ministry of outreach, evangelism, and work among the poor. He gave himself totally to house-to-house visitation and to the establishment of Sabbath schools, including a Sabbath evening school of two thousand children. The impression he made in preaching was described as follows:

> The eyes are light in color and have a strange dreamy heaviness which contrasts [when] expanded in their sockets and illuminated into all their flame and fervor in some moment of high entranced enthusiasm . . . but the shape of the forehead is perhaps the most singular part of the whole visage . . . wide across the eyebrows . . . immediately above the extraordinary breadth of this region . . . an arch carrying out the summit boldly and roundly . . . unquestionably I have never heard, whether in England or in Scotland, any preacher whose eloquence is capable of producing an effect so strong and irresistible as his . . .[5]

In time he moved on to the chair of moral philosophy at St. Andrews (1823–1828), where he influenced students such as Alexander Duff (cf. 8.4.5). He preached at Edward Irving's opening at the Scottish Church in London (1827). Uncommonly nervous before speaking, Chalmers continued his battle for principles even against opposing faculty colleagues. In 1828 he took the chair of theology at the University of Edinburgh and sat as chair of the General Assembly in 1832. He poured out such writings as his four volumes on Romans. He epitomized the evangelical move that culminated in the Disruption in 1843 and the formation of seven hundred Free Churches, and his own assumption of the principalship at New College, Edinburgh, where he finished out his ministry.

Chalmers has been called a solar man, he was like the sun in prominence and power. He had a marked affection for the Scripture and a great dedication to study.[6] He counted as his friends Sir Walter Scott, Prime Minister Gladstone, Thomas Carlyle, and many such others. But his preaching of the Word was his forte. He testified, "There is no continuous passage which I read with greater delight than Isaiah 53. I can remember when I made at least one perusal of it a daily task. The very cadence of its sentence is dear to me."[7]

He was not without his critics. Hazlitt said, he "catches at truth with his fists like a monkey catching an apple." His voice was husky and his Scottish brogue heavy. Yet he used words so magnificently and with such intensity, his audience had to listen. People of all classes waited with bated breath for his preaching. His sermons were best-sellers. Chalmers was yielded to the supremacy of Scripture, claiming "I give myself over in my whole mind and whole person to the authority of a whole Bible."[8]

Both Pascal and Jonathan Edwards influenced Chalmers, but he was the quintessential Puritan in preaching sin and grace. He appealed to would-be preachers,

"Close with Christ, and accept of Him as he is offered to you in the Gospel," and warned of the danger that "the invitations of God's tenderness will give place and that speedily to the terrors of a vengeance which will burn all the more fiercely because of a slighted gospel and a rejected Saviour."[9]

Chalmers skillfully used rhetorical questions. His great sermon "The Expulsive Power of a New Affection" is typical, with both very short and very long sentences. This sermon is not like "a mighty maze and quite without a plan," but the classic example of a one-point sermon. Robert Hall suggested it was like a rocking horse, it "moves but does not go on." The congregation was "like a forest bending under the power of a hurricane."[10] Said one listener, "We went home quieter than we came."

---

1. Nigel M. de S. Cameron, ed., *Dictionary of Scottish Church History and Theology* (Downers Grove, Ill.: InterVarsity Press, 1993), 505.
2. Hugh Watt, *Thomas Chalmers and the Disruption* (Edinburgh: Thomas Nelson, 1943). An excellent study.
3. W. G. Blaikie, *Thomas Chalmers* (Edinburgh: Oliphant Anderson, 1896), 33. The definitive biography with complete bibliography is Stewart J. Brown, *Thomas Chalmers and the Godly Commonwealth in Scotland* (Oxford: Oxford, 1982).
4. Ibid., 41. Karl Marx dubbed Chalmers "the arch-parson Chalmers."
5. Ibid., 77.
6. Adam Philip, *Thomas Chalmers: Apostle of Union* (London: James Clarke, 1929), 36.
7. Ibid., 111.
8. G. D. Henderson, *The Burning Bush: Studies in Scottish Church History* (Edinburgh: St. Andrew, 1957), 201.
9. Ibid., 202. For an assessment of Chalmers' impact upon the politics and economics of his time, see Boyd Hilton, *The Age of Atonement: The Influence of Evangelicalism on Social and Economic Thought, 1795–1865* (Oxford: Clarendon, 1988), 55ff.
10. T. Harwood Pattison, *The History of Christian Preaching* (Philadelphia: American Baptist Publication Society, 1903), 297.

9.1.5 Andrew Thomson—Leaning on the Shepherd

The framework of our Church may be better moulded, and its parts put into goodlier adjustment than before; but, like the dry bones in the vision of Ezekiel, even when reassembled into the perfect skeleton, and invested by a covering of flesh and skin, with the perfect semblance and beauty of a man—so our Church, even when moulded into legal and external perfection by human hands, may have all the inertness of a statue, and with the monumental coldness of death upon it, till the Spirit of God shall blow into it that it may live.

—Thomas Chalmers

In the succession of those who believed that prayer and revival were the remedies above all others, Thomas Chalmers stepped into the leadership role which had been long carried by **Andrew Thomson** (1779–1831). Chalmers described Thomson as a man of "colossal mind, wielding the weapons of spiritual warfare" with "an arm of might and voice of resistless energy," carrying "as if by storm the convictions of his people."[1] When William Cunningham first spoke to the Assembly, "It was said of him that it was Andrew Thomson come again to hammer the Moderates."[2]

Thomson was born in a pastor's home in Dumfriesshire and educated at Edinburgh. After serving in Kelso and Roxburghshire, he ministered in Perth. He became known for his scintillating expositions of Scripture, and in 1814 he was called to the new St. George's on Shandwicke Place in Edinburgh. He won the hearts of his people, visited and catechized among them, and edited the controversial *Edinburgh Christian Instructor* (which greatly aided the evangelical cause). He also led the battle against inclusion of the Apocrypha in editions of the Bible and against slavery. His boldness turned the tide in favor of evangelism. When he died, his friend and admirer Chalmers stated in his funeral message:

> If our next war is to be a war of principles, then before the battle has begun, the noblest of our champions has fallen. Yet we dare not give up to despondency a cause which has truth for its basis and the guarantee of heaven's omnipotence for its complete and everlasting triumph.[3]

Thomson died of a heart attack on his own doorstep after a church meeting, but the set of the sail had been made. He was known for his love of music and arrangements of the Psalms, and he took up the cudgel willingly against the universalism of **Thomas Erskine** of Linlathen[4] and **John McLeod Campbell.** He maintained solid ties with some in the Secession Church and used their writers in his publication. The implosion of his preaching was characterized by Maclagan:

> But the preaching of Dr. Thomson was like a bombshell falling among the people. Not only did he give constant prominence to the distinctive gospel doctrines of grace and redemption by an atonement, but in terms of great directness and plainness of speech he denounced the customs of a society calling itself Christian; and in a marvelously short time, by his zeal and faithfulness under God, a remarkable change was effected in the habits and pursuits of many of his people . . .
>
> —from the history of St. George's[5]

Thomson was called by some "the gladiator of the intellect."[6] One analysis of his preaching concluded, "He brought culture back into the pulpit without in the least degree obscuring the cross." Perhaps something of the charm and vigor of the man is seen in his retort to the fellow minister who wondered why with his gifts of ready speech he spent so much time preparing his sermons. The minister said that he had on many occasions prepared a sermon and killed a salmon before breakfast. Thomson replied, "Well, sir, I would rather have eaten your salmon than listened to your sermon."[7]

1. Nigel M. de S. Cameron, ed., *Dictionary of Scottish Church History and Theology* (Downers Grove, Ill.: InterVarsity Press, 1993), 820.
2. Ibid.
3. Adam Philip, *Thomas Chalmers: Apostle of Union* (London: James Clarke, 1929), 55.
4. Nicholas R. Needham, *Thomas Erskine of Linlathen: His Life and Theology, 1788–1837* (Edinburgh: Rutherford House, 1990). A nephew of John Erskine (cf. 8.3.7), he drifted away from the center and denied any reprobating purpose in God. Robertson said to him, "The God whom you have chosen is agreeable to your feelings, but has it never occurred to you that you may not have chosen the God of the Bible?" (458).
5. A. E. Garvie, *The Christian Preacher* (New York: Scribner's, 1923), 224.
6. For a general overview, see Henry F. Henderson, *The Religious Controversies of Scotland* (London: T & T Clark, 1905).
7. T. Harwood Pattison, *The History of Christian Preaching* (Philadelphia: American Baptist Publication Society, 1903), 289.

9.1.6 JOHN DUNCAN—LEARNING THE BASICS

We must observe this enclosing language of Holy Scripture; we must not look beyond, but in the Scripture, and we will find that every passage either proves itself or is proved by parallelism. Hereby we know that we know him, by his Spirit that he hath given to us; the things revealed by the Spirit the Apostles spake. God employs human speech, but he himself selects the words that are to express his thoughts. He leaves not man to put words on them; the words are as much the Spirit's as the ideas, and the Apostle Paul studiously avoids other words.

Oh, it is a pitiable thing for a poor silly puppy of a scilist to stand up in the pulpit vexing the people by shaking their confidence in our good English translation.

I was a very popular preacher till I began to preach on the work of the Spirit, then the church grew thin.

—John Duncan

Bolstering the outbreak of so much solid, Spirit-anointed preaching in Scotland were gifted and godly scholars like **John Duncan** (1796–1870). Duncan was a conscientious conservator of the Bible, who came out of an Original Secession background in Aberdeen. He was born the son of a shoemaker, and lapsed into infidelity and Sabellian and Socinian errors (unsound views of the Trinity and the deity of Christ) early in his life. Duncan was converted at Divinity Hall when Dr. Cesar Malan of Geneva (converted under the ministry of Robert Haldane) visited and preached. When Malan left he said of the young Duncan, "That man will soon be before you all; he believes the Word of God."[1]

Duncan preached in a rural chapel in Perthshire before moving on to lectureships in English at the Duke Street Gaelic Chapel. He was called *rabbi* by his students because of his long white beard. Elsewhere he drew notice as a gifted but absentminded preacher. Because of his brilliance in Hebrew, he was commissioned to a ministry among the Jews in Buda and Pesth in Hungary.[2] In 1843 he was invited to take the chair of Old Testament and Hebrew in New College in the wake of the Disruption. Duncan accepted and brought with him a recent convert, Alfred Edersheim, who went on to become author of the popular *Life and Times of Jesus the Messiah.*

Duncan exerted a powerful influence through his teaching and preaching and touched McCheyne, William Burns, A. Moody Stuart, and an entire generation of preachers-to-be. He loved evangelism and delighted to preach. "Preaching is the delivery of a message," he insisted.[3] Suffused with a deep personal piety and dedication to prayer (on occasion his opening prayer in class consumed half the period), he battled depression all his life. Fond of anecdote, he was in great demand as a visiting preacher, particularly in communion seasons. Dr. John Kennedy of Dingwall reported of a sermon:

> I stole quietly into the church, and heard a sermon that did not seem to have been prepared on earth, but felt as if one of the old Prophets had come from within the veil to tell us what was going on there. Nothing more heavenly did I ever hear from human lips.[4]

Duncan once stated, "Hyper-Calvinism is all house and no door: Arminianism all door and no house."[5] Liberalizing young theologues fresh from nests of skepticism on the Continent sought to deprecate him and his scholarship. When some of his students began to move toward higher criticism, the lifeline of biblical preaching was cut and preaching began to decline.[6] But Duncan's authenticity and obvious mastery of Hebrew made an immeasurable impact.

---

1. A. Moody Stuart, *The Life of John Duncan* (Edinburgh: Banner of Truth, 1872), 23.
2. For a sketch of Duncan's ministry in Hungary, see John S. Ross, "A Pioneer in Jewish Mission: Rabbi Duncan," *Christian Witness/Israel Herald* (June–August 1991): 10ff. Shows his great linguistic skills and movingly describes the conversion of Adolph Saphir, who became a leading Presbyterian minister in Scotland.
3. Ibid., 210.
4. F. R. Webber, *A History of Preaching in Britain and America* (Milwaukee: Northwestern, 1955), 2:322.
5. Ibid., 2:323.
6. Richard Allan Riesen, *Criticism and Faith in Late Victorian Scotland* (Lanham, Md.: University Press of America, 1985).

9.1.7 EDWARD IRVING—LED ASTRAY

No man that I have known had a sunnier type of character or so little hatred toward any man or thing. Noble Irving! He was the faithful elder

brother of my life in those years—generous, wise, beneficent all his dealings and discoursings were.

—Thomas Carlyle after Irving's death

He was unquestionably, by many degrees, the greatest orator of our times.
Of him indeed, more than any man whom I have seen throughout my
whole experience, it might be said with truth and emphasis, that he was
a Boanerges, a son of thunder.

—Thomas De Quincy

He put me in mind of the devil disguised as an angel of light.

—Sir Walter Scott

The path to preaching prowess is a slippery slope, and dangers lurk on every
side. **Edward Irving** (1792–1834) exemplified the amazingly gifted preacher
who stumbles and falls down that slope. Irving was born in Annan near Dumfries
and studied at Edinburgh, supporting his work in divinity by teaching school in
Haddington and Kirkaldy. He had decided to go to America when Thomas
Chalmers asked him to assist him in ministry in the slums of Glasgow.

Mrs. Oliphant's *Life of Edward Irving* is particularly moving in its depiction
of Irving's compassion and his marked influence among the disenfranchised of
society. His millennialism was contagious. In 1822 he took a call to London to
serve a small group of Scots living there. The ministry was so successful that the
beautiful National Scottish Church at Regent Square was built for him in 1827.

Tall and strapping, handsome and willowy, Irving took London by storm. A
vast influx of hearers came to hear his brilliant rhetoric: "Statesmen, philosophers, poets, painters, and literary men; peers, merchants and fashionable ladies
in abundance."[1] Stoughton opined:

Never since George Whitefield had anyone so arrested attention; and Irving went far beyond Whitefield in attracting the respectful, even the admiring, notice of lords, ladies and commons. His name was on every lip.
Newspapers, magazines and reviews discussed his merits; a caricature
in shop windows hit off his eccentricities.[2]

Another had the impression that "He has a powerful voice, feels always warmly,
is prompt in his expression, and not very careful of his words."[3] In the first quarter of Irving's ministry in London, seatholders increased from fifty to fifteen
hundred.

This was indeed gratifying to an ambitious man but exceedingly dangerous. His
sermons became long and ranting. He expressed heterodox views on the sinless
humanity of our Lord. Wilks says he fed his soul on Chrysostom, Jeremy Taylor,
and Hooker but regarded no contemporary as able except for Chalmers.[4] He was
impatient with the old paths, and espoused extreme views on prophesying and on
speaking in tongues, although he himself never used the gifts publicly.

Irving's views became highly sacramentarian, and he established the Catholic

Apostolic Church. Warfield attributed his subsequent defrocking and collapse to "his over-weening confidence in himself."[5] His earlier sermons are worthy of emulation, but he soon moved "beyond the sermon" to the "oration," so much better suited to the higher class of person he was reaching. He flaunted his success shamelessly.[6]

Something seemed to have snapped inside of Irving. The influence of the romantic Samuel Taylor Coleridge did not help (cf. 8.2), and his disappointment in love (Jane, for whom he cherished a great affection, married Thomas Carlyle) fueled his instability. Dallimore bemoans that Irving began using a text as a peg for speculative ideas rather than opening the text expositorily.[7] He died at forty-two without ever fulfilling the exciting promise his gifts seemed to portend. McCheyne eulogized him at his passing:

> I look back upon him with awe, as on the saints and martyrs of old. A holy man in spite of all his delusions and errors. He is now with his God and Saviour whom he wronged so much, yet I am persuaded, loved so sincerely.[8]

---

1. Nigel M. de S. Cameron, ed., *Dictionary of Scottish Church History and Theology* (Downers Grove, Ill.: InterVarsity Press, 1993), 436.
2. A. E. Garvie, *The Christian Preacher* (New York: Scribner's, 1923), 227.
3. T. Harwood Pattison, *The History of Christian Preaching* (Philadelphia: American Baptist Publication Society, 1903), 299.
4. Arnold Dallimore, *Forerunner of the Charismatic Movement: The Life of Edward Irving* (Chicago: Moody, 1983), 28.
5. Ibid., 52.
6. Ibid., 54. An important analysis is found in Gordon Strachan, *The Pentecostal Theology of Edward Irving* (Peabody, Mass.: Hendrickson, 1973), who points out that Karl Barth acknowledges Irving as the forerunner of those holding to a radical Christology, in this case believing Christ has a fallen nature; see *Church Dogmatics*, 1.2 (153–54).
7. Ibid., 74.
8. Cameron, *Dictionary of Scottish Church History and Theology*, 437.

9.2 THE AMERICAN WHIRLPOOL

> The great engine for maintaining the effectiveness of religion in national life was not dogma at all but revivalism, intense, immediate and personal.
> —Robert Bellah in *The Broken Covenant*

The Second Great Awakening (1776–1810) touched both America and Europe. Bebbington correctly remarks, "Preaching the gospel was the chief method of winning converts."[1] We see this in the itinerations of **Henry Alline** (1748–1784) in Nova Scotia (although Alline stumbled toward the end of his ministry).

The powerful tides of deism and skepticism washed in on the newly independent colonies through the speeches and writings of **Thomas Paine** (1737–1809). Paine was a Methodist lay preacher at one time. Born in Thetford in England, he is mentioned in the journals of John Wesley as ministering in Sandwich.[2] Yet he became hostile toward all doctrine, and developed a particular contempt for the Bible and the cross of Christ. His every effort was bent toward the demolition of "the Christian view of revelation."[3]

But the resurgence of the Second Awakening counteracted his efforts and greatly Christianized the United States.[4] Indeed, democracy owes a great debt to Colonial preaching. It is our purpose to explore this relationship and its concomitants.[5] Of course there was transatlantic dialogue. Chalmers was indebted to Thomas Reid's commonsense realism, whose influence filtered across the ocean and helped shape Princeton Seminary.

---

1. D. W. Bebbington, *Evangelicalism in Modern Britain* (London: Allen and Unwin, 1989), 5.
2. John Keane, *Thomas Paine: A Political Life* (Boston: Little, Brown, 1995), 46.
3. Ibid., 498.
4. Ibid., 500ff.
5. George Mecklenburg, *Bowing the Preacher Out of Politics* (New York: Revell, 1928), N.B. chapter 6, "The Debt of Democracy to Colonial Preaching," 48–60; also Ellis Sandoz, ed., *Political Sermons of the American Founding Era: 1730–1805* (Indianapolis: Liberty Press, 1991). The concern is that the new nation be "under God."

9.2.1   TIMOTHY DWIGHT—BRIGHTENING THE HORIZON

The plain meaning is the true meaning.

The trophies of the Cross are being multiplied.

—Timothy Dwight

Siren voices sought to lure spiritual leaders in the new republic away from their biblical roots. Among those who succumbed were the Unitarians, who repudiated core doctrines such as inerrant biblical authority,[1] or offbeat movements like the Shakers of Ann Lee with their eschatological proclamation that "Christ has come a second time" and who paid scant attention to preaching.[2]

Against these threats stood **Timothy Dwight** (1752–1817), the son of Jonathan Edwards' daughter. Young Timothy read Scripture with ease at four years of age and was studying Latin at six. Entering Yale at thirteen, he gave himself to revelry and card playing, but soon grew serious in his studies and became a tutor at Yale. At the time, homiletical training was largely an indoctrination in classical rhetoric. This was helpful for Dwight because he was hesitant in his speech. He became accomplished at style and composition, using Ward's *System of Oratory*.

In 1774 Dwight was converted. He joined the church and shortly after was married. For thirteen months he served as a chaplain in the Continental Army. After his ordination he took a congregation in Greenfield, Connecticut, and inveighed strongly against the Half-Way Covenant. He gave himself to preaching for the salvation of men "in a way that is subservient to the divine glory."[3] Eventually Dwight ministered in Greenfield for twelve years and established Dwight's Academy to supplement his annual income of five-hundred dollars. He also wrote hymns. His "I Love Thy Kingdom, Lord" is still one of the richest we have.

Tall, with an impressive appearance and voice, Timothy Dwight was elected president of Yale in 1795. Spirituality was at low ebb when he came and found, as he said, "a most ungodly state." His objective was to break the enemy's grip on Yale even though there were few Christians there. Lyman Beecher, who was converted in those years, describes the situation:

> Most of the class before me were infidels. They thought the faculty was afraid of free discussion; but when they handed Doctor Dwight a list of subjects for class disputation, to their surprise he selected this: "Is the Bible the Word of God?" and told them to do their best. He heard all they had to say, answered them, and there was an end. He preached incessantly for six months on the subject and all infidelity skulked and hid its head.[4]

A great outpouring of the Holy Spirit came and infidelity was routed. "No weeds of infidelity throve there," he noted. Beecher reported hearing him preach from Jeremiah 8:20. To use his words, "A whole avalanche rolled down on my mind. I went home weeping every step."[5] The series of sermons he preached to the class remain in his *Theology*.

Revivals came to Yale in 1808, 1812 to 1813, and 1814 to 1815. On one day fifty-two students came for prayer, and one hundred students were converted in the last visit. The revival spread to Princeton, where eighty of the one hundred five students there were converted and twenty-five went into the ministry.

Dwight's health collapsed in 1816. He died the following year of cancer of the bladder. His eloquent and forceful preaching challenged the fashionable infidelity and skepticism and caused "these things to lose their influence."[6]

---

1. John Fea, "Theodore Parker and the Nineteenth-Century Assault on Biblical Authority," *Michigan Theological Journal* 3 (1992): 65–80. Fea argues: "Parker's understanding of orthodoxy not only supports the fact that the infallibility of Scripture was dominant in the nineteenth century, but that this conservative position on the Bible was operative throughout all of church history. Parker's description of nineteenth-century bibliology seems not only to refute Sandeen's understanding of the history of this doctrine, but also makes a dent in the proposal expounded by those who would argue that the entire Christian Church never held to a view of infallibility in areas of science and history" (78).

2. Stephen J. Stein, *The Shaker Experience in America* (New Haven, Conn.: Yale University Press, 1992). Although later under the influence of American revivalism, Shakers began to pay attention to the Bible, and in their Shaker Manifesto have a column on the Bible and using expository methods (329). Shakers went to hear both Henry Ward Beecher and D. L. Moody.

3. Charles Cunningham, *Timothy Dwight: 1752–1817* (New York: Macmillan, 1942), 110.
4. T. Harwood Pattison, *A History of Christian Preaching* (Philadelphia: American Baptist Publication Society, 1903), 364.
5. Cunningham, *Timothy Dwight,* 334.
6. F. R. Webber, *A History of Preaching in Britain and America* (Milwaukee: Northwestern, 1957), 3:153. For important insights on the theological struggle at this time, cf. Joseph Conforti, *Samuel Hopkins and the New Divinity Movement: Calvinism, the Congregational Ministry and Reform in New England Between the Great Awakenings* (New York: Christian University Press, 1981).

9.2.2 JOHN WITHERSPOON—BUILDING THE BODY

So very sacred a thing indeed is truth, that the very shadow of departure from it is to be avoided. . . . Let me therefore recommend to you a strict universal and scrupulous regard to truth; it will give dignity to your character, it will put power into your affairs, it will excite the most unbounded confidence, so that whether your view be your own interest, or the service of others, it promises you the most assured success.

—John Witherspoon

Dr. Witherspoon is a character well known. He is a man of considerable abilities, a little tinctured with fanaticism of the Whitefieldian complexion. Some years ago we had frequent occasion of mentioning his writings published while he was a minister in Scotland, his native country. He is now become an eminent preacher among the Americans . . . his doctrines breathe a spirit so candid and so agreeable to the moderation of the Christian character that, excepting a few passages tending to encourage the Americans in their scheme of independency, this animated and pious discourse might have been delivered with great acceptance and possibly with good effect before any Fast Day audience in the Kingdom without subjecting the preacher to the imputation of disloyalty or disaffection to the government.

—*The Monthly Review*

The formative influence of preachers and preaching on the American Revolution and the subsequent emergence of the republic is generally acknowledged.[1] Such a shaper of men—and the only clergyman to sign the Declaration of Independence in 1776—was the illustrious preacher and longtime president of the College of New Jersey (later Princeton), **John Witherspoon** (1723–1794).

Witherspoon was born in a devout minister's home in Gifford, four miles southeast of Haddington. He entered Edinburgh at age thirteen. Ordained in 1743, he began his ministry in Beith in Ayrshire. Imprisoned briefly by the forces of the Pretender, he moved on to Paisley. A champion of orthodoxy and a preacher of the fundamental core of the gospel, he enjoyed twenty-four years of ministry and publishing. His *Essay on Justification* had wide circulation in Scotland. Through the influence of John Erskine, Witherspoon made contact with the board of the College of New Jersey. The emissary from America had difficulty in persuading Mrs. Witherspoon, but finally Witherspoon accepted the call to the presidency in 1768.

Just as Timothy Dwight was an archfederalist, Witherspoon rapidly became an American. None doubted he stood on the Colonial side. His celebrated sermon on "Christian Magnanimity," preached from 1 Thessalonians 2:12 on the occasion of commencement in 1775, was a defining moment.[2] Another sermon preached on the fast day in May 1776 was widely heralded. He was appointed as a delegate to the Continental Congress and presented his credentials on June 28, 1976.

The College of New Jersey grew rapidly. Nine of its graduates were delegates to the Constitutional Convention—fully one-sixth of the entire delegation. Aaron Burr and James Madison were both among the alumni.[3]

During debate in the Continental Congress, a dissenter ventured that the colonies were not ripe for independence, "Dr. Witherspoon rose to his great height and retorted in his strong Scottish brogue, 'In my judgment, sir, we are not only ripe but rotting.'"[4] When the British soldiers neared Princeton, Witherspoon closed the college. The Redcoats billeted in Nassau Hall and destroyed the college library. The college suffered abysmally from neglect during these years.[5]

During the war, Witherspoon was returned to Congress year after year and sat on the war board in some of the most critical phases of the rebellion. He sat on several committees with his former student, James Madison, whose gifts and convictions were increasingly decisive in deliberations. He regularly preached in Philadelphia and, on one occasion, expounded the text "redeeming the time" with a number of his fellow members of Congress present.[6]

After retiring from Congress, Witherspoon devoted his life to recouping the fortunes of the college. He made one bold trip back to Scotland and England, where he did some preaching but could raise no funds. At commencement in 1783, virtually the whole Congress and General George Washington were present. Washington presented a gift of fifty guineas to the college and sat for a portrait which still hangs at Princeton.[7]

When Witherspoon's daughter died, he preached a series of sixteen sermons on submission to God's will from Luke 22:42. He died in 1794 in his seventy-second year.

How significant that a stalwart champion of the Bible as "the unerring standard" and the gospel as the solution to the human predicament should have such opportunity to influence the founding days of our country. Here indeed is a light set upon a hill.

---

1. Bernard Bailyn, *Faces of Revolution: Personalities and Themes in the Struggle for American Independence* (New York: Knopf, 1990). In a poignant section Bailyn shows an obscure Connecticut minister, Stephen Johnson, who in 1765 published six newspaper articles and a sermon that anticipate "almost the entire range of arguments that would be debated in the coming decade."

2. Varnum Lansing Collins, *President Witherspoon* (Princeton, N.J.: Princeton University Press, 1925), 1:178.
3. John Eidsmoe, *Christianity and the Constitution: The Faith of Our Founding Fathers* (Grand Rapids: Baker, 1987), 83.
4. Merle Sinclair and Annabel Douglas McArthur, *They Signed for Us* (New York: Hawthorne, 1957), 43.
5. Collins, *President Witherspoon*, 118. A choice sermon by John Witherspoon is "On Ministerial Character and Duty" from 2 Corinthians 4:13, "We also believe and therefore speak" in *Sermons by the Late John Witherspoon* (Edinburgh, 1798), 1–19.
6. Ibid., 22.
7. Ibid., 135–36.

9.2.3 *Francis Asbury—Emblazoning the Gospel*

July 28: Arose, as I commonly do, before five o'clock to study the Bible. I find none like it; and find it of more consequence for a preacher to know his Bible well than all the books and languages in the world—for he is not to preach these, but the Word of God.

Sunday, July 20, 1880, Lynn, Massachusetts: There had been a long drought here, and nature seemed as if she were about to droop and die. We addressed the throne of Grace most fervently and solemnly, and had showers of blessings. Whilst I was preaching, the wind came up and appeared to whirl around every point, and most gracious rain came on; this I considered as a most signal instance of divine goodness.

—from Francis Asbury's journal

In his stimulating *The Democratization of American Christianity,* Nathan Hatch argues that the Second Great Awakening tended to be antielitist, anticlerical, and in many cases anti-Calvinistic. As the population surged over the Alleghenies, the tilt was away from Episcopal, Congregational, and Presbyterian toward Methodist, Baptist, and Christian (Campbellite) expressions of spiritual fervor.

Methodist strength was minimal at the time of the Revolution, but by 1820 membership had reached a quarter of a million and by 1830 was twice that. Baptists multiplied ten times in the three decades following the revolution.[1] In all of this, Hatch sees the inversion of authority, the "withering of establishments," and "the triumph of vernacular preaching" in a climate that saw the "birth of American gospel music."[2] At the very forefront of this magnificent advance was what Hatch calls "the spartan mission of Francis Asbury."[3]

Francis Asbury (1745–1816) was born in Hamsted Bridge near Birmingham in England in modest circumstances. As a youth he was apprenticed to a blacksmith. His Welsh mother taught him the Scriptures and encouraged him to hear the itinerant Methodist preacher who visited their town. Praying in his father's barn at the age of fourteen, Asbury was converted and almost at once began to preach three, four, or five times a week.[4] He took his first circuit in 1766 and ultimately volunteered to go to America, sailing in 1771.

At his first conference, there were ten preachers representing about six hundred Methodists in America; at his last conference seven hundred preachers represented 218,000 registered communicants. He was first cosuperintendent with **Thomas Coke** (1747–1814). When Coke returned to England in 1784, Asbury was elected bishop.

Asbury embodied what Hatch calls "an ethic of sacrifice." He worked indefatigably and preached in excess of 16,500 sermons until he died at Spotsylvania in 1816.

Asbury was a school dropout and a simple gardener's son, yet he had more power than any other figure in religion in his time. A plain preacher, Asbury was poor, unworldly, and celibate all his life. He feared those who wanted to become great without work and sacrifice. "Don't be a gentleman," he urged, "be a common man." His heart's longing was "Lord, keep me from all superfluity of dress, and from preaching empty stuff to please the ear, instead of changing the heart." He discarded Wesley's liturgical and sacramental style, even doing away with clerical dress.

Revival fires began to burn after 1800 and camp meetings proliferated.[5] Again Asbury took to the circuit. As he charged his preachers: "When you go into the pulpit, go from your closets . . . take with you your hearts full of fresh spring water from heaven, and preach Christ crucified and the resurrection, and that will conquer the world."[6]

Half of the circuit riders died before they were thirty. Yet Asbury rode on. Often in ill-health, he traveled on horseback twenty-five to fifty miles a day. His remarkable journal is an endless reiteration of "I preached" and "I preached."

Wednesday, June 6: We had twelve miles to R.'s, along a busy, hilly road. A poor woman with a little horse, without a saddle, outwent us up and down the hills, and, when we came to the place appointed, the Lord met with and blessed her soul. . . . [Later he preached to three hundred people] but there were so many wicked whiskey-drinkers, who brought with them so much of the devil, that I had little satisfaction in preaching.[7]

In his journal we have outlines of two hundred sermons and texts for another seven hundred. He did not aspire to be nor was he ever an orator, but steeped in Scripture as he was, he would always take a text and preach it with authority. He preached on Galatians 6:14, endeavoring to show:

1. What it is for a man to glory in a thing;
2. What men glory in, which is not the cross of Christ;
3. What is glory in the cross of Christ;
4. How a person may know when he glories in the cross of Christ—namely, by the world being crucified to him and he to the world.[8]

One contemporary wrote that Asbury's sermons were the result of sound wisdom and good common sense and were "delivered with great authority and gravity, often attended with divine unction, which made them as refreshing as the dew of heaven."[9] Usually he preached an hour even when he was old and frail and had to be literally carried to the pulpit. He wrote:

> I preached at the chapel, to about four hundred serious people, from John 4:48: I spoke for two hours; perhaps it is the last time . . .[10]

He delighted in preaching on the beauties of the Book of Revelation. He read the Scripture effectively, and people were moved in its presentation by itself.[11] He had haunting dreams of heaven and hell. In his notes to the Discipline, he urges his preachers "to convince sinners of their danger, to set forth the atoning blood, to keep engagements and that on time, to be deeply serious, to be cautious of allegorizing, to avoid awkward gestures, to beware of writing for the press on the advice of a few enthusiastic friends."[12] He used vivid illustrations and was particularly effective in ordination sermons and at funerals.

The memorial statue of Asbury in Washington, D.C. is that of a weary old man and a tired horse with a drooping head. Yet the statue breathes "dogged determination." In dedicating the monument in 1924, President Coolidge paid tribute to Asbury as "one of the builders of our nation, this circuit rider who spent his life making strong the foundation on which our Government rests."

---

1. Nathan O. Hatch, *The Democratization of American Christianity* (New Haven, Conn.: Yale University Press, 1989), 3. Note also Hatch's important redefinition of the Second Great Awakening, Appendix 1.
2. Ibid., 125.
3. Ibid., 81ff.
4. James Lewis, *Francis Asbury: Bishop of the Methodist Episcopal Church* (London: Epworth, 1927), 16.
5. A. K. Curtis, ed. "Spiritual Awakenings in North America," *Christian History* 8, no. 3, issue 23. An important source. In his disappointing *Revivals and Revivalism* (Edinburgh: Banner of Truth, 1994), Iain H. Murray is too dismissive of camp meetings, the altar call, and "decisionist evangelism." Where is evangelical catholicity?
6. Charles Ludwig, *Francis Asbury: God's Circuit Rider* (Milford, Mich.: Mott Media, 1984), 165.
7. Lewis, *Francis Asbury,* 87.
8. Ibid., 126.
9. Herbert Asbury, *A Methodist Saint: The Life of Bishop Asbury* (New York: Knopf, 1927), 281.
10. L. C. Rudolph, *Francis Asbury* (Nashville: Abingdon, 1966), 81.
11. Ibid., 93.
12. Ibid.

9.2.4 EDWARD GRIFFEN—BREATHING THE SPIRIT

This pulpit was not erected to hurl anathemas against men who to their own master must stand or fall. . . . The business to be transacted here lies

not between us and our brethren of different names or opinions, but between God and our own souls.
—Sermon on the occasion of the dedication of Park Street Church

But let any man continually carry about him a full and distinct image of God, exhibiting all the truths of His Word, all the strictness of His law, all the guilt and danger of sinners—carrying reproof to everything selfish, everything proud, everything vain, everything that does not make God the supreme object—and let him moreover be constituted by his age or office a reprover; and there is not a community of worldly men in Christendom who will not be offended . . . This must be true or the "carnal mind" is no longer "enmity against God."
—Edward D. Griffin

While Nathan Hatch's thesis as to the democratization of Christianity in the burgeoning new nation has validity, there is yet the moving of the Spirit in the more traditional and establishment-type churches. The effective preaching ministry of **Edward D. Griffin** (1770–1837) surely demonstrates this. Griffin was born into a home of comfortable means and studied at Yale. His parents had no particular spiritual profession, but young Edward had "religious impressions" from very early in his life. After an illness at Yale, he sought the Bible and discovered the Sermon on the Mount in which "the whole character of Christ as a preacher opened to my view."[1] The upshot was "I chose to be a minister . . . I hugged the cross."

Griffin studied theology with **Jonathan Edwards Jr.** (1745–1801), who denied imputation and advanced the governmental view of the atonement. Griffin himself was thoroughly orthodox. Strikingly handsome, Griffin was tall, with a powerful voice and effective gesture. Initially he did supply preaching at Park Street, or "Brimstone Corner," as it was called. Henry James called it "the most interesting mass of brick and mortar in America."[2] He soon took a pastorate in New Hartford, followed by a charge in Newark, New Jersey. He served briefly as Bartlett Professor of Pulpit Eloquence at the new Andover Theological Seminary, founded to set forth orthodoxy more clearly and compellingly. Griffin went on to the pastorate of historic Park Street Church in Boston (1809–1815).

After some tensions over finances in Boston, Griffin went back to the strategic pulpit in Newark and then in 1821 on to the presidency of Williams College, where the famous Haystack Prayer Meetings took place. When his health failed in 1837, he returned to Newark where he died.

Griffin always had a strong missionary impulse. He was part of the American Board of Commissioners for Foreign Missions, which sent out Adoniram Judson, Samuel Newell, Samuel Nott, Gordon Hall, and Luther Rice, and was one of the founders of the American Bible Society.

His Park Street lectures on the theological issues of the day show him to be a strong, traditional Calvinist.[3] His method of pulpit preparation was unique. He wrote out numerous pages of content and text without any particular care for logical order. He would then organize the material.[4] His sermons show various patterns in structure, including the interrogative type outline as in the sermon he preached at the dedication of Park Street Church on the corner of Park and Tremont on the Commons on January 10, 1810, from 2 Chronicles 6:18: (1) Does the omnipresent God dwell in any one place? (2) Will God dwell with men on the earth? and (3) Can it be presumed that he will dwell in this house which we have built? His answer was in the affirmative.[5] The collected sermons are a rich repository, especially "Adam, Our Federal Head" from Romans 5:12–19,[6] "Returning from Crucifixion" from Luke 23:47–49,[7] and "The Brazen Serpent" from John 3:14–15.[8]

His ministry and preaching were always revivalistic. From his very first sermon, "His preaching was almost immediately attended by manifest tokens of the presence of the Holy Spirit."[9] The cross of Christ and the blood of the Savior were constant themes. His former view of the atonement (governmental) was abandoned: "God has declared that he will accept this sacrifice for men, and we must believe him, and must expect to discover the reality and glory of the atonement by faith and not by speculation."[10]

Griffin was a pastor who not only visited conscientiously but also preached passionately. He exhibited a warm and tender generosity to his flock and always preached for conversions. His biographer claims, "It would be difficult to name the individual in our country since the days of Whitefield who has been instrumental of an equal number of hopeful conversions."[11] In one stirring of the Spirit in Newark, ninety-seven people joined the church in one day.[12]

Strong biblical and doctrinal preaching built the nation and changed lives. They will still do so today.

---

1. William B. Sprague, *Sermons of Edward D. Griffin and a Memoir of His Life*, vol. 1 (Edinburgh: Banner of Truth, 1987), 5.
2. H. Crosby Englizian, *Brimstone Corner: Park Street Church Boston* (Chicago: Moody, 1968), 11.
3. Ibid., 59.
4. F. R. Webber, *A History of Preaching in Britain and America* (Milwaukee: Northwestern, 1957), 3:174.
5. Englizian, *Brimstone Corner,* 38.
6. Sprague, *Sermons of Edward D. Griffin,* 305.
7. Ibid., 597.
8. Ibid., 2:15.
9. Ibid., 8.
10. Ibid., 70.
11. Ibid., 259.
12. Ibid., 90.

9.2.5 ARCHIBALD ALEXANDER—BRACING THE FOUNDATIONS

He appeared absolutely overpowered by the truths he was presenting and his every feature was illuminated and glowing with the fire within.
—Comment by someone listening to Archibald Alexander preach

The pulpit is no place for historical, philosophical or political discussions . . . Sometimes a preacher becomes so enveloped in criticism or metaphysics that plain people cannot understand him. The minister should be a critic and a metaphysician but carry only the result to the pulpit . . . Preaching the Gospel is not to gratify a refined taste . . . but the preacher should avoid disgusting men of taste . . . It is a grievous fault to speak nonsense in the name of the Lord . . . the main object is to make preaching useful to the souls of men.

—Archibald Alexander

The first president of Princeton Theological Seminary, and the man who set the course for the school so dominant in theology and homiletics, was born in Valley of Virginia, Tidewater country, in 1772. **Archibald Alexander** (1772–1851) was the third of ten children in a prosperous farmer's home. He studied in Liberty Hall, which later became Washington College, but interrupted his schooling to serve as a private tutor for a while. He was converted at seventeen after studying with William Graham, reading John Flavel, and listening to Baptist preachers during what would be called "The Revival of 1789."[1]

Though ultimately a leader of the Old School, Alexander had known "great outpourings of the Holy Spirit" and "the internal evidences of Christianity."[2] Deeply tinctured with the Common Sense Realism of Thomas Reid from Scotland, he sought to set a course between the sterilities of the Enlightenment and the theological mushiness in vogue in much of Pietism. He believed with Edwards that the affections direct the will.

Alexander preached his trial sermon in 1791. Appropriately, the text was from Jeremiah 1:7. He soon served several smaller congregations and itinerated widely as an increasingly sought-after preacher.

He preached with great rapidity ("I ran on until I was perfectly out of breath") and had a habit of "looking steadily down upon the floor." His voice was powerful and clearly heard even in a large room, but "I was so conscious of my own defects that often after preaching, I was ashamed to come down from the pulpit."[3] Two great orators contemporary with Alexander influenced him: Patrick Henry, who lived just six miles away, and John Randolph of Roanoke.[4]

At twenty-five he became president of Hampden-Sidney College, but in a stringent shortage of ministers was called to the pastorate of Third Presbyterian Church in Philadelphia (Pine Street Church). The church flourished and grew 50 percent in his time there. He was elected Moderator of the General Assembly. Throughout his years in Philadelphia, Alexander's neighbor was the English nonconformist and chemist **Joseph Priestly,** who pastored the Universalist congregation where John Adams and other members of Congress attended.

Alexander took a preaching tour of New England. He preached for the eminent Dr. Emmons as well as in Dr. Hopkins' pulpit. (Both Alexander and his successor, Charles Hodge, were Hopkinsian postmillennialists and expected that missions would convert the world.[5]) Alexander's text was John 14:21: "Whoever has my commands and obeys them, he is one who loves me." His outline diverged from the Puritan model, reverting to the more classical type:

I. The foundation of love to Christ as it relates both to the object and subject of the affection;
II. The properties of love to Christ: sincerity, supremacy, constancy;
III. The evidences of love to Christ: a desire of pleasing and fear of offending; a desire of conforming to his character; a desire of communion and sorrow on account of absence; a desire to promote his glory.

Alexander related, "I insisted strongly on the position that love must terminate on the true character of the object beloved."[6]

In 1812 he accepted the call to establish Princeton Seminary. He also served as professor of didactic and polemical divinity. Here the foundations were laid for Princeton Theology, a vital response to the Scottish moderate Hugh Blair's sacred rhetoric at Harvard (which had a damaging impact on Ralph Waldo Emerson). Alexander's "less formal pulpit vitality" reigned at Princeton.[7]

For thirty-nine years Alexander presided over Princeton and the accompanying trend toward expounding larger passages of Scripture. Though short of stature, Alexander was commanding in the pulpit with his "crown of iron-gray hair, uncombed" and his old-fashioned rectangular glasses.[8] For his part, his sermons were not theological lectures but the opening of a text and the division of the same with theological and doctrinal integrity.[9] His evening sermons to students, preached from scraps of paper, were the occasion of many conversions and were typical of "all those qualities which made him eminently popular among the common people, who preferred his free and often irresistible invitations. His lively and penetrative voice was a welcome contrast to the more staid and scholastic addresses which smell of the lamp and sacrifice religious to literary merit."[10]

1. James A. Alexander, *The Life of Archibald Alexander* (New York: Scribner's, 1854), 39ff.
2. Lefferts A. Loetscher, *Facing the Enlightenment and Pietism: Archibald Alexander and the Founding of Princeton Theological Seminary* (Westport, Conn.: Greenwood, 1983), 21.
3. Ibid., 50.
4. One of the best studies of this incomparable orator is that of Russell Kirk, *John Randolph of Roanoke: A Study in American Politics* (Indianapolis: Liberty Press, 1951).
5. John Wheeler Auxier, "Princetonian Eschatology 1812–1878: The Neglect of the Apocalypse" (M.A. thesis, Trinity Evangelical Divinity School, 1986).
6. Alexander, *The Life of Archibald Alexander,* 247.
7. Loetscher, *Facing the Enlightenment and Pietism,* 237.
8. F. R. Webber, *A History of Preaching in Britain and America* (Milwaukee: Northwestern, 1957), 3:187.
9. Alexander, *The Life of Archibald Alexander,* 683. The breadth of Alexander's legacy is seen in his student, Charles Hodge, who spent 1826–1828 in Europe, where he was taught German by George Müller at Halle and contacted Tholuck, Hengstenberg, Olshausen, Krummacher, Neander, Monod, Ewald, and heard Charles Simeon preach in England (A. A. Hodge).
10. Ibid., 377.

9.2.6 LYMAN BEECHER—BEQUEATHING THE LEGACY

When I've nothing to say I always holler.

I went home expecting, and the word was sent up from the Springs that the Lord had come down on the previous Sunday, and that a meeting was appointed for Tuesday evening, and I must not disappoint them. I went and preached. I saw one young man with his head down. I wanted to know if it was an arrow of the Almighty. I came along after the sermon and laid my hand upon his head. He lifted his face, his eyes all full of tears; I saw it was God. Then I went up to the Northwest and the Lord was there; then to Ammigansett and the Lord was there; and the flood was rolling all around. Oh, what a time it was!

I soon found myself harnessed to the Chariot of Christ, whose wheels of fire have rolled onward, high and dreadful to his foes, and glorious to his friends. I could not stop.

—Lyman Beecher

The progenitor of the great house of preaching Beechers was **Lyman Beecher** (1775–1863). Beecher was born in New Haven to a line of blacksmiths and farmers. When his mother died in his third year, he was transplanted to Guilford in Connecticut, where he was raised, and then on to Yale, where he was converted during the presidency of Timothy Dwight (cf. 9.2.1). Already under conviction by thoughts of his hometown inebriate's destiny in hell, Beecher was "defenseless" before President Dwight's sermon on Jeremiah 8:20, "The harvest is past, the summer is ended and we are not saved."[1] "A whole avalanche rolled down," reported Beecher, and he went home "weeping every step." Throughout his ministry, Henry observes, "Hell was dreadfully important to Lyman Beecher."[2] He graduated from Yale in 1797 and studied theology with Dwight.

Beecher was a Calvinist but reacted against what he called "the sloughs of high-Calvinism." He was impatient for revival, and while serving in his first pastoral charge in East Hampton, Long Island (1800–1810), he suffered a total collapse that left him unable to preach for a year. Subsequently he moved to Litchfield, Connecticut, where his ministry was richly blessed.

Beecher was totally dedicated to the temperance cause and preached an epochal series of six sermons which are doubtless some of the strongest preaching on the use of beverage alcohol ever preached.[3] Interestingly, the Old Light Charles Hodge thought that both abolition and temperance were not movements in which Christian ministers should be involved because they were not authorized in the Scripture. But Lyman Beecher thundered out the message:

Oh! were the sky over our heads one great whispering gallery, bringing down about us all the lamentation and woe which intemperance creates, and the form of earth one sonorous medium of sound, bringing up around us from beneath the wailings of the damned, whom the commerce in ardent spirit had sent thither—those tremendous realities assailing our senses would invigorate our conscience and give decision to our purpose of reformation.[4]

When Alexander Hamilton was killed in a duel with Aaron Burr, Beecher preached against dueling. His message helped lead to legislation outlawing dueling. He also preached a notable series at Park Street Church in Boston in 1823 with revival fires burning, and ultimately his son Edward came to serve that congregation as its pastor. His famous sermon on "The Bible as a Code of Laws" was preached first in Litchfield in segments, the final manuscript running to more than fifty pages.

From 1826 through 1832 he served the Hanover Street Church in Boston. Beecher led an overt challenge to the Unitarian tide sweeping New England. The Unitarians were led by the articulate and able **William Ellery Channing.** But Beecher, "in the prayer and in the sermon that seemed like the rolling in of the Atlantic upon the beach," raised a bulwark. His preaching was heavily doctrinal but extremely vital. One contemporary spoke of him "as a thunderbolt—you never knew where it would strike, but you never saw him rise to speak without feeling that so much electricity must strike."[5]

In 1832 Beecher moved west to take the presidency of Lane Seminary in Cincinnati and the pastorate of Second Presbyterian Church, the most distinguished in that city. The Albert Barnes heresy trial in 1831 (charging Barnes with taking up the New Theology and the governmental view of the atonement) ended with Barnes being "provisionally censured."[6] Beecher faced a heresy trial as well. The germs of New England theology lay in his drift from infant damnation and Calvinism toward "a more optimistic anthropology" and an insistence on man's moral ability. He clashed with Charles G. Finney on "the new measures," but agreed with Finney in terms of theological direction. With attorney Salmon P. Chase defending him, Beecher was vindicated. Chase, a member of Second Church, would later join Lincoln's cabinet.

The years at Lane were sometimes turbulent because of controversies over slavery. Theodore Weld, who had been converted by Finney, led debates on the issue. These were eventually banned by the trustees. Professor Asa Mahan led the students up to Oberlin where he became president and Finney Professor of Theology. During the schism between New School and Old School Presbyterians (1835–1846), Beecher desperately sought to save the school from financial ruin.

In 1851, Beecher walked away from Lane and moved to Maine, where his daughter Harriet and her husband, Calvin Stowe, were living. His children were one of his chief legacies, especially Harriet, "a genius in a family of eccentrics," whose *Uncle Tom's Cabin* was so influential in pre-Civil War America. Harriet testified, "I have sat under preaching which didn't hit and didn't warm and did not comfort."[7] It was not her father's "sledgehammer sermons" that she was describing. Son Henry Ward also gained preaching notoriety. His unfortunate leanings will come into focus in the next chapter.

Much in Beecher was modeled on Jonathan Edwards, including the stern stress on God's offended holiness. Beecher was a true revivalist and a hard preacher.

"Cut and thrust, hip and thigh, and [don't] ease off,"[8] he liked to say. He prepared his sermons shortly before the service time and would then rush to the church. On at least one occasion he dispensed with all hymns and prayers.[9] He would expound Scripture, face objections, and then make application. Out on the frontier he preached to thousands in camp meetings and outdoor services and was frequently the agent of multiplied conversions.

When someone asked him what the greatest pursuit was, he replied, "It is not theology; it is not controversy; but it is to save souls."[10] In his declining years Beecher moved to Boston. Once, when reference was made to his failing strength, he leaped up and preached an impassioned sermon as of old.

Lyman Beecher died before his son Henry's scandals blurred Beecher's remarkable legacy.

1. Stuart C. Henry, *Unvanquished Puritan: A Portrait of Lyman Beecher* (Grand Rapids: Eerdmans, 1973), 40.
2. Ibid., 41.
3. Ronald G. Walters, "Strong Drink," in *American Reformers, 1815–1860* (New York: Hill and Wang, 1978), 123–43.
4. T. Harwood Pattison, *The History of Christian Preaching* (Philadelphia: American Baptist Publication Society, 1903), 366.
5. Ibid., 367.
6. Henry, *Unvanquished Puritan,* 107.
7. Joan D. Hedrick, *Harriet Beecher Stowe* (New York: Oxford University Press, 1994), 370.
8. Edward F. Hayward, *Lyman Beecher* (Boston: Pilgrim, 1904), 26.
9. Milton Rugoff, *The Beechers: An American Family in the Nineteenth Century* (New York: Harper, 1981), 76.
10. Pattison, *The History of Christian Preaching,* 367.

9.2.7 ASAHEL NETTLETON—BUDDING OF HOLINESS

It is no use to preach, if the church does not pray.

—Asahel Nettleton

I suppose no minister of his time was the means of so many conversions. . . . He . . . would sway an audience as the trees of the forest are moved by a mighty wind.

—Francis Wayland, president of Brown University, 1827–1855

Often overlooked in the history of preaching is **Asahel Nettleton** (1783–1844), possibly the greatest evangelist New England saw since George Whitefield. Nettleton was God's instrument in bringing more than twenty-five thousand converts to Christ. He was born on a farm in Killingworth, Connecticut, near New Haven, at a time when the excesses of past revivals, the extreme behavior of the Davenportites, and the roving evangelists made most church people leery of revival. The "New Divinity" preachers did call for immediate repentance[1] (as opposed to the "Old," who maintained that God would do it in his own time).

At about eighteen, Nettleton had ominous thoughts of divine judgment after a Thanksgiving ball in his community. After hearing sermons by his pastor, Josiah Andrews, on regeneration and the danger of quenching the Spirit, he had a genuine conversion.[2] Soon after, he felt called to missionary service. Nettleton went on to Yale in 1805 and witnessed the moving of the Spirit there under President Dwight. Touched by the teaching that came out of Yale, Nettleton saw that "man has the power and duty to repent."[3] He was licensed and began to preach as an evangelist, experiencing remarkable visits from heaven in locales like Newington where converts swelled the membership from 64 to 132.

Stocky in build and ruddy in complexion, Nettleton was not the highly refined preacher that some of his compatriots were. Yet he had a dramatic flair, using a theatrical introduction and employing "the vacant people" to good effect, often likened to the rustic John Bunyan.[4] In all of the preaching by American-trained preachers at this time we see a marked move away from the Puritan style, influenced by the more classical rhetorical instruction, back to the modified form espoused by Hyperius and Henry Smith (cf. 6.1). Classical emphases were mixed with a religious intellectualism after the colonial period, and a marked English influence crept in.[5]

Nettleton's friend Bennet Tyler preserved specimens of Asa's preaching. His sermon on John 4:29, "Come, see a man which told me all things that ever I did," is a typical example:

I. The duty of preachers. It is to tell sinners their hearts. "He told me . . ."
II. Preaching which discloses the hearts of sinners is likely to be remembered. "He told me all things . . ."
III. The preacher who tells sinners their hearts is not likely to want for hearers. The invitation will be given, "Come, see the man which told me . . ."
IV. The conversion of one sinner is likely to be followed by the conversion of others. The invitation was complied with and a great spiritual harvest followed.[6]

Some of these messages are remarkably creative as "Some who are living, greater sinners than some who are in Hell," from Luke 13:1–5.[7] Dr. Wayland of Brown, who had heard Chalmers, gave Nettleton high marks for logical coherence, positive use of questions, and doctrinal thoroughness. His voice was "piercing," and his eyes are described by one thoughtful hearer:

But his eye, after all, was the master power in his delivery. Full and clear and sharp, its glances, in the most animated parts of his discourses, were quick and penetrating, beyond almost anything I recollect ever to have witnessed. He seemed to look every hearer in the face, or rather to look into his soul, almost at one and the same moment.[8]

He pleaded and persuaded in such a manner that even Thornbury concedes that he scarcely sounded like a Calvinist. In fact, he introduced inquiry meetings and anxious services for those exercised in conviction.

In 1822 Nettleton was drastically limited for two years by typhus fever. During that confinement he produced his *Village Hymns,* which was sorely needed in New England, and introduced such jewels as Tappan's "Tis Midnight and on Olive's Brow" and many others. He never truly recovered from his illness but did resume itineration particularly in the South. In 1831 he visited Scotland and Europe, where no auspicious response attended his preaching but where he had excellent opportunity to network with such as John Angell James of Carr's Lane, Birmingham, William Jay, Robert Murray McCheyne, and Andrew Bonar. Both of the latter were divinity students at Edinburgh at the time.[9]

Not only was Nettleton dogged by ill health, but slanderous charges of immoral behavior dulled the luster of his last years, and he was constantly embroiled in controversy. He was troubled by reports of the Western revivals, particularly under Charles G. Finney, whose "new measures" greatly perturbed him. Nettleton's concerns included the anxious seat, women praying in public in mixed assemblies, praying for individuals specifically by name, hasty recognition of individuals as converted, and severe language in preaching.[10] The two antagonists met several times without resolving their differences, but both made clear they doubted neither the converts nor the sincerity of the other.

Deepening tensions over the New England Theology of Nathaniel Taylor were foreshadowing the tragic American denial of sin and depravity as well as imputation. This would all have a negative effect on Phillips Brooks and Henry Ward Beecher, and indeed persists to our own time. Oddly enough, both Samuel Hopkins and Charles Finney denied imputation, and poor Lyman Beecher tried to bridge all parties. Even Nettleton was veering toward the governmental view of the atonement and denying that a price had to be paid, though he stood against Beecher and Taylor in the crucial encounters. New England theology was in crisis.

In 1834, Bennet Tyler established a training school in protest against New England Theology which later became the Hartford Seminary. Tyler became the first president, and Nettleton became professor of pastoral duty. As a tribute to his biblical learning, the Nettleton Rhetorical Society was founded. The Society served as a memorial to "his defense of the faith and dedication to a style and vivacity of thought which was able to arrest, interest and instruct."[11]

We have just the skeletons of Nettleton's sermons, but sufficient testimony remains of the rich illustrative material and vocabulary employed by this precious servant of Christ. Nettleton finally succumbed to his physical ailments and died in 1844.

---

1. Sherry Pierpont May, "Asahel Nettleton: Nineteenth-Century American Revivalist" (Ph.D. dissertation, Drew University, 1969), 23.
2. Bennet Tyler, ed., Andrew A. Bonar, *Nettleton and His Labours* (Edinburgh: Banner of Truth, 1854), 23ff.
3. May, "Asahel Nettleton," 48.
4. J. F. Thornbury, *God-Sent Revival: The Story of Asahel Nettleton and the Second Great Awakening* (Welwyn, Herts, England: Evangelical Press, 1977), 19, 73.

5. Warren Wiersbe and Lloyd M. Perry, *The Wycliffe Handbook of Preachers and Preaching* (Chicago: Moody, 1984), 118ff.

6. Tyler, *Nettleton and His Labours,* 176.

7. Ibid., 185.

8. Thornbury, *God-Sent Revival,* 106.

9. Ibid., 206.

10. May, "Asahel Nettleton," 106.

11. Thornbury, *God-Sent Revival,* 222.

9.2.8   GARDINER SPRING—BATTLING FOR THE TRUTH

Few know how much they are under obligations to the pulpit. They boast of other influences but overlook this simple institution of heavenly wisdom. But for this single institution, what a world would this earth of ours have been! Blessed are the people that "know the joyful sound." Favored is the man who bears even nothing more than the mark of the pulpit upon his conscience, exciting his fears, restraining his vices, and reaching forth its hand to keep him from the gulf of perdition before the time!

Different ages of the world and different lands and different departments of the Christian church are a sort of transcript of the pulpits that have instructed them, and bear their peculiarities to the present hour.

Oh, if ministers only saw the inconceivable glory that is before them, and the preciousness of Christ, they would not be able to refrain from going about, leaping and clapping their hands for joy, and exclaiming, I am a minister of Christ! I am a minister of Christ!

—Gardiner Spring

Gardiner Spring (1785–1872) was born into the home of a prominent clergyman, Samuel Spring, in Newburyport, Massachusetts, the town in which George Whitefield died. The elder Spring had been a chaplain in the Continental Army. Gardiner Spring was raised in this godly environment and went on to Yale and then to Bermuda briefly while studying for the law. He was admitted to the bar. Yet he felt God's call to ministry and went on to Andover Seminary (of which his father was a founder). He was ordained to the ministry in 1810 as he began his ministry at the Brick Presbyterian Church in New York City. He remained in that charge for sixty-two years until his death.

Spring was a staunch Calvinist with a slight Hopkinsian tinge. He was a critic of what he called "spurious revivals." Indeed we have the spurious and the genuine described in Scripture, an example of a spurious revival under Joash (2 Chron. 24), and a genuine revival under Hezekiah (2 Chron. 29ff.). A close friend of Nettleton, he was in the middle of much of the turmoil in the nineteenth century. His first four years in New York City were uneventful, but then waves of revival swept over pastor and people. He wrote widely and was active in many missionary endeavors. One of his choice volumes, *The Power of the Pulpit,* is an example of an able preacher's serious reflection on the craft. He believed preaching to be the preeminent task of the pastor.[1]

Here is a capable preacher who pondered everything from the indispensable message to the urgent necessity of "feeling his subject." He pleaded for integrity, and urged that the preacher's heart "be a transcript of his sermons, and then he will be a chosen vessel to carry to lost men his name who was crucified."[2] Preaching is what angels wished to do, he alleged, and insisted that those who train preachers be deeply versed in the pastoral office. Preachers have a duty to enjoy their office, for indeed:

> It is the Saviour's voice by whom this message is uttered. He bows the heavens and comes down. He walks amidst the golden candlesticks. When his ministers speak in his name, he is with them; when his people meet together, he is there. He will be sanctified in them that come nigh him, and before all the people will he be glorified.[3]

Spring was of the conviction that the preacher should "preach as though he were in sight of the cross and heard the groans of the Mighty Sufferer of Calvary." The centrality of the cross and samples of his style may be examined in his priceless volume *The Attraction of the Cross*.[4]

Spring held that all things are tributary to the cross and that "the cross was designed to be the most compendious and vivid expression of all religious truth."[5] In a time when many were slipping from the penal and forensic view of the sacrifice at Calvary, Spring stood steadfastly for propitiation. The wave of the future would be New England Theology and the governmental view, but Spring pointed out the intertwining of sin, repentance, and substitutionary atonement. He trumpeted the cross as "the only propitiation," a transaction by which Christ bore our sins in his own body. In his W. H. Griffith Thomas Lectures at Dallas Theological Seminary in 1987, David Wells aptly demonstrates how crucial the debate over the atonement was in the nineteenth century. He quotes A. A. Hodge on the point at hand:

> The two great doctrines just at present most generally brought into question, and which have suffered most at the hands of Rationalistic criticism, are those concerning the nature and extent of biblical Inspiration, and the nature of the redemptive work of Christ. These naturally stand or fall together. For if the inspiration of the Scriptures is plenary, then the church doctrine as to the nature of the Redemption remains impregnable. But if the authority of the Scriptures may be abated, the way is open, of course, in due proportion, to theories of Redemption adjusted to "the finer feeling," the "moral intuitions," and the administrative experiences of mankind.[6]

Gardiner Spring was a strong and discerning champion of theological orthodoxy in a time of considerable erosion and declension, and one who magnified the preaching office in a time of mediocrity.

1. Gardiner Spring, *The Power of the Pulpit: Thoughts Addressed to Christian Ministers and Those Who Hear Them* (Edinburgh: Banner of Truth, 1848, 1986), 109.
2. Ibid., 154.
3. Ibid., 239.
4. Gardiner Spring, *The Attraction of the Cross* (New York: M. W. Dodd, 1859).
5. Ibid., 35.
6. David F. Wells, "The Debate over the Atonement in Nineteenth-Century America," *Bibliotheca Sacra* 144, no. 575 (July–September 1987): 247. These four lectures are of extraordinary importance. The diminution of clarity with respect to scriptural authority or the atoning work of Christ is disastrous for preaching as later events would show in Scotland. Biblical authority and the blood atonement are the special objects of satanic fury and hostility.

9.3 THE ENGLISH WATERFALL

. . . the age was one of religious seriousness.

—A. R. Vidler

Not only a modified Sunday observance, but Bible reading and family prayers were common until near the end of the century.

—G. M. Trevelyan

If one asks how nineteenth-century English merchants earned the reputation of being the most honest in the world (a very real factor in the nineteenth-century primacy of English trade), the answer is: because hell and heaven seemed as certain to them as tomorrow's sunrise, and the Last Judgment as real as the week's balance-sheet. This keen sense of moral accountancy had also much to do with the success of self-government in the political sphere.

—R. C. K. Ensor

The post-Napoleonic years were commonly called the Victorian Age, although Queen Victoria did not ascend the throne until 1837. It was a time of expanding empire, an era of immense literary productivity (with the likes of Dickens, Jane Austen, Thomas Carlyle, Thomas and Matthew Arnold, Lord Tennyson, Robert Browning, and Anthony Trollope). Frederick Karl's magisterial biography of George Eliot (Mary Ann Evans) speaks of her as the "voice of a century."[1] Profoundly religious and even evangelical early on, Eliot moved to secular humanism and a morally deficient life. She slowly defected from her evangelical reading, church attendance, and old friends. In the face of a tradition-driven society, she found her own way. Eliot exemplifies the trend of the times.

---

1. Frederick R. Karl, *George Eliot: Voice of a Century* (New York: Norton, 1995). A treasury of Victoriana.

9.3.1 JOHN ANGELL JAMES—RAISING THE STANDARD

> Oh . . . how delightful is it, notwithstanding the humbling and sorrowful consciousness of defects and sins, to look back upon a life spent for Christ.

> Preach as in full view of all the wonders of Calvary, and let it be as if, while you spoke, you felt the Saviour's grace flowing into, and filling your soul, and as if at that moment you were sympathizing with the apostle in his sublime raptures—"God forbid I should glory, save in the cross of our Lord Jesus Christ."

> While yet a youth engaged in secular concerns, I had been deeply susceptible of the power of an awakening style of preaching, which was strengthened by the perusal of the rousing sermons of Dr. Davies of New Jersey. From that time to the present I have made the conversion of the impenitent the great end of my ministry.
>
> —John Angell James

One of the honored deans of nonconformity in early Victorian England and first in the noble succession of James, R. W. Dale, and J. H. Jowett at Carr's Lane Chapel in Birmingham was **John Angell James** (1785–1859). Birmingham came to prominence with a great influx of nonconformists after the Restoration, and Carr's Lane came into existence as a protest against Unitarianism. Arthur Porritt, Jowett's biographer, argued that "the position occupied by Carr's Lane Church in the life of Birmingham has perhaps no parallel in any other English city."[1] During the tenure of James, which began in 1804 and lasted until 1859, the church became a powerful center of biblical preaching and missionary outreach and vision.

The man who entered such large responsibility at age nineteen was born in Dorset. Apprenticed to a draper for several years, James converted under strong gospel preaching. He began to teach Sunday school and then attended Dr. Bogue's school at Gosport, which had been established under the auspices of the Haldanes. Carr's Lane was small when he commenced his labors, and for the first seven years not much seemed to happen. James testified that first he learned to preach and then he began to learn to pray and in the eighth year there came a turn. Soon a new church edifice was needed to seat eighteen hundred people.

When asked why he didn't preach his Calvinism, James responded, "Because I do not seem to find much about Calvinism in the Bible."[2] He prepared thoroughly for his preaching with great attention to the text. Composed and serious in his delivery, he wanted to avoid both "the contortions of an epileptic zeal" and "the numbness of a paralytic one." "He attached the utmost importance to the proper reading of the Holy Scriptures . . . it was quite a feast to hear him."[3] James stressed Christian character as the outcome of Christian conversion, and indeed, "The motto of all his discourses, as of all his works was 'Holiness to the Lord!'"[4] His preaching was not eloquent in the learned sense but good old Anglo-Saxon, as when he made three prescriptions for preachers: (1) brains, (2) bowels (compassion), and (3) bellows (lungs).[5]

James' written legacy goes to seventeen volumes, including his influential *The Anxious Inquirer after Salvation* (600,000 copies!) where he quotes widely from bishops and Adam Clarke. He read widely and had broad interests. One significant piece from his hand and heart is a "Review of the Character" of Richard Knill, whose ministry in India but particularly in St. Petersburg was outstanding, in which he was the forerunner of the great Lord Radstock.[6] James was determined to preach law first and was convinced that exegesis should be augmented by persuasion and pleading. As he so characteristically put it:

> It is delicious, I know, to hear a fine, eloquent and richly theological descant upon a redeeming love and pardoning mercy—to have the imagination and heart regaled with rhetoric, radiant with the glories of the cross and redolent with the odour of that Name which is above every name: it is gratifying to the thinking mind to have the intellect pleased with logical dexterity, and the fine abstractions of clear and strong thinking: it will be well enough also to have the subjects of moral obligation discussed in vague generalities and by elegant composition—but it is not so acceptable to have all the special and difficult duties of the Christian's life, or man's conduct to his fellows, set clearly before the understanding and enforced upon the conscience. Men do not so well like to be followed through all the labyrinths of the heart's deceitfulness, beaten out of every refuge of lies, and made to feel the obligations to love where they are inclined to hate and to forgive where they desire to revenge. And we ministers pander too much to this taste.[7]

James was known for finishing his sermons well. He initiated his successor, Robert W. Dale, into the work and saw many conversions attending his ministry. Years later, Joseph Parker observed that "a kind of Pentecostal effect" was part of his ministry and that "he reaped a harvest second to none."[8] In advanced age, James reflected:

> Ministers may think too little of this now, and the work of conversion be lost sight of too much, in their eager desires and ardent ambition after popularity and applause; but the time is coming when these, except as they give a man a wider sphere for his converting work, will be thought worthless and vain. Amidst the gathering infirmities of old age, and the anticipations of eternity—much more at the bar of Christ, and in the celestial world—it will be deemed a poor and meagre reflection to a minister of Christ, that he was once followed and applauded by admiring crowds.[9]

---

1. Arthur Porritt, *John Henry Jowett* (London: Hodder and Stoughton, 1924), 70.
2. F. R. Webber, *A History of Preaching in Britain and America* (Milwaukee: Northwestern, 1952), 3:467.

3. John Campbell, *John Angell James* (London: John Snow, 1860), 45.
4. Ibid., 51.
5. Ibid., 77.
6. James' chapter is in C. M. Birrell, *The Life of Rev. Richard Knill of St. Petersburg* (London: Religious Tract Society, 1859), 255–70. Knill knew Carey and Judson and preached widely abroad. He was close to William Jay in Bath. He ultimately served the church in Chester earlier served by Matthew Henry.
7. Campbell, *John Angell James,* 188.
8. Webber, *A History of Preaching,* 3:468.
9. Campbell, *John Angell James,* 240.

9.3.2 *THOMAS BINNEY—AFFIRMING THE BASICS*

Truth cannot be injured by fair and full discussion, and by open and un-compromising statements. I have no hesitation about saying that I am an enemy to the Establishment . . . I confess as a matter of deep serious religious conviction that the Established Church is a great national evil . . . that it destroys more souls than it saves.

That there is a grandeur investing our position, may be further felt by adverting to the fact of our aim and solicitude being precisely those of the Saviour himself . . . we sustain that office which He sustained and are discharging its functions as representatives of Him.

It is an inestimable blessing to possess these "writings;" to draw near to them as to a "holy oracle;" and to learn, immediately and directly from themselves what the Lord God has "made known" to man or "requires" of him. Still, a living agency, official teaching, a ministerial "steward-ship of the mysteries of God," is a necessary and permanent institution. It is necessary for the preservation, improvement and perseverance of Christians themselves, for it is "the gift" of Christ for the "edifying of his body," and "the perfecting of the saints;" for far more is it necessary for the promulgation of the Truth, and through that, for the extension, enlargement and triumph of the Church.

—Thomas Binney

Another of the defining mentors of Victorian dissent was **Thomas Binney** (1798–1874), who modeled a straightforward style of preaching for many non-conformists. Binney initially considered Spurgeon an upstart, but he came to admire and commend the younger man.[1] Born in Newcastle-on-Tyne in Northumbria, Binney was instructed in Latin and Greek by an old Presbyterian minister. He developed a great love for books while working in a book store. He attended Coward College (the Congregational seminary) in Wymondly, which was maintained by the Reverend Thomas Morell.

After serving briefly in Bedford and on the Isle of Wight, in 1829 he took the pastorate of the King's Weigh-House Chapel in London, where he served for over forty years. The chapel was in a sense the nonconformist cathedral in London and drew many persons of wealth and from the middle class. Like Isaac Watts in an earlier generation, Binney dedicated himself to raising the level of congregational worship and singing. A new sanctuary was necessary to accommodate the growing throngs which gathered to hear the forceful biblical preaching of Thomas Binney.

He was an early pamphleteer, putting his strong convictions into print for a widening audience. As a preacher, he was a master of accent and eloquent in his own way, with a great power to paint a picture and to be alternately "fiend or angel."[2] Browning, who had nonconformist roots, certainly would have found in Binney what he longed for in a chapel preacher, as reflected in his "Christmas Eve and Easter Day." He was criticized for lack of culture but adhered to the highest view of the authority of Holy Scripture. He had drunk deeply at the springs of Augustine, Calvin, Howe, Charnock, and Baxter.[3] Some of his noted sermons were his address to the London Missionary Society on "Messiah Suffering and Messiah Satisfied" and his memorable funeral sermon for Algernon Wells, "Light and Immortality Brought to Light by the Gospel."

The great Alexander Maclaren testified that it was Binney who taught him how to preach. Like South and Latimer before him, Binney was, according to Hood, "The most charming humorist in the pulpit of our time."[4] He always preached without notes and used humor effectively. Yet he tended to be nervous and was a man of considerable eccentricity. Some likened him to Lacordaire, the French preacher of consummate skill (cf. 6.3.2.3). Listeners occasionally had difficulty because of his habit of dropping his voice at the end of a sentence. We have a sterling example of good division of a text and skillful impartation of its truth in "The Ultimate Design of the Christian Ministry" delivered to the London Missionary Society, and then also in his brilliant "The Christian Ministry Not a Priesthood."[5] One hearer recorded his impression at Weigh-House:

> The moment we saw a gentleman ascending the pulpit stairs, we felt assured, from the description we had previously been favored with that he must be the minister of whom we had heard so much; he was tall and large-chested, but the head and face were the most strikingly intellectual in their developments we had ever looked upon. In a tone of voice so low as to be heard with great difficulty, even by us who were so near him, he read a chapter . . . there is no familiarity, no bawling, no hurry; all is calmness, earnestness and quiet supplication . . . that he is excessively nervous is easily perceptible from the anxious look which he directs to some part of the chapel, whence a slight noise proceeds, and by the occasional twitching of his facial muscles . . . we listen with the utmost attention lest a word should escape us . . . in spite of his peculiarities, he is a very great preacher.[6]

---

1. G. Holden Pike, *The Life and Work of Charles Haddon Spurgeon* (Edinburgh: Banner of Truth, 1894, 1991), 1:134.

2. E. Paxton Hood, *Thomas Binney: His Mind, Life and Opinions* (London: James Clarke, 1874), 54.

3. Ibid., 84.

4. Ibid., 118.

5. Thomas Binney, *The Ultimate Design of the Christian Ministry* and *The Christian Ministry Not a Priesthood* (London: Jackson and Walford, 1849).

6. Hood, *Thomas Binney,* 148–50.

9.3.3 JOHN HENRY NEWMAN—RISKING ALL

Definiteness is the life of preaching. Nothing that is anonymous will preach, nothing that is dead and gone.

Lead, kindly Light, amid th' encircling gloom, Lead Thou me on! The night is dark, and I am far from home; Lead Thou me on! Keep Thou my feet; I do not ask to see. . . . The distant scene; one step enough for me.

—John Henry Newman

He was interested in everything that was going on . . . in science, in politics, in literature. Nothing was too large for him, nothing too trivial, if it threw light on the central question what man really was and what his destiny . . . He had read omnivorously, and studied modern thought in all its forms, and with all its many-colored passions.

—J. A. Froude

In the front ranks of English preachers is **John Henry Newman** (1801–1890). The son of a London banker and a Huguenot mother, Newman came under evangelical influence while a student of fifteen at Ealing. One of his classics teachers, the Reverend Walter Mayers, "an ardent Evangelical and a Calvinist," influenced both John Henry and his brother Francis. Mayers encouraged the Newmans to read Thomas Scott, Philip Doddridge, and Beveridge's *Private Thoughts.*[1]

Francis joined the Plymouth Brethren[2] but lost his faith on the mission field under the corrupting influence of Bishop Colenso and his higher critical extremism.[3] John Henry often spoke of his conversion in this time-frame. It was a time of some uneasiness in the Church of England with evangelicalism evincing unexpected strength. Could evangelicalism hold the ground for orthodoxy in the face of mounting antisupernaturalistic influence from Germany, or would the Bible become a casualty, with the authority of Rome offering ecclesiastical security in the raging storms?

John Henry went on to Oriel College at Oxford, where his own evangelicalism gradually faded. He followed E. B. Pusey, Keble (the preacher and hymnwriter), and his friend Froude into the Oxford Movement, or Tractarianism. The Oxford Group was largely an offshoot from evangelicalism. In the British Isles as well as America, preaching drifted away from the Puritan and post-Puritan models.[4] Newman would eventually go with Henry Manning into the Roman Catholic Church itself (his friend F. W. Faber, who wrote "Faith of our Fathers," went with him).

Newman was a remarkably serious follower of Christ and student of the Bible early on. His prayer was "Give me grace—make me holy."[5] He felt called to the ministry and began to preach at St. Clement's in Oxford. While at Oxford he came under the spell of **Richard Whatley** (1787–1863), his principal at Merton College and an expert in logic and mathematics. Whatley was also a Broad churchman, and later became archbishop of Dublin. His rhetorical theory advanced the notion that reasonable and logical proof consists not of "invention" but rather pursuing a proposition with the support of varying kinds of testimony. Both Newman and F. W. Robertson were molded to some degree by Whatley. Newman assisted Whatley in the preparation of *Elements of Logic* in 1826.[6] In 1828 he was appointed Vicar of St. Mary's, Oxford, the university church, where his outstanding preaching became increasingly well known. While on a Mediterranean trip he became ill, and on board ship wrote his stately hymn "Lead, Kindly Light."

His earlier preaching in St. Mary's was strongly biblical and focused on Christ and his cross:

> The doctrine of Christ crucified is the only spring of real virtue and piety, and the only foundation of peace and comfort . . . Comfort is a cordial, but no one drinks cordials from morning to night. . . .[7]

For twenty years Newman drifted toward Rome. When he finally converted in October of 1845, he took over the Oratory in Birmingham. His last sermon in St. Mary's, "The Parting of Friends," left his friends and his church stunned. The defection of such a prince to Rome shook the foundations. He worked in Ireland from 1854 to 1862 in order to establish a national Catholic university. Thereafter he was made a cardinal in 1879, and he preached and wrote until his death.

The sermons of Newman, particularly his earlier efforts, have an extraordinary power and beauty. All of the sermons in his famous *Parochial and Plain Sermons* come prior to 1843. Dean Lake described the preaching and its effect:

> There was first the style, always simple, refined and unpretending, and without a touch of any thing which could be called rhetoric, but always marked by a depth of feeling which evidently sprang from the heart and experience of the preacher, and penetrated by a suppressed vein of the poetry which was so strong a feature in Newman's mind and which appealed at once to the hearts and the highest feelings of his hearers . . .[8]

In the succeeding days he often preached on the Second Coming and the challenge of the Antichrist as did the Tractarians generally. After preaching once on "The Incarnate Son, a Sufferer and Sacrifice,"[9] Newman's magnetism is described:

> Newman had described closely some of the incidents of our Lord's Passion; he then paused. For a few moments there was a breathless silence. Then in a low, clear voice, of which the faintest vibration was audible in

the farthest corner of St. Mary's, he said: "Now I bid you recollect that He to whom these things were done was Almighty God." It was as if an electric stroke had gone through the church, as if every person present understood for the first time the meaning of what he had all his life been saying. I suppose it was an epoch in the mental history of more than one of my Oxford contemporaries.[10]

In growing increasingly high church, Newman became harder and more ve-hement in his preaching with "an under-current of pessimism and gloom." We see this in his famous sermons "Christian Nobleness" and "Feasting in Cap-tivity."[11] Samuel Wilberforce spoke of "the general tone of the Sermons is that of requisition."[12] Always veering toward the severe and the ascetic, Newman's listeners heard less and less of the joyful sound. He was a gifted and great preacher but he lost something essential: "The glorious gospel of our Blessed God!"

1. David Newsome, "The Evangelical Sources of Newman's Power," in *The Recovery of Newman: An Oxford Symposium,* ed. John Coulson and A. M. Allchin (London: SPCK, 1967), 11, 13. A good overall treatment of the life and ministry of Newman is Brian Martin, *John Henry Newman: His Life and Work* (Oxford: Oxford Univer-sity Press, 1982).
2. William Robbins, *The Newman Brothers* (Cambridge, Mass.: Harvard University Press, 1966), 30.
3. B. B. Warfield, "Some Perils of Missionary Life," in *Selected Shorter Writings* (Philipsburg, N.J.: Presbyterian and Reformed, 1973), 2:502ff.
4. O. C. Edwards, "Newman and Robertson," in *Concise Encyclopedia of Preaching* (Louisville: Westminster John Knox, 1995), 219. Newman always preached his proposition; see Lewis O. Brastow, *Representative Modern Preachers* (New York: Macmillan, 1904), 302.
5. Dr. Zeno, *John Henry Newman: His Inner Life* (San Francisco: Ignatius, 1987), 28.
6. R. D. Middleton, *Newman at Oxford: His Religious Development* (London: Oxford University Press, 1950), 44.
7. Zeno, *John Henry Newman,* 40.
8. Middleton, *Newman at Oxford,* 94.
9. John Henry Newman, *Parochial and Plain Sermons* (San Francisco: Ignatius, 1987), VI, 1220. Eight volumes of his sermons (169 sermons) beautifully bound together.
10. Middleton, *Newman at Oxford,* 96ff. Newman read his sermons, but Gladstone said his matter overcame his manner.
11. David Newsome, *The Parting of Friends: The Wilberforces and Henry Manning* (Grand Rapids: Eerdmans, 1966), 180–81.
12. Ibid., 202. In his *Newman: An Appreciation* (Edinburgh: Oliphant, 1901), Alexander Whyte shares his great fondness for Newman, with whom he spent some time, but also voices his regret that the gospel message doesn't sound clearly and authenti-cally in Newman.

9.3.4 SAMUEL WILBERFORCE—RELISHING THE FELLOWSHIP

> My own belief is that things will grow worse and worse . . . I think that
> the Church will fall within fifty years entirely and the State will not sur-
> vive it much longer.
>
> —Samuel Wilberforce

> Charles Simeon and Samuel's father-in-law, John Sargent, visited the
> Wilberforces on the Island of Wight, reporting a conversation after an
> evening service—Simeon, contrasting this time with Whitefield's and
> Wesley's, spoke of the coldness now: "Such men as Daniel Wilson,
> Marsh, etc. laboring, with little or no fruit. There's a dew everywhere
> but a shower nowhere."

Along with Simeon, the name of Wilberforce alone stands to the fore as we
consider the pioneers of the evangelical renaissance in the early nineteenth century. **William Wilberforce** (1759–1833) was the gifted orator and spiritual leader
of the Clapham Group, which spearheaded the abolition of slavery, improvement
of prison conditions, and revocation of the Corn Laws.[1] William was a devout
Anglican, and spent two hours daily before breakfast studying Scripture and praying. He served in a Parliament that from 1784 to 1832 boasted 112 evangelicals.
Evangelicals also obtained their first bishops—Ryder in Gloucester, C. R. Sumner
in Llandaff, and his brother J. B. Sumner in Chester, later archbishop of Canterbury
(1848–1862).[2]

Yet the harsh winds of German rationalism[3] and Darwinian theories of origin were threatening the foundations of orthodoxy.[4] With fully one-third of the
Anglican clergy being evangelical, the evangelical understanding of salvation
was dominant until the 1840s. The coming collapse of evangelical orthodoxy
would involve a move away from eternal punishment and the vicarious atonement, a move from Jesus the Lamb to Jesus the Man, what F. D. Maurice described as "a shift of the center of gravity from the atonement to the
incarnation."[5] These are the views enshrined in the popular volume *Lux Mundi*
edited by Charles Gore.

And how would the rising generation meet the challenge to orthodoxy? Some
as we have seen opted for the trek to Rome; others became concessive Broad
churchmen. Many remained evangelical. Some, like **Samuel Wilberforce** (1805–
1873), son of William Wilberforce, were torn in various directions.

Raised in a pious home, Samuel went to Oxford. One of his dear friends there
was Francis Lyte, who wrote "Abide with Me." Samuel was married in 1828 to a
daughter of John Sargent, close friend and confident of Charles Simeon, who
performed the marriage. After a curacy near Oxford, he moved to Brighstone on
the Island of Wight, where his preaching soon gave him a widening reputation.
Worried much about the antinomianism of the dissenters, Samuel preached vigorously and directly on smuggling and other sensitive topics on the island. His
sermons were lengthy:

Extra services and classes were at once begun, not only in the parish church, but the outlying hamlets; and to this day the villagers remember how no weather stopped him; while as to his preaching, a story is yet current how at evening service he would sometimes go on till it grew dark, so that you could not see him; but, it is added, "the people would have sat all night listening."[6]

Wilberforce was not an original thinker, but he was a reader and activist with an amazing capacity for work. He was out front on all of the critical issues of the day and close to Prime Minister Gladstone. He tended toward high church, and preached a series of sermons at the University Church in Oxford. He felt that Hook preached essays rather than sermons in that pulpit. Wilberforce preached without notes and with such adaptability that he was asked to explain his style:

He replied that he owed his facility of speech mainly to the pains his father had taken with him. His father used to cause him to make himself well acquainted with a given subject, and then speak on it, without notes, and trusting to the inspiration of the moment for suitable words. Thus his memory and his power of mentally arranging and dividing his subjects were strengthened.[7]

In 1841 he was assigned Alverstoke and the archdeanery of Surrey. At this time he was made chaplain to Prince Albert, preaching in the Royal Chapel at Windsor.[8] Shortly after moving to Alverstoke, his beloved wife passed away. He never remarried. Wilberforce was deeply troubled over Maurice's views on the atonement,[9] and endured the debacle of a debate with T. H. Huxley.[10] He saw his daughter, his three brothers, his son-in-law, and four brothers and sisters-in-law leave the Church of England and take up spiritual residence in the Church of Rome. As the Oxford Group continued toward Rome, Samuel broke with Pusey, denying that the Eucharist had any salvific value.

Wilberforce's critics thought he was evasive and too adroit. They called him "sly Sam" or "soapy Sam," ostensibly because he would wring his hands as he spoke. He saw his brother-in-law Henry Manning and Newman become Catholic bishops.[11] He parted ways with Newman and declined to write for his publication.

We do not possess many of Wilberforce's sermons, but his writings suggest a direct manner with a clear concern to let the text speak.[12] The publication of his brother Robert's work on the incarnation of Christ demonstrates the basic soundness in theology inherited from their father, since the mediatorial work of Christ as sin-bearer and perfect sacrifice on the cross is made very clear.[13] Samuel Wilberforce faltered and wavered on many issues, but on balance he held the banner of biblical preaching high, as he reflects about a visit to Ryde and the curate there:

He seems to me to be a sincere and humble Christian, but very slow indeed, and his sermons from all accounts are of just the lunar rainbow sort of inefficiency and generalization, which you would expect to find from an X superstructure upon so foggy a foundation. . . . The more I see the more I am convinced of the evil of general preaching, of the evil of cold preaching, and of the infinite superiority of the X's over the Z's (X being Evangelical and Z being High and Dry).[14]

Samuel Wilberforce was made dean of Westminster and then bishop of Oxford in 1845, serving in that capacity until 1870, when he was made bishop of Winchester. He died in 1873 when he fell from his horse.

1. William Wilberforce, *Real Christianity Contrasted with the Prevailing Religious System* (Portland, Oreg.: Multnomah, 1982). Note Charles W. Colson, "Standing Against All Odds," *Christianity Today* (September 6, 1985): 26ff.
2. G. R. Balleine, *A History of the Evangelical Party in the Church of England* (London: Longman, Greens, 1908), 196.
3. John Louis Haney, *The German Influence on Samuel Taylor Coleridge* (New York: Haskell House, 1966). A sample tracing of an important theological and cultural influence.
4. Charles Coulston Gillispie, *Genesis and Geology: The Impact of Scientific Discoveries Upon Religious Beliefs in the Decades Before Darwin* (New York: Harper Torchbooks, 1951). An important study of pre-Darwinian development.
5. Boyd Hilton, *The Age of Atonement: The Influence of Evangelicalism on Social and Economic Thought, 1795–1865* (Oxford: Clarendon, 1988), 5.
6. A. R. Ashwell and Reginald G. Wilberforce, *The Life of Samuel Wilberforce* (New York: Dutton, 1883), 18.
7. Ibid., 47.
8. Ibid., 70. For a moving description of Wilberforce's friendship with Richard Trench, whose studies on the miracles and the parables have been such an enrichment over the years, see Warren Wiersbe, *Living with the Giants* (Grand Rapids: Baker, 1993), 29. Trench followed Whatley as archbishop of Dublin at a difficult time.
9. Ibid., 228.
10. William Irvine, *Apes, Angels and Victorians: Darwin, Huxley and Evolution* (New York: McGraw-Hill, 1955), 5–8. This is a caustic but essentially accurate description of this unfortunate encounter, when Bishop Wilberforce turned to Huxley and "begged to know, was it through his grandfather or his grandmother that he claimed his descent from a monkey." Huxley slapped his knee and softly said to his neighbor, "The Lord has delivered him into my hand." Huxley saw that by using ridicule, Wilberforce opened himself up to the same.
11. David Newsome, *The Parting of Friends: The Wilberforces and Henry Manning* (Grand Rapids: Eerdmans, 1966). This book is a treasure, a most genteel and thoughtful tracing of complex relationships in a troubled time.
12. Samuel Wilberforce, *Heroes of Hebrew History* (London: W. H. Allen, 1896).
13. Archdeacon Robert Wilberforce, *The Doctrine of the Incarnation of Our Lord Jesus Christ* (London: Mozley and Smith, 1879).
14. Newsome, *The Parting of Friends,* 170.

9.3.5 F. W. Robertson of Brighton—Reaching for the Idea

The preacher's preacher!

—John Bishop

The one great preacher in the history of the English Church.

—Canon Charles Smith

Save yourself from sectarianism; pledge yourself to no school; cut your life adrift from all party; be a slave to no maxims: stand fast, unfettered and free, servants only of the truth . . .

I believe I could have become an orator, had I chosen to take pains. I see what rhetoric does and what it seems to do, and I thoroughly despise it . . . and yet perhaps I do it injustice; with an unworldly noble love to give it reality, what might it not do!

—F. W. Robertson

There was much preaching in Victorian England and much boring preaching and indeed much boring evangelical preaching. Anthony Trollope wrote in *Barchester Towers*, "There is perhaps no greater hardship inflicted on mankind in civilized and free countries than the necessity of listening to sermons."[1] Trollope was not alone in deploring the "tedium of sermons," and what was among the evangelicals exceedingly dreary "if not subversive." His characters like Reverend Samuel Prong and Rev. Joseph Emilius (a wife-beater and a bigamist), to say nothing of Archdeacon Grantley, whose "frolics were of a cumbrous kind," reinforce Trollope's childhood impression of "trashy sermons in ludicrously theatrical manner."[2]

But there were exceptions, such as the brief but stellar ministry of **Frederick W. Robertson** (1816–1853), of whom Dean Church said, "He has become beyond question the greatest preacher of the nineteenth century." Robertson was born in a family that had long been in the military. His commission was delayed so long that his father urged him to enter the ministry. Five days later the commission came, but he was already at school.

Robertson was a frail and sensitive young man whose first brief charge was at Cheltenham, then for a short time at the English church in Heidelberg in Germany, then St. Ebbe's in Oxford, and then for six years at Trinity Chapel in the resort city of Brighton. Only one of his sermons was published before his death at age thirty-seven, but quickly his remarkable sermons began to circulate and his stature was recognized. On his monument in Brighton are written the words: "He awakened the holiest feelings in poor and in rich, in ignorant and in learned. There is he lamented as their guide and comforter."

Here is preaching that made a difference. Robertson was a staunch evangelical who had moved away from an earlier transcendentalism and Shelley's "atmosphere of profligacy" to the more Wordsworthian and Shakespearean tradition compatible with the evangelicals in the Church of England.[3] Poets like Tennyson and writers like Ruskin (with whom he debated in the Oxford Union) were his friends rather than the philosophers. Perhaps he overreacted against rationalism, but he treasured and memorized Scripture constantly.[4]

Robertson occasionally recoiled from evangelical cant. He walked a solitary path, and both liberals and hard-shell conservatives found fault with him. Yet he sustained a steady and conscientious course and could not tolerate the liberal vivisection of Scripture. The chapel in Brighton overflowed.

At an early stage, Robertson had been taken by Newman but he soon regained his poise. His preaching was always biblical and textual. His sermons, invariably with two divisions, were dedicated to saying what the text of Scripture says. He labored diligently in his preparation. He ordinarily preached forty-five minutes and spoke quite calmly, calling fluency the "fatal gift."[5] "To preach Christ," he said, "was to preach the doctrines of Christ, that men may be saved."[6] He eschewed emphasis on memory:

> All public speakers know the value of method. Persons not accustomed to it imagine that a speech is learnt by heart. Knowing a little about the matter, I will venture to say that if any one attempted that plan, either he must have a marvelous memory, or else he would break down three times out of five. It simply depends upon correct arrangement. The words and sentences are left to the moment; the thoughts methodised beforehand; and the words, if the thoughts are rightly arranged, will place themselves. But upon the truthfulness of arrangement all depends.[7]

He preached from a very small piece of paper and wrote up the sermon on the next day. Stopford Brook, his principal biographer, gathered six volumes of sermons.

Because he was a master of illustration and application, his sermons have a remarkable literary quality even in the abbreviated form in which we have them. His famous sermon on "The Loneliness of Jesus" from John 16:31–32 is almost autobiographical:

> There are two kinds of solitude; the first consisting of isolation in space; the other isolation of the spirit.

His first main division treats Christ's loneliness, and then he moves on to the loneliness of the obedient follower of Christ. He was a suffering soul, first from debilitating illness, then from misunderstanding and criticism which he did not handle well, and then from self-doubt and feelings that he was a failure. His deep melancholy was evident to the Swiss preacher Malan, who told him: "You will have a sorrowful life and a sorrowful ministry." Robertson chose his direction:

> I would rather live solitary on the most desolate and the most solitary crag, shivering, with all the warm wraps of falsehood stripped off, gazing after unfound truth . . . than sit comfortably on more inhabited spots,

where others were warm in a faith which is true to them, but which is false to me.[8]

Every preacher should dip into Robertson's life and letters[9] and read some of his sermons. They are for the ages. The main volume of his sermons was published by Harpers in 1870 and has been continuously in print ever since. His exegesis was radioactive. A typical sermon is "The State of Nature and the State of Grace" from Ephesians 2:3–5 with two obvious divisions. An unusual sermon on "The Three Crosses on Calvary" from Luke 23:33 has three points with Christ on the cross being the first and then on to each of the malefactors.[10] Some have claimed him as the forerunner of the psychological preachers, but this is only to underscore the great pastoral instincts and applicatory skills that Robertson brought to the preaching task.[11] How sad that Anthony Trollope never got to hear the likes of F. W. Robertson.

---

1. Victoria Glendinning, *Anthony Trollope* (New York: Knopf, 1993), 230.
2. Ibid., 93.
3. Lewis O. Brastow, *Representative Modern Preachers* (New York: Macmillan, 1904), 51, 59.
4. James R. Blackwood, *The Soul of Frederick W. Robertson* (New York: Harpers, 1947), 14. Robertson discussed with Wilberforce his inability to hold to or preach baptismal regeneration when he was offered St. Ebbe's in Oxford on a permanent basis; see David Newsome, *The Parting of Friends* (Grand Rapids: Eerdmans, 1966), 333.
5. Ibid., 88.
6. Ibid., 107. For a fine study consult Gilbert E. Doan's introduction to *The Preaching of F. W. Robertson* (Philadelphia: Fortress, 1964).
7. Ibid., 113. For Robertson, obedience is the organ of spiritual knowledge.
8. Ibid., 142.
9. Stopford Brooke, ed., *Life and Letters of Frederick W. Robertson* (London: Henry S. King, 1872).
10. Frederick W. Robertson, *The Human Race and Other Sermons* (New York: Harper, 1870), 115.
11. Charles Smyth speaks of him as "the first and greatest psychological preacher in the Church of England," because he coupled with his "exact and extensive knowledge of the Bible" such a "deliberate referencing to modern conditions—so personal," cf. *The Art of Preaching: A Practical Survey of Preaching in the Church of England 747–1939* (London: SPCK, 1940), 230. Robertson's "passionate devotion to Christ" is also part of the mix.

9.3.6 The Bickersteths—Reiterating the Advent

If ever a Church Missionary was filled with the Spirit, that secretary was Edward Bickersteth.

—Eugene Stock

The Scripture, in the Old and New Testament alike, detaches our ultimate confidence from man, the creature, and attaches it to God, the Creator. Scripture, in the Old and New Testament alike, requires us to repose our ultimate confidence in the Lord Jesus Christ.

—Edward Henry Bickersteth

With the waning of Simeon and Wilberforce, leadership among evangelicals largely fell to **Edward Bickersteth** (1786–1850), the son of a doctor, whose remarkable family was so squarely evangelical and who provided the Church of England with two bishops, an archdeacon, and a son-in-law, Thomas Birks, who was the first secretary of the Evangelical Alliance. Evangelicalism was not strong in scholarship, although it was represented by Bishop Ellicott of Gloucester and Bristol, who wrote significant Bible commentaries, Alexander M'Caul, who was Hebrew professor at King's College in London, Cyril Garbett, who edited the *Record* and refuted Darwin, and John William Burgon (1813–1888), the champion of the Textus Receptus and later dean of Chichester, all of whom were solid biblical preachers of note and effect.

Edward Bickersteth came from old Lancashire stock tracing back to Bickerstaffe in the twelfth century. He became secretary of the Church Missionary Society in 1824 and is described by Professor Chadwick as "the most colorful and godly of the Evangelical clergy."[1] He traveled widely abroad (especially in Africa) and preached constantly in the homelands and always at Wheler Chapel, Spitalfields, when not otherwise engaged. In 1830 he became rector of Watton near Hertford, where he had an outstanding ministry of systematic biblical exposition although still traveling extensively for the CMS. He also published *Christian Hymnody* in 1830 and was known as the evangelical Keble. He wrote four books on Bible prophecy reflecting the view of the imminent return of Jesus Christ for his church:

He was led to believe that the second coming of Christ will precede the Millennium; that the first resurrection is literal, and that Christ will establish a kingdom of righteousness on earth at His return, before the resurrection of the wicked and their final judgment.[2]

He believed the Jews would return to Palestine in the complex of end-time events. He joined with John Angell James in establishing the Evangelical Alliance in 1845.

Anthony Ashley Cooper, later Lord Shaftesbury (1801–1885), successor to William Wilberforce as lay leader of the evangelicals and the great Christian philanthropist, resided near Watton and studied prophecy with Bickersteth, who convinced him that "Christ would come suddenly and soon."[3] Together they became early advocates of Christian Zionism in Britain. His buoyancy and warmth infused his preaching and it was said that "the waves of vehement argument were often calmed down by the oil of Mr. Bickersteth's affection."[4]

Bickersteth's only son, **Edward Henry Bickersteth** (1824–1906), early on took a living on Shaftesbury's estate, where he was known for his pastoral and evangelistic zeal.[5] He labored then for thirty years as Vicar of Christ Church, Hampstead, went on to be dean of Gloucester in 1885, and then bishop of Exeter. Like his father, he wrote hymns and published a hymnal called *Hymnal Companion to the Book of Common Prayer* (1870), of which Dr. Julian in the *Dictionary of Hymnology* says: "Bishop Bickersteth's work is at the head of all hymnals in the Church of England, and in keeping with this unique position it has also the purest texts."[6] His own hymns include "Peace, Perfect Peace," "Till He Comes," "Not Worthy, Lord, to Gather Up the Crumbs," and "O Brothers, Lift Your Voices." He was also known for his effective outdoor preaching.

The high quality and richly biblical and doctrinal content of Bickersteth's sermons are also reflected in the several volumes that he wrote on the inspiration of Scripture and his superb piece on the Holy Trinity.[7] Evangelical churchmanship was also upheld by his cousin Robert, who was bishop of Ripon,[8] and by another cousin Edward, who was dean of Lichfield. Other worthy successors in following generations carried the torch of truth ignited early in the Bickersteth lineage.

1. Michael Hennell, *Sons of the Prophets: Evangelical Leaders of the Victorian Church* (London: SPCK, 1979), 29.
2. Ibid., 44.
3. John Pollock, *Shaftesbury: The Poor Man's Earl* (London: Hodder and Stoughton, 1985), 53. For a significant treatment of one of Shaftesbury's ardent sympathizers, see Cecil Woodham-Smith, *Florence Nightingale* (New York: McGraw-Hill, 1951). For consideration of the place of Bible prophecy at this time, see J. F. C. Harrison, *The Second Coming: Popular Millenarianism 1780–1850* (New Brunswick, N.J.: Rutgers University Press, 1979); also W. H. Oliver, *Prophets and Millennialists: The Uses of Biblical Prophecy in England from the 1790s to the 1840s* (Auckland, New Zealand: Auckland University Press, 1978). Herein is traced the influence of the famous Albury Conferences sponsored by the banker Henry Drummond starting in 1826. Edward Irving was involved early but was destroyed by his excesses. Hugh McNeile, later dean of Ripon, was a leader in the movement, as was Edward Bickersteth. Keble and Newman were as concerned about the last days as was Bickersteth (142). Newman argued: "He will very soon be here, that is quite certain and He has given us all notice." He has sermons on "Watching" and "Waiting for Christ."
4. D. N. Samuel, ed., *The Evangelical Succession in the Church of England* (Cambridge, Mass.: James Clarke, 1979), 73.
5. Pollock, *Shaftesbury,* 102. Shaftesbury was aroused about the poor after viewing a pauper's funeral.
6. G. R. Balleine, *A History of the Evangelical Party in the Church of England* (London: Longmans, Green, 1908), 282.
7. Edward Henry Bickersteth, *The Rock of Ages* (New York: The Bible Scholar, n.d.). A very rich study.
8. Montagu Cyril Bickersteth, *Robert Bickersteth* (New York: Dutton, 1887). Interestingly, Robert was saved from drowning by Dean Henry Alford of Canterbury, a venerable name in evangelical scholarship (21).

9.3.7 CHARLES KINGSLEY—ASSESSING THE EMPHASIS

Let us read the Bible as we never read it before. Let us read every word, ponder every word; first in its plain human sense. . . . In the present day a struggle is coming . . . a question must be tried—is intellectual Science or the Bible, truth; and All Truth?

If, however, I found it in Scripture, I should believe it: what I want is— plain, inductive proof from texts.

For if we once lose our faith in the Old Testament, our faith in the New will soon dwindle to the impersonal "spiritualism" of Frank Newman, and the German phosophasters [those who turned to salt].

The value of the Bible teaching depends on the truth of the Bible story. That is my belief. Any criticism which tries to rob me of that, I shall look at fairly, but very severely indeed."

—Charles Kingsley

Evangelicals were filling the land with a rhapsodic diversity of preaching. They ranged from the perennially popular convert from Catholicism **William Blake Kirwan** (1754–1805) to **Henry Melvill** (1800–1871), who particularly influenced Ruskin and Browning and whom Spurgeon called "a Demosthenes among preachers."[1] The Broad church preachers (comparable to the mediating school in Germany) were often reared as evangelicals, like **Frederick Denison Maurice** (1805–1872), who was always at the center of controversy. Coleridge and the German school of Schleiermacher exerted much influence on these thinkers, although Maurice was electrifying in his preaching. One listener said of him, "He seemed to be the channel of communication, not the source of it." A close friend of Maurice was the irrepressibly robust **Charles Kingsley** (1819–1875), who one day walked fifty-two miles.

Kingsley was born into an evangelical minister's home. He was something of a prodigy, preaching a sermon on "Following God" at the age of four. The sermon was transcribed by his mother.[2] She sent it to the bishop of Peterborough, who predicted a bright future for its author. Quite shy and never popular while growing up, he had a cumbersome hesitation in his speech, yet it never manifested itself while he preached.[3] After his studies at Cambridge, he took the curacy at Eversley near Hampshire, a neglected rural parish where he spent the next thirty-three years. Like Baxter at Kidderminster, Kingsley made the parish. When he arrived, the alehouses were full and the church was empty, but Kingsley set himself to a vigorous ministry that changed the whole community.

A glutton for work, Kingsley tended to wear himself out until he needed a leave of absence. He served first as professor of English literature and composition at Queen's College and then filled the chair of modern history at Cambridge vacated by William Wilberforce's son-in-law, **Sir James Stephen.**[4] He would teach one day per week. He introduced an evening service at Eversley, as Samuel

Wilberforce had done on the Isle of Wight. Kingsley was a great lover of the Bible, and was deeply committed to preaching the text. He regarded David Strauss, whose *Leben Jesu* went so far as to deny the historicity of Jesus, as "the great false prophet of the day, who must be faced and fought by the clergy."[5] Through all of his hyperactivity, he kept his focus: "One thing I do know, that I have to preach Jesus Christ and Him crucified."

Kingsley identified with the impoverished rural folk in his parish and led the Chartist charge for social reform. He was a prolific writer of novels, poetry, and drama. Although prolix in style, his great sea story *Westward Ho* is one of the best. *The Water Babies* and the plight of Tom, the little chimney-sweep, deeply moved Lord Shaftesbury, and *Alton Locke* was heralded by Thomas Carlyle as "a new explosive or red-hot shell against the devil's dung-heap."[6] His novel *Hypatia* concerns the conflict between the early Christians and Alexandrian philosophy. His description of decadent religion as "the opiate of the people" was seized by Karl Marx as apt for his purposes.

Kingsley's literary feats led him to significant friendships with Frederica Bremer, who visited the Kingsleys, as well as Harriet Beecher Stowe and John Greenleaf Whittier. The Kingsleys on occasion vacationed with the Tennysons.[7] He fought the Tractarians, and his attack on Newman precipitated Newman's famous *Apologia Pro Vita Sua*. The Roman Catholic convert and poet Gerard Manley Hopkins said that Kingsley had "the air and spirit of a man bouncing up from the table with his mouth full of bread and cheese and saying that he meant to stand no blasted nonsense." He became one of the queen's favorite preachers and engaged in correspondence with **Adolph Saphir**, the Jewish convert who preached so magnificently and made clear his belief "as firmly as any modern interpreter of prophecy, that you are still the nation, and that you have a glorious, as I think a culminating part to play in the history of the race."[8] Doubtless to his physical disadvantage, he took on additional roles and assignments, first as canon of Chester in 1869 under the godly Dean Howson and then as canon of Westminster. He regularly preached in these famous cathedrals.

We are blessed with various collections of his preaching, including village sermons and sermons from Westminster. One observer commented:

> In preaching he would try to keep still and calm, and free from all gesticulation; but as he went on, he had to grip and clasp the cushion on which the sermon rested, in order to restrain the intensity of his own emotion; and when, in spite of himself, his hands would escape, they would be lifted up, the fingers of the right hand working with a peculiar hovering movement, of which he was quite unconscious; his eyes seemed on fire, his whole frame worked and vibrated. It was riveting to see him as well as hear him, as his eagle glance penetrated every corner of the church, and whether there were few or many there, it was enough for him that those who were present were human beings standing between two worlds, and that it was his terrible responsibility as well as high privilege, to deliver a message to each and all.[9]

Kingsley was a renaissance man with wide interests and love for nature. He was a wonderful father to his children and husband to his dear wife, Fanny. Unstinting in his preparation, he often talked about his next week's text on Sunday evening after a busy Lord's Day and started promptly on Tuesday in his work, allowing it to simmer through the week until providing the finishing touches on Friday. He traveled to the West Indies and later to America, where he had special joy in his visits with William Cullen Bryant. He was a man who could sleep at anytime or anywhere and derive much benefit from a brief rest.

Among his best sermons are those preached on "The Mystery of the Cross" and "The Word of God" from Psalm 119:89–96.[10] These are hearty, sound messages well applied. In the latter he begins by saying:

This text is of infinite importance, to you, and me, and all mankind. For if the text is not true; if there is not a Word of God, who endures [and] is settled forever in heaven: then this world is a miserable and a made place; and the best thing, it seems to me, that poor ignorant human beings can do, is to eat and drink, for tomorrow we die.

He argues here for the indissoluble unity of the written and the living Word of God. In his "Good News of God" he shared his typical preaching, simply structured, and full of Christ and his cross. He ranged over the whole of Scripture and was concerned to expose the text and its meaning for all of his hearers. When asked the secret of his inner life, he responded: "I had a friend!" Charles Kingsley died at fifty-six after a full and energetic life lived for his Lord and Master.

1. T. Harwood Pattison, *The History of Christian Preaching* (Philadelphia: American Baptist Publication Society, 1903), 305ff.
2. Fanny Kingsley, ed., *Charles Kingsley: His Letters and Memories of His Life* (London: Kegan Paul, 1882), 1:5.
3. Ibid., 1:13, 245.
4. Ibid., 1:115, 2:107. A delightful sketch of Stephen may be found in Michael Hennell, *Sons of the Prophets: Evangelical Leaders of the Victorian Church* (London: SPCK, 1979), 91–103.
5. Kingsley, *Charles Kingsley,* 1:193.
6. Johnstone G. Patrick, "A Fighter for the Faith: Centenary Salute to Charles Kingsley," *Life of Faith* (January 25, 1975): 3–4. Kingsley would often say, "Never lose an opportunity to see something beautiful!"
7. Kingsley, *Charles Kingsley,* 1:89.
8. Ibid., 1:280.
9. Ibid., 1:283.
10. Charles Kingsley, *Westminster Sermons* (London: Macmillan, 1884); *The Good News of God* (London: Macmillan, 1908). We happily possess quite a battery of books containing the sermons of Charles Kingsley.

9.4 THE CONTINENTAL CATARACT

And the whole nineteenth century was dominated by this apostasy from Christianity.

—Kurt Aland

After the French Revolution and the Napoleonic era, all of central Europe was reorganized. Under the aegis of **Frederick William III** of Prussia (a devout Calvinist), the Lutheran and Reformed churches in Germany came into union in 1817. But as Germany moved to unification, unbelief and skepticism about the Bible swept through the universities. "Kant is our Moses," chortled Holderlin, as he heralded deliverance from orthodoxy via Kant's epistemological bifurcation. But Kant left Christian faith in the shifting realm of the subjective.[1] Burgeoning secularism deadened the churches. Hegel and his disciple Karl Marx lost God in the dialectic of history, and Ludwig Feuerbach's *The Essence of Christianity* in 1841 concluded that God was only the projection of the human mind.

As we have seen, there were those particularly in the Broad church party in England who were taken with the new styles in thinking. George Eliot, Frank Newman (the cardinal's brother), and J. A. Froude hustled into the vanguard of those who took their signals from the Continent. F. D. Maurice and Benjamin Jowett, the great Oxford don, couldn't jettison the categories of orthodoxy fast enough. When the notorious *Essays and Reviews* of 1860 were published, Samuel Wilberforce observed, "Trains of German doubt intended to blow up the Church."[2]

Yet there were champions of historic Christianity who came to the fore, such as the redoubtable **E. W. Hengstenberg,** the Berlin professor, editor, and prolific writer joined more traditional and pietistic forces to do battle for orthodoxy.[3] (Hengstenberg's massive *The Christology of the Old Testament* and his commentaries continue to be a great blessing today.) A powerful revival of confessionalism rose to counteract the tidal waves of infidelity pouring out of the universities. Bible societies, the Inner Mission, and foreign missionary societies began to proliferate. Movements like the Basel Mission Society, founded in 1815, and the Rhenish Mission Society, founded in 1828, were committed to the propagation of the gospel of Christ.[4] God was not without his witnesses in this tempestuous time.

---

1. James J. Sheehan, *German History* (Oxford: Clarendon, 1989), 242. The best recent survey.
2. M. A. Crowther, *Church Embattled: Religious Controversy in Mid-Victorian England* (London: David and Charles, 1970). Shows the negative but also the positive under men like Olshausen, Stier, Dorner, and those who came together in the Evangelical Alliance where Krummacher gave one of his most memorable addresses.
3. Sheehan, *German History,* 561.
4. Kurt Aland, *A History of Christianity* (Philadelphia: Fortress, 1986), 2:352.

9.4.1 F. W. KRUMMACHER—THE DYNAMISM OF PREACHING

There have fallen again the tongues of fire which bear witness for Christ; from the pulpits there is heard more and more in new and distinct utterances the proclamation of the old good Word; there are flourishing mission schools under the shelter of the gentle royal scepter; Bible societies in full and unwearied activity; institutions aiming at the promotion of the welfare of the neglected and the criminal, and what is yet more than all this there are considerable bands of men continually increasing in number in all districts of the land who have sworn that they will never bow the knee to Baal; a company of praying men encompassing the land as a chain, diffusing blessings all around.

—F. W. Krummacher

The leading preacher in this rekindling of evangelical zeal in an age of torpor was **Friedrich Wilhelm Krummacher** (1796–1868). Krummacher was born in a line of preachers from both his father's and mother's families. John Ker likens him to Thomas Guthrie "in appearance and in his pulpit manner, as well as in the tone of his mind."[1]

The Krummacher family must be recognized as pivotal in a spiritual awakening along the lower Rhine.[2] Krummacher later wrote of his father's sermons:

I do not remember ever to have heard anyone preach the Gospel in a more loving tone and with a more dignified mien, or in a more heart-winning manner, than he did. Were I to give a motto to his sermons which would at once characterize their spirit and their general theme, I would present these words of the apostle, which naturally suggest themselves—"But after that the kindness and love of God our Saviour toward man appeared, not by works of righteousness which we have done, but according to His mercy He saved us, by the washing of regeneration, and renewing of the Holy Ghost." He discerned his commission as a preacher especially in these words of Isaiah—"Comfort ye, comfort ye my people, saith your God. Speak ye comfortably to Jerusalem, and cry unto her, that her warfare is accomplished, that her iniquity is pardoned." And he remained true to this commission to the end of his days, only with ever-increasing penetration into the mysterious ground on which the command rested.[3]

Young Krummacher studied at both Halle and Jena universities. By this time Semler and Gesenius were inducting students at Halle into a cold rationalism. Rationalism would not be countered until the ascendancy of Tholuck in 1827. Krummacher says of his seminary experience:

We saw the Lord of Glory stripped of all His supernatural majesty, shrivelled into the rank of a mere Rabbi, noble indeed, and high gifted, but yet always entangled by the prejudices of his time. He had never performed a miracle, and had neither risen from the dead nor ascended up

into heaven. We saw also the whole contents of the Gospel, after being
stripped of its particularistic and mythic veilings, reduced to a mere moral
system, for the manifestation of which no divine revelation was at all
needed.[4]

Luther's works steadied Krummacher, and his family and friends upheld him.
He survived what carried away thousands of students and "doomed many congregations to this day to spiritual famine because they have presented to them
only the husks and chaff which were there gathered and stored up by his
[Wegscheider's] students."[5] Krummacher went on to serve five fulfilling years
as assistant in Frankfort-on-Main and then to several happy years as pastor of
the Reformed congregation at Ruhrort, of which he later spoke:

> Oh, how incomparably happy was the time which was granted to me in
> dear Ruhrort. I not only preached to a congregation hungering for the
> Word of God, which received from my lips with eyes beaming with de-
> light whatever I had to offer them from the treasury of the gospel; but I
> also felt myself as if borne up by the affections and by the prayers of
> considerable circles of experienced and well-informed Christians who
> gathered around me. . . .[6]

He spent nine fruitful years at Barmen and then went on to Elbersfeld, where
the blessing of God was poured out most lavishly upon his preaching. While there
he preached the sermon on Galatians 1:8–9 which he called "the torch of war
into the midst of the church life." It was a sermon that raised a clarion call against
rationalism and unbelief. At this time he declined the call to the faculty of the
Mercersburg Seminary in Philadelphia. Instead he recommended Dr. Philip
Schaff, who accepted the position and went on to a noteworthy career in the United
States. Schaff described Krummacher's preaching:

> Krummacher does not make a pleasing impression at first sight. He is
> not good looking. He is built like a lion, and his eloquence corresponds
> with his build. An imposing, strong figure, massive facial features, a wild
> confused head of hair, gray eyes, the man vanishes, so to speak, in the
> pulpit orator. The solemn bass voice which itself sounds forth like thun-
> der upon his congregation, the rushing torrent of his figures, the bold
> but controlled gestures, the tossing of the head from side to side, the
> contents of the sermon itself, which is always original and, clothed in
> splendid garb, unlocks the depths of sin and grace, now breaking to pieces
> the fabric of the old man and the pleasures of the world, now comforting
> and with magic softness wooing to the source of salvation . . .[7]

By this time his sermons and books were in widening circulation. His work
with the Evangelical Alliance extended his influence around the world, and he
was called to the great Trinity Church in Berlin. Schleiermacher had once
preached in Trinity, and now the church was empty. Soon it was filled, but

Krummacher realized what devastation higher criticism had wrought. He spoke in terms of "a new fall of man" and used the Lamentations for his jeremiads of doom. In 1853 the king called him to be court preacher at Potsdam, where he ministered until his death. The king wrote him on one occasion, "That advent sermon which you preached surpassed all I have ever heard," and ordered copies. But when warned of the king's displeasure if he did not conform to a certain controversial edict, Krummacher responded, "Tell his Imperial Majesty that I am ready at any time to lay my head on the block at His Majesty's command; but when His Imperial Majesty presumes to be lord of the gospel, I despise His Imperial Majesty!" (M. Niemoller, cf. 12.6.1).

Krummacher's introductions were brief and his divisions of the text were clear. Ker likens his sermons to "a gallery of paintings." He was so graphic and detailed in sketching the death of John the Baptist that some in the audience shrieked and fainted.[8] Sterling examples of his expositions are his popular sermons on Elijah and Elisha.[9] Good samples of his prose style include his peerless meditations on the last days of Christ, of which the eminent evangelical bibliographer, Wilbur Smith, once said: "I believe that the greatest single volume written during the entire nineteenth century is *The Suffering Saviour,* by Friedrich Wilhelm Krummacher."[10] The organizational schema and his chapters on "Lord, Is It I?" and "It Is Finished" are without equal. Smith's work contains a complete listing of the works of Krummacher translated into English. His brief introduction to a sermon from 1 Kings 8:65 on "Solomon's Feast" displays some of his charm:

> The words we have read place us in one of the happiest times in the history of Israel. They introduce us to a feast. The joyful songs of these fair days have been silenced for thousands of years. But if we listen, they renew themselves in our hearts with loftier tones. Let us try to catch their echoes by thinking, first, of the object of the feast, and, secondly, of the feast itself.[11]

---

1. John Ker, *Lectures on Preaching* (New York: Armstrong, 1889), 357.
2. Kurt Aland, *A History of Christianity* (Philadelphia: Fortress, 1886), 2:339.
3. F. W. Krummacher, *Friedrich Wilhelm Krummacher: An Autobiography* (New York: Robert Carter, 1869), 29–30. Preface by John Cairns.
4. Ibid., 52.
5. Wilbur M. Smith, "Biographical Introduction" to F. W. Krummacher, *The Suffering Saviour* (Chicago: Moody, 1952), xv.
6. Ibid., xvii.
7. Ibid., xx.
8. Ker, *Lectures on Preaching,* 363.
9. F. W. Krummacher, *Elijah the Tishbite* (Grand Rapids: Zondervan, n.d.); *Elisha* (Grand Rapids: Zondervan, n.d.); of special delight and fragrance, *Cornelius the Centurion* (Edinburgh: Fraser and Crawford, 1839).
10. Smith, "Biographical Introduction," xi.
11. Ker, *Lectures on Preaching,* 367.

9.4.2   *RUDOLF STIER—THE DEMANDS OF THE TEXT*

I solemnly pledge myself to preach to you nothing else than what stands in the Bible; to derive everything from the sacred text; to make the Bible clear to you; to initiate you so into it that you may yourselves be able to see the only true and best preaching in the very text itself.

—E. Rudolph Stier at his installation at Frankleben, 1829

Preserve unto us, above all things, thy Holy Word and Gospel, and may they ever be preached more fruitfully among us, that our devotion and true knowledge may ever grow hand in hand! Constantly accompany our music and song with the power of thy Spirit upon all hearts, and may we also be ever consecrated to thee. Let whoever shall hear this organ be reminded thereby of thee, and of the eternal glory to which thou invitest us all! And let whoever shall pass by this house of God on worldly business be exhorted, by the tones he shall hear, to give heed to thy word, and to humble himself before thee that he may be saved!

—E. Rudolph Stier's prayer at the organ dedication in Frankleben

A peasant said to his pastor that the people could understand him because he preached "just as it was in the Bible, and if they did not do right now, the fault could not be his."[1] That pastor was **Ewald Rudolf Stier** (1800–1862), well known for his Bible commentaries and biblical preaching. He was born the second child in a Lutheran Prussian family and early made quite a record for himself in school. He began to study law at the University of Berlin but decided against a legal career because of his love for poetry. Then he shifted to theology under the famous Neander, even in the face of his father's opposition.

From 1815 to 1818, Stier sat under Schleiermacher and DeWette. He studied also under Gesenius and Wegscheider, but was not swept into antisupernaturalism. The influence and example of his grandfather, who was an old-time preacher, and his uncle helped spare him from the poison of their rationalism. The death of his fiancée Pauline, along with his reading of Thomas à Kempis, also inclined him to spiritual things. At this time Tholuck became his good friend.

Further moved by the Bible exposition sponsored by Baron von Kottwitz,[2] Stier made "his full and radical self-consecration to God."[3] He became convinced "that Scripture cannot be holy Scripture and the norm of faith unless it have the character of strict inspiration."[4] Finishing his training at the University of Wittenberg, Stier preached his first sermon on the death of Christ for needy sinners.

For a while Stier taught in Lithuania and pursued a beautiful courtship with Ernestine, daughter of the venerable Dr. K. I. Nitszche of Bonn. Upon their marriage, he accepted a call to teach Old and New Testament in the original languages at the Mission Seminary in Basle, where he was associated with President Christian Gottlieb Blumhard. In that same year his first book, *Hints on the Believing Interpretation of the Scriptures,* was published; in it he argues that the Bible is the source of all true knowledge.

The school was a beehive of activity for evangelical missionaries, but after four years Stier's health collapsed. He was virtually an invalid from the beginning of his clerical career and often preached sitting down. The death of his wife was a heavy blow to his already weakened frame, but he remarried and went on to produce his famous Polyglot Bible and a highly acclaimed series of sermons on Old Testament saints.

After a year's leave, he took a pastoral assignment in Frankleben (1829), where he wrote his *Keryktics* on the science of preaching. He then went on to Wichlinghausen (1838), where his penchant for the fusion of exegetical and practical became well known. His series of expository sermons on James was attended by large and appreciative crowds. He took the opposite of Luther's view on the importance of James.[5]

Ker says of his preaching:

> But Stier went to the Bible alone, and to all the Bible, and in approaching it he sought to strip himself of everything that would prevent him from receiving its full impression and from reflecting it in its rounded completeness on his fellow-men. This is why we have called him a biblical preacher . . . the Bible is one book with a pervading plan—the history of salvation— and with the living breath of the Holy Ghost through it all. No part, therefore, can be interpreted by itself; each part must be taken in the light of the whole, and has always some reference to the whole.[6]

His sermons implemented a brief introduction and a focus on the development of the main principle in the text which then must be applied. To Stier, all sermons were to be both scriptural and personal.[7] His classic works have widely influenced many, particularly his *Words of the Lord Jesus*,[8] *Words of the Apostles*,[9] and *Words of the Risen Saviour*.[10] All of these volumes were translated into English and circulated broadly. He was also known for the hymnbook he produced. He gathered ministers together for the purpose of digging into the Scripture.

From 1847 to 1850, Stier lived in retirement at Wittenberg, but subsequently took pastoral superintendencies in Schkeuditz near Magdeburg and at Eisleben, where he died. On his gravestone is inscribed: "But the Word of our God shall stand forever."[11]

Here was a preacher deeply rooted in the text of Scripture. God was yet at work, and even out of the world's hotbed of rationalism and skepticism came streams of living water.

---

1. John P. Lacroix, *The Life of Rudolf Stier* (New York: Nelson and Phillips, 1874), 211.
2. Ibid., 47ff.
3. Ibid., 55ff.
4. Ibid., 61.
5. Ibid., 279.
6. John Ker, *Lectures on the History of Preaching* (New York: Armstrong, 1889), 352.
7. Ibid., 356.

8. Rudolf Stier, *Words of the Lord Jesus* (Edinburgh: T & T Clark, 1872).

9. Rudolf Stier, *Words of the Apostles* (Edinburgh: T & T Clark, 1889).

10. Rudolf Stier, *Words of the Risen Saviour* (Edinburgh: T & T Clark, 1887). The translator is William B. Pope, the British Methodist from Manchester whose *A Higher Catechism of Theology* is a mature Wesleyan statement. All three of Stier's books are rich, careful exegetical treatments of key passages.

11. Lacroix, *The Life of Rudolf Stier,* 332.

9.4.3   THE BLUMHARDTS—THE DEVOTION OF THE PREACHER

When Blumhardt preached, it was out of a vision . . . he himself lived in the powers of the kingdom which he proclaimed, and therefore he could say: "One needs to have experienced something of heaven, then one knows what the kingdom is."

—R. Lejeune

It was not ability, not art, not fluency of speech—it was a power of the Saviour that made my father a preacher . . . If only people had prayed with my father, we would have had a different theology a long time ago . . . to him the Kingdom of God was something immensely greater, more eternal and more effective for body and soul than anything he saw in Christianity.

—Christoph Blumhardt

Even in the stygian darkness of unbelief, there were those who were watchers in the night. Among those who stood against "the bold mocking spirit of the age" were **Gerhard Tersteegen,** the sweet singer from the previous century whose great hymns John Wesley translated. "O Thou Hidden Love of God" was thought by Oliver Wendell Holmes to be the greatest hymn in the English language. **E. W. Hengstenberg** (1808–1869), was staunch in defense of Scripture at Berlin. **August Tholuck,** whom we have already seen spearheading a remarkable renaissance of pietism at Halle,[1] drew John Ker, Charles Hodge, and Calvin Stowe, husband of Harriet Beecher Stowe, to that university.[2] And **Julius Muller** (1801–1878) of Marburg was a champion of orthodox faith and biblical exposition.

In the vanguard of those who had a truly spiritual ministry in this dire time were **Johan Christoph Blumhardt** (1805–1880) and his son **Christoph Blumhardt** (1842–1919). The elder Pastor Blumhardt, as he was called, was born near Stuttgart and trained for ministry at Tubingen. He then served a brief vicarate, after which he taught at the Basle Mission Seminary for six years.[3] After serving another assistantship, he took the pastorate of the Mottlingen parish, where three phenomena took place:

1. Blumhardt experienced what he called "the battle," the confrontation with evil and the demonic that focused on one of his parishioners, Gotliebin Dittus, who had dabbled in magic arts when young and was now demon-possessed and suicidal;[4]

2. The movement of repentance and awakening that reached out to many in all parts of Germany;
3. The ministry of prayer and healing that led him ultimately to leave Mottlingen and purchase Bad Boll, to which the sick and hopeless of all classes resorted for the ministry of the Word and prayer.

At his death, his son Christoph became his successor in the ministry.[5]

Like his father, Christoph was a gifted and powerful preacher. After serving several parishes, he joined his father and went on extensive preaching missions throughout the nation. He preached twenty times to thousands in Berlin in 1888. He shared the "Jesus is Victor!" emphasis of his father and increasingly ministered outside traditional circles. "Die and Jesus will live" epitomized his thrust. He became involved in political affairs and strove for social justice, serving in the legislative assembly in Wurtemberg from 1900 to 1906.[6] Blumhardt focused on the Second Coming of Christ and proclaimed that "Jesus is on the way!" The fullness of his now/not yet tension came to be widely celebrated by Eduard Thurneysen, who introduced him to his appreciative friend Karl Barth. Barth affirmed the preaching on the "old texts" and wrote approvingly of Blumhardt in 1916.[7] Bonhoeffer, Moltmann, Jacques Ellul, and many others have acknowledged the positive influence of the Blumhardts. Their writings and sermons have been kept available through the efforts of Hutterian Brothers in New York and Connecticut.[8]

The sermonic style is simple and direct; the use of the text is striking and dominant. A passion and warmth are apparent. Such messages as "Jesus among the Wretched" from Romans 10:10[9] and "The Saviour Is Coming" from Matthew 24:36–42 are typical of the gripping nature of Blumardt's preaching.[10] We are very much reminded of what Jessie Penn-Lewis, Watchman Nee, and T. Austin-Sparks were to do later.

Above all, Blumhardt's Christocentricity and faithful commitment to biblical preaching kept the work from spilling over into the serious pathology often characteristic of experience-oriented movements.

---

1. We shall consider George Müller among the English Plymouth Brethren, but he came from the Halle circle in Germany, where he tutored Charles Hodge for a time; see A. T. Pierson, *George Muller of Bristol* (London: Pickering and Inglis, 1899). Franke's orphanages were Müller's. Again we see a fascinating networking.
2. Andrew L. Drummond, *German Protestantism Since Luther* (London: Epworth, 1951), 128.
3. Kenneth Scott Latourette describes the critical founding of the Basle Mission Society in *A History of the Expansion of Christianity* (Grand Rapids: Zondervan, 1941, 1969), 4:90–91; the theological course of the mission and its now defunct training schools are traced by Jacques Weber, "The Basel Mission: Its Historic Deviations from and/or Its Adherence to Its Founding Principles" (M.A. thesis, Trinity Evangelical Divinity School, 1982).
4. Frank S. Boshold, trans., *Blumhardt's Battle: A Conflict with Satan* (New York: Thomas E. Lowe, 1970).

5. Alo Munch, *Johan Christoph Blumhardt, ein Zeuge des gegenwartligen Gottes* (Basel, Switzerland: Brunnen-Verlag Giessen, 1949); Hans Fredrich Lavater, *Bad Boll durch 350 Jahre und Beide Blumhardt* (Basel, Switzerland: Brunnen-Verlag Giessen, 1951).
6. R. Lejeune, *Christoph Blumhardt and His Message* (Rifton, N.Y.: Plough, 1938, 1963), 71.
7. Karl Barth, *Action and Waiting* (Rifton, N.Y.: Plough, 1969).
8. Johan Christoph Blumhardt and Christoph Friedrich Blumhardt, *Now Is Eternity* (Rifton, N.Y.: Plough, 1976); Vernard Eller, ed., *Thy Kingdom Come: A Blumhardt Reader* (Grand Rapids: Eerdmans, 1980).
9. Lejeune, *Christoph Blumhardt and His Message,* 186.
10. Ibid., 220.

9.4.4 *JOHAN TOBIAS BECK—DARING IN THE PULPIT*

It is Scripture, in union with nature and life, faithfully appropriated on all sides, and realized in a man's own experience, which makes the theologian and preacher, the teacher and pastor, capable of striking out a course for eternal truth amid the rocks and currents of opinion in his time, in every sphere both small and great, and fashioning men of God, characters meet for the kingdom of heaven.

—J. T. Beck in *Pastoral Theology of the New Testament*

The curate in Charles Kingsley's novel *Yeast* observed from his standpoint that all Germans were pantheists. This was of course not true, but Hegel's influence made it seem that way at times. Radical scholarship seemed to be in the driver's seat in most of the universities. Names like Ewald, Wellhausen, and his successor Harnack, whose *What Is Christianity?* epitomized liberal thought, dominated the scene. Hermann and Ritschl, whose thinking on the atonement was anthropocentric,[1] all were part of a great swell of unbelief and skepticism.

Of course there were pockets of conservatism and orthodoxy such as at Leipzig, where the renowned Orientalist **Franz Delitzsch** (1813–1888), known as the Christian Talmudist, stood firmly for the supernatural and established the *Instituta Judaica*. His collaborator on the still widely-used Old Testament commentary series, **Karl Friedrich Keil,** a student of Hengstenberg, likewise took a firm stand on the miraculous.

Another orthodox wheelhorse important in the company of the preachers is **Johan Tobias Beck** (1804–1879), born near Stuttgart and educated at Tubingen, where Strauss and Baur carried the day with their advocacy of a purely historical study of the Bible. They acknowledged only Romans, Corinthians, and Galatians as genuine Pauline letters. His close friendship with **Wilhelm Hofacker** and others helped him fend off hypercritical views. He fed deeply on Bengel and Oetinger and served well in several smaller parishes where he gained quite a reputation for his biblical exposition.

Beck was called to teach as assistant professor and preacher in Basel, leaving us six volumes of his sermons from that time period. His plain, simple lifestyle and his dedication to the text made a great impression. His sermons were almost all homilies, and he always sustained a passionate emphasis on missions and evangelism.

In 1843, Beck took the appointment to Tubingen, where F. C. Baur favored him because of a long-standing feud with Ewald, who opposed Beck.[2] He stepped into the vacuum at Tubingen and served a noble purpose, enjoying popularity among the students. The impact upon Wurtemberg and southern Germany cannot be overstated. Ker reports of Beck's attractiveness:

> He had laid not only his understanding but his heart, conscience, his spirit, close to the Bible, having made it the unbroken study of his life. He knew it as a man knows the home in which he has lived for years, and was "a man of the Word," as few have been since the days of the Apostles.[3]

Beck had a reputation for preaching in the classroom and teaching from the pulpit. *Ideae Scripturariae* must be above *ideae academicae*. He saw Strauss, Baur, and Renan as "anatomists" who missed the life of the organism.[4] His classic *Pastoral Theology of the New Testament* represents his mature thinking. It is drenched with Scripture and points to Christ as the pattern. The models for ministry in the New Testament, according to Beck, are prescriptive in a principal sense. He explores the preaching of Jesus and the apostles for clues relevant to our preaching.[5] Beck also left major commentaries on Romans and the Pastorals. Here is a preacher-scholar blooming in an arid venue.

1. Andrew L. Drummond, *German Protestantism Since Luther* (London: Epworth, 1951), 143. It is worthwhile to peruse Albrecht Ritschl's *The Christian Doctrine of Justification and Reconciliation* (Edinburgh: T & T Clark, 1900) just to perceive the disastrous theological defection that had taken place.
2. Horton Harris, *The Tubingen School: A Historical and Theological Investigation of the School of F. C. Baur* (Grand Rapids: Baker, 1975, 1990), 43, 52.
3. John Ker, *Lectures on the History of Preaching* (New York: Armstrong, 1889), 384.
4. Ibid., 385.
5. J. T. Beck, *Pastoral Theology of the New Testament* (New York: Scribner and Welford, 1885). Old but choice.

9.4.5 C. E. LUTHARDT—DRIVE IN THE PULPIT

> A bridge must be thrown over the abyss that separates the holy God from sinful people. God must come to us, in order that we may come to him: "Where sin abounded, grace did much more abound" in Jesus who appeared as Mediator between God and us.
>
> —C. E. Luthardt

Beautiful Leipzig in Saxony claimed cultural distinction in musicians like Bach, Schumann, Mendelssohn, and Wagner, as well as the philosopher Leibniz and the poet Goethe. Its university, founded in 1409, maintained its strength in

the onslaught of rationalism in the nineteenth century, not only in biblical studies with Delitzsch but also in systematics with **Christoph Ernst Luthardt** (1823–
1902). Luthardt was born near Nuremberg and studied at Erlangen and Berlin.
Not only was he a strong exegete—his commentary on the Gospel of John is still
used—but he was an ecclesiastical statesman of repute, the author of a major
dogmatics, and a powerful preacher. He taught at Erlangen and Marburg and went
on to an illustrious career at Leipzig from 1856 to 1902.

Luthardt's exegetically oriented systematic theology has exerted a lasting influence on many Lutherans.[1] He took the position over against Schleiermacher
and others that, while the material principle of dogmatics is fellowship with God
through Christ's atonement, the normative principle is the Holy Scripture and
"that Scripture is the authentic original record of divine revelation, and as such
the Christian is sure of its truth."[2] What establishes the truth of Scripture above
all else is the internal witness of the Spirit. Luthardt not only taught this but
preached it eloquently and effectively. Dargan refers to his appeal to the emotions as he preached,[3] and Ker speaks of him as "a distinguished [preacher] who
never fails to find an audience . . . his aim is to reach the heart and conscience,
but his sermons are marked by a union of simplicity with elevation, and by
thoughtfulness compressed often into short, sententious sentences."[4]

A recent issue of *Decision* carried the gist of a sermon on "Jesus Christ: the
God-Man," which is a moving example of biblical preaching coupled with a strong
sense of theological construct. What a tribute and testimony to God's gifted servant. "He being dead, yet speaks."[5]

---

1. R. F. Weidner, *An Introduction to Dogmatic Theology based on Luthardt* (New York:
   Revell, 1888).
2. Ibid., 82.
3. E. C. Dargan, *A History of Preaching* (New York: Hodder and Stoughton, 1912), 2:382.
4. John Ker, *Lectures on the History of Preaching* (New York: Armstrong, 1889), 385.
5. Christoph Ernst Luthardt, "Was Jesus Christ Really God and Man?" *Decision* (December 1995): 26–27.

9.4.6   THEODOR CHRISTLIEB—DESIGNER OF THE CRAFT

The great work of the Christian preacher is not to be an orator but an
interpreter, to teach the people how to read and use the Word of God. He
is a conveyance-pipe to draw the water from the fountain and pour it on
grass and flowers to make them grow, also on consuming fires of sin to
extinguish them.

—Dr. John Ker

Dr. John Ker, who lectured on preaching and practical theology for his United
Presbyterian Church school in Glasgow, himself had served several congregations
and was a preacher "of rare and manifold faculty."[1] He gave particular attention to
German preaching, having spent time in Germany and seeing certain negatives:

There are some preachers who cut down the tree of life, and deal it out in hard dry planks, sometimes even presenting hard knots and sawdust— abstract doctrines without sap or sympathy. Others give flowers from parasitical plants which they have attached to it, things which have no fruit and no healing leaves. The first is the deadly formal; the second, the equally deadly fanciful.[2]

Such was not the preaching of **Theodor Christlieb** (1833–1889). Born in Birkenfeld and trained at Tubingen under Beck and Baur, Christlieb was decisively influenced by the former. He always placed the strongest stress on conversion. Christlieb served the German church in London for a time. This exposure to the larger Christian family encouraged him to be active within the Evangelical Alliance. He opposed the sterile rationalism that permeated the churches and universities and served as university preacher and professor of theology at Bonn with great distinction. Christlieb believed so strongly in the unique endowment of evangelists for Christ's church that he led in the purchase of a redundant Presbyterian Chapel in Bonn that was used for the training of evangelists. The school later moved to Bremen.

The brilliance of Christlieb's scholarship is seen in his magisterial *Modern Doubt and Christian Belief,* a peerless apologetic address to the burning issues of his time.[3] No one faced Hegelian pantheism and deistic rationalism more boldly or deftly than did Christlieb. He waded into the battles over the bodily resurrection of Christ and the miracles of the Bible. But further, Christlieb lectured and wrote on the homiletical issues necessary for the communication of the historic gospel. Dargan uses twenty-four footnotes from Christlieb in his treatment of German preaching, and Christlieb's *Homiletic: Lectures on Preaching* is a classic summons to build the sermon on the text itself.[4] While recognizing that expository preaching can never be independent of rhetoric, he yet saw the sermon as *sui generis* (unique). His treatment of the special occasions for preaching such as baptism, confirmation, marriage, and the funeral are exceedingly rich. He also spoke to preaching in connection with the observance of the Lord's Supper.[5] His thinking on preaching was sound and influential and the example of his own evangelistic sermons is particularly striking.

1. John Edwards, *Nineteenth-Century Preachers and Their Methods* (London: Charles Kelly, 1902), 65.
2. Ibid., 73.
3. Theodor Christlieb, *Modern Doubt and Christian Belief* (New York: Scribner, Armstrong, 1874), 549 pages. The best biographical data are in *Theodor Christlieb of Bonn: Memoir by His Widow and Sermons* (Edinburgh: Hodder and Stoughton, 1892). Other strong commentaries from this era are by Johan Peter Lange (1802–1884) and H. A. W. Meyer (1800–1873). Conservatives produced a vital literature at this time of assault on faith.
4. Theodor Christlieb, *Homiletic: Lectures on Preaching* (Edinburgh: T & T Clark, 1897).
5. Ibid., 291–307.

9.4.7   ABRAHAM KUYPER—THE DREAM OF THE KINGDOM OF GOD

> In a sermon on Revelation 3:11 on Hold that fast which thou hast: Do not bury our glorious orthodoxy in the treacherous pit of a spurious conservatism.

> Everything depends, therefore, upon a true and certain knowledge that our Refuge and Mediator really poured out His blood for us.
>
> —Abraham Kuyper

The Netherlands, so often crushed between great powers, has seen a remarkable church life down through the centuries and has produced many significant preachers, not the least of whom is **Abraham Kuyper** (1837–1920). Radicals like Kuenen and moderates like Van Oosterzee, who himself was an able expositor of Scripture, seemed to be carrying the day. It was then that the poet Bilderdikj and two Jewish converts of his, Isaac da Costa and Cappadose, "denounced with glowing fury the general declension" from orthodoxy.[1]

Kuyper's pastor father stayed in the state church when the secession of conservatives took place in 1834, while the young Kuyper at the University of Leiden drifted away from his orthodox moorings.[2] He was moved spiritually by a mediocre English novel by Yonge titled *Heir of Redclyffe* and by an old peasant woman whose stubborn orthodoxy struck him with the strange persistency of orthodoxy in the face of all comers. He soon broke completely with modernism and served significant pastorates in Utrecht and in Amsterdam. His watchword was ever "God is absolutely sovereign."

Kuyper was acclaimed as a preacher who loved to open the Scripture in the ministry of the Word. His sermon "The Antithesis Between Symbolism and Revelation" left no doubt that he regarded ritualism and symbolism as replacing revelation and moving dangerously from conscious to unconscious religion. Indeed, he astutely saw such a move as taking the faithful along the road to Asia not Calvary.[3]

Kuyper entered politics and as early as 1874 took a seat in Parliament, where he spoke on behalf of the poor and disenfranchised.[4] In 1875 he attended one of the D. L. Moody meetings in Brighton. He founded the Free University of Amsterdam in 1880, where he sought to further the strength of orthodoxy and where he served as professor of theology. In 1892 a merger of the church of the secessionists (including Kampen and Bavinck) with the main body formed the Netherlands Reformed Church. In 1898 he gave the Stone Lectures at Princeton on Calvinism, and in the same year he issued his princely *Encyclopedia of Sacred Theology*.

Kuyper wrote two hundred volumes and for many years edited a daily newspaper and a religious journal. In 1899 his beloved wife of thirty-six years died, and he did not remarry. In 1901 he was invited by Queen Wilhelmina to become Prime Minister of the Netherlands, where he served until 1905.

Above all in his lustrous career, Kuyper wanted to be known as a preacher of the Word of God. Turnbull argues that his primary burden was the exposure of the text.[5] Kuyper's studies on women in the Scriptures and his masterful work on the Holy Spirit give us a sense of the genius and giftedness of this devoted servant of Christ for whom the very reading of the Scripture in public was an interpretation of the Scripture.

Kuyper repeatedly stressed the necessity of "drawing near to God."

> The fellowship of being near unto God must become reality, in the full and vigorous prosecution of our life. It must permeate and give color to our feeling, our perceptions, our sensations, our thinking, our imagining, our willing, our acting, our speaking. It must not stand as a foreign factor in our life, but it must be the passion that breathes throughout our whole existence. . . . Stress on creedal confession, without drinking of these waters, runs dry in barren orthodoxy, just as truly as spiritual emotion, without clearness in confession standards, makes one sink in the bog of sickly mysticism.[6]

1. E. C. Dargan, *A History of Preaching* (New York: Hodder and Stoughton, 1912), 2:420.
2. The best biography available is Frank Vandenberg, *Abraham Kuyper* (Grand Rapids: Eerdmans, 1960).
3. Abraham Kuyper, *The Antithesis Between Symbolism and Revelation* (Edinburgh: T & T Clark, n.d.).
4. James W. Skillen, ed., *Abraham Kuyper's The Problem of Poverty* (Grand Rapids: Baker, 1891, 1991).
5. Ralph G. Turnbull, *A History of Preaching* (Grand Rapids: Baker, 1974), 3:367–68.
6. Abraham Kuyper, *Near to God* (Grand Rapids: Eerdmans, 1961).

9.5 THE SWISS-FRENCH BROOK

> The gospel is believed when it has ceased to be to us an external and has become an internal truth, when it has become fact in our consciousness. Christianity is conscience raised to its highest exercise.
>
> —Alexandre Vinet

> Whoever speaks, let him speak, as it were, the utterances of God.
>
> —1 Peter 4:11a (NASB)

After the revocation of the Edict of Nantes in 1685, two hundred thousand of the approximately nine hundred thousand Huguenots fled France for more distant parts. Persecution began to abate after the death of Louis XIV, but life in the Church of the Desert was arduous. Outbursts of intolerance, the defection of the Camisards, and inner turmoil in the nation upended stable growth.[1] Then came the traumas of the French Revolution and the Napoleonic wars. As late as 1815 to 1816, a wave of terror was directed at French Protestants. Protestants were dwindling.

In the nineteenth century such pulpit giants as **Henri Dominique Lacordaire,** who stood in the tradition of the great court preachers of the seventeenth century (cf. 6.3.2.3), held forth in Notre Dame and elsewhere in widely acclaimed discourses on redemption and upright living.[2] Lacordaire was supported especially by the bishop of Orleans, **Felix Dupanloup** (1801–1878), whose book *The Ministry of Preaching* is one of the better homiletics of the time. Although there were proportionately few preachers of note, there always were some who espoused popular preaching of the Scriptures to the flock. Steeped in all the classical sources, Dupanloup pressed his preachers "to put into the preaching of the Word that fire and vividness which go direct to hearts because they come from the heart; which take hold of and penetrate souls, which enlighten, soften, win over and convert them."[3] The Bible was for him "the very Word of God," and he advanced the thesis that a good pastor must seek to be a good preacher. He wanted subjects that led to conversion.[4] Dupanloup urged that sermons be characterized by clearness, vivacity, directness, movement, warmth, simplicity, and "familiarity . . . but never to the point of vulgarity."[5] He spoke against the dogma of papal infallibility at the Vatican Council in 1870. Here is evidence of clear thinking in an unexpected place and time.

Another medium for the propagation of the Word was through the outreach of the British and Foreign Bible Society. The saga of **George Borrow** (1803–1881) was legendary. An uneducated man from Norwich, Borrow was exceptionally gifted in linguistics, reading the Bible in thirteen languages. He was hired to translate a Manchu-language Scripture, and from 1833 to 1835 was posted to St. Petersburg. For the next five years he traveled in Portugal and Spain with a special burden for the Gypsies and the desire to translate the Bible into Romany. His book *The Bible in Spain*[6] and his collected letters[7] tell an absorbing story of heroism in preaching and testifying for Christ. The Reverend **R. B. Girdlestone** paid tribute on behalf of the society for his translations and ministry.[8] Thus was the Word transmitted in even the dreariest of settings.

---

1. John D. Woodbridge, *Revolt in Pre-Revolutionary France: The Prince de Conti's Conspiracy Against Louis XV* (Baltimore: Johns Hopkins University Press, 1995).
2. H. L. Sidney Lear, *Henri Dominique Lacordaire* (London: Rivingtons, 1882), 186.
3. Felix Dupanloup, *The Ministry of Preaching* (London: Griffith Farran, 1893), liii.
4. Ibid., 121.
5. Ibid., xix.
6. George Borrow, *The Bible in Spain* (London: Thomas Nelson, 1893).
7. T. H. Darlow, ed., *Letters of George Borrow* (London: Hodder and Stoughton, 1911).
8. Ibid., 471. Girdlestone wrote *The Grammar of Prophecy* (Grand Rapids: Baker, 1955).

9.5.1 Cesar Malan—Spearheading the Revival

Thank God the gospel has been once more preached in Geneva!
—Robert Haldane to Malan in Geneva, 1817

Rationalism had left a significant residue of resistance to the supernatural gospel, but a movement of revival emanating from Switzerland called the Reveille surged in a dramatic renewal of biblical preaching between 1820 and 1850. The exposition of Romans by Robert Haldane (cf. 9.1.1) in early 1817 fanned "the dying embers of Moravian pietism into a new flame."[1] Several new congregations were formed, including one led by **Merle d'Aubigne** (1794–1872), whose writings on Calvin continue to be a mainstay, and another led by **Cesar Malan** (1787–1864). A descendant of the Waldenses and the great-grandson of Reformation martyrs, Malan was steeped in Voltaire and Rousseau but went on toward ordination in 1810 and did some teaching. In 1816, under the influence of the Moravian Brethren, he was converted, and in the following year came into contact with the teaching of Haldane. Immediately he dedicated his life to preaching justification by faith alone wherever he could—which did not ingratiate him with the Reformed church in the canton.

Malan traveled extensively in Europe and in England and Scotland preaching with large effect. In appearance he was "apostolic," it was said, "with his hair long, forehead bare, and on each side a few little curls."[2] His preaching was characterized by what was called winning sweetness. This really was the beginning of the Free Evangelical churches of Switzerland. In 1831, the Societe Evangelique was formed to unify adherents of the revival under the leadership of **Professor Louis Gaussen** (1790–1863) and d'Aubigne. Gaussen was known for his great work on the full inspiration of Scripture and for his strong biblical commentaries.[3] Malan gathered an anthology of hymns for worship in 1834 which was titled *Chants de Sion*.[4] When he was in England he met a young woman, Charlotte Elliott, who seemed unclear on the way to salvation. He told her "Come just as you are, Charlotte," and of course she then wrote the great gospel invitation hymn, "Just as I am, without one plea, but that Thy blood was shed for me."[5]

Even though violence was directed against Malan and his followers, his popularity as a preacher continued to grow. His son Salomon was a gifted linguist in the Indian missionary movement and also wrote a definitive work on Gregory the Illuminator (256–332) in old Armenia. Malan's sermon on "The Piety of the Young Daniel" is a model of simplicity, biblicality, and spiritual passion.[6]

---

1. Stuart Piggin and John Roxborogh, *The St. Andrews Seven* (Edinburgh: Banner of Truth, 1985), 19.
2. Ibid., 19.
3. S. R. L. Gaussen, *The Inspiration of the Holy Scriptures* (Chicago: Moody, 1949). Gaussen contends: "Not only was the Scripture inspired on the day when God caused it to be written, but that we possess this word inspired eighteen hundred years ago; and that we may still, while holding our sacred text in one hand, and in the other all the readings collected by the learned in seven hundred manuscripts, exclaim with thankfulness, 'I hold in my hands my Father's testament, the eternal word of my God!'" (197). See also S. R. L. Gaussen, *The Prophet Daniel Explained*, 2 vols. (London: J and C Mozley, 1873) and *The World's Birthday: A Book for the Young* (London: T. Nelson, 1891). Gaussen served as professor of systematic theology, Oratoire, Geneva.

4. H. Daniel-Rops, *Our Brothers in Christ 1870–1959* (London: J. M. Dent, 1965), 245.
5. E. C. Dargan, *A History of Preaching* (New York: Hodder and Stoughton, 1912), 2:452.
6. Ibid., 452.

9.5.2   ALEXANDRE VINET—SPEAKING IN THE REVIVAL

> . . . that ugly man who becomes beautiful when he speaks.
> —the comment of a woman who listened to Alexandre Vinet

Preacher par excellence and homiletician of the revival was the celebrated **Alexandre Vinet** (1797–1847). Vinet was born near Lausanne, the son of descendants of Huguenot refugees. Early in life he was a connoisseur of literature and the arts. By age twenty he was a professor in a gymnasium and then at the University of Basel. He came to know Christ through the ministry of Cesar Malan and quickly took his place among the *momiers* or *mummers*, the epithet used to taunt the evangelicals. He gained notoriety in 1826 for his prize-winning essay calling for full religious freedom, titled "Memoir in Favor of Liberty of Cults."[1] He was consequently excluded from professorial chairs and served for ten years as professor of practical theology at Lausanne. He was highly respected and extended his significance beyond Switzerland to France.[2] Even the Roman Catholic Daniel-Rops pays him tribute:

> Beneath a calm exterior there lay a fiery soul. He followed in the steps of Pascal, with a stern conscience, a love for saintliness and a wide-ranging mind capable of seizing on essentials. He was prepared to sacrifice everything for his convictions. He demonstrated the painful void of the heart, which only the revelation of God incarnate and sacrifice can fill . . .[3]

Widely known for his *Treatise on Homiletics* and his *History of Preaching among the Reformed During the Seventeenth Century,* Vinet advocated careful biblical exposition and practiced it. He illustrated skillfully, and his view of speaking style was well expressed:

> Neither an anathema on art, nor art for art's sake, but art for God's sake, is what we insist upon. It results, as it seems to us, from what we have said, that good style is necessary, and that good style does not come of itself.

Significantly, America's two premier homileticians of the nineteenth century both show awareness of and indebtedness to Vinet. Austin Phelps of Andover makes eight references to Vinet,[4] and John Broadus of Southern Baptist makes twenty-six references.[5] As late as 1923 A. E. Garvie cites Vinet six times.[6]

Alexandre Vinet made a mark not only in his time but for eternity.

1. A. H. Newman, *A Manual of Church History* (Philadelphia: Judson, 1902), 2:572.
2. Paul T. Fuhrmann, *Extraordinary Christianity: The Life and Thought of Alexandre Vinet* (Philadelphia: Westminster, 1964).
3. H. Daniel-Rops, *Our Brothers in Christ 1870–1959* (London: J. M. Dent, 1965), 167.
4. Austin Phelps, *The Theory of Preaching* (London: Richard D. Dickinson, 1882).
5. John A. Broadus, *A Treatise on the Preparation and Delivery of Sermons* (New York: Armstrong, 1898).
6. A. E. Garvie, *The Christian Preacher* (New York: Scribner's, 1923).

9.5.3   *ADOLPHE MONOD—STRENGTHENING THE REVIVAL*

> Great artist by temperament, Monod was so also by conscience; for he considered it a duty to take all the literary care of which he was capable to convince and persuade men of the truth which saves.
>
> —Professor Paul Stapfer

Frederick L. Godet (1812–1900) provided sound exegesis to Francophones and to the world with commentaries on Romans, Luke, and the Gospel of John. Born in Neuchatel, Switzerland, but educated in Berlin and Bonn, Godet pastored churches, served as preceptor of the crown prince of Prussia for three years, and ultimately went on to professorships in his native land until his death. His *Commentary on Romans* has been immensely influential, with a strong insistence on the "moral liberty of man."[1] Godet was associated with the Free Evangelical movement and Pastor Otto Stockmeier.

The crowning expression of the Reveille in terms of preaching can be seen in **Adolphe Monod** (1802–1885). Four sons were born to Pastor Jean Monod: Frederick, Adolphe, William, and Horace. All four became preachers.

Adolphe was born in Copenhagen, where his father was serving the French Reformed Church. His brother Frederick was the prime mover in the formation of the Paris Evangelical Missionary Society in 1882.[2] Young Adolphe studied both in Paris and Geneva but was chilled by the rationalistic environment. He was converted in 1825 under the influence of Malan and d'Aubigne.[3] After pastoring briefly in Naples, he went to Lyons and lectured at the seminary in Montauban. Monod finished his ministry as pastor of the Church of the Oratory, the leading Reformed church in Paris until his demise. Christ-centered in his preaching, Monod was known for his humor and godly piety. Professor Stapfer considered Bossuet and Monod to represent French preaching at its apex.

In his widely noted lecture on "The Delivery of Sermons," Monod characteristically asserts:

> Take your position as the ambassador of Jesus Christ, sent by God to treat with sinful men; believe that He who sends you will not leave you to speak in vain; labor for the salvation of those whom you address, as if it were your own; so forget yourself to see only the glory of God and the

salvation of your hearers; you will then tremble more before God, but less before men.[4]

In a superb sermon on Luke 4:1–13 on "The Weapon in Christ's Conflict" (in which he acknowledges his indebtedness to Krummacher), Monod takes us through the temptations of Christ. This message is one in a series given to the seminary students at Mantauban and breathes a radiant confidence in the Scripture. One senses the nerve and the verve of the preacher.[5]

Another remarkable preacher is **Eugene Bersier** (1831–1889). Although he was born in Switzerland, Bersier served with enormous distinction in Paris. He nearly lost everything theologically while on an extended visit to the United States, but recovered while studying under d'Aubigne in Geneva. He led in building a great independent congregation that drew many in Paris and always had many visitors, and he saw the Eglise de l'Etoile build "a noble edifice near the Arc de Triomphe."[6] Yet another special ministry belonged to **Robert W. McAll** (1820–1893), an English preacher of ability, who left his pastorate and came to Paris for evangelistic work. He established the McAll Mission where his moving gospel preaching saw in one year "over one million hearers in its halls and 10,000 scholars in its Sunday Schools."[7] Thus even in a time of considerable spiritual sterility, the gospel message was heard.

---

1. Frederick L. Godet, *Commentary on the Epistle to the Romans* (Grand Rapids: Zondervan, 1883, 1956).
2. Kenneth Scott Latourette, *The Great Century: Europe and the United States* (Grand Rapids: Zondervan, 1969), 92.
3. E. C. Dargan, *A History of Preaching* (New York: Hodder and Stoughton, 1912), 2:457.
4. H. C. Fish and D. W. Poor, eds., *Select Discourses* (New York: Sheldon and Lincoln, 1860), 400.
5. Ibid., 150–79. Monod was a favorite at the Keswick Convention, where it was said of him: "Small of stature, with an aesthetic appearance and vivacious personality, he spoke fluently in English—but with many a quaint turn of phrase." The volume *Keswick's Authentic Voice* edited by Herbert F. Stevenson (London: Marshall, Morgan, and Scott, 1959) contains Monod's stirring message "With the Whole Heart" from Jeremiah 32:41, delivered in 1882 (248, 281–86).
6. Dargan, *A History of Preaching*, 2:469.
7. T. Harwood Pattison, *The History of Christian Preaching* (Philadelphia: American Baptist Publication Society, 1903), 222.

9.6 THE SCANDINAVIAN STREAM

May the Lord be praised! Gladdening news is reaching us from many areas of our land of an awakening of spiritual need and life. The long, cold, dark winter of indifference and security is yielding to the warm rays of the Sun of Righteousness.

—C. O. Rosenius of Sweden in *Pietisten,* 1850

During the winter 1850–51 there was considerable expansion of the spiritual revival among us. It was felt everywhere. From many directions we heard that the "dead bones" were coming alive.

—Matilda Foy

The Scandinavian countries followed Luther in the Reformation, but "the tidal waves caused by the revolt of Martin Luther had flattened out by the time they reached Scandinavian shores."[1] Olaus Petri, the great Swedish Reformer, studied at Wittenberg from 1516 to 1518. Awakened pastors like Nils Grubb (1681–1724) and Jacob Otto Hoof (1769–1839), who as a minister was dramatically converted out of drunkenness, were fiery preachers whose influence extended well beyond their home province.[2] The American Presbyterian Robert Baird visited Sweden in 1836 and launched a vigorous temperance movement, and George Scott the English Methodist spent ten years in Sweden stirring revival fires. Representatives of the Haldane brothers visited Scandinavia, and the translated pamphlets of Doddridge, Fuller, and Angell James had profound effect.[3] We have already noted the able preaching of Schartau (cf. 8.2.7), which had particular impact on southern Sweden. While Schartau shrank back from Herrnhuter emphasis, Moravian pietism was pervasive in the revival movement, particularly with its "The Spirit always answers to the blood" foundation. Professor Montgomery titled one of his books *The Wind from the Spirit in Sweden and Norway.* In this gracious time of visitation, preaching was pivotal.

---

1. Leslie Stannard Hunter, ed., *Scandinavian Churches: The Development and Life of the Churches of Denmark, Finland, Iceland, Norway, and Sweden* (Minneapolis: Augsburg, 1965), 15.
2. Karl A. Olsson, *By One Spirit* (Chicago: Covenant, 1962). This compendious study is most worthwhile.
3. Gunnar Westin, *The Free Church Through the Ages* (Nashville: Broadus, 1958), 280.

9.6.1 *Hans Nielsen Hauge—The Irrepressible Preacher*

The worst temptation I have to resist is this that when I speak to those who have a desire to hear and a will to follow my admonitions, and who may by the power of God even amend their lives, then I am given the praise and thanks for it. This is bad for me as the evil spirit thereby fills my mind and corrupt flesh with thoughts that I am exceedingly good, have great reward with God, and am better than others. But God does not forbid me to speak and this gives me confidence.

By the grace of God, nothing shall ever draw me away from the truth of the Holy Scriptures. After many trials, I have found that Scripture alone is able to give true peace, blessed joy, power to conquer sin, comfort in death, and a constant hope of eternal life. In this life it furnishes the mind with all Christian virtue.

—Hans Nielsen Hauge

The revival in Norway was especially sweet and was contained almost entirely within the established state church. To this day the Free Church movement is relatively small. From 1536 Norway was part of Denmark until the Treaty of Kiel in 1814, when Denmark handed Norway over to Sweden. Independence was not achieved until 1905. Through this period, German rationalism and the fallout of the Enlightenment took a negative toll on the churches.[1]

The visit of the Spirit in the Norwegian revival was focalized in the ministry of **Hans Nielsen Hauge** (1771–1824), who was born on a farm near Thun in southeastern Norway. He had little formal schooling but was deeply imbued with the Bible and Luther's Catechism in his home, and as well was exposed in large doses to Arndt, Pontoppidan, and Kingo. Though often terrified by his violation of the law of God and almost perishing on occasion, Hauge was not converted until 1796 while at work in his father's field:

> My heart was so uplifted to God that I do not know nor can I express what really took place in my soul. As soon as my senses returned to normal, I regretted that I had not served the loving and all-gracious God; now I felt that no worldly thing was of importance. It was a glory which no tongue can express; my soul felt something supernatural, divine and blessed . . . I had a completely transformed mind, a sorrow over all sins, a burning desire to read the Scriptures, particularly Jesus' own teachings, as well as new light to understand them and the teachings of godly men; toward the one goal, that Jesus Christ has come to be our Savior, that we should be born again by his spirit, be converted and sanctified more and more in godliness to serve the triune God alone, in order to improve and prepare our souls for the eternal blessedness.[2]

Hauge then embarked on a series of preaching missions throughout Norway (1796–1804). He often encouraged trade activities among his converts. He loved to sing hymns and preach the Word. He wrote thirty-three books and supervised their printing and their distribution. He was imprisoned for breaking the Conventicle Act by preaching as a layman.[3] His health broken by conditions during his imprisonment from 1804 to 1814, he continued to preach and indeed preached from his deathbed to the salvation of lost souls.[4] The ecclesiastical authorities were scandalized by his success and his direct, simple message. "But," he testified, "I discovered that there was a power of God in the foolishness of preaching, as Paul says in 1 Corinthians 1:31."[5] He was a zealous soulwinner and could not obey the edicts to keep quiet about Jesus and the gospel.

Hauge's conversion was paradigmatic for him, and he never ceased to marvel how deep the well was from which he drew the water of salvation. He felt the fire burning in him to preach. He preached even to the bailiff's wife when he was on trial.[6] Several times he traveled to Copenhagen for ministry, and while many were eager to hear the Word, there were many who rebuffed him and his message. At Tromso both Norwegians and Finns wept "and were open to persuasion."[7] He explained to the dean of Stavanger, who came to hear him, that "I can only express those things that coming to my heart and mind from the text of the Bible I am convinced and believe are right."[8]

The Haugean movement in Norway and in this country would be described as "a Low-Church form of orthodox Lutheranism, conservative in matters of biblical criticism and once powerful enough to found the private Theological Faculty at Oslo in protest against the liberal school dominant at the University at the beginning of the century."[9] The long-time teacher and the founder of the school was the widely-read **Ole Hallesby** (1879–1961), whose books on prayer, conscience, and *Why I Am a Christian* remain part of the rich legacy of this movement. Other professors of note from this school, which still provides training for one-third of the ministers of the state church in Norway, are **Olaf Moe** (whose volumes on the apostle Paul are sterling),[10] and **Olav Valen-Sendstad** (whose *The Word That Can Never Die* is a scholarly refutation of modernistic incursions in today's theology).[11] The Haugean influence is also to be seen in the founding of missionary societies and the Bible society as well as in the Inner Mission lay movement which is still very strong in Norway. The scholarly ministry of **Gisle Johnson** at the University of Oslo and the Johnsonian revival of confessionalism in the last half of the century must be seen as a further impetus of the Haugean impulse. Norwegian pietism is a somber pietism (as we pick it up in the novels of Alexander Kielland) but is a vital and a strong spiritual movement.

1. T. K. Derry, *A History of Modern Norway* (Oxford: Clarendon, 1973).
2. G. Everett Arden, *Four Northern Lights: Men Who Shaped Scandinavian Churches* (Minneapolis: Augsburg, 1964), 57.
3. Joel M. Njus, trans., *Autobiographical Writings of Hans Nielsen Hauge* (Minneapolis: Augsburg, 1954), 12.
4. Ibid., 14.
5. Ibid., 47.
6. Ibid., 103.
7. Ibid., 118.
8. Ibid., 122.
9. Leslie Stannard Hunter, ed., *Scandinavian Churches* (Minneapolis: Augsburg, 1965), 177.
10. Olaf Edward Moe, *The Apostle Paul: His Life and Work* (Grand Rapids: Baker, 1923). Volume 2 is on the Epistles.
11. Olav Valen-Sendstad, *The Word That Can Never Die: A Scriptural Critique of Theological Trends* (St. Louis: Concordia, 1949). Argues that the humble form of Scripture is analogical to the perfect humanity of Christ.

9.6.2   PAAVO HENRIK RUOTSALAINEN—THE INEXTINGUISHABLE PREACHER

Let trouble and sorrow drive you to seek the revealed and despised Savior in his Word . . . No matter how cold and unresponsive you may feel yourself to be, diligently hear and use the Word whence comes the hidden light for those who yearn for light . . . The Word awakens in the heart a desire for Christ, and this desire moves the heart to pray and long for the well-spring of life, and ere you are conscious of it, the Christ-life has been born within you.

—Paavo Henrik Ruotsalainen

Always considered a Scandinavian country but with a language and history so different (although 8 percent of the people are Swedish-Finns), Finland became Protestant in the Reformation, and in the Vasteros Edict of 1527 it was stipulated: "The pure Word of God is to be preached throughout the land."[1] Bishop Agricola in this time characterized most preaching as "both nasty and lazy."[2] To this day 92 percent of the Finns are Lutheran but not very spiritually lively. Most are nominal.[3] This deadness and formalism have been challenged from time to time by movements of revival but none quite like that led by **Paavo Ruotsalainen** (1777–1852). Other movements among the Swedish-Finns in the west joined forces with Ruotsalainen, while Henry Renqvist inclined more to a prayer movement and F. G. Hedberg turned from Ruotsalainen to follow Rosenius.[4] Some Finns followed the Swedish revivalist Laestadius in an emphasis on mutual confession and absolution. Theologically the Church of Finland was much influenced by J. T. Beck of Tubingen (cf. 9.4.4). After long union with Sweden, in 1809 Finland was seized by Russia and was a Russian duchy until 1917, when she declared her independence. The heroism of the Finnish people will long be remembered as they so stoutly resisted Russian incursion in 1939 in the Winter War under their gallant General Carl von Mannerheim.

Ruotsalainen was born into a poor peasant family and learned to read but never learned to write. All that we have from him in print was dictated. The revivals came sweeping through Finland as through Norway and Sweden. Young Paavo was gripped by what took place and began to read the Bible, Luther's Shorter Catechism, and the writings of John Bunyan, Pontoppidan, and other confessional Lutherans. He heard of a blacksmith, Jacob Hogman, who lived some distance away who had an authentic walk with the Lord, and he journeyed to meet him, begging food and lodging along the route. Hogman had a simple word of advice for him: "One thing you lack and therewith you lack all else: the inner awareness of Christ."[5] This was his tower experience, and it set the serious, almost grave tone for his subsequent life and ministry. When excesses of glossalalia threatened the movement, Ruotsalainen pulled things back to the center. He was a powerful preacher "who had the knack of communicating his thoughts so clearly and directly that the old Gospel truths of which he spoke were luminous with new light and meaning."[6] He was the architect of a spirituality which to this day represents an alternative to overinstitutionalized formalism. He placed great emphasis on the assurance of salvation and inner peace.

To him whose conscience has been awakened you shall say that he must never think too highly of himself, but must not therefore doubt or hesitate. He must lay hold of God's gracious promises and with patience look unto Christ as his helper, until the Holy Spirit bears witness to him that he really possesses the righteousness of Christ.[7]

This peace is not spiritual euphoria and ecstasy chiefly, but the reality of the living Christ within and slow, patient learning in the school of the cross. He argued that "the objective reality of a gracious, redeeming, loving God is there at the center of life itself, quite apart from any tangible or palpable human experience."[8] In Ruotsalainen we have another revivalistic lay preacher whose message shook and shaped a nation.

1. John H. Wuorinen, *A History of Finland* (New York: Columbia University Press, 1965), 61.
2. Ibid., 65.
3. Leslie Stannard Hunter, ed., *Scandinavian Churches* (Minneapolis: Augsburg, 1965), 68–75.
4. Conrad Bergendoff, *The Church of the Lutheran Reformation* (St. Louis: Concordia, 1967), 222.
5. G. Everett Arden, *Four Northern Lights: Men Who Shaped Scandinavian Churches* (Minneapolis: Augsburg, 1964), 25.
6. Ibid., 25.
7. Ibid., 29.
8. Ibid., 39.

9.6.3 CARL OLOF ROSENIUS—THE INDEFATIGABLE PREACHER

When fruitlessly exerting all your powers in the desperate attempt to do the will of God, you shall ultimately be impelled to pray for the Spirit of God to help you. Then shall you in the school of experience receive the true light upon the Word of God—the light from heaven. Without this experience, the highbrows and scribes are blind as bats in things spiritual. Without the Holy Spirit, the Word of God is not understood. Luther says: "When God gave His Word, He said: I shall let it be plainly written and preached, but I shall so arrange matters, that it shall depend upon my Spirit as to who shall understand it. Hence we see that they who think that they are able to understand the saving doctrine of their own mental astuteness, remain in spiritual darkness."

—Carl Olof Rosenius

The vapid rationalism that wasted the other Scandinavian countries had a similar impact upon Sweden. An intellectual like Emanuel Swedenborg (1688–1772), whose father was bishop of Skara, had attempted to fuse science and mysticism into a religious system that still has followers today, even though it is a cultic denial of the Christian faith. Under the influence of the Moravian Brethren and older Swedish Pietists like the gifted preacher **Anders Rutstrom** and **Peter Murbeck**, revival fires began to glow in Sweden as in Norway and Finland.

The embodiment of Pietistic orthodoxy is to be seen in **Carl Olof Rosenius** (1816–1868), born in a parsonage in Lulea in Norrland. His father was clearly in the camp of the evangelical revivalists, and young Carl was nurtured in the context of this life movement. He was converted at the age of fifteen and conducted his first Bible meeting shortly thereafter.[1] With the unrest and anxiety accompanying rapid industrialization and a changing society and economy, many were more open to the gospel. Rosenius studied for a while at Uppsala but became a private tutor until he joined with the English Methodist George Scott. Their ministry of evangelism and outreach "promoting the revival of pure Christianity" centered in the independent Bethlehem Chapel in Stockholm. Early in 1840 Rosenius "attempted his first Bible exposition," and Scott immediately recognized the rich gifts of his somewhat bewildered young friend.[2] The salary of Rosenius was paid by an American organization called the Foreign Evangelical Society of New York City. Rosenius was soon the preaching equal of Scott. In 1842 *Pietisten,* the immensely popular periodical, was established with Rosenius as its editor, and he became a household name in Sweden.[3] He preached in the dialect of the people and was dubbed by some as a mystical fanatic. He traveled widely and while always faithful to confessional Lutheranism, he ministered in a church within a church, existing to this day as Evangeliska Fosterlandsstiffelsen (the Evangelical Patriotic Society). His writings reflect his careful and meticulous biblical scholarship and his vigorous confidence in Scripture and insistence on conversion.[4] Colporteurs and criers moved through the countryside. Signs and wonders were not uncommon. "Preaching sickness" would come on children and youth and people of both sexes. One of my grandparents was converted when a dying boy in the parish preached law and gospel with prophetic vision.[5]

The sermons of Rosenius were fruitful and productive. In reaction against "the dull, deadening theological status in the universities," Rosenius trumped the condemnation of law and then the healing balm of "saved by grace through faith alone." Music by Ahnfelt, the Lutheran Sankey of Sweden, and others resounded through the land. Rosenius particularly loved Romans (and ran a six-year series on Romans in the paper). Professor Hult comments on his probing "into the interior of the text with astounding patience . . . such intense scanning of the inner heart and organism of the Word of God."[6] But all of this, we must be assured, was predicated on the premise: "The Church work of Rosenius was—to save souls!"[7] Analysis of his sermons shows them not to be highly structured but filled with Scripture and warm exhortation.

Following in the succession in Swedish revivalism must be **Lektor Paul Peter Waldenström** (1838–1917), a Ph.D. from Uppsala, who brought together most of the Free Church people into what was organized as the Swedish Mission Covenant in 1878. Unfortunately tinged with a Ritschlian view of the atonement, Waldenström was a preacher of considerable force and power.[8] "Where is it written?" became the watchword of the Mission Friends in Sweden and in America. He visited the United States five times and served in the Swedish Parliament from 1894 to 1905.[9] His sermons were biblical and forceful and he became more conservative as he grew older.[10] The biblically and theologically rich preaching of Waldenström did not characterize all of his successors in the pietistic institutionalization that he led.[11] Quite clearly biblical preaching is of the essence in the revivals in Sweden that have had such powerful impact on Scandinavian Free Church movements on this side of the Atlantic.

1. G. T. Rygh, Preface to C. O. Rosenius, *A Faithful Guide to Peace with God* (Minneapolis: Augsburg, 1923), 10.
2. Karl A. Olsson, *By One Spirit* (Chicago: Covenant, 1962), 50. For the impact of industrialization and the agricultural crisis that so upended society, see Ingvar Andersson, *A History of Sweden* (Westport, Conn.: Greenwood, 1968), 351–74.
3. G. Everett Arden, *Four Northern Lights: Men Who Shaped Scandinavian Churches* (Minneapolis: Augsburg, 1964), 124.
4. Carl Olof Rosenius, *A Faithful Guide to Peace with God.* Especially rewarding sections on law, conversion, the revelation of the mystery, etc.
5. Olsson, *By One Spirit*, 60.
6. Adolf Hult, trans., *C. O. Rosenius, The Believer Free from the Law* (Minneapolis: Lutheran Colportage, 1923), 16.
7. Ibid., 19.
8. John Wordsworth, *The National Church of Sweden* (London: Mowbray, 1911), 375.
9. Ragnar Tomson, *Den Radikale Waldenström* (Stockholm: Missionsforbundets Forlag, 1945).
10. P. P. Waldenström, *Biblisk Troslära* (Stockholm: Svenska Missionsforbundets Forlag, 1918).
11. J. G. Princell, trans., P. P. Waldenström, *The Lord Is Right: Meditations on the Twenty-fifth Psalm* (Chicago: John Martenson, 1889). Eric G. Hawkinson has a sensitive treatment on the centrality of preaching among the Scandinavian immigrant churches in *Images in Covenant Beginnings* (Chicago: Covenant, 1968) in which he observes: "Preaching was seen as the very heart of the mission of the fathers . . . the Bible was the trustworthy Word of God. Its message had to do with what God had done in Jesus Christ for man's salvation. It was for man—when he saw what God had done—to accept this grace and believe. The texts were as often chosen from the Old Testament as the New. The Bible was one book and spoke of one grace. The burden was to discover what the Bible had to say to man" (130). See also Herbert E. Palmquist, trans., *The Word Is Near You* (Chicago: Covenant, 1974).

9.6.4 *NIKOLAI F. S. GRUNDTVIG—THE INCANDESCENT PREACHER*

Then it was brought home to them that faith itself is the work of the Holy Spirit, and they ceased from all righteousness in their own conceit, and denied themselves, and took up their cross and followed Jesus. That, my friend, is the way, the truth and the life. If we acknowledge our own impotence and unworthiness, and the necessity of becoming altogether new human beings through spiritual rebirth, of becoming members of Christ's body, having no life, no salvation apart from him, then we shall sigh until we learn to pray, think, until we learn to feel. We shall journey and rest with the thought that God sees us, that only Jesus can save us, that only the Holy Spirit can enlighten, move and strengthen us.

—N. F. S. Grundtvig

Beautiful little Denmark, like the other Scandinavian countries, was in the grip of sweeping change in the nineteenth century, with her imperial possessions stripped away, the loss of Schleswig-Holstein to Germany, and the impact of new and high-powered economic change. Religiously Denmark was much affected by Enlightenment rationalism, and notwithstanding the new Danish Constitution of 1849 guaranteeing religious freedom, the Danish Folk-Church was in a state of abysmal torpor. The earlier Pietistic influence on the royal court, which resulted in sending out missionaries to India (cf. 8.4.1), had dissipated, and historic doctrines of the Trinity and the Atonement were abandoned in favor of a toothless religion of gentle Jesus and good deeds.[1] Of course there were exceptions, and beacon lights like the south Jutlander **Bishop Erik Pontoppidan** and **Hans Adolph Brorson** (who wrote "Behold the Host Arrayed in Light") were mighty preachers of conversion and sanctification.[2]

The mighty revivals that cascaded across the northern countries did not come in such force among the more sedate and self-sufficient Danes, but there was a little springtime led by **J. P. Mynster** (1775–1854) and **N. F. S. Grundtvig** (1793–1877). The latter was born and nurtured within a parsonage. He was something of a romantic in reaction against rationalism but quite critical of the Pietists for their individuality. He leveled devastating critiques against the Church of Denmark. He studied at the University of Copenhagen and afterwards tutored in a wealthy family until he went to be associate to his father. His first sermon in 1810 in this role was titled "Why Has the Word of the Lord Vanished in His House," which was a withering blast against the rationalism of the clergy.[3] His questioning of the spiritual status quo led to his own spiritual awakening. Grundtvig specifically attacked Professor H. N. Clausen and was sued and found guilty and subsequently fined. Many left him in "the Church Struggle," but in 1839 he took the pastorate in Vartov, which was really the chaplaincy of a home for aged women.[4] Here he preached and counseled and wrote until his death, becoming the center of a spiritual stirring that reached all of Denmark. He wrote one thousand hymns, including the classic "Built on the Rock the Church Doth Stand." He initiated popular education in Denmark. He was highly sacramental and because his followers stayed in the church they influenced the church greatly in this regard. At some theological points Grundtvig deviated from orthodoxy, being concerned at times overmuch to foster a happy Christianity. One secular historian speaks of Ansgar as the prophet of the north in the ninth century and Grundtvig as the prophet of the north in the nineteenth century.[5]

Also challenging the largely moribund state church was **Soren Kierkegaard** (1813–1855), who scathingly attacked the church in which he argued "Christianity has ceased to exist." In such strong reaction against Hegalian rationalism, he is one of the fathers of modern existentialism. He loved to read sermons aloud, and his *Edifying Discourses,* including the peerless *Purity of Heart Is to Will One Thing,* are really unpreached sermons.[6] He advocated a leap of faith in his brilliant treatment of the Abraham and Isaac story in *Fear and Trembling* and in his address to despair in *The Sickness Unto Death.* Kierkegaard savaged **Bishop H. L. Martensen** (1808–1884), denying that he could have been a "truth-witness." This was extreme because Martensen was an able preacher of Christ concerning whom he said late in his life, "Nothing is for me more certain than the risen, ascended Christ and the heavenly kingdom."[7] Kierkegaard also has significance in the history of preaching for his notion of indirect address, which Fred Craddock has picked up in his *Overhearing the Gospel*. In this a subtle, nondeclamatory approach is advocated for preaching.

Kierkegaard's assaults did inspire **Vilhelm Beck** (1829–1901) to join with others in founding the Inner Mission. He was stirred by Kierkegaard's scathing critique of the worldliness of the church. He was converted in 1859 and began to preach with great power and eloquence. He differed from Grundtvig with respect to biblical inerrancy, holding to a conservative formulation. He preached revivals through Jutland emphasizing "Conversion and Faith." He is seen by some as "the last of the great Danish preachers of the nineteenth century."[8] At the time of his death there were four hundred meeting houses in the movement, but they stayed within the state church.

A more separatistic stance was taken by **Niels Pedersen Grunnet** (1827–1897), who was influenced by a Moravian Pietist to go to Basle and study there at the Mission-Seminary. He married a Swiss woman, Maria Vatter, in 1856 and came back to Copenhagen to lead in founding the Evangelical Lutheran Free Church in 1855. Grunnet founded churches throughout the country and served and preached with effectiveness at Martin's Church on Martin's Road in Copenhagen. He wrote many treatises such as "Some Truths and Testimonies Against the Teaching of the Conversion after Death" (1857) and a collection of eighteen sermons titled "Come Jesus Christ to Mind" (1889). Only seven of these congregations remain, but Martinskirken is still well worth a visit in Copenhagen. This was a small come-out group, but in the main the evangelical movement was kept within the state church.

---

1. The classic delineation of this view is seen in Adolph Harnack, *What Is Christianity?* (New York: Putnam). Supernaturalism has been effectively surrendered.
2. Jens Christian Kjaer, *History of the Church of Denmark* (Blair, Neb.: Lutheran Publishing House, 1945), 68ff.
3. Ibid., 84.
4. G. Everett Arden, *Four Northern Lights: Men Who Shaped Scandinavian Churches* (Minneapolis: Augsburg, 1964), 95.
5. J. H. S. Birch, *Denmark in History* (Westport, Conn.: Greenwood, 1938, 1975), 358.
6. Douglas V. Steere, trans., Soren Kierkegaard, *Purity of Heart Is to Will One Thing* (New York: Harpers, 1938, 1948). For a choice analysis of Kierkegaard, see E. J. Carnell, *The Burden of Soren Kierkegaard* (Grand Rapids: Eerdmans, 1965). Neglected by his contemporaries Kierkegaard was rediscovered in our century and has profoundly shaped existential theology with its tragic denial of supernatural and metaphysical approaches to theology. The consequences of Kierkegaard's "truth is subjectivity" is painfully apparent in Catholic, Protestant, and atheistic varieties of existential theology. There is no "true principium" here for the construction of theology.
7. Kjaer, *History of the Church of Denmark,* 107. See Thomas Oden, ed., *Parables of Kierkegaard* (Princeton, N.J.: Princeton, 1979).
8. Ibid., 109.

CHAPTER TEN

Starbursts and Sidetracks
of the Victorian Pulpit

Part Two: The Raging River

And at his appointed season he brought his word to light through the preaching entrusted to me by the command of God our Savior.
—Titus 1:3

You must teach what is in accord with sound doctrine. . . . so that no one will malign the word of God.
—Titus 2:1, 5b

For we also have had the gospel preached to us, just as they did; but the message they heard was of no value to them, because those who heard did not combine it with faith. . . . For the word of God is living and active. Sharper than any double-edged sword, it penetrates even to dividing soul and spirit, joints and marrow; it judges the thoughts and attitudes of the heart.
—Hebrews 4:2, 12

See to it that you do not refuse him who speaks. If they did not escape when they refused him who warned them on earth, how much less will we, if we turn away from him who warns us from heaven?
—Hebrews 12:25

He chose to give us birth through the word of truth, that we might be a kind of firstfruits of all he created. . . . Therefore, get rid of all moral filth and the evil that is so prevalent and humbly accept the word planted in you, which can save you. Do not merely listen to the word, and so deceive yourselves. Do what it says.

—James 1:18, 21–22

Preaching is indispensable to Christianity. Without preaching, a necessary part of its authenticity has been lost. For Christianity is, in its very essence, a religion of the Word of God.

—John R. W. Stott

Apart from blunt truth, our lives sink decadently amid the perfume of hints and suggestions.

—Alfred North Whitehead

The Bible is not telling us about human preachers; it is telling us about preaching. Furthermore, the prior Greek history gives no specific meaning to *kerux* (to proclaim). The New Testament knows nothing of sacred personages who are inviolable in the world. . . . The messengers are like sheep delivered to wolves (Matthew 10:10). As the Lord was persecuted, so His servants will be persecuted (John 15:20). The servants of Christ are, as it were, dedicated to death (Revelation 12:11). But the message does not perish with the one who proclaims it. The message is irresistible (2 Timothy 2:9). It takes its victorious course through the world (2 Thessalonians 3:1). Hence *kerussein* (what is proclaimed) is more important then the *kerux* in the New Testament.

—Kittel and Friedrich

The nineteenth century was a self-conscious time of transition. John Stuart Mill observed in 1831 that "mankind have outgrown old institutions and old doctrines, and have not yet acquired new ones."[1] Bulwer-Lytton moaned, "The age then is one of destruction! . . . Miserable would be our lot were it not also an age of preparation for restructuring."[2] Charles Kingsley offered the opinion that "few of us deeply believe anything."[3] The rationalism and the romanticism of the Enlightenment were making hash out of accepted orthodox belief.

The likes of David Hume and Herbert Spencer were drawing many to doubt and denial. Tennyson's *In Memoriam* is not belief or unbelief; it is doubt. Matthew Arnold's *Dover Beach* is a melancholy review of the recession of faith. George Eliot cut off her evangelical roots because of biblical criticism and went on to be an advocate of free love. Auguste Comte's religion of humanity tantalized many on the Continent. Ruskin tried desperately to hold on to theism in some sense. Thomas Carlyle in *Past and Present* celebrates his heroes but is "full of contradictory notions and beliefs." Once planning to study for the ministry, he became a teacher and then a writer, and in this 1843 volume becomes "the Victorian prophet of the great fight."[4] Lytton Strachey's *Eminent Victorians* is a mishmash.[5] Friedrich Wilhelm Nietzsche was the son of a German minister but developed doctrines of the superman and the will to power. Before dying of paresis, he conceded, "A man of spiritual depth needs friends, unless he still has God as a friend. But I have neither God nor friends."[6]

In her novel of a clergyman, *Robert Elsmere,* Mrs. Humphrey Ward, a niece of Thomas Arnold and editor of *Amiel's Journal,* depicts characters who "have a hunger for life and its satisfactions, which the will was more and more powerless to satisfy."[7] A vacuum was emerging. The optimisms of empire and the new age of science were doomed to disillusionment in the quagmire of suicidal war, the Holocaust, and the horrors of the atomic age. Meanwhile, the faithful preaching of the supernatural gospel and the exposition of Holy Scripture continued to make a significant impact in Europe and America and indeed around the world. The Christian church was becoming an international community of the blood-bought and the born-again.

---

1. Walter E. Houghton, *The Victorian Frame of Mind* (New Haven, Conn.: Yale University Press, 1957), 1.
2. Ibid., 3.
3. Ibid., 22.
4. Ibid., 206.
5. Lytton Strachey, *Eminent Victorians* (Garden City, N.Y.: Garden City Publishing, 1917).
6. Kurt F. Reinhardt, *The Existential Revolt: The Main Themes and Phases of Existentialism* (Milwaukee: Bruce, 1952), 59. See also Carl Pletsch, *The Young Nietzsche: Becoming a Genius* (New York: Free Press, 1991).
7. Houghton, *The Victorian Frame of Mind,* 65.

10.1   THE TRIBUTARY OF THE EVANGELISTS

He who descended is the very one who ascended higher than all the heavens, in order to fill the whole universe. It was he who gave some to be . . . evangelists.

—Ephesians 4:10–11

Evangelistic preaching is a special genre. During this complex time, the outburst of powerful evangelistic preaching on every continent was to become a vital part of history.

10.1.1   CHARLES G. FINNEY—THE LAWYER IN THE PULPIT

The question of the inspiration of the Bible is of the highest importance to the Church and the world, and that those who have called in question the plenary [total] inspiration of the Bible, have, sooner or later, frittered away nearly all that is essential to the Christian religion.

I gave myself to a great deal of prayer. After my evening services, I would retire as early as I could; but rose at four o'clock in the morning, because I could sleep no longer, and immediately went to the study, and engaged in prayer. And so deeply was my mind exercised, and so absorbed in prayer, that I frequently continued from the time I arose at four o'clock till the gong called for breakfast at eight o'clock. My days were spent, so long as I could get time, in searching the Scriptures. I read nothing else, all that winter, but my Bible; and a great deal of it seemed new to me . . . the whole Scriptures seemed to me all ablaze with light.

—Charles G. Finney

Called the father of American revivalism and the originator of a new style of pulpit oratory, **Charles Grandison Finney** (1792–1875) saw five hundred thousand professions of Christ in his ministry. He played a crucial part in the western revivals that led to the Great Prayer Meeting Revival of 1857–58.[1] His "new measures" were innovative in evangelism. Perry Miller pays high tribute to Finney's *Lectures on Revivals of Religion* as the key exposition of the movement and to Finney himself. Miller wrote, "No religious leader in America since Edwards had commanded such attention; no one was to do it again until Dwight Moody."[2]

Finney was born in an old New England family in Connecticut but moved to New York. In time he studied law and led the choir in a Presbyterian church pastored by George Gale, a Princetonian of the Old School who later founded Knox College in Galesburg, Illinois, which is named after him.

Finney had been deeply moved by a man he heard praying, and this left a profound mark on him. For Finney, prayer was always uppermost, and he was unusually sensitive to what he called "an earnest spirit of prayer." After much reading of Scripture, he went out into the woods, declaring, "I will give my heart to God or I will never come down from there." What he called "waves of liquid love" flowed over him. He struggled with the Old School passivity and reluctance to invite sinners to come to Christ, and in 1824 he began to preach in the "burned-over district" in which he lived.[3]

His preaching was extempore and sometimes impromptu, "throwing manuscripts away."

In delivering a sermon in this essay style of writing, the power of gesture and looks and attitude and emphasis is lost. We can never have the fullness of the gospel till we throw away our written sermons.

He remembered an old preacher who read his sermons and made no impression whatever on anyone's mind. Not so Finney! But even more controversial was his theology. Ever since the days of Solomon Stoddard, Calvinists had been torn by revivals—how did they fit into the scheme of things? Finney chose to build on Jonathan Edwards and the New England theology that grew out of his thinking.[4] Edwards' disciples went much farther than the master, as when Nathaniel Taylor denied original sin. Finney followed on this track and moved to a governmental view of the Atonement. His new measures created a furor, but the one most vociferously opposed was Finney's insistence that women participate in the prayer meetings. Warfield, while acknowledging that Finney "conducted the most spectacular evangelism activities the country has ever witnessed," was not unfair with respect to the serious nature of Finney's theological lapses.[5] Later accretions of perfectionism and the development of Oberlin perfectionism would come via J. H. Noyes and the Oneida Community in New York.

The climax of Finney's itinerant ministry was in the great Rochester Revival in 1830–31, which saw thousands come to Christ and the forces of evil put on the run. In 1831 he published his *Revival Lectures,* and in 1835 began to preach in the Broadway Tabernacle in New York City. He crossed the Atlantic several times and had a fruitful ministry, yet everywhere he went he fomented opposition. Samuel Tregelles, the Brethren New Testament scholar in Britain, spotted the chinks in his armor, and the Old School were against him. He and Lyman Beecher wrangled, but Beecher himself gave way to the new theology when all was said and done. The Universalists and Unitarians could not abide Finney's strong preaching on hell. Drummond argues that Finney "mellowed" on several of the theological matters, particularly regarding human ability.[6] Evidence for this claim is sparse at best.

Social and societal issues were always important for Finney, and he led in the abolitionist cause long before it was popular. He pushed temperance issues and anti-Masonry. Finally he became a professor at Oberlin, Ohio, and was eventually elevated to president of that school.

But as a preacher, Finney was rapierlike in his lawyerly logic and clarity. He had a resonant voice, yet not as powerful as Whitefield, and great dramatic ability. As he preached "an awful solemnity" would fall on the audience. People wilted before the preaching of the Word of God, which often went two hours in length. Many testified to his "unforgettable eyes . . ." "his prominent forehead and those remarkable, hypnotic eyes . . . large and blue, at times mild as an April sky and at others, cold and penetrating as polished steel."[7]

Many have argued that what Andrew Jackson was in politics, Finney was in religion. He could be denunciatory. He called for immediate response, and sometimes seekers started toward the mourner's bench or inquirer's room even before he finished the sermon.

Finney's language in preaching was spare, and he could outline a sermon well.[8] In a great sermon on Luke 16:2 simply titled "Stewardship," Finney launched from the text, "Give an account of your stewardship." He drew seven applications and fashioned a concluding section for hell-bound sinners from the clause, "You shall no longer be my steward." Finney always preached with "spiritual travail" and leaned on and expected the anointing of the Holy Spirit. As late as 1871 he preached a great sermon on "The Gift of the Holy Spirit" to the National Congregational Council meeting at Oberlin.[9] He reflected on his long years pastoring at First Congregational in Oberlin: "I ploughed my church up every year." He believed that the problem for sinners in coming to Christ was not "cannot" but "will not." He advised, "The Almighty God awaits your consent."

---

1. Though very critical, see William G. McLoughlin, *Modern Revivalism* (New York: Ronald Press, 1959).
2. Keith J. Hardman, *Charles Grandison Finney: Revivalist and Reformer* (Syracuse: Syracuse University Press, 1987), x. Finney's *Revivals of Religion* (Chicago: Moody, 1962) is available in paper and is most worthwhile—a stirring read.
3. James E. Johnson, "Father in American Revivalism," *Christian History* 7, no. 4, issue 20: 6ff. The entire issue is on Finney.
4. Allen C. Guelzo, *Edwards on the Will: A Century of Theological Debate* (Middletown, Conn.: Wesleyan, 1989). Charles Hambrick-Stowe argues that Finney sought evangelical consensus, cf. his *Charles G. Finney and the Spirit of American Evangelicalism* (Grand Rapids: Eerdmans, 1997). He overstresses Finney's Calvinistic ties.
5. B. B. Warfield, *Perfectionism* (Philadelphia: Presbyterian and Reformed, 1967), 166ff. Finney doubtless had an important influence on the higher life movement, but Warfield is unnecessarily severe on Keswick theology, which does not partake of the serious errors of Finney in his denial of original sin and imputation of righteousness. For an important analysis of Finney, see Jay E. Smith, "The Theology of Charles Finney: A System of Self-Reformation," *Trinity Journal,* 13 n.s. (1992): 61–93. A neglected dimension in Finney and others is excavated by Donald W. Dayton, *Discovering an Evangelical Heritage* (New York: Harper, 1976), 15–24.
6. Lewis A. Drummond, *The Life and Ministry of Charles G. Finney* (Minneapolis: Bethany House, 1983), 115.
7. Hardman, *Charles Grandison Finney,* 35. See V. Raymond Edman, *Finney Lives On* (New York: Revell, 1951).
8. Louis Gifford Parkhurst Jr., ed., *Charles G. Finney, Principles of Revival* (Minneapolis: Bethany House, 1987). We are in the debt of Bethany House and Parkhurst for republishing so many of Finney's sermons and articles.
9. J. Gilchrist Lawson, *Deeper Experiences of Famous Christians* (Anderson, Ind.: Warner, 1911), 243ff.

10.1.2 PETER CARTWRIGHT—A FRONTIERSMAN IN THE PULPIT

> Many nights, in early times, the itinerant had to camp out, without fire or food for man or beast. It is true we could not, many of us, conjugate a verb or parse a sentence, and murdered the king's English almost every lick. But there was a Divine unction attended the word preached and thousands fell under the mighty power of God, and thus the Methodist Episcopal Church was planted firmly in this western wilderness, and many glorious signs have followed, and will follow, to the end of time.
>
> —Peter Cartwright

In the great westward movement into and beyond the valley of the Mississippi, God too was moving mightily. This historic epoch was a time of great revival.[1]

One of the key preachers in this breakthrough was **Peter Cartwright** (1785–1872), who served as a presiding elder in the Methodist Episcopal Church for fifty years, preached more than fifteen thousand sermons, baptized twelve thousand persons, received ten thousand into the church, twice served in the Illinois State Legislature, and was defeated for the U.S. Congress in 1846 by Abraham Lincoln.[2] This thickset, muscular man was born in Virginia into the home of a soldier who had fought in the American Revolution. His family moved to Kentucky by packhorse into an area known "Rogue's Harbor." Here was born the camp meeting and an incendiary movement of the Holy Spirit.

Peter heard preaching in the family cabin when he was nine and later was converted out of a life of sin. Francis Asbury was a potent factor in the explosive growth of the Methodist church, and influenced the Gasper River and Cane Ridge Camp Meetings which were such a significant part of the Second Great Awakening.[3] This was known as the Cumberland Revival.

Called by some the Kentucky boy, Cartwright said, "I took my text and preached." First appointed as an exhorter and then put into "the traveling connection," Peter would preach up to three hours and sometimes two or three times a day as he traveled.[4] He was directed by his presiding bishop to a course of study, but his texts were usually one verse, as when he preached on Isaiah 26:4, "Trust ye in the Lord forever: for in the Lord Jehovah is everlasting strength." Cartwright reported that the Lord gave light, liberty, and power, and the congregation melted into tears with conversions.[5] Sometimes he would stay for protracted meetings, notwithstanding rowdies (whom he dealt with handily), denominational tensions, and critics. One learned preacher tried to humiliate him by using Greek words, which Cartwright did not understand. Cartwright responded in German, which this minister thought was Hebrew and commended Cartwright for his erudition.[6] The mighty power of God fell on the meetings with great regularity. He feared no one, not even the famous General Andrew Jackson, who appreciated Cartwright for his forthrightness.

Because of his aversion to slavery, Cartwright asked for transfer to Illinois, which was just beginning to break open. He settled his family in Sangamon County where his forty-mile days continued and the conversions multiplied. He faced Arians, deists, Universalists, skeptics, Shakers, and—at nearby Nauvoo—Mormons. One winter he led a five-month revival. "I preached, exhorted, sung, prayed and labored at the altar," said Cartwright. "I need not say several times a day or night, but almost day and night for months together."[7]

He also did extensive evangelism among the Indians. When he went back to General Conference in Boston in 1852, he expounded on great texts such as Hebrews 10:22 and Job 22:21. But none evoked as much stir as when he took Matthew 11:12 and was simply "the old pioneer of the west."[8] There was in his own style what he called "animal excitement." He attributed his immense physical strength to a simple regimen: "Keep your feet warm, your head cool, your bowels well regulated, rise early, go to bed early, eat temperately and drink no spirits." Peter Cartwright was a rough-hewn instrument, available and dispensable in God's hands.

1. Stephen E. Ambrose, *Undaunted Courage: Meriwether Lewis, Thomas Jefferson and the Opening of the American West* (New York: Simon and Schuster, 1995). Provides a feel for the burgeoning west and the movement to it.
2. F. R. Webber, *A History of Preaching in Britain and America* (Milwaukee: Northwestern, 1957), 3:217.
3. A. K. Curtis, ed. "Spiritual Awakenings in North America," *Christian History,* 8, no. 3, issue 23:24ff.
4. W. P. Strickland, ed., *Autobiography of Peter Cartwright: The Backwoods Preacher* (Cincinnati: Jennings and Graham, 1856), 54.
5. Ibid., 68.
6. Ibid., 80.
7. Ibid., 406.
8. Ibid., 477.

10.1.3 LORENZO DOW—THE ECCENTRIC IN THE PULPIT

The language of my heart is, "What is past, I know; what is to come, I know not. Lord, bless me in the business I am set out upon."

Justification by faith is what God does for us, through the death of his Son; but regeneration or the new birth, also called sanctification, is what God does in us by the operation of his Holy Spirit. The first work is pardon, the latter is purity. One is to forgive, the other is to make holy.
—Lorenzo Dow in *Babylon to Jerusalem*

The preacher called Crazy Dow was born **Lorenzo Dow** (1777–1834) in Coventry, Connecticut. He was part of the first surge from the East that spilled westward. Johnny Appleseed (born John Chapman in Massachusetts in the same time frame) went into the Ohio Valley spreading apple seeds and sprouts and the teachings of Swedenborg. Lorenzo Dow, eccentric but grippingly effective as a preacher, headed west spreading the gospel.

Asthmatic from childhood, through his whole life Dow had visions and dreams beyond the ordinary. He had a long beard and hair to his shoulders. His clothing was usually ragged and he was sometimes shoeless, yet he was heard widely, making three preaching tours to Ireland and England. In appearance he was "tall and fragile, stoop-shouldered with thin legs and arms, a thin nose and bright blue eyes in a pallid face. He was generally wrapped in a black cloak . . . his voice was harsh from continual use and he spoke in gasps with difficulty, his shoulders moving convulsively up and down, as he worked his vocal organs as laboriously as a man would work at a dry pump, although with a little more success."[1] He rode or walked many miles each day, usually preaching about noon daily in a meeting house, a bar, or the open air. Sometimes he preached without preliminaries, taking a text and always including his personal testimony. He carried and sold Methodist books and preached many one-week camp meetings. He introduced the camp meeting to English Methodists and thereby provoked a split between the Primitive Methodists and the main body.

Dow was converted under the preaching of Hope Hull, the Methodist evangelist. He was called to preach in a dream he had about John Wesley. In April of 1796, he preached his first sermon. He later wrote of it:

> I being both young in years and ministry, the expectations of many were raised, who did not bear with my weakness and strong doctrine, and would not consent that I should preach there again for some time.[2]

From 1799 to 1801, he ministered in Ireland with considerable effect, returning in 1802 to marry Peggy, whom he always affectionately called "my rib." He made a great swing down through Georgia and preached "the first Protestant sermon in Alabama." He did five hundred to eight hundred meetings a year. Because of his idiosyncratic ways, he was always in and out of acceptance in Methodist circles. He had the unfortunate tendency to pick peculiar texts and controversial titles like "Good News from Hell." It was Dow who preached against women's hairstyles from the text "Top-knot come down" (Matt. 24:17 actually says, "Let him who is on the housetop not come down"). He was known to have jumped out the window after a meeting just to move on a little more rapidly. Critics spoke of "the taint of vulgar popularity" which tended to adhere to "Lorenzo," or "the cosmopolite," as he called himself. The shaggy stranger was not only a pamphleteer but gave himself to peddling "Lorenzo Dow's Family Medicine."

Dow would occasionally stuff miscellaneous information into his sermons. His preaching became increasingly dominated by lurid prophecies of woe. Once when preaching about those "cast into hell" he heaved a young boy across the room.[3] He gave himself increasingly to the popularization of the "popish menace." But his famous "watch sermon" made effective visual use of the timepiece.

His dear Peggy died of consumption after fifteen years of marriage. Although he soon remarried, Dow himself died in 1834 at the age of fifty-six. He wrote twenty-five books and dreamed of establishing a city of peace, Loren, in western Wisconsin.

The heart of his conviction is reflected in words he wrote "On the Ministry":

> How shall one know whether it be his own duty to preach or not? There are but three evidences by which he may be able to judge and determine concerning him on that subject: (1) Divine evidence in his own soul; or (2) by the fruits of his labor; or (3) the witness of his word with power.[4]

Because of his strong dependence on the Holy Spirit he was accused of being "Quakerized."[5] But the truth of the matter was that his word was with great power. Despite his many eccentricities, Crazy Dow was part of that noble army who brought Christ to the farthest reaches of the frontier.

---

1. Charles Coleman Sellers, *Lorenzo Dow: The Bearer of the Word* (New York: Minton, Balch and Company, 1928), 5.
2. Lorenzo Dow, *The Life, Travels, Labors and Writings of Lorenzo Dow, Including*

His Singular and Erratic Wanderings in Europe and America (New York: R. Worthington, 1881), 27.

3. Sellers, *Lorenzo Dow*, 214.

4. Dow, *The Life, Travels, Labors and Writings*, 396. Earle E. Cairns gives Dow a prominent place in *An Endless Line of Splendor*.

5. J. Gilchrist Lawson, *Deeper Experience of Famous Christians* (Anderson, Ind.: Warner, 1911), 223.

10.1.4 *Phoebe Palmer—A Sister in the Pulpit*

> This Revelation—holy, just and true—
> Though oft I read, it seems forever new;
> While light from heaven upon its pages rest,
> I feel its power, and with it I am blest.
>
> —Phoebe Palmer, age eleven

Walter Palmer (1804–1890), himself a well-known physician, and his wife **Phoebe Palmer** (1807–1874) traveled much in churches and camp meetings and saw more than 25,000 persons receive pardon. Phoebe came to prominence in the spiritual stirring often called the Third Awakening. This great work sprang out of a vital prayer movement in New York City, as ten thousand people met daily for prayer from 1857 to 1859.

The Palmers ministered with powerful impact in Canada, the United States, and in the British Isles. Phoebe Palmer also established the Five Points Mission in the Bowery in New York City, reinforcing Timothy Smith's important thesis tying revivalism in with social and benevolent concerns.[1]

Phoebe Worrall Palmer was born in New York City in a devout home and converted at an early age. She married Dr. Palmer at age nineteen and was "quickened in the divine life" at a revival in the Allen Street Methodist Episcopal Church after the death of her firstborn son. With her sister she initiated "The Tuesday Meeting" in the interest of a deeper Christian life.[2] She began to probe the Scriptures and to develop an "altar theology" that became part of her enlarging Bible teaching ministry. She wrote extensively on sanctification and prophecy and on the return of the Jews to Palestine. Palmer had a marked influence on Bishop Matthew Simpson and William and Catherine Booth.

As one not ordained, it was quite a while before Phoebe acknowledged that her speaking was in fact preaching. Close inspection of her writings and sermons shows how much John Wesley and John Fletcher shaped her thinking and style. She was steeped in the biblical commentaries of Adam Clarke. She was indefatigable in her promotion of scriptural holiness, arguing that revival was "only a return to primitive Christianity untrammeled by mere human opinions and church conventionalisms."[3] She could discourse for an hour without her voice tiring. The fruit was gathered at the altar.

Palmer's sermonic structure was simple and direct, her content rich with a heavy overlay of exhortation. Her record of overseas itineration is particularly moving, and the richness of her work *The Way of Holiness* is wonderfully evident.[4] The Methodist church in the United States increased by more than two hundred thousand members from 1842 to 1850. God was working mightily, and Phoebe Palmer was undeniably one of his remarkable instruments.

1. Timothy L. Smith, *Revivalism and Social Reform: American Protestantism on the Eve of the Civil War* (Nashville: Abingdon, 1957; rev. 1980). A classic study in which the Palmers loom large.
2. Charles Edward White, *The Beauty of Holiness: Phoebe Palmer as Theologian, Revivalist, Feminist, and Humanitarian* (Grand Rapids: Francis Asbury/Zondervan, 1986), 9ff.
3. Ibid., 166. See John D. Hannah, "The Layman's Prayer Revival of 1858," in *Bibliotheca Sacra* 134, no. 533 (January–March 1977): 59.
4. Thomas Oden, ed., *Phoebe Palmer: Selected Writings* (Mahwah, N.J.: Paulist, 1988), 165ff.

10.1.5 CHRISTMAS EVANS—IMAGINATION IN THE PULPIT

You will observe that some heavenly ornaments and power from on high are visible in many ministers when under the Divine irradiation, which you cannot approach by merely imitating their artistic excellence, without resembling them in their spiritual taste, fervency and zeal, which Christ and His Spirit "work in them." This will cause, not only your being like unto them in gracefulness of action and propriety of elocution, but will also induce prayer for the anointing of the Holy One, which worketh mightily in the inward man. This is the mystery of effective preaching. We must be endued with power from on high.

—Christmas Evans

In his classic *Handbook of Revivals,* Henry C. Fish advanced the thesis that "foremost among the instumentalities for saving men is the pulpit."[1] Fish cites historical examples and Elder Jacob Knapp and A. B. Earle in his own time as corroboration. A sterling historical instance is certainly **Christmas Evans** (1766–1838), who was born on Christmas Day in South Wales. Evans was called the John Bunyan of Wales, "the one-eyed man from Anglesea," and the "prophet sent from God."

His father was a poor cobbler who died when Christmas was nine. Evans himself lived a rough life with several miraculous escapes from death before his conversion in 1783. At the time of his salvation experience he could neither read nor write. He taught himself to read both Hebrew and Greek so he could truly exegete a text. In 1787, he was waylaid by former carousing friends and lost one of his eyes. He was ordained in 1789 and served two years in North Wales, borrowing most of his sermons from Beveridge and Rowland. Evans then itinerated for several years, preaching five times on Sunday "and walking as far as twenty miles a day."[2] In 1791 he began an extended ministry on the Isle of Anglesea.

Although he was an Arminian Presbyterian early on, Evans became a Calvinistic Baptist. He was one of the greatest Welsh preachers ever. To speak Welsh, it is said that one must have a cold in the head, a knot in the tongue, and a husk of barley in the throat. Evans had to combat the Sandemanian heresy. A blessed filling of the Holy Spirit led to a great revival on the island, and Evans relates, "Thus the Lord delivered me and the people of Anglesea from being swept away by the evils of Sandemanianism."[3] Eventually Evans learned to preach in English and read theology voraciously. Reference to his sermons shows he organized and structured his messages with assiduous care.

Perusal of his remarkable sermons, even though some of the subtleties in the Welsh original cannot be translated, discloses some of the finest sermons ever. Eight of the twenty-two sermons in Joseph Cross' splendid selection treat the meaning of Jesus' death on Calvary. His "covenants" with God are models of entire consecration.[4] He was richly doctrinal and went right to justification by faith and the Christological issues as foundational for everything Christian. He frequently took two mains, as in his superb message on "One God and One Mediator" from 1 Timothy 2:5.[5] In "The Sufferings of Christ" from 1 Peter 2:24, Evans gave meticulous attention to the text and drew subs as well as mains from it.

He preached with unusual imagination, evoking both laughter and convulsive tears in his hearers. Above all, "Jesus Christ and him crucified" was "the alpha and the omega" of Christmas Evans' utterance.[6]

---

1. Henry C. Fish, *Handbook of Revivals* (Harrisonburg, Va.: Gano, 1874, 1988), 254.
2. Earle E. Cairns, *An Endless Line of Splendor: Revivals and Their Leaders from the Great Awakening to the Present* (Wheaton, Ill.: Tyndale House, 1986), 139.
3. J. Gilchrist Lawson, *Deeper Experiences of Famous Christians* (Anderson, Ind.: Warner, 1911), 206.
4. Christmas Evans, *Sermons and Memoirs of Christmas Evans* (Grand Rapids: Kregel, 1986), 265.
5. Ibid., 54.
6. Ibid., 299.

10.1.6 BILLY BRAY—ABOUNDING JOY IN THE PULPIT

You must know that the Devil is not deaf either, and yet his servants make a great noise. The Devil would rather see us doubting than hear us shouting . . . If they were to put me in a barrel, I would shout "glory" out through the bunghole. I can say glory, glory; I can sing glory, glory; I can dance glory, glory.

—Billy Bray

God had his mouthpiece even in the far reaches and wilds of Cornwall, England. This was Methodist country after Wesley's escapades in quest of the tin miners, but **Billy Bray** (1794–1868) was the man God used to dot the landscape with chapels for the preaching of the Word of God. The area desperately needed his spiritual fervor.

The noted scholar and skeptic of this century, A. L. Rowse, has chronicled his own Cornish childhood and noted how the local rector had preached a particularly moralizing sermon one Sunday and then the next day decamped with the church organist. The successor was "intolerably tedious," with a penchant for the pyramids, British Israelism, and Christadelphianism.[1]

Small in stature but great in heart, Billy Bray was born in Twelveheads near Truro and became a drunken and dissolute man. Like the vast majority of his people, he was a tin miner and several times was nearly killed in his dangerous work.

Bray was soundly converted after reading Bunyan's *Visions of Heaven and Hell* and began to preach in chapels and in fields. He soon became one of Cornwall's "most illustrious sons."[2] Bray worked with the Wesleyans and the Primitive Methodists but was a part of the Bible Christian movement (Bryanites) that built chapels all over the countryside. This joyous, loving, trusting believer truly walked with the living Christ.[3] The remarkable answers to his prayers and his childhood confidence in the Lord made him a legend in his own time.

He never stopped working in the mines, but traveled weekends in his somber clerical black. He preached three times on a Sunday, singing loudly en route and back. Often he was joined by happy pilgrims.[4] The Bible was Bray's only textbook, and his sermons were simple explanations of Scripture with appropriate appeal. His illustrations were common but effective—"a farmer digging potatoes, the fall of a rock in a tin mine, an auction sale of household goods, the sight of a burning cottage, and even a woman caring tenderly for a sickly barnyard fowl."[5] In preaching to a group of miners on Jesus' words, "I am the Bread of Life," Bray said:

> Precious loaf this! The patriarchs and prophets ate of this loaf, and never found a bit of crust about it. The apostles and martyrs ate of this loaf, too, for many long years, and never found a bit of "vinny" in it. And bless the Lord! Poor old Billy Bray can eat it without teeth and get fat on it![6]

Bray was a man of such absorbing prayer and intercession "who set the Lord always before him." He had a strong influence on the Anglican minister **William Haslam** (1818–1905), who was converted and became a flaming preacher through the whole of England, "admonishing the people against a mere outward loyalty to externals rather than trust in the Lamb of God that taketh away the sin of the world."[7] When Haslam preached his fervent message on this theme in St. Paul's Cathedral in 1874, he nearly broke up the furniture in his zeal. The theme and thrust of Billy Bray lived again!

Billy Bray caught the fancy of both Spurgeon and Queen Victoria. Mark Guy Pearse maintained that "from one end of Cornwall to another, no name is so familiar as Billy Bray."[8]

1. A. L. Rowse, *A Cornish Childhood* (London: Clarkson L. Potter, 1942), 136.
2. F. R. Webber, *A History of Preaching in Britain and America* (Milwaukee: Northwestern, 1952), 1:727.

3. John Tallach, *God Made Them Great* (Edinburgh: Banner of Truth, 1974), 69ff.
4. Webber, *A History of Preaching,* 1:730.
5. Ibid., 1:731.
6. Ibid., 1:744.
7. F. W. Bourne, *Billy Bray: The King's Son* (London: Epworth, 1877), 29.
8. Ibid., 31.

10.1.7 DWIGHT LYMAN MOODY—FLAMING FIRE IN THE PULPIT

I know perfectly well that, wherever I go and preach, there are many better preachers known and heard than I am; all that I can say about it is that the Lord uses me.

—D. L. Moody

If you will stop preaching your own words and preach God's Word, He will make you a power for good.

—Henry Moorhouse to D. L. Moody

Dwight Lyman Moody (1837–1899) was known for murdering the king's English. He could pronounce Nebuchadnezzar in two syllables. Yet his evangelistic preaching missions in the United States and Britain were part of a virile spiritual quickening in the 1870s and afterward, which strongly defied the incursions of secularism and unbelief.

William G. McLoughlin is quick to dismiss Moody as "a young tycoon of the revival trade,"[1] as is Sidney Mead. And Iain Murray, from the standpoint of imperial Calvinism, looks askance at Moody as a mere promoter of "revivalism" (as he does to Wesley and Finney) rather than as a leader in "godly revival" because of the tilt toward Arminianism.[2] But serious historians like Gundry and Findlay see Moody's powerful impact as much more than "a backward look at a simpler America."

The fifth of nine children, Moody was born in Northfield, Massachusetts. His father was a heavy-drinking brickmason who died when Dwight was four. The impoverished family was aided by the Unitarian Congregational Church.[3] At seventeen, Moody went to Boston to sell shoes for his uncle, an arrangement contingent upon his attending church at the Mt. Vernon Congregational Church. His Sunday school teacher from that church, Edward Kimball, came to his shoe store and led him to Christ in 1855. Moody never before had heard of the new birth. His acceptance into membership was deferred a year because of his abysmal ignorance of the Scripture. In 1856 he moved to Chicago to sell shoes and met Emma Revell, who was to be his wife, at the Wells Street Mission of the First Baptist Church. In the swell of revival in the city, he organized the North Market Sabbath School. His amazing gifts as a soulwinner soon became evident. He became known as Crazy Moody because of his zeal, and soon built attendance to fifteen hundred boys and girls.

John Farwell of First Methodist Episcopal Church saw how Moody could tell a Bible story and influence these children. He cast his substantial resources into the cause that ultimately became the Moody Church. Henry Sloan Coffin heard Moody preach on "Dan'l" at Northfield and felt it so vividly that he later said, "He made us feel we were right on the spot." Abraham Lincoln was invited by Farwell to attend on one occasion and spoke briefly, protesting "I have never preached a sermon in my life."

Moody did Civil War duty working with Union soldiers in the border states, returning to Chicago to work with the YMCA and his Sunday school. In 1867 Moody visited Britain to meet and study the methods of Charles Spurgeon and George Müller. In England and Scotland, Spurgeon, the Bonars, and R. W. Dale were strong supporters, the latter testifying that what drew him to Moody was the fact that he never talked about lost souls without tears in his eyes. A convert in England was C. T. Studd's father. While in Dublin, Moody heard **Henry Varley** issue the challenge: "The world has yet to see what God will do with and for and through and in and by the man who is fully consecrated to him." Also formative in his influence was the English boy preacher **Henry Moorhouse** (1840–1880), who preached for Moody in Chicago and urged him to be more inductive in his study of Scripture and to give "Bible readings." Moorhouse preached night after night from John 3:16. Moody was moved.[4]

While raising funds in the East after the great Chicago fire of 1871 had destroyed the tabernacle and his home, Moody had a deepening touch and anointing of the Holy Spirit.[5] About this time **Ira D. Sankey** (1840–1908), whom Moody met at a YMCA convention in Indianapolis, began to travel the world with him. Moody traveled more than a million miles and preached to more than a million people with converts by the thousands.[6]

Moody's theology was simple and direct: ruined by the fall, redeemed by the blood, regenerated by the Spirit. His famous sermon on the new birth was preached 183 recorded times from 1881 to 1899.[7] Undoubtedly Plymouth Brethren preachers like John Nelson Darby, Henry Moorhouse, C. H. McIntosh, and George Müller influenced Moody theologically, especially in his eschatology.[8] While the campaigns around the world were always controversial, the great Chicago Revival of 1876 was typical. Out of a population of four hundred thousand people, half of the city was unchurched. In the three-and-one-half months of the campaign, a tabernacle seating eight thousand was built; more than nine hundred thousand attended with six thousand names added as converts. Moody spent the first two weeks of the campaign on the Christians. The song service linked the people together, and then Moody got up to preach in his "locomotive style of delivery."[9] No offering was taken until the end, and the offering was then given to the YMCA. At the last service four hundred converts sat together. He always used the inquiry room for seekers.

As the years passed, Moody added considerable weight to his bullish frame. Yet he was first of all a "muscular Christian" with an extraordinary sensitivity to his audience. His sermons were simply constructed and delivered without great emotional volatility. Sometimes he would preach from the wordless book with the black, red, white, and gold leaves. He would gather material for his sermons, which were more topical than textual, in envelopes. He used interleafed Bibles with his handwritten notes intercalated. He read Scripture slowly but accelerated as he preached to about 220 words per minute. He held unswervingly to biblical inerrancy but fellowshiped with believers who did not share his way of stating his conviction. He invited many of them to the great Northfield Conference he established. Both R. A. Torrey in his famous *Why God Used D. L. Moody* and Charles Erdman in his splendid study attribute a great part of Moody's success in ministry to the character and quality of his dedication to biblical preaching.[10] His great book of messages on heaven is peerless as an exposition of where heaven is, who its inhabitants will be, and how to get there.[11] In his classic message on "The Results of True Repentance," he draws out five specific consequences of genuine repentance, but he does not always have such a clear outline.[12] He often preached on the blood of Christ,[13] and many of his sermons are included in the Sword of the Lord series of *Great Sermons*.[14] After Moody's death, John R. Mott (himself a convert of Moody's meetings) observed:

> I can safely say that I have not visited a country in Europe, Asia or Africa, where the words of Mr. Moody are not bearing fruit. Next to the words of the Bible, and possibly those of Bunyan, his words have been translated into more tongues than those of any other man. Oh, the infinite possibilities of the surrendered, subjugated, consecrated tongue . . .[15]

1. William G. McLoughlin, *Modern Revivalism* (New York: Ronald Press, 1959), 216.
2. Iain H. Murray, *Revival and Revivalism: The Making and Marring of American Evangelicalism, 1750–1858* (Edinburgh: Banner of Truth, 1995). This unfortunate book is well reviewed by Mark Noll, "How We Remember Revivals," in *Christianity Today* (April 24, 1995): 31ff., in which Noll points out that such heroes of Murray as Charles Hodge were critical of all revivals, including those very dear to Murray. Such a matter is not mentioned in Murray.
3. The best Moody biography must still be that of John Pollock, *Moody: The Biography* (Chicago: Moody, 1963, 1983).
4. William R. Moody, *The Life of Dwight L. Moody* (New York: Revell, 1900), 137. Pollock's *Moody* shows Moody's adaptation of the "Bible Reading" from Moorhouse (90). In chapter 11 we shall deal at length with the development of the "Bible Reading" or renewal of the ancient homily among the Brethren.
5. J. Gilchrist Lawson, *Deeper Experiences of Famous Christians* (Anderson, Ind.: Warner, 1911), 348.
6. Ira D. Sankey, *My Life and the Story of the Gospel Hymns* (Philadelphia: Sunday School Times, 1906). The conversion of the noted medical missionary, Wilfred Grenfell, is chronicled in *A Labrador Doctor: Wilfred Thomas Grenfell,* in which he tells how he came to Christ in 1885 in a Moody-Sankey tent.
7. Stanley N. Gundry, *Love Them In: The Life and Theology of D. L. Moody* (Chicago: Moody, 1976).
8. James F. Findlay, *Dwight L. Moody: American Evangelist* (Chicago: University of Chicago, 1969), 125.

9. Darrel M. Robertson, *The Chicago Revival: 1876* (Metuchin, N.J.: Scarecrow, 1989). A rich study.
10. Charles R. Erdman, *D. L. Moody: His Message for Today* (New York: Revell, 1928).
11. D. L. Moody, *Heaven* (Chicago: Moody, 1880).
12. D. L. Moody, *The Overcoming Life* (Chicago: Moody, 1986, 1994), 40.
13. Wilbur M. Smith, ed., *Great Sermons on the Death of Christ* (Natick, Mass.: W. A. Wilde, 1965), 33ff.
14. Curtis Hutson, ed., *Great Sermons on the Holy Spirit* (Murfreesboro, Tenn.: Sword of the Lord, 1988), 49.
15. Smith, *Great Sermons on the Death of Christ*, 44.

10.1.8 BROWNLOW NORTH—GENTLEMAN IN THE PULPIT

God helping me, I will stand or fall by the Lord Jesus Christ. I will put my trust in His truth, and in His teaching as I find it in the written Word of God; and doing that, so sure as the Lord Jesus Christ is the truth, I must be forgiven and saved.

Don't think that I am intruding into the office of the holy ministry. I am not an authorized preacher, but I'll tell you what I am; I am a man who has been at the brink of the bottomless pit and has looked in, and as I see many of you going down to that pit, I am here to "hollo" you back and warn you of your danger. I am here, also, as the chief of sinners, saved by grace, to tell you that the grace that saved me can surely save you.

—Brownlow North

As D. L. Moody was never formally ordained, neither was the gentleman evangelist **Brownlow North** (1810–1875). This was a time of great spiritual awakening. From 1762 to 1862 there were fifteen outstanding revivals in Wales alone. In these stirrings, 110,000 converts were added to the churches.[1]

Brownlow North was born into a Scottish noble family. He was a grandnephew of Lord North, who was Prime Minister under George III, and his grandfather was bishop of Winchester. North attended Eton and graduated from Magdalen College at Oxford. He had a wild spirit, but his godly mother prayed unceasingly for him. The death of a friend in a horseback riding accident sobered him. North spent some time in Ireland, married, and later settled in Aberdeenshire. In November of 1854 he fell under great conviction of sin while playing cards and was converted. The duchess of Gordon led him into a remarkable mastery of the Word and into ministry. He became a dedicated winner of souls and an evangelistic preacher of unusual power.

Called by some the John the Baptist of the revival of 1859, Brownlow North was known for his great earnestness. One newspaper in Stirling gave this account:

The intense earnestness of his manner, indicative of the deepest feeling of compassion for the perishing, was obviously the grand secret of his tremendous moral power. The most common truths appear to be unheard-of-realities, because they are manifestly the utterance of a mind to which they are real, present, and momentous, and they enter many a startled ear because pronounced with burning lips as a message from the Majesty of heaven.[2]

He ministered through the British Isles with one object: "the preaching of the Word and gaining souls for the Master."[3] His intense reverence for the Scriptures and their plenary authority was foundational. Early in 1859 a great wave of the Spirit broke out in Northern Ireland (Ulster) in which one hundred thousand converts were added to the churches. His expositions from Luke 16:19–31 were often preached to thousands in the open air. Five thousand persons listened in the marketplace at Londonderry, eleven thousand at Ballymena, and twelve thousand at Newtonlimavady. Sermons on such engaging themes as "How the Beggar Became Rich," "How the Rich Man Became Poor," and the classic "Earnest, Heart-felt, Too-late Prayer" capitalized on the story line in the narrative as North argued that no one is lost because he is rich or saved because he is poor. "The cups of both were filled to the brim,"[4] he stated. His preaching was rooted deeply in the text and his confidence in the sufficiency of the Scriptures.

---

1. Efion Evans, *Revival Comes to Wales* (Cardiff: Evangelical Press of Wales, 1979), 97, 99.
2. K. Moody-Stuart, *Brownlow North: His Life and Work* (London: Banner of Truth, 1878, 1961), 57.
3. Ibid., 69. An important study: R. F. Foster, *Paddy and Mr. Punch: Connections in Irish and English History* (London: Penguin, 1995). An Irish historian dismantles "the romantic myth" of Irish enslavement.
4. Brownlow North, *The Rich Man and Lazarus* (London: Banner of Truth, 1960), 15.

10.2 THE SURGING FLOW OF THE MISSIONARIES

Therefore go and make disciples of all nations, baptizing them in the name of the Father and of the Son and of the Holy Spirit, and teaching them to obey everything I have commanded you.

—Matthew 28:19–20

Go into all the world and preach the good news to all creation.

—Mark 16:15

Spiritual awakening, biblical preaching, and the gracious visits of the Holy Spirit not only counteracted a flood-tide of error and unbelief but also quickened evangelization both at home and abroad. An inevitable concomitant of spiritual renewal was the fueling of missionary expansion on all fronts. In his massive treatment of the history of missions, Kenneth Scott Latourette calls the period from 1815 to 1914 "the great century." Volume 4 particularly zeroes in on the factors which ignited an unparalleled expansion of the Christian faith among the nations.[1] This was, as Ruth Tucker points out, "the Protestant Era," and commercial expansion and colonialism were interwoven with gospel extension in a complex mix. Nevertheless this was a period when preaching went global and the harvest was vast.[2]

---

1. Kenneth Scott Latourette, *The Great Century,* vol. 4 (Grand Rapids: Zondervan, 1941, 1969).
2. Ruth A. Tucker, *From Jerusalem to Irian Jaya* (Grand Rapids: Zondervan, 1983), 109ff.

10.2.1 OPENING UP AFRICA—DAVID LIVINGSTONE

19 March 1872—Birthday. My Jesus, my King, my life, my All; I again dedicate my whole self to Thee. Accept me and grant, O gracious Father, that ere this year is gone I may finish my task. In Jesus' Name I ask it. Amen, so let it be. David Livingstone.
—written in his diary shortly before his death

Unduly lionized by some and unreasonably lambasted by others as an agent of imperialism, **David Livingstone** (1813–1873) was foremost a missionary of the cross and secondarily an explorer and an antagonist of the slave trade.[1] His ancestors came from the island of Ulva off Scotland and settled in Blantyre in the Scottish Highlands, where Livingstone was born. His father was a poor but devout man who sold tea from door to door. The elder Livingstone left the highly Calvinist kirk for an independent Congregational church in nearby Hamilton. He sent his son Charles to Finney's school at Oberlin in the U.S. because he agreed with Finney that "The Holy Spirit is given to all who ask."[2] A similar independency characterized his son David, who leaned more to the Church of England later in his life but never joined it.

David Livingstone started working at age ten as a cotton-spinner in a factory. He used to say his parental home was the mirror image of *The Cotter's Saturday Night,* and David knew considerable spiritual conviction early on. After reading Dick's *Philosophy of a Future State,* he was converted and sensed a call to missions overseas. "He could now see that all he needed to do was to seek God with all his heart, hand over to him the penitent soul, and accept the pardon purchased by Jesus' blood on Calvary."[3] Livingstone studied medicine in Glasgow and applied to serve under the London Missionary Society. He was strongly evangelical and decidedly influenced by the ideas of **Vinet** (cf. 9.6.4).[4] Trained as a preacher by Richard Cecil, who stressed memorization of the manuscript, Livingstone's first effort was a disaster. He began reading his text and then said abruptly, "Friends, I have forgotten all I had to say," and fled.[5] Yet he was ordained in 1840 and sailed for the Cape of Africa the next year. He commenced his mission work with **Robert Moffat** (cf. 8.4.7), whose daughter Mary he would marry.

Livingstone spent thirty years in Africa, returning home twice for only two years. While on his first furlough in 1857, he published his famous *Missionary Travels,* which built some of the myth around the man. He was five foot six inches tall—slender and sinewy. Once he was severely mauled by a lion and thereafter was unable to raise his right arm. He often knew great loneliness in the bush along with weakness through fever and hunger. One of his sons, Robert, served with the Union Army in the American Civil War and died in a prisoner-of-war camp in Atlanta in 1865. But truly he was an indefatigable servant of Christ. Blaikie describes Livingstone's preaching:

> Livingstone was in the habit of preaching to the natives and conversing seriously with them on religion, his favorite topics being the love of Christ, the Fatherhood of God, the resurrection, and the last judgment. His preaching to them, in Dr. Moffat's judgment, was highly effective. It was simple, scriptural, conversational, went straight to the point, was well fitted to arrest the attention, and remarkably adapted to the capacity of the people. To his father he writes (July 5, 1848): "For a long time I felt much depressed after preaching the unsearchable riches of Christ to apparently insensible hearts; but now I like to dwell on the love of the great Mediator, for it always warms my own heart, and I know that the gospel is the power of God—the great means which He employs for the regeneration of our ruined world."[6]

He loved to speak of Jesus but was often spurned and he felt it deeply. In traveling twenty-nine thousand miles—discovering Victoria Falls and many other key sites—he undoubtedly preached to more Africans than many missionaries ever dreamed. One of his early converts was Chief Sechele, who with Setefano was among the earliest baptized.

Livingstone said, "I am a missionary, heart and soul. God had an only Son, and He was a missionary and a physician. A poor, poor imitation of Him I am, or wish to be. In this service I hope to live, in it I wish to die." His wife died at Shapanga in 1862 and left him with motherless children.

Livingstone's second term out was not under the London Missionary Society but directly under the British government. In this term he was lost from all contact for two years, and the Welsh journalist, **Henry M. Stanley,** went out and found him. At that time Livingstone had no book but the Bible in his possession. Livingstone's life and testimony won Stanley to Christ in the heart of Africa.[7]

He was truly an evangelist, pleading with the townspeople of Blantyre on a visit home "to accept God's offers of mercy to them in Christ and give themselves wholly to Him. To bow down before God was not mean; it was manly. His one wish for them all was that they might have peace with God and rejoice in the hope of the eternal inheritance."[8]

Livingstone was always sound, differing from Bishop Colenso's liberal and critical views of Scripture.[9] "I cannot leave Africa with my work unfinished," he stated. His faithful valet Susi found him dead, kneeling in prayer by his bed, on

April 29, 1873. We possess few of his sermons, but we sense how his proclamation of the gospel remains as one of the most heroic chapters in the saga of the preaching of the grace of God.

1. The conclusion of "David Livingstone and Africa," a seminar at the Centre of African Studies at the University of Edinburgh held on the centenary of Livingstone's death, May 4–5, 1973, and published with the proceedings.
2. Tim Jeal, *Livingstone* (New York: Putnam, 1973), 12. The most solid recent treatment of Livingstone, but a work that does not truly understand his spiritual ministry. A lavishly illustrated study is Elspeth Huxley's *Livingstone and His African Journeys* (New York: Saturday Review Press, 1974).
3. Jessie Kleeberger, *David Livingstone: Missionary Explorer of Africa* (Anderson, Ind.: Gospel Trumpet, 1925), 10.
4. W. G. Blaikie, *The Personal Life of David Livingstone* (New York: Revell, 1880), 40.
5. Kleeberger, *David Livingstone,* 14.
6. Blaikie, *The Personal Life of David Livingstone,* 110. Blaikie's study is old but the most inwardly sensitive to the spirit of the man.
7. Charles J. Finger, *David Livingstone: Explorer and Prophet* (Garden City, N.Y.: Doubleday, 1927), 257.
8. Blaikie, *The Personal Life of David Livingstone,* 240. Of immense interest are *Livingstone's Family Letters* (Westport, Conn.: Greenwood, 1959), in 2 volumes.
9. Ibid., 362. Frank Boreham's great sermon on "David Livingstone's Text" on the Great Commission which contains his famous words, "It is the word of a gentleman," is to be found in *A Bunch of Everlastings* (New York: Abingdon, 1920), 129ff. Colenso was a radical missionary bishop who adversely effected John Henry Newman's brother (cf. 9.3.3).

10.2.2 PIONEER IN CHINA—J. HUDSON TAYLOR

Perishing China so filled my heart and mind that there was no rest by day and little sleep by night, till health gave way.

The secret was that Jesus was satisfying the deep thirst of heart and soul.

I did long to be able to tell them the Glad Tidings.

—J. Hudson Taylor

Another cross-cultural crusader for Christ whose preaching was pivotal was **James Hudson Taylor** (1832–1905), the great pace-setting missionary who opened up the heart of China to the gospel. Born in Yorkshire to praying parents, he was reared as a Methodist. His father was a somewhat disaffected class leader who moved into the Methodist Free Church while young Taylor increasingly fellowshiped with the Plymouth Brethren. James was converted in 1849 when his mother was on her knees interceding for him as he read a booklet on the finished work of Christ.[1]

At an early age, Taylor spoke of God's call to go to China. China was a troubled country, with its Western influence confined to the treaty ports.[2] Taylor worked as a dispenser for Dr. Richard Hardey and began medical school with the help of the Chinese Evangelization Society founded by Dr. Gutzlaf of Hong Kong. While still in Hull in England he preached his first sermon. The call of God burned in his being. He wrote his sister of the experience:

> On Tuesday I went to preach at Royston. The room was crowded; there would be from fifty to sixty present. I never was so blessed in my life. We had a prayer-meeting afterwards in which ten or twelve took part. One little girl of about thirteen came to the penitent-form and professed to find peace. She is young, but Jesus can keep her.[3]

At age twenty-one he sailed for China on a five-and-a-half month voyage. During the trip he held sixty services on board, systematically opening Scripture beginning with Romans 4.[4] Arriving in China he first heard preaching in the Shanghai dialect and set himself to language study. We must bear in mind that most of these missionaries did their preaching in languages which were not easy to learn.

Dressing as a Chinese—to the disapproval of most of the other missionaries— Taylor began his preaching tours in 1855 and baptized his first convert.[5] Excited crowds gathered, and he gave himself to his itinerant vision of "preaching where Christ was not named."[6] On his fifth journey, Taylor recorded his search for an appropriate pulpit from which to preach and used a bronze incense vase. He described the response:

> At the lowest computation, five or six hundred persons must have been present, and I do not think it would be over the mark to say a thousand. As they quieted down, I addressed them at the top of my voice, and a more orderly, attentive audience in the open air one could not wish to see. It was most encouraging to hear one and another call out . . . pught- ts's, pugh-ts's . . . not wrong, not wrong, as they frequently did when something said met with their approval.[7]

Taylor anguished over the death of his wife, Maria, and several of his children. He struggled for personal holiness, resolving his quest to a large degree with his discovery of the believer's union with Christ. Taylor exclaimed, "I am one with Christ." He endured conflict with other missionaries over such things as baptism. Taylor himself was eventually rebaptized among the Brethren in Hull. The Anglican leader, George Moule, was upset, but ultimately many Anglicans became part of the China Inland Mission founded by Taylor on his first furlough.

The China Inland Mission (OMF today) sprang out of the Great Revival of 1859 and "the hidden years" (1860–1864) when Taylor stayed in England. In all of this time he had great joy in preaching and was heard often at Keswick, where he enjoyed a lifelong association. It was at Keswick that he led F. B. Meyer into the truth of the Spirit-led life. Taylor held to the inerrancy of Scripture and the imminency of Christ's return involved with the return of the Jews to Palestine. He visited America and preached at both the Niagara Conference and at Northfield. He developed deep ties with Lord Radstock in the raising of funds for sending out personnel and rejoiced at Radstock's later revival ministry among Tsarist nobles in Russia.[8]

Taylor was associated with the young evangelist H. Grattan Guiness in meetings in Dublin. Good samples of his preaching in the Western world are to be found in his studies in the Song of Solomon titled *Union and Communion*.[9] These messages were widely heard and a trifle allegorical—not strange to Plymouth Brethren ears.

Yet his life and ministry were mainly in China, where he would often preach to workers in English on Sundays and then go on his journeys into the interior during the week. "I never made a sacrifice," he would say, but he faced bandits, uprisings, hostilities, and great dangers with his beloved Savior and his dear old harmonium to accompany singing. By 1900 the China Inland Mission had 750 missionaries under call. The summons was to men and women "to live and preach Christ openly!"[10]

---

1. Dr. and Mrs. Howard Taylor, *Hudson Taylor's Spiritual Secret* (London: China Inland Mission, 1932), 13–14.
2. J. C. Pollock, *Hudson Taylor and Maria* (Grand Rapids: Zondervan, 1962), 22. The best modern biography.
3. Dr. and Mrs. Howard Taylor, *Hudson Taylor: The Early Years— The Growth of a Soul* (London: China Inland Mission, 1911), 1:105. The large two-volume work is classic and every page brimming with blessing. The leader of the Assembly in Hull was Andrew Jukes, whose *The Law of the Offerings* (London: Lamp Press, 1954) is immensely helpful.
4. Ibid., 1:192.
5. Pollock, *Hudson Taylor and Maria*, 51.
6. Taylor, *Hudson Taylor*, 1:186.
7. Ibid., 1:279.
8. Pollock, *Hudson Taylor and Maria*, 130; also Taylor, *Spiritual Secret*, 83.
9. J. Hudson Taylor, *Union and Communion: Thoughts on the Song of Solomon Relating to Personal Fellowship with Christ* (Chicago: Moody, n.d.). Fifty thousand copies are in print; introduction by J. Stuart Holden.
10. Taylor, *Spiritual Secret*, 149.

10.2.3 BEACON IN SOUTHEAST ASIA—ADONIRAM JUDSON

In the great country of America, we sustain the character of teachers and explainers of the contents of the sacred Scriptures of our religion. And since it is contained in those Scriptures, that, if we pass to other countries, and preach and propagate religion, great good will result, and both those who teach and those who receive the religion will be freed from future punishment, and enjoy, without decay or death, the eternal felicity of heaven—that royal permission be given, that we, taking refuge in the royal power, may preach our religion in these dominions, and that those who are pleased with our preaching and wish to listen to and be guided by it, whether foreigners or Burmans, may be exempt from government molestation, they present themselves to receive the favor of the excellent king.

—Adoniram Judson in 1819 to the emperor of Burma at Ava

Another valiant emissary of the cross of Christ was **Adoniram Judson** (1788–1850). He was born the oldest of four children in Malden, Massachusetts, to an old-line Congregational minister who opposed New England theology. Adoniram means "Lord of Height," and very early in his life he excelled, learning to read the Bible at three and preaching to other children at four. His favorite childhood hymn was "Go preach my gospel, says the Lord."

Judson went to Brown University, where he graduated valedictorian of his class in 1807, but in the process lost his faith to French infidelity and deism. In 1808, while he was staying in a country inn after a raucous indulgence, he was deeply troubled over the agony of a man in the next room. The next day he was stunned to learn the man had died. That man was Jacob Eames, a compatriot of his in profligacy.[1] Shortly thereafter he was converted and matriculated at Andover Theological Seminary. There he found common cause with a group of young men who had been part of the Haystack Prayer Meetings at Williams College (cf. 9.2.4).

A sermon by Dr. Claudius Buchanan of Bristol inflamed him for missions and caused him to exclaim, "The New Testament is all missions!"[2] Rather than taking the call to be associate to Dr. Griffin at Park Street Church, Boston, Judson took his bride and sailed for India. His penchant for evangelistic preaching had been demonstrated earlier when he was imprisoned by a French privateer. In Bayonne, France, as a prisoner, he pleaded with his hearers to receive Christ with "just the sort of sermons he later preached in Burma."[3] Shortly thereafter they released him.

Although they were sent out by the American Board in 1812, Judson and his wife were moved to shift their views on baptism and were immersed in India. Still, William Carey was dubious about them and sent them on to the Isle of France in the Mauritius Islands, where Judson preached to the English soldiers. About to be sent home, he and his wife hopped on a ship to Rangoon and launched the American Baptist Missionary Union work in Burma.

The Judsons and the small band of workers who joined them worked seven years before their first convert was received. The "extravagant idealism and nihilism" of the Hinayana Buddhism of Burma presented "no God to save, no soul to be saved and no sin to be saved from." Progress was exceedingly slow.

Yet within the first year, the Judsons had commenced public worship and preaching. The Buddhists had zayats, which were covered areas where lay teachers could sit on a raised platform and where people could come to rest and talk. Judson built a Baptist zayat and there preached the gospel.[4] A primary objective in his life was to translate the Bible into Burmese, a task he finished in January 1834. Judson and his family endured brutal persecution, and he was cruelly imprisoned. He lost two wives and two children and was survived by his third wife only a few years in his own passing. He loved to preach, and his wife in *Wayside Preaching* describes his messages:

> His preaching was concrete. He did not deal in vague abstractions. Truth assumed in his mind statuesque forms . . . Behind his words when he preached lay the magnet of a great character.[5]

When Judson was home on furlough he preached biblical messages that sometimes disappointed the crowds, who wanted exciting stories of danger and heroism.[6] Yet his "vigorous sermons tinged with humor" always made a clear mark on the hearers.

Adoniram died after a long illness while out at sea off Burma in a French ship and was buried at sea. His wife, assisted by Dr. Francis Wayland, president of Brown University and a gifted preacher in his own right, developed his memoirs.[7] In tribute to him are Judson churches, Judson Press, Judson College—but more significantly, many souls which shine as stars in the heavens to the praise of our God. At the time of his death in 1850 there were seven thousand converts (both Burmans and Karens, a mountain people in Burma) with sixty-three different congregations and an outreach stretching into Siam and to the Jews.

---

1. L. Helen Percy, *Adoniram Judson: Apostle of Burma* (Anderson, Ind.: Gospel Trumpet, 1926), 19.
2. J. Mervin Hull, *Judson the Pioneer* (Philadelphia: American Baptist Publication Society, 1913), 25.
3. Ibid., 43.
4. Courtney Anderson, *To the Golden Shore: The Life of Adoniram Judson* (Boston: Little, Brown, 1956), 219.
5. Harlan P. Beach, *Knights of the Labarum* (New York: Student Volunteer Movement, 1898), 33.
6. Anderson, *To the Golden Shore,* 457, 462. For the rigor and romance of translation, see Eunice Pike, *Words Wanted* (Chicago: Moody, 1958).
7. Francis Wayland, ed., *Memoirs of Adoniram Judson,* 2 vols. (Boston: Sampson, 1855).

10.2.4 Finding the Key—John Livingstone Nevius

The Holy Spirit was gradually but continually shedding light into my soul, and taking of the things of Christ and showing them to me. In a word, I am changed . . . I now feel my utter inability to take the first step in the Christian life without divine aid. Sinfulness and selfish motives are mixed with all I do. My only hope is in God's mercy through faith in the Lord Jesus Christ.

What should be my gratitude to being able so soon to have the oversight of a flock of Christ's sheep in this far-off wilderness; to speak to them in their own tongue of the wonderful works of God; and to point inquiring souls "to the Lamb of God who taketh away the sins of the world"!

—John Livingstone Nevius

John Livingstone Nevius (1829–1893) had two special joys—horses and street preaching. Born in Seneca County in western New York within a staunchly Presbyterian family, Nevius was of Dutch descent. His family possibly dates back to the French Huguenot refugees. His father died when he was two, but his hardworking mother helped him attend Union College in Schenectady. After graduating, he spent a year teaching in Georgia. At this time he came under deep conviction for sin and came to Christ.[1] Then, sensing God's call on his life, he went on to Princeton Theological Seminary in 1850.

During his seminary days he felt especially close to Charles Hodge and was profoundly moved by the preaching of Archibald Alexander.[2] He was always an avid Bible student and gave himself unstintingly to Scripture and to the mastery of "the cardinal doctrines of the Bible."[3] Teaching Sunday school and taking services in the neighboring communities, he felt keenly disappointed in his own preaching but preached on occasion before the president and faculty with increasing approbation.[4] After reading Mrs. Adoniram Judson's memoirs of missionary work in Burma, he responded to the call to China.

In 1853 Nevius sailed for China with his physically fragile bride. They were first stationed for language study at Ningpo, where the church consisted of one hundred disciples. Helen Nevius had to return home for a year and a half, and both of them suffered permanent debilitation from the strange fevers that vexed their bodies. Nevius was made pastor of the native church and preached the Word with facility in Chinese. While Hudson Taylor believed wearing Chinese native dress was advantageous, Nevius felt such effort was futile. Yet the Lord greatly blessed both men with real harvest despite their divergent convictions on this issue. Mrs. Nevius reported:

My husband's sermons preached on these occasions were carefully prepared, and were listened to with deepest attention.[5]

Their ministry shifted to Hang-Chow and then north to Shantung province and the city of Tung-Chow. This is the area made famous by Langdon Gilkey's *Shantung Compound,* the story of World War II incarceration. Here Nevius continued to preach, travel, and write a systematic theology. The Neviuses made a voyage to England, where they fellowshiped with the Hudson Taylors, and then went on to the United States, where they spent three years before returning to China.

The work in China was growing significantly in spite of famines, rebellions, and the perennial shortage of workers. At this time he was writing his still classic study on demon possession. He translated Luke 8–23 and James 3 to Revelation

2 for the Chinese Bible. He was moderator of the Shanghai Missionary Conference in 1890, when more than four hundred missionaries gathered for prayer and strategizing.

John and Helen Nevius visited "the hermit kingdom" of Korea in 1890 as well as Japan. But it was in Korea that the Nevius Method of "self-governing, self-supporting and self-propagating" missions was most impressively implemented. The Korean revival (1904–1910), saw a 300 percent growth rate in the church.[6]

Nevius was known for his incisive and biblical missionary addresses at home and abroad. He and his wife sailed once again for China in 1892 on the *Empress of China,* and he died there in the following year at the age of sixty-four. He had been a stalwart preacher and a gifted man of vision.[7]

1. Helen S. Nevius, *The Life of John Livingstone Nevius* (New York: Revell, 1895), 56ff.
2. Ibid., 73.
3. Ibid., 97.
4. Ibid., 83, 107.
5. Ibid., 160.
6. Roy E. Shearer, *Wildfire: Church Growth in Korea* (Grand Rapids: Eerdmans, 1966); See also "The Koreans' Formula: Independence, Dependence," *The Presbyterian Journal* (February 19, 1969): 9ff.
7. Other significant statements of missionary strategization must include that of another North China missionary, Roland Allen, *Missionary Methods: St. Paul's or Ours* (Chicago: Moody, 1912, 1959) and the definitive work of Johannes Warneck of the Rhenish Mission, *The Living Christ and Dying Heathenism* (Grand Rapids: Baker, 1954), written over against the remarkable response of the Battaks of Sumatra.

10.2.5 PRESSING THE PARAMETERS—MARY SLESSOR

There is nothing small or trivial, for God is ready to take every act and motive and work through them to the formation of character and the development of holy and useful lives that will convey grace to the world.

It was the dream of my childhood to be a missionary to Calabar.

All is dark except above . . . Calvary stands safe and secure.
—Mary M. Slessor

One of the most courageous chapters of missionary expansion was written by **Mary Slessor** (1848–1915), who carried the Word of God into situations of indescribable difficulty. Born in Aberdeen, Scotland, the second of seven children, she was reared by a godly mother who despite a cruel and drunken husband directed her children aright. The preaching of the fires of hell drove Mary to Christ,[1] and the reality of the Savior sustained her as from age eleven she toiled from six to six in the mills.

The mission of the United Presbyterian Church in Calabar (now Nigeria) early gripped her imagination, and the death of Livingstone clinched her call. At age twenty-eight she sailed for the field to work as a missionary teacher in "the white man's graveyard." Already on the coast there were 174 members and one thousand people meeting on the Lord's Day. Her personal text was "Learn of Me," and she opened Scripture with deftness and clarity. The menace of slavers and the darkness of witchcraft and sorcery pressed in upon her, but she visited the hovels and sought to win the respect of both the native chiefs and the governing authorities.

Slessor first learned to speak Efik, the trade language, and at her first opportunity preached on John 5:1–24. She spoke of "their need of healing and saving, of which they must be conscious through their dissatisfaction with this life, the promptings of their higher natures, the experience of suffering and sorrow, and the dark future beyond death, and asking the question 'Wilt thou be made whole?' pointed the way to peace."[2] Slessor developed a considerable ease with the language, conducting large Sunday school classes. "Preaching the love of Christ was her passion."[3] Her visits home were not easy. As she put it:

> I am pained often at home that there is so little of depth, and of God's Word, in the speeches and addresses I hear. It seems as if they thought anything will do for children, and that any kind of talk about coming to Christ and believing on Christ will feed and nourish immortal souls.[4]

Slessor remained convinced that the great need was for the systematic teaching of the Bible.

She almost married on one visit home, but chose to return to Africa when her fiancé was deemed not physically strong enough for service overseas. Upon returning to Calabar, her ministry moved inland to the Okoyongs, a people given to violence and unspeakable cruelty. "No man can do anything with such a people," she conceded, but she saw God perform the impossible. Dressed unlike the other Europeans and without shoes, Slessor marched into the bush to preach Christ. She presented the story of Jesus and persisted in the simple, direct gospel message.[5] She fought malarial fever and terrible boils, claiming Romans 8:11 as her life verse. She served as judge in the courts and as consul for her government, but her obsession was to share the Word wherever she went. Robert Glover in his classic survey of worldwide missions says:

> It is a question if the career of any other woman missionary has been marked by so many strange adventures, daring feats, signal providences, and wonderful achievements.[6]

1. W. P. Livingstone, *Mary Slessor of Calabar: Pioneer Missionary* (London: Hodder and Stoughton, 1917), 3.
2. Ibid., 26.

3. Ibid., 34.

4. Ibid., 46.

5. Ibid., 67, 112.

6. T. J. Bach, *Vision and Valor* (Grand Rapids: Baker, 1963), 81.

10.2.6 *INTO PERIL—JOHN G. PATON*

Nothing known to men under Heaven could have produced their new character and disposition except only the grace of God in Christ Jesus. Though still marred by many of the faults of heathenism, they were at the roots of their being really new creatures, trying, according to their best light, to live for and to please their new Master, Jesus Christ.

What power in the gospel! O God, give me health and long life that I may teach the gospel to these people.

—John G. Paton

Those who are wise will shine like the brightness of the heavens, and those who lead many to righteousness, like the stars for ever and ever.

—Daniel 12:3

The news of the martyrdom of **John Williams,** the apostle to Polynesia, stunned the Christian world, but such was the tidal wave of gospel advance that many sought to take his place or came forward as willing to pay the price wherever the Lord would send. Among these "of whom the world was not worthy" was **John G. Paton** (1824–1906), who came from the old covenanting Reformed Presbyterian Church of Scotland. Though poor—his father was a stocking weaver—family prayers were made morning and evening in his home and the Scripture was central.

For nine years, Paton served the Glasgow City Mission, reaching the lost through outdoor preaching and furthering the cause of total abstinence.[1] Sensing the call to preach the gospel, he sailed in 1828 with his new wife to the New Hebrides, thirty small islands northeast of Australia. "The wail of the perishing heathen in the south seas" was inescapable.[2] The environment was physically hostile. Both his wife and baby died the first year, and the darkness threatened to swallow him up as he stood between the warring inland people and the harbor people. The constant movement of armed men and the shrieks of women being sacrificed took a heavy toll. Nonetheless, he would not be deterred, and he held meetings in the villages to preach against idolatry.[3]

Returning with his second wife, Paton settled in Aniwa, where he established credibility by digging a well and obtaining much-needed water in this unheard-of way.[4] The missions ship *Dayspring* helped them move among the islands, and Paton went back and forth to both sides of the continuing conflict. Cannibals began to praise God—up to six thousand converts in number.[5] The first communion service on Aniwa was memorable. As always the Word was given, "a short and careful exposition of the Ten Commandments and the way of salvation according to the gospel."[6] Paton also translated the Gospel of Mark into the aboriginal tongue.

Itinerating in the homeland was an important opportunity for Paton, and he spoke to fourteen hundred different audiences in a two-year period. Sponsoring him were J. Oswald Dykes, the British Presbyterian, J. Hood Wilson of Edinburgh, Lord Radstock, F. B. Meyer in Leicester, and John Hall of Fifth Avenue Presbyterian in New York City. He was especially effective at the Mildmay Conference in England.

Spurgeon called John Paton the king of the cannibals. How many others there are who ought to be included in this narrative, who like Paton preached the everlasting gospel without fear or favor.

---

1. J. J. Ellis, *John G. Paton: The Story of a Noble Life* (London: Pickering and Inglis, n.d.), 20.
2. John G. Paton, *Autobiography* (New York: Revell, 1898), 85, 87. Appreciation by A. T. Pierson.
3. Bessie L. Byrum, *John G. Paton: Hero of the South Seas* (Anderson, Ind.: Gospel Trumpet, 1924), 96.
4. Ellis, *John G. Paton,* 90; Paton, *Autobiography,* 178–79.
5. Byrum, *John G. Paton,* 108.
6. Paton, *Autobiography,* 221. An extraordinary document.

10.2.7 AROUND THE WORLD—FREDRIK FRANSON

> That which is biblical is everywhere appropriate, for all countries and all peoples.
>
> Fellowship with Jesus and work for Jesus are two preoccupations that we can never assess too highly.
>
> —F. Franson

"The crowds of listeners that streamed to Franson's meetings . . . can be counted in the tens of thousands, and thousands of people came to faith in Christ through his preaching."[1] That fiery preacher was **Fredrik Franson** (1852–1908), not known widely outside of Scandinavia. Yet he was the founder and strategist of a missionary movement of awesome power.

Franson was born into a godly home in Westmanland in Sweden. The revivals kindled by Rosenian pietism fostered an atmosphere of the awareness of sin and grace, but Franson was not converted until emigrating to Nebraska. After a bout with malarial fever, Franson came to Christ in a Swedish Baptist congregation in his community. Feeling God's call, he attached himself as an apprentice to D. L. Moody and joined the Moody Church in Chicago. Franson traveled as an evangelist working in Mormon country. Many Scandinavians had come to Utah under the aegis of the Mormons.

His motto was "Have faith in God," and he broke free from ethnic bonds and preached widely on all continents except Australia. He attended the Evangelical Alliance conference in Copenhagen in 1884; there he met Professor Christlieb (cf. 9.4.6) and heard his great message in German on "The Religious Indifference and the Best Means to Combat It."[2]

Franson's vision for outreach led to the formation of the Scandinavian Alliance Mission in Chicago, known now as the Evangelical Alliance Mission. He networked with both J. Hudson Taylor and A. B. Simpson.[3] He was a great lover of the truth of the Lord's return, but unfortunately in his book, *Himlauret, The Heavenly Clock,* he set a date for the rapture. Franson was close to Andrew Murray in South Africa.[4] He traveled widely in South America and planted churches there that still bear remarkable fruit.

Several societies still vital in Scandinavia trace their lineage to Franson. He must be seen as one of the premier missiologists of his time and a preacher who had great strength in presenting and applying the Scriptures. He said:

> What a difference between Stockholm and Copenhagen! It seems as if the true religion of Jesus has caught hold among both the higher and lower levels of society, and the Gospel is being preached . . . in a great many meeting places. Nevertheless, regardless of how much one works and preaches, it seems as if it is hard to meet the ever growing cravings of the people to hear the Word of God. One must adjust oneself to preach three to four times on Sunday. On coming Ascension Day, I expect to have to speak at five or six meetings.[5]

Fredrik Franson died at fifty-six in Idaho Springs, Colorado, after crossing over to the United States from Mexico to take a short rest from his evangelistic travels.

---

1. Edvard Torjesen, *Fredrik Franson: A Legacy* (Wheaton, Ill.: TEAM, n.d.), 11. Torjesen is *the* Franson scholar today.
2. O. C. Grauer, *Fredrik Franson* (Chicago: Scandinavian Alliance Mission, n.d.), 54.
3. Ibid., 75. To my knowledge, Mrs. J. G. Princell's excellent biography was never translated into English.
4. Ibid., 188. For the choicest on the Swedish situation, see David Nyvall, *My Father's Testament* (Chicago: Covenant, 1974), 197.
5. Edvard Torjesen, *Fredrik Franson: A Model for Worldwide Evangelism* (Pasadena, Calif.: William Carey, 1983), 54.

10.3 THE SWELL AND THE UNDERTOW OF AMERICAN PREACHING

> Two inestimable advantages Christianity has given us: first the Sabbath, the jubilee of the whole world; whose light dawns welcome alike into the closet of the philosopher, into the garret of toil, and into prison cells, and everywhere suggests, even to the vile, the dignity of spiritual being. . . . And secondly, the institution of preaching in the speech of man to man—essentially the most flexible of all organs, or all forms. What

hinders that now, everywhere, in pulpits, in lecture rooms, in houses, in fields, wherever the invitation of men or your own occasion lead you, you speak the very truth, as your life and conscience teach it, and cheer the waiting, fainting hearts of men with new hope and new revelation.
—Ralph Waldo Emerson's address to the senior class at Harvard Divinity School in 1838

As we turn to consider American preachers in the latter half of the nineteenth century, we must brace for some shock and disappointment. Certainly there were solidly biblical servants of the Word, and we shall note them with appreciation and gratitude. But there was an undertow that arose out of New England theology and its denial of original sin, its depreciation of imputation, and its devaluation of an Anselmian or substitutionary aspect of the atonement. As early as 1831, de Tocqueville, the inveterate French observer, said of American preachers:

It is often difficult to ascertain from their discourse whether the principal object of religion is to procure eternal felicity in the other world or prosperity in this.

In his invaluable *Cosmos in the Chaos: Philip Schaff's Interpretation of Nineteenth-Century American Religion,* Stephen Graham shares the overview of the great church historian **Philip Schaff** (1819–1893). Schaff came from Germany to teach at Mercersburg Seminary in Pennsylvania and at Union in New York. He was trained at Halle, Tubingen, and Berlin, and took a pietistic stand against Enlightenment rationalism. Schaff also affirmed the authority of Scripture.[1] Yet he was inordinately critical of the Puritans and revivalists, although he liked D. L. Moody.[2] Schaff was antislavery but pro-evolution. He favored biblical revision and oversaw the translation of the Lange commentaries and the assembling of the great *Schaff-Herzog Encyclopedia.* He was a strong advocate of the total abstinence movement and Sabbath societies.

The anguish of the Civil War and the opening of the west must be thoroughly worked into our perspective on the American pulpit at this time.[3]

---

1. Stephen R. Graham, *Cosmos in the Chaos: Philip Schaff's Interpretation of Nineteenth-Century American Religion* (Grand Rapids: Eerdmans, 1995), 74.
2. Ibid., 154.
3. Schaff admired Lincoln's stand. Out of the vast literature, I believe one of the most helpful pieces for our purposes is Elton Trueblood, *Abraham Lincoln: Theologian of American Anguish* (New York: Harper, 1973). Not to be underestimated is Lincoln's own paradigm of communication, particularly the *Gettysburg Address,* 272 words "which remade America"; see Garry Wills, *Lincoln at Gettysburg* (New York: Simon and Schuster, 1992). Lincoln according to Wills was a student of the Word. His use of vernacular rhythms is striking.

10.3.1 *Horace Bushnell—Rudderless in the Pulpit*

I have been greatly blessed in my doubtings.

I really did not expect to remain in the ministry long. I thought if I could sometime be called to a professorship of moral philosophy, it would be a more satisfactory field of exertion.

—Horace Bushnell

Without question a brilliant preacher and person of huge intellectual capacity, **Horace Bushnell** (1802–1876) must yet be seen as a tragic figure in American pulpit annals. He was born in Litchfield, Connecticut. His father was a Methodist and his mother an Episcopalian, but he was a member of the only local church, the Congregational.

Bushnell started at Yale in 1823, and after graduating did stints in teaching and in newspaper work in New York. He was not happy, nor was he ever healthy. He returned to Yale to attend law school and remained aloof when revival came to the campus in 1831.[1] His hero was Samuel Taylor Coleridge. Neither sin nor the cross were central in Bushnell's thinking. Nonetheless in 1833 he took the pastorate of North Church, Hartford, where he stayed until he was forced to retire for reasons of health in 1859.

Bushnell has been called the father of liberalism, and indeed in moving beyond New England theology he lurched very close to Unitarianism. Certainly in *God in Christ* he lapsed into Unitarian thinking, espousing a modal view of the Trinity. In his *Vicarious Sacrifice* and *Forgiveness and Law,* Bushnell jettisoned transactual and propitiatory aspects of the atonement. In a reaction against revivalism, he opted for gradualism rather than conversion in his book *Christian Nurture*. Neither did he believe a child to be depraved. He believed the child was to grow up never knowing that he or she is other than a Christian.

Charles Hodge spoke of his views as "less than Christian."[2] For Bushnell the Bible was essentially figurative. In 1866 he indicated his leaning toward understanding the fall in Eden as a myth. Jesus was teacher rather than the crucified and suffering God. His were "orthodox memories, Unitarian hopes."[3] The old wine had not survived being transferred to new bottles.[4] He scoffed at the idea of the Second Coming.[5] He was very theological but he did not preach sound doctrine.

Yet Bushnell was a preacher's preacher. There was a virility in his style and a fire inside him, but the common people were not drawn to his variety of naturalism. Early on, he gained a reputation as a public speaker of note, and his ability to title sermons is dramatic. Little wonder he was offered the presidency of the College of California (later the University of California at Berkeley), which he turned down.[6]

Bushnell's celebrated sermon on "Unconscious Influence" is based on John 20:8, "Then went in also that other disciple." But for Bushnell this had nothing to do with the resurrection or Jesus Christ. He did not do exegesis, and even Brastow speaks of his interpretations as often "fanciful" and lacking "the support of recognized exegetical canons."[7]

Bushnell may have been "a homiletical genius," but he was not a biblical preacher, and his influence upon successive generations has been unfortunate. His sermons were in fact "an essay in social psychology," as David Smith observes.[8] Bushnell's own reflections on preaching are unrelievedly horizontal.[9] If his sermons were on every preacher's shelves in Scotland, we can begin to grasp why Scotland was in such a theological tailspin in the nineteenth century.

---

1. Barbara M. Cross, *Horace Bushnell: Minister to a Changing America* (Chicago: University of Chicago Press, 1958), 10.
2. David L. Smith, *Symbolism and Growth: The Religious Thought of Horace Bushnell* (Chico, Calif.: Scholars Press, 1981), 78.
3. Ibid., 104. For a critique of Bushnell on the atonement, see H. D. McDonald, *The Atonement of the Death of Christ* (Grand Rapids: Baker, 1985), 299. "The penal doctrine was specially anathema."
4. Ibid., 140. On Bushnell's subjective view, see David Wells, "The Collision of Views on the Atonement," *Bibliotheca Sacra* 144, no. 574 (October–December 1987): 374ff.
5. Mary Bushnell Cheney, *Life and Letters of Horace Bushnell* (New York: Arno, 1969), 99.
6. Howard A. Barnes, *Horace Bushnell and the Virtuous Republic* (Metuchen, N.J.: Scarecrow, 1991), 10.
7. Lewis O. Brastow, *Representative Modern Preachers* (New York: Macmillan, 1904), 150.
8. Smith, *Symbolism and Growth*, 49.
9. Horace Bushnell, *Pulpit Talent: Training for the Pulpit Manward* (London: Richard Dickinson, 1882).

10.3.2 HENRY WARD BEECHER—THE PULPIT WITH A POPULAR SHOWMAN

I am, in the providence of God, so circumstanced in reference to public speaking, which seems to be my specialty, that I put my whole strength into that and give up everything else to it.

—Henry Ward Beecher

It was one of the most signal triumphs of oratory in the history of human speech . . . it was also one of the most significant exhibitions of the power of a great personality as the unofficial representative of a nation.
—Lewis Brastow on Beecher's travels in Britain
and on the Continent in 1863

Dubbed "the most eloquent preacher of his day" (O. C. Edwards), "the most popular preacher in the Greater New York metropolitan area" (F. R. Webber), and "the greatest preacher of America and of our century . . . the greatest preacher Protestantism has ever produced" (Phillips Brooks), **Henry Ward Beecher** (1813–1887) did indeed build America's largest church at the time and a national pulpit as have few others. However we assess him as a preacher, none will contest William McLoughlin's description of him as "the high priest of American religion."

Beecher was deeply indebted to and influenced by Horace Bushnell, putting Bushnell's message on the wings of a highly emotional oratory. But he was at bottom the exponent of an American religion that was, as Alan Bloom saw it, "a kind of Emersonian gnosticism." "His work was to secularize the American pulpit."[1] Listed by even the gentle Ralph Turnbull under those of "liberal convictions," we have a preacher over whom Spurgeon and Joseph Parker disagreed sharply, with Parker welcoming Beecher into the pulpit of the City Temple in London.[2]

Beecher was the seventh of eight living children in the Lyman Beecher manse (cf. 9.2.6). In a sense he continued on where his New School Presbyterian father left off. He created a romantic Christianity, becoming himself an "effective role model for liberal preachers in the early part of the twentieth century, especially for one like the Reverend Harry Emerson Fosdick."[3] His six brothers all became preachers. Little in Henry's early life indicated an orator was in process. He was so backward in his studies that he was not sent to Yale but to Amherst and then to Lane Seminary to study during his father's agonies there. He served two churches in Indiana, and in the Second Presbyterian Church of Indianapolis (1839–1847) he came into his own as a pulpiteer, publishing his famous *Lectures to Young Men* on issues such as gambling, cheating, and intemperance.

Beecher's successes in the West brought him to the attention of Henry Bowen and John Howard, who were establishing the first Congregational church in the growing New York suburb of Brooklyn. From the outset Beecher promised he would "wear no fetters" in his pulpit, and two years later he led in rebuilding after a fire destroyed the old building in Brooklyn Heights. The congregation built a new sanctuary seating thirty-two hundred with no pulpit but a small desk. The structure still stands in Brooklyn Heights.

While we must give Beecher credit for speaking against slavery when many were mute, we must also recognize that his secular agenda overshadowed spiritual priorities. He made his pulpit into a center of antislavery propaganda, using the mock auction of slaves as a technique. He was admittedly the P. T. Barnum of the pulpit. Numerous boats, called Beecher's barges, came over from Manhattan to hear him. The crowds that flocked to his services would vanish when he was not present.

Beecher's innovative delivery, powerful voice, fervent excoriation of the wealthy, and adept humor filled Plymouth twice every Sunday and brought seven or eight hundred back on Fridays for a lecture and questions. He became the most sought-after lecturer in America.[4] He spent forty years at Plymouth and was unquestionably the Shakespeare of the modern pulpit.[5]

Beecher preached "a new experimental Christianity with God as love" as the center.[6] This effectively did away with the "stern God of justice" and hell and conversion as such, substituting for it the gradual growth of character in the Bushnellian sense, as if the two were mutually exclusive. The Bible was the finger pointing to truth, but nature was an even more significant revelator of the majesty of God. This was a gospel of success, and as McLoughlin observes, Beecher became "a prophet of reassurance for a nation that wants to be loved and to love itself."

Strongly influenced by Herbert Spencer of England and enamored with the evolutionary vision, Beecher was "obsessed to add to his own popularity."[7] Webber opines that it was hard for him to be serious.[8] His was a message of "the father-hood of God and the brotherhood of man,"[9] in which edification gave way to entertainment. Although his gift was not organization, he carried discourse through his great dramatic gifts, the concreteness of his illustrations, and his extraordinary phrasing.[10] Harriet reported that her brother lectured at Tremont Temple in Boston with "unreportable pyrotechnic splendors."

Beecher began preparing his morning sermon an hour before the service and did his evening sermon on Sunday afternoon. He preached virtually extempora-neously with much ad-libbing. He had the most unusual "verbal memory." Beecher published a novel, *Norwood,* which brought him money but much pan-ning in the press. One of his last books, *Evolution and Religion* (1885), sums up everything: modified Socinian, very little Bible, derision of conversion, and the repudiation of any transactualism in the Atonement.[11]

In his years of ministry Beecher lived through many national crises. After the war, in an era of scandals and a major depression,[12] he himself knew the disaster of debt and a trial for adultery, demonstrating how dangerous the gospel of love and its theme of freedom can be. A series of reports and allegations did great damage to Beecher before the Tilton affair (the charge by one of Beecher's best friends that he had an adulterous affair with his wife), but his omission of the authority of Scripture in doctrinal statements and his watering down of scriptural authority were enhanced by his "role in the erosion of traditional authority."[13]

Henry Ward Beecher is a profound study in accommodation in message and method. Under his aegis the Lyman Beecher Lectures on preaching at Yale were inaugurated, and he himself gave the first three series. R. W. Dale of Birmingham spoke of Beecher as "the greatest preacher of the Christian Church," but such euphoria had lost touch with reality. We face the same issues today.

---

1. William G. McLoughlin, *The Meaning of Henry Ward Beecher: An Essay on the Shifting Values of Mid-America 1840–1870* (New York: Knopf, 1970), ix. See also *Henry Ward Beecher as His Friends Saw Him* (Boston: Pilgrim, 1904).

2. G. Holden Pike, *The Life and Work of Charles Haddon Spurgeon* (Edinburgh: Ban-ner of Truth, 1894, 1991), 5:67, 337.

3. Halford R. Ryan, *Henry Ward Beecher: Peripatetic Preacher* (Westport, Conn.: Greenwood, 1990), 7. Volume 5 in the "Great American Orators Series." American presidents and world statesmen took the counsel of Beecher.

4. Ibid., 75.

5. Lewis O. Brastow, *Representative Modern Preachers* (New York: Macmillan, 1904), 137.

6. Clifford E. Clark Jr., *Henry Ward Beecher: Spokesman for Middle-Class America* (Urbana: University of Illinois, 1978), 4. Beecher's oration at the rededication of Ft. Sumter in 1865 must be seen as a classic.

7. Ibid., 254. Clark describes how Lyman Abbott took over Beecher's journalistic tasks. Abbott was to follow Beecher at Plymouth to a congregation reduced by half (1887–1899). His messages were largely secular, and like Beecher he was much into

evolutionary theology. He jettisoned a literal second advent and the resurrection of the body. He was uncertain about the virgin birth. Phillips Brooks attended his installation council. See Ira V. Brown, *Lyman Abbott: Christian Evolutionist—A Study in Religious Liberalism* (Westport, Conn.: Greenwood, 1953).

8. F. R. Webber, *A History of Preaching in Britain and America* (Milwaukee: Northwestern, 1957), 3:360.

9. Daniel Dulany Addison, *The Clergy in American Life and Letters* (London: Macmillan, 1900), 313.

10. Brastow, *Representative Modern Preachers,* 140.

11. See the multiple volume *Plymouth Pulpit* (New York: Ketcham, 1893). Also *Beecher in England* (London: Clark, 1886).

12. Ari Hoogenboom, *Rutherford B. Hayes: Warrior and President* (Lawrence: University Press of Kansas, 1995).

13. Altina L. Waller, *Reverend Beecher and Mrs. Tilton* (Amherst: University of Massachusetts Press, 1982), 70. Waller shows how Beecher "packaged ideas and style in response to the market" (27). Here we have an early version of the popular American "audience-centered preaching" intending to "mass-produce personal religion."

10.3.3 PHILLIPS BROOKS—THE PULPIT WITH A POWERFUL PERSONALITY

To be dead in earnest is to be eloquent.

Preaching is the communication of truth by man to men. It has two essential elements, truth and personality . . . Preaching is the bringing of truth through personality.

There must be a man behind every sermon.
—from Phillips Brooks' Beecher Lectures, sixth in the series, 1877

If listening to Beecher was like trying to drink water from a fire hydrant, **Phillips Brooks** (1835–1893) was like a deft surgeon, a skilled artist, a refined craftsman. Brooks drew great audiences, and his thoughts on preaching as set forth in his Beecher Lectures are considered one of the highlights of that series.[1] He was born in Boston as the ninth generation of cultured Puritan stock. Brooks always had a kind of Puritan reserve, but was baptized a Unitarian and reared an Episcopalian by doting parents who moved increasingly to serious doctrinal definition. He graduated from Boston Latin School, Harvard, and Virginia Theological Seminary in Richmond, where he felt somewhat out of place, scorned "anti-intellectualism of the Evangelicals," and drank deeply of Schleiermacher.[2] Brooks' teaching experience at Boston Latin was a disaster, so he turned to pastoring. His pulpit prowess in Philadelphia and then at Trinity Church, Boston, began to attract considerable attention. Elected bishop of Massachusetts in 1891, after only fifteen months in office he died of a diphtheroid disease. He was fifty-seven.

Brooks traveled widely, and as he never married, he was unencumbered and financially independent. At six feet four inches tall and three hundred pounds, he was an imposing figure. His two most memorable sermons, "Our Mercies of Reoccupation" on Thanksgiving Day and "The Life and Death of Abraham Lincoln" in 1865, qualify as literature.[3] "Harvard Commemoration," from the end of the Civil War, is an oratorical tour de force.[4]

"He made an overwhelming impression" was the universal verdict. People went away saying "How good it is to be alive" and "How easy it seems to be heroic."[5] Brooks was a topical preacher, only very rarely textual. Yet he used the historic present to give a dramatic immediacy in his preaching. There was "no touch of self-consciousness."[6] He sought a principle in the text but did not feel controlled by it. The four rivers in Eden would give him occasion to speak of four aspects of any subject. He could preach at Christmas on John 1:14 and talk about shepherds but not about the angel's announcement of the redemption story.

Thus although all agree he was a great man and a great preacher, we are concerned about his impatience with theology. He held to the Thirty-nine Articles and the Creeds and he urged preaching of doctrine in his lectures,[7] yet he disparaged expository preaching and did not himself preach much doctrine. Those who influenced him were Schleiermacher, Maurice, Coleridge, Carlyle, and Ruskin. He loved Milton, Tennyson, and Browning but eschewed preaching a theological system. Barstow calls him "the Christian humanist" because he sensed his vocation to be "to interpret men to themselves."[8] Brooks loved the church because "it represented ideal humanity."[9] He saw the moral significance of Christ to be the completion of "the realization of the ideal in humanity."[10] Redemption was by revelation, and the Bible "is not authority but the record of authority."[11] Soteriology was in the Incarnation. His successor as bishop, William Lawrence, relates in his biography of Brooks his mother's concern:

> His mother had in the earlier years of his ministry feared for his faith, and she had prayed mightily that he might remain true. She warned him against a certain volume of sermons, "They tear the view of Christ's vicarious suffering all to pieces. I hope you do not own the book, but if you do, I want you to burn it with Frederick [his brother] present to witness and exult over it." No, my dear child; remember, you have promised to preach Christ and Him crucified in the true meaning of the words, and I charge you to stand firm.[12]

But T. J. Jackson Lears correctly perceives that rather "he blunted all the sharp edges in Protestant tradition and produced a bland religion of reassurance."[13] Woolverton is right that "The Bible did not dominate his idealism," nor did he "explore the singularity of the Scriptures."[14] His exquisite Bohlen Lectures on "The Influence of Jesus" are without any focus on redemption.[15] His preaching is artistic but disappointingly horizontal. Here in the succession of Bushnell and Beecher we have "feel-good theology" and "feel-good preaching" but little substance. Where is the Word of God?

A. B. Bruce and a vast horde pay lavish tribute to Brooks.[16] To be sure, he exerted a positive influence, but compare him with the other Episcopalian preacher of note in early America, George Whitefield. Brooks' sermons were carefully prepared and read without melodrama. Brooks' preaching voice was not strong,[17] and he took voice lessons to improve.[18]

Brooks' serious modification of theology, however, meant, as Hethcock remarks, that "He, more than any other of his century, integrated homiletics and preaching into the liberal project in America."[19] Roger Lundin argues that "his romanticism emasculated Christianity," and he laments, "If only Brooks had sided more with Edwards than with Channing."[20] George Marsden has recently described both Beecher and Brooks as liberals, citing the latter's "believe in yourself" approach and his view that "the ultimate fact of human life is goodness and not sin" as prima facie evidence of a grave deficiency.[21]

Phillips Brooks was a remarkable preacher, and before he was thirty-two he wrote the magnificent Christian hymn, "O Little Town of Bethlehem." But, like his preaching, even the hymn lacks strong Christological affirmation. The American pulpit was in serious danger of selling its birthright.

1. On the history of the Beecher Lectures, see Edgar Dewitt Jones, *The Royalty of the Pulpit* (New York: Harper, 1951), biographical analysis; Batsell B. Baxter, *The Heart of the Yale Lectures* (New York: Macmillan, 1947).

2. John V. Woolverton, *The Education of Phillips Brooks* (Urbana: University of Illinois Press, 1995), 70, 75.

3. Daniel Dulany Addison, *The Clergy in American Life and Letters* (London: Macmillan, 1900), 342.

4. Ibid., 350.

5. Ibid., 355.

6. Alexander V. G. Allen, *Phillips Brooks* (New York: Dutton, 1907), 581. Hagiographic but voluminous.

7. Phillips Brooks, *Lectures on Preaching* (Grand Rapids: Zondervan, n.d.), 129.

8. Lewis O. Brastow, *Representative Modern Preachers* (New York: Macmillan, 1904), 204.

9. Ibid., 198.

10. Ibid., 214.

11. Ibid., 229.

12. William Lawrence, *Life of Phillips Brooks* (New York: Harper, 1930), 125f.

13. Woolverton, *The Education of Phillips Brooks*, 6.

14. Ibid., 105.

15. Phillips Brooks, *The Influence of Jesus* (London: Allenson, 1879); see Brooks' *Addresses* (Chicago: Henneberry, n.d.). This collection contains the Lincoln sermon and other beautiful expressions.

16. Allen, *Phillips Brooks*, 580.

17. Raymond W. Albright, *Focus on Infinity: A Life of Phillips Brooks* (New York: Macmillan, 1961), 141.

18. Ralph M. Harper, "Phillips Brooks' Voice Lessons," *Church Management* (January 1947).

19. William Hethcock on "Phillips Brooks" in *Concise Encyclopedia of Preaching* (Louisville: Westminster/John Knox, 1995), 48.

20. Roger Lundin quoted in Woolverton, *The Education of Phillips Brooks,* 112–13.
21. George Marsden, *Understanding Fundamentalism and Evangelicalism* (Grand Rapids: Eerdmans, 1991), 19.

10.3.4 MATTHEW SIMPSON—THE PULPIT WITH A BIBLE-PREACHING BISHOP

> The preacher—His throne is the pulpit; he stands in Christ's stead; his message is the Word of God; around him are immortal souls; the Savior, unseen is beside him; the Holy Spirit broods over the congregation; angels gaze upon the scene, and heaven and hell await the issue. What associations and what a vast responsibility!
>
> —Matthew Simpson

Many have preached in the tradition of the Enlightenment—anthropocentrically and horizontally—but **Matthew Simpson** (1811–1884) was a Methodist bishop who preached in the tradition of the Reformation: in God-centered and Christ-centered terms. The youngest and largest of America's denominations, Methodism at this time was preaching full and free salvation in a spiritual explosion on the frontiers. Simpson was born in Cadiz, Ohio, in a settler's home where he learned to read at the age of three. Educated at Madison College (later Allegheny College) near Pittsburgh, he read voraciously and learned to love Latin, Greek, and Hebrew. Simpson was a tall, gangling young man who was converted in a camp meeting in 1829. He studied medicine, and in 1834 felt the call to preach. Assigned to Pittsburgh, he preached two or three times each Sunday. His voice was never strong and his words suffered from that pious suffix, "uh."[1] He set out to improve, and even delivered a commencement address in Hebrew at Allegheny College. He successively served some brief pastorates, then professorships, and became founding president of Indiana Asbury University at Greencastle.

An example of his expository preaching was a great study of Ezekiel 47 given in his twenty-seventh year on the occasion of the one hundredth anniversary of John Wesley's founding of the Methodist Society.[2] How refreshing to follow the text of Scripture! Simpson then served as editor of the Western Christian Advocate out of Cincinnati, as his church was in the throes of agony over the slavery issue and ultimately was torn in two. This national trauma was undoubtedly a serious distraction for all of the preachers of the era, but Simpson was not to be diverted from preaching the gospel.

Simpson was elected a bishop in 1852 at the age of forty-two. Soon thereafter he preached his famous "King sermon" in Corvallis, Oregon, on Paul's great autobiographical "But none of these things move me" out of Acts 20:24.[3] He and his family successively moved to Chicago, Philadelphia, and Washington, D.C., where he preached before Congress and knew Secretary Chase and President Lincoln well. He preached in the House of Representatives after the second inaugural.[4] Bishop Simpson preached the funeral sermon for President Lincoln at Springfield, Illinois, having ministered to the Lincoln family after the assassination.

He was through and through an old-time Methodist preacher who could "put on the rousements." Frances E. Willard, founder of the Women's Christian Temperances Union, heard Simpson give his renowned sermon on "The Victory of Faith" from 1 John 5:4[5] to more than eight thousand at the Des Plaines Camp Meeting outside of Chicago. Willard was ecstatic in her endorsement:

> I have heard great preachers, Beecher, Talmage, Spurgeon in England, Pere Hyacynthe in France, but to my thought, no flight was ever so steady, so sustained, so lofty, as that of Bishop Simpson on that memorable day.[6]

In 1878, Simpson followed Beecher at the Opera House in San Francisco, and while he could not equal the old war horse in theatrics, his timely and logical message on "Is Christianity a Failure?" was reported in the *Chronicle* with glowing terms:

> In the outward graces of oratory, Beecher was "incomparably the superior"; but for "intellectual depth and grasp" the palm must be according to the Bishop. The tall, lean, thin-faced old man with the shrill, piping voice was extraordinarily moving. As he began to speak his face lighted up, his eyes flashed and he carried men away on a "sparkling stream of thought" that made them forget his ungainly figure and uncouth gesture. The great audience listened with deep attention, broken only by expressions of approval, sobs and shouts. He was the "old man eloquent."[7]

Simpson's Beecher Lectures at Yale in 1878 and 1879 developed the thesis that "Preaching is the chief work but not the only work of the Christian minister."[8] How delightful to hear his ringing call for Christ-centered preaching! He reiterated the centrality of the Scripture and the importance of preaching the biblical text.[9] While Simpson saw arrangement as critical, and while he urged preaching extempore,[10] he warned of the danger of "being drawn into the political canvass."[11] His two strongest lectures are "The Influence of the Pastorate Upon the Pulpit" and "Is the Modern Pulpit a Failure?"

In his collected sermons we relish especially his two magnificent sermons on Christ's resurrection. He skillfully divided the sermon in "Our Times in God's Hands" from Psalm 31:15 and others. He preached on "The Great Commission" and appealed to sinners to be converted.[12] He preached clearly on "Glorying in the Cross" and left no one in any doubt that he saw Christ as a sacrifice for our sin.[13] He pressed such a message as "What Think Ye of Christ?" and spoke of the eschaton and the Lord's return.[14]

Not all American preachers were given to the vagaries and vanities of pious platitudes. Matthew Simpson offered strong and convicting preaching for hungry souls.

---

1. Robert D. Clark, *The Life of Matthew Simpson* (New York: Macmillan, 1956), 36.
2. Ibid., 77.
3. Ibid., 188.

4. Ibid., 246.
5. George R. Crooks, ed., *Sermons of Bishop Matthew Simpson* (New York: Harper, 1885), 193ff.
6. Clark, *The Life of Matthew Simpson,* 272.
7. Ibid., 302.
8. Matthew Simpson, *Lectures on Preaching* (New York: Phillips and Hunt, 1879), 11.
9. Ibid., 73, 100, 108.
10. Ibid., 173.
11. Ibid., 306.
12. Crooks, *Sermons of Bishop Matthew Simpson,* 111.
13. Ibid., 253.
14. Ibid., 293.

10.3.5 *JOHN HALL—THE PULPIT WITH A GIFTED ULSTERMAN*

Remember, that the great business of your life is to be the exegesis of the holy Word.

A verse rightly put and rightly repeated, will often fix a truth better than a whole sermon.

If it please God to put you into the ministry, prepare your sermons from the Word, and order your work with a view to the conversion of men.

The main thought of the text should be the main thought of the sermon.
—John Hall in his Beecher Lectures, 1875

Upon a preaching scene awash with eloquent artifice but little scriptural substance, came a call from an Ulsterman located in New York City. "What prevents our ministers from adopting, more generally than they do, the practice of expository preaching?"[1] asked **John Hall** (1829–1898). Hall was the son of Scottish immigrants who settled in County Armagh, Northern Ireland. Also from Ulster came such preaching giants as **Alexander Carson** (1776–1844), who was called the Jonathan Edwards of Ireland and whose masterful studies on divine providence are classic.[2] Evangelist **William P. Nicholson** (1876–1959) hailed from Ulster as well. Despite his unorthodox methodology, he brought many to Christ.[3]

Reared on a farm in modest circumstances, John Hall studied at the Royal College in Belfast before attending seminary. He was classically educated, and throughout his life wrote Latin prayers for his notebooks and his sermon conclusions.[4] His first pastoral charge was in Connought, in the west of Ireland, during the potato famine. In 1852 he moved on to the First Presbyterian Church of Armagh and then to a tenure at Scott's Church, Mary's Abbey, Dublin. Eventually he took the successor post at Rutland Square Church, Dublin, where his strong biblical preaching drew great throngs and necessitated the building of a new church.

Hall was consumed with a great missionary zeal and was a participant in the powerful stirring of the Spirit in Ulster in 1859. Although he was a reserved Presbyterian, some thought he more closely resembled a Methodist because of the prayer meetings he led and the extra preaching services he conducted.[5] He was known for his careful and faithful pastoral visitation. He even preached aboard ship while traveling to America. Upon his arrival, he itinerated widely and was so appreciated that he was called to Fifth Avenue Presbyterian Church in New York City.

Hall was close to Charles Hodge and at the same time deeply involved with the American Sunday School Union.[6] He had tensions with Henry Ward Beecher over theology, as might be expected, but Hall was always a Christian gentleman in his defense of the faith. The heresy of Dr. Charles Briggs, who was brought finally to trial, deeply pained him.[7]

Hall preached strong biblical sermons at Fifth Avenue, a prestigious Old School congregation, and once again saw the congregation grow until a new church was built to accommodate the crowds. He ministered for thirty years in his increasingly famous pulpit, but his last years were clouded somewhat by controversy over his loyalty to a Jewish missionary he felt had been falsely accused. Hall eventually resigned and returned to Ireland, where he died.

Hall was committed unequivocally to the inerrancy of the Scriptures, the substitutionary atonement, and the future conversion of the Jews. He delivered the Beecher Lectures at Yale in 1874 and 1875 using as his theme "God's Word Through Preaching." His stately lectures exuded great confidence in the Word of God and its power to convict of sin and change lives.[8]

Known as a slow starter in his own preaching, Hall pleaded with his listeners at Yale for consecutive book exposition. Like his friend, the distinguished lawyer Richard J. Storrs, Hall argued for preaching extempore. Homiletically, Hall stood with Hoppin of Yale and Phelps of Andover for clear division of the text and sermon along the lines of the more classical style of Claude and Simeon.[9]

This gracious preacher had "both weight as well as movement"[10] in his preaching and stood as a champion of biblical exegesis.

---

1. John Hall, *God's Word Through Preaching* (New York: Dodd, Mead, 1875), 104. The Beecher Lectures 1874–1875.

2. Alexander Carson, *The History of Providence as Explained in the Bible* (Grand Rapids: Baker, 1977). Choice.

3. James Beatty, "Memories of Evangelist W. P. Nicholson," *Banner of Truth* (June 1984): 30ff.

4. F. R. Webber, *A History of Preaching in Britain and America* (Milwaukee: Northwestern, 1957), 3:409.

5. Thomas C. Hall, *John Hall: Pastor and Preacher* (New York: Revell, 1901), 93.

6. Charles Hodge wrote a book for the Sunday School Union that treats basic doctrines so clearly that any evangelical Arminian would have no difficulty subscribing; see *The Way of Life: A Handbook of Christian Belief and Practice* (Grand Rapids: Baker, 1977). Good on sin and justification, repentance and faith.

7. Hall, *John Hall,* 185. While he was at Fifth Avenue, Hall tenderly ministered to the Theodore Roosevelt family in several of their times of need; see David McCullough, *Mornings on Horseback* (New York: Simon and Schuster, 1981), 140, 185, 284.

8. Hall, *John Hall,* 242.
9. James Hoppin, *Homiletics* (New York: Dodd, Mead, 1881); Austin Phelps, *The Theory of Preaching* (London: Richard Dickenson, 1882). Both emphasize the division of the text and the sermon.
10. T. Harwood Pattison, *The History of Christian Preaching* (Philadelphia: American Baptist, 1902), 390.

10.3.6 THEODORE CUYLER—THE PULPIT WITH A CRUSADING DUTCHMAN

"Preach my word" does not signify the clapping of a few syllables as a figure-head on a long treatise spun out of a preacher's brain. The best discourses are not manufactured; they are a growth. God's inspired and infallible Book must furnish the text. The connection between every good sermon and its text is just as vital as the connection between a peach-tree and its root.

Whatever makes the Gospel or Jesus Christ more clear to the understanding, more effective in arousing sinners, in converting souls, in edifying believers and in promoting pure honest living is never out of place in the pulpit.

Sometimes a sermon may produce but little impression, yet the same sermon at another time and place may deeply move an audience and yield rich spiritual results. Physical condition may have some influence on a minister's delivery; but the chief element in the eloquence that awakens and converts sinners and strengthens Christians is the unction of the Holy Spirit. Our best power is the power from on high.

—Theodore L. Cuyler

An especially effervescent and sprightly Presbyterian preacher of the time was **Theodore Cuyler** (1822–1909). Born of Dutch ancestry in Aurora, New York, south of Auburn, Cuyler was reared by a widowed mother of great devotion to Christ who taught her only child the Bible and the catechism. Cuyler went on to Princeton, where he confessed Christ publicly as his Savior and then, after his call to preach, on to Princeton Seminary, where he feasted on the viands served up by the Alexanders and Hodge. A. A. Hodge was in Cuyler's graduating class of 1841. At the age of twenty Cuyler traveled to Europe and met with Wordsworth, Dickens, and Carlyle, not all of whom were easy to access.[1] Over the years, he was on intimate terms with Newman Hall, Charles Spurgeon, Beecher, John Hall, B. M. Palmer, Charles G. Finney, and many more. His impressions of his contemporaries are invaluable.

Cuyler's ministerial life began in Pennsylvania, but he served for a much longer time in Burlington, New Jersey. Then, in 1853, he began a significant pastorate at Market Street Dutch Reformed Church in New York City, where he labored and preached with distinction until 1860. He was deeply involved in the great stirring in 1859, and urged his readers:

Every pastor ought to be constantly on the watch, with open eye and ear, for the first signs of an especial manifestation of the Spirit's presence. Elijah, on Carmel, did not only pray, he kept his eyes open to see the rising cloud. The moment that there is a manifestation of the Spirit's presence, it must be followed up promptly.[2]

In 1860 he became the first pastor of the Lafayette Street Presbyterian Church in Brooklyn, where he served for thirty years and built the membership to 3,103 souls. While he was there the Lord visited the congregation with what he called "spiritual downpour." One such revival started with the Universal Week of Prayer during the first full week of January (still observed in some communions and frequently a time of revival). At one point 320 souls were added, including one hundred heads of household. The agony of the Civil War was meaningfully reflected in his writings and preaching,[3] and his personal travail in the death of two of his children was related as part of the Lord's dealing with him. He was a gifted preacher known for his unusually effective illustrations and imagery.[4] He generally took a short text and used often startling introductions. Cuyler wrote twenty-two books and four thousand religious articles for publication. His written style reflects his lively imagination, as in his "Cedar Christians" and "The Honey of God's Word."[5]

Cuyler's lively spirit caused some to call him a Methodistical Presbyterian. He was always dutiful in his pastoral ministry, believing strongly that what a preacher does outside of his pulpit bears heavily on what he can do in his pulpit.[6] His objective was ever to preach strong gospel sermons. His splendid sermon on "Jesus Only" from Matthew 17:8 focuses clearly on Jesus' identity as Savior and sin-bearer.[7] Preaching from Joshua 10:14 on "The Pivot Battles of Life," he divided the sermon in pursuit of his big idea from the text, "And there was no day like that before it or after it."[8]

Theodore Cuyler stands as a friend of biblical preaching and the supernatural gospel.

---

1. Theodore L. Cuyler, *Recollections of a Long Life* (New York: Baker and Taylor, 1902), 12ff., 37ff., 170ff., 190ff.
2. Ibid., 84.
3. Ibid., 144.
4. Ibid., 70.
5. Theodore L. Cuyler, *Beulah-Land* (New York: American Tract Society, 1896), 34ff., 135ff.
6. Theodore L. Cuyler, *How to Be a Pastor* (London: James Nisbet, 1891), 9.
7. Theodore L. Cuyler, *The Presbyterian Pulpit: A Model Christian* (Philadelphia: Presbyterian Board, 1903), 97ff.
8. Ibid., 43ff.

10.3.7 Thomas De Witt Talmage—The Pulpit with a Trumpet Blast

The most memorable scene in my childhood was that of father and mother at morning and evening prayers.

A live church must be a soul-saving church. The Gospel of Jesus Christ must be preached in it. A church may be built around one man who shall read an essay, the church may be built around one man who shall preach something other than the Gospel, and there may be large congregation; but after a while the man dies, and the church dies.

—Thomas DeWitt Talmage

He was variously called the Spurgeon of America or the cultured Billy Sunday. It was said of him that "there was no ecclesiastical starch in his collar." His sermons were in three thousand newspapers and read around the world. Yet Pattison says of him:

He was a master of sensational rhetoric, who too easily mistook assertion for proof and illustration for argument; a scene-painter rather than an artist; a trafficker in words, who himself as much as any one of his hearers, was the victim of a florid and ill-balanced judgment.[1]

Yet the esteemed **J. Gregory Mantle** pays him high tribute for his freshness as a preacher, his fearlessness, and his fidelity to truth.[2] Who is right?

Thomas DeWitt Talmage (1832–1902) was the twelfth child of farmer folks, born in Bound Book, New Jersey. His father, though an invalid, was precentor at the local church and with his wife read the Bible daily with their children. Though very poor, young De Witt attended the University of the City of New York. He had been converted at eighteen in the revivals of the time.[3] Called to preach, he graduated from New Brunswick Seminary of the Dutch Reformed Church and served congregations at Bellville, New Jersey, Syracuse, New York, and the First Reformed Church of Philadelphia (1862–1868). He was a gospel preacher and when he was warned he wouldn't get calls from churches he replied, "If I cannot preach the gospel in America, then I will go to heathen lands and preach it."[4] The death of his first wife in a boating accident seemed almost to destroy him, but through the grace of God he rebounded from this tragedy.

Talmage was approached by the old Central Presbyterian Church in Brooklyn, now known as the Brooklyn Tabernacle, to become their pastor. Once strong and vital, the church had dwindled to nineteen members rattling around in their twenty-nine hundred seats. He accepted the task in 1869 and called for the building of a new sanctuary seating five thousand, with fine acoustics, free pews, a great organ, and only congregational singing. Two of his great tabernacles burned down, and each was rebuilt larger than the previous one. His Tabernacle in Brooklyn had the largest seating capacity of any in America. He had a theatrical style and was much criticized. On occasion he preached with police protection because of threats on his life. Yet when he traveled abroad, he was always received by great audiences.[5] His was a commanding pulpit presence:

A tall, stalwart man, slighting stooping; broad-shouldered, long-armed, bony and spare of flesh; a massive, superbly developed head, bald on top; an expansive brow; rather small and deeply-set blue eyes, that now laughed like sunbeams and now blazed like forked lightnings; a large, mobile mouth; a square, pugnacious jaw, trimmed with spare sandy side-whiskers; the whole figure clad in plain black. He was not a handsome man, nor the miracle of ugliness the caricaturists have tried to make him. He was a commanding and intellectual figure, compelling respect and inviting confidence and affection.[6]

Talmage was anchored squarely in the authority of Holy Scripture. He preached "the old, sweet story of Christ's love and Calvary's sacrifice."[7] "I shall take all of the Bible or none," he insisted. Hicks summarizes the whole of his theology: "No theme can afford such consolation in sorrow, such hope in despondency, such strength in weakness, such light in darkness, as the Cross of Christ."[8] Talmage preached without notes for about half an hour. He testified that "to think in metaphor is natural for me."[9] He wrote best-selling books on his tour of the Holy Land,[10] and was the founding editor of *The Christian Herald* magazine. He was also chaplain of the famous Thirteenth Regiment in Brooklyn. Like Cuyler, he loved to visit notables abroad, leading a massive effort to feed the starving Russian people and dining with the Tsar. He crusaded against vice, drinking, and dissipation. Taking the First Presbyterian Church of Washington in 1895, he served "the Church of the Presidents" until 1899. He then lived in retirement until his death in 1902.

Some of Talmage's sermons do seem disorganized and use too many illustrations. Yet his message on Queen Esther in which he gives a ringing call to greater Christian aggressiveness, using the theme "The Christian for the Times,"[11] is powerful. His sermon on "Attacks on the Bible" is a masterpiece.[12] His sermon on "The Highway from Earth to Heaven," based in Isaiah 35:8–10, is choice, and his study of "Easter Joy" out of 1 Corinthians 15 is carefully divided.[13] He was not an expositor in great depth, but he was a faithful servant of the Word.

One visitor to the Brooklyn Tabernacle described the scene:

His style of delivery and action are somewhat uncommon. He stands upon the bare platform without desk, with the small Bible in hand, and without any note whatever speaks most feelingly . . . He suits the action to the word—wriggles and twists about, starting and pausing, raising and lowering his voice in a most striking and arresting manner.[14]

Talmage preached with zeal and passion. His message was Christ and salvation, and his torrid sermons are still widely read and circulated. He made his mark for God.

1. T. Harwood Pattison, *The History of Christian Preaching* (Philadelphia: American Baptist Publication Society, 1903), 390.
2. J. Gregory Mantle, introduction to W. Percy Hicks, *Life of Dr. Talmage* (London:

Christian Herald, 1902). He was an English Methodist who later moved within the
orbit of A. B. Simpson, founder of the Christian and Missionary Alliance. He was
on the committee that recommended the young Campbell Morgan not enter the ministry, but some of his remarkable collections of sermons such as *The Way of Humiliation: The Way of the Cross* and *The Counterfeit Christ* are themselves rich and
rewarding.

3. Hicks, *Life of Dr. Talmage,* 44.
4. Ibid., 51.
5. T. Dewitt Talmage, *The Life and Letters of Rev. T. Dewitt Talmage* (Kansas City:
Topeka Book Co., 1902), 39.
6. Ibid., 40.
7. Hicks, *Life of Dr. Talmage,* 144.
8. Ibid., 146.
9. Ibid., 76.
10. T. Dewitt Talmage, *The Palestine Sermons of T. Dewitt Talmage* (Chicago: Rhodes
and McClure, 1890).
11. Hicks, *Life of Dr. Talmage,* 166.
12. Ibid., 199.
13. T. Dewitt Talmage, "Easter Joy," in *Great Sermons on the Resurrection* (Murfreesboro,
Tenn.: Sword of the Lord, 1984), 11.
14. Hicks, *Life of Dr. Talmage,* 70.

10.3.8 WILLIAM TAYLOR—THE PULPIT WITH A SCOTTISH GENTLEMAN

In truth there is nothing more absurd than this clamor against doctrine,
for they who raised it do not seem to see that there is beneath the cry
itself a doctrine, to the effect that it makes no matter what a man believes, if he only says he is resting upon Christ . . . but the Christ that
saves is the Christ that is revealed in the Gospels.

Exposition is the presentation to the people, in an intelligible and forcible manner, of the meaning of the sacred writer which has been first
settled by the preacher for himself, by the use of those grammatical and
historical instruments with which his preparatory training has furnished
him.
—William M. Taylor in his Beecher Lectures of 1875–1876

In the glittering galaxy of pulpiteers in the New York City area was heard the
gentle Scottish burr on the tongue of **William M. Taylor** (1829–1895). Taylor
preached at the old Broadway Tabernacle where Charles G. Finney had once
stood. Born in Kilmarnock in a shopkeeper's home, Taylor graduated from
Glasgow University in 1849. He went on to divinity studies at the United Presbyterian Hall in Edinburgh, receiving his degree in 1852.

Taylor pastored briefly in Ayrshire and then took the call to Derby Road
Church, a congregation of seafarers and their families and others in the mari-
time, located in a suburb of Liverpool.[1] He became very well known during his

seventeen years there, and after filling Dr. Storr's Church of the Pilgrims in Brooklyn for a summer was in demand in the United States. In 1872 he accepted a call to fill the pastoral vacancy at Broadway Tabernacle at Broadway and 34th Street. Taylor preached it full morning and evening for twenty years. Although he manuscripted his sermons and wrote forty books, his preaching seemed extempore. Just after his twentieth jubilee at Broadway, he suffered a stroke. He longed to preach again but was unable to do so.

In a lectureship titled "The Ministry of the Word," Taylor laid the stakes for biblical preaching. He argued strenuously for the preacher's study and use of the original languages.[2] He also called for expository preaching of the text on five grounds:

1. It brings the preacher and hearers into immediate contact with the mind of the Spirit;
2. It secures variety in the ministrations of the preacher;
3. The preacher will be compelled to treat many subjects from which otherwise he might have shrunk;
4. Biblical intelligence among the people will be promoted;
5. In the process of preparing expository discourses the preacher will acquire a great store of resources which he can use for many other purposes.[3]

Taylor also laid bare the potential weaknesses and vulnerabilities in expository preaching. He warned against making exposition dense with content and cautioned about lack of organic unity.[4] Twice the massively built Scot was invited to deliver the Beecher Lectures, an honor extended only to Beecher himself, Washington Gladden, and C. R. Brown. His second course of Beecher Lectures was a rare historical survey on the theme "The Scottish Pulpit from the Reformation to the Present Day."[5] These are not the equal of Professor Blaikie's classic treatment, but they are a solid argument for the supremacy of the authoritative Word of God.

One of the most popular series of books at the time was his series of sermon volumes on great characters of the Bible. His twenty-six discourses on Moses, for instance, are spiced with superb background material, choice quotations and illustrations, and good practical application.[6] His more typical sermons include "Contrary Winds," from Matthew 14:24, preached November 28, 1880.[7] The sermon is divided into a two-point problem/solution outline. "Pleasures of Sin," from Hebrews 11:25, is in four divisions and is true to the text.[8]

Along with John Hall, William Taylor must be considered one of America's finest preachers out of Europe.

---

1. F. R. Webber, *A History of Preaching in Britain and America* (Milwaukee: Northwestern, 1957), 3:406.
2. William M. Taylor, *The Ministry of the Word* (New York: Anson Randolph, 1877), 160.
3. Ibid., 161ff. Taylor would preach one expository sermon and one topical sermon each Lord's Day.

4. Ibid., 178.

5. William M. Taylor, *The Scottish Pulpit* (London: Charles Burnet, 1887).

6. William M. Taylor, *Moses the Law-Giver* (London: Sampson Low, 1888).

7. William M. Taylor, *Contrary Winds* (New York: Hodder and Stoughton, 1883), 7ff.

8. Ibid., 121ff. Taylor also authored significant, meaty, and solid volumes on the parables and miracles of Jesus.

10.3.9 A. J. GORDON—THE PULPIT WITH A YANKEE CLIPPER

> Every phrase of the New Testament has a meaning definite and single—
> a meaning that can be accurately ascertained and clearly expressed ac-
> cording to fixed and settled laws of human speech. . . . [From Professor
> Hackett he got] that reverent regard for divine revelation which, on the
> one hand, brooks no mystical importation of human fancies into the
> sacred text and, on the other, does not permit the smallest Greek ar-
> ticle or conjunction to be treated as an idle or ambiguous thing in that
> Word, which holy men of old wrote as they were moved by the Holy
> Ghost.
>
> The sincere milk of the Word may be dispensed from the pulpit, yet given
> out so frigidly and unfeelingly as to make it very hard to receive. In Si-
> beria, the milkmen sometimes deliver their milk in chunks, not in quarts,
> it being frozen solid and thus carried about to the customers. Alas! is not
> this the way many pulpits deliver the milk of the Word?
> —Adoniram Judson Gordon

The ministry of **Adoniram Judson Gordon** (1836–1895) was transformed by a dream of Christ visiting his service. Gordon subsequently wrote *How Christ Came to Church.*[1] For twenty-five years he served as pastor of the Clarendon Street Baptist Church of Boston.

Born in New Hampshire and nurtured spiritually in the home of the owner of a woolen mill, he yielded to Christ after a sleepless night and went on to study at Brown University in Providence. Gordon sensed God's hand on him to preach, and at Newton Seminary he ministered to many small churches in the area. Timid in the parlor but not in the pulpit, Gordon took his first pastoral charge at Jamaica Plain, where he authored the delightful work *In Christ,* a study of the believer's position and union with the Savior.[2]

In 1869 he assumed the pastorate at Clarendon Street, a fashionable church in Boston, which he led to pristine heights. He was a prime mover in the American Baptist Missionary Union and revamped the worship and music at Clarendon until it was among the best in the Boston area. In an atmosphere of liberalism and Unitarianism, Gordon did not pull his punches. When "repent" and "sin" were not heard, his son relates in his satisfying biography of his father:

> He proclaimed without flinching the helplessness of man, the impotence
> of the unrenewed will, the destiny of sorrow and punishment to which

the unconverted are drifting. And where the knife probed, the ointment followed. For while there was no abatement of stern truths, there was in his preaching, as in the gospels, no want of tenderness.[3]

Gordon counseled with his neighboring Episcopalian rector, **William R. Nicholson,** later bishop of the Reformed Episcopal Church,[4] and many Plymouth Brethren friends. He was an intimate of **Uncle John Vasser,** the outstanding winner of souls,[5] and was once arrested for preaching in Boston Common. Gordon led the support of the Moody campaign in 1877, and so many drunkards were saved in his church that the congregation abandoned the use of real wine for the communion in deference. He led an important crusade against the false teaching of Mary Glover Baker Patterson Eddy, centered in Boston. Dr. James McCosh, president of Princeton, often had him to the college for special meetings with the students. He traveled extensively and preached at the Mildmay Conference in England and was especially close to the great preacher of prophecy, Dr. Guiness.

Gordon's preaching voice was peerless. His illustrations were "palpitating with actuality." He had what Shedd called "the homiletic habit" and was, according to A. T. Pierson, one of the most faithful biblical expositors of his acquaintance.[6] His style was terse and clear, his preaching clearly under "the administration of the Holy Spirit." Gordon urged, "Let us lay down the cudgel and take up the cross." Listen to the lilting sentences that poured from his blazing heart:

> What a solemn expression is this, "Making the cross of Christ of none effect!" No power or might of man can sweep the stars from the sky or blot the sun from the heavens or efface the splendid landscape; but one wound in the eye can destroy the sight and make all those things as though they were not. So the atonement of Christ can never pass into eclipse or cease to be a fact; but there is such a thing as the eclipse of faith—unbelief filming the soul so that the cross and the atonement shall become a great blank—vacant, lifeless, meaningless. O eyes that are becoming dim, but not with age; blinded, but not with tears; hard of seeing, but not with use—hear the Lord speaking from heaven, "Anoint thine eyes of eye-salve, that thou mayest see." It is not that God has need to do greater things for us, but that we should open our eyes and see what he has done.[7]

Gordon preached "the blessed hope"[8] and was staunchly premillennial, as were his fellow Baptists, Keach, Gill, and Spurgeon. He loved the Jewish people and saw them as a barometer for the future. Pierson was "as flint to steel" in a very close friendship.

Adoniram Gordon wrote the music for the great hymn, "My Jesus, I love Thee, I know Thou art mine." His several volumes of collected sermons yield such gems as "The Repulsions of Christianity" from Acts 5:13, and such symmetrical sermons as the title sermon "Grace and Glory" from Psalm 84:11.[9] "The Two

Heredities" from John 3:6 is a masterpiece,[10] and his study of sanctification titled "The Two-fold Life" is for the ages.[11]

---

1. A. J. Gordon, *How Christ Came to Church: A Spiritual Autobiography* (Philadelphia: American Baptist, 1895).
2. A. J. Gordon, *In Christ: The Believer's Union with His Lord* (Chicago: Moody, rev. from 1872).
3. Ernest B. Gordon, *Adoniram Judson Gordon* (New York: Revell, 1896), 275ff.
4. Bishop William R. Nicholson was an outstanding preacher in his own right and is known for his studies in Colossians, *Oneness with Christ* (Grand Rapids: Kregel, rev. from 1903) and his unique little volume of sermons, *The Six Miracles of Calvary* (Chicago: Moody, 1927). "Revivals to Life in the Calvary Graveyard" is special.
5. Thomas E. Vasser, *Uncle John Vasser* (New York: American Tract Society, 1931). A. J. Gordon wrote the introduction to this book. See also "John E. Vasser: Minister in Homespun," Decision (August 1995): 11.
6. Gordon, *How Christ Came to Church,* xff.
7. Ibid., 292.
8. A. J. Gordon, *Ecce Venit: Behold He Cometh* (New York: Revell, 1889). Great preaching on prophecy.
9. A. J. Gordon, *Grace and Glory* (Boston: Howard Gannett, 1880), 133ff., 1ff.
10. A. J. Gordon, *Yet Speaking* (New York: Revell, 1897), 37ff. Gordon also wrote on divine healing.
11. A. J. Gordon, *The Twofold Life or Christ's Work for Us and Christ's Work in Us* (Chicago: Moody, rep. 1883).

10.4 THE SOUTHERN RAPIDS IN AMERICAN PREACHING

So face with calm that heritage and earn contempt before the age.
—Allen Tate in 1932

The southern and border states have a unique heritage in the history of preaching, perhaps because those in the South "clung to [their] belief in the supernatural" more stubbornly, as Richard Weaver suggests.[1] The decades leading up to the Civil War had already sundered the largest denominations, and the war itself claimed 360,000 Union lives and 260,000 Confederates. The anguish, alienation, and agony were appalling. Studies of leaders and studies of the common people disclose the unimaginable trauma of war in egregious social, political, and economic dislocation.[2]

Even though there were deep movings of the Spirit among the troops on both sides of the fratricidal nightmare, the issues of abolition and emancipation divided the north ideologically and became consuming and distracting in a way that had a deleterious effect on preaching. In dealing recently with the moral trauma of slavery and the Civil War, Andrew Delbanco has argued that the Civil War was the great divide between the culture of faith and the culture of doubt in America.[3] He shows that the United States went into the war believing in providence and emerged from the war with only a hope for luck. Yet biblical faith and preaching were alive in the border and Southern states before, during, and after the carnage.

---

1. George M. Curtis III and James J. Thompson Jr., eds., *The Southern Essays of Richard M. Weaver* (Indianapolis: Liberty Press, 1987), xi. Note Weaver's illuminating essay on "The Older Religiousness in the South" (134).
2. Gene Smith, *Lee and Grant: A Dual Biography* (New York: McGraw-Hill, 1984). For a further feel of the wartime and postwar situations, see Charles Bracelen Flood, *Lee: The Last Years* (Boston: Houghton-Mifflin, 1981).
3. Andrew Delbanco, *The Death of Satan: How Americans Have Lost the Sense of Evil* (New York: Farrar, Strauss, 1995), 98, 138. I am indebted to my friend and former student Dr. Dorrington Little III for this book recommendation.

10.4.1 Alexander Campbell—Preacher on the Frontier

Imitate the Apostles and primitive preachers—preach the gospel, which, when received, produces repentance not to be repented of . . . preach Christ crucified, in whom is manifested the wrath and judgment of God against sin; and his condescending love, mercy and grace to the sinner.
—Alexander Campbell

The name of **Alexander Campbell** (1788–1866) is essential to a history of preaching not only because he was an electrifying preacher but because he also played an integral role in launching the Restoration Movement, which had such an influence in the South. Campbell was born in Ireland and came to America at the age of twenty-one. His father had preached in a Seceder Presbyterian Church near the family farm, and directed Alexander in extensive learning and much memorization of Scripture. Alexander studied one year at the University of Glasgow. He had been converted in his early teens and upon coming to the United States felt called to preach. At the age of twenty-two Campbell preached his first sermon from Matthew 7:24–27. Throughout his life he often preached polemical sermons among those who wanted unity in Christ rather than in man-made ecclesiastical structures. He founded Bethany College in West Virginia, where he was president for twenty-five years. He was a member of the Virginia Constitutional Convention and preached to Congress in 1850. He labored tirelessly, writing sixty volumes, editing the *Millennial Harbinger,* and debating Baptists and Roman Catholics.

We do not have many of Campbell's sermons because he preached extempore. We do have his great sermon from Romans 8:3 in which he contrasts the law of Moses with the gospel of Christ. Campbell often preached outdoors and usually spoke for an hour or more. In 1829 he debated the Scottish infidel Robert Owen in Cincinnati and spoke for twelve hours. The first sentence of his sermons was riveting, observers said.[1] President Madison, who was often with him on various councils, said of him:

It was my pleasure to hear him very often as a preacher of the Gospel, and I regard him as the ablest and most original expounder of the Scriptures I have ever heard.[2]

Dr. Humphrey, president of Amherst, recalled Campbell's preaching on the clauses "justified in the spirit, received into glory," and observed:

I never remembered to have listened to or to have read a more thrilling outburst of sacred eloquence than when he came to the scene of the coronation of Christ, and quoted the sublime passage from the twenty-fourth Psalm, beginning, "Lift up your heads, O ye gates, and be ye lifted up, ye everlasting doors, that the King of Glory may come," when he represented all the angels, principalities and powers of heaven as coming together to assist, as it were, in placing the Crown on the Redeemer's head.[3]

He did not gesticulate or pound the pulpit or speak vociferously. He used language artfully. Very few of the phenomena often seen in the great revivals of Kentucky and Tennessee were to be found in his meetings. His voice was ringing and clear and at times in crescendo. McLean says of Campbell's driving purpose:

His aim was to set forth what the Word of God taught, and not to prove that it is true, or that some notions held were true because they are supported by texts of Holy Writ . . . His familiarity with the language of the Bible enabled him to employ its glorious expressions and beautiful similes with great effect. . . . Bible themes, Bible thoughts, Bible terms, Bible facts, were his materials, and these he wrought up with consummate skill into intellectual and spiritual palaces of glorious beauty, in which every listener desired to prolong his stay.[4]

Christ was the center and the circumference of his message. We might well say of the Restoration Movement, as we might say of many of our movements, if all who followed had stayed with the basics as did our founders, we would be better off today. General Robert E. Lee paid him high tribute:

He was a man in whom were illustriously combined all the qualities that could adorn or elevate the nature to which he belonged; knowledge of the most various and extended virtue that never loitered in her career or deviated from her course.[5]

---

1. Archibald McLean, *Alexander Campbell as a Preacher* (Nashville: Reed and Company, rev. 1973), 11. I am indebted to my former student Dr. Sellers Crain Jr. for bringing this and other material on Alexander Campbell to my attention.
2. Ibid., 11. The problem in Restoration preaching was proof-texting—it was thematic and not very often exegetical.
3. Ibid., 14–15.

4. Ibid., 34.

5. Ibid., 45. In a study of remarkable candor, Bill Love of the Churches of Christ laments: "It was our preaching which was anemic—what we preached showed little correspondence to the richness, depth and power of the New Testament core gospel." Although there have been laudable exceptions, he regrets the lack of the preaching of the cross. See Bill Love, *The Core Gospel: On Restoring the Crux of the Matter* (Abilene: Abilene Christian University, 1992), 258.

10.4.2 JOHN A. BROADUS—THE PREACHER WHO TAUGHT PREACHERS

Deliver me, O Lord, from wrong ambitions, from every improper desire to be first among my brethren. May I be enabled to subordinate all my desires and plans and hopes to Thy will, and when I labor and strive for success and eminence and fame, may I do all for the glory of God.

An expository discourse may be defined as one which is occupied mainly, or at any rate very largely, with the exposition of Scripture . . . it may be one of a series or stand by itself. We at once perceive that there is no broad line of distinction between expository preaching and common methods, but that one may pass almost insensible gradations from textual to expository sermons.

The greatest privilege of earthly life is to give some fellow creature the blessed word of God, and then try by loving speech and example, to bring home to the heart and conscience . . . the truth it contains.

—John A. Broadus

Truly one of the Olympians in the history of preaching, **John A. Broadus** (1827–1895) is called by some the father of American expository preaching. Broadus was born of Welsh extraction in Culpepper County, Virginia. Converted at sixteen in "a protracted meeting," he went on to study classics at the University of Virginia. Influenced by a sermon he had heard, Broadus announced, "The question is decided; I must try to be a preacher." An able student and master of detail, he was influenced much by Dr. McGuffey, a Presbyterian minister, professor of moral philosophy at the university, and author of *McGuffey's Reader.* Broadus was fluent in eleven languages. He preached in Charlottesville and tutored and taught at the university, where he could have had the chair of Greek. Instead, he was drawn to share in the formation of the Southern Baptist Seminary in Greenville, North Carolina. Always frail, his health snapped in the shock of war. The fledgling seminary closed, and during these hard years Broadus wrote his justly famous commentary on Matthew.

Stonewall Jackson urged him to come to the front and preach.[1] He did so, and sent dispatches to newspapers from the front. He continued to preach in many small churches throughout the war. After the conflict, the seminary reopened with just six students. Broadus' first course of lectures on preaching, which later became his widely used text,[2] was delivered to one blind student. Ultimately the seminary relocated to Louisville. In all, Broadus served there for thirty-six years, the last several of which were as president.

Towering even in a field of Southern Baptists where preaching has always been strong and central,[3] Broadus was never lacking in opportunities to take pastorates and teach elsewhere. He turned down invitations from Calvary Baptist, New York City, First Baptist, Richmond, and the University of Chicago, Brown University as president, Vasser, Newton Seminary, and Crozer Seminary. In 1867 he preached the baccalaureate sermon at Washington College at the insistence of the president of the school, his good friend Robert E. Lee. He read widely in all literary genre and was totally committed to the trustworthiness of Scripture, not "embracing the higher criticism of the nineteenth century."[4]

Broadus supported the long ending of Mark's gospel and was cited as a source in that position by John William Burgon, its chief exponent.[5] In 1870 he spent a year abroad to regain his health. His meetings with Spurgeon, H. P. Liddon, Lightfoot, Eadie, Alford, Westcott, and Hort are graphically recounted in his letters.[6] He coauthored 1 and 2 Samuel in the Lange commentaries with C. H. Toy of the Southern Baptist faculty[7] and gave five lectures on the history of preaching at Newton Seminary. He worked for many years on the old International Sunday School Lesson Committee and wrote for *The Sunday School Times*. Broadus turned down a call to the First Baptist Church of Chicago but spoke regularly at Northfield and Chatauqua. He gave the Beecher Lectures at Yale in 1888.[8] And in all of this, "his health trembled in the balance."[9]

Not only was Broadus a gifted homiletical theoretician, but also he was an immensely popular and able preacher. His more classical approach is derided today on many sides for his "discursive" and "conceptual" flavor, but in 1870 he spoke more about narrative than did Haddon Robinson in 1980. Broadus argued for the sermon taking its shape from the text.[10] He always preached extempore, his task being to expose the text. He used few gestures and tended to preach conversationally. His hallmark was clarity. His fine sermon on John 4:32–38 divides the text and the sermon into four parts.[11] The classic message on "The Habit of Thankfulness" from 1 Thessalonians 5:18 has two divisions and some subdivisions.[12]

E. C. Dargan came to help him in homiletics at Southern and eventually succeeded him. Broadus wrote a unique *Harmony of the Gospels,* served as a regent of the Kentucky School of Medicine, and kept up a prodigious correspondence with many, including General Lew Wallace, author of *Ben Hur.* Broadus was "always looking for the coming of Christ"[13] and strongly supported the Moody-Sankey campaigns. He declined writing on the Pastorals for the ICC series but turned down little else.

By the time of his retirement, the seminary had close to three hundred students. In his last class meeting, one of his students recalled his words, which so beautifully capture this man and his message:

> "Young gentlemen, if this were the last time I should ever be permitted
> to address you, I would feel amply repaid for consuming the whole hour
> in endeavoring to impress upon you these two things: true piety and, like

Apollos, to be men 'mighty in the Scriptures.'" Then pausing, he stood for a moment with his piercing eye fixed upon us, and repeated over and over again in that slow but wonderfully impressive style peculiar to himself, "mighty in the Scriptures," "mighty in the Scriptures," until the whole class seemed to be lifted through him into a sacred nearness to the Master. That picture of him as he stood there at that moment can never be obliterated from my mind.[14]

---

1. A. T. Robertson, *Life and Letters of John Albert Broadus* (Harrisonburg, Va.: Gano, rev. 1987), 197.
2. John A. Broadus, *A Treatise on the Preparation and Delivery of Sermons* (New York: Armstrong, 1907). Dargan revised the original on suggestions by Broadus; J. B. Weatherspoon later revised it; and Vernon L. Stanfield again revised it.
3. Al Fasol, *With a Bible in Their Hands: Baptist Preaching in the South 1679–1979* (Nashville: Broadman, 1994).
4. Raymond H. Bailey, "John A. Broadus: Man of Letters and Preacher Extraordinaire," *Preaching* (November–December 1993): 58ff. Bailey paints Broadus as the "gentleman-scholar-preacher."
5. John William Burgon (1813–1888), bishop of Chichester, born in Ixmir (Smyrna), Turkey, was himself a fine preacher. See Edward M. Goulburn, *John William Burgon: A Biography* (London: John Murray, 1892). Analyzes the textual issue.
6. Robertson, *Life and Letters of John Albert Broadus,* 243–44. Everett Gill's fine *A. T. Robertson* (1943) is invaluable because it shows how one of Broadus's students "got hold of preaching" in his class. Robertson married Ella Broadus, the youngest daughter.
7. The tragedy of C. H. Toy was seen in his drift from orthodoxy and his departure from Southern Baptist Seminary for Harvard and infidelity.
8. Bailey, "John A. Broadus," 60, on the Beecher Lectures, which were never published as such but incorporated in various books and articles by Broadus. David McCant calls them "The Lost Yale Lectures on Preaching."
9. Robertson, *Life and Letters of John Albert Broadus,* 323. Robertson's own fine sermons are in *Passing the Torch* (New York: Macmillan, 1943).
10. Steve Reagles, "One Century after the 1889 Lectures: A Reflection on Broadus' Homiletical Thought," *Preaching* (November–December 1989): 35.
11. V. L. Stanfield, ed., *Favorite Sermons of John A. Broadus* (New York: Harper, 1959), 14ff.
12. Ibid., 21ff.
13. Robertson, *Life and Letters of John Albert Broadus,* 417.
14. Ibid., 430.

10.4.3 R. L. DABNEY—THE TEACHER WHO COULD PREACH

My charge hangs on my hands like a growing burden, heavier and heavier continually. They listen to my preaching very attentively, and often with fixed interest; but it always feels to me like the interest of the understanding and imagination only, and not of the spiritual affections.

My preaching seems to human eyes to be utterly without effect; bad for
me, and bad for them.

—R. L. Dabney of some of his early struggles at
Tinkling Spring Church

You now perceive that when once the inspiration of the Scriptures is established, they become practically the great storehouse of proofs for pulpit
argument. . . . The only hope for Protestants is the work of the Holy Ghost
. . . to the objection that didactic preaching is dry, I answer, that if it ever
seems to be so, this is the fault of the preacher and not of the truth. . . .
The exact mind of the Spirit in the text must then be ascertained before
you preach on it.

It is a noble thing to make the truth beautiful!

—R. L. Dabney

A notable company of Southern Presbyterian preachers came together around
the time of the Civil War. Their dean, **James Henley Thornwell** (1812–1862),
was called by D. Martyn Lloyd-Jones "one of the greatest preachers that America
has ever produced." His teaching and pastoral work were chiefly done in Columbia, South Carolina.[1] "The glory of the Southern Pulpit" was an accolade
heaped on **Benjamin M. Palmer** (1818–1902), described as "an insignificant-
looking little fellow." He succeeded Thornwell in Columbia and then served First
Presbyterian Church in New Orleans for forty-six years. Palmer preached free-
style and knew episodic visits of the Spirit in revival.[2] His *Theology of Prayer* is
in a class by itself. His tongue was "fire-tipped" and his homiletics outstanding.

The third member of this dauntless trio was **Robert Lewis Dabney** (1820–
1898), who came from Louisa County near Richmond. In a revival in his home
church he made his profession of faith. He was trained by Hampden-Sidney
College and the University of Virginia, where he took his M.A. Dabney resolved
to enter the ministry and studied at Union Seminary, then located at Hampden-
Sidney.[3] The school had eighteen students at the time. After serving the Scots-
Irish Church in Tinkling Spring, he accepted a call to teach at the seminary, now
down to twelve students, and served concurrently as copastor of the College
Church for some thirty years.

Dabney was hungry for revival in the churches.[4] He preached at Fifth Avenue
Presbyterian Church in New York and at Princeton and was moderator of the
Synod of Virginia in the fateful year of 1860. Stonewall Jackson wanted his services at the front as adjutant general, and out of that relationship came Dabney's
biography of the great general.[5]

Dabney's outstanding sermon to Synod in 1881 from Colossians 2:8 on "A
Caution Against Anti-Christian Science" left a profound impression. But controversies at Union Seminary led him to the chair of mental and moral philosophy at the University of Texas. Due to some misunderstandings, he resigned
after eleven years and became one of the founders of the Austin Presbyterian
Seminary.

His preaching was didactic and packed with content but also imaginative and full of word pictures. John Broadus heard his sermon from John 4:35 on "The World White to the Harvest; Reap, or It Perishes" at a large missions meeting in New York and pronounced it "one of the most powerful sermons with which he was acquainted."[6] Dabney was a staunch defender of plenary inspiration, although properly recognizing the use of phenomenal language in Scripture.[7] Dabney was cautious, as his article on "Aesthetics as a Substitute for Christianity" indicates.[8] Nonetheless, many listeners were struck by "the energy and power of his constructive imagination."[9]

His lectures on sacred rhetoric are outstanding and touch the danger of fragmentary preaching. He underscored the need for "one burning focus," division of the text, pleasing transitions, a clear announcement of the proposition, and the desirability of beginning softly![10] In this, like Hoppin and Broadus, he was Aristotelian and thus anathema to many contemporaries. Yet while emphasizing that unity implies parts and eulogizing "lucid order," he treated the narrative genre, pushed continuous application and the use of many illustrations.[11] Yet he distinguished his position from scholastic preaching[12] and emphasized imagination and preaching extempore for maximum effect. Dabney quoted a French writer who characterized American orators as "very ingenious and fluent, but his conclusion is too much like that of the pointer dog, who when he wishes to sleep turns around and around following his own tail, and at last lies down just where he began."[13]

Too much of Aristotle may indeed be problematic, but the idea of rhetoric as the application of style for the purpose of persuasion and the law of contradiction are good even if they emanate from a Greek pagan. Logical investigation and rational judgment are also Aristotelian but, like Robert Dabney's preaching, are eminently defensible.[14]

---

1. B. M. Palmer, *The Life and Letters of James Henley Thornwell* (Edinburgh: Banner of Truth, 1875, 1986).

2. Thomas C. Johnson, *The Life and Letters of Benjamin Morgan Palmer* (Edinburgh: Banner of Truth, 1987).

3. Thomas C. Johnson, *The Life and Letters of Robert Lewis Dabney* (Edinburgh: Banner of Truth, 1903, 1977), 80.

4. Ibid., 111.

5. Ibid., 261ff.

6. Ibid., 167.

7. Ibid., 342.

8. Ibid., 518.

9. Ibid., 545.

10. R. L. Dabney, *R. L. Dabney on Preaching: Lectures on Sacred Rhetoric* (Edinburgh: Banner of Truth, 1870, 1979), 310.

11. Ibid., 197, 254.

12. Ibid., 217–18.

13. Ibid., 178.

14. Jean Dietz Moss, ed., *Rhetoric and Praxis: The Contribution of Classical Rhetoric to Practical Reasoning* (Washington, D.C.: Catholic University of America Press, 1986). A thoughtful case.

10.4.4 B. H. CARROLL—THE PREACHER ON THE PRAIRIES OF TEXAS

I certainly understand the passage [2 Timothy 3:17] to teach the plenary inspiration of the Holy Scriptures—the Old Testament directly, the New Testament by implication. That, being inspired, they are authoritative and inerrant. That as such they constitute an all sufficient standard of human belief, conduct, and destiny.

The only way to find pardon for past offenses is in Christ. Will you come to Him? Here now, press through this throng—make a way—come up here now and let us unite our prayers that God today will give you the Holy Spirit that you may be led to repentance toward Him and faith in the Lord Jesus Christ.

—B. H. Carroll

The centrality of religion and the importance of preaching before, during, and after the American Civil War are abundantly clear.[1] As a young man, **Benajah Harvey Carroll** (1843–1914) was carried off the battlefield with a rifle ball in one of his legs. He went on from that close call to enjoy an especially blessed ministry.

Born in Mississippi, Carroll and his family moved to Texas when he was fifteen. He attended Baylor University, fought in the war, and then received Christ as his Savior at a Methodist camp meeting.[2] He started as assistant pastor at the First Baptist Church in Waco, Texas, and in 1871 became its pastor, a post he filled for thirty years. Carroll was the founder of the Southwestern Baptist Theological Seminary, probably to this day the largest seminary in the world and a fountainhead of the kind of preaching emphasis that has made the Southern Baptist Convention a leading influence in the United States and abroad.

Carroll wrote his *Interpretation of the English Bible* in 13 volumes. To him the preaching of the Word was of the essence in the church and the pastor's task.

Just think of it seriously. Eternal interests hinge on every sermon. Every sentence may be freighted with eternal weal or woe. Every word may be the savor of life unto life or death unto death.[3]

Of the 241 sermons we possess from Carroll, 157 are expository, 55 topical and 24 textual. His outlines were terse and clear.[4] In a searching message on "The Conquering Word of God" from Jeremiah 23:28, Carroll faced head-on the misuse of the Word of God by the false prophets who presented a counterfeit Word which "had the semblance of wheat, in order to deceive."[5] His illustrations and quotations are sparkling and effective.

Following Carroll and shaping Southern Baptist preaching in Texas and westward was **Jefferson Davis Ray** (1860–1951), who served as professor of preaching at Southwestern from 1907 to 1944. He was known especially for his powerful reading of the Scripture, and he epitomizes the preaching Carroll modeled for his students. In arguing for expository preaching, Ray pleaded for preachers to probe the text for "the juicy inner substratum meaning of the Word of God."[6] He was clearly an advocate of what we have called the classical expository sermon, with unity and an orderly structure. Ray wrote movingly of the calling of the local pastor of a smaller church.[7] He helped fulfill the vision of B. H. Carroll in the founding of Southwestern. He wanted "knowledge on fire."

1. Richard J. Carwardine, *Evangelicals and Politics in Antebellum America* (New Haven, Conn.: Yale University Press, 1993).
2. Al Fasol, *With a Bible in Their Hands: Baptist Preaching in the South 1679–1979* (Nashville: Broadman, 1994), 84.
3. Ibid., 85.
4. Ibid., 87.
5. B. H. Carroll, *Revival Messages* (Nashville: Broadman, 1939), 115.
6. Jeff D. Ray, *Expository Preaching* (Grand Rapids: Zondervan, 1940), 60.
7. Jeff D. Ray, *The Country Preacher* (Nashville: Sunday School Board of the Southern Baptist Convention, 1925).

10.5 THE SCOTTISH WATERFALL

> The priestlike father reads the sacred page, How Abram was the friend of God on high;
> Or, Moses bad eternal warfare wage with Amalek's ungracious progeny . . .
> Perhaps the Christian volume is the theme, How guiltless blood for guilty man was shed;
> How He, who bore in Heaven the second name, Had not on earth whereon to lay His head.
> —Robert Burns in *The Cotter's Saturday Night*

Apart from the special place the Bible had in the Scottish heart and home, it is hard to understand the remarkable outcropping of biblical preaching that flourished in Scotland in the nineteenth and early twentieth centuries. The Scottish church clung tenaciously to an educated ministry, but there was tragedy in the offing that had its genesis in concessions made to higher criticism and skepticism in the centers for ministerial training. It will be our task to trace the zenith as well as the recession of biblical preaching in this small, pastoral land.

Adam Phillip (b. 1856), one of the biographers of Chalmers and a parish pastor of long experience, in his Warrack Lectures in 1930 urged preachers to make points "which like peaks, catch attention."[1] The concern of the preacher must be to know "the gales of the Spirit."[2] In a land where confidence in preaching is now low, we must look carefully at what made the Scottish pulpit soar, and at which crossroad the wrong turn was taken.

---

1. Adam Phillip, *Thoughts on Worship and Preaching* (London: James Clarke, 1930), 128.
2. Ibid., 154.

10.5.1 Thomas Guthrie—The Preacher Who Painted a Picture

I am a painter . . . only I paint in words. While this faculty is not to be allowed to run away with a man, it is a telling one, and valuable for the highest ends. Mind the three P's: In every discourse the preacher should aim at proving, painting and persuading; in other words, addressing the Reason, the Fancy and the Heart.

Jesus Christ is the propitiation for our sins; and not for ours only, but also for the sins of the whole world. The whole world . . . ah! some would say that is dangerous language. It is God's language; John speaking as he was moved by the Holy Ghost. It throws a zone of mercy around the world. Perish the hand that would narrow it by a hair's breadth.

—Thomas Guthrie

Considered second only to Chalmers as a Scots preacher in the nineteenth century, **Thomas Guthrie** (1803–1873) was born in Brechin in Angus. He trained at Edinburgh, which he entered at twelve and from which he graduated at sixteen. Guthrie inherited a warmth for the Seceders from his mother. He tried medical studies in Paris (1826–27) but yielded to God's call to preach. His first charge was at Arbirlot and then Greyfriars in Edinburgh in 1837 and the new St. John's near Cowgate.

Guthrie was a social reformer with great compassion for the poor. His homespun manner and illustrations went straight to the hearts of the common people. He participated in the Disruption, serving afterwards at Free St. John's. He succeeded Candlish as moderator of the Free Church in 1862. Not only the poor flocked to hear him, but such as Sir James Simpson, inventor of chloroform, were his members. He worked ceaselessly for the working class "ragged schools." In the auspicious row of statues in the park along Prince's Street in Edinburgh, Guthrie's is the only one of a clergyman.

Guthrie was "not in the strictest sense of the term, a refined and intellectual preacher,"[1] but his "vivid imagination and quick sympathies" made him a magnet for the multitude.[2] He seemed to have an inexhaustible fund of anecdotes. James M'Cosh called him "the pictorial preacher of the age," very much like another Scot, Peter Marshall, in his sermons in the book *Mr. Jones, Meet the Master.* As one observed:

The swing of the broad shoulder, the head bent forward, the look of earnestness of the flushed countenance, all tell of a man who feels he has come forth on an important errand, and is straitened till it be accomplished

. . . an unusually tall and commanding person, with an abundance of easy and powerful gestures; a strongly expressive countenance; a powerful, clear and musical voice, the intonations of which were varied and appropriate, managed with an actor's skill, though there was not the least appearance of art.[3]

Such were Guthrie's gifts. He could have spoken impromptu, for "the oil which he brought into the sanctuary was 'beaten oil.'"[4] He was a pastoral evangelist who poured through the commentaries in his meticulous preparation.[5] His magnificent messages in *The Gospel in Ezekiel* unfold Ezekiel 36 in a painstaking but most pleasurable form. A typically effective message is "The Nature, Necessity and Power of Prayer" from Ezekiel 36:37, "I will yet for this be inquired of by the house of Israel, to do it for them." The sermon is divided under five heads.[6] Guthrie argued that our good and God's glory ever run in the same direction. His studies in Colossians were widely read, under the theme *Christ and the Inheritance of the Saints* from Colossians 1.[7] His books like *Man and the Gospel*[8] and a collection of his stories like *Out of Harness,*[9] with a most intriguing sermon on "The Rechabites" from Jeremiah 35, are eminently worthwhile.

A heart ailment finally forced Guthrie to retire. What a monumental pulpit ministry of the Word!

---

1. Thomas Guthrie, *Life of the Rev. Thomas Guthrie,* compiled mostly from his own lips (Glasgow: John S. Marr, n.d.), 105.
2. Thomas Guthrie, *Autobiography of Thomas Guthrie and Memoir by His Sons* (London: Daldy, Isbister, 1876), 188.
3. Ibid., 197ff.
4. John Edwards, *Nineteenth-Century Preachers and Their Method* (London: Charles H. Kelly, 1902), 59.
5. Lewis O. Brastow, *Representative Modern Preachers* (New York: Macmillan, 1904), 368.
6. Thomas Guthrie, *The Gospel in Ezekiel Illustrated in a Series of Discourses* (Grand Rapids: Zondervan, n.d.), 340ff. He quotes from John Wesley and uses illustrations from ancient history and from nature.
7. Thomas Guthrie, *Christ and the Inheritance of the Saints Illustrated in a Series of Discourses from the Colossians* (Edinburgh: Adam and Charles Black, 1858). Dwells minutely on each phrase from Colossians 1:12–20.
8. Thomas Guthrie, *Man and the Gospel* (New York: E. B. Treat, n.d.). Clarence Macartney in his Stone Lectures at Princeton in 1928 highlights Guthrie as a pictorial preacher who addresses himself with model effectiveness to the average person; see *Sons of Thunder* (New York: Revell, 1929).
9. Thomas Guthrie, *Out of Harness: Sketches, Narrative and Description* (New York: E. B. Treat, n.d.). His depictions of French Protestantism are most enlightening (108ff.), and his chapter on "Dr. Chalmers and the Cowgate" describes the encouragement Guthrie received from the great Chalmers in the poorest section of Edinburgh.

10.5.2 WILLIAM CUNNINGHAM—THE THEOLOGIAN WHO TOOK A STAND

> The Reformers were all led by God to give careful attention to the study of the sacred Scriptures . . . Their strength and success arose very much from their familiar and intimate acquaintance with the word of God—the whole word of God. They were familiar with the meaning and application of its statements, and they were deeply imbued with its spirit. The word of God dwelt in them richly. There is reason to fear, that, since the period of the Reformation, the careful study of the word of God itself has not received the share of time and attention which its importance deserves . . . We know but little of the word of God as it ought to be known.
>
> —William Cunningham in *The Reformers and the Theology of the Reformation*

Described by Webber as "one of the most majestic preachers of Disruption days" and one of the confidantes of Chalmers and Candlish, **William Cunningham** (1805–1861) was a key leader in the Free Church of Scotland. Born in Hamilton and trained at Edinburgh, which he entered at fifteen, he was licensed in 1828. Walker says of Cunningham, "As a student he was known as an omnivorous reader and also a vigorous thinker and effective speaker."[1]

Cunningham was apparently a moderate initially, but under Andrew Thompson (cf. 9.1.5) and the fiery evangelical preaching of **Robert Gordon** (1786–1853), he became a strong evangelical. After serving at Greenock, Cunningham went to Edinburgh in 1834 to teach at Trinity College. Although he gave up much, he was with Chalmers in the Disruption and was one of the first to march out of St. Andrew's Church that fateful May 18, 1843.[2] He was the first professor of theology at New College and then moved over to church history, succeeding Chalmers as principal. Cunningham also moderated the General Assembly in 1859.

Dealt a heavy blow in the death of their champion, Thomas Chalmers, the Free Church looked to Cunningham and Candlish, who did not see all issues alike. Cunningham was a deep-dyed Calvinist[3] but wrote significantly on the history of theology. He was unswerving in his commitment to the authority of Scripture for which he argued both on the grounds of rational evidence and the witness of the Spirit. Though holding to particular atonement, he strongly advocated the free offer of the gospel:

> It is right that these offers and invitations should be freely and indiscriminately addressed to men of all characters and in all circumstances, without exception, condition or qualification.[4]

John J. Bonar (1803–1891) said of Cunningham that "the splendour that surrounds his name was quickly eclipsed as Scottish churchmen opted for the theology of the Enlightenment in preference to that of the Reformation. If that situation is ever reversed people will again take seriously Cunningham's claim to be Scotland's greatest theologian."[5]

Cunningham visited the United States to preach and was awarded an honorary doctorate at Princeton. He traveled with Guthrie to England to interpret developments. His powerful sermon on the cross at the opening of the General Assembly in 1860 was epochal. J. W. Alexander described him:

> A stout but finely formed man . . . powerful reasoning and sound judgment . . . a walking treasury of facts, dates and ecclesiastical law. I heard him for an hour on Friday . . . indescribable Scottish intonation, but little idiom and convulsion of body, but flowing elegant language and amazing power in presenting an argument . . .[6]

The rise of higher criticism would ultimately spell disaster for Scottish preaching. The sad story is chronicled by Riesen.[7] The silence of A. B. Davidson, the radical thinking of William Robertson Smith, and the concessions of George Adam Smith were the death knell. Riesen purports to see the seeds of this sedition even in the Free Church fathers Chalmers, Cunningham, and Bannerman.[8] Nicholas Needham sets that record straight.[9] We shall return to the gloomy account of the spiritual declension that ravaged the Scottish church. In his preaching and teaching, however, Cunningham stood fast for "the faith once for all delivered to the saints."

---

1. Norman L. Walker, *Chapters from the History of the Free Church of Scotland* (Edinburgh: Oliphant, 1895), 92.
2. Henry Wellwood Moncrief, *The Free Church Principle: Its Character and History* (Edinburgh: Macniven, 1883).
3. William Cunningham, *The Reformers and the Theology of the Reformation* (London: Banner of Truth, 1862, 1967).
4. D. Macleod, "William Cunningham," in *Dictionary of Scottish Church History and Theology*, ed. Nigel M. de S. Cameron (Downers Grove, Ill.: InterVarsity Press, 1993), 230.
5. Ibid., 230. The Cunningham Lectures were in his memory and among the most prestigious in Scotland.
6. F. R. Webber, *A History of Preaching in Britain and America* (Milwaukee: Northwestern, 1955), 2:352.
7. Richard Allan Riesen, *Criticism and Faith in Late Victorian Scotland* (Lanham, Md.: University Press of America, 1985).
8. Ibid., 377.
9. Nicholas R. Needham, *The Doctrine of Holy Scripture in the Free Church Fathers* (Edinburgh: Rutherford House, 1991). Needham demonstrates that the Free Church fathers were not the unwitting precursors of Robertson Smith. Riesen seems to tar Charles Hodge himself with the same brush, which undercuts his entire case (400).

10.5.3 ROBERT CANDLISH—THE PASTOR, PROFESSOR, AND PREACHER

Do we not need as a people, a new and fresh interposition of Divine power, to quicken and revive our spiritual life, a new outpouring of the Spirit, a new baptism from above! Oh! that it might please Him who, when He ascended up on high, received gifts for men . . . to shed forth His saving and unerring grace, in such manner and measure as might be seen and heard. Oh! that it were thus owned and blessed by some signal tokens of the Spirit's power, in unquestionable instances of sinners converted, backsliders reclaimed, anxious inquirers comforted and humble followers of the Saviour filled with every new joy and peace in believing.

—Robert S. Candlish

At the apogee of Scottish biblical preaching, onslaughts against soundness and scripturality were mounted. **John McLeod Campbell** (1800–1872) denied scriptural authority and penal substitution. In this he was influenced by the maverick **Thomas Erskine of Linlathen.**[1] Campbell went to trial in 1831 and was deposed from his charge at Row to spend his last twenty-five years at a small, independent chapel in Glasgow. Likewise, the celebrated capitulation of the brilliant young **William Robertson Smith** (1846–1894) to the blandishments of higher criticism and the ensuing trial were a dark hour for the Free Church of Scotland.

Among the stalwart defenders of orthodoxy at this time was the able **Robert S. Candlish** (1806–1873), who was closely allied with Cunningham and Chalmers. Candlish was born in Edinburgh. His father was a teacher of medicine. Both of his parents were related to the Scottish poet Robert Burns. Candlish tutored at Eton for a time. Early on he had a reputation as a moderate and served associateships under such auspices. Then he won the call to St. George's, the largest in Edinburgh, over Cunningham. St. George's was a parish with eight thousand souls, and among his assistants there were Andrew Bonar, the famous oratorical preacher J. Oswald Dykes, and Alexander Whyte. He was offered a professorial chair at New College but canceled his acceptance when the new pastor-designate died. Candlish stayed at St. George's—known as Free St. George's after the Disruption—for the rest of his life.[2]

Thus Candlish both taught and preached for many years. In 1862 he was appointed principal of New College. Although he never had finished his theological studies, Princeton gave him a D.D. in 1841. His decorous sermons before the General Assembly were memorable, and his funeral sermon for Dr. Guthrie was a classic. His study and desk were neat, as were his sermons.[3] In appearance he was slight with a large head and "a great shock of unruly hair." Before the close of the pulpit hymn he would almost jump up and move quickly to the pulpit to unleash a tidal flow of passionate discourse.[4] Three volumes of his lectures on Genesis are still read, and his masterful studies in 1 John are peerless. His work on *Reason and Revelation* is significant and is exceeded only by Professor James Bannerman's six-hundred-page treatise on the authority of Scripture.

Alexander Whyte spoke of the exposition of Candlish in the following terms:

He would set himself to unwind and unweave its texture, filament by filament, and fibre by fibre, with the most minute analysis and the most practiced exegetical skill. And then how he would address himself to the reweaving of it all again, and that into a rich web of evangelical doctrine.[5]

In his exposition of 1 John 4:4–6, "The Spirit of Christ in us greater than the Spirit of Antichrist in the world," he uses two divisions very simply—he who is in the world is great; but he who is in us is greater because he is the Lord Almighty.[6] Especially arresting in this series are the messages on "The Test of Antichrist" and "Passing Away of the World." This is solid biblical fare which wore well for many years. Today the highlight of the week at St. George's West on Shandwicke Place is the senior citizens' lunch. At St. George's, the battle over the Bible was lost and great preaching went with it.[7]

1. George M. Tuttle, *John McLeod Campbell on the Atonement* (Edinburgh: Handsell Press, 1986). Sympathetic.
2. Jean L. Watson, *Life of Principal Candlish* (Edinburgh: James Gemmell, 1882), 124.
3. Ibid., 163. See also the massive work by William Wilson, *Memorials of Robert Smith Candlish* (Edinburgh: Adam and Charles Black, 1880).
4. F. R. Webber, *A History of Preaching in Britain and America* (Milwaukee: Northwestern, 1955), 2:360.
5. Quoted by Wilbur M. Smith in his biographical preface to Robert S. Candlish, *1 John* (Grand Rapids: Zondervan, n.d.).
6. Ibid., 367ff.
7. "What Are We to Say?" A Church of Scotland pastor writes to his congregation of devout Highlanders about the drift away from the Word of God in our time, *Christian Heritage Magazine* (November 1977): 4ff.

10.5.4 JOHN EADIE—THE PREACHER WHO TAUGHT EXEGESIS

I have, as I dare say you will bear me witness, preached the Gospel, and the great central truth of the Gospel—salvation by the cross; and I have uniformly done this, I can plead to no neglect or indifference in this. This crown I will let no man take from me. I was "separated to preach the Gospel," and that Gospel I have endeavored to preach with all freedom and fullness . . . I have preached more than a thousand sermons from a thousand texts . . . and yet I mourn not the want of themes; I feel in no danger of falling into monotony. I find the riches of Christ to be unsearchable.

—John Eadie on his 25th Anniversary at
Cambridge Street Church, Glasgow

Times of thriving preaching are also times of the writing and publication of many sound commentaries on Scripture. A superb example of this is the preach-

ing and writing of **John Eadie** (1810–1876) from the minuscule United Secession Church, which also gave us Orr and Cairns. Born in Sterlingshire and educated at Glasgow, Eadie entered the divinity hall at sixteen and was soon
conspicuous for his gift of speech.[1] He also gained renown for his feats of memory,
being able to recite all of *Paradise Lost*. Often called to lecture on temperance,
he gave himself unstintingly to "the scientific exposition of Scripture."[2] In 1835
he took the call to the Cambridge Street Church in Glasgow, where he ministered for twenty-eight years to a working class audience of seven hundred. Eadie's
first message was from Acts 10:39. Following that, he went through book by book
with his flock. Not surprisingly, he preached from memory.

In 1843 Eadie was elected to the chair of biblical literature in Secession Hall,
where his deep reverence for the text strengthened the strong tradition of exegetical
preaching in his communion. His exposition had dramatic power. His aim was
"a faithful attempt to unfold the real meaning of Scripture and apply it to the
practical wants of daily life."[3] Along with his teaching and preaching he published prodigiously, including a biographical memoir of the deaf English scholar,
John Kitto (1804–1854).[4] He also produced a condensation of Cruden's concordance, a biblical encyclopedia (1848), an *Analytical Concordance* (1856), an
Ecclesiastical Encyclopedia (1861), and a family Bible. We have already referred
to his *Paul the Preacher* (1854 cf. 2.3.3), and while not as strong in grammar as
he was in exegesis, he wrote substantive and valuable commentaries on Ephesians,
Colossians, Philippians, and the Thessalonian correspondence published after his
death. His commentary on Galatians is especially strong.[5]

Not at all sectarian, Eadie loved all believers. In 1861 he planted a new church
in Lansdown in Glasgow, where he sought to introduce some changes in worship, including response to prayers with an audible "amen" from the congregation. He visited the U.S. in 1871 and developed a lasting friendship with William
Cullen Bryant, the American poet. Eadie also preached for John Hall and enjoyed good fellowship with Professors Schaff at Union and Charles Hodge at
Princeton. He spoke at John Wanamaker's Bethany Sabbath School in Philadelphia, and was an integral part of the revision of the Scripture (RV). In 1876 his
health broke, and his ministry was unexpectedly over.[6] Yet his dedication to the
explication of Bible truth remained. One writer observes:

> Because Eadie held to the highest view of the New Testament text as
> inspired by the Holy Spirit, he also had the highest conception of the
> task of the biblical exegete. For the same reason he rejected the subjec-
> tivism of much of the rationalistic scholarship of his day.[7]

---

1. John Brown, *Life of John Eadie* (London: Macmillan, 1878), 38.
2. Ibid., 47.
3. Ibid., 172.
4. John Eadie, "A Critical Estimate of Dr. Kitto's Life and Writings," in J. E. Ryland,
   Memoirs of John Kitto (Edinburgh: William Oliphant, 1856), 667ff. S. P. Tregelles,
   the Plymouth Brother, also made contribution to this volume.

5. John Eadie, *Commentary of the Epistle of Paul to the Galatians* (Grand Rapids: Zondervan, 1869, 1894).

6. Brown, *Life of John Eadie,* 370.

7. Nigel M. de S. Cameron, ed., *Dictionary of Scottish Church History and Theology* (Downers Grove, Ill.: InterVarsity Press, 1993), 270.

10.5.5 *Norman Macleod—A Popular Preacher Who Wrestled with Principle*

> I was ordained here. You know what an awful thing it is. I feel as if the weight of those hands is still upon my head, crushing me with responsibility. But it was a delightful scene. I got well over my first sermon, "Now are we ambassadors." Once or twice nearly overcome; and this day I have preached twice. I have been then, in the parish a week, have been over it all, visited each day from ten till five. . . . It is in a terrible state . . . there is in all the parish an awful want of spiritual religion.
>
> —Norman Macleod in a letter, March 25, 1838

Norman Macleod (1812–1872) came from a distinguished line of clergy out of the island people of the Highlands. Known popularly as Macleod of Barony and ultimately as "the chief ecclesiastic of the Church of Scotland" (Dean Stanley), he was raised in the seaport of Campbeltown, where he learned Gaelic. Macleod loved literature and had a powerful imagination.[1] Studying at Glasgow and then at Edinburgh, he acknowledged that Chalmers made "an ineradicable impression on him." The death of his younger brother James also proved to be a spiritual turning point.

The springtime of Macleod's ministerial life was the five-year period he served his first parish in Loudoun in Ayrshire. In some respects he was Bunyan's Mr. Facing-both-ways, and the Disruption in 1843 found him in the middle. At a time when some would "peril their all for conscience sake,"[2] Macleod stayed in the Church of Scotland. He was identified with the "forty" who did not want to be identified with the moderates or the evangelicals, whom he called those "firebrands."[3] Although he loved Christ and the Word, he found it hard to maintain the middle ground.

In 1843 he transferred to Dalkeith near Edinburgh and was sent to North America with a team to interpret the Disruption to Scottish churches and immigrants. His sermons were growing elaborate by now, but his preaching was always well received.[4] Although he endeavored to restrain his descriptive bent, as he matured, his preaching developed a higher teaching component and was more "homely talk."[5]

On the death of Dr. Black, Macleod assumed the pastorate of the Barony Church in Glasgow in 1851, the same year in which he married. The population of the parish was more than 87,000, and he gave himself with great abandon to reaching them. He established Sunday schools, savings banks and a special service for the poor, and edited a periodical called *Good Words.* He assumed denominational leadership of the India Mission and became a chaplain and advisor to Queen Victoria. His stand against the traditional Scottish Sabbath involved him in a hurricane of controversy. He was active in the Evangelical Alliance and served as moderator of the General Assembly in 1869.

Although lovable and congenial, Macleod's aversion to taking a stand undercut his preaching ministry, and nowhere in his massive two-volume memoirs do we hear about a passion for conversions. Yet he was known as an able preacher who "could swing with a wide cable." He was most influenced by Thomas Arnold (the English broad churchman) and by his cousin John Macleod Campbell, with whom he walked every Saturday evening. He regarded the discipline of Campbell as "barbarous intolerance,"[6] and saw his own theological views "expanding" and moving way from any penal sense in the atonement.[7]

Macleod was increasingly uneasy about requiring any subscription to theological standards and felt this should be left to the individual.[8] He did not see the Second Coming of Christ as "objective," and though he was shocked by infidelity, he believed "the infidel is nearer the kingdom of God than many an Orthodox minister."[9] Condemnation after death was to be a process of education. In this he was with Thomas Erskine and F. D. Maurice, two of his best friends. He advocated reducing all standards to the Apostles' Creed and overlooking other differences. Webber accurately reflects Macleod's theological imprecision in his observation:

> Men who have heard him preach have said that he was inclined at times, when preaching an expository sermon, to skip from verse to verse, causing an attentive hearer to regret that certain truths had not been developed more fully.[10]

Yet despite all of this vacillation, Norman Macleod was a winsome and popular preacher.

---

1. Donald Macleod, *Memoir of Norman Macleod* (London: Daldy, Isbister, 1876), 1:100.
2. Ibid., 1:170.
3. Ibid., 2:228.
4. Ibid., 2:249.
5. Ibid., 2:231.
6. Ibid., 1:275.
7. Ibid., 2:116, 118, 138.
8. Ibid., 1:302.
9. Ibid., 1:315.
10. F. R. Webber, *A History of Preaching in Britain and America* (Milwaukee: Northwestern, 1955), 2:388.

10.5.6 JOHN KENNEDY OF DINGWALL—THE PREACHER WHO WAS FIRM AS A ROCK

> My style of preaching has been described as antiquated, as ignoring the superior enlightenment of these bright times, as making no use of the wondrous results of recent scientific researches. . . . As I judge the position of the age, I desire my preaching to be behind it; for I think that, in

these days, the preacher's work is to be calling back his generation to "the old paths" in which the Lord was found and followed by the fathers. Nor can I discover any difference between the men of this age and those of another as sinners, and I cannot, therefore, see how the gospel which suits the one can be unsuitable to the other.

—John Kennedy of Dingwall

At this time a surge of biblical preaching was complementing an outpouring of rich theological reflection. **James Buchanan** (1804–1870) had a thriving preaching ministry in North Leith. He succeeded Chalmers, and bequeathed us masterpieces of solid theology on the Holy Spirit and on justification by faith alone.[1] Another preaching theologian in the Free Church was **George Smeaton** (1814–1889), who wrote powerful and profound works on the Holy Spirit and two magnificent tomes on the atonement. Another in this brave legion was **S. D. F. Salmond** (1837–1904), principal at Aberdeen and author of *The Christian Doctrine of Immortality,* a lucid and convincing statement of the doctrine of everlasting punishment. Another in this camp who stayed in parish ministry and was known as the prince of Highland preachers was **John Kennedy** of Dingwall (1819–1884), called by some the greatest preacher of his generation in Scotland.

Kennedy was born in a Scottish manse and studied at Aberdeen. He became serious about spiritual things and ministry upon his father's death. Up to that time he had been "clear as an icicle and equally cold."[2] He went out in the Disruption to serve his only charge, the Free Church in Dingwall, where the Lord gave him a ministry in which "He exercised a peculiar fascination over the minds of the Highland population."[3] Kennedy preached services in both Gaelic and English every Lord's Day. It was said he spoke Gaelic as if he knew no English and English as if he knew no Gaelic.[4] He became immensely popular as the speaker for the communion services in the north. Spurgeon himself came up for the dedication of the new Free Church. As early as 1869, Kennedy was troubled with diabetes and traveled extensively to regain his health. Upon visiting the United States, he bonded with Charles Hodge and shrank from Beecher, who so downplayed sin and the Atonement.[5]

Kennedy loved paintings, music, and Shakespeare. He opposed union with the United Presbyterians and had grave reservations about the Moody and Sankey meetings. He was not naturally feisty or combative, as his good friend **Hugh Martin** (1822–1885) observed: "What a pity that our brother Kennedy's modesty muzzles him on the floor of the Assembly."[6] He believed in spoken not read prayers and that preaching was central in worship. His own messages were solidly constructed and described in the *Daily Review:*

> The sermon was built up, block upon block, of granite reasoning. Each of those fundamental propositions was presented with intense and overpowering earnestness. The blocks were laid upon each other red hot. . . . As the discourse went on, and the reasoning became molten into fiery flood . . . the labouring breath struggled into voice and rang over the hillside like a clarion . . . and the whole responding multitude bent forward.[7]

Vintage Kennedy is heard in the following from his sermon "The Preaching of Christ Crucified":

> Pauline preaching is becoming, in the estimation of many, an antiquated kind of thing, which, in an age such as ours, should be quite laid as a fossil on the shelf. And what do they propose to substitute? We preach Christ crucified, and in doing so we preach peace to sinners through "the blood of His cross." O what a blessing is peace with God to a sinner condemned to die! The sinner himself can do nothing to meet the Law's claims . . . but Christ crucified hath done and suffered all that is required in order to a free and full exercise of divine mercy such as shall be to the praise of the divine glory. In preaching Christ crucified there is presented to the sinner this one ground on which he is called to take his stand before the mercy, free and infinite, of God, to receive "with money and without price" the blessing of everlasting peace with God.[8]

---

1. James Buchanan, *The Doctrine of Justification* (Grand Rapids: Baker, 1867, 1955). Included in the Cunningham Lectureship, this volume still stands as the single best treatment of this vital Reformation doctrine.
2. Maurice Roberts, "Dr. John Kennedy—A Memorial Sketch," *Banner of Truth* (August–September 1984): 4.
3. Ibid., 3.
4. Donald Beaton, *Some Noted Ministers of the Northern Highlands* (Glasgow: Free Presbyterian, 1929, 1985), 274.
5. Alan P. F. Sell, *Defending and Declaring the Faith: Some Scottish Examples 1860–1920* (Exeter: Paternoster, 1987), 19. John Kennedy is the first of eight notable defenders of the faith analyzed in this glowing work. Hugh Martin's volumes of preaching on Jonah and *The Shadow of Calvary* are among the finest of the wheat.
6. Roberts, "Dr. John Kennedy," 20.
7. Ibid., 2.
8. F. R. Webber, *A History of Preaching in Britain and America* (Milwaukee: Northwestern, 1955), 2:408–9.

10.5.7 William B. Robertson of Irvine—The Poet-Preacher

> The doctrine of the Atonement might be called the doctrine of Scripture; and woe be to them that would swerve in the least away from that. It was very sad to think that earnest, gifted men like the late Robertson of Brighton, should swerve from this soul-saving truth, and go their weeping, woeful way, in darkness.
>
> —William B. Robertson

One of the truly soaring spirits in the Scottish pulpit at this time as agreed by all hands was **William Bruce Robertson** of Irvine (1820–1886). The old-timers would often say of even a good preacher that "the vintage was not equal to the gleanings in Robertson's time." He spent his entire ministerial life in Irvine, where David Dickson (cf. 7.5.2) had such a signal ministry. Robertson was born near Stirling and educated at Glasgow, where he was deeply influenced by Candlish and Chalmers. He entered the divinity hall of the United Secession Church in Edinburgh in 1838. One of his classmates was **John Ker** (1819–1886), who was to become professor of practical training for the ministry.[1] Ker recalled the originality and imagination of young Robertson as he preached on King Ahaz and the "eerie awesomeness" of the impression.[2] Robertson also knew De Quincey and went with Ker to study at Halle under Tholuck and Neander.

Licensed in 1843, he began his preaching in the Cotton Row Church (U.P.) in Irvine, a kind of sleepy hollow of not six thousand souls. One who saw him mount the pulpit in those days was indignant that one so young should dare to preach. But that same observer reported, "[When] I heard him pray, I felt that the most aged might sit at his feet."[3] A doctrinal preacher, Robertson gave moving expository lectures as well as sermons. His lifting sermon from Exodus 24:11, "They saw God and did eat and drink," had three heads:

I. To eat and drink and not see God is sin.
II. To eat and drink and not see God because of tears is sorrow.
III. To eat and drink and see God, that is salvation.[4]

He presented an unforgettable series on "The Silences of the Bible" that gave a "sense that he spoke from immediate inspiration." He loved to preach on praise to God and was in great demand for the communion seasons. Robertson held devoutly to a view of the premillennial return of Christ. At times some felt his sermons were "a little too luscious in their ripeness and unformed in their splendor."[5] His magnificent sermon on Ephesians 4:30 on not grieving the Holy Spirit, however, is straight as an arrow:

I. A great period: "the day of Redemption";
II. A great privilege: "being sealed by the Holy Spirit of God";
III. A great practical requirement: "grieve not the Holy Spirit of God";
IV. The grand persuasion to the performance of the requirement—that which knits up the whole: "grieve not the Holy Spirit of God by whom ye are sealed."[6]

Robertson loved poetry and wrote much of it himself. Some called him the modern Jeremy Taylor. Imagination was a dominant faculty in his preaching, and his picture images were most rare. He enjoyed preaching in the open air. His congregation was rocked by the great revival of 1859, and to hold the influx of people a new building, called Trinity Church, was constructed. After a long illness, William Robertson died in Mentone, France, just as Spurgeon had.

1. John Edwards, *Nineteenth-Century Preachers and Their Methods* (London: Charles Kelly, 1902), 65ff. We have already benefited from Ker's pioneering lectures on preaching and especially on German preaching.
2. Arthur Guthrie, *Robertson of Irvine: Poet-Preacher* (Edinburgh: Menzies, 1889), 25, 209, 318.
3. Ibid., 56.
4. Ibid., 74.
5. Ibid., 122.
6. Ibid., 125ff.

10.5.8 *ADOLPH SAPHIR—THE HEBREW CHRISTIAN WHO REALLY PREACHED CHRIST*

There subsists an essential and vital connection between the eternal Word of God and the written Word which testifies of Him, of His person and work, of His sufferings and glory. . . . It is impossible for us to understand the nature of Scripture unless we view it in relation to the Son of God, the Messiah of Israel, the Redeemer of God's people; for He is the centre and kernel of the inspired record.

—A. A. Saphir

The background of the startling ministry of **Aaron Adolph Saphir** (1831–1891) was the Church of Scotland mission to the Jews of Budapest. This was conceived providentially in Candlish's proposal, McCheyne's trip to Palestine (cf. 9.1.3), and the ministry in Budapest opened by Rabbi "Rab" Duncan (cf. 9.1.6).

From a distinguished old Jewish family, Adolph Saphir avowed faith in Jesus the Messiah. Saphir went with Duncan and Alfred Edersheim, another convert, back to Edinburgh to perfect his English.[1] From 1844 to 1848 he studied in Berlin, where he was received by Neander and Hengstenberg. He later recalled this time: "I suffered for years from the teachings of Scheiermacher's disciples when I was about seventeen."[2]

In 1854 Saphir was ordained a Free Church missionary to the Jews and served briefly in Hamburg. Always coping with physical infirmity, he served a succession of English Presbyterian churches and launched his amazing writing ministry, out of which came such widely-read titles as *Conversion, Christ and the Scriptures* and *The Divine Unity of Scripture*. Thoroughly premillennial, Saphir watched constantly for Christ's imminent return. His expository lectures on Hebrews are classic and give a clue to the richness of his preaching.[3] Always meticulously prepared, he preached extempore. He later wrote:

The preaching of the gospel, however legitimately allied to natural and mental acquirements, must always retain the mark of crucifixion. It does not become us to be orators. There is an element in human eloquence, which is not according to the gospel of Christ. Preaching is more than an exposition of Scripture; it is a reproduction of Scripture . . . the gospel is preached with the Holy Ghost sent down from heaven . . .[4]

Franz Delitzsch of Leipzig, a friend of evangelism to the Jews, wrote the introduction to Saphir's influential tract "Who Is an Apostate?" Saphir convened a Free Church Conference on the Jews in 1889, where Andrew Bonar also spoke. "The future of Israel is bright and glorious," Saphir proclaimed. The future restoration of Israel is a certainty.[5] A typical exposition of his is "The Christian's Hope" from 1 John 3:2. Here Saphir nicely divides the text and the sermon:

I. We shall see Christ as he is
    A. The object of our vision
    B. The manner of our vision
        1. How we have it at present
        2. How we shall have it in the future
II. We shall be like Christ
    A. We shall know him as we are known
    B. We shall be healed[6]

When Saphir's wife died, he was so frail that he could not attend the funeral. William Wingate stayed with him. A day later, Aaron Adolph Saphir was taken home also.

---

1. Gavin Carlyle, *Mighty in the Scripture: A Memoir of Adolph Saphir* (London: John Shaw, 1894), 17. The report was by the missionary, the Reverend William Wingate, grandfather of Lt. Gen. Orde Wingate, a well-known British military genius and lover of the "hope of Israel." On the Scottish mission, see David L. Larsen, *Jews, Gentiles and the Church: A New Perspective on History and Prophecy* (Grand Rapids: Discovery House, 1995), 129.
2. Ibid., 64, 251.
3. Adolph Saphir, *Epistle to the Hebrews* (Grand Rapids: Kregel, 1874, 1983). Nine of his titles are published in this series. Arno Gaebelein of *Our Hope* magazine picked up Saphir's writings and popularized them in the U.S.
4. Carlyle, *Mighty in the Scripture*, 354.
5. Ibid., 299, 303.
6. Ibid., 303.

10.5.9 *JOHN R. MACDUFF—THE PREACHER WITH A POWERFUL PEN*

The righteousness of that law must be "fulfilled;" its requirements must be met, and its sanctities upheld, either in the person of the sinner or of his divine Surety . . . by His voluntary substitution and suretyship He has once and for ever solved the momentous problem—settled the awful alternative, condemn or not condemn.

—John R. MacDuff

Here is a preacher who touched many lives through his more than seventy-five books and his preaching of the Word with effect and power. **John R. MacDuff**

(1818–1895) was born in the parish of Scone in Perthshire. He was brought to evangelical conviction and experience through Dr. Chalmers while studying at Edinburgh. MacDuff served several congregations, including the Sandyford Church in Glasgow, "where he had a large, handsome church building and a large, intelligent congregation."[1] His books are sermonic in nature but are richly biblical and devotional. Among many favorites is his series of studies on John 4 under the title *Noontide at Sychar*.[2] Sermons such as "The Gift of God and Living Water" and "The Heavenly Food and the Field of Harvest" are especially tantalizing. Also of note is his volume on *In Christo* or *The Monogram of St. Paul*.[3] These studies of the "in Christ" formula in the apostle Paul are doctrinally probing and practical.

---

1. F. R. Webber, *A History of Preaching in Britain and America* (Milwaukee: Northwestern, 1955), 2:400.
2. John R. MacDuff, *Noontide at Sychar* (London: James Nisbet, 1877).
3. John R. MacDuff, *In Christo* (London: Charles J. Thynne, n.d.).

10.5.10 HENRY DRUMMOND—THE UNIVERSITY PREACHER WHO TOUCHED STUDENTS

> Evangelism was the master-passion of his life . . . He found the heart of Christianity in a personal friendship with Jesus Christ, and it was his ambition as an evangelist to introduce men to Christ. It was a simple message; but delivered with the thousand subtle influences radiating forth from his strong and rich personality, it evoked a wonderful response in the crowded meeting and in the quiet talk in the streets or in young men's lodgings.
>
> —Rev. D. M. Ross

A singular spirit among the preachers at the end of the century was **Henry Drummond** (1851–1897), who had an unusually effective outreach ministry to university men in Scotland and beyond. He touched Arthur James Balfour, later British Prime Minister and Foreign Secretary, Von Moltke of Germany, and countless others. Drummond was born in Stirling in a traditional Scottish Free Church home. After studying at the University in Edinburgh starting at age fifteen, he entered New College for the divinity course.

Drummond had been moved by F. W. Robertson's sermon on "The Loneliness of Christ" (cf. 9.3.5) and joined with classmates such as James Stalker, George Adam Smith (who later wrote a fine biography of Drummond), and John Watson (Ian Maclaren).[1] While he was somewhat influenced by A. B. Davidson's concessions to biblical criticism, Drummond was soon caught up in the Moody-Sankey mission of 1873 to 1875. He organized meetings for students with Stalker and spoke to thousands about Christ. He became a deep friend of D. L. Moody.[2] Returning to school, Drummond finished his course. Meanwhile, the Moody campaigns filled the theological halls of Scotland. While appointed as lecturer in natural science in the Free Church College in Glasgow, Drummond assisted both Hood Wilson in Barclay Church in Edinburgh early on and then Marcus Dods in Renfield Church in Glasgow.

The Free Church had come into existence in large part because the sermons of the moderates "might have been preached in a heathen temple as fitly as in St. Giles."[3] Drummond was torn, and though he had no comment on the Robertson Smith case in 1879, he did not know which way to turn. He traveled widely, visiting America several times and ministering at Northfield, where his ideas on evolution were a problem.[4] He pursued geologic and evangelistic aims in Africa and ministered in Australia and the South Seas. His sermon from 1 Corinthians 13 on "The Greatest Thing in the World" was one of Moody's favorites.[5] It is a classic of exposition and elegance. Drummond spoke in house meetings to the cream of British society. He also worked with C. T. Studd of Cambridge in the great Edinburgh Students' Revival of 1884 and 1885.[6] His distinctive style is recalled for us:

> Attired in a well-cut frock-coat . . . with a voice that reached the farthest seat in the auditorium in tones of sweet reasonableness . . . frequently lasting fifty minutes . . . his vocabulary was a rich one . . . he had read widely in belles lettres as well as in science and theology; he had traveled much; and enriched by fitting figures of speech or apt illustration, he spoke under the influence of the master-passion of his life.[7]

I can well remember the impression of reading Drummond's three great sermons on the will of God in my own early collegiate years. His majestic sermon on "Ill-Temper: The Elder Brother" is peerless, and his message on "The Eccentricity of True Religion" from Mark 3:21 is unforgettable. He preached on "The Christian's Clairvoyance" out of 2 Corinthians 4:18 and masterfully on the facts of sin and salvation.[8]

In his last years, Drummond became very ill and died of a malignant disease of the bones. He had never married. Henry Drummond was a light that burned brightly and then sadly flickered out in such physical extremity.

---

1. James Y. Simpson, *Henry Drummond in Famous Scots Series* (Edinburgh: Oliphant Anderson, 1901), 32.
2. Ibid., 43, 45.
3. W. Robertson Nicoll, *The Ideal Life* (New York: Dodd Mead, 1898), 6.
4. Cuthbert Lennox, *The Practical Life Work of Henry Drummond* (New York: James Pott, 1901), 152ff.
5. Henry Drummond, *Addresses* (Chicago: Revell, 1891), 7ff.
6. Lennox, *The Practical Life Work of Henry Drummond,* 96.
7. Ibid., 100.
8. These sermons are all found in Nicoll, *The Ideal Life.*

10.5.11 PRINCIPAL RAINY—THE PREACHER-PROFESSOR WHO DEFINED A MOVEMENT

> Learn to serve Christ on the great scale, and even, if the scene of your work be narrow or obscure, serve Him on the grand principles which make life strong, noble and spacious. Never look at any period of the past with a timid or a cringing heart. From the greatest and most impressive of past services and departed servants turn to your own work with the thought—I also, I too, am a servant of Christ Jesus.
>
> —Robert Rainy

Nineteenth-century Scotland saw a brilliant array of scholars and preachers. **Robert Flint** (1834–1910) was born in a shepherd's cottage, served as assistant to Norman Macleod, and followed William Milligan at Kilconquhar. While his sermons "occasionally flew over their heads like birds of paradise," Flint was indeed noteworthy.[1] **A. B. Davidson** (1831–1902) succeeded Duncan at New College, but who was "doubting at every pore."[2] Yet Stalker spoke of Davidson's gripping preaching, and many a student and congregant could testify, "His prayer revived my drooping feelings."[3] Both **Andrew Fairbairn** and **Patrick Fairbairn** were able preachers and scholars, and **George Milligan,** minister in Caputh in Perthshire, produced an outstanding commentary on 1 Thessalonians.[4]

But chief among these is **Robert Rainy** (1826–1906), who after Cunningham and Candlish presided at the defining hours of the Scottish Free Church. The son of a professor of medicine in Glasgow, Rainy was related to William E. Gladstone and the Balfours. He served the Free Church in Huntly, where George MacDonald had his roots. He attracted notice for his solid preaching at the High Free Church in Edinburgh over eight years. Still, his chief biographer acknowledges, "He did not have the exuberant oratory with which Dr. Guthrie drew a crowd of all classes, nor even the immense nervous force with which Dr. Candlish kept his great congregation at St. George's."[5] Rainy tended to be a bit heavy, but his sermons are luminous and direct.[6] My particular favorite is "Mutability and Endurance" based on 1 Peter 1:24–25.

In 1862 Rainy took Cunningham's chair in church history, which he filled for thirty-eight years. As principal he had to handle the Robertson Smith case. The brilliant young Smith had studied with Wellhausen and had given way to higher critical views, including the abolition of predictive prophecy. Salmond defended him, A. B. Davidson remained silent, and Andrew Bonar moved for Smith's suspension from teaching after a rebuke achieved no alteration. Bonar's motion carried by one vote. Although Rainy was evangelical ("I remain orthodox on the atonement," he claimed), he tried to walk both sides of the street and found himself successively defending Marcus Dods, Henry Drummond, A. B. Bruce, and George Adam Smith. The soul of the Free Church was at stake. K. R. Ross notes of Rainy, "Personally he did not find criticism a major issue and he underestimated the degree to which it provoked questions regarding biblical authority."[7]

In the ensuing discussion of preaching, Rainy distinguished between the moralistic preaching of the moderates—which was, as Lord Roseberry described it, "flat as decanted champagne"—and the evangelical preaching of the gospel.[8]

Three times Rainy was moderator of the General Assembly and finally in 1900 steered the merger of the Free Church with the United Presbyterians. Asked how he managed to maintain any semblance of equanimity in all of this conflict, Rainy's oft-quoted response rings a chord: "Oh, man, I am happy at home."[9]

Although Rainy was a successor to the fathers of the Disruption, he catalyzed the liberalization of the Free Church. Ross observed that Rainy was unduly set on building a consensus "when something more prophetic was needed. . . . The fact that his leadership was characterized by complacency and opportunism, rather than initiative and conviction, accounts in part for the loss of ground which the Free Church suffered in his time."[10]

---

1. Donald Macmillan, *The Life of Robert Flint* (London: Hodder and Stoughton, 1914). Flint went on to teach at St. Andrews, Edinburgh (where he succeeded Thomas J. Crawford, whose *Doctrine of the Atonement* was sound. Flint's Baird Lecture in 1876 on theism (Edinburgh: Blackwood, 1887) is a classic.
2. James Strahan, *A. B. Davidson* (London: Hodder and Stoughton, 1917) shows how his study with Ewald at Gottingen and the influence of Driver in the U.S. made him "a noncommittal article."
3. Richard Allan Riesen, *Criticism and Faith in Late Victorian Scotland* (Lanham, Md.: University Press of America, 1985), 322.
4. George Milligan, *St. Paul's Epistles to the Thessalonians* (Grand Rapids: Eerdmans, 1908, 1952).
5. Patrick Carnegie Simpson, *The Life of Principal Rainy* (London: Hodder and Stoughton, 1909), 1:128.
6. Robert Rainy, *Sojourning with God and Other Sermons* (London: Hodder and Stoughton, 1902).
7. K. R. Ross, "Robert Rainy" in *Dictionary of Scottish Church History and Theology,* ed. Nigel M. de S. Cameron (Downers Grove, Ill.: InterVarsity Press, 1993), 690.
8. Simpson, *The Life of Principal Rainy,* 1:417ff.
9. Ibid., 2:92.
10. Ross, "Robert Rainy," 690.

10.6 THE ENGLISH ESTUARY

Depend on it, my friends, that there is no security whatever except in standing upon the faith of our fathers and saying with them that the Blessed olde Book is "God's Word written" from the very first syllable down to the very last, and from the last to the first.

—Lord Shaftesbury

It aimed at bringing back, on a large scale, and by an aggressive movement, the Cross, and all that the Cross essentially implies.

—Prime Minister William E. Gladstone speaking of the Evangelicals

Meanwhile, the religious climate in England, Wales, and Ireland was much like that of Scotland, albeit even more fissured and fractured. Evangelicals in and out of the Church of England were burdened to stress the authority of the Word of God, clear teaching on original sin, and the necessity of conversion and justification by faith alone. Other vital doctrines included eternal punishment, millenarianism and the return of our Lord, special providence, and the assurance of salvation.[1] Strong emphasis was also placed on liturgical piety, the family and the home, missionary and philanthropic endeavor, and the response to the world. An impressive array of evangelical scholars began turning out solid commentary and theology. A magnificent host of preachers from many backgrounds entered the fray to do battle for the gospel.

Authors of fiction occasionally reflected certain of these concerns as seen in "the apocalyptic mood of late romanticism," but on the whole writers either misunderstood biblical faith or were downright hostile to it. Thackery's "wild onslaught upon sermons and preachers" is a case in point.[2] George Eliot understood the truth but mocked it, and Samuel Butler showed suspicion of emotional conversion. Trollope was generally disdainful. Dickens assaulted evangelicalism. Charlotte Yonge's novels carried the Tractarian message, and George MacDonald detested evangelicalism. Nonetheless, Gladstone endorsed Mrs. Humphrey Ward's concern about negative scholarship as seen in *Robert Elsmere*.[3]

Amid this maelstrom of confusion and religious pandemonium, God graciously raised up some of the best and most biblical preaching the British Isles ever saw.

---

1. Elizabeth Jay, *The Religion of the Heart: Anglican Evangelicals and the Nineteenth-Century Novel* (Oxford: Clarendon, 1979). She underestimates the evangelical scholarly enterprise as if T. R. Birks were the only one (40).
2. Ibid., 122.
3. Robert Lee Wolff, *Gains and Losses: Novels of Faith and Doubt in Victorian England* (New York: Garland, 1977). Cf. also my upcoming, *The Irresistible Rewards of Reading: A Theological Guide to Great Literature* (Grand Rapids: Kregel, 1999).

10.6.1 Marcus Rainsford—The Irish Anglican Who Excavated the Text

> For centuries there has not been a time of so much practical, hearty work, so much earnest preaching, so much instruction and consolation given, so much care for the poor and for the young.
>
> —Gladstone to the queen, 1874

As in the United States and Scotland, by midcentury in England a massive attack was mounted on the authority of Scripture. Rebellion against the preaching of repentance and substitutionary atonement was rampant. Benjamin Jowett at Oxford hated imputation, and the move away from teaching on hell quickened. **John William Colenso** (1814–1883), who became bishop of Natal in South Africa, attacked "penal substitution—liberating God from the charge of being a 'blood-thirsty pagan tyrant.'"[1] Prime Minister Gladstone commendably held to depravity and the cross and maintained good rapport with evangelicals. He allied with Wilberforce in reforming aspects of the Church of England.

In the face of it all, "The sermon was still an effective means of persuasion."[2] **John Bird Sumner** was the strongly evangelical archbishop of Canterbury starting in 1828 and **Archibald Campbell Tait,** conciliatory to nonconformists and evangelicals, was first bishop of London and in 1868 became archbishop of Canterbury. The son of Scottish Presbyterians, he was persuasive but not eloquent. Five of his six children died of scarlet fever in 1856. Tait was called the layman's bishop. He made many positive appointments, including the partisan evangelical, J. C. Ryle to be bishop of Liverpool. His Presbyterian low-church views were encouraging to evangelicals in the Church of England.[3]

One of the choicest examples of strong biblical preaching in the Church of England at this time was **Marcus Rainsford** (1820–1897). Rainsford had the decisive influence on **W. H. Griffith Thomas** and was much sought after by D. L. Moody, with whom he developed some remarkable "gospel dialogues."[4] Though descended from Norsemen who settled in Lancashire, Rainsford's ancestors had moved to Ireland, where he was born. At age sixteen he was startled by a dream and sought the Lord, early finding Romaine's *Life of Faith* to show him the way. He graduated from Trinity College, Dublin, and began serving in 1850 as vicar in Dundalk, a town of some ten thousand mostly Roman Catholic inhabitants.[5]

The revival of 1859 deeply touched Rainsford's ministry and his churches. In 1866 he took the call to St. John's, Belgrave Square in London, a strong and fashionable church. His biblical preaching stirred up a storm—the Prince of Wales was often there, as was Gladstone, and the Lord Chancellor became a member. After working so closely with Moody in London, Rainsford was invited to Northfield and made a memorable impression there. He preached the imminent return of Christ and sought conversions in each of his sermons.

His son William described Rainsford's "fine, carrying voice and Irish eloquence" and "his precious devotion to close and systematic study of the Holy Scriptures."[6] Sadly, William abandoned the views of his father.

Rainsford's expository studies in John 17, titled *Our Lord Prays for His Own,* exceed even Thomas Manton's glorious study.[7] His books of lectures on the believer's standing in Christ from Romans 5, 6, and 7 moved Griffith Thomas.[8] Another fine collection of his sermons shows them to be "soaked through and through with the Word of God." A glowing message on "Did I Receive the Holy Spirit When I Believed?" from Acts 19 is divided into six parts.[9] His exegesis is painstaking and rich. Marcus Rainsford offers Anglican biblical preaching at its best.

1. Boyd Hilton, *The Age of Atonement: The Influence of Evangelicalism, 1795–1865* (Oxford: Clarendon, 1988), 383.
2. P. T. Marsh, *The Victorian Church in Decline: Archbishop Tait 1868–1882* (Pittsburgh: University of Pittsburgh, 1969), 6. This book shows how after Newman's secession, Liddon and Stanley "exerted winning influence."
3. Sidney Dark, *Seven Archbishops* (London: Eyre and Spottiswoode, 1944), 197ff.

4. Marcus Rainsford, *Our Lord Prays for His Own* (Chicago: Moody, 1876, n.d.), 244ff.

5. S. Maxwell Coder, "Biographical Introduction" in Rainsford, *Our Lord Prays for His Own,* 13.

6. Ibid., 15.

7. Ibid. Every chapter is a gem. The first message is on "Father, the hour is come" (25).

8. Marcus Rainsford, *Lectures on Romans 5* (London: John Hoby, n.d.); *Lectures on Romans 6* (London: Charles Thynne, 1898); *Lectures on Romans 7* (London: John Hoby, n.d.).

9. Marcus Rainsford, *The Fullness of God* (London: S. W. Partridge, 1898), 62ff.

10.6.2 JOHN CHARLES RYLE—THE BISHOP WHO PREACHED AND BUILT

You preach the Gospel of Jesus Christ so fully and clearly that everybody can understand it. If Christ crucified has not His rightful place in your sermons, and sin is not exposed as it should be, and your people are not plainly told what they ought to be and do, your preaching is no use.

—John Charles Ryle

With evangelicalism taking hits from rationalism, hedonism, and ritualism, one outstanding preacher and writer was the first Anglican bishop of Liverpool, **John Charles Ryle** (1816–1900). Ryle embodied the pastoral strengths important to evangelicals.[1] Millions of copies of his tracts and other writings, such as his *Expository Thoughts on the Gospels,* have made a substantial impact. As a moderate Calvinist, Ryle believed in general rather than particular atonement and was a staunch premillennialist. A bit skittish about the Keswick deeper life teaching, he also felt that the ritualism of the Tractarians was incongruous with the essentially Protestant nature of the Church of England.

Methodist by background, Ryle studied at Eton and Christ Church, Oxford. While out hunting one day, an old Eton friend rebuked him for his profanity. He was sobered by the incident, and later was converted in the face of the truth of Ephesians 2:8–9.[2] Immediately he began to gobble up books by Wilberforce, John Angell James, John Newton, and Bickersteth. Upon graduation he served as curate in Exbury and then took pastoral appointments in Winchester, Helmingham, and Stradbrooke. Although he had a somewhat antisocial disposition, his preaching filled these places to "suffocation," as he put it.[3] Again and again he was named select preacher at both Cambridge and Oxford. In 1880, this man "who lived to be missed" was named the first bishop of Liverpool, by now a teeming city of seven hundred thousand, which had come into such dominance during the surging days of empire-building.

Ryle's preaching style was increasingly plain and direct, with short sentences that allowed only one subordinate clause. He carefully divided the text and discourse with strong bridging to daily life and the adept use of telling illustrations. He was a tall, well-built man. As one reporter testified, Ryle spoke to a crowd of four thousand "with a force and earnestness which have been rarely equalled, and which riveted the attention of the vast audience from commencement to finish."[4]

His friend Tollemache, when he felt that Ryle had preached long enough, would occasionally stand up in the service and look at his watch. Ryle's style was earthy and true to his Reformed convictions; he refused to dress "in an embroidered cope and mitre and carry a pastoral staff."[5] He railed at "the enormous folly of baptismal regeneration" but purred at what he called "the unspeakable beauty and excellence of the doctrine of the Second Advent."

In 1883 he welcomed D. L. Moody and company to Liverpool. Twelve years later Ryle sponsored the Liverpool General Christian Mission with W. Hay Aitken. Among his close friends were Canon **Cyril Garbett,** who preached at his enthronement as bishop,[6] **Bishop W. Boyd Carpenter** of Ripon,[7] and **Hugh MacNeil,** the impetuous Irish flame-thrower who preached without notes and only a small pocket Bible in his hand.

Of his children only his daughter shared his views, and his favorite son Herbert, who became a bishop, went off in another theological direction, as did his descendants Martin and Gilbert Ryle, men of auspicious scientific accomplishment but no faith.

Ryle's tracts such as "Are You Converted?" and "Are You Free?" had immense circulation. A collection of his tracts on divisive matters, titled "Knots Untied," argues that controversy is a positive duty on key issues.[8] Likewise his messages on "The New Birth" and "Practical Religion" were widely read, as was his "No Uncertain Sound," earlier known as "Charges and Addresses." Vintage Ryle is *Holiness: Its Nature, Hindrances, Difficulties and Roots.* The laudatory foreword by D. Martyn Lloyd-Jones, who speaks of him as "always scriptural and expository," is worthwhile. Messages in this collection on "Sanctification" and "The Ruler of the Waves" show careful organization and faithful adherence to the text.[9]

J. C. Ryle's strength was "His steadfast theological convictions which did not perceptibly change throughout his life."[10] Here is a preacher of purpose and pertinacity.

---

1. D. N. Samuel, ed., *The Evangelical Succession in the Church of England* (Cambridge, Mass.: James Clarke, 1979), 76.
2. J. C. Ryle, *A Self-Portrait* (Swengel, Pa.: Reiner, 1975), 40.
3. Peter Toon and Michael Smout, *John Charles Ryle: Evangelical Bishop* (Swengel, Pa.: Reiner, 1976), 37.
4. Ibid., 46.
5. Ibid., 76.
6. Cyril Garbett wrote the classic defense of biblical infallibility, *God's Word Written* (New York: E. P. Dutton, 1879).
7. Bishop William Boyd Carpenter was one of the most eloquent and biblical preachers among the Victorian prelates. See H. D. A. Major, *The Life and Letters of William Boyd Carpenter* (London: John Murray, 1925), 115ff. His noted lectures on preaching given at Cambridge are worthwhile: *Lectures on Preaching* (London: Macmillan, 1895).
8. J. C. Ryle, *Knots Untied,* 31st ed. (London: James Clarke, 1954). "A man of granite with the heart of a child."

9. J. C. Ryle, *No Uncertain Sound* (Edinburgh: Banner of Truth, 1903, 1978). Ryle released his own son as examining chaplain in Liverpool because of the latter's concessions to higher criticism. J. C. Ryle, *Holiness* (Grand Rapids: Kregel, 1956). The thesis of these sermons is simply, "No holiness, no happiness."

10. Ibid., 104. The cathedral he longed to construct in Liverpool was not built until the time of Bishop F. J. Chavasse.

10.6.3 ALEXANDER MACLAREN—EXPOSITOR WITHOUT PEER

I cannot ever recall any hesitation as to being a minister. . . . It just had to be.

To efface oneself is one of a preacher's first duties.

I thank God for the early days of obscurity and struggle.

I have always found that my own comfort and efficiency in preaching have been in direct proportion to the depth of my daily communion with God. I know no way in which we can do our work but in fellowship with God, in keeping up the habits of the student's life, which needs some power of saying "No" and by conscientious pulpit preparation. The secret of success is trust in God and hard work.

—Alexander Maclaren

Known as the prince of expositors and described as "the supreme example, the perfect type, of the classic Protestant tradition of expository preaching," **Alexander Maclaren** (1826–1910), is one of our best models in commending strong biblical preaching. Born in Glasgow of Highland stock and reared in a merchant's home, Maclaren of Manchester followed his parents under the influence of the Haldanes into the Baptist church. He was a classmate of Robert Rainy (cf. 10.5.11) at the University of Glasgow, from which he went to Stepney College in London (forerunner of Regents Park College) to study for the Baptist ministry in 1842. The tall, shy, silent Scot did not impress the examiner, but he dug into Hebrew and Greek and mastered "the holy tongues." "Binney taught me to preach," he would say later, referring to the notable preacher of the old Weigh House Chapel (cf. 9.3.2).[1]

Maclaren's dedication to exegeting the original text was a lifelong hallmark. When asked to fill in briefly at the Portland Chapel in Southampton, he found a barnlike building seating eight hundred with fifty on the roll and twenty in attendance. He began to preach and the people kept coming for the rich biblical fare for the next twelve years.

As was his habit throughout life, he gave himself much to study, refusing many invitations beyond his own flock. He would visit his own church families two nights a week. In 1858 he took the call to the Union Chapel in Manchester, where he served for forty-five years. A new church was built during his ministry that seated fifteen hundred people. The sanctuary was typically jammed with two thousand souls. Maclaren's preaching ministry had a long radius. His sermons were printed on Mondays in the *Manchester Guardian.*

Maclaren's listeners were drawn to his beautiful and faultless diction. It was said he served up the Bread of Life on a "three-pronged fork." As Robertson Nicoll exquisitely phrased it: "Maclaren touched every text with a silver hammer and it broke up into three natural and memorable divisions."[2] The sermons we read were preached extempore and transcribed as he preached them. They seldom required editing. "Burn your manuscripts," he counseled preachers. Ernest Jeffs in his *Princes of the Modern Pulpit* recalls it well:

> The charm of Maclaren's preaching was intellectual and artistic. It lay in the logical closeness and firmness of his exposition, the architectural culmination of proof and argument, the warmth and richness of his metaphor and illustration; and under all this was the stern challenge to righteousness and repentance, bringing into the sunshine, so to speak, when the emphasis changes from the God who judges to the Jesus who redeems . . .[3]

Maclaren stayed with his text. He preached for about forty minutes, his sermon delivered in a "rich, musical voice, clear and penetrating," and always with that delightful Scottish brogue.[4] He read Carlyle ravenously, as well as the English poets, Shakespeare, and the Puritans. In that inevitable introspection that follows a message delivered from the heart, Maclaren would say, "Well, I can't help it, I did my best and there I leave it."[5] His commitment was to the infallible Word, and he never "turned from the old conception of a vicarious atonement."[6]

Nicoll surmises that in some respects Maclaren's expositions have never been superseded. His thirty-two original volumes of *Expositions of Holy Scripture* are exceedingly rich—Genesis and Colossians are considered the best. He also did Psalms for the Expositor's Bible. His absolutely astonishing *The Life of David Reflected in the Psalms* is my all-time favorite. His several volumes *Sermons Preached in Manchester* were described by F. B. Meyer as: "a great cathedral, so exquisitely constructed were they, and so entirely complete in proportion." These do, however, present one problem. As some have observed, it can be dangerous to read a Maclaren outline before one preaches. The temptation to preach his outline is too great.

When Binney heard Maclaren preach on "The Lord said by the hand of Moses," he went home and wept. One of the hundreds of sermons we possess, "Mahanaim: The Two Camps" from Genesis 32 is especially recommended:

I. The angels of God meet us on the dusty road of common life.
II. The angels of God meet us punctually at the hour of need.
III. The angels of God come in the shape we need.[7]

He closed the sermon with a great illustration about Gordon of Khartoum. In preaching on "no more sea" from Revelation 21:1, he projected the sea as standing for mystery, frightening power, unrest, distance, and separation.[8] Departing from his custom of staying at home as he grew older, he was twice president of the Baptist Union (breaking with Spurgeon in the Downgrade Controversy) and first president of the Baptist World Alliance (1905), to whose delegates he addressed the following searching words:

> We are crying out for a revival. Dear friends, the revival must begin with each of us by ourselves. Power for service is second. Power for holiness and character is first, and only the man who has let the spirit of God work His will upon him, and do what He will, has a right to expect that he will be filled with the Holy Ghost and with power. Do not get on the wrong track. Your revival, Christian ministers, must begin in your study and on your knees. Your revival must be for yourselves with no thought of service. But if once we have learned where our strength is, we shall never be so foolish as to go forth in our own strength, or we shall be beaten as we deserve to be.[9]

No sermons from the nineteenth century are so thoroughly worth reading as Maclaren's.

1. John C. Carlile, *Alexander Maclaren: The Man and His Message* (New York: Funk and Wagnalls, 1902), 27ff.
2. Johnstone G. Patrick, "A Prince of Preachers: A Ter-Jubilee Tribute to Dr. Alexander Maclaren," *Life of Faith* (February 7, 1976): 7. Also John Bishop, "Alexander Maclaren: A Great Expositor," *Preaching* (July–August 1987): 51–52.
3. John Pitts, "Alexander Maclaren: Monarch of the Pulpit," *Christianity Today* (June 5, 1964): 8.
4. Carlile, *Alexander Maclaren,* 71.
5. E. T. McLaren, *Dr. McLaren of Manchester* (London: Hodder and Stoughton, 1911), 209. E. T. McLaren was the cousin and sister-in-law of Alexander Maclaren and explains the change in the spelling of the name.
6. Carlile, *Alexander Maclaren,* 147.
7. Alexander Maclaren, "Mahanaim: Two Camps" in *Christ in the Heart and Other Sermons* (London: Macmillan, 1887), 195. Maclaren reads well but we are assured that he spoke better than he wrote.
8. Alexander Maclaren, *Sermons Preached in Manchester* (New York: Funk and Wagnalls, 1905), 2:325.
9. McLaren, *Dr. McLaren of Manchester,* 241.

10.6.4 CHARLES HADDON SPURGEON—THE PRINCE OF ALL THE PREACHERS

> The preaching of Christ is the whip that flogs the devil. The preaching of Christ is the thunderbolt, the sound of which makes all hell shake.

> I must and I will make men listen.

> —as a boy preacher

The revealed Word awakened me; but it was the preached Word that saved me.

—Charles Haddon Spurgeon

Spurgeon was called the people's preacher. He had preached a thousand sermons by the time he reached the age of twenty-one. His printed sermons sold twenty-five thousand copies a week. No preacher up to this time had so influenced the masses. He is unique in the history of preaching.[1] He recommended that young preachers "make the pulpit your first business." He said he would rather be a preacher of the gospel than the angel Gabriel. He called the pulpit the Thermopolyae of Christendom. He saw the Reformation as the liberation of the Bible. He added fourteen thousand members in his thirty-seven years at the Metropolitan Tabernacle. Brastow calls him "the Puritan pastoral evangelist . . . the most impressive and permanently successful evangelistic preacher of the age."[2] Prime Minister David Lloyd George called him "the greatest preacher of his age." Ruskin, Gladstone, Florence Nightingale, and General James Garfield, later president of the United States, came to his working-class church to hear him. Helmut Thielicke, the German theologian of the twentieth century, counseled: "Sell all you have and buy Spurgeon." Vincent Van Gogh, the Dutch artist, began ministry preaching in the London slums using Spurgeon's sermons.[3]

Preaching was Spurgeon's life. He claimed to have seen the devil preaching in one of his dreams. When the devil was asked how it was he preached so capably, he replied: "I cannot further mine own cause better than by preaching without unction." Charles Haddon Spurgeon was a Bible preacher with unction.

---

1. G. Holden Pike, *The Life and Work of Charles Haddon Spurgeon* (Edinburgh: Banner of Truth, 1894, 1991), 5:16. The two massive volumes by Pike, who had edited *Sword and Trowel* for Spurgeon, are the best. The single volume without peer is Lewis Drummond, *Spurgeon: Prince of Preachers* (Grand Rapids: Kregel, 1992). For a modest introduction for a beginner, Arnold Dallimore, *Spurgeon* (Chicago: Moody, 1984).
2. Lewis O. Brastow, *Representative Modern Preachers* (New York: Macmillan, 1904), 383–84.
3. Irving Stone, ed., *Dear Theo: Autobiography of Vincent Van Gogh* (New York: Signet, 1937), 16, 19, 38.

The Progress of the Pilgrim

Born in Essex, the oldest of seventeen children, **Charles Haddon Spurgeon** (1834–1892) was the son and grandson of Congregational ministers of Flemish descent. Charles spent the bulk of his childhood with his grandparents and was exposed to Puritan writers, Foxe's *Book of Martyrs,* and especially Bunyan's *Pilgrim's Progress,* which he read through twice a year over his lifetime.

Spurgeon possessed a photographic memory. He attended several schools and began to feel "the evil of sin." He did not share this churning inner turmoil with his parents, but while visiting the small Artillery Street Primitive Methodist Church in Colchester, Spurgeon heard an unidentified preacher pour out his heart to the tiny congregation. The minister spoke from Isaiah 45:22, "Look unto me and be ye saved, all the ends of the earth, for I am God and there is none else."[1] Spurgeon danced all the way home, and recalled, "I wanted to tell the cows!" He immediately began to teach Sunday school, was baptized as a Baptist, and joined the St. Andrew's Street Baptist Church in Cambridge. His mother was clearly disappointed in the latter development, saying, "We had not prayed you would be a Baptist."

For two years Spurgeon preached at the Baptist Church in Waterbeach. His preaching gifts were already in evidence, and his voice unusual. One elderly listener addressed him after a service, "You are the sauciest dog that ever barked in a pulpit."[2] Here also he began his lifelong smoking habit. Spurgeon was never ordained and had no formal training, largely through the mistake of a maid when he missed appointment with the tutor of Stepney College, Dr. Joseph Angus. He did make a point to hear preachers like John Jay and John Angell James and modeled many things well. When he was nineteen he began his ministry at the New Park Street Baptist Church in London, following **Benjamin Keach, John Gill,** and **John Rippon.** On the south side of the river, the church neighborhood reminded Spurgeon of "the black hole of Calcutta" The congregation was down to eighty or so attendees in twelve hundred seats.[3] From the outset of the ministry, a praying nucleus and a passionately preaching pastor experienced an outpouring.

> When I came to New Park Street Chapel it was but a mere handful of people to whom I first preached, yet I could never forget how earnestly they prayed. Sometimes they seemed to plead as though they could really see the Angel of the Covenant present with them, and as if they must have a blessing from him. More than once we were all so awe-struck with the solemnity of the meeting that we sat silent for some moments while the Lord's Power appeared to overshadow us; and all I could do on such occasions was to pronounce the benediction, and say, "Dear friends, we have had the Spirit of God here very manifestly tonight; let us go home and care not to lose His gracious influence." Then down came the blessing; the house was filled with hearers, and many souls were saved.[4]

Hayden attributes the blessing to "sound doctrine" and "loving invitation." Spurgeon never gave an outward invitation, as his friend D. L. Moody did. Although he was a firm Calvinist, he was not systematic in his commitment and held tenaciously to the necessity of human response in repentance and faith. "You don't have to reconcile friends," he replied when he was asked how he handled divine sovereignty and human responsibilities. He was totally committed to evangelism and the need for making "a bee-line" for the cross and Christ's substitutionary death. Yet he was never fully accepted by the Strict Baptists.

The Pattern of the Preaching

Spurgeon knew his Bible and had a personal library of twelve thousand volumes. Although he did not come to his morning sermon until Saturday night or his evening sermon until Sunday afternoon, he was primed to preach to his great urban congregation as the result of much study, compulsive reading, and fervent prayer. "My people pray for me," was his own explanation of what took place. Soon they had to move to Exeter Hall, which seated five thousand people, while the new Metropolitan Tabernacle, which seated six thousand, was being built.

Spurgeon rejected many conventionalities in preaching; he was humorous, dramatic, used catchy titles ("Turn or Burn" on Psalm 7:12), and employed sense appeal particularly in his marvelous illustrations.[5] His voice was natural and easily reached six thousand hearers. His fresh style and forceful Anglo-Saxon discourse connected, and clearly Whitefield was his model. Craig Skinner, who has written widely on Spurgeon, sees his sermonic appeal in his fresh style, his uncommon clarity, his solid doctrine "upon which people could base their lives," and his ability to bridge to people's needs.[6] Some accused him of showmanship, and he did believe in advertising and promotion, but it was because, to use his own words, "I would preach standing on my head if I thought I could convert your souls."[7]

Strictly speaking, Spurgeon was not a classical expositor as was Maclaren. Regarding the Puritans in their eminently textual style, Spurgeon eschewed their "far-fetched similitudes and long-winded sentences."[8] He loved to break a text and was only occasionally textual-topical. Joseph Parker, who loved Henry Ward Beecher, admitted of Beecher that "I could not smell so much as a text in his velvet-collared coat." But Spurgeon regarded Beecher as an evil influence because he did not preach the gospel.[9] Spurgeon's commentary on Matthew was published posthumously, but this was as close as he ever came to expounding the natural thought unit.

Assuaging some of our concerns here is the fact, not frequently noted, that as Spurgeon read the Scripture lesson, he gave a running commentary. Some thought this was as good as the preaching.[10] He always preached without paper, and greatly admired Charles Simeon's ability to outline.[11] But Spurgeon must be read, especially in thematic anthologies, if we are to pick up his thinking on great doctrines.[12] He used to advise giving the people something worth hearing and they would listen like a woman hearing a will read or a condemned man hearing his sentence given by the judge. Spurgeon gave what was worth hearing.

The Power of the Pen

Spurgeon is epochal in the history of preaching not only because of his sermons in London and throughout the British Isles, but also because what he preached he published. Three hundred million copies of his printed works have been in circulation, chiefly his printed sermons.[13] Five hundred thousand copies of his *Lectures to My Students* have been printed, the product of his Friday afternoon lectures and visits to the Pastor's College.[14] Three hundred thousand copies of the quaint *John Ploughman's Talks* have been issued, and 150,000 sets of his massive *Treasury of David* have sat on Bible students' shelves. Two hundred churches in England were planted under the aegis of his ministry and students. Twenty social ministries were established, the chief of which was the great Stockwell Orphanage. He turned down an astronomic financial offer to come to America to preach.

Spurgeon addressed political issues widely in the pages of *Sword and Trowel,* and was a close follower of Gladstone and the Liberal Party until the issue of Irish home rule. He was an avowed pacifist, and spoke out for total abstinence from alcohol. He had a strong aversion to instrumental music but was known for his remarkable soliloquies at the Lord's Table and was a convinced premillennialist. Spurgeon spoke so vehemently against slavery that American publishers occasionally excised his comments on the subject. What an extraordinary influence and impact for the preacher—God blessed His Word as it was preached and then printed.

The Poise of the Person

Like Moody, who attended the Tabernacle and was invited to preach there, Spurgeon was physically "without angles" and very heavy.[15] He was blessed with a happy marriage to Susannah Thompson, but she became an invalid at age thirty-three and was seldom able to attend services after that. They were parents of twin boys, Thomas, who succeeded his father as pastor of the Tabernacle after serving in Auckland, New Zealand, and Charles Jr., who managed the orphanage.[16]

Often lecturing ten times a week, he spoke rapidly—140 words per minute for forty minutes at a time. He took heavy hits from such tragedies as the Royal Surrey Gardens stampede, which happened while he was praying. Seven were killed in that incident and twenty-eight hospitalized. He also suffered from "fainting fits" and depression. From 1871 he was virtually an invalid.[17] He had chronic kidney problems from early on (Bright's disease) and rheumatic gout. Sent abroad repeatedly to recover his health, he died at Mentone in southern France at the age of fifty-seven.

Spurgeon broke with Parker over some theological issues and the theater. He was embroiled in a great controversy over baptismal regeneration, which alienated him perhaps unnecessarily from some of his good friends in the Church of England. The famous Downgrade Controversy led to his resignation from both the Evangelical Alliance and the Baptist Union. He also parted ways with Angus and Maclaren. The Downgrade Controversy was a sticky affair in which he had problems with his own brother James, who was associate pastor at the Tabernacle. Spurgeon made his move essentially out of a growing concern for liberal incursions and inroads into the Baptist Union.

In a beautiful issue on Spurgeon, *Christian History* magazine properly comes to the conclusion that Charles Haddon Spurgeon was the greatest preacher in the nineteenth century. The sixty thousand people who passed his coffin after his death bore testimony to that assertion.

1. Lewis Drummond, *Spurgeon: Prince of Preachers* (Grand Rapids: Kregel, 1992), 116.
2. G. Holden Pike, *The Life and Works of Charles Haddon Spurgeon* (Edinburgh: Banner of Truth, 1894, 1991), 1:69.
3. Eric W. Hayden, *A History of Spurgeon's Tabernacle* (Pasadena, Tex.: Pilgrim Publications, 1962, 1971).
4. Eric W. Hayden, *Spurgeon on Revival: A Biblical and Theological Approach* (Grand Rapids: Zondervan, 1962), 14. See also Iain Murray, *The Forgotten Spurgeon,* 2d ed. (Edinburgh: Banner of Truth, 1973). A bit tilted.
5. Drummond, *Spurgeon,* 282. Jay Adams, *Sense Appeal in the Sermons of Charles Haddon Spurgeon* (Grand Rapids: Baker, 1975). Studies both titles and sermons. A most revealing study.
6. Craig Skinner, "The Preaching of Charles Haddon Spurgeon," *Baptist History and Heritage* (October 1984): 16–26.
7. Drummond, *Spurgeon,* 283.
8. Pike, *The Life and Works of Charles Haddon Spurgeon,* 5:83.
9. Ibid., 3:71; 5:67.
10. Ibid., 2:177; 3:37, 67.
11. Drummond, *Spurgeon,* 295.
12. Charles Haddon Spurgeon, *The Passion and Death of Christ* (Grand Rapids: Eerdmans, n.d.).
13. *The Metropolitan Tabernacle Pulpit* in 57 volumes is the most popular set; *Spurgeon's Sermons* by Funk and Wagnalls was also widely distributed.
14. C. H. Spurgeon, *Lectures to My Students* (Grand Rapids: Zondervan, 1972) has gone into many printings.
15. Pike, *The Life and Works of Charles Haddon Spurgeon,* 5:80.
16. Craig Skinner, *Spurgeon and Son* (Grand Rapids: Kregel, 1999). Traces how James Spurgeon, the brother and sometimes associate (also pastor of the Croyden Tabernacle), promoted A. T. Pierson, an American Presbyterian, and baptized him in West Croydon, but his son Thomas took the call in 1894. The Tabernacle burned in 1898, and a new building was constructed. The health of Thomas, who served for fourteen years, finally broke, and A. C. Dixon came from America to serve from 1911 to 1919.
17. Pike, *The Life and Works of Charles Haddon Spurgeon,* 5:24.

10.6.5 JOSEPH PARKER—THE PREACHER WITH PERSONALITY

Sunday is my festival day. I love Sunday. All the days of the week lead up to it and I hold high festival with my God and my people every Sabbath.

You must study the idea of your text: try to pierce it to its very heart and, having seized the truth, expound it with all simplicity and earnestness.
—Joseph Parker

To him, preaching was "dignified conversation" and a propulsive passion. When asked what his hobby was, he replied "preaching." When pressed what else beside preaching, he insisted: "Preaching, nothing but preaching. Everything with me ministers to preaching."[1] Sometimes called the "Beecher of England," **Joseph Parker** (1830–1902) came from Hexham in the far north of England, the son of a stonemason (as were Thomas Carlyle and D. L. Moody). He had only common school education but taught himself Greek in his late teens. His stalwart and stubborn father led the family from the Independent (or Congregational) church to the Methodists. Converted at the age of twelve, Parker later visualized the scene:

> I remember the Sunday night when, walking with my father and a most intelligent Sunday School teacher, I declared my love to Christ, and asked him to take my child-heart into His own gracious keeping . . . It was a summer evening, according to the reckoning of the calendar, but according to a higher calendar it was in very deed a Sunday morning, through whose white light and emblematic dew and stir of awakening life I saw the gates of the Kingdom and the face of the King.[2]

At eighteen Parker felt the call into the Lord's vineyard and preached his first sermon most unexpectedly on the text in Matthew which reads: "It shall be more tolerable for Tyre and Sidon in the judgment than for you."[3] Being a Congregationalist at heart, he wrote Dr. Campbell, pastor of the Whitefield's Tabernacle, Moorlands, for help in finding a place of service. Campbell invited him to London, took him under his wing, and force-fed him theology and exegesis for nine months.[4] From 1852 to 1859 Parker served in Banbury in Oxfordshire, grew in stature and reputation as a preacher, had a famous debate with an atheist, and dedicated a new building with R. W. Dale as preacher.

For the next eleven years Parker preached in the Cavendish Chapel, Manchester, a chief nonconformist center. The church had a congregation of 350 in a sanctuary seating 1,700. He soon filled the church, and his remarkable gift of prayer, both public and private, was a matter of notice.[5] He received a D.D. from the University of Chicago in 1862. In 1869 he moved to London, assuming the pastorate of the old Poultry Chapel where he served powerfully for thirty-three years. This was the church Thomas Goodwin (cf. 7.3.2.3) had founded and which had come on hard times in a commercial neighborhood.[6] Parker led in the building of a new City Temple in Holborn Viaduct in 1874 with the Corporation of London donating a massive white pulpit. He saw it filled to three thousand persons morning and evening on Sunday and averaging one thousand at a Thursday noon service. At the Thursday services he usually spoke, but to the rostrum he also invited such speakers as Prime Minister Gladstone, Newman Hall of Christ Church, Westminster Road, and many others. Parker read extensively and founded an Institute of Homiletics in 1871. His book *Ad Clerum* addressed aspects of preaching and pastoring. He made four trips to the United States, was close to Beecher, and became a confidant of John B. Gough, the famous temperance lecturer. Newman's sermons also influenced him.

Parker wrote many books, including a choice piece on the Holy Spirit. He also wrote verse and fiction. He was an expansive, creative soul who took a stand on prison reform and preached strongly against gambling. He was immensely dramatic in his delivery. Here he is described in action in the City Temple pulpit:

> His massive figure and leonine head at once fixed the attention and his voice, rich as an organ, held his audience spell-bound. It rose and fell in sonorous periods as he poured out his perfectly-phrased sentences. He was a superb actor and he delivered his thoughts with a dramatic force that kindled each sentence . . . the gleaming eyes, the vigorous gesture, the constantly changing inflection of his voice, now soft as a whisper, then challenging as a trumpet.[7]

Although he was close to Beecher, who gave up textual analysis in preaching, Parker gave himself to preaching through the Bible in about seven years. This resulted in the twenty-five-volume *People's Bible* and about one thousand sermons from Genesis to Revelation. Studded with his prayers, these sermons do not see the division of the text but do deliver what the passage as a whole says. A good sample is "On the Building of Babel" from Genesis 11.[8] His illustrations are more suggestions than sequential stories. He also published *The People's Family Prayer Book*. Parker was rather ecumenical and spoke repeatedly to the Scottish Free Church assemblies.[9] Yet he stood with the conservatives when he addressed the Free Church Assembly in the imbroglio over high criticism.

Parker was sound on the Bible. "It is not as many think, a mere record containing the Word of God, but the Word of God itself, speaking with a divine voice in divers manners, authoritatively and finally."[10] He was solid on the Atonement, and said that if he ever preached in Westminster or at St. Paul's he would preach nothing but salvation through the blood of Jesus.

Yet Parker had a somewhat dismissive attitude toward theology and its importance and sometimes sounded mincing and mediating.[11] His successor, R. J. Campbell, espoused the "new theology" and denatured the Atonement entirely. Campbell was finally forced out in 1915 because of his socialistic views and replaced by the liberal Joseph Fort Newton. Later incumbents were F. W. Norwood and Leslie Weatherhead, a gifted Methodist but a preacher who psychologized the gospel.

City Temple was destroyed in World War II and rebuilt. Even though Leonard Griffith served for a time (1960–66), the congregation has died. After Spurgeon's death, the succession question became ugly and divisive. Did Parker's depreciation of doctrine and Beecherish association make the succession a fatality?

Robertson Nicoll gave Joseph Parker's funeral address with Principal P. T. Forsyth joining the procession. Campbell and J. H. Jowett preached the memorial sermons at City Temple.

---

1. John Bishop, "Joseph Parker: Poet, Seer, Preacher," *Preaching* (November–December 1988): 43.
2. William Adamson, *The Life of Joseph Parker* (New York: Revell, 1902), 12–13.
3. Ibid., 23.

4. Ibid., 38.

5. Ibid., 126. He stressed preaching the meaning of the text, not the text as such.

6. Arthur Clare, *The City Temple: 1640–1940* (London: Independent Press, 1940). The tercentenary volume.

7. Bishop, "Joseph Parker," 45. This is the recollection of Alexander Gamme.

8. Joseph Parker, *The People's Bible: Discourses on Holy Scripture* (London: Richard Clarke, 1885), 1:176ff. He also wrote and published six volumes of *Studies in Texts*. Both series have been reissued by Baker.

9. Adamson, *The Life of Joseph Parker,* 255.

10. Ibid., 238.

11. Ibid., 163.

10.6.6 H.P. LIDDON—SURGEON OF THE SOUL AND OF THE SCRIPTURES

Brethren, Jesus Christ has been with us Englishmen as a nation for at least some sixteen or seventeen hundred years. As a nation, do we know Him? Are our laws—our marriage laws, our poor laws, for instance— all of them, in clear agreement with His law of high and pure morality? Are our habits, our great currents of opinion, our national enthusiasms and aversions, such as become His disciples? Is He our King, not merely recognized in our temple, but honoured in our streets, in our organs of national opinion and feeling, in our great representative assemblies, in our halls of science, as well as in our sanctuaries?

If we believe that He is the true Light of the world, we shall close our ears against suggestions impairing the credit of those Jewish Scriptures which have received the stamp of His Divine authority.

—Henry Parry Liddon

At the three-quarter mark of the century Spurgeon was speaking to ten thousand people each Sunday, Parker to six thousand, but a great variety of others were "fatally uninteresting" or unorthodox.[1] But near Parker in majestic St. Paul's, "ministering to the wise," was **Henry Parry Liddon** (1829–1890), "whose sweet and gentle melancholy" in preaching made such a lasting impression on so many. Services had been held in the choir for a long time but then moved out into the nave, where thousands listened to sermons that invariably took an hour.

Liddon's father was an officer in the Royal Navy. When Henry went up to Oxford, he became associated with the Tractarians and wrote the life of E. B. Pusey, who led the high-church forces and authored an outstanding commentary on the Minor Prophets. Ordained in 1852 and serving as assistant curate at Wantage, Liddon was appointed by Bishop Wilberforce as vice principal of the Theological College, Cuddesdon. He never married.

Liddon had a first-rate mind and was returned to be vice principal at St. Edmund Hall, Oxford, where he gave his famous Bampton Lectures on The Divinity of Our Lord in 1866. These lectures were the bane of all Unitarians.[2] Liddon's trenchant themes of "the divine personality of the Eternal Son" and "the virtue of His atonement" pressed his hearers to acknowledge Christ as the Son of God or dismiss him as a flagrant deceiver. He railed at negative higher criticism as undercutting the Savior's infallibility. His basic argument was that Christ could not err.

Serving also as Ireland Professor of Exegesis, Liddon gave a series of popular Bible readings and expositions. In 1870 he was appointed canon of St. Paul's and came down to preach Sundays. Stanley said, "Liddon took us straight up to heaven and kept us there for an hour." Interestingly, Liddon refused to preach in Westminster because of Dean Stanley's fellowship with liberals and rationalists.[3] Donaldson describes "his appearance as striking, his voice sweet and penetrating, his influence magnetic . . . yet there was about him a holy self-restraint that kept in check the explosive forces of that sensitive physique."[4] Some said that Spurgeon was Isaiah and Liddon was Jeremiah.

Liddon in some ways emulated the French court preachers. His introduction was classic, and he usually used three heads. His magnificent sermon on "Profit and Loss" from Mark 8:36 was needed in the City of London. "The Cleansing Blood" was likewise right on the mark. His analytical outlines on Romans are unique and indispensable for the serious student.[5]

His health began to falter early on, and when Pusey died Liddon resigned his post at Oxford. He never felt strong, and on April 18, 1863, before his first sermon at St. Paul's, he characteristically wrote:

> Feel very unequal to preaching at St. Paul's tomorrow, both spiritually and physically. Oh, Lord Jesus, help me, a poor sinner.

The Bible was to him "power—the power of an Infallible Spirit teaching the souls of men from pages which have been preternaturally preserved from the taint of error, and with a living force which bridges the centuries that have passed since its latest books were written."[6] Just before his sudden death in 1890, he took a trip with his sister to Palestine and Egypt. It was to her that he dedicated his glorious magnificat which comes from his *Advent in St. Paul's.* Its twin, *Easter in St. Paul's,* is without an equal in our language.[7]

Liddon trumpeted the trustworthiness of the Old Testament, which he loved and preached. His sermon on the disobedient prophet is a treasure. He often spoke of the Holy Spirit as the "great preacher of the Godhead."[8] Such earnestness was owned of God. Dr. Bright queried of the man: "What made Liddon so vitalizing a preacher? What but his supreme devotion to a Christ alive forevermore."[9]

1. C. Maurice Davies, *Unorthodox London: Phases of Religious Life in the Metropolis* (London: Tinsley Bros., 1875).

2. H. P. Liddon, *The Divinity of Our Lord and Saviour Jesus Christ* (London: Rivingtons, 1885).

3. Aug. B. Donaldson, *Henry Parry Liddon* (London: Rivingtons, 1905), 38.

4. Ibid., 33. For some interesting footnotes on Liddon, see *Autobiography of Robert Gregory, Dean of St. Paul's, 1819–1911* (London: Longmans, Green, 1912). Reflects on Liddon's extraordinary prowess as a preacher.

5. H. P. Liddon, *Explanatory Analysis of St. Paul's Epistle to Romans* (Grand Rapids: Zondervan, 1876, 1961). Dr. Merrill Tenney calls this "A model of analytical work in the Greek text."

6. Donaldson, *Henry Parry Liddon,* 107.

7. H. P. Liddon, *Easter in St. Paul's* (London: Longmans, Green, 1895).

8. Donaldson, *Henry Parry Liddon,* 139.

9. Charles Smyth, *The Art of Preaching: A Practical Survey of Preaching in the Church of England 747–1939* (London: SPCK, 1940), 247.

10.6.7 ROBERT W. DALE—THE PREACHER WHO LOVED DOCTRINE

He has his arena down at Birmingham, where he does his practice with Mr. Chamberlain and Mr. Jesse Collings and the rest of his band; and then from time to time he comes up to the metropolis, to London, and gives a public exhibition of his skill. And a very powerful exhibition it often is.

—Matthew Arnold

I advise you to read every book on preaching that you can buy or borrow, whether it is old or new, Catholic or Protestant, English, French or German. If your experience corresponds with mine, the dullest and most tedious writer on this subject will remind you of some fault that you are committing habitually, or of some element of power which you have failed to use.

Exposition will do something to protect you from the desultoriness and want of method which is one of the gravest faults of modern preaching, and which is one of the chief causes that it conveys so little definite and systematic instruction. Our practice of preaching from texts has accustomed people to try what they can discover in single sentences and even single phrases, of the Bible, and to disregard the general current and structure of the argument or history.

—Robert W. Dale

Robert William Dale (1829–1895) "put his pulpit first." Born and reared in London, Dale and his family were spiritually nurtured at Moorlands Tabernacle. He started teaching school at age fourteen and was captured by John Angell James' (cf. 9.3.1) *Anxious Inquirer After Salvation.* He preached his first sermon at age sixteen and attended a small college in Birmingham, taking his degree at the University of London in 1853. Dale became an assistant to James while a student. Upon James' death after fifty-six years at Carr's Lane Chapel, Dale assumed the pastorate and remained there for forty-two years. He was known above all as a fervent and effective doctrinal preacher even though he had been warned Carr's Lane would not stand for it. His reply was, "They will have to tolerate it."

Dale was not at ease with hyper-Calvinism and particularly resisted restricted grace. At first hesitant, he soon sensed when Moody and Sankey came to Birmingham in 1875 "that the work was most plainly of God."[1] He saw authentic life-change in the great after-meetings and became an ardent backer.

Dale often reflected that what drew him above all else to Moody was that he never spoke about hell and lost souls without tears in his eyes. The Moody-Sankey visit provided a year of powerful impact in the services. This was the year that Dale gave his masterful lectures on the Atonement at the Sunday evening services in which he so adroitly argued the case for objective atonement. It was also the time when Dale's ministry was quickened as he wrote his Easter sermon and realized: "Christ is alive! Alive! Alive!" An Easter hymn was sung at Carr's Lane every Sunday thereafter. Dale's sermons on *The Laws of Christ for Common Life* show Christian ethics applied. Moody's revival ministry was bearing fruit.[2]

Dale typically preached from a manuscript for about an hour. Robertson Nicoll described his style as "one of the most perfect in the whole range of English literature."[3] Edmund Burke was his model, and like Burke he made few concessions to his audience. There was little personalization but meticulous preparation. Before he preached the centenary of Wesley's death in City Road Chapel in London, he read through the complete works of Wesley.

In 1877 Dale gave the Beecher Lectures at Yale, published as *Nine Lectures on Preaching*. These are poignant and powerful lectures and were considered some of the best in the early history of the lectureship. He rewrote his lectures four or five times in order to perfect them.[4] Dale shunned fancy or clever sermons and could be intense. Close examination of his lectures on the atonement of Christ reveal the mettle of the man as a preacher. He opened up the Atonement as Turretin called it, "The chief part of our salvation, the anchor of Faith, the refuge of Hope, the rule of Charity, the true foundation of the Christian religion, and the richest treasure of the Christian Church."[5]

Dale saw the atoning sacrifice of Christ as the key, even more than Christ's teaching or His life. He intended to show in his discourses the relationship between Christ's sacrifice and the remission of sin. "The real truth is that while He came to preach the gospel, His chief object in coming was that there might be a gospel to preach,"[6] said Dale. He engaged the thinking of the clever Unitarian, James Martineau, and was unflinching in asserting that in propitiation, "His [Christ's] face is turned toward God, not toward man."[7] He tracked the substitutionary atonement through all the documents of the New Testament and through church history. As Paul deployed his message, clearly it was essentially "Christ died for our sins."

> The Death of Christ, as the objective ground of the Divine forgiveness of human sin, was the substance of Paul's preaching; it was the central idea of his theology; it was the spring of the mightiest motives by which he was animated in his apostolic work.[8]

And how did Birminghamites take such preaching? One member said, "If Dr. Dale preaches like that I shall not come to hear him, for I cannot stand it; it goes through me."[9] What a giant for God! What a spokesman for God! What a trumpeter for truth!

1. D. W. Lambert, "The Scholar and the Evangelist: R. W. Dale and D. L. Moody," *Life of Faith,* (February 15, 1975): 3.
2. Ibid.
3. John Bishop, "Robert William Dale: Interpreter of Evangelical Truth," *Preaching* (September–October 1989): 40.
4. John Edwards, *Nineteenth-Century Preachers* (London: Charles Kelly, 1902), 37.
5. R. W. Dale, *The Atonement* (London: Congregational Union, 1897), 3.
6. Ibid., 46.
7. Ibid., 165.
8. Ibid., 264.
9. Bishop, "Robert William Dale," 41.

10.6.8 F. W. FARRAR—THE PREACHER WHO EXEMPLIFIED VERSATILITY

> Thousands came to be fed by a man [Farrar] who believed in righteousness, and was not afraid of thundering against those who did not. Upon the whole I think his most helpful sermons were those which explained a book of the Bible in its broadest outlines . . . a sermon on the Book of Job haunts me today.
>
> —Bishop Montgomery

If Ryle was low church and Liddon was high church, then Dean **Frederic William Farrar** (1831–1903) was broad church. Born in Bombay, India, the son of a chaplain, Farrar was a gifted and forceful preacher in the Church of England. His voracious appetite for books was manifest early, and in 1847 he entered King's College, Cambridge, where F. D. Maurice became his mentor. Farrar taught at Marlborough and Harrow under C. J. Vaughn, a noted preacher and leader in his own right.[1] He returned to Marlborough as headmaster, and his chapel sermons there began to attract attention. In 1875 he was appointed rector of St. Margaret's, adjacent to Westminster and the church of the House of Commons. He was soon chaplain to the queen and then dean of Canterbury in 1895.

An accomplished writer of many books, Farrar was best known for his massive *Life of Christ* and *Life of St. Paul*. Although he lamentably had given up the biblical teaching of a universal flood in Noah's day and had stepped forward as a defender of Bishop Colenso, both his teaching and preaching about Christ were thoroughly orthodox.[2] As one described him:

> But the crowning impression for me that afternoon was when the time came for the second lesson, which, I believe, is always read by the Dean, when he is present, as his regular part of the service. In the same absorbed manner, as if seeing nothing around him, but wholly devoted to the thing he was doing, he went up to the reading-desk, found the lesson of the day, and began to read words which, of all Scripture, were to me the most perfect and wonderful to express what I was feeling . . . I sat spell-bound.[3]

Farrar's style was vigorous (some felt vehement at times). He loved to preach in series. Illustration was his forte. For Farrar, the purpose of preaching was always "to utter and interpret, to feel and to know that God was in Christ reconciling the world to Himself, not imputing their trespasses to them."[4] In a sermon delivered in the royal chapel in 1872, Farrar preached from Micah 6:6–8 on "What God Requires." He drew the mains from the text in its natural order and made bridges to the New Testament with skill and effect.[5] His Victorian rhetoric was at times "audacious," as when he spoke of "the luminous wand of the milky way" or "the glorious conflagration of the earth's decay."[6]

Farrar wrote *The History of Interpretation* for his Bampton Lectures of 1875. He also penned several Bible commentaries, biographical novels of giants such as Chrysostom, and more than seventy other volumes. He veered toward universalism as the years went by, a heresy that plagued the well-known American Quaker, Hannah Whitall Smith, and others. Farrar's daughter Maud married Bernard Law Montgomery, son of a bishop and later to be celebrated as General Montgomery of Alamein.[7] Scandal and sorrow among his sons and other considerations denied him preferment, but F. W. Farrar was a remarkably articulate preacher, "admired by many, intensely disliked by a few."[8]

---

1. C. J. Vaughn was a prolific and controversial schoolman and preacher. Bishop B. F. Westcott read one of Vaughn's sermons every Sunday afternoon for thirty years.
2. F. W. Farrar, *The Life of Christ* (Hartford, Conn.: S. S. Scranton, 1918), 656ff.
3. R. A. Farrar, *Life of Dean Farrar* (New York: Thomas Crowell, 1904), 320.
4. John Edwards, *Nineteenth-Century Preachers and Their Methods* (London: Kelly, 1902), 54.
5. F. W. Farrar, *The Silences and the Voices of God* (London: Macmillan, 1892), 71ff. Another volume of typical sermons is F. W. Farrar, *Sermons—The Contemporary Pulpit Library* (London: Swan, Sonnenschein, 1890).
6. F. R. Webber, *A History of British and American Preaching* (Milwaukee: Northwestern, 1952), 1:595.
7. Nigel Hamilton, *Monty: The Making of a General* (New York: McGraw-Hill, 1981), 1:3–4, 19. Montgomery was an eccentric genius but bore witness to the bodily resurrection of Christ; see *Prophetic Witness* (November 1983): 11.
8. Ibid., "Grandfather Farrar," 20ff.

10.6.9 Hugh Price Hughes and Mark Guy Pearse—The Team That Made a Mark

Look at it. Think of it. A hundred and twenty men and women, having no patronage, no promise of earthly favor; no endowment, no wealth— a company of men and women having to get their living by common daily toil—and yet they are to begin the conquests of Christianity! To them is entrusted a work which to turn the world upside down! None so exalted but the influence of this lowly company shall reach to them, until the throne of the Caesars is claimed for Christ . . . a thing impossible, absurd, look at it as you will, until you admit this—they are to be filled with the Holy Ghost. Then the difficulties melt into the empty air. Their strength is as the strength of the Almighty. This is Christ's idea of Christianity; the idea not of man—it is infinitely too sublime—the idea of God.

—Mark Guy Pearse

The vitalities in preaching in Britain at this time were not reserved for one theological perspective or denomination; the networking encompassed the heirs of John Wesley as well. There was huge theological defection in Methodism, as seen in the drastic concessions to higher criticism made by **A. S. Peake** (1865–1929), who taught at Manchester and himself came from the Primitive Methodists. Although he had been reared with great reverence for the Word by his godly preacher father, Peake followed Wellhausen, gave up the Virgin Birth, and clashed with James Denney on the meaning of Christ's atoning death.[1] This is the stream that led to Weatherhead and Donald Soper and extreme liberalism. Thank God there was another stream in the likes of Professor G. G. Findley and Samuel Chadwick that led to William Sangster and Alan Walker in Australia and others.

But mightily used of God in a unique preaching ministry at this time were two gifted individuals, **Hugh Price Hughes** (1847–1902), from Wales, and **Mark Guy Pearse** (1842–1930), who hailed from Cornwall. Hughes was a doctor's son who was converted and felt the call to preach. At age fourteen, on a Sunday when the preacher did not show up, young Hughes walked to the pulpit and preached a creditable sermon. After training in London, he served three years in Dover. At his first service eighteen people professed salvation.[2] Pearse was a medical student when God tabbed him to preach, and he subsequently served several pastoral charges, beginning in Leeds. In 1887 these two preachers began a copastorate in West London which met at St. James Hall in a more informal setting with music that targeted the people in Piccadilly. Spurgeon preached at the opening with the proviso that there be no instrumental music. Pearse knew Spurgeon especially well and was greatly influenced by him.

Hughes was a spellbinding preacher. His sermons in *Essential Christianity* include a moving address on "The All-Sufficiency of Christ" from John 14:6.[3] His series on *Ethical Christianity* was widely heard and read, as was his well-known sermon, "The Christian Extra" from Matthew 5:47, "What do ye more than others?"[4] Both Hughes and Pearse were essentially evangelists. The attendance at the West London Mission was consistently more than three thousand.

Charles Bradlaugh, the notorious freethinker, once challenged Hughes to a debate. Hughes accepted with a counterchallenge: I'll bring one hundred whose lives have been changed by the gospel; you bring one hundred whose lives have been changed through your testimony. Bradlaugh never showed up, and Hughes turned the occasion into a great testimony meeting.

Pearse was an aggressive, somewhat cycloid preacher, known as the apostle of good cheer. His gift was imagination in preaching that painted a picture. His messages on *The Christianity of Jesus Christ* are direct and engaging.[5] Pearse patterned himself after Billy Bray (cf. 10.1.6), whose biography he wrote.

Copastorates have not on the whole been very successful, but Pearse's ministry in West London with Hughes was outstandingly fruitful. Here is the fulfillment of the desire and dream of the Wesleys for soul-saving stations everywhere. As John Wesley insisted in the first *Methodist Discipline:* "You have nothing to do but to save souls. Therefore spend and be spent in this work."[6] To that end Pearse preached:

> I cannot consecrate myself to the Lord. My purpose falters and fails in changing circumstances; I am fickle, forgetful, false. My lofty desires of today, tomorrow cease to soar, and sink beneath the clouds again, and rest once more with wearied wings indifferent upon the earth. The only consecration possible is not with me or with my will. It is the entrance of the Lord himself, his possessing and claiming and using me; that is the only true consecration. It is not my giving so much as my receiving; not so much my surrender to him so much as my acceptance of him, on which my mind is to be stayed.[7]

---

1. John T. Wilkinson, *Arthur Samuel Peake: A Biography* (London: Epworth, 1971) 6, 115ff., 119. The primary source here is A. S. Peake's own disappointing *The Nature of Scripture* (London: Hodder and Stoughton, 1922).
2. F. R. Webber, *A History of British and American Preaching* (Milwaukee: Northwestern, 1952), 1:641.
3. Hugh Price Hughes, *Essential Christianity* (New York: Hunt and Eaton, 1894), 73ff.
4. Hugh Price Hughes, *Ethical Christianity* (New York: Dutton, 1891), 1ff.
5. Mark Guy Pearse, *The Christianity of Jesus Christ* (Cincinnati: Jennings and Pye, n.d.).
6. For an exposition of this point, see Robert E. Coleman, "Nothing to Do but Save Souls," *John Wesley's Charge to His Preachers* (Grand Rapids: Francis Asbury/Zondervan, 1990).
7. Pearse, *The Christianity of Jesus Christ,* 187.

CHAPTER ELEVEN

The Glory and Agony of Twentieth-Century Preaching

Part One: Vitality or Entropy?

It was revealed to them that they were not serving themselves but you, when they spoke of the things that have now been told you by those who have preached the gospel to you by the Holy Spirit sent from heaven.

—1 Peter 1:12

For you have been born again, not of perishable seed, but of imperishable, through the living and enduring word of God. For, "All men are like grass, and all their glory is like the flowers of the field; the grass withers and the flowers fall, but the word of the Lord stands forever." And this is the word that was preached to you.

—1 Peter 1:23–25

For certain men whose condemnation was written about long ago have secretly slipped in among you. They are godless men, who change the grace of our God into a license for immorality and deny Jesus Christ our only Sovereign and Lord. . . . "In the last times there will be scoffers who will follow their own ungodly desires." These are the men who divide you, who follow mere natural instincts and do not have the Spirit.

—Jude 4, 18–19

The Word proclaimed is a divine word and as such it is an active force which creates what it proclaims.

—G. Friedrich

True preaching from start to finish is the work of the Holy Spirit.
—John Knox

When we built Redeemer Church in Atlanta, we had carved on the front of the pulpit the cry of Jeremiah, "O earth, earth, earth, hear the word of the Lord." To preach the Word of the Lord is to preach on a text from the Bible. Like a blooming flower that opens its petals to the sun, a preacher takes a text and lets it unfold with authority and certainty. People recognize it as coming from God and respond, "You'd better believe it" or "You'd better do it!"
—John Brokhoff

How is the Kingdom of Heaven opened and shut by the preaching of the holy gospel? In this way: the Kingdom of Heaven is opened when it is proclaimed and openly testified to believers, one and all, according to the command of Christ, that as often as they accept the presence of the gospel with true faith all their sins are truly forgiven them by God for the sake of Christ's gracious work. On the contrary, the wrath of God and eternal condemnation fall upon all unbelievers and hypocrites as long as they do not repent. It is according to this witness of the gospel that God will judge the one and the other in this life and in the life to come.
—Heidelberg Catechism (1563), Lord's Day 31, Q & A 84

With the dawn of the twentieth century, humankind was awash in optimism and euphoria. The Darwinian vision was overwhelmingly positive. Science was on the way to leading the human race to utopia. As Carl F. H. Henry put it, "From Descartes to Dewey one finds the same confidence that man, apart from any reference to a special supernatural revelation, can solve his problems."[1] The underpinnings of this mindset were (1) the inevitability of human progress; (2) the inherent goodness of man; (3) the absolute uniformity of nature; (4) the ultimate reality of nature; and (5) the ultimate animality of man.[2]

But all of this was doomed as modern civilization experienced two fratricidal world wars, uncontrolled worldwide economic depression, the horror of the Holocaust, and the advent of the atomic age. Even the fall of state socialism in the former Soviet Union and her satellites has unleashed narrow new nationalisms that torment the nations. The sexual revolution and AIDS, the war in Vietnam, the insoluble challenges in the Middle East, and the increasing gulf between the "haves" and the "have nots" in the "two-thirds world" have ripped societies and stabilities asunder. In all of this the Word has been preached, and in the face of the theological turmoil and ecclesiastical tension, the gospel goes forth. To this unstable and mottled time we turn.

---

1. Carl F. H. Henry, *Remaking the Modern Mind* (Grand Rapids: Eerdmans, 1948), 22. Still the classic analysis. Note also Henry's *The Drift of Western Thought* (Grand Rapids: Eerdmans, 1951). For an astute study of the collapsing moral foundations

of Western civilization, see Donald G. Bloesch, *Crumbling Foundations: Death and Rebirth in an Age of Upheaval* (Grand Rapids: Academie Books, Zondervan, 1984).
2. Ibid., 26ff. Nothing excels Henry's massive six-volume work on *God, Revelation and Authority* (Waco, Tex.: Word, 1976).

11.1   THE PLYMOUTH BRETHREN AND DISPENSATIONAL WORTHIES

What we are about to consider will tend to shew that, instead of permitting ourselves to hope for a continued progress of good, we must expect a progress of evil; and that the hope of the earth being filled with the knowledge of the Lord before the exercise of His judgment, and the consummation of this judgment on the earth, is delusive. We are to expect evil, until it becomes so flagrant that it will be necessary for the Lord to judge it . . . I am afraid that many a cherished feeling dear to the children of God, has been shocked; I mean, their hope that the gospel will spread by itself over the whole earth, during the actual dispensation.
—J. N. Darby, "Progress of Evil on the Earth," 1840

Preaching among the so-called Plymouth Brethren is usually overlooked in the history of preaching, but this is unfortunate. The Brethren have been avid students of Scripture. Their history began with Darby and his associates and our indebtedness to them should be reviewed. These New Testament "restorationists" have some twelve hundred assemblies in North America and have been strong in Britain and Germany (the late Erich Sauer is included among them).[1]

While every believer who does not offer animal sacrifices is in a sense a dispensationalist, the seeds of an interpretive system are found in Augustine (*"distingue tempora et scripturae concordabint"*), Joachim of Fiore, Cocceius, Isaac Watts, and in Thomas Bernard's Bampton Lectures for 1864 on *The Progress of the Gospel in the New Testament.*[2] Dispensationalism as a system has come more from the Brethren than from anyone else, and thus their influence extends far beyond what their actual numbers would lead us to project.

Homiletically, the Brethren generally reacted against all traditional ideas of form and tended to revert to the ancient homily with its running commentary on the text. So Edith Blumhofer has recently written of Darby and the Plymouth Brethren:

Replacing the typical sermon with a "Bible reading," they devised a preaching form that dismayed some of the era's pulpiteers but had enormous influence on popular evangelicalism.[3]

George Needham spoke for the Brethren in presenting himself as "a plain man, telling a plain story, in a plain manner."[4] D. L. Moody and many others took this form (i.e., took "a string of related texts or passages with brief comments").[5]

Though admiring the biblicality of this kind of preaching, President Francis L. Patton of Princeton warned his homiletical students "against supposing that you have given an adequate substitute for a sermon when, with the help of

Cruden's Concordance, you have chased a word through the Bible, making a comment or two on the passages as you go along."[6] Patton well argued that a sermon is a "rhetorical organism evolved by a genetic process from the text" with careful hermeneutical discipline.[7]

---

1. Thomas Stewart Veitch, *The Story in the Brethren Movement* (London: Pickering and Inglis, n.d.); Robert Baylis, *My People: The History of Those Christians Sometimes Called Plymouth Brethren* (Wheaton, Ill.: Harold Shaw, 1995). I am indebted to my student Mark Stevenson for lending me this book—a rewarding study. For a study of present Brethren losses in Britain, cf. Peter Brierley et al, *The Christian Brethren as the Nineties Began* (Carlisle, U.K.: Partnership, 1993).
2. Thomas D. Bernard, *The Progress of Doctrine in the New Testament* (Grand Rapids: Eerdmans, 1949). Bernard argues the case for progressive revelation (i.e., the gradual process of divine self-disclosure).
3. Edith R. Blumhofer, *Restoring the Faith* (Urbana/Champaign: University of Illinois Press, 1993), 16.
4. Ernest R. Sandeen, *The Roots of Fundamentalism: British and American Millenarianism, 1800–1930* (Grand Rapids: Baker, 1970, 1978), 137.
5. J. C. Pollock, *Moody: the Biography* (Chicago: Moody, 1963, 1983), 90. Compare 10.1.7.
6. Sandeen, *The Roots of Fundamentalism,* 137. F. F. Bruce, himself a Plymouth Brother, contrasts preaching a coherence and a sequence with "a mere stringing together of gospel texts" as was common; see *In Retrospect* (Grand Rapids: Eerdmans, 1980), 15.
7. John L. Patton, *Presbyterian and Reformed Review* 1 (1890): 36–37.

11.1.1 *JOHN NELSON DARBY—THE PROPHET AMONG THE RUINS*

Oh, the joy of having nothing and being nothing, seeing nothing but a living Christ in glory, and being careful for nothing but His interests down here.

I love not only to preach, but to be in direct communication with souls as to their relation with God—saints, and sinners yet more.

It is no mistake to be always expecting the Lord to return. The object of the conversion of the Thessalonians was to wait for God's Son from heaven. People fancy that the truth of the Lord's return is a bit of knowledge at the top of the tree; but instead of that, it is what the Thessalonians were converted for, and meanwhile they are to serve God.

—John Nelson Darby

Born in London, the sixth son of eight children in an old English family of Leicestershire, **John Nelson Darby** (1800–1882) is considered the founder of the Plymouth Brethren movement. He was early separated from his mother when his parents parted company. Educated in Westminster Public School, in 1815 he went to Trinity College, Dublin, where he studied to become a barrister. One of his close friends was J. G. Bellett, who later joined him in the early days of the Brethren.

A series of "spiritual awakenings" led to Darby's conversion at twenty-one.[1] He was ordained a deacon and then a priest in the Church of Ireland (by Archbishop Mager), yet he was without peace.[2] Thrown from his horse in a violent accident, he came to assurance of salvation and found "deliverance" from the condemnation of the law.[3] "The absolute, divine authority and certainty of the Word" became his compass, and he began to meet with others for the breaking of bread and the exposition of Scripture.

The Brethren movement sprang from a pessimism about the organized church. The church was seen as in ruins and the assemblies were "the little flock." Christ was the focus of the exposition as the crucified and risen Savior, now ascended and seated, about to return for his bride, the church. Evangelism was primary, but prophecy was also important. The great prophetic meetings at Powerscourt and Darby's broken engagement which had such a personally shattering effect upon his life were all integral to this amazing story.

There was a shyness in Darby's public speaking; he was "original but not obtrusive."[4] He never displayed his knowledge of the original languages but continued to pour forth scriptural exposition not only in Britain but also in America, where he preached for Moody, in France, Germany, and particularly in Geneva, Switzerland. Darby was an assiduous student of the Hebrew and Greek Scriptures. His collected writings run to 34 volumes. The best of his exposition is found in his extensive *Synopsis of the Books of the Bible.*[5]

Robert Louis Stevenson wrote of Darby's influence in his *Travels with a Donkey in the Cevennes,* and Tolstoy refers to the Plymouth Brethren whom he came to know through Lord Radstock. Interestingly, Darby was a lifelong paedo-Baptist.

Darby wrote much poetry and many hymns and translated the Bible into three languages. His message was driven home again and again:

> As an external body, the Church is ruined [has drifted into apostasy]; and though much may be enjoyed of what belongs to the Church, I believe from Scripture that the ruin is without remedy, that the professing church will be cut off. I believe that there is an external professing Christendom, holding a most important and responsible place, and which will be judged and cut off for its unfaithfulness. The true body of Christ is not this. It is composed of those who are united by Christ by the Holy Ghost, who, when the professing church is cut off, will have their place with Him in heaven.[6]

---

1. Max S. Weremchuk, *John Nelson Darby* (Neptune, N.J.: Loizeaux Brothers, 1992), 33.
2. Ibid., 42.
3. Ibid., 48.

4. Ibid., 189.
5. John Nelson Darby, *Synopsis of the Books of the Bible* (London: G. Morrish, n.d.).
   The Word "is more immediately of God" than mere abstract truth, 3:10.
6. John Nelson Darby, *Collected Works,* 14:417. For examples of his poetry, *Spiritual
   Songs* (Kingston-on-Thames: Stow Hill Bible and Tract Depot, n.d.).

11.1.2 GEORGE MÜLLER—PRACTITIONER OF FAITH AMONG THE DESOLATE

Immediately upon beginning to expound "Blessed are the poor in spirit . . ."
I felt myself greatly assisted; and whereas in the morning my sermon had
not been simple enough for the people to understand it, I now was listened
to with the greatest attention, and I think I was also understood. My own
peace and joy were great. I felt this was a blessed work.

—George Müller

Thus is described the initial preaching experience of **George Müller** (1805–
1898) in the environs of Halle, where he was studying for the ministry. He was
born in Prussia and lost his mother when he was fourteen. Though reared in a
religious environment and undergoing confirmation, Müller had no concept of
God. He drank, played cards, and at sixteen was in jail as a libertine and a thief.[1]

Despite his dissipated lifestyle, he commenced study for the ministry at Halle.
While there, he was invited to a cottage Bible study and prayer meeting where
he was converted in November of 1825. The well-known Professor Tholuck was
his mentor (cf. 8.2.6). To help pay his way through the university, Müller tutored
Americans in German, one of whom was Charles Hodge. He went to England as
a missionary to the Jews under the auspices of the Church of England, but soon
sundered his ties with the established church and moved into the orbit of the rapidly growing Plymouth Brethren movement.

The Second Coming of Christ was a frequent subject of his preaching. His
expositions of Romans particularly commended him to the Brethren.[2] Müller was
called to minister to the congregation at Ebenezer Chapel in Teignmouth, though
they were somewhat divided over him. He remained there for two and a half years,
preaching with a strong German accent.

Müller became a great lover of the Word, usually reading his Bible on his knees.
He spoke of learning "the preciousness of the Word of God." Soon he moved to
Bristol where he shared in preaching and ministry at several chapels, chiefly
Bethesda, where he reached this conclusion:

We ought to receive all whom Christ has received, irrespective of the
measure of grace or knowledge to which they have attained.[3]

Müller and **Henry Craik** alternated in the preaching. They set aside evenings
when people could come to the vestry for individual conversation and counsel.[4]
Deep tensions tore the movement apart when Darby and Müller broke fellowship.
The split launched the Closed Brethren (Darby) and the Open Brethren (Bethesda
and Müller). In all of this Müller founded the orphanages accommodating two

thousand children, a ministry which continues to this day. His life of faith compelled him never to take a salary or ask for money.

Müller preached an average of three sermons a week, more than ten thousand in his lifetime. He could preach fluently in seven languages. His method is described like this:

> Expository preaching . . . instead of a solitary text detached from its context, he selects a passage, it may be of several verses, which he goes over consecutively clause by clause. His first care is to give the meaning of the passage, and then to illustrate it by other Scriptures, and afterwards apply it.[5]

Müller utilized the typical Brethren homiletic with great impact, preaching into his ninety-third year. He traveled to America several times, where he preached for Talmage in Brooklyn, met with President and Mrs. Hayes at the White House, and preached at Moody's Church in Chicago. In England he worked untiringly with the Moody-Sankey meetings and preached for Spurgeon. Shaped above all by Scripture but also by the biographies of Francke, John Newton, and George Whitefield, George Müller shook his generation for Christ. If indeed 1849 to 1914 was the great age of liberalism, this oft-divided but resilient movement of Darby, Müller, William Kelly, and F. C. Grant faithfully held forth the Word of Life.

------

1. Roger Steer, *George Müller: Delighted in God,* rev. ed. (Wheaton, Ill.: Harold Shaw, 1981), 15.
2. Basil Miller, *George Müller: Man of Faith and Miracles* (Minneapolis: Bethany, 1941), 25.
3. Thomas Stewart Veitch, *The Story of the Brethren Movement* (London: Pickering and Inglis, n.d.), 37.
4. A. T. Pierson, *George Müller of Bristol and His Witness to a Prayer-Hearing God* (New York: Revell, 1899), 88.
5. Steer, *George Müller,* 220.

11.1.3 CHARLES HENRY MACKINTOSH—THE PREACHER WHO LOVED LEARNING

> The Word of God was rejected. . . . remember the words of the Lord Jesus Christ, how He said, "As it was in the days of Noah, so shall it be in the days of the Son of Man . . ." Some would have us believe that ere the Son of Man appears in the clouds of heaven, this earth shall be covered from pole to pole with a fair mantle of righteousness. They would teach us to look for a reign of righteousness and peace, as the result of agencies now in operation; but the brief passage just quoted cuts up by the roots, in a moment, all such vain and delusive expectations. How was it in the days of Noah?
>
> —C. H. M. (as he was known among the Brethren)

Many Plymouth Brethren Bible students were amazingly productive. They include George Wigram in *Englishman's Hebrew and Chaldee Concordance,* Samuel P. Tregelles in textual criticism,[1] F. W. Grant in his *Numerical Bible,* which influenced H. A. Ironside so decisively, and William Kelly's New Testament commentaries to which F. F. Bruce and Spurgeon paid such high compliment.[2]

Another astute Bible teacher was **Charles Henry Mackintosh** (1820–1896), born in Ireland and moved by Darby's "Operations of the Spirit," in which the case is made for our assurance on the basis of Christ's work for us. Mackintosh ran a school in Westport for ten years and then gave himself to the ministry of the Word. He was in the thick of the revival that swept over Ireland in 1859 and 1860 and is known for his *Notes on the Pentateuch.*[3] He spoke and wrote in a strong and perspicuous style, although a given interpretation may be forced. He was among those who remained totally loyal to Darby. Andrew Miller correctly said of his work:

> Man's complete ruin in sin, and God's perfect remedy in Christ are fully, clearly and often strikingly presented.[4]

---

1. George H. Fromow, *B. W. Newton and S. P. Tregelles: Teachers of the Faith and the Future* (London: Sovereign Grace Advent Testimony, 1969).
2. F. F. Bruce, *In Retrospect: Remembrance of Things Past* (Grand Rapids: Eerdmans, 1980), 293.
3. C. H. Mackintosh, *Notes on the Pentateuch* (New York: Loizeaux Brothers, 1879). My experience of delight with these five small volumes in my youth directly parallels Warren Wiersbe's *Giant Steps* (Grand Rapids: Baker, 1981), 133. C. H. M. demonstrates so vividly that there is meaning for us in "the old, old story."
4. Hy Pickering, *Chief Men among the Brethren* (London: Pickering and Inglis, 1918), 111.

11.1.4 C. I. SCOFIELD—DOYEN OF THE DISPENSATIONALISTS

> If you're going to do it, and do it for God, there is only one way—not a smooth, easy way, but as unto the Lord.
>
> —C. I. Scofield

> We commend him to you as one who delights to hide behind the uplifted cross of Jesus; one who will preach a full and free salvation through the shed blood of God's Lamb; one who will lead you into the deep things of the Word, and one who teaches and who preaches the whole truth of God.
>
> —Letter on the occasion of Scofield's dismissal from the
> First Congregational Church of Dallas in 1895

Although not of the Brethren but of the dispensational family, no one is more pivotal in the progress of this movement than **Cyrus Ingersoll Scofield** (1842–1921). Born in Michigan and reared in Tennessee, Scofield served in the

Confederate Army under General Robert E. Lee. After the war he read for the law and was admitted to the bar in 1869 in Kansas, where he was then elected to the State House of Representatives. Scofield was active in politics and named U.S. Attorney for Kansas when he was thirty. Many enemies of his theological system have written scurrilously about his personal life, and much of it may be true, before his conversion.

A friend led him to Christ when he was thirty-six, and he testified, "the passion for drink was taken away."[1] Then the young lawyer living in St. Louis came under the teaching of **Dr. James H. Brookes,** Presbyterian pastor and Bible teacher.[2] Brookes led him deeply into the Scripture, and in 1882 Scofield was called to the First Congregational Church of Dallas. Scofield's solid Bible preaching was used of God to build the membership from fourteen to 551 members.

D. L. Moody had met Scofield in St. Louis and invited him to speak at Northfield and the Niagara Conferences. In 1895 he invited Scofield to come as pastor of Moody's home church in Northfield, where he labored for seven years. As early as 1888, Scofield wrote his famous *Rightly Dividing the Word of Truth* and soon after the equally well-known Scofield Correspondence Course. He also founded the Central American Mission.

Returning to Dallas in 1902, he worked on the *Scofield Reference Bible,* of which Brookes was a consulting editor. R. A. Torrey suggested the use of subheads. Oxford University Press was and is the publisher of the famous Bible study tool. Always when Scofield visited Oxford in connection with his editorial work, he and Mrs. Scofield found fellowship in a Plymouth Brethren gathering.[3]

Scofield was an energetic and effective preacher on any biblical theme but especially on the victorious Christian life.[4] His preaching style was similar to that of the Brethren in that he seldom divided the text or the sermon. His illustrations were practical and memorable. He could be aggressively evangelistic or pastorally didactic.[5]

---

1. Charles G. Trumbull, *The Life Story of C. I. Scofield* (New York: Oxford University Press, 1920), 31. Trumbull, editor of the *Sunday School Times,* was the son of Henry Clay Trumbull, who with John Wanamaker bought the *Times.* The elder Trumbull gave the Beecher Lectures at Yale on the Sunday school in 1887 and 1888. The younger Trumbull became a protégé of Scofield and himself wrote messages on the victorious life which were widely heard and read. Philip E. Howard (a son-in-law and later editor) wrote *The Life's Story of Henry Clay Trumbull* (Philadelphia: Sunday School Times, 1905).
2. Ibid., 35. Cf. David Riddle Williams, *James H. Brookes: A Memoir* (St. Louis: Presbyterian Board of Publications, 1897).
3. Ibid., 108. The linkage of Scofield to Darby via Walter Scott, Gaebelein, and Brookes is judiciously explored in David J. MacLeod, "Walter Scott, A Link in Dispensationalism Between Darby and Scofield," *Bibliotheca Sacra* 153, no. 610 (April–June, 1996): 155ff.
4. C. I. Scofield, *The New Life in Christ Jesus: Messages of Joy and Victory* (Chicago: Moody, 1915).
5. C. I. Scofield, *In Many Pulpits with C. I. Scofield* (Grand Rapids: Baker, 1922, 1966).

11.1.5 A. C. Gaebelein—Dean of the Dispensationalists

> Laodicea is all about us. It is the final state of Protestant Christendom, lukewarm, indifferent and modernistic. Yet the work of the true servant of God is not to denounce the professing Church, but to go and bear a loving, faithful testimony to those in Laodicea.
>
> One of the temptations of a busy life of ministry is the neglect of study, and especially of that which is most essential, the study of the Word of God and prayer.
>
> —Arno Clemens Gaebelein

Born in Thuringia in Germany, coming to the United States, and settling in Lawrence, Massachusetts, **Arno Clemens Gaebelein** (1861–1945) was always close to the Brethren and is certainly one of the founts of dispensational truth. He was converted at twelve, dedicated to Christ's service at eighteen, and became a preacher in the German Methodist Conference in Baltimore, Harlem, and Hoboken. He started to study Hebrew to reach the Jews for Christ.

In 1892 he preached a series of sermons on "Joseph and His Brothers" which were published and widely distributed.[1] In close touch with A. B. Simpson, founder of the Christian Missionary Alliance, James M. Gray, Rector of First Reformed Episcopal Church of Boston and later dean and president of Moody Bible Institute,[2] and C. I. Scofield, Gaebelein soon launched *Our Hope* magazine. He also began an itinerant Bible preaching ministry that crisscrossed the United States over the next forty years.

Gaebelein left the Methodist church in view of the merciless onslaughts of higher critical thought. When S. Parkes Cadman trumpeted that inerrancy was "no longer possible of belief among reasonable men" and that the New Testament "contains contradictions," Gaebelein left.[3] Gaebelein contributed to *The Fundamentals* (1910–1912) and participated in Plymouth Brethren conferences, the Niagara Bible Conference, and the great Chicago Prophecy Conference of 1914. His lucidly written commentaries on Psalms, Daniel, Joel, Zechariah, Matthew, Acts, and Revelation along with his extensive *Annotated Bible* contain the substance of his communication over the years. Speaking in his German accent, he was one of the first to foresee the Bolshevistic threat in Russia.[4]

His preaching style was clear and calm and always utilized helpful illustrations. Wilbur M. Smith recalled the impression Gaebelein made from the pulpit:

> Dr. Gaebelein spoke before about 2,000 [in Bethany Presbyterian Church of Philadelphia] on the phrase: "We wait for thy salvation O God." I do not remember five occasions in my life when I was so lifted as I was that morning. There was no desire to take notes. I did not even care to remember what he was saying. I felt my soul cleansed and refreshed and my whole being ennobled. I went out of that auditorium determined to be a different kind of preacher and student than I had ever been before.[5]

The lead editorial in *Our Hope* was always focused on the Lord Jesus. So Gaebelein in the morning service would preach Christ and then move to Bible prophecy in the evening. I believe the list of his close compatriots shows how influential he was. He wrote sixty books, including *The Christ We Know* (in answer to Bruce Barton's *The Man Nobody Knows*), *The Lord of Glory, The Conflict of the Ages, The Harmony of the Prophetic Word, Hopeless—Yet There Is Hope.* Gaebelein would speak topically on occasion and in his exposition followed the Brethren verse-by-verse style very well. How many have been converted and blessed through the faithful proclamation of the Word by this servant of Christ!

---

1. Arno Clemens Gaebelein, *Half a Century: The Autobiography of a Servant* (New York: Our Hope, 1930), 29.
2. Dr. James M. Gray was himself a gifted preacher; see *Salvation From Start to Finish* (Chicago: Moody, n.d.). In a beautiful exposition on Titus 3:3–8, Gray nicely divides the text and the sermon into three classic main points.
3. David A. Rausch, *Arno C. Gaebelein: Irenic Fundamentalist and Scholar* (Lewiston, N.Y.: Edwin Mellen Press, 1983), 60.
4. Ibid., 107. His analysis of Marxism is in *The Conflict of the Ages* (New York: Our Hope, 1933).
5. Ibid., 231. A. C. Gaebelein's gifted son, Frank E. Gaebelein, became an evangelical icon and gifted writer.

11.1.6 Sir Robert Anderson—The Sermonizer from Scotland Yard

One day soon after my conversion I received a letter from a friend telling me that he was unable to keep an engagement to address a Gospel meeting, and asking me to take his place. The messenger waited for an answer and I promptly replied that I could not take such a position. But then I fell a-thinking. I had been praying that God would give me work to do for Him; might not this be the answer? So I hurried after the messenger to tell of my change of mind. And the next day I preached my first Gospel sermon.

The Coming of Christ is not some strange thing that faddists have imported into Christianity. No one has any right to call himself a Christian who denies the Coming of the Lord Jesus Christ . . . you ought not to be merely a person who holds the doctrine of the Advent; if you are a Christian you should hold it as a living hope in the heart.

—Sir Robert Anderson

Representative of lay preachers who were so prominent in the Brethren ranks are such names as Dr. A. T. Schofield, the well-known Harley Street physician,[1] F. W. Baedeker, brother of the travel-book man who with Lord Radstock opened such a remarkable door to Russia, and **Sir Robert Anderson** (1841–1918), who had high office in the Metropolitan Police of London and in Scotland Yard.

Born in Dublin, Anderson called himself an "anglicised Irishman of Scottish extraction." He studied at Trinity College, Dublin, where the eminent historian of morals, W. H. E. Lecky, was his friend and classmate. He returned to Trinity to study after the law but was converted at the age of nineteen in the ripple effect of the Great Revival of 1859.[2] He soon began to preach both evangelistically in gospel meetings and in serious expositions of the deeper things of Scripture.[3] Through his long lifetime he continued to preach in many venues, frequently among the Brethren, although he fellowshiped with Adolph Saphir's ministry in Notting Hill. He took a position with the British Home Office and then became head of the Criminal Investigation Department of the London Police and Scotland Yard in the wake of the Jack the Ripper scare.

Nonetheless, Sir Robert's first love was gospel ministry. He once said he could not understand anyone standing up with the Bible in his hand and failing to be interesting.[4] Tinged with humor, his messages always exalted the grace of God in Christ. He was well received at Mildmay and other conferences, being close to A. C. Dixon, Ada Habershon (who wrote so memorably on the names and titles of the Lord of Glory), J. Stuart Holden, Professor Henry Drummond, and W. F. Moulton, the New Testament scholar. He was much influenced by F. E. Marsh and the rather idiosyncratic Church of England Bible teacher Dr. E. W. Bullinger.[5] In his large circle of friends was also the delightful Bishop Taylor Smith and Professor Hechler from Vienna, who had a great influence on Theodore Herzl, founder of Zionism.[6] None other than Horatius Bonar first interested him on the doctrine of the Second Coming.

A great stream of books and pamphlets flowed from Anderson's pen. Not least of these is his magisterial *The Coming Prince,* which treats the prophecy of the seventy sevens in Daniel 9:24–27.[7] He made the case for the accuracy and historical reliability of Daniel.[8] The Sir Robert Anderson Library Series is still in print and is well worth reading.[9] His study *The Bible and Modern Criticism* was commended by Bishop Moule in its preface, and his notable piece on *Daniel in the Critics' Den* (a reply particularly to Professor Driver at Oxford) was endorsed by Spurgeon, Gaebelein, and Griffith Thomas.

1. A. T. Schofield, *Behind the Brass Plate* (London: Sampson, Low, n.d.). Dr. Schofield lived 1846–1929.
2. A. P. Moore-Anderson, *Sir Robert Anderson and Lady Agnes Anderson* (London: Marshall, Morgan, 1947), 18–19.
3. Ibid., 27.
4. Ibid., 121.
5. Ibid., 82. Dr. Bullinger wrote some scholarly and searching books, particularly on *The Apocalypse* and *The Gifts and the Giver* (a masterpiece on every reference to the Holy Spirit in the New Testament), but he lurched into extreme dispensationalism. Compare H. A. Ironside, *Wrongly Dividing the Word of Truth* (New York: Loizeaux, n.d.).
6. Ibid., 98.
7. Robert Anderson, *The Coming Prince: The Marvelous Prophecy of Daniel's Seventy Weeks Concerning the Antichrist* (Grand Rapids: Kregel, 1957).

8. Robert Anderson, *Daniel in the Critics' Den* (Grand Rapids: Kregel, 1990).
9. The library published by Kregel contains such notable volumes as *The Silence of God, Forgotten Truths, The Gospel and Its Ministry,* and *Types in Hebrews.*

11.1.7 H. A. IRONSIDE—THE ALL-AROUND BIBLE PREACHER

"Pray for us . . ." Who can tell how much each servant of Christ is indebted to the prayers of God's hidden ones? To bear such up before Him is a wondrous ministry, the fullness of which will only be manifested in that day when every secret thing will be revealed according to his own service. Let none think it is a little thing to pray. There is no higher ministry, no more important office, than that of intercessor.

—H. A. Ironside

Henry (Harry) Allan Ironside (1876–1951) was a short, rotund, bald-headed man of calm and humble bearing. Yet he was a mightily used preacher of the Word. Sometimes called the archbishop of fundamentalism, Ironside was born in Toronto, where his father was a street preacher known as the eternity man.

John Ironside died at twenty-seven, when Harry was only two years of age. Mrs. Ironside then moved with her two sons to Los Angeles, where Harry was converted at twelve following one of D. L. Moody's meetings.[1] At fifteen he left home to become a Salvation Army officer and was commissioned a lieutenant.[2] Ultimately he left the Army because of his inner struggle for perfection (as related in his *Holiness: The True and the False*). Helped by George Cutting's little book, *Safety, Certainty and Enjoyment,* H. A. I., as he was called, soon found himself among the Brethren and deeper and deeper into the Word.

He worked in evangelism for awhile with **Henry Varley,** who had given Moody the epigram, "The world has yet to see what God will do with a man who is fully yielded to him."[3] This was the Golden Age of Independent Brethren, and Ironside traveled the next thirty years preaching the Word in simple and direct ways to thousands. His sermons exuded Scripture as he preached his typically Brethren verse-by-verse exposition with stories and anecdotes.

Ironside had a long connection with Dallas Theological Seminary, where his style was appreciated early on. He was known for book-by-book studies, all of which found their way into print.[4] His favorite sermon was from Philemon and was titled "Charge That to My Account."[5]

In 1930 Ironside shocked the Brethren world by accepting the call to pastor the great Moody Memorial Church in Chicago. From that year until 1948 he preached to full houses of four thousand morning and evening. He was especially known for his studies on the Lord's return from Daniel, Revelation, and his signature volume, *The Great Parenthesis.*[6]

In his standard collections of sermons, Ironside did not divide the text, nor did he divide the sermon.[7] With their teaching charts, Brethren preachers traveled and preached, the finest of them Ironside, August Van Ryn,[8] Frederick Tatford, and Neil Fraser.

1. E. Schuyler English, *H. A. Ironside: Ordained of the Lord* (Grand Rapids: Zondervan, 1946), 33.
2. H. A. Ironside, *Random Reminiscences* (New York: Loizeaux, 1939), 9. A great story of exposition in a Pullman, (68ff.).
3. English, *H. A. Ironside,* 83.
4. H. A. Ironside's lectures on Jeremiah, Romans, Revelation, and almost every Bible book were given at schools and preached from pulpits all over the country and around the world.
5. "Charge That to My Account" is the lead sermon in a book by that title but is also found in English, *H. A. Ironside,* 181ff.
6. H. A. Ironside, *The Great Parenthesis* (Grand Rapids: Zondervan, 1943). This title has been maligned as depreciating the church in God's plan, but Ironside spoke of the interval from the standpoint of Israel.
7. Especially choice are *The Lamp of Prophecy, Great Words of the Gospel,* and *Care for God's Fruit Trees.*
8. August Van Ryn, *Sixty Years in His Service* (Waynesboro: Ga.: Christian Missions Press, n.d.).

11.1.8 Arthur W. Pink—The Troubadour of Gospel Truth

God has said in his Word, "He that believeth shall not make haste" (Isa. 28:16), and if ever there was a time when his children needed to give special heed to this admonition it is now. The children of God are infected with the spirit of the world. The mad rush which characterizes everything around us, the awful hustle and bustle of the ungodly as they rush headlong to eternal death, has affected the members of the household of faith . . . the irreverent speed with which the Holy Scriptures are read in the average pulpit; the rate at which sacred songs are commonly sung; the unholy manner in which many rush into the presence of the Most High God, and gabble off the first words that come to their lips, are so many examples of this infection . . . stand, sit, wait, tarry.

—Arthur W. Pink

If a Christian can be a curmudgeon, **Arthur W. Pink** (1886–1952) was such a person. Better known through his extensive writings and his magazine, *Studies in the Scriptures,* Pink preached to large conferences and was a vigorous and effective preacher. He was born in Nottingham in England and reared in a godly home but got tangled up in Theosophy, opening a correspondence with Annie Besant.[1] His concerned father gave him Proverbs 14:12, and he stayed in his bedroom under such conviction that he was converted three days later.[2]

In 1910 he traveled to Chicago and began studies at Moody Bible Institute, but seemed bored and stayed only two months. He moved on to a brief pastorate in Silverton, Colorado, where his first recorded sermon was on "Beholding the Crucified Christ," from Matthew 27:35–36, incisive on imputed righteousness and the atonement. He moved on to California, where a man in Oakland was saved hearing a message on thanksgiving from Hebrews 13:15 because he realized he had never praised God! During ministry in a small church in Kentucky, he met and married his wife, Vera Russell, who worked with him on the editing of *Studies in the Scriptures,* which he launched in 1922.

Although of independent frame of mind, Pink was close to the Brethren and used many Brethren writers in the earlier issues of the magazine. Enduring frequent bouts of discouragement and depression, the Pinks served a Baptist Church in Spartanburg, North Carolina, but then in 1925 moved to Australia. After much reading in the Puritans, Pink began to move toward a narrow Calvinism and away from his premillennial and dispensational roots.[3] His preaching became more and more doctrinal. He was determined not to fuss over people and was very quick to rebuke.

Pink was addicted to typology, demonstrated when he developed 101 ways in which Joseph prefigures Christ.[4] Still, his rich *Gleanings from Genesis, Gleanings from Exodus, Gleanings from Joshua,* and *Gleanings from Paul* were nourishment for saints and stimulation for preachers.

The Pinks went back to England, and "cut off from visible fellowship," tried again in the United States, back to England, and then to Scotland. Their last years were in Stornoway on the Island of Lewis in the Outer Hebrides, where they did not understand Gaelic, nor did they fellowship in any church. Murray analyzes this disconsolate time when a man who had formerly preached three hundred times a year now did not preach at all. He calls him "the unwanted preacher."[5] Still the flow of rich expository materials continued, as Pink produced three incomparable volumes on John, *The Life of David,* theological tomes on the inspiration of Scripture and the attributes of God. His messages on the Seven Last Words, unlike most of his preaching, do see the division of the sermon in a more classical mode because the texts were very brief.[6] His magazine dropped in circulation to less than nine hundred in 1938, but Mrs. Pink finished several issues after his death in 1952. But here was a preacher of the Word!

---

1. Pink's ensnarement in Theosophy reminds us of the enormous influence of this pseudo-eastern religion on Yeats, James Joyce, Jack London, D. H. Lawrence, Mahler, Sibelius, and Shirley McLaine. For the best overall resource to survey the subject, see Sylvia Cranstrom, *The Extraordinary Life and Influence of Helena Blavatsky* (New York: Putnam, 1993).
2. Iain H. Murray, *The Life of Arthur W. Pink* (Edinburgh: Banner of Truth, 1981), 7.
3. A. W. Pink, *The Antichrist* (Swengel, Pa.: Bible Truth Depot, 1923). Acceptable to any dispensational interpreter.
4. A. W. Pink, *Gleanings from Genesis* (Chicago: Moody, 1922), 142ff.
5. Murray, *The Life of Arthur W. Pink,* 100ff.
6. A. W. Pink, *The Seven Sayings of the Savior on the Cross* (Grand Rapids: Zondervan, 1951).

11.2 THE SCOTTISH GIANTS IN THE EARLY TWENTIETH CENTURY

The William Robertson Smith case in the Free Church of Scotland, which was of so much interest to Americans, marked the beginning of a new relationship between British evangelicals and biblical criticism. Smith freely applied the criticism of the Continent to the Old Testament, but he did so while maintaining a belief in miracles, personal divine revelation, and the supernatural. At the end of a complicated series of hearings, Smith lost his professorship in 1881, but retained his status as an ordained minister. Of this action it was said that the Free Church secured its liberty in biblical criticism by the sacrifice of one individual.

—Mark A. Noll

Bible-believing Christians in Scotland won the battle but effectively lost the war. Their traditional views gave way because practitioners of the new criticism, which savaged the Bible, ultimately presented themselves as part of the community of faith and piety.[1] Cambridge scholars like H. C. G. Moule, B. F. Westcott, and J. B. Lightfoot all defended the Scripture's integrity. Preachers like Spurgeon, Liddon, Jowett, Morgan, and Meyer upheld inerrancy. James Denney defended the substitutionary atonement against Ritschl's subjective view.[2]

A parallel situation in the United States found Charles Augustus Briggs, a Presbyterian who taught Old Testament at Union Seminary in New York, under charges of wholesale concessions to modern criticism on issues like Pentateuchal authorship, the unity of Isaiah, and Daniel's authorship of the prophecy bearing his name. He was suspended from Presbyterian standing but became an Episcopalian, and Union became independent to keep him on the faculty. Briggs lost, but his views became dominant.[3] The fallout soon became all too apparent.

---

1. Mark Noll, *Between Faith and Criticism* (New York: Harper and Row, 1986), 72.
2. Ibid., 79.
3. Mark S. Massa, *Charles Augustus Briggs and the Crisis of Historical Criticism* (Minneapolis: Fortress, 1990).

11.2.1 ALEXANDER WHYTE—THE MASTER OF THE PULPIT

The pulpit is a jealous mistress, and will not brook a divided allegiance.

Somehow a great Gospel text is always the most difficult text for me to preach on, so as to make it fresh and interesting. But difficult or easy, I must preach more on such texts, and so must you. It is for such texts, above all else, that we have our pulpits committed to us.

Never think of giving up preaching. The angels around the throne envy you your great work. You say you scarcely know how or what to preach. Look into your own sinful heart, and back into your sinful life, and around

on the world full of sin, and open your New Testament and make application of Christ to yourself and your people and you will preach more
freshly and more powerfully every day.

—Alexander Whyte

From the depths of obscurity to the peaks of prominence and popularity was
the road that **Alexander Whyte** (1836–1921) took, but Scotland's most distinguished preacher of his time took it all with becoming humility before God
and man. Whyte was born in Kirriemuir, a weaving community. His parents
were never married.[1] At the time of Alexander's birth his father was not a Christian, and his mother, a believer, would not compound her disobedience. His
father was later converted and died in America serving with the Union Army
at Bull Run.

In the morning, young Whyte would accompany his mother to the South Free
Church and in the afternoon go with his grandmother to the Relief Church (known
to readers of Sir James Barrie, who wrote *The Little Minister* and who was a
contemporary of Whyte). Whyte was apprenticed in a shoemaker's shop, and,
according to G. F. Barbour's incomparable biography of him, he would read
Milton in the kirkyard during his breaks.[2] Whyte attended King's College, Aberdeen, where he was on the debating society. In the revival of 1859, he showed
great power of preaching in surrounding churches and then went on to New College, Edinburgh, for divinity, where he studied under Rainy, Candlish, and
Davidson and talked theology with his friend Marcus Dods. He spent his time
studying four volumes of Henry Alford and twelve volumes of Thomas Goodwin.
His struggle was as much against "inward depression as it was against hindering
circumstances."[3]

Here are a few milestones that mark his meteoric ascension.

- Worked as a student under Dr. Moses Stuart at Free St. Luke's.
- Preached on Ezekiel 37:1–14 which Candlish criticized, "Not a bad sermon
  if it had been a little more on the text."
- Was an assistant at Free St. John's (1866–1870) in Glasgow under Dr. John
  Roxburgh, where Chalmers had been; saw the rejuvenation of the prayer
  meeting; was a consistent soul-winner; explored Shorter Catechism.
- Became a colleague (1870–1873) of Dr. Candlish, who was nearing retirement at the cathedral of the Scottish Free Church, Free St. George's,
  Shandwicke Place. Here he first met the young William Robertson Smith.
- Took full charge at St. George's (1873) and shared in the revival of 1874
  when Moody and Sankey ministered.
- In the ten-year controversy over Robertson Smith, stood loyally with Smith,
  who was declared "unsettling and unsafe" by the General Assembly. Yet even
  his biographer admits, "He was by no means satisfied that Smith had sufficiently considered the wider bearings of certain statements he had used."[4]
  His own preaching was sound.
- Married Jane Barbour (1881); became a total abstainer; almost died in a serious coach accident.

- Shared ministry with several associates, including Hugh Black, whose brother James succeeded Whyte and wrote the book from his Warrack Lectures which is titled *The Mystery of Preaching,* John Kelman (after Hugh Black went to Union Seminary in New York City, where he taught until 1948), and George H. Morrison of "Wellington" (N.B. 11.2.7).
- Added the duties of principal at New College when Rainy died; pushed church union; resigned the church at eighty and the principalship at eighty-two; died in his sleep in 1921.

Whyte was gregarious and a loyal friend. He interviewed and appreciated Cardinal Newman (which evoked quite a ruckus), liked Joseph Parker, and was close to Professor Henry Drummond. He was a good friend to Baron Von Hugel,[5] and was especially close to his nephew by marriage, **Hubert Simpson**. Simpson served Westborne United Free Church in Glasgow and was invited to succeed Dr. Kelman at Free St. George's but went rather to Westminster Chapel in London.[6]

In his study at 7 Charlotte Square, Whyte read extensively and had a brilliant grasp of a huge body of data, but he always complained about a proverbially bad memory. Here he prepared his five weekly presentations at St. George's, among which were his famous lectures on Bunyan, St. Teresa, William Law, Samuel Rutherford, and Tauler's sermons for Whyte's classes.[7]

Although somewhat shy, he was leonine in the pulpit. Even early in his career his preaching was described as on the highest evangelical level, "awakening, arresting, interesting, scintillating with imaginative insight."[8] His was a most extraordinary imagination, and he studied with Roget's *Thesaurus* ever at his elbow. He used a manuscript in the pulpit to pace himself but was more effective when he spoke extempore. His preaching was "personal, ethical, inward and it dealt but sparingly with speculative or social problems."[9]

Whyte preached against sin with great vehemence, but along with this preaching of righteousness "he did not heal the wound of the people slightly."[10] His trademark was "his scourging of depraved human hearts in the pulpit."[11] Barbour argues that he mellowed with the years.[12] Heart attacks slowed him down but even at seventy-eight, when Chapman and Alexander came for an Edinburgh crusade, the old war-horse filled the pulpit when Chapman became ill.

Whyte was portrayed as "a man of deep and various silences."[13] Admittedly, he was sympathetic to Christ-centered mysticism (to use Deissman's frame of reference), but his sermons were powerful expositions. His *Bible Characters*[14] is greatly loved, as are his beautiful messages on the life of our Lord and on the apostle Paul. Especially favored are his twenty-three sermons on prayer. "The Psalmist—Setting the Lord Always Before Him," from Psalm 16:9, is particularly noteworthy.[15] The last sermon which he preached was "A Study on the Swelling of the Jordan" from Jeremiah 12:5.[16]

Whyte may not have discerned all of the issues being faced by the Free Church in terms of Enlightenment biblical criticism, but he himself was a giant of a preacher—so clear on sin and the need for salvation. Whyte of St. George's had received the commission from the Lord:

What seemed to me to be a divine voice spoke with all-commanding power in my conscience, and said to me as clear as clear could be, "No, go on and flinch not! Go back and finish the work that has been given you to do. Speak out and fear not. Make them, at any cost, to see God's holy law as in a glass. Do you that, for no one else will do it. No one else will so risk his life and his reputation as to do it. And you have not much of either left to risk. Go home and spend what is left of your life in your appointed task of showing my people their sin and their need of my Salvation."[17]

1. G. F. Barbour, *The Life of Alexander Whyte* (London: Hodder and Stoughton, 1923), 15.
2. Ibid., 30–31.
3. Ibid., 49.
4. Ibid., 206.
5. Baron Von Hugel was a Roman Catholic mystic, though his mother was reared a Scottish Presbyterian. Von Hugel was very clear in his warnings about the dangers of subjectivity and pantheism; see Michael De La Bedoyere, *The Life of Baron Von Hugel* (New York: Scribner's, 1961). "Holiness is sanctified courtesy" was a favorite saying.
6. Hubert L. Simpson, *The Intention of His Soul* (London: Hodder and Stoughton, 1921). Note especially "Abigail Voices."
7. Alexander Whyte, *Bunyan Characters* (Edinburgh: Oliphant Anderson, n.d.); two volumes on *Pilgrim's Progress* and one on *The Holy War.* I have treasured my copies of these extraordinarily creative sermons. Spurgeon also preached on Bunyan's characters; cf. C. H. Spurgeon, *Pictures from Pilgrim's Progress* (Grand Rapids: Baker, 1982).
8. Barbour, *The Life of Alexander Whyte,* 164.
9. Ibid., 304. See Wilbur M. Smith, "Some Lesser-Known Pages from Dr. Alexander Whyte," *Chats from a Minister's Library* (Boston: W. A. Wilde, 1951), 103ff.
10. Ibid., 305.
11. Ibid., 373.
12. Ibid., 532.
13. Ibid., 371.
14. Alexander Whyte, *Bible Characters* (Grand Rapids: Zondervan, 1952).
15. Alexander Whyte, *Lord, Teach Us to Pray: Sermons on Prayer* (New York: Ray Long, 1931), 90.
16. Alexander Whyte, *In Remembrance of Me* (Grand Rapids: Baker, 1906, 1970), 83, 95.
17. Ralph G. Turnbull, *Dargan's History of Preaching* (Grand Rapids: Baker, 1974), 3:511.

11.2.2 JOHN KELMAN—THE PREACHER ASTRIDE THE ATLANTIC

The true aim of any one sermon is to be suggestive rather than exhaustive in its treatment of its subject. One great object of preaching is to startle men and women into thinking, to suggest even by opposition, to stimulate thought by exaggeration. There is all the difference in the world between the exaggeration which is the habit of the untruthful mind, and that which the art of a skillful master of persuasive speech.

—John Kelman in the Beecher Lectures

Known for his long and loyal association with Alexander Whyte at Free St. George's (1907–19), **John Kelman** (1864–1929) became known as a influential pulpiteer in his own right. Born in a Free Church manse, he studied at New College in Edinburgh and then three years at Ormand College in Melbourne, Australia. He returned to Scotland to work under **George Adam Smith** (1856–1942) at Queen's Cross, Aberdeen.[1] Later under Whyte he achieved some visibility as a preacher and gave the Beecher Lectures at Yale on "The War and Preaching."[2]

Kelman did war work in France for the YMCA for which he received the O.B.E., but the lectures, like many of his sermons, seem a bit thin. Instead of succeeding Whyte as had been supposed, Kelman took the call to Fifth Avenue Presbyterian Church in New York City after Jowett's departure. But he came to Fifth Avenue as a "worn-out, prematurely old man of fifty-five."[3] With his health breaking, he resigned and returned to Britain to serve a Presbyterian church in Hampstead. He died in Edinburgh at the age of sixty-five.

Yet Kelman had remarkable gifts. He took pages out of Smith's book and used poetry and other literature with skill. He wrote a book on the religion of Robert Louis Stevenson, the fabled Scottish poet and novelist who had a heritage of biblical knowledge and was familiar with Bunyan. (Stevenson's defense of Father Damien was noble, but he had little spirituality himself.)[4]

Kelman's fifty-two abstracts of sermons from Fifth Avenue were published as *Things Eternal*. A reviewer at the time lamented his avoidance of controversial issues, and mused over the lack of reference to redemption.[5] The reviewer wrote, "It will leave the readers waiting for the next work before they can decide on Dr. Kelman's position and power as a preacher."[6] One of the better sermons in the collection is from 2 Kings 5:11, 15 and is titled "Opinion and Knowledge." The text contrasts "Behold I thought" with the consequent "behold now I know."[7]

Kelman's hesitancy in matters of theological commitment mirrors the effect of the general equivocation seen in the Free Church at the time. Theology filters down to the pulpit.

---

1. George Adam Smith studied under both Delitzsch and von Harnack but followed the latter in a more evolutionary approach to biblical origins. His *Historical Geography of the Holy Land* was widely used. His sermons in *Forgiveness of Sins* (1904) are poetic and strong. The sermons on the Gideon cycle from Judges are especially suggestive (London: Hodder and Stoughton, n.d.), 192ff. He also wrote *Life of Henry Drummond* and worked with John Buchan on a history of the Scottish kirk.

2. John Kelman, *The War and Preaching* (London: Hodder and Stoughton, 1919).

3. F. R. Webber, *A History of Preaching in Britain and America* (Milwaukee: North-western, 1955), 2:514.

4. John Kelman, *The Faith of Robert Lewis Stevenson* (Edinburgh: Oliphant Anderson, 1903), 88.

5. Anonymous, "Review of *Eternal Things*," *The Evangelical Christian* (February 1921): 34f.

6. Ibid.

7. John Kelman, *Eternal Things* (New York: George H. Doran, 1920), 157ff.

11.2.3 James Stalker—The Scholar and Statesman in Good Balance

It is no good sign of the times that controversy should be looked down upon.

The preacher must be a master of human words . . . The message from God which we carry is to become a message to men, and therefore we must know how to introduce it successfully to their notice. Strong as our own conviction may be, yet it may be crude and formless; and before it can become the conviction of others, it must take a shape which will arouse their attention. It may belong to a region of thought with which they are unfamiliar, and it has to be brought near, until it enters the circle of their own ideas.

—James Stalker

In the face of the howling gales of rationalistic and evolutionary thought, the divinity halls in Scotland were laid waste. Yet some preachers still stood, as did **James Orr** (1844–1913) of the United Presbyterian Church. Orr's position was conservative and effective in polemics (although he did not stand with Warfield on inerrancy).[1] With him stood **James Denney** (1856–1917) of the Cameronians or Reformed Presbyterians, who like Orr taught at the Free Church College in Glasgow. He was particularly effective in relation to the doctrine of the atonement.[2] Similar in position but more gifted as a preacher was the long-time professor at Aberdeen, **James Stalker** (1848–1928). He was born in Perthshire and studied at Edinburgh, Berlin, and Halle. Stalker pastored in Kirkaldy and then for fifteen glowing years at St. Matthew's in Glasgow. He was known as a more effective preacher than teacher, and was so steady in a time of theological vacillation. Stalker had proportion and balance in whatever he did.[3]

His beautiful study books (coedited with Alexander Whyte) on *The Life of Jesus Christ* and *The Life of St. Paul* were to be in many homes on both sides of the Atlantic. His delightful *Imago Christi: The Example of Jesus Christ* gives a sample of his style and directness. His volume titled *The Atonement* asserts emphatically that "The Bible does not speak of a limitation of the Atonement."[4] He faulted Macleod Campbell and Ritschl for being "insensible to the element in sin which we call guilt and therefore to the process by which this is put away."[5] His matchless devotional study, *The Trial and Death of Jesus Christ,* is compelling.[6] His

Beecher Lectures of 1891 are among the best of the last century. Titled *The Preacher and His Models,* even the outline is worthwhile:

    I. Introductory
   II. The Preacher as a Man of God
  III. The Preacher as a Patriot
  IV. The Preacher as Man of the World
   V. The Preacher as a False Prophet
  VI. The Preacher as a Man
 VII. The Preacher as a Christian
VIII. The Preacher as an Apostle
  IX. The Preacher as a Thinker[7]

In preaching on New Year's Day, Stalker took Psalm 73:24 and divided it as follows: (1) Thou shalt guide me; (2) Thou shalt guide me with thy counsel; and (3) Thou shalt guide me with thy counsel, and afterward . . . "[8] James Stalker knew what it was to dig into the Word of God, and his ministry of teaching and preaching was a blessing to many in a day of widespread drift and defection.

---

1. Glen D. Scorgie, *A Call for Continuity: The Theological Contribution of James Orr* (Ph.D. dissertation, St. Andrews, 1986). His outstanding work includes his article on the Virgin Birth for *The Fundamentals* as well as other articles; his editorship of *International Standard Bible Encyclopedia;* James Orr, *Revelation and Inspiration* (New York: Scribner's, 1916); James Orr, *God's Image in Man* (Grand Rapids: Eerdmans, 1948).
2. James Denney, *The Death of Christ* (London: Tyndale, 1951). This is choice. Also, *The Atonement and the Modern Mind* (London: Hodder and Stoughton, 1903) and *Studies in Theology* (New York: Armstrong, 1895). These are his lectures at the University of Chicago. Denney's wife thought his preaching needed more pathos. She introduced him to the writings of Spurgeon, and he became Christ-centered and evangelistic.
3. Ralph C. Turnbull, *Dargan's History of Preaching* (Grand Rapids: Baker, 1974), 3:479. One of Stalker's colleagues at Aberdeen, Sir William M. Ramsay (1851–1939), made a strong contribution toward the appreciation of the integrity of the Book of Acts over against the Tubingen emphasis. See W. Ward Gasque, *Sir William Ramsay: Archaeologist and New Testament Scholar* (Grand Rapids: Baker, 1966).
4. James Stalker, *The Atonement* (London: Hodder and Stoughton, 1908), 105.
5. Ibid., 122.
6. James Stalker, *The Trial and Death of Jesus Christ* (Grand Rapids: Zondervan, 1894). Well-divided sermons.
7. James Stalker, *The Preacher and His Models* (Grand Rapids: Baker, 1967). Here Stalker shares what McMillan of Ullapool gave him: "Begin low; proceed slow; rise higher; take fire."
8. James Stalker in *Sermons and Outlines for Special Occasions* (Grand Rapids: Baker, 1952), 9ff.

11.2.4 GEORGE MATHESON—THE BLIND PREACHER WHO HELPED PEOPLE SEE

At the beginning of the week it [his sermon] was without form and void,
but at the end he was always able to pronounce it very good!
—of George Matheson and often said by him

Outbursts of genuinely moving preaching took place in the Church of Scotland itself,[1] and considered one of the two best preachers in Edinburgh along with Alexander Whyte was **George Matheson** (1842–1906). Born in a wealthy Glasgow merchant's home, he suffered from severely impaired vision which was congenital and progressive. His eldest sister helped him with his studies and throughout his life, though he did learn to use Braille.

At seven Matheson preached to his family.[2] In divinity hall he received honors and was drawn to Professor John Caird, who, like his brother Edward (who went on to teach at Oxford), became a stout defender of Hegelian absolute idealism.[3] This perspective tinged Matheson's thought throughout his life. Matheson preached his first homily on "Precious in the Lord's sight is the death of his saints," immediately marking him as a great preacher in embryo.[4] A born actor, Matheson was also a poet and wrote the well-known hymns "O Love That Will Not Let Me Go" and "Make Me a Captive, Lord."

His first pastoral charge was as assistant to J. R. MacDuff at Sandyford (cf. 10.5.8), where his first sermon had beauty of style but not much spirit. In 1867 he became pastor at the resort village of Innellan. Matheson had a clear, ringing voice, and for eighteen years he drew throngs to hear his striking twenty-minute sermons and original prayers. He would choose his text for the next Sunday morning on Sunday afternoon after preaching and then ponder it for a few days. Blessed with a remarkable memory, he would write it out completely and memorize it. He did this until one unforgettable day when he went blank in the pulpit and had to sit down. From then on he mastered his material more generally and preached extempore. His reading of Scripture was such that strangers had no idea he was blind. As one visitor wrote:

There is a power of eloquence wielded by Dr. Matheson which places him on a level with any or all of them [referring to Guthrie, Caird, Macleod, and Tullock], while in originality of conception, and forcible, quaint expression, he excels them all.[5]

Matheson wrote some philosophical books and gave the Baird Lectures in 1881. He was noncommittal on evolution at this time but later came to disbelieve in it. He wrote fourteen books in all, the later of which were richly devotional messages. Tennyson was very fond of Matheson for his writings.[6]

In 1885 Matheson preached before the queen at Balmoral. Rather than her customary signed portrait, she presented the sightless Matheson with a small bust of herself as a remembrance of the occasion.

In 1886 he took the pastoral charge for St. Bernard's in Edinburgh, a congregation of some fifteen hundred members, where he served with great distinction for thirteen years. He never preached a sermon to his congregation for a second time. In addition to his pulpit work he was known for his Bible classes and addresses to teachers. For years he employed a secretary and helper with his own funds. In his prime he was an indefatigable visitor—blindness was never an excuse for him. He had a special relationship with Joseph Parker and often exchanged pulpits with Alexander Whyte from Free St. George's. Also of encouragement to Matheson was his old friend Dr. Hugh Macmillan of Greenock.[7]

Matheson's books of brief sermon summations are exceedingly rich and suggestive, though some show a tendency to overlook the essential context. His messages on "seek that you may excel" from 1 Corinthians 14:12, and "The Peaceableness After Purity" from James 3:17, "First pure, then peaceable," are powerful.[8] So too, his studies of men and women of the Bible are well worth perusing. His gripping turn of phrase and his trenchant exposition can be seen in his last book, *Rests by the River*. Favorites include "The Abuse of Noble Things" from Matthew 6:23, "If the light that is in you be darkness, how great is that darkness!"[9] Another is his remarkable "The Temporary Loss Involved in Eternal Gain," from John 4:28–29 on the woman's forgotten waterpots.

Always frank and outspoken, he was yet much loved by his parishioners. When he retired in 1899 at the age of fifty-seven, the sorrow of his people knew no bounds. He died on holiday in 1906. We are richer preachers ourselves because of the insights of the preacher who could never observe his congregation.

---

1. An outstanding example is James MacGregor, who served forty years at St. Cuthbert's in Edinburgh. Lady Frances Balfour has given us a splendid biography of this preacher who always "felt dull in the forenoon." See *Life and Letters of James MacGregor* (London: Hodder and Stoughton, 1912).
2. D. Macmillan, *The Life of George Matheson* (London: Hodder and Stoughton, 1907), 20.
3. Alan P. F. Sell, *Defending and Declaring the Faith* (Exeter: Paternoster, 1987), 64ff.
4. Macmillan, *The Life of George Matheson*, 50.
5. Ibid., 111.
6. Macmillan, *The Life of George Matheson*, 215.
7. A very choice study on John 15 is one of the legacies of Hugh Macmillan, *The True Vine* (London: Macmillan, 1879).
8. George Matheson, *Times of Retirement* (New York: Revell, 1901), 77, 143.
9. George Matheson, *Rests by the River* (Cincinnati: Jennings and Graham, 1906), 305, 356.

11.2.5 GEORGE MACDONALD—THE PREACHER WHO WROTE FANTASY AND NOVELS

But you can begin at once to be a disciple of the Living One—by obeying Him in the first thing you can think of in which you are not obeying Him. We must learn to obey Him in everything, and so must begin somewhere. Let it be at once, and in the very next thing that lies at the door of our conscience! Oh fools and slow of heart, if you think of nothing but Christ, and do not set yourselves to do His words! You but build your houses on the sands.

—George MacDonald

Known for his influence on C. S. Lewis and upon his circle, **George MacDonald** (1824–1905) was born in rural Aberdeenshire and studied science at Aberdeen. His mother died when he was very young. MacDonald reacted strongly against the high Calvinism of his father but retained a close and communicative relationship with him until the old man's death in 1858.[1] MacDonald became a Congregational minister and served the congregation at Arundel, in Sussex, where his denial of heathen condemnation was argued and he was ultimately starved out of the manse.[2] For a while he preached in Manchester. He started writing to supplement the income for his large family, and the widow of Lord Byron began to assist him financially. He moved to London and ultimately joined the Church of England and moved to Italy. Always sickly, he yet toured and lectured in America extensively in 1873. He was close to F. D. Maurice and John Ruskin and was acquainted with Dickens, Carlyle, and Trollope.

MacDonald's original works were not easy to read. Many had rambling sentences of 100 to 150 words in length and some in excess of 200 words. Many of his books have been rewritten and simplified and are widely read today, one of the most popular being *The Minister's Restoration,* the story of a minister's sin and the way back.[3] In all, he wrote twenty-nine realistic novels, all of which have the conventional happy ending. He also wrote books of fantasy which may have been a model for the *Chronicles of Narnia.* His imaginative fiction gave T. S. Eliot his wasteland motif.

MacDonald's preaching was Christocentric and clear. He argued that "correct opinions are no substitute for obedience,"[4] but he was unfortunately influenced by rationalistic German theology and by Blake, Swedenborg, and Boehme. MacDonald kept working to bring the focus clearly on the person of the Lord Jesus but veered off toward universalism. He taught that hell is not eternal, there is a second chance after death, and even Satan will ultimately repent. C. S. Lewis argues against this lurch to universalism in *The Great Divorce.*

George MacDonald's sermons breathe the fresh air of creativity and beauty, but his belief system eroded sadly.

---

1. Rolland Hein, ed., George MacDonald, *Life Essential: The Hope of the Gospel* (Wheaton, Ill.: Harold Shaw, 1974).
2. Richard H. Reis, *George MacDonald* (New York: Twayne, 1972).
3. George MacDonald, *The Minister's Restoration* (Minneapolis: Bethany House, 1988). The Scottish novel uses the Scottish dialect, which is a treat to read.
4. Rolland Hein, ed., George MacDonald, *Creation in Christ* (Wheaton, Ill.: Harold Shaw, 1876). Especially sermons 1, 2, and 3.

11.2.6 JOHN WATSON (IAN MACLAREN)—THE PREACHER WHO COULD TELL GREAT STORIES

Of the parishioners in Logiealmond in the Highlands: I am in the ministry today because of the tenderness and charity of those country-folk, those perfect gentlemen and Christians.

The critical and influential event in the religious week is the sermon . . . whenever preaching falls into low esteem, the Church becomes weak and corrupt . . . it is impossible to exaggerate the opportunity given to the preacher when he ascends the pulpit and faces his congregation.

—John Watson (Ian Maclaren)

Inheriting from his mother a fiercely patriotic, Highland Jacobite, and Roman Catholic background, and from his stern father a Free Church upbringing, **John Watson** (1850–1907), or **Ian Maclaren,** as he called himself in many of his writings, carved a unique niche for his ministry.[1] He was born in England, where his father was a civil servant, but was reared in Perthshire. His minister there was the Reverend John Milne of the McCheyne school of evangelistic piety. Watson was fed on Spurgeon's sermons and learned of Henry Drummond while at Stirling High School.[2] In 1866 he began studies at Edinburgh, where he sat under the ministry of Horatius Bonar at the Grange Free Church and became a student for Free Church ministry. In his studies under A. B. Davidson and Principal Rainy, "the determined orthodoxy of the Free Church began to yield."[3]

Watson studied briefly at Tubingen under Beck and then spent three miserable months at Barclay Church in Edinburgh. The fit was just not right. This was followed by three idyllic years in Logiealmond in Perthshire, which he later memorialized in his charming books like *Beside the Bonnie Brier Bush.*[4] In 1877 he took pastoral responsibility in Free St. Matthew's in Glasgow. During this time he stood firmly in the premillennial advent camp.[5] Conservative in his instincts, he was an established churchman in theory and broad in his sympathies.

His preaching style began to embrace a wider message and appeal, and this he brought to his famous twenty-five years at Sefton Park Presbyterian Church in Liverpool. The church grew rapidly, and he soon visited America, where he gave the Beecher Lectures in 1896.[6]

Not a high Calvinist by any means, he was a sentimentalist in his characterization of rural Scottish idylls. Many loved to hear him, including Matthew Arnold, who worshiped at Sefton Park on the day that he died. Watson himself retired in 1906 and died in America on his way to deliver a lectureship at Vanderbilt University.[7]

We see in Watson the incipient dilution of the orthodox insistence on the deity of Christ and the doctrines of grace as based on the trustworthy documents of Scripture. He did not deny the doctrines but backed off from any strong assertion of biblical authority.[8] Watson believed that the Word was *contained* in the Bible and was not to be equated with it. Although he did not follow the logical consequences of his position, Watson opened the door to the trend that would gut Scottish evangelicalism and its preaching even to the present day.

1. Ian Maclaren is not to be confused with the also very able Ian Macpherson, who delivered the important lectures on preaching, *The Burden of the Lord* (Nashville: Abingdon, 1955). See Macpherson, *Kindling* (Old Tappan, N.J.: Revell, 1969).
2. W. Robertson Nicoll, *Ian Maclaren: The Life of John Watson* (London: Hodder and Stoughton, 1908), 26. Nicoll was a gifted preacher in his own right who spent his life in England as an editor and founder of *The British Weekly.* He was quite evangelical and edited both *The Expositor's Bible* and *Expositor's Greek Testament.*
3. Ibid., 49.
4. Ian Maclaren, *Beside the Bonnie Brier Bush* (Chicago: E. A. Weeks, 1894). Drumtochty is of course the Logiealmond of his own experience. The most well-known chapter is "His Mother's Sermon," in which the liberally touched young dominie is urged by his dying mother to "say a gude word for Jesus." Another book of the rural Scottish pastorate is the more recent *Highland Shepherds* by Arthur Hewitt (1939).
5. Watson's Glasgow stories are found in the delightful *St. Jude's* (London: Religious Tract Society, 1907).
6. John Watson, *The Cure of Souls* (New York: Dodd, Mead, 1896). Several chapters on preaching are convincing.
7. John Watson, *God's Message to the Human Soul* (New York: Revell, 1907). The Cole Lectures that he never delivered.
8. Ibid., 164.

11.2.7 GEORGE MORRISON—SILVER-TONGUED EXPOSITOR OF WELLINGTON CHURCH, GLASGOW

Young preachers will do well to guard against the tendency to rush, which is the bane of modern life. The habit of unprofitable bustle and rush, the present-day preoccupation with small affairs and engagements, is withholding many good things from us. For myself, it is essential that I have leisure to brood and meditate.

I simply get my message, then I prepare my heart and mind to deliver it, sit down and write it, and on Sunday give it to my people.

—George Herbert Morrison

Just as Alexander Whyte captured Edinburgh, **George Herbert Morrison** (1866–1928) took Glasgow. People lined up to get into his evening services.[1] He was born in Glasgow, the youngest of seven children in a line that traced back to the Island of Lewis. His father was a schoolman and Free Church elder, and his mother, who died when he was only five, named him George Herbert after the celebrated preacher/poet (cf. 6.2.3).

In 1883 George commenced study at Glasgow, where he was influenced by the Cairds and where C. Sylvester Horne (cf. 11.3.7) was a classmate and a confidant. Henry Drummond deeply influenced him at this time, and he worked for two years under Sir James Murray on the *Oxford English Dictionary.*[2] Both James Denney (who would later be his member at Wellington) and James Candlish (son of the great old warhorse of the faith) tilted him conservatively. Morrison strongly supported the doctrine of substitutionary atonement.

Morrison served as city missionary at Oakshaw Free Church and then as assistant to Whyte at St. George's. Here he helped develop the evening service. In 1894 he began a four-year pastorate in Thursoway in the North and first came to the attention of the General Assembly when he reported on the revival in that region. In 1898 he moved to St. John's in Dundee, where his weak voice was at great disadvantage in a sanctuary notorious for poor acoustics. His health was never robust, and he was forced to take a respite. When he returned to work, it seemed as if he was more compassionate and companionable than before. As always, he engaged in a strenuous pastoral ministry as well as a rigorous regimen for his preaching. Despite his health problems, he never took Monday off. His book of sermons titled *Flood-Tide* came out of these difficult years.[3]

The Morningside Church in Edinburgh coveted his services, and Rainy proposed him for Fifth Avenue in New York, but Morrison stayed put. He also turned down the new Stevenson Memorial Church in Glasgow, where W. M. Clow then took the call. In 1902 Morrision did accept an invitation to the Wellington Church in Glasgow, which sits like a Greek temple on the edge of the university. Here he served for twenty-six glorious years until his death at age sixty-two.

The Wellington Church was an original secession congregation but had become the largest United Free Church in the city. Morrison moved the afternoon service to the evening. The worship services were strongly Presbyterian. Morrison typically preached a traditional expository series in the morning, moving to a textual-topical style in the evening. He held a popular Bible class after the evening service, and in June gave Monday night lectures which claimed considerable attention for many years. Typical series on the life of Abraham and the Book of Nehemiah show his strengths.[4] Communion services at Wellington were memorable. His favorite hymn, "When I Survey That Wondrous Cross," was invariably sung at those services. His prayer meeting addresses were also well-remembered,[5] and Morrison was known for his children's sermons. He also had the distinction of preaching the first Scottish sermon over the radio.

Morrison had a modest and gentle spirit. He was an inveterate reader of sermons, selecting one to read each day. He had a personal library of more than six thousand volumes and possessed "great dexterity in quotation."[6] His facility with words was most attractive, but his sermons were pastoral and devotional—not the best models on how to handle a text. He had a tendency to do much with obscure texts, such as Job 5:23, "Thou shalt be in league with the stones of the field," or Revelation 12:16, "The Earth Helped the Woman," using the theme "How Science Helps Religion."[7]

In 1926 Morrison was elected moderator of the General Assembly and traveled the next year in Africa. Shortly after returning, he became critically ill and died suddenly. Gammie describes Morrison and how he appealed to the young who populated his evening services: "The man in the pulpit with the soft voice, the quiet, effortless style, and the subtle elusive charm."[8]

1. Many noted preachers were in Glasgow, including the stately W. M. Macgregor whose sermons *Scholar as Preacher* were well known, as later became the case with his Warrack Lectures on *The Making of a Preacher.*
2. Alexander Gammie, *Dr. George H. Morrison: The Man and His Work* (London: James Clarke, 1928), 34–35.
3. George H. Morrison, *Flood-Tide* (Grand Rapids: Baker, 1971). The George Morrison Library has six volumes.
4. George H. Morrison, *Morning Sermons* (Grand Rapids: Baker, 1971).
5. Gammie, *Dr. George H. Morrison,* 112.
6. Ibid., 48.
7. Examples of this abound as "The Message of the Colt," in *Wind on the Heath* (Grand Rapids: Kregel, 1994), 79ff. What should be emphasized is that Palm Sunday is about Jesus Christ not the colt.
8. Alexander Gammie, *Preachers I Have Heard* (London: Pickering and Inglis, n.d.), 180.

11.3 THE ENGLISH CHAMPIONS

Let us not give up the great principles of plenary inspiration.
—Bishop J. C. Ryle

With the death of Queen Victoria and the move into the Edwardian age, even the novelist Henry James was moved to remark, "The wild waters are upon us now."[1] **Thomas Hardy** (1840–1928), the famous novelist and poet, is an example of the currents flowing. A lifelong Anglican who early had aspiration for holy orders, he knew the Bible better than any other writer of his time. Even though he became an unbeliever and gave up the supernatural entirely, he continued communing.[2] Influenced by positivism and the indifferent God of Darwinianism, he kept going to church as a habit, interested only in a Christ without dogma. Even though he had praying Christian friends like the Baptist Henry Brastow (whom he caricatures in "A Laodicean") and Horace Moule from his Dorchester days (of the well-known Moule family from which Bishop H. C. G. Moule comes), Hardy's poems "The Funeral of God" and "God-Forsaken" say it all. Yet even in the face of massive and militant unbelief, there were preachers who stood mindful of the example of Spurgeon and the exhortation of Ryle.

1. After Strachey's *Eminent Victorians* (Garden City, N.Y.: Garden City Publishing Co., n.d.), cf. Piers Brendon's *Eminent Edwardians* (New York: Houghton Mifflin, 1980); also John Paterson, *Edwardians: London Life and Letters, 1901–1914* (New York: Ivan Dee, 1995).
2. Martin Seymour-Smith, *Hardy: A Biography* (New York: St. Martin's, 1994), 28, 30. Key to this distinguished writer.

11.3.1 WILLIAM L. WATKINSON—THE PREACHER WITH ARCHITECTONIC GENIUS

> Preaching is a subject of which we are never weary; it has for us an abiding charm. For my own part, I love a book on homiletics as much as ever I did in my life. I read with eager expectation the last published lectures on the art of preaching, trusting to know how to do it before I die.
>
> I see no reason why our preaching should not display the same skill that is brought into the artistic world, the same power, the same delivery, the same perfection of finish. If an artist puts all the labor and pains that he does into a picture, should we put any less into our sermons?
>
> —William L. Watkinson

The spiritual heirs of the Wesleys were particularly hard hit by the tidal waves of skepticism and unbelief that pilloried the people of God at this time, but there were still resolute voices that spoke and knees that did not bow. Among these is **William L. Watkinson** (1838–1925). Watkinson was born in Hull in Yorkshire, where his father was a chapelkeeper at Kingston Methodist Church. We know little about him apart from a book of letters exchanged between him and a friend in their declining years. Watkinson started to preach at age eighteen. He was so tall and thin and frail in appearance that he was turned down for overseas service in India and narrowly approved for the itinerant Methodist ministry.[1] He spent only six weeks in training college and then was thrust into a needy vacancy. He served Methodist preaching points, most notably in Liverpool, and was then editor and president of the Wesleyan Methodist Conference. Watkinson made one extensive tour of the United States and was well received at Moody Bible Institute, where he preached from John 6.

Hugh Sinclair marks Watkinson as a preacher known for "the explicit, architectural manner of preaching, which is almost a lost art in these impressionistic days."[2] He read voraciously and crafted his massive discourses most carefully. He read Gibbon's *Decline and Fall of the Roman Empire* three times aloud to himself in order to ingest its striking lucidity and style. Watkinson loved to preach through a biblical book and distribute outline summaries. He used irony (and few have ever used it well) and occasionally allowed humor to get away from him. He was known for his illustrations and for the timeliness of his preaching.

One book of Watkinson's preaching gives a searching and scathing exploration of what sin is.[3] His oratory occasionally was a bit too florid and turgid but such was characteristic of the Edwardian Age. Especially poignant is his message on "The Plea of Evil," from the man with an unclean spirit who cried "Let us alone!" This is a thoughtful exposé of the masochistic nature of sin.[4]

Like George Morrison, he had a penchant for unusual texts and short texts. He tended to be moralistic and hortatory, which may have become the general rule in his movement rather than the exception.[5] John Bishop is accurate in his assessment:

> The chief criticism that can be made of these sermons is that there is too little of Christ in them, and too much of man, his character and conduct.

There is a man-centeredness in his sermons as the very titles of his books suggest. They are uniformly exhortatory or didactic. Exhortation and instruction are honorable forms of preaching in the New Testament but they are definitely subordinate forms. They rise out of the Kerygma. In these sermons we are instructed about character and conduct, but rarely are we given a vision of God.[6]

What appeared as a hairline fracture in Watkinson would become a shattered bone in the movement of which he was a part.

---

1. John Bishop, "W. L. Watkinson: The Touch of Reality," *Preaching* (March–April 1990): 41.
2. F. R. Webber, *A History of Preaching in Britain and America* (Milwaukee: Northwestern, 1952), 1:621.
3. W. L. Watkinson, *The Transfigured Sackcloth* (New York: Dutton, 1906).
4. Ibid., 87ff. Watkinson wrote many volumes of published sermons.
5. W. L. Watkinson, *Frugality in the Spiritual Life* (New York: Revell, 1908). The title sermon comes from the text in John 6:12, which tells of gathering up the leftovers. This misses the aorta of the passage, which is Jesus and the great hunger.
6. Bishop, "W. L. Watkinson," 44. Another example of this type of evasion of authorial intent in a text is the famous Lenten series brought by Rev. William Havergal (father of Frances Ridley Havergal) on the Queen of Sheba.

11.3.2 DINSDALE T. YOUNG—ONE OF THE LAST OF THE SHOUTING METHODISTS

Preaching as an ordinance is part of God's good pleasure. There has been no revocation of this supreme ordinance. It is the sacrament. Of all the acts of worship it is the most helpful. The churches grieve God's Spirit when they depreciate preaching.

Preaching which has taken the deity out of Christ, the Atonement out of the Cross, faith out of the method of salvation, and the indwelling of the Divine Spirit out of Christian experience, is "cut down like the grass and withereth."

No preacher is permanently popular if he does not make people uncomfortable. We must wound with the sword of the Spirit. We must show them all the mercy by showing them all the sin.

—Dinsdale T. Young

One of London's most popular preachers in his day, but a man of direct and simple speech, **Dinsdale T. Young** (1861–1938) was born in Northumbria (as was Joseph Parker). Young's father was a prominent physician. Dinsdale was converted and called to the ministry, beginning to preach at fifteen. He was ordained in 1879, the youngest person until then ever ordained to the Methodist ministry.

Young trained at Headingley College in Leeds and served with growing reputation in places like Nicholson Square Wesleyan Methodist Church in Edinburgh. In 1906 to 1914 he served Wesley Chapel, City Road, in London, and then was assigned to Westminster Central Hall, where he preached to full houses for twenty-four years until just weeks short of his death in 1938. Young spoke to the largest congregations in London during those years, and though he was not nearly as gifted a preacher as Jowett, it was said that "Jowett gets Dinsdale Young's overflow."[1] Liberals in and out of his denomination did not think he would last because he was such a fundamentalist, but he continued to preach seven or eight times weekly and travel ten thousand miles a year. He graciously never attacked his opponents but neither did he deviate from the old gospel.

Dressed always in frock coat and silk hat, Young was increasingly picturesque as he grew old, his "white locks streaming out behind him as if he were Liszt, while two triangles of white hair flanked the high pink dome of his forehead."[2] He was a preacher of the old school and yet attracted many young people. He had a great speaking voice and was a skillful communicator. Young loved to dig into commentaries—one of his favorites was Thomas Goodwin—and he reread Bonar's diary every year. A great lover of Trollope, Young was an "inveterate homiletician."

He usually struck three mains and extolled expository and evangelistic preaching. Occasionally his predilection for unusual texts got him off track, as did his sermon on "Religious Solidity" from Song of Solomon 1:17, "The beams of our house are cedar."[3] Young did preach the gospel of sin and grace unflinchingly. One observer said that he was so orthodox that he had become a heretic.[4] Young's classic message on "The Protevangelium" from Genesis 3:15 breaks down into two sections:

I. The Savior's Injury of Satan
II. Satan's Injury to the Savior

The emphasis is strongly on redemption.[5] The reader may chafe at his use of such short snippets of texts, yet one cannot but marvel at the insights of a sermon like "The Consistency of Character and Conduct" from John 10:13, "The hireling flees because he is a hireling."[6]

Young addressed the largest audiences in Britain right up until World War II. He apparently indulged a little foray into British Israelism, but remained loyal to the everlasting gospel. In his last moments of consciousness, he sang over and over, "Just as I am without one plea." His last words were, "I triumph."[7]

---

1. John Bishop, "A Champion of Orthodoxy: Dinsdale T. Young," *Preaching* (November–December 1987): 46.
2. Alexander Gammie, *Preachers I Have Heard* (London: Pickering and Inglis, 1945), 145.
3. Dinsdale T. Young, *Sermons on Unfamiliar Texts* (Grand Rapids: Baker, 1899, 1970), 117ff.

4. F. R. Webber, *A History of Preaching in Britain and America* (Milwaukee: Northwestern, 1952), 1:679.

5. Dinsdale T. Young, *The Enthusiasm of God* (Cincinnati: Jennings and Graham, n.d.), 79ff.

6. Dinsdale T. Young, *The Crimson Book and Other Evangelical Sermons* (Grand Rapids: Baker, 1903, 1974), 206ff.

7. Bishop, "A Champion of Orthodoxy," 47.

11.3.3 G. Campbell Morgan—The Expositor of Expositors

For two years my Bible was shut; two years of sadness and sorrow. Strange, alluring materialistic theories were in the air, and to these I turned . . . I became well-versed in the philosophies that were the vogue in England at that time, but from them I got no relief. In my despair I took all the books that I had, placed them in a cupboard, turned the key, and there they remained for seven years. I bought a new Bible, and began to read it with an open mind and a determined will. That Bible found me. The Book gave forth a glow which warmed my heart, and the Word of God which I read therein gave to my troubled soul the relief and satisfaction that I had sought for elsewhere. Since that time I have lived for one end— to preach the teachings of the Book that found me.

It is my conviction that the Scriptures, as originally committed to writing, were safeguarded in every word by the Holy Spirit. . . . There is nothing I desire more in my dealing with the Bible than to lead people to a personal appreciation and understanding of it . . . We are out to storm the citadel of the will and seize it for Jesus Christ.

—G. Campbell Morgan

Called the Prince of Expositors, the greatest expository preacher of his time, **George Campbell Morgan** (1863–1945) held great masses of people spellbound by his preaching for sixty years. Born in Tetbury, England, he was known on both sides of the Atlantic as "a specialist in the interpretation of God's Blessed Book." His parents reared him in Cardiff, Wales, where he was part of the Roath Road Wesleyan Methodist Church. His father was an independent Baptist of strong views who came under the influence of George Müller and the Plymouth Brethren. Young George preached sermons in his home as a boy of seven, and was deeply troubled with the death of his beloved sister, Lizzie. At thirteen he preached his first public sermon in Monmouth on salvation. The sermon had four main points:

   I. A great salvation (Hebrews 2:3)
  II. A common salvation (Jude 3)
 III. An eternal salvation (Hebrews 5:9)
 IV. A present salvation (2 Corinthians 6:2)[1]

At nineteen he had a deep crisis with respect to the authority of the Word. This was resolved in favor of faith and an unflinching confidence in the Scripture.[2] He taught for three years at a Jewish college for boys in Birmingham, an exposure that greatly enriched his understanding of the Old Testament. Yet Morgan had no formal education.

Morgan's Career

In 1888, to his great anguish, his trial sermon before the Methodist establishment in Birmingham did not meet muster.[3] He preached the sermon in a hall seating more than one thousand, but only seventy-five listeners were present. Morgan would harbor lifelong negative feelings toward small crowds. Despite this rebuff, Morgan remained close to Methodists like Dinsdale Young, William Watkinson, Samuel Chadwick, and even J. Gregory Mantle, who had been one of the examiners.

Morgan nearly joined the Salvation Army, but after a thirteen-month mission in Hull (where his lifelong friendship with Gypsy Smith began), he was ordained by the Congregationalists and entered into a distinguished and well-heard ministry.

From 1889 to 1891, Morgan pastored in Stone. His first text was Matthew 28:20, which was also used for his last sermon at Westminster. From 1891 to 1893, he served Heron Court Congregational Church in Rugeley, where his expository method began to jell. In the years 1893 to 1897, Morgan served at Westminster Road Church in Birmingham, where he enjoyed much fellowship with R. W. Dale. In 1897, Morgan took the call to New Court Church, Tollington Park North, where he served until 1899. Here also is where Manton, Baxter, and Goodwin had preached.

The great numbers of converts in the Moody-Sankey meetings both in Britain and in America needed to be built up in the Word. This was the wave which Morgan rode to such eminence. When Moody died in 1899, Morgan was invited to come to Northfield and spearhead the extension and conference ministry. In a series of farewell meetings before he left for America, Morgan was surrounded by his close friends J. D. Jones, F. B. Meyer, and Joseph Parker, who took occasion to observe:

> You may depend upon one thing, the only ministry that will last, and be as fresh at the end as it was at the beginning, is a biblical and an expository one. Mere anecdotes fail and in the long run exhaust themselves, the Word of the Lord abideth forever.[4]

Morgan traveled extensively in North America from 1901 to 1904. "The nomad in his blood" drove him to exhaustion. From 1904–1917, Morgan served at Westminster Chapel, London, "the white elephant of Congregationalism." Westminster had never filled its twenty-five hundred seats since the new building was dedicated in 1865 but was filled from Morgan's first Sunday twice every Lord's Day.

The Welsh Revival of 1904–05, in which Morgan was involved, was part of the cascading impact of his ministry. He went on to serve conjointly as president of Chestnut College, Cambridge, which unfortunately sped the collapse of his health. In 1917, Morgan was forced to resign this post due to one of his episodic health breakdowns. He then served Highbury Quadrant Church, which lost eighty of its sons in World War I. (Interestingly, Nonconformist bore disproportionate losses in both world wars.)

In 1919, Morgan returned to America for frenetic itineration. He served terms at the Bible Institute of Los Angeles (BIOLA), Gordon in Boston, and brief pastorates in Cincinnati and at Tabernacle Presbyterian in Philadelphia. He enjoyed tremendous response to his studies. Then in 1933, it was back to Westminster at age sixty-nine (though not all in the church favored it). He ministered there for a decade, endured the horrors of the blitz, and retired.

In all, Campbell Morgan made fifty-four crossings of the Atlantic and wrote seventy-two books by 1930. His first book, *Discipleship,* came in 1897; his strong book *The Ten Commandments* was issued in 1901. In 1915 came *The Living Messages of the Books of the Bible,* which shows his genius for synthesis as his commentaries demonstrate his brilliance in analysis.[5] His work on Jeremiah is one of the best, as are his commentaries on Matthew and Acts.[6]

Morgan's Communication

"He made the Bible come alive!" was the verdict on his preaching. Standing tall and slender, frail and almost gaunt in the pulpit, his voice (which may be heard on recordings) was amazingly strong and deeply resonant. John Hutton, who had a vastly influential ministry at Westminster in the 1920s, observed, "Morgan always spoke with authority."[7] Morgan felt that the grave danger for the preacher was to use scriptural fragments out of context. His method applied the contextual principle in Bible study.[8] He was dispensational from early on, seeing that Israel is different from the church.[9]

Morgan loved new translations, particularly modern-language versions like Weymouth's. "This man believes the Bible!" his listeners agreed. He built his great Friday evening Bible classes with more than fifteen hundred in attendance. The charts and analysis we have in *The Analyzed Bible* first saw the light of day in that setting.

Morgan rarely used illustrations and almost stands alone in his general disdain for application, believing that application is the work of the Holy Spirit. Painting word pictures was his special strength (as in *The Great Physician* and *The Parables and Metaphors of Our Lord*). In his Sprunt Lectures at Union Seminary in Richmond, published as *The Ministry of the Word,* he showed the close relationship between the preacher and the pastor in ministry. In "Biblical Homiletics" he put his oar into the water on the behalf of his method and called for the essentials: truth, clarity, and passion.[10]

The "one thing" for Morgan was preaching and its careful preparation. His public reading of the Scripture was momentous, and his choice of hymns was careful, though he was fond of the newer genre of music, gospel songs.[11] His monumental *Westminster Pulpit* is still well worthwhile for the expositor. He used various patterns in dividing the sermon, but his progression was always natural and logical. The text remained supreme and structure was never bony. Even to the end, when his sermons were under thirty minutes, his published works on Job, the Corinthian correspondence, and his studies in the Psalms are scintillating. "Let the text make its statement," was his plea. One of the aristocrats of the pulpit, Morgan was eloquent yet substantial. Horton Davies said of him, "He proves conclusively the varied spiritual wealth that is at the disposal of the preacher who mines the deep lodes of the Bible."[12] Even a secular journalist found himself taken with the man and his message during a memorable ministry in Baltimore.[13] Who has ever led us into Hosea as has Morgan in his *Hosea—The Heart and Holiness of God*? Most would agree that they are seldom left unmoved by this venerable practitioner of the craft.

Morgan's Commitment

Wilbur Smith described Morgan's preaching as "a mystic spell" and "the intangible atmosphere of union between teacher and taught." In probing for the secret of Morgan's extraordinarily fruitful ministry in the Word, we find both Smith and Warren Wiersbe attributing his success to hard work.[14] He truly gave himself to unremitting toil and concentration on the task of exegesis and sermonics. Those who have written about him speak of his "capacity for friendship." Although somewhat unapproachable in manner, Morgan built and sustained rich, warm friendships that ennobled his insights and inspiration. His dear friend and longtime associate Albert Swift, his soul brother Len Broughton from Atlanta, and his colleague Dr. John MacInnis, for whom he left BIOLA out of loyalty, are but samples of the breadth and depth of his relationships. His association with D. Martyn Lloyd-Jones, whom he brought from Wales to share his pulpit beginning in 1938, testifies to this particularly in view of the sharp differences between the two on Calvinism-Arminian issues. Lloyd-Jones's remarks at Morgan's memorial service demonstrate a genuine friendship.[15]

Always an impeccable dresser, Morgan was sometimes accused of being a free spender and of traveling too luxuriously. Yet he was generous and kind, self-effacing and genuinely humble. A significant testimony to Morgan is the fact that all four of his sons became preachers, three Presbyterian and one Anglican. Some have wanted him to be more doctrinal but he was never one to subordinate the text to a doctrine. His priority was ever to release the Word of God. As such a champion, he must be accorded a large place in this history.

When he preached at Moody Bible Institute, he gave the people Malachi, and when he was at Northfield one season, he gave them what we have in his work on the Minor Prophets. Oh for such a steady and solid diet today! How many would love to be so nourished.

---

1. John Harries, *G. Campbell Morgan: The Man and His Ministry* (New York: Revell, 1930), 27.
2. Jill Morgan, *A Man of the Word: Life of G. Campbell Morgan* (New York: Revell,

1951), 39. An outstanding work by his daughter-in-law. Also of great interest is Morgan's *This Was His Faith: The Expository Letters of G. Campbell Morgan* (London: Pickering and Inglis, n.d.). One of his grandsons has also written an intriguing article in which he studies three sermons delivered in Westminster Chapel in times of great crisis as examples of "holistic preaching." See Richard Lyon Morgan, "Preaching as Pastoral Moment: A New Slant on G. Campbell Morgan," *Preaching* (September–October 1987): 29ff.

3. Ibid., 58ff.
4. Harries, *G. Campbell Morgan,* 65.
5. Wilbur M. Smith, "The Life and Writings of Dr. G. Campbell Morgan," in *A Treasury of Books for Bible Study* (Grand Rapids: Baker, 1960), 133.
6. G. Campbell Morgan, *Studies in the Prophecy of Jeremiah* (Westwood, N.J.: Fleming H. Revell, 1955).
7. Jill Morgan, *A Man of the Word,* 245. Wiersbe says he tries to read this book every year.
8. Don C. Wagner, *The Expository Method of G. Campbell Morgan* (Westwood, N.J.: Revell, 1957), 69.
9. G. Campbell Morgan, *God's Methods with Man* (New York: Revell, 1898), along with a colored chart of God's plan for the ages; also *The Spirit of God* (Westwood, N.J.: Revell, 1953), 81ff.
10. G. Campbell Morgan, *Preaching* (New York: Revell, 1937), 37ff.
11. Jill Morgan, *A Man of the Word,* 251.
12. John Bishop, "George Campbell Morgan: A Man of the Word," *Preaching* (March–April 1991): 59–60.
13. William G. Shepherd, *Great Preachers as Seen by a Journalist* (New York: Revell, 1924), 173ff.
14. Smith, "Life and Writings," 131; Warren W. Wiersbe, *Living with the Giants* (Grand Rapids: Baker, 1993), 185.
15. *The Westminster Record* 19.7 (July 1945) gives the transcript of the memorial service, including the praise of Lloyd-Jones for "the wonderful campaigns of Moody and Sankey in this country" and a moving description of his close association with Morgan and "never the slightest suspicion of difference between us." Lloyd-Jones says of Morgan that "preaching was the supreme passion of his life" and that the only poor sermon he had ever heard Morgan deliver was a topical sermon (60ff.).

11.3.4 *F. B. MEYER—A BAPTIST FOR ALL THE BELIEVERS*

What we need is the old, old story preached by new, new men! Ethics by all means; but the fair temple must have its foundations set deep in the death which destroyed Him that had the power of death, and delivered them who throughout their lives had been subject to bondage.

It is impossible to preach to men unless you know men.

My earnest advice to all young ministers is—to mix freely with the people; to visit systematically and widely; to study men as well as books;

to converse with all classes and conditions of men: always on the alert to learn from some fresh pages of the heart opened to the view of the sympathetic soul.

—F. B. Meyer in *The Bells of Is*

The founder of Bible Study Fellowship with branches all over the world, **A. Wetherell Johnson** (1907–1984) was reared in Leicester in England and recalls Andrew Murray, Evan Roberts of the Welsh Revival, and Mrs. Jessie Penn-Lewis, but especially **Frederick Brotherton Meyer** (1847–1929), their pastor. Johnson recalls:

A rather fragile looking man, with a very fresh complexion, clear blue eyes, a face wrinkled like a russet apple. His expression was that of a gentle radiancy. You felt that you had come into contact with a man who lived with God and who was a friend of God. His voice was quiet, yet it reached into every part of the large hall or chapel. While he spoke, there came a sense of stillness, and we seemed to hear the strong, virile voice of God which reached to the deepest part of one's being.[1]

F. B. Meyer was called the Christian cosmopolitan, the archbishop of nonconformity, the ubiquitous Dr. Meyer, and the evangelical opportunist. He was born in London—his successful great-grandfather came from Germany and worshiped at Charlotte Baptist Chapel in Edinburgh while living in that city; his mother came from staunch Quaker stock. The family attended Bloomsbury Chapel, where Dr. Brock had a strong influence on the young lad, who very early had an awareness of "the constant interchange between Him [the Lord] and me."[2] While he was yet very young, he preached to his family and the servants. He attended Brighton College and preached his first public sermon (from Psalm 84:11) at sixteen. Sensing a deep call to ministry, Meyer worked two years for a tea merchant—a positive experience for certain of his future Christian enterprises. Meyer then went on to Regent's Park College and took his B.A. from London University in 1869.

The Wellsprings of F. B. Meyer

While he was at school, in addition to enjoying a high profile in the debating society, Meyer served the nucleus that would become the Duke Street Baptist Chapel in Richmond. Turning down a call to Portland Chapel in Southampton, where Alexander Maclaren had served, he went in 1870 to be associate of Dr. C. M. Birrell of Pembroke Chapel, Liverpool. Birrell was a dedicated exegetical preacher who taught the fledgling preacher much, but Meyer had to unlearn delivery by memoriter. After two years he took the call to the Priory Street Baptist Chapel in York, where he came into contact with **James Parsons** (1799–1877) at Salem Congregational Church. Parsons was known throughout England as the barrister preacher, whose eccentric style and constantly twitching face and blinking eyes could not foreclose two passionate hours of extraordinary discourse.[3] In York, Meyer was the first English preacher to welcome D. L. Moody and Ira Sankey. It was in this stirring in 1873 that Frances Ridley Havergal, the well-known hymn writer, came to a deepening of her spiritual life. In 1874 Meyer moved on to the Victoria Road Church in Leicester, where the leadership was not in harmony with his evangelistic thrust. One well-to-do deacon protested by saying, "We cannot have this sort of thing here. This is not a Gospel shop!"[4]

Meyer went on to establish a new church in Leicester, Melbourne Hall, which would seat twelve hundred persons. Here he enjoyed a great prison ministry and preached his first character studies on Jacob and Joseph. In 1887 he accepted the call to the wealthy Regent's Park Chapel in London, then in 1892 followed the well-known Newman Hall at Christ Church, Westminster Road in Lambeth, south of the river, known as the Cathedral of Nonconformity. **Newman Hall** (1816–1902) had taken Surrey Chapel, once served by Rowland Hill, and made it into Christ Church, with a morning service like low Church of England and an evening service that was typical nonconformity.[5]

In 1909 Meyer went back to Regent's Park; in 1915 he returned to Christ Church, where John McNeill and Len Broughton had served in the meantime. Meyer became minister emeritus in 1921 and died in 1929 at the age of eighty-two. He lived at such a fast pace that some called him "St. Francis with Bradshaw's Railway Guide."[6]

The Well-Crafted Sermons of F. B. Meyer

Meyer did not have the great intellectual depth of Campbell Morgan nor the brilliant eloquence of Jowett, but his was a tireless expenditure of energy and a love affair with Scripture. Birrell had advised him that topical sermons were limited by the number of topics possible and therefore, "Become an expositor of Scripture. You will always retain your freshness and will build up a strong and healthy church."[7] He defined expository preaching as "the consecutive treatment of some book or extended portion of Scripture."[8] Meyer warned against recapitulation ("last Sunday I was saying") or any kind of forecasting. Let each sermon stand independently on its own even if it is in a series.[9]

He had a clear voice that conveyed tender compassion. Nor were there any "hammer-marks" on his sermons. While there could occasionally be a little Prussian autocracy in his manner, the Quaker softness and sweetness prevailed. He decried lack of fervor yet was known for the brevity of his public prayers. His illustrations were graphic and luminous. Hugh Sinclair's assessment reflects this:

> His preaching is expressive of his personality, suggesting spiritual fastidiousness and a sweet, sun-washed serenity of soul. So simple and intimate is his utterance that many hearers will scarcely divine the art that conceals art, but the practiced will soon realize with what consummate ease and subtle mastery of effect he handles speech and thought, and how enchantingly he plays upon an instrument whose limitations are known and accepted by him.[10]

Meyer preached some sixteen thousand sermons. Called by his intimates the Skipper, he experienced new impact on his ministry subsequent to a filling of the Holy Spirit under the tutelage of Hudson Taylor at Keswick during the time he was in Leicester.[11] One of his hearers exclaimed, "It's good just to see him!" Spurgeon said, "Meyer preaches as a man who has seen God face-to-face." His good friend Joseph Parker remarked that Meyer always brought a benediction along with him, and he called him his father confessor.

One firm sold 2,545,000 copies of his books. He was very popular in Sweden, and twenty volumes were translated into Swedish. His marvelous Bible biographies are representative of his preaching at its best. Abraham and Jeremiah are favorites.[12] His two volumes on Exodus and his two volumes on John are superb. He also produced rich studies in Hebrews and Zechariah. His sermon "Reckon on God's Faithfulness," from Mark 11:22–24, picked up the theme of his ministry. Beginning with three biblical illustrations, he proceeded to show how we need to reckon on God for forgiveness of sin, for answers to prayer, and for guidance.[13] Although he always spoke of himself as a two-talent person, he was also a man who aspired to please God and proclaim Christ.

The Works and Service of F. B. Meyer

Meyer was visible at Keswick for many years and active in its cause. He was president of the Free Church Council in 1904 and involved in the serious protest movement on educational issues thereafter. His Quaker gentility further involved him in objecting to a prize fight in London in much the same way as Telemachus challenged gladiatorial combat in the early church. He was great for holding lantern slide meetings for the poor and building a Brotherhood movement to involve men. For a brief time he was principal of All Nations Bible College and was closely tied to Regions Beyond Missionary Union led by the Guiness family. He established a children's home, as did Spurgeon, and took leadership in the Advent Testimony Movement which was especially vocal at the time of the Balfour Declaration in 1917 and which trumpeted the imminent return of Christ for his church. He even got Mrs. Emmeline Pankhurst, a militant suffragette, worked up about the Second Coming. He established the Window Cleaning Brigade for his converted convicts and put his business prowess to good use.

Christ Church had its "teetotaler corner" and its "consecration corner," and here the exposition of Scripture was at the core of all this outreach and ministry. Here he preached on "God Is Near" and "A Vision of the New Life" from Acts 26:19; "The Power of Appropriation" and "Reigning in Life" from Romans 5:17; and "Living the Life of Christ" from John 6:57.[14] Though president of the Baptist Union, Meyer's heart was in the dark alleys of Lambeth described so vividly by Somerset Maugham in 'Liza of Lambeth. His ministry was to the conversion of the notorious Hooligan family and the like.[15] What a servant! What a preacher!

---

1. A. Wetherell Johnson, *Created for Commitment* (Wheaton, Ill.: Tyndale House, 1982), 28.

2. W. Y. Fullerton, *F. B. Meyer* (London: Marshall Morgan and Scott, 1929), 9. Fullerton also wrote a biography of Spurgeon as his longtime assistant and later followed Meyer at Melbourne Hall. Called the happy warrior of the London pulpit, his own *Sunset Sermons* (Philadelphia: Judson, 1929) are done well in the Keswick style.
3. F. R. Webber, *A History of Preaching in Britain and America* (Milwaukee: Northwestern, 1952), 1:482.
4. A. Chester Mann, *F. B. Meyer: Preacher, Teacher, Man of God* (New York: Revell, 1929), 45.
5. Newman Hall drew the plans for the striking "pile" called Christ Church, which seated twenty-three hundred people. We have a sample of his fine preaching in *The Lord's Prayer: A Practical Meditation* (Edinburgh: T & T Clark, 1883).
6. Fullerton, *F. B. Meyer,* 70. Two exquisite little books by Meyer describe his early and later city ministries, *The Bells of Is* (New York: Revell, 1894) and *Reveries and Realities: Life and Work in London* (London: Morgan and Scott, n.d.). He was heard both by the poor in London and at Northfield with rapt attention.
7. Mann, *F. B. Meyer,* 74. Some his finest expositions are in *The Directory of the Devout Life, Matthew 5–6–7.*
8. F. B. Meyer, *Expository Preaching: Plans and Methods* (London: Hodder and Stoughton, 1912), 29.
9. Ibid., 32–33. His expositions on 1 Peter, *Tried by Fire,* are particularly outstanding.
10. Mann, *F. B. Meyer,* 71.
11. The first series of sermons Meyer preached at Carnegie Hall, New York, and in Tremont Temple, Boston, are published as *The Christ-Life for the Self-Life* (Chicago: Moody, 1897). A copy of this book of sermons given to my mother by her Sunday school teacher came into my hands in my early teens and led to a deep crisis of consecration.
12. F. B. Meyer, *Jeremiah: Priest and Prophet* (New York: Revell, 1894). These are eleven Bible biographies that I regard as superior to those of either Alexander Whyte or George Matheson—much stronger exegetically and in their bridging from then to now. Meyer's study on Psalm 23, *The Shepherd Psalm,* is one of the best.
13. F. B. Meyer, *Five Musts of the Christian Life* (New York: Revell, 1927), 91ff.
14. F. B. Meyer, *Meet for the Master's Use* (New York:. Revell, n.d.).
15. Mann, *F. B. Meyer,* 60. Meyer's *Our Daily Homily* and his daily notes on each biblical chapter are superb.

11.3.5 JOHN HENRY JOWETT—THE WORDSMITH WHO PREACHED GRACE SO GLORIOUSLY

If the pulpit is to be occupied by men with a message worth hearing, we must have time to prepare it.

I have a conviction that no sermon is ready for preaching, not ready for writing out, until we can express its theme in a short, pregnant sentence as clear as crystal. I find the getting of that sentence is the hardest, the most exacting, and the most fruitful labour in my study. To compel oneself to fashion that sentence, to dismiss every word that vague, ragged, ambiguous, to think oneself through to a form of words which defines the theme with scrupulous exactness—this is surely one of the most essential factors in the making of a sermon: and I do not think any sermon ought to be preached or even written, until that sentence has emerged, clear and lucid as a cloudless moon. Do not confuse obscurity with profundity, and do not imagine that lucidity is necessarily shallow. Let the preacher bind himself to the pursuit of clear conceptions, and let him aid his pursuit by demanding that every sermon he preaches shall express its theme and purpose in a sentence as lucid as his powers can command.

—J. H. Jowett

Called by many on both sides of the Atlantic the greatest living practitioner of the homiletic art, **John Henry Jowett** (1863–1923) was a slight, frail, bald man, and so mightily used of God. He was born in Halifax, in the north of England in the moorland country of the Bronte novels. His father was a tailor and a draper. How shall we understand his usefulness?

What Shaped Jowett?

"I was blessed with the priceless privilege of a Christian home," Jowett testified.[1] His parents were not leaders in the Square Congregational Church of Halifax, but Jowett learned to pray at his mother's knee and "she taught me to see." He also said, "When I think of a Christian man, I think of my Father."[2] Through his lifetime he started work in his study at 6 A.M. because he had seen in his youth how all the tradesmen started early. His pastor, Dr. Enoch Mellor, made a deep impression with his pulpit oratory, but they never really met. His Sunday school teacher, Mr. Dewhirst, a humble carpenter, challenged young Jowett when he was inclined to the law with the words God used to redirect his life, "I had always hoped you would go into the ministry."[3] The vivid learning experience in his Sunday school class was never effaced. Jowett preached his first sermon from 1 Samuel 3:19 during an evangelistic outreach sponsored by his Sunday school class.

He matriculated at Airedale College in Bradford, where **Dr. Andrew Fairbairn** (1838–1912) had a profound effect on his thinking.[4] When Fairbairn heard Jowett preach in class, he remarked, "Behind that sermon is a man." Jowett then moved on to Edinburgh where he often heard Alexander Whyte and George Matheson preach and where the prince, Henry Drummond, drew him ever deeper into discipleship and "many a time sent me home to my knees."[5] In his student pastorates, "He learned the necessity of interesting his congregation." In 1888 and 1889 he spent two terms at Mansfield College, Oxford, with his beloved Fairbairn, where he also met one of his dearest friends, C. Sylvester Horne, who went on to serve a significant tenure in Kensington.

What Set Jowett Apart?

Right out of school, Jowett unusually was accorded a call to the important St. James Congregational Church in Newcastle-on-Tyne. St. James was packed from the beginning of his ministry, and he spent six satisfying years here. In 1889 he was ordained here with **Charles Berry,** who was later called to succeed Beecher in Brooklyn.[6]

Immediately Jowett's "originality of thought and rhetorical power" were in evidence in his preaching. He was painstaking and methodical in his Bible study, pasting a page of text on one side of a large book and entering exegetical notes and observations on the other side.[7] He and his wife had a great ministry to children, and he strongly espoused the temperance cause. He believed in conversion and preached for a verdict.[8] He had what he called "the wooing note" as he preached grace, the center of his message.

In 1895 he was tapped to succeed R. W. Dale at Carr's Lane, Birmingham, which A. T. Pierson called "the finest church in the world." From the outset Jowett determined to be himself. The difference was well put: "Dale's congregation could pass an examination in the doctrines and Jowett's in the Scriptures."[9] Nicoll reported:

> In Dr. Jowett everything preaches. The voice preaches, and it is a voice of great range and compass, always sweet and clear through every variety of intonation. The eyes preach, for though Dr. Jowett writes every word of his sermons, he is extraordinarily independent of his manuscript. The body preaches, for Dr. Jowett has many gestures, and not one ungraceful. But above all, the heart preaches. I have heard many great sermons, but never one at any time which so completely seized and held from start to finish a great audience . . . Above all preachers I have heard, Dr. Jowett has the power of appeal . . . at times the tension of listening, the silence, and the eagerness of the crowd were almost oppressive . . . it was all very wonderful and very uplifting.[10]

Besides his two Sunday services, Jowett had a great Thursday night service and a class for the Sunday school teachers. Although he was only thirty-one when he came to Carr's Lane, he was soon in widespread demand. In 1906 he was chair of the Congregational Union, having earlier preached his famous sermon, "Apostolic Optimism" from Romans 12:12 on "rejoicing in hope" to them. In 1911 he was president of the Free Church Council after visiting America and ministering at Northfield.

Also in 1911, he faced three overtures from Fifth Avenue Presbyterian Church in New York City and finally accepted, although he never felt at home in New York. When he came to New York, he insisted on taking no more than his salary at Carr's Lane. His preaching was well received—"Yet I wish I were in England."[11] He turned down the call to Free St. George's and enjoyed his happiest season in 1913 and 1914, when he gave one of the finest series in the history of the Beecher Lectures at Yale.[12]

Finding it hard to contend with endless distraction and so many invitations, Jowett was open when City Temple, London, approached him. He did not accept the call because of his conservative stand in the furor over R. J. Campbell's views, but then took the call to Westminster Chapel in London, succeeding Campbell

Morgan. It was not easy for an Englishman to be absent from his native country during the crisis of the first world war. Even Prime Minister Lloyd George urged him to come home. His ministry in London was brief but much appreciated. Jowett suffered a total collapse of health; what seemed to be a mysterious illness turned out to be pernicious anemia. He led and spoke at the great armistice service in Albert Hall with the king and queen present and also spoke at a highly controversial interdenominational service in Durham Cathedral. Yet he was "a bird with a broken pinion," and he soon resigned.

What Sustained Jowett?

Jowett's secret was first of all his commitment to the spacious and grand themes of Scripture and of the Christian faith. As he prepared, he would ask himself how other preachers he knew would treat the text and how the people would handle it. Jowett had both heat and light. He avoided topical preaching and did not care much for apologetics from the pulpit. When he returned from England he ventured more into application for national life. But he was in fact an unashamed "old-fashioned preacher."[13] He was the stylist of preachers of his time and may have used the English language more effectively than did any other preacher in the twentieth century. He loved to read the dictionary and was committed to Saxonisms rather than Latin. He was a planner *par excellence* and was always punctual. He began preparing his sermons on Tuesday and when taking the train into Birmingham on Sunday morning, he would read Spurgeon for the atmosphere. He had a great sense of humor, and while he walked with kings, he never lost the common touch.

Jowett wrote voluminously, but it was mainly his sermons that were published. He divided sermons brilliantly. Whether it is his *The Passion for Souls, The Silver Lining,* his arresting expositions of *The Whole Armour of God,* or his *Life in the Heights: Studies in the Epistles,* this is great preaching.[14] Who but Jowett could turn a phrase like "Faith is not a safe orthodoxy but a hazardous adventure" or, in speaking of worship, see the great danger of luxuriating in our own emotion. Some favorite Jowett sermons are in *The School of Calvary.*[15] Let the reader respond to his prayer: "Open our eyes to discern the footprints of our Lord."

---

1. Arthur Porritt, *John Henry Jowett* (London: Hodder and Stoughton, 1924), 4. Introduction by Archbishop Davidson.
2. Ibid., 6.
3. Ibid., 21.
4. Andrew Fairbairn (not to be confused with Patrick Fairbairn, who wrote the great volume on typology) came out of the United Secessationists and gave the 1891–1892 Beecher Lectures, "The Place of Christ in Modern Theology." He had wrestled with issues of faith and doubt but had been much helped in Germany by Tholuck and Hengstenberg. He was brilliant but long, often preaching an hour and twenty minutes.

5. Porritt, *John Henry Jowett,* 35. It was said of Whyte and his associate Hugh Black that "in the morning Whyte painted the people black and in the evening Black painted the people white."

6. Charles M. Berry (1852–1899) declined calls to both Brooklyn and Westminster Chapel. He is known for his conversion at the bedside of a dying lady, "I got her in," he declared to Jowett, "and I got in myself." His son Dr. Sidney Berry succeeded Jowett at Carr's Lane Chapel in Birmingham.

7. Porritt, *John Henry Jowett,* 62.

8. Ibid., 63.

9. John Bishop, "John Henry Jowett: A Preacher of Grace," *Preaching* (January–February 1987): 54.

10. Porritt, *John Henry Jowett,* 76.

11. Ibid., 172.

12. J. H. Jowett, *The Preacher: His Life and Work* (New York: Hodder and Stoughton, 1912). Excellent and elegant.

13. John Pitts, "John Henry Jowett: Prince of Preachers," *Christianity Today* (December 6, 1963): 13.

14. J. H. Jowett, *The Whole Armour of God* (Grand Rapids: Baker, 1916, 1969); *Life in the Heights* (Grand Rapids: Baker, 1925, 1973).

15. J. H. Jowett, *The School of Calvary* (Grand Rapids: Baker, 1956).

11.3.6 *J. D. JONES—THE WELSH PREACHER WHO DREW YOUNG AND OLD*

> In the deepest sense of all a man cannot be taught to preach. The Word must be like a fire in a man's bones if he is to become an effective preacher. But a man can be taught how to put his message forcibly, he can be taught how to stand and how to speak and how to arrange his matter.
>
> Preachers often seem to me to fight shy of the big themes and to be content with secondary and subsidiary topics. Since I have had the opportunity of sitting more often in the pew, I have heard sermons on social justice, on peace, on ethical subjects, but I can't recall a single sermon on such a central theme as the Incarnation. We are never going to build strong churches that way. To make strong vigorous churches we must launch out into the deep.
>
> —J. D. Jones

Undeniably there was at this time a great swell of powerful preaching in the churches of nonconformity. Yet there was still strong preaching in the established church, such as by **Henry Scott Holland**, for twenty-six years canon of St. Paul's in London and close to Liddon.[1]

Another sparkling example from the nonconformity was **John Daniel Jones** (1865–1942), who was born in Wales, the grandson of a Wesleyan preacher and the son of a schoolman who obtained quite a name for himself in Welsh hymnody. After the early death of his father, Jones was reared in the Calvinistic Methodism of his mother. He heard much strong preaching and was a "thricer" (i.e., attended church Sunday morning and evening with Sunday school in the afternoon). He served as organist in his home church and in due time was converted and joined the church. Jones testified that the ministry really chose him rather than vice versa. When he preached his first sermon, the service was moved outdoors and the wind blew his manuscript away. This led him to his conviction that preaching without a manuscript is preferred.[2] He went on to Owen's College in Manchester and then took his B.D. at St. Andrews.

His first pastoral charge was the Congregational church at Newland, Lincoln, where he spent nine happy years. The church held twelve hundred people, and Jones filled it. Jones was known for the uniform excellence of his messages. His preaching was even and calm, in contrast to the "fiery eloquence and dramatic" power of his predecessor in the Richmond Hill Congregational Church in the seaside resort city of Bournemouth, to which he went in 1898. Jones spent thirty-nine years as pastor of this outstanding church and turned down many opportunities to move. He became a fixture in the life and affairs of the community and was greatly loved. Every Sunday there were 350 to 500 strangers in the services. His Tuesday morning studies were very popular and a four-volume devotional commentary on the Gospel of Mark affords insight into the reason for that popularity. His sermons were well designed, but his sentences were not oratorically polished. Twenty volumes of his sermons have been published, and half of the sermons are from the Old Testament. He loved Scripture and used many Scripture quotations as well as quotations from literature and biography. There were "no dramatic moments" in Jones, but part of his strength resided in the fact that he was a great pastor.[3] One observer commented on a sermon he preached in Tremont Temple in Boston:

> It was "different" from an American sermon, exegetical and expository rather than topical, quiet and simple, but holding the throng as the preacher made them sit in the heavenly places with Christ Jesus . . .[4]

Jones was active in denominational affairs in the Congregational Union of England and Wales and made many trips to the U.S. and Australia in connection with Congregationalism. In 1899 he heard D. L. Moody preach at Plymouth Church in Brooklyn (Moody himself being a Congregationalist). J. D. Jones gives his experience:

> I remember how he announced his text. "My text," he said, "is all the way from Genesis to Revelation." What he was really intent upon was to show that the idea of atonement ran through the whole Scripture. "I guess," he said at the beginning of his sermon, "I shall make some of you mad this morning." And I daresay he did—for he preached a theology to which I fancy Ward Beecher's and Dr. Hillis' people were not accustomed . . . and though he stated the old substitutionary theory in the baldest way, he got down to the quick of things and we felt the power of his speech. I am glad I got a grip of his hand.[5]

Out of his contact with Moody came invitations to speak at Northfield, which he fulfilled several times. In his own sermon at the Second International Council of Congregationalists, his message was well received. Indeed, he "dispensed with his paper," but in his own view, P. T. Forsyth's great message on the cross was the spiritual high moment. "He flamed, he burned," was Jones' vivid recollection.[6] One cannot escape the sense in Jones that already Enlightenment rationalism was driving a serious wedge in the Congregational fabric not only in America but also in Britain.[7] Jones was clearly evangelical and found Forsyth's theology of the cross preferable to George Gordon on "The Glories of Congregationalism," which he thought was "puff pastry" or "a bee buzzing about in vacuity."[8]

Jones knew the deep valley of sorrow as his wife died in 1917, and his only son was twice wounded and severely gassed in France, recovering but then dying in Africa. He retired in 1937 and moved to Wales, where his ministry continued in other forms. He was a steady biblical influence in his time. A splendid example of biblical preaching can be seen in his *The Lord of Life and Death,* a series on John 11.

Described as "a burly figure with white hair with a rich silvery voice," Jones demonstrated his careful work in the Greek text.[9] Some his messages are classic, such as "When the Half-Gods Go, the Gods Arrive," from 1 Corinthians 13:10, "The Originality of Jesus" from John 7:46, and "The Reserve of Jesus" from Matthew 12:19.[10] It was J. D. Jones who urged his friend Campbell Morgan to bring D. Martyn Lloyd-Jones to London. J. D. Jones, "the unmitred bishop of Congregationalism," urged Lloyd-Jones to step into the deepening leadership vacuum in that fellowship.[11]

---

1. Henry Scott Holland (1847–1918) was close to Liddon but not homiletically what Liddon was. He served Christ Church, Oxford, before and after his twenty-seven years at St. Paul's and later became Regius Professor at Oxford.

2. J. D. Jones, *Three Score Years and Ten* (London: The Book Club, 1940), 26–27. Arthur Porritt, a close friend, also wrote a brief memoir of Jones.

3. John Bishop, "J. D. Jones: 'Man with the Mouth of Gold,'" *Preaching* (May–June 1989): 53.

4. Jones, *Three Score Years and Ten,* 174.

5. Ibid., 126.

6. Ibid., 132.

7. Note A. E. Garvie's own view of the Bible at this time: "The Bible is not the Word of God but contains the Word of God," in *The Christian Preacher* (New York: Scribner's, 1923), 350. Garvie was Congregationalism's ecumenist.

8. Jones, *Three Score Years and Ten,* 171. George Gordon (1853–1929), born in Scotland, served Old South Church, Boston. His liberalism totally denuded Christ and the Bible of anything supernatural. In his autobiography, *My Education and Religion* (Boston: Houghton Mifflin, 1925), he shares how his friend Phillips Brooks disdained Jonathan Edwards (301). Gordon could preach, as his sermon "The Lilies on Top of the Temple" suggests, but he had no gospel message.

9. J. D. Jones, *The Lord of Life and Death* (Grand Rapids: Baker, 1972). On his grave: "Preacher of the Gospel."

10. J. D. Jones, *The Gospel of the Sovereignty* (London: Hodder and Stoughton, 1914), 44ff., 74ff., 134ff.
11. Iain H. Murray, *David Martyn Lloyd-Jones: The Fight of Faith* (Edinburgh: Banner of Truth, 1990), 61ff. J. D. Jones lamented the general loss of the great preachers, asserting that the average was raised but not the "great ones."

11.3.7 *CHARLES SYLVESTER HORNE—WITH THE SWEEP OF A TORNADO*

The one supreme qualification for the ministry is a soul of flame.

Nobody ought ever to go into a pulpit who can think and talk about sin and salvation, and the Cross of Christ, which is for all true men the symbol of hope and service, without profound emotion and passion.
—C. Sylvester Horne

Embodying and personifying that flame of passion of which he spoke, **Charles Sylvester Horne** (1865–1914) was a meteorite that streaked across the heavens and was too soon gone. Born in Sussex, the son of a Congregational minister, Horne was educated at Glasgow, where his radiant personality and plethora of gifts were already evident. He then went to Mansfield College, Oxford, under Fairbairn. His forensic and oratorical abilities were marked early and came into fruition in two distinct phases of pastoral ministry.

First, he spent ten years in Kensington, London, where he preached amid high society and fashion. He was an unusual preacher. Webber is right in describing him as "winsome, eager, radiant, fascinating and glowing."[1] Gammie said, "No platform speaker could excel Sylvester Horne at his best . . . grasping his coat lapels as he began quietly, he gradually gathered momentum until the sparks were flying and the whole atmosphere became electric. With shafts of humour, pungent phrases, and the glow of a burning passion, he could rouse an audience to an enthusiasm which brought them to their feet time and again."[2]

Then Horne underwent a drastic change of venue and style. For another ten years he moved to Whitefield's Tabernacle on Tottenham Court Road among the poor and the downtrodden. In this time he also served as a member of Parliament from Ipswich, and while he did not bring politics into his sermons as such, he preached to great Sunday afternoon rallies on current issues. In 1914 he sailed for America to give the Beecher Lectures at Yale, after which he died suddenly of a massive coronary while sailing with his wife into Toronto harbor. He was forty-nine.

There was a scholarly side to Horne that bespoke his fine mind and that can be seen in his splendid history of the Free Churches. In the epilogue of this work he refers to the Welsh revival of 1904, which began with prayer meetings in Newcastle Emlyn and spread like a prairie fire throughout Wales, resulting in thousands of accessions in the Free Churches.[3] One wishes that more exegetical foundation were visible in his sermons as published. His Beecher Lectures in 1914 give us a significant window into the soul of the preacher as he sought to inculcate a wondering sense of "The Romance of Preaching," as the lectures were titled.[4] The approach is historical and yet a clear call for conversion rings out in his last lecture, as he insisted, "Amid all changes of thought and phrase the wonder of conversion remains, to be the supreme joy and glory of the preacher."[5]

The theological tensions among Congregationalists over the new theology and R. J. Campbell were becoming increasingly acute (Campbell finally left for the Church of England). An important symposium on *The Old Faith and the New Theology* drew contributors who, in a gentlemanly way, spoke of Campbell's drift, among whom were Peter Forsyth, J. D. Jones, and Sylvester Horne. Horne's piece was a sermon from Romans 1:16 on "The Power Unto Salvation," in which he ranged over the entire first chapter of Romans and was clear on sin and the atonement.[6] He openly challenged Campbell on the sinlessness of Jesus and pleaded with him "to believe with the rest of us, in a sinless Saviour, a Lamb without blemish and without spot."[7] Yet others in the anthology made dangerous concessions, and the increasingly schizoid composition of nonconformity was clear.[8] More than romance or ecstatic extroversion was needed. Clear, cogent doctrinal exposition of Scripture was the need of the hour.

---

1. F. R. Webber, *A History of Preaching in Britain and America* (Milwaukee: Northwestern, 1902), 1:703.
2. Alexander Gammie, *Preachers I Have Heard* (London: Pickering and Inglis, n.d.), 69.
3. C. Sylvester Horne, *A Popular History of the Free Churches* (London: James Clarke, 1903), Epilogue.
4. C. Sylvester Horne, *The Romance of Preaching* (Boston: Pilgrim's Press, 1914).
5. Ibid., 275.
6. Charles H. Vine, ed., *The Old Faith and the New Theology: A Series of Sermons and Essays on Some of the Truths Held by Evangelical Christians and the Difficulties of Accepting Much of What is Called the "New Theology"* (New York: Eaton and Mains, 1907).
7. Ibid., 59.
8. Ibid., 220, 227.

11.3.8 John Hutton—On the Edge of Greatness

The teachers of our new theologies are never under a greater mistake than when they imagine that it is the preaching of this old Gospel of the grace of God—old, yet ever new—which is alienating the modern world from the Churches. It is not the preaching of this Gospel which is emptying the churches, but the want of it.

—James Orr

Apart from Morgan and Meyer, the tendency to take a microtext seemed to be prevailing. Jowett talked about "fat texts" but they tended to be short "fat texts." Of course there is a time for a minitext, but exposition requires a natural thought unit. Not only do we sense some decline in biblicality (with the small texts) but as well a waning of sharp, clear affirmation of biblical authority. Few of these preachers wanted to enter the lists of controversy and engage the poisonous currents which were sucking supernaturalism out of discourse.

This troubles us about **John Hutton** (1868–1947), but it was he who, in his brief pastorate at Westminster Chapel after Jowett, captivated the young Martyn Lloyd-Jones. "This man's preaching appealed to me tremendously," he recalled. Iain Murray says of him, "Hutton's preaching was uneven in effect. He was not expository, and his best efforts were occasional rather than regular . . . he believed in rebirth and regeneration."[1]

Hutton was born in Scotland and studied at Glasgow. He came out of the old United Presbyterians and served parishes in Scotland and then in the Presbyterian Church of Scotland in Newcastle. In 1923 he took the call to Westminster and "took London by storm." He was warmhearted and effective in the pulpit, filling Westminster morning and evening for the brief time he was there. When J. M. E. Ross, editor of the influential *British Weekly,* died, Hutton was called as editor and served from 1925 to 1946 in that capacity. He was often featured at Moody's Northfield Conference and at Morgan's Mundesley Conference in Norfolk. His analytic skills were described by Joseph Fort Newton, who was even thinner theologically than Hutton but who heard him in City Temple:

> The faces of the great congregation became ashen grey as Dr. Hutton described Antichrist, wearing the robes of the Christian Church and grappling with the Lord Jesus Christ. Dr. Newton declares that his sentences flashed like lightning as he crouched in the pulpit, his face livid. Then, rising triumphantly, with ringing sentences he described the incredible love of the Saviour in His death on the Cross for the sins of the world . . . he spoke without manuscript, and under the excitement of the moment there was, at times, an energetic fervor that the printed page cannot reproduce.[2]

On occasion Hutton could probe into Scripture, as in his studies titled *The Tragedy of Saul.*[3] These are among the finest studies ever done on Saul. Hutton's personal love for the poets Browning and Francis Thompson sometimes threatened to preclude anything biblical, as in his curious messages at Mundesley published as *The Winds of God.*[4] His works on Paul in *Finally* are ably strategized, but he does not seem to pull the cord.[5] Undeniably there are rich gifts here, and there were moments of effective ministry, but what might have been if Hutton had really opened Scripture?

1. Iain Murray, *D. Martyn Lloyd-Jones: The First Forty Years, 1899–1939* (Edinburgh: Banner of Truth, 1982), 61.
2. F. R. Webber, *A History of Preaching in Britain and America* (Milwaukee: Northwestern, 1952), 1:525–26.
3. John A. Hutton, *The Tragedy of Saul* (New York: George H. Doran, 1926).
4. John A. Hutton, *The Winds of God* (New York: Hodder and Stoughton, 1911).
5. John A. Hutton, *Finally: With Paul to the End* (New York: Harper, n.d.). My favorite

sermons, *The Fear of Things* (New York: George H. Doran, 1911), include "The Fear of the Threshold" and "The Love of God in the Embarrassments of Life."

11.4 THE AMERICAN VENTURERS

The majestic testimony of the Church in all time is that its advances in spiritual life have always been toward and not away from the Bible, and in proportion to the reverence for, and power of realizing in practical life, the revealed Word.

—Casper Wistar Hodge

The disuse of the Bible is always a scourge, and the iconic use of the Bible is a travesty, but Bible-believing preachers were now facing not only the buffetings of unbelief and skepticism but also new forms of agnosticism. Liberalism and its naive optimism about humankind were collapsing in the face of the unmitigated horrors of the so-called enlightened twentieth century. Two individuals symbolize the two extremes.

Thomas Edison (1847–1931) represents the venturesome American spirit of enterprise and energy. Born of Dutch extraction in Milan, Ohio, and reared in Port Huron, Michigan, Edison was "a singular genius" whose "Napoleonic zeal" and prodigious creativity made him famous and wealthy. Though an instance of the Puritan work ethic, he drew his philosophy from Emerson:

> If a man can write a better book, preach a better sermon or make a better mousetrap than his neighbor, though he builds his house in the woods, the world will make a beaten path to his door.[1]

An omnivorous lifelong reader, he loved Thomas Paine's *Age of Reason* and found Hume and Gibbon very much to his liking.[2] Although he recited portions of the Bible over his new phonograph, he dabbled in Theosophy and Swedenborg. He was "intoxicated by the expansive rhetoric of social Darwinianism."[3] Like his friend, John Burroughs, the New England Transcendentalist, he was "seduced by Emerson, Thoreau and Whitman."[4] Though toward the end of his incredibly productive life he was preoccupied with thoughts about existence after death, he did not turn to the Bible but rather to Blavatsky. There is something very American about Edison.

In contrast stood a small, brilliant New Testament scholar named J. Gresham Machen (1881–1937). In this time, even the sardonic H. L. Mencken saw it clearly:

> What survives under the name of Christianity, above the sub-stratum of the mob, is no more than a sort of humanism with little more supernatural in it than you will find in mathematics or political economy.[5]

Machen, whose father was an outstanding attorney and whose mother was related to the Southern poet Sydney Lanier, studied classics at Johns Hopkins. His "Uncle Henry" Van Dyke, who taught at Princeton and served the Brick

Church in New York City, turned viciously on Machen in the controversies at Princeton.[6] Machen took his stand against "the claims of the new scholarship." He supported the 1910 stand of the General Assembly of the Presbyterian church, which "reaffirmed inerrancy as an essential article of faith." He was brushed off as a "high-brow fundamentalist" but argued persuasively that liberalism was essentially dishonest in tailoring the gospel to fit the modern mood and was "nothing more than positive thinking in modern garb."[7] In his masterful *The Origin of Paul's Religion,* he went straight to the solar plexus, and in *The Virgin Birth of Christ*, published by Harper and Row, he worried over "the Christless Christianity" peddled from many pulpits.

Dismissed from Princeton because he refused to allow theology to be reduced to matters of polity, Machen saw Princeton, the bastion of Warfield and the Hodges, reorganized in 1929. The center no longer held, and uncheered by what neo-orthodoxy offered in place of a discredited liberalism, Machen went on to found Westminster Seminary. Casper Wistar Hodge called him "The greatest theologian in the English-speaking world." A portion of the evangelical resurgence after World War II must be attributed to the clarity of his vision and the doughtiness of his courage. It was in the dialectic between Edison and Machen that American preaching took place in this century.

---

1. Neil Baldwin, *Edison: Inventing the Century* (New York: Hyperion, 1995), 66.
2. Ibid., 26.
3. Ibid., 230.
4. Ibid., 327ff.
5. D. G. Hart, *Defending the Faith: J. Gresham Machen and the Crisis of Conservative Protestantism in Modern America* (Grand Rapids: Baker, 1994), 2.
6. Van Dyke resented his relative so much that when Machen was stated supply in First Presbyterian Church in Princeton, Van Dyke would not attend to hear him preach. Van Dyke's very thin Beecher Lectures in 1895 were published as *The Gospel for An Age of Doubt.* The companion volume was titled *The Gospel in an Age of Sin.* Infinitely preferable is Machen's volume, *Christianity and Liberalism* (New York: Macmillan, 1923). Walter Lippmann pays Machen high tribute in *A Preface to Morals* (New York: Macmillan, 1929), 30–32. Lippmann calls Machen a "scholar and a gentleman" and asserts that the liberals never answered Machen.
7. Hart, *Defending the Faith,* 81.

11.4.1 ARTHUR T. PIERSON—BALANCED AND BIBLICAL

Preaching is a divine art, and therefore the finest of the fine arts. There is, about the logical structure of a true sermon, that which suggests all that is most beautiful in architecture; about the elaboration of its rhetorical features, all that is most symmetrical in sculpture; and about the use of imagination in illustration and metaphor, all that is most fascinating in painting; while oratory, itself a fine art, suggests that other kindred art of music, to which it is so closely allied in the utilization of all that is

most attractive and persuasive, melodious and martial, in the human
voice. As Paul Veronese said of painting, preaching is a "gift from God."
—Arthur T. Pierson

The first subject in this section is a servant of Christ distinguished not only as
a preacher but as a missionary statesman who held the highest view of the verbal
inspiration of Scripture and therefore the highest view of preaching. His lectures
on preaching at Spurgeon's College are pithy and pointed.[1] His motto was that
of the Waldensian church, *Trituntur mallei, remanet incus* (the mallets or ham-
mers are broken, but the anvil still stands).[2] The ministry of **Arthur T. Pierson**
(1837–1911) was on both sides of the Atlantic and rather than inching toward
accommodation, he is one who became progressively more committed to orthodox formulation.

Born in New York, Pierson was educated at boarding school, Hamilton College,
and Union Seminary in New York City, which he entered in 1857 and which had
120 students and five faculty at the time. He was a student there when the revival
of 1859 erupted, and this genuine moving of God's Spirit marked him for life.

Pierson's first pastorate was in First Congregational Church in Binghamton
(two-and-a-half years); here his increasingly conservative ideas were attacked,
and he went into a brief eclipse of confidence but emerged all the stronger after a study of Christian evidences, particularly the argument from prophecy.[3]
His next pastorate was a six-year stint at the Presbyterian church in Waterford,
New York. He was an intense preacher of a somewhat nervous temperament,
but his preaching was truly developing, as was his lifelong commitment to the
world missionary task. His Sunday afternoon Bible class usually numbered 150
to 200.[4]

In 1869 Pierson took a call to the Fort Street Presbyterian Church in Detroit.
(He declined the call to the chair of systematics at McCormick Seminary in Chicago.)[5] The congregation had 238 members and met in a sanctuary which seated
eight hundred. Pierson had a great evangelistic urge and saw much growth. "Always tell men the truth" was his credo.

After a brief interlude in Indianapolis in 1882, he resigned because of impatience in the situation,[6] but out of this time came his choice *Many Infallible Proofs:
The Evidences of Christianity* (London: Morgan and Scott, 1882). This work has
some of the best treatment of the fulfillment of prophecy in the destruction of
Jerusalem in 70 A.D. of which I am aware.

At forty-six, Pierson became pastor of the Wanamaker church in Philadelphia,
Bethany Presbyterian, where he had six glorious years. Active in prophetic Bible
conferences, he was at times weighed down by too much introspection.[7] He began espousing the imminence of Christ's premillennial coming.

Pierson then moved on to a more international ministry and filled in for
Spurgeon when the latter was ill (1891–93). He had been influenced much by
George Müller, whose biography he had written. In the tensions after Spurgeon's
death there were those who called for Pierson's assumption of the pastorate.
Indeed, this staunch Presbyterian was baptismally immersed in that interest,
but he was passed over in favor of Thomas Spurgeon. Pierson continued to travel

and write in an expanding arena of usefulness and fruitfulness. He died at seventy-six, spending his last years with Brooklyn as headquarters.

Pierson was deeply involved in ministry at the Keswick Convention in the Lake Country in northern England and in the Keswick emphasis on the victorious life around the world. Some of his finest preaching was done under these auspices.[8] His preaching was always anchored in the biblical text.[9] He believed that preaching is more the discovery of what the Bible says than it is the invention of ideas for discourse. An example of his analysis of the believer's relationship to the world is set forth in his sermon on our Lord's high-priestly prayer in John 17:

1. Believers are in the world;
2. Believers are not of the world;
3. Believers are chosen out of the world;
4. Believers are sent into the world.[10]

Charles Inwood, the Methodist preacher from Ulster who gave himself full-time to the Keswick message, described services in Belfast conducted by Pierson:

> The great Grosvenor Hall, accommodating over 3,000, was crowded every night and his address on Foreign Missions was by far the most eloquent and soul-moving missionary address I ever heard. Many features of his character and work have left an indelible and sacred impression on me—his knowledge, his gifts, his warm and guileless love, his holy and blazing indignation where the honour of his Lord and His Word were at stake . . . most of all I was impressed with his absolute abandonment of his whole personality to the ministry of the moment; every cubic inch of his being was in every message, in every sentence, in every word, every tone, every look as he spoke.[11]

Pierson was close to D. L. Moody and was influential on John Mott and Robert Speer in the Student Volunteer Movement. One of his biographers, J. Kennedy Maclean, opines, "At Keswick, perhaps more than anywhere else, he possessed his kingdom and occupied the sphere fitting his great gifts. There he dominated the Convention by his spiritual and intellectual gifts and thousands hung upon his words with great eagerness for instruction and help that was never disappointed."[12]

---

1. Arthur T. Pierson, *The Divine Art of Preaching* (New York: Baker and Taylor, 1892), 84ff.
2. Ibid., 94.
3. Delaven Leonard Pierson, *Arthur T. Pierson* (New York: Revell, 1912), 81.
4. Ibid., 93.
5. To sense how such institutions shift and change, cf. George L. Robinson, *A Short Story of a Long Life* (Grand Rapids: Baker, 1957). Robinson was a distinguished and principled Old Testament scholar at McCormick.

6. Pierson, *Arthur T. Pierson,* 162.

7. Ibid., 181.

8. J. Kennedy Maclean, *Dr. Pierson and His Message* (New York: Association Press, 1911), 34ff. For a good sample of his Keswick ministry, see Arthur T. Pierson, *A Spiritual Clinique* (New York: Gospel Publishing House, 1907).

9. Pierson, *Arthur T. Pierson,* 238.

10. Ibid., 265–66.

11. In Herbert F. Stevenson, ed., *The Ministry of Keswick* (Grand Rapids: Zondervan, 1963), 1:101–2.

12. Ibid., 103ff.

11.4.2 CHARLES E. JEFFERSON—GENTLEMAN WITH A BIBLICAL MESSAGE

How is it possible for a young man reared in the world of books to take a hearty and genuine interest at once in a world so stupid and belated? It is by no means easy for a young man to become a shepherd, and he ought not to be discouraged if he cannot become one in a day, or a year. An orator he can be without difficulty. A reformer he can become at once. In criticism of politics and society he can do a flourishing business the first Sunday. But a shepherd he can become only slowly, and by patiently traveling the way of the cross.

It is surprising how stoutly and stubbornly the church insists upon preachers knowing how to preach. They will forgive almost anything else, but they will not forgive inability to preach.

—Charles E. Jefferson

High praise was always given to **Charles Edward Jefferson** (1860–1937). He was typical of a growing company of able preachers who tilted toward a mediating position with reference to the historic faith. Frederick Keller Stamm speaks of him as "the greatest American preacher,"[1] and it was generally conceded that "he was always at his best."

Jefferson was born in Ohio and trained for teaching and indeed taught oratory at Ohio Wesleyan and Ohio State Universities. When he heard Phillips Brooks preach, he felt called to preach himself and prepared at Boston University School of Theology. Brooks, who claimed that F. D. Maurice, the English immanentist, influenced him as none other, shaped Jefferson. When Jefferson asked Brooks if he had to believe in the miracles and the resurrection, Brooks retorted, "I should not say you must, I should say you may."[2] After serving several smaller churches, Jefferson took the call to the Broadway Tabernacle in Manhattan, where he served for the next thirty-one years. This is the church where Finney and William Taylor served. In 1905 a new church was built at Broadway and 56th. The congregation does not now exist as such.

Some have compared Jefferson to Alexander Maclaren in his reserved and shy appearance and his "penetrating seriousness" about ministry and preaching. He was a man of the study,[3] simple and direct in his style. He felt that the sermon should be as long as necessary, which for him was about an hour.[4] He always preached extempore. His Beecher Lectures at Yale in 1910 on "The Building of the Church" sought to put the preacher's task in an ecclesiological context. In this lectureship, Jefferson resoundingly called for more personal preaching and summoned preachers to public Bible reading. He advanced the sensible idea that "It is possible to work too long on a sermon."[5]

Jefferson's twin volumes on *The Minister as Prophet* and *The Minister as Shepherd* were given as lectureships at Bangor Seminary in Maine. Perhaps no one in modern times has spoken or written as movingly about the shepherd character of ministry as has Jefferson.[6] His studies of *Cardinal Ideas of Isaiah* and *Cardinal Ideas of Jeremiah* show the range and depth of Jefferson's mind.[7] He spoke wisely and well to younger preachers and those just entering the ministry.[8] He always saw indolence and idleness as the demon for young aspiring preachers.

Although he would not get on the antidogma bandwagon, Jefferson made some painful concessions to the modern mood. He went so far as to blur the uniqueness of the Christ-event.[9] While he lamented the decline of preaching on the cross of Christ, he rejected substitutionary atonement in favor of something new and undefined. Jefferson set up a false dichotomy of options regarding the authority of Scripture and set dictation against illumination as the choice. He accepted an evolutionary account of biological and spiritual origins and clearly held to degrees of inspiration.[10] Along the same line, Jefferson gave up the idea of a literal second coming of Christ.[11] These concessions led ultimately to the mutilation of the gospel in Protestant preaching on a grand scale. Many like Jefferson had a sentimental attachment to the old paths, but little by little they jettisoned the supernatural elements of Christian faith on the alleged basis of scholarly criteria. The result was disastrous for the mainline, notwithstanding the gifted preachers. It would be disastrous for evangelicals as well.

---

1. Frederick Keller Stamm, *The Best of Charles E. Jefferson* (New York: Thomas Y. Crowell, 1960), 3.
2. Ibid., 75. Jefferson would read the Bible and Shakespeare aloud annually.
3. John Bishop, "Charles Edward Jefferson: Preaching the Great Doctrines," *Preaching* (September–October 1991): 61ff. Jefferson was part of the "preach positively" school, which wanted to flush away all negatives.
4. Stamm, *The Best of Charles E. Jefferson,* 10.
5. Charles E. Jefferson, *The Building of the Church* (New York: Macmillan, 1923), 294.
6. Charles E. Jefferson, *The Minister as Prophet* (New York: Grosset and Dunlap, 1905); *The Minister as Shepherd* (New York: Thomas Y. Crowell, 1912). The latter kindled the crisis of commitment to pastoral/preaching ministry in my life as a seminary senior. This book is warm and so alive!
7. Charles E. Jefferson, *Cardinal Ideas of Isaiah* (New York: Macmillan, 1925).
8. Charles E. Jefferson, *Quiet Talks to Growing Preachers in My Study* (New York: Thomas Y. Crowell, 1901).
9. Charles E. Jefferson, *Doctrine and Deed: Expounded and Illustrated* (New York: Thomas Y. Crowell, 1901).

10. Stamm, *The Best of Charles E. Jefferson,* 15. Jefferson goes so far as to state, "The Bible is not the only book. God has revealed himself through other men than the Jews. English literature contains a revelation" (*The Minister as Prophet,* 89). To say that the Bible contains the Word of God is to move away from the absolute uniqueness of divine revelation in Holy Scripture. Unknowingly, I believe, the store was being given away.

11. Ibid., 58.

11.4.3 *George C. Lorimer—Massive Messages*

There is only one answer possible: Death, sacrifice, blood, an offering made once for all in the end of the old ages for the redemption of the world. The knowledge of it and faith in it were needed in the past; they are needed still; and impotent and faithless the Christian message whenever its significance is minimized or lost. St. Paul gloried in the cross; and it will be a bitter day for humanity when the church shall hide it, apologize for it, and explain away its only possible meaning as though it were her shame.

—George C. Lorimer

Preaching in the United States was veering farther and farther away from anything exegetical. Among the conservatives, preaching was moving toward the oratorical and ornamental. A prime example is the Baptist preacher, **George C. Lorimer** (1838–1904). He was born in Edinburgh but came to the U.S. at the age of seventeen and traveled as an actor. While he was playing in Louisville, he was converted. He studied for the ministry and served churches in Harrodsville, Paducah, Walnut Street Baptist Church in Louisville, and First Baptist in Albany, New York. While serving the Shawmut Avenue Baptist Church in Boston, Lorimer came into contact with a group who purchased the old Tremont Theater across the street from Park Street Church in order to offer a vigorous evangelical ministry with free seats.[1] A magnificent structure was built, which burned down three times and was subsequently rebuilt. It stands yet today on Tremont Street, with its giant pipe organ with consoles on two levels. Here Charles Dickens gave his readings. The interior of the church is equal to the eight-story buildings beside it.

In 1873 Lorimer did his first ministry at Tremont. The thriving work bore ample testimony to his gifts as a preacher. To the disappointment of his people, he left for a successful ministry at two churches in Chicago (there is still a Lorimer Baptist Church in a southern suburb of Chicago). In 1891 he returned for a second ministry at Tremont Temple that lasted ten years. Lorimer then took a call to the old Madison Avenue Baptist Church in Manhattan, where he served until retirement.

Lorimer was dramatic, massive in content, and generally sound. His memory was exceptional; he had only to read his manuscript once and then could preach it without referring to it.[2] He wrote a noted biography of Spurgeon and penned many books. His son, George H. Lorimer, was the longtime editor-in-chief of the *Saturday Evening Post.*

But as was increasingly common, we find little exegesis in Lorimer's sermons. A text was taken almost as a pretext. At best it supplied the motif or main idea of the sermon. Is this enough?[3] No doubt Lorimer was essentially committed to Christ and the historic gospel, but where is the gospel and any appeal to sinners in these sermons?[4] They were intellectual, heavy with literary and historical quotation but desperately short of Bible truth.[5] In the absence of gospel dynamic, the tendency is to be moralistic. His heavy critiques of Harnack do not altogether assuage our anxiety because of such sentiments as "The Bible of verbal inspiration is not the true Bible."[6]

Yet even in such a prestigious Baptist theologian as A. H. Strong, we see modifications in historic orthodoxy in an attempt to accommodate evolutionary and higher critical ideas.[7] Other noted preachers were similar, including **Newell Dwight Hillis** (1858–1929), who served Plymouth Church in Brooklyn,[8] and the articulate **Cortland Myers** (1864–1941), who had notable ministries in the Baptist Temple in Brooklyn and at Tremont Temple.[9] Their thoughts were ordered and compelling but bereft of the Bible. No wonder that the Plymouth Brethren and their compatriots were drawing followers with their more exegetical preaching (cf. 11.1).

---

1. F. R. Webber, *A History of Preaching in Britain and America* (Milwaukee: Northwestern, 1957), 3:448.
2. Ibid., 3:449.
3. Defining a current trend along these lines is Harold T. Bryson, *Expository Preaching* (Nashville: Broadman and Holman, 1995), 32. Bryson seems to argue that only the point need come from the text, not the mains and subs.
4. George C. Lorimer, *The Modern Crisis in Religion* (New York: Revell, 1904); *Messages of Today to the Men of Tomorrow* (New York: George H. Doran, 1896).
5. George C. Lorimer, *Argument for Christianity* (Philadelphia: American Baptist Publication Society, 1894).
6. Lorimer, *The Modern Crisis in Religion,* 270.
7. Carl F. H. Henry, *Personal Idealism and Strong's Theology* (Wheaton, Ill.: Van Kampen, 1951), 77.
8. Newell Dwight Hillis, *A Man's Value to Society: Studies in Self-Culture and Character* (New York: Revell, 1896). These are more the essay-sermon of Tillotson, but for all their beauty they have no anchorage in Scripture.
9. Cortland Myers, *Making a Life* (New York: Revell, 1900); *Dangers of Crooked Thinking* (New York: Revell, 1924); *The Real Holy Spirit* (New York: Revell, 1909). Sound and popular but no wrestling with a text, no modeling of how Scripture is relevant. Brilliant but encouraging spectatorism.

11.4.4 *Russell H. Conwell—Name It and Claim It Early On*

You must keep in mind the question, "Will Jesus come here and save souls?" You must carefully eliminate all that will show irreverence for holy things or disrespect for the church. You must carefully introduce, wherever you can, the direct teachings of the Gospel, and then your entertainments will be the power of God unto salvation. The entertainments of the church need to be carefully guarded; and if they are, the church of the future will control the entertainments of the world. Then the theater that has its display of low and vulgar amusement will not pay because the churches will hold the best classes and, for divine and humane purposes, will conduct the best entertainments. There will be double inducement that will draw all classes, and the institutional church of the future will be free to use any reasonable means to influence men for good.

—Russell H. Conwell

The American entrepreneurial spirit and policy of manifest destiny were part of what made the U.S. the great frontier and a success story without parallel. This was reflected in preaching, especially in a charismatic figure like **Russell H. Conwell** (1843–1925). Born on a New England farm, Conwell was suckled on the sermons of Beecher and, as a young boy, did plays on *Uncle Tom's Cabin*. He would preach to the chickens.[1] He ran away from home at fifteen and worked his way to Europe. Eventually he attended a Methodist academy and entered Yale, where he did not seem to mind his shabby clothes. He took a dip into atheism but turned back to Christianity after attending a service in Plymouth Church, where Beecher auctioned off a runaway slave in a famous public-relations gambit.[2]

Enlisting in the army, Conwell fought in the Civil War and was wounded at Kenesaw Mountain. He was converted while he was in the army hospital. After the war he studied law at Albany University of New York State. (He could repeat the two volumes of Blackstone's commentaries from memory.) Admitted to the bar, he moved to Minneapolis, where he worked in legal and journalistic enterprises. He was a mover and a shaker. At thirty-seven he moved to Boston and took a position on the Boston *Traveler.* He traveled widely and interviewed Bismarck, Von Moltke, Tennyson, Garibaldi, Dickens, Gladstone, Victor Hugo, Beecher, and John Greenleaf Whittier. Conwell became popular as a lecturer on these persons and taught a large Sunday school class of two to three thousand at Tremont Temple.

With the death of his wife, Conwell turned anew to the Bible.[3] Remarried and living in Newton Centre, he ingested the influence of Newton Seminary nearby and took the pastorate of a virtually defunct little Baptist church in Lexington. His methods were sensational and highly controversial, but he averred, "Woe be to me if I preach not the Gospel!" He was an electrifying speaker who was "not limited for lung power."[4] He took a call to a floundering little church in North Philadelphia called Grace Baptist Church. He did little actual preparation of his messages, which were "simple, direct, full of homely illustrations that stayed in the memory and enabled his hearers to make the spiritual truths he preached a part of their everyday lives."[5]

A man of tremendous energy, Conwell led in breaking ground for a new church called the Baptist Temple, which seated 3,135 in the sanctuary and another 2000 in the lower Temple. Nine thousand people attended on the day the Temple was opened. Dues were charged regular attendees. The seats were soft, and Conwell had designed an uncustomarily user-friendly environment. He reiterated his conviction that "The mission of the Church is to save the souls of men."[6] The frenetic pace always threatened to distract, as Temple University was founded and then Samaritan Hospital. Gordon-Conwell Seminary represents a merging of several of these interests. Conwell did baptize more than ten thousand people in his thirty-three years as pastor at the Temple, and yet in all those years there was never a case of church discipline. The music was outstanding, with Professor David Wood, the blind organist, being a great drawing card. Prayer meetings were large and participative. Conwell was a social crusader who vigorously combatted evil. He was one of the original Chatauqua lecturers and itinerated constantly. His great lecture on "Acres of Diamonds" was given six thousand times to a total of thirteen million people and earned him eight million dollars, which he ploughed back into the work. "Only in America," one is tempted to say. This lecture is the idea that the diamonds we seek are in our own back yards, and the message is very much the "you can do it!" notion so quintessentially American, but so Pelagian.

Conwell wrote biographies prolifically, including a popular biography of Spurgeon. He claimed John Wanamaker as a close friend and was an advocate of Gladstone's "Do It Now Club." His glorification of prosperity reflected the American ethos of the time, but how biblical was it?[7] A sermon outline on Acts 16:31 focuses our concern:

1. Belief in a person means belief in his character;
2. If we believe in a man's character, we desire to be like him;
3. If we desire to be like him, we will naturally act like him [my response: reading of Christ's innocence makes us innocent?];
4. To be like him is to be saved.

Whatever Conwell might protest to the contrary, we miss the Cross and redemption entirely. He preached the spirit of the age.[8] Much American preaching at this time and on into our own day is such an amalgam of patriotism, self-help, and positive thinking. We saw this at the great Central Church in Chicago, established by **David Gram Swing** (1830–1894), who left the Presbyterian church under duress and charges of heresy and established a church which met in Orchestra Hall, seating three thousand. This influential and affluent congregation was subsequently served by Newell Dwight Hillis, who went on to Plymouth Church in Brooklyn. **Frank Gunsaulus** (1856–1921) was literally crippled by overexertion but preached brilliantly. No one answered the agnostic Robert Ingersoll as effectively as did Gunsaulus, yet there was no gospel of the grace of God in what he said.[9] Another preacher at Central Church, **Frederick Shannon** (1877–1947), was a homiletical craftsman of spectacular skill, and yet his sermons had no exegesis or biblical substance.[10] We sense something so American in this preaching, but there is so little that is biblical or theological. This pervasive tradition continues in our own time.

1. Agnes Rush Burr, *Russell H. Conwell and His Work* (Philadelphia: John Winston, 1926), 63. This is the authorized biography of Conwell and quite hagiographic.
2. Ibid., 107.
3. Ibid., 167.
4. Ibid., 176.
5. Ibid., 188.
6. Ibid., 207.
7. F. R. Webber, *A History of Preaching in Britain and America* (Milwaukee: Northwestern, 1957), 3:472.
8. Burr, *Russell H. Conwell and IIis Work,* 391.
9. Frank W. Gunsaulus, *Paths to Power* (New York: Revell, 1905); *Paths to the City of God* (New York: Revell, 1906). Gunsaulus admirably takes a text but its use is only to supply his motif rather than his outline. He gave the Beecher Lectures at Yale in 1911 on "The Minister and the Spiritual Life." David Swing had been converted at fifteen in a Methodist revival meeting; see Joseph Fort Newton, *David Swing* (Chicago: Unity Publishing Co., 1909).
10. Frederick F. Shannon, *A Moneyless Magnate and Other Essays* (New York: George H. Doran, 1923). The essay-type sermon is polished and brilliant but textually lacking in acuity. The Central Church has long since ceased to be.

11.4.5 A. B. SIMPSON—THE BIBLE PREACHER AND SWEET SINGER OF THE GOSPEL

I am no good unless I can get alone with God.

Every fiber in my soul was tingling with the sense of God's presence.
—A. B. Simpson

I traveled with him in conventions and what he preached he lived . . . He was the greatest heart preacher I ever listened to. He preached out of his own rich dealings with God.
—Paul Rader, who followed Simpson as head of the CMA

I count Dr. A. B. Simpson the foremost in power to reach the depths of the human soul. And his message was so bathed in love that it was always redolent of the personality of Him who having not seen we love.
—C. I. Scofield

Born and raised on King Edward Island in Canada, **Albert Benjamin Simpson** (1844–1919) was a Scot by extraction. He was strongly influenced by his mother, who prayed he would enter the ministry.[1] Simpson testified that he knew from age fourteen that God wanted him to preach. During his early years he devoured Scripture with "unspeakable ecstasy."[2] He pleaded with his austerely Calvinistic father to allow him to become a preacher. At seventeen Simpson made a remarkable nine-hundred-page "Covenant with God" and then went on for thorough training at Knox College in Toronto. When he preached while he was home one Christmas, everyone realized that his was to be "the prophet's mantle."[3]

At twenty-two, Simpson took the pastoral office at Knox Presbyterian Church in Hamilton and served there eight years, seeing 750 accessions to membership. Then he moved on to the Chestnut Street Presbyterian Church in Louisville, where his vision for worldwide evangelism began to enlarge. He spearheaded an evangelistic crusade with Major Whittle and P. P. Bliss. The churches benefited greatly, but Simpson had to come to terms with his own problem of self and arrogance. He yielded to the Lord and experienced powerful fillings of the Holy Spirit. Subsequently, he founded the Christian and Missionary Alliance (CMA).

Simpson oversaw the building of an evangelistic tabernacle in Louisville, but in 1879 he moved on to the Thirteenth Street Presbyterian Church in New York City. Sharing his vision for missions was not easy in this fashionable church, and after a year he had a total health breakdown. While up at Old Orchard Conference in Maine, Simpson received a healing touch from God. Jesus as healer has remained a focus in the CMA ever since.

After an amicable parting with Thirteenth Street Church, Simpson began an independent evangelistic ministry in Caledonian Hall, which ultimately became the Gospel Tabernacle at Eighth Avenue and West Forty-forth Street, just off Time Square. Called by some the Cave of Adullum, the Tabernacle became an extraordinary center of ministry and missions in the heart of New York City. An early German service was held each Sunday, and an Episcopalian communion service was officially sanctioned.

Simpson never expected to found a denomination as such, but the conventions he promoted, the magazines he edited, the school he started (Nyack Missionary Training School), and his extensive ministry resulted in a worldwide fellowship of churches that authentically carried forth the vision of the founder. Deeply committed to premillennialism, Simpson heralded the fourfold message of Jesus as Savior, Sanctifier, Healer, and coming King.[4]

D. L. Moody said of Simpson, "No one gets at my heart like that man."[5] He was truly a man who knew and walked with God. He published more than seventy books, including his classic pair of volumes on the Holy Spirit in the Bible as well as his twenty-four-volume commentary, *Christ in the Bible*.[6] He was also the composer of many hymns, some of which are timeless.[7]

Simpson was providentially led to part company with John Alexander Dowie of Zion, Illinois, whose obsession with healing would have distracted Simpson and his movement.[8] One of his closest heart-brothers was F. E. Marsh of Bristol, with whom he had many meetings.[9]

Weariness and fatigue began to plague him, and in Simpson's final years, as Tozer described it, "He lost the sense of the presence of the well-beloved."[10] But those shadows could not eclipse the remarkable Bible preaching of this stalwart soldier of the Cross who, along with **I. M. Haldeman** at First Baptist Church at Seventy-nineth and Broadway, exemplify the soundest and most exegetical preaching being done in New York City.[11] With respect to the burgeoning ministry of the Alliance, Tozer's analysis is that "The true headquarters was the pulpit of the Gospel Tabernacle."[12] "He was a minstrel . . . preaching was melodious and musical when it fell from his lips," Leon Tucker observed.[13] Tozer describes the preacher in action:

> Mr. Simpson steps forward, pauses for a moment, and then in a low reverent tone announces his text. The tense silence is broken only by the voice of the speaker. His early training has given him a quiet reserve. His manner is relaxed and natural as he faces his hearers. Large framed, impressive and dignified, his very appearance gives promise of a great message to follow. He begins to speak with the Bible out-spread on one hand and the other hand resting lightly upon his hip. At first the words come slowly, spoken in a rich baritone of remarkable range and power. As he warms to his theme the speed of utterance increases, his voice takes on mounting degrees of emotional intensity, while his body sways back and forth rhythmically . . . his gestures are few, but when moved more than usual he lays his Bible down, places both hands on his hips and shakes his great head to emphasize a point. The lofty truth he is proclaiming, the strong, magnetic quality of his voice, the swift flow of his language, all combine to produce an impression so profound that when he is through speaking and the benediction is pronounced the listeners sit in hushed silence, unable or unwilling to break the spell of the sermon . . .[14]

A. B. Simpson's sermons were "models of structural perfection." He loved to use biblical illustrations and did so with great skill. His printed sermons glowed, and his devotional pieces are radiantly incandescent.[15] He may have been as one described him, "a cadaverous-looking minister," but he was vibrantly alive in the Spirit.

---

1. A. W. Tozer, *Wingspread: Albert B. Simpson—A Study in Spiritual Altitude* (Harrisburg, Pa.: Christian, 1943), 18.
2. Ibid., 27.
3. Ibid., 33.
4. Ibid., 105.
5. Daniel J. Evearitt, "A. B. Simpson, the Man," *Alliance Life* (November 10, 1993): 7.
6. A. B. Simpson, *The Holy Spirit or Power from on High,* 2 vols. (Harrisburg, Pa.: Christian, 1896, 1924). Powerful!
7. Tozer, *Wingspread,* 117. N.B. A. B. Simpson, *Songs of the Spirit* (Harrisburg, Pa.: Christian, 1920).
8. Ibid., 134.
9. Ibid., 137. Cf. F. E. Marsh, *Night Scenes of the Bible* (Grand Rapids: Baker, 1904, 1967), N.B. 4.2.3, note 21.
10. Ibid., 141.
11. I. M. Haldeman (1845–1933) has given some mighty scriptural studies on the Tabernacle and sacrifices of the Old Testament, against liberalism and various cults, and on prophecy; see *The Coming of Christ: Premillennial and Imminent* (New York: Charles C. Cook, 1906).

12. Tozer, *Wingspread,* 111.

13. Ibid., 114.

14. Ibid., 114f.

15. A. B. Simpson, *The Christ-Life* (New York: Alliance, 1925); *Wholly Sanctified* (New York: Alliance, 1925); *The Life of Prayer* (New York: Alliance, 1925); *Days of Heaven Upon Earth* (New York: Alliance, 1925). His daily readings.

11.4.6 DAVID JAMES BURRELL—BIBLE PREACHER AND HOMILETICIAN

> Just here it becomes apparent why the much exploited New Theology is not adequate to the business at hand. In eliminating the divine factor from the Scriptures it undermines the only reliable authority for the fundamental facts of the Gospel and drives one to the logical conclusion that conversion is a figment of the imagination and that revivals are out of date.

> In all my life I have never asked a man or woman to come to church or to join the church. I have stood on my platform and told the truth to all who came. I held Him before them, because I knew that the power came from Him, not from me.

> I don't believe in taking Christianity half-way. If Christianity is not good for every day in the year and for every minute in the day; if it isn't good in business as well as in church; if it doesn't make a burdened man or woman happier and hopeful and a business man honest and clean-conscienced, then I don't want anything more to do with it. But it does. I know it does. For over half a century I have proved that it does.
>
> —David James Burrell

David James Burrell (1844–1926) was born in Pennsylvania but was reared in Freeport, Illinois. He attended Phillips Academy and then went on to Yale, where he lost his faith. His mother expected him to go into the ministry, and he could not admit to her that he had become an unbeliever, so he went to Union Seminary in New York City. While working among impoverished boys near Washington Square, he was called to assist a dying Scotsman who had drifted from the faith himself but who interrogated Burrell about his faith. Lying repeatedly to the dying man, Burrell at last capitulated. Having come into the room a skeptic, he left "a fanatic for Christ."[1] He went on to work with his wife for four years in the slums of Chicago and then spent eleven years as pastor of the Second Presbyterian Church in Dubuque, Iowa.

In 1887 Burrell moved to the prestigious Westminster Presbyterian Church of Minneapolis, which he brought to a strength of more than two thousand members. In 1891 he accepted a call to the Marble Collegiate Church (Reformed Church in America), which he pastored until his death in 1926. There were only 115 members left in this historic church when he arrived, but his strong biblical preaching soon built a mighty flock. Marble Collegiate was at one time a great center of gospel preaching. During four of those years he filled a vacancy in the chair of homiletics at Princeton Seminary, traveling by train to Princeton for lectures.

He gave the first of the Sprunt Lectures at Union Seminary in Richmond; they were published as *The Sermon: Its Construction and Delivery.* This distillation of his teaching and practice registers his clear preference for expository preaching.[2] Classically oriented, he devoted fifty-eight pages to the argument in the sermon (developing the body). While stressing the importance of the exordium (introduction), he is particularly pointed on the urgency of the peroration:

> The peroration winds up the argument . . . the peroration is intended to clinch it. For this reason, the preacher should devote more careful and prayerful attention to the close of the sermon than to any other portion of it. He cannot safely trust to the moment for his last words.[3]

While disliking "vulgar buffoonery" in the pulpit, his dislike for dullness was even greater. He did not entirely exclude appropriate use of humor. Burrell preached well-packaged doctrinal sermons in which he effectively argued that the Bible is not "a mingled tissue of truth and falsehood or as merely 'containing' a less or greater modicum of truth."[4] A sample of his probing expository work can be seen in his practical exposition of John 13–17 in the *Short Course Series* of T & T Clark. His message here on "The Dispensation of the Holy Ghost" from John 16:5–15 is especially noteworthy.[5] Examples of his versatility and verve in preaching are observed in splendid messages on "Watchman, What of the Night?" from Isaiah 21:11–12 and "A Sensational Gospel" from 1 Corinthians 1:21, which concludes with an impressive flourish and invitation.[6] Both the texts and body of these sermons are well-divided, and the preacher is careful to practice what he enjoins in his own lectures on the nature of preaching.

Shepherd said Burrell reminded him "of a great stone, set in a certain place to hold a burden. His square chiseled face, his broad shoulders and his medium stature gave me a sense of his solidity; the grayness that comes of his eighty years gave me an impression of the hoariness that settles through the centuries on an immovable stone."[7]

1. F. R. Webber, *A History of Preaching in Britain and America* (Milwaukee: Northwestern, 1957), 3:482. Though not acknowledged by Webber, these insights appear to be sourced from William G. Shepherd, *Great Preachers as Seen by a Journalist* (New York: Revell, 1924), 20–21.
2. David James Burrell, *The Sermon: Its Construction and Delivery* (New York: Revell, 1913), 63, 71.
3. Ibid., 188.
4. David James Burrell, *Why I Believe the Bible* (New York: Revell, 1917), 15.
5. David James Burrell, *In the Upper Room* (Edinburgh: T & T Clark, 1913), 87ff.

6. David James Burrell, "The Morning Cometh," in *Talks for the Times* (New York: American Tract Society, 1893), 5ff., 56ff.

7. Shepherd, *Great Preachers as Seen by a Journalist,* 16.

11.4.7 *A. Z. Conrad—Preacher and Promoter in Boston*

Religiously, Boston, like other cities, has undergone a considerable change in its attitude toward the church and the spiritual activities represented by the church. A considerable indifference toward church attendance has been painfully apparent. A sense of religious responsibility has seemed to grow more and more feeble. As a corrective of these tendencies the church has been importuned to popularize its services. But the effort in this direction has not seemed to stem the tide outward. The church has been importuned to rationalize her preaching. But every added elimination of the supernatural has only accentuated the disinterestedness of the people in the church. The church has been urged to institutionalize herself and devote her attention increasingly to the material interests of the people. In Boston, as elsewhere, where an honest effort to answer the demand has been made, it is perfectly apparent that this has not solved the problem. Indeed it has been in this very period when the church has been trying all these various devices to stem the outward tide, that the decline in church attendance has been most in evidence.

—A. Z. Conrad

To address the above-described need, 166 churches representing 120,000 members from many denominations united in simultaneous evangelistic crusades early in 1909, the central movement being led by Dr. J. Wilbur Chapman and Charles M. Alexander. The general chairman of this massive concerted effort was **Arcturus Zodiac Conrad** (1855–1937), for thirty-two years the pastor of historic Park Street Church at the head of Boston Common. The response was overwhelming, with hundreds professing Christ and joining the churches. The united prayer meetings were indescribably beneficial.[1] Many of the central meetings were held in Tremont Temple, which was without a pastor at this time.[2] Conrad gave revitalizing leadership to the movement in the greater Boston area as he was giving strong leadership at Park Street Church. Other revivals followed, including one in 1928 with Dr. Biederwolf.

Conrad was born in Indiana, where his father was a Presbyterian minister. He graduated from Carleton College in Minnesota and from Union Seminary in New York, where he also did doctoral study at New York University. He served congregations in Brooklyn and in Worcester, turning down a call to serve a church in London, England. In 1905 he began his ministry at Park Street. This historic church (cf. 9.2.8) was at low ebb at the time of his coming. Conrad was an activist and gave himself unsparingly to the rejuvenation of the Sunday school, the work among youth, and overseas missions. He was an able and a fighting preacher:

We are too much afraid of open collision. We spend our time parleying about consequences. The apostles told the truth and told it straight without such adjustment as emasculates the truth declared.[3]

Conrad's sermons were thoroughly biblical and often controversial. He tackled topics like "Proven But Not Persuaded: The Word That Defies Dungeons, Demons and Death," and "When the World Slams the Door in Your Face and Goes Back to Bed." He certainly rang the changes in his sermon from Mark 4:39 and 5:8 on "Civilizing, Socializing, Christianizing the World," but the sermon is not very exegetical.[4] One obtains a similar impression from other collections of his sermons.[5] A deeper expository ministry would await the coming of Conrad's successor, Harold John Ockenga.

During the last fourteen years of Conrad's ministry, both Sunday services were broadcast over a local radio station. At age seventy-six he remarried a twenty-seven-year-old[6] and died of cancer in his eighty-second year.

---

1. A. Z. Conrad, *Boston's Awakening* (Boston: King's Business Publishing, 1909), 13ff.
2. Tremont Temple would soon be occupied by gifted preachers such as J. C. Massee (1871–1965), who was an able evangelist himself; see *Revival Sermons* (New York: Revell, 1928) and *Evangelism in the Local Church* (Philadelphia: Judson, 1939). Massee was in the forefront of those concerned about the theological drift in the Northern Baptist Convention; see L. Rush Bush and Thomas J. Nettles, *Baptists and the Bible* (Chicago: Moody, 1980), 355. Later preachers of spiritual power to preach from the Tremont pulpit were Sidney Powell and Gordon Brownville.
3. H. Crosby Englizian, *Brimstone Corner: Park Street Church* (Chicago: Moody, 1968), 221.
4. A. Z. Conrad, *Comrades of the Carpenter* (New York: Revell, 1926), 123ff.
5. A. Z. Conrad, *Radiant Religion* (New York: Harper, 1930).
6. Englizian, *Brimstone Corner: Park Street Church*, 223.

11.5   THE EVANGELISTIC WHEELHORSES

He sends his command to the earth; his word runs swiftly.
—Psalm 147:15

Evangelists have always nudged the church toward the cutting edge. If, as Archbishop William Temple insisted, "Evangelism is the winning of men to acknowledge Christ as their Savior and King, so that they may give themselves to His service in the fellowship of His Church," we must say that the evangelists in the United States (apart from B. Fay Mills) did some of the soundest and most effective biblical preaching of this time.

Kerygmatic preaching is of the essence whether it is done by the local pastor/teacher or a visiting evangelist.[1] The marks of solid evangelistic preaching, as the late Methodist preacher and editor Roy Short crystallized them so clearly, are (1) authoritative; (2) scriptural; (3) hopeful; (4) urgent; (5) far-reaching.[2]

Without the evangel, nothing can be right. As Vincent Taylor put it so well, "The test of a good theologian is—can he write a tract?"[3]

---

1. David L. Larsen, *The Evangelism Mandate: Restoring the Centrality of Gospel Preaching* (Wheaton, Ill.: Crossway, 1992). This work surveys the nature and history of evangelistic preaching.
2. Roy Short, *Evangelistic Preaching* (Nashville: Upper Room, 1946). Longtime editor of The Christian Advocate.
3. William Barclay, *Fishers of Men* (Philadelphia: Westminster, 1966), 103.

11.5.1 SAM JONES—THE GOSPEL VOICE FROM THE SOUTH

It is considered vulgar now, really vulgar, for a man to get up and preach hell to sinners . . . It is not polite to believe that way, and many a little fellow has scratched that out of his creed; but he won't be in hell more than fifteen minutes before he will revise his creed and having in it nothing but hell.

Quit your meanness!

—Sam Jones

Samuel P. Jones (1847–1906) was born in Alabama and moved about with his Southern Methodist family during the Civil War. To the great sorrow of his family, young Jones became a heavy drinker and not until he was converted in 1871 did he stop.[1]

Traveling as an itinerant evangelist for the North Georgia Conference, Jones was unimpressive in appearance. He was much influenced by Spurgeon's sermons but tended to theological weakness on sin and the atonement. He emphasized repentance more than faith. Sam Jones hated sham and pretense, and "His fiery sermons in plain, simple Anglo-Saxon, with a sprinkling of the homely colloquialisms of the common people, attracted attention."[2] He was a lifelong Methodist, but testified, "I like loose-fitting denominational garments." He was brutally blunt if not downright insulting at times—"skin 'em in rabbit-fashion" was his counsel. Yet he cautioned, if someone has a sore throat, you say "open your mouth," but you don't throw in the whole medicine case.

Jones maintained a frenetic pace, preaching at 6:00 A.M., 10:00 A.M., 3:00 P.M., and 7:00 P.M. daily. In his great Nashville crusade, fifteen hundred people confessed Christ. He went North to do a great crusade with Talmage in Brooklyn in 1885. E. O. Excell (who wrote "Since I Have Been Redeemed" and put "Count Your Blessings" and "Jesus Wants You for a Sunbeam" to music) was frequently his musician. He ventured North again for a great crusade in Chicago, but his ministry was mainly Southern. It was estimated that in 1885 and 1886 seventy thousand souls were added to the roles of the Methodist Episcopal Church South as the result of his ministry.

R. G. Lee's father said that Sam Jones was the greatest master of an audience he had ever heard. He made "sinners smell sulphur." Robert Ingersoll, the great freethinking orator, would not debate him. As Methodism increasingly became "indifferent to creed," Jones clashed with the bishops and identified with the dissidents. He did seem to become more coarse toward the end, and he was beside himself because of troubles in his family. Bishop Ivan Lee Holt heard him as a university student and recalled that "there were tears in all our eyes and hearts."[3] He was every bit as popular on the Chatauqua circuit as was William Jennings Bryan.[4] When he died, thirty thousand people passed by his casket in Atlanta, where he was buried.

"Fighting the Devil," based on Acts 17:16, is a typical sermon. Jones preached as few local pastors would dare to preach. Half of his sermons were illustrations, and he used sarcasm devastatingly, but he also used ancillary Scriptures effectively.[5] He brought the great audience in St. Louis to the Cross and closed with Wesley's moving hymn, "I saw one hanging on the tree," put to music by Excell. "Men Pay Dearly for Eternal Damnation" from Mark 8:36 is another example of his fearless preaching.[6] He excoriated people who earned money from liquor and gambling, which he called blood money. A gambler offered him five hundred to test him, and Sam took the proffered contribution. "The devil's had it long enough," was his quick retort. Jones was a highly controversial preacher but effective for God and faithful to the Word.

---

1. Kathleen Minnix, *Laughter in the Amen Corner* (Athens: University of Georgia, 1993), 7. This understanding study must be seen as the definitive biography of Sam Jones. It probes his deep depressions and instability.
2. F. R. Webber, *A History of Preaching in Britain and America* (Milwaukee: Northwestern, 1957), 3:492.
3. Ivan Lee Holt, "A Genius in the Pulpit," in *Great Pulpit Masters: Sam Jones* (Grand Rapids: Baker, 1950), 9.
4. Bryan, the perennial populist of American politics, was a gifted lay preacher and gave the tenth of the Sprunt Lectures in Richmond titled *In His Image* (New York: Revell, 1922). They have a sermonic ring.
5. Sam Jones, "Fighting the Devil" in *Sam Jones' Sermons* (Chicago: Rhodes and McClure, 1888), 68ff.
6. Ibid., 290ff.

11.5.2 WILBUR CHAPMAN—THE GOSPEL VOICE WHICH MOVED MEN

When the great evangelist called for an after-meeting I was one of the first to enter the room and to my great joy Mr. Moody came and sat down beside me. I confessed that I was not quite sure that I was saved. He handed me his opened Bible and asked me to read John 5:24. He said to me: "Do you believe this?" I answered: "Certainly." He said: "Are you a Christian?" I replied: "Sometimes I think I am and again I am fearful." "Read it again," he said. Then he repeated his two questions and I had to answer as before . . . he spoke sharply: "Whom are you doubting?" and then it came to me with startling suddenness. "Well, are you a Christian?" and I answered: "Yes, Mr. Moody, I am." From that day to this I have never questioned my acceptance with God.

—J. Wilbur Chapman

An evangelist with striking appeal to men, **J. Wilbur Chapman** (1859–1917) was a choice servant of Christ and an unusual preacher. Born in Indiana, he was raised in a godly home. His mother was related to Senator Sumner and Archbishop Sumner. Chapman's earliest surrender to Christ took place in his Sunday school class in the Methodist Episcopal Church.[1] He went on to study at Oberlin and Lake Forest College, from whence he went into Chicago and heard Moody preach. (Lake Forest College is also where B. Fay Mills attended, who ultimately become the reprobate Unitarian evangelist.)

In 1879 Chapman went to Lane Seminary in Cincinnati, from which he graduated, and took with his new bride yoked parishes, a circuit of several local charges. In 1883 he answered the call to the Reformed church in Schuylerville, New York, where his emphasis on ministry to men was in clear evidence.[2] For five years he served the First Reformed Church in Albany, where a genuine evangelistic breakthrough, with Sankey's songs and inquirers' meetings, took place in the rather staid and traditional setting. Five hundred members were added. In 1890 Chapman went on to the great Bethany Presbyterian Church in Philadelphia (succeeding A. T. Pierson), where in the two years he worked with John Wanamaker more than eleven hundred members were added. In 1899 he took the pastorate of Fourth Presbyterian in New York City.[3]

In 1903 Chapman went full-time into evangelism and built the Chapman/Charles Alexander team which held numerous crusades and simultaneous evangelistic campaigns in North America, "under the Southern cross," and through the Orient and Europe. He was closely identified with summer conferences which were beginning to thrive in such places as Niagara-on-the-Lake, Winona Lake, Montreat, and Stony Brook. The ministry of "Praying Hyde," the American Presbyterian minister, was deeply intertwined with Chapman's.[4] Chapman served as moderator of the Presbyterian General Assembly in 1917 but failed in health and died on Christmas morning in 1917 at the age of fifty-eight.

His was an unbending defense of the full inspiration of the Scriptures. The imminent return of Christ for his church was a precious article of faith for Chapman.[5] He took a steadfast stand for "the full authority and integrity of God's Word," manifest in his view and practice of preaching. He created quite a stir when he advocated recalling all overseas missionaries who did not hold to inerrancy.[6]

What was it that held such vast audiences spellbound as if eternity itself were closing round them? It was the simple story of Jesus. Never in all these meetings did Dr. Chapman or any member of the part make a single apology for the Word of God. They believed in it, in its inspiration from Genesis to Revelation, and preached it as men preach who believe themselves to be ambassadors of Christ and messengers of the Most High God to a world of sinners.[7]

Chapman was steady and even-tempered. He had "a commanding presence" and a "rich, deep and musical voice." He also had a rare sense of humor.[8] The lucidity and clarity of his prose style is apparent in "Conversion Is a Miracle."[9] His evangelistic sermons are well outlined, such as his famous "And Judas Iscariot" from Mark 3:19,[10] and his deeply moving "And Peter" from Mark 16:7.[11] One of his most effective messages was to Christians and was titled "The Power of a Surrendered Life" or "Turning Back at Kadesh-Barnea."[12] Well illustrated and deftly applied, J. Wilbur Chapman's sermons were models for many young preachers, including Billy Sunday, who got his start with him. Those sermons serve as excellent examples for us yet today.

---

1. Ford C. Ottman, *J. Wilbur Chapman: A Biography* (New York: Doubleday, 1920), 22.
2. Ibid., 47. Ottman was an American Presbyterian minister best known for his superb writings on Bible prophecy.
3. Ibid., 68ff.
4. V. Raymond Edman, *They Found the Secret* (Grand Rapids: Zondervan, 1960), 81.
5. Ottman, *J. Wilbur Chapman,* 308.
6. Ibid., 203. The associate song leader, Henry Barraclough, wrote "Ivory Palaces" from a sermon from Psalm 45:8.
7. Ibid., 256.
8. Ibid., 317.
9. J. Wilbur Chapman, *The Personal Touch* (New York: Revell, n.d.), 149.
10. J. Wilbur Chapman, *And Judas Iscariot* (New York: George H. Doran, 1906), 11ff.
11. J. Wilbur Chapman, *And Peter* (Chicago: Moody, n.d.), 38ff.
12. J. Wilbur Chapman, *The Power of a Surrendered Life* (Chicago: Moody, n.d.), 32ff.

11.5.3 REUBEN ARCHER TORREY—THE GOSPEL VOICE TO INTELLECTUALS

> I have no dread of preaching now; preaching is the greatest joy of my life, and sometimes when I stand up to speak and realize that He [the Holy Spirit] is there, that all the responsibility is upon Him, such a joy fills my heart that I can scarce restrain myself from shouting and leaping.
> —R. A. Torrey

From very early in his life, **Reuben Archer Torrey** (1856–1928) was haunted by a sense of call to preach. Born in Hoboken, New Jersey, R. A. was raised in Brooklyn in a devout Congregational home of considerable means. His father made and lost several fortunes and was active in Democratic party affairs. The wife of President William Howard Taft was a Torrey.

It was his mother's prayers that were decisive for young R. A.[1] Wanting to be a lawyer, he entered Yale at fifteen in 1871. He was struggling and thought to take his own life when he decided to yield to God: "I will preach."[2] Torrey was utterly at sea at Yale Divinity School but claimed John 7:17. D. L. Moody taught him to win souls during a visit to Yale. Upon graduating, Torrey took his first pastoral charge in Garrettsville, Ohio. At this time he was not altogether clear on inerrancy, was still a universalist like his father, and was hazy on the Second Coming. Under the stimulus of Finney's revival sermons, he aggressively sought to win souls to Christ and even held revival meetings in saloons.[3]

In 1882 Torrey and his family spent a year studying in Germany, primarily with Delitzsch and Luthardt at Leipzig and with Frank and Zahn at Erlangen. In this time he came to clear focus on the inerrancy of Scripture and soon the premillennial return of Jesus Christ.[4] Torrey had a brilliant mind and wrestled with all of these issues in profound depth.

Torrey returned to the U.S. in 1883 to plant a new church in Minneapolis and a second new church as well. Soon he came to see the need for the endowment of the Holy Spirit for life and ministry, normally called "the filling of the Spirit" but which he called "the baptism of the Holy Spirit."[5] In 1889 he went to Chicago as the first superintendent of the Moody Bible Institute (as it was later called) and the pastorate of what was to be the Moody Church. His indefatigable labors in personal evangelism saw particular fruit at the World Colombian Exposition in Chicago in 1893 when he brought evangelist John McNeill for a six-month period. Torrey broke with D. L. Moody's son, Will R. Moody, over the latter's espousal of George Adam Smith's high critical views.[6] Yet the mantle of Moody fell on Torrey at the conclusion of the Kansas City Crusade, which was Moody's last. A. C. Dixon took the pastorate of Moody Church in Chicago, and R. A. Torrey went full-time into evangelism. Tremendous response to the crusades was reported around the world.

Traveling with Torrey was Charles Alexander with "the Glory Song" signature.[7] Grace Saxe was part of the team to set up follow-up Bible classes. Midday meetings were held in the grinding regimen of the campaigns. In launching the Chicago meetings, he said:

> You, who think we need a new Bible; something better than the Bible, the old Bible; an expurgated Bible; take heed to our experiences. Eighteen months of preaching its Gospel, thirty thousand men and women won to Christ, proves that the Bible, the old Bible, is what the world needs, what the twentieth century needs.[8]

One of his chief backers over the years was the Quaker Oats layman, Henry Crowell.[9] Vitriolic opposition from such as S. Parkes Cadman was only a further stamp of God's approval on the man and his message. In his great Toronto crusade, Oswald J. Smith and his brother came to Christ.

By 1908 Torrey became the founding dean of the Bible Institute of Los Angeles (BIOLA) and the first pastor of the Church of the Open Door. Among his students at BIOLA were Charles E. Fuller, Donald Gray Barnhouse, and A. A. MacRae. "Strong currents of unbelief" and apostasy in the mainline denominations continually confronted conservatives. Slashing attacks by Dean Shirley Jackson Case and Shailer Matthews of the University of Chicago Divinity School were common. Torrey repeatedly gave his great message on "Why I Believe the Bible is the Word of God."[10]

Torrey had an unusual mind. He read Scripture in five languages. His messages were solidly biblical, logical, and clear in their form and presentation. He had no great eloquence or fanciness, yet he was impressive in appearance. He is described here at age forty-six:

> His erect figure, his broad shoulders, the manly face with its massive brows give an impression of great strength . . . and his face, when seen close at hand, with its bright complexion and clear eyes and a certain radiancy of smile, has still the freshness of youth.[11]

Some his most memorable sermons were "What Are You Waiting For?" and "The Need of a Hiding Place." One of his best-selling books has been his sound and powerful work, *What the Bible Teaches.*[12] In a typical sermon on "The Great Judgment Day" from Acts 17, Torrey characterized the judgment under five headings:

I. The certainty of it
II. The universality of it
III. The basis of it
IV. The administrator of it
V. The issues of it[13]

An especially thoughtful message he shared is "God's Roadblocks on the Road to Hell" from 2 Peter 3:9 and John 3:16.[14] Torrey was also known for his magnificent preaching on the resurrection of Christ, an example of which is "Up from the Grave He Arose!" from 1 Corinthians 15.[15]

Torrey was one of the founders of the World Christian Fundamentals Association and one of the prime movers in the publication of *The Fundamentals.* In 1924 he concluded his ties in Los Angeles and went home to glory in 1928. Will Houghton of Atlanta's Baptist Tabernacle preached the funeral sermon.

1. Roger Martin, *R. A. Torrey: Apostle of Certainty* (Murfreesboro, Tenn.: Sword of the Lord, 1976), 25.
2. Ibid., 34. A provocative study on Torrey, the best we have.
3. Ibid., 51.
4. Ibid., 69.
5. Ibid., 118. I possess documents which seem to prove that Torrey later clarified his use of the terms.
6. Ibid., 124.
7. Helen C. Alexander and J. Kennedy Maclean, *Charles M. Alexander: A Romance of Song and Soulwinning* (London: Marshall, 1920). When Alexander went with Chapman, Homer Hammontree became songleader.
8. Martin, *R. A. Torrey,* 164.
9. Richard Ellsworth Day, *Breakfast-Table Autocrat: The Life Story of Henry Parsons Crowell* (Chicago: Moody, 1946). Crowell's anguish over the drift of his denomination is exceedingly poignant.
10. Martin, *R. A. Torrey,* 244; the content of the lecture is on 281ff.

11. Ibid., 140.

12. R. A. Torrey, *What the Bible Teaches* (New York: Revell, 1898). See page 144 on the atonement. Solid!

13. R. A. Torrey, "The Great Judgment Day," in *Great Preaching on Judgment* (Murfreesboro, Tenn.: Sword of the Lord, 1990), 159ff.

14. R. A. Torrey, "God's Roadblocks on the Road to Hell," in *Great Preaching on Hell* (Murfreesboro, Tenn.: Sword of the Lord, 1989), 195–96.

15. R. A. Torrey, "Up from the Grave He Arose!" in *Great Preaching on the Resurrection* (Murfreesboro, Tenn.: Sword of the Lord, 1984), 155ff. One of Torrey's significant books was *The Higher Criticism and the New Theology* (1911).

11.5.4 BILLY SUNDAY—THE GOSPEL VOICE THROUGH A ROUGHNECK

I am an old-fashioned preacher of the old-time religion, that has warmed this cold world for two thousand years.

This Bible is God's inspired Word, and every word in it from cover to cover is God's Word. If you try to tell me that some old beer-soaked Higher Critic says otherwise, and that the consensus of "modern scholarship" says otherwise, then I can only tell you and your professor and the consensus of modern scholarship that they are going to perdition.

—Billy Sunday

Such a character, so often uncouth and rough-and-tumble, Billy Sunday was a powerful preacher of the gospel of Christ! **Dr. Maitland Alexander,** pastor of First Presbyterian Church of Pittsburgh, testified how the Sunday campaign shook the whole community. Nine department stores in the city held daily prayer meetings before business. His own church seating thirty-two hundred was filled for the special services for lawyers and doctors, and the tabernacle seating twenty thousand was jammed with steel workers night after night. After the crusade, 419 joined his congregation on their profession of faith.[1]

William Ashley Sunday (1862–1935) was born in Ames, Iowa. His father died while serving with the Union Army. When he was ten, Sunday was sent by his mother with another brother to an orphanage because she was unable to provide for them. Never graduating from high school, Billy Sunday at eighteen went to work in Marshalltown, where he played baseball. In 1883, Cap Anson of the Chicago White Stockings called him up to the big city to play ball. His remarkable speed made him a valuable player.

While playing for Chicago for five years, Billy was confronted with the claims of Christ by the Gospel Wagon from the Pacific Garden Mission. Upon invitation, he went to the mission, where he went forward and gave his life to Christ.[2] Although he continued to play for Chicago and subsequently signed contracts with Pittsburgh and Philadelphia, his heart and the heart of his dear bride from Jefferson Park Presbyterian Church, where he attended, were increasingly drawn to the Lord's work. He quit baseball, giving up good money to work and speak for the YMCA.[3]

As Dorsett points out, "It was becoming voguish to question the veracity of

Scripture,"[4] but Billy Sunday was anchored to the old gospel. In a marvelous networking, he became J. Wilbur Chapman's advance man for two years and served an apprenticeship that prepared him for his own crusades on "the saw-dust trail." Besides Chapman, who gave him his homiletics course, the writings of F. B. Meyer and E. M. Bounds shaped him to be the man of God he became.

When Chapman went back to Bethany Presbyterian in Philadelphia, Sunday was unemployed. He received an invitation to do his first crusade in Garner, Iowa.[5] God blessed the "baseball evangelist" with his relentless message of "get right with God!" In 1898 he was licensed by the Presbyterians to preach. The first eleven years were tough, but Billy Sunday preached on.

Sunday was quite theological in style. "Although he joked, used homey illus-trations, and relied on barnyard metaphors [recall Zwingli, 5.4.1, 2], he was no buffoon. His Christology was strong and his knowledge of Scripture impressive."[6]

Billy Sunday preached to more than one hundred thousand people from 1908 to 1920. Even New York City responded to the preacher who preached with ev-ery muscle in his body. Carnegie Hall was filled and thousands milled about outside. Not even Andrew Carnegie himself could get in! Sunday's songleaders were Homer Rodeheaver and Harry Clark. He led great crusades against liquor and special interests. He preached in a time of growing urbanization and under-stood where so many of his hearers came from. His warnings about immorality and the dangers of the city were needed and in many cases heeded.

But Sunday's call was to salvation and forgiveness of sin through repentance and faith. He was "the midwestern storyteller," who could live out the Bible sto-ries, enacting five-minute segments which made them vivid and alive.[7] People crowded every inch of the Moody Church at his funeral (the auditorium has 4,400 seats) with Dr. John Timothy Stone, former pastor of Fourth Presbyterian Church in Chicago, giving the funeral sermon in which he urged those present who were not Christians to repent: "Don't put off accepting Christ until the end of this fu-neral service."[8]

If there was a flaw in Sunday, it might be that as he become well known and a good friend of John D. Rockefeller, neither he nor his children handled money or fame well. So too, his platform gymnastics and acrobatic preaching scandal-ized some. But he was a born actor and remarkable in his repartee:

> You say, "Mr. Sunday, the Church is full of hypocrites." So's hell. I say to you if you don't want to go to hell and live with that bunch forever, come into the Church, where you won't have to associate with them very long. There are no hypocrites in heaven.
> You say, "Mr. Sunday, I can be a Christian and go to heaven without joining a church." Yes, and you can go to Europe without getting on board a steamer. The swimming's good—but the sharks are laying for fellows who take that route. I don't believe you. If a man is truly saved, he will hunt for a church right away.[9]

In some crusades the response was phenomenal. Billy had a great day at the University of Pennsylvania, with amazing fruit. In Columbus, Ohio, the eighteen thousand converts included the chief of police and all of the policemen detailed to duty at the tabernacle. Members in congregations this author has served date their conversion to a Billy Sunday meeting. Gordon H. Clark, the noted apologist and philosopher, was converted under Billy Sunday.

A typical Billy Sunday sermon is his textual-topical message on "Heaven Is a Place," in which he pulls out the stops.[10] The text is John 14:1–6 and the sermon is saturated with Scripture. One can visualize Billy Sunday preaching—

> I'm against sin. I'll kick it as long as I've got a foot, and I'll fight it as long as I've got a fist. I'll butt it as long as I've got a head. I'll bite it as long as I've got a tooth. And when I'm old and fistless and footless and toothless, I'll gum it till I go home to glory, and it goes home to perdition!

1. William T. Ellis, *Billy Sunday: The Man and His Message* (Philadelphia: John Winston, 1914), 174.
2. Lyle W. Dorsett, *Billy Sunday and the Redemption of Urban America* (Grand Rapids: Eerdmans, 1991), 26.
3. Ibid., 30–31.
4. Ibid., 47.
5. Ibid., 58.
6. Ibid., 77.
7. Roger Bruns, *Preacher: Billy Sunday and Big Time American Evangelism* (New York: Norton, 1992), 82.
8. Dorsett, *Billy Sunday and the Redemption of Urban America,* 145.
9. Ellis, *Billy Sunday,* 150–51.
10. Billy Sunday, "Heaven Is a Place," in *Great Preaching on Heaven* (Murfreesboro, Tenn.: Sword of the Lord, 1987), 93ff.

11.5.5 Aimee Semple McPherson—The Gospel Voice with Spiritual Static

She was an actress whether she liked it or not.

—Charlie Chaplin

Whatever one may think of **Aimee Semple McPherson** (1890–1944), and there are shadows and reproaches to be sure, two recent major works have focused attention on her ministry and on the issues it raises for our time. That she used effects and was dramatic is not unique in these annals (remember Whitefield). She was fundamental and orthodox in her doctrine. "If the Scriptures tell one lie, they lie like a sieve" she would say. Many who packed the fifty-three hundred seats night after night in Angeles Temple in Los Angeles were genuinely converted as they listened to the simple gospel message. Paul Rader, William Edward Biederwolf, and William Jennings Bryan filled her pulpit. Anthony Quinn (*Zorba the Greek*) worked closely with her for a time.[1] Charlie Chaplin and she took walks together in Marseilles.

Yet there were scandals, and her ministry was always close to "show business."[2] Angeles Temple in Echo Park resembled a theater, and Sister Aimee epito-mized Hollywood stardom. She argued it was simply "being all things to all men," but the question must be raised as to whether there are not some canons of good taste which must be observed. How user-friendly can we properly become with-out mutilating the gospel? How much is legitimate?

She was born Aimee Kennedy in Ontario into a Methodist home, but her mother, Minnie, had joined the Salvation Army before Aimee's birth. Young Aimee was early drawn to the Pentecostals, and in 1902 she won a gold medal in the WCTU public speaking contest. In 1908 she married Robert Semple, a Pen-tecostal minister, and went with him to Hong Kong for missionary service. He died in 1910 just before the birth of her first child. McPherson returned to New York and began a nationwide revival ministry. In 1921 she was ordained by the First Baptist Church of San Jose just after groundbreaking for Angeles Temple. The time was ripe for evangelism as the huddled masses crowded into the cities of America and population grew by one-third.

Unlike Billy Sunday, McPherson tapped into the American tradition of preach-ing of love and light and joy. "Let's forget about hell," she advised.[3] There was an erotic quality to her preaching from early on, and while the morning services were more traditional in form and preaching (and healing was always handled out of the large rallies), Sunday night was showtime.[4] Hers was "a ministry of performance."[5] In the 1930s she had a series of fairy-tale sermons. Despite hor-rific blowups with her mother and her daughter, there was "never an empty seat on Sunday night."[6] Numbers correlated with God's favor. Certain familiar mo-tifs surely make her a forerunner of thinking and theory today.

Sister Aimee's institutions have long survived her, and the Church of the Four-square Gospel has immense vitality in this country and overseas. She saw Chris-tians as "end-time people," and the gift of the Spirit entrusted to Pentecostals was to be shared with all believers. Occasionally her hermeneutic was outland-ish.[7] She had a richly melodic, somewhat incantatory voice, and mixed piety with pageantry.[8] Aimee Semple McPherson brought drama into the lives of those who were bored. She adapted the use of technology to mass evangelism as did no one else up to her time. Blumhofer says in conclusion:

> That legacy involved not only presentation but content. In significant ways, Sister's user-friendly gospel anticipated Norman Vincent Peale's positive message and Robert Schuller's media extravaganzas blending the Bible, patriotism and the stage.[9]

---

1. Edith L. Blumhofer, *Aimee Semple McPherson: Everybody's Sister* (Grand Rapids: Eerdmans, 1993), 343–44.
2. Daniel Mark Epstein, *Sister Aimee: The Life of Aimee Semple McPherson* (New York: Harcourt, Brace, 1993), 383.
3. Blumhofer, *Aimee Semple McPherson*, 383.
4. Ibid., 125.
5. Ibid., 389.

6. Ibid., 422.
7. Epstein, *Sister Aimee*, 62ff.
8. Blumhofer, *Aimee Semple McPherson*, 231.
9. Ibid., 390.

11.5.6 *WILLIAM EDWARD BIEDERWOLF—A PLAIN AND POWERFUL GOSPEL VOICE*

I am here to fight the devil tooth and nail, wherever he may be found. I am going to hunt out Satan.

I'd rather be a dog with gratitude enough to wag his tail, a foul-featured orangutan of the jungle, a leather-hided rhinoceros, my jaws dripping red with the blood of slaughtered prey, a dodo, an ichthyosaurs, a big hippopotamus, or any sort of a cloven-hoofed, web-footed, sharp-clawed creature of God's earth, than to be a man with a soul so contemptibly mean as to sit down at the table three times a day and gulp down the food that God has provided and never once lift my heart in thanksgiving to God who gives it all.

—William Edward Biederwolf

Almost patrician in his propriety and precision, **William Edward Biederwolf** (1867–1939) was born in Montecello, Indiana, to German emigrant parents. As a boy of fifteen he ran away but was soon converted and made public confession of his faith in Christ. He attended Wabash College and then Princeton University for his M.A.

The husky young man worked summers in mission work in the Bowery of New York City with Jerry McCauley. After finishing Princeton Seminary, he traveled a year with evangelist B. Fay Mills and then used his New Testament Greek Fellowship to study for a year in Berlin and Paris. While serving his first pastoral charge in the Broadway Presbyterian Church of Logansport, Indiana, Biederwolf spent one year as a chaplain with the U.S. Army in Cuba. In 1900 he entered evangelism, working at first with J. Wilbur Chapman and then going out on his own.[1] He used magical illusions in the early days to draw attention and illustrate biblical truth.

Biederwolf was a refined Billy Sunday and preached on sin, as did the master; he proposed to "clean up the town!" His famous sermon on "The White Life" from Psalm 119:9 appeals to people to live the overcoming life.[2] He flayed the cults, such as Christian Science, and was agile enough to do stunts to draw the students at the University of Southern California. Like others, he did shop meetings while in a local crusade. Occasionally he would do single-church crusades, as in the memorable series at Temple Baptist in Los Angeles with Dr. James Whitcomb Brougher.[3] One of the great burdens of his life was his leper project in Korea.

Like Chapman and Torrey, Biederwolf traveled widely. His erudition was reflected in his volumes *Illustrations from Mythology* and *Illustrations from Art*. His massive *Millennial Bible* is an amazing repository of data from Scripture on the Second Coming.[4] He also directed the Winona Lake Conference and the Winona Lake School of Theology. In his later years he pastored the affluent Royal Poinciana Community Chapel in Palm Beach, Florida. He also directed the Family Altar League and did a one year copastorate of the famous Cadle Tabernacle in Indianapolis.

Biederwolf was a fiery preacher. He had "a forensic style, an expressive voice and an unusually fine vocabulary."[5] He was skilled in the dramatic pause, and his illustrations were well blended and effective. His outlines are clear and memorable, reflecting Burrell's influence at Princeton.

Many of Biederwolf's evangelistic sermons had real doctrinal substance, as his mighty message on "The Atonement" from Hebrews 9:26.[6] He took full advantage of the narrative in preaching on "Determined to Find Christ" on Luke 19:1–10.[7] An impressive series of messages for believers has as its apex an unusual message on "Arrested Development and Spiritual Dwarfage" from John 15:2. This is splendidly nuanced.[8] Biederwolf is akin to Chapman and Torrey and was greatly available to the Lord, who used him mightily.

1. Ray E. Garrett, *William E. Biederwolf* (Grand Rapids: Zondervan, 1948), 26ff.
2. Ibid., 45.
3. Ibid., 41.
4. William Edward Biederwolf, *The Millennium Bible* (Grand Rapids: Baker, 1924, 1964). This runs to 728 pages.
5. Garrett, *William E. Biederwolf*, 40.
6. William E. Biederwolf, *Biederwolf's Evangelistic Sermons—Doctrinal Series* (Chicago: Glad Tidings, n.d.), 55ff.
7. William E. Biederwolf, *Later Evangelistic Sermons* (Chicago: Moody Colportage, 1925), 75ff.
8. William E. Biederwolf, *The Growing Christian* (Grand Rapids: Eerdmans, n.d.), 67ff.

11.5.7 Gypsy Smith—The Gospel Voice Out of the Gypsy Wagon

Then he said to his servants, "The wedding banquet is ready, but those I invited did not deserve to come. Go to the street corners and invite to the banquet anyone you find." So the servants went out into the streets and gathered all the people they could find, both good and bad, and the wedding hall was filled with guests.

—Matthew 22:8–10

To this point we have considered American evangelists who often had extensive overseas involvement. Mention must also be made of **John McNeill** (1854–1933), sometimes called "the Scottish Spurgeon."[1] Not to be omitted are the inimitable **Evan Roberts** and **Rhys Bevan Jones,** who were so used in the Welsh revival of 1904 and 1905.[2]

Born in England but with a world evangelistic ministry was **Rodney "Gypsy" Smith** (1860–1947). Even with minimal education (he taught himself to read and write), Gypsy was known as one of the finest exponents of Anglo-Saxon speech in his time.[3] He was born in a gypsy tent and lost his mother very early. His father was not converted until sometime later, but young Rodney Smith was saved when the gypsy wagon was in Bedford, where John Bunyan had lived. "By the grace of God, I will be a Christian and meet my mother in heaven!" Smith exclaimed.[4] Immediately he began to study the Bible intensively and to preach and sing to the turnip fields.[5]

At seventeen, Smith became an evangelist for William Booth and the Christian Mission, which became the Salvation Army. He was dismissed from the Army over a misunderstanding and then launched a four-year mission in Hanley, "the nearest place to the bottomless pit" in all of England.[6]

Though often scorned and ridiculed, there was a disarming charm about the little rotund gypsy. "When you sing 'Throw out the Life-line,' be sure you make more room in the boat," he liked to say. He spoke of butterflies as "God's flowers on wings."[7]

Smith preached simply but directly from Scripture, and the invitations began to pour in. He made repeated trips to America, where he was very popular. He led the great Manchester Wesleyan Mission in which F. B. Meyer and G. Campbell Morgan assisted him. In 1893 and 1894 he preached the great Glasgow Mission Campaign and then conducted a mission for Alexander Maclaren in Union Chapel, Manchester, the only special series Maclaren ever had in his long pastorate there.[8] Six hundred converts resulted. In America, Smith was a favorite at Ocean Grove and had a most fruitful ministry at Harvard University. He sang some of the compositions of the blind hymn writer Fanny Crosby to the composer herself.

Smith's messages are basic but biblical. One favorite is "The Hope of Glory" from Colossians 1:27–28 in which he contrasts the cry, "educate-educate-educate" with Christ's word, "regenerate-regenerate-regenerate."[9] "What crowd do you belong to?" he liked to ask. Often there was great joy among the angels when Gypsy Smith preached.

---

1. John McNeill was of humble origin but his sermons, like "David in the Dumps," were heard around the world. The best collection of his addresses is *The Passionate Pilgrim* (London: Pickering and Inglis, n.d.). Vivid preaching.
2. Cf. George T. B. Davis, *When the Fire Fell* (Philadelphia: Million Testaments Campaign, 1945), 63ff.; a most remarkable study is D. M. Phillips, *Evan Roberts: The Great Welsh Revivalist and His Work* (London: Marshall, 1906).
3. G. Campbell Morgan in *Gypsy Smith, An Autobiography* (New York: Revell, 1907), 6.
4. Ibid., 79. I remember hearing Gypsy Smith give his life story and preach in the Minneapolis Armory in the early 1940s. He was along in years but irrepressibly winsome. He taught us to sing, "Let the Beauty of Jesus Be Seen in Me." He radiated a Christ-like warmth which has been irrevocably etched upon my memory.
5. Ibid., 85.
6. Ibid., 142–43.
7. Ibid., 178.
8. Ibid., 285.

9. Gypsy Smith, *Evangelistic Talks* (London: Epworth, 1922). Largely given in the Nashville, Tennessee, crusade.

11.5.8 John R. Rice—The Gospel Voice That Never Swerved

Do the work of an evangelist.

—2 Timothy 4:5c

Called the Will Rogers of the pulpit and the dean of American evangelists, **John R. Rice** (1895–1980) represents those who have become independent Baptists and independent fundamentalists and have maintained a concentration on evangelistic preaching. Such would include Bob Jones Sr. (an old-fashioned Methodist by background), B. R. Lakin (who preached for years in the Cadle Tabernacle in Indianapolis, which seated ten thousand), Sam Morris, and countless others.[1]

John R. Rice was born in Gainesville, Texas, and was, as they used to say of him, "born to preach." He was saved at age nine when he went forward after hearing a sermon on the prodigal son, but nobody dealt with him. Hence, he used to say he was "saved for certain at age twelve."[2] Rice lost his mother early and taught school before going off to college. Deeply moved by R. A. Torrey's *How to Pray*, Rice went to study at Decatur Baptist College and served a brief stint in the army at the end of World War I. He taught English at Wayland Baptist College and then studied at Baylor and the University of Chicago. He surrendered for the ministry at Pacific Garden Mission in Chicago and went on to Southwestern Baptist Seminary, where he graduated in 1921.

For a while Rice served as associate pastor at First Baptist, Plainview, but then went on for two years to Shamrock, Texas, where the church under his preaching grew from 200 to 460 in two years. He loved to preach, blistering and blessing the congregation as he did. He was known for his copious weeping in his early preaching.[3]

In his early years he was close to J. Frank Norris, the controversial pastor of First Baptist in Fort Worth and at the same time, for a period of time, pastor of the Baptist Temple in Detroit, both large churches. Rice broke with Norris over Rice's insistence on a powerful Holy Spirit enduement for preaching. He soon left the Southern Baptist Convention over doctrinal deviation in some of the schools.

In 1926 Rice entered evangelism. In 1934 he founded *The Sword of the Lord* paper, which continues as an influential organ in the interest of soulwinning and great evangelistic preaching.[4] He founded several independent Baptist churches, including the great Galilee Baptist Church of Dallas, which grew to seventeen hundred members in seven years. In 1940 he moved to Wheaton, Illinois, to concentrate on the publishing ministry but continued to do citywide campaigns with J. Straton Shufeldt, Harry Clark, and others. In 1946 he joined with Bob Jones Sr. and Paul Rood of California in a great Chicago crusade which was mightily blessed.

In his earlier days, Rice did united crusades but eventually broke with Billy Graham and others over the issue of inclusivity in sponsorship and became increasingly separatistic and critical. His writing was prolific and extended to millions of copies. His little book *Soulwinner's Fire* kindled evangelistic passion in many a pastor and layman.[5] Who could ever forget his sermons on "All Satan's Apples Have Worms," or "Trailed by a Wild Beast" from "Be sure your sin will find you out," or his tender "Watching Jesus Die."

Rice fought worldliness, lodges, and wrote a book on *Bobbed Hair, Bossy Wives and Women Preachers*. The resultant fracture of fellowship with this wing of the gospel cause has been painful and the splintering has seemed endless, but we must not allow that to obscure the great biblical preaching that has often come from these brothers. Often we could wish for more exegetical care and a more rigorous hermeneutic, as in Rice's sermon that makes the gates in Nehemiah 3 representative of the steps to salvation, but here is love for Christ and for the lost. Inspection of Rice's sermons is rewarding and richly worthwhile.[6]

---

1. Dallas F. Billington, *God Is Real* (New York: David McKay, 1962). The story of Akron Baptist Temple, is very typical. The new Baptist Temple built after World War II could seat five thousand. This story has been duplicated many times over.
2. Robert L. Sumner, *Man Sent from God: A Biography of Dr. John R. Rice* (Grand Rapids: Eerdmans, 1959), 29. Viola Walden, Rice's longtime secretary, has also given us a fine biography.
3. Ibid., 69.
4. I am aware that Sumner and the Sword people parted company over another controversy later.
5. John R. Rice, *The Soulwinner's Fire* (Chicago: Moody, 1948).
6. John R. Rice, "Jesus May Come Today," in *Great Preaching on the Second Coming* (Murfreesboro, Tenn.: Sword of the Lord, 1989), 212–13. I heard Rice preach from the old Broadway Temple in North Minneapolis years ago. Excellent expostulation. Another superbly biblical evangelist, Harry Vom Bruch, *Modern Prodigals* (Mt. Morris: Kable, n.d.), 211ff. on Hebrews 12:1ff.

11.6 *METHODISTIC AND HOLINESS AMBASSADORS FOR CHRIST*

How far have we gotten with our various substitutes? Look over our churches: they are full of people, who have been brought up on these substitutes, are strangers to those deeper experiences without which there had been no New Testament and no Church of Christ.

—Professor Edwin Lewis

We have acted and spoken as though our pluralism permits us to pick and choose which part of the gospel we will employ and enjoy and which part we will reject and put aside.

—Bishop Roy Short

The twentieth century has seen a general spiritual and theological drift in world Methodism and the proliferation of smaller and more conservative bodies which have sought to preserve and perpetuate the biblical supernaturalism championed by John Wesley. Says one prominent Methodist leader, "Methodism so easily turned to schemes of world betterment and social uplift as a substitute for the declining evangelistic urge."[1] The theology of immanence with its antisupernatural theology of meaningfulness laid great waste to biblical preaching. "The supernatural character of the Gospel is the vital issue."[2]

Yet there are those who have cherished and treasured the everlasting gospel as encased in Holy Scripture. We now highlight several of these as well as a few representatives of those who left Methodist structures for a broader ministry in the Salvation Army.

---

1. R. P. Marshall, "Trends in Modern Methodism," *Christianity Today* (January 4, 1960): 9ff.
2. Kenneth Hamilton, *Revolt Against Heaven: An Inquiry into Anti-Supernaturalism* (Grand Rapids: Eerdmans, 1965), 181–82. How this applies to the Methodist scene is fine-lined by Ira Gallaway, *Drifted Astray* (Nashville: Abingdon, 1983); Jerry L. Walls, *The Problem of Pluralism: Recovering United Methodist Identity* (Wilmore, Ky.: Good News Books, 1986).

11.6.1 LOUIS ALBERT BANKS—A SPOKESMAN FOR THE LIVING GOSPEL

The stories Jesus told and the stories which are related concerning the people whom He healed and who were converted under His ministry, are a constant source of power and inspiration to Christian people today. We get faith and courage to cast out devils from men now because of the picture we have of that redeemed man of Gadara whom Christ transformed and sent forth to tell to his friends the good news of salvation.

—Louis Albert Banks

Across the years there have been godly Methodist bishops who were great biblical preachers, such as Bishop Quayle of Minnesota and Bishop Moore of Georgia.[1] Pastors and evangelists loyal to the historic faith have been dwindling in number, but they have fearlessly proclaimed the Word in the face of much criticism and great opposition.[2]

One of these giants was **Louis Albert Banks** (1855–1933). He was born in Corvallis, Oregon. His roots were in the old United Brethren Church. At age eleven he entered Philomath College with grown men and ultimately went on to Boston University. In the intervening years he served as a circuit rider on the Oregon frontier and saw changed lives and the power of God capture even a city for Christ.[3] Though always engaged in evangelistic itineration, he served Methodist churches in South Boston, Kansas City, the great Trinity Methodist Church in Denver, and the huge First Methodist Church of Cleveland, Ohio, where the Spirit visited with a powerful revival. In 1893 he ran as candidate of the Prohibition Party for governor of the state of Massachusetts.

The first sermon Banks preached lasted only eight minutes. Thereafter he spoke longer and much more eloquently. The sermons of his maturity were spacious, bright, alive, and direct. Many volumes of his collected sermons were published, and they were widely disseminated. Especially impressive is a series of evangelistic messages delivered from Galatians starting with "The Key-Note of Christ's Gospel" from Galatians 1:3–4 and including such other messages as "The Tragedy of Frustrating the Grace of God" from Galatians 2:21 and a clear word on "Christ Cursed for Us" from Galatians 3:13.[4] Banks' discourse abounds with pertinent illustrations and quotes from a wide range of sources. Strong hortatory preaching can be seen in his fine sermon "The Emphatic Date in Human Life" from Hebrews 3:15, "Today if you hear his voice . . ." His passionate evangelistic message, "The Greatest Thief in the World Is Neglect," from Hebrews 2:3, "How shall we escape if we neglect to great salvation?" is equally dramatic.[5] What is so deeply satisfying in Banks' preaching is his wrestling with the text. For most preachers, the text was becoming chiefly a pretext. Banks was not a scintillating exegetical preacher, but he was strong in telling us what the text really said.

---

1. Bishop William Quayle was a gifted preacher (as in *The Hidden Shadow* [New York: Abingdon, 1923] and other works) who reflected helpfully on the craft, as in his fine *The Pastor-Preacher* (Cincinnati: Eaton and Mains, 1910). Bishop Arthur J. Moore could also deliver the evangel, as in *The Mighty Saviour* (New York: Abingdon, 1952), which he preached at First Methodist Church in Atlanta. Moore sought scripturally to stem the tide that for years had sought to humanize God, deify man, and minimize sin. His outstanding lectures on the Christian world task as given at Southern Methodist University were published as *Immortal Tidings in Mortal Hands* (New York: Abingdon, 1953).
2. An example of a truly effective preacher who had an outstanding ministry in Detroit for over twenty years was Merton S. Rice, whose magnificent sermons can be studied in *The Advantage of a Handicap* (New York: Abingdon, 1925, more biblical) and in *Diagnosing Today* (New York: Abingdon, 1932, more cultural/analytical and brilliantly developed). Rice had "Preach the Word" engraved in stone on his desk and every ten days telegraphed that message to his preacher son. Another engaging but controversial preacher was Robert P. ("Fighting Bob") Shuler who pastored the great Trinity Methodist Church at 12th and Flower in Los Angeles for twenty-six years. His sermons in *What New Doctrine Is This?* (New York: Abingdon, 1946) are stirring. Shuler ran for governor of California.
3. Louis Albert Banks, *Soulwinning Stories* (New York: George H. Doran, 1902), 95.
4. Louis Albert Banks, *The Sinner and His Friends* (New York: Funk and Wagnalls, 1907), 28ff., 82ff., 104ff.
5. Louis Albert Banks, *Paul and His Friends* (New York: Funk and Wagnalls, 1898), 150ff., 182ff. From his Cleveland days.

11.6.2 CLOVIS G. CHAPPELL—A SPOKESMAN TO REASONABLE PEOPLE

We ought to major on preaching because it is our job . . . because we are God's one chance at our congregation . . . because preaching is a necessity. Every great day of the Church has been a great day of preaching.

On Jesus rescuing Peter from sinking: "That mighty hand that is always feeling for yours and mine in calm and in tempest, in the daylight and in the dark, gripped the uplifted hand of Simon and lifted him out of defeat into victory. So it may happen to us. Let us reach our hands to him in the faith that his hand is reaching to ours."

—Clovis G. Chappell

Charming, biblically solid, well heard, and widely read, the sermons of **Clovis G. Chappell** (1877–1972) are among the best in Methodism.[1] Born and reared in Flatwoods, Tennesee, of farmer folk, Chappell studied only briefly at what would become Duke and then at Harvard. The youngest of six children, he had a Puritan father and a sweet Irish mother. He later testified that his father left him no worldly goods to speak of, but "He left me that kind of faith and it made all the difference in my world."[2]

Family worship each day was the center of life, and out of those homely scenes and situations came so much of the picturesque language and anecdotes that Chappell's gentle humor utilized so aptly. Called Muttonhead in his hometown, Chappell's "intellectual conversion" took place at Webb School Academy, where he carried his class by rising at 3:45 A.M. daily to study.

Chappell taught school for several years and soon began to preach in a series of pastorates which brought him to effective service in Washington, D.C., Birmingham, Memphis, Dallas (where George W. Truett was one of his best friends), Houston, Oklahoma City, Jackson, Mississippi, and finally Charlotte, North Carolina. These were downtown churches on the whole, and Chappell used the public invitation to receive Christ and come forward wherever he preached.[3] He was wed to the text of Scripture. Finney's logic was his model, but there was a winsome pleading, what one called "the gentle persuasions of Christ." Everywhere he preached he saw people coming to Christ. But the preaching was under the divine anointing, and later he pointed back to his source:

Today was the greatest day in my life. For a long time I had been longing and praying for the Holy Spirit. He came today. What a wondrously joyous experience. I am so glad I found the secret.[4]

In lectures on preaching, which he gave at Candler School of Theology, Chappell had much to say about the techniques of crafting, but he mainly spoke to the preacher's own call and spiritual maintenance under the Spirit.[5] He used illustrations with consummate skill. He could dramatize the biblical story masterfully, as in his great sermon "The Prodigal Wife" on Gomer, the spouse of Hosea, perhaps equaled only on this text by Donald Grey Barnhouse. His outline on 2 Timothy 1:11–12 is simple but unbeatable:

I. I believe
II. I commit
III. I know[6]

Chappell's sermons on "The Lost Book" from 2 Chronicles 34 and on "A Glimpse of the After Life" from Luke 16:19–31 are especially appealing.[7] But of course he is best known for his sermons on Bible characters.[8]

A withering blast has been directed at preaching Bible biographies by Sidney Greidanus in our time. Greidanus' point is important because in preaching about humankind we can horizontalize and psychologize to the point that God is left out.[9] Yet the peril of missing the vertical exists in the preaching of any literary genre. On the whole Chappell avoided this pitfall and almost always focused sharply on the Lord, as in "The Supreme Question—the Philippian Jailer" from Acts 16:30–31.[10] The jailer in question is the point of contact, and the subject of the sermon is raised by the jailer's question.

Chappell was deemed one of the top ten in a survey on America's most popular and influential preachers. He was always thoroughly prepared and preached the Word effectively.

---

1. Ralph Sockman once said over his nationwide broadcast that he considered Clovis G. Chappell the "outstanding biblical preacher in America." Though Sockman, who pastored Christ Church (Methodist) in Manhattan for many years, and his successor, Harold A. Bosley, were well-known and published, neither had the evangelical warmth, the essential biblicality, and the unflagging burden for evangelism and conversion that Chappell had.
2. Wallace D. Chappell, *Clovis Chappell: Preacher of the Word* (Nashville: Broadman, 1978), 11. Wallace Chappell is Clovis Chappell's nephew.
3. Ibid., 31.
4. Ibid., 28.
5. Clovis G. Chappell, *Anointed to Preach* (New York: Abingdon-Cokesbury, 1951). Great on "Keeping Fit," 106ff.
6. Chappell, *Clovis Chappell,* 64.
7. Clovis G. Chappell, *The Village Tragedy and Other Sermons* (Nashville: Cokesbury, 1925), 128ff., 79ff.
8. Clovis G. Chappell, *Sermons on Biblical Characters* (New York: George H. Doran, 1922); *Faces About the Cross* (Nashville: Abingdon-Cokesbury, 1941). Chappell wrote and published some thirty different books of sermons.
9. Sidney Greidanus, *The Modern Preacher and the Ancient Text* (Grand Rapids: Eerdmans, 1988), 162ff. See also Andrew W. Blackwood, *Biographical Preaching for Today* (Nashville: Abingdon, 1954). After all, the Bible does use historical figures as models and exemplars: see Hebrews 11, James 5:11 (Job), and James 5:17 (Elijah). I wish Greidanus' concern were shared more clearly in Blackwood and Roy E. De Brand, *Guide to Biographical Preaching* (Nashville: Broadman, 1988). The whole move to emphasis on narrative needs to face the challenge of God-centeredness.
10. Chappell, *Sermons on Biblical Characters,* 129ff.

11.6.3 General William Booth—Spokesman to the Disenfranchised

> Booth died blind and still by faith he trod
> Eyes still dazzled by the ways of God.
> Booth led boldly and he looked the chief
> Eagle countenance in sharp relief,
> Beard a-flying, air of high command
> Unabated in that holy land.
> —Nicholas Vachel Lindsay in "General Booth Enters Heaven"

A fighter against the sufficiency of religious formality and a true evangelist was **General William Booth** (1829–1912), who with his wife, Catherine, founded the Salvation Army and who with his sons and daughters spearheaded the worldwide extension "through blood and fire." Booth was born in Nottingham, England, and was apprenticed out when he was thirteen. His father died that year and left the family in grinding poverty. Trying his luck in London, William was spiritually stirred at Wesley's chapel and was moved from the premise that with regard to the Bible, it is all or nothing.[1] He made up his mind that God would have all of him, and he would argue that his conversion made him a preacher.[2] Booth began lay preaching and took a charge in Lincolnshire for eighteen months. He rejoiced to see people coming forward and testified:

> I shall always remember the week that I spent at Swineshead Bridge, because I prayed more and preached with more of the spirit of expectation and faith, and then saw more success than in any previous week of my life. I dwell upon it as, perhaps, the week which most effectually settled my conviction forever that it was God's purpose by my using the simplest means to bring souls into liberty, and to break into the cold and formal state of things to which His people only too readily settle down.[3]

Booth sought knowledge and continued campaigns so vigorously that the charge he held in Brighouse/Gateshead was called "a converting shop." He wanted to travel for the Lord, but the Liverpool Conference gave a resounding no. Deprived of Methodist backing, Booth did eventually travel and establish the Christian Mission in London's East End on Whitechapel Road amid much squalor. He had bands play in the streets and then march to the hall followed by the seekers. Booth's goal was the glory of God and the salvation of souls. His was "a perpetual motion to the Cross." He preached long sermons—sometimes an hour and a half—and expected and saw old-fashioned conversions.[4] One hearer said:

> At one moment he is full of humor and robust talk, a genial, merry, shrewd-eyed old gentleman; at the next—at the mention of real sin—his brows contract, his eyes flash, and his tongue hisses out such hatred and contempt and detestation as no sybarite could find on the tip of his tongue for anything superlatively coarse or ill-favored.[5]

Booth preached between fifty and sixty thousand times. The stringent disciplines he exacted from the soldiers and officers he more than required of himself. His wife was also an eloquent preacher, and together they fostered inner empowerment through an ever-deepening experience of the Holy Spirit.[6] His messages were biblical and direct and simple.

Booth's son and successor Bramwell recalled that his voice was not his greatest asset. He customarily began like a lamb, would project two or three points from the text, and then move with cyclonic force. "What is your Delilah?" he would ask. "What is your Delilah?"[7] All of his offspring preached, and the story of his daughter, *The Marechal,* who opened France and Switzerland for the gospel, is but one of many that could be told.[8]

No one denied that William Booth was a bit of a sensationalist, but he spoke appropriately for the needy masses. "It is as a preacher of Jesus Christ and His Salvation, with a direct and arresting message, that he will be most remembered in all the lands that he visited."[9]

---

1. George S. Railton, *General Booth* (London: Hodder and Stoughton, 1912), 13. The statement on biblical inspiration as found in the Statement of Doctrine of the Salvation Army is a strong and high statement.
2. Ibid., 17.
3. Ibid., 34.
4. Harold Begbie, *Twice-born Men: A Clinic in Regeneration* (New York: Revell, 1909). Begbie collected vivid and moving instances of transformed lives. My favorite has been "Lowest of the Low," 169ff.
5. Railton, *General Booth,* 210. Railton was Booth's first commissioner.
6. J. Gilchrist Lawson, *Deeper Experiences of Famous Christians* (Anderson, Ind.: Warner, 1911), 355ff.
7. Bramwell Booth, *Echoes and Memories* (London: Salvationist Publishing, 1925), 21.
8. James Strahan, *The Marechal* (London: Hodder and Stoughton, 1914). Strahan authored a great study of Job.
9. Booth, *Echoes and Memories,* 24.

11.6.4 SAMUEL LOGAN BRENGLE—THE SPOKESMAN TO THE SEEKERS

I find Satan tempting me to seek rapid promotion—it's on the lines of my old ecclesiastical ambitions. Dear Lord, save me from it. Would you be disappointed very much, my sweet wife, if I should take a low rank in The Army? I want to be useful. God save me from wanting to be famous. He does save me from it, bless His Name.

Did either Luther, Fox, Wesley or the Founder . . . ask what special message he should bring to his age? I hardly think so. Each one of these men first got a definite, burning experience of redeeming love and grace, that filled his own heart with peace, with flaming love to God, restful confidence in Jesus, tender compassion for his fellowmen, and then, after diligent searching of the Scripture, and after much prayer, he spake as he was moved by the Holy Ghost.

—Samuel Logan Brengle

Sharper than a Damascene blade for Christ and his kingdom was the Lord's servant, **Samuel Logan Brengle** (1860–1936). Born in Fredrickburg, Indiana, in a family of Presbyterian and Methodist preachers, his schoolteacher father never recovered from the wounds he sustained at Vicksburg. His mother remarried, and Brengle was reared on a farm where the situation was extremely lonely for the young boy.

Brengle turned to study and reading, including an absorbing obsession with the dictionary. Although he had a reverential fear of God, he sought conversion and went five nights to the altar in a revival, but no one dealt with him. He finally received the "witness" of his personal relationship to God through Christ.[1] Going on to Indiana Asbury University (now DePauw), he gave himself to oratory studies and won prizes in that field. Although intending for the law, in one oratorical contest on the East Coast he said to the Lord: "If you let me win, I will preach!"[2] He did start to preach, memorizing his messages as he would an oration. Brengle was consumed with ambition to be a great preacher.

Going on to Boston University School of Theology, he was led into a deeper experience of death to self at the Cross through his mentor, Professor Daniel Steele (whose *Half Hours with St. Paul* and other works touched so many). Of this crisis, General Evangeline Booth later wrote, "The Christ of the Cross summoned a soldier of Salvation to His bleeding side and sent him forth."[3] Brengle was now willing to say, "Let me stammer and stutter if that be your will."[4]

In 1885 Brengle heard General Booth at Tremont Temple in Boston and was deeply stirred. In seeking the hand of Elizabeth Swift, a young Salvationist, he had to weigh the call to the prestigious Studebaker Methodist Church in South Bend against going to London to train as a cadet in the Salvation Army. His will was yielded to the Lord and he went to London. His first assignment, to clean muddy boots, tested his submission.[5]

Upon returning to the States, Brengle and his wife took officership in a series of assignments, including Boston #1, where he was violently attacked and permanently injured. Yet increasingly his powerful preaching of the gospel and of holiness moved him to strategic leadership in both District and Provincial Office in places like Chicago and San Francisco. Ultimately he was given the post of "National Spiritual Special" and traveled almost constantly, preaching within and outside the Army for the rest of his life.

Brengle was always known as a long-winded preacher.[6] His sense was that the problem he faced in preaching to the culture was "failure to believe in the vitality of the Word."[7] He was so immersed in Scripture that he was sometimes called the talking Bible. He usually read the Scriptures on his knees. As a preacher he was graphic and pictorial. "Vast things simply" was his motto.[8] Logical in his organization and with little pulpit manner in his delivery, he was known as the "psychologist of the heart." The goal in his preaching was Christ and the penitent form.

"Sanctified sanity" is the best description of Brengle and his preaching. His dear friend and confidante Professor Doremus Hayes shared with him a great thirst for the deeper things.[9] He was often assigned to troubleshoot tensions engendered by the tongues movement. In Bergen, Norway, on one occasion, he had to counteract a new theology and its onslaught against the historic faith. Brengle's famous Atonement sermon on this occasion is a classic on the substitutionary death of Jesus.[10]

In 1915 his wife died, but Brengle carried on and was made commissioner in 1926. He exerted extraordinary influence outside of the Army as well as in the case of his friendship with J. Stuart Holden, whom we shall meet in the next chapter. There was never any change in his doctrine. He held to the faith when even in the Army social concerns threatened to overmatch spiritual concerns, and was much blessed of God for it. Other sermons indicate an intellectual rigor which relied on the Holy Ghost for insight and passion. This made Brengle one of the choicest spokesmen of his time. But at core, as he put it, "The honey pots were spilled into his own heart."

---

1. Clarence W. Hall, *Samuel Logan Brengle: Portrait of a Prophet* (New York: Salvation Army, 1933), 28.
2. Ibid., 40.
3. Ibid., v.
4. Ibid., 49.
5. Ibid., 74.
6. Ibid., 127.
7. Ibid., 112.
8. Ibid., 123.
9. Professor Hayes of Garrett Biblical Institute was a New Testament scholar who has given us the exquisite *The Most Beautiful Book Ever Written* (New York: Methodist, 1913) and *Paul and His Epistles* (New York: Methodist, 1915). The former is a priceless study of the Gospel of St. Luke.
10. Samuel Logan Brengle, *The Guest of the Soul* (London: Marshall, Morgan, and Scott, 1934), 9ff. Other sermons also are included here including a searching study of the work of the Holy Spirit, "The Guest of the Soul," 58ff.

11.6.5 SAMUEL CHADWICK—THE SPOKESMAN FOR TRUE HOLINESS BEFORE GOD

I would rather preach than do anything else I know in this world. I have never missed a chance to preach. I would rather preach than eat my dinner, or have a holiday, or anything else the world can offer. I would rather pay to preach than be paid not to preach. It has its price in agony of sweat and tears and no calling has such joys and heartbreaks, but it is a calling an archangel might covet; and I thank God that of His grace He called me into this ministry. Is there any joy like that of saving a soul from death? Any thrill like that of opening blind eyes? Any reward like the love of little children to the second and third generation? Any treasures like the grateful love of hearts healed and comforted? I tell you it is a glorious privilege to share the travail and the wine of God.

If this be my last word in the name of my Master, I could say with all due solemnity and earnestness, there is no other Gospel, there is no other Saviour. But if you reject this Gospel of Jesus Christ you will be lost, you will be damned, and that forever.

—Samuel Chadwick

Samuel Chadwick (1860–1932) was one of English Methodism's greatest preachers. The foreword to his biography was written by former British Prime Minister D. Lloyd George, who visited at Cliff College. He heard Chadwick, whom he termed "a pulpit giant," speak at Brighton and said of him, "I never saw a man so hold his audience."[1] Chadwick preached on occasion for three hours and prayed publicly for twenty-five minutes.

Chadwick was small and slightly built and was ailing most of his life. His head was big with a prominent nose. He was known as "champion of the oppressed and advocate of revivalism."[2] Born in Burnley in a strong Methodist home, Chadwick signed the Pledge when he was eight. He worked in the cotton mill from six to six as a boy and never got much education. At ten he was converted in an anniversary service and from the start committed himself to a regimen of daily prayer. He always loved chapels and cathedrals. At sixteen he began to preach, having admired his dear pastor as "a master of exposition."[3] Chadwick visited a sick friend every Sunday afternoon and read him the sermons of Talmage.

When he was twenty-one, Chadwick became lay pastor at Stacksteads, where he formed a prayer league. He came with fifteen sermons and after preaching twelve of them still saw no revival. He stopped leaning on his sermons, entered into what he called "a crisis of obedience," and saw his first converts. In this time he took some classwork at the Methodist College, where he made some of his best lifelong friends: **Frederick Luke Wiseman** (later president of the Methodist Conference and pastor of Wesley Chapel); **W. B. Pope** (greatest Methodist theologian of the time);[4] and **Herbert B. Workman** (whose epochal work on the persecution of the early church we have already referred to early on in this book cf. 3.1.3).

Chadwick went on to serve successively the Nicholson circuit in Edinburgh, Clydebank (where he was known for his outdoor preaching), in two very powerful ministries in Leeds separated by a brief time in Shoreditch in London. He was known as the most loved and the most hated man in Leeds. At Wesley Leeds Hall, the chapel was full a half-hour before the service, and at Oxford Place on the other side of the river the crowds kept coming for thirteen years.

Chadwick loved to preach doctrine and saw conversions every Sunday and often every day.[5] He preached on subjects like "God's Lions," "Two Right Hands," "Angels and Asses," "Devil Making," and "Buried Alive." In 1907 he shared a memorable series of expositions from the Book of Revelation. He served for twenty-five years as editor of *Joyful News* magazine,[6] and at forty-seven he became tutor in biblical and theological studies at Cliff College. After a five-year interval in the coal fields he became principal of Cliff College upon the death of Thomas Cook.[7]

As an expositor, Chadwick was without a peer. His lectures on preaching were legendary. He drove his preachers into the Word and gave an exam to them on themes such as, "Write an epitome of the call of the prophet Ezekiel." In his sermon clinic, he would listen to the students preach in what they called "the inquest." In giving what he called "the canons" of preaching, he insisted on fidelity to the text, unity of discourse, and order in presentation.[8] As he would say, "In every text there is a unique feature, and the unique feature of the text becomes the subject of the sermon and unifies the whole."

His own preaching was well heard in America, which he visited seven times. Large congregations heard him at Northfield, in Atlanta where he preached for Len Broughton, and at Winona Lake. In 1917 he served as chairman of the Methodist Conference and in 1922 as president of the Free Church Council. He held a great evangelistic crusade in Edinburgh, the first service of which he preached in Free St. George's.

In a weighty book of sermons (he averaged an hour in preaching), Chadwick shared the kind of strong biblical preaching which built up the work of God. His sermon on "The Divine Servant" from Matthew 12:18–21 is a good sample:

I. The Divine Servant and His Lord
II. The Servant's equipment
III. The Servant's mission

The exegesis is rich and deep, and the application is strong.[9] His message on "The Standard Miracle" from Ephesians 1:18–20 on Christ's resurrection as the paradigm for God's power working in human life is arresting and suggestive. In Samuel Chadwick we see the godly life and powerful preaching in God-glorifying balance.

---

1. Norman G. Dunning, *Samuel Chadwick* (London: Hodder and Stoughton, 1933), 104ff.
2. Ibid., 16.
3. Ibid., 28.
4. William Burt Pope, *A Higher Catechism of Theology* (New York: Phillips and Hunt, 1884). Strong on the Atonement.
5. Dunning, *Samuel Chadwick,* 50.
6. Samuel Chadwick, *The Way to Pentecost* (London: Hodder and Stoughton, 1921). This meaty study of the person and work of the Holy Spirit consists of articles that he wrote for *Joyful News.* Good on names of the Holy Spirit.
7. E. W. Lawrence, "Samuel Chadwick: God's Servant," *The Free Methodist* no. 6 (November 22, 1960): 766.
8. Samuel Chadwick, *Humanity and God* (New York: Revell, n.d.), 92ff., 136ff.
9. Ibid., 92ff.

11.6.6 E. M. BOUNDS—THE SPOKESMAN FOR PRAYER AND THE LIFE OF SANCTITY

Hold fast to the old truths—double-distilled.

Have a high standard and hold to it . . . we hold definitely without compromise in the least to the plenary inspiration of the Scriptures.

The preaching that kills may be, and often is, orthodox . . . dogmatically, inviolably orthodox. We love orthodoxy. It is good. It is the best. It is the clean, clear-cut teaching of God's Word, the trophies won by truth in its conflict with error, the levees which faith has raised against the desolating floods of honest or reckless misbelief or unbelief; but orthodoxy, clear and hard as crystal, suspicious and militant, may be but the letter well-shaped, well-named and well-learned, the letter which kills. Nothing is so dead as dead orthodoxy, too dead to speculate, too dead to think, to study or to pray.

—E. M. Bounds

A massive flow of soundly scriptural and aggressive preaching emanated from the Methodist Episcopal Church, South, in this country before and after the turn of the century. We have already identified the evangelist Sam Jones, who lodges in this category, and there are many others.[1] Not the least of these is **Edward McKendree Bounds** (1835–1913), who traced the relationship between lively Bible preaching and old-fashioned, on-your-knees praying more compellingly than did anyone in the history of preaching.

Bounds was born in Shelby County, Missouri, where he was given a middle name in honor of the first American-born Methodist bishop who was such a force for God on the frontiers of America. Even though his father died when he was fourteen, Bounds gave himself to studying the law and at nineteen was admitted to the bar in Missouri. Though converted earlier, the young and successful Bounds came to the crisis of surrender in 1859 and yielded to God's call to preach.[2] After voracious study he was licensed to preach the following year. Although two older brothers served in the Union Army, he was a chaplain with the Confederates.

Only five feet five inches tall and with a receding hairline, Bounds showed great courage with Hood's forces. In the battle of Franklin, he was captured by the Union army and spent a year and a half in a federal prison. Yet the fiery-eyed preacher was never bitter or vindictive. He served the Methodist church in Franklin, Tennessee, after the war. In one week of revival under the pastor's preaching, 150 souls were converted.[3]

Appointment was made to Selma, Alabama, and then to two different parishes in St. Louis. First Bounds served St. Paul's Methodist Episcopal and then First Methodist Episcopal, before returning to St. Paul's. His strong biblical preaching led to conversions and growth.

Bounds then took editorial responsibility for *The Christian Advocate* and itinerated widely in and beyond the St. Louis conference. His preaching on *The Resurrection and Heaven* reflect something of the Christian solace Bounds and his wife found in the experience of losing two of their sons.[4] In the face of mounting liberalism and its denial of hell and original sin and Christ as the only way, Bounds (like Sam Jones) was increasingly at odds with the ecclesiastical hierarchy. His analysis is astute:

> John Wesley said that if Methodism was ever destroyed, it would be destroyed by the love of money. He wrote his last sermons and spent his last years in warning the Methodist people against the love of money. He knew that the enterprising and hearty genius of Methodism would tend to make our people rich, and he foresaw that unsanctified wealth would corrupt.[5]

Resistance to evangelism drove Bounds to seek voluntary location, and he thus became a minister to the nation. Moving from Nashville to Georgia, he continued to rise at 4 A.M. to pray, as he did throughout his lifetime. He was so immersed in his studies that on occasion he forgot to eat. Bounds ministered at great revivals at Asbury College and Seminary in Wilmore, Kentucky, and many other places. His best-known book, originally *Preacher and Prayer* (slightly altered and issued as *Power Through Prayer*), made an immense impact. In all he wrote eight volumes on prayer.

He often said he was willing to be "crazy for God," and Bounds was confessedly eccentric. Homer Hodge, who saw to the publication of Bounds' works, said of him: "He was one of the most intense eagles of God that ever penetrated the spiritual ether."[6] His studies of Satan were notable in their time.[7] The platform for his praying and his preaching could not have been made more clear:

> The true ministry is God-touched, God-enabled, and God-made. The Spirit of God is on the preacher in anointing power, the fruit of the Spirit is in his heart, the Spirit of God has vitalized the man and the word; his preaching gives life; gives life as the spring gives life; gives life as the resurrection gives life; gives ardent life as the summer gives ardent life; gives fruitful life as the autumn gives fruitful life. The life-giving preacher is a man of God, whose heart is ever athirst for God.[8]

---

1. Representative of the vigor and vibrancy of this heritage is William Elbert Munsey (1833–1877), who preached on hell and everlasting punishment as have very few; see "The Awfulness of Eternal Punishment" from Mark 9:43–48 in Curtis Hutson, ed., *Great Preaching on Hell* (Murfreesboro, Tenn.: Sword of the Lord, 1989), 151ff.; also Henry Clay Morrison, *Some Chapters of My Life Story* (Louisville: Pentecostal Publishing Co., 1941). Morrison was an evangelist, pastor, editor, and longtime president of Asbury College in Wilmore, Kentucky.
2. Lyle Wesley Dorsett, *E. M. Bounds: Man of Prayer* (Grand Rapids: Zondervan, 1991), 16.
3. Ibid., 16.
4. E. M. Bounds, *Heaven: A Place, A City, A Home* (Grand Rapids: Baker, rep. 1966).

5. Dorsett, *E. M. Bounds,* 42.

6. Ibid., 59.

7. E. M. Bounds, *Satan: His Personality, Power and Overthrow* (Grand Rapids: Baker, rep. 1933).

8. Dorsett, *E. M. Bounds,* 66. His best-known work is *Power Through Prayer* (Chicago: Moody, n.d.). My favorite of his messages on prayer is *Purpose in Prayer* (Chicago: Moody, n.d.).

11.6.7 WILLIAM E. SANGSTER—THE SPOKESMAN FOR BIBLICAL PREACHING AT ITS BEST

Commissioned of God to teach the Word! A herald of the great King! A witness of the eternal gospel! Could any work be more high and holy? To this supreme task God sent his only begotten Son. In all the frustration and confusion of the times, is it possible to imagine a work comparable in importance with that of proclaiming the will of God to wayward men?

I believe that I was born to be a minister. I cannot recall a time in my life when I was without a sense of holy vocation. It did not derive from any conviction in the mind of my parents who had never so much as entertained the thought. But I felt the pressure of a directing hand upon me from my tenderest years.

—William E. Sangster

In the forefront of English preachers in this century and an avid student of the craft of preaching was **William Edwin Sangster** (1900–1960).[1] Sangster exceeded his Methodist cohorts Leslie Weatherhead,[2] who tended more to psychology than Scripture, and Donald Soper, who was consumed in radical politics.

Though his parents were in the established church, Sangster was an unabashed evangelical, having come to Christ at the Radnor Street Mission (Methodist) in London.[3] After serving in the army at the end of World War I, he committed himself to the ministry and trained at Richmond College, Surrey, where C. Ryder Smith influenced him particularly, and where his preaching gifts were in evidence to his classmates and to the faculty.[4] He then ministered consecutively in Wales (1926–1929), in Liverpool (1929–1932), at Central Hall in Scarbourough (where he had four churches in his charge), and then succeeded Weatherhead at Brunswick in Leeds, where he had an unusual ministry.

In 1938 Dinsdale Young of Westminster Central Hall died, and after Dr. Luke Wiseman filled in for a year, Sangster came to serve in 1939, thus beginning a sixteen-year ministry of unusual depth and proportion. Westminster Central Hall, right across from the Abbey, seated three thousand people. Sangster had a five-year ministry there during the London blitz, when he virtually lived in the great bomb shelter beneath the church.

A saintly and resilient soul, Sangster was heard on both sides of the Atlantic and left Westminster reluctantly to spearhead the entire evangelistic thrust of

British Methodism as the head of home missions. He always endorsed the Billy Graham crusades and worked with Alan Redpath, Stephen Olford, and the bishop of Barking in a great evangelistic campaign.[5] His son Paul, who has given us a classic volume on the preacher's declamatory skills, wrote a biography of his father which ranks among the most candid and richly-layered preacher biographies ever written. In the chapter "Warts and All," which Dr. Sangster told his son must be written if the book were to be published at all, young Sangster sketched his father's life and manner:

> In appearance: tall, strong, manly; talked incessantly with his hands; scrupulous but old-fashioned in his dress.
>
> Of great natural dignity seeming at times pompous to some, but very kind and understanding of people in fact.
>
> Driven by a great energy and strong will, "Impatience was his greatest blemish," but he learned this in his illness.
>
> He never passed a church without going into it; tremendous enthusiasm; dramatic in all things.
>
> Tended to be Puritanical and a bit severe with regard to worldliness reflected in his great sermon "This Britain" in 1953.
>
> Possessed a keen sense of humor; a prodigious memory; people mattered much to him. Totally God-obsessed.
>
> His illness with onset in late 1957 was probably his greatest sermon although for the last year he could not speak.[6]

Young Sangster spoke of his father as "a preacher curious about the craft of preaching."[7] Not all effective preachers are reflective of their craft, but Sangster not only preached well but has given us several volumes of significant worth on preaching itself and one of the best books ever written on sermon illustration.

Those who knew him spoke of his evangelistic intensity, brief introductions and conclusions, short, staccato sentences with memorable structure.[8] One of his early books of sermons begins with a gem, "When I Survey the Wondrous Cross."[9] The richness of his preaching can be gauged by his widely-read daily devotional extracts.[10] The finest of the wheat from his Westminster days can be assayed in Sangster's *Special Day Sermons* and *Can I Know God?* which contain such capital messages as "Christ Has Double Vision" from John 1:42 and "The Homesickness of the Soul" from 2 Corinthians 5:8. One could wish he would take a bigger piece of text more frequently, but there is a lilt and scriptural practicality in his sermons, as in the three sections of "The Secret of Radiant Life":

  I. The Life—the person I could be
 II. The Truth—the person I am
III. The Way—the path between[11]

Sangster became ill with a progressively debilitating disease known as muscular atrophy and could not speak at all during the last year of his strenuous and productive life. To catch the flavor and the fervor of this life poured out as a drink offering for God, read the mighty memorial address given by Sangster's lifelong friend, Professor H. Cecil Pawson. Pawson pointed out that Sangster's sermon as president of the Methodist Conference was titled "Offering Christ to the People."[12] A fitting epitaph for a Spirit-filled life.

---

1. The American Methodist who most closely approximates this double-giftedness must be G. Ray Jordan, who taught at Candler in Atlanta. His most influential book was *You Can Preach* (New York: Revell, 1958), and his typical good preaching is seen in such books as *We Face Calvary and Life* (Nashville: Cokesbury, 1936).
2. Weatherhead went on to serve City Temple in London for twenty-four years and led the march toward the psychologization of preaching. He could really preach, as we see in *That Immortal Sea,* but even his Beecher Lectures in 1948 were published as *Psychology, Religion and Healing.* Yet most often he took no text.
3. Paul Sangster, *Doctor Sangster* (London: Epworth, 1962), 33.
4. W. E. Sangster, *The Path to Perfection: An Examination and Restatement of John Wesley's Doctrine of Christian Perfection* (London: Epworth, 1943). His 1954 title *The Pure in Heart* is less technical.
5. Sangster, *Doctor Sangster,* 67.
6. Ibid., 311ff.
7. W. E. Sangster, *The Craft of Sermon Construction and Illustration* (Grand Rapids: Baker, 1981) combines two books. Sangster preached forty minutes to an hour.
8. John Bishop, "William Edwin Sangster: An Evangelical Greatheart," *Preaching,* September-October 1987, 48.
9. W. E. Sangster, *He Is Able* (London: Wyvern, 1936). Dedicated to his wife, Margaret, with the lovely words, "With whom it is as easy to keep in love as fall in love."
10. Frank Cumbers, ed., *Daily Readings from W. E. Sangster* (New York: Revell, 1966).
11. W. E. Sangster, *The Secret of Radiant Life* (New York: Abingdon, 1957).
12. W. E. Sangster, *Sangster of Westminster* (London: Marshall, Morgan, and Scott, 1960), 59.

11.7 THE KESWICK CONNECTION ON THE DEEPENING OF THE SPIRITUAL LIFE

Preaching is the art of making a sermon and delivering it? Why, no, that is not preaching. Preaching is the art of making a preacher and delivering that.

—Bishop William Quayle

It is fair to say that in the face of all her foes and the swirling ideological currents which beat upon her, humanly speaking the church of Jesus Christ should have been long dead and theological orthodoxy but a corpse long since interred. As Paul Johnson has observed, "The most extraordinary thing about the twentieth century was the failure of God to die!"[1] The vaunted death-of-God theologians molder in a theological grave, while a faithful gospel preacher like Billy Graham flourishes. Noted scholars speak about "Wesley's World Revolution" in which "throughout the Third World and the former Communist bloc, a vibrant Protestant Christianity is radically remaking people's lives."[2]

A catalyst for the preservation and propagation of biblical Christianity has been the Keswick conventions, in which worship and preaching are central. Controversial since its founding in 1875 and centering on annual conventions in Keswick in the English Lake Country, Keswick has drawn from a broad span of denominational bodies and has as its theme "All One in Christ Jesus." Anglican in its inception, Keswick emphasizes on successive days the nature and holiness of God, the sin of man, redemption through Christ, the lordship of Christ, and the fullness of the Spirit.[3] Outreach and mission as inescapable concomitants are of the essence.[4] We shall examine some representative preachers in this renewal movement and see the criticality of their preaching.

---

1. Paul Johnson, *The Quest for God: A Personal Pilgrimage* (New York: Harper/Collins, 1996), 6.
2. David Martin, "Wesley's World Revolution," *National Review* (December 31, 1995): 26.
3. Of the several histories of Keswick, I think the best is J. C. Pollock, *The Keswick Story* (Chicago: Moody, 1964).
4. An instance is the legendary Anglican Temple Gairdner, who surrendered his life for missions at Keswick in 1893 and burned himself out in ministry to the Muslims in Cairo. Close to Samuel Zwemer. See Constance E. Padwick, *Temple Gairdner of Cairo* (London: SPCK, 1929). His patron saint was General Gordon of Khartoum.

11.7.1 EVAN H. HOPKINS—THE THEOLOGIAN OF KESWICK

Many can give Bible expositions who are not able to help seeking souls into the fullness of the blessing. We must keep to the original lines of the Movement; in other words, we must set forth definitely Sanctification by faith.

—Evan H. Hopkins

I ask Thee not for subtle thought, for pictures exquisitely wrought,
For speech of grand or graceful turn, for tones that thrill and words that burn;
But let me touch Thy garment's hem, and bear the fragrance unto them.
—trans. from the French of Theodore Monod,
a very close friend of Hopkins

Keswick has been more than spiritual gourmandism. The movement arose out of a concern that orthodoxy had become "iron-cold, hard and dull." The message of full salvation in Christ was intended to be bread not confection, not a time for discussion so much as a time for decision.

Rising out of higher life meetings at Broadlands, Oxford, and Brighton, the prime mover of Keswick was Canon **Thomas Dundas Harford-Battersby** (1822–1883), who had been living in St. John's in Keswick for the last thirty-two years of his life. He presided at the first convention.[1] Although not at the first convention but at the next forty was Harford-Battersby's good friend **Evan H. Hopkins** (1837–1918). Hopkins, who spoke Spanish fluently, was born in South America, the son of a British mining engineer. After returning to England, he worked as a mining engineer in Dorset, but while there was converted and began to preach. He matriculated at King's College, London, where the strong biblical teaching of E. H. Plumptre especially moved him. He was ordained in 1865 and served a curacy at what became St. Paul's, Portman Square, and counted Lord Cairns and Lord Shaftesbury among its constituents.[2] From 1870 to 1893 Hopkins served Holy Trinity, Richmond, in Surrey. One said:

> I can see him now, in his old black gown, with the quiet manner, the well-sustained voice, the clear-cut divisions, the simple well-illustrated teachings, making the things of God real and practical to a schoolboy. I remember the hush of expectation, when all faces were turned toward the pulpit.[3]

Hopkins' messages were richly expositional.[4] In this time he not only led in the development of Keswick but also established the Church Army. He dealt with misunderstanding and criticism of Keswick in the recognition that some were puzzled, some provoked, and some were persuaded. Among these "converts" were Bishop Moule, R. W. Dale, D. L. Moody, who attended conventions, and even J. C. Ryle, who never spoke at Keswick but did seem to modify his earlier hostility.[5]

Understanding sanctification as both crisis and process, Hopkins' exposition of the Keswick message stands as the classical statement.[6] In 1893 he moved to St. Luke's in South Kensington, a church that seated twelve hundred people. He regularly used the aftermeeting for the care of souls under conviction.[7]

Whether in the tent at Keswick or elsewhere, Hopkins' ministry was astonishingly across denominational lines. He visited Sweden and held seven meetings under the aegis of Prince Oskar and Princess Ebba Bernadotte. Along with Lord Radstock, he was called to anoint Archdeacon Basil Wilberforce according to James 5.[8] He visited the Holy Land several times and, along with Alfred Eidersheim, was the prime mover in raising funds for the Jerusalem Garden Tomb Maintenance Fund.[9] He was likely the first preacher who used the differentiation of faith-fact-feeling to positive advantage.

Hopkins was dedicated to preaching not only justification but sanctification as well. Above all, in his preaching and leadership, Hopkins was the foremost exponent of full salvation in Britain at this time. He retired in 1906 and moved to Woburn Chase in Surrey. At his funeral, Prebendary Webb-Peploe, his closest associate in Keswick, and Bishop Taylor Smith spoke. The hymn that Keswick inspired Frances Ridley Havergal to write "Like a River Glorious" made an apt musical tribute.

---

1. J. Elder Cumming, *Holy Men of God* (Chicago: Moody, rev. 1961), 227–37. Cumming, a Scottish Presbyterian, was also well heard at Keswick and led the Keswick convention that was held in Glasgow.

2. Alexander Smellie, *Evan Henry Hopkins* (London: Marshall Brothers, 1920), 33. Smellie, himself from the Reformed Presbyterian Church, wrote *Men of the Covenant* and gave memorable messages at Keswick, especially his 1919 Bible readings on "We Beheld His Glory," in Herbert Stevenson, ed., *The Ministry of Keswick* (Grand Rapids: Zondervan, 1963), 1:327ff.

3. Ibid., 36.

4. Ibid., 46.

5. The most caustic onslaught of all time was led by B. B. Warfield in his *Perfectionism* (Philadelphia: Presbyterian and Reformed, rev. 1967). The attack on Keswick is largely *argumentum ad hominem* in relation to the Pearsall Smiths, though Warfield does hold out an olive branch to the "Arminian" James McConkey and his well-known work *The Three-fold Secret of the Holy Spirit* (Pittsburgh: Silver, 1897). McConkey, a graduate of Princeton University, like many other North Americans imbibed the Keswick message; see Louise Harrison McCraw, *James H. McConkey: A Man of God* (Grand Rapids: Zondervan, 1939), 46ff. The message is union with, yielding to, and abiding in Christ.

6. Evan H. Hopkins, *The Law of Liberty in the Spiritual Life* (Philadelphia: The Sunday School Times, 1952).

7. Smellie, *Evan Henry Hopkins,* 119.

8. Ibid., 192.

9. Ibid., 174.

11.7.2 *H. C. G. Moule—The Compass of Keswick*

We want preachers so filled with Christ, by the Holy Ghost, that they cannot get away from Him as their theme; that they know they have in Him the Word, the Message, authentic from the throne, for every need of the human soul. We want those to preach to us who are never tired of exploring the written Word for the glories of the living Word, and who come out from their exploration to set Him forth, in all the power of faith, in the spoken Word.

Let us preachers be, in a profound sense, "men of one Book," and above all, "men of one Name," and we shall never lack listeners.

—H. C. G. Moule

Initially he was cautious about the Keswick message, but after he attended and experienced drastic spiritual rejuvenation, **Handley G. C. Moule** (1841–1920) became a strong leader of Keswick and one of the mainstays of the platform speakers. Moule was born into a Dorsetshire vicarage in a family which gave many clergy, scholars, and missionaries to the cause of Christ (cf. 11.3). He studied at Cambridge and served two curacies with his father.

For nineteen years Moule was dean of Ridley Hall at Cambridge, a divinity training school founded for evangelically-minded candidates for the Church of England.[1] He often preached at Simeon's old church, Holy Trinity, endeavoring "to maintain the fine evangelical traditions of that great leader."[2] He then served as Norrisian Professor of Divinity at Cambridge and in 1901 became bishop of Durham as successor to Westcott, who in turn had succeeded J. B. Lightfoot in the tradition of Bishop Butler. Both Westcott and Lightfoot were also professors at Cambridge and shone brightly in this remarkable constellation of conservative thinkers there.[3]

Moule was known for his scintillating expositions of the Greek text, which he gave nightly at Cambridge. Later he gave these expositions at an early hour in the chapel at Ridley Hall, influencing more than one thousand young men. Moule's "dark wavy hair, prominent nose and full lips" made him look like the half-Huguenot that he was.[4] He played a pivotal role in Moody's mission at Cambridge and had an insatiable hunger for holiness.

Moule became convicted that his critical attitude to Keswick involved a great deal of "mixed motive, jealousy and prejudice."[5] In response to the strong biblical preaching of Evan Hopkins, Moule and his wife were deeply stirred and both stood in surrender to Christ. Even after Moule moved into his nineteen-year bishopric in Durham and his remarkable ministry to miners during the world war, his profile at Keswick was commanding. It was said of Moule's hearers, "They came expecting to be led to the Cross and to hear of Christ, and they were never disappointed."[6]

Moule's role in the Cambridge Greek New Testament, the Cambridge Bible, and the Expositor's Bible (he did Romans) is well known. His commentary on the Greek text of Philippians, for instance, is most helpful in the CGNT,[7] and his devotional commentaries on Ephesians and Colossians are rich.[8] His messages on the Pastorals are outstanding,[9] as are his studies on the Holy Spirit.[10]

Moule's messages on ecclesiastical occasions never disappoint. He trumpets for conscientious work in the text and for intimacy with Christ as absolutely essential:

> "That they might be with Him, and that He might send them forth to preach." There is the first, the deepest, the absolutely vital qualification of the preacher who is to be true; "that he should be with Him." Personal knowledge of the Lord Jesus Christ, "nothing between," is the first requisite for the preaching apostle; and it is the first requisite assuredly for the man who, in any sense instinct with life and power, would be the preaching apostle's successor.[11]

A typical jewel is "The Cross and the Spirit," an exposition of Galatians that captured the Keswick theme so poignantly.[12] His first message at Keswick in 1886 was titled "The 'Total Abstinence' of the Gospel," from Ephesians 4:1–2, 31–32.[13] From a message to ministers out of Luke 1:19 on the subject "Essential Principles of Christian Service," he drew three mains: (1) in the presence of God; (2) standing in the presence of God; and (3) "I am sent"; words well worth weighing for the servants of Christ.[14]

At the end of Moule's long involvement at Keswick, one seasoned listener said, "In some ways, the most impressive speaker I ever heard at Keswick was Dr. Handley Moule. His very presence seemed to express the beauty of the Lord. He had a rich, cultured voice, and his spiritual intensity was so great that tiny beads of moisture covered his brow."[15] Dr. Moule left a legacy of orthodoxy and truth.

1. As evidence of his stand, see H. C. G. Moule, *The Evangelical School in the Church of England* (London: Nisbet, 1901).

2. F. R. Webber, *A History of Preaching in Britain and America* (Milwaukee: Northwestern, 1952), 1:634.

3. Arthur Westcott, *The Life and Letters of Brooke Foss Westcott* (London: Macmillan, 1903). Westcott's great commentaries on the Johannine corpus, on Hebrews, and on Ephesians are choice. He had a weak voice but took great pains in articulation. The scholarly fecundity of this circle is amazing—Westcott's domestic chaplain, Charles H. Boutflower, has given us a splendid study on the Book of Daniel. For a measured evaluation of J. B. Lightfoot's scholarly stature, see Warren W. Wiersbe, *Living with the Giants* (Grand Rapids: Baker, 1993), 47ff. Lightfoot on Galatians, Philippians, Colossians, and the Fathers is peerless.

4. J. C. Pollock, *The Keswick Story* (Chicago: Moody, 1964), 68.

5. Ibid., 69.

6. Webber, *A History of Preaching,* 1:635.

7. H. C. G. Moule, *Philippians in the Cambridge Greek Testament* (Cambridge, Mass.: Cambridge University Press, 1897).

8. H. C. G. Moule, *Ephesian Studies* (London: Pickering and Inglis, n.d.); *Colossian and Philemon Studies* (New York: Revell, n.d.). Though strong in the great text, these are in the valued genre of devotional commentaries.

9. H. C. G. Moule, *The Second Epistle to Timothy* (Grand Rapids: Baker, 1952).

10. H. C. G. Moule, *Veni Creator: Thoughts on the Person and Work of the Holy Spirit* (London: Hodder and Stoughton, 1890).

11. H. C. G. Moule, *My Brethren and Companions and Other Sermons* (London: Nisbet, 1905), 23f.

12. H. C. G. Moule, *The Cross and the Spirit* (London: Pickering and Inglis, n.d.).

13. H. C. G. Moule, "The 'Total Abstinence' of the Gospel," in *Keswick's Authentic Voice* (London: Marshall, Morgan, and Scott, 1959), 51ff.

14. Ibid., 521ff.

15. Ibid., 27.

11.7.3 W. H. Griffith Thomas—The Scripturality of Keswick

Preachers must know this Book if they are to preach acceptably. If we go to our people with "Thus saith the Lord," this Book must be in mind and heart and life. There is no Christianity worthy of the name that is not based upon this Book. By this Book we stand; on it we rest; with it we fight; through it we shall conquer, because it is the Word of God which liveth and abideth forever.

There is another criticism, the Highest Criticism. Here it is. "To this man will I look, even to him that is of a contrite spirit and trembleth at my word." I now refer to the criticism of the humble soul. You will find that text in Isaiah 66:2. Also another text: "The Word of God is a critic of the thoughts and intents of the heart" (Heb. 4:12). If the soul of man will allow God's Word to criticise it, if we will do a little more of that trembling at God's Word; that will be the Highest Criticism and it will be the criterion that will settle almost everything for us.

—W. H. Griffith Thomas

The Bible-based and Christ-centered nature of Keswick preaching is seen at its quintessential best in **William Henry Griffith Thomas** (1861–1924), whose varied gifts and multiplied ministries brought great blessing to the church. Few things were positive in his early life. His father died before he was born. He was reared by Grandfather Griffith for a while, but by fourteen he had to leave school because of the financial stringencies of the family. When he was sixteen, Thomas was asked to teach Sunday school in Oswestry, Shropshire, his hometown, but was not at the time a converted person. His teaching efforts were frustrated, but through the witness of two young men he came to know Christ at eighteen. He testified:

When I awoke the next morning, my soul was simply overflowing with joy, and since then I have never doubted that it was on that Saturday night, I was born again, converted to God.[1]

Thomas went up to London to work for an uncle and began to study Greek. Bishop Frederick Temple admonished him "never to neglect his Greek New Testament for a single day."[2] Offered a lay curacy at St. Peter's, Clerkenwell, where he attended, he was able to take studies at King's College with distinction and was ordained in 1885. From 1888 to 1896 he was curate at St. Aldgate in Oxford. With the decline of Canon Christopher, he did most of the preaching and pastoral work and was able to win the Junior Septuagint Prize and obtain his B.D. with first class honors at Christ College. He went on to be vicar of St. Paul's, Portman Square (where Sherlock Holmes and Dr. Watson of Baker Street would have attended, had they had a mind to do so, it being very close) and a congregation where later J. Stuart Holden, Bishop Goodwin-Hudson, Prebendary Colin Kerr, Canon Harry Sutton, and others have served with such distinction.

From 1905 to 1910 Thomas went back to Oxford as principal of Wycliffe Hall, an evangelical Anglican training college. He exerted an immense influence for the historic faith as "the icy blasts of Higher Criticism were blowing from Germany, and shaking the faith of many."[3] Lawrence of Arabia and his brothers attended his Sunday afternoon classes on the Greek New Testament on occasion. In 1910 he took a professorial chair at Wycliffe College, Toronto, but when he arrived it turned out not to be systematic theology but Old Testament. Still he filled the chair competently and extended his ministry on both sides of the Atlantic.

Thomas' staunch midday messages on "The Bible and the Spiritual Life" at Keswick in 1914 are deep and compelling.[4] With Lewis Sperry Chafer and A. B. Winchester of Knox Presbyterian Church in Toronto, he founded Dallas Theological Seminary, but his death in Duluth, Minnesota, in 1924 precluded his ever teaching there.

What strikes one about Thomas' preaching is his solid biblical content and his keen sense of theological construct. His Stone Lectures at Princeton in 1913 on the Holy Spirit would have to be included in any list of ten key works on the subject.[5] His prolific output has put us in his debt particularly for his devotional commentaries on Genesis,[6] the works of the apostle John,[7] and the works of the apostle Peter.[8] His writings on Hebrews formed the basis for his highly touted Keswick Bible Readings in 1922.[9] His devotional commentary on Romans is likewise "the finest of the wheat."[10]

He would say to preachers, "We cannot make up for failure in our devotional life by redoubling energy in service."[11] The breadth of his own study is seen in his delightful compendium of Christology titled *Christianity Is Christ*. Typically he makes the case for the objective reality of the resurrection of Christ.[12] Samples of his sermons show clearly outlined messages with mains and subs drawn from the text and an obvious ability to preach it home with pointed application and illustration.[13]

Although Thomas was of such size that he had to have a bicycle especially made for him, he cast a much larger spiritual shadow. In G.T., as he was called, we have a pulpit giant.

---

1. Warren W. Wiersbe, *Living with the Giants* (Grand Rapids: Baker, 1993), 168.
2. Ibid., 169. These sketches put into book form a series of articles in *Moody Monthly*.
3. Herbert F. Stevenson, *The Ministry of Keswick* (Grand Rapids: Zondervan, 1963), 1:197.
4. Ibid., 199ff. "The messages are The Bible as (1) Revelation; (2) Authority; (3) Message; (4) Power."
5. W. H. Griffith Thomas, *The Holy Spirit of God* (Grand Rapids: Kregel, 1986). Great chapter on modernism.
6. W. H. Griffith Thomas, *Genesis: A Devotional Commentary* (Grand Rapids: Eerdmans, 1946).
7. W. H. Griffith Thomas, *The Apostle John: Studies in His Life and Writings* (Grand Rapids: Eerdmans, 1946).
8. W. H. Griffith Thomas, *The Apostle Peter: A Devotional Commentary* (Grand Rapids: Kregel, 1984).
9. W. H. Griffith Thomas, *Let Us Go On: The Secret of Christian Progress in Hebrews* (Grand Rapids: Zondervan, 1944).
10. W. H. Griffith Thomas, *St. Paul's Epistle to the Romans: A Devotional Commentary* (Grand Rapids: Kregel, 1974).
11. Wiersbe, *Living with the Giants*, 172.
12. W. H. Griffith Thomas, *Christianity Is Christ* (Grand Rapids: Kregel, 1981). Impressive bibliography as always.
13. W. H. Griffith Thomas, *The Christian Life and How to Live It* (Chicago: Moody, 1919). Pay close attention to "What We Believe" from Titus 3:4–7 as a sterling example of expository preaching with finesse. A sparkling little gem is the final message in the collection on "God's Surprises" from Genesis 48:11.

11.7.4 J. Stuart Holden—The Rock of Keswick

> At the heart of all human fellowship with God is a cross. He was never so near to the heart of the world's sin and need as when Christ Himself said, "My God, why hast Thou forsaken me?" And this is the centre of faith for us; not the mount on which the Teacher stood, not even the manger in which the Brother lay, but the cross on which the Saviour hung and died. It is this fact, and this recognition which transform sin into penitence and life into glad devotion to the Lord.
>
> —J. Stuart Holden

F. B. Meyer and G. Campbell Morgan were eagerly heard at Keswick, but the dominant figure and the key leader of the movement for many years was the exceptionally able preacher **John Stuart Holden** (1874–1934). Thus while the aforementioned were Baptist and Congregational, and while there were Brethren (George Goodman) and Methodists (Charles Inwood and J. Gregory Mantle), the core of leadership at Keswick was quite consistently Anglican.

Holden was born in Liverpool and converted at sixteen. He studied at Liverpool College and worked in a bank for five years. Some patrons made it possible for him to attend Cambridge, where H. C. G. Moule took him under his wing. After graduating in 1899, Holden was ordained to a curacy at Bath. For some years he traveled with the parochial Anglican evangelist, Canon W. Hay Aitken, also a Keswick preacher in considerable demand. Holden married in 1901. In 1905 he succeeded Griffith Thomas at St. Paul's, Portman Square, where he ministered for almost thirty years. Immediately he moved evening prayers to Sunday afternoon and established a Sunday evening evangelistic service. He also organized a well-attended Bible school.

His "mellifluous voice and polished oratory" and his eminently biblical and rich preaching made him a perennial favorite at Keswick, in North America, and in his West London pulpit.[1] "Dapper little Holden" as he was called, first appeared at Keswick in 1901 and served as chairman of the council from 1924 to 1930 at a time of some innovation. At the same time he was home director of the China Inland Mission, president of the Missionary School of Medicine, one of the founders of the Evangelical Union of South America (which came into being after the World Missionary Conference at Edinburgh when a false ecumenicity refused to regard South America as a missionary continent), and editor of *The Christian* (1915–1920). His honorary D.D. was bestowed by Westminster College in Fulton, Missouri.

Strong-voiced **J. Russell Howden** was one of Holden's truest compatriots.[2] Howden had notable ministries at Tunbridge Wells and at one of the Wren churches, St. Andrews, Holborn, and gave the Bible readings at Keswick five times. **Jessie Penn-Lewis** of Wales, whose husband was a former parishioner of Evans Hopkins, was also close to Holden, who appeared with her at the first Keswick in Wales.[3]

Holden's Bible readings at the Portstewart Convention in Northern Ireland broke new ground and furnished a sample of the kind of exposition of which he was so capable.[4] In 1914, just before the war, he gave a sermon at Keswick from Daniel 3:18, "But if not," which made a profound impression and seemed almost prophetic.[5]

At times we wish Holden would expose more text than he does, though his sermon "God's Voice in the Whirlwind" on Job is superb.[6] His analysis of the enemies of the heart in Matthew 6:19–21, the moth, rust, and the thief, is truly classic.[7] Holden had a knack for titling sermons, giving us such gems as "When Nothing Seems to Happen," from 1 Kings 18:43, or "The Polestar of the New Life," from Psalm 16:8, or "The Transformation of the Unlikely" from 1 Samuel 22:2.[8]

The Holdens were independently wealthy and childless, but there were some conflicts within the council, most of them related to leadership style, during the 1920s when he was at his zenith.[9] Yet Intervarsity Fellowship was founded in large part under a Keswickian influence as Norman Grubb, nephew of Keswick stalwart George Grubb, was quick to point out.[10] The steady biblical sermons of J. Stuart Holden helped keep Keswick on course. He died just short of his sixtieth birthday.

Fascinatingly, he and Mrs. Holden had been booked on the *Titanic* for her ill-fated voyage, in earlier years, but were unable to make the trip because of illness.[11]

<hr />

1. Herbert F. Stevenson, *The Ministry of Keswick* (Grand Rapids: Zondervan, 1963), 1:245.

2. Herbert F. Stevenson, *The Ministry of Keswick* (London: Marshall, Morgan, and Scott, 1964), 2:57–58. Holden's series on "A Man's Foes: The World, the Flesh, and the Devil; and the Way of Victory" given in 1924 may be found in this anthology. See also his unusual *Life Indeed: The Victorious Life in Four Aspects* (London: Pickering, 1933).

3. Mrs. Penn-Lewis' gifts are to be seen in her justly noted *War on the Saints* in collaboration with Evan Roberts (Parkstone, Dorset: Overcomer Literature Trust, n.d.). Some of her best expositions include *The Conquest of Canaan: Sidelights on the Spiritual Battlefield; The Story of Job;* and *The Hidden Ones: Union with Christ traced in the Song of Songs. The Overcomer* magazine she founded continues to be published by the Overcomer Trust.

4. J. Stuart Holden, *Some Old Testament Parables* (London: Pickering and Inglis, 1934). His last public utterances.

5. J. Stuart Holden, *Your Reasonable Service* (London: Marshall Brothers, 1921), 162ff. The following year (1915), Holden delivered a remarkable series, "Perplexities of the Divine Providence," in Herbert F. Stevenson, ed. *Ministry of Keswick,* 1:247ff.

6. J. Stuart Holden, "God's Voice in the Whirlwind," in *Keswick's Triumphant Voice* (Grand Rapids: Zondervan, 1963), 269.

7. J. Stuart Holden, "Life's True Values," in *Your Reasonable Service,* 97ff.

8. J. Stuart Holden, *Redeeming Vision* (London: Robert Scott, 1908), 22ff., 56ff. The latter is one of the best sermons I know on the Cave of Adullam, although J. C. Massee's is I think better; cf. *Seven Sunday Night Talks* (Chicago: Moody, 1926).

9. J. C. Pollock, *The Keswick Story* (Chicago: Moody Press, 1964), 145ff.

10. Ibid., 141. Norman Grubb married the daughter of C. T. Studd of "The Cambridge Seven." Grubb became a missionary and director of Worldwide Evangelization Crusade. He was a great teacher of the deeper life but came dangerously close to pantheism in his last years; see his life story, *Once Caught, No Escape* (Ft. Washington, Pa.: CLC, n.d.).

11. Other collections of sermons by J. Stuart Holden, *The God-lit Road* (London: Marshall Brothers, 1926); *A Voice for God* (London: Hodder and Stoughton, 1932); *The All-round Christian Life* (London: Pickering and Inglis, 1954).

11.7.5 *ANDREW MURRAY—THE COMET OF KESWICK*

My first text is: "We preach Christ crucified." 1 Cor. 1:23. May it be true! But I feel it very difficult not to preach myself, by attending too much to the beauty of thought and language and feeling too little that God alone can teach me to preach.

> —from Andrew Murray's first sermon after
> returning home from study abroad

Would that the spiritual prosperity of the Church were as encouraging as its numbers increase in my congregations. I begin to fear that the state of a great majority of members is much sadder than I at first realized, and I feel in some little measure that nothing but God's mighty Spirit is able to conquer the deep enmity of the unconverted heart. I rejoice at the proposal of a weekly concert of prayer throughout the Church.

> —Andrew Murray

His weekday English services are mainly for the young. I am obliged to listen very attentively to all his sermons for he makes me his critic and always expects to know just what I think. I tell him it is good for him that he has a simple congregation for whom he must bring down his ideas to their comprehension. He is obliged to clip his wings or else . . . I think he would be in some danger if he had a clever and intellectual congregation; he would become too fanciful or too new, if I may use this expression, in his sermons. Now they must be plain and practical, and shorn of the new, varied, and perhaps a little wild interpretations and symbolic meanings that he favors me with.

> —Emma Murray

He visited Keswick as early as 1882 when seeking a cure for his throat, returning only once to speak in a never-to-be-forgotten appearance in 1895. The South African Dutch Reformed preacher **Andrew Murray** (1828–1917) both embodied and emblazoned the Keswick message in his preaching. He led the South African Keswick movement, and his numerous writings continue to be a blessing around the world. In his classic biography, Professor Du Plessis shows why Murray must be seen as "the mountaineer of the higher Christian life movement."[1] The story of Andrew Murray is the gripping chronicle of a mighty man of God who transcended ecclesiastical controversy and national crisis in a worldwide ministry of preaching, Christian education, writing, and the pastorate.

Murray was born in South Africa, his father being a Scottish immigrant pastor of the old-light secessionistic Presbyterians. The elder Murray served the Dutch Reformed Church in Graaf-Reinet for forty-five years. Andrew's mother was of German-Calvinistic Dutch ancestry. In this pious home, visits from Livingstone and Moffat were well remembered. Because of the paucity of good schools, Andrew and his older brother John were sent to Scotland for schooling, first to Aberdeen, where they lived with their preacher uncle, John Murray. This was a time of much reading for young Andrew, and both sons came under the influence of Chalmers, Candlish, the Bonars, and McCheyne.[2] Other discernible influences were the writings of William Law, Madame Guyon, Professor J. T. Beck (cf. 9.4.4), and Count Zinzendorf.

After receiving their M.A. degrees at Aberdeen, the Murrays went on to Utrecht in Holland for divinity studies, since they would be ministering in the Dutch language. Here Andrew was converted.[3] The Haldane influence from Scotland tended to temper his Reformed thinking and a meeting with Pastor Blumhardt left an indelible impression upon Murray. Here the seeds were planted for his continuing emphasis on the healing of the body (cf. 9.4.3).[4] The unfolding scenario of Murray's ministry follows.

At twenty-one, he was inducted as pastor in Bloemfontein and stayed eleven years. He was the first regular pastor in a parish of fifty thousand square miles. Murray made repeated trips across the Vaal to the seven thousand immigrant Dutch farmers.[5] At the end of this time, he was part of a delegation to protest the withdrawal of British sovereignty north of the Orange River. Asked to fill Surrey Chapel in the months prior to the coming of Newman Hall, Murray felt unable to do so and spent the next two years in Europe.[6]

Murray married Emma Rutherford, the daughter of Church of England immigrants. Emma transcribed all of his books.[7] The couple took their honeymoon in an oxcart journey to the field. The Anglo-Boer War isolated him, but Murray continued to write and speak and travel as he was able. The Murrays served in Worcester, one hundred miles east of Cape Town (1860–1864), and had a tremendous visit of the Spirit in revival. They were able to reach the native Africans as well, and fifty young men went into Christian service out of this one congregation.[8]

Eventually Murray took a joint pastorate in the large Dutch Reformed Church in Cape Town (1864–1871). When he retired at seventy-eight, Murray served the Wellington pastorate (1871–1906). He established here the Huguenot Seminary to train more than one thousand young women as schoolteachers (after the Mt. Holyoke, Massachusetts, model) as well as a Missionary Training Institute. Dr. Daniel Malan, later Prime Minister of South Africa, was one of his students.

Murray built a place at Wellington called Clairvaux for retirement. It was said that "meals with the Murrays were like the Holy Communion."[9] Alexander Whyte called him "a happy man."

Always physically frail, Murray lost his voice for two years. Out of this "time of silence" (particularly through the counsel of Pastor Stockmeier, the Swiss-German pastor who also spoke at Keswick; cf. 9.5.3) there came a spiritual deepening and the writing of several of his many books on prayer.[10]

Murray's preaching was steeped in Scripture. His incomparable devotional commentary on Hebrews delves deeply into the text.[11] His message at Keswick in 1895 from Mark 10:35ff. on "The Pathway to the Higher Life" had a phenomenal effect. His mains were

I. The blessing which consecration seeks
II. The mistakes that consecration makes
III. The consecration which Christ demands
IV. The consecration yielded
V. The contention of the disciples about it
VI. Their relationship to their fellow men[12]

Murray's style was intense. He was gifted with "no peculiar charm or poetry or sentiment or willing sweetness;" his words were "naked and unadorned" but "full of weight and power." He could be vehement in the pulpit, but even when he was almost deaf and quite stooped in old age, one listener remarked, "What a voice for such a body!"[13]

Murray was an evangelist who introduced D. L. Moody's aftermeeting into the very staid Dutch Calvinism. He came to this after preaching on hell and sensing such response that many needed to be counseled and prayed with.[14] He fought liberalism and rationalism with great vigor. He preached a widely chronicled series of thirteen sermons against the liberal and Unitarian ideas that were seeping in.[15]

Murray preached the holiness message of Keswick and was ablaze with missionary passion. Few have spoken so clearly to the needs of our hearts as has Andrew Murray.

---

1. J. Du Plessis, *The Life of Andrew Murray of South Africa* (London: Marshall Brothers, 1919).

2. W. M. Douglas, *Andrew Murray and His Message: One of God's Choice Saints* (New York: Revell, n.d.), 26–27.

3. Ibid., 37.

4. Leona Choy, *Andrew Murray: Apostle of Abiding Love* (Ft. Washington, Pa.: CLC, 1978), 45.

5. Douglas, *Andrew Murray and His Message,* 60.

6. Ibid., 72ff.

7. Choy, *Andrew Murray,* 63.

8. Ibid., 85.

9. Ibid., 221.

10. Ibid., 139. N.B., *The Ministry of Intercession* (New York: Revell, 1898); *With Christ in the School of Prayer* (Philadelphia: Henry Altemus, n.d.); *The Prayer Life* (London: Marshall Brothers, 1913). He wrote 240 books.

11. Andrew Murray, *The Holiest of All* (Westwood, N.J.: Revell, n.d.); also *The True*

Vine (Chicago: Moody, n.d.); *Abide in Christ* (New York: Grosset and Dunlap, n.d.); *Waiting on God* (New York: Revell, 1895).

12. Andrew Murray, "The Pathway to the Higher Life," in *Keswick's Authentic Voice* (London: Marshall, Morgan, and Scott, 1959), 292ff. Another gifted preacher who served in Johannesburg and was well heard at Keswick was Gerald B. Griffiths, who also served Spurgeon's Tabernacle, Charlotte Chapel in Edinburgh and in Toronto. His messages at Keswick in 1958 and his printed sermons are remembered: *My Brother's Keeper* (London: Marshall, Morgan, and Scott, 1962); also "Operation Uplight" from Exodus 17:8–13 in *World Vision Magazine* (October 1965): 4ff.

13. Douglas, *Andrew Murray and His Message*, 131.

14. Choy, *Andrew Murray*, 98.

15. An earlier book of great charm, *The Children for Christ: Thoughts for Christian Parents on the Consecration of the Home Life* (New York: Revell, n.d.). See also *The Lord's Table* (Chicago: Moody, n.d.); *The School of Obedience* (Chicago: Moody, 1898); *Absolute Surrender* (Chicago: Moody, n.d.). A compilation of nine typical sermons.

11.7.6 BISHOP J. TAYLOR SMITH—THE CHARACTER OF KESWICK

I cannot give any decisive answer until I have consulted my Lord and Master.

Heaven is more real to me than earth.

The stream of power comes from the enthroned Christ in Heaven and in us.

Many read, few feed. . . . You cannot be noble unless you love your Bible.
                                                                —Bishop J. Taylor Smith

"He became one of the most popular preachers of his day, ever keeping the conversion of souls as the centre of his theme and illustrating his sermons by incidents drawn largely from his own experience."[1] This was the thumbnail evaluation of **Bishop John Taylor Smith** (1860–1937), who came out of modest circumstances. Born in Kendal in England, his father was a coal agent who took steps to set his two sons up in the jewelry business. At age twelve young Smith was converted.[2] Immediately he set up his lifelong custom of "the morning watch"—breakfast, time in the Word, and prayer. He was very athletic, and at seventy-five still astounded friends with his ability to do a backward somersault into the water—notwithstanding his considerable girth. Smith was serious about the Christian life and, despite ridicule and scorn, knelt by his bed morning and evening in his dormitory. He was also a dedicated soulwinner.

Smith trained not at the universities but at Highbury College, vigorously Protestant and evangelical. He lived his whole life with the deep sense of God ordering his goings. "As then, so now," was his motto. He served as curate in St. Paul's in the London suburb of Upper Norwood, where he built a great Sunday school and youth work.[3] Smith ultimately became president of the Children's Special Service Mission. At first he preached extempore but was urged to seek greater cohesion.

> He never failed to realize that the sermon, carefully prepared beforehand and then preached with or without a few pulpit notes, has a much greater hold on most people than a read sermon.[4]

In 1891, after considerable trysting before God and having an almost mystical experience in the Livingstone niche in Westminster Abbey, he surrendered to become a canon-missioner in Sierra Leone, West Africa, called by some the white man's grave. He was consecrated bishop of Sierra Leone and the Canary Islands in 1897 in St. Paul's Cathedral in London under the aegis of Archbishop Frederick Temple. Through an intriguing set of providential circumstances, he became a favorite preacher of Queen Victoria and, at the urging of King Edward VII, was appointed Chaplain-General of the British military. For more than twenty-three years "this tubby, serene, approachable bachelor bishop remained a potent influence in the British Army."[5] Despite criticism, the question he always pressed was, "What would you say to a man who was fatally wounded, but conscious, and only ten minutes to live?"[6] Smith gave himself unstintingly to Scripture distribution among the forces and to the cause of total abstinence from alcohol and nicotine.

Often called "the bishop of the merry soul," Smith faced the massive postwar problems and then took retirement at sixty-five. Yet he still spoke at Swedish Keswick under the sponsorship of Prince Bernadotte and his wife,[7] and conducted children's meetings at Royal Albert Hall. He never wrote a book, but what he wrote on the wide margins of his great Bible has been published and is a veritable encyclopedia of spiritual riches.[8]

Pollock is right that Smith was more an excavator of biblical gems than a true expositor.[9] His sermon introductions were often striking and there was a freshness and an originality in his preaching.[10] He was a graphic artist in preaching and such a character! Stevenson conjures up the picture of the "portly figure in ecclesiastical garb (gaiters and apron), surmounted by a kindly, shrewd, humorous countenance, with twinkling eyes behind rimless pince-nez."[11]

Smith did much personal counseling at Keswick. His sermon on "The Blessed Life" on the Beatitudes in 1913 was long cherished by those who heard it.[12] His 1922 message on Samson, titled "How to Overcome Temptation," is typical.[13] A true Christian gentleman exuding honesty, humor, courtesy, kindness, and generosity, J. Taylor Smith made a great impact on those whom he met. While returning home from Australia, bowing his head at breakfast somewhere in the Mediterranean, he was suddenly called home.[14]

---

1. Maurice Whitlow, *J. Taylor Smith: Everybody's Bishop* (Grand Rapids: Zondervan, 1938), 35.
2. Ibid., 185. This appendix gives an address in which Smith gives his own account of his conversion and struggles.

3. Ibid., 30.
4. Ibid., 35.
5. J. C. Pollock, *The Keswick Story* (Chicago: Moody, 1964), 144.
6. Whitlow, *J. Taylor Smith*, 97.
7. Ibid., 113.
8. Percy O. Ruoff, *Gems from Bishop Taylor Smith's Bible* (London: Marshall, Morgan, and Scott, n.d.).
9. Pollock, *The Keswick Story*, 144.
10. Whitlow, *J. Taylor Smith*, 139.
11. Ibid., 141.
12. J. Taylor Smith, "The Blessed Life," in *Keswick's Authentic Voice* (London: Marshall, Morgan, and Scott, 1959), 209.
13. J. Taylor Smith, "How to Overcome Temptation," in *Keswick's Triumphant Voice* (Grand Rapids: Zondervan, 1963), 193.
14. Whitlow, *J. Taylor Smith*, 109, 184. I heard Wilbur Smith describe Bishop Smith's visit to the Moody centenary. He was so ill he could not speak, but the huge audience in Moody Church was blessed by just a look at his face.

11.7.7 W. GRAHAM SCROGGIE—THE DISTANCE CARRIER OF KESWICK

Preachers will take for texts, phrases which convey a moral or spiritual suggestion, and will develop that thought along one or other of many lines. But one may do that kind of work for half-a-century and yet leave his audience in appalling ignorance of the Bible. Such sentences can be found by the hundred thousand in the world's literature, and a very instructive course of sermons could be preached from the dicta of Confucius; but that is not the business of the Christian preacher.[1]

Is the Bible the Word of God? It seems to be—it claims to be—it proves to be.

—W. Graham Scroggie

Continuous cross-pollination between Keswick and America took place as European preachers crossed the Atlantic and as strong preachers like A. T. Pierson and S. D. Gordon came from America to preach at Keswick. Still the heavy preaching load year after year was carried by the British and by no one more regularly than the Scottish Baptist who gave the Bible readings twelve times at Keswick over a forty-two-year period. **William Graham Scroggie** (1877–1958) was born in Malvern, England, of Scottish parents who ministered as evangelists. He was reared in an ambiance of rich Christian experience.[2] Scroggie took his training at Spurgeon's College and served a succession of churches, including Leytonstone Church in London (1899–1901); Trinity Church in Halifax (1902–1905); Bethesda Free Church in Sunderland (1907–1916); and a most fruitful tenure at Charlotte Chapel, Edinburgh (1916–1933).[3] He, like Campbell Morgan, gave himself first to a mastery of the English Bible and was known for his clear-cut and well-outlined expositions of Holy Scripture. After leaving Charlotte,

Scroggie traveled the world in conference ministry for several years and then served Spurgeon's Tabernacle during the war years (1938–1944).[4]

Listeners marveled at the solid Bible content of his preaching.[5] Scroggie wrote Scripture Union and Sunday school materials for *The Sunday School Times* for years, efforts that gave him a firm footing in Scripture.[6] He also took great pains in careful and appropriate application.

He had a delightful dry wit and "his measured voice and somewhat stern mien masked warmth of affection."[7] In his years at Charlotte, thirty-two men entered the ministry and fifty-one missionaries were sent overseas. In recognizing his effectiveness as a preacher and missioner in bestowing an honorary doctorate, the University of Edinburgh paid tribute to him for his "devotion to the study and teaching of the Bible in its two-fold character of a Divine Revelation and great Literature."[8]

Scroggie led thousands through a Bible correspondence course. He was a strong premillennialist and looked for a special work of God among the Jews at the end of the age.[9] He was equally adept at analysis and synthesis. Several of his favorite Bible readings at Keswick show his gifts as an expositor and preacher. Especially memorable were his studies on *Paul's Prison Prayers, Paul's Hymn of Love, Christ in the Creed,* and *Salvation and Behavior* (Romans). A favorite is *The Land and Life of Rest* (Canaan and the Heavenlies). Scroggie was neat and concise in his layout.[10] His skill in arrangement is in clear evidence:

I. Contemplating the Land
II. Entering the Land
III. Conquering the Land
IV. Possessing the Land
V. Interpreting the Land

The Keswick movement has seen a theological and a methodological ripple effect around the world. W. Graham Scroggie personifies the best aspects of that legacy.

---

1. W. Graham Scroggie, "The Preparation of Addresses," in Ralph Turnbull, ed., *A Treasury of W. Graham Scroggie* (Grand Rapids: Baker, 1974), 192ff. Scroggie agonized over how Phillips Brooks and G. H. Morrison use the cubic dimensions of the Holy City in Revelation 21:16 to speak of Christian character, or Brooks' use of Matthew 24:27, "the lightning out of the East and West," to speak of the spread of the gospel westward. Well-taken cautions.
2. Mrs. James J. Scroggie, *The Story of a Life in the Love of God* (Edinburgh: Pickering and Inglis, 1938).
3. Charlotte Chapel was bathed in revival under the ministry of Joseph Kemp. When he came in 1902, only thirty-five members attended his induction; by 1907 the membership was 609 and 830 by 1914. The chapel was enlarged in 1912 to seat one thousand. In 1915 Kemp went on to a ministry in New York and then on to the Auckland Tabernacle in New Zealand. Described in Brian H. Edwards, *Revival: A People*

Saturated with God (Durham, N.C.: Evangelical Press, 1990), 204–5. Pastors like Kemp, Scroggie, Gerald Griffiths, Sidlow Baxter, Alan Redpath, and Derek Prime have all contributed to the strength of Charlotte Chapel as a preaching center.

4. Eric W. Hayden, *A History of Spurgeon's Tabernacle* (Pasadena, Calif.: Pilgrim, 1971), 46ff.

5. Of great substance is W. Graham Scroggie, *A Guide to the Gospels* (Grand Rapids: Kregel, 1995).

6. The two volumes of his notes on the gospels were published by Ark Publishing in London in 1981.

7. J. C. Pollock, *The Keswick Story* (Chicago: Moody, 1964), 142.

8. Nigel M. de S. Cameron, ed., *Dictionary of Scottish Church History and Theology* (Downers Grove, Ill.: InterVarsity Press, 1993), 763–64.

9. W. Graham Scroggie, *The Great Unveiling: An Analytical Study of Revelation* (Grand Rapids: Zondervan, 1979); his work, *What About Heaven?* (London: Pickering and Inglis, 1940) is most comforting. His analysis of the Psalter is choice (*A Guide to the Psalms,* 4 volumes in one, Grand Rapids: Kregel, 1995).

10. W. Graham Scroggie, *The Land and Life of Rest* (London: Pickering and Inglis, 1950).

CHAPTER TWELVE

The Glory and Agony of Twentieth-Century Preaching

Part Two: Resurgence or Senescence?

How may we have within ourselves that which shall impart to our preaching the right sort of authority, the conviction and confidence which lacks neither a proper respect for the hearer nor the humility of a sinful man, which is neither overridingly dogmatic nor weakly diffident? I suppose in the end the secret lies in the quality of our own spiritual life and the extent to which we are ourselves walking humbly with God in Christ.

—H. H. Farmer

But Micaiah said, "As surely as the LORD lives, I can tell him only what the LORD tells me."

—1 Kings 22:14

I saw under the altar the souls of those who had been slain because of the word of God and the testimony they had maintained.

—Revelation 6:9

Then I saw another angel flying in midair, and he had the eternal gospel to proclaim to those who live on the earth—to every nation, tribe, language and people.

—Revelation 14:6

He who was seated on the throne said, "I am making everything new!"
Then he said, "Write this down, for these words are trustworthy and true."
—Revelation 21:5

The angel said to me, "These words are trustworthy and true. The Lord,
the God of the spirits of the prophets, sent his angel to show his servants
the things that must soon take place."
—Revelation 22:6

There is a false belief abroad that only gentle, tender, loving persuasions
are in harmony with the New Testament times. It is all a mistake! Never
in the world's history were fearless, resolute, whole-souled prophets
called for and needed more than today. This age needs Jeremiahs to tell
the truth, the whole truth, please or displease, dungeon or no dungeon,
mire or no mire!
—General William Booth

Unless he has spent the week with God, and received Divine communi-
cations, it would be better not to enter the pulpit or open his mouth on
Sunday at all.
—James Stalker

Coming down the stretch of the tumultuous twentieth century, the tensions of
the Cold War yielded to the reassertion of old tribalisms and state terrorism; the
growing affluence and deepening materialism of a very small segment of the West
and parts of Asia; the reinvigoration of radical Islam and Hinduism; the continued decline of mainline Protestantism and the cultural erosion of evangelicalism;
as well as the increasing theological confusion of Roman Catholicism.
Evangelicals seem to be victimized by the pervasive shift toward "self-seeking,
self-indulgence and self-gratification" as profoundly as any.[1] Religion generally
is trivialized and marginalized in American law and politics.[2] Christian exclu-
sivity is increasingly seen as the one untenable and unacceptable position on the
spectrum. Exaggerated individualism continues unabated at century's end even
as Bellah and associates diagnosed it earlier.[3] The Europeanization of American
Christianity is in mounting evidence.

The biblical message is proclaimed not simply in a post-Christian age but in
an anti-Christian age. In the postmodern pluralistic climate, fact and opinion are
seen as no different. D. A. Carson brilliantly traces the modern turn to subjectivity (remember Kierkegaard's steadfast refusal to define revelation as communication of doctrine) and what he characterizes as "the drift into intellectual
nihilism."[4] This proceeds through the domestication of Scripture through higher
criticism or the substitution of "spirituality" for theological construct as in "new
age" and higher types of neo-gnostic hubris. The ground which must be maintained if we are to be true to "the word of our testimony" (Rev. 12:11) was articulated by Max Warren shortly before he died:

It is all too easy . . . to talk of different roads to the summit, as if Jesus were in no particular and distinctive sense "the Way, the Truth and the Life." Of course where this point is reached, the Great Commission is tacitly, if not explicitly, held to be indefinitely in suspense if not quite otiose. This is the view forcefully propounded by some Christians holding professorial chairs in Britain and across the Atlantic. Are they right? Is courtesy always to preclude contradiction? Is choice now just a matter of taste, no longer a response to an absolute demand? Is the Cross on Calvary really no more than a confusing roundabout sign pointing in every direction, or is it still the place where *all* men are meant to kneel?[5]

This is the context and milieu of biblical preaching as the twentieth century concludes.

1. James Lincoln Collier, *The Rise of Selfishness in the United States* (Oxford: Oxford University Press, 1991).
2. Stephen L. Carter, *The Culture of Disbelief* (New York: Basic Books, 1993). America spinning out of control.
3. Robert N. Bellah et al., *Habits of the Heart* (New York: Harper, 1985). Bellah's latest study indicates that the pathologies he identified earlier on are more pronounced today; see "Individualism and the Crisis of Civic Membership," *The Christian Century* (May 8, 1996): 510ff.
4. D. A. Carson, *The Gagging of God: Christianity Confronts Pluralism* (Grand Rapids: Zondervan, 1996).
5. Ibid., 94–95.

12.1 EMISSARIES IN THE WORLDWIDE EXPANSION OF THE GOSPEL

I still see the cross of Jesus as the one place in all the history of human culture where there is a final dealing with the ultimate mysteries of sin and forgiveness, of bondage and freedom, of conflict and peace, of death and life . . . I find here a point from which one can take one's bearings and a light in which one can walk, however stumblingly. I know that guiding star will remain and that that light will shine till death and in the end. And that is enough.

—Bishop Lesslie Newbigin[1]

Despite the dilution of the mandate to preach the gospel to every creature through an epidemic of universalism and theological relativism, there were those like Newbigin who stayed with the historic gospel. Andrew Murray wrote a burning response to one of the early conferences. His focus was on prayer and the ministry of the Word:

I know that it is no easy task to speak humbly, wisely, lovingly and yet faithfully and effectually, of what appears lacking or sinful in the Church.

And yet I am sure that there are many who would welcome help in answering the questions: Is there any real possibility of such a revival in the Church that in every congregation where the full gospel is preached, her most important aim will be to carry the gospel to every creature? What is the path that will lead to this change? And what steps should be taken by those who lead the missions of the church?[2]

In response to the modernistic book by Hocking, *Rethinking Missions,* and its endorsement by Pearl S. Buck, J. Gresham Machen led in setting up the Independent Board for Presbyterian Foreign Missions in 1933.[3] The battle was over the uniqueness of Christ and his Cross for salvation.

---

1. Lesslie Newbigin, *Unfinished Agenda: An Autobiography* (Grand Rapids: Eerdmans, 1985), 254. Newbigin relates how the vision of Christ crucified changed his life (11) and how a careful study of Romans brought him to clarity on the objective nature of Christ's atoning work on the Cross (30).
2. Andrew Murray, *A Key to the Missionary Problem* (Ft. Washington, Pa.: CLC, 1979), 27.
3. D. G. Hart, *Defending the Faith: J. Gresham Machen and the Crisis of Conservative Protestantism in Modern America* (Grand Rapids: Baker, 1994), 149.

12.1.1 SAMUEL M. ZWEMER—THE MISSION TO MUSLIMS

If the Cross of Christ is anything to the mind, it is surely everything—the most profound reality and the sublimest mystery. One comes to realize that literally all the wealth and glory of the gospel centres here. The Cross is the pivot as well as the centre of New Testament thought. It is the exclusive mark of the Christian faith, the symbol of Christianity and its cynosure.

—Samuel M. Zwemer

Kenneth Scott Latourette speaks of him as "frankly a conservative evangelical" and saw something of the Old Testament prophet's fearlessness and forthrightness in him. He was part of the Student Volunteer Movement which rose in dedication to "the evangelization of the world in this generation."[1] **Samuel Marinus Zwemer** (1867–1938) was born the third of fifteen children in a Dutch Reformed manse in Vriesland, Michigan. He was the descendent of French Huguenots who had fled to the Netherlands. Four of the five Zwemer brothers became ministers.

Zwemer trained at Hope College and the New Brunswick Seminary (RCA), preaching his first sermon in 1888 to a small African-American congregation.[2] He felt the call to missions and especially to follow the great missionary to the Muslims, Raymond Lull. Zwemer and his friend Cantine founded the Arabian Mission and went to Beirut to learn Arabic and explore Muslim lands.[3] Establishing work in Bahrain, Zwemer traveled for three years on behalf of the Student Volunteer Movement. In 1912 the United Presbyterians and the Church Missionary Society jointly called Zwemer to Cairo, where his "acquisitive and inventive mind" quickly catapulted him to become the "leading authority on Islamics from a Christian perspective."[4] He traveled to every Islamic nation and blanketed the world with conference ministry. In Cairo he received the young William Borden of Yale, a wealthy visionary who had targeted Tibet for his service but who shortly died of spinal meningitis. Zwemer conducted the funeral.

Increasingly he became a platform crusader for Christ and the missionary cause. A staunch champion of verbal inspiration, Zwemer took a strong stand against Hocking's *Rethinking Missions* and published a rejoinder titled *Thinking Missions with Christ.*[5] "He had little patience for the higher critics of Scripture," his biographer says.[6]

Zwemer was a strong and insightful preacher who spoke at Northfield, Winona Lake, and three times at Keswick in England. A ravenous reader and disciplined student, he published a trilogy of books on the birth, death, and resurrection of Christ.[7] Joining the Princeton Seminary faculty in 1929, he became a popular teacher. His Smyth Lectures from Columbia Seminary in Decatur, Georgia, are a measure of his scholarly bent.[8]

Interestingly, with all his lifelong dedication to Muslim missions, Zwemer had an absorbing burden for the Jews as well.[9] Twice widowed, he retired in 1938 and then taught at Biblical Seminary in New York City and at the Alliance Missionary Training Institute (Nyack). In advanced years he continued to preach even to the convalescents in the nursing home where he died at eighty-four.[10]

What influence and impact he had and how grateful we are for the flame of concern for the Muslim world which he kindled. Over a billion Muslims in our time! How many will hear of our Savior?

1. Kenneth Scott Latourette, Introduction to J. Christy Wilson, *Apostle to Islam* (Grand Rapids: Baker, 1952).
2. Ibid., 31.
3. Samuel M. Zwemer and James Cantine, *The Golden Milestone: Reminiscences of Pioneer Days Fifty Years Ago in Arabia* (New York: Revell, 1938).
4. Wilson, *Apostle to Islam,* 84, 92. Cf. Zwemer's classic, *The Moslem Doctrine of God* (Edinburgh: Oliphant, Anderson and Ferrier, 1905). This book is dedicated to his minister father, Adrian Zwemer.
5. Ibid., 67, 199.
6. Ibid., 241.
7. His 1937 messages at Keswick are charming and challenging; see *No Solitary Throne* (London: Pickering and Inglis, 1937), in response to Gandhi's comment: "I am unable to place Jesus Christ on a solitary throne." The trilogy consists of *The Glory of the Manger* (New York: American Tract Society, 1940); *The Glory of the Cross* (London: Oliphants, 1954); *The Glory of the Empty Tomb* (New York: Revell, 1947).
8. Samuel M. Zwemer, *The Origin of Religion* (New York: Loizeaux Brothers, 1945). These lectures are dedicated to Professor Wilhelm Schmidt of Vienna to whom

Zwemer was indebted for his anthropological case for primitive monotheism. For a more recent assessment, see Ernest Brandewie, *Wilhelm Schmidt and the Origin of the Idea of God* (Lanham, Md.: University Press of America, 1983).

9. Wilson, *Apostle to Islam,* 241.
10. Beside J. Christy Wilson and J. Dudley Woodberry, the other great evangelical scholar in Islamic law and custom in our time has been Sir Norman Anderson, *An Adopted Son: The Story of My Life* (Leicester: Inter-Varsity, 1985).

12.1.2 E. STANLEY JONES—MISSION TO INDIA AND THE WORLD

I'm only a Christian in the making.

But when you ask us to accept the basis that all religions are equally true, we are sorry, but we cannot. For we believe that there is something unique in Jesus Christ. And that uniqueness is the Person himself!

On Hebrews 9:26: "'At the climax of history . . .' All history moved on to this climactic moment when we saw God sacrificing himself on a cross. That was the climax of history and the climax of revelation . . . this is the climax; this is the Voice, all else is echo. . . . So my contact as a Christian missionary with a non-Christian nation has led me more and more to the cross."

—E. Stanley Jones

Listening to **Eli Stanley Jones** (1884–1973) was like trying to drink from a fire hydrant. The hyperenergetic preacher delivered more than sixty thousand sermons and always pressed himself to the limit—with a series of nervous breakdowns as a consequence. Born in Baltimore, Jones' home situation was difficult. But he had a praying mother and was converted at the age of fifteen in an evangelistic crusade at Memorial Methodist Church:

I had him—Jesus—and he had me. We had each other. I belonged. My estrangement, my sense of orphanage were gone. I was reconciled. As I rose from my knees, I felt I wanted to put my arms around the world and share this with everybody.[1]

Immediately Jones got into the Wesleyan class meetings and began to grow. He had leanings to the law but went on to Asbury College after hearing Henry Clay Morrison preach. At Asbury he surrendered to missionary service. Hannah Whithall Smith's *The Christian's Secret of a Happy Life* brought him to yield all to Christ and to be filled with the Holy Spirit.[2] He had several very shaky starts in his preaching. In his first sermon, he drew a complete blank but then recovered sufficiently to give his testimony of new life in Christ, and his ministry was launched.[3] Jones went to India.

Arriving in Bombay in 1907, Jones served as pastor in Lucknow during language study, but it soon became clear that evangelism was his calling. At first he reached out to the outcasts in his district of one million souls but then gave himself to a ministry to the intellectuals. He used roundtables with Hindus and Muslims and he started Christian ashrams (spiritual retreats) where the Bible hour was central. Early on he became a bit taken with some Marxist ideas and ruefully acknowledged later how mistaken he was.[4] Jones was an evangelist and an unashamed supernaturalist, Christocentric in an almost radical sense. He preached "Jesus Christ and him crucified," and his book *Conversion* stands as a classic.[5] Often in his assertion that "Jesus is Lord!" he stressed the importance of living out the sermon. Yet his obsession with experience and his lack of training led him to a systematic de-emphasis on theology and a unfortunate turn away from the Old Testament and a strong view of biblical inspiration.[6]

Jones traveled the world as an evangelist with especially great meetings in Japan. Twenty thousand people heard him in Madison Square Garden and eighty-two hundred stayed afterward for surrender. He became a champion of racial reconciliation and federal union among churches and yet would not be deterred from his main evangelistic purpose. In 1928 he was elected a bishop of the Methodist church but resigned twenty-four hours later because he felt he was a missionary and an evangelist and not a bishop!

Jones wrote twenty-nine books and several times was nominated for the Nobel Prize for peace.[7] His glowing personality was contagious. After a serious stroke, E. Stanley Jones insisted on going back to India where he died. His sermon "The Divine Yes" from 2 Corinthians 1:19–20 effectively brings out Christ as the "yea and amen" and emphasizes spiritual rebirth, cleansing from sin, and the fullness of the Holy Spirit.[8]

---

1. E. Stanley Jones, *A Song of Ascents: A Spiritual Autobiography* (Nashville: Abingdon, 1968), 26ff., 28.
2. Ibid., 52. Another great preacher out of Asbury was J. C. McPheeters, who served as president. Note his strong expositions on Corinthians in the Proclaiming the New Testament series (Grand Rapids: Baker, 1964).
3. Ibid., 65.
4. Ibid., 148.
5. E. Stanley Jones, *Conversion* (Nashville: Abingdon, 1949). He argues here that liberals know everything but change nothing.
6. E. Stanley Jones, *The Divine Yes* (Nashville: Abingdon, 1975), 39.
7. Books of daily reading like *Abundant Living* (Nashville: Abingdon, 1942) and *Growing Spiritually* (Nashville: Abingdon, 1953) have been immensely popular and are very Scripture-driven.
8. Many missionaries to India have become great preachers (as we hark back to Carey and Duff) even into this century with Bishop J. Waskom Pickett and Donald McGavran, who founded the Church Growth Movement. Jones is true to this text without going over the edge like Henry Ward Beecher who was critiqued by an English Wesleyan "for giving too little prominence in his teaching to redemption in the blood of Christ," cf. David Bebbington in George A. Rawlyk and Mark Noll, *Amazing Grace* (Grand Rapids: Baker, 1993), 85; or without suffering total shipwreck

like Norman Vincent Peale, cf. his *The True Joy of Positive Living* (New York: William Morrow, 198); or the maceration of Pauline theology in Robert Schuller's *Self-Esteem: The New Reformation* (Waco: Word, 1982). Where is the gospel in all of this? Jesus vs. Paul is a wrong-headed false dichotomy.

12.1.3 ROWLAND V. BINGHAM—MISSION TO AFRICA AND CANADA

Not to create a sentiment of peace in a world that is in rebellion against God, but to secure the acceptance of the One who made peace through the blood of His cross, is the business of the preacher.

The normal life of the Christian is a triumphant life. The provision made for triumph is such that it is disloyal to consider defeat. We are "always" to triumph; to be more than conquerors.

—Rowland V. Bingham

Founder of Canadian Keswick, longtime editor of *The Evangelical Christian* in Canada, **Rowland V. Bingham** (1872–1942), was the prime mover in the Sudan Interior Mission. Bingham was born in Sussex in England, the second of eight children who were financially devastated by their father's death when Rowland was thirteen. The family was nominally Anglican, but Rowland was soundly converted in a Salvation Army Hall under the ministry of a believing Jew.[1]

Bingham soon lost his meager teaching position because of his dissenting loyalties. Immediately he began to win souls.[2] Because he did not feel he could sell smoking materials in his mother's shop, he decided to migrate to Canada.[3] "God made it clear that he wanted me to preach the Gospel," he wrote, and surrendered for missionary service. With two friends he visited the Sudan in Africa, and though he was shaken by their deaths, he went on to study medicine and then Bible at Simpson's school in New York City.

Facing seemingly insurmountable odds, Bingham and his associates launched beachheads of gospel advance in hard places. Dr. Thomas Lambie led out in Ethiopia, as did the remarkable Dr. Andrew Stirrett among the Hausas in Nigeria.[4] Bingham was not only a missionary statesman and leader but also an able preacher, itinerating widely. He was a student of doctrine. His concentration on spiritual warfare and what the Bible says about demons and divine healing was salutary. He was "a man of one Book" who was "unflinchingly loyal to the sacred Word."[5] His lecture on "Prophecy Proved by Photography" strengthened the faith of many.[6]

Bingham's love for the deeper recesses of Christian experience led to the founding of Canadian Keswick at Muskoka. Here he expounded Scripture with others like Griffith Thomas, Graham Scroggie, Charles Trumbull, Canon Dyson Hague, and Gordon Watt from England.[7] Many did not agree with Bingham's eschatological positions, but his spirit was kind and genial, and he wrestled with the issues in depth.[8]

At the heart of the great Sudan Interior Mission (currently with more than thirteen hundred missionaries on the field) is the steady biblical preaching and vision of a man who sought after the Lord and reveled in the presence of the mighty God.

1. J. H. Hunter, *A Flame of Fire: The Life and Work of Rowland V. Bingham* (Toronto: Sudan Interior, 1961), 43.
2. Ibid., 46.
3. Ibid., 48.
4. Douglas C. Percy, *Stirrett of the Sudan* (Toronto: Sudan Interior, 1948). A truly remarkable saga.
5. Hunter, *A Flame of Fire,* 275.
6. Ibid., 276.
7. Ibid., 259. For a good sample of this English preacher, cf. Gordon Watt, *The Cross in Faith and Conduct* (Philadelphia: The Sunday School Times Company, 1924).
8. Rowland V. Bingham, *Matthew the Publican and His Gospel* (London: Marshall, Morgan, and Scott, n.d.). Bingham tends to build straw men in prosecuting his case. He is persuaded that all dispensationalists end up with Bullinger. To recognize that Matthew's gospel has a particular appeal to the Jew does not make it unusable by others.

12.1.4 JONATHAN GOFORTH—MISSION TO CHINA

Like his Master, Goforth had a great compassion for the needy and helpless and a two-edged flashing sword for the self-satisfied Christian Pharisee. It was probably this searching penetrating method of preaching to bodies of even Christian workers that caused opposition to his being sent, as was urged years later, on a Mission tour in India as he had in China.

—Dr. John Buchanan of India

This I can say that on no occasion where we stood with our backs to a wall and used the Word of God did we fail ultimately in gaining a victory.

—Jonathan Goforth

Adjudged to be "China's most outstanding evangelist" by Dr. J. Herbert Kane, **Jonathan Goforth** (1859–1936) was one of our time's most adept China hands, mightily used of God in China, Manchuria, and Korea.[1] Born in Thorndale, Ontario, he was the seventh child of eleven.

Goforth was converted in the local Presbyterian church under the ministry of a pastor who called for decisions at the end of every service.[2] Life was hard for the young farm boy. Many times in his life he miraculously escaped death.[3] But the lessons of sowing and reaping were never lost on him, and Goforth's love for the mission field is not surprising. He was raised on Scripture, and as a lad stood fascinated before maps.[4] After reading Robert Murray McCheyne, Goforth laid his life on the altar of missionary service.

Tutored by his pastor, he began to serve and preach. Again, his life was touched for missions.[5] He went on to study at Knox College in Toronto, where he was ridiculed and humiliated but was unswerving in his commitment. He worked in the slums, jails, and missions of the city. Soon he was walking sixteen to eighteen miles every Sunday, preaching three times. Eventually he shared the platform at the Niagara-on-the-Lake Conference with William E. Blackstone, author of *Jesus Is Coming!* with whom Goforth shared a strong premillennial conviction.

Then he met his beloved Rosalind. Rosalind saw that the shabby man was a sharp arrow for the Lord, and they made a great team. The Goforths would be the first North Americans to volunteer for the China Inland Mission. Ironically it was the students of Knox who helped raise the money enabling the Goforths to leave for China. They were commissioned at historic Knox Presbyterian Church in Toronto, where a plaque commemorating the occasion still can be seen on the wall.[6]

Taking Hudson Taylor's watchword to go forward on their knees, the Goforths endured unspeakable adversity. They narrowly escaped death in the Boxer Rebellion. Their personal effects were burned, and they lost several of their children in death. Yet Goforth continued his endless preaching tours. He had a great passion for preaching and often took as his theme "The Sacrifice of Christ."[7] His dedication was to preach Christ with an open Bible even though his cohorts warned him against so direct an approach. Sinners came to Christ from the very first.[8]

After the Boxer Rebellion, the Goforths returned to do family evangelism with great effectiveness. Meanwhile, under the influence of Finney's *Lectures on Revival,* Goforth began the revival ministry that God was opening for him. Preaching on the text from 1 Peter, "He bore our sins in His own body on the tree," he enjoyed an extraordinary response.[9] Returning for a furlough, Goforth preached in this vein at Keswick in England in 1910. He was invited to stay and itinerate for Keswick for a year, but he had to return to China.[10]

Goforth was also in the center of the spiritual conflagration that ignited in Korea. His book *By My Spirit* gives the full story. The text he used in the breakthrough service in Shansi Province in China was Revelation 3:15, the words to the church in Laodicea.[11] In 1918 he preached to General Feng's army and saw many conversions, ultimately seeing the general himself take up preaching.[12]

Goforth had considerable conflict with Roman Catholic incursion in his areas, and he fought the incessant growth of higher critical ideas and the resultant waning authority of Scripture in the lives of many of the new missionaries arriving on the field. His wife relates, "He felt powerless to stem the tide and resolved to preach, as never before, salvation through the Cross of Calvary and demonstrate its power in his own life."[13]

On their furlough in 1916, Mrs. Goforth was led into a deeper experience of the Holy Spirit through Dr. Charles G. Trumbull of *The Sunday School Times.* This opened new doors of ministry at the American Keswick in New Jersey and other places.[14]

As the years passed, Dr. Goforth lost the sight of both of his eyes and Mrs. Goforth lost her hearing. Up to that time he had his Scofield Bible in English and his Chinese Bible always before him. Rosalind Goforth testified:

> Jonathan Goforth *loved* the Word. To him the simple reading of it was a delight. It was sacred, divine. How often have I seen him, when taking up his Bible to read, first uncover his head and in an attitude of deepest

reverence remain so a few moments before beginning his reading. In this simple act we see the secret of his life. Before he crossed the Borderland he stated that he had read the Bible seventy-three times from cover to cover.[15]

At long last the Goforths had to come home to stay in 1935. In the last eighteen months of his life he spoke more than five hundred times, including American Keswick and Ben Lippen conferences. The fiery preacher went home to glory in October of 1936.

1. Ruth A. Tucker, *From Jerusalem to Irian Jaya* (Grand Rapids: Zondervan, 1983), 188.
2. Rosalind Goforth, *Goforth of China* (Grand Rapids: Zondervan, 1937), 24. Her book *How I Know God Answers Prayer* is a missionary and devotional classic.
3. Ibid., 19.
4. Ibid., 21.
5. Ibid., 28.
6. Knox Presbyterian Church in Toronto is adjacent to the campus of the University of Toronto and has been a great center of biblical exposition, most signally in this century by Dr. William Fitch.
7. Goforth, *Goforth of China,* 105.
8. Ibid., 83.
9. Ibid., 181.
10. Jonathan Goforth, "Power from on High" from Acts 1:14 in *Keswick's Triumphant Voice* (Grand Rapids: Zondervan 1963), 364ff. "Revival is no pleasant process; it just means Gethsemane and Calvary," 368.
11. Goforth, *Goforth of China,* 194.
12. Ibid., 253.
13. Ibid., 214.
14. Ibid., 230.
15. Ibid., 315.

12.1.5 ROBERT E. SPEER—MISSION TO NORTH AND SOUTH AMERICA

Work without prayer is ashes; prayer without work is a dream.
—Robert E. Speer

At Northfield Dr. Speer would stand before us on the high platform in the auditorium, straight as a spruce tree against the sky, usually grave but frequently smiling too, never talking down, never given to colloquialisms, an intellectual making simple the deep things of the spirit, his fine voice matching the eloquent flow of his ordered thought. Echoes come back across the years: "The Gospel is either true for all or it is not true at all."

—W. Reginald Wheeler

A pivotal missions strategist, **Robert E. Speer** (1867–1947), for forty-six years the secretary of the Board of Foreign Missions for the PCUSA, was possibly the greatest motivational preacher missions has ever had. John Mackay heard him at Edinburgh in 1910 and concluded that Speer "was the greatest personality I have ever known."[1]

Speer was born into a staunchly Presbyterian home in Huntingdon, Pennsylvania, one of five children, where the father was an attorney and two-term Democratic congressman. His mother died when he was nine, but she had elicited from him the promise that he would never use alcohol. His upbringing was Puritan, and his Bible-teaching father required that his children learn both the Shorter and Larger Catechism. Young Speer attended Andover Academy (he remembered Principal Fairbairn's ministry) and then Princeton University, where he was valedictorian of his class and played football for four years.

Speer was caught up in the Student Volunteer Movement and often visited Northfield to hear Moody and others. He became known as a forceful speaker on purity of life and character at student meetings.[2] He often traveled with John Mott, who came from Cornell.[3] Speer attended Princeton Seminary, but left in his middle year when he was invited to become secretary of the Board of Foreign Missions. Only twenty-four, he took on the large responsibility of an enterprise with 598 missionaries and 28,000 native workers. He traveled constantly, married in 1893, traveled to Mexico, and the next year to Keswick in England.

Speer was a great storyteller. He had a grave earnestness about him, but this was tempered by a sense of humor as well. He was a top administrator and promoter and a powerful preacher with immense appeal to students. Reading from his "tiny, well-worn New Testament," he would open the Scripture. He was considered "tops in exposition and application."[4]

Speer was a man who read constantly and expressed himself expertly and clearly.[5] His instincts were sound and doctrinally conservative. "He believed with Chrysostom that the cause of all our evils lies in our not knowing the Scriptures."[6] He was unreservedly a supernaturalist and at length defended the Virgin Birth of our Lord. His well-known Stone Lectures on *The Finality of Jesus Christ* are classic.[7]

He wrote scathingly of the liberally tilted Laymen's Foreign Missions Inquiry Report of 1932. He contributed several key articles to *The Fundamentals*. In all, Speer wrote and edited sixty-seven books. He profoundly influenced so many who in turn exerted great influence, such as Samuel Shoemaker, the Episcopalian missionary to China who then served parishes in New York City and Pittsburgh.[8] Speer was prophetic in his interest and vision for Latin America and in his "Brazil Plan" for the indigenization of Hispanic missions.

The center of Robert Speer's life and ministry was biblical preaching. Thus, when he was elected moderator of the General Assembly in 1927, conservatives were encouraged. The church was in turmoil and the inroads of modernism and liberal theology were gnawing away at the vitals of the communion. Here Speer failed. Was it lack of training in theology or was it the congeniality of the man or was it the bias of the organization man? Speer did not see the dangers of the Barthian denial of propositional revelation.[9] He believed he could unite the liberals and the conservatives. J. Gresham Machen felt that Speer betrayed the missionary cause and Princeton Seminary.[10] When Speer died of leukemia near eighty years of age, his lifelong friend Henry Sloan Coffin of Union Seminary in New York conducted the funeral service.[11]

At what point does the man in the middle need to take the plunge? Machen and Speer believed alike doctrinally but drew sharply different ecclesiological conclusions. We remember Robert Speer as a layman whose Christlike personality and preaching made a vast difference for many.

---

1. W. Reginald Wheeler, *A Man Sent from God: A Biography of Robert E. Speer* (New York: Revell, 1956), 9.

2. Ibid., 49.

3. John R. Mott (1865–1955) was, like Speer, a consecrated layman. He did not contribute to *The Fundamentals,* and his biographer develops the thesis that while Speer remained theologically steady, Mott accommodated. See C. Howard Hopkins, *John R. Mott* (Grand Rapids: Eerdmans, 1979). President Wilson wanted Mott to become U.S. ambassador to China. He also won the Nobel Peace Prize.

4. Wheeler, *A Man Sent from God,* 127. Speer's *John's Gospel: The Greatest Book in the World* (New York: Revell, 1915) was a widely used study book and is typical of his rich Bible study. His book of sermons from Northfield gives typical fare; see *Remember Jesus Christ* (New York: Revell, 1899). These are beautiful and moving sermons.

5. Robert E. Speer, *How to Speak Effectively Without Notes* (New York: Revell, 1918). With this little gem, Speer addresses the issue of the advantages of extempore preaching in a manner similar to such heavies as Richard S. Storrs (who served Brooklyn's Church of the Pilgrims for fifty-three years); Clarence E. Macartney; and Charles W. Koller, whose *Expository Preaching Without Notes* (Grand Rapids: Baker, 1962) has influenced so many.

6. Wheeler, *A Man Sent from God,* 143.

7. Robert E. Speer, *The Finality of Jesus Christ* (New York: Revell, 1933). These are the Stone Lectures from Princeton given in 1932 and 1933 and the Gay Lectures from Southern Baptist Seminary delivered in the same year.

8. Wheeler, *A Man Sent from God,* 138–39.

9. Ibid., 97.

10. D. G. Hart seems to feel that Speer "bore the brunt of the Board's lubricity." See *Defending the Faith: J. Gresham Machen and the Crisis of Conservative Protestantism in Modern America* (Grand Rapids: Baker, 1994), 149; Ned B. Stonehouse, *J. Gresham Machen: A Biographical Memoir* (Grand Rapids: Eerdmans, 1954) expresses much stronger disappointment in Speer's unwillingness to draw the line in the Pearl Buck case and to speak out (469ff.).

11. Henry Sloan Coffin (1843–1929) was baptized by Pastor John Hall at Fifth Avenue Church. His father was treasurer of Moody's New York campaign. In his long pastorate at Madison Avenue Church in New York City (1905–1926) and his presidency at Union Seminary, he moved steadily left. He disavowed the work of Billy Sunday and was a prime mover in the Auburn Affirmation of 1923–1924. See Morgan Phelps

Notes, *Henry Sloan Coffin* (New York: Scribner's, 1964). The Robert Speer story dramatically demonstrates the dilemmas of the organization man.

12.1.6 *FRANK LAUBACH—MISSION TO THE ILLITERATES*

Oh, if we only let God have His full chance He will break our hearts with the glory of His revelation. That is the privilege which the preacher can have above others. It is his business to look into the very face of God until he aches with bliss.

Deeper yet, O Christ, deeper, deeper, yet into Thy broken heart let me bury my will, that from Thy heart I may draw the power of Pentecost. Help me stay. Help me abide. Nothing else in the world matters but that.
—Frank Laubach

Sometimes called the apostle of literacy, **Frank C. Laubach** (1884–1970) was born and reared in Benton, Pennsylvania. He trained at Princeton University and Colombia University as well as Union Seminary in New York City. He was a missionary educator and preacher among the Muslim Moros on Mindanao in the Philippine Islands and served as dean of Union College in Manilla.

While handling the tough assignment among half a million hostile Moros, Laubach experienced a most extraordinary breakthrough of the sense of the Lord's presence as he prayed.[1] Prayer was for him "the mightiest force in the world." Laubach went on to lead the "Each one reach one" campaign of winning the world for Christ. This involved using his method for teaching people to read the Word of God.[2]

He had a doctorate in sociology from Colombia but soon realized that people needed the transformation that only God can give through his Word. But what is the Bible for those who cannot read? Laubach saw the answer. He wrote or co-authored more than two hundred primers for illiterate adults in more than 165 languages in fifty-one countries.

Laubach was more of an exhorter than an expositor. A dynamic preacher in his own right, he was deep into the Scriptures.[3] His delivery was rapid-fire, and he seemed to sweep over all resistance as he poured forth his heart and the great need. Pieces of his sermons show the biblical thrust from the launching pad and his artistic arc to application for life.[4]

---

1. Frank Laubach, *Practicing His Presence* (Auburn, Me.: Christian Books, 1973); *Letters by a Modern Mystic* (New York: Revell, 1937).
2. Frank Laubach, *How to Teach One and Win One for Christ* (Grand Rapids: Zondervan, 1964).
3. Frank Laubach, *Frank Laubach's Prayer Diary* (New York: Revell, 1964). Each day is anchored in a Bible portion.
4. Frank Laubach, *Living Words* (Grand Rapids: Zondervan, 1967); *Wake Up or Blow Up* (New York: Revell, 1951).

12.1.7 F. J. HUEGEL—MISSION TO MEXICO

There has been now for some years a decided turning away from the Cross on the part of these ambassadors of Christ. They are going to most every source, biblical and extra-biblical, for their sermon material. But in the main they are not going to Calvary's Cross. This has been outmoded. The bloody Cross of the Crucified Redeemer for them is hardly a fit thing for exaltation in our churches.

Calvary is the greatest moment in the moral history of God.
—F. J. Huegel

Many able missionary preachers have been primarily exhorters, but there are those who have sought after and preached the "deep things of the Spirit of God." Among these is **F. J. Huegel** (1889–1971).[1] His brilliant mind led him to stray in philosophy, although he was reared in a Christian home. At the University of Wisconsin he was converted while reading F. W. Farrar's *Life of Christ*.

Huegel ministered within the Christian Church, or the Disciples of Christ as they have been called. In World War I, he was a chaplain to the American Expeditionary Force in France and then for twenty-five years was a missionary to Mexico. He taught on the faculty of Union Seminary in Mexico City and had a remarkable evangelistic ministry in the prisons of Mexico. In the anguish of a great trial, the Lord showed him the centrality of the Cross as the means of victory over Satan and sin.[2]

Huegel also acknowledged a great debt to the teaching of Jessie Penn-Lewis.[3] Known on both sides of the Atlantic for his preaching on the Cross and the victorious life, Huegel also had a great influence on L. E. Maxwell and Eugenia Price, to name but two. His language is colorful, his illustrations pungent, and his preaching drips with nourishment. Few preachers have probed so painfully but used the Balm of Gilead so generously.[4]

---

1. Another example would be L. L. Legters, cofounder with W. Cameron Townsend of Wycliffe Bible Translators; see *Partakers* (Philadelphia: Pioneer, 1936); *Freedom Through the Cross* (Philadelphia: Pioneer, 1937).
2. F. J. Huegel, *The Cross of Christ—The Throne of God* (Minneapolis: Bethany Fellowship, 1935), 137ff.
3. Jessie Penn-Lewis, *The Centrality of the Cross* (Parkstone, Dorset: Overcomer Trust, n.d.). Messages from the Swanwick "Message of the Cross Conference," April 19–24, 1920.
4. Huegel's messages are in *Bone of His Bone* (Grand Rapids: Zondervan, n.d.); *That Old Serpent, the Devil* (Edinburgh: Marshal, Morgan and Scott, 1954); *Calvary's Wonderful Cross* (Grand Rapids: Zondervan, 1949); *The Cross Through the Scriptures* (Grand Rapids: Zondervan, 1966); *John Looks at the Cross* (Grand Rapids: Zondervan, 1957); *Forever Triumphant* (Minneapolis: Bethany, 1955); *Prayer's*

Deepest Secrets (Minneapolis: Bethany, 1959). My dear friend, Dr. Gordon Johnson, president emeritus of Rio Grande Bible Institute in Edinburgh, Texas, possesses an unpublished biographical memoir of Huegel by his son.

12.1.8 *Amy Carmichael of Dohnavur—Mission to South India*

If I am afraid to speak the truth, lest I lose affection, or lest the one concerned should say, "You do not understand," or because I fear to lose my reputation for kindness; if I put my own good name before the other's highest good, then I know nothing of Calvary love.

> Pour through me now: I yield myself to Thee,
> Love, blessed Love, do as Thou wilt with me.

—Amy Carmichael

"Still climbing!" was the description she wanted of her life and ministry. "We have heard the preaching, but can you show us the life of your Lord Jesus?" a Hindu asked. **Amy Carmichael** (1867–1951) both taught and wrote (thirty-six books), but above all she exemplified and embodied the reality of the living Christ.

Born in Northern Ireland, Carmichael was early touched by the gospel and by the Keswick message. She became the adopted daughter of Robert Wilson, one of the early leaders of Keswick. She held children's meetings in Belfast and then reached out to working girls and required a hall seating more than five hundred, which the Lord miraculously provided.[1] A similar ministry followed in Manchester. She became the first missionary sent out by Keswick and visited Japan and Ceylon before sensing God's call to work among the Tamils in South India, particularly among the temple prostitutes.

"Amma" (Tamil for mother), as she was called in the Dohnavur Fellowship, went through incredible trials in her fifty-five years without a furlough, but she was confident:

I think God wants to make me pure gold, so He is burning out the dross, teaching me the meaning of the fire, the burnt offering, the death of the self-part of me.[2]

Hers was not fashionable Christianity. The rich maturity of her insight and utterance did not derive from the lowering of the threshold but from "the ordination of the pierced hands." Hers was the Order of Epaphroditus (Phil. 2:30). In the last twenty years of her ministry she was an invalid, having fallen into a pit in the dark. In this time she was "climbing unawares."

Both Elizabeth Elliot and Bishop Houghton have given us invaluable studies of this woman of God. Sherwood Eddy, who knew her, spoke of the "beauty of her character," as "the most Christlike character I ever met. . . . Her life was the most fragrant, the most joyously sacrificial, that I ever knew."[3] When she left Keswick in 1895, her theme was "Nothing Too Precious for Jesus." The Fellowship still thrives at Dohnavur (now under Indian leadership entirely), and the goal is still the same: "We preach Jesus Christ as Lord and ourselves as your servants for Jesus sake."[4] Her books are still in extensive circulation.

---

1. Frank Houghton, *Amy Carmichael of Dohnavur: The Story of a Lover and Her Beloved* (Ft. Washington, Pa.: CLC, n.d.), 25ff.
2. Elizabeth Elliot, *A Chance to Die: The Life and Legacy of Amy Carmichael* (Grand Rapids: Revell, 1987), 145.
3. Ruth Tucker, *From Jerusalem to Irian Jaya* (Grand Rapids: Zondervan, 1983), 239.
4. Elliot, *Chance to Die,* 382.

12.1.9 RUTH PAXSON—MISSION TO CHINA AND THE WORLD

How should you and I begin the day? From a position of victory. Where should we begin each day? Yonder seated with Christ in the heavenlies, far above all principality and power and might and dominion. "All things are under his feet." What does that mean? Whose feet are they? Whose body? We can have all things under our feet too, if we will; instead of that, we go through each day with everything on top of us: we are underneath most of the time. Can you get higher up than "far above all principality and power and might and dominion"?

—Ruth Paxson

A disproportionate amount of gospel proclamation on the mission fields of earth has been done by single women missionaries. Another who is representative of these is the American **Ruth Paxson,** who served as a missionary to China under the China Inland Mission for many years. Her base of ministry was Shanghai.

Paxson often spoke at the Pei Tai Ho Convention in North China and gave a noted series to women at Keswick in England in 1936. Like her beautiful *Rivers of Living Water,* the Keswick series is so clearly and logically outlined:

I. Oneness with Christ
II. Likeness to Christ
III. Fullness of Christ
IV. Wrestlers for Christ[1]

This reminds us of her most renowned series of messages on Ephesians, *The Wealth, Walk and Warfare of the Christian,* which she subtitles "The Grand Canyon of Scripture." Her ability to chart and visualize, her lucid and clear style, her "comparing spiritual things with spiritual" are most engaging.[2]

But of course her masterpiece is the three-volume work *Life on the Highest Plane,* which she gave to "pastors, evangelists, teachers and other Christian leaders in Conferences held in China."[3] R. A. Torrey paid her high tribute when he said, "Her knowledge of Scripture I have rarely seen paralleled." Upon returning to this country, she had a fruitful ministry in boys' and girls' schools and conferences. Dr. Clarence S. Roddy, in his renown sermon on Romans 6, acknowledged his great indebtedness to Ruth Paxson. Here is biblical exposition of a high order.

1. Ruth Paxson, *Called Unto Holiness* (London: Marshall, Morgan, and Scott, 1936).
2. Ruth Paxson, *The Wealth, Walk and Warfare of the Christian* (New York: Revell, 1939).
3. Ruth Paxson, *Life on the Highest Plane* (Grand Rapids: Kregel, 1996).

12.2 BAPTIST STALWARTS WHO TAKE A STAND AGAINST SECULARISM

Essentially I mean the moment you consider man's real need, and also the nature of the salvation announced and proclaimed in the Scriptures, you are driven to the conclusion that the primary task of the Church is to preach and to proclaim this, to show man's real need, and to show the only remedy, the only cure for it.

—D. Martyn Lloyd-Jones

The decomposition of the Judeo-Christian foundations of Western culture has gained momentum as the century has advanced. Peter Berger describes believers as a "'cognitive minority' whose standards of knowledge deviate from what is publicly taken for granted."[1] As P. T. Forsyth foresaw earlier, the critical issue in the twentieth century is the issue of authority. In postmodernism, the very idea of truth has dissolved. Man has become his own god, and in thus conforming truth to desire, he has bankrupted modern culture.[2] Some within the ranks of orthodoxy have given way to "the cultural relativizing of revelation."[3] Others saw in the evolutionary vision and in the concessions to antisupernaturalistic premises a dangerous threat to the historic Christian faith. We shall see the spokesmen for a vigorous biblical apologetic emerging from many quarters, but at this point, we want to shift the spotlight to some Baptist preachers who model for us clarity of conviction and great courage.

1. Wolfhart Pannenberg, "How to Think About Secularism," *First Things* (June/July 1996): 27.
2. E. Michael Jones, *Degenerate Moderns: Modernity as Rationalized Sexual Misbehavior* (San Francisco: Ignatius, 1993). Jones makes essentially the same point as Paul Johnson makes in *Intellectuals* (New York: Harper, 1988).
3. Carl F. H. Henry, "The Cultural Relativizing of Revelation: A Review of Charles Kraft's Christianity in Culture," *Trinity Journal* 1 n.s. (1980): 153–64. Kraft asserts that even "biblically informed believers have no universally valid information about God." Kraft follows the neo-orthodox notion that revelation is personal rather than informational. Not both?

12.2.1 JOHN ROACH STRATON—TAKING A STAND IN THE HEART OF NEW YORK CITY

While many Protestant churches in this city—literally scores of them—have died in recent years because of unbelief and unbiblical methods of work, and while other modernist churches are fanatically striving "to hold the young people" by having dances, theatricals, etc. and are straining to keep up attendance on Sundays by introducing into their services "dramatics," movie "stars" speaking in the pulpits and such other novelties, and even by having bare-legged girls dancing in the sanctuary on the Lord's Day with vari-colored lights playing on them, Calvary Church has prospered and built up on the Old Gospel and spiritual methods of work. The "novelties" finally play out—and have no power even while they are playing in—but the "word of God endureth forever."

—John Roach Straton

One of the central citadels of biblical preaching in New York City for one hundred fifty years has been Calvary Baptist Church in two locations, on Twenty-third Street and in two buildings on Fifty-seventh Street.[1] The seventh pastor at Calvary was a crusader and a communicator. **John Roach Straton** (1875–1929) served Calvary for twelve years. He was a preacher's son and was raised in the South, though he was born in Evansville, Indiana.

Backsliding into skepticism, Straton was soundly converted in a revival meeting in the First Baptist Church of Atlanta. He went on to study at Mercer University in Macon and Southern Baptist Seminary in Louisville. So outstanding were his oratorical gifts that he took further study at the Boston School of Oratory and then taught oratory and literature at Mercer and at Baylor University in Waco, Texas.

But the call to preach was incessant, and he served successively Second Baptist Church of Chicago, Seventh-Immanuel Baptist Church of Baltimore, and First Baptist Church of Norfolk, Virginia. At age forty-three he came to New York, "slender, handsome, dynamic and an orator who immediately attracted attention."[2] Straton crusaded against white slavery, the liquor industry, gambling, pornography, and prize fighting. His somewhat sensational methods brought him great attention; then he moved in with the gospel message with all of his might. Unable to obtain radio time, he established the first church-owned radio station in the nation. He cried:

The Church of God is not a hospital to nurse sick saints into heaven. The church is rather an armory for the training of soldiers to fight for righteousness and to strive for the salvation of souls. . . . Christianity means heroic self-renunciation, or it means nothing at all.[3]

The Sunday school trebled and the evening service attendance soared to two thousand. In the summer he toured the streets with his portable automobile pulpit. He was a flaming evangelist and invited William Biederwolf, George Truett, and Mordecai Ham (the Southern Baptist under whose preaching Billy Graham came to Christ) to hold great crusades at Calvary. He championed the cause of historic orthodoxy against evolution and higher criticism and took the case into a series of public debates at Carnegie Hall. Straton also went after the Ku Klux Klan.

In all of this, Calvary flourished, and Straton led in the demolition of the old church and the building of a combination church and hotel which still stands on the Fifty-seventh Street location. His lecturing and preaching reached their zenith in the 1928 presidential campaign, when he focused his shot against Al Smith and Tammany Hall. He was struck down with a heart attack and then a stroke that took him from the battles of this life at the early age of fifty-four.[4]

After interviewing the liberal Harry Emerson Fosdick, a New York journalist then interviewed Straton. If the former spoke to his head, the latter spoke to his heart. He told the newspaper man "the old, old story of Jesus and His love."[5] The journalist concluded that Straton had a religion for men and women who were troubled in a troubled world.

The sermonic strategy of Straton (who bore a striking resemblance to Woodrow Wilson) was to burrow down in a great text. His message on "The Modern Need of a Great God" from Isaiah 6 is exegetically weak, but the progression of thought in the passage prevails.[6] The sermon on "How the Fisherman Captured Rome," based in Acts 2:46–47, is more loosely strung but delineates the message, the method, and the might of the early church.[7] The sermon on "The Empty Place" from 1 Samuel 20:18 is moving, but builds a temple where the Scripture only has a tent.[8] His illustrations are crisply developed and his style is not florid. Straton clearly loved to preach on the Second Coming of Christ and on the Cross of Christ and its meaning. His vibrant and enthusiastic delivery was doubtless a potent factor in the great impact this preacher of the Word made upon the city.

---

1. William R. De Plata, *Tell It from Calvary* (New York: Calvary Baptist, 1972). This study traces the growing years under Dr. Robert S. MacArthur (1870–1911); the call to Joseph Kemp of Charlotte Chapel, Edinburgh, and his brief ministry before going to New Zealand; the great ministry of Will Houghton, who followed Straton (cf. Wilbur M. Smith, *A Watchman on the Wall: Life Story of Will H. Houghton* (Grand Rapids: Eerdmans, 1951); and the pulpit eloquence of William Ward Ayer, who served Calvary from 1936 to 1949 (see his sermons, *Marked Men* [Grand Rapids; Eerdmans, 1947] and his lectures on evangelism at Bob Jones University, *Flame on the Altar* [Grand Rapids: Zondervan, 1952]).

2. F. R. Webber, *A History of Preaching in Britain and America* (Milwaukee: Northwestern, 1957), 3:577.

3. De Plata, *Tell It from Calvary,* 47.

4. Ibid., 53.

5. William G. Shepherd, *Great Preachers as Seen by a Journalist* (New York: Revell, 1924), 72.

6. John Roach Straton, *The Old Gospel at the Heart of the Metropolis* (New York: George H. Doran, 1925), 17ff.

7. Ibid., 36ff.

8. Ibid., 201ff.

12.2.2 WILLIAM BELL RILEY—TAKING A STAND IN THE MIDWEST FOR THE BIBLE AND THE SUPERNATURAL

The reason there are so many poor preachers is because there are so few who are willing to put gray matter into the preparation of sermons.

When we remember these mighty conflicts and see that the ultimate issue has ever been on the side of truth, we wonder at the arrogance of that heterodoxy which under many forms of liberalism is today disturbing the evangelical creeds of Europe, England and America. We are also surprised that the religious age should seem alarmed at these freaks of faith! Why not remember, and so remind them, that the procession of orthodoxy has left buried in its triumphal track greater names than even theirs, and still sweeps on, conquering and to conquer, till the time shall come when the paean of eternal triumph shall be shouted once for all?

—W. B. Riley

Standing tall and straight as an arrow with his shock of snow-white hair, he was an unforgettable figure in the pulpit. William Jennings Bryan called him "the greatest Christian statesman in the American pulpit." **William Bell Riley** (1861–1947) was reared in Boone County, Kentucky, where he worked hard as a young lad on his father's farm. Of Irish-Scotch, English, and Dutch pedigree, Riley had early impressions of the nation torn and divided and earned his first substantial money as a tobacco trader.

In August of 1878, Riley was converted in a revival, followed the Lord in baptism, and made public profession of his newfound faith.[1] He was driven by a motivation he could not understand to seek education. He enrolled at the Normal School in Valparaiso, Indiana, where he paid $1.45 per week for food and owned but a $13.00 suit for school. By 1880 he had his teaching certificate and was set to go in Possum Ridge, Owen County, Kentucky. A wealthy farmer wanted to pay his way through Hanover College at this time, and to help with expenses, Riley traveled by horse and buggy to fill preaching places. He did not want to be a preacher—debate and oratory were his obsessions—but God would not let him go.[2] Riley served a string of congregations while he studied at Southern Baptist Seminary in Louisville under the great John Broadus and John Sampey.

It was while Riley was at Louisville that the higher critical views of the promising young Crawford H. Toy compelled his leaving school. Riley became part of D. L. Moody's Louisville crusade and early on was an evangelist himself.

In 1888 Riley gave the ringing graduation address at Southern Seminary on "The Triumph of Orthodoxy." One senses in reading it that the sail is set.[3] Dr. George Lorimer of Chicago preached his installation sermon at New Albany, Indiana, from whence young Riley went to serve a successful pastorate in Lafayette, Indiana. Here he met and married a young Methodist. Riley went on to Bloomington, Illinois, and then to Calvary Baptist Church on the south side of Chicago. Here he bumped into the liberalism of President William Harper at the University of Chicago and became a thorn in the side of those who denied the gospel. Along with his high-profile activism in the community, he evolved a dream of building something like the Tremont Temple at the heart of a great city, but by then Chicago was too vast and sprawling.[4]

The opening of opportunity came remarkably in 1897, when he accepted the call to the First Baptist Church of Minneapolis. There he was to be the pastor for the next forty-five years and the pastor emeritus for three years. Immediately a power bloc in the church was antagonized by Riley's outspoken opposition to pew rents, church fairs, and bazaars. His enemies hired a private detective, but after five years of struggle, 146 of them left to found their own congregation on Lowrey Hill. Riley led into battle the Bible-believing forces of the Twin Cities against evolution, liquor interests, and gambling. Able and articulate, his debates spread around the country. He was one of the prime movers with A. C. Dixon and William Jennings Bryan in founding the World Christian Fundamentals Association.[5] In all of this time, he gave himself to the rebuilding of the First Baptist Church, which had 2,640 seats. He also founded Northwestern Schools (Bible School and Seminary), where Billy Graham succeeded him as president.

Riley held evangelistic crusades and Bible conferences around the world and always brought in the finest of biblical preachers to fill his pulpit when he was absent. He believed that if a sermon is worth preaching, it should be printed. He preached through the entire Bible from 1923 until 1933, and these sermons can be found in the forty-volume *Bible of the Expositor and the Evangelist.* The more expositional messages for Sunday morning are here along with the evangelistic addresses from Sunday night (remember that the "seekers' services" were then held on Sunday night). His sermons are well researched and well illustrated. He clipped from his reading and pasted into scrapbooks. In all, Riley had seventy volumes of these three-hundred-page scrapbooks and drew upon them freely. Almost all of his sermons have a respectable set of mains and subs. Listeners were seldom aware that the preacher was working from a fully written manuscript.

Riley was in the middle of the tensions and turmoil in the Northern Baptist Convention, from which he withdrew near the end of his life. His good friend and colleague, Earle V. Pierce, chose the more mediating way and served as president of the convention. (Pierce performed the wedding of Riley and his second wife.)[6] Even with the huge responsibilities of church and school and the broader ministry, Dr. and Mrs. Riley paid pastoral calls and never lost sight of the people.

Although usually he exposed a good piece of text, Riley once preached a series on "The Seven Things God Hates" from Proverbs 6:16ff.[7] He was a preacher's preacher who fitted strong content to appropriate form. Perhaps he pursued issues like evolution too far, too much, but he was always on the cutting edge of a society and culture cast loose from their moorings. He was a great preacher of Bible prophecy, and his books, though dated, are well worth obtaining and reading.

---

1. Marie Acomb Riley, *The Dynamic of a Dream: The Life Story of W. B. Riley* (Grand Rapids: Eerdmans, 1938), 43.

2. Ibid., 31.
3. Ibid., 53ff.
4. Ibid., 63.
5. Riley was succeeded in the presidency of the WCFA by the founder of the Bryan Bible League and his close friend Dr. Paul Rood, pastor of Beulah Covenant Church, Turlock, California, and later pastor of the Church of the Open Door and President of BIOLA. Rood was a mighty preacher in his own right; see *When the Fire Fell* (Grand Rapids: Zondervan, 1939). I heard Rood preach the memorial address at the Minnesota Fundamentals Conference following the homegoing of W. B. Riley in 1947.
6. Earle V. Pierce served Lake Harriet Baptist Church in Minneapolis and was a most engaging preacher; see *The Conflict Within Myself* (New York: Revell, 1942). "A Kiss That Did Not Count" from Ruth 1:14 is exceptional; also see *The Church and World Conditions* (New York: Revell, 1943); *The Supreme Beatitude* (New York: Revell, 1947). The latter is one of the best books of sermons preached on stewardship.
7. W. B. Riley, *The Bible of the Expositor and the Evangelist,* 40 vols. (Cleveland: Union Gospel Press, 1926 and on). I came into possession of the entire set through the kindness of the late Mr. and Mrs. Dan Bren; *Youth's Victory Lies This Way* (Grand Rapids: Zondervan, 1936); *Christ the Incomparable* (New York: Revell, 1924); *The Seven Churches of Asia* (New York: Christian Alliance, 1900); *Seven New Testament Converts* (Grand Rapids: Eerdmans, 1940); *Re-Thinking the Church* (New York: Revell, 1940). These are my favorite titles.

12.2.3 A. C. DIXON—TAKING A STAND FOR THE SAVING GOSPEL ON BOTH SIDES OF THE ATLANTIC

God's work in God's way with God's power to God's glory.

My delight is in the Lord, and not in what man may think or say about me. My constant prayer is that my heart may be perfect toward God. . . . I desire to be Christ's in body and mind and heart and time and purse.

How I do long to preach Jesus to the lost, and to see them saved! May God prepare us for our future work. We are in His hands for success or failure, and it is blessed to rest just there. I have a vision of my own selfish, sinful soul, which has crushed me into the dust, but I have also the glorious vision of Christ and His Word.

—A. C. Dixon

The motto of **Amzi Clarence Dixon** (1854–1925) was "The whole Christ in the whole Bible for the whole world." He had a commanding love and loyalty for Scripture. It was said of his preaching, "He quoted Scripture with the readiness and alacrity of a lover quoting poetry."

This confidence in the Word seemed to be in his blood, born as he was in Shelby, North Carolina, the son of a farmer-lay preacher. His early years were caught up in the maelstrom of the Civil War, but Dixon was converted in a revival at nearby Old Buffalo Church under his father's preaching from Acts 16:31. Ninety-seven others were baptized the day he was.[1]

Dixon attended Wake Forest College and on one occasion was forced to preach when the assigned speaker failed to come. Out of this experience came his sense of call to preach and an insatiable desire to master the Greek New Testament.[2] He wrote to Charles Spurgeon in London about the feasibility of taking his seminary work at the College in London, but Spurgeon counseled that Dixon study at home. He began seminary studies at the Baptist Seminary in Greenville, South Carolina (since moved to Louisville), and particularly benefited from John Broadus as a teacher.

Dixon was a pastor-evangelist by calling. He never finished seminary but took the pastorate of First Baptist in Chapel Hill, North Carolina, where he launched his ministry with a series of protracted meetings in which revival fell upon the congregation. On one occasion when he was ill, he recovered dramatically when a country lad was saved.[3] He moved on to Asheville, North Carolina, where there was almost continual revival for the two-and-a-half years he was there. One young carpenter whom Dixon led to Christ in turn led a lad to Christ of whom we shall hear much—George W. Truett.

Systematic visitation was a key thrust in Dixon's strategization. He moved on to the Immanuel Baptist Church of Baltimore, where he had a gracious ministry. Crusading against liquor was important to Dixon, and he dealt much with "the dangerous lure of some popular amusements." In Baltimore he led in the building of a new tabernacle seating twelve hundred and began to visit Northfield and other venues of biblical preaching.

"The trend away from biblical authority" was very apparent and grievous to Dixon.[4] He spoke out against Roman Catholic heresy even in Baltimore. While speaking at the World Sunday School Convention in 1889, Dixon became well-acquainted with Spurgeon, who invited him to speak at the Metropolitan Tabernacle. Dixon analyzed Spurgeon's strength as "The fact that he has the anointing of the Holy Spirit, and preaches God's Word, relying on Him to bless it."[5]

Dixon's next charge was the Hanson Place Baptist Church in Brooklyn (1890–1901). Its second pastor, Dr. Robert Lowry, wrote such hymns as "Up From the Grave He Arose," "Shall We Gather at the River?" and "I Need Thee Every Hour." Dixon brought Fanny Crosby in to speak to the youth. He promoted large prophetic conferences and a training institute at which Dr. Nathaniel West spoke effectively on "The Pentateuch and Higher Criticism." Dixon was so outspoken against the forces of unbelief that the famous skeptic Robert Ingersoll sued him. Although Beecher was gone, Dixon had to face the legacy of his equivocation on Scripture, the Atonement, and future punishment.[6] Clearly apostasy was spreading.[7]

In 1893 he was invited to be part of the evangelical pulpit team that ministered at the Chicago World's Fair. The team consisted also of David Burrell (cf. 11.4.6) and Theodore Cuyler (cf. 10.3.6). After resistance to expansion, Dixon took the call to Ruggles Street Baptist Church in Boston. Here he entered into an ongoing sparring match with Christian Science. He spoke at the first Baptist World Congress in London in 1905, as did F. B. Meyer, and preached for Campbell Morgan at Westminster Chapel and for Thomas Spurgeon at the Metropolitan

Tabernacle. He had fine opportunity for fellowship with his dear friend Sir Robert Anderson of Scotland Yard (cf. 11.1.6). Dixon also made the first of two visits to preach at Keswick on this visit abroad.

In 1906 he began an eventful five-and-a-half year ministry at the Chicago Avenue Church, which later became the Moody Church. During this time he played a vital role in the writing of *The Fundamentals.* In 1911 he began his ministry at the Metropolitan Tabernacle in London, a ministry he continued until 1919. The ministry at Elephant and Castle more than held its own during these trying years, and Dixon ministered in Norway, Scotland (preaching for Joseph Kemp at Charlotee Square in Edinburgh), and elsewhere with great energy. In one twelve-month period, seven hundred souls were converted at the Tabernacle.

Dixon, together with Campbell Morgan, F. B. Meyer, Dinsdale Young, and Stuart Holden, hailed the signing of the Balfour Declaration in 1917 as having prophetic significance.[8] Upon returning to the United States after the war, he traveled in conference ministry and taught at the Bible Institute of Los Angeles. He returned to Baltimore and a ministry at the new University Baptist Church near John Hopkins University.

He and Mrs. Dixon then went to China. While ministering there, she suddenly died. He came back to Baltimore for a last shot, challenging high criticism, Bolshevism, and evolution. He brought such scholars as Robert Dick Wilson from Princeton (who worked in twenty-six languages)[9] and Melvin Grove Kyle from Xenia Seminary in Pittsburgh to defend historic Christianity.[10]

Early in his ministry in London, Dixon held a three-week evangelistic crusade, and his sermons from that effort were published as *The Glories of the Cross.* These sermons are biblically based, some expository and some textual, imagistic, and pictorial. He illustrated extensively and well. Several of the messages are like the Plymouth Brethren and F. E. Marsh Bible readings.[11]

Dixon had a simple and direct style. On occasion, we wish he would probe further into the passage, yet he divided a text well, sometimes with as many as seven or eight mains. Truly a man of great humility and one who was indifferent to popular approval, Dixon's life text was, "Worthy is the Lamb that was slain to receive power and riches and wisdom and strength and honor and glory and blessing." A. C. Dixon was plain but powerful, and he was always biblical![12]

---

1. Helen C. A. Dixon, *A. C. Dixon: A Romance of Preaching* (New York: Putnam's, 1931), 31.
2. Ibid., 38. The second Mrs. Dixon was the widow of Torrey's song leader, Mrs. Charles Alexander.
3. Ibid., 41.
4. Ibid., 95.
5. Ibid., 107.
6. Ibid., 127.
7. Ibid., 181.
8. See my book *Jews, Gentiles and the Church* (Grand Rapids: Discovery House, 1995), 169ff.

9. Robert Dick Wilson, *A Scientific Investigation of the Old Testament* (Chicago: Moody, 1959).

10. Melvin Grove Kyle, *Mooring Masts of Revelation* (New York: Revell, 1933). Dixon's successor at University Baptist was Russell Bradley Jones, whose sermons *Gold from Golgotha* on the seven last words are a classic series.

11. A. C. Dixon, *The Glories of the Cross* (Grand Rapids: Eerdmans, 1962), 69ff.

12. A. C. Dixon, *Through Night to Morning* (Grand Rapids: Baker, 1969); *The Bright Side of Life* (New York: George H. Doran, n.d.); *Heaven on Earth* (Greenville, S.C.: Gospel Hour, n.d.).

12.2.4 *LEN G. BROUGHTON—TAKING A STAND FOR CHRIST IN ATLANTA AND ON THE THAMES*

> But there is coming a time when the Gentile dispensation is coming to an end; when the church shall have done its work in proclaiming Jesus Christ as the Savior of the world; and when the Gentile period, or church period of the world is at an end, then Israel will be restored, and she will take her rightful place as the favorite of God, proclaiming the Messiah to a lost and ruined world . . . the Jew as a nation is going to receive Jesus Christ.
>
> —Len G. Broughton

One of the most eagerly awaited preachers of the Word at this time was the six-foot, 118-pound physician-evangelist **Leonard G. Broughton** (1864–1936). Born in Wake County, North Carolina, Broughton received his medical education at the University of Kentucky. He was practicing medicine in Reidsville, North Carolina, when the call of God to be a physician of souls took priority above all else. He studied theology, was ordained in 1893, and then pastored successfully in Knoxville, Tennessee, and in the Grove Avenue Baptist Church of Richmond, Virginia.

In 1898 Broughton came to Atlanta, then a city of sixty-five thousand, and founded the Baptist Tabernacle. It would ultimately become the largest Southern Baptist church of its time. Broughton's vision came to fruition in a great sanctuary seating thirty-three hundred. He also established the Tabernacle Hospital and Training School for Christian Nurses.[1] In 1914 he went to Christ Church, Westminster Road, in London (cf. 11.3.4), where he enjoyed an astounding ministry until his health collapsed. Webber gets to the heart and soul of Broughton's preaching:

> Dr. Broughton was not the first American who filled a London pulpit, but few have attracted the attention he did. In a day when it was customary for the majority of London's clergymen to take at least a neutral attitude toward biblical criticism and the New Theology, later known as Modernism, Dr. Broughton did not hesitate for a moment to make his theological position clear. He took it for granted that Genesis is of Mosaic authorship, that the world was created as the Bible states, that the

Book of Isaiah was written by Isaiah. . . . He believed in eternal life for the true believer and endless punishment for the wicked and the unbelieving. Once more the people of London flocked across Westminster Bridge, almost as they had done in the days of Spurgeon, whose Metropolitan Tabernacle was not far from Dr. Broughton's church.[2]

Broughton preached the Second Coming of the Messiah and an end-time scenario in which the Jews return to Palestine and come to Christ (Romans 11).[3] His style was electrifying and explosive. He preached the old-time religion with great charm and warmth. "Possessed of a ringing voice of pleasant quality, he won men instantly by his preaching . . . His eloquence had a note of the Southern grandiloquence now and then."[4] Clear outlines were not his forte; rather, he made use of the dramatic story, "the American anecdote."

Analysis of his sermons shows them to be no models of tight organization, but the great personal magnetism of the preacher leaps off the printed page. Contagious warmth and pastoral tenderness radiate from "He Lifted Him Up" from Mark 9:26–27 and from "The Cup of Cold Water" from Matthew 10:42.[5] Pungent address to practical issues emanates from "Forgiveness" out of Matthew 18:21; genuine exegetical analysis is evident in "The Things That Defile" from Mark 7:15.[6] He argued emphatically that great preaching and great practice must be in parallel. Loved at Northfield as much as in the Bible belt in the deep South, Leonard Broughton was an unusual preacher who made a remarkable impact.

---

1. Among the strong preachers who led the Baptist Tabernacle on to even greater heights was John W. Ham, whose unusually fine preaching is reflected in his *Present-Tense Salvation* (Chicago: Moody, 1927) and in *Good News for All Men* (New York: Doubleday, Doran, 1928). These sermons are well outlined and illustrate what became the dominating type of sermon in Southern Baptist preaching—the stirring evangelistic or kerygmatic sermon.
2. F. R. Webber, *A History of Preaching in Britain and America* (Milwaukee: Northwestern, 1957), 3:565.
3. Len G. Broughton, *Where Are the Dead?* (Atlanta: Phillips-Boyd, n.d.). His *Revival of a Dead Church* is famous.
4. Webber, *A History of Preaching,* 3:566.
5. Len G. Broughton, *Christianity and the Common Place* (London: Hodder and Stoughton, 1914), 23ff., 41ff.
6. Ibid., 105ff., 119ff.

12.2.5 GEORGE W. TRUETT—TAKING A STAND IN THE OPEN SPACES OF TEXAS

When I see the varied temperaments and relative needs of my church members, sermons come to me like birds in flocks. [Yet "His preaching always leaves the impression that it is founded on and fortified by the Word of God."—Powhatan W. James]

I have sought and found the shepherd's heart.

Think of a preacher being a moral coward! We are to be willing to pay the price for spiritual power. It is a great price. We must be crucified with Christ. We must die to self. We must live unto the Lord without evasion or reservation, if we are to be the witnesses, the prophets, the advocates of the Gospel of Christ that we ought to be . . . What manner of men preachers should be! Good men. Not goody good men. Good men. God's men, impassioned and empowered by the living Spirit. What manner of men we ought to be!

—George W. Truett

The distinguished historian Douglas Southall Freeman wrote of **George W. Truett** (1867–1944), "It would be difficult to exaggerate the influence of Dr. Truett's positive preaching on American ministers in a critical age."[1] Truett was born in Clay County in the rugged blue hills of North Carolina, the seventh child of a farmer, Charles Truett and his wife, Mary. He and his siblings attended Hayesville Academy because the parents desperately wanted their progeny well educated. Because his brother Spurgeon was deaf and was taught to lip-read, young George developed unusually good enunciation.[2]

In his childhood, "the big-faced boy of Charlie Truett," as he was known, gave an eloquent oration on the death of a pet squirrel.[3] He was converted in a revival meeting. He started to teach school and established a successful academy but moved with his parents when they emigrated to Texas. Folk frequently asked him, "Oughtn't you to be preaching?" The church in Whitewright, Texas, moved to ordain him. At first he objected, but finally yielded when he realized that God was indeed calling him to preach.

In 1890, B. H. Carroll (cf. 10.4.4) approached him to raise funds for the almost defunct Baylor College. Young Truett virtually lived with the Carrolls during this time and indeed saved Baylor (and the seminary, which moved to Fort Worth and is now known as Southwestern Baptist Seminary). From 1893 to 1897, he studied at Baylor and served as a student pastor in East Waco. When he graduated from Baylor, the First Baptist Church of Dallas (with 715 members) called him. He served that great church for forty-four years, leading them to seven thousand members and an enlarged auditorium seating four thousand persons.

Accidentally killing his best friend, the sheriff of Dallas County, in a hunting mishap, almost drove Truett from the ministry. He went on with the support of God, his wife and family, and strong friends like the gifted preacher and executive of Texas Baptists, J. B. Gumbrell.[4] He preached to cowboys and in evangelistic crusades around the world. Three times he was president of the Southern Baptist Convention (1927–1929) and of the Baptist World Alliance (1934). Still, First Baptist of Dallas was his home and haven.

Known as the "devout dogmatist," Truett always preached Christ crucified. Books were his hobby. He averaged one sermon or lecture per day for forty years. The tall, raw-boned preacher was popular on college and seminary campuses. His preaching was like a cavalry charge; his "short, smashing sentences" were well suited to Texas. His eyes were "blue-gray . . . his voice was pleading and clear as a bell."[5] Yet the Bible in its perfection and power was basic to everything he did.

Truett preached to the troops in Europe both before and after the armistice. He preached an annual two-week revival in his own church, and the noon services in a theater broke new ground in evangelism and outreach. Together with Merton Rice of Detroit (cf. 11.6.1 note 2) Truett was among the leaders in "America's Preaching Mission" in 1936 and 1937.

Yet unlike his successor, W. A. Criswell, Truett was not expository. He preached the main thought of his text but did little exegesis. His biographer explains:

> He will be accorded this place in the Hall of Fame, not for profundity of thought, nor brilliance of rhetoric, or originality of exegesis, nor cleverness of homiletics, but for his simplicity of language, his singleness of purpose, force of delivery, depth of compassion, ability to reach humanity's heart and will, and power to exalt Christ as Savior and Lord. It will be said of him as he said of Spurgeon: "The pulpit was his throne and he occupied it like a king."[6]

Truett's gestures were limited. His titles were simple and seldom announced beforehand. He put his notes for preaching on the back of envelopes with his personal abbreviations. "He trusts his memory and it seldom betrays him. He prefers to stumble a bit, if need be, with repetitions and inverted sentences, rather than to fall back on his written notations."[7] Yet he could be dazzlingly eloquent, as when he spoke to fifteen thousand on the steps of the United States Capitol on "Baptists and Religious Liberty."[8]

Truett's pastoral prayers were especially powerful. His outlines were sound, but his written sermons cannot begin to match the charm of what was preached. His basic pattern was to prompt the audience to think, move them to feel, and motivate them to choose.[9] Explanation and argumentation were not large parts of his style. Yet the George W. Truett Library, with its 108 sermons and fifteen hundred pages of his preaching, is well worth owning and perusing. He never preached in series, but his messages on the person and work of Christ in *Who Is Jesus?* are typical.[10] In sample Old Testament sermons as found in *On Eagle Wings,* two messages on the Word are particularly moving—"The Bible Lost and Found" from 2 Kings 22:8 and "Mutilating God's Word" from Jeremiah 36:23.[11]

All of these sermons are replete with strong, winning illustrations and good application. The focus always shifts to commitment to Christ before bridging to the public invitation. His son-in-law biographer phrased it well: "He was gifted with access to the human heart."[12]

---

1. Powhatan W. James, *George W. Truett* (Nashville: Broadman, 1939), viii.
2. Ibid., 17–18.
3. Ibid., 22.
4. Al Fasol, *With a Bible in Their Hands: Baptist Preaching in the South 1679–1979* (Nashville: Broadman, 1994), 102ff.

5. James, *George W. Truett*, 105.
6. Ibid., 235.
7. Ibid., 249.
8. Ibid., 1.
9. Ibid., 255.
10. George W. Truett, *Who Is Jesus?* (Grand Rapids: Baker, 1952).
11. George W. Truett, *On Eagle Wings* (Grand Rapids: Baker, 1953), 65ff., 77ff.
12. James, *George W. Truett*, 246.

12.2.6 ROBERT G. LEE—TAKING A STAND FOR THE BIBLE IN THE MID-SOUTH AND BORDER STATES

> The Bible is our greatest national asset—that supreme Book, supernatural in its origin, divine in authorship, human in penmanship, infallible in authority, inexhaustive in its adequacy, a miracle book of diversity in unity, infinite in scope, universal in interest, eternal in duration, personal in application, inspired in totality, regenerative in power, inestimable in value, immeasurable in power, unsurpassed in literary beauty, unequalled in simplicity of expression, immortal in its hopes, the masterpiece of God.
>
> —Robert G. Lee

Preaching has always enjoyed primacy in the Southern Baptist Convention.[1] No one exemplifies the old-time Southern Baptist preacher better than **Robert G. Lee** (1886–1978). Lee was born in a log cabin where his devout parents were sharecroppers who earned an annual wage of $250. He was educated in a one-room school and was converted in a protracted revival meeting in 1898.[2] He had a passion for reading but was obsessed with the Book of all books. When Lee heard Dr. Edwin Poteat, president of Furman University, preach, he sensed God's call.[3] Attempting to raise funds to go to college, he went to work on the Panama Canal and almost died of black fever. Returning to graduate from Furman in 1913, he served twelve student pastorates and grew in his reputation as a preacher. Studying further at Tulane, Lee was offered the Latin chair at Furman but declined it because the school stipulated he could not pastor and teach.

In 1918 Lee took the call to First Baptist Church in Edgefield, South Carolina, where Senator Strom Thurmond's father, the district attorney, was a member. Here for the first time he gave his famous sermon, "Pay Day, Some Day," which he preached one thousand times. It is the narrative of Ahab and Naboth's vineyard in eight scenes. At this time he completed a doctoral degree in law by correspondence at the Chicago Law School. Starting in 1921, he spent sixteen months at First Baptist in Chester, South Carolina, where he introduced tent revivals and many other innovations. Four hundred and fifteen members were added to the church while he preached there. On one day alone, five thousand people saw him baptize 120 converts.

In 1922 Lee began a ministry at First Baptist Church, New Orleans (where Dr. J. D. Grey and others were to have such distinguished ministries). But he worked himself into a breakdown of health and needed a ten-week reprieve in which to recover. In 1925 he took the Citadel Square Baptist Church of Charleston, where E. C. Dargan had served. Despite a struggle with the church's debt, a revival broke out.[4]

By 1927 he began what would be a thirty-two-year pastorate at the Belleview Baptist Church in Memphis, Tennessee. The church took in 600 new members in his first year, and he built the membership to 6,106 by 1942. Lee was a dutiful pastor and visited constantly to win souls. He taught the men's Bible class forty-four Sundays of the year, wrote thirty books, traveled widely, and served as president of the Southern Baptist Convention for three terms.

Yet with all of this, preaching had priority for Robert G. Lee. He was at his best when he was preaching about Jesus Christ![5] Twenty-five percent of his sermons were about the atoning work of Christ on Calvary; two-thirds were textual-topical. The sermons of Talmage and Edwin Poteat shaped his style. His forty-five-minute sermons were ornate, much like Halford Luccock's "confectioner's sermon." He had a vast vocabulary and used alliteration adeptly, speaking about 110 words per minute.[6] As Paul Gericke observes in his study of Lee's preaching, Lee was "attracted to the English language—he gave special attention to the meaning of words and the construction of sentences." His titles were unique like "A Grand Canyon of Resurrection Realities"; "Glory Today for Conquest Tomorrow" (from Matt. 17:1–7, 14–18); "The Menace of Mediocrity"; "When We Bleed, We Bless"; "Chasing Fleas and Dead Dogs" (from 1 Sam. 24:14); and "Boo!" (from Ezek. 25:3–4).

A typical sermon is "Christ Above All," which he based on the thought of John 3:32. His outline was:

  I. Christ is above all as to His Source;
  II. Christ is above all in relation to Creation;
  III. Christ is above all in the way he made entrance into the world;
  IV. Christ is above all as to his revelation of God;
  V. Christ is above all in his supernatural power;
  VI. Christ is above all in his teaching;
  VII. Christ is above all in his sacrificial suffering;
  VIII. Christ is above all in his relation to death;
  IX. Christ is above all as to his promised return.[7]

What is missed in Lee and some other Southern Baptist preaching is suggested by Gericke: "Lee understood New Testament Greek but not Hebrew. However, he did not use it much in his study. . . . He did not study commentaries much, but when he did, he favored the commentaries of Matthew Henry and Jamieson, Fausset and Brown."[8]

What Lee did read was sermons, endless sermons, and literature generally, which tended to inflate his style. Neither was his style sufficiently enriched with strong exegesis. After considerable "picturizing" of the sermon, Lee preached it without notes. Gericke characterizes Lee's strong points as being clarity, energy, elegance, imagination, and humor.[9]

Robert G. Lee was a powerful influence for the historic gospel, but there is little digging into Scripture in this preaching.[10] We read Lee not as a model but as an example of a period piece.

---

1. O. Eugene Mims, "The Importance of Biblical Preaching in Southern Baptist Churches," *Proclaim,* 1994, 4ff. There was some poison in the water even after the Toy affair. Fasol shows how E. Y. Mullins, longtime president of Southern Baptist Seminary, Louisville, was influenced by Schleiermacher (see *With a Bible in Their Hands,* Nashville: Broadman, 1994), 99; cf. E. Y. Mullins, *Why Is Christianity True?* (Philadelphia: American Baptist Publication Society, 1905); for a study of the Mullins Preaching Lectures at Southern Seminary, see Don M. Aycock, *The E. Y. Mullins Lectures on Preaching with Reference to the Aristotelian Triad* (Washington, D.C.: University Press of America, 1980).
2. John E. Huss, *Robert G. Lee* (Grand Rapids: Zondervan, 1967), 29. E. Schuyler English wrote an earlier study.
3. Al Fasol, *With a Bible in Their Hands: Baptist Preaching in the South 1679–1979* (Nashville: Broadman, 1994), 116.
4. Huss, *Robert G. Lee,* 123.
5. Ibid., 141, 144.
6. Paul Gericke, *The Preaching of Robert G. Lee* (Orlando: Christ for the World Publishers, 1967), 98ff.
7. Clarence S. Roddy, ed., *We Prepare and Preach* (Chicago: Moody, 1959), 86ff.
8. Gericke, *The Preaching of Robert G. Lee,* 119.
9. Ibid., 140ff. One of Lee's successors, Adrian Rogers, is more exegetical; see *The Secret of Supernatural Living* (Nashville: Thomas Nelson, 1982). Belleview has relocated and has more than thirteen thousand members.
10. For sample collections of sermons, see Robert G. Lee, *This Critical Hour* (Grand Rapids: Zondervan, 1942); *Great Is the Lord* (New York: Revell, 1955). Doctrinally sound preaching on justification and the return of our Lord—but there is little exegesis.

12.2.7 ROBERT THOMAS KETCHAM—WARRIOR FOR CHRIST

The scriptural injunction is, "Be ready to give an answer to everyone that asketh for the hope that lies in you"; and when a man is asked in all Christian courtesy if he believes that Jesus Christ is God, pre-existent with the Father and born of a virgin, and that His death upon the cross bore the wrath of God against our sins, and he refuses to answer, he cannot blame his questioner if he assumes that his reason for silence is due to the fact that he does not believe it.

—R. T. Ketcham

All of the mainline denominations were facing the massive inroads of liberalism. Nowhere was the battle hotter than in the Northern Baptist Convention as W. B. Riley, J. C. Masse, and Cortland Myers led the champions of the fundamentals. Leading for the liberals were Cornelius Woelfkin and Harry Emerson Fosdick.[1]

Coming up out of the trenches as point man for the conservatives was **Robert Thomas Ketcham** (1889–1978). Ketcham was born in modest circumstances in a Methodist home in Nelson, Pennsylvania. His mother died when he was seven, and his father married a Baptist widow. Hence, in the providence of God, the children were raised Baptist. Leaving home as a rebel when he was sixteen, young Ketcham nonetheless yielded to Christ in meetings at Galeton Baptist when he became enamored with messages by W. W. Rugh on the types in the tabernacle in the Old Testament.[2]

Surrendering his life to Christ, at age twenty-three Ketcham took a call to pastor the Roulette Baptist Church, comprised of twenty-eight women and five old men. His first message was out of Matthew 1 in which he found an extra virgin birth.[3] He had only two books in his library: his Scofield Bible and a volume of sermons for special occasions. Ketcham gave himself to a study of the cults which were thriving about him and started correspondence courses at Crozer, a Baptist seminary. Quickly he learned of liberal advances in the convention and saw them even at his own ordination council.[4]

In the thirty-four months he was at Roulette, six hundred percent growth occurred as the membership moved up to two hundred. Yet already his chronic eye problems, which would finally leave him blind, were apparent. Throughout his ministry, he memorized his text and the hymns and then pretended to read. Occasionally he held his Bible upside-down.

In 1915 Ketcham moved to First Baptist, Brookeville, Pennsylvania, where he had a fine ministry and wrote a pamphlet challenging the New World Movement, a unified budget program of the convention. W. B. Riley was so impressed he ordered twenty thousand copies. Taking the call to First Baptist in Butler, Pennsylvania, Ketcham became more and more embroiled in the liberal/fundamentalist controversy. About this time his first wife died, leaving him with two daughters. He later remarried, and to that union one son was born.

In one convention after another, the conservatives were outfoxed or defeated. Serving in Niles, Ohio, and then at First Baptist in Elyria, Ohio, following R. E. Neighbor, Ketcham was increasingly recognized as an able spokesman for historic Christianity. After the 1927 convention in Chicago, Ketcham saw the handwriting on the wall and told Riley, "I am never coming back."[5] He left the convention.

In 1932 the Ketchams took up a new ministry at Central Baptist Church in Gary, Indiana, following William Ward Ayer. Here he was part of the leadership of the new General Association of Regular Baptists (GARB). Total separatism did not end the turmoil, as Ketcham and J. Frank Norris (who pastored First Baptist, Fort Worth, and Temple Baptist, Detroit, simultaneously) continued to feud for many years. In 1939, when young Pastor P. B. Chenault was killed, Ketcham became pastor of the Walnut Street Baptist Church of Waterloo, Iowa, where God mightily blessed the Word. In 1948, though virtually blind, he was appointed national representative of the GARB. For his remaining years he sustained an amazing profile of activity and ministry even in seriously declining health, preaching as much as 283 times a year.

R. T. Ketcham was a preacher of unusual charm and effectiveness. He could be tender but was always tough-minded. He was hard-hitting but from the heart. His famous series on the Twenty-third Psalm titled "I Shall Not Want" must stand among the classic sermons preached on the shepherd psalm. His illustrations were riveting and revealing. But like some other gifted preachers, Ketcham was not always reflective on the preaching process—indeed, he occasionally disparaged homiletics.[6] When he stayed with a text he was outstanding, but occasionally he rambled, speaking the truth but not supporting it with sound hermeneutics. Several of his published sermons show this weakness.[7] Yet anyone who heard him preach could only concede that he was eminently able.

---

1. Harry Emerson Fosdick (1878–1969) was unusually gifted as a preacher but was in no sense biblical. He testified: "The stereotyped routine into which old-fashioned expository preaching had fallen was impossible to me, i.e. the elucidation of a scriptural text, its application and then exhortation." See Lionel Crocker, *Harry Emerson Fosdick's Art of Preaching: An Anthology* (Springfield: Charles C. Thomas, 1971). His espousal of "life-situation preaching," which does not begin with the Bible, is a method not unpopular among evangelicals today. The theoretical base for this approach can best be traced in the works of Charles F. Kemp; see *The Preaching Pastor* (St. Louis: Bethany Press, 1966). Kemp's example sermons have two sermons by Fosdick.
2. J. Murray Murdoch, *Portrait of Obedience* (Schaumburg, Ill.: Regular Baptist Press, 1979), 24f. I am indebted to my doctoral student Gilbert Parker for this book.
3. Ibid., 31.
4. Ibid., 47.
5. Ibid., 117.
6. Ibid., 248.
7. R. T. Ketcham, "Did You Leave Something on the Stairs?" in Murdoch, *Portrait of Obedience,* 301ff. This is an allegorization of the Song of Solomon every bit equal to that of Bernard of Clairvaux; see also "The Course and End of Satan's World System," in Warren W. Wiersbe, *Classic Sermons on Spiritual Warfare* (Peabody, Mass.: Hendrickson, 1992), 29ff. This is a powerful statement of truth, but when a sermon is not text-driven, we sacrifice the clear advantage of the most effective demonstration of biblical truth; see Walter C. Kaiser Jr., "The Crisis in Expository Preaching Today," *Preaching* (September/October 1995): 4ff.

12.3 SCHOLARS AND TEACHERS WHO STOOD IN THE BREACH

The postmodernist rejection of objectivity pervades the evangelical Church . . . This downplaying of doctrine and objective thinking . . . This openness to personal feelings and experience is a point of contact with postmodernism, which has gone on to exaggerate the role of subjectivity beyond anything that a "hot gospeler" of the nineteenth century would ever recognize.

—Gene Edward Veith Jr.

Subjectivity is in vogue as we head into the new millennium. A. E. Garvie had protested, "In view of many tendencies towards an excessive subjectivity, what needs to be asserted is that the Christ of the faith of the Church is a constant objective reality, and that the preacher is Christian only as he recognizes and respects the distinctiveness of the faith he preaches as historical."[1] Likewise, the patriarch of American evangelical theologians, Carl F. H. Henry, laments "the loss of the objective reality of God and the objective truth of His revelation, which has been replaced in our society by a looming skepticism and a despairing hedonism."[2]

The emphasis today is mood, not mind. We have opinions but not facts. In the face of this drift, many scholars and teachers among conservatives have stood steadfastly and resolutely for the truth, often taking their stand along the lines of the Lausanne Covenant:

> We affirm the divine inspiration, truthfulness and authority of both Old and New Testament Scriptures in their entirety as the only written word of God, without error in all that it affirms and the only infallible rule of faith and practice.

Few wrote more cogently or compellingly than did Francis Schaeffer of L'Abri Fellowship in words that point to the watershed issue for biblical preaching:

> There is the danger of evangelicalism becoming less than evangelical, of its not really holding to the Bible as being without error in all that it affirms. We are then left with the victory of the existential methodology under the name of evangelicalism. Holding to a strong view of Scripture or not holding to it is the watershed of the evangelical world.[3]

We now look at several representatives of the learned academy who used the pulpit as well as the classroom for the articulation of "the faith once for all delivered."

---

1. A. E. Garvie, *The Christian Preacher* (New York: Scribner's, 1923), 278. Garvie's own call came while he was reading Stalker's *Life of Paul,* "and there came home to me the world's need of the preacher. As though I heard a voice, the words possessed my mind—'Woe be to me if I preach not the Gospel'—I sat down and wrote my decision to my Father." From Ralph G. Turnbull, *A Minister's Obstacles* (Grand Rapids: Baker, 1946).
2. Carl F. H. Henry, *Chicago Tribune,* November 20, 1982, 17.
3. Francis A. Schaeffer, *No Final Conflict: The Bible Without Error in All that It Affirms* (Downers Grove, Ill.: InterVarsity Press, 1975), 48. Schaeffer himself came to Christ in a tent meeting where he went forward; see Louis Gifford Parkhurst, *Francis Schaeffer: The Man and the Message* (Wheaton, Ill.: Tyndale House, 1985). He was an able preacher, and a selection of his sermons, *No Little People* (Downers Grove, Ill.: InterVarsity Press, 1974) shows he is biblical but not text-driven.

12.3.1 PETER TAYLOR FORSYTH—CONTENDING FOR THE BIBLE AND ITS AUTHORITY

> The key to history is the historic Christ above history, and in command of it, and there is no other.

> Preaching is the Gospel prolonging and declaring itself. The gift of God's grace was, and is, his work of Gospel. And it is this Act which is prolonged in the word of the preacher and not merely declared.

> There is penalty and curse for sin, and Christ consented to enter that region . . . Christianity is not the sacrifice we make but the sacrifice we trust. An undogmatic Christianity is a contradiction in terms.
>
> —P. T. Forsyth

The brilliant **Peter Taylor Forsyth** (1848–1921) has a slot in the history of preaching not only as a fine preacher and a theorist of preaching (in his Beecher Lectures at Yale in 1907 titled *Positive Preaching and the Modern Mind*) but also as a liberal who turned back to Christ and the Bible. He became a pillar and a rock for the faith. Listen to him lamenting the "lost note of authority" in the contemporary church:

> Without a real authority Protestantism is not only a blunder but deserves to be a failure. We need an authority more than anything else . . . There is only one thing greater than liberty, and that is authority.[1]

Forsyth was notoriously reticent about his personal life, but we know he was born in Aberdeen, Scotland, the son of very poor people. He never knew birthdays or presents in his upbringing but was brought up devoutly and joined the Blackfriars Street Congregational Church. Always physically precarious, he was a brilliant student at Aberdeen, where he studied under Andrew Fairbairn, and he went to Germany to study under Ritschl at Gottingen. He lapped up Ritschl's subjectivity in doctrine and returned to England to serve several churches.[2] While he was at Leicester he realized the bankruptcy of liberalism and moved from "being a Christian to being a believer, from being a lover of love to an object of grace."[3] He then served Emmanuel Congregational Church in Cambridge, a low ebb time for him with the death of his wife, and was made principal of Hackney College in 1901, teaching at the University of London at the same time.

His theological conversion was profound. He returned to orthodoxy and defended the gospel against R. J. Campbell and the New Theology. His critique of liberalism was devastating. As a liberal he had denied substitution in the Atonement, but now stressing the centrality of the cross, he insisted on "the need of an objective expiatory idea of the Atonement."[4] He felt that the pulpit in nonconformity had lost its power "because it has lost intimacy with the Cross, immersion in the Cross."[5] Forsyth asserted the radicality of evil and felt that Americans tended to a Pelagian superficiality in thinking about sin. His ripest work was probably his masterpiece on *The Person and Place of Jesus Christ*.[6]

Basic in all of this was his insistence on the priority and authority of the Word of God. Conservative German scholars such as Adolph Schlatter now weighed heavily with Forsyth. Coupled with his resurgent orthodoxy was the conviction that "a man's life is seen at the level of his prayer life."[7] Yet Forsyth still retained some vestiges of liberal thinking, most especially his universalism. Soren Kierkegaard also influenced him.

Forsyth wrote twenty-five books. Always epigrammatic in his writing and preaching, he was sharp-featured with a "fine forehead, with a large moustache and deep piercing eyes."[8] Donald Miller says that trying to follow the majestic stream of Forsyth's thought is like standing beside Niagara with a tin cup.[9] Forsyth felt that the great danger of the preacher was in so preaching *to* their age they might well *preach* their age. He urged preachers to take a substantial piece of text for their expository sermons. We possess few of Forsyth's sermons, and so it is difficult to know how well he practiced his own counsel.[10] Of this we are sure: his stand for Christ and Scripture was unexpected and is still influential. He said:

> How can we hope to regain the influence the pulpit has lost until we come with the surest Word in all the world to the guesses of science, the maxims of ethics, and the instincts of art.[11]

1. Robert McAfee Brown, *P. T. Forsyth: Prophet for Today* (Philadelphia: Westminster, 1952), 94. Archbishop Donald Coggan's intriguing endorsement of Forsyth's lectures, "Under-estimated Theological Books" in his *Christian Priorities* (New York: Harper and Row, 1963), 149ff. Coggan's ringing conservatism is a great encouragement.

2. To assay this, see Albrecht Ritschl, *The Christian Doctrine of Justification and Reconciliation* (Edinburgh: T & T Clarke, 1900); for a sympathetic view, see Albert T. Swing, *The Theology of Albrecht Ritschl* (New York: Longmans, 1901).

3. Robert S. Paul, "P. T. Forsyth: Prophet for the Twentieth Century," in *P. T. Forsyth* (Pittsburgh: Pickwick, 1981), 63. He traces this radical move from liberalism in *Positive Preaching and the Modern Mood* (281–85).

4. Ibid., 57. A. M. Hunter also shows how Forsyth retained the penal idea; see *P. T. Forsyth* (London: SCM, 1974), 120.

5. P. T. Forsyth, *The Cruciality of the Cross* (Grand Rapids: Eerdmans, 1909). The issue: sympathy or salvation?

6. P. T. Forsyth, *The Person and Place of Jesus Christ* (Grand Rapids: Eerdmans, 1909). A sad example of a Scottish professor who went to more liberal and concessive thinking would be the prolific and often helpful William Barclay (1907–1978). N.B. Clive L. Rawlins, *William Barclay* (Grand Rapids: Eerdmans, 1984); also William Barclay, *A Spiritual Autobiography* (Grand Rapids: Eerdmans, 1975). His commentaries are homiletically pregnant but antisupernatural (he holds the "little brown paper bag theory" on feeding the five thousand and denies the Virgin Birth).

7. P. T. Forsyth, *The Soul of Prayer* (Grand Rapids: Eerdmans, 1916). Some have waxed eloquent that Forsyth was "Barth before Barth," but while they both rediscovered sin, Barth would never have extolled biblical authority like this.

8. Hunter, *P. T. Forsyth,* 21.

9. Donald G. Miller, *P. T. Forsyth: The Man* (Pittsburgh: Pickwick, 1981), 16.

10. P. T. Forsyth, *Revelation Old and New: Sermons and Addresses* (London: Independent Press, 1962).

11. P. T. Forsyth, *Positive Preaching and the Modern Mind* (Pittsburgh: Pickwick, repr. 1981), 184.

12.3.2 J. Gresham Machen—Contending for Historic Orthodoxy

The Bible is not a ladder; it is a foundation. It is buttressed, indeed, by experience; if you have the present Christ, then you know that the Bible account is true. But if the Bible were false, your faith would go. You cannot, therefore, be indifferent to biblical criticism. Let us not deceive ourselves. The Bible is at the foundation of the Church. Undermine that foundation and the Church will fall. Two conceptions of Christianity are struggling for the ascendancy; the question that we have been discussing is part of a still larger problem. The Bible against the modern preacher. . . . The Church is in perplexity. She is trying to compromise. God grant that she may choose aright. God grant she may decide for the Bible!

—J. Gresham Machen

We have already introduced **J. Gresham Machen** (1881–1937) as one of the key figures in the pitched battle between modernism and historic orthodoxy (cf. 11.4). He belongs in the body of this study not only because of his immense and impressive scholarship, but also because he was a believer in preaching.

Machen was a brilliant teacher who was early stirred by the preaching of Dr. Hoge and later by Dr. Harris Kirk at his home church, Franklin Street Presbyterian Church in Baltimore. Hesitating over his vocation, he felt called to go to Princeton, where he learned preaching under David J. Burrell and was grounded in the Word under B. B. Warfield and Francis Patton (who had prosecuted David G. Swing in 1874).[1] He went on to study at Gottingen and Marburg in Germany and felt the attraction of the liberalism of Julicher at the former and William Hermann's Ritschlianism at the latter, but he held his ground.[2] He hoped to do more study in Germany, but his mother was worried he would lose his faith. He therefore took the opportunity at Princeton Seminary to be the junior colleague of Professor William Park Armstrong in New Testament. His earliest efforts at preaching put his listeners to sleep, but he was soon infected with a great love for preaching, particularly the Old Testament.[3]

Machen early on took a strong stand for inerrancy, and his brilliant scholarship earned him widespread respect. He used Galatians in exegesis, and his classic text in beginning Greek has been the guide for thousands of expositors over the years.[4] Unafraid to take on the hard questions, Machen was yet sensitive to the cultural issues. He observed, "The great questions may easily be avoided . . . many preachers are avoiding them."[5]

As early as 1914 signs of Princeton being on the slippery slope were discernible, but by and large the church was indifferent to this bold prophet's warnings.

His detractors spoke of his "high-brow fundamentalism." He did associate with W. B. Riley and the WCFA and spoke to them, though he was not a member.[6] He spoke also at Northfield and had a sympathetic view of Billy Sunday even though a greater contrast between two servants of Christ can hardly be imagined.[7]

Machen began to want to preach more widely. He appreciated Jowett in New York City but blanched at what Parkhurst, Coffin, and Fosdick were doing with Scripture. Around the time of World War I, he left Princeton to work for the YMCA in France. In 1924 he returned to the battle for the soul of Princeton and stood with Clarence Macartney of Arch Street Presbyterian Church in Philadelphia in the General Assembly. The fundamentalists faced Fosdick, who had just put forth his nasty sermon, "Shall the Fundamentalists Win?" and the thirteen hundred signers of the Auburn Affirmation, which attacked inerrancy and viewed all doctrinal formulation as theorization.[8]

In the inevitable reorganization of the seminary, Machen was out. With others he founded Westminster Seminary and the Independent Board of Foreign Missions, which ultimately led to his ecclesiastical trial in 1936 and his expulsion. He was never given a chance to defend his views. In the following year he died of pneumonia at the untimely age of fifty-six while on a preaching tour in Bismarck, North Dakota.

A steady stream of his powerful books, published chiefly by mainline secular houses, kept coming through all of those difficult years. His *What Is Faith?* (1925) argued effectively against the separation of religious experience from theology.[9] A sparkling series of radio addresses show how serious theology can be communicated.[10] The collection of his major addresses has many treasures.[11] Dr. Stonehouse has done all of us a great service in gathering some of the choice sermons together, including significant messages on such subjects as "God Transcendent" from Isaiah 40:22, "The Gospel and Modern Substitutes" from Romans 1:16, and "The Separateness of the Church" from Matthew 5:13. The sermons are not long and show a simple organizational schema.[12] When Machen left Princeton, he encapsulated his experience:

> If you decide to stand for Christ, you will not have an easy life in the ministry . . . You will graciously be permitted to believe in supernatural Christianity all you please if you will only act as though you did not believe in it, if you will only make common cause with its opponents. Such is the program that will win the favor of the church. A man may believe what he pleases, provided he does not believe anything strongly enough to risk his life on it and fight for it. "Tolerance" is the great word. Men may ask for tolerance when they look to God in prayer. But how can any Christian possibly pray such a prayer as that? What a terrible prayer it is, how full of disloyalty to the Lord Jesus Christ.[13]

---

1. Ned B. Stonehouse, *J. Gresham Machen: A Biographical Memoir* (Grand Rapids: Eerdmans, 1954), 64.
2. Ibid., 105.

3. D. G. Hart, *Defending the Faith: J. Gresham Machen and the Crisis of Conservative Protestantism in Modern America 1881–1937* (Grand Rapids: Baker, 1994), 30.
4. J. Gresham Machen, *New Testament Greek for Beginners* (New York: Macmillan, 1923, 1952). In its twenty-fifth printing.
5. Stonehouse, *J. Gresham Machen,* 188.
6. Hart, *Defending the Faith,* 66. Cf. Mark Noll, ed., *The Princeton Theology 1812–1921* (Grand Rapids: Baker, 1983).
7. Stonehouse, *J. Gresham Machen,* 223. Another strong spokesman for the faith is T. J. McCrossan, *The Bible: Its Christ and Modernism* (New York: Alliance, 1925). He was examiner in Greek and Hebrew for the Presbytery of Minneapolis.
8. Stonehouse, *J. Gresham Machen,* 364. Unaccountably this dastardly sermon is held up as "a model sermon for today's preachers" in Long and Plantinga, *A Chorus of Witnesses* (Grand Rapids: Eerdmans, 1994), 243.
9. Hart, *Defending the Faith,* 91. N.B. J. Gresham Machen, *What Is Faith?* (Grand Rapids: Eerdmans, 1925).
10. J. Gresham Machen, *The Christian Faith in the Modern World* (Grand Rapids: Eerdmans, 1936).
11. J. Gresham Machen, *What Is Christianity?* (Grand Rapids: Eerdmans, 1951). Compare this with von Harnack's *What Is Christianity?* (New York: Putnam's, 1904) and its pabulum of the fatherhood of God and brotherhood of man.
12. J. Gresham Machen, *God Transcendent and Other Sermons* (Grand Rapids: Eerdmans, 1949).
13. David Otis Fuller, *Valiant for Truth: A Treasury of Evangelical Writings* (New York: Lippincot, 1961), 450.

12.3.3 WALTER A. MAIER—CONTENDING FOR GRACE AND MERCY

Culinary clatter and dramatic razzle-dazzle called "church work" are drowning out the testimony of the saving Gospel.

Picture the cancerous growth of modern infidelity as ego-complexed pulpiteers, disguising the breed of the wolf beneath silk cassocks . . . read from the Scriptures with crossed thumbs, tongues in cheek and with mental reservations, who place the Bible on the level with heathen philosophies . . . Think of the smooth, oily surrender of the deity of our Savior . . . I still repeat the cry, "Back to Luther!"

—Walter A. Maier

Time called him "the Chrysostom of American Lutheranism." Billy Graham labeled him the greatest evangelist of this century. Daniel Poling spoke of him as "the preeminent voice of Protestant faith and practice." We know **Walter A. Maier** (1893–1950) as the speaker on "Bringing Christ to the Nations." He was the founder and preacher of this broadcast, which aired on 1,236 stations in 120 countries in thirty-six languages with some twenty million hearers. He was "a preacher of the old-fashioned religion."[1] He also held a doctorate in philosophy in Old Testament and Semitics from Harvard and was a professor at Concordia Seminary in St. Louis.

Maier defended the reliability and trustworthiness of Scripture and preached it with power. He was born in Boston of German immigrant parents. His father was an organ builder. He attended Concordia Collegiate Institute in Westchester County, New York, where he early on loved Latin, Greek, Hebrew, and German.[2] Graduating as valedictorian of his class, he went on to finish his B.A. at Boston University. Maier continued on to Concordia Seminary in St. Louis, where such giants as Franz Pieper and J. Theodore Mueller defended the old gospel, and then on to Harvard Divinity School and Graduate School for his doctoral studies. At this time he won the Billings Prize in Oratory.[3] Imbued with a great heart for missions and evangelism, Maier served for two years as executive secretary of the Walther League, the youth branch of the Missouri Synod.

In 1922 he became professor of Old Testament at Concordia Seminary in St. Louis. There he trumpeted the genuine gospel and the need for a forthright facing of the problem of human sinfulness. He found that his message was in high demand all over the country. Holy Week in 1922, he preached to great throngs in the American Theater Noonday Services and so contemporized the events of the first Holy Week that he spoke "as if he had witnessed them himself."[4]

Maier had a vision for the inner city and helped found St. Stephen's in a blighted area of St. Louis. Then he became the leader of the Lutheran Hour broadcast, which received two hundred thousand letters per week. He filled Soldier's Field in Chicago for a great Lutheran Hour rally and similarly the Hollywood Bowl in 1948. Maier was Lutherlike and potent in his biblical citation. With rapid-fire delivery and vehemence, he opened Scripture and fearlessly applied it. He believed "firmly in a verbally inspired Bible . . . Gifted with an exceptionally keen mind, he had weighed the arguments of the Higher Critics and the Modernists and had come to the conclusion that these men are religious mountebanks."[5] He was a creationist (and we are indebted to the Missouri Synod for such preceptors as Rehwinkel, Zimmerman, and Klotz for scholarship in this area). He challenged the efforts of the modernist Federal Council of Churches to obtain a monopoly on the religious airwaves.[6]

Ordinarily Maier's sermons were two points, problem and solution. His introductions were brief and direct. He used all of the rhetorical tools available to the skilled communicator.[7] He was the author of thirty-one books, including an influential study of marriage, *For Better Not For Worse*. Of his Lutheran Hour sermons, 509 have been published in twenty volumes. "Jesus Christ Is Your God" from John 14 divides into two parts: (1) Believe in God; (2) Believe also in Christ.[8] "Join the Jury Trying Jesus" and "Follow Christ on the Calvary Road" are sterling examples of his preaching. His commentary on Nahum is the best ever done on that great Old Testament book.[9]

This is the heart of a preacher from a liturgical tradition who in the onslaught of liberal and neo-orthodox challenges did not lower the flag. He had defended his doctoral dissertation in a citadel of unbelief before the likes of Robert Pfeiffer and Paul Foot Moore. No wonder both Machen and Maier died at fifty-six! They poured forth their all in loyalty to the historic gospel. Successors like Oswald C. J. Hoffmann would carry on the ministry of the Lutheran Hour.

1. F. R. Webber, *A History of Preaching in Britain and America* (Milwaukee: Northwestern, 1957), 3:594.
2. Paul L. Maier, *A Man Spoke, A World Listened: The Story of Walter Maier* (New York: McGraw, 1963), 17.
3. Ibid., 25.
4. Ibid., 75.
5. Webber, *A History of Preaching,* 3:594.
6. Maier, *A Man Spoke, A World Listened,* 188. Other great radio preachers were Charles E. Fuller, M. R. DeHaan, and Theodore Epp.
7. Ibid., 206–7. Kenneth Hartley Sulston, "A Rhetorical Criticism of the Radio Preaching of Walter Arthur Maier" (doctoral dissertation, Northwestern University, 1958); Lester Erwin Zeitler, "An Investigation of the Factors of Persuasion in the Sermons of Dr. Walter A. Maier" (St. Louis: M.S.T. dissertation, Concordia Seminary, 1956). For a recent sample of Missouri Synod homiletics, see Francis Rossow, *Preaching the Creative Gospel Creatively* (St. Louis: Concordia, 1983).
8. Walter A. Maier, *Global Broadcasting of His Grace* (St. Louis: Concordia, 1949), 88ff.
9. Walter A. Maier, *The Book of Nahum: A Commentary* (St. Louis: Concordia, 1959). A masterpiece. He shows twenty-two respects in which the prophetic predictions of Nahum were historically and actually fulfilled, 114ff.

12.3.4 *A. T. Robertson—Contending for the Bible and Its Accuracy*

Some people appear to rest their minds when they preach.

What on earth can I do that I haven't done to inspire those men to learn this book? What are they thinking about? Why do they not master it? How can they expect to preach the book unless they know it?

The greatest proof that the Bible is inspired is that it has stood so much bad preaching.

Never get out of a text what was never in it.

—A. T. Robertson

For twelve seasons a favorite preacher at the Northfield Conference, whose preaching sent F. B. Meyer into "ecstasies," was **Archibald Thomas Robertson** (1863–1934), or Dr. Bob as he was called. He was a key figure who, as Machen argued, combined "scholarship and popular power" in a trenchant way.[1] Well received at Winona Lake as well, Robertson was a teacher of six thousand students at Southern Baptist Seminary and the author of forty-five books. He preached with his Greek New Testament in his hand—and wore out a dozen of them in the process. In this he resembled the English Quaker, Dr. J. Rendal Harris of Birmingham, who was so scintillating in his expositions.[2]

Robertson was born in Pittsylvania, Virginia, the son of a doctor whose fortune was broken. Young "Archie" moved with his family to North Carolina when he was twelve. He sensed a change of heart in 1876 and was greatly influenced by his pastor, J. B. Boon, who wondered if he had not thought of preaching.[3] Enrolling at Wake Forest College, Robertson tried to overcome a speech impediment. "I am like Demosthenes," he said, "in that I have a hesitation in my speech when I grow nervous." But he entered into debating societies and other activities and became "an impressive speaker." He developed great prowess in Greek, though he tended to overwork himself and was through his lifetime subject to infection and exhaustion.[4]

"He wanted to be a preacher and he became one of the great expository preachers of his day."[5] Entering Southern Baptist Seminary in Louisville in 1885, he "got hold of preaching," and became the much appreciated supply preacher at First Baptist in Covington, Kentucky. Upon his graduation, he was made assistant to John Broadus (cf. 10.4.2) in Greek and homiletics and stayed on at Southern for forty-six years.

Preaching was a vital part of his ongoing ministry. While he deliberately avoided denominational office, Robertson was one of the founders of the Baptist World Alliance. He made several trips to Europe and knew Maclaren, Spurgeon, and Professor Zahn in Leipzig.[6] Although demanding, Robertson was a great teacher with whom "The New Testament became a new and glowing book."[7] In academic circles his work was highly respected, but it was thought he talked too fast and was hyperorthodox. His most significant scholarship was as a philologist and textual critic.

His first writings were the critical notes for Broadus' *Harmony.* He challenged the radical notions of President Harper of the University of Chicago, a fellow Baptist. In 1894 Robertson married the youngest daughter of Dr. John Broadus. Upon the death of Broadus four months later, he was made full professor of New Testament Greek at Southern. Robertson eventually wrote the definitive biography of John A. Broadus.

He advanced from the premise that the Bible is true. In the face of the massive doses of negative higher criticism, the cause of classical biblical Christianity needed scholars who would give their genius to the state of the biblical text as received. This Robertson did in *An Introduction to the Textual Criticism of the New Testament* and his twenty-six-year project, a fifteen-hundred-page "big grammar," *A Grammar of the Greek New Testament in the Light of Historical Research.* Here he argues conclusively, as Rendal Harris had earlier, that the Greek of the New Testament is the koine of the average person and the papyri. His work was praised by Warfield, Zahn, Stalker, Souter, and many others. He knew and worked with Sir William Ramsay, A. H. Sayce, Principal Fairbairn, and Walter Lock. His six-volume work, *Word Pictures in the New Testament,* has assisted many expositors. Twice he gave the Stone Lectures at Princeton, the last of which in 1926 was his splendid *Paul and the Intellectuals: The Epistle to the Colossians.*[8] When he died, he was working on a new translation of the New Testament.

Robertson's written and spoken style befits his ancestral Scottish trait of economy in words, and he never lost his passion for preaching. Early on he tended to be subject-centered, but he became increasingly text-driven. His sermons were described as "spritely" and thus quite consistent with his character. He hated "sham and pretense" and confessed on one occasion that "I have been too ambitious for personal fame."

The death of his daughter, Charlotte, left Robertson devastated with the question as to why the Lord who raised the daughter of Jairus would not raise his daughter, but he yielded, "Not my will but Thine be done." He loved to preach revivals and do evangelism. Some thought him a bit severe because he was so blunt and direct, but he had a delightful sense of humor as he described Deacon Skinflint and Sister Sharp-tongue and Rabbi Smell-fungus and Pastor Dry-as-dust. He exulted in *The Glory of the Ministry* and skillfully delineated *Types of Preachers in the New Testament.* The collection of his sermons demonstrates his ability to use appealing illustration.[9]

Robertson loved to hear great preaching, and he listened with appreciation to Mark Guy Pearse in England and Hugh Black in Scotland. He compared notes with Ellicott, Lightfoot, Alford, Westcott, and Hort at a luncheon it would have been marvelous to attend. Here was a man of valor and virtue who stood steadfastly in a culture on the brink.

---

1. Everett Gill, *A. T. Robertson: A Biography* (New York: Macmillan, 1943), 132.
2. For a sample of J. Rendel Harris' preaching, see *As the Hart Pants* (London: Hodder and Stoughton, 1924).
3. Gill, *A. T. Robertson,* 31.
4. Ibid., 49.
5. Ibid., 50.
6. Ibid., 70.
7. Ibid., 116. A typical book by Robertson, *The Mother of Jesus: Her Problems and Her Glory* (Grand Rapids: Baker, 1963).
8. A. T. Robertson, *Paul and the Intellectuals: The Epistle to the Colossians* (Nashville: Broadman, 1956). In his *Studies in the Text of the New Testament* (New York: George H. Doran, 1969 rep. College Press, Joplin, Mo.), Robertson makes a strong case for the preacher's ongoing reading and studying, 106.
9. A. T. Robertson, *Passing on the Torch and Other Sermons* (New York: Revell, 1934). Particularly impressive are the sermons titled "The One Talent Man" from Matthew 25:13–30 and "Buying Up the Opportunity" from Colossians 4:5 and Ephesians 5:16. Another significant Baptist scholar and preacher was H. Wheeler Robinson (1872–1945), long associated with Regent's Park College in London and Oxford. His works on *The Cross of Job, The Cross of the Servant, The Cross of Jeremiah*, and *The Christian Experience of the Holy Spirit* make some concessions but are homiletically rich. Note Ernest A. Payne, *Henry Wheeler Robinson* (London: Nisbet, 1946). Robinson points out the perennial danger for the preacher when the introduction and exegesis take all of his time and he never "gets to the real sermon" (40).

12.3.5 WILBUR M. SMITH—CONTENDER FOR THE SUPERNATURAL GOSPEL

Wilbur Smith believes that Christians have a supernatural gospel, that it can transform lives through the work of the Holy Spirit, that we learn about it in the inerrant Scriptures, and that it ought to be constantly preached and taught . . . He is a man who tried to apply these principles and has been successful in doing so.

—Paul Woolley

The pulpit was the one place for which I really lived.

—Wilbur Moorehead Smith

One of the century's foremost bibliographers and a bibliophile of the first order, **Wilbur Moorehead Smith** (1894–1977) was a special gift to Bible-believing Christians. As a man of encyclopedic knowledge on many religious subjects and an honored professor at three prestigious evangelical institutions, Smith was a powerful preacher in his own right. His indefatigable reading uncovered a gem by a biographer of E. W. Hengstenberg, who wrote:

> [Hengstenberg] saw that the entire literature of religion stands or falls with the early documents which are its elements and alphabet: that if these individual books were not written by the men to whom the later Scriptures ascribe them—if they do not record facts that are historical— if the New Testament inspiration is not really an approval and guarantee of an Old Testament inspiration—if the Scriptures of the old and new covenants contradict each other—if, in short, there is not a perfect unity in the grand and complete record, then Christianity is undermined and ready to fall, bringing down with it the hopes of mankind.[1]

Smith was born into a wealthy Chicago home. His parents were active in the Moody Church. His father was called the apple king because of his large orchards in Michigan. Yet young Smith had little formal education apart from a brief stint at Moody Bible Institute and a short tenure at Wooster College in Ohio. Upon his marriage, he assumed the pulpit in a series of Presbyterian churches in Wilmington, Delaware; Ocean City and Baltimore, Maryland; Covington, Virginia; and the large Presbyterian church in Coatsville, Pennsylvania (1930–1937). Coatsville was a church of more than eighteen hundred members, where he followed the fine incumbency of Dr. Roy Brumbaugh.[2] In 1933 he preached at Moody Founder's Week in Chicago, the first of seventeen appearances over the years. His gifts as an expositor were increasingly recognized, and he began to write and review for the *Sunday School Times* and to write the commentary on the International Sunday School lesson, which he maintained for thirty-five years. Pastors built their libraries on the bibliographies in *Peloubet's Notes*. His years of teaching at Moody Bible Institute, Fuller Theological Seminary (in English Bible and apologetics), and later at Trinity Evangelical Divinity School were exceedingly positive.[3]

Smith built a personal library of more than thirty thousand volumes and was "tireless" in his reading, writing, and preaching. His burden was what he perceived to be "terrible errors menacing evangelical Christianity today."[4] His primary focus was:

1. The effect of the Bible on history, translations of the Bible, and Bible dictionaries.
2. The defense of the bodily resurrection of Christ. His *Therefore Stand* was a great encouragement in its day.[5]
3. The historicity of Christ's nativity. *The Supernaturalness of Christ: Can We Still Believe in It?* was most timely.[6]
4. The literal interpretation of biblical prophecy. His works on *Egypt in Biblical Prophecy, World Crises and the Prophetic Scriptures,* and *Israeli/Arab Conflict and the Bible* are balanced contributions.[7] His widely praised *The Biblical Doctrine of Heaven* is in a unique category.[8] He owned 284 commentaries on Revelation.
5. The impact of science on Christian faith as in his 1945 study, *The Atomic Bomb and the Word of God.*[9]
6. Preaching and sermons in his editing of the "Great Sermons on" series and his invaluable radio talks for pastors as published cannot conceal his great excitement and enthusiasm for the Word of God and its infinite treasures.[10]
7. The subject of revival, particularly his fine study on the revival in the days of King Hezekiah.[11]

Roger Phillips assesses Smith as a bibliographer, and Smith's own memoirs afford many insights into his friendships and involvements over the years. The close association between Smith and Machen is fascinating.[12] Smith served on the Scofield Bible Revision Committee and was offered the post as first editor of *Christianity Today.*

Always fresh and prepared in the lecture hall or pulpit, Smith impressed some as abrupt and a bit fussy. His "excessive use of superlatives" became a trademark and for some a hindrance. Yet those who got past the somewhat crusty veneer found a wondrously gentle and generous follower of Christ. His wit and humor, his passion in preaching, his rich content impress us with the hard work he put into preaching.[13] Tributes by his colleagues and contemporaries put him into scale.[14] Typical sermons are those he preached at Keswick in England in 1952 on *The Word of God and the Life of Holiness.*[15] These sermons follow no set rules but both burn and bless their readers as they did the listeners who first hung on the words as spoken. In many ways Smith is not to be a model for preachers, but he was always a motivator.

---

1. Wilbur M. Smith, *A Treasury of Books for Bible Study* (Grand Rapids: Baker, 1960), 202. One of the most popular of all Smith's writings and still read is his *Profitable Bible Study* (Boston: W. A. Wilde, 1939).
2. Roger Wendell Phillips, *Wilbur Moorehead Smith: A Profile and Bibliography* (thesis for the M.L.S. degree at Emporia Kansas State College, 1976), 18ff., 84.
3. Smith was one of the four original faculty (the others being Harold Lindsell, Carl F. H. Henry, and Everett F. Harrison). The story of why he left Fuller and one point of view on the changes in Pasadena is given by George Marsden, *Reforming Fundamentalism: Fuller Seminary and the New Evangelicals* (Grand Rapids: Eerdmans, 1987).

4. Phillips, *Wilbur Moorehead Smith*, 6.

5. Wilbur M. Smith, *Therefore Stand: A Plea for a Vigorous Apologetic in This Critical Hour of the Christian Faith* (Boston: W. A. Wilde, 1945). Josh McDowell, in his popular work on the resurrection, quotes this book twenty-three times.

6. Wilbur M. Smith, *The Supernaturalness of Christ: Can We Still Believe in It?* (Boston: W. A. Wilde, 1940).

7. Wilbur M. Smith, *Egypt in Biblical Prophecy* (Boston: W. A. Wilde, 1957); *World Crises and the Prophetic Scriptures* (Chicago: Moody, 1952); *Israeli/Arab Conflict and the Bible* (Glendale, Calif.: Gospel Light, 1967).

8. Wilbur M. Smith, *The Biblical Doctrine of Heaven* (Chicago: Moody, 1968). All of Smith's writing are quite homiletical.

9. Wilbur M. Smith, *The Atomic Bomb and the Word of God* (Chicago: Moody, 1945).

10. Wilbur M. Smith, *Chats from a Minister's Library* (Grand Rapids: Baker, 1951); *The Minister in His Study* (Chicago: Moody, 1973). The latter work is a series of lectures given at Trinity Evangelical Divinity School in 1972.

11. Wilbur M. Smith, *The Glorious Revival under King Hezekiah* (Grand Rapids: Zondervan, 1937).

12. Wilbur M. Smith, *Before I Forget: Memoirs* (Chicago: Moody, 1971). Some remarkable byways in memory lane.

13. Wilbur M. Smith, "No Set Rules," in *We Prepare and Preach,* ed. Clarence S. Roddy (Chicago: Moody, 1959), 160ff.

14. Kenneth Kantzer, ed., *Evangelical Roots: A Tribute to Wilbur Smith* (Nashville: Thomas Nelson, 1979).

15. Wilbur M. Smith, *The Word of God and the Life of Holiness* (Grand Rapids: Zondervan, 1957). I recall hearing Wilbur Smith speak at a seminary convocation in the fall of 1953 on "Preach the Word" from 2 Timothy 4:2, a sermon which will always be for me one of the most dynamic and inspirational expositions I have ever heard.

12.3.6 *Theodor Zahn—Contender for the Integrity of the Word of God*

Men may receive much grace, and yet go forth empty. It is the undeserved grace of reconciliation itself that we have to accept aright. The one gracious Word of God, the love of God, revealed on the Cross, must do all for us; we must accept it again and again, and allow it to work in us that for which it has the power. Then our lives will also show forth the fruits of grace.

—Theodor Zahn

The providential networking of Bible-believing servants of Christ took place all over the world, even in the den of German rationalism (cf. 9.4). An important link in the defense of the gospel was the distinguished New Testament and patristics scholar, **Theodor Zahn** (1838–1933).

Zahn's grandmother, Anna Schlatter, came out of the pietistic "awakening" *(Erweckung)* in St. Gallen, Switzerland.[1] It is interesting to note that the Iron Chancellor himself, Otto Van Bismarck, though caught in the coils of pantheism, professed conversion and read the Bible morning and evening through the influence of his first wife, a Lutheran fundamentalist.[2]

Zahn taught at several universities but chiefly at Erlangen (1892–1909), Leipzig, and Berlin, where A. T. Robertson heard him.[3] Their friendship ripened, and Zahn paid tribute to Robertson's range of knowledge of German literature.[4] Wilbur Smith called Zahn "One of the greatest New Testament scholars of our time," and paid special tribute to his three-volume *Introduction to the New Testament*.[5] Few of his magnificent commentaries have been translated.

In his widely used work, *Introduction to the New Testament*, Henry Clarence Thiessen of Wheaton makes thirty-five references to Zahn. His work on the Greek text and his strong defense of Lucan authorship of the third Gospel and the Book of Acts and Paul's authorship of the Pastorals have been like a guiding star for conservatives.[6] His multivolume history of the canon is superb.

Zahn was university preacher at Gottingen and was eagerly heard at the other universities where he taught. One volume of these sermons has been translated. As a "loyal Lutheran" he used the pericope; the lucidity of his discourse is marvelous. His sermon for Palm Sunday, "The Beauty of Praise," is well divided and does not dodge the difficult issues.[7] His Lenten sermon on "Death in Sin or Death in Grace" is built on the expression found three times on the lips of Jesus in John 8:21–30, "dying in your sins." He admonishes:

> I know well that this is a hard saying, but it is the word of my Lord, who is Lord of us all. Let philosophers philosophize, let poets romance, let fine orators speak of what they do not know and do not believe! But woe be to the Christian preacher, who here in the pulpit, or by the sick-bed, or at the grave, speaks otherwise than he has heard the Lord speak . . . The great alternative: either we die in faith in the Vanquisher of death or we die in our sins.[8]

God has never been without his witness. His faithful messengers have spoken for him even in the greatest of difficulty. May we be so faithful in our time.[9]

---

1. Another influential conservative scholar with the same grandmother was Adolph Schlatter (1852–1938), whose chief goal was "the opening of Scripture" and whose Tubingen sermons were a high priority. He has given us four hundred publications. He appreciated Karl Barth's attention to Romans but lamented his "ahistorical tone, subjectiveness, and irrationality." Werner Neuer, *Adolph Schlatter* (Grand Rapids: Baker, 1995), 135.

2. Edward Crankshaw, *Bismarck* (New York: Viking, 1981), 30.

3. Everett Gill, *A. T. Robertson: A Biography* (New York: Macmillan, 1943), 70.

4. Ibid., 208.

5. Wilbur M. Smith, *Chats from a Minister's Library* (Grand Rapids: Baker, 1951), 134.

6. Henry Clarence Thiessen, *Introduction to the New Testament* (Grand Rapids: Eerdmans, 1954), 35, 149–52, 256–57.

7. Theodor Zahn, *Bread and Salt from the Word of God* (Edinburgh: T & T Clark, 1905), 93ff. Another striking book of published sermons by Zahn is *The Apostle's Creed* (London: Hodder and Stoughton, 1899).
8. Ibid., 59.
9. Another significant German teacher and preacher is Erich Sauer of the Bible School in Wiedenest, Rhineland, Germany. His works include *The Dawn of World Redemption* (commended by F. F. Bruce), *The Triumph of the Crucified, From Eternity to Eternity,* and *The King of the Earth,* translated by G. L. Lang. His sermons on Hebrews 12 titled *In the Arena of Faith: A Call to the Consecrated Life* (Grand Rapids: Eerdmans, 1956) are the highest quality exposition with careful divisions of the text. A prominent French-speaking Swiss preacher was Rene Pache of Emmaus Bible School in Lausanne; his major works, *The Inspiration and Authority of Scripture, The Return of Jesus Christ, The Future Life* and *The Person and Work of the Holy Spirit,* have been circulated in ten languages.

12.3.7 C. S. LEWIS—CONTENDER FOR THE SKEPTICAL MIND

It would seem that Our Lord finds our desires not too strong, but too weak. We are half-hearted creatures, fooling around with drink and sex and ambition when infinite joy is offered us, like an ignorant child who wants to go on making mud pies in a slum because he cannot imagine what is meant by the offer of a holiday at sea. We are far too easily pleased.

—C. S. Lewis

What an extraordinary gift to classical biblical Christianity was given in the person and genius of **Clive Staples Lewis** (1898–1963). Emanating from the halls of Oxford and Cambridge through his inimitable prose and his often forgotten preaching was "a voice for old-fashioned Christian orthodoxy." Born and reared in Northern Ireland, sent to England at the age of nine after his mother's death, Lewis has been the subject of numerous biographical probings. His life as represented in the film *Shadowlands* has spoken deeply to millions. Even a secular biographer like A. N. Wilson has to face the conversion experience of Lewis: first his move to theism in 1929 ("It really happened!") and then his personal commitment to Christ two years later.[1]

Lewis' personal testimony is this: When he started for Whipsnade Zoo in the sidecar of his brother's motorcycle, he "did not believe that Jesus Christ is the Son of God and when [they] reached the zoo [he] did."[2] His full conversion "released literary flow," as the torrent of his brilliant works of fiction and nonfiction bear striking witness. His discovery of George MacDonald and his friendship with Tolkien and the Inklings are all part of the mysterious mix which made the man. We would be in his immense debt only for the works on literature, the Narnia stories, *Till We Have Faces, The Screwtape Letters, The Problem of Pain, Miracles, The Pilgrim's Regress, The Great Divorce,* and on and on. C. S. Lewis was such an encouragement to persons of faith in the supernatural in a time of increasing denial and drift from orthodox positions and formulation.

As a lay theologian, his *Reflections on the Psalms* are especially helpful with a section on the imprecatory psalms. His magnificent piece on prayer titled *Letters to Malcolm* and *A Grief Observed* are classics. His poignant work on the illness and loss of his wife, Joy Davidman (whose work on the Ten Commandments, *Smoke on the Mountain,* is special), is timeless. What is less frequently recognized is that Lewis was a preacher, not only on the broadcast talks which launched him into prominence during the war (and were published as *Mere Christianity*) but also in churches and gatherings as time and schedule allowed. He so ably addressed what he called "the inconsolable longings" of humanity. Lewis was wounded in the First World War and loved to preach to the troops in the Second.

George Sayer's truly fine biography of Lewis has a chapter on him as "Preacher and Broadcaster." Here Sayer traces not only those aided by Lewis in toddling steps of faith but also those—especially among his colleagues—who were offended by his apologetic efforts.[3] Lewis was gifted in being personal and good at expressing emotion, yet "he strongly admonished preachers to not 'accommodate to the world' and preach a watered-down gospel."[4]

Usually when he spoke, he wore clericals but with a regular suit to let the audience know "he was one of them."[5] His major collection of sermons is given its title by the first sermon that Lewis preached in an Oxford church in 1941, "The Weight of Glory," from 1 Corinthians 4:16–18. The sermon is biblical, theologically sound, and aptly and personally applied.[6] Another sermon in this brief anthology is called "Transposition" and was preached on Whitsunday 1944 in Magdalen College Chapel, Oxford, on the subject of spirituality. Lewis was so moved that he stopped preaching. A hymn was sung while the preacher collected himself, and then he resumed and concluded. Eric Routley, the theologian and hymnologist, heard him often and described his preaching as not only showing "superb delivery and wonderful command of language but also the ability to capture his hearer's hearts by his love of Christ and his obvious enjoyment of preaching."[7] C. S. Lewis wrote and spoke as one who was raised up to protest the relativization of Christ and promote the supernatural Christ of the historically reliable and trustworthy New Testament documents.[8]

---

1. A. N. Wilson, *C. S. Lewis: A Biography* (New York: Fawcett Columbine, 1990), 133.
2. C. S. Lewis, *Surprised by Joy: The Shape of My Early Life* (London: Fontana, 1955), 189.
3. George Sayer, *Jack: C. S. Lewis and His Times* (San Francisco: Harper and Row, 1988), 168–74.
4. Perry Bramlett, "The Weight of Glory: C. S. Lewis as Preacher," *Preaching* (September–October 1994): 45.
5. Ibid., 45.
6. C. S. Lewis, *The Weight of Glory* (Grand Rapids: Eerdmans, 1949), 1ff.
7. Bramlett, "The Weight of Glory," 45.
8. Another English man of letters who created a stir in roughly the same time frame was J. B. Phillips, whose *New Testament in Modern English* and *Four Prophets,* as well as his *Your God Is Too Small* and his sermons *Making Men Whole* (London: Fontana, 1952) had considerable impact. His impressions of the power of the text and the "historicity

and reliability of the New Testament" are given in his fine piece, *The Ring of Truth* (New York: Macmillan, 1967). Phillips' personal struggle with depression is reflected in his autobiographical *The Price of Success* (Wheaton, Ill.: Harold Shaw, 1984).

12.4 BRITISH PRACTITIONERS OF CREATIVITY AND CAPABILITY

The archbishop of Canterbury at the coronation of a British monarch in the presentation of a Bible: "Our gracious King [or Queen]: we present you with this Book, the most valuable thing that this world affords. Here is wisdom; this is the Royal Law; these are the oracles of God."

For centuries the Word of God was respected and revered in Britain as it was in most of the Western world.[1] How do we account for "the almost incredible disappearance of the knowledge of the Bible," as Sir Charles Marston spoke of it, not only in Britain but also in America? The diminution of the preaching and teaching of the Word of God in the churches is simultaneously symptom and cause of the secularizing of a shrunken Christianity.

The twentieth century has been traumatic for the once mighty and proud British Isles with its massive wars, loss of empire, moral decline, and naturalistic temper. Sporadic glimmers of the old faith surface, as when Margaret Thatcher gave unequivocal witness to her belief in the Bible and Christianity to the General Assembly of the Church of Scotland.[2] We now identify some of the preachers who have stood firmly for classical biblical Christianity through this turbulent century. For a good backdrop on the mood and movements of this relativistic period, I refer the reader to Johnson's *Modern Times*.[3]

---

1. For a fascinating documentation of this thesis, see Barbara W. Tuchman, *Bible and Sword: England and Palestine from the Bronze Age to Balfour* (New York: Ballentine, 1956). Chapter 5, "The Bible in English," is key.
2. Margaret Thatcher, "Sow and Ye Shall Reap for All," *The Wall Street Journal,* 31 May 1988, and Paul Johnson's insightful commentary on it, "Thatcher Captures Moral Initiative," 9 June 1988.
3. Paul Johnson, *Modern Times: The World from the Twenties to the Eighties* (New York: Harper, 1983).

12.4.1 ARTHUR JOHN GOSSIP—THE PREACHER WITH RARE SKILL

Always it has been through preaching that revivals have come and always by preaching that the Spirit has made the tired Church young again.

Preach to your own heart, and many startled passers-by will stop to listen, feeling you are addressing them. Draw anonymously on the story of your life, and they will sit astonished in the pews, asking, "Who has been telling him about me?"

—Arthur John Gossip

He did not have a very good voice; he did have a heavy accent; his gestures were "often ungainly"; he was not strong in outlining his sermons; and he clearly needed to be more exegetical. Nonetheless, **Arthur John Gossip** (1873–1954) belongs in Britain's Westminster Abbey of preachers. He was born and reared in Glasgow, educated at Edinburgh University where he sat under the ministry of Alexander Whyte, and served four Free Churches with distinction (Liverpool, Forfar, St. Matthew's in Glasgow, and Beechgrove, Aberdeen). He was a military chaplain with the Glasgow Highlanders in the First World War. In 1928 he was chosen to be professor of practical theology and ethics at Trinity College, Glasgow, until his retirement in 1945.

Gossip was as intense and "headlong as a Highland torrent."[1] One memorial tribute put it this way:

> He often spoke in breathless sentences in which clause was piled on clause, and the bonds of syntax were strained in a way no grammarian would have allowed; and yet each clause added its own quota to fan the fires of eloquence until every heart in a congregation was warmed to a generous glow.[2]

He was a master of illustration and the apt quotation. Four books of his choice sermons have been published and are eminently readable.[3] Pastoral and caring in his preaching, Gossip could write titles and topics such as "How to Face Life with Steady Eyes," "On the Art of Thinking in Terms of the Cross," and "What Christ Hates Most." His "A Peep at the Last Page" is a message on Moffat's translation of Romans 10:11–12, "No one who believes in Him, the Scripture says, will ever be disappointed. No one." Gossip practiced preaching without notes and was known for his children's sermons, which were published in *The Expository Times*.

Gossip loved to quote Pere Didon, "Your influence over a soul is conditioned by the depth of your love for it." He made his listeners feel the genuineness of his caring. When his dear wife was suddenly snatched from his side by death, he preached his famous sermon from Jeremiah 12:5: "But When Life Tumbles In, What Then?" He begins the sermon:

> Here is a man who, musing upon the bewilderments of life, has burst into God's presence, hot, angry, stunned by His ordering of things, with a loud babble of clamorous protest. It is unfair, he cries, unfair! And frowningly he looks into the face of the Almighty. It is unfair! And then suddenly he checks himself, and putting this blunt question to it, feels his heart grow very still and very cold.[4]

Rounding out his remarkably versatile ministry as a teacher of young preachers, he gave a memorable course of the Warrack Lectures in 1925, published as *In Christ's Stead*.[5] In his lectures, he admits us into the nooks and crannies of his own soul. He is like Chalmers "slowly catching fire." We wince as he gives us James I on his court preacher, "It is not preaching, it is playing with his subject." It was said of Arthur John Gossip, "Never has preaching been more full of Christ."[6]

---

1. John Bishop, "Arthur John Gossip: A Passion for Preaching," *Preaching* (May–June 1988): 52.
2. Ibid., 52.
3. Arthur John Gossip, *The Galilean Accept* (Edinburgh: T & T Clark, 1926); *From the Edge of the Crowd* (New York: Scribner's, n.d.). Gossip is epigrammatic as when he says "Novelty and progress are not necessarily synonymous." His last book of sermons is titled *Experience Worketh Hope* (New York: Scribner's, 1945).
4. Arthur John Gossip, *The Hero in Thy Soul: Being an Attempt to Face Life Gallantly* (New York: Scribner's, 1933), 106.
5. Arthur John Gossip, *In Christ's Stead* (Grand Rapids: Baker, 1925). Other notable Warrack lectureships must include James Black's *The Mystery of Preaching* (1923); R. E. McIntyre's *The Ministry of the Word* (1949); and David MacLennan's *Entrusted with the Gospel* (1955). J. Paterson Smyth's *The Preacher and His Sermon,* given at Trinity College, Dublin, in 1922 is also most helpful. The renowned Warrack lectureship has fallen into leaner times.
6. Bishop, "Arthur John Gossip," 51.

12.4.2 WILLIAM M. CLOW—THE PREACHER WITH A RELENTLESS THEME

> The missing note in the preaching of today is the note of persuasive urgency . . . a sociological message is being delivered . . . Yet it sometimes suggests that Christianity is little more than a movement for the social betterment of the people . . . There has been a neglect of the counsel to "do the work of an evangelist."
>
> —William M. Clow

Of one preacher it was said, "He went down deeper, stayed down longer and came up drier than anyone else," but this could never be said of **William McCallum Clow** (1853–1930).

Born and reared in Glasgow, Clow was educated at the University of Glasgow and the United Free Church College. He had a significant pastoral ministry in Aberdeen at the South Church, in Edinburgh at the Barclay Church in Glasgow, from which he was called in 1911 to serve as professor of practical theology and ethics at the United Free Church College. Here he was closely associated with A. B. Bruce, its principal, to whom we are indebted for his seminal *The Training of the Twelve*.[1] Clow later became principal of the college and continued his unusually effective preaching ministry in many locales.

Though he is not usually considered in the ranks of Scotland's foremost preachers, Clow is compelling for two reasons: he was more exegetical than Alexander Whyte or George Morrison and works in a text without abandoning serious application; he was dedicated to the centrality of Christ's atoning work. "The atonement was the primary message of Clow."[2] His preaching can be described as "beautiful" but substantive.

Clow's series of messages titled *The Idylls of Bethany* is an unparalleled study of the Bethany household where "the light always falls on the figure of Jesus."[3] His sermons on Matthew 16–17, beside being singular in their attention to the transfiguration of our Lord, are profound and gripping.[4] A splendid sample of his evangelistic preaching is found in his bracing collection of sermons, *The Evangel of the Strait Gate*. These twenty-six messages are divided into five sections:

I. The Parable of the Gate
II. Led into the Way
III. Passing Through the Gate
IV. Finding Life
V. End of the Broad Way

His quotes are from Augustine, Bunyan, Tennyson, John Bright, Matthew Arnold, Robert Burns, Henry Martyn, George Whitefield, and Frances Ridley Havergal, to name a few.[5] His outlines are exemplary. But his priceless masterpieces are his two volumes of sermons on the cross of Christ, which vie with those of Krummacher and Schilder. This ranks his preaching on the Cross with the best in English in several centuries. The first volume is "a course of sermons on the men and women and some of the notable things of the day of the crucifixion of Jesus," published as *The Day of the Cross*.[6] Unlike some treatments of this type, Clow avoids being distracted from the cross of Christ and the Christ of the cross.

Preeminent among Clow's preaching is his companion volume of twenty-five sermons coming out of his Glasgow pastorate. These he called *The Cross in Christian Experience*.[7] The forewording sermon is "Simply to Thy Cross I Cling," based on Romans 5:1; the afterwording sermon is "The Primacy of the Atonement," built on 1 Corinthians 15:3. The meat in the sandwich between these two delicious morsels include such striking studies as "The Dark Line in God's Face," "Love in Four Dimensions," "Receiving the Atonement," and "Christ's Last Gospel Message"—something unique from Acts 26:18. His guiding thesis is, "The Cross is never out of sight of the Christian soul."[8]

1. Alan P. F. Sell, *Defending and Declaring the Faith: Some Scottish Examples 1860–1920* (Exeter: Paternoster, 1987), 89, 92. Bear in mind that the Church of Scotland and the United Free Church merged in 1929.
2. Ralph G. Turnbull, *A History of Preaching* (Grand Rapids: Baker, 1974), 524. The updating of Dargan's work.
3. W. M. Clow, *The Idylls of Bethany* (London: Hodder and Stoughton, 1919; repr. 1969).
4. W. M. Clow, *The Secret of the Lord* (London: Hodder and Stoughton, n.d.)
5. W. M. Clow, *The Evangel of the Strait Gate* (New York: George H. Doran, 1916). Another Scot burdened for evangelism tells his story from his experience at North Kelvinside in Glasgow. See Tom Allan, *The Face of My Parish* (London: SCM, 1954). He inveighs strongly against "the acceptable sermon."
6. W. M. Clow, *The Day of the Cross* (London: Hodder and Stoughton, 1909).

7. W. M. Clow, *The Cross in Christian Experience* (London: Hodder and Stoughton, 1908).
8. Ibid., 11. Clow also edited *The Bible Reader's Encyclopedia and Concordance* (London: Collins, 1930).

12.4.3 JOHN MACBEATH—THE PREACHER WITH A ROBUST WORD

The Bible is the preacher's warrant and first reference library. There is no book that takes so much knowing, and there is no book that is so rewarding to the questing mind. Out of its fullness it is the preacher's prerogative to bring things new and old.

—John Macbeath

Another engaging Scottish Baptist preacher on the order of Graham Scroggie and J. Sidlow Baxter was **John Macbeath** (1881–1967). Born in Edinburgh and schooled at Glasgow University and the Baptist Theological College of Glasgow, he served congregations in St. Andrews, Cambuslang, Fillebrook Church in London, Hillhead Church in Glasgow, and Haven Green Church in Ealing, London. His preaching was biblical, his delivery winsome. As Turnbull observes, "His literary bent was unmistakable and all the riches of his literary knowledge shone through in allusion, quotation, and interpretation of themes expounded."[1] Macbeath broke loose from his manuscript.[2] He was widely heard in training schools, on broadcasts, and on nine visits to preach in the U.S. and Canada.

Sane and sound exposition can be sampled in a brief series of sermons on Ephesians. Here we see his ability to divide and outline the text well and move that registration of truth efficiently to an appetizing sermon outline.[3] Evidence of his charm and creativity is clear in an extended series in which he preaches sermons on twenty-four hills or mounts in Scripture under four headings:

I. Hills of Testimony
II. Hills of Trial
III. Hills of Tragedy
IV. Hills of Triumph[4]

---

1. Ralph G. Turnbull, *A History of Preaching* (Grand Rapids: Baker, 1974), 450.
2. Turnbull is not right on this point; cf. John Macbeath in *My Way of Preaching* (London: Pickering and Inglis, n.d.), 106. This symposium, edited by Robert J. Smithson, is like those edited by Donald MacCleod (1952), Clarence Roddy (1959), and Richard Bodey (1992).
3. John Macbeath, *The Life of a Christian* (London: Marshall, Morgan, and Scott, n.d.).
4. John Macbeath, *The Hills of God* (London: The Religious Tract Society, 1930). A touch of revival struck the Hebrides Islands off the west coast of Scotland after World War II under the ministry of Duncan Campbell. His strong biblical preaching is found in *God's Standard* and *God's Answer* (Ft. Washington, Pa.: CLC, 1964, 1960).

12.4.4 Oswald Chambers—The Preacher with a Radiant Testimony

All He wants from me is unconditional surrender.

After I was born again as a lad I enjoyed the presence of Jesus Christ wonderfully, but years passed before I gave myself up thoroughly to His work. I was in Dunoon College as tutor of Philosophy when Dr. F. B. Meyer came and spoke about the Holy Spirit. I determined to have all that was going, and went to my room and asked God simply and definitely for the baptism of the Holy Spirit, whatever that meant.

My mind still grows impatient at much of the success-lusting desire of Christian workers. How many patrons had Jeremiah or the apostles! Alone for God is the greater calling of a man.

—Oswald Chambers

If only for his devotional classic, *My Utmost for His Highest,* he would be a household word among Western Christians! **Oswald Chambers'** (1874–1917) extensive writings and preaching were posthumously compiled and guarantee him a portico in this temple of biblical preaching.

Many find Chambers hard to understand, while others find him so fresh and fragrant in his utterance as to be without peer.[1] His life was cut short while he was with the British military in Egypt in 1917. However, Chambers lived to the hilt.

- 1874–1889, born in Aberdeen; his father was a Baptist minister and raised his family there and in Perth. Both of his parents were baptized by Charles Haddon Spurgeon. His father's economizing ways grated upon young Oswald.[2]
- 1889–1895, left home at fifteen, already an accomplished musician; studied art; active in Rye Lane Baptist Church.
- 1895–1897, studied at the University of Edinburgh; enjoyed the preaching of Matheson and Whyte. He was destitute. His lodgings in Edinburgh had just been vacated by John Henry Jowett. He was a gifted painter.[3]
- 1897–1905, tutor in philosophy at Dunoon College. He struggled much with the "dark night of the soul," but in a "crisis of self-surrender" yielded to the Lord's call to ministry. He became a much sought-after preacher. Dinsdale T. Young discovered him and greatly influenced him "toward a more evangelical attitude."[4]
- 1906–1907, associated with the Japanese holiness evangelist Nakada, he traveled and taught in both America (God's Bible School in Cincinnati) and in Japan. His ties in Japan were with the Cowmans, the Oriental Missionary Society, and Dr. James Cuthbertson's Japan Evangelistic Band.[5] (Cuthbertson has given some of the finest expositions on the Song of Solomon ever heard.)
- 1907–1911, associated with the Pentecostal Prayer League. Met Gertrude (Biddy) Hobbs onboard ship to the U.S. in 1908; married in 1910. He traveled much in preaching missions to Ireland and all about.

- 1911–1915, founded the Bible Training College in Clapham, London. Many of his books were developed out of the lecture notes his wife took at this time (which accounts for their highly condensed form). His famous *Biblical Psychology* shows the influence of J. T. Beck's work on psychology; (see 9.4.4).
- 1915–1917, accepted by the YMCA (much as J. Gresham Machen was in Europe) for work in the desert camps in Egypt as survivors of Gallipoli and the British disaster in the Dardenelles fell back upon Egypt. His family was permitted to join him.

Although he was somewhat mystical and at times imprecise, Chambers' basic theological stance was this:

> The true pattern for the experience of the Christian, is the life of Christ. The Christian ideal is not the outward and literal imitation of Jesus, but the living out of the Christ life implanted within by the Holy Spirit.[6]

Both P. T. Forsyth and James Denney shaped Chambers' thinking on the meaning of Christ's death. Forsyth wrote the foreword to one of his books. Rendel Harris was in Egypt after being torpedoed and found much in common with him. Archbishop Donald Coggan payed him eloquent tribute as truly "a man of one book."[7] Samuel Zwemer preached his funeral.

His preaching was exceedingly idiosyncratic and creative. A report from Egypt indicated:

> Mr. Oswald Chambers' address on the subject "Has History Disproved the Song of the Angels?" was a convincing defense of Christianity; he was listened to with rapt attention and much appreciation by the audience, soldiers and civilians alike.[8]

Two favorite books of his messages are built on the schema of the believer's life in parallel with the life of Jesus. They are *Bringing Sons Unto Glory* and *The Psychology of Redemption,* prolific and productive to the end. His messages on the life of Abraham are highly condensed but show his penchant for the alliterative outline, tight structure, meaty exposition, and memorable application.[9] As a poet of some ability he was used to compressing language, and this shows in his prose style.

Chambers had just finished his talks on Job and was beginning his studies in Ecclesiastes when his health crisis came.[10] "Drench us with humility" was the lifelong prayer of this servant of Christ whose life and work in the Scriptures have made so many of us his beneficiaries.

---

1. Some of Chambers' opaqueness could be due to his early dabbling in Swedenborg, the cultic Swedish mystic; see David McCasland, *Oswald Chambers: Abandoned to God* (Grand Rapids: Discovery House, 1993), 88. Also, Biddy Chambers, *Oswald*

Chambers: His Life and Work (London: Simpkin, Marshall, 1933), 62. The deleterious influence of Swedenborg on William Blake is traced at length in Peter Ackroyd's *Blake: A Biography* (New York: Knopf, 1996).

2. McCasland, *Oswald Chambers*. This is a magnificent study. Highly recommended.
3. D. W. Lambert, *Oswald Chambers: An Unbribed Soul* (Ft. Washington, Pa.: CLC, 1968), 14.
4. Chambers, *Oswald Chambers*, 63.
5. For a fine study of the Cowmans and their work, see B. H. Pearson, *The Vision Lives On* (Los Angeles: Cowman, 1961). Mrs. Cowman will always be remembered as the author of the widely used *Streams in the Desert*.
6. Lambert, *Oswald Chambers*, 59.
7. F. D. Coggan, *Stewards of Grace* (quoted in Lambert, ibid., 45–46). Coggan's careful and inspiring study on *The Ministry of the Word* (London: Canterbury Press, 1945) is a solid and substantial piece.
8. McCasland, *Oswald Chambers*, 242.
9. Oswald Chambers, *Not Knowing Whither: The Steps of Abraham's Faith* (London: Marshall, Morgan, and Scott, 1957). "God's call is a command that asks us, that means there is always a possibility of refusal on our part" (11).
10. Oswald Chambers, *Baffled to Fight Better* (London: Marshall, Morgan, and Scott, 1955); *Shade of His Hand* (London: Simpkin, Marshall, 1947). Both series were given in the YMCA Hut in Zeitoun, Egypt, in 1917.

12.4.5 James S. Stewart—The Preacher with a Remarkably Rich Endowment

There are rich rewards of human gratitude waiting for the man who can make the Bible come alive.

Stint no toil to achieve clear thought, fit language, true construction, decisive appeal.

Imagination is one of the preacher's essential weapons. Put yourself and your people into the heart of what you are preaching about. Imagination is a living quality. Its place is among the attributes of God.
—James S. Stewart

The waning of biblical Christianity in Scotland is tragical and lamentable. At the present rate of attrition the Church of Scotland will virtually cease to exist in the next century. Yet there has been a movement in the interest of expository preaching through whole books of Scripture led by William Still of Gilcomston South Church in Aberdeen.[1] Certainly Scotland's "premier preacher" of the last half of the twentieth century has been "thoroughly orthodox" and an extraordinarily gifted Bible preacher.[2] We refer to **James S. Stewart** (1896–1990), who was born in Dundee.

Stewart received M.A. and B.D. degrees from St. Andrews and did postgraduate study at Bonn. His father was converted under D. L. Moody, sold his business, and became a well-known Bible teacher for the YMCA. Stewart pastored at

Auchterarder in Perthshire, the Beechgrove Church in Aberdeen, and then with such conspicuous favor at the North Morningside Church in Edinburgh.[3] For the next twenty-two years, he was professor of New Testament at New College, Edinburgh. His best-selling book, *The Life and Teaching of Jesus Christ,* sold more than one hundred thousand copies in the United States. His serious study of *A Man in Christ: The Vital Elements of St. Paul's Religion* (his Cunningham Lectures) continue to be well worth reading, as he argues that "Paul's is a conversion theology." His Warrack Lectures on preaching in 1945, published as *Heralds of God,* ranks as one of the finest in that prestigious series and displays a great acuity and sensitivity to the preaching task.[4] His Beecher Lectures in 1952 focus on the great doctrines of the gospel and come to us under the title *A Faith to Proclaim.* They are rich and show no signs of what has become an increasing aversion to doctrine and the cognitive in our time.

It has been Stewart's published sermons that have vaulted him into such an exclusive circle of admiration. Always grounded deeply in the text, his sermons are those of a preacher's preacher. Festooned with choice titles ("Hearsay or Experience," "Sport of Fate or Plan of God?" and "Rumor or Reality?"), they are outlined with such memorable divisions, applied with fine illustrations, and facilitated with skillful transitions. Longenecker underscores his brilliant blending of "rigorous scholarship, reverential reading of Scripture and effective communication of the gospel."[5] He recalls vividly when Professor Stewart—who tended to be "unimposing and shy"—would "start expounding on a subject in a pedantic and discreet manner, then get so carried away with his subject that it began to take control of him, so that, without any rise in pitch or volume, there would be an increase in emotional intensity and a crescendo of descriptive detail and lyrical expression, and finally, when he had exhausted his subject, he would drop back to his discreet manner. His hearers often experienced that buildup and drop—sometimes inadvertently expressing their empathy in a gasp."[6]

Stewart's printed sermons, titled *The Strong Name, The Gates of New Life, The Wind of the Spirit,* and *River of Life,* are worth owning, reading, rereading, and digesting thoroughly. His lectures on *Thine Is the Kingdom: The Church's Mission in Our Time* clearly indicate his commitment to the evangel around the world.[7] Here is a preacher who preaches out of the overflow.

Bishop expresses special joy over Stewart's sermon, "The Strengthening Angel," from Luke 22:43.[8] The text is a bit meager, but the outline is magnificent:

I. The strengthening angel today is often some shining word out of the Book of God
II. The strengthening angel today may be some fellow creature
III. The strengthening angel today may be the Lord himself[9]

Even more are we drawn to his regal "The Triumphant Adequacy of Christ" from Romans 15:29:

I. I am coming to you with Christ
II. I am coming to you with the gospel of Christ

III. I am coming to you with the blessing of the gospel of Christ
IV. I am coming to you with the fullness of the blessing of the gospel of Christ[10]

Stewart models an effective preacher who could serve as chaplain to a local professional soccer club, preach regularly at the rescue mission, or lecture around the world.[11] His was not an "intellectual isolation" but a powerful engagement with the Word of God and with the times in which he lived.

---

1. Douglas F. Kelly, "The Recovery of Christian Realism in the Scottish Expository Ministry Movement," in *Pulpit and People: Essays in Honour of William Still on His 75th Birthday,* ed. Nigel M. de S. Cameron and Sinclair B. Ferguson (Edinburgh: Rutherford House, 1986), 17ff. Also, *Evangelicals Now,* June 1995, "William Still— A Modern Simeon."
2. Richard Longenecker, "Missing One of Scotland's Best," *Christianity Today* (July 22, 1991): 11.
3. John Bishop, "James S. Stewart: Passionate Intensity, Evangelical Fervor," *Preaching* (January–February 1988): 61.
4. James S. Stewart, *Heralds of God* (New York: Scribner's, 1946).
5. Longenecker, "Missing One of Scotland's Best," 61.
6. Ibid., 61.
7. James S. Stewart, *Thine Is the Kingdom: The Church's Mission in Our Time* (New York: Scribner's, 1959).
8. Another intriguing sermon on this text by Clarence Macartney's successor at Arch Street Presbyterian Church in Philadelphia, G. Hall Todd, *O Angel of the Garden* (Grand Rapids: Baker, 1961), 11ff.
9. James S. Stewart, *The Wind of the Spirit* (Nashville: Abingdon, 1968), 103ff.
10. James S. Stewart, *The Strong Name* (Grand Rapids: Baker, 1972), 90ff.
11. Longenecker, "Missing One of Scotland's Best," 61.

12.4.6 WILLIAM TEMPLE—THE PREACHER WITH RARE ACUMEN

To worship is to quicken the conscience by the holiness of God, to feed the mind with the truth of God, to purge the imagination by the beauty of God, to devote the will to the purpose of God.

—William Temple

Lunch-hour talks! In church! During August Bank Holiday Week! In Blackpool! On the Revelation! Most of us felt he was batting on a sticky wicket, and despite extensive postering not more than forty or fifty people turned up. The next day there were over two hundred, and for the remaining days the church was packed, a queue outside stretching almost down to the Front, waiting to get in—a wonderful example of his judgment and an amazing testimony to his power of exposition!

—A missioner from the Blackpool mission of 1922
(conducted along "rather old-fashioned evangelical lines")

The desperate plight and sad state of the Church of England are well known to us. Yet in the Stott-Lucas wing of the church there has been vigorous biblical preaching.[1] Even in the broad church, or centrist branch, we have the intellectual and spiritual giant **William Temple** (1881–1944). His father, **Frederick Temple,** was also a schoolman who became archbishop of Canterbury in his seventy-sixth year.

Frederick Temple lived with his mother until he was fifty-five and then married as the bishop of Exeter. He had two sons, one of whom followed in his footsteps. William eventually served as headmaster of Repton, rector of St. James in Picadilly, bishop of Manchester in 1921, and then successively archbishop of York after Cosmo Lang and archbishop of Canterbury. William was a large, rotund man, and a spokesman for religion in both world wars. He was unforgettable in his preaching and could preach to scholars and the common people with equal effectiveness and seeming effortlessness. This "Pickwickian figure," was without pretension. Even though he was the primate of England, he could be seen queuing up for a bus after addressing meetings at Royal Albert Hall.[2]

Of course Temple was a Rugby man, where his father and Thomas Arnold had been headmasters, and went to Balliol at Oxford. Here he was tutored by Benjamin Jowett and shaped by Edward Caird, the Scottish Hegelian. Temple was never well, suffering his first attack of gout when he was two years of age.[3] His eight Sunday evenings at Oxford in 1931 became the spiritual crossroad for many a soul.[4] From 1932 to 1934, he gave the Gifford Lectures in Edinburgh, published as *Nature, Man and God.* In them he argued for the transcendence of immanence and the immanence of transcendence.

Temple was supremely a preacher and a teacher and served as president of the Oxford Union.[5] He took a strong stand for the Virgin Birth of Christ and the bodily resurrection of our Lord.[6] His favorite preaching portion was John's gospel, which he attributed to the disciple of Jesus. His incomparable *Readings in John's Gospel* came out of his years at St. James, Picadilly.[7] Iremonger, his chief biographer, calls this "the greatest devotional treatise since William Law's *A Serious Call to a Devout and Holy Life.*[8]

He enjoyed facing off with H. G. Wells on the issue of a finite God and joined with Dick Sheppard in heading up the Life and Liberty Movement, which concerned life in the Church of England rather than secular confinement.[9] While he was canon at Westminster and bishop of Manchester (with six hundred parishes), he preached incessantly and had particular effect with his great university missions.[10] As early as 1931, he warned of the danger of Marxist communism[11] and always felt Pelagianism was damnable.[12] Still he was adamant in maintaining that Christianity had immense implication for society and culture.[13]

Temple's speaking voice was not outstanding, nor was his oratory finished, but he had a presence and an ability to think on his feet. Even with only fifty percent vision, he read constantly and wrote thirty-five books. It was said of him that "he spoke pamphlets." He had great spontaneity but prepared well, though he never prepared the words he would use. Dean W. R. Matthews of St. Paul's described "the believing quality of his mind."[14] Iremonger was of the opinion that "he moved more and more to the right during his later years."[15] His sermons were not startling compositionally, but they were direct, biblical, and steeped in an honesty and a practicality that consistently made their mark.[16] His friend, A. E. Baker, said of his preaching:

> He combined, in a quite unique way, the knowledge of the student of ideas and affairs, the understanding of the thinker, and the prophet's power to speak to and move the spirit of the nation.[17]

---

1. A superb example of strong biblical exposition was Canon Guy H. King of Christ Church, Beckenham, successor to the Reverend Harrington Lees, who went on to be archbishop of Melbourne. King's sermons are meticulous with the text and appear in such volumes as *A Belief That Behaves* (James), *Joy Way* (Philippians), *Crossing the Border* (Colossians), and *A Leader Led* (1 Timothy). An American Episcopalian of great evangelical influence was the celebrated Dr. Sam Shoemaker, who served parishes in New York and Pittsburgh; see his *Extraordinary Living for Ordinary Men* (Grand Rapids: Zondervan, 1965). Paul Rees said he had fireball not mothball theology.
2. Alexander Gammie, *Preachers I Have Heard* (London: Pickering and Inglis, n.d.), 188ff.
3. Charles W. Lowry, *William Temple: An Archbishop for All Seasons* (Washington, D.C.: University Press of America, 1982), 18.
4. Lowry, *William Temple*, 48–49.
5. Ibid., 22.
6. Ibid., 24.
7. William Temple, *Readings in John's Gospel* (Wilton, Conn.: Morehouse Barlow, 1985 ed.).
8. F. A. Iremonger, *William Temple: Archbishop of Canterbury, His Life and Letters* (London: Oxford, 1948), 176. This is the official biography of Temple, who was often called the people's archbishop.
9. Lowry, *William Temple*, 35. Sheppard was quite a preacher in his own right; see R. J. Northcott, *Dick Sheppard and St. Martin's* (London: Longmans Green, 1937); another friend of Temple was G. A. Studdert-Kennedy, whose sermons on the Apostles' Creed, *I Believe*, were widely heard but tended to be weak and vague.
10. Iremonger, *William Temple*, 377.
11. Ibid., 82.
12. Joseph Fletcher, *William Temple: Twentieth-Century Christian* (New York: Seabury, 1963). Lowry correctly feels that Fletcher is "too eager to show the modernity of Temple" (146).
13. William Temple, *Christianity and the Social Order* (London: Penguin, 1942). N.B. Robert Craig, *Social Concern in the Thought of William Temple* (London: Gollancz, 1963); Owen C. Thomas, *William Temple's Philosophy of Religion* (London: SPCK; New York: Seabury, 1961); W. R. Rinne, *The Kingdom of God in the Thought of William Temple* (Abo, Finland: Abo Akademi, 1966).
14. Craig, *Social Concern in the Thought of William Temple*, 12.
15. Iremonger, *William Temple*, 512.
16. William Temple, *Fellowship with God* (London: Macmillan, 1920), preached in Westminster; *Studies in the Spirit and Truth of Christianity: University and School*

Sermons (London: Macmillan, 1914). Particularly moving is his sermon on "Faith and Doubt" based in 2 Timothy 4:6–8 and Mark 15:34, 17ff. This last book is dedicated to Charles Gore, who had an unusual influence on Temple. Gore was bishop of Oxford and the force behind the Lux Mundi volume.
17. A. E. Baker, *William Temple: An Estimate and an Appreciation* (London: James Clarke, 1946), 100.

12.4.7 *DAVID MARTYN LLOYD-JONES—THE PREACHER WITH A RESOUNDING MESSAGE*

To me the work of preaching is the highest and greatest and the most glorious calling to which anyone can ever be called.

Every preacher should believe strongly in his own method . . . I can say quite honestly that I would not cross the road to listen to myself preaching, and the preachers whom I have enjoyed most have been very different indeed in their method and style. But my business is not to describe them but to state what I believe to be right, however imperfectly I have put my own precepts into practice. I can only hope that the result will be of some help, and especially to young preachers called to this greatest of all tasks, and especially in these sad and evil days.

—D. Martyn Lloyd-Jones

He was called by Wilbur M. Smith "the greatest Bible expositor in the English-speaking world." The Doctor, as he was often referred to, exerted a powerful and profound influence at the heart of London with reverberations all around the world. His ministry was essentially the opening of Scripture to a vast congregation three times a week. **David Martyn Lloyd-Jones** (1899–1981) and his preaching silence those who claim that the preaching of historic orthodoxy under the unction of the Spirit makes no impact in postmodern times. The current panic to market-driven preaching and abandonment of text-driven preaching needs to come to terms with how God used Lloyd-Jones.

The Building of the Preacher

Lloyd-Jones was a Welshman born in Cardiff, the middle son of three born to Henry and Maggie Lloyd-Jones. Part of the Calvinistic Methodist (or Presbyterian) Church, he narrowly escaped death as a boy when his father's general store burned down. When his father went bankrupt, they moved to London. Here they attended the Welsh Chapel, although Lloyd-Jones often heard Campbell Morgan or John Hutton at Westminster Chapel.

Lloyd-Jones was reluctant to speak about himself or his own conversion in public.[1] He began to study medicine at St. Bart's Hospital Medical School and became a protégé of the world-famous Lord Horder. Soon he married a fellow medical student, Bethan Phillips. Yet his practice of medicine after his graduation in 1921 did not satisfy him, and he increasingly struggled with what seemed to be God's hand on him to preach. The newlyweds left Harley Street to take the pastorate of the Bethlehem Forward Movement Mission Church in Sandfields, Aberavon, a congregation of miners, dockworkers, and metalworkers, which numbered ninety-three when he came. In just over eleven years, Aberavon grew to a membership of 530, with attendance at 850. Many came as new converts.[2]

Though not theologically trained, Lloyd-Jones was a student and a logician of the first magnitude, using Horder's Socratic method.[3] In 1938 he accepted Campbell Morgan's invitation to come as associate pastor at Westminster. Though they were so different, the two men worked together harmoniously. They alternated morning and evening services monthly until Morgan retired in 1943 under the acute strains of old age and war.[4] After the war, attendance began to build and soon twenty-five hundred people filled Westminster morning and evening with twelve hundred for the Friday night Bible study. Westminster was one of the largest congregations in London. The lofty attendance continued until the Doctor retired in 1968.

The Burden of the Preacher

In the early days at Westminster, Lloyd-Jones did not always follow consecutive book exposition but developed series like "God's Plan for World Unity" and "A Preview of History" from Revelation 4–5. He early on did a series on 2 Peter, followed by his famous extended series, *Studies in the Sermon on the Mount.*[5]

While Campbell Morgan tended to be Arminian, Lloyd-Jones was staunchly a Calvinist and a great admirer and student of the Puritans, who were models for him in many respects. He decried "concessions made to so-called scholarship" and the "slide toward a liberal view of the Scriptures."[6] He saw clearly that what was at stake was "the loss of a doctrine of the full inspiration and inerrance of Scripture." During the war years, Lloyd-Jones was president of Inter-Varsity in Britain and was a part of the vital leadership the movement took in pointing the way back to classical biblical Christianity. The need for revival was a lifelong burden of his.[7] Although he was an amillennialist, Lloyd-Jones was of the conviction that God had something special for the Jews at the end of the age. He said, "I feel increasingly that we may be in the last times."

Lloyd-Jones established the Westminster Library and the Westminster Ministers' Fraternal, which made a great impact.[8] His pneumatology was a bit of a strain on his followers since he held that a believer "could have more than one baptism of the Spirit" and that the sealing of the Spirit was subsequent to conversion.[9] He was quite a separatist and did not support the Graham crusades. He broke with Stott, insisting that Anglican evangelicals leave the Church of England.[10] He was always waspish with regard to Keswick and probably misunderstood the movement. His critique of S. D. Gordon's preaching was unfair.[11] Yet having pointed out the flyspecks in the marble of the Parthenon, we can only rejoice that this preacher stood so stalwartly and strongly for the historic Christian faith. He was eminently theological in his mindset and in this sets an important standard.

The Brilliance of the Preacher

Lloyd-Jones loved to preach; the circulation of his sermons in print and by tape is without parallel in our time. His multivolume series on Romans is epochal; his eight volumes of Sunday morning preaching from Ephesians is equally impressive. His sermons on *Spiritual Depression* have aided and assisted thousands.[12] His expository studies from Psalm 73 under the title *Faith on Trial* are spectacular.[13] His Sunday morning sermons on *The Kingdom of God* during the Profumo scandal show the startling relevance of the Word to the contemporary situation.[14]

In the strict sense Lloyd-Jones's preaching was almost always textual-topical because he exposed such a small piece of text (like the Puritans, whom he emulated in so many ways). He used an inverted pyramid, moving from a small piece of text to what the Scripture as a whole taught on the subject and what its theological ramifications were. Lloyd-Jones could pray publicly for thirty-five minutes at a time. He was not expository in the sense of taking a natural thought unit and modeling how one moves through the thought of the author in the sermon. Occasionally, as in his famous sermon on Peter healing Aeneas (based on Acts 9:33–34), in which he made the miracle a parable about what must happen in the church, he moved to a kind of odd allegorization.[15] Neither has his idiosyncratic interpretation of Romans 7 found many followers. At times his views of preaching and worship are a bit cranky; he sounds like he is death on illustration and quotation in the sermon and would not have a choir or special music. Yet he used more methodological aids than he was willing to concede. But nothing can obscure the driving passion of his soul for preaching the Word of God. Who could more trustworthily be our guide in considering the vexed issue of the phenomena of revival than Lloyd-Jones? Who could preach on grace as he could? Something in the sober, serious manner of the Doctor captivated multitudes in a response that, humanly speaking, should not have taken place. But it did. God spoke through his servant.

The Blessing of God on the Preacher

Although he is an Anglican, J. I. Packer was greatly shaped as a young listener in Westminster Chapel. R. V. G. Tasker, the brilliant New Testament lecturer at King's College, University of London, came under Lloyd-Jones's message Sunday evenings at Westminster Chapel and forsook liberalism because he became convinced of original sin and the wrath of God.[16] Sunday night was the evangelistic service, and the Doctor at Westminster as at Aberavon would be available to talk to seekers afterward as he was indeed available Sunday morning. (Who says being seeker-focused is new?) An Indian journalist, Sunder-Rao, reported:

> What impressed me was not the personal aspect of the great preacher, though that made no uncertain impact. It was that as the preacher unfolded the theme he seemed to have been possessed, or to be discreet, motivated by One greater than himself, in Whom he lived, moved and

had his being. All great preaching becomes a sacrament, nay, a miracle, when in and through it, it holds forth the indications and intimations of the presence of God.[17]

In D. Martyn Lloyd-Jones we have described the imparting of the Spirit, "the sacred anointing," a spiritual work much needed today.[18]

1. Iain H. Murray, *D. Martyn Lloyd-Jones: The First Forty Years 1899–1939* (Edinburgh: Banner of Truth, 1982), xiii. Murray's two massive biographical volumes are pure gold. Reading almost every page is a spiritual experience.
2. Bethan Lloyd-Jones, *Memories of Sandfields 1927–1938* (Edinburgh: Banner of Truth, 1983). His glorious messages from this period are found in *Evangelistic Sermons* (Edinburgh: Banner of Truth, 1983).
3. Christopher Catherwood, *Five Evangelical Leaders* (Wheaton, Ill.: Harold Shaw, 1985), 61.
4. *The Westminster Record,* vol. 17, no. 7 through vol. 25, no. 2 with the G. Campbell Morgan Memorial Issue.
5. D. Martyn Lloyd-Jones, *Expository Sermons on 2 Peter* (Edinburgh: Banner of Truth, 1983); *Studies in the Sermon on the Mount* (Grand Rapids: Eerdmans, 1959) in two volumes.
6. Interview with Carl F. H. Henry, "Martyn Lloyd-Jones: From Buckingham to Westminster," *Christianity Today* (February 8, 1980): 17ff. Reprinted in Christopher Catherwood, ed., *Martyn Lloyd-Jones: Chosen of God* (Wheaton, Ill.: Crossway, 1986), 95ff.
7. D. Martyn Lloyd-Jones, *Revival* (Wheaton, Ill.: Crossway, 1987). Sermons on the one hundredth anniversary of the British revival.
8. D. Martyn Lloyd-Jones, *The Puritans: Their Origins and Successors* (Edinburgh: Banner of Truth, 1987).
9. D. Martyn Lloyd-Jones, *Preachers and Preaching* (Grand Rapids: Zondervan, 1971), 308. Lectures at Westminster Theological Seminary in Philadelphia.
10. Iain H. Murray, *D. Martyn Lloyd-Jones: The Fight of Faith 1939–1981* (Edinburgh: Banner of Truth, 1990), 535ff.
11. D. Martyn Lloyd-Jones, *Knowing the Times: Addresses 1942–1977* (Edinburgh: Banner of Truth, 1989), 264. Cf. 12.7.4
12. D. Martyn Lloyd-Jones, *Spiritual Depression: Its Causes and Cure* (Grand Rapids: Eerdmans, 1965).
13. D. Martyn Lloyd-Jones, *Faith on Trial* (Grand Rapids: Eerdmans, 1965).
14. D. Martyn Lloyd-Jones, *The Kingdom of God* (Wheaton, Ill.: Crossway, 1992). The more standard homiletical form is seen in Geoffrey King, who for twenty years served West Croydon Tabernacle in London; see *The Forty Days* (Grand Rapids: Eerdmans, 1949), recommended by James Stewart; *Truth for Our Time* (Grand Rapids: Eerdmans, 1957), especially a sermon like "The Sterner Side of the Twenty-Third Psalm" (89).
15. Murray, *The First Forty Years,* 328, 334.
16. Interview with Carl F. H. Henry, "Martyn Lloyd-Jones," 29.

17. Murray, *The Fight of Faith,* 198.
18. Tony Sargent, *The Sacred Anointing: The Preaching of Dr. Martyn Lloyd-Jones* (Wheaton, Ill.: Crossway, 1994).

12.5 AFRICANS, AFRICAN-AMERICANS, NATIVE AMERICANS, AND ASIANS PREACHING THE WORD OF HIS GRACE

> It has always been my ambition to preach the gospel where Christ was not known, so that I would not be building on someone else's foundation.
> —Romans 15:20

The devastating and erosive effects of Enlightenment rationalism have been seen not only in the centers of Western Christendom but also in all parts of the earth. The viciousness of this plague can be seen even in Judaism, within which a perceptive scholar like Eugene Borowitz bemoans Judaism's "love affair with modernity." He sees that "modernization has become our Messiah," that is, liberal religion with its deification of the self has accommodated itself to culture.[1] With Abraham Heschel, Borowitz he accepts the accuracy of the biblical record—its content is accurate and binding. On this basis he believes that the covenant between God and Israel continues in full force.[2] He sees the Documentary Hypothesis in shambles and finds liberalism wanting in its notions that revelation is discovery, sin is error, judgment is self-criticism, and atonement is self-sacrifice. He asserts on the basis of Scripture that Israel is a nation covenanted with God and therefore will survive in historic continuity until messianic days and "the culmination of the Covenant in the days of the Messiah."[3] Similar confidence in the Bible has given impetus to the worldwide proclamation of the gospel with amazing fruit among the nations. Yet Western fads and theological bypaths have made deep inroads into the growing churches of the two-thirds world, the part of the world that is non-Western. We now sample some of the vitalities in other ethnic settings.

---

1. Eugene B. Borowitz, *Renewing the Covenant* (New York: Jewish Publication Society, 1991), 19.
2. Ibid., 45.
3. Ibid., 298.

12.5.1 JOHN JASPER—THE ROOTS OF AFRICAN-AMERICAN PREACHING

> In the black church, if you do not have a Jesus Punch Line, you have not preached.
> —T. Hoyt

> On the power of proclamation: "It is not in the tone of voice. It is not in the eloquence of the preacher. It is not in the gracefulness of his gestures. It is not in the magnificence of his congregation. It is in a heart broken, and put together, by the eternal God!"
> —Gardner C. Taylor

Black Christianity in the United States rose among slaves who found the theme of liberation in the exodus from Egypt and in the gospel story. The African-American pulpit tradition reflects the centrality of the church in the black community. Preaching is critical for leadership in the black church.[1] The rhythms of black worship and the exhortations of the preacher in sync with the congregation make us realize that the cultural roots of this remarkably vibrant people are deep in Africa.[2] The penchant for narrative in the black sermon is reflected in African-American preaching today.[3] Preachers like Henry Mitchell, Gardner Taylor, and others have helped us understand the genius of black preaching as well as its susceptibilities.[4] All of this can be seen in the preaching of a remarkable pioneer, **John Jasper** (1812–1901).

John Jasper was the twenty-fourth and last child born to slaves named Philip and Tina Jasper. His father was "an exhorter" and died before his birth. His mother called him John after John the Baptist. Working as a slave in a tobacco factory, he was gloriously converted. His master, Sam Hardgrave, a deacon at First Baptist Church in Richmond, Virginia, sent him on his way to preach the Good News with the advice to "Fly like an angel, John!"[5] He soon became pastor of the Sixth Mount Zion Baptist Church in Richmond, where he drew large audiences. Without education, he was tutored in the Word and in preaching by the Reverend William E. Hatcher of Grace Street Baptist Church, who said of Jasper:

> He was a theater within himself, with the stage crowded with actors. He was a battlefield—himself the general, the staff, the officers, the common soldiery, the thundering artillery and the rattling musketry. He was the preacher.[6]

White people as well as black came to hear Jasper preach. He could tell a story and paint a picture. In his sermon "The Stone Cut Out of the Mountain," based on Daniel 2:45, he depicts Nebuchadnezzar troubled by his dream and the imagery of the great stone not cut out with human hands rolling and rolling and rolling.[7] His most famous sermon, which he preached about the country 250 times, was "The Sun Do Move" from Joshua 10:12–14. His message on "Frogs, Frogs, Frogs" from Exodus 8 is graphic beyond imagination. These are not homiletically polished expositions, but we can imagine the postwar Richmond audience hearing these sermons built off the dynamic storyline of Scripture. He concluded his sermon out of Joshua 10 unforgettably:

> The chariot that will come to take us to our Father's mansion will sweep out by them flickerin' lights and never halt till it brings us to clear view of the throne of the Lamb. Don't hitch your hopes to no sun nor stars; your home has got Jesus for its light, and your hopes must travel up that way![8]

---

1. C. Eric Lincoln and Lawrence H. Mamiya, *The Black Church in the African-American Experience* (Durham, N.C.: Duke University Press, 1990). For beautiful insight into a typical, more rural local black church experience, see Alex Haley, *Easter in Henning*

(New York: Doubleday, 1985), about the New Hope Colored Methodist Episcopal Church.

2. Bengt Sundkler, *Zulu Zion* (New York: Oxford University Press, 1976). A fascinating study of how this now independent church in Swaziland owes its origins to John Alexander Dowie (1847–1907) and the Christian Catholic Church of Zion, Illinois. The ministry of Simon Kimbangu, the African prophet, is also fascinating. He died in 1951 as a martyr.

3. Brad Hill, "Preaching the Word in the CEUM: Toward a Theology of Obedience," *The Covenant Quarterly* (February 1987): 37–44. Hill analyzes such varied narrative forms as "the diminishing spiral model; the pin-cushion model; the sunburst model; the linear-progression model."

4. Henry Mitchell, *Black Preaching* (San Francisco: Harper, 1979); Gardner C. Taylor, *How Shall They Preach* (Elgin, Ill.: Progressive Baptist Publishing, 1977). His 1976 Beecher Lectures. See the interview, "The Pulpit King," *Christianity Today* (December 11, 1995): 25ff. For his sermons, see *The Scarlet Thread* (Elgin, Ill.: Progressive Baptist Publishing, 1981).

5. Al Fasol, *With a Bible in Their Hands: Baptist Preaching in the South 1679–1979* (Nashville: Broadman, 1994), 74–75.

6. William E. Hatcher, *John Jasper: The Unmatched Negro Philosopher and Preacher* (Chicago: Revell, 1908), 9.

7. Fasol, *With a Bible in Their Hands,* 74.

8. Quoted in Richard Lischer, "John Jasper," in *Concise Encyclopedia of Preaching* (Louisville: Westminster John Knox, 1995), 279. Richard Ellsworth Day also has a lovely book, *Rhapsody in Black: The Life Story of John Jasper* (Philadelphia: Judson, 1953).

12.5.2 MARTIN LUTHER KING JR.—THE RAGE OF AFRICAN-AMERICAN PREACHING

Our ultimate allegiance is not to this nation. Our ultimate allegiance is to the Almighty God and this is where we get our authority . . . When God speaks, who can but prophesy?

There are two aspects of the world which we must never forget. One is that this is God's world and He is active in the forces of history and the affairs of men. The second is that Jesus Christ gave his life for the redemption of this world and as his followers we are called to give our lives continuing the reconciling work of Christ in this world.

I'm a Baptist preacher and that means I am in the heart-changing business.
—Martin Luther King Jr.

James Welldon Johnson's great poem, "God's Trombones," affords us insight into the amazing imaginative skills of the African-American preacher. Very few such sermons are in print, and even if they were available, the printed page cannot convey the electrifying aliveness of the preaching situation. In a day of dismal oratorical performance generally, we need to consider the arousing effectiveness of a Jesse Jackson or a Malcolm X. Rhetorical skill is not dead.

We see this in a Christian context in the preaching of **Martin Luther King Jr.** (1929–1968). His father had been a country preacher. At the age of fifteen, the elder King had put himself through school and became pastor of Ebenezer Baptist Church in Atlanta after the death of his father-in-law, who was its second pastor. Martin Sr. was known for his "hard preaching" and "sulfurous evangelism," and he would on occasion "walk the benches" when the poetic and musical crescendo mounted into an almost unbearable climax.[1]

Martin Luther King had unusual gifts as a preacher—we mark his rage, his tremendous sense of climax, his rhetorical genius, his near-hypnotic rhythm, his masterful use of irony, his use of the focal instance, his instinct for symbolic action. But he is included in this narrative because, unlike many, he came back from liberalism to his roots as a Christian and as a Bible preacher.

The younger King was schooled by theological liberals but was strongly influenced by Gardner Taylor, who held to "an explicitly evangelical doctrine of salvation centered in the substitutionary atonement of Christ."[2] King preached his trial sermon and was ordained when he was eighteen. Successive scholarships allowed him to study at Morehouse College in Atlanta, Crozer Seminary near Philadelphia, and at Boston University, where he did his doctoral work. Although embracing much of Enlightenment liberalism's vocabulary, Lischer argues, King did not become a liberal.[3] He learned the love ethic from Beecher and Brooks out of the previous century, but toward the end of his ministry that liberal optimism was blown away, "exposing once again the bedrock of black eschatology," which insists that not human idealism but God's mighty power will accomplish what needs to be done.[4] But at this time King was dipping heavily into Fosdick, Wallace Hamilton (the Methodist),[5] Howard Thurman of the Church of All Nations in San Francisco, Paul Tillich, and Chuck Templeton.[6] His failure to acknowledge his sources was a lifelong problem.

In 1954 he became pastor of the prestigious Dexter Avenue Baptist Church of Montgomery, Alabama. His intern, J. T. Porter, characterized King's early preaching at Dexter Avenue as a "very positive, Schuller type thing."[7] The boycott battles pushed King back into the more confrontational "smite 'em" style of his outstanding predecessor, Vernon Johns, who had "vanquished the power of positive thinking."[8] This was more the style of Jonathan Edwards than of Phillips Brooks. His seminary education had turned him away from the Bible, and he had lapped up the BOMFOG (brotherhood of man and fatherhood of God) thinking.[9] Lischer astutely observes:

> He did not notice that the historical criticism he was learning stifled the Christian impulse to get close to the Scripture, to live it, and did nothing to bridge the gap between the cultures. In fact, higher criticism only magnified the distance between the Book and its modern readers.[10]

In 1960 King moved to a one-hundred-month copastorate with his father at Ebenezer, where he preached what Lischer calls "the Ebenezer gospel." Churches without a sense of mission he called "entertainment centers." Increasingly his reference was to the supernatural, the Christological foundation, the meaning of the cross. His 1966 sermon on "the acceptable year of our Lord" from Luke 4 is explosively eschatological.[11]

King believed in original sin and that only God's pardon can rectify the human predicament.[12] The base of all is the nature and character of God, who is the Father of the Lord Jesus Christ. He was clearly evangelical on Jesus and salvation,[13] and used the altar call as an invitation to accept Christ.[14] He and his staff consulted with the Billy Graham crusade.[15]

We must see King in the cultural and social trauma of the racial revolution of the 1960s. Certainly there are aspects of his life and ministry that we cannot understand, but here was a man who preached Christ. His was a tragic loss for all Americans and in a very particular sense for all Christians in America, black or white, when he was killed in his thirty-ninth year. "But the Word of our God stands forever."

---

1. Richard Lischer, *The Preacher King: Martin Luther King, Jr. and the Word that Moved America* (New York: Oxford University Press, 1995), 45. An important study. See also Paul Scott Wilson, *A Concise History of Preaching* (Nashville: Abingdon, 1992), 170ff.

2. Lischer, *The Preacher King,* 51.

3. Ibid., 53.

4. Ibid., 57.

5. J. Wallace Hamilton is in the Peale-Schuller genre; see his sermons in *Where Now Is Thy God?* (New York: Revell, 1969); *What About Tomorrow?* (New York: Revell, 1972). He told good stories, but the well was dry.

6. Lischer, *The Preacher King,* 104. Templeton was a tragic cul-de-sac with his abandonment of friendship with Billy Graham, abandonment of the ministry, and abandonment of the faith; see Charles Templeton, *An Anecdotal Memoir* (Toronto: McClelland and Stewart, 1983). Paul Tillich likewise could put thoughts together memorably (although when I heard him his heavy accent made him somewhat difficult to follow), but he was not even a theist. See his popular books of sermons, *The Shaking of the Foundations* (New York: Scribner's, 1943); *The Eternal Now* (New York: Scribner's, 1956). Tillich was also a notorious philanderer. Lischer faces this issue in *The Preacher King,* 168ff.

7. Lischer, *The Preacher King,* 81.

8. Ibid., 85.

9. Ibid., 199, 148.

10. Ibid., 199.

11. Ibid., 235.

12. Ibid., 224.

13. Ibid., 226.

14. Ibid., 240. Lischer speaks of his "reversion from the philosophical method he learned in graduate school to his native theological assumptions" (202). His was a growing disillusionment with white liberals.

15. Ibid., 243.

12.5.3 Toyohiko Kagawa—The Reach of Asian Preaching

By the truth as man thinks of it, we cannot come to understand the redeeming blood of Christ. Even by means of the philosophy of the eighteenth and nineteenth centuries, it could not be understood. When we come to have the feeling of the God of the whole universe, that is, the heart of the suffering Christ, only then can we come to comprehend the atonement.

The theology of the nineteenth century left out the atonement . . . a certain church almost entirely left out the atonement . . . But in the Bible it is not so. If we ask why the doctrine of the atonement is left in many chapters of the Bible, it is because of the existence of the great problem of sin.

When one man is converted there flows out a river of influence by which many people receive life. By the conversion of Jerry McCauley, Bradley was saved. By this influence, Merle [sic] Trotter, who had served ten sentences in prison, was saved.[1] Then Billy Sunday was saved and by his influence tens of thousands were converted. That is what it means for rivers of living water to flow from us. It is not merely influence. It is the influence of the Holy Spirit which draws the lineage to one after another, until it is wonderful to trace.

—T. Kagawa

The twentieth century has seen the modernization of Japan, the breaking of Japan on the wheel of World War II, and its postwar rejuvenation into a mighty economic and political power. The Christian minority is minuscule here, but exerts a significant influence. Japan's greatest biblical preacher beyond question has been **Toyohiko Kagawa** (1888–1960). Kagawa was born in Kobe to a wealthy and politically significant Samurai and his geisha concubine.[2] When he was four years of age both of his parents died, and he was sent to live with his father's legal wife and a foster grandmother. Here he knew only abuse. Kagawa studied in the Buddhist temple and was forced to work very hard in the Kagawa enterprises. He was often taunted as the "concubine child."[3] While he was a student, he came under the influence of American missionaries, H. W. Myers and C. A. Logan, who led him to Christ. He went on to the Presbyterian College in Tokyo and ultimately took his B.D. at Princeton. Frail in health and tubercular, Kagawa spent fifteen years living and ministering in the infamous Shinkawa slums of Kobe. Always "a flaming evangel," he had to take a year off in "a rendezvous with death."[4]

Some scholars have questioned aspects of Kagawa's theology. He was well read in both Asian and Western classics, and his faith was so contextualized that the mode of his expression seems a bit strange to us. Yet his favorite hymn was "Jesus, Keep Me Near the Cross," and his *Meditations on the Cross* (1935) are sound. He preached vigorously against sin in all of its forms and the blood of

Christ as the antidote.[5] Clearly he was a Trinitarian and Nicaean in his Christology and was strong on the divinity of our Lord and Christian experience through the Holy Spirit.[6] Kagawa was part of the Kingdom of God Movement and its simultaneous evangelistic crusades in six major Japanese cities in which verbal proclamation loomed large. Of his preaching:

> His addresses are characterized by quiet fervor and moving power. He sways the multitudes who everywhere gather to hear him. Himself a man of action, his addresses lead men to action. Throughout his messages there are the delicate touches of a poet and the telling action and gestures of an actor. However, the most vivid and abiding impression left with the listeners is that of a mind alert, a soul on fire, an overwhelming passion in possession of the disease-riddled body all dedicated to one high, unselfish purpose and working together in absolute harmony toward its realization.[7]

Even when Kagawa was studying at Princeton (imagine him listening to Warfield), he worked in the Bowery among the needy in New York City. His wife, Haru, would join him after he returned to Japan in preaching to beggars and gamblers in the alleys of the slums.[8] His book *Psychology of the Poor* made a deep impression. He was imprisoned for siding with the oppressed workers. The great earthquake of 1923 gave him great opportunity for ministry, but the darkness of Pearl Harbor and World War II and imprisonment brought him to desolation. He spent much of the conflict consigned to a tubercular colony he had founded on the Inland Sea. After the war, he had opportunity to preach before the emperor and the empress. Indeed the first public appearance of the emperor after the war was a visit to the center where Kagawa established a ministry to twenty thousand refugees.[9] The life and message of the man can be summed up:

> As in a single Word, Christ's Love-Moment
> Is summed up in the Cross. The Cross is
> The whole of Christ, the whole of love . . .[10]

---

1. I think Kagawa means Melvin Trotter, a trophy of grace who founded a Grand Rapids rescue mission and represents all of these faithful preachers in this setting. See Melvin Trotter, *These Forty Years* (Grand Rapids: Zondervan, 1939). Campbell Morgan and H. A. Ironside write appreciative forewords to this volume.
2. Charlie May Simon, *A Seed Shall Serve: The Story of the Spiritual Leader of Modern Japan* (London: Hodder and Stoughton, 1959), 8.
3. Ibid., 26.
4. William Axling, *Kagawa* (New York: London, 1932), 19–23.
5. Ibid., 123.
6. Toyohiko Kagawa, *Meditations on the Holy Spirit* (Nashville: Cokesbury, 1939), 111ff.
7. Axling, *Kagawa,* 119.

8. Simon, *A Seed Shall Serve,* 114.
9. Ibid., 147. Kagawa wrote more than one hundred fifty books.
10. Ralph G. Turnbull, *A History of Preaching* (Grand Rapids: Baker, 1974), 401. Turnbull indicates "To Kagawa there was never any doubt concerning the validity of the scriptural records" (403).

12.5.4 WATCHMAN NEE—THE RICHNESS OF ASIAN PREACHING

What matters is the effectiveness of the word proclaimed.

No servant of Christ should be satisfied with present attainment. Anyone who is content with what is, is a loser of opportunities. I believe those God is now giving us are far beyond anything we can conceive. Every day God is giving us opportunities and the aggregate who can assess? To redeem the time is to seize today the opportunities God has appointed for us today. When the church buries a talent there is serious loss.
—Watchman Nee, after the Communist takeover of China

Whether shackled by foes or hampered by circumstances, whether totally paralyzed or walled up in solitary darkness, we can pray, we can appeal to Him, we can ask. We shall surely receive. God will act again. If we will go on asking, our sorrow will be turned to surpassing joy.
—Watchman Nee

The long history of missionary preaching in China has been touched at several points in this narrative, but it is important to see that part of the fruit of missionary enterprise has been the multiplication of gifted and able Chinese preachers. These include Leland Wang, Andrew Gih,[1] Marcus Cheng,[2] and most signally, **Watchman Nee** (1903–1972).

Nee was born in Swatow, the third of nine children; his father was a soft-spoken man, a cloth merchant, and his mother was very strong-willed. She became a forceful Methodist preacher in her own right. Nee's parents were converted under the ministry of evangelist Dora Yu. When in the aftermath of her conversion, his mother confessed to Watchman that she had beaten him unjustly (an unheard-of loss of face in China), he too was converted at the age of eighteen and attended Yu's Bible school.[3]

Missionary Margaret E. Barber, who was supported by Pastor D. M. Panton's Surrey Chapel in Norwich, had an immense influence on him. Under her counsel he was baptized.[4] She introduced him to the writings of Madame Guyon, the French mystic who had a marked influence on the home meetings in which young Nee was now increasingly involved. These gatherings evolved into the Little Flock Movement. Barber also initiated him into the thinking of Mrs. Jessie Penn-Lewis on the Cross, who came out of the Calvinistic Methodists of Wales and the Welsh revival. He traveled with his mother in special services in Malaysia after graduating from Anglican Trinity College in Foochow. His insightful biblical preaching and his work as editor of *Revival* (later *The Christian*) brought him into prominence and usefulness. Although he had a brief Presbyterian connection, he moved more and more to the practice of local assemblies independent of mission societies and unsalaried ministers.

He was diagnosed as having tuberculosis but left the issue of his healing in the discovery of the truth that Christ is victor![5] He spoke ceaselessly in Overcomer Conferences along the Keswick line. Kinnear describes Watchman Nee's strength:

> The appeal of Watchman's own preaching lay first of all in his gift of making so plain the way to God that relies solely upon Christ's finished work. All too many Christians were striving after a salvation based on good works of their own, a way little removed in principle from Buddhism. They had been told it was presumptuous to say confidently that they were saved. The preaching of new life as God's free gift startled them therefore with its novelty. Nor did Watchman stop with the good news of righteousness by faith. He was finding now much personal help from the writings of Andrew Murray and F. B. Meyer on the practical life of holiness and deliverance from sin. He read, too, all he could of Charles G. Finney and of Evan Roberts and the Welsh spiritual awaking of 1904–5, and he delved into Otto Stockmeier [cf. 9.5.3] and Jessie Penn-Lewis on the questions of soul and spirit and triumph over Satanic power.[6]

Many of us would have a problem with his ecclesiology. But Nee had an incredible knowledge of the biblical text. He walked back and forth as he spoke with "his hands behind his back, just speaking from his heart."[7] Yet again:

> Standing there in his dark-blue cotton gown he held their attention with his gentle manner, his simple but thorough reasoning and his apt analogies. No one ever saw him use any notes for he could reproduce anything he read. To illustrate a thing visually he could draw a swift imaginary sketch in the air (which a young worker might reproduce on poster paper afterwards) and if to illumine some point he told a personal anecdote it was nearly always a story against himself. His keen sense of humour sent frequent ripples of laughter round the hall and "you never got sleepy in his meetings." But from start to finish he never strayed from his subject.[8]

He visited Britain and America in both 1933 and 1938. Unable to fit easily into the coils and complexities of Western polities, he nonetheless enjoyed his contacts with George Cutting in England, the author of *Safety, Certainty and Enjoyment,* which at that time had run to thirty million copies. Nee also found a soul brother in T. Austin Sparks, a former Baptist preacher whose ministry at Honor Oaks Farm and through the printed page were a tonic to Nee.[9] He visited Keswick in 1938, where both his prayers and his presence made a deep impression. On his way back to China, Nee delivered a memorable set of messages in Denmark.[10]

During this time, in harmony with his conviction on ministerial compensation, Nee managed the family chemical enterprise.[11] In 1947 he came to a new emphasis on brokenness of heart and spirit.[12] He enjoyed good fellowship with two young pioneers, Geoffrey Bull and George Patterson, who were going to the Tibetan frontier.[13]

With the Chinese communist takeover in 1949, the Little Flock Movement was under strong pressure to become part of the Three Self Movement sanctioned by the government. In resisting, Nee was first arrested in 1952. In anticipation of the situation, he had sent his somewhat authoritarian colleague Witness Lee to Taiwan.[14] He visited there himself but chose to return to mainland China. Accused of being "a running dog of the imperialists," criminal charges were preferred in 1956. With a great flow of invective, he was found guilty and was sentenced to fifteen years of hard labor. Amid cruelty and persecution, Watchman Nee yet worked for the Lord in the prison and won men to Christ. In 1972 he died in prison at the age of sixty-nine, five years beyond the sentence given to him. The martyr's seed has given much fruit; the church in China, numbering one million when the missionaries were expelled in 1949, may now number seventy million. And Nee is read everywhere.

1. Andrew Gih, *Launch Out Into the Deep* (London: Marshall, Morgan, and Scott, 1938). Gih is highly commended by J. Edwin Orr, whose revival and preaching ministry have been crucial. See Newman Watts, *Edwin Orr: The Ubiquitous Ulsterman* (Croydon, England: Uplift Books, 1947). Orr not only wrote the history of revival but also preached revival mightily.
2. Edla Matson, *Peter Matson: Covenant Pathfinder in China* (Chicago: Covenant, 1951), 157ff. Cheng was the gifted professor at Kingchow Seminary.
3. Angus I. Kinnear, *Watchman Nee: Against the Tide* (Ft. Washington, Pa.: CLC, 1973), 18, 37.
4. Ibid., 42–43. See *The Autobiography of Madam Guyon* (Chicago: Moody, n.d.). There is a strain of Christ-mysticism (to use Deissman's phrase) in Watchman Nee, and we sense the same in Guyon, whose work he valued.
5. Ibid., 73–75. Cf. Dana Roberts, *Understanding Watchman Nee* (Plainfield, N.J.: Haven, 1980). Quite critical. He uses the word *pietism* pejoratively and tars Watchman Nee. This is to misrepresent historic pietism.
6. Ibid., 64.
7. Ibid., 141. Nee's studies on Ephesians are gripping, *Sit, Walk and Stand* (Bombay: Witness and Testimony, 1957); *The Normal Christian Life* is his best-known work (London: Witness and Testimony, 1958); *What Shall This Man Do?* (Ft. Washington, Pa.: CLC, 1961); *The Latent Power of the Soul,* in which he contrasts the spiritual with the soulish (New York: Christian Fellowship, 1972); *Love Not the World* (Ft. Washington, Pa.: CLC, 1968); *Twelve Baskets Full* (Hong Kong: Church Book Room, 1966). In these multiple text sermons we see artistic and aesthetic Asian logic in full force.
8. Ibid., 118. Roberts alleges that some of his close followers made sounds in prayer like Nee's clicking dentures.
9. The works of T. Austin Sparks are many. Some of the best, in my opinion: *The Stewardship of the Mystery* in two volumes (London: Witness and Testimony, 1939);

Rivers of Living Water (London: Witness and Testimony, n.d.); *God's Reactions to Man's Defections* (London: Witness and Testimony, 1956); *Fundamental Questions of the Christian Life* (London: Witness and Testimony, n.d.). The publication of *Toward the Mark* has recently ceased.

10. At the invitation of Pastor Fjord Christensen of Copenhagen, where he gave The Normal Christian Life studies for the first time, Kinnear *(Watchman Nee,* 113).

11. Ibid., 126–27, 140.

12. A similar message was preached in the West by Roy and Revel Hession. See his books, *The Calvary Road* (Ft. Washington, Pa.: CLC, 1950); *We Would See Jesus; Be Filled Now.* I shall never forget sermons I heard Hession deliver many years ago. See his autobiography, *My Calvary Road* (Grand Rapids: Zondervan, 1978).

13. Kinnear, *Watchman Nee,* 140. Geoffrey Bull's magnificent *When Iron Gates Yield* (Chicago: Moody, 1955) and *The City and the Sign: An Interpretation of the Book of Jonah* (Grand Rapids: Baker, 1970) are "must" reading.

14. Charges of doctrinal irregularity against Witness Lee have been reconsidered by many critics. See J. Gordon Melton, *An Open Letter Concerning the Local Church, Witness Lee and the God-Men Controversy* (Santa Barbara: Institute for the Study of American Religion, 1985). For a thoughtful survey of the ministry situation in Taiwan after 1949, see Allen J. Swanson, *Taiwan: Mainline Versus Independent Church Growth* (South Pasadena, Calif.: William Carey Library, 1970).

12.5.5 *THE KOREAN PULPIT—THE REVIVAL AND PREACHING*

The Bible is the Word of God. Therefore, when we understand the truth of the Bible through the Holy Spirit, we can feel the power of life in the Bible. Preaching is not a lecture or an apologetic speech. Preaching is the product of a spiritual life. It is the fruit of the Holy Spirit through prayer, study of the Bible and obedience to the Word.

—Yune-Sun Park

This has been a turbulent century for Korea, once called the hermit kingdom. Within the Chinese family of nations, Korea remained tightly closed until the arrival of Christian missionaries.

Korea has been called "the banner mission field in the world." We have already spoken of Nevius and Goforth and the revival that came early in the century. The spiritual resurgence there has been largely Presbyterian, with strong Baptist, Holiness, and Pentecostal work as well. In fact, the largest Presbyterian, Methodist, and Pentecostal local church congregations are in Korea. Yet Japanese occupation and cruelty (1910–1945) saw many martyrs and intensified purity in the church. Then came the Korean War with all of its suffering. The postwar years brought the partition of the peninsula, the communization of the North, and a hodgepodge American policy, termed by the late Sumner Wells as "one of the most serious crimes of the twentieth century." Despite all the turmoil, the urbanization and industrialization of the nation have taken root.[1] But prosperity does not bode well for the church. The life of prayer, which had been so striking in the Korean church, does not easily survive Western influence.

Under governmental encouragement, many Koreans have emigrated around the world. Two million Koreans still reside in China, and many are flocking to the U.S. The Korean church in America is facing some serious issues, many related to generational tensions.[2]

Koreans have been known as good speakers and preachers. Very little sermonic literature has been translated, but a new study of Korean preaching has just been published in this country, and several leading preachers can be identified.

Sun-Joo Kil (1869–1935) preached in the revivals of 1907, when converts increased by thirty percent. Strongly evangelistic and tending toward allegorization, Kil was strongly dispensational and premillennial.[3] He established sixty churches despite becoming blind.

Ihk-Doo Kim (1874–1950) was a notorious hoodlum who was converted and read the Bible one hundred times before his baptism. Signs of the Spirit often accompanied his powerful preaching.[4] His main themes were the Cross, the blood, and repentance.

Sung-Bong Lee (1900–1965) was often called the D. L. Moody of Korea. He was an evangelist for the Holiness Church of Korea. Persecuted by the communists, he was faithful in a ministry that was owned of the Spirit and saw many converts. He often sang a hymn while preaching.[5] Lee provided strong preaching on the Second Advent.

Hwa-Sik Kim (1894–1947) was imprisoned by both the Japanese and the communists. Although frail in health, he was an unusually gifted preacher, sometimes called the Spurgeon of Korea. Dr. Chung remarks, "We can feel a mother's warm hand in his preaching."[6] He used lively introductions and was a poet. Kim loved John Bunyan and often quoted him. In 1947 he was killed in prison.

Ki-Chul Choo (1897–1944) preached fearlessly when Shinto shrine worship was an issue (1930–1945). The Japanese required all citizens to participate in shrine ceremonies. Many Christians complied, but others led by Choo felt that participating was idolatrous. His sermons were God-centered.[7] He died in prison.

Yang-Won Sohn (1902–1951) was incarcerated for six years by the Japanese over the shrine issue, and saw two of his sons martyred in the communist revolt of 1948. He was captured by the communists and was shot three years later. His ministry had a great focus on lepers. He was called "Korea's atom bomb of love."[8] Sohn led Korean Christians by his life and example but also through his penetrating biblical preaching. Clearly the historic biblical faith and its faithful proclamation are at the heart of this dear people.

---

1. In my opinion the best history is Robert T. Oliver, *A History of the Korean People in Modern Times* (Newark, N.J.: University of Delaware Press, 1993). The postwar Korean president, Syngman Rhee, was a Methodist.
2. For interesting insight into émigré mentality, see K. Connie Kang, *Home Was the Land of the Morning Calm* (New York: Addison/Wesley, 1995) The danger for the émigré is allowing the church to be the celebration of ethnicity.
3. Sung-Kuh Chung, *The Korean Church and Reformed Faith: Focusing on the Historical Study of Preaching in the Korean Church* (Seattle: Times Publishing, 1996),

45, 51. Dr. Chung is the former president of Chongshin College and is now a professor at Chongshin Theological Seminary. The publication of Chung's study makes an inestimable contribution.

4. Ibid., 56.
5. Ibid., 66.
6. Ibid., 75.
7. Ibid., 106.
8. Ibid., 120.

12.5.6 *Sadhu Sundar Singh—The Risks of Indian Preaching*

We shall never get a second opportunity of bearing the Cross after our life on earth . . . so now is the time to bear the Cross joyfully. Never again will an opportunity be given us of bearing this sweet burden.

Other religions say, "Do good and you will become good." Christianity says, "Be in Christ and you will do good." The meaning of the Atonement and the Blood that washes away our sins is that we are grafted into Christ.

I don't sit down and write out my sermons. As I pray, I get texts, subjects and illustrations. Preachers ought to get their message from God. If they get it from books instead, they do not preach their own gospel; they preach the gospel of others. They sit on other people's eggs and hatch them and think they are their own.

—Sundar Singh

The masses of the subcontinent of India (India, Pakistan, and Bangladesh), buffeted by the renewal of native religions, tribal and religious warfare, precarious economies, and population explosion, desperately need the gospel. We have noted some of the early missionaries who have been augmented by gifted indigenous preachers, and in some areas there has been a remarkable response. Yet the teeming millions seem relatively impervious to the gospel of Christ.

One of the gifted and able preachers in this century for all too brief a time was **Sadhu Sundar Singh** (1889–1933?). He was born in a devout Sikh family in Rampur in the Punjab. Sikhism was founded by Nanak (1469–1538) as a conscious compromise between Hinduism and Islam. Their holy book, the Granth, a collection of poems, is virtually worshiped at the central shrine in Amritsar.[1] Many lawyers, military men, and police officers in India are Sikhs. Young Sundar was very religious and in fact memorized the Gita of the Hindus by the age of seven. He was searching: "I wanted to save myself! But I could not achieve it for myself."[2] Both his mother and his older brother died, and he became desperate for meaning. He had contact with an American Presbyterian mission school and had the New Testament, but he burned it publicly and became a ringleader of those who pelted the village preachers with stones.[3] Determined to take his own life, Singh had a vision of Jesus coming into his room and asking him in Hindustani, "Why do you persecute me?"[4] He became a Christian even though this meant being disowned by his father and excommunicated by the Sikhs. He was baptized at sixteen and became a sadhu, a homeless wanderer, suffering and proclaiming Christ.

There is something quintessentially Indian about this Christian mystic. Archbishop Soderholm of Sweden observed, "Sundar is the first to show the whole world how the Gospel of Jesus Christ is reflected in unchanged purity in an Indian soul."[5] Singh did spend some time studying at St. John's Divinity College in Lahore, but the lure of the road was too strong. He traveled over the whole world but was especially burdened to capture the great Buddhist strongholds in Tibet and Burma. Making several trips to the West, he was deeply disillusioned by the materialism and disunity in the church. Singh made repeated forays over the Himalayas to Tibet and was often persecuted. Even when his funds were wiped out in a bank failure, he was determined to return to preach in Tibet. In 1929 he moved out in quest for converts in Tibet and beyond and was never seen again. In 1933 the Indian government, assuming him dead, probated his will.

Sundar Singh was a great lover of the Bible, professing that "the Bible, like a lump of sugar, is sweet to me at whatever point I taste it."[6] He particularly treasured the Gospel of John and loved to share it. Repelled by modern rationalistic criticism of the Bible, Singh called it "spiritual influenza" resulting in denigration of Christ as Lord and God.[7] He had problems with any mechanistic theory of inspiration and knew and felt the power of the Holy Spirit in and through the Word. One report had it as follows:

> A few weeks ago a Christian Sadhu by name Sundar Singh came about preaching the Gospel in the villages round about Narkanda and suffered a great deal of persecution. We were sitting and chatting . . . when a farmer by name Nandi came up and said: "A very strange thing has happened in our village. We were reaping the corn in a field and a Sadhu came up to us and began to preach religion. We all felt very annoyed at this interference in our work and showered curses on him; but little heeding our curses and threats the man went on with his talk. At this my brother took up a stone and hit the man on the head. But this good man, unmindful of the insult, closed his eyes and said, 'O God, forgive them.' After awhile my brother who had flung the stone was suddenly caught with a splitting headache and had to give up reaping. At this the Sadhu took my brother's scythe and started reaping the corn. We all marveled and said, 'What manner of man is this Sadhu, that, instead of abusing and cursing us in return, he prays in our favor.' Then we took him to our house where he told us many nice things. After he had gone, we noticed an amazing thing. The field where this good man had reaped has never yielded so much corn as it has this year; we have gathered two maunds above the average this time."[8]

He knew the philosopher Tagore and he knew Gandhi, but Sadhu Sundar Singh's consuming passion was to be known as "a witness to the saving power of God in Jesus Christ."

1. Robert E. Hume, *The World's Living Religions* (New York: Scribner's, 1955), 94ff.
2. C. F. Andrews, *Sadhu Sundar Singh: A Personal Memoir* (London: Hodder and Stoughton, 1934), 64.
3. Ibid., 68.
4. Cyril J. Davey, *Sadhu Sundar Singh* (Bromley, Kent: STL Books, 1950), 32ff.
5. Andrews, *Sadhu Sundar Singh,* 131. He attended the Keswick Convention in 1922.
6. B. H. Strecter and A. J. Appasamy, *The Sadhu* (London: Macmillan, 1927), 196.
7. Ibid., 200.
8. Ibid., 209. A maund is an Indian unit of weight measuring about 82.28 pounds.

12.5.7 BLACK ELK—THE RESILIENCE OF NATIVE AMERICAN PREACHING

Without an adequate sermon, no clue is given to the moral purpose at the heart of the mystery, and reverence remains without ethical content.
—Reinhold Niebuhr

In recent centuries, the Roman Catholic church and Eastern Orthodoxy have been so involved in liturgy that preaching of substance has been eclipsed. The unmatched television effectiveness of Bishop Fulton J. Sheen in the 1950s (who can forget his piercing blue eyes?) held millions spellbound, but his message was practical not biblical, relational not salvific. Since Vatican II, there has come a renaissance of interest in preaching in Catholicism both stateside and abroad.[1] In areas where Catholicism has been dominant, preaching has been recessive, but with the Protestant explosion in Latin America, for instance, a rising new generation of Roman Catholic preachers of ability and skill is coming into view.

A true gospel preacher who came out of the Jesuit outreach at the St. Francis Mission in Rosebud, South Dakota, and the Holy Rosary Mission in Pine Ridge, South Dakota, was the Native American known as **Black Elk** (d. 1950). Black Elk was known technically as a catechist.[2] He lived in the world of the Lakota Sioux Indians, where for many years he was "a kind of preacher" who preached the Bible and Christian doctrine to his people for the greater part of his life.

Government Indian policy has been one of the great scandals of our national history. In 1868 the American government signed the Laramie Treaty, giving all of South Dakota west of the Missouri River to the Sioux. This treaty was broken by General George Custer in 1874 in connection with the gold rush in Deadwood and Lead, South Dakota. Uprisings led by Black Elk's cousin, Crazy Horse, and Sitting Bull resulted. At the Battle of Wounded Knee, two hundred Indians—men, women, and children—were massacred. In these years, Black Elk was a native medicine man and was partially blinded at Wounded Knee.

After these years of warfare, Black Elk was converted by the "blackrobes," as contrasted with the Episcopalians, who were called "whiterobes," or the Presbyterians, who were called "shortrobes." Black Elk's Christianity did not compromise or stultify his Indianness. Of his conversion it was said, "The Son of God called him to lead a new life."[3] He sensed God's call to "instruct the people out of the Scriptures."[4] His forte was Bible stories, and his own reading of the

Bible was legendary.[5] Black Elk faced many obstacles, including the American Indian Movement, whose members would tear down the signs advertising Black Elk's meetings. In his missionary work, he challenged the use of peyote in Native American worship, and "he converted a lot of those people."[6]

It was said of Black Elk that "on any occasion he can arise and deliver a flood of oratory." His heart was full of Christ. Literally hundreds came to the Lord through his preaching ministry. His favorite theme was the two-road map. We must remember that in Indian religion, no personal relationship exists with a personal Savior.[7] But Black Elk relentlessly hammered away with the message, "Believe in Jesus Christ."[8] We recall him with the tribute, "He practiced a Christian life."

---

1. For a European sample, see Otto Semmelroth, *The Preaching Word: On the Theology of Proclamation* (New York: Herder and Herder, 1965). The significant American work is Walter J. Burghardt, *Preaching: The Art and the Craft* (New York: Paulist, 1987). The approach of some Roman Catholic preachers is more conservative, such as Cardinal Lustiger of Paris or Joseph Cardinal Ratzinger, *Dogma and Preaching* (Chicago: Franciscan Herald Press, 1985), or more radical and liberal, such as John Dominic Crossan of Chicago, *Jesus: A Revolutionary Biography* (New York: Harper/Collins, 1994), in which he argues that dogs ate the body of Jesus (154). In contrast, the late Henri Nouwen was one of the most captivating preachers I have ever heard.
2. Michael F. Steltenkamp, *Black Elk: Holy Man of the Oglala* (Norman: University of Oklahoma, 1993), xvii.
3. Ibid., 36.
4. Ibid., 47.
5. Ibid., 47.
6. Ibid., 62. For a thoughtful statement on the issue here, see Samuel Shangchi Pan, *Some General Principles for Sermon Preparation in Cross-Cultural Preaching* (Th.M. thesis, Trinity Evangelical Divinity School, 1986).
7. Ibid., 145.
8. Ibid., 74.

12.6 GERMAN, DUTCH, SWEDISH, AND SWEDISH-AMERICAN PREACHERS IN A TUMULTUOUS TIME

From the beginning, then, Christianity, being concerned with the Event which by definition has no parallel, God being agent in it as He is not in other happenings, was committed to preaching, to proclamation. Whoso said Christianity said preaching. There was no choice between that and absolutely ceasing to be, with not the least chance of ever occurring again.

—H. H. Farmer

Western Europe in the twentieth century has become more and more a "spiritual ice-belt." The savage assaults of Enlightenment unbelief have been succeeded by postmodern "radical relativism and skepticism that rejects any idea of truth, knowledge or objectivity" (Gertrude Himmelfarb). The catastrophic loss of Christian understanding and influence in recent years has left church attendance at between two and three percent. Authority was lost when authoritarianism was dismissed by autonomous man, with no willingness to recognize the critical difference. Even so fine a preacher as F. W. Dillistone became so enamored with Lloyd Morgan's emergent evolution that he concluded we must embrace the modern scientific worldview posthaste.[1] Whether or not there is any real difference between Karl Barth's neo-orthodoxy and Jacques Derrida's deconstructionism may be argued, but there were preachers who, even in the Sahara of subjectivity, had a message from God.[2] This is what we need now even in the United States, where pragmatism is the potentate.[3]

---

1. Charles Raven, *F. W. Dillistone* (Grand Rapids: Eerdmans, 1975). He did reject "the robots of modern behaviorism."
2. Graham Ward, *Barth, Derrida and the Language of Theology* (Cambridge, Mass.: Cambridge University Press, 1996).
3. Marva J. Dawn, *Reaching Out Without Dumbing Down: A Theology of Worship for the Turn-of-the-Century Culture* (Grand Rapids: Eerdmans, 1995). She argues that there is "normative truth" which calls the community into being.

   The fierce struggle among the Jesuits against total horizontalization in which unbelief is assumed to be an option is almost paradigmatic in our time. See Malachi Martin, *The Jesuits: The Society of Jesus and the Betrayal of the Roman Catholic Church* (New York: Simon and Schuster, 1987). The whole notion of "salvation" is virtually lost as meaning is sought in the world, not from Scripture; the "new fabric" does not involve preaching "Christ crucified" (429).

12.6.1 MARTIN NIEMOLLER—PREACHING IN THE BELLY OF THE BEAST

We can see how God's Word is being put into chains and imprisoned from the list of undesirable books on which figures nearly all the desirable Christian literature, to the prison-cells which close behind the messengers of Jesus Christ, even to the prayers . . . that God may give our people back the free and unimpeded preaching of the gospel.

The gospel must remain the gospel; the church must remain the church; the creed must remain the creed; Protestant Christianity must remain Protestant Christianity.

—Martin Niemoller

That ours is a spiritual battle against demon hordes is especially clear when we consider preachers who engaged in defiance of totalitarian regimes, such as **Martin Niemoller** (1892–1984). Born in Westphalia, the son of a Lutheran pastor with some Reformed proclivities, Niemoller early had a childlike devotion to Jesus.[1] His father was strong follower of Pastor Johan Wichern's Inner Mission movement, which aimed at the spiritual renewal of Germany through the huge Kirchentags and other approaches. This was a movement with which the younger Niemoller was closely associated for many years. He graduated from the German Naval Academy at Kiel and served as a U-boat commander in World War I. His exploits and adventures in sinking and destroying shipping earned him the Iron Cross.[2] Yet his thoughts were more and more turning to God. For a while after the war he farmed, but he was not content. God was calling him to preach.

Niemoller was terrified at the thought of standing before a congregation and speaking.[3] Still he could not escape the divine compunction:

> I had been taught as a child that belief in Christ as Lord and Saviour and diligent attention to God's Word can transform men and give them freedom and strength. That lesson I had never forgotten, for my own experience had proved it to be true. I now became convinced that the best and most effective help I could give to my countrymen in the national calamity would be to share that knowledge with them.[4]

He took up studies at Munster and was chiefly taken with Professor Karl Heim. Here he overcame his fears of speaking and did a curacy. He worked in Westphalian home missions from 1923 to 1931. From 1931 to 1936, he served the strategic Dahlem Church in a well-to-do suburb of Berlin and developed a deep friendship with Gerhard Jacobi, the Jewish Christian who served the Kaiser Wilhelm Church. With the advent of Hitler and the National Socialists, Niemoller found that he was one of the earliest opponents of Nazism and Hitler's dedication to create a "positive Christianity."[5] He spearheaded the formation of the Pastor's Emergency Union and quickly became the spokesman of the German churches in opposition to Hitler.

Not all clergy were so disposed. Some became Nazis, or at least strong advocates of Hitler's policies, such as Heidegger, Althaus, Kittel, and Hirsch. But the thrust of Niemoller's preaching was "God is my Fuehrer!" Not surprisingly, he had a personal confrontation with Hitler.[6] Dr. Hjalmer Schacht, the Nazi economic csar acquitted at Nuremburg, was a member of Niemoller's congregation, and the von Ribbentrops attended, but Niemoller refused to baptize their children. In 1936 he was arrested by the Gestapo and removed from his charge, but he would not be muzzled. During the war, he spent time in a number of prisons, including Sachsenhausen and Dachau. We have in printed form his letters from Moabit Prison and sermons which he preached at Dachau.[7] That any preaching at all was allowed at Dachau during the four years he was kept there is a remarkable story in itself. These strongly biblical messages are deeply moving considering the circumstances in which they were delivered.[8]

After the war, Niemoller acted as representative of the German churches, and he traveled widely in England, the United States, and Russia. He was also president of the Protestant church (Lutheran/Reformed) in Hessen, Nassau, and Frankfurt-am-Main. His wife Else was killed in an automobile accident. Nihilism was threatening to devour the populace. Writers like Gunter Grass and Herman Hesse tried to find something to say to the questions and guilt of the

German people. He remarried and continued significant ministry in the vacuum of postwar Germany until his death in 1984.

The main collection of his sermons from Dahlem days (where he had ten thousand members) shows that, while grounded firmly in a biblical text, Niemoller seldom divided the text carefully. As good Lutheran sermons, they certainly are Christ-centered and emphasize the grace of God.[9]

When his father had been deposed from his pulpit, he preached in a dance hall, filling it to the rafters for the proclamation of the gospel of Christ.[10] "The Bible is not bound," said the elder Niemoller. Martin Niemoller learned that lesson well.

---

1. James Bentley, *Martin Niemoller: 1892–1984* (New York: Free Press, 1984), 3.
2. Basil Miller, *Martin Niemoller* (Grand Rapids: Zondervan, 1942), 22–73. The truth is stranger than fiction!
3. Bentley, *Martin Niemoller,* 22.
4. Quoted in Dietmar Schmidt, *Pastor Niemoller* (Garden City, N.Y.: Doubleday, 1959), 65.
5. Bentley, *Martin Niemoller,* 237.
6. Ibid., 85. Cf. Robert P. Ericksen, *Theologians Under Hitler* (New Haven, Conn.: Yale University Press, 1985).
7. Hubert G. Locke, ed., *Exile in the Fatherland: Martin Niemoller's Letters from Moabit Prison* (Grand Rapids: Eerdmans, 1986). The life of another typical wartime hero-preacher is chronicled in Yerasmus Zervopoulos, *Kostas Metallinos: God's Messenger to Greece* (Chicago: Wordsmith, 1983). Dr. Metallinos was director of the Government Office of Accounting and led the Free Evangelical Church movement. He was the greatest preacher in Greece in this century and a dedicated student of the Scripture. He translated Godet and was an especially avid student of eschatology.
8. Martin Niemoller, *Dachau Sermons* (New York: Harper, 1946), 1ff.
9. Martin Niemoller, *Here Stand I!* (Chicago: Willet, Clark, 1937). Great preaching on the suffering and death of Jesus.
10. Miller, *Martin Niemoller,* 14.

12.6.2 KARL BARTH—PREACHING IN THE SHAMBLES OF WAR AND IN THE SUNLIGHT OF PEACE

Preaching is the Word of God which he himself speaks, claiming for the purpose the exposition of a biblical text in free human words that are relevant to contemporaries by those who are called to do this in the church that is obedient to its commission.

Theology as a church discipline ought in all its branches to be nothing other than sermon preparation in the broadest sense.

If a sermon is biblical it will not be boring.

> The need is not so much to get to the people as to come from Christ . . .
> then one automatically gets to the people.
>
> —Karl Barth

Appropriately called the theological titan of this century, **Karl Barth** (1886–1968) shows us both the appealing strengths and the grave weaknesses of neo-orthodoxy, one of the primary theological movements of our time. The son of Fritz Barth, a theologian from Basel, Karl Barth was reared largely in Bern and was, like so many, very liberal in his theology. He studied under Wilhelm Herrmann at Marburg and von Harnack at Berlin.

Old liberalism was built on Immanuel Kant's denial of any intellectual comprehension of objective truth. Usually the alternative was Schleiermacher's theology of experience and subjectivity. The utter bankruptcy of liberalism became apparent to Barth as he served two industrial parishes in the German Reformed Church before and after the First World War.[1] He then turned to Scripture itself:

> I sat under an apple tree and began to apply myself to Romans with all the resources that were available to me at the time. I had already learnt in my confirmation instruction that this book was of crucial importance. I began to read it as though I had never read it before. I wrote down carefully what I discovered . . . point by point . . . I read and read.[2]

Aided especially by the writings of J. T. Beck (more than by Schlatter), Barth began to develop his dialectical theology, the theology of crisis or the theology of the Word, as it came to be known. Always exercised about the preaching task, he began to preach about the sinfulness of humanity and the grace of God. He shed his former liberalism and socialism and wrote his famous *Romans*. "The mighty voice of Paul was new to me," he exclaimed and found the rest of Scripture likewise new to him. Barth's rediscovery of sin and the Word have been refreshing and salutary for many. As he went on to a teaching career at Basel and shared his *Church Dogmatics* and other works, he extended his influence widely to capture evangelical institutions and thinkers, as well as others (Bernard Ramm and Donald Bloesch are two examples).[3]

Barth's neo-orthodoxy hoped to blend enough orthodoxy with Enlightenment thinking on the Bible as to make effective appeal to contemporary culture, but it is Barth's faulty and deficient view of scriptural authority that aborts his overall objective. Barth retained his critical view of Scripture. The Word of God is not to be equated with the words of Scripture in the orthodox sense. The Word is found in Christ, in the Scripture, and in preaching. "The Word is not per se Scripture, but rather what Scripture has to communicate to man from God."[4] The Bible becomes God's Word as it speaks to us, as Barth sees it, but nothing preserves Scripture from the "pick-and-choose" approach as to what is reliable and factual.[5] Barth and Bultmann parted company, but in terms of Barth's system, what can he say to Bultmann's radical antisupernaturalism?

Clearly Barth has a high view of preaching in this schema and argues strongly that "the task of the sermon is to create space for the Word of God."[6] But the

Word of God for Barth is not Scripture as such but what Scripture becomes in the divine/human encounter. In seminars held at Bonn in 1932 and 1933, before he was sacked by Hitler, Barth vigorously critiqued homiletical practice in his time. He was particularly critical of Bauer, who did not insist on a biblical text in preaching. Barth scoffed at deciding what is to be preached in terms of what attracts and what repels (hear! hear!) and summoned the preacher to preach not *about* the Bible but *from* the Bible.[7] He spoke of regard for the text, confidence in the text, and the relevance of the text in searching and challenging words. Yet the contention that the Bible is a record of divine self-disclosure and not the revelation itself perpetuates the false dichotomy between the personal and the propositional. The Bible is certainly both.

Barth in his own preaching always used the pericope, though as he grew older he often trimmed the preaching portion. Earlier on he stayed closer to the text. Because he did not accept natural revelation, he did not believe a sermon should have an introduction or a conclusion. Since there was no point of contact between God and people (a view not unlike that of Cornelius Van Til but hardly in line with Romans 1:18–32), the sermon could never serve an apologetic purpose.

Barth's preaching was Christocentric.[8] After 1954 he did most of his preaching in the Basel prison. Many of these sermons are remarkable reading, as are *Deliverance to the Captives* (1961) and *Call for God* (1965). Yet Barth was critical of Billy Graham's preaching and bemoaned what he heard at St. Jacob Stadium as "heating up hell."[9] This perhaps reflected his own strong "move toward universalism," which really stemmed from his reservations on scriptural authority.[10]

Lovers of preaching can only adulate the high place Karl Barth and many of his followers have given to preaching. They do preach! But their rejection of "objective intelligible revelation" causes them to founder at key places in doctrinal formulation (no Satan in his theology) and practical ministration (no real evangelism and no "conversion").[11] For Barth, "revelation is revelation only if it is recognized, acknowledged and accepted by man."[12]

1. Karl Barth, *Protestant Thought: From Rousseau to Ritschl* (New York: Harper, 1959). Barth's own critique.
2. Eberhard Bush, *Karl Barth: His Life from Letters and Autobiographical Texts* (Grand Rapids: Eerdmans, 1976), 97ff.
3. Bruce L. McCormack, *Karl Barth's Critically Realistic Dialectical Theology: Its Genesis and Development 1909–1936* (Oxford: Clarendon, 1995). Argues for the essential continuity of Barth's postliberal theology.
4. John Wick Bowman, "The Barthian Theology and the Word of God," *The Presbyterian* (September 3, 1936): 1ff. For another early analysis, see H. R. Mackintosh, *Types of Modern Theology: Schleiermacher to Barth* (New York: Scribner's, 1937). Major evangelical critiques are found in Van Til, Gordon Haddon Clark, Carl Henry, Klaas Runia.
5. Emil Brunner veered even further in doctrinal deviation and denied the Virgin Birth. Brunner was very popular in the U.S. and taught at Zurich. His sermons are of interest;

see *The Great Invitation and Other Sermons* (Philadelphia: Westminster, 1955). The flagrant and bizarre results of "our deciding" what is to be believed in Scripture can be seen in Hans Kung, *Judaism: Between Yesterday and Tomorrow* (New York: Crossroad, 1992). In eagerness for Jewish/Christian dialogue, Kung urges us to come without "trinitarian presuppositions," without a preexistent Savior, and without expiatory sacrifice. So ultimately nothing will be held back from concession to modernity.

6. Karl Barth, *Homiletics* (Louisville: Westminster/John Knox, 1991), 122.
7. Ibid., 49. An incisive analysis of Barth is in Addison H. Leitch, *Winds of Doctrine* (Westwood, N.J.: Revell, 1966), 20ff.
8. Karl Barth, *Come Holy Spirit* (New York: Round Table, 1933).
9. Bush, *Karl Barth*, 446. Bush faces the sad situation in Barth's home over the years, 185ff.
10. Well analyzed by D. A. Carson, *The Gagging of God* (Grand Rapids: Zondervan, 1995), 143f.
11. Carl F. H. Henry, *God, Revelation and Authority* (Waco, Tex.: Word, 1976), 2:158ff.
12. Herbert Hartwell, *The Theology of Karl Barth: An Introduction* (Philadelphia: Westminster, 1964), 69.

12.6.3 *HELMUT THIELICKE—PREACHING IN THE NIGHTMARE OF A NATION*

Having its origin in oral proclamation, Scripture presses back to its origin, i.e. to the presentation of its message by the spoken word. It seeks to be preached . . . to preach it is to understand it. Sermons are not just recitation but exposition. Exposition is possible only when the scope and emphases of what is to be expounded are taken from the text and hermeneutically evaluated.

As a preacher I am involved in an unending dialogue with those to whom I must deliver my message. Every conversation I engage in becomes at bottom a meditation, a preparation, a gathering of material for my preaching. I can no longer listen disinterestedly even to a play in a theater without relating it to my pulpit . . . Thus life in all its daily involvements becomes for me a thesaurus in which I keep rummaging, because it is full of relevant material for my message.

—Helmut Thielicke

Strongly drawn to Karl Barth when he was young, **Helmut Thielicke** (1908–1985) was thoroughly tinged with Barthian thought, especially on Scripture.[1] He was a theologian who loved to preach and was heard appreciatively in a wide circle. Born in Wuppertal-Barmen, Thielicke attended the famous gymnasium there. He then went on to Griefwald, where he was seriously ill, then on to Marburg, Erlangan, and Bonn for his training.[2] From 1936 to 1940, he taught at Heidelberg until he was dismissed for criticism of Nazi policies. He was then ordained and served in Ravensburg and then in Stuttgart.

Thielicke was Lutheran, and law/gospel was central in his message. After the war, he held the chair of systematic theology at Tubingen and in 1954 became the first Protestant rector of the University of Hamburg. As dean of the theological school, he saw the enrollment quickly move from 90 to 260 students. The essential charm and good sense of the man is seen in his delightful *A Little Exercise for Young Theologians*.[3] Evangelicals have always purred that he was so taken with Spurgeon.[4]

Through a unique arrangement, for many years Thielicke preached to four yearly services which he arranged from the high pulpit of the great S. Michaeliskirche in Hamburg. Even in the peak of the tourist season, the attendance here averages 150 to 400, but in his services Thielicke packed the 2,550 seats and the great galleries. Many were converted to Christ.[5] This success was somewhat controversial, as may be imagined, and those who attended were called "Thielicke Christians."

The sermons that we have from Genesis in *How the World Began*[6] and his messages on the Sermon on the Mount titled *Life Can Begin Again* are samples of what he did in the cathedral.[7] His famous sermons on the Lord's Prayer in shattered Stuttgart in the closing days of the war have been widely circulated under the title *The Prayer That Spans the World*.[8]

There is a strong biblicality in these sermons. We treasure what must be one of the finest sermons ever preached from Luke 15:11ff., "The Waiting Father," which truly captures the meaning of the text. It is in a volume of masterful sermons on the parables of Jesus.[9] The sermons are not exegetical but must be called textual-topical, or textual-thematic. Dirks has analyzed his lay appeal and found that he ranked very high in personality, originality, and use of illustrations. He was lower in credibility, confrontation with decision, and thought-provoking quality.[10] His titles are unusually arresting, and he uses questions very adeptly. He even has a book of sermons on difficult texts.[11] At so many key points we can identify with this able preacher who drew more listeners than did any other in postwar West Germany, not least when he says:

> Where is the man who can accomplish all this and who among those who are faced with this enormous assignment does not despair of accomplishing it? The only man who can assume such a bold and hazardous task is one who convinced that he need not beware the responsibility for its success and that Another is there interceding for him. He knows that not he but only the Spirit of God himself is able to reach and open the hearts of his hearers.[12]

---

1. Helmut Thielicke, *The Evangelical Faith* (Grand Rapids: Eerdmans, 1982) 3:191ff.; *Between Heaven and Earth* (Greenwood, S.C.: Attic, 1967). N.B. "Historical Criticism of the Bible," 14ff.
2. Marvin J. Dirks, *Laymen Look at Preaching: Lay Expectation Factors in Relation to the Preaching of Helmut Thielicke* (North Quincy, Mass.: Christopher, 1972), 73.
3. Helmut Thielicke, *A Little Exercise for Young Theologians* (Grand Rapids: Eerdmans, 1962).
4. Helmut Thielicke, *Encounter with Spurgeon* (Philadelphia: Fortress, 1963). The essence of his lectures.
5. Dirks, *Laymen Look at Preaching,* 59.

6. Helmut Thielicke, *How the World Began* (Philadelphia: Muhlenberg, 1961). Dirks analyzes the sermon on Cain (206).
7. Helmut Thielicke, *Life Can Begin Again: Sermons on the Sermon on the Mount* (Philadelphia: Fortress, 1963).
8. Helmut Thielicke, *The Prayer That Spans the World* (Greenwood, S.C.: Attic, 1953). From the Stuttgart years.
9. Helmut Thielicke, *The Waiting Father: Sermons on the Parables of Jesus* (New York: Harper, 1959). Strongly endorsed by Paul Scherer, another Lutheran, who taught homiletics at Union and preached brilliantly. His Yale Lectures in 1942 and 1943, *For We Have This Treasure,* are outstanding. His lectures/sermons on Isaiah are likewise remarkable but are vitiated by higher critical presuppositions; see *Event in Eternity* (New York: Harper, 1945).
10. Dirks, *Laymen Look at Preaching,* 284.
11. Helmut Thielicke, *Faith the Great Adventure* (Philadelphia: Fortress, 1985).
12. Dirks, *Laymen Look at Preaching,* 191.

12.6.4 Dietrich Bonhoeffer—Preaching in a Time of Testing

> Preaching was the great event in his life; the hard theologizing and all the critical love of his church were all for its sake, for in it the message of Christ, the bringer of peace was proclaimed. To Bonhoeffer, nothing in his calling competed in importance with preaching.
>
> —Eberhard Bethge

> A truly evangelical sermon must be like offering a child a beautiful red apple or holding out a glass of water to a thirsty man and asking, "Wouldn't you like it?"
>
> —Dietrich Bonhoeffer

Dietrich Bonhoeffer (1906–1945) loved to preach, and he preached the night before the Nazis hanged him in Flossenburg Prison just hours before Allied liberation. He was born into an upper-class German family where religion was perfunctory. He began his study at the University of Berlin, where his father was a professor of psychiatry, and his dissertation on "The Communion of Saints" was acclaimed by Karl Barth as "a miracle." Serving the German church in Barcelona briefly, Bonhoeffer returned to teach in Berlin at the age of twenty-six. He spent the year 1930 on a study fellowship at Union Seminary in New York City and taught Sunday school in Harlem. As early as 1933, he denounced Hitler over the radio and pressed hard the issue of "The Church and the Jewish Question."[1] In 1935 he took the leadership of the Confessing church seminary at Finkenwalde on the Baltic, during which time he finished his classic *The Cost of Discipleship.*[2] By late 1937, Hitler had closed down the seminary and arrested twenty-seven students.

Visiting the U.S. at the time the war began, Bonhoeffer could have stayed in safety but was determined to return home to become part of the struggle against Hitler. While in New York City, he longed to hear a sermon that was truly biblical.

At several prestigious churches he heard "quite unbearable rubbish, forced application, no exposition of a text." Then he visited Broadway Presbyterian Church and heard Dr. John McComb preach a solid biblical message.[3] He reacted with a passionate desire, "I eagerly want to preach once again!"[4] He returned to Germany and was incarcerated by Hitler in 1943 and eventually martyred.[5] Despite his pacifism, Bonhoeffer was part of the bomb plot to kill the Fuehrer.

Theologically Bonhoeffer has been claimed by "the death of God" theologians and radicals, and some evangelicals have been overzealous in making him one of their own.[6] The fact is he was quite thoroughly Barthian and did not disclaim higher critical thinking. But he was at the same time sufficiently Lutheran and pietistic—especially through Schlatter's commentaries—as to be Christ-centered and personally devout.[7]

Our special interest in Bonhoeffer stems from his great commitment to the preaching of the Word as the instrument of the Spirit's renewal of the church. He often said the importance of preaching the Bible cannot be overestimated.[8] American preaching he felt was sugared water with too much personal experience and "marginal notes on current events."[9] He saw the only answer to the increasing desecration and secularization of the Lord's day to be the renewal of preaching.[10] To him the preaching office was supreme.

Early on Bonhoeffer was long-winded and preached over the people's heads. His docent in homiletics urged him "to cultivate plain, noble simplicity from time to time in the presentation of the most important idea in the text."[11] Later he taught preaching at Finkenwalde and grappled with the issue of the necessity of preaching for the life of the church. He was an advocate of *lectio continua* (preaching in series) and greater use of the Old Testament. "The goal of the individual sermon is that the text must be orally expressed," he said.[12]

Bonhoeffer greatly stressed the work of Andrew Hyperius as the first Protestant homiletician (cf. 6.1.1). His reflections on the restlessness of the preacher after he has preached and his "sense of total emptiness" are classic and seldom verbalized. His challenges to "cheap grace" and "easy Christianity" were at the heart of his preaching and are themes greatly needed in pulpit communication in our time.

---

1. David P. Gushee, "Following Jesus to the Gallows," *Christianity Today* (April 3, 1995): 29.

2. Dietrich Bonhoeffer, *The Cost of Discipleship* (New York: Macmillan, 1949). "When Christ calls a man, he bids him come and die." This book and *Life Together* were published just before his leaving Germany and explain his discomfiture in both Hitler's Germany and materialistic America. His *Temptation* and *Ethics* are also important.

3. Clyde E. Fant, ed. and trans., *Bonhoeffer: Worldly Preaching* (Nashville: Thomas Nelson, 1975). Lectures at Finkenwalde. John Hess McComb (1898–1981) was a dear friend of mine. He wrote several books of biblical exposition, the last of which was privately published: *Reborn to a Living Hope: Peter's Message to God's Pilgrim Band* (1983). McComb served Broadway Presbyterian Church from 1935 to 1959.

4. Ibid., 23.
5. Dietrich Bonhoeffer, *Letters and Papers from Prison* (London: Fontana, 1953). Bethge edited a larger edition.
6. Georg Huntemann, *The Other Bonhoeffer: An Evangelical Reassessment* (Grand Rapids: Baker, 1993). The author has taught at Lovain and Basel and certainly makes a good if somewhat overstated case.
7. Bruce A. Demarest, "Devotion, Doctrine and Duty in Dietrich Bonhoeffer," *Bibliotheca Sacra* 148, no. 592 (October–December 1991): 399ff. Another good analysis is that of Klaas Runia, "Dietrich Bonhoeffer: The Man and His Beliefs," *Eternity* (December 1965): 11ff. It is important to see that Bonhoeffer did not hold to inerrancy or verbal inspiration.
8. Fant, *Bonhoeffer,* 3.
9. Ibid., 14.
10. Ibid., 31.
11. "A Translation of the Evaluation of D. Bonhoeffer's Examination Sermon," *Dietrich Bonhoeffer Verke* (Munich: Ch. Kaiser Velag, 1986), 9:183–6 (Nr. 114). (*Collected Works of Dietrich Bonhoeffer.*)
12. Fant, *Bonhoeffer,* 157.

12.6.5 KLAAS SCHILDER—PREACHING IN A POLITICAL CAULDRON

There is not an inch of human life about which Christ, who is Sovereign over all, does not proclaim, "Mine."

—Klaas Schilder

Rationalism and the ravages of higher criticism took a heavy toll on Christian witness in the Netherlands, and gospel preaching was at low ebb in the nineteenth century. Counteracting this abysmal situation were the establishment of the new theological school at Kampen and the ministry of Abraham Kuyper (cf. 9.4.7). Kuyper led those who longed to hear the Word of God proclaimed. The splinter he founded, the De Gereformeerde Kerken (GKN), was weakened not only by Kuyper's death in 1920 but also by the departure of Herman Bavinck from Kampen in favor of the Free University.[1] Challenges were raised about the historicity of the early chapters of Genesis, and the doughty champion of full scriptural integrity was the brilliantly endowed **Klaas Schilder** (1890–1952). Always a man of controversy, he was a popular preacher who served six congregations.

Both in his preaching and in his lectures on diverse topics, he always showed that he was well prepared. No one opened the Word of God to the people of that day as K. Schilder did. His knowledge of literature and philosophy staggered the imagination of both friend and foe.[2]

Schilder's preaching voice was problematic, and he did vocal exercises "all of his adult life."[3] From the 1920s, he helped edit key periodicals and was often supported by Dr. F. Grosheide of the Free University and author of the commentary on 1 Corinthians in the New International Critical Commentary. Schilder early on saw the dangers of Barthianism. He wrote his doctoral dissertation at Erlangen in German on the use of paradox in theology, a matter dear to Karl Barth. In 1934 Schilder was installed as professor at Kampen.

Even his friends conceded that Schilder was overly polemical at times, but that his burden was the weakening of doctrine under Barthian influence. His redemptive-historical teaching and his strong emphasis on expounding the text had wide effect.

> With this type of preaching, of which Schilder was a master, the minis-
> ter in the pulpit would do justice to the text and to its place in the long
> process of revelation. As a result of Schilder's emphasis on these mat-
> ters, preaching was rejuvenated in many of the churches.[4]

He also wrote bitingly about the development of Hitler's National Socialism in Germany. He traveled in the U.S. and found much common ground with Cornelius Van Til at Westminster Seminary and Geerhardus Vos at Princeton. Those who observed him in America noticed how profusely he perspired as he preached.

During the war years of the 1940s, he was arrested by the Nazis and kept in a prison cell in Arnhem. Because of his adamant and uncompromising stand on doctrinal issues, his own synod deposed him as minister and professor. Dr. G. C. Berkouwer presided over these actions.[5] Two hundred churches and ten thousand members separated from the GKN at this time, and Schilder took the lead in founding a new school in Kampen. Ultimately the GKN acknowledged its error in suspending him. He died in 1952.

The most enduring monument to the remarkable preaching of Klaas Schilder is his massive three-volume work on the suffering and passion of Jesus, translated by Henry Zylstra. These volumes of sermonic literature, *Christ in His Suffering, Christ on Trial,* and *Christ Crucified,* must stand as the most extensive work of its kind and surely rank close to Krummacher and Clow as the most outstanding in terms of quality and depth. Such a message as "Satan at the Pulpit of the Passion" from Matthew 16:23 is striking.[6] There are great moments in his sermon "The Unimpaired Majesty of Jesus" of the mocking of Christ.

Although Schilder's style is typically Dutch and quite heavy, he offered some fresh insights as he reflected on how "Christ had already prepared the wood for the sacrifice" and how Satan "threw Christ a life-line," in the matter of Barabbas. In his message on "Christ's Last Ministration of the Word," from Luke 23:27–31, Schilder did not divide the text in the traditional manner but depicted our Lord on his way to "the dunghill of the world," faithful in presenting God's Word until the last.[7]

---

1. Henry Vander Kam, *Schilder: Preserver of the Faith* (New York: Vantage, 1996), 17.
2. Ibid., 23. J. Geertsema has also edited a volume of essays of Schilder, *Always Obedient* (Phillipsburg, NJ: Presbyterian and Reformed, 1996), on his life and thought.

3. Ibid., 23.
4. Ibid., 45.
5. Ibid., 76.
6. K. Schilder, *Christ in His Suffering* (Grand Rapids: Eerdmans, 1938), 15ff.
7. K. Schilder, *Christ Crucified* (Grand Rapids: Eerdmans, 1944), 55ff.

12.6.6 *Frank Mangs—Preaching in the Maelstrom of Scandinavian Secularism*

The expositor is only to provide mouth and lips for the passage itself so that the Word may advance . . . The really great preachers are in fact only the servants of the Scripture. When they have spoken for a time— the Word gleams within the passage itself and is listened to: the voice makes itself heard . . . the passage itself is the voice, the speech of God; the preacher is the mouth and the lips and the congregation the ear in which the voice sounds.

—Gustaf Wingren

Even secular writers in Scandinavia recognized how higher critical ideas had displaced biblical authority, as when the young Danish novelist Peter Hoeg relates of a certain distinguished professor of theology:

He established on scientific grounds the falsity of the biblical texts while at the same time testifying to their profundity.[1]

Of course there were defenders of classical biblical faith. Professor Olav Valen-Sendstad was closely associated with O. Hallesby and Olaf E. Moe at the Independent Seminary in Oslo.[2] Professor Gustaf Wingren critiqued Barth for "employing the language of Scripture in a system which is totally foreign to the Bible."[3] But the typical Swedish attitude toward spiritual things was that of the inventor Alfred Nobel, who came from "the barren and God-fearing province of Smaland." Nobel inherited "high standards of right and wrong," but his ties with the church were nominal and only formal. Archbishop Soderblom preached his funeral.[4] "My life is woven out of torment," Nobel bemoaned. Fittingly, his favorite poet was Lord Byron.[5]

Certainly there were Bible preachers who moved multitudes. One of them was Lewi Pethrus, who preached in the great Filadelfia Church in Stockholm which seated five thousand. Pethrus also edited a daily newspaper in Stockholm. Another solid preacher was Knut Svensson, president of the Swedish Alliance Mission (1953–1968), whose sermons published as *En for Alla (One for All)* are exemplary. Trygve Holm-Glad of the Norwegian Mission Covenant was also a biblical preacher of moving power. But without question, the towering giant of the Swedish pulpit in this century was **Frank Mangs** (1897–1994).

Mangs was born a part of the ten percent Swedish minority on the West coast of Finland, a residue from the years that Sweden was one with the Finns. (General Mannerheim and the composer Sibelius were also Swedish Finns). Mangs served congregations in the Mission Covenant Church of Sweden, for many years the largest Free Church body in Sweden. He was a large man with a strong and commanding voice. He turned to evangelism and traveled extensively throughout Scandinavia. The existence of the Norwegian Mission Covenant and the once-great Bethlehem Church of Oslo were due to revival fires kindled through Mangs' preaching.[6] He visited the United States many times and held unforgettable midnight meetings in the old Lyccum Theater in Minneapolis with large numbers seeking after the Lord.[7] He used English passably, and after preaching under great fervor he would sit down at the piano and sing "Have You Forgotten God?" with great effect. Even until late in his life he was heard at the great summer gathering place at Torp in the interest of revival and renewal in the Christian life and in the Swedish churches.

Mang's three-volume autobiography is a commentary on a century of religious decline in Scandinavia, with but occasional and sporadic outbursts of renewal.[8] Most of his books of sermons have not been translated, but we do have his *The Master's Way* and a series of studies from Luke 5 titled *Out of Dismal Failure into Glorious Success*. The sermons are not structurally complicated. In the former volume he pursues the general order of the life of Jesus and continually urges his hearers to heed the Savior's words, "Follow me."[9] These messages are intensely personal in tone. His illustrations are apt.[10] This preaching was owned by the Spirit of God on several continents.

Frank Mangs was something of a maverick, but his great voice, now silenced, is sorely missed.

---

1. Peter Hoeg, *The History of Danish Dreams* (New York: Farrar, Strauss and Giroux, 1995), 59.
2. Olav Valen-Sendstad, *The Word That Can Never Die* (St. Louis: Concordia, 1949); O. Moe, *The Apostle Paul: His Life and His Work* (Minneapolis: Augsburg, 1950). One-third of the ministers of the Church of Norway are trained at the Independent Seminary in Oslo founded by O. Hallesby, noted devotional author and gifted preacher.
3. Gustaf Wingren, *Theology in Conflict* (Philadelphia: Muhlenberg, 1958), 125. See also his *The Living Word* (Philadelphia: Fortress, 1965), 201–3. Wingren was professor of systematic theology at Lund.
4. Charles J. Curtis, *Nathan Soderblom: Theologian of Revelation* (Chicago: Covenant, 1966); in another treatment of Soderblom, *Soderblom: Ecumenical Pioneer* (Minneapolis: Augsburg, 1967), Curtis faults Soderblom for what he calls "the sentimental, almost-sick, blood-of-Jesus piety of nineteenth-century evangelical revivalism" (132). At this point it would seem the archbishop is reflecting historic Christianity.
5. Kenne Fant, *Alfred Nobel* (New York: Arcade, 1991). This wealthy man never escaped melancholy or misanthropy.
6. "An Interview with Frank Mangs on His 90th Birthday," *Betlehem Misjonskirkes Menighetsblad,* July/August 1987, nr. 7/8, side 9ff. Mangs retained close ties to the Oslo congregation which rose out of the revival.
7. I heard Mangs preach both in Swedish and English in Sweden and in the United States. Powerful! Mangs had close ties with A. B. Simpson.

8. Frank Mangs, *Hogst Personlicht,* 3 vols. (Stockholm: Harrier, 1980). "Highly personal."
9. Frank Mangs, *The Master's Way* (London: Marshall, Morgan, and Scott, n.d.).
10. Frank Mangs, *Out of Dismal Failure into Glorious Success* (Chicago: privately published, n.d.).

12.6.7 GUSTAF F. JOHNSON—PREACHING IN THE AMBIGUITY OF IMMIGRATION AND INTEGRATION

Preaching was seen as the very heart of the mission of the fathers. Their sermons were both Bible-centered and man-centered. The Bible was the trustworthy Word of God. Its message had to do with what God had done in Jesus Christ for man's salvation. It was for man—when he saw what God had done—to accept this grace and believe. The texts were as often chosen from the Old Testament as the New. The Bible was one book and spoke of one grace. The burden was to discover what the Bible had to say to man.

—Eric G. Hawkinson

The masses of immigrants from countless cultures largely replicated the religious situation of their homelands. Sometimes disruption and privation made the newcomers more open to the gospel. Many Swedish migrants came out of the revival fires of the old country (cf. 9.5.3) and planted Mission Covenant congregations in the United States. The pioneer preachers of this movement were a sturdy lot who loved Scripture and continually asked, "Where is it written?"[1]

Erik August Skogsbergh (1850–1939), known as the Swedish Moody, had tremendous preaching ministries at the Chicago Tabernacle and in both the large Minneapolis and Seattle tabernacles, the latter two of which he saw built.[2] The Evangelical Free Church, the sister denomination and in a sense daughter of the Covenant, had some exceedingly able preachers such as its longtime president, **E. A. Halleen,** and its foremost evangelist, **A. J. Thorwall.**[3] Though largely contained within the Scandinavian evangelical movement, perhaps the best-known of these immigrant preachers was the always controversial but always impactful **Gustaf F. Johnson** (1873–1959).

"Texas" Johnson, as he was known early in his ministry, was born in Nasjo in Smaland in Sweden but migrated with his parents to Texas when he was nine years of age. He was converted in a Methodist church in Brushy, Texas, where his parents were members, but he soon joined the Swedish Free Church in Austin. He was ordained by Pastor C. O. Sahlstrom in Deckar, Texas, and at the age of eighteen went to Japan in the first contingent of missionaries sent by Fredrik Franson (cf. 10.2.7).[4] While he was in transit on the Pacific going to and returning from Japan, Johnson mastered the plays of Shakespeare, a fact that in part explains his excellent English diction. He served several Swedish Free Churches and was responsible under God for the rapid growth of the Free Church in Rockford, Illinois, an important center of Swedish immigration, where he served from 1901 to 1913. In 1914 he moved to the Swedish Tabernacle of Minneapolis, where he preached to huge throngs for twenty-five years. He then served thirteen years as the founding pastor of the Park Avenue Covenant Church until his retirement in 1952.

Johnson was a deep student of Scripture and was mightily used in evangelism and in the exposition of the prophetic word particularly. Many of the immigrant preachers were exhorters and devotional in their approach to the text, but Johnson opened a text with care, as did others in the movement.[5] He was pictorial and vivid, alternating humor and the sense of the incongruous with scathing jeremiads. His titles were artful: "Spiritual Geography," "A Select Band of Vagabonds" on the cave of Adullam, and "Light Burdens for Weak Shoulders" on Acts 15. One listener recorded his reaction to Johnson's preaching:

> When sixteen, I can remember attending a Sunday evening service in the First Covenant Church of Duluth to hear the Rev. Gustaf F. Johnson conclude an evangelistic series. The impact on me was not only moving; it was frightening. My hair stood up stiff on my head. Yet as much as I would not dream of another encounter of that kind, I knew I would have to return if such an event recurred.[6]

Even in translation the sermons have a tang, a colorful flow, and strong personal application.[7] In his well-known study of Luke 24, "Hearts Aflame," Johnson calls preachers:

> Many a beautiful sermon containing wonderful truth and dressed in eloquent language falls to the ground like a bird shot down in flight. What is lacking? No heart! Nothing is wrong with its theology. The teaching is correct, and truth is spoken. Scripture after Scripture is quoted. The presentation is quiet and orderly, and the language is dignified and stately. Despite all this, not a soul is gripped by the message. Why is this? Simply because the preacher has neglected to make what he says a vital issue for himself. He is like a record player which grinds out what has been cut into the record of the memory during the previous week. This is not preaching. This is merely making a speech.[8]

Johnson was both loved and hated, but no listener was ever indifferent to the message.

---

1. Eric G. Hawkinson, *Images in Covenant Beginnings* (Chicago: Covenant, 1968), 130ff.; Erik Wallgren, *A Swedish-American Preacher's Own Story* (Chicago: Covenant, 1963); A. H. Jacobson, *Adventures of a Prairie Preacher* (Chicago: Covenant, 1960).
2. Erik Dahlhielm, *A Burning Heart: Erik August Skogsbergh* (Chicago: Covenant, 1951). He was an orator (196).
3. E. A. Halleen, *The Wonders of the Cross* (Chicago: Chicago Bladet, 1929); LaReau Thorwall, *And Light New Fires: The Life of A. J. Thorwall* (Minneapolis: Free Church Press, 1969).
4. John Carlstig, *Gustaf F. Johnson: mannen med det brinnande hjartat* (Jonkoping,

Sweden: SAM Forlaget, 1965). We need a strong and reflective biography of this preacher's preacher.

5. Erik Dahlhielm, "The Value of Expository Preaching," *The Covenant Quarterly* (August 1943): 3ff.
6. Arthur W. Anderson in Glen V. Wiberg, "Is There a Covenant Way of Preaching?" *The Covenant Quarterly* (August 1996): 10.
7. Gustaf F. Johnson, *Hearts Aflame,* trans. Paul R. Johnson (Chicago: Covenant, 1970); *From a Shepherd's Heart* (Minneapolis: Free Church Publications, 1960). The latter is a collection of brief meditations.
8. Gustaf F. Johnson, *The Word Is Near You,* ed. Herbert E. Palmquist (Chicago: Covenant, 1974), 163.

12.7 EVANGELICAL HEADLINERS IN A CULTURE OF DECOMPOSITION

The crisis is here in all its stark and unquestionable reality. We are in the midst of an enormous conflagration burning everything into ashes. In a few weeks millions of human lives are uprooted; in a few hours century-old cities are demolished in a few days, kingdoms are erased. Red human blood flows in broad streams from one end of the earth to another. Ever-expanding misery spreads its gloomy shadow over larger and larger areas. The fortunes, happiness, and comfort of untold millions have disappeared. Peace, security and safety have vanished. Prosperity and well-being have become in many countries but a memory; freedom, a mere myth. Western culture is covered by a blackout. A great tornado sweeps over the whole of mankind.

—Pitirim A. Sorokin

Oswald Spengler in his *Decline of the West* and Sorokin in *The Crisis of Our Age* have meaningfully sketched "the agony of the West." This has increasingly become the milieu of preaching in our time. Along with Allan Bloom, Harold O. J. Brown has analyzed "the degenerative phase of the sensate culture" in which there is mounting challenge to "the objective meaning of any text."[1] Religion is shunted to the fringes of culture, and a chaotic syncretism has led to the general breakdown of authority.[2] Yet the Word of God is still being blessed by the Holy Spirit.

1. Harold O. J. Brown, *The Sensate Culture: Western Civilization Between Chaos and Transformation* (Dallas: Word, 1996), 54. Involved in the decline is "the gradual abandonment of Christian heritage" in the West.
2. Ibid., 70. This study of "late second millennium culture" is most critical for gospel communicators in our time.

12.7.1 MARK A. MATTHEWS—THE PREACHER AS BUILDER

> Hide me behind the Cross; lift me out of self; teach me to speak the truth
> as He taught it.
>
> —the prayer Mark Matthews prayed just before his
> exposition of the Word of God

> The country is in its present condition—to some extent at least—because
> the ministers were not firm, fundamental and persistent in preaching the
> great truths necessary to lead an individual to Christ and stabilize a na-
> tion . . . If we are to have a revival it must begin in the pulpit . . . Let us
> get back to the business of preaching, to the technique of preaching, to
> the art and power of preaching, to the mastery of preaching . . . The way
> to cure it [dullness in the pulpit] is for ministers to study the Bible and
> learn how to do expository preaching . . . Let us master the technique of
> expository preaching . . . The revival will follow and sinners will be saved
> and the saints revived.
>
> —Mark A. Matthews

"Preacher of the Word of God and Friend to Man" is embossed on the statue
of **Mark A. Matthews** (1867–1940) in Denny Park in Seattle, Washington. Like
that of Thomas Guthrie in Edinburgh (cf. 10.5.1), the ministry of Matthews shook
an entire city. Of Scotch-Irish extraction and Presbyterian-Methodist roots,
Matthews was born in a poor home in Calhoun, Georgia. Converted at the age of
thirteen, he never graduated from high school, college, or seminary but was from
childhood an avid student and reader.

He preached his first sermon at seventeen, doing constant supply preaching
while working at a dry-goods store. At twenty he was ordained and served in
Dalton, Georgia, and then Jackson, Tennessee, where the membership doubled.[1]
In 1900 he passed the bar in Tennessee in an examination conducted by William
Howard Taft.[2] He was a gangling youth and grew to six feet six inches in height,
had long, flowing hair, and publicly appeared in top hat and morning coat.

In 1902, at the age of thirty-four, Matthews was called to be the pastor of First
Presbyterian Church in Seattle, Washington. At that time, the sparkling city on
Puget Sound had a population of eighty thousand. Matthews began with four
hundred members and served the church for thirty-eight years until his death at
seventy-two. In that time, he received more than twenty-five thousand new members, the majority of them new converts. The church grew to nine thousand members, the largest in the world at that time.

In 1906 a new edifice was constructed at Seventh and Spring, seating more
than three thousand, the largest capacity of any church in the city. Even with these
large numbers of constituents, he was known for his amazing memory for names
and faces. With his 107 elders and 60 deacons he not only served his large membership but also reached out through the city in various crusades of civic righteousness. He brought his "Nineteen Symptoms of Graft" before the city council
and gave his temperance lectures around the country.[3]

Matthews' church was the first to own a radio station. He established twenty-eight branch churches and Sunday schools around Seattle in a pattern many imitated as "The Mark Matthews Plan." He was active in the conservative strategy in the Presbyterian church struggles and was moderator of the General Assembly in 1912. With youth from all the branches pouring downtown for the great Sunday evening service, Matthews had a Sunday evening ministry every bit as dynamic as his Sunday morning expositions. He fought the so-called New Era program (an official denominational program of the Presbyterian Church) and stood shoulder to shoulder with the fundamentalists in the battle of the 1920s. He was one of the founders of the Day Care Movement for the weekday care of children.[4]

Like Spurgeon, Matthews did not use a pulpit when he preached but paced back and forth during his forty-five-minute message. Often called the "Tall Pine of the Sierras," he had a "pleasing and flexible voice."[5] He used no notes and was often thematic with strong reliance on the texts of Scripture. He could use "pulpit pyrotechnics" in the oratorical tradition of his day.

Matthews did not shrink from preaching the great doctrines of the Bible, particularly the doctrines of the Holy Trinity, the Atonement, and the Second Coming.[6] His sermon on "The Great Foundation" from 1 Corinthians 3 is well outlined and meaty.[7] In a prize-winning book on the church, we see the depth of his thinking and the soundness of his theological method.[8] He was truly a pastor-evangelist with a great commitment to making the way of salvation plain in every sermon. This focus is explained:

> The minister must teach absolute loyalty to the Bible, the Infallible Word of God, the only text-book of the church, the court of last resort. The minister must also present the full Gospel of Jesus Christ as the only means of salvation. The minister must determine to know only one thing, namely—the Blood of Jesus Christ. He must present the cross of Christ on which the Son of God was sacrificed for the redemption of the world, by which sacrifice His Blood was shed for the regeneration of a soul. It is the eternal purpose of that sacrifice that must be preached if the full Gospel of Christ is to be presented.[9]

After suffering a massive heart attack, Mark Matthews died in the hospital while dictating the next Sunday's sermon to his secretary. The company of the preachers was richly enhanced by the gifts and endeavors of this greatly used servant of Christ.

---

1. Ezra P. Giboney and Agnes M. Potter, *The Life of Mark A. Matthews* (Grand Rapids: Eerdmans, 1948), 19ff.
2. Ibid., 21.
3. Ibid., 31.
4. Ralph G. Turnbull, *A History of Preaching* (Grand Rapids: Baker, 1974), 242. Turnbull, a delightful Scottish preacher, was a later pastor of First Presbyterian

Church, Seattle, and oversaw the building of a new structure after an earthquake severely damaged the old building. Turnbull's work was an effort to update and complete Dargan.

5. Giboney and Potter, *The Life of Mark A. Matthews*, 44.
6. Mark A. Matthews, *Gospel Sword Thrusts* (New York: Revell, 1824). Matthews carried on a great battle against the liberals at Union Theological Seminary in New York prior to World War I; N.B. Lisa S. Nolland, "The Uniqueness of Mark Matthews, Fundamentalist: A Study of His Social Concerns," (M.C.S. thesis at Regent College, Vancouver, 1984, 53–54); also *Amazing Grace: Evangelicals in Australia, Britain, Canada and the United States,* ed. George A. Rawlyk and Mark A. Noll (Grand Rapids: Baker, 1993).
7. Giboney and Potter, *The Life of Mark A. Matthews*, 107.
8. Mark A. Matthews, *Building the Church* (New York: American Tract Society, 1940).
9. Ibid., 159.

12.7.2 *FRANK W. BOREHAM—THE PREACHER AS STORYTELLER*

A man is naturally fluent or he is not. If he is not, the constant creation of manuscript will overcome his handicap. In the act of writing, the mind is ceaselessly groping for words. Every word that it captures becomes from that moment part of its stock in trade. The word, never employed before, remains within easy reach, and when he is speaking or preaching, it will be ready to his hand. A halting and hesitating speaker will, if he takes it in time, cure this slovenly and repulsive habit by persistent writing.

Dr. Parker and Dr. Meyer taught me that the only remedy for this kind of thing [people not comprehending the message] lies in sane and judicious repetition. It is the duty of the pulpit to say the same things over and over again. They must be clothed in different phraseology, and illumined by fresh illustration, and approached by a new line of thought, but the things that are really worth saying must be said repeatedly.

—Frank W. Boreham

The moderator of the Church of Scotland once introduced this preacher as "the man whose name is on all our lips, whose books are on all our shelves, and whose illustrations are in all our sermons."[1] That is quite a bit to say about any preacher, but it certainly was true of **Frank W. Boreham** (1871–1959). Although he was born in Tunbridge Wells, Kent, England, the greater part of his unusual ministry was in Australia. He was born into an old Anglican family that moved into the nonconformity of Emmanuel Church on Mount Ephraim of the Countess of Huntingdon's Connection.

The visit of Moody had made quite an impression on the family, but young Boreham focused on a secular future until a serious accident in the brickyard where he was working consigned him to hospital for an extended stay. He was left with a lifelong limp. The call of God took hold of him when he went up to

London and sat under the ministry of such as Newman Hall, Marcus Rainsford, Joseph Parker, and F. B. Meyer.[2] Boreham conferred at length with Hudson Taylor about his suitability for missionary work in China, but his injury led Taylor to urge upon him a ministry in the homeland.[3] He became a Baptist and graduated from Spurgeon's College, where he was much influenced by Arthur T. Pierson (cf. 11.4.1) and by D. L. Moody on his last visit to England in 1893.[4]

Boreham did much street preaching under the Open Air Mission and in several student pastorates. When Thomas Spurgeon came back from New Zealand in 1894, Boreham responded to the call to pastor a congregation of Scottish settlers in Mosgiel, New Zealand. Just as John Watson (Ian Maclaren) shared Scottish church life in *Beside the Bonnie Brier Bush* (cf. 11.2.6), so Boreham described his ministry and the people whom he pastored in essays and articles he wrote as the editor of *The New Zealand Baptist*.

Here is another preacher who could really tell a story.[5] Boreham's books of essays are dotted with choice exegetical insights and beautiful word pictures. His famous Sunday evening preaching on "Texts That Made History" have a freshness about them.[6] He wrestled with making a public appeal for decision at the end of the service and finally opted to do so.[7]

In 1970 Boreham moved to Hobart, Tasmania, where he spent nine years. Eventually he experienced a serious breakdown in his health and "spasms of lassitude." His last pastorate was for ten years with the Armdale Baptist Church in Melbourne. After thirty-four years in parish ministry, he turned to an international ministry or "gypsying," as he called it. Often he occupied significant pulpits for an extended period of time, such as Methodist Central Hall in Melbourne for six months. In 1931, Boreham delivered the Bevan Lectures on Preaching in Australia.

While at times we might wish Boreham grappled more with a text, we find his insights and structure engaging. His more than forty books never leave the reader feeling cheated. His Christmas materials catalyzed some breakthroughs toward saying the old truth in a new way.[8] Titles like "The Danger of Diffusion" on worship or "Consolation for the Disillusioned" came from Boreham. No one offers more help with Lamentations 3:27 and "Bearing the Yoke in Youth" than does Boreham.[9] His message for young preachers titled "On Frightening Timothy" from 1 Corinthians 16:10 is a classic.[10] Some of his illustrations are usable today. His lucid style, literary breadth, absolute soundness, and warmth of heart draw us to him. In our time when so much interest is attaching to narrative, we would do well to take another look at Boreham.

---

1. F. W. Boreham, *My Pilgrimage* (London: Epworth, 1940), 251. The last milestone almost up to his death.
2. Ibid., 61ff. Happily, Kregel Publications of Grand Rapids is reissuing many of Boreham's titles.
3. Ibid., 79.
4. Ibid., 95.
5. F. W. Boreham, *The Luggage of Life* (Grand Rapids: Kregel, 1995).

6. F. W. Boreham, *A Bunch of Everlastings* (Grand Rapids: Kregel, 1994) expounds Chalmer's text and those of Luther, Latimer, Bunyan, Knox, etc. In *A Casket of Cameos* (Grand Rapids: Kregel, 1994) he tackles Brainerd, Shackleton, John Bright, Melancthon, R. W. Dale, and a host of others. Different!
7. Boreham, *My Pilgrimage,* 212ff. His sermons on the Beatitudes are outstanding: *The Heavenly Octave* (New York: Abingdon, 1936), reprinted by Baker in 1968.
8. F. W. Boreham, *My Christmas Book: A Handful of Myrrh, Aloes and Cassia* (Grand Rapids: Zondervan, 1953).
9. F. W. Boreham, *The Crystal Pointers* (New York: Abingdon, 1925), 99ff.
10. F. W. Boreham, *Mountains in the Mist* (Grand Rapids: Kregel, 1995), 21ff.

12.7.3 ALAN WALKER—THE PREACHER AS SOULWINNER

> God-sent men never fail.
>
> —Alan Walker's father's word to him

> Proclamation by preaching was Christ's chosen method. Here is the supreme reason why preaching is central to the strategy of mission. "Jesus came preaching." In the communication of truth, nothing is so powerful as a human personality incandescent with the love and power of God. Unpredictable, wonderful things happen when a man stands up to preach. This has been shown a thousand times through the history of the Christian church. . . . Preaching sets people marching!

> Effective worship requires the vigor and thrust of preaching. History is stained with unethical religion. Religious practices and ritualistic services can easily lack ethical challenge. They can communicate a sense of the holy, yet become escapist and irrelevant. Religious worship without effective preaching can be so general and vague that it fails to thrust the gospel with any sharpness into the mind and conscience of those who worship. Preaching completes an act of public worship.
>
> —Alan Walker

Preaching in Australia has always been supported by the solid bedrock of evangelical Anglicanism such as is represented by the archbishops of Sidney—men like Howard Mowll, Harrington Lees, and Marcus Loane, and scholars like Leon Morris.[1]

Another Aussie whose preaching ministry encompassed the whole world came out of Methodism, **Alan Walker,** born in 1911 in Sidney. He stood thirteenth in a succession of Methodist ministers in his family. His two sons also entered the ranks. Walker was a descendant of John Joseph Walker of Hull, England, who was sent to the penal colony established in Australia in 1806.

Walker was converted under his father's preaching.[2] He saw much poverty and privation in places where his father ministered. In 1928, Alan went with his father to visit Gypsy Smith, who was conducting a crusade in the area. In this encounter and a time of prayer, Walker sensed the call to preach.[3] He entered theological college in 1930 and worked his way through by operating a fruit and vegetable run, all the time handling the Hornsby preaching circuit. With his wife, Walker spent a year in England. There he was much influenced by William Sangster, who shared with him his excellent filing system, and Norman Dunning. Dunning was "an evangelist of the old school, pietistic rather than prophetic, calling people to commitment to Christ more in personal than in social terms."[4] He tended to balance off Donald Soper, who convinced Walker of pacifism, and William Temple, whose studies on John were key to his warm, devotional approach to Scripture.

Back home, Walker took up the ministry at Cessnock, a mining town, and there started a radio broadcast called "The Friendly Road" which attracted considerable attention. While in something of a personal funk, Walker discovered Vincent Taylor's trilogy on the death of Christ while he was preparing Holy Week sermons in 1941.[5] This was a turning point in his ministry. Among his many books of lecture-sermons, a perennial favorite has been his choice work *The Many-Sided Cross of Christ.*[6] Walker and his wife faced many struggles, both ecclesiastically and with their deaf daughter, Lynette. He moved on to the Waverley Church in a suburb of Sydney, where great growth ensued and revival came. On one night, fifty came to Christ.[7]

Walker was at the forefront of crusades against liquor, gambling, and the nuclear threat. He served as advisor to the Australian delegation to the United Nations, headed up the Mission to the Nation in Australia, and did many university crusades in the U.S. and Britain. From 1958 to 1978, he served as superintendent of the great Central Methodist Mission in Sidney, where his emphasis on the priority of preaching and resultant public witness by those seeking Christ became lasting hallmarks of a significant urban ministry. His earlier work on preaching, now published under the title *Evangelistic Preaching,* well encapsulates his conviction that "the preacher's theme is the whole gospel of Jesus Christ."[8] He gave a ringing call to preach for a verdict. Walker became a strong supporter and friend of Billy Graham in his remarkable crusades "down under."

A fine book of his typical sermons is included in the American "Preaching for Today" series and contains a well-divided study of Romans 7 under the title "The Conquest of Inner Space."[9] His sermons are artfully illustrated and always practical and well applied. Walker came into increasing prominence as a preacher and was knighted by the queen in 1981, but characteristically said, "I prefer still to be known by the sufficient title of Reverend Alan Walker. For a Christian there can be no greater title than that of a minister."[10] Walker was director of evangelism for the World Methodist Council, preached in over sixty countries and was the first to hold evangelistic crusades in the Soviet Union.

---

1. Certainly one of the critical books for evangelicals after midcentury was Leon Morris, *The Apostolic Preaching of the Cross* (Grand Rapids: Eerdmans, 1955) with its vigorous defense of the substitutionary atonement. John Stott's later work on *The Cross of Christ* (Downers Grove, Ill.: InterVarsity Press, 1986) is similarly strong and substantive on this theme.

2. Harold R. Henderson, *Reach for the World: The Alan Walker Story* (London: Collins, 1981), 7.

3. Ibid., 12.

4. Ibid., 30.

5. Vincent Taylor, *Jesus and His Sacrifice: A Study of the Passion-Sayings in the Gospels* (London: Macmillan, 1951). Taylor gives us rich studies in his three volumes, but his emphasis on Christ as our representative tends to crowd out Christ as our substitute. See H. D. McDonald, *The Atonement of the Death of Christ* (Grand Rapids: Baker, 1985), in which a thoughtful critique of Taylor is made (329–30).

6. Alan Walker, *The Many-Sided Cross of Christ* (Nashville: Abingdon, 1962). Christ is victim and victor! Occasionally Walker speaks with some theological imprecision, but in the main he follows James Denney (40ff.).

7. Henderson, *Reach for the World,* 63, 68. How the Spirit of God was "very near" all day and then came the "break."

8. Alan Walker, *Evangelistic Preaching* (Grand Rapids: Francis Asbury/Zondervan, 1988).

9. Alan Walker, *God Is Where You Are* (Grand Rapids: Eerdmans, 1962). The title sermon is from Psalm 139:7–10.

10. Henderson, *Reach for the World,* 215.

12.7.4 S. D. Gordon—The Preacher as Empathizer

A great sorrow has come into the heart of God. Let it be told only in hushed voice—one of his words is "a prodigal." Hush your voice yet more—ours is that prodigal world. Let your voice soften down still more—we have consented to the prodigal part of the story. But, in softest tones yet, He has won some of us back with His strong tender love. And now let the voice ring out with great gladness—we won ones may be the pathway back to God for the others. That is His earnest desire. That should be our dominant ambition. For that purpose He has endowed us with peculiar power.

—S. D. Gordon

One of the most underrated and neglected preachers of modern times is **Samuel Dickey Gordon** (1860–1936). He was often called "Quiet Talk Gordon" because he deliberately spoke softly, believing that people listened better if they had to strain a bit. Some have spoken derisively and unfairly of his preaching because his sermons were put in a series of volumes called "Quiet Talks."[1] In fact, his trademark was the question, "Are you listening?"

While Mr. Gordon, as he liked to be called, was not a classical expositor, he was deeply into the text of the Word as his inimitable *Quiet Talks on John's Gospel* and *Quiet Talks on the Crowned Christ of Revelation* conclusively prove. One of his books of messages that had a searing effect on my soul in my early years was his *Quiet Talks on Power.* He was a layman and not trained for ministerial work but was a YMCA worker like others in this saga, including Moody and Machen.

Gordon served in Philadelphia and spent nine years as YMCA secretary for Ohio before beginning an itinerant ministry of preaching. There was a certain charm and power in his more reserved manner, and the Spirit mightily blessed his preaching and his writings. He traveled extensively in Europe and spent a year in the Far East. His two visits to Keswick were well remembered, as in 1910 and again in 1931 he "captured the hearts of his hearers" by his informal and intimate style. His "quiet talk" on "The Incoming of Power" was especially blessed.[2]

He had a gentle spirit, and his "quaint phrases" stuck in the mind so that Pollock observes that he "remains one of the very few pre-1914 speakers widely read."[3] In 1895, Gordon gave a notable series of lectures at Moody Bible Institute. About this time his first "Quiet Talk" book was published. *Quiet Talks on Prayer* has become one of the classics on that subject and is drenched with the Word. Gordon properly sees prayer as "The Greatest Outlet of Power."[4]

Gordon touched the heart. He drew people to himself and the truth he shared with deft skill. He could image a biblical text like John 7:37–39, where we sense the liquidity of "the rivers of living water."[5] His message on "The Price of Power," expounding Matthew 16:24, is among the finest ever preached on this text.[6] His depiction of "Phil," a person of an illustration he develops, and his dad tug at the heart.[7] The richness of his pictures is particularly evident in *Quiet Talks on Following the Christ,* in which he began with "The Lone Man Who Went Before" and went on to trace "What Following Means" in terms of "A Look Ahead," "The Main Road," "The Valleys," and "The Hilltops."[8]

Gordon was especially gifted in reaching youth.[9] He did not dodge the relevance of the gospel to modern issues.[10] He spoke helpfully to eschatological concerns, and has given us a marvelous study on life after death.[11] S. D. Gordon is more than a period piece in the history of preaching. He modeled pastoral and preaching strengths convincingly. He died at his home in Winston-Salem, North Carolina, on June 26, 1936.

---

1. D. M. Lloyd-Jones, *Knowing the Times* (Edinburgh: Banner of Truth, 1989), 264. Lloyd-Jones judges Gordon by the titles of his books which he says "did great harm." Lloyd-Jones completely misunderstands.
2. Herbert F. Stevenson, ed., *Keswick's Triumphant Voice* (Grand Rapids: Zondervan, 1963), 321, 379ff.
3. J. C. Pollock, *The Keswick Story* (Chicago: Moody, 1964), 131–32.
4. S. D. Gordon, *Quiet Talks on Prayer* (Westwood, N.J.: The Christian Library, 1984 Revell). A truly stimulating treatment. Other smaller works on prayer include his *Prayer Changes Things* and *Five Laws That Govern Prayer.*
5. S. D. Gordon, *Quiet Talks on Power* (New York: Revell, 1903), 21. Great on "Making and Breaking Connections."
6. Ibid., 87.
7. S. D. Gordon, *Quiet Talks with World Winners* (New York: Revell, 1908), 24ff.
8. S. D. Gordon, *Quiet Talks on Following the Christ* (New York: Revell, 1913). Messages from his travels.

9. S. D. Gordon, *Quiet Talks with Eager Youth* (New York: Revell, 1935). One of his last books.

10. S. D. Gordon, *Quiet Talks on the Crisis and Afterwards* (New York: Revell, 1926); *Quiet Talks on Personal Problems* (New York: Revell, 1906). Especially fine on "The Problem of Self-Mastery."

11. S. D. Gordon, *Quiet Talks on Life After Death* (Chicago: Moody, n.d.). Exceedingly tender.

12.7.5 CLARENCE E. MACARTNEY—THE PREACHER AS CONSERVATOR

Put all the Bible you can into it!
—Clarence Macartney to his brother, who was going out to preach

Before I preach I must irrigate my soul with the joys and sorrows of my people.

As the years go by, we think less about preaching a good sermon, and more about preaching a sermon that will do good.
—Clarence E. Macartney

When he was to be installed as pastor of the First Presbyterian Church of Pittsburgh to succeed Dr. Maitland Alexander, who had served for twenty-nine years, the church received a letter from Dr. Francis L. Patton, longtime president of Princeton, which read:

The new minister of your church will come with a message and not a query, and will be fully conscious that zeal in the pulpit will never grow out of doubt in the study.[1]

Well said of **Clarence E. Macartney** (1879–1957). He was the youngest of seven children and one of four preacher brothers born to a Scot-Irish immigrant minister of the Covenanters, John Longfellow Macartney, and his Huguenot wife, Catherine Robertson.

Born in Northfield, Ohio, but reared on the campus of Geneva College in Beaver Falls, Pennsylvania, of which his father was one of the founders, Macartney was raised in the Reformed Presbyterian Church with its twenty-three-minute-long prayers and one-hour sermons. He never forgot the solemnity of the semiannual communion services and his praying to receive Christ at eleven years of age and then joining the church.[2]

Moving west with his family when his father sought renewal of health, Macartney was trained at Pomona College. Here a lecturer turned him on to the fascination of biography.[3] Macartney then attended the University of Denver and the University of Wisconsin, where he majored in English and was distinguished for his achievements as a debater. After a year's break of travel, he began his studies at Princeton Seminary. Macartney was particularly drawn to B. B. Warfield in theology and Robert Dick Wilson in Old Testament. He served several summer pastorates in Prairie du Sac, Wisconsin, and out of these years traced deep and lasting friendships with Woodrow Wilson of Princeton and the LaFollette brothers of Wisconsin politics. His homiletician was David J. Burrell (cf. 11.4.6), who was just at his peak at the Marble Collegiate Church in New York City and would come over to Princeton each Monday to teach preaching. He advised Macartney to have a clear outline and to preach without notes.[4]

Macartney served three congregations:

- First Presbyterian Church, Paterson, New Jersey (1905–1914). The downtown property of this historic church was on the market when young Macartney came. God blessed the Word and the whole direction changed.
- Arch Street Presbyterian Church, Philadelphia (1914–1927). "He is digging his grave," it was said when Macartney took the call to this downtown hulk, but "the old church began to show signs of life . . ."[5]
- First Presbyterian Church, Pittsburgh (1927–1953). Here he was known above all for his Tuesday Noon Club for men and his great Sunday evening services. He filled five regular preaching and teaching preparations each week.

Macartney never married but traveled extensively and read voraciously, especially history, in which he concentrated on the American Civil War and Abraham Lincoln. In this field he wrote a number of significant works.

Macartney was pivotal as moderator of the General Assembly in 1924, to which post he was nominated by William Jennings Bryan. This was the crucial action that led to the withdrawal of Harry Emerson Fosdick from the pulpit of First Presbyterian Church of New York City. Macartney was a champion of orthodoxy, as his vigorously doctrinal sermons indicate.[6] When Fosdick's famous sermon, "Will the Fundamentalists Win?" shook the denomination, Macartney replied with "Will Unbelief Win?" Macartney backed Machen in the founding of Westminster. His ripened thought on preaching may be found in *Preaching Without Notes*. His volume of printed illustrations, though now archaic, display his wide reading and erudition.[7]

Macartney is at his biblical best in his series on the Lamb in Revelation and in his sermons on the blood of Christ.[8] He often used four points in his sermons. No one can use another preacher's method, but his steps in sermon preparation are as instructive as any. From early on he exploited the interest in preaching Bible characters.

"Biographical preaching strikes a popular chord," he asserted.[9] We have already noted some of the dangers in biographical preaching (cf. 11.6.2, note 9), and some of that concern must register with Macartney's tendency to fixate on a minor matter in the text and enlarge it beyond any sense of the author's intention.[10] In his famous sermon on "Come Before Winter," from 2 Timothy 4:21, a poignant evangelistic appeal, he makes a somewhat incidental request into the fulcrum for a strong gospel appeal. Is there not a platform text for a sermon on working together with God better suited than Acts 9:25, "and let him down in a basket?"[11] Notwithstanding this caveat, we must heartily underscore the strength and soundness of Macartney, particularly when he takes a more spacious text.[12]

Frank Gaebelein speaks of a certain grandeur in his preaching: "High seriousness, powerful directness, intentive conviction, mastery of the Scriptures, and knowledge of the human heart marked his sermons. In his imaginative illustrations and in his ability to reach the minds of his listeners, he had few equals."[13]

---

1. Clarence E. Macartney, *The Making of a Minister* (Great Neck, N.Y.: Channel, 1961). A posthumous work.
2. Ibid., 66, 68.
3. Ibid., 91.
4. Ibid., 129.
5. Ibid., 173. His Stone Lectures, *Sons of Thunder,* describe certain eminent preachers who were much used of God.
6. Clarence E. Macartney, *Twelve Great Questions About Christ* (Grand Rapids: Baker, 1956). A clarion call!
7. Clarence E. Macartney, *Preaching Without Notes* (Nashville: Abingdon, 1946); *Macartney's Illustrations* (Nashville: Abingdon, 1945) includes fifteen hundred classified stories, anecdotes, and quotes for sermons.
8. Clarence E. Macartney, compiled by Richard Allen Bodey, *The Lamb of God* (Grand Rapids: Kregel, 1994).
9. Macartney, *The Making of a Minister,* 150.
10. Clarence E. Macartney, *Peter and His Lord* (Nashville: Abingdon, 1937).
11. Donald Macleod, *Here Is My Method* (Westwood, N.J.: Revell, 1952), 113ff.
12. Clarence E. Macartney, *The Greatest Questions of the Bible and of Life* (Grand Rapids: Kregel, 1995); *Great Interviews of Jesus* (Grand Rapids: Kregel, 1996); "Christian Giving" (a sermon from 1 Corinthians 16:1); "Now Concerning the Collection" (Grand Rapids: Zondervan, 1936). Takes off on Jowett's great idea from this text.
13. John Bishop, "Clarence E. Macartney: Evangelize or Perish," *Preaching* (September–October 1990): 51.

12.7.6 *Andrew W. Blackwood—The Preacher as Interpreter*

What busy preacher does not need to keep up his study of preaching as an art? Many of us approached homiletics in school as a science. Now we know that our work was too theoretical. The way to study an art is through its choicest products.

The best way to improve one's pulpit work is through the study of sermons. At some early stage almost every master preacher has made a study of printed sermons by former divines. In the classroom I have felt the need of some one volume of sermons for use in "laboratory work" . . . Men will learn more about preaching if they dig down into each sermon and discover the secrets of its effectiveness . . . Instead of admiring sweeping surveys by distant critics, why not get down and dig?

—Andrew Watterson Blackwood

He was called Mr. Homiletician! One teacher of preaching said of him, "For the years of his service in Princeton Seminary he probably had as much influence as any teacher of homiletics has had."[1] **Andrew W. Blackwood** (1882–1966) "was the best-known and most widely published homiletician in America in the twentieth century," and he was an excellent preacher as well.[2] He was born into a physician's family in Clay Center, Kansas, of Reformed Presbyterian (Covenanters) stock. Moving about with his family, he then took baccalaureate degrees from both Franklin College in Ohio, with a background in classics and humanities, and Harvard, where he was active in debating and where he was negatively influenced by prevailing Unitarian ideas.

Sensing nonetheless a call to ministry, Blackwood enrolled at Princeton in 1905. Under the aegis of B. B. Warfield and John Davis, he became staunch in his orthodoxy. Taught to preach by David Burrell, he was largely unimpressed by the pure lecture method in teaching preaching and in Burrell's independent spirit as shown by his disdain of preaching from a pulpit.[3] After his first year, Blackwood had the first of several physical and emotional breakdowns and transferred to Xenia Seminary in Ohio, closer to home. He was ordained in 1908 under the United Presbyterians and took some early charges in Kansas. Preaching his first sermon in "a clear, resonant voice," he took the text in John 12:32 on "The Magnetic Christ."[4] His ministerial career prepared him well for the teaching of preaching:

- Sixth United Presbyterian Church, Pittsburgh (1911–1914). He did substitute teaching at Xenia Seminary.
- First Presbyterian Church, Columbia, South Carolina (1914–1921). He began his deep study of classical preachers and sermons.
- Indianola Avenue Presbyterian Church, Columbus, Ohio (1921–1925). He continued to produce articles, believing it was important to write.
- Chairman of English Bible at Louisville Presbyterian Seminary (1925–1930). He taught the Bible homiletically.
- Professor of preaching, Princeton Theological Seminary (1930–1950). He used the "coach method" in teaching.
- Professor of homiletics, Temple University School of Theology (1950–1958). He had *carte blanche* to effect change.

Blackwood's homiletic was built on a sound rhetorical foundation and tended to be quite traditional in its taxonomy of sermons. He insisted on the distinction between a textual and an expository sermon in which the natural thought unit is considered rather than a microtext. Yet, as Jay Adams shows, he was innovative in adding many new courses.[5] In his avid study of preachers and preaching, Blackwood introduced a highly personalized one-on-one approach to teaching— even though the classes at Princeton included more than one hundred students.[6] While at Princeton, the Blackwoods were neighbors of the Albert Einsteins; they had little spiritual success with the scientific genius but led Mrs. Einstein to Christ on her deathbed.[7]

Feeling increasingly isolated theologically at Princeton, Blackwood moved on to Temple, where he continued to develop his theory of imagination.[8] Even after retiring, he continued to preach and lecture and write for *Christianity Today* and did five more books. He advocated strong use of active verbs and avoidance of "excessive Latinization" in speaking.[9] His strong biblicality is manifested in *Preaching from Samuel.* Here we have probing insights into the biblical text and choice samples of splendid application.[10]

Not as exegetically or theologically nuanced as we might sometimes desire, Blackwood still is a champion of expository preaching that is more than explaining the passage.[11] His studies of doctrinal and biographical preaching were blazing new trails.[12] One of the most influential of his works was his unmatched work on planning our preaching.[13] No one has given us as helpful a guide on the difficult matter of public prayer.[14] Blackwood as a preacher or as a teacher was no dynamo, but he was steady and sound. As Matthew Arnold said of Sophocles, "He saw life steadily and he saw it whole," also applies to Andrew Blackwood. Fewer and fewer of his students are still actively preaching, but we are all beneficiaries of his legacy and patrimony. He must take an honored place in this chronicle.

---

1. Jay E. Adams, *The Homiletical Innovations of Andrew W. Blackwood* (Grand Rapids: Baker, 1975), 101.
2. William H. Willimon and Richard Lischer, eds., *Concise Encyclopedia of Preaching* (Louisville: Westminster/John Knox, 1995), 37.
3. Adams, *Homiletical Innovations,* 108ff.
4. Ibid., 46.
5. Ibid., 84.
6. Ibid., 61. Note his collection of master sermons in *The Protestant Pulpit* (Nashville: Abingdon, 1947).
7. Ibid., 85.
8. Ibid., 124ff.
9. Ibid., 114ff. I think Dr. Lloyd M. Perry of Northern, Gordon, and Trinity succeeded Blackwood as doyen of homiletics.
10. Andrew W. Blackwood, *Preaching from Samuel* (Nashville: Abingdon, 1946). Titles were never his strong suit.
11. Andrew W. Blackwood, *Expository Preaching for Today* (Nashville: Abingdon, 1953).
12. Andrew W. Blackwood, *Doctrinal Preaching for Today* (Grand Rapids: Baker, 1956); *Biographical Preaching for Today* (Nashville: Abingdon, 1954). We have already noted a caution on the latter; cf. 11.6.2, note 9).
13. Andrew W. Blackwood, *Planning a Year's Pulpit Work* (Grand Rapids: Baker, 1942, 1975).
14. Andrew W. Blackwood, *Leading in Public Prayer* (Nashville: Abingdon, 1958). One of several pastoral works.

12.7.7 DONALD GREY BARNHOUSE—THE PREACHER AS EXPOSITORY TEACHER

Expository preaching is the art of explaining the text of the Word of God, using all the experiences of life and learning to illuminate the exposition.

The prime factor in expository preaching is the belief that the Bible is the Word of God. When I take the Bible into my hands I think of it as originating with God, given by Him to every man in the very order, terms, phrases and words in which He wanted us to have it.

I glory in all that scholarship has accomplished in lower criticism, establishing an ever more accurate text of the original languages. I give practically no consideration to anything that has been done in the field of higher criticism, although I have spent hundreds of weary hours plowing through the critics, trying to find out what they are driving at, and finally rejecting their conclusions because they proceed on the false premise that the Bible originated with man and that it is the record of man's thoughts about God.

—Donald Grey Barnhouse

Reflective of a genuine resurgence of classical expository preaching in the last half of the twentieth century is the strikingly effective preaching of **Donald Grey Barnhouse** (1895–1960). A large and gravelly-voiced man, Barnhouse combined high-density exposition of the text with the most remarkable illustrations and a blunt, almost overbearing manner with a most delightful sense of humor and the incongruous.[1] He was born in Watsonville, California, and came under the influence of R. A. Torrey at the Bible Institute of Los Angeles (BIOLA). Exceedingly intelligent and probing as a student, he went to study at Princeton Seminary, the University of Grenoble in France, the University of Chicago, and the University of Pennsylvania, where he was a faculty assistant. He had a Th.M. from Eastern Baptist Seminary and a Th.D. from the seminary in Aix-en-Provence in France. After World War I, he had a positive ministry in war-torn Belgium and France.[2]

In 1918 Barnhouse was ordained into the Presbyterian ministry. In 1927 he began a thirty-three-year ministry at Tenth Presbyterian Church in Philadelphia, a congregation which was never huge but which had a most extraordinary influence on students and leaders in the city. From 1928 on, he had a radio ministry called the "Bible Study Hour" and later a television outreach. He edited *Revelation* and *Eternity* magazines successively and wrote prolifically. He began his ministry with three and a half years of close exposition of Romans and later expanded these messages to the radio congregation, now published in ten magnificent volumes.[3] By special arrangement, Barnhouse preached twenty-six Sundays a year at Tenth and then traveled the nation in popular Bible conferences the rest of the year. He also had a weekly New York Bible class for many years.

Staunchly Calvinistic and almost gruff in his manner, he yet enjoyed close fellowship with Billy Graham and was passionately evangelistic to the point that his appeals seemed inconsistent with his doctrine. His wife's biography documents the mellowing of Barnhouse over the years if not some softening in doctrinal precision.

Barnhouse's first book was a guide for instructing young Christians and consisted of eighty lessons on doctrine accompanied with visual sketches. This work has been translated into many languages and shows the visual tilt of Barnhouse's wonderful mind.[4] His steps in preparation of sermons are helpful because we see the importance of outline for his preaching even if he never formally emphasized structure as such in presentation.[5] He often made extensive comments on points in the scriptural text as he read it, not unlike Spurgeon.[6] Barnhouse was very much aware of the reality of spiritual warfare in the preaching process from beginning to end.[7]

His great strength was his biblical content. After all, the elaboration of a triviality is still trivial. Barnhouse was so rich in the text, as is shown in his unique devotional expositions in Genesis.[8] His creative work in John's gospel is outstanding.[9] And who else ever thought of using 1 John as a commentary on the Upper Room Discourse?[10]

Despite his "inexhaustible energy" and "pugnacious controversialism," Barnhouse became an all-time favorite at Keswick in England starting in 1935.[11] From his BIOLA days, he was an outspoken dispensationalist and pretribulation rapturist.[12] Illustrations from yesterday are often not worth reading, but Barnhouse's knack for the startling story makes his collected illustrations still valuable.[13] His tool for evangelism, *Your Right to Heaven,* was instrumental in the conversion of Dr. D. James Kennedy and is at the core of his Evangelism Explosion approach so used of God and owned of the Spirit in our time.[14] To hear Barnhouse was never to forget the experience!

---

1. The only preacher I ever heard who was more adept at this than Barnhouse was the Scottish pulpiteer, Dr. James McGinlay, who served Central Baptist Church in London, Ontario, and the Baptist Temple in Brooklyn; see *The Birthday of Souls and Other Sermons* (Grand Rapids: Eerdmans, 1939). Also, John W. Drakeford, *Humor in Preaching* (Grand Rapids: Zondervan, 1986).
2. Margaret N. Barnhouse, *That Man Barnhouse* (Wheaton, Ill.: Tyndale House, 1983), 104. This volume is written in the spirit of candor and openness which started with Elizabeth Elliot's *Who Shall Ascend: The Life of R. Kenneth Strachan of Costa Rica* (New York: 1968). A strategy of concealment and cover-up is invariably self-defeating.
3. Donald Grey Barnhouse, *God's Wrath: Expository Messages on the Whole Bible Taking the Epistle to the Romans as a Point of Departure* (Wheaton, Ill.: Van Kampen, 1952). There are ten volumes in this series.
4. Donald Grey Barnhouse, *Teaching the Word of Truth* (Grand Rapids: Eerdmans, 1940). A most useful piece.
5. Clarence S. Roddy, ed., *We Prepare and Preach: The Practice of Sermon Construction and Delivery* (Chicago: Moody, 1959), 33ff. Roddy was himself a great preacher, pastor of the Baptist Temple in Brooklyn at one time, professor at both Eastern Baptist in Philadelphia and Fuller in Pasadena. He was "my homiletician."
6. Barnhouse, *That Man Barnhouse,* 154. Both Mariano di Gangi and James Montgomery Boice, his successors at Tenth Presbyterian Church, have been strong expositors of the Word. Boice has been strongly in his mold.
7. Ibid., 369. Barnhouse's best book in my opinion and his last, *The Invisible War* (Grand

Rapids: Zondervan, 1966).

8. Donald Grey Barnhouse, *Genesis: A Devotional Exposition,* 2 vols. (Grand Rapids: Zondervan, 1970, 1971).

9. Donald Grey Barnhouse, *The Love Life* (Glendale, Calif.: Regal/Gospel Light, 1973). Vintage Barnhouse.

10. Barnhouse, *That Man Barnhouse,* 257.

11. J. C. Pollock, *The Keswick Story* (Chicago: Moody, 1964), 161ff.; see *The Ministry of Keswick: Second Series,* ed. Herbert F. Stevenson (London: Marshall, Morgan, and Scott, 1964), 155ff. A most searching series given in 1948 on "Baptized into Christ." Called "the most controversial speaker in Keswick's history," but a "genius" who drew great crowds. He loved repartee and debate. Bishop Houghton spoke of him as "a man mighty in the Scriptures." His superlative afternoon studies at Keswick in 1938 are *God's Methods for Holy Living* (Grand Rapids: Eerdmans, 1951).

12. Especially drawn out in his work *His Own Received Him Not and Revelation* (Grand Rapids: Zondervan, 1971).

13. Donald Grey Barnhouse, *Bible Truth Illustrated* (New Canaan, Conn.: Keats, 1979); *Words Fitly Spoken* (Wheaton, Ill.: Tyndale House, 1969). Barnhouse used simple everyday matters to illustrate great truth.

14. Donald Grey Barnhouse, *Your Right to Heaven* (Grand Rapids: Baker, 1977). "What right do you have to enter my heaven?" The incisive issue for everyone of us is addressed in the justifying work of Christ through Calvary.

12.7.8 *Harold John Ockenga—The Preacher as Visionary Leader*

You can't stand and converse with people from the pulpit; you'll lose them. If you have a strong pulpit ministry, you're going to have a strong church, no matter what else is lacking. If you have a strong counseling church without a strong pulpit, you'll have a weak church. Preaching has got to be there, or people are not going to come. It has to be enlightening, interesting and challenging. Conversational preaching is a mistake. You've got to develop certain points, like a syllogism. You have to develop something people can follow, an outline with alliteration. When you get through, people can say, "That's what he said about this and that's what he said about that."

—Harold John Ockenga

Continued strong emphasis on expository preaching continued among evangelicals in the last half of the twentieth century. One of the conspicuously excellent practitioners of the craft was **Harold John Ockenga.**[1] Ockenga was born in 1905 in Chicago and reared in the Methodist Church by a godly mother. His father was not converted until later in life. Always sickly and frail as a child but aggressive and enterprising (establishing a monopoly on box kites in his neighborhood), he announced at age nine, "I'm going to be a preacher and see the world."[2] Through the interest of a consecrated woman in his Olivet Methodist Church, Ockenga made his commitment to Christ and dedicated himself to the Christian ministry.[3] He worked his way though Methodistic Taylor University, where he excelled in forensics. Because he loved to preach, he preached four hundred times during college days and saw souls come to the Savior.[4]

From 1927 to 1929, he was at Princeton Seminary but finished at the new Westminster, where he met Macartney. After serving several Methodist charges, he became Macartney's assistant. With this pedigree, he became a strong Calvinist. Eventually he moderated his views, coming to believe in the freedom of human response to the gospel while also retaining his Methodistic emphasis on the deeper spiritual life. Ockenga eschewed any kind of perfectionism.[5] At his Presbyterian ordination in 1931, Macartney gave the charge and Machen preached.[6] From 1931 to 1936, he served Point Breeze Presbyterian Church in Pittsburgh and earned a doctorate in philosophy at the University of Pittsburgh.

In 1936, upon the recommendation of Macartney and Machen, Ockenga was called to pastor the historic Park Street Church in Boston, succeeding the venerable A. Z. Conrad, who had just died (cf. 11.4.6). This congregation had stood firmly against "the Unitarian landslide" that had almost engulfed New England. Ockenga's ministry was needed. For thirty-three years the pulpit was primary in the steady growth and expanding influence of this great congregation.[7]

Ockenga was a man of the Book, with a keenly logical mind, clear outlines, and long introductions. Deeply committed to evangelism, he witnessed on Boston Common and preached from the outdoor Geneva pulpit. "He loses himself in his preaching," it was often said for he had tremendous driving force and flow as he preached. Ockenga had a great missions emphasis and brought Oswald J. Smith from Toronto for six years to advance it (cf. 12.8.2).

Ockenga founded Boston Evening School of the Bible with Dr. Howard Ferrin of Providence Bible Institute, and he was one of the prime movers and first president of the National Association of Evangelicals founded in 1942. He was one of the minds behind *Christianity Today* and cofounder of Fuller Seminary with Charles E. Fuller, of which he was president in absentia for many years. Fuller's early conservative stand was one of Ockenga's contributions.

Ockenga catalyzed and envisioned the Billy Graham Crusade in Boston in 1949, which saw so many converts. The fruit was quickly seen; in 1950, 186 converts of the crusade joined Park Street Church.

Ockenga was heard morning and evening over a fifty-thousand-watt Boston radio station. He fully manuscripted and memorized his messages. The story of God's blessing reaching out from the ministry of Park Street Church is an exciting reinforcement of the insistence on the primacy of preaching.[8] Many churches sought to secure his services, but he turned them down. He nearly went to Seattle First Presbyterian Church to succeed Mark Matthews, but declined.[9]

His published expositions are meaty messages. His books on 2 Corinthians, Ephesians, and 1 Thessalonians were enormously popular. His expository addresses on Romans are typically superb samples of taking a good piece of text. He did not use a microtext, as did Lloyd-Jones or Barnhouse, but he took the larger natural thought unit. Ockenga covered Romans in twenty-four sermons. His message on Romans 1:1–17 is titled "The Gospel of which to be Proud":

I. The gospel of God makes us debtors;

II. The gospel of God makes us bold and daring;

III. The gospel of God brings us salvation.[10]

This is Harold Ockenga in his prime, and he was one of the best.

_____

1. The move to exposition was led by William Evans of Moody and James Braga at Multnomah, by Faris Whitesell of Northern Baptist and Lloyd Perry at Trinity, and by the Dallas succession of Haddon Robinson, Donald Sunukjian, and Timothy Warren. We have already seen that strong support came from Andrew Blackwood at Princeton.
2. Harold Lindsell, *Park Street Prophet: The Story of Harold Ockenga* (Wheaton, Ill.: Van Kampen, 1951), 15.
3. Ibid., 20–21.
4. Ibid., 25. At this time he had what he called "a personal appropriation of the Pentecostal gift." See Clarence S. Roddy, *We Prepare and Preach* (Chicago: Moody, 1959), 114. Always a strong emphasis for him.
5. Ibid., 93. "The Calvinism of the classroom has been probably molded to a degree by the experiences of the pastorate and by intimate contacts with people."
6. Ibid., 33. A towering intellectual, he later became president of Gordon College and Gordon-Conwell Divinity School.
7. Cf. Earl V. Comfort, "Is the Pulpit a Factor in Church Growth?" *Bibliotheca Sacra* 140, no. 560 (January–March 1983): 64–70. This research concludes that sermons, with high biblical content, are the most significant factor in growth.
8. H. Crosby Englizian, *Brimstone Corner: Park Street Church Boston* (Chicago: Moody, 1968), 228ff. The novelist Henry James spoke of Park Street Church as "The most impressive mass of brick and mortar in the United States."
9. Lindsell, *Park Street Prophet,* 60–61.
10. Harold John Ockenga, *Every One That Believeth* (New York: Revell, 1942), 11ff.

12.8 EVANGELICAL POINT MEN AMID THE COLLAPSE OF CIVILIZATION

> The remnant . . . will know whose word will stand, Mine or theirs. My words will surely stand against you.
> —Jeremiah 44:28b, 29b (NASB)

The Christian communicator has always confronted enormous challenges, making the supernaturalism of the task essential. But as the century draws to a close, he or she now faces the death of truth in a spiritual and moral free-fall of staggering proportions. Even secular diehards have lamented the loss of "the common culture" of the Bible in the rush toward nihilism and relativism.[1] Judge Bork traces "the descent of popular culture into vulgarity and obscenity," into "gleeful sadism," in which "narcissistic nihilism" and "the resistance to restraints" have triumphed.[2] He was not the first to identify radical individualism and radical egalitarianism as twin demons in our time.[3] The Canadian philosopher Mark Kingwell documents the "brink culture" of which we are a part and how rationality is totally out of fashion.[4] But the "net-culture" is also beset with an "extraordinary rise in anxiety" and much fear of the future. So the stage is set again and again for "the ministry of the word and prayer."

1. Allan Bloom, *The Closing of the American Mind* (New York: Simon and Schuster, 1987), 58.
2. Robert H. Bork, *Slouching Toward Gomorrah: Modern Liberalism and American Decline* (New York: HarperCollins, 1996). Also weighty, Stephen L. Carter, *The Culture of Disbelief: How American Law and Politics Trivialize Religion* (New York: Basic Books, 1993). Quotes Martin Marty, "The public sphere does not welcome particularized witness."
3. On the former especially, Robert N. Bellah et al., *Habits of the Heart: Individualism and Commitment in American Life* (New York: Perennial Library, Harper and Row, 1985). Bellah's updates show that the situation has gotten worse.
4. Mark Kingwell, *Dreams of Millennium: Report from a Culture on the Brink* (Toronto: Viking/Penguin, 1996). I am indebted to my friend and former teaching fellow, the Reverend Timothy Callaway, for this invaluable source.

12.8.1 *T. T. SHIELDS—THE PREACHER AS FIGHTER FOR THE TRUTH*

Preaching is the biggest business I know. It is a far bigger job than being Prime Minister. I don't believe there is any occupation in the world that makes a bigger demand upon all that a man has or may become, than preaching.

After a disappointing Sunday morning experience in London, but then hearing Dinsdale Young at Westminster Central Hall: "The service began with an invocation, and he put the cross right in the center. He spoke of the Mercy Seat, of Christ, of his imputed righteousness, His blood, and I just heaved a sigh and said, 'Thank the Lord, I have come to church!'"

I have a vivid recollection, even now, of an experience I had more than thirty years ago. I was working on a sermon, and the bush burned with fire. I can think of nothing this side of heaven, unless it be the actual delivery of the sermon, than to be shut up with one's Bible in one's study, no extra duties calling, feeling that you are just in the proper place to await God, and let God speak to you, and just prayerfully to work out some great theme of the gospel. I would not change places with any king upon his throne when I have that really ecstatic experience.

—T. T. Shields

Some saw clearly the situation developing in the flight from authority in our culture, and their baleful warnings were not always appreciated or heeded. Such a preacher was the often feisty and combative **Thomas Todhunter Shields** (1873–1955), who pastored the premier Baptist church in Canada, the great Jarvis Street Baptist Church in Toronto, for forty-five years.

Some called him the Canadian Spurgeon, and there are striking similarities between the two. Others called him the John Bunyan of Canada. Shields was born in Bristol, the fifth of eight children. His father was a Primitive Methodist clergyman who became a Baptist and emigrated to Canada. The elder Shields was his teacher of Latin and Greek but especially of proper English usage.[1]

Shields was converted in 1891 under the preaching of a visiting speaker who pressed 1 John 1:9 on his hearers, and young T. T. "rested in the Word of God."[2] He was a tall, stately man who often carried a walking stick. Shy and reserved, he could not resist the call to the ministry. He preached his first sermon in 1894 and served several smaller Baptist churches until he enjoyed significant ministries in Hamilton and at the Adelaide Baptist Church of London, Ontario (1904–1910). Here he sought to implement the pattern of Ephesians 4:11 and saw a considerable spiritual impact.[3]

Although he could have gone to the Hanson Place Baptist Church in Brooklyn (where A. C. Dixon had served, cf. 12.2.3), Shields took the call to Jarvis Street Baptist Church in Toronto, whose fifteen hundred seats he filled morning and evening. On his regular visits to England, he filled the pulpit at Spurgeon's Tabernacle, and his reputation for strong biblical preaching was growing. He was approached at one time to take the pastoral leadership in Spurgeon's Tabernacle, but he declined. About this time, Shields received honorary doctorates both from McMaster (the Baptist school) and Temple University from Russell Conwell.

Like W. B. Riley and R. T. Ketcham in the U.S., Shields fought heavy battles in the drift toward liberalism. A considerable disruption over his views took place at Jarvis Street in 1921, but "great years" followed under his "solid Bible exposition and evangelism" Sunday by Sunday.[4] In 1924 revival came in a summer series of meetings with J. Frank Norris in which the vast Massey Hall was filled. He soon built the largest Sunday school in Canada.

Shields' preaching was first and foremost biblical and always Christ-centered. His "Christ in the Old Testament series" was one of most intently followed series he ever gave. He said:

> Take the Bible as a whole, learn the Book. Fill your mind with the Book. Whatever else you read, be sure that you master the Bible. Learn the whole Bible so that you know your way about.[5]

This he did himself, and when a storm cut off the power just as he started to read his text in a service, he recited the balance of the passage from memory in the darkened auditorium. His sermons were well outlined and abounded with effective illustration. He was frank in his speech and could never be accused of being "Mr. Facing-both-ways."[6] He preached for a verdict and was known for being pastoral.

Shields founded the Toronto Baptist Seminary and often insisted to his students that above all the preacher must be "a good man."[7] He had a striking way about him, as when he preached from John 1:29, "Behold the Lamb of God who takes away the sin of the world," and used as his title, "Jesus Christ, the Scavenger of the World." His sermons appeared every two weeks in the sixteen pages of the *Gospel Witness,* which he edited throughout his ministry.

One of the sermons in Tarr's biography reflects Shields's leadership of the Canadian Protestant League. Titled "One Sacrifice Forever," it is based on Hebrews 10:11–13.[8] His book of sermons on *The Prodigal and His Brother, or The Adventures of a Modern Young Man* present a high level of well-structured preaching.[9] His sermon on "Songs in the House of My Pilgrimage" from Psalm 119:54 for New Year's shows his skill in the appropriate use of hymn stanzas and poetry.[10] His Christmas message on Galatians 4:4–7 confirms the sound patterns of rich content, sound form, and engaging points of contact in illustration and allusion.[11] His ecclesiology and separatism distract some, but here is a preacher who did evangelism with dignity and fostered reverence toward God and His Word faithfully in a time when many veered on to the steep slippery slopes of concession.

---

1. Leslie K. Tarr, *Shields of Canada: T. T. Shields 1873–1955* (Grand Rapids: Baker, 1967), 19.
2. Ibid., 27.
3. Ibid., 46.
4. Ibid., 86.
5. Ibid., 152.
6. Ibid., 162.
7. Ibid., 183.
8. Ibid., 194ff. Shields is assessed in *Amazing Grace: Evangelicals in Australia, Britain, Canada and the United States,* ed. George Rawlyk and Mark A. Noll (Grand Rapids: Baker, 1993), 364ff.
9. T. T. Shields, *The Prodigal and His Brother, or The Adventures of a Modern Young Man* (Toronto: Gospel Witness, n.d.). Shields analyzes the Oxford Group Movement and Russellism, among others.
10. T. T. Shields, "Songs in the House of My Pilgrimage," *Sword of the Lord* (December 19, 1995): 1ff.
11. T. T. Shields, "A Christmas Message," in *Great Preaching on Christmas,* ed. Curtis Hutson (Murfreesboro, Tenn.: Sword of the Lord, 1988), 143ff. This is volume 10 of the worthwhile "Great Preaching" series.

12.8.2 OSWALD J. SMITH—THE PREACHER AS PROMOTER OF MISSIONS

God has laid on me a burden for revival, and in order to accomplish this I must have His blessed Spirit. Oh, God, strip me of all that hinders the filling of Thy Holy Spirit.

God is giving me sermons by His Holy Spirit. When least expected they flash before me; I grab my notebook and take down the headings as fast as I can, all within about three or four minutes. This morning as I was reading in John 3, within ten minutes I had the outline for three new addresses.

The Bible is becoming the Book of books to me; the message that I have to proclaim is clearer, more definite and more glorious than ever before, but I am fully conscious that unless I have the Unction, the Enduement of Power, my message will be unavailing and profitless. . . . But I must first experience it myself.

—Oswald J. Smith

One of the foremost proponents of worldwide evangelization in the twentieth century was **Oswald J. Smith** (1889–1986). He was born into modest means on an Ontario farm. Very sickly as a child and a poor scholar, he nonetheless read constantly, devouring all of Henty's books of historical fiction for boys. He began to sense a call to preach even before he was converted.[1]

The death of one of his sisters, in addition to the conversion of the community drunk and the good influence of an aunt in Toronto, led him and his brother to travel to Toronto to attend the Torrey-Alexander meetings in Massey Hall, where they were both saved.[2] He began to study the Bible in earnest and prepared sermons to preach to the birds.

Smith felt called to foreign missionary service and began to take night classes at the Toronto Bible Training Institute. He was at the farewell service for the Goforths as they ventured forth to China (cf. 12.1.4). Turned down again and again for overseas ministry because of lack of preparation, he entered into colportage work with the Bible society and traveled extensively in British Columbia, especially among the Indians and the loggers. His preaching was in demand, and he conducted his first evangelistic campaign at age twenty-one. He then went on to study at McCormick Seminary in Chicago. Always a writer of poetry and verse and a gifted musician, Smith wrote more than a thousand hymns in his lifetime, including "Then Jesus Came," "The Savior Can Solve Every Problem," "With Thy Spirit, Fill Me," and "The Song of the Soul Set Free."

The thin, gangling preacher did a stint in the Kentucky hills and served First Presbyterian in South Chicago while finishing seminary. At the advice of Dr. Henry Hepburn of Buena Memorial Presbyterian Church, he returned to Toronto, where he served as associate to J. D. Morrow at Dale Presbyterian Church and met a young deaconess who became his wife. Fired with a great missionary passion, he was influenced much by Charles Finney and John Fletcher.[3] Warring factions at Dale closed that door for him after three and a half years, although revival touched the church profoundly but not the core leadership.

Smith preached for a while at Beulah Tabernacle just off Yonge Street downtown in Toronto. At this time he was much under the writings of Charles Trumbull (cf. 11.1.4, note 1) and William R. Newell. He took his stand on Romans 6:11 and on Galatians 2:20.[4] He then went with Shantyman's Mission, working especially among lumberjacks. He worked part-time for Roland Bingham as an editor for *The Evangelical Christian* but broke with Bingham over the nature of his poetry.

Smith set up his own church in the needy Dovercourt area and merged with Parkside Tabernacle of the CMA. He was close to Paul Rader, who was president of the CMA at this time. Smith was then called to the mother church, the Gospel Tabernacle in New York City. Because he felt his preaching would not carry the challenge of the work, he brought in much outside talent, like the famous Cleveland Colored Quintet.

He traveled incessantly and had a blessed ministry in Latvia and Russia, but had problems in the local church because so much money was flowing out of the treasury into non-Alliance causes.[5] For a while he served as superintendent of the central and eastern CMA churches. He was on the road all the time, and his little family suffered.

In 1927 he took the call to be pastor of the Los Angeles Gospel Tabernacle and had an unusual ministry there, but the next year he resigned and went back to Toronto. He had resigned three thriving pastorates; what was next?[6] In this time frame, both he and Rader left the Alliance, a decision he subsequently regretted.

In 1928 Smith started the Cosmopolitan Tabernacle in Toronto in a great series of meetings in Massey Hall, which seated thirty-four hundred people. Later called the Toronto Gospel Tabernacle and ultimately the People's Church, this was the church that missions built. With Rader's bankruptcy, Smith had to move into missionary management. The church grew, but often had to use rented quarters. Gypsy Smith was a personal friend and held great crusades with many saved. His son Paul worked with him, ultimately succeeded him, and built a great new church in 1962.

Oswald Smith was not an imposing presence. Thin as a rail with a birdlike physique, he was a nervous but powerful preacher. Of a frugal lifestyle, he poured everything into missions. He introduced the faith promise challenge in Toronto and around the world.[7] He preached more than twelve thousand sermons and kept at it up into his nineties. He was disciplined to take a two-hour rest each afternoon, which doubtless kept him going notwithstanding a lifelong pattern of much illness. Perhaps his frequent traveling and relentless schedule kept him from digging deeper into the Scripture.

Smith's books of sermons have had huge circulation. His message on saving faith was given many times and in many forms.[8] Tending to be a bit thin, the messages are still sound and Scripture-based, if not Scripture-shaped, and they reverberate with passion.[9] His messages on prophecy show satisfying familiarity with the relevant texts, although in the 1930s he ventured too far in speculative identification.[10]

His 1954 lectures at Bob Jones University on "The Consuming Fire" capture the man and his preaching.[11] No one has wrestled more thoroughly with the relationship between evangelism and revival than did Oswald J. Smith. I heard him over many years and up almost to the last and never failed to be deeply stirred by the singleness of his vision and the vitality of his preaching. A news report from his ministry in South Australia said:

> Let him open his mouth to speak and the outward frailty vanishes. Smith becomes a man of robust spirit, bursting with life and energy, a man on

fire. The flame of his zeal reaches you, then your neighbor, and presently the whole congregation is engulfed in a spiritual conflagration.[12]

1. Lois Neely, *Fire in His Bones: The Official Biography of Oswald J. Smith* (Wheaton, Ill.: Tyndale House, 1982), 24.
2. Ibid., 26.
3. Ibid., 95ff.
4. Ibid., 103.
5. Ibid., 147.
6. Ibid., 155.
7. Ibid., 231ff.
8. Oswald J. Smith, *From Death to Life* (New York: Christian Alliance Publishing, 1925), 67ff.
9. Oswald J. Smith, *The Enduement of Power* (London: Marshall, Morgan, and Scott, 1933); *The Man God Uses; The Work God Blesses; The Battle for Truth* (London: Marshall, Morgan, and Scott, 1953). He also wrote books for children. He was well read and felt at liberty to return to the enjoyment of the classics.
10. Oswald J. Smith, *Prophecy—What Lies Ahead?* (London: Marshall, Morgan, and Scott, n.d.).
11. Oswald J. Smith, *The Consuming Fire* (London: Marshall, Morgan, and Scott, 1954).
12. Neely, *Fire in His Bones,* 277. Smith's congregation at the People's Church was about two thousand for each service.

12.8.3 J. VERNON MCGEE—THE PREACHER AS COMMUNICATOR TO THE COMMON PEOPLE

It was fortunate for me that during my college days I met a very scholarly minister who had the knack of taking the profound truths of theology and translating them into the simple language of the ordinary person. I asked him for his secret. He assured me that this priceless gift was one that needed to be developed and cultivated. His formula went something like this: In the preparation of the sermon every effort should be made to attain simplicity—then go over the sermon the second time to reduce it to the simplest common denominator. Go over the sermon again and again until you are ashamed of its simplicity, then preach the sermon so the children can understand it. Afterward, one of the spiritual saints will come up to remark about the depth and profundity of the message.

—J. Vernon McGee

No preacher has had such an avid following in a through-the-Bible exposition of Scripture over radio as did **J. Vernon McGee** (1904–1988). His broadcasts continue today, long after his homegoing. He was a great preacher and student of the Word.

McGee was a quaint, colloquial preacher who seemed to cultivate his Texas-Oklahoma twang as the years passed. Born in Hillsboro, Texas, he graduated from

Southwestern University in Memphis and Columbia Theological Seminary, taking both his Th.M. and his Th.D. from Dallas Theological Seminary. A staunch Southern Presbyterian in his early days, he served pastorates in Nashville, Tennessee, and in Cleburne, Texas. For over eight years, he pastored the Lincoln Avenue Presbyterian Church in Pasadena, where he followed Oscar Raymond Lowery. In 1949 he became pastor of the great Church of the Open Door at Sixth and Hope in downtown Los Angeles, succeeding Dr. Louis T. Talbot.

McGee consistently drew great audiences but was especially known for the thousands who came to follow his Thursday night through-the-Bible expositions, Genesis to Revelation.[1] He was much in demand at Bible conferences around the country and the world, and continued three weekly and daily radio programs through his long tenure at Church of the Open Door.

Not advocating simply verse-by-verse progression but insisting on "a logical division and method of presentation in each message," McGee captivated audiences with his unusually rich content and uncanny ability to apply the text to world conditions and everyday life. Hundreds of thousands were McGee addicts and needed the daily "fix" this gifted expositor could furnish. His marvelous studies in the Book of Ruth are peerless, as one could also say of his work on Esther.[2]

His printed sermons have tang and pop to them, uncommon when a character as colorful as McGee puts the spoken message into printed form.[3] Such sermons as "'Twas the Prayer Before Christmas" from Luke 1:5–17 or "The Power of Negative Thinking" from Proverbs 3:5–7 show McGee at his best.[4] The danger for one who is so down-home and so chatty is of course occasional demagoguery. McGee had special skill and ability in handling biblical prophecy, and his collected sermons contain such gems as "From the Top of the Mount of Olives You Can See Forever" from the Olivet Discourse of Matthew 24–25 or his "The Amazing, Alarming and Awful Apostasy" from Jude 1–4 are superb examples.[5] Any open-minded listener always got the Word of God from J. Vernon McGee. There may have been a little cornpone with it, but it was delicious and always deeply satisfying.

---

1. J. Vernon McGee's "Thru-the-Bible" books span all of Scripture. His *Moving Through Matthew* and *Reveling Through Revelation* are typical. These have enjoyed incredible circulation. W. A. Criswell of First Baptist Church, Dallas, also used the consecutive through-the-Bible approach over most of his many years in Dallas.
2. J. Vernon McGee, *Ruth: The Romance of Redemption* (Wheaton, Ill.: Van Kampen, 1954). Other fine sermon series on Ruth include Philip Mauro, *Ruth: The Satisfied Stranger* (Swengel, Pa.: Bible Truth, 1963); Charles E. Fuller, *Ruth: A Life of Love and Loyalty* (Westwood, N.J.: Revell, 1969); M. R. DeHaan, *The Romance of Redemption* (Grand Rapids: Zondervan, 1958); Carl McIntire, *Better Than Seven Sons* (Collingswood, N.J.: Christian Beacon, 1954). McIntire's classmates at Princeton were agreed that he was one of their most gifted preachers.
3. J. Vernon McGee, *The Fruit of the Sycamore Tree and Other Sermons* (Wheaton, Ill.: Van Kampen, 1952).
4. J. Vernon McGee, *The Best of J. Vernon McGee* (Nashville: Thomas Nelson, 1988), 107ff., 81ff.

5. J. Vernon McGee, *On Prophecy: Man's Fascination with the Future* (Nashville: Thomas Nelson, 1993), 111ff., 143ff.

12.8.4 Paul S. Rees—The Preacher as Ambassador of Holiness

> On consulting other preachers who have published sermons on the text, or, at any rate, the subject one has chosen: "Manifestly, this is not for the purpose of imitating them but rather of catching inspiration from them. I have met a few ministers who say they never read other men's sermons. I find it impossible to share their feeling. Currently I have between seven and eight hundred volumes of sermons in my library. My incurable interest in expository preaching leads me, understandably enough, to the works of men who are saturated with the Word of God and endowed with the ability to expound it."
>
> —Paul S. Rees

He has been described as "a mind aflame," in recognition of both the brilliance of his preaching in its content and form and the warmth and passion of his heart. **Paul Stromberg Rees** (1900–1991) was nurtured in the arms of the Holiness movement. His father, Seth Rees, was first a Quaker and then prominent in the Church of the Nazarene and finally one of the founders of the Pilgrim Holiness Church.[1]

Young Rees had an inquiring mind and compiled an outstanding record as an undergraduate at the University of Southern California. But he did not pursue doctoral studies at the request of his father because of the negative spiritual effects of doctoral studies on a brother. The unusual preaching skills of the young preacher were in conspicuous evidence as at first he helped his father at the Pilgrim Tabernacle in Pasadena, California. He then served as ministerial superintendent of the Detroit Holiness Tabernacle, an enterprise sponsored by Methodistic laymen who were burdened about spiritual decline. Rees preached at the Tabernacle and then in an increasingly wide circle of camp meetings, conferences, and evangelistic series. From 1938 to 1958, he served as pastor of the great First Covenant Church in downtown Minneapolis with an amazing outreach to college and university students and people of all denominations. In 1958 he became preacher at large for World Vision and continued to travel around the world in effective ministry almost up until his death at nearly ninety-one years of age. He was widely used in the Billy Graham crusades with the ministers, and his written products were many and highly valued everywhere.

Paul Rees was a preacher's preacher. His reading was varied, and he was quite literary in his style. He wrote full manuscripts and largely memorized his material. His reproduction was so precise that a secretary transcribing his sermon from tape found virtually no difference between the original manuscript and the ultimate delivery.[2] His vocabulary, use of illustration, appropriate literary allusion, and exegetical conscience combine to make him a memorable preacher. Popular at Keswick conventions around the world (he was featured at the Japan convention many years in a row), he visited English Keswick again and again. His Bible readings there beginning in 1956 show him at his expository best (e.g., his series on the prayers of Paul in 1956, which he titled "Prayer and Life's Highest";[3] his superb expositions from Philippians in 1958 called "The Gospel and Humanities";[4] and his careful exegetical work in 1 Peter under the theme "Triumphant in Trouble,"[5] which he did in 1961). Rees was a Christian gentleman, a gracious and godly man. It was not hard to hear him preach about holy things. Occasionally his voice had a little sob in it, but he was genuine.

Probably his most famous sermons were textual, in which genre he specialized. A typical example would be his sermon "The Rain of Righteousness," from Hosea 10:12, which reads, "It is time to seek the Lord, till he comes and rains righteousness upon you." His outline aids us in seeing his special capability:

I. Spiritual recovery and revival require man's response to God's call;
II. Spiritual recovery and revival require man's reception of God's gift;
III. Spiritual recovery and revival require man's recognition of God's time.[6]

Rees seldom preached in series, but one he did do was particularly outstanding. The series focused on "The Radiant Cross" and consisted of studies of ten brief texts related to the Cross.[7] Heavier theologically is his Trinitarian approach in *Stand Up in Praise to God* with its multiplied triads.[8] In structure, alliterative outline, and polished components, Rees had few equals. At times there seemed to be overcontrol. His Bob Jones Lectures in 1951 on *Stir Up the Gift* allowed vent for the more scholarly Rees to express himself, in connection with which he has a stirring lecture on *The Re-Validation of the Sermon.*[9] His strength in application can be appreciated especially in his sermons on *Christian: Commit Yourself!* projected in a year of denominational mobilization for evangelism.[10]

Broadcasting his morning sermons live for many years, Rees touched thinking people through the upper Midwest and around the country in his itinerant ministry. Such masterpieces as "The Hallowing of the Heart" from 1 Peter 3:15[11] or "The Victor Unveiled" from Hebrews 2:9 explain his appeal.[12]

Paul Rees did his homework. His preparation was disciplined. He stands for us as the personification of pulpit effectiveness and prowess.

---

1. Paul S. Rees, *Seth Cook Rees: The Warrior-Saint* (Indianapolis: Pilgrim, 1934). A beautiful study. See also Carl Bangs, *Phineas F. Bresee: His Life in Methodism, the Holiness Movement and the Church of the Nazarene* (Kansas City: Beacon Hill, 1995). Also, Frank Bartleman, *Azusa Street* (South Plainfield, N.J.: Bridge, 1980).
2. Clarence S. Roddy, ed., *We Prepare and Preach* (Chicago: Moody, 1959), 147.
3. Paul S. Rees, *Prayer and Life's Highest* (Grand Rapids: Eerdmans, 1956). Rees knew the literature.
4. Herbert F. Stevenson, ed., *The Keswick Week,* 1958 (London: Marshall, Morgan, and Scott, 1958) 33ff.
5. Herbert F. Stevenson, ed., *The Keswick Week,* 1961 (London: Marshall, Morgan, and Scott, n.d.), 31ff.

6. Paul S. Rees, *Things Unshakable and Other Sermons* (Grand Rapids: Eerdmans, 1947), 45ff.
7. Paul S. Rees, *The Radiant Cross* (Grand Rapids: Eerdmans, 1955).
8. Paul S. Rees, *Stand Up in Praise to God* (Grand Rapids: Eerdmans, 1960).
9. Paul S. Rees, *Stir Up the Gift* (Grand Rapids: Zondervan, 1962), 131ff.
10. Paul S. Rees, *Christian: Commit Yourself!* (Chicago: Covenant Press, 1957).
11. Paul S. Rees, *Heart Throbs from a City Pulpit* (Minneapolis: Covenant Tabernacle Church, 1945), 39ff.
12. Paul S. Rees, *The Hope That Hallows* (Louisville: Pentecostal Publishing Company, n.d.), 22ff.

12.8.5 Walter L. Wilson—The Preacher as Encourager

If there is a definitive characteristic of his [Wilson's] ministry, it has been its remarkable simplicity. Every message he preached, every book he wrote, every class he taught—all were geared for complete understanding and digestion by any member of his audience. This is not to imply that he dealt only with the elementary milk of the Word. On the contrary, he had the remarkable gift of making the most meaty portions of scripture palatable for the untrained spiritual appetite. He could, as Spurgeon admonished his students to do, "put the cookies on the lower shelf where the children can reach them."

—Kenneth O. Gangel

Walter L. Wilson (1881–1969) was a unique and singular force for God. He was born in Aurora, Indiana, into a strong Christian home. His father was a Methodist minister and a practicing physician. His mother died in 1882, and Wilson was reared by his grandparents in Ft. Smith, Arkansas.

He wanted to become a preacher and a doctor like his father.[1] Later he was taken to Kansas City by his father and his new mother. Here he joined a church but by then had been a member of two churches and was not yet converted. His employer and future father-in-law took him to a Plymouth Brethren Tent on Ninth and Agnes Streets in Kansas City, where the evangelist John Moffat preached clearly night after night successively on Romans 4:5, Titus 3:5, Ephesians 2:8–9, and on Isaiah 64:6. Wilson was under deep conviction and six months later gave in. He was converted![2] When he was sixteen, a dying Scottish preacher named Donald Ross placed his hands on him to anoint him to take his place.

Wilson began to do street preaching, faithfully attending the Gospel Hall and studying the Word deeply and constantly. He went to University Medical School in Kansas City and he and his new bride began to practice in Webb City, Missouri. He worked also with his father-in-law in the tent manufacturing business. He sold the big tops to Ringling Brothers Circus.

His great love was for preaching, and he had legendary gifts as a personal soulwinner. In 1920 he established the Central Bible Church in Kansas City. The first meetings were in a tent, but the work flourished. Under Wilson's evangelistic and expository ministries, Central Bible Church became a powerful center of

Christian witness and testimony. Many conversions took place. He began radio ministry as early as 1924 over WOQ, and he founded the Flagstaff Indian Mission to the Navajos. In 1932 he founded Kansas City Bible Institute, which later merged with Midwest Bible College of St. Louis to become Calvary Bible College in Kansas City.

Wilson was unusually gifted in doing object lessons. He was interested in nature and the relationship of science to biblical Christianity. In his teaching he made a strong emphasis on knowing the Holy Spirit personally.[3] He was excellent in repartee and was a popular youth and children's speaker.[4] His evangelistic preaching tingles with spiritual passion and warmth and is solidly based on the great texts of Scripture.[5] His expositions were rich in biblical insight, as his series of pocket commentaries indicates.

Wilson's major contribution to biblical scholarship is his famous *Dictionary of Bible Types*. Given the tendency we have noted in some Bible preachers to overdo typology, it is of interest to sense the return to consider a proper biblical typology under such scholars as Leonard Goppelt and others. Wilson classified his lengthy survey of typological material under three headings: (1) the overtly typical as indicated by Scripture itself, about which there is no question; (2) those materials which seem appropriate as types, such as Noah's ark or the cities of refuge in the Old Testament, although they are not identified as such in Scripture; (3) those material about which there is considerable doubt.[6]

Almost eighty-eight years of a life wholly given to the Lord in the midsection of America—the name of Walter Wilson is synonymous with an irenic Bible teaching ministry and aggressive evangelism that touched many.

---

1. Kenneth O. Gangel, *Walter L. Wilson: The Beloved Physician* (Chicago: Moody, 1970), 18.
2. Ibid., 23ff.
3. Ibid., 89.
4. Walter L. Wilson, "There Is a Double Need," *In Green Pastures: Ten Messages to Young People* (Findlay, Ohio: Fundamental Truth Publishers, 1937), 13ff. Here he joins others such as Dan Gilbert, Percy Crawford, and Paul Rood.
5. Walter L. Wilson, *The Doctor's Best Love Story* (Chicago: Moody, 1936). Like Moorhouse on John 3:16.
6. Walter L. Wilson, *Wilson's Dictionary of Bible Types* (Grand Rapids: Eerdmans, 1957). A compendium.

12.8.6 ALAN REDPATH—THE PREACHER AS MOTIVATOR

It is my conviction that the message, which lives and burns as a fire in the heart of the preacher, is that which he has received from the Lord Himself in his own personal quiet time and waiting upon God. Commentaries and other textbooks may be useful additions, but this surely is the supreme thing in all ministry. We are not intended to be copies of other people in the truth we present, but rather to be original. God has an individual pattern of ministry for every one of us. For that reason I find that a "Seed-Thought Notebook" is a most valuable part of the equipment of my personal devotional life. As the Word of God speaks in a quiet time, I register in the book some verse or promise which has stood out and then leave it there, remembering that our devotional life is not the time for the preparation of sermons but rather the time for feeding our own hearts. To return to the "Seed-Thought Notebook" for further study and to work at the text as the carpenter works among the shavings on his bench is to find the material beginning to burn and take fire in one's own heart. Complete dependence on the Holy Spirit is essential.

—Alan Redpath

Over the years there has been much pulpit exchange between the United States and Britain. Certainly one of the more vibrant instances was the significant tenure of **Alan Redpath** (1907–1988) in historic Moody Church on Chicago's near north side.

He was born in Newcastle-on-Tyne in England and was a chartered accountant at Imperial Industries, the largest industrial combine in Britain.[1] Redpath obtained training at Durham University and later at Wycliffe Hall, Oxford, and increasingly felt the call of God upon his life for ministry and the preaching of the Word. He spent four years in itinerant ministry with Christian Youth Movement and then took the pastorate for thirteen years at Duke Street Baptist Church in Richmond, Surrey (where Stephen Olford followed him and had such a significant ministry). In 1953 Redpath took the call to the Moody Church, where he labored into the 1960s until returning to Britain. His proximity to Moody Bible Institute and other training schools brought large audiences to his passionate pulpit ministry.[2] His ministry was worldwide, and he was eagerly received at Keswick in England.[3] Redpath followed J. Sidlow Baxter as pastor of Charlotte Baptist Chapel in Edinburgh. Even after a serious stroke, he continued a remarkably diffuse ministry with special emphasis on the deeper things of the Spirit and the victorious Christian life.[4]

Alan Redpath was always disciplined to bring a hot coal out of each biblical text. His discourse was like a lava flow and sizzled with fire from deep within the preacher. At times his intensity was overmastering, but his moral earnestness was radioactive and seismic. One senses this in a collection of sermons preached in a particularly difficult time in this urban church, especially in the messages on forgiveness and powerlessness.[5]

The biblicality of Redpath's preaching can be seen in his marvelous expositions from Joshua; no one has ever preached this book more adeptly. His outlines are helpful and not obtrusive.[6] Likewise his studies in Nehemiah, such as "Building and Battling" from Nehemiah 4:11–23, are sparkling.[7] His illustrative material is in good blend and does not overshadow his work in the text. Most attractive are his courageous messages from First Corinthians in which he faces all of the issues head-on.[8]

Most typical of Redpath are his studies on the Lord's Prayer in which we sense the secret to his immense spiritual passion.[9] The severe acculturation of the North American and British churches was hard on such a sensitive follower of Christ as Alan Redpath. But the sheer consistency of his devotion to the Word and to

Christ was itself part of the very great legacy and gift he left to us who follow and carry on.

---

1. Clarence S. Roddy, *We Prepare and Preach* (Chicago: Moody, 1959), 134, on Alan Redpath.
2. The president of MBI during these years was Dr. William Culbertson, earlier a bishop of the Reformed Episcopal Church and a preacher of great insight and pastoral sensitivity. His Keswick messages from 1957 titled *God's Provision for Holy Living* (Chicago: Moody, 1957) and his keynote sermons from Founder's Week called *The Faith Once Delivered* (Chicago: Moody, 1972) are outstanding. See also Warren Wiersbe, *William Culbertson: A Man of God* (Chicago: Moody, 1974). Laid back in comparison with Redpath, he yet had a quiet, compelling word.
3. Alan Redpath, "When Jesus is Enthroned," in *Keswick's Triumphant Voice,* ed. Herbert F. Stevenson (Grand Rapids: Zondervan, 1963), 401ff. A thoughtful exposition of 2 Samuel 5.
4. Herbert F. Stevenson, ed. *The Keswick Week: 1975—Centenary Year* (London: Marshall, Morgan, and Scott, 1975), 75ff. A typical Redpath sermon titled "The Christian Revolution" is based on a probing exposition of Colossians 3:1ff.
5. Alan Redpath, *Learning to Live* in the Preaching for Today series (Grand Rapids: Eerdmans, 1961), 77ff., 39ff.
6. Alan Redpath, *Victorious Christian Living: Studies in the Book of Joshua* (Westwood, N.J.: Revell, 1955).
7. Alan Redpath, *Victorious Christian Service: Studies in the Book of Nehemiah* (Westwood, N.J.: Revell, 1958), 94ff.
8. Alan Redpath, *The Royal Route to Heaven: Studies in 1 Corinthians* (Westwood, N.J.: Revell, 1960).
9. Alan Redpath, *Victorious Praying: Studies in the Family Prayer* (Westwood, N.J.: Revell, 1957).

12.8.7 *VANCE HAVNER—THE PREACHER AS EXHORTER*

What kind of preaching do we need today? We need the same kind we've always needed. Nothing important has changed. Just because we've split the atom and sent a man to the moon doesn't mean we need a new kind of Christianity. We have a new kind of preacher in some quarters, but we don't need him. . . . You can't preach it like it is if you don't believe it like it was. If you don't believe that the Scriptures are God-breathed and that Jesus Christ was virgin born, that he died for our sins and rose bodily from the grave and is coming again, you can't preach it like it is. You can't preach "Jesus Christ the same yesterday" today, if you don't believe what He was yesterday. For what He was then He is now.

—Vance Havner

A revivalist and an itinerant exhorter to the churches, he was sometimes called the Will Rogers of the American pulpit. **Vance Havner** (1901–1986) filled a unique niche among biblical preachers for a generation, and he has no successor. Billy Graham said of him, "He knew how to preach" and labeled Havner "The most quoted preacher in America."[1]

Havner's Tarheel drawl and his "sanctified sarcasm" are as unforgettable for those who heard him as his piercing, probing soul surgery. He was born in 1901 in Jugtown in Catawba County in the Blue Ridge Mountains of North Carolina. His godly parents had three sons, all of whom became preachers. Havner was converted at age ten, when after a revival meeting he went into the woods and sought after the Lord.[2] He began to study the Bible and at age twelve was a preacher. He stood on a chair behind the pulpit. As the years went by he had a foray into "the marshlands of liberalism," but through reading Machen's *Christianity and Liberalism* he saw the futility of a desupernaturalized gospel and came back to the old faith.[3]

Spending brief periods at Catawba College near home, at Wake Forest College, and one year at Moody Bible Institute, Havner took his first pastorate at Weeksville, North Carolina. In 1934 he took the pastorate of the oldest Baptist church in the south, the historic First Baptist Church of Charleston, South Carolina. He had an effective ministry to this run-down congregation and while there had his first of fifteen invitations to address Moody Founder's Week. He also found his stride as an effective writer. His *Rest Awhile* essays were written after a vicious bout with insomnia, and through his life he alternated essays with volumes of sermons.[4]

In 1940 Havner began an itinerant ministry of awakening and renewal in the churches, and the following year he was married. He headquartered at first in Minneapolis and then later and permanently in Greensboro, North Carolina. He was especially close to Donald Grey Barnhouse, W. B. Riley, and Will Houghton at Moody during these years. The great burden of his heart was for revival in the churches.

His sermons were not structured traditionally but were anchored in a text which the preacher developed in his creative and pictorial manner. He painted the picture. He made it come alive. His study of the need for fire from heaven is movingly developed in "Road to Revival" from 1 Kings 18.[5] Havner's sermon on the man from Matthew 22:1–14 who came but went to hell can never be erased from the hearer's mind. "And he stood speechless . . ."[6] The pithy, tangy discourse and his ability as a semanticist to find the arresting epigram are part of what made people listen and say, "He can really keep people awake."[7] He could be more expository and exegetical as in his famous sermon on the Book of Amos in one message. He was persuaded along with Finney that "We must have exciting and powerful preaching or the devil will have the people."[8]

Havner could be very tender as well as searing.[9] He was designated Preacher of the Year by *Decision* magazine in 1973. Over his lifetime, he conducted more than one thousand revival campaigns and conferences and preached more than thirteen thousand times. Half a million of his books were sold to untold blessing. The homegoing of his wife left him devastated, and the sermon he preached on the day she died and then afterward is on a par with Arthur John Gossip's similar message (cf. 12.4.1).[10]

But there is more here than a theology of nostalgia. Havner's rapid-fire, blunt, severe call for repentance is exactly what the contemporary church and all Christians today need. He is right that for many congregations the pastor's preaching time could be described as "how tedious and tasteless the hours." He is correct that while we sing "Throw out the Lifeline" we don't seem to have enough pep to hang out the clothes.

Vance Havner's own testimony was steady: "I just love to point Him out!"[11] He wanted his epitaph to be, "Just a preacher."

1. Douglas M. White, *Vance Havner: Journey from Jugtown* (Old Tappan, N.J.: Revell, 1977), 164.
2. Ibid., 25.
3. Ibid., 51, 68.
4. Vance Havner, *Rest Awhile* (New York: Revell, 1941). A great chapter on "Country Preaching," 13ff.
5. Vance Havner, *Road to Revival* (New York: Revell, 1940), 9ff. See also *It Is Time* (New York: Revell, 1943).
6. Vance Havner, *Blood, Bread and Fire* (Grand Rapids: Zondervan, 1939), 70ff.
7. White, *Vance Havner,* 124.
8. Havner, *Blood, Bread and Fire,* 124.
9. Vance Havner, *Peace Like a River* (New York: Revell, 1942); *Rest for the Weary* (New York: Revell, 1946).
10. Vance Havner, *Just a Preacher: Selected Messages from a Doctor of Souls* (Chicago: Moody, 1981), 17ff.
11. Vance Havner, *The Best of Vance Havner* (Old Tappan, N.J.: Revell, 1969), 43.

12.8.8 A. W. Tozer—The Preacher as Disturber

But for the searching of the Scripture and true knowledge of them, an honorable life is needed, and a pure soul, and that virtue which is according to Christ; so that the intellect guiding its path by it, may be able to attain what it desires and to comprehend it, in so far as it is accessible to human nature to learn concerning the word of God. For without a pure mind and a modeling of the life after the saints, a man could not possibly comprehend the words of the saints. He that would comprehend the mind of those who speak of God needs begin by washing and cleansing his soul.

The best rule is: Go to God first about the meaning of any text. Then consult the teachers.

A church can wither as surely under the ministry of soulless Bible exposition as it can where no Bible is given at all.

Many a splendid church has drifted into modernism because its leaders would not insist on the everlasting importance of the basic doctrines of the faith; and many a church split has resulted from an undue attachment to nonessentials.

—A. W. Tozer

Known variously as oracle, seer, sage, gadfly, Christian mystic, and the conscience of American evangelicalism, **A. W. Tozer** (1897–1963) called himself a minor prophet. He was born the third of six children on a farm near what is now called Newburg in the hills of western Pennsylvania. His paternal grandmother, a Scotch-Irish Presbyterian, was God's chief voice to young Tozer. The family moved to Akron, Ohio, where at eighteen he was converted and joined the Methodist church, though he was immersed in the Brethren Church.[1] He had the joy of leading his mother and sisters to Christ.[2]

Almost at once he began open-air preaching. Becoming *persona non grata* with the Methodists, Tozer joined the Christian and Missionary Alliance Church. For two summers he traveled through West Virginia preaching in schoolhouses with his sister's husband. During World War I, Tozer served in the army.

In 1919 Tozer took appointment as pastor in Nutter Fort, West Virginia. Subsequently he had good charges in Morgantown, West Virginia; Toledo, Ohio; and Indianapolis, Indiana. He and his wife, Ada, prayed for the filling of the Holy Spirit, and the clear touch of God was on his ministry.[3]

In 1928 he was recommended by R. R. Brown, then superintendent of the western district, to become pastor of the relatively new Southside Alliance Church in Chicago.[4] The church met in a remodeled garage and grew considerably during the thirty-one years of his remarkable preaching ministry. A new church seating eight hundred was eventually built, but he never drew huge crowds—his Sunday morning attendance averaged between four and five hundred.

Tozer did not do pastoral work at all and was rather antisocial except to a small group of friends. He cherished solitude and really quite neglected his wife and seven children.[5] He disliked organizations, though he served on the CMA board of managers for many years. In 1950 he began his celebrated editorship of the *Alliance Weekly,* later the *Alliance Witness* and now *Alliance Life.* Many subscribed to the magazine just to read his editorials. One of his last editorials was titled "The Waning Authority of Christ in the Churches."[6]

Leonard Ravenhill was not sure that Tozer was the greatest preacher he had ever heard, but he did believe Tozer had greater intimacy with God than any other person he had known.[7] For Tozer "the exaltation of the Triune God" was primary. His works on *The Pursuit of God* and his more theological *The Knowledge of the Holy* are classics.[8] He boasted that he never took a vacation or a day off, but he did seek the solitudes.[9] He never owned or drove a car—instead he bought books.[10] He loved the classics and read deeply in the mystics. He read *Paradise Lost* through four times aloud in order to strengthen his voice since it was not a strong preaching voice. Tozer wrote poetry and his song-leader, Raymond McAfee, put some of his verse to song.

Tozer was concerned about sound doctrine.[11] He correctly saw that figures of speech and metaphors can illustrate truth but not originate it.[12] He claimed that he was a Calvinist when he prayed and an Arminian when he preached.[13] Curiously he did seem to believe in the indefectible ability of a person even as a sinner to obey God's commandments (like Finney).[14] He was a maverick and a character. Slightly built and spare, he stood on his toes when preaching, holding his Bible in his left hand when he got going in the sermon. He used much humor (more when he was tired) and was "an incurable tease," though his humor and his illustrations are for the most part edited out of his printed sermons.

Having studied cartooning when young, Tozer's "lively imagination and eloquent descriptive powers" were striking. "Get the idea clear" was his consuming drive, and he always seemed to have just the right word. He was a great storyteller, loved music and nature, and had a long radio ministry. But as a result of overextending himself, he had a heart attack in 1952.

When the Southside Alliance Church faced the issue of relocation, Tozer felt they needed another type of leader. He resigned and took the pastorate of the large central city Avenue Road Church in Toronto, continuing with his writing and editorial duties. This was a hard decision for him, but he had good years in this pulpit. Interestingly he and D. Martyn Lloyd-Jones in London were good friends in the kind of exemplary evangelical networking that is needed today.

Tozer lambasted book digests, religious movies, gospel choruses, "hillbillyism in religion," social climbing, and a host of other issues which tended to make people uncomfortable and which, he reported to Lloyd-Jones, had preached him right off most stateside conference platforms.[15] His critics found him insufficiently loyal to the Alliance and spearheaded an effort to depose him from his editorship. They accused him of being overly cynical, too negative, hypercritical, severe, and aloof. His answer was always, "Everything is wrong until God sets it right."[16]

Yet whatever is said, Tozer preached with a laser, as Warren Wiersbe has said. He spent three years leading his congregation through John's gospel. His expositions from Hebrews in two volumes are outstanding.[17] His sermons on the Holy Spirit (edited by Gerald B. Smith) are a tonic.[18] Many of his forty books were edited after his passing. He had the burden for the shallowness of evangelical worship long before the present resurgence.[19] His love for the mystics adumbrated the current renewal of interest of classic devotional works.[20] Tozer is always good for us and works us over instead of serving up self-esteem pablum.[21] His analysis of the cult of entertainment, the cult of imitation, and the cult of celebrity are even more current and relevant than when he first shared it. Although he has been many years dead, thousands still read the preaching and writing of A. W. Tozer. The Word speaks the truth of it: "Those who impart wisdom will shine like the brightness of the heavens, and those who lead many to righteousness, like the stars for ever and ever" (Dan. 12:3).

1. David J. Fant Jr., *A. W. Tozer: A Twentieth-Century Prophet* (Harrisburg, Pa: Christian Publications, 1964), 14.
2. James L. Snyder, *The Pursuit of God: The Life of A. W. Tozer* (Camp Hill, Pa.: Christian Publications, 1991), 41.
3. Ibid., 44.

4. Ibid., 208. R. R. Brown, who pastored the Omaha Gospel Tabernacle for many years, had an early and effective radio ministry. He was himself an unusually gifted and lively preacher with a great sense of humor.

5. Ibid., 8.

6. Fant, *A. W. Tozer,* 88.

7. Ibid., 1.

8. A. W. Tozer, *The Pursuit of God* (Harrisburg, Pa.: Christian Publications, 1948); *The Knowledge of the Holy* (New York: Harpers, 1961). Under family pressure, Tozer published "his crowning literary achievement" with a secular house. See Snyder, *The Pursuit of God,* 127. This is a study of the attributes of God suffused with the spirit of true worship and awe.

9. Fant, *A. W. Tozer,* 63, 80.

10. Snyder, *The Pursuit of God,* 182.

11. A. W. Tozer, *A Treasury of A. W. Tozer* (Grand Rapids: Baker, 1980), 174ff.

12. Fant, *A. W. Tozer,* 81.

13. Ibid., 67. To hold to man's moral ability is to deny human depravity. Even Reinhold Niebuhr saw "the relevance of an impossible ethical ideal"; see *An Interpretation of Christian Ethics* (New York: Living Age Books, 1956), 97ff.

14. A. W. Tozer, *Paths to Power* (Harrisburg, Pa.: Christian Publications, n.d.), 29ff.

15. Snyder, *The Pursuit of God,* 112.

16. Fant, *A. W. Tozer,* 24. Another preacher very much like Tozer was L. E. Maxwell, longtime head of Prairie Bible Institute, Three Hills, Alberta, Canada. To have both Tozer and Maxwell on the same platform was a heavy dose. Maxwell's works, *Born Crucified, Crowded to Christ,* and *Abandoned to Christ,* are incendiary.

17. A. W. Tozer, *Jesus, Our Man in Glory* and *Jesus, Author of Our Faith* (Camp Hill, Pa.: Christian Publications, 1988).

18. A. W. Tozer, *Ten Sermons on the Ministry of the Holy Spirit* (Harrisburg, Pa.: Christian Publications, 1968).

19. A. W. Tozer, *Worship—The Missing Jewel of the Evangelical Church* (Harrisburg, Pa.: Christian Publications, 1961).

20. A. W. Tozer, *The Christian Handbook of Mystical Verse* (Harrisburg, Pa.: Christian Publications, 1963).

21. Snyder, *The Pursuit of God,* 122.

The history of faithful and effective biblical preaching continues on to this hour. The record is unfinished until Christ completes his chosen bride and translates her from this earth to heaven. Our preaching of this week may be part of the chronicle as we treasure God's Word and trust his Spirit.

EPILOGUE

The Prospects for Preaching

Look in the scroll of the LORD and read.

—Isaiah 34:16

On what are you basing this confidence of yours?

—Isaiah 36:4b

The word of our God stands forever.

—Isaiah 40:8b

From Whence We Have Come

Preaching is to be taken seriously as proclamation of the living Word of the regnant Christ . . . In its essence it is nothing less than an eschatological event, an act in which, for a moment, the kingly Christ stands revealed among men, and He is shown forth before them as indeed Christus Victor. It is altogether proper to speak of the pulpit as the throne of the Word of God and of the sermon as the "Monstrance of the Evangel."

—Daniel Jenkins

Certain general principles can fairly be drawn from our extended historical inquiry.

1. When preaching has been strong in the Christian church, the church has been strong; when preaching has been weak, the church has been weak. Preaching is by no means the only factor, but it is an obvious and a critical one.
2. A high view of scriptural authority leads to and sustains a high view of preaching. What we believe about the Bible and its authority will shape our view of preaching.
3. Only a high view of Scripture and of preaching focuses on and sustains the

proclamation of the *kerygma* (i.e., the saving death and resurrection of Jesus Christ). Liturgy may contain the gospel, but the gospel must be supported by preaching.

4. Rhetorical forms used in preaching are many and diverse and are culturally conditioned, but as in all contextualization of truth, assiduous care must be taken to avoid distortion. "The author (or preacher) cannot choose to avoid rhetoric; we can only choose the kind of rhetoric we shall employ."[1] Rhetoric is how we speak. Among the various rhetorical forms used in the history of preaching, the chief are the classical homily and its derivative, the Bible reading; the essay sermon of neoclassicism; the university or scholastic sermon; the modified modern sermon; and the Puritan sermon (please note appendix 3).

5. Many shoals and reefs loom before preachers, threatening disaster. These obstacles may be doctrinal, spiritual, moral, or relational. The history of preaching lays bare our human frailty and our unceasing need for dependence on the Holy Spirit in every aspect of our lives and endeavors. Much wreckage is strewn along the way.

6. At the most unexpected times and in the most unpromising of circumstances, the rediscovery of the power of the Word of God and its proclamation have been blessed of God to the renewal and the reviving of the Christian church.

7. The centers of ecclesiastical power have often been indifferent to the primacy of the preached Word and have been seduced to a fixation on other programmatic emphases, but frequently the despised and disparaged have risen with the anointing of God upon their preaching and have been catalytic in spiritual renaissance and transformation.

8. The history of preaching discloses an amazing and unpredictable networking of the Spirit, like Tozer and Lloyd-Jones. God brings it about!

Where We Are

This hearing of the Word of God, hearing what the Lord of the Church wants to say to His Church in its actual situation, is the primary task of the Church, the basic human action in worship.

—C. E. B. Cranfield

The most effective preachers, those whose preaching is life-changing, are expository preachers. They tell and interpret the biblical story.

—Lyle Schaller

With the complete collapse of the dream of the secular city, our society is in a mood of perpetual crisis. The West is in moral and spiritual crisis. While elements of the religious core of our culture remain, Woody West is correct that consensual truth, agreed-upon standards, and institutions that demand and deserve allegiance have largely disappeared. He quotes David Gelernter's re-creation of the United States in 1939 to the effect that "The most marked difference from this country today, nearly sixty years down the slope, is the absence of authority."[2] Before he died, Norman Cousins lamented the disrespect for coherent thought process and the resultant "communication collapse."[3]

Many in the homiletics of the left have capitulated to the new hermeneutic and abandoned any serious effort to break the lock of the original meaning of the biblical text.[4] Evangelicals, conversely, have been tempted by user-friendly and market-driven considerations to give up on a truly serious effort to transmit a biblical passage in its context with strong application for life. Taking the thought out of a text and preaching it rather than preaching the biblical text is now passing for expository preaching.[5] In either case, the danger is a cultural accommodation which is at best a mutation of the gospel. Even H. Richard Niebuhr saw this danger for preaching in the "Christ of culture" approach:

> The point of contact they seek to find with their hearers dominates the whole sermon; and in many instances the resultant portrait of Christ is little more than a personification of an abstraction. Jesus stands for the idea of spiritual knowledge; or of logical reason; or of the sense of the infinite; or of the moral law within; or of brotherly love.[6]

Others stand somewhat defensively, echoing the existentialist and neo-orthodox insistence that reality not ideas must be our primary concern and that the personal must be stressed over the propositional. This presents something of a challenge to the pulpit communicator. Clearly a false dichotomy is being advanced, since our choice is not between reality and ideas nor between the personal and the propositional. Yet many earnest preachers feel torn between teaching the Bible and addressing the hurts and manifest needs of humankind. Many practitioners are laid low by doubts about the craft and are confused in the face of conflicting counsel. The history of preaching shows that while these dilemmas have particular poignancy in our time, they are not new issues or concerns. Again and again, in its ministry in local parishes or around the world in a missionary context, these tensions have been felt acutely. Our study has repeatedly rehearsed God's faithfulness to bless his Word.

Anthony Trollope in 1875 spoke the truth when he averred in *Barchester Towers* that "There is, perhaps, no greater hardship at present inflicted on mankind in civilized and free countries, than the necessity of listening to sermons." This must be seen as a reflection not upon the craft but upon the craftsmen. The problems in preaching are not the problem of the Word but of those who work with the Word. In a time of massive societal, intellectual, and religious change, preachers find themselves awash in discussions about preaching and its future. Shifting paradigms on every side raise crucial questions about the craft. One leader insists that "Jesus never preached an expository sermon or a doctrinal sermon" with lamentable and dangerous conclusions. This is to cave in to the "feel-good factor" and the "look-good factor." The result is country-club Christianity with lavender-water theology. This is where we are today.

Whither Shall We Go?

The supreme work of the Christian minister is the work of preaching.
This is a day in which one of our great perils is that of doing a thousand
little things to the neglect of one thing, which is preaching.

—G. Campbell Morgan

Preaching in America is not going to improve until the preachers once
again believe in preaching, both in its content and its method.

—John R. Brokhoff

Of course we cannot enter the new century and the new millennium (should our
Lord tarry) by looking through the back mirror. The study of any past era or the
vain attempt to recapture a bygone time will not suffice—an insight missed by some
of our neo-Puritan enthusiasts. How then shall we face what one news commentator described as "a new form of popular religion, the rock-and-roll church with its
nocturnal, narcissistic, mischievous anti-authoritarian creed"?[7] The history of biblical preaching leaves us with some clear directives. Our duty is to:

1. Stand staunchly with classical biblical faith and its worldview, espousing
   confidence in the Scriptures through its positive proclamation and a vigorous apologetic.
2. Uphold the cruciality of systematic biblical exposition with a strong dedication
   to modeling the study of a passage in its context with appropriate application.
3. Loyally practice the necessary wedding of sound exegesis to lively exposition.
4. Increasingly become devotees of the most careful and responsible hermeneutic with its relentless commitment to finding the original meaning of the
   text with the help of all available tools and resources.
5. Continue to seek to know the filling of the Holy Spirit, the divine author of
   Scripture, upon whom we must totally rely at every stage of sermon preparation and delivery.
6. Remain avid students of the craft of preaching, seeking to grow in every aspect of its practice.
7. Be open to cultivate skills in new forms, as in the present renewal of interest
   in the narrative portions of Scripture and their more effective presentation.
8. Be unwavering in our conviction of the essential Christ-centeredness of
   preaching and to neglect no portion of revealed truth and to avoid no doctrine, for all is profitable.
9. Never step back from the quest for excellence as those called by God to
   preach.
10. Conscientiously and wholeheartedly seek that integrity and uprightness of
    character and conduct which will never bring the gospel or our Lord into
    disrepute.[8]
11. Remember humbly that we are heirs of faithful heralds through the ages and
    that we stand on their shoulders as we fulfill the task of our time.

12. Rest in the power of Almighty God, our divine sovereign, whose we are and whom we serve. "The battle is the Lord's," and he will have the victory over all principalities and powers through the blood of our Lord Jesus Christ and "the word of our testimony" (Rev. 12:11). The outcome is not in doubt. Thus preaching has a great and glorious future.

Now to him who is able to establish you by my gospel and the proclamation of Jesus Christ, according to the revelation of the mystery hidden for long ages past, but now revealed and made known through the prophetic writings by the command of the eternal God, so that all nations might believe and obey him—to the only wise God be glory forever through Jesus Christ! Amen.

—Romans 16:25–26

---

1. Wayne C. Booth, *The Rhetoric of Fiction* (Chicago: University of Chicago Press, 1961, 1983), 149.
2. Woody West, "Decline in Authority . . . Demise of Democracy," *Insight* (November 18, 1996): 48.
3. Norman Cousins, "The Communication Collapse," *Time* (December 17, 1990): 114.
4. Craig A. Loscalzo, in *Hermeneutics for Preaching,* ed. Raymond Bailey (Nashville: Broadman, 1992). He shows that David Buttrick rejects the idea that biblical texts "are locked up tight in a vault labeled 'Original Meaning' . . . The world assembled before the cross is ever different, and patterns of being-saved-in-the-world are thus ever-changing" (116). Thomas Long's abandonment of classical exegesis is similar; see "The Use of Scripture in Contemporary Preaching," *Interpretation* (October 1990): 341ff.
5. As an example, Harold T. Bryson, *Expository Preaching* (Nashville: Broadman, 1995), 32.
6. H. Richard Niebuhr, *Christ and Culture* (New York: Harper, 1951), 109. Niebuhr asserts, "It seems impossible to remove the offense of Christ and his cross even by means of these accommodations; and cultural Christians share in the general limitation all Christianity encounters whether it fights or allies itself with the 'world'" (108).
7. Tom Brokaw in John Howard, *A Sure Compass* (Rockford, Ill.: Rockford Institute, 1992), 5. We have seen the stubborn persistence of moralistic and at times Pelagian preaching in the American pulpit. Kurt Hamsum, the Norwegian Nobel Prize winner of some years ago, observed that the sermons he heard in the U.S. "did not contain theology but morality . . . they do not develop the mind, though they are entertaining." God help us.
8. Billy Graham, quoted in Craig A. Loscalzo, *Evangelistic Preaching That Connects* (Downers Grove, Ill.: InterVarsity Press, 1995), 12. Graham's most timely word is "Our world today is looking primarily for men and women of integrity, communicators who back up their ministry with their lives." Graham's own unflinching stand for biblical inerrancy and the centrality of the cross of Christ in preaching is well known. See Stephen F. Olford, *A Passion for Preaching: Reflections on the Art of Preaching* (Nashville: Thomas Nelson, 1989), 126.

Nominations for the Fifteen Most Significant Sermons in Church History

1. Jesus Christ, The Sermon on the Mount (Matthew 5–7).
2. The apostle Peter, Sermon on the Day of Pentecost (Acts 2).
3. The apostle Paul, Sermon on the Areopagus in Athens (Acts 17).
4. Chrysostom (John of Antioch), "Homily Concerning the Statues" (Genesis 3).
5. Bernard of Clairvaux, "On Conversion: A Sermon to Clerics" (Acts 13:44; Luke 19:10).
6. Martin Luther, "The Gift of God" (John 3:16–21).
7. John Wesley, "The New Birth" (John 3:7).
8. George Whitefield, "Christ the Believer's Wisdom, Righteousness, Sanctification and Redemption" (1 Corinthians 1:30).
9. Jonathan Edwards, "Sinners in the Hands of an Angry God" (Deuteronomy 32:35).
10. William Carey, "Sermon to the Association at Nottingham" (Isaiah 54:2–3; see 8.4.3).
11. Charles Haddon Spurgeon, "Christ the Cure of Troubled Hearts" (Luke 24:38).
12. Lyman Beecher, "The Bible as a Code of Laws" (see 9.2.6).
13. J. Stuart Holden, "But if not . . ." (Daniel 3:18, preached just before World War I; see 11.7.4).
14. William E. Sangster, "This Britain: What Would a Revival Do for Britain?" (This sermon hit front-page headlines in big type at a particularly vexing time for Britain; see 11.6.7).
15. Robert G. Lee, "Pay Day, Some Day" (1 Kings 21; preached one thousand times; see 12.2.6).

Appendix Two

Nominations for the Greatest Sermons in Literature

Many writers, among them Charles Dickens, Anthony Trollope, and Susan Howatch have written insightfully about preachers, but in some literature preaching itself is highlighted:

1. Father Mapple's sermon from Jonah 1 in Herman Melville's *Moby Dick.* Something of the range of diverse interpretation of the sermon is reflected in D. Bruce Lockerbie, "The Greatest Sermon in History," *Christianity Today* (November 8, 1963): 9ff.
2. Dr. Primrose's unusual sermon "On Providence," preached in prison where he is incarcerated because of debt in Oliver Goldsmith's *The Vicar of Wakefield.*
3. Father Zossima's sermon on John 12:24 from Dostoevsky's *The Brothers Karamazov.* For an appreciation of this sermon, see Eugene H. Peterson, *Under the Unpredictable Plant: An Exploration of Vocational Holiness* (Grand Rapids: Eerdmans, 1992) 49, 66–67.
4. The Reverend Cyril Maitland's two sermons in Maxwell Gray's *The Silence of Dean Maitland,* the first where under his guilt he is unable to finish his sermon (an experience Arthur Dimsdale in *The Scarlet Letter* never had), and his later sermon (and his last) in the little church at Malbourne, where he confesses his sin.
5. The Reverend Robert Elsmere's sermon on Jesus' first sermon from Luke 4:14ff. in Mrs. Humphry Ward's novel, *Robert Elsmere.* The story traces the inward spiritual and intellectual struggle of this Oxford clergyman in the Victorian/Edwardian tensions between faith and reason. The author describes his preaching on this occasion: "The preacher forgot all but his Master and his people."

6. The ambitious Pastor Theron Ware's magnificently well-received conference sermon in Harold Frederic's *The Damnation of Theron Ware* did not get him the big church he had hoped for and indeed only hastened his downfall.

7. The army chaplain preached a great sermon from Ezekiel 37, on the resurrection of dry bones, in Anthony Powell's gripping *The Valley of the Bones,* volume 7 in his twelve-volume Music of Time series. This sermon was preached to the troops facing the oppression of the German initiative. With Kipling and Proust as his models, Powell magnificently traces one hundred characters in slow motion.

8. Most unexpectedly, in A. N. Wilson's *Gentlemen in England,* Father Cuthbert preaches on "the old, old story of Jesus and his love" and confronts his audience with the contemporary Christ. Lionel Nettleship "realized he had never accepted Jesus Christ, God and Man, as his personal Savior. He had never opened his heart to Jesus and let him in, to change and purify his whole life. And now during the singing of the hymn he did so, and he felt his whole being suffused with a glow which he knew to be the sure token of our Lord's presence with him" (61, 63).

9. In William Faulkner's *The Sound and the Fury,* which traces the incredible confusion in the Compson family in Yoknapatawpha, Mississippi. The one stable figure appears to be the black servant, Dilsey, whose poise and perspective on Easter Sunday of 1928 are guided and enlightened by an Easter sermon she heard preached in St. Louis. She shares it.

10. Archbishop Thomas Becket's sermon preached on Christmas morning in Canterbury Cathedral, 1170, from Luke 2:10–11. The sermon in T. S. Eliot's play *Murder in the Cathedral* serves as an interlude between Act I and Act II. It centers on Christ's birth and the implication of his death.

11. George MacDonald treats several sermons in his clergy novels from Scotland including the Reverend James Blatherwick preaching before Isy in *The Minister's Restoration* and more notably the young cleric's sermon in *The Curate's Awakening.*

12. Corporal Trim reads the sermon by the Rev. Yorick from Hebrews 13:18 at York in Laurence Stern's pioneering novel *Tristam Shandy* (1759).

13. In the American poet Sidney Lanier's great early poem, "Jacquerie," a Franciscan father, Friar John, preaches a memorable sermon out of Revelation 6 on the seals of the Apocalypse, in which he indicts war, praises the martyrs (like Savonarola), and calls for a "vast undoing of things" (Book 2).

14. In George Eliot's *Adam Bede,* the woman Methodist preacher, the Rev. Dinah Morris, preaches a sermon on the village green and the entire chapter is given up to it (chapter 11).

15. In *The Portrait of an Artist as a Young Man,* James Joyce shares the rebellion of the young Stephen Daedalus and what is doubtless the greatest sermon on hell ever recorded in fictive literature.

The Basic Taxonomy of Sermonic Form Through Church History

Classical Homily

Chrysostom 3.3
Augustine 3.4

Leo the Great 4.1.1
Gregory the First 4.1.2

University or Scholastic Sermon

St. Bernard 4.2.1

Alan of Lille 4.3.1

Neo-classical Essay Sermon	**Modified Modern Sermon**	**Reformers**	**Puritan Sermon**
	Andrew Hyperius 6.1.1	Luther 5.2	Wm. Perkins 6.1.3
	Henry Smith 6.1.2	Calvin 5.3	
Tillotson 6.2.7		Zwingli 5.4	
	Jean Claude 6.1.4		
	Charles Simeon 8.5.4		
Schleiermacher 8.2.4			

10.4.2
Broadus
Phelps
Perry
Robinson

Bible Reading

Plymouth
Brethren 11.1

Lloyd-Jones 12.4.7

Scripture Index

Subject Index

Author Index